AMERICA'S
PAST AND PROMISE

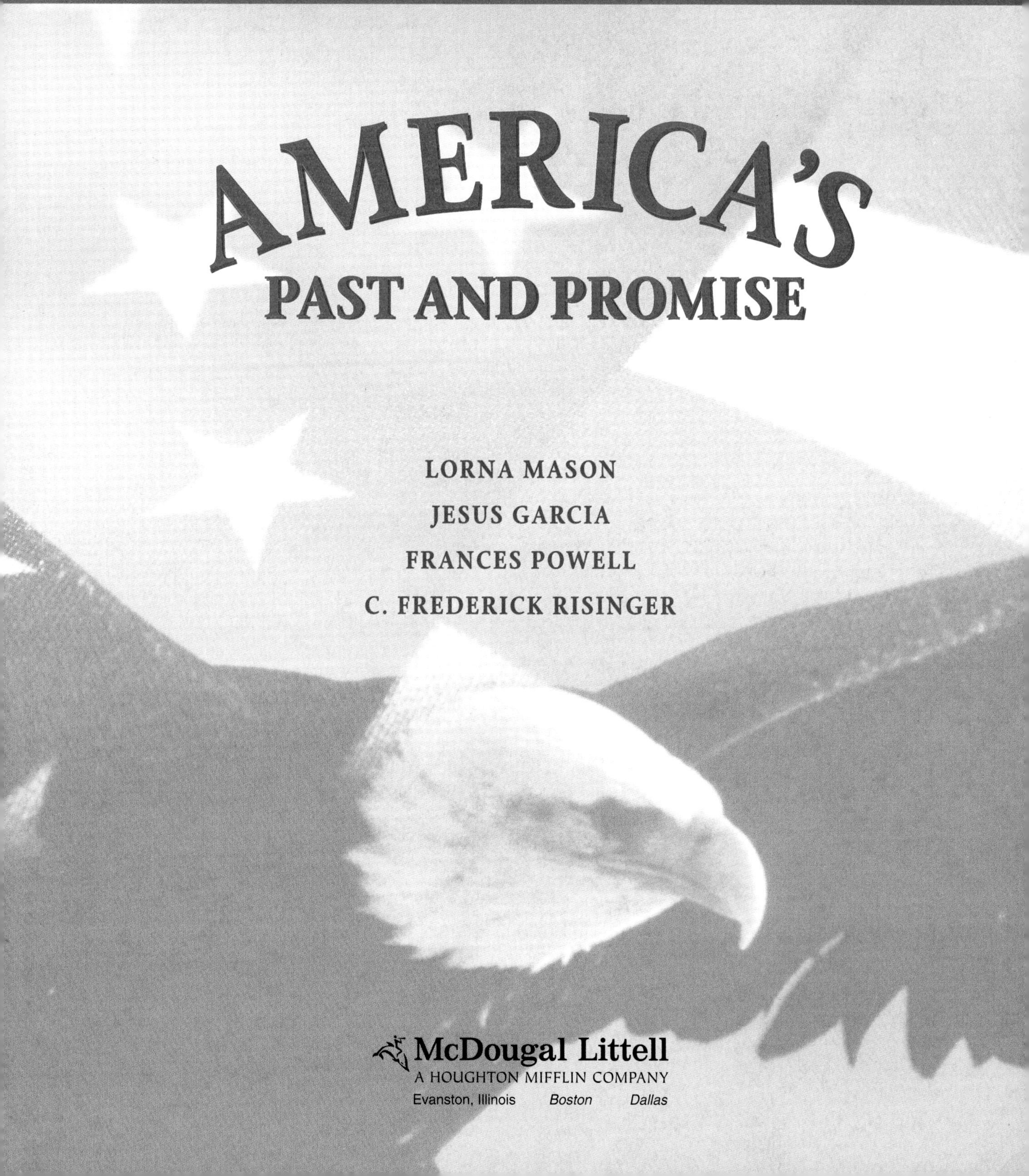

AMERICA'S
PAST AND PROMISE

LORNA MASON

JESUS GARCIA

FRANCES POWELL

C. FREDERICK RISINGER

McDougal Littell
A HOUGHTON MIFFLIN COMPANY
Evanston, Illinois   Boston   Dallas

The Authors

LORNA C. MASON is a professional writer and editor. Mrs. Mason has taught social studies at both the secondary and junior college levels. She is author of several social studies textbooks. Most recently Mrs. Mason has been a consultant to a series of children's books on multicultural themes.

JESUS GARCIA is Professor of Social Studies Education at the University of Illinois at Urbana-Champaign. A former elementary and secondary social studies teacher, Dr. Garcia co-authored an elementary social studies program. He has written extensively on issues relating to multicultural education.

FRANCES J. POWELL is Professor of History and Political Science at Montgomery College, Takoma, Maryland. Dr. Powell taught secondary social studies in Washington, D.C., for 18 years before becoming Curriculum Director for Social Studies in the District of Columbia public school system.

C. FREDERICK RISINGER is Associate Director of the Social Studies Development Center at Indiana University. He is a former social studies teacher and a recent president of the National Council for the Social Studies. Currently Mr. Risinger serves on the coordinating committee for the National History Standards Project.

Student's Edition ISBN: 0-395-86707-X

Copyright © 1998 by McDougal Littell Inc. All rights reserved. Printed in the United States of America.

1 2 3 4 5 6 7 8 9 10–VH–03 02 01 00 99 98 97

To the Student

Welcome to American history! We hope that the year ahead will be one of discovery for you. In about five years you will have the rights and responsibilities of an adult citizen of the United States. The United States has lasted more than 200 years because each generation has helped it to do so. Soon it will be your turn to help shape the future of our country.

A wise man once said, "He who knows only his own generation remains always a child." Understanding the past, in other words, helps you prepare for adulthood and for the future. This book will introduce you to a variety of Americans, some famous and some not-so-famous, and their role in the events and ideas that have helped shape this nation. To help you on this journey into the past, we have worked to make this textbook exciting to use.

America's Past and Promise deals primarily with this nation's past. Yet you, its reader, represent the future promise of America. We hope that by knowing America's past, you will help fulfill America's promise.

Lorna C. Mason

Jesus Garcia

Frances J. Powell

C. Frederick Risinger

Contents

UNIT 5   EXPANSION AND CHANGE (1810–1860)   362

MAPS

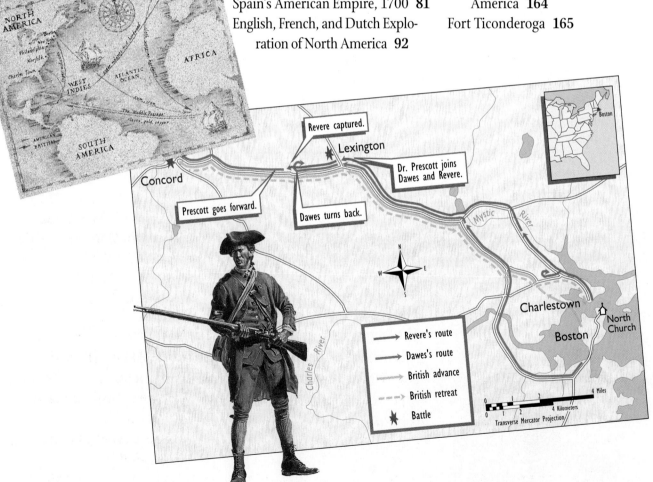

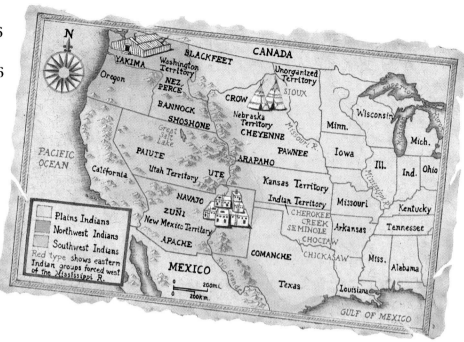

CHARTS AND GRAPHS

GEOGRAPHY IN THIS BOOK

In addition to the scores of maps throughout the book, the following special pages will sharpen your map-reading skills and show in detail how geography affects history.

SKILLS IN THIS BOOK

Each chapter contains a skill lesson in which you will learn, practice, and apply a different skill. There are a variety of skills for a variety of situations.

PRIMARY SOURCES IN THIS BOOK

Through primary sources you can hear the voices of those who made history. Primary sources are woven into the narrative of this book. Historical documents appear at the end of the book. Skill lessons help you interpret primary sources.

Primary Sources

135,000 SETS, 270,000 VOLUMES SOLD.
UNCLE TOM'S CABIN
FOR SALE HERE.
The Greatest Book of the Age.

Historical Documents

Skill Lessons

CIVICS IN THIS BOOK

Learning your nation's history is an important step toward becoming a responsible citizen. These pages provide special information on the United States, its people, and its government.

Skill Lessons

Documents

Civics Handbook

THE THEMES OF THIS BOOK

An American history course contains a tremendous amount of information. How can you pull all this information together into a usable form? How can you apply the lessons of the past to the future—and to your own future? One way is to recognize the broad themes that run through American history. Here are the five themes of this textbook. Following each is a question that will guide you in exploring the theme. As you read this textbook, keep these themes in mind. You will find that while each time period is unique, these five themes occur again and again throughout American history.

⭐ Society

How has the interaction of different cultures strengthened America?

⭐ Politics

How have Americans progressed toward achieving democracy for all?

⭐ Economics/Technology

What factors have made the United States a land of economic opportunity? How have new technologies changed the way Americans live and work?

⭐ Ideas and Images

How does American culture reflect the diversity of the American people?

⭐ International Relations

How and why has the role of the United States in world affairs changed over time?

About Your Book

Why is this book so special? It is about people—the people of our nation's past. You'll hear them speak, see how they lived, and follow them through history as they build the United States. Why is this book fun to use? Read it and see!

Several chapters make up a unit. At the start of each unit is a graphic organizer. It previews each chapter and shows how the chapters are related to each other.

"The Spirit of '76" captures the proud determination of Patriot fighters: Troops march on as a fallen comrade salutes. The Patriots defeated a powerful British army and won America's independence.

1775	1777	1779	1781
1776 Battle of Trenton		1779 Spain joins the war	1780 British capture Charleston
1777 Battle of Princeton			
1777 Battle of Saratoga		1781 Articles of Confederation adopted	
1778 France joins the war		1781 Battle of Yorktown	

CHAPTER 10

Americans Win Independence (1776–1787)

1 Early Years of the War

SECTION GUIDE

Main Idea
During the Revolutionary War, inexperienced Patriot forces struggled with a lack of supplies and a divided society.

Goals
As you read, look for answers to these questions:
1. What difficulties did Washington face as head of the American army?
2. What were the major battles of the war in the North?
3. How did foreign nations affect the war?

Key Terms
enlist
mercenary
rendezvous
Battle of Saratoga

N 1776 MERCY OTIS WARREN published *The Blockheads*, a play set in Boston during the British occupation. In the play a British officer, General Puff, complains, "We are shamefully confined within the bounds of three miles, wrangling and starving among ourselves."

The Country Divided

General Puff's complaint reflects the British situation throughout the Revolutionary War. The British were able to take and hold every city, except for Boston, that they wanted. They could do so because of their superior firepower, trained troops, and supply ships from Britain. However, British troops went into the countryside at their peril. As another character in Warren's play observed, "These Yankee dogs . . . divert themselves by firing at us, as at a flock of partridges. A man can scarcely put his nose over the entrenchments without losing it."

The Americans had problems of their own. Only a minority of Americans actively supported the Revolution. About two-fifths of them were Patriots. One-fifth were Loyalists, also called Tories. The rest did not take sides.

The American Revolution was thus a civil war that bitterly split families and neighbors. Patriots and Loyalists alike came from all walks of life and from all parts of America. In general, however, New England and Virginia had the greatest share of

1783	1785	1787
		1787 Northwest Ordinance
	1785 Ordinance of 1785	
1783 Treaty of Paris		

201

When did it happen? The timeline at the beginning of each chapter lists the events that made history and when they took place.

Like a road map, the Section Guide box leads you through the section. The Main Idea summarizes the section. Goals and Key Terms tell you what to look for as you read.

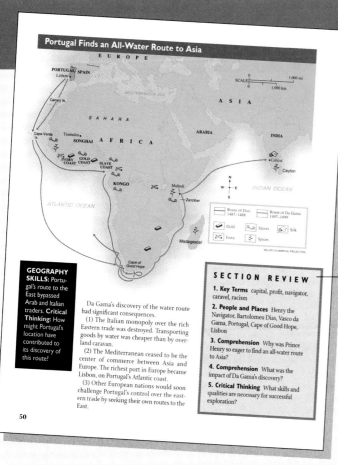

Portugal Finds an All-Water Route to Asia

GEOGRAPHY SKILLS: Portugal's route to the East bypassed Arab and Italian traders. **Critical Thinking:** How might Portugal's location have contributed to its discovery of this route?

Da Gama's discovery of the water route had significant consequences.

(1) The Italian monopoly over the rich Eastern trade was destroyed. Transporting goods by water was cheaper than by overland caravan.

(2) The Mediterranean ceased to be the center of commerce between Asia and Europe. The richest port in Europe became Lisbon, on Portugal's Atlantic coast.

(3) Other European nations would soon challenge Portugal's control over the eastern trade by seeking their own routes to the East.

50

SECTION REVIEW

1. Key Terms capital, profit, navigator, caravel, racism

2. People and Places Henry the Navigator, Bartolomeu Dias, Vasco da Gama, Portugal, Cape of Good Hope, Lisbon

3. Comprehension Why was Prince Henry so eager to find an all-water route to Asia?

4. Comprehension What was the impact of Da Gama's discovery?

5. Critical Thinking What skills and qualities are necessary for successful exploration?

After you've read the section, stop and review what you've read. You'll define the key terms and describe important people and places. The last question will give you a chance to apply what you've learned.

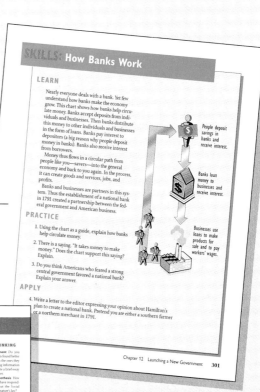

SKILLS: How Banks Work

LEARN

Nearly everyone deals with a bank. Yet few understand how banks make the economy grow. This chart shows how banks help circulate money. Banks accept deposits from individuals and businesses. Then banks distribute this money to other individuals and businesses in the form of loans. Banks pay interest to depositors (a big reason why people deposit money in banks). Banks also receive interest from borrowers.

Money thus flows in a circular path from people like you—savers—into the general economy and back to you again. In the process, it can create goods and services, jobs, and profits.

Banks and businesses are partners in this system. Thus the establishment of a national bank in 1791 created a partnership between the federal government and American business.

People deposit savings in banks and receive interest.

Banks loan money to businesses and receive interest.

Businesses use loans to make products for sale and to pay workers' wages.

PRACTICE

1. Using the chart as a guide, explain how banks help circulate money.

2. There is a saying, "It takes money to make money." Does the chart support this saying? Explain.

3. Do you think Americans who feared a strong central government favored a national bank? Explain your answer.

APPLY

4. Write a letter to the editor expressing your opinion about Hamilton's plan to create a national bank. Pretend you are either a southern farmer or a northern merchant in 1791.

Chapter 12 Launching a New Government **301**

The skills you'll need—for school and for life—appear in every chapter. They all follow a three-step process of Learn, Practice, and Apply.

CHAPTER **22** SUMMARY AND REVIEW

Summary

1. The United States experienced a huge wave of immigration in the late 1800s and early 1900s. Immigration from southern and eastern Europe increased. New York's Ellis Island was the first stop for many European immigrants. Most then moved to the cities of the industrial United States.

2. New immigrants, such as Jews fleeing mistreatment in eastern Europe, struggled to adjust to life in the United States. Free education helped immigrants, but working and living conditions were often difficult.

3. Immigration helped fuel the expansion of cities. Electric street cars and bridges helped cities expand outward. Political machines controlled a number of city governments. They stayed in power by buying votes. Women began to enter the workforce in larger numbers. Many women also worked in settlement houses, which helped immigrants. The Social Gospel encouraged people to help the poor.

4. Advances in technology and advertising increased the circulation of newspapers. Department stores offered large varieties of goods. Sports and entertainment helped make city life exciting.

Graphic Summary

Review

KEY TERMS

Define the following terms.
1. political machine
2. nationality
3. vaudeville
4. suburb
5. tenement
6. pogrom
7. settlement house

COMPREHENSION

1. What factors encouraged southern and eastern Europeans to immigrate in the late 1800s?
2. Where did four states rank in half of all immigrants in the early 1900s? Why did immigrants settle there?
3. What was the relationship between padrones and immigrants?
4. Why did so many eastern Europeans Jews come to the U.S. in the late 1800s and early 1900s?
5. What factors caused tension between adult immigrants and their children?
6. What role did electricity play in the expansion of cities in the late 1800s?
7. What role did ward bosses play in the running of political machines in cities?
8. How did the role of women change in the late 1800s?
9. How did advertising help the newspaper business?
10. Why was baseball a popular sport among immigrants?

Places to Locate

Match the letters on the map with the places that are listed below. Then explain the importance of each place.
1. Ellis Island 3. Detroit 5. Chicago
2. St. Louis 4. Pittsburgh 6. Minneapolis
Geographic Theme: Place Why do you think immigrants to the United States settled mostly in cities? Explain.

Skill Review

Study the street map of Chicago in 1890 and answer the questions below.

1. In what box does the Chicago River flow into Lake Michigan?
2. Which two streets intersect in box D2?
3. In what box does the South Branch of the Chicago River cross 22nd Street? In what box does it cross 12th Street?
4. If you walked down Milwaukee Ave. toward the lake, through what boxes would you pass?

CRITICAL THINKING

1. **Making a Judgment** Do you think that immigrants found better lives in America than the ones they had left behind? Using information from the chapter, write a brief essay explaining your answer.
2. **Forming a Hypothesis** How might Jane Addams have responded to the charge that the Social Gospel went against nature's law?

PORTFOLIO OPTIONS

1. **Civics Connection** Imagine you are an immigrant from Europe in the late 1800s with no family or friends in America. Where could you turn for help in finding a job and a place to live? Discuss your options with the class.
2. **Writing Connection** Make a list of problems cities faced in the late 1800s and early 1900s. Then write a newspaper editorial expressing your opinion on how to solve one of the problems.
3. **Contemporary Connection** Millions of people still immigrate to the United States each year. Do you think that immigration should be restricted? Organize a class debate on the issue.
4. **Timeline Connection** Copy the chapter timeline. What do you think the Statue of Liberty symbolized to immigrants arriving at Ellis Island? Add other events from the chapter you think should be included and explain why.

550

Chapter 22 The Rise of American Cities **551**

Show what you know. At the end of each chapter are text and graphic summaries. Then come questions and activities that test your understanding of the terms, events, and skills presented in the chapter.

Also Featuring

Some special pages show up only once in every unit. They enrich the story by letting you explore a topic in greater detail. Other special features point out links across time and space or introduce you to the people who made history.

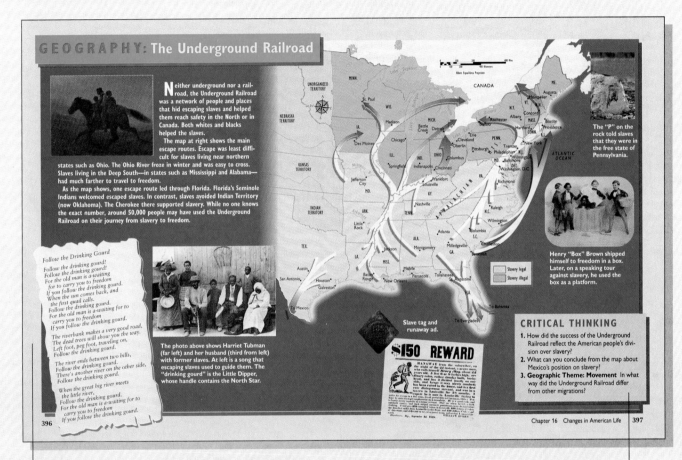

GEOGRAPHY: The Underground Railroad

Neither underground nor a railroad, the Underground Railroad was a network of people and places that hid escaping slaves and helped them reach safety in the North or in Canada. Both whites and blacks helped the slaves.

The map at right shows the main escape routes. Escape was least difficult for slaves living near northern states such as Ohio. The Ohio River froze in winter and was easy to cross. Slaves living in the Deep South—in states such as Mississippi and Alabama—had much farther to travel to freedom.

As the map shows, one escape route led through Florida. Florida's Seminole Indians welcomed escaped slaves. In contrast, slaves avoided Indian Territory (now Oklahoma). The Cherokee there supported slavery. While no one knows the exact number, around 50,000 people may have used the Underground Railroad on their journey from slavery to freedom.

Follow the Drinking Gourd

Follow the drinking gourd!
Follow the drinking gourd!
For the old man is a-waiting
for to carry you to freedom
If you follow the drinking gourd.
When the sun comes back, and
the first quail calls,
Follow the drinking gourd.
For the old man is a-waiting for to
carry you to freedom
If you follow the drinking gourd.

The riverbank makes a very good road,
The dead trees will show you the way.
Left foot, peg foot, traveling on,
Follow the drinking gourd.

The river ends between two hills,
Follow the drinking gourd.
There's another river on the other side,
Follow the drinking gourd.

When the great big river meets
the little river,
Follow the drinking gourd,
For the old man is a-waiting for to
carry you to freedom
If you follow the drinking gourd.

The photo above shows Harriet Tubman (far left) and her husband (third from left) with former slaves. At left is a song that escaping slaves used to guide them. The "drinking gourd" is the Little Dipper, whose handle contains the North Star.

The "P" on the rock told slaves that they were in the free state of Pennsylvania.

Henry "Box" Brown shipped himself to freedom in a box. Later, on a speaking tour against slavery, he used the box as a platform.

Slave tag and runaway ad.

$150 REWARD

RANAWAY from the subscriber, on the night of the 2d instant, a negro man, who calls himself Henry Mng...

CRITICAL THINKING

1. How did the success of the Underground Railroad reflect the American people's division over slavery?
2. What can you conclude from the map about Mexico's position on slavery?
3. **Geographic Theme: Movement** In what way did the Underground Railroad differ from other migrations?

More than just maps, geography affects where and how we live, work, and play. In these special geography pages you'll read about slaves' passages to freedom, the battle that decided the fate of this nation, America's vacation highway, and much more.

Thinking critically means using information, not just repeating it. Critical thinking questions appear throughout the book.

American LITERATURE

Johnny Tremain
ESTHER FORBES

Johnny Tremain, by Esther Forbes, tells the story of a fourteen-year-old apprentice silversmith in Boston during the early years of the American Revolution. Johnny becomes a spy for the Committee of Public Safety, a Patriot group preparing to fight the British. In the excerpt below, Johnny tries to get information about a British plan to stop the Patriots.

The very night—crow darkness—the men would move, but in what direction? And who would obey catchlines? Surely

Analyzing Literature

1. What is the importance of the colonel's choice of saddles?
2. Does Johnny want Dove to talk by asking direct questions? Explain.

Tell it in a story—or a poem or a song. Every unit contains literature excerpts that reflect the time period covered.

Daily Life

OF NATIVE AMERICANS TODAY

There are almost 2 million Native Americans in the United States. They live in cities and on reservations, hold modern jobs and practice ancient traditions. The photographs on these pages give a taste of the diversity of Native American life today.

This class is meeting in a school on a Hopi reservation in Arizona. For a long time, American Indians had little say in the education of their children and the management of their reservations. In recent years, laws have given Indians more control over their lives and lands.

In 1993 Ben Nighthorse Campbell became the first American Indian to serve in the Senate since 1929. Campbell traces his roots to the Northern Cheyenne.

Centuries ago Iroquois teams played lacrosse on giant fields for days on end. Today the Iroquois National team (shown above playing England) follows modern rules. The team proudly marches under its own flag in the world championships.

The Northwest Indians no longer rely on their great wooden canoes, but they have not lost their skill at carving them. Forty canoes made from ancient cedar trees participated in the "Paddle to Seattle" Celebration shown below.

In the 1800s American Indians were told to give up their languages and become English speakers. Today they are once again studying traditional languages. Durbin Feeling, shown right, teaches Cherokee to his grandson using an alphabet first developed in the 1820s.

Celinda McKelvey combines two ancient Navajo traditions to create a new one. The designs on her pots are inspired by sandpaintings, which are part of the Navajo healing ceremony. Celinda learned this style of pottery from her mother, Lucy.

What was it really like to live in colonial Boston or to be a Civil War foot soldier or to work in a sweatshop? These Daily Life pages show the lives of average Americans at different times in our history.

Links with the present and with world events are part of every chapter.

CONNECTING WITH THE PRESENT   WOMEN IN VIETNAM

They were said to have young faces and old eyes. The thousands of U.S. Army nurses who served in Vietnam walked among mangled bodies and felt the impact of falling bombs. Like other veterans, they received no hero's welcome when they returned home.

On Veteran's Day, in November 1993, a bronze statue (left) was dedicated in Washington, D.C. It shows two women helping a wounded soldier. At the ceremony, one veteran noted, "It took a long time to figure out that what we did during the Vietnam War was very important."

The decal above reminds Americans of the Vietnam War's POWs (Prisoners Of War) and MIAs (soldiers Missing In Action)

South Vietnamese army. It also meant bombing targets in North and South Vietnam, to prove that the United States remained committed to the South. In the end, more bombs were dropped on Vietnam—a country the size of New Mexico—

involved in foreign conflicts. Relatives of MIAs—soldiers listed as Missing In Action—would pray for years that their loved ones would return alive. For all of these reasons, the Vietnam War remains a painful scar in American history.

History comes to life when we see how it touches us. The History and You pages show how events became real for those who lived through them or for later generations.

HISTORY AND YOU

Alligator Stampede!
Spanish Words in English

The language we use daily mirrors our society. When customs and ideas from different cultures become part of our lives, the language we speak changes. For example, over many generations our Spanish heritage has brought new words into American English. "Taco," "burrito," and "salsa" might come quickly to mind. Other words, such as "plaza," "tornado," and "cigar," also have Spanish origins. *El lagarto* means "the lizard" in Spanish. If you say the two Spanish words quickly so that they run together, you can hear how the English word "alligator" came about.

Imagine the crashing sound of a cowherd in a headlong rush. Amid the noise, your Spanish friends yell *estampeda!* You can hear only part of the word. You shout to your English-speaking friends, "stampede!"

Spanish culture and language shaped the American West, from Texas to the Pacific Coast. Like lands in central Spain, the western plains suited cattle raising. Spaniards brought horses to this new countryside and practiced ranching. Vaqueros, or cowboys, herded cattle on horseback (and sometimes saw stampedes). Several words now used in English come from this way of life—"ranch" (from *rancho* and *ranchero*), "bonanza," "lasso," "lariat," "corral," "bronco," "mustang," and "rodeo," for example.

Many place names in the United States reflect our Spanish heritage. City names, such as El Paso, Santa Fe, San Diego, Los Angeles; and state names, such as Texas, Colorado, California, Florida, and Montana, are a few examples. In 1513, even before Spanish explorer Ponce de León got off his ship, he named the new land he saw "Florida." From the ship, he could see the blooms of hundreds of flowers, or flora.

CRITICAL THINKING
1. What words and phrases from different languages do you use in everyday speech?
2. Why would you expect American English to contain words from many different languages?
3. Is the diversity of American English a strength or a weakness? Explain.

566

Mary Antin remembered:

❝ Jews who escaped the pogroms came to Polotsk with wounds on them, and horrible, horrible stories. . . . Only to hear these things made one sob and sob and choke with pain. People who saw such things never smiled any more, no matter how long they lived: and sometimes their hair turned white in a day, and some people became insane on the spot. ❞

Eager to leave, Mary Antin's father made his way from Polotsk to Boston, Massachusetts. Three years later when Mary was thirteen, she and the rest of her family joined him.

The Importance of Education
More than anything, Mary Antin's father wanted his children to receive an education. He believed that education was "the treasure no thief could touch, not even misfortune or poverty."

The American school system was expanding even faster than the nation's population in these years. In time, schools took over some of the tasks that had once belonged to parents and churches. Schools were expected to teach children citizenship, proper social behavior, and the skills to earn a living.

After 1870, cities and states began to pass laws requiring children to attend school until they reached a certain age. The number of children attending school more than doubled between 1870 and 1900.

Educators faced a difficult task. They had to educate children who came from different backgrounds and spoke different languages. To help schools become more efficient, educators looked to the factory as a model.

One result of this was a system of grades that organized students by age. Standards

CULTURAL MOSAIC

IRVING BERLIN
(1888–1989)

A Russian child named Israel Baline grew up to become one of America's great songwriters—Irving Berlin. Berlin's family fled the pogroms and came to New York City when he was a child. As a young man, he taught himself music and began writing popular songs. He was drafted into the army in 1918, where he entertained troops with his music. Americans sang his patriotic tunes during World Wars I and II, and his musicals were hits on Broadway. In his lifetime, Berlin wrote over 1,000 songs, such as "You'll Be Surprised" (below). His holiday classic, "White Christmas," is one of the most popular songs of all time.

were set for each grade. The marking system, courses, and textbooks became standardized. Schools also added vocational courses. Classes in carpentry, metalwork, and sewing were offered.

Many working families needed the money earned by their children. So, despite new school attendance laws, these families chose not to send their children to school. In Mary Antin's family, the oldest daughter, Frieda, went to work so that Mary could go to school. Mary understood the sacrifice her sister made for her.

People you'll remember. Songwriters, generals, poets, inventors, spies, and more are described in these biographies.

Basic Map Skills: UNDERSTANDING A MAP

Though maps can be quite different, they all have certain features that are alike. Every part of a map tells you something important. You can understand maps better once you know how to use these features.

The **title** tells you the place shown on the map. Usually, the title also tells you what kind of map you are using.

The **grid** is made up of lines that form a pattern of squares on a map. The lines have numbers or letters to help you find a place. This map's grid is made up of lines of **latitude** and lines of **longitude**. Lines of **latitude** run east to west around the globe. Lines of **longitude** run around the globe from the North Pole to the South Pole.

An **inset** is a small map inside a larger one. The inset shows a different area or gives different information than the larger map does. On this map, Alaska and Hawaii are in insets. They are so far away from the other states that they do not fit on the larger map.

United States: Years of Entry into the Union

The map below is a historical map of the United States. It gives information about an earlier time in history. From this map, you'll learn when each state entered the Union. You'll also learn about some important map parts.

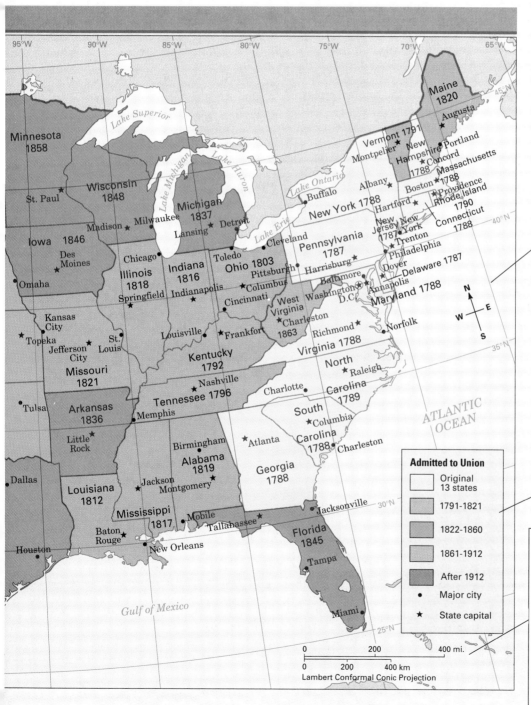

The **compass rose** shows which way the directions north (**N**), south (**S**), east (**E**), and west (**W**) point on the map.

The **legend,** or **key,** tells what the symbols and colors on the map mean. On this legend each color shows one time period when some states entered the Union.

Admitted to Union
- Original 13 states
- 1791-1821
- 1822-1860
- 1861-1912
- After 1912
- • Major city
- ★ State capital

The **scale** tells how much smaller the map is than the area it shows. The scale helps you measure distances on the map. This scale shows that one and one-half inches on the map equal 400 miles on earth.

Basic Map Skills: GLOSSARY OF GEOGRAPHIC TERMS

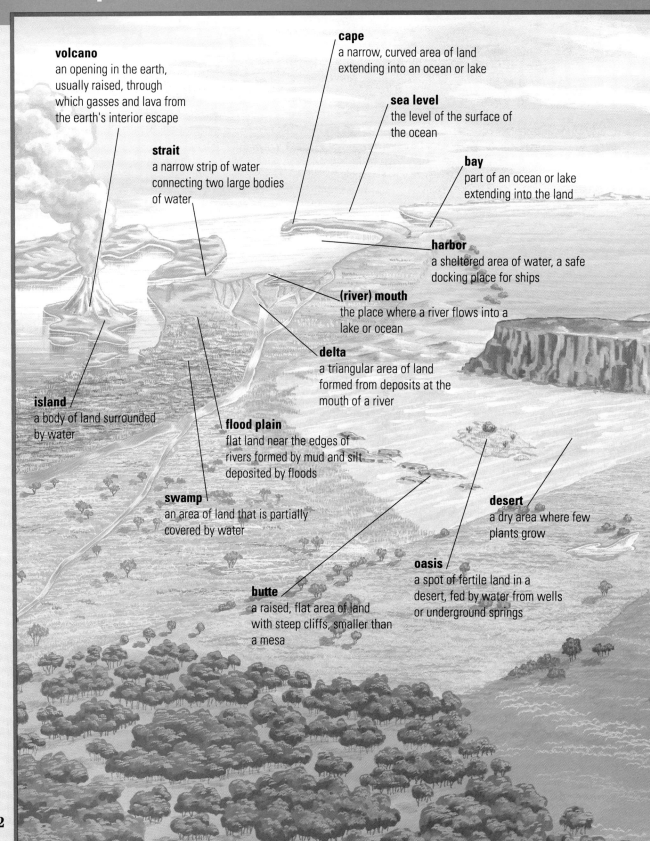

volcano
an opening in the earth, usually raised, through which gasses and lava from the earth's interior escape

cape
a narrow, curved area of land extending into an ocean or lake

sea level
the level of the surface of the ocean

strait
a narrow strip of water connecting two large bodies of water

bay
part of an ocean or lake extending into the land

harbor
a sheltered area of water, a safe docking place for ships

(river) mouth
the place where a river flows into a lake or ocean

delta
a triangular area of land formed from deposits at the mouth of a river

island
a body of land surrounded by water

flood plain
flat land near the edges of rivers formed by mud and silt deposited by floods

swamp
an area of land that is partially covered by water

desert
a dry area where few plants grow

oasis
a spot of fertile land in a desert, fed by water from wells or underground springs

butte
a raised, flat area of land with steep cliffs, smaller than a mesa

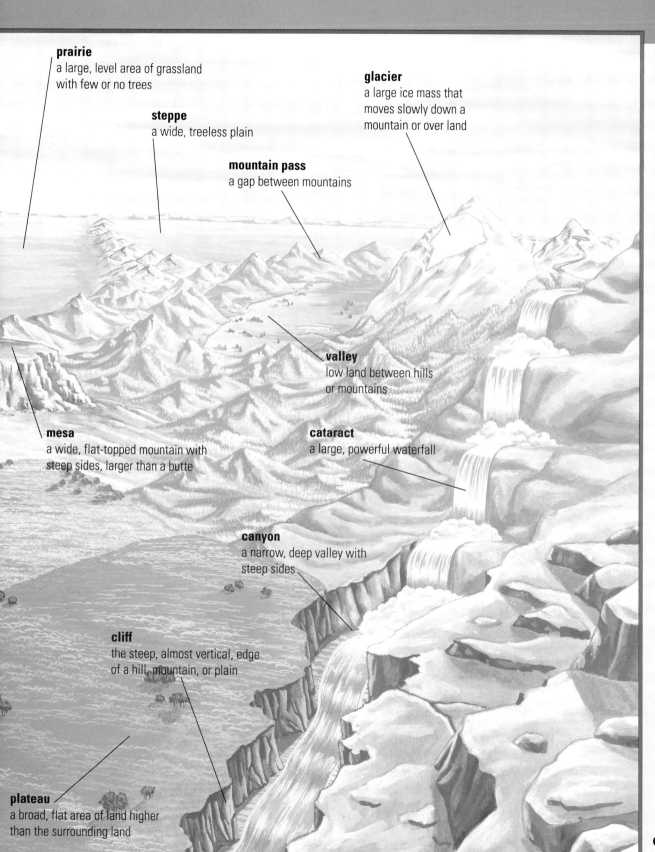

prairie
a large, level area of grassland with few or no trees

glacier
a large ice mass that moves slowly down a mountain or over land

steppe
a wide, treeless plain

mountain pass
a gap between mountains

valley
low land between hills or mountains

mesa
a wide, flat-topped mountain with steep sides, larger than a butte

cataract
a large, powerful waterfall

canyon
a narrow, deep valley with steep sides

cliff
the steep, almost vertical, edge of a hill, mountain, or plain

plateau
a broad, flat area of land higher than the surrounding land

Map Projections

A flat map cannot show how the earth curves. It stretches out some land and water areas. When a mapmaker draws the whole earth, it is a projection of the earth's surface. Different mapmakers have created different projections. Gerhardus Mercator drew the Mercator Projection in 1569. German mapmaker Arno Peters drew the Peters Projection in 1974.

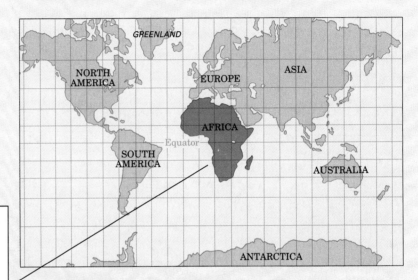

The Mercator Projection shows most of the continents as they look on a globe. However, the projection stretches out the lands near the North Pole and South Pole. Africa is highlighted in red. Compare the different size of Africa on this projection and on the one below.

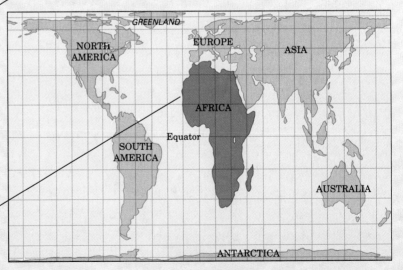

Compare the shapes of the continents on this Peters Projection with those on a globe. This projection's continents are the right size but the shapes of the continents are not as they appear on a globe. Compare the shape of South America to its shape on a globe.

The Five Geographic Themes

One way that geographers think about their subject is in terms of major themes, or ideas that run through teaching and learning about geography. They are described in greater detail below.

As you continue to learn about geography—and to see how it applies to history, science, and many other parts of everyday life—try to become aware of these themes. "Thinking geographically" can give you a new outlook on the world around you.

 ## Location

This theme can be expressed as, "Where in the world are we?" One way to answer this question is through the coordinates of latitude and longitude on the grid system. These can give you the accurate, *absolute* location of any place on earth.

In ordinary speech, you are more likely to describe location in a different way. To the question, "Where is it?" people often answer in terms of something else: next door, or south of the Mason-Dixon Line. Phrases like these point out *relative* location.

 ## Place

Place and *location* mean about the same thing in ordinary speech but have special meanings in geography. The idea of "place" goes beyond the idea of where something is. It includes the special characteristics that make one place different from another. *Physical* characteristics of any place are its natural features, such as landscape, physical setting, plants and animals, and weather. *Human* characteristics include the things people have made—from language and philosophy to buildings.

 ## Interactions

For millions of years, people have interacted with their natural environment. Sometimes they have changed it, leveling hills to build highways or plowing the prairies to plant wheat. Sometimes the environment has changed them, forcing them to invent ways of coping with extremes of hot or cold, natural disasters, floods, and other problems.

 ## Movement

People in different places interact through travel, trade, transportation, and communication. For much of the 1800s, the United States relied on its natural defenses of two great oceans to protect itself from potential enemies. Today, even if Americans wished to isolate themselves, this would be impossible. Computers, television, satellite hookups, and other forms of communication have increased the movement of people, things, and ideas from place to place.

 ## Regions

Just as you cannot study an entire subject at once, geographers do not try to study the whole world. They break it into regions. A region can be as large as a continent or as small as a neighborhood, but it has certain shared characteristics that set it apart. The simplest way to define a region is by one characteristic, such as political division, type of climate, language spoken, or religious belief.

Review of Basic Map Skills

KEY TERMS

Define the following terms.
1. latitude
2. longitude
3. inset
4. projection
5. key
6. scale
7. plateau
8. mesa

COMPREHENSION

Use the maps and other information in this section to answer the following questions.

1. In the map below, what information does the key provide?

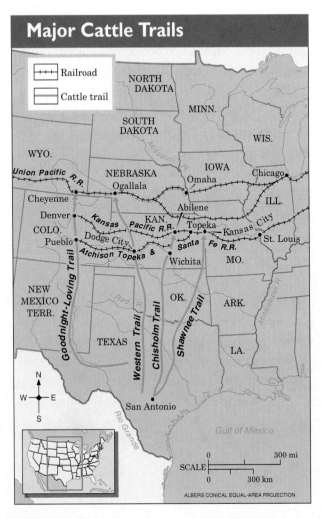

Major Cattle Trails

Railroad

Cattle trail

2. Using the map on this page, list the names of three railroads and three cattle trails.
3. What is the purpose of a map grid?
4. What is the capital of Tennessee?
5. What states joined the Union in 1889?
6. Which is the capital of New Mexico, Albuquerque or Santa Fe? How do you know?
7. Which two states do not border any other U.S. state?
8. Was New York one of the original thirteen states? How do you know?
9. What are the five geographic themes?
10. What is a region?

CRITICAL THINKING

1. Look at the map on page G1. Why are different scales provided for both of the inset maps as well as the main map? What do the scales tell you about the relative sizes of Alaska and Hawaii?
2. Why do different map projections make the sizes and shapes of continents look different?
3. Choose a place, such as your home or school, and describe its physical and human characteristics.
4. Describe the theme of movement from the point of view of someone who lived in the 1500s. Then describe the theme from the point of view of someone alive today.

ACTIVITIES

1. Find the grid coordinates for your community. Then find the "opposite" places in the eastern and southern hemispheres.
2. Make a poster display showing the geographic characteristics of your state. The display should include an outline map of your state plus such information as the location of your state capital, notable natural features, and neighboring states.

HISTORICAL ATLAS OF THE
UNITED STATES

The following series of maps allows you to see the growth of the United States just as it took place, by stages. The map on the next page shows the geography of the United States: its mountains, plains, and valleys. The green part of the map shows the area of the United States in 1790. Below the map is a graph listing the U.S. population at that time.

By turning the transparent overlays one at a time, you can see how this nation expanded. The maps record political as well as territorial growth, listing new states and the years in which they joined the Union. Also shown are increases in population over time.

The last map in this Historical Atlas shows the United States as it appears today. On the other side of that map is a timeline of American expansion. The events listed there and shown on the maps help you see that the United States grew from 13 states to 50, from 4 million people to more than 250 million, and from a small to a mighty nation.

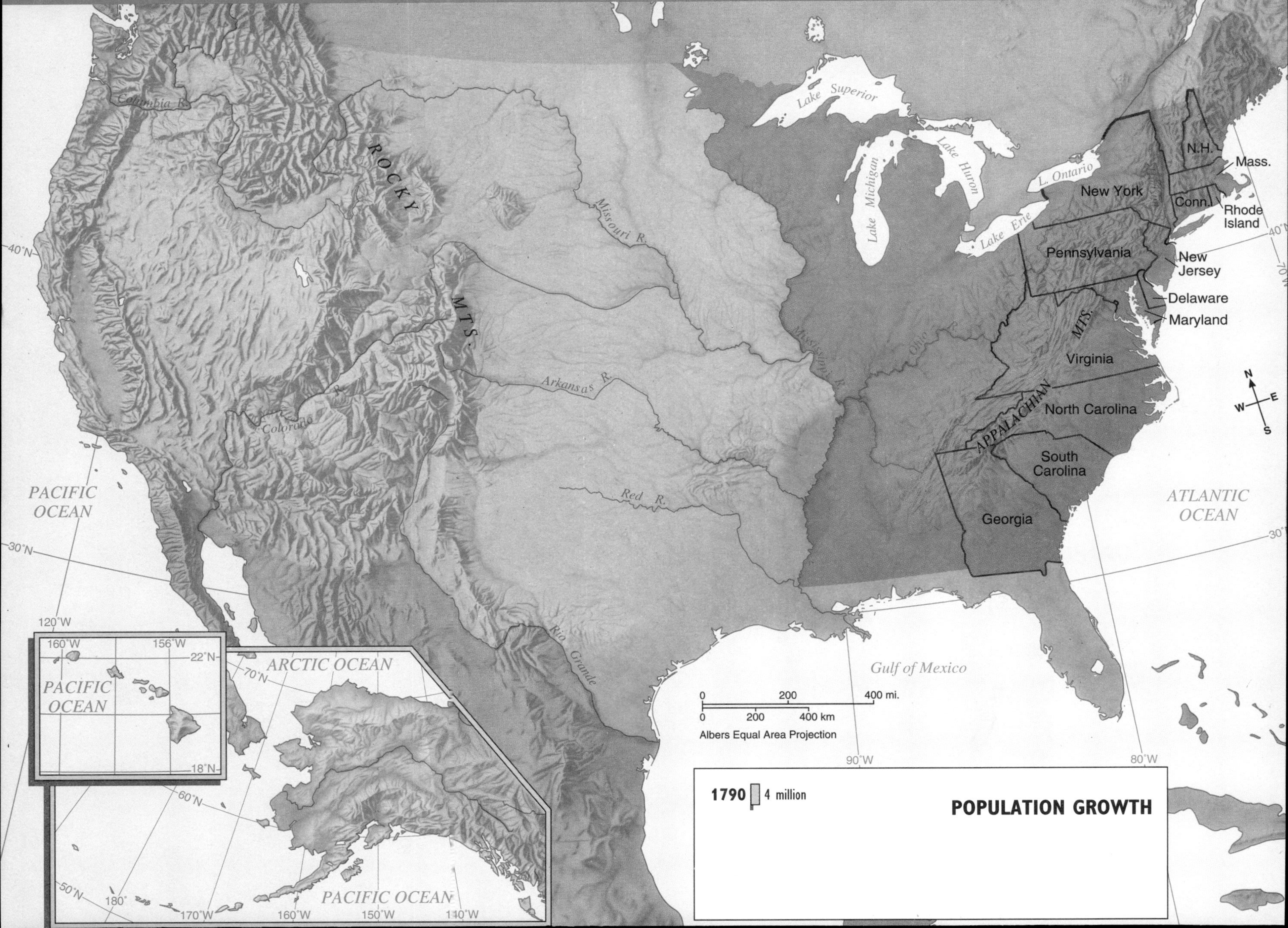

POPULATION GROWTH

1790 ▨ 4 million

400 mi.

400 km

200

200

0

Albers Equal Area Projection

ATLANTIC OCEAN

N.H.
Mass.
Conn.
Rhode Island
New Jersey
Delaware
Maryland
New York
Pennsylvania
Virginia
North Carolina
South Carolina
Georgia

APPALACHIAN MTS.

L. Ontario
Lake Erie
Lake Huron
Lake Michigan
Lake Superior

Gulf of Mexico

Mississippi R.

Missouri R.

Arkansas R.

Red R.

Rio Grande

Colorado R.

ROCKY MTS.

PACIFIC OCEAN

ARCTIC OCEAN

PACIFIC OCEAN

70°W
80°W
90°W
40°N
30°N
30°W

22°N
18°N
156°W
160°W
120°W
60°N
70°N
130°W
150°W
160°W
170°W
180°
50°N

The United States—Today

N E
S

ATLANTIC OCEAN

Maine
Mass.
Rhode Island
N.H.
VT.
Conn.
New York
New Jersey
Delaware
Maryland
Pennsylvania
Virginia
West Virginia
North Carolina
South Carolina
Georgia
Florida
Ohio
Kentucky
Tennessee
Alabama
Mississippi
Louisiana
Indiana
Illinois
Michigan
Wisconsin
Minnesota
Iowa
Missouri
Arkansas
Oklahoma
Texas
Kansas
Nebraska
South Dakota
North Dakota
Montana
Wyoming
Colorado
New Mexico
Arizona
Utah
Nevada
Idaho
Oregon
Washington
California

ROCKY MTS
APPALACHIAN MTS

Lake Superior
Lake Michigan
Lake Huron
Lake Erie
Lake Ontario
Hudson R.
Ohio R.
Mississippi R.
Missouri R.
Arkansas R.
Red R.
Rio Grande
Columbia R.

Gulf of Mexico
PACIFIC OCEAN
ARCTIC OCEAN

Albers Equal Area Projection

0   200   400 mi.
0   200   400 km

POPULATION GROWTH

1790 — 4 million
1820 — 9.6 million
1860 — 31.4 million
1920 — 105.7 million
1990 — 250 million

Alaska 1959

70°N
60°N
160°W
150°W
140°W
PACIFIC OCEAN

0   300   600 mi.
0   300   600 km

Hawaii 1959
22°N
20°N
18°N
160°W   156°W
PACIFIC OCEAN

0   150 mi.
0   150 km

40 N
70 W
80 W
90 W
30 N
40 N
120 W

AMERICA'S
PAST AND PROMISE

UNIT
1

A New Atlantic World
(Beginnings–1700)

UNIT OVERVIEW

Christopher Columbus's voyage to the Americas in 1492 helped lead to contacts among the peoples of the Americas, Africa, and Europe.

Chapter 1

The First Americans (Beginnings–1492)
North and South America were home to a diverse group of Native American peoples.

Chapter 2

Peoples of West Africa (Beginnings–1591)
Trading kingdoms of West Africa established ties with Europe beginning in the 1400s.

Chapter 3

Europeans Reach Outward (400–1522)
Searching for new trade routes, Europeans voyaged to Asia and the Americas.

Chapter 4

Spain Builds an Empire (1493–1700)
Spain followed Columbus's discoveries by invading and colonizing parts of the "New World."

Illustration: Cortés's conquest of Mexico.

Long before Christopher Columbus sailed west from Europe, people had settled the Americas. This photograph, taken around 1900, shows James A. Garfield Velarde. Velarde was a Jicarilla Apache, one of America's many Indian peoples.

| 12,000 B.C. | 10,000 | 8000 | 6000 |

c. 9500 B.C. Clovis people

c. 12,000 B.C. Ocean covers Beringia

The First Americans
(Beginnings–1492)

1 People Arrive in the Americas

SECTION GUIDE

Main Idea
People first arrived in the Americas many thousands of years ago. Over time they developed new ways of life, such as farming.

Goals
As you read, look for answers to these questions:

1 How did people first arrive in the Americas?

2 How did people's lives change once they had a stable food supply?

Key Terms
Paleo-Indian
artifact
migrate
culture
domestication
civilization

R ISING HIGH ABOVE the dry plains of New Mexico is a great sandstone rock—El Morro, or Inscription Rock. At the foot of the rock is a spring and a small pond of fresh water—the only water for miles around. On the sheer sandstone walls one can see where past travelers have carved their names. They include Spanish explorers from the early 1600s and American explorers from the 1800s. The oldest carvings, however, are those of American Indians. Few places in North America make it so clear that a study of American history must start with the history of the Native Americans, the first settlers of this continent.

The Paleo-Indians

We now know a good deal about the first people in the Americas. Those people are called **Paleo-Indians** from palaios, the Greek word for "ancient." Scientists have examined skeletons and **artifacts** —items made by humans. They have also studied American Indians, the descendants of the first Americans. (The term Indian, used in this book to describe Native Americans, comes from a mistake made by Christopher Columbus when he first reached the Americas. He thought he had arrived in the Indies of Asia, so he called the people he saw Indians.)

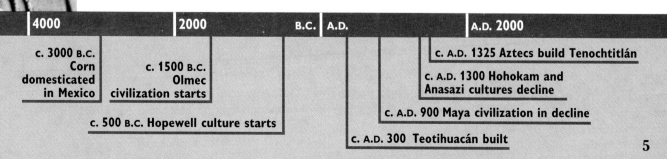

4000	2000	B.C.	A.D.	A.D. 2000

c. 3000 B.C. Corn domesticated in Mexico

c. 1500 B.C. Olmec civilization starts

c. 500 B.C. Hopewell culture starts

c. A.D. 300 Teotihuacán built

c. A.D. 900 Maya civilization in decline

c. A.D. 1300 Hohokam and Anasazi cultures decline

c. A.D. 1325 Aztecs build Tenochtitlán

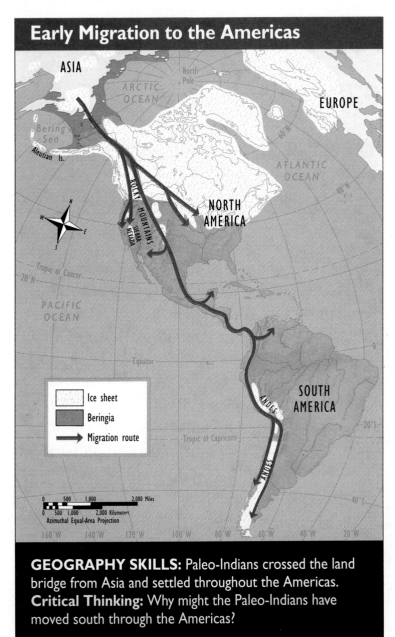

Early Migration to the Americas

GEOGRAPHY SKILLS: Paleo-Indians crossed the land bridge from Asia and settled throughout the Americas.
Critical Thinking: Why might the Paleo-Indians have moved south through the Americas?

sands of years. During this time much of the world's water froze. The level of the oceans dropped, uncovering land between western Alaska and eastern Russia. As a result, the continents of Asia and North America were connected by a 1,000-mile-wide "bridge." Beringia, the name given this bridge, existed where the Bering Strait is now. Then the earth warmed, and the rising ocean covered up Beringia. The ice age ended about 10,000 years ago.

Some scientists think that Paleo-Indians may have come by boat as well as by land. In any case, there are signs that suggest that people were living in the Americas more than 25,000 years ago.

The Hunters

Scientists do agree that a group of big-game hunters they call the Clovis people thrived in North America from about 11,500 to 11,000 years ago. The Clovis people worked together to hunt such elephant-like animals as the mammoth and mastodon. To do so they used spears with sharp, carefully crafted spearpoints.

Then, about 11,000 years ago, North America's largest mammals, including mammoths, became extinct. No one knows exactly why the big animals died off. One theory is that the climate was warming too fast for the animals to adapt. Another theory is that the Clovis people killed off the mammoths. The Clovis people disappeared at about the same time.

Growing Diversity

Whatever caused the mammoths to disappear, people had to change in order to survive. Hunters began to make different spear points with which to hunt a broader range of animals, including bison (buffalo). People also fished.

A hunting-gathering **culture** began to take shape. (A culture is a way of life shared by people who have similar arts, beliefs, customs, and methods of doing things.)

After looking at blood types, human genes, teeth, and languages, many scholars have decided that the first Americans probably came from northern Asia. Most Native American cultures teach that their people originated in the Americas. Even scientists are not sure when or how the ancient Indians **migrated** (moved) from Asia.

Paleo-Indians may have walked to North America during the last ice age. This was a time of extreme cold that lasted for thou-

Hunter-gatherers learned from observation. A woman collecting grass seeds, for instance, would have seen that seeds sprout in moist and fertile soil. From that understanding it was but one step to planting seeds. Over time, many hunter-gatherers became farmers. The result was the domestication of a wide variety of plants. (Domestication is breeding plants or animals to meet specific human needs, such as food and transportation.) In time the Indians domesticated more than 100 plants. Of these, corn was one of the most important.

About 5,000 years ago people in central Mexico began to sow the seeds of wild corn. From wild corn the size of a strawberry, farmers developed a corn cob like the one today. This corn had a closed husk that prevented birds from eating the kernels. Dried, the corn would last months and even years. The domestication of corn meant a more stable food supply.

A Hopi woman (left) grinds corn as her ancestors did thousands of years ago. Since then, an ear of corn has grown in size and quality (below). **Critical Thinking:** Why was the domestication of corn important in American history?

A Settled Life

The development of a stable food supply brought huge changes in the way people lived. If people did not have to move in search of food, they could stay in one place, building permanent settlements. They also had more leisure time, since farming allowed people to build up stocks of food.

As farming improved, more food was produced. Some people were freed to do other things. They could become expert at making pots in which to store food. Others could become excellent weavers. A few could devote themselves to serving as religious leaders. The culture became more complex. A society with cities, specialized jobs for different people, and a complex culture is known as a civilization.

Farming was the most common way to ensure a stable food supply. However, some societies achieved the same result by harvesting sea life. Still other societies used trade as the basis of a settled life. As societies became more complex, their governments became more complex as well.

SECTION REVIEW

1. Key Terms Paleo-Indian, artifact, migrate, culture, domestication, civilization

2. Places Bering Strait, Mexico

3. Comprehension Where was Beringia and why does it no longer exist?

4. Comprehension How did people's way of life change when their main source of food, the mammoth, died off?

5. Critical Thinking Why do many historians consider the development of farming to be one of the great revolutions in human history?

2 Ancient North America

SECTION GUIDE

Main Idea
Highly advanced Indian societies developed in North America.

Goals
As you read, look for answers to these questions:

1. Why are the Olmec called the "mother culture" of Mesoamerica?

2. How did civilizations develop in the Valley of Mexico?

3. What cultures developed in North America?

Key Terms
empire
famine
irrigation

NOT FAR FROM Mexico City there rises a pyramid twenty stories high, nearly as large at its base as the greatest of Egypt's pyramids. Like those in Egypt, it has a core of mud bricks surrounded by walls of stone. Known as the Pyramid of the Sun, it is but one of the monuments built by ancient peoples of the Americas. The Pyramid of the Sun is a symbol of how advanced ancient Americans became. Only a well organized people who understood mathematics and engineering could have built such a monument.

The Olmec

The first civilization in the Western Hemisphere arose in Mesoamerica. This region of North America extends from central Mexico south to the Isthmus of Panama. (This isthmus, or narrow strip of land, separates North and South America.)

The "mother culture" of Mesoamerican civilizations was that of the Olmec. The Olmec culture developed on the Gulf of Mexico. This was a rain forest, humid and swampy. In this area, starting at about 1500 B.C., the Olmec introduced traditions and skills that would influence Mesoamerica for centuries.

The Olmec built, not cities, but large religious centers that featured earthen temple mounds. They were the first in this hemisphere to use symbols and images to express words and ideas. They may also have been the first to develop a calendar system. The Olmec traded by land and sea with other parts of the hemisphere. In this way their culture spread.

The Maya

Among those influenced by the Olmec were the Maya. The Maya lived in the tropical rain forest of what is now Guatemala. They too had ceremonial centers. These centers were home to the priests and nobles who controlled the surrounding coun-

Olmec artists produced giant stone statues. This helmeted head may have been a priest or ruler.

tryside. The power of these leaders probably came from their knowledge of astronomy and the calendar. The Maya were the first in the world to invent a symbol for zero. The Maya calendar was one of the most accurate ever developed.

The Maya also developed a game that used a rubber ball. The game became popular with later cultures as well. Ruins of the playing courts, with their low, sloping walls, can be found throughout Mesoamerica. The contest, in which players scored points by hitting markers or hoops, was often a religious observance. Ballgames were still being played when the Spanish arrived. Impressed by the sport, the Spaniards introduced Europeans to the use of rubber balls in games and team play.

Maya culture declined in the Guatemala lowlands starting about A.D. 900, perhaps because of wars between Maya cities. The culture continued for centuries more, however, at sites in the Yucatán Peninsula.

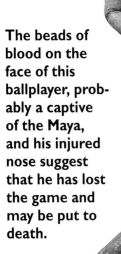

The beads of blood on the face of this ballplayer, probably a captive of the Maya, and his injured nose suggest that he has lost the game and may be put to death.

The Goddess of Teotihuacán was worshiped as the ruler of nature, fertility, and water. **Critical Thinking:** Why might the artist have painted her with flowers in her hands?

In the Valley of Mexico

Meanwhile, people living in the Valley of Mexico were also developing a complex society. By A.D. 300 they had built the city of Teotihuacán (tay-uh-tee-wah-KAHN). Three hundred years later it was one of the largest cities in the world. It was also a planned city, with neighborhoods for people of different jobs and different backgrounds.

The priest-rulers of the city lived in great stone-and-plaster houses decorated with carvings and murals. A common image on the murals is that of the Goddess of Teotihuacán, shown above.

One temple within Teotihuacán was dedicated to the god Quetzalcóatl (ket-sahl-ko-AHT-ehl), symbolized by a feathered serpent. Quetzalcóatl was considered the defender of good against evil. To keep such gods happy, the people of Teotihuacán made sacrifices of birds, animals, flowers, and, on occasion, humans.

No amount of sacrifice, however, could protect the city forever. The city collapsed about A.D. 750. Evidence points to a violent end with rulers murdered and temples burned. Scholars think the city was destroyed by a revolution of its own people, not by conquest.

The Aztecs

In the early 1200s the Aztecs, invaders from the north, came to the Valley of Mexico. In about 1325 they settled a snake-infested island in Lake Texcoco (tay-SKOH-koh). A practical people, they ate the snakes. They built a city, Tenochtitlán (teh-nawch-TEE-tlahn). Then they began to conquer their neighbors. The conquered peoples were forced to pay offerings of goods and produce to the Aztecs. With these offerings flowing in, the Aztecs did not have to work for food. They were free to expand their army and conquer more peoples. In this way, most of central Mexico became part of the Aztec **empire.** (An empire is a number of peoples or lands controlled by one nation or ruler.)

About 1450 a drought of four years struck the Valley of Mexico. This period of low rainfall led to a terrible **famine,** or shortage of food. For the Aztecs, it also meant a loss of power. In an appeal to the gods to end the drought, the frantic Aztecs began a practice of mass human sacrifice.

After the drought ended, Aztec power again grew. Tenochtitlán became one of the great cities of the world. In 1500, few places could rival in beauty or size this island city of about 250,000 people.

Peoples of the Southwest

The Aztecs and other peoples of Meso-america influenced their neighbors to the north. About 4,000 years ago, people living in the deserts of the American Southwest began raising corn and squash. Later they learned to grow beans. Over time, they developed farming cultures that depended on what American Indians called the "Three Sisters"—corn, squash, and beans.

Agriculture in the desert is difficult without a steady source of water. The Hohokam people of what is now central Arizona adapted to this environment. They built dams to collect water and dug canals to bring that water to their crops.

This practice of bringing water to crops, called **irrigation,** influenced the Anasazi people of the Colorado Plateau. The Anasazi began to build small dams and ditches to water their crops. Like many farming peoples of North America, the Anasazi also hunted game and gathered wild plants, seeds, and nuts.

Over time, Anasazi society became quite complex. They built entire towns in the walls of canyons. They also built Pueblo Bonito, a ceremonial and trading center in

Chaco Canyon, New Mexico. Roads 30 feet wide went out from Pueblo Bonito. A thousand years ago people traveled these roads carrying wood, pottery, cloth, baskets, and turquoise. The turquoise most often ended up in the markets of faraway Mexico, where it was highly valued.

After A.D. 1300 both the Hohokam and Anasazi cultures went into decline. No one knows why. Some scholars think that a terrible drought caused a breakdown of these societies. The people moved to other places, such as the Rio Grande Valley and present-day Hopi and Zuni lands. Their descendants live there still.

Mound Cultures

Cultures also developed in the Eastern Woodlands of North America. These woodlands extend from the Atlantic Ocean to the Great Plains. The most complex of these cultures was the Hopewell culture in the Ohio Valley. It lasted more than a thousand years, from about 500 B.C. to A.D. 700.

The religion of the Hopewell culture focused on death rituals. The people buried their leaders in huge mounds. With the dead, the Hopewell people buried all the wealth that the deceased would need in the next world. In one burial site alone, archeologists found thousands of pearl beads, necklaces of grizzly-bear teeth, and copper ornaments.

About A.D. 700 the Hopewell people took to the hills, where they built large earthworks for defense. Obviously there was unrest in the land, perhaps an invading people. These earthworks are the last evidence of the Hopewell culture.

In Chaco Canyon, New Mexico, the ruins of Pueblo Bonito illustrate the advanced culture of the Anasazi. Their engineering skills ensured that doorways, such as those shown upper right, line up perfectly. **Critical Thinking:** How could a drought destroy a society?

This painting from 1850 shows the cross section of a mound being dug up in Louisiana. **Critical Thinking:** Why might the Indians have held religious ceremonies on top of the mounds?

Mississippian Culture

About the same time, another mound culture emerged in the Southeast and the Mississippi Valley. This is known as the Mississippian culture.

The Mississippian people built towns on the river flood plains. Such locations were good for farming because floods constantly enriched the soil. The rivers also made it easy for traders to come and go by canoe. Mississippian towns featured large flat-topped mounds on which were built temples, meeting houses, and the homes of chiefs and priests. (The mounds were also a refuge in times of flood.)

The culture had clear ties with Mexico. Common symbols in Mississippian art were the falcon and the jaguar. Both of these animals had long been honored in Mesoamerica.

The jewel of the Mississippian culture was Cahokia, in what is now western Illinois. Cahokia once boasted 30,000 residents and more than 100 mounds. The tallest mound at Cahokia rises ten stories from a sixteen-acre base. Near the mound, archeologists discovered a circular pattern of posts. The shadows cast by the posts may have served as a kind of calendar for the people. By keeping track of the sun's position, priests could tell farmers when to sow crops.

Parts of the Mississippian culture lasted to about 1700. Thus we know something about the culture from the Europeans who first traveled in the lower Mississippi Valley. These explorers caught a glimpse of the splendor of Mississippian culture.

Later Indians of the region could not say who built the mounds. Yet there seems little doubt that many of the Southeast Indian cultures are descendants of the mound builders.

SECTION REVIEW

1. Key Terms empire, famine, irrigation

2. Peoples Olmec, Maya, Aztecs, Hohokam, Anasazi, Hopewell, Mississippian

3. Comprehension What are some achievements of the ancient societies of Mesoamerica?

4. Comprehension How were the Hopewell and Mississippian cultures alike? How were they different?

5. Critical Thinking What kinds of events might lead to the decline and collapse of a society? Explain.

SKILLS: Reading a Timeline

LEARN

When you began this chapter, one of the first things you saw was a timeline. A timeline is a list of events and dates shown in the order in which they occurred. There is a timeline at the start of every chapter in this book. Each one gives you a preview of the main events in the chapter. Reading the timeline should be your first step toward organizing the information in the chapter.

Look at the timeline below. It focuses on one culture from this chapter's timeline. Notice that the earliest date is at the left and the latest is at the right because we read from left to right. A timeline may also run up and down. In that case the earliest date is usually at the top.

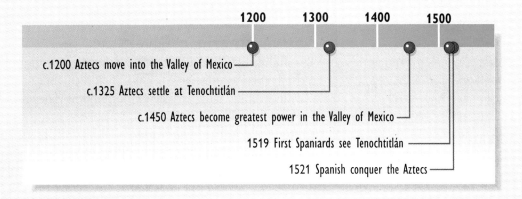

1200   1300   1400   1500

c.1200 Aztecs move into the Valley of Mexico

c.1325 Aztecs settle at Tenochtitlán

c.1450 Aztecs become greatest power in the Valley of Mexico

1519 First Spaniards see Tenochtitlán

1521 Spanish conquer the Aztecs

PRACTICE

1. What is the subject of the timeline shown above?

2. Which came first, the settlement of Tenochtitlán or the arrival of the Spanish?

3. How many years does the timeline cover?

APPLY

4. Choose one of the Native American peoples discussed in the chapter. Draw a timeline showing at least three events in the history of that culture. Use information from your textbook and from other reference books.

SECTION GUIDE

Main Idea
A variety of Indian groups lived in North America in 1492. Each had its own distinct culture.

Goals
As you read, look for answers to these questions:

❶ How did the geography of North America influence the way American Indians lived?

❷ How were the peoples of North America different? How were they similar?

Key Terms
tundra
technology
totem
slash-and-burn
constitution

IN 1492 THREE SHIPS led by Christopher Columbus landed in the Americas. The history of these continents took a dramatic turn that day. This section gives a snapshot of life in the different regions of what is now the United States at the time Columbus arrived. Though it is written in the past tense, this way of life has not completely disappeared. Many Native Americans continue to uphold the traditions and beliefs of their people. A glimpse of Native American life in the United States today follows this section.

Native American Diversity

Throughout their long history, Native American groups have moved from region to region. As they did so, they changed their ways as needed to live in a new environment. They also changed as they learned from each other.

Over time, Native Americans developed different languages and organized their societies in different ways. They were alike in one important way, however. Native Americans looked upon themselves as part of the environment in which they lived. They felt a spiritual connection to the animals, plants, and natural forces on which they depended. This connection was celebrated in the stories, songs, dances, prayers, and art of the different groups.

Dogs provided the power for transport over the ice and snow of the Eskimos' environment. Dogsleds are still part of the culture of the Far North.

Hunters of the North

One of the most challenging environments in the world is the Far North. The Eskimos, which in Alaska include the Inupiat and Yupik, lived in the arctic **tundra.** The tundra is a treeless region where the subsoil is permanently frozen. In the winter the temperature is below freezing and there is no sun for weeks at a time. Summer brings only a surface thaw of a foot or so.

Farming was impossible in this climate. The Eskimos hunted such land animals as polar bears and caribou (large deer related to the reindeer). They also hunted sea mammals by rowing out in the icy waters in kayaks, small boats with enclosed decks.

The Northwest Coast

Like the Eskimos, the Northwest Coast Indians looked to the sea for their food. Along the narrow coastal region from Alaska to California, summer and fall were a time of harvest—a sea harvest. Every year millions of salmon returned from the ocean to the coastal streams where they were born. As the salmon headed up the streams, Indians caught them with nets, spears, and traps. Cut in strips and dried, the salmon would form a principal part of the diet in the year to come.

In general the Northwest Coast was a region rich in marine (sea) foods. In addition to salmon, there were shellfish and marine mammals, such as seals, otters, and whales.

Trees of great height and diameter grow along the Northwest Coast. They include the redwoods of northern California and, farther north, cedars and firs. The Northwest Coast Indians therefore based much of their technology on the use of wood. (Technology is the use of tools to do things.) Their houses were made of wooden planks. Their ocean-going boats were hollowed out of huge logs and could be as long as 45 feet and as wide as 6 feet. They made capes and mats by weaving strips of bark. Their hats were wooden. They even cooked in wooden boxes by adding hot stones to the food.

The men were excellent woodcarvers, decorating their boats, houses, and boxes with intricate shapes. Many of the shapes represented **totems**—the animal spirits to which the carver claimed a special bond. Carvers also made huge totem poles to stand in front of their houses.

Wealth was very important to the Northwest culture. Status—one's standing in society—depended on how much wealth one had and how much wealth one could give away. At the great feasts called "potlatches," the host was expected to give presents to all the invited guests. The higher the status of the guest, the more valuable was the present.

Western Indians

The Indian people of the Columbia Plateau, the Great Basin, and California were also hunter-gatherers. Unlike their neighbors to the northwest, they did not rely on the sea. They hunted deer, elk, antelope, rabbits, and waterfowl. They also fished. In addition to nuts, they harvested berries, edible roots, and grass seed.

The Northwest Coast Indians used wooden boxes (left) for cooking as well as storage. Beautifully carved totem poles (far left) served as symbols of family background and history. **Critical Thinking:** What kinds of symbols do people use today to show their status?

A Pomo woman in northern California weaves a basket in the traditional way. As the baskets to the right show, western Indians often wove designs and figures into their work.

Hunter-gathers migrated with the seasons. When fall came, for instance, the people of the Plateau were most likely camped along the rivers, where they caught and dried salmon. People of the Great Basin could be found in the mountains collecting nuts. In California people were collecting a year's supply of acorns from the native oaks.

The hunting-gathering cultures of the West excelled in making baskets that were beautiful as well as useful. They used baskets for gathering and storing food. Tightly woven baskets could hold water or be used for cooking. Basket weaving was also used to make hats, capes, and mats.

Indians of the Southwest

In the dry Southwest, hunting and gathering was difficult. Indians there turned to farming. They built permanent communities. When Spanish explorers entered the Southwest, they saw Indians living in villages of many-storied houses. The Spanish called them Pueblo Indians. *Pueblo* means "village" in Spanish.

The Pueblo Indians farmed along the Rio Grande. In addition to corn, squash, and beans, they raised cotton. They did some gathering and hunting. The animals they hunted added meat to their diet as well as provided the materials for tools and clothing.

Pueblo Indian society was highly structured. Religious ceremonies were a way to stay in harmony with the natural world. For example, after the fall harvest the Pueblo peoples would hold a ceremony that could last a week. The ceremony would include both dances in the plaza and prayers in the kivas. Kivas are underground rooms used by the Pueblo Indians for religious purposes.

In general, the tasks of men were farming, hunting, building rooms, and weaving. The women prepared food, repaired and replastered the mud-brick houses, and made pottery.

In the late 1400s other groups of Indians were also entering the Southwest. They included the Apache and the Navajo, who had moved in small bands southward.

A Pueblo woman fills a water jug. **Critical Thinking:** Why might the Indians of the desert Southwest have relied on pottery rather than wooden boxes for storage?

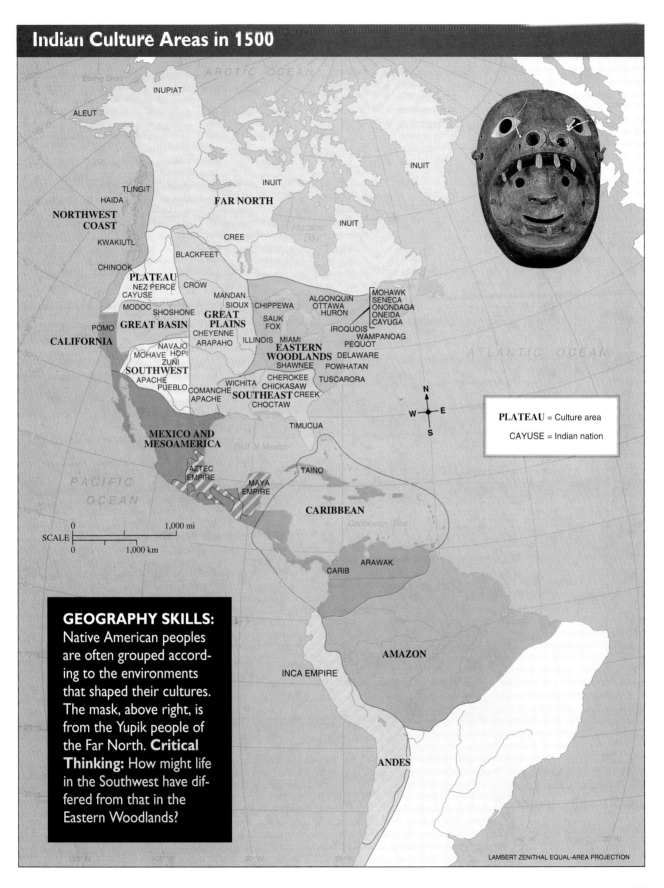

ARCTIC OCEAN

INUPIAT

ALEUT

INUIT

FAR NORTH

INUIT

TLINGIT

HAIDA

NORTHWEST COAST

INUIT

Hudson Bay

KWAKIUTL

CREE

CHINOOK

BLACKFEET

PLATEAU

NEZ PERCE   CROW

CAYUSE

MODOC   SHOSHONE   MANDAN

SIOUX   CHIPPEWA   ALGONQUIN   MOHAWK

GREAT PLAINS   OTTAWA   SENECA

SAUK   HURON   ONONDAGA

POMO   **GREAT BASIN**   FOX   ONEIDA

CHEYENNE   IROQUOIS   CAYUGA

CALIFORNIA   ARAPAHO   ILLINOIS   MIAMI   WAMPANOAG

NAVAJO   **EASTERN**   PEQUOT

MOHAVE   HOPI   **WOODLANDS**   DELAWARE

ZUNI   SHAWNEE   POWHATAN

SOUTHWEST

APACHE   CHEROKEE   TUSCARORA

PUEBLO   WICHITA   CHICKASAW

COMANCHE   **SOUTHEAST**   CREEK

APACHE   CHOCTAW

TIMUCUA

ATLANTIC OCEAN

N

W   E

S

PLATEAU = Culture area

CAYUSE = Indian nation

MEXICO AND MESOAMERICA

Gulf of Mexico

PACIFIC OCEAN

AZTEC EMPIRE   TAINO

MAYA EMPIRE

CARIBBEAN

Caribbean Sea

0   1,000 mi

SCALE

0   1,000 km

ARAWAK

CARIB

AMAZON

INCA EMPIRE

ANDES

GEOGRAPHY SKILLS: Native American peoples are often grouped according to the environments that shaped their cultures. The mask, above right, is from the Yupik people of the Far North. **Critical Thinking:** How might life in the Southwest have differed from that in the Eastern Woodlands?

LAMBERT ZENITHAL EQUAL-AREA PROJECTION

Plains Indians

The Apache were from the Great Plains. Life there in 1492 was very different from the image shown in movies and on television westerns. Plains Indians did not chase buffaloes on horses. There were no horses in North America until European explorers brought them. Five centuries ago most Plains Indians lived in river valleys at the edge of the Plains. They were farmers, growing corn, squash, beans, sunflowers, and tobacco. Women did all the farming except for tobacco. Raising tobacco was the job of older men.

Younger men did the hunting. Hunting buffalo was a cooperative effort in which men on foot drove buffalo into corrals or stampeded them over cliffs. Before going out on a hunt, the Indians were likely to seek the help of the buffalo spirits through song and dance.

Some Plains Indians lived in circular lodges that were partly underground. Such lodges gave protection against the extreme heat, cold, and wind of the Plains.

One group that was learning to live almost full-time on the Plains was the Apache. These immigrants from the Canadian forests were great walkers, who used pack trains of dogs to carry their burdens. The Apache spent much of the year on the Plains following the buffalo. In fall they headed toward more settled areas such as Pecos, a Pueblo town of about 2,000 people on the edge of the Plains. There the Apache would spend the winter and trade. The Apache traded their buffalo hides and dried meat for cotton clothing, turquoise, and food crops.

Before the Spanish introduced horses to North America, dogs were used to carry and pull packs across the Great Plains. Though many Plains Indians were farmers, buffalo hunting played an important role in their cultures. The headdress shown above was made to be worn in a buffalo dance. **Critical Thinking:** What in the picture shows that these Apache hunted?

Farmers of the Southeast

East of the Plains, in the South, Indians were farmers. Unlike the Pueblo farmers, however, the Southeast Indians lived in a region of abundant rain. This was the region of the Mississippian culture. In 1492 that culture was in decline. The farmers of the flood plains were leaving large centers to build villages in river valleys. There such groups as the Choctaw, Chickasaw, and Creek Indians continued the farming traditions of their ancestors. Others, such as the Cherokee, moved to the area and adopted their way of life.

During the summer, the women took care of the crops. The men helped harvest the crops in the fall. Then, the men prepared for winter hunting. They might spend months in the woodlands hunting deer. Most clothing of the eastern Indians was made of buckskin (deer hide).

Villages were built around a central square used for ceremonies and celebrations. One of the most important festivals was the Green Corn Dance, a kind of New Year's celebration. Old pots were thrown away and old quarrels forgotten to symbolize a new beginning. The nations of the Southeast feasted on such dishes as bear ribs and corncakes and played a brutal, two-stick version of lacrosse.

The Creek Indians were organized into leagues of red towns and white towns. The red towns supplied war leaders. The white towns handled peaceful activities and supplied the principal chiefs. As with many Indian peoples, the most powerful leaders were older, wiser people than the warriors. Leaders had only as much authority as the group was willing to give. They made important decisions only after speaking with other village leaders.

Indians of the Northeast

As in the South, the Indians of the Northeast enjoyed an environment rich in wildlife, trees, and water. These Indians

CULTURAL MOSAIC

WILMA MANKILLER
(1945–   )

At age 12, her father's farm destroyed by a drought, Wilma Mankiller and her family left the Cherokee reservation in Oklahoma for San Francisco. At that time the U.S. government was encouraging Indians to leave their reservations. After she grew up, Mankiller moved back to Oklahoma. She built a house and started a program to improve life on the reservation. "My goal has always been for Indians to solve their own economic problems," she says. In 1985 she became principal chief of the Cherokee. She is the first woman chief of a major North American Indian nation.

practiced slash-and-burn agriculture. In slash-and-burn farming, the Indians killed and burned trees to create fields. The ashes helped fertilize the soil. After about eight years the soil would wear out, and the Indians would leave the field for another.

Northeast Indians also set fires in the woods to destroy underbrush. These were low-heat fires that swept through an area quickly, sparing stronger trees. One effect of these fires was to make ashes that added nutrients to the soil. Another effect was that grass, berries, and new shrubs were likely to grow on the fire-cleared ground.

The new growth in turn attracted animals such as deer, bears, and wild turkeys. Thus, Indians created an environment for the wildlife they hunted. The cleared woods were also easier to travel.

Most Indians of the Northeast belonged either to the Algonquin or to the Iroquoian language group. The Algonquin lived in round, bark-covered shelters called wigwams. Iroquois people called themselves "People of the Longhouse." Their longhouses were shared by eight to ten families. Algonquin fields were small, like gardens. In contrast, the Iroquois fields were larger and more important as a source of food.

In both societies, the women did the farming. As in the Southeast, men were primarily hunters and warriors. Both hunting and war allowed men to show courage and gain status.

League of the Iroquois

There came a time, however, of too much war and too much bloodshed. Therefore, at least 500 years ago, five groups of the northern Iroquois—the Cayuga, Mohawk, Oneida, Onondaga, and Seneca—joined together in a league.

Binding the League of the Iroquois was the Great Law of Peace, a code of justice. According to Iroquois history, the Great Law of Peace was the idea of a prophet called the Peacemaker. The orator Hiawatha promoted the Peacemaker's vision.

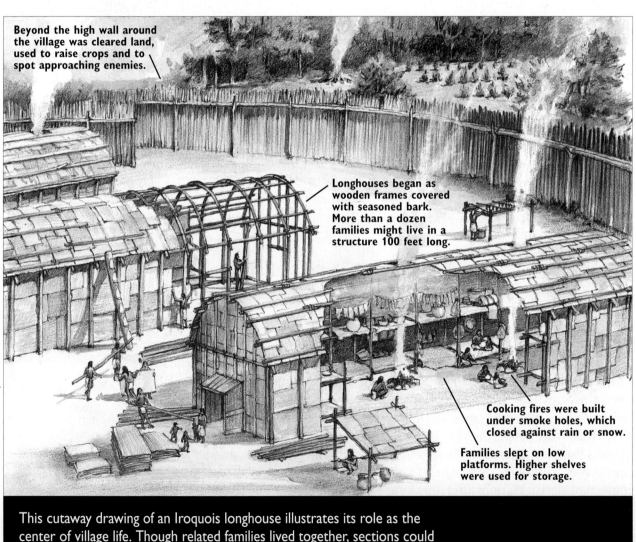

Beyond the high wall around the village was cleared land, used to raise crops and to spot approaching enemies.

Longhouses began as wooden frames covered with seasoned bark. More than a dozen families might live in a structure 100 feet long.

Cooking fires were built under smoke holes, which closed against rain or snow.

Families slept on low platforms. Higher shelves were used for storage.

This cutaway drawing of an Iroquois longhouse illustrates its role as the center of village life. Though related families lived together, sections could be curtained off for privacy. **Critical Thinking:** What does the longhouse show about the Iroquois attitude toward family?

The Mohawk Nation Council meets in a longhouse in New York State. The Mohawk follow the Great Law of Peace, their 500-year-old constitution.

©1993 Steve Wall

The Peacemaker created a framework for government, or **constitution,** that was very democratic. It was led by the Grand Council. The Grand Council was made up of chiefs from the tribal councils.

Women had title to the land through families and clans. It was the women of the League who nominated political and religious leaders. They required that the leaders be honest and have the best interests of the people in mind.

According to the Great Law of Peace, clan mothers could remove a chief who abused his office. The Great Law also guaranteed women's and children's rights, freedom of religion, and the right of appeal before the Grand Council. The Grand Council consulted the people directly on major issues.

Our Indian Heritage

American Indians today are seeking to transmit their language, their knowledge, and their world view to their children. Scholar George P. Horse Capture writes:

❝ No longer is our history locked away in isolation. Today we are familiar with our past, and it fills us with pride and stabilizes our journey into the future. ❞

The American nation shares in the Indian heritage. As the pictures in this chapter show, it is a heritage of skill and art in the making of beautiful things. The Indian heritage is also one of ideas. One of those ideas is living in harmony with the environment. If we take care of the earth, it will take care of us. Another of those ideas is liberty and the right of people to create and control their government. The pages that follow show how these ideas and skills continue to enrich American Indian life today.

SECTION REVIEW

1. Key Terms tundra, technology, totem, slash-and-burn, constitution

2. Comprehension How did the geography of the Northwest Coast affect the way of life of American Indians living there?

3. Comprehension What was the Great Law of Peace?

4. Critical Thinking How might American Indians of the past feel about today's movement to protect the environment? Explain your answer.

Daily Life

OF NATIVE AMERICANS TODAY

There are almost 2 million Native Americans in the United States. They live in cities and on reservations, hold modern jobs and practice ancient traditions. The photographs on these pages give a taste of the diversity of Native American life today.

©1987 Steve Wall

Centuries ago Iroquois teams played lacrosse on giant fields for days on end. Today the Iroquois National team (shown above playing England) follows modern rules. The team proudly marches under its own flag in the world championships.

The Northwest Indians no longer rely on their great wooden canoes, but they have not lost their skill at carving them. Forty canoes made from ancient cedar trees participated in the "Paddle to Seattle" Celebration shown below.

In the 1800s American Indians were told to give up their languages and become English speakers. Today they are once again studying traditional languages. Durbin Feeling, shown right, teaches Cherokee to his grandson using an alphabet first developed in the 1820s.

This class is meeting in a school on a Hopi reservation in Arizona. For a long time, American Indians had little say in the education of their children and the management of their reservations. In recent years, laws have given Indians more control over their lives and lands.

In 1993 Ben Nighthorse Campbell became the first American Indian to serve in the Senate since 1929. Campbell traces his roots to the Northern Cheyenne.

Celinda McKelvey combines two ancient Navajo traditions to create a new one. The designs on her pots are inspired by sandpaintings, which are part of the Navajo healing ceremony. Celinda learned this style of pottery from her mother, Lucy.

Summary

1. The first humans migrated to the Americas thousands of years ago. These people, called Paleo-Indians, lived by hunting large game animals. As these animals became extinct, the Paleo-Indians began to hunt smaller game and to gather plant foods. About 5,000 years ago, the Indians learned how to farm. This led to the development of village life and the growth of more complex cultures.

2. Highly advanced civilizations, including those of the Olmec, Maya, and Aztecs, arose in Meso-america. Other cultures were influenced by contact with Mesoamerican civilizations. These include the Anasazi of the Southwest as well as the moundbuilders of the Eastern Woodlands.

3. In 1492 North American Indians were very diverse, though, in general, Indian societies believed that there was a strong spiritual relationship among all living things. Influenced by their different environments, American Indians of the Far North, Northwest Coast, West, Southwest, Plains, Southeast, and Northeast developed different cultures and societies.

Graphic Summary

Paleo-Indians →

Mesoamerican Cultures
Olmec   Maya   Aztec

North American Cultures
Anasazi   Hopewell   Mississippian

Far North
Northwest Coast
West
Southwest
Plains
Southeast
Northeast

Review

KEY TERMS

Define the following sets of terms.
1. artifact; culture
2. domestication; civilization
3. irrigation; famine
4. technology; slash-and-burn
5. empire; constitution

COMPREHENSION

1. Where did the first people in the Americas come from? How did they arrive?
2. What change forced the Paleo-Indians to develop into hunter-gatherers?
3. How and when did agriculture develop in the Americas? How did it change the Indians' way of life?
4. What was the "mother culture" of Mesoamerica?
5. What other civilizations developed in Mesoamerica?
6. How did the Hohokam and Anasazi people survive in the desert Southwest?
7. What were the distinctive features of the Hopewell and Mississippian cultures?
8. Describe the Indians' view of their relationship with the natural environment.
9. How did Indians on the Northwest Coast get most of their food? How did Indians in the Southwest get their food?
10. What was the Great Law of Peace? How was it achieved?

Places to Locate

Match the letters on the map with the places listed below.
1. Northwest Coast Indians
2. Eastern Woodlands Indians
3. Bering Strait
4. Aztec empire
5. Great Plains Indian cultures

Geographic Theme: Interactions How did the Indian groups of the Northwest Coast and the Southeast adapt their lifestyles to fit their environment?

Skill Review

Study the timeline below. Then answer the questions that follow.

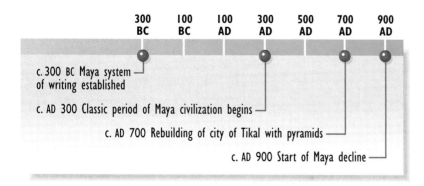

1. What is the subject of the timeline?
2. Which came first, the building of Tikal or the development of the Maya system of writing?
3. Approximately when did the Maya civilization start to decline?
4. Which event on the timeline do you think is the most important? Explain.

CRITICAL THINKING

1. Inferring Why does the discovery of artifacts in the graves of Paleo-Indians lead scholars to infer that these early Americans believed in an afterlife?

2. Understanding the Main Idea Reread the paragraphs under the heading "League of the Iroquois" in Section 3. Then tell in your own words the main ideas in those paragraphs.

PORTFOLIO OPTIONS

1. Civics Connection How might the role of the individual in Indian society of the 1500s differ from the role of an individual in today's society? Discuss your ideas with the class.

2. Writing Connection Chief Seattle said, "Whatever befalls the earth befalls the sons of the earth. Man did not weave the web of life, he is merely a strand in it." Put that statement in your own words and then write a paragraph explaining why you agree or disagree with it.

3. Contemporary Connection In this chapter you read about the spread of agriculture in the Western Hemisphere. What are examples of the spread of knowledge and customs in the world today?

4. Timeline Connection The "c." before the dates in the timelines in this chapter stands for *circa*. Look that word up in the dictionary, and then explain why it is used on the timelines.

Most African Americans trace their heritage to the peoples of West Africa. In the city of Mali called Mopti, people still come to pray at the Friday Mosque (below). Just as in ancient Mali, students today study the Qur'an (the Islamic holy book) by memorizing passages from it.

B.C.	7000	5000	3000	1000

6000 B.C. First cultures in Nile Valley develop in Nubia and Egypt

3100 B.C. Egyptians unified under a pharaoh

750 B.C. Nubians organize kingdom of Kush

Peoples of West Africa
(Beginnings–1591)

1 Ancient Africa

A.D. 1000

1591 Moroccans invade Songhai

1482 First Portuguese trading post in West Africa

1324 Mansa Musa journeys to Mecca

T HE AFRICAN AMERICAN poet Countee Cullen wrote these lines about 60 years ago:

> **One in three centuries removed
> From the scenes his fathers loved,
> Spicy grove, cinnamon tree,
> What is Africa to me?**

Today over 30 million Americans are descended from Africans. Their ancestors, brought to the Americas to become slaves, were told to forget their past. They did not. Their African heritage became part of a new African American culture, which in turn became part of America. Yet most Americans today know little about Africa itself. What had African life been like before Africans came to the Americas? What contributions did Africans make to world civilization? What events were to link African history with that of the United States?

The Birth of Humanity
The story starts in the remote past of prehistory —that is, before written history. Most scholars believe that Africa was the original home of human beings. Humans emerged in Africa over two million years ago. About 1.5 million years ago, humans began migrating from the continent to Asia, and then to Europe. Later, as you have read, people crossed from northeast Asia into the Americas and spread across those continents.

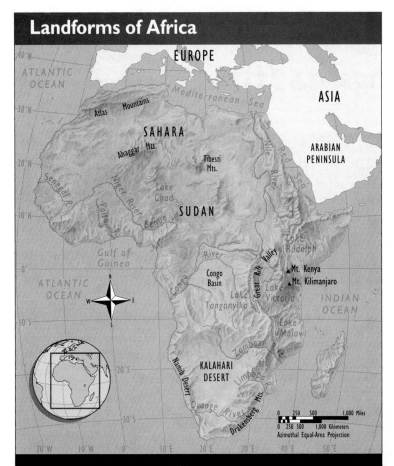

Landforms of Africa

GEOGRAPHY SKILLS: This map shows the various landforms of Africa. **Critical Thinking:** Which landforms might have made migration out of the Sahara more difficult for the ancient Africans? Explain.

In Africa most early humans lived in the savannas, or grassy plains regions. These regions had a mild climate and nutritious plant food. Their varied wildlife provided meat and skins for clothing. Yet about 5,000 or 6,000 years ago, one part of the savanna region began drying up. This was the birth of what would become the world's largest desert, the Sahara.

When their surroundings change, people must change as well if they are to survive. You read that the Paleo-Indians changed from big-game hunting to hunting and gathering when the big-game animals became extinct. In Africa, as the Sahara became desert, the people living there headed for lands that could sustain them.

The drying of the Sahara led to the development of distinct peoples and cultures. People left the Sahara in every direction. These people were the seeds of Africa's future. Their sons and daughters would build the kingdoms and empires of the Nile Valley, of North Africa, and of West Africa.

Kingdoms of the Nile

Those who went east out of the desert settled in the fertile Nile Valley. They joined peoples who had already settled along the Nile River thousands of years earlier. Over time many cultures emerged along the Nile, among them the great civilizations of Nubia (NOO-bee-uh) and Egypt.

Nubia

The first culture of the Nile Valley began in Nubia around 6000 B.C. In prehistoric times Nubians lived by hunting, fishing, and herding cattle. Later the Nubians learned to farm. Nubia had other resources as well. The land was a treasure-trove of gold and minerals. Around 750 B.C., Nubians built their strongest and longest-lasting kingdom, Kush.

Kush expanded through trade. Skilled at ironworking, Nubians traded iron as well as ivory, ebony, ostrich feathers, and gold. Caravans —groups of traders and their pack animals loaded with trade items— carried these goods to ports on the Red Sea and Mediterranean Sea. From there the goods went to Arabia, India, and even China, half a world away.

By the first century A.D., however, Kush had begun to decline. The spread of ironmaking skills throughout Africa made Kush's iron products worth less. The rival empire of Aksum began raiding Kush's trade routes, which were its lifeline. In A.D. 350, Aksum invaded and later destroyed Kush.

Senkamenisken ruled Nubia in the 600s B.C.

Ancient Egypt

To Nubia's north, closer to where the Nile reaches the Mediterranean, the people of Egypt built perhaps the greatest civilization of the ancient world. Egypt began shortly after Nubia. Around 3100 B.C. the Egyptians were unified under one ruler, called a **pharaoh** (FAYR-oh).

Under the pharaohs, Egypt built an empire through conquest. It would in time collapse, like all empires. Egypt's gifts to world culture, however, would endure. The Egyptians invented a system of mathematics and a system of writing and record-keeping. They were the first to organize an entire country under one government. Using hundreds of thousands of laborers, they built by hand the huge stone pyramids, whose size and beauty still amaze people today.

For well over 2,000 years other peoples of the eastern Mediterranean region marveled at Egypt. The Greeks, who also developed a remarkable civilization, were influenced by Egyptian mathematics, medical knowledge, and religion.

Africa South of the Sahara

In the year 1000 B.C. the entire population of Africa was about 6.5 million. Roughly half of these people lived in North Africa (mostly in Egypt). By about A.D. 1000, Africa's population had grown to about 33 million. By then, however, nearly 70 percent of all Africans lived south of the Sahara. What caused the growth and shift of population?

(1) When the Sahara became desert, the people who moved south found no river valleys as rich as the Nile. However, using newly learned skills such as wheat growing, they could live well on their new land. Africans south of the Sahara began to cultivate crops that grew better in their climate regions. People could count on having a more reliable food supply.

(2) Ironmaking skills spread across

The pyramids in Giza, Egypt, were built about 4,500 years ago.

Africa. Now more and more Africans learned how to make iron tools and weapons. With these stronger tools to use in farming and other activities, more people lived longer and better lives. Also, iron weapons were more effective against enemies.

The impact of these changes on people living south of the Sahara was enormous. Populations and new skills continued to grow. Soon trade with peoples outside of Africa expanded. In the next section, you will read how these changes helped give rise to mighty empires in West Africa.

SECTION REVIEW

1. Key Terms prehistory, savanna, caravan, pharaoh

2. Places Sahara, Nile Valley, Nubia, Egypt

3. Comprehension How did the drying of the Sahara lead to the birth of great cultures and empires in Africa?

4. Comprehension Why was the spread of ironmaking skills in Africa important?

5. Critical Thinking How might the history of Africa have been different if the Sahara had not turned into desert?

2 Empires of West Africa

SECTION GUIDE

Main Idea
A profitable gold trade across the Sahara allowed prosperous states and empires to develop in West Africa.

Goals
As you read, look for answers to these questions.

1 What brought about the rise to power of Ghana, and what led to its decline?

2 What were the outstanding features of Mali and Songhai?

3 What was family and religious life like in Africa?

Key Terms
monopoly   kinship
Muslim   pilgrimage
mosque

West African empires grew wealthy from gold. Gold is still an important resource in that region. A woman pans for gold (left). Gold necklaces (right) have been worn for centuries.

HOW MUCH would you pay for a pound of salt, or a pound of gold? The price of something depends on supply and demand. When the supply of an item is large or the demand low, its price drops. If the supply decreases or the demand increases, the price rises. In the humid climate of West Africa, the supply of salt was low and the demand high. Trading salt for gold—a lousy bargain in the United States today—was sensible. This trade of salt for gold helped make three West African empires prosper.

Ghana

Ghana (GAH-nuh) began its rise sometime after A.D. 300. It was the creation of the Soninke (so-NIN-kay) people, who lived on the southern edge of the Sahara. Ghana dominated West Africa for some three hundred years. It reached the peak of its power in the early 1000s.

Trade was a source of strength for Ghana. In Ghana traders from north and south met to exchange gold and salt. Traders from North Africa brought salt from mines in the Sahara. Salt was worth its weight in gold in the lands south of the Sahara. The people living in West Africa's warm tropical climate lost salt in perspiration and needed to add it to their diets to stay healthy. From areas south of Ghana, gold was mined and brought to the empire. For hundreds of years the rulers of Ghana were the main suppliers of gold for North Africa and Europe.

Ghana had a monopoly on the critical gold-salt trade. In other words, it controlled that trade. Ghana made all traders pay high taxes on both the buying and selling of salt. These taxes brought the empire great wealth, thereby supporting Ghana's army and government.

Gold was not the only valuable item brought to Ghana for trade. Merchants sent ivory, skins, kola nuts, honey, cotton, and slaves in camel caravans north over the trading routes to North Africa.

Empires of West Africa, A.D. 1000–1600

GHANA
Kumbi

MALI
Timbuktu
Djenné

SONGHAI
Timbuktu
Djenné

GEOGRAPHY SKILLS: The West African empires developed in the grasslands region south of the Sahara. **Critical Thinking:** Why did the major cities develop near the Niger River?

The Spread of Islam

During the time of Ghana's greatness, the religion of Islam was expanding into Africa. Islam was founded by Muhammad in the 600s in Arabia. People who follow the teachings of Islam are called Muslims. (There are about one billion Muslims in the world today.) Like Jews and Christians, Muslims believe in one God. They regard Jesus and the Hebrew prophets as messengers of God. They believe that Muhammad was the last and greatest of the prophets.

Islam quickly spread westward from Arabia across North Africa to the shores of the Atlantic Ocean. Brought by traders crossing the Sahara, it spread southward in Africa sometime after the year 1000.

Rulers in Ghana wanted to further expand their trade with the wealthy Islamic empires of North Africa. They eagerly welcomed Muslim traders. Ghana's rulers even allowed the traders to build a mosque —Muslim place of worship—in the capital. However, the people of Ghana (and the rest of Africa south of the Sahara) were slow to accept the religion. Most saw Islam as a foreign religion and continued to follow their traditional religions.

Slavery

With the spread of Islam, the African slave trade increased. Slavery had existed in Africa for centuries. A person could become enslaved in many ways, such as being kidnapped, captured in war, sold for debt, or traded for food during a famine. Criminals could also become slaves.

Slaves had some rights. Slave children were usually not sold and were often freed. Slaves could marry, own property, and freely worship their own religion. A few slaves became high officials in West African empires.

Every year thousands were taken from lands south of the Sahara. Lined up in columns, they marched barefoot across the Sahara behind the camel caravans.

These slaves were sold and taken to Arabia, Persia, and other Muslim lands. Some wound up in India, others as far away as China.

The Fall of Ghana

Ghana brought law and order to a large part of Africa. Traders knew they could do business in safety. In turn, thriving trade made Ghana wealthier and more powerful. Success brought Ghana both friends and enemies.

In 1076 an army of Muslims from northwestern Africa conquered Ghana and its capital, Kumbi. As Ghana lost power, its hold on its lands weakened. A number of local leaders took advantage of that weakness to build up their own small kingdoms. By the end of the 1200s, the empire of Ghana ceased to exist.

Mali

The Mandinka (man-DIN-ka) people of West Africa finally ended Ghana's greatness. The Mandinka had built a small state called Mali (MAH-lee) on the Upper Niger River in the 600s. Some six centuries later, Mali's Muslim leader, named Sundiata (suhn-dee-AH-tuh), defeated Ghana and turned Mali into an empire. Conquering new lands, he took over the caravan trade. Unlike the people of Ghana, many people of Mali (mostly merchants and officials) converted to Islam.

In the early 1300s one ruler of Mali, Abu Bakari II, dreamed of sending a fleet of boats out to sea to explore the world. His fleet headed down the Senegal River to the Atlantic, but was never heard from again.

Mansa Musa

Mali's most famous ruler, Mansa Musa (MAHN-sah MOO-sah), came to power in 1312. He made Mali one of the world's largest empires at that time. The Mali city of Timbuktu was famous for its mosques, royal palace, and for its schools, which became centers of Muslim learning.

Like every Muslim, Mansa Musa was supposed to make a **pilgrimage** to Mecca, the holy city of Islam in Arabia. (A pilgrimage is a journey to a sacred place.) His show of wealth in his journey to Mecca in 1324 made news far and wide. A caravan of 60,000 people, all dressed in Persian silk, escorted him. Riding on horseback, Mansa Musa was followed by 500 slaves, each carrying a staff of gold weighing about 5 pounds. Then came his baggage train of 100 camels, each loaded with bags of gold dust to pay the king's expenses on the long journey.

Mansa Musa's wealth had a great impact all along the 3,600 miles of his pilgrimage. He spent and gave away so much gold that the price of gold dropped and stayed down in Cairo, Egypt, for about twelve years.

After his return from Mecca, Mansa Musa expanded Timbuktu's trade connections in North Africa. He also promoted culture and learning throughout the empire. When Mansa Musa died in 1337, Mali was a powerful empire.

Mali then began to decline. Small kingdoms and states broke away from the empire. Enemies pressed in at its borders. In the late 1400s much of Mali was conquered by the Songhai people. Songhai then replaced Mali as the most powerful state in West Africa.

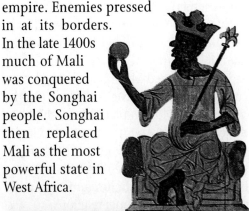

Observers commented that Mansa Musa's glittering procession to Mecca in 1324 put the sun to shame.

32

SKILLS: Reading for the Main Idea

LEARN

Have you ever watched someone giving a speech and asked yourself, "What's the point?" You were listening in vain for the main idea. The main idea is a statement that summarizes the main point of a speech, a magazine article, a section in a history book, or even just a paragraph.

Main ideas can be stated or unstated. The stated main idea of a paragraph is often the first or last sentence. If it is the first sentence, it is followed by supporting details. If it is the last, the details build up to the main idea at the end. To find an unstated main idea, you must use the details of the paragraph as clues. For example, if each detail describes a different kind of boat used in ancient Africa, the main idea probably is "Ancient Africans used a variety of boats."

When you read, look for main ideas. Then focus on how the details support the main ideas. This simple strategy is the key to getting the most out of what you read.

PRACTICE

Read the paragraph at the right.

1. Is the main idea stated or unstated?

2. What is the main idea?

3. Name two details that help support or explain the main idea.

APPLY

4. Write a paragraph about Mansa Musa's rule of Mali. Be sure your main idea is clearly stated.

5. Write another paragraph about Mansa Musa's rule of Mali with a clear—but unstated—main idea.

Trade was a source of strength for Ghana. In Ghana traders from north and south met to exchange gold and salt. Traders from North Africa brought salt from mines in the Sahara. Salt was worth its weight in gold in the lands south of the Sahara. The people living in West Africa's warm tropical climate lost salt in perspiration and needed to add it to their diets to stay healthy. From areas south of Ghana, gold was mined and brought to the empire. For hundreds of years the rulers of Ghana were the main suppliers of gold for North Africa and Europe.

Songhai

As Mali had been a part of Ghana, so had Songhai been a part of Mali. In 1465, led by the Muslim general Sunni 'Ali, Songhai took control of Mali. Sunni 'Ali greatly extended the empire's reach, leading his army against many other peoples in West Africa. He captured Timbuktu and then lay siege to the famous learning and trade center of Djenné (jen-NAY). According to legend, Djenné held out for seven years, seven months, and seven days. Finally it surrendered. With this victory, Sunni 'Ali was able to establish Songhai's control over all the major trading cities of the region.

Sunni 'Ali died in 1492. A general who became known as Askia the Great declared himself emperor. During the reign of Askia the Great (1493–1528), the Songhai empire grew even larger.

Askia was a devout Muslim. His pilgrimage to Mecca from 1495 to 1497 was said to rival that of Mansa Musa in glitter and generosity. Under Askia, Timbuktu became an even greater and better-known Muslim cultural and learning center. People from all over West Africa, North Africa, and Arabian lands gathered in Timbuktu. There they studied law, literature, theology, grammar, geography, mathematics, and surgery. Leo Africanus, a traveler and historian in the early 1500s, described the city:

> **There are numerous judges, professors, and holy men. . . . More profit is made from selling books in Timbuktu than from any other branch of trade.**

The Songhai Empire thrived for more than a hundred years. By the late 1500s, however, Songhai had come under attack by outsiders. The rich empires of West Africa had been the envy of North African rulers for centuries. These rulers dreamed of taking over the empires and their profitable gold trade. In 1591 the Moroccans of North Africa invaded and eventually destroyed the Songhai Empire.

Called the "meeting point of the camel and the canoe," Timbuktu stood at the crossing point of the trans-Sahara trade routes and the Niger River.

Family and Religion in Africa

Even among the peoples of Ghana, Mali, and Songhai, there were many differences in customs and beliefs. In Africa as a whole, the variety was greater still. Yet the peoples of Africa did have many things in common.

Kinship was central to African life. Kinship is a relationship based on common ancestors. People of the same kin lived together. To most Africans, the kinship unit was more important than an individual.

Family ties were part of Africans' religious beliefs as well. People looked to the spirits of their dead ancestors for help in their lives. They honored their ancestors with ceremonies of dance, song, drum music, and prayer. The oldest man of the family served as the priest and ran the religious ceremonies.

As you have read, Islam entered North Africa and spread to lands south of the Sahara after 1000. Africans south of the Sahara were slow to accept Islam at first. Some kingdoms rejected Islam outright. In other areas, the ruler converted but many of the people did not. To avoid angering their people, many African Muslim rulers combined Muslim and traditional practices.

Gradually, more and more West Africans accepted Islam. The reasons included:

(1) The Islamic world was rich and powerful. Many people saw becoming Muslim as a way to gain a higher status in society.

(2) Most African languages were not written ones. As contact with Muslim traders increased, more and more Africans learned to read and write Arabic—the language of Islam. (Today Arabic is the official language of all North African countries, as well as the Republic of Sudan. Arabic is also widely spoken in many parts of East and West Africa.)

(3) Many aspects of Islam were compatible with traditional African practices. For

Ancient family traditions continue today. A family in Timbuktu bakes bread early in the morning.

example, both Islam and many traditional African customs allowed a man to have more than one wife.

Islam was not the only foreign religion to reach Africa. Christianity was first introduced in Aksum in East Africa in the 300s. The Portuguese brought Christianity to West Africa in the 1500s. Some areas of West Africa embraced Christianity. However, most Africans responded to Christianity, as they first did with Islam, with caution.

SECTION REVIEW

1. Key Terms monopoly, Muslim, mosque, pilgrimage, kinship

2. People and Places Mansa Musa, Askia the Great, Ghana, Mali, Songhai

3. Comprehension How did Ghana's control of the gold-salt trade play a part in its rise to prosperity and power?

4. Comprehension Why did Islam spread within West Africa?

5. Critical Thinking West Africa had no written languages for centuries. How might the early history of this region be known?

Daily Life

CELEBRATING KWANZAA

"The first step forward is a step backward to Africa and our roots." Professor Maulana Karenga used these words to explain why he created the Kwanzaa festival in 1966. An African American, Karenga based Kwanzaa on harvest festivals that occur in parts of Africa. ("Kwanzaa" means "first fruits of harvest.") Kwanzaa takes place over seven days at the end of the year. As this page shows, each day is devoted to a different value important in African cultures. Millions now celebrate Kwanzaa as a way to honor their African heritage.

7 Faith

6 Creativity

5 Purpose

4 Cooperative economics

3 Collective work and responsibility

1 Unity

2 Self-determination

3 Contacts with Europe

SECTION GUIDE

Main Idea
The arrival of Portuguese ships and traders along the West African coast in the 1400s would have far-reaching consequences for this region.

Goals
As you read, look for answers to these questions:

1. Why did the Portuguese send ships along the West African coast?

2. What type of relationship did West Africa and Portugal have?

Key Term
trading post

Portuguese contact influenced many aspects of West Africa, including its art. This ivory mask from the mid-1500s shows Portuguese men on the crown.

SINCE THE 1100s the story of a man named Prester John had traveled around Europe. According to legend, Prester John was a Christian ruler of a faraway land that was surrounded by Muslims. No one, however, knew exactly where Prester John's kingdom was. Perhaps it was in Africa, about which Europeans knew very little. Might Europeans find Prester John and his kingdom?

Arrival of the Portuguese

In the 1400s Europe began an age of exploration that would carry voyagers to Africa, Asia, and the Americas. As you will read in the next chapter, they were looking for new trade routes to Asia, for gold, and for ways to spread Christianity. Some were also looking for Prester John. (Historians think that while Prester John never existed, the legend refers to the ancient East African kingdom of Aksum.)

Portugal began this period of exploration. A Portuguese prince, who became known as Henry the Navigator, started sending ships south along the northwest coast of Africa. In the 1440s Portuguese voyagers had reached the mouth of the Senegal River. In 1482 they had built a fort on the west coast of Africa. Along the way they set up **trading posts** —fortified stations where they exchanged goods with local traders.

Gold was not the only product that interested the Portuguese. They also loaded their ships with cargoes of ivory, pepper, and animal skins, and they bought slaves from traders. Soon they were shipping enslaved Africans to Spain and Portugal at the rate of a thousand a year.

Descendants of these slaves—born in Spain and Portugal—were among the first blacks to see the Americas. These black explorers, soldiers, and slaves took part in European voyages to the Americas.

Europeans would later bring millions of enslaved Africans to the Americas. They would justify this by claiming that Africans were inferior. Yet when the Portuguese first met Africans, they did not see them as inferior. In fact, Portuguese traders were impressed by the power of the African rulers and the wealth of

ALEX HALEY
(1921–1992)

Alex Haley wrote a book that made history—and changed it. From stories passed through generations of slaves, he traced his family to a village in West Africa and wrote *Roots: The Saga of an American Family*. The book came out in 1976, broke sales records, and won many awards. Millions watched the Roots television series. Like Haley, people wanted to know more about African American history. Many were curious about their own ethnic backgrounds. Haley opened the way for new voices to be heard in American history.

peoples in the interior of Africa. The arrival of the Portuguese made the West African coast, in the words of one historian, a "frontier of opportunity." In return for items like gold and ivory, greatly valued by the Europeans, African traders bought products made of metal and cloth.

Sometimes African leaders looked to Europeans for help against African rivals. Europeans, in turn, often tried to benefit from tensions among African peoples, or tried to bully weaker African rulers. In one case a Portuguese commander asked to build a house to store trade products. The local African ruler agreed. Yet what the Portuguese built was not a house but a fort, which they refused to leave.

Still, Europeans and Africans dealt with each other mainly through trade rather than war. Most African states were strong enough to defend themselves. They, as well as the Europeans, knew that through trade, Africa and Europe both could profit from these new contacts. Little did either side know that the demand for slaves in the Americas would soon bring enormous change to Africa.

their royal courts. The first Africans taken to Portugal were treated with honor. Some were asked to serve as guides on later expeditions to the African coast.

Dealing with Newcomers

"Go and do business with the king of Timbuktu and Mali," the traveler Leo Africanus advised. First Portugal, then other European nations, took his advice. Europe had much to gain from trade with Africa. What did Africa stand to gain in return?

Trade brought wealth to the African coastal states as well as the Europeans. These states had traded mostly with the

SECTION REVIEW

1. Key Term trading post

2. People and Places Henry the Navigator, Portugal

3. Comprehension Why did the Portuguese set up trading posts along the west coast of Africa?

4. Comprehension Explain how both the African coastal states and Europe benefitted from trade.

5. Critical Thinking Trading relationships usually work better if the two sides possess equal strength. Explain why this is so.

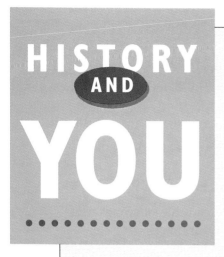

Looking Back at Slavery

Slavery in the United States was abolished by the Thirteenth Amendment to the Constitution. Yet its wounds are still visible today. This account comes from an African college student, a descendant of a slave.

In Africa, every high school kid knows about the transatlantic slave trade and the methods used to capture our ancestors. No other topic my history teachers taught, no other story told by my parents caused me such fear and pain.

Once, my dad took me and my three brothers to the Cape Coast Castle located in Central Ghana. This castle . . . is where the captives were brought to wait for the ships.

As we climbed down the narrow passageway and deeper into the darkness of the dungeon, I heard my dad cough. He pulled a handkerchief from his pocket and dabbed his eyes. I was surprised and perplexed. I had never seen my dad cry. In Africa, men are not supposed to cry.

Many years later, when I was visiting Nigeria, I stopped at the town of Badagri, where there are ancient sets of chains that date back to the 1600s. Slave chains, ordinary pieces of metal fashioned to hold humans, powerful enough to yank away freedom, strong enough to kill. Chains for the hands, feet, and neck. Chains for punishment. Chains even for children.

I stood frozen as our guide told how they were used. "This one with the wedge at the end was for captives who became too exhausted to continue the long walk from the interior," he says. "They were taken into the bush, where this wedge was hammered into a tree and they were left to die."

He offered the neck shackle to me to try on. I said no. The tools of slavery, I thought, are nothing to play with. Suddenly, I had to get out of there. The walls seemed to be closing in on me. As I turned to leave, I said to myself, "I will not cry."

But, as with my father, tears flowed freely.

CRITICAL THINKING

1. Why, in your opinion, did the topic of slavery cause the author "fear and pain"?
2. Why did the author not want to cry when he was viewing the slave chains? Why, in your opinion, did he cry?

Summary

1. Scholars believe that Africa was the original home of human beings. Most early humans lived in the savanna region of Africa. One part of the savanna, the Sahara, dried out, forcing people to migrate in all directions. The population south of the Sahara grew larger due to a reliable food supply and the spread of ironmaking skills.

2. Between the 300s and 1500s, three empires rose and fell in West Africa. These empires—Ghana, Mali, and Songhai—profited from their control of the gold-salt trade. In West Africa, as in other parts of Africa, family ties extended beyond the immediate family to include all kin. Traditional religious beliefs were tied to kinship as well. Yet in many parts of Africa the religion of Islam gained followers.

3. In the 1400s Europeans arrived in West Africa and built trading posts along the coast. Gold and ivory were the major items of trade. In return, Africans received metal and cloth. Both Africa and Europe profited from trade.

Graphic Summary

Beginnings–6,000 B.C.

Origins of humans in Africa; migration across continent; ancient Nile Valley civilizations.

A.D. 300s–1500s

West African empires: Ghana, Mali, and Songhai.

1400s

Trade established between West Africa and Portugal.

Review

KEY TERMS

Define the following terms.
1. caravan
2. kinship
3. monopoly
4. mosque
5. Muslim
6. pilgrimage
7. pharaoh
8. prehistory
9. savanna
10. trading post

COMPREHENSION

1. Why was the savanna region of Africa an ideal environment for early humans?
2. How did the drying of the Sahara lead to the development of distinct peoples and cultures in Africa?
3. What factors led to the decline of the Nubian kingdom of Kush?
4. What impact did the Egyptians have on the world?
5. What led to the growth of population in areas south of the Sahara?
6. Describe Ghana's role in the gold-salt trade.
7. What were some notable features of Mansa Musa's rule of Mali?
8. Describe family life and religion in many African cultures.
9. What factors led to the acceptance of Islam in areas south of the Sahara?
10. Why did the Portuguese come to Africa?

Places to Locate

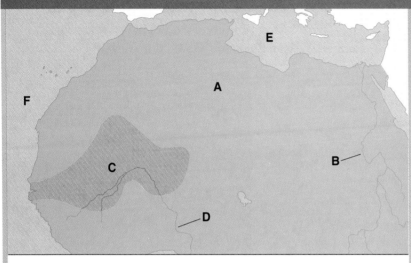

Match the letters on the map with the places listed below. Then explain the importance of each place.

1. Nile River   **3.** Sahara Desert   **5.** Songhai Empire
2. Niger River   **4.** Atlantic Ocean   **6.** Mediterranean Sea

Geographic Theme: Movement Explain how the movement of people in Africa helped shape the history of the continent.

Skill Review

Reread this paragraph from the section "Arrival of the Portuguese."

Europeans would later bring millions of enslaved Africans to the Americas. They would justify this by claiming that Africans were inferior. Yet when the Portuguese first met Africans, they did not see them as inferior. In fact, Portuguese traders were impressed by the power of the African rulers and the wealth of their royal courts. The first Africans taken to Portugal were treated with honor. Some were asked to serve as guides on later expeditions to the African coast.

1. What is the main idea of this paragraph? Is it stated or unstated?
2. Write a paragraph describing the early relations between West Africans and the Portuguese. Use a stated main idea.
3. Write another paragraph, this time with an unstated main idea.

CRITICAL THINKING

1. Forming a Hypothesis People in the cities of the Mali and Songhai converted to Islam, while village dwellers, on the whole, did not. Why might villagers have kept to their traditional religions?
2. Economics Explain how Mansa Musa's generosity with gold during his trip to Mecca could cause the price of gold in the world to drop.

PORTFOLIO OPTIONS

1. Civics Connection Compare the importance of an individual in an African kinship unit with the importance of an individual in American society.
2. Writing Connection Imagine you are a reporter in 1324 covering Mansa Musa's journey to Mecca. Write an article describing his procession. Consult books from the library to obtain more information if necessary.
3. Contemporary Connection Look at a modern-day map of Africa to see which countries are located in the former boundaries of the empires of Ghana, Mali, and Songhai. Research and write a short report on those countries and their relations with the United States.
4. Timeline Connection Copy the chapter timeline. Add other events from the chapter you think should be included. Which event do you think had the greatest impact on Africa and its people?

Three ships, the *Niña, Pinta,* and *Santa Maria,* brought Columbus and his crew to the Americas in 1492. Almost 500 years later, these three ships re-enacted that famous voyage. This 1555 map, though far from accurate, shows how early European explorers such as Columbus viewed the Western Hemisphere.

400   550   700   850   1000

400s Middle Ages begin

1000s Vikings reach North America

800s Norsemen attack western Europe

Europeans Reach Outward (400–1522)

1 An Awakening Europe

SECTION GUIDE

Main Idea
After a period of chaos, western Europe started regaining strength around A.D. 1000. This led to a new interest in learning and discovery.

Goals
As you read, look for answers to these questions:

1. What was European society in the Middle Ages like?

2. What were the effects of the Crusades?

3. How did the Renaissance change life in Europe?

Key Terms
Middle Ages   Crusades
feudalism   nationalism
self-sufficient   Renaissance
middle class

IMAGINE THAT all trade in and out of your state came to a halt. Also imagine that at the same time warriors entered your state robbing, killing, and burning. What might happen to government, to towns, to the food supply? How would your community survive?

Western Europe Declines
The collapse of trade and savage invaders ushered in the Middle Ages in Europe. The Middle Ages, or the medieval period, separates ancient and modern times. The Middle Ages were roughly the years between the 400s and the 1400s.

The last of the ancient empires was the Roman Empire, which controlled the Mediterranean Sea and the lands bordering it. The empire established stability and trade throughout the Mediterranean. By about A.D. 500, however, Germanic peoples from the north had successfully toppled the western half of the Roman Empire.

With the Germanic invasions, new languages and new ways took hold in Europe. The invaders, for instance, were not sea traders. Thus, with the rise of Islam in the 600s, most Mediterranean trade would come under the control of the Muslims.

The invasions brought turmoil and hard times to Europe. Under Germanic rule, agriculture became more important and trade less important. Without trade, there was little money. Without money (and taxes), kingdoms fell apart.

1150	1300	1450	1600

1300s Renaissance begins

1519 Magellan begins expedition around the world

1498 Da Gama finds all-water route to Asia

1492 Columbus sails to America

This dragon head from a Viking ship shows why western Europeans feared "the fury of the Northmen."

The Dreaded Norsemen

To make things worse, in the 800s invaders began to attack from the north. These were the Norsemen. Also called Vikings, the Norsemen came from Scandinavia—the lands of Sweden, Denmark, and Norway. These sea-faring adventurers were fierce warriors as well as fine sailors.

Wherever the Norsemen landed, their hit-and-run raids devastated the land and its people. In western Europe, church services added a new prayer: "From the fury of the Northmen, good Lord deliver us."

Rise of Feudalism

Threatened both by invasions and the collapse of trade, western Europeans came up with a way to survive. This was the social, economic, and political system known as feudalism. In effect, it provided a way for people to live off the land.

The land was divided into large estates called "manors." A manor included one or more villages, a manor house, fields, and woods. Those who owned manors were lords, members of the noble class. Those who worked the land of the manors were most often serfs. Serfs worked for the lords and were not allowed to leave the manor. With no markets to buy goods and little trade, the manors were forced to become self-sufficient. In other words, they produced everything they needed.

Everyone in feudal society was bound by duties and rights. For instance, a lord had power over his serfs but also the duty of protecting them. Lords built castles where people could go when threatened. Lords also gave land to warriors who would fight for them. The most important warriors were knights. When armored knights began to fight from horseback in the 900s, they were awesome—as awesome as the first armored tanks 1,000 years later.

New technology made mounted troops possible. By the late 700s European cavalry were using stirrups. Stirrups increased a warrior's ability to fight from horseback and not be toppled by the first blow. Of course, it took a huge horse to carry the weight of an armored man. By about 900, Europeans had bred such horses.

Influence of the Church

The Roman Catholic Church steadily grew in power during the Middle Ages. At a time of political disunity, it was the great unifying force throughout Europe. Even rich lords feared the power of the Church. If a lord failed to obey his bishop, he might be forced out of the Church. Such a person, the Church said, stood no chance of going to heaven.

As kingdoms fell apart, the Church took over jobs once carried out by the government. The Church also became the largest landholder in western Europe. Kings and lords gave land to the Church in exchange for its services.

Two important parts of Church life were the monks and the nuns. Monks lived together in places called "monasteries" to serve God through prayer and work. Similarly, nuns lived together in convents. Both monks and nuns kept learning and the arts alive. They also aided the poor and sick and homeless.

Nuns treat the sick in a hospital. Monks and nuns played an important role in medieval society.

Castles, like the one shown here, provided nobles with protection against attack by their enemies. Towns often needed similar protection. Stone walls with guarded towers could be found around many medieval towns.

Revival of Trade and Towns

In general, the 800s and 900s were a time of chaos and almost constant warfare. The average person lived only 30 difficult years.

During the 1000s (the eleventh century), however, life began to get better. For one, the Norsemen were no longer so threatening. Faced with fighting armored knights, Norsemen stopped raiding and began trading for the things they wanted.

They also sailed into the Atlantic Ocean and settled in Iceland and Greenland. About A.D. 1000, Viking adventurers explored the coast of North America. One group, led by Leif Ericson, set up an outpost there. Other Norsemen became Christians and settled into European society.

Life in Europe improved in other ways. New farming methods produced a surplus of food and a boom in population. These led to increased trade. As a result, old towns were revived and new towns sprang up near castles, crossroads, and harbors.

Life in a medieval town differed greatly from life on a manor. Townspeople had freedom to travel and make their own laws. Instead of working to serve a lord, people in towns worked as merchants and artisans. Artisans practiced a variety of trades, from shoemaking to metalwork. The merchants and artisans made up a new social class, the middle class. They had more freedom and wealth than the serfs but less than most lords.

To express their Christian faith, townspeople built beautiful churches. The artistic glory of these centuries of hope was the Gothic cathedral, whose spires soared toward the heavens.

Trade with the East

Trade increased within Europe, but also with places outside Europe. The leader in the expansion of this trade was the Italian city of Venice. Venice had always been a city of shipping and commerce. Venetian traders had maintained contact with Constantinople, then the greatest city of the Mediterranean world.

Venice was thus in a position to profit from the Crusades. Beginning in 1096, the Crusades were a series of wars to recapture the Holy Land from the Muslims. (The Holy Land is the area of the Middle East where Jesus lived.) From all over Europe, Christian knights assembled in Venice to board ships for the Holy Land.

The Crusades failed to take back the Holy Land. However, they did increase contacts between East and West. Crusaders brought home knowledge of the advanced way of life in the East. Demand for the East's luxury goods rose.

From China came silk and dyes, as well as the dishes the Europeans called "china." Among the most precious goods from the East were spices such as pepper, nutmeg, cloves, cinnamon, and ginger. Spices added flavor to foods and helped keep food from spoiling. In exchange for Asian goods, the Europeans sold leather, tin, swords, and woolen cloth.

The most famous of Italy's merchants was Marco Polo. When he was only 17, Marco Polo's father and uncle took him on an overland journey to China. Marco Polo lived and traveled in Asia for 24 years.

This illustration from the 1300s shows Marco Polo leaving Venice for his journey to Asia. His travels helped open European eyes to the wonders of Asia.

A New Spirit of Curiosity

With peace and prosperity, a new spirit of curiosity arose. Scholars eagerly read the writings from ancient Greece and Rome. Artists created beautiful works of art. Contacts with Islamic culture in Spain brought Europeans greater knowledge of science, philosophy, and medicine.

This period of scientific curiosity, return to classical learning, and praise of humanity came to be called the Renaissance (rehn-ih-SAHNS). *Renaissance* is a French term meaning "rebirth." The start of the Renaissance in northern Italy in the 1300s marked the beginnings of the modern age. By the 1400s, the Renaissance had spread throughout Europe.

The growth of knowledge was fed by a new invention, the printing press. In 1454 Johannes Gutenberg, a German goldsmith, perfected a press that used movable metal type. No longer was it necessary to copy a book by hand. Books could be made more quickly and cheaply. As books became available, new ideas spread rapidly. One of the most popular new books was *The Travels of Marco Polo.* By now Europeans were interested in faraway places. They were ready to believe Marco Polo's tales.

After his return home, Marco Polo told his adventures to a writer. Their book described the treasures Marco Polo had seen: splendid carpets, precious stones, and fine weapons. At the time, few Europeans believed Marco Polo. Imagine a black stone (coal) that burned! Imagine a parade of 5,000 elephants, each draped in cloth of silk and gold!

The Decline of Feudalism

The growth of trade and the rise of towns during the Middle Ages weakened the feudal system. Many serfs ran away from the manors to live in the towns. To keep laborers on the land, lords began to contract with them. As a result, hired labor began to replace serf labor. Lords traded more with towns, and manors became less self-sufficient. Thus the nobility began to lose power, and the townspeople gained power.

With the weakening of feudal lords, strong rulers emerged in Europe. Kings in England, France, and Portugal built especially strong governments. These rulers won the support of townspeople because they could raise large armies to enforce order. As countries became safer, people began to travel more. Trade flourished. For the first time in history, Europeans experienced a feeling of nationalism —love for and loyalty to one's country.

SECTION REVIEW

1. Key Terms Middle Ages, feudalism, self-sufficient, middle class, Crusades, nationalism, Renaissance

2. People and Places Norsemen (Vikings), Marco Polo, Johannes Gutenberg, Venice

3. Comprehension What led to the rise of feudalism?

4. Comprehension What caused the end of feudalism?

5. Critical Thinking How was the Renaissance an age of discovery?

2 The Search for New Sea Routes

SECTION GUIDE

Main Idea
The growth of trade led to a new economic system in Europe. Competition for trade routes increased knowledge of world geography.

Goals
As you read, look for answers to these questions:

1. Why did Europeans seek new sea routes to Asia?

2. What discoveries made voyages of exploration possible?

Key Terms
capital   **navigator**   **racism**
profit   **caravel**

A worker receives his pay in a fifteenth-century Italian bank.

IMAGINE THE BOOT SHAPE in the Mediterranean Sea that is Italy. Then imagine boot straps high up on each side of the boot. The easternmost strap marks the location of Venice. The westernmost strap marks the location of Genoa. In the 1400s these two cities were among the richest and most powerful cities in Europe, for the Mediterranean Sea was the crossroads of the Western world.

New Forms of Finance
Both Genoa and Venice were city-states, or self-governing cities. Both had grown from small fishing villages into sea powers. The two city-states became gateways through which rare goods—spices, dyes, African wool, gold, and silks—reached the far corners of Europe.

Italian merchants needed large amounts of money to finance the growing trade. This led to a revolution in how business was done. Italian bankers devised a new form of business arrangement: the joint-stock company. The joint-stock company made it possible to collect a large amount of **capital,** or money for investment, because a number of people combined their funds. By the mid-1400s, Genoa's Bank of St. George had branches throughout Europe.

Rivalry over Trade
The Italians' long presence in Muslim cities on the Mediterranean had given them good connections to those in power. This allowed them to have a special relationship with the Muslim traders who brought goods from China, India, and other lands. The result was that Italians enjoyed a monopoly on the Asian trade, as seen in the Trade Networks map on page 48.

Other European countries were jealous of the Italian cities. The Italians sold Asian goods for much more than they paid. As a result, they made huge **profits** —money left after costs are paid. Merchants in other parts of Europe had no chance to share in the trade routes monopolized by the Italians. If, however, they could discover another way to reach Asia, they too might become wealthy and powerful.

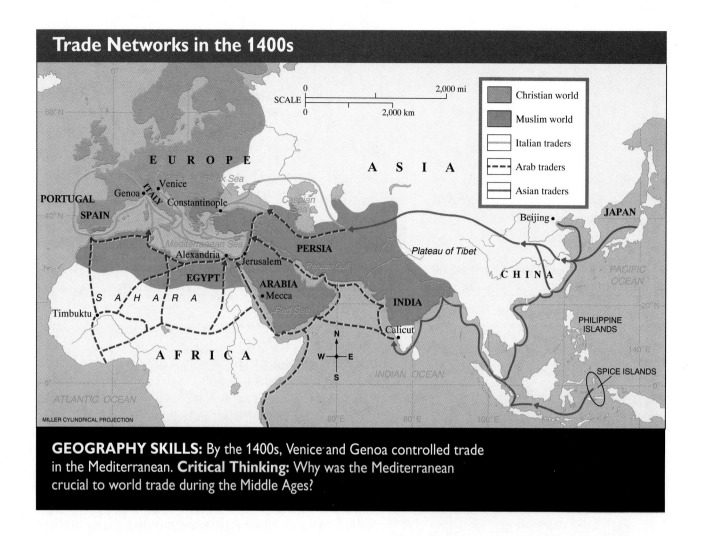

Trade Networks in the 1400s

Legend:
- Christian world
- Muslim world
- Italian traders
- Arab traders
- Asian traders

SCALE 0 — 2,000 mi / 0 — 2,000 km

MILLER CYLINDRICAL PROJECTION

GEOGRAPHY SKILLS: By the 1400s, Venice and Genoa controlled trade in the Mediterranean. **Critical Thinking:** Why was the Mediterranean crucial to world trade during the Middle Ages?

Portuguese Discoveries

Portugal led the search. The Portuguese king's power had grown with the decline of feudalism. Early in the 1400s Prince Henry (whom you read about in the last chapter) became interested in the unknown ocean on Portugal's coastline. Many people at that time believed that the sea boiled at the equator and that it was filled with ferocious sea monsters.

Why did the ocean interest Prince Henry so?

(1) He hoped to find an all-water route to the trading centers of Asia. This would break Italy's monopoly on trade with the East.

(2) A powerful navy would help him defeat Muslim forces in North Africa.

(3) He wished to spread Christianity beyond Europe's borders.

(4) As a child of the Renaissance, he also wanted to learn more about the ocean and what lay beyond it.

As you read, Prince Henry began sending ships south from Portugal down the coast of Africa. He did not actually sail with the Portuguese expeditions himself. Because he sponsored them, however, he became known as Henry the Navigator. A **navigator** is someone who can plan and control the course of a ship.

To his castle Henry invited geographers, astronomers, mapmakers, and sailors of many lands and religions. They reviewed each expedition's reports. Then they drew charts that allowed each expedition to go a little farther than the one before.

Henry's shipbuilders designed a double-rigged ship, the **caravel.** Using triangular sails it could sail into the wind, and with square sails it could sail with the wind at its back. Such a ship gave sailors confidence. They knew they could get home again no matter how the winds blew.

Portugal continued exploring the West African coast. The Portuguese found the

West Africans, who had been trading with North Africans for centuries, willing to trade. At first the Portuguese traded mostly for gold and ivory. By the early 1440s, however, they began to trade for slaves.

The Changing Slave Trade

Slavery was not new. From the earliest times slavery had been part of societies the world over. Slaves taken from Eastern Europe had long been a major part of Mediterranean trade. In fact, the word *slave* comes from *Slav*—eastern Europe's largest ethnic group. Slavery was no longer common in western Europe in the 1400s, but it still existed in eastern Europe and the Middle East, as well as in Africa.

This form of slavery is not what we usually think of when we hear the word "slavery." Slaves were seen as unlucky individuals, not as members of an inferior group or race. Because slaves often performed skilled tasks, they were generally treated with respect. A slave could marry a free person and could raise a family. The children of slaves were born free persons, not slaves.

Slavery changed, however, with a new and rising demand for field laborers on sugar plantations. In the 1400s the Portuguese began raising sugar cane on the Cape Verde Islands off the West African coast. Growing and harvesting sugar cane, a tropical plant, required intense labor in a hot climate. The Portuguese turned to African slaves, whom they bought from local traders.

In their desire for masses of agricultural laborers, the Portuguese laid the foundation for a new kind of slavery. The traditional idea of slaves developing their talents and being treated with respect was discouraged. Plantation slavery became a system tied to a race. **Racism** — the belief that one's own racial group is superior to others—kept slaves in an inferior position.

New technology helped European explorers expand their understanding of the world. The painting at left shows men captivated by navigational tools. The astrolabe (below) helped ships determine their location.

A Water Route to Asia

The Portuguese first sailed across the equator in 1473. Then, in 1487, Bartolomeu Dias (DEE-ahs) sailed around the tip of Africa. The king of Portugal hoped that Dias had found a route to India. He named the tip of Africa the Cape of Good Hope.

In 1497 another Portuguese explorer, Vasco da Gama (DUH GAM-uh), set out to fulfill the king's hope. Da Gama followed Dias's route around the Cape of Good Hope and then continued north along the eastern coast of Africa to Malindi, in present-day Kenya.

In Malindi lived a community of East Indians—people from India. There Da Gama hired a pilot for his ship. The pilot, a Muslim named Abu Majid, was one of the most experienced of his day. With Abu Majid in charge, Da Gama's expedition sailed across the Indian Ocean straight for the port of Calicut. Finally, the Portuguese had found an all-water route to Asia!

Portugal Finds an All-Water Route to Asia

E U R O P E

PORTUGAL SPAIN

Lisbon

MEDITERRANEAN SEA

Canary Is.

SCALE

0   1,000 mi

0   1,000 km

S A H A R A

Nile R.

A S I A

ARABIA

INDIA

Cape Verde Is.

Timbuktu

SONGHAI

A F R I C A

Calicut

Ceylon

Niger R.

IVORY COAST

GOLD COAST

SLAVE COAST

KONGO

Congo R.

Malindi

Zanzibar

N
W   E
S

INDIAN OCEAN

ATLANTIC OCEAN

Zambezi R.

Madagascar

Cape of Good Hope

	Route of Dias 1487–1488		Route of Da Gama 1497–1499
	Gold		Slaves		Silk
	Ivory		Spices	

MILLER CYLINDRICAL PROJECTION

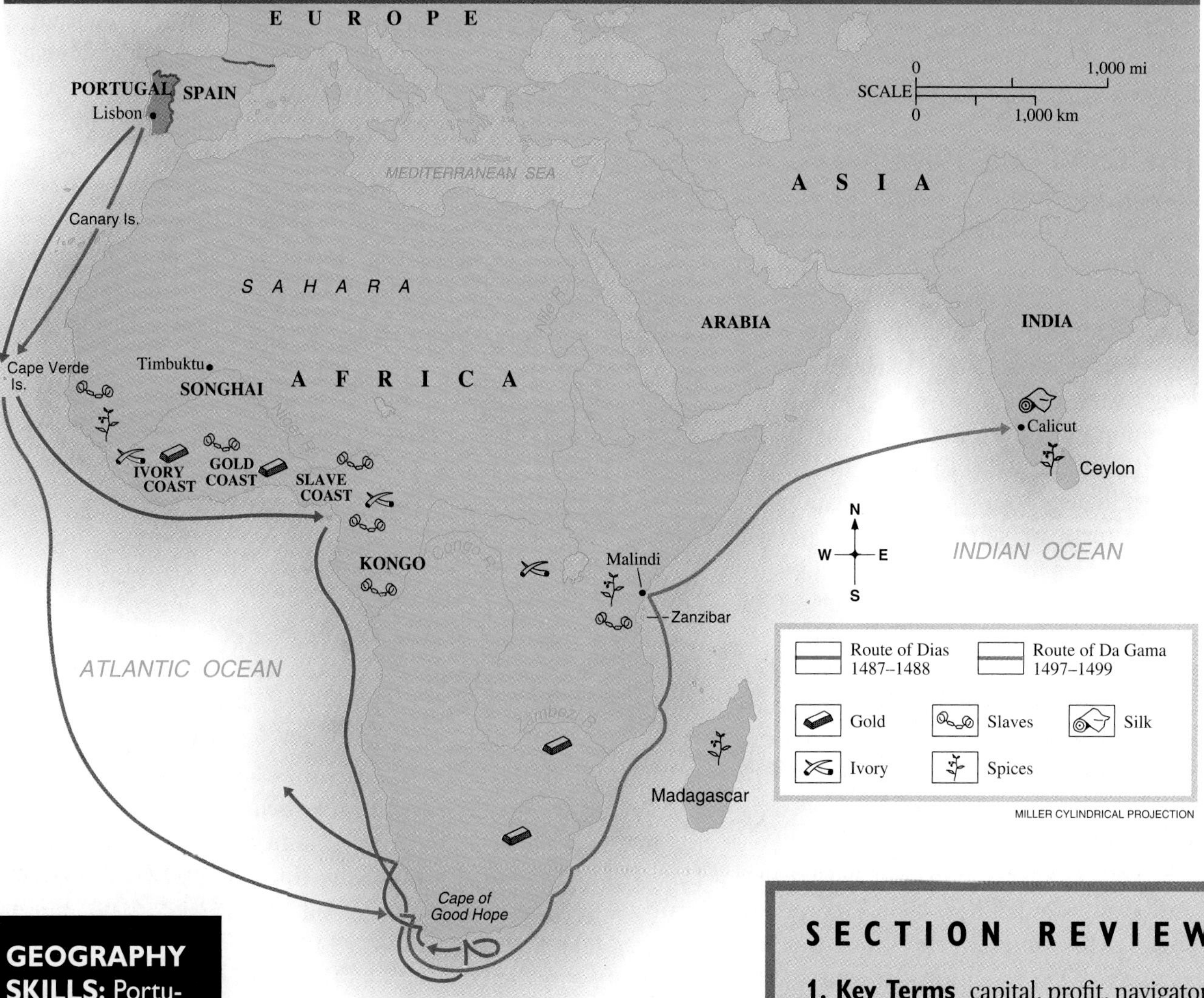

GEOGRAPHY SKILLS: Portugal's route to the East bypassed Arab and Italian traders. **Critical Thinking:** How might Portugal's location have contributed to its discovery of this route?

Da Gama's discovery of the water route had significant consequences.

(1) The Italian monopoly over the rich Eastern trade was destroyed. Transporting goods by water was cheaper than by overland caravan.

(2) The Mediterranean ceased to be the center of commerce between Asia and Europe. The richest port in Europe became Lisbon, on Portugal's Atlantic coast.

(3) Other European nations would soon challenge Portugal's control over the eastern trade by seeking their own routes to the East.

SECTION REVIEW

1. Key Terms capital, profit, navigator, caravel, racism

2. People and Places Henry the Navigator, Bartolomeu Dias, Vasco da Gama, Portugal, Cape of Good Hope, Lisbon

3. Comprehension Why was Prince Henry so eager to find an all-water route to Asia?

4. Comprehension What was the impact of Da Gama's discovery?

5. Critical Thinking What skills and qualities are necessary for successful exploration?

3 The Voyages of Christopher Columbus

SECTION GUIDE

Main Idea

Spain's desire to gain wealth and to spread the Catholic religion led it to support a voyage of exploration by Christopher Columbus.

Goals

As you read, look for answers to these questions:

1. What changes were going on in Europe at the time of Columbus's birth?

2. What did Columbus learn that prepared him for his famous voyage?

3. Why did King Ferdinand and Queen Isabella decide to finance Columbus's voyage?

Key Terms

monarch
Reconquista

CHRISTOPHER COLUMBUS grew up in the Italian city-state of Genoa, where he was drawn to the city's busy waterfront. At age 14 he began going on trading voyages. One such voyage would change his future. Columbus was 25 when his ship was sunk by a hostile fleet off the coast of Portugal. He survived by holding on to an oar and swimming to shore. He made his way to Lisbon, where his brother worked as a mapmaker. In Lisbon he would acquire the knowledge that would lead him west across the Atlantic.

Columbus's Education

Columbus learned mapmaking from his brother and taught himself to read and write Spanish. He also learned Latin, the language of most books at the time. Among the books he read were the works of Ptolemy, a mathematician and geographer who worked in ancient Egypt. Columbus also read *The Travels of Marco Polo*. Marco Polo's tales of the wealth of Asia sparked Columbus's imagination. Columbus was excited by Marco Polo's description of Japan, which was based only on rumor. "Many of the apartments," Marco Polo wrote, "have small tables of pure gold." Marco Polo also claimed that the entire roof of the ruler's palace was covered with gold.

Columbus had landed in the best place in the world to learn the science of ocean navigation. Yet Portugal's knowledge of navigation was considered a government secret. By marrying the daughter of a Portuguese sea captain, however, Columbus received what today would be considered a top-secret security clearance. He carefully studied his father-in-law's charts and maps. In this way, Christopher Columbus learned of the great advances Portugal had made in ocean exploration.

The bountiful spices of Asia lured many explorers. Here Marco Polo helps a group in India harvest pepper.

In 1492 Queen Isabella (below) achieved her goal of a united Spain. By sponsoring the first voyage of Columbus (right), she linked Europe and the Americas and launched the mighty Spanish empire.

Columbus also learned the skills of deep-sea navigation. He sailed south with a Portuguese fleet to Guinea, on Africa's Gold Coast. During the voyage he gained experience in sailing a caravel. Columbus also noticed that the winter winds off North Africa blew from the east. That observation would help ensure his future success.

Columbus's Vision

Within ten years of his soggy arrival on the Portuguese coast, Columbus formed the idea that became his life's passion: Why not sail *west* around the world to reach the Indies? (*The Indies* was the term used to describe the lands of East Asia.) At one time, many people believed that the earth was flat. By the 1400s, however, most educated Europeans knew that the earth was round. It made sense that by heading west, a ship would eventually circle the globe and arrive in the east. As far as Europeans knew, no one had tried before. The Viking voyages had been forgotten.

Europeans believed that the ocean was too big to cross. Yet Columbus took heart from Biblical teachings, which stated that God made the world six parts land and one part water. From this Columbus decided that the ocean was not nearly as wide as people supposed. The riches of the Indies

lay, Columbus said, not too far west across the ocean.

In 1484 Columbus approached the king of Portugal with his idea. The king's scientists found his math faulty. More importantly, the Portuguese were making good progress exploring the African coast and were not to be distracted. Neither was Columbus. He believed that God wanted him to make great discoveries in order to spread Christianity. As one writer put it, he "had developed in his heart the unshakable [belief] that he would find what he said he would find, as if he had it locked away in a trunk somewhere."

Help from Spain

Columbus took his son Diego and went to neighboring Spain. There he talked with the monarchs King Ferdinand and Queen Isabella about his ideas. (A monarch is a king or queen.) They were interested in the proposed voyage, for they saw that it might bring Spain both gold and an advantage over rival Portugal. Isabella, a deeply religious Catholic, also believed it was the duty of Spain to spread Christianity around the world.

Columbus's timing was poor. Ferdinand and Isabella were fighting to expel the Moors (North African Muslims) from the city of Granada, their last stronghold in Spain. The struggle to win back Spain was known as the Reconquista (ray-kahn-KEES-tuh)—Spanish for "reconquest."

The *Reconquista* was a holy war against the Muslims. Its goal was a Spain unified under one religion, Christianity. The *Reconquista* had occupied Ferdinand and Isabella's ancestors for centuries, and they were set on completing the job. The monarchs' quest for Christian unity affected Jews as well. All Jews who refused to be baptized were ordered to leave Spain.

In 1492, after six years of waiting, Columbus was about to give up on Spain and offer his services to France. At last, however,

Ferdinand and Isabella's armies took Granada and defeated the Moors. The monarchs had achieved their dream of an entirely Christian Spain. Now they were ready to consider Columbus's dream. Isabella called for Columbus.

Columbus proved a hard bargainer. This weaver's son insisted on being made a nobleman and given a coat of arms. He demanded the right to rule any lands he conquered. He asked for 10 percent of all wealth from those lands, and the grand title of Admiral of the Ocean Sea. After three months, the king and queen agreed. "You are going at our command," they told Columbus, "to discover and subdue the islands and continent in the ocean. It is only just and reasonable that since you expose yourself to danger to serve us, you should be rewarded for it."

An enthusiastic Columbus assembled his expedition at the Spanish port of Palos. At dawn on Friday, August 3, 1492, three ships—the *Niña* (NEE-nyuh), *Pinta*, and *Santa Maria*—left the harbor on a south-west course. Columbus wanted to reach the latitudes where, he remembered, the winds blew toward the west. In the Canary Islands to the west of Morocco, he restocked his ships with wood, water, and meat. Then he gave his crew the course: "West; nothing to the north, nothing to the south." The great voyage had begun.

Reaching the Americas

Columbus and his crew of about 90 sailors, many of them teenagers, had a long and difficult voyage. Conditions were rough. Cooking was done on the ship's decks. Only a few officers had bunks.

As the voyage dragged on, the crew grew nervous. Many began to fear they would never see Spain again. Columbus began to keep a false record. It showed the ships' daily progress to be less than it really was. Columbus kept to himself the true distance his ships were from Spain. Even this trick was not enough to calm the sailors. On October 10, after ten weeks at sea, the crew requested that Columbus turn back. He

Crew member during the 1991 re-enactment of Columbus's first voyage to the Americas.

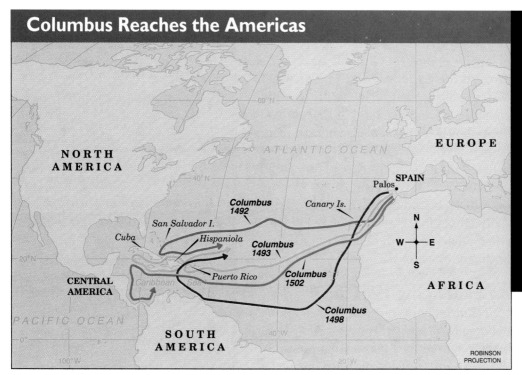

Columbus Reaches the Americas

NORTH AMERICA

ATLANTIC OCEAN

EUROPE

San Salvador I.

Cuba

Hispaniola

Columbus 1492

Canary Is.

Palos SPAIN

Columbus 1493

Puerto Rico

Columbus 1502

CENTRAL AMERICA

Caribbean Sea

Columbus 1498

AFRICA

PACIFIC OCEAN

SOUTH AMERICA

ROBINSON PROJECTION

GEOGRAPHY SKILLS: Columbus eventually sailed three more times to the Americas following his famous 1492 voyage. **Critical Thinking:** Why was he unable to reach Asia as originally planned?

This painting from the 1800s shows how one artist viewed Columbus's landing in the Americas. **Critical Thinking:** Do you think a Native American would have painted the scene differently? Explain.

convinced them to sail west for three more days. Just after midnight on October 12, the lookout on the *Pinta* sighted land.

No one is sure exactly where Columbus landed. It may have been Samana Cay, a tiny island in the Bahamas. Columbus named the island San Salvador. He did not find the golden palaces he was seeking. Instead he met "simple and honest" people who were "liberal [generous] with all they have." Columbus was impressed by their canoes, which he noted were "swifter in movement" than his rowboats.

Believing that the golden-roofed palaces of Japan were near, Columbus zigzagged through the Caribbean Sea in search of Marco Polo's Japan. He finally found enough gold on the island of Hispaniola (his-puhn-YO-luh) to convince himself that he had reached Asia. He did not realize that he had landed at the edge of the continents of North America and South America. Indeed, he did not suspect that these continents even existed. In January 1493 he sailed homeward with hopeful reports for Ferdinand and Isabella.

An Expanding Horizon

For centuries Europeans had looked upon the ocean as a barrier. For centuries there had been no contact between Europe and the Western Hemisphere. With one voy-

age, Columbus changed that. The Atlantic Ocean became a "bridge" instead of a barrier. The Atlantic bridge would end up connecting Europe, Africa, and the Americas. Within a short time the Atlantic replaced the Mediterranean as the heart of European trade. This would forever change life on all the continents involved.

As for Columbus, he had little notion of what he had actually achieved. Still believing he had reached Asia, he searched for the golden-roofed palaces of Japan. Altogether he would make four trips to explore the Caribbean Sea.

He brought back geographic knowledge but not the riches of his dreams. Although Queen Isabella too had wanted riches, she also wanted to bring Christianity to new peoples. Thus she was angry to hear that Columbus had begun to enslave the native Arawak Indians on Hispaniola. To punish him, the rulers of Spain took away Columbus's power to govern the lands he discovered. Then, after his fourth voyage, they stopped supporting him altogether. In 1506 Columbus died, bitter at his treatment by the monarchs.

SECTION REVIEW

1. Key Terms monarch, *Reconquista*

2. People and Places Christopher Columbus, King Ferdinand, Queen Isabella, Genoa, Guinea, Gold Coast, Palos, San Salvador, Hispaniola

3. Comprehension On what ideas did Christopher Columbus base his plans for reaching Asia?

4. Comprehension Why did Spain decide to support Columbus's voyage?

5. Critical Thinking What Renaissance ideas probably influenced Columbus? Explain your answer.

SKILLS: Cause and Effect

LEARN

Cause and effect is all around you. Here is an example: If you don't clean up your room regularly, it will look messy. The cause—not cleaning up your room—makes something happen. The effect—the messy room—is what happens. Effects, in turn, can become causes. What happens when a parent sees that your room is a complete mess? The messy room is now the cause, and the parent's reaction is the effect.

History works the same way. To understand European exploration of the Americas, you need to find out what caused it. You also need to find out what effect it had. In your search you may uncover multiple causes and effects. You can follow the trail of causes and effects to discover the impact of any major historical event.

CAUSES
- Renaissance spirit of curiosity
- Desire for adventure, glory, and riches

EUROPEAN EXPLORATION

EFFECTS
- European settlement of the Americas
- Expanded knowledge of world geography

PRACTICE

Study the cause-and-effect chart above.

1. Name one of the causes and one of the effects.

2. What is another cause of European exploration? What is another effect?

3. Turn one of the effects into a cause. Then suggest one or two possible effects of the new cause.

APPLY

4. Draw a simple cause-and-effect chart to represent the events in the following statement: Contact with Asia during the Crusades led to greater European demand for Asian goods.

5. Choose another event from this chapter. Draw your own chart showing as many causes and effects of that event as you can find.

4 On to the Pacific

SECTION GUIDE

Main Idea
Explorers gradually learned that Columbus's new lands were another continent, not part of Asia.

Goals
As you read, look for answers to these questions:

1. Why did Spain claim most of the Americas?

2. How did explorers prove that the Americas were not Asia?

Key Terms
Line of Demarcation
strait
convert
circumnavigate

WHAT HAPPENS when two people want the same thing? They may fight over it. One person may give in to the other. Or, they may divide it. Nations are no different.

Dividing the World

Columbus's first voyage to the Americas triggered an intense dispute between Spain and Portugal over the new lands. Portugal had a monoply on trade with the African coast, where it traded for slaves and gold. Portugal wanted to continue exploring the South Atlantic. Spain insisted, however, that it had the right to the lands Columbus had discovered.

Spain and Portugal turned to the Pope for a solution to their dispute. At the time, the Pope claimed the right to place non-Christian lands under the protection of Christian rulers.

In 1493 the Pope established a **Line of Demarcation** —an imaginary line around the earth, running north and south. The Line of Demarcation divided the world in half. Portugal could claim all non-Christian lands to the east of the line. Spain could claim such lands to the west.

Spain and Portugal thought they were only dividing Asia. No one knew at the time that the Line of Demarcation also gave Spain the rights to most of North and South America. (See the map on the next page.)

Cabral and Vespucci

After Vasco da Gama's report on a route to India around Africa, Portugal quickly made plans for a follow-up voyage. Its captain would be Pedro Álvares Cabral.

Da Gama, trying to avoid terrible winds, had made a huge swing into the South Atlantic during his voyage to India. Cabral made an even wider swing. Instead of reaching India, he landed on the coast of Brazil. He sent back a report to the king of Portugal arguing for a settlement there. Cabral thought it might be a good stopping point on the way to India.

This painting shows the signing of the Treaty of Tordesillas in 1494. The treaty positioned the Line of Demarcation.

56

Early Spanish and Portuguese Voyages

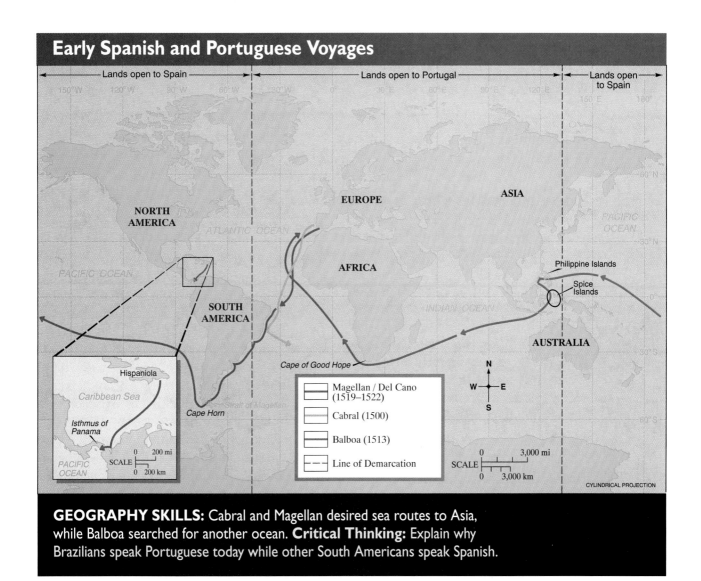

GEOGRAPHY SKILLS: Cabral and Magellan desired sea routes to Asia, while Balboa searched for another ocean. **Critical Thinking:** Explain why Brazilians speak Portuguese today while other South Americans speak Spanish.

The mariner who then explored South America's coast for Portugal in 1501 was Amerigo Vespucci (ves-POO-chee). He realized that what he saw was not Asia but a new continent. He was quoted as saying:

> **❝I have found a continent more densely populated and abounding in animals than our Europe, Asia, and Africa. We may rightly call this continent the New World. ❞**

Impressed by these words, a German mapmaker named the new continent "America" after Amerigo Vespucci.

For the next half century, the name America was given only to South America. Maps of the time showed North America to be a vast peninsula connected to Asia.

Balboa Finds the Pacific

Vasco Núñez de Balboa was one of the many Spanish adventurers who followed Columbus to the Americas. He went to the new Spanish settlement at Darién, on the Atlantic side of the Isthmus of Panama. There Balboa heard Indian reports of another ocean. To find it, Balboa organized a large expedition in 1513.

CATHOLICISM IN THE PHILIPPINES

Magellan's voyage eventually took him to a group of islands later named the Philippines, in honor of King Philip II of Spain. As Spain established its rule over the islands, it began to convert the local people to Catholicism. To do so, Spanish clergy known as friars were sent to the islands. They soon gained a powerful role within the colonial government.

The friars vigorously discouraged native religious practices on the islands. Muslims in the south, known as Moros, successfully resisted Spanish rule and remained untouched by Catholicism. Most Filipinos, however, converted, and the Church became an important part of Filipino society.

Moving southward, the group hacked their way through thick jungle. At last Balboa reached the top of the mountains that run along the Isthmus of Panama. Before him stretched the Pacific Ocean (or, as Balboa named it, the "South Sea"). Four days later he touched the ocean surf with his sword and claimed the ocean for Spain. Somewhere on the other side of that ocean, people now realized, lay Asia.

Magellan's Remarkable Voyage

Meanwhile, the Spanish looked glumly on as Portuguese ships returned from the Indies laden with spices, silks, and jewels. The Line of Demarcation prevented Spain from following the Portuguese route around Africa to the East. Yet a continent stood in the way of the Spanish reaching the Indies by sailing west.

In early 1518 the king of Spain was introduced to Ferdinand Magellan. Born in Portugal, Magellan was a navigator who had sailed with Portuguese ships to India and the Spice Islands. After he and King Manuel of Portugal quarreled, he offered his services to the king of Spain.

Magellan laid out a plan to sail west to the Indies. He told the king that he could find a water passage around the Americas by sailing south. Excited by what he heard, the king of Spain agreed to sponsor Magellan's voyage.

In September 1519 Magellan set out from Spain with 5 ships and about 240 men. The ships crossed the rough Atlantic and then turned south along the coast of South America. As they continued south, the weather grew stormier and more bitter. So did tempers. When some of his sailors tried to mutiny (rebel), Magellan put down the mutiny and executed its leader.

The expedition spent the winter on the coast near the tip of South America. In the spring they set out again. Despite terrible storms and winds, Magellan found what he was looking for—a **strait** (narrow passage of water) between the two oceans. He knew it was a strait, not a river, because the water remained salty. This is the waterway now called the Strait of Magellan.

Before heading into the strait, Magellan sent men out to gather food for the long voyage ahead. When they had gathered enough, the ships lifted anchor and headed into the strait. Four days later they sailed into Balboa's South Sea. The ocean seemed so calm that Magellan renamed it the "Pacific," meaning "peaceful."

Circling the Globe

For the next several months, Magellan and his crew sailed across the Pacific. The ocean was far wider than Magellan had guessed. The voyage seemed endless. The fresh food lasted only a month. Hunger, thirst, and disease tortured the sailors.

We know all this because of Antonio Pigafetta. The Spanish king had allowed Pigafetta, an adventurous Italian nobleman, to tag along on the voyage. Of those terrible days on the Pacific, Pigafetta wrote, "We ate biscuit, which was no longer biscuit, but powder of biscuits swarming with worms. . . . often we ate sawdust from boards. Rats were sold for [gold], and even then we could not get them."

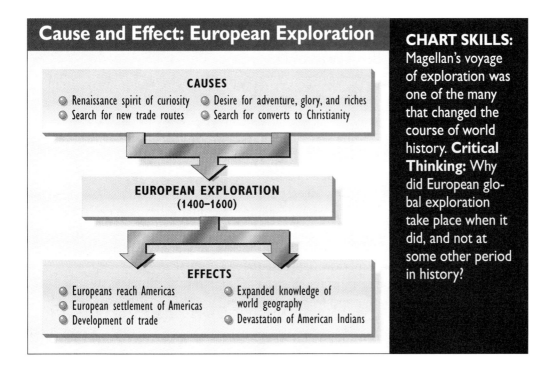

Cause and Effect: European Exploration

CAUSES
- Renaissance spirit of curiosity
- Desire for adventure, glory, and riches
- Search for new trade routes
- Search for converts to Christianity

EUROPEAN EXPLORATION
(1400–1600)

EFFECTS
- Europeans reach Americas
- European settlement of Americas
- Development of trade
- Expanded knowledge of world geography
- Devastation of American Indians

CHART SKILLS: Magellan's voyage of exploration was one of the many that changed the course of world history. **Critical Thinking:** Why did European global exploration take place when it did, and not at some other period in history?

Nearly dead, the sailors at last reached the islands later named the Philippines. There, fresh food and fresh water helped them begin to regain their health.

In the Philippines, Magellan was pleased to *convert* a chief to the Catholic faith. (To convert is to change someone's beliefs, especially religious beliefs.) Anxious to help the chief, Magellan became involved in a local war. He decided to fight the friendly chief's enemy. Magellan wanted to show how powerful the Spanish were and thereby demonstrate the power of their God. It was a costly mistake. In a beach assault, Magellan's forces were met by a hail of bamboo spears, and he was killed.

Despite the death of their leader, the expedition sailed on. The crew headed south to the Spice Islands, where they picked up cloves and other spices.

Only one ship completed the journey. This was the *Victoria,* whose captain was Juan Sebastián del Cano. Del Cano sailed across the Indian Ocean, around Africa, and then north in the Atlantic. In 1522, three years after leaving Spain, the *Victoria* and its crew of Europeans and four Indians arrived home. The expedition had been the first to *circumnavigate* —sail around— the earth. The spices on board more than paid for the cost of the expedition.

The expedition gave the first real proof that the earth was round. Mapmakers went back to their drawing boards.

SECTION REVIEW

1. Key Terms Line of Demarcation, strait, convert, circumnavigate

2. People and Places Amerigo Vespucci, Vasco Núñez de Balboa, Ferdinand Magellan, Juan Sebastián del Cano, Isthmus of Panama, Strait of Magellan

3. Comprehension What did Magellan know about the Western Hemisphere? What did he guess at?

4. Comprehension What did Magellan's voyage prove?

5. Critical Thinking How are explorers like scientists?

Summary

1. In the 400s western Europe entered the Middle Ages, a period of foreign invasions and declining trade. Feudalism, based on control by local lords and the work of serfs, emerged. The growth of trade led to the decline of feudalism and to the rise of powerful monarchs. Beginning in the 1400s the Renaissance brought to Europe a new spirit of curiosity, learning, and praise of humanity.

2. Newly powerful European nations searched for overseas routes to end the Italian monopoly on the Asian trade. Portugal made advances in navigation and found an all-water route to Asia. Needing more farm labor, Portugal also began the slave trade with Africa.

3. Europe in the 1400s was filled with energy and new ideas. Columbus set out to reach Asia by sailing westward from Spain. His 1492 voyage took him to islands off the coast of the Americas. The Atlantic Ocean became a "bridge" instead of a barrier for European explorers.

4. In 1493 the Pope established the Line of Demarcation to divide non-Christian lands between Spain and Portugal. Explorations by Cabral, Vespucci, Balboa, and Magellan increased Europeans' knowledge of world geography. The explorers proved the world was round and showed that the Americas were separate from Asia.

Graphic Summary

The collapse of trade and invasions cause western Europe's decline. Feudalism develops to help people survive. Increased trade and new towns weaken feudalism.

The Renaissance leads to a new spirit of curiosity. Europeans search for new trade routes. In its desire for agricultural laborers, Portugal begins trading for African slaves.

Columbus journeys to the Americas in his search for a westward route to Asia. Other Europeans begin exploring the Americas. Magellan's expedition circumnavigates the globe.

Review

KEY TERMS

Define the terms in each of the following pairs.
1. Middle Ages; feudalism
2. capital; profit
3. strait; circumnavigate

COMPREHENSION

1. What factors caused the rise of feudalism in medieval Europe?
2. Describe the importance of the Roman Catholic Church during the Middle Ages.
3. Why did Europeans seek new trade routes to Asia?
4. Why did the Portuguese begin the slave trade with Africa?
5. Why was Da Gama's expedition so important?
6. What did Columbus notice on his voyage to Africa that would later help him on his voyages across the Atlantic Ocean?
7. Why did the Spanish monarchs decide to finance Columbus's first voyage?
8. Explain the significance of Columbus's first voyage to find a westward route to Asia.
9. What role did the Pope play in establishing European claims over newly explored lands?
10. What was the purpose of Magellan's voyage around the world? What happened to Magellan on that voyage?

Places to Locate

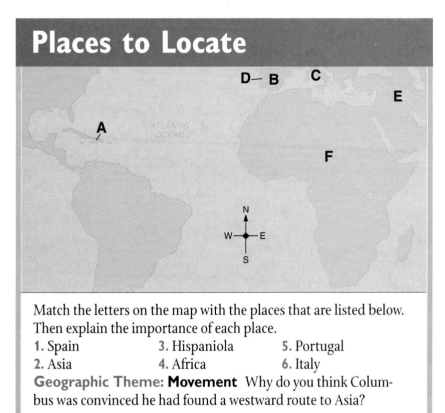

Match the letters on the map with the places that are listed below. Then explain the importance of each place.

1. Spain
2. Asia
3. Hispaniola
4. Africa
5. Portugal
6. Italy

Geographic Theme: Movement Why do you think Columbus was convinced he had found a westward route to Asia?

Skill Review

Copy the chart below onto a separate sheet of paper. Then complete the chart by filling in the missing causes and effects.

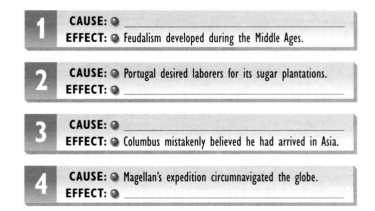

1
CAUSE: ◉ _____
EFFECT: ◉ Feudalism developed during the Middle Ages.

2
CAUSE: ◉ Portugal desired laborers for its sugar plantations.
EFFECT: ◉ _____

3
CAUSE: ◉ _____
EFFECT: ◉ Columbus mistakenly believed he had arrived in Asia.

4
CAUSE: ◉ Magellan's expedition circumnavigated the globe.
EFFECT: ◉ _____

CRITICAL THINKING

1. Relating Past to Present Explain the ways in which trade helps people. What examples of trade do you see every day? How can trade help us learn about other cultures?

2. Forming a Hypothesis In what ways did slavery change in the 1400s? Why did these changes occur?

PORTFOLIO OPTIONS

1. Civics Connection Describe the system of government that existed in Europe during the Middle Ages. How did it change with the growth of trade and towns?

2. Writing Connection Imagine that you are a sailor on Magellan's expedition around the Americas. Write a series of journal entries detailing your experiences. Be sure to include descriptions of the ocean voyage, places visited, and people encountered.

3. Contemporary Connection Consult magazines, newspapers, and encyclopedias to learn what unexplored areas remain in today's world. How, in your view, should people approach those areas? Prepare a report on one of these areas and present it to the class.

4. Timeline Connection Copy the chapter timeline. Which of the voyages listed do you think was most important? Explain. Now add two other events from your reading of the chapter that you think should be included and explain why.

Spain, realizing that the Americas were not a part of Asia but a vast new resource, began to conquer and colonize them. Christopher Columbus's brother founded Santo Domingo on the island of Hispaniola, shown here, and it remains the oldest permanent European settlement in the Americas.

CIVITAS S. Domingi sita in Hispaniola Insula Angliæ magnitudine fere æquali, ipsa urbs elegantior ab Hispanis privata, et omnibus circumiacens insulis, suam dat.

1480   1505   1530   1555

1493 Columbus colonizes Hispaniola

1508 Ponce de León explores Puerto Rico

1521 Cortés conquers Mexico

1541 De Soto reaches Mississippi River

1528 Narváez expedition begins

Spain Builds an Empire
(1493–1700)

1 Caribbean Beginnings

SECTION GUIDE

Main Idea

Spain's colonization of the West Indies brought great change to Europe and Africa as well as the Americas.

Goals

As you read, look for answers to these questions:

❶ How did the arrival of Europeans affect life in the Western Hemisphere?

❷ What was the effect of the slave trade on Africa? On the Western Hemisphere?

Key Terms

Columbian exchange
conquistador
missionary
plantation
African diaspora

IF 600 YEARS AGO you wanted to eat lunch, you would not have been able to order a pizza. Nowhere would you have found an all-beef hamburger with french fries. You would not even have been able to get a simple peanut butter sandwich.

The Columbian Exchange

Why were those foods unavailable in the 1400s? The reason has nothing to do with the lack of fast-food restaurants in those days. The real problem would have been that you wanted to combine foods that came from two different—and totally separate—worlds. Wheat, the basic ingredient of pizza crust and sandwich bread, was grown in the "Old World" of Europe, Africa, and Asia. Cattle too were raised only on those continents. People in the "New World" of the Americas knew nothing of those food sources. However, they grew tomatoes, potatoes, and peanuts. These plants, necessary for pizza sauce, french fries, and peanut butter, had never been seen in the Old World. Then in 1492, the Old and New Worlds met, changing forever the way people on earth lived and ate.

Our modern foods are just one of many examples of the Columbian exchange. The Columbian exchange refers to the transfer of plants, animals, and diseases between the two hemispheres. The Geography Feature on the next two pages describes the effects of that exchange.

1580	1605	1630	1655	1680

1609 Santa Fe founded

1680 Pueblo Indians force Spanish from New Mexico

GEOGRAPHY: The Columbian Exchange

Is an ocean more like a wall or a highway? Before Columbus, the Atlantic Ocean served as a wall, dividing the Americas from Africa and Europe. After Columbus, the ocean served as a highway, linking the continents.

The ocean highway even had "lanes" for travel. Sailing ships relied on winds and ocean currents to power them across the water (see map below). Ships crossed the Atlantic on these currents, bringing people, plants, animals, and diseases from one side of the ocean to another. Examples of this transfer, called the Columbian Exchange, are shown on these pages.

The plants and livestock brought by the Spaniards enlarged the food supply of the Americas. The plants that Europeans carried from the Americas changed diets around the world. Corn and potatoes—both developed by American Indian farmers—fed a rapidly growing world population.

The Europeans also carried germs across the ocean. Such germs caused diseases that killed millions of Indians. Thus weakened, Indian societies found it hard to resist European invaders.

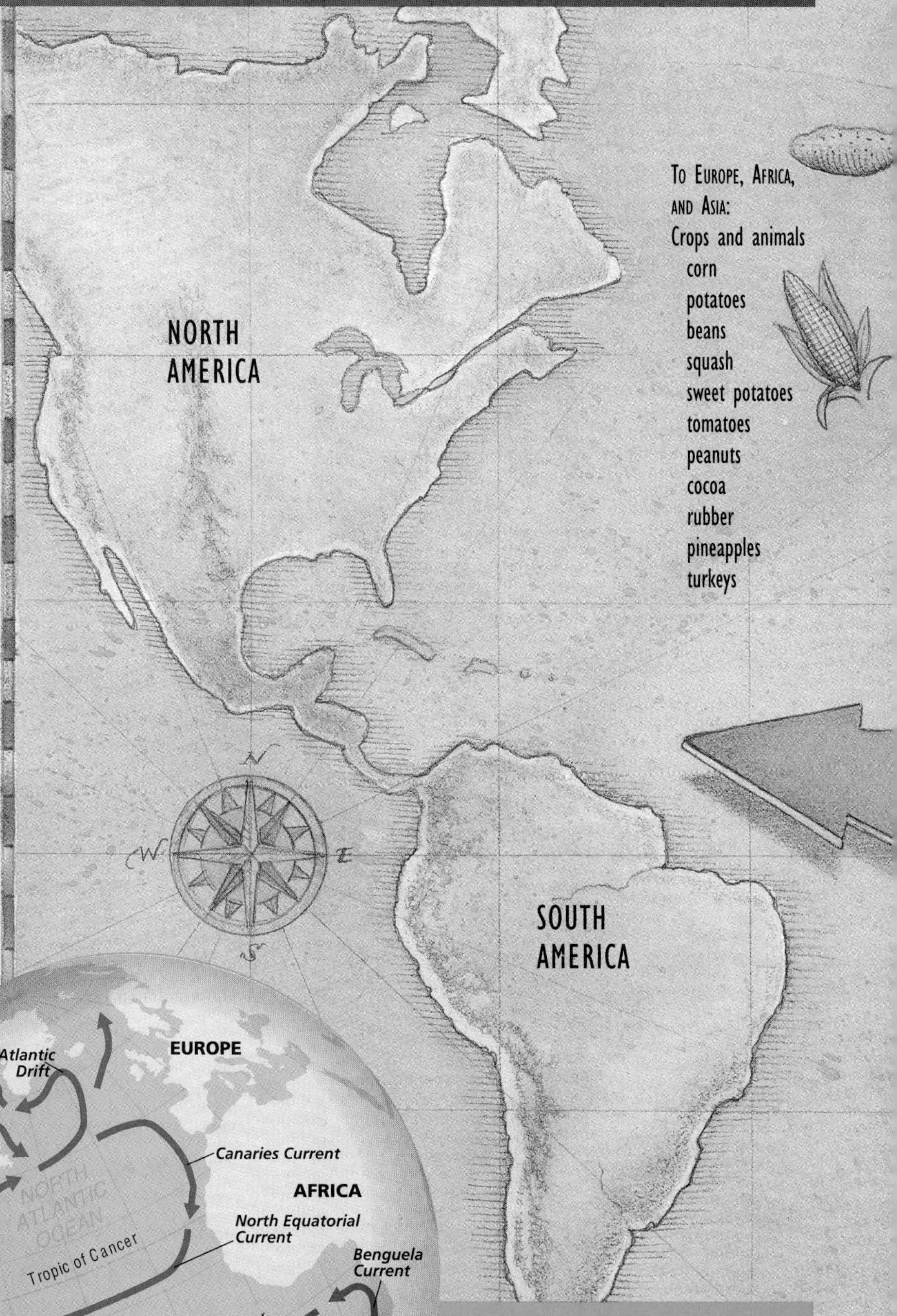

NORTH AMERICA

SOUTH AMERICA

TO EUROPE, AFRICA, AND ASIA:
Crops and animals
corn
potatoes
beans
squash
sweet potatoes
tomatoes
peanuts
cocoa
rubber
pineapples
turkeys

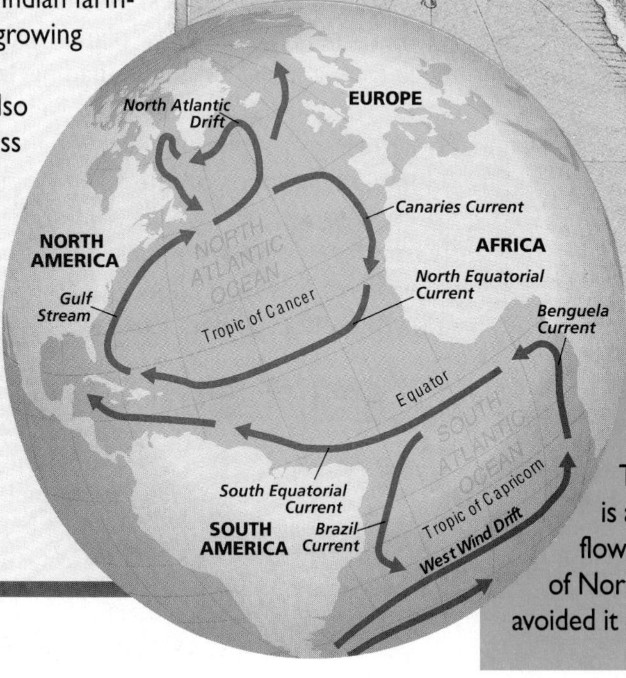

EUROPE

North Atlantic Drift

Canaries Current

NORTH AMERICA

AFRICA

North Equatorial Current

Gulf Stream

Benguela Current

Tropic of Cancer

Equator

South Equatorial Current

SOUTH AMERICA

Brazil Current

Tropic of Capricorn

West Wind Drift

This map shows the major currents of the Atlantic Ocean. The Gulf Stream, for example, is a "river" of warm water that flows north along the eastern coast of North America. Sea captains avoided it on their way to the Americas.

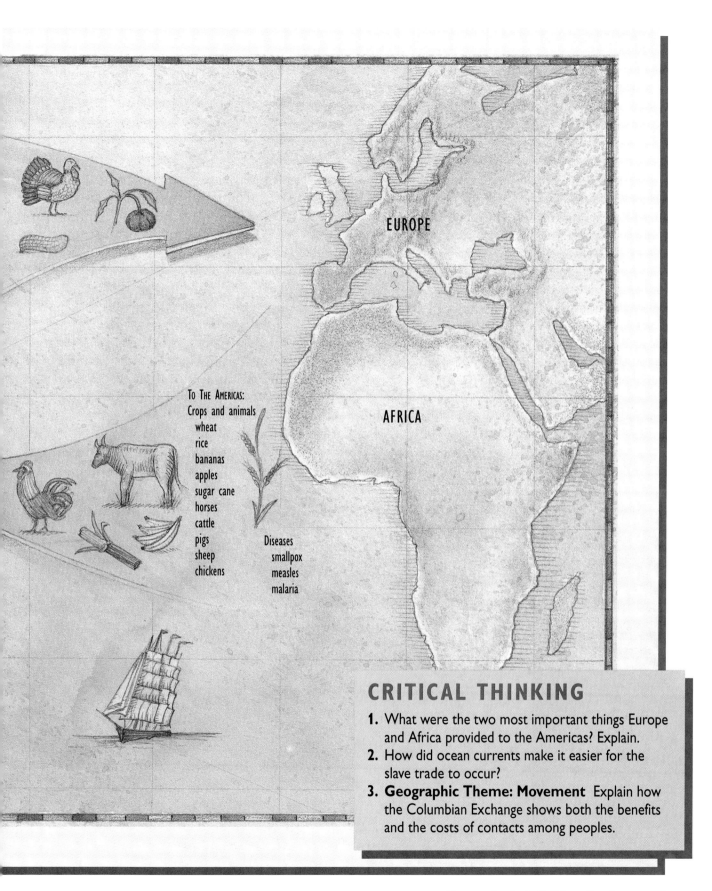

EUROPE

AFRICA

To The Americas:
Crops and animals
   wheat
   rice
   bananas
   apples
   sugar cane
   horses
   cattle
   pigs
   sheep
   chickens

Diseases
  smallpox
  measles
  malaria

CRITICAL THINKING

1. What were the two most important things Europe and Africa provided to the Americas? Explain.
2. How did ocean currents make it easier for the slave trade to occur?
3. **Geographic Theme: Movement** Explain how the Columbian Exchange shows both the benefits and the costs of contacts among peoples.

Another result of Columbus's voyage was a European shift of focus toward an Atlantic world. Until this time the Mediterranean had served as the center for European trade. After Columbus, European commerce focused on Atlantic ports. The continents of Europe, Africa, and the Americas became bound together in a way that changed life on both sides of the Atlantic. In time the changes would extend to Asia as well.

The Spanish Explorers

The restless young men of Spain who returned with Columbus to Hispaniola had high ambitions. They dreamed of finding gold and glory. They dreamed of being conquistadors (kahn-KEES-tuh-dorz)—conquerors.

The conquistadors fought not only for gold and glory but also for God. Spain was deeply committed to Christianity and to the Roman Catholic Church. Spain had just expelled its Moors and Jews. Now the Spanish hoped to convert non-Christian peoples in the Americas to the Roman Catholic faith. Every Spanish expedition included missionaries, people sent to do religious work. Most were friars, religious "brothers" who had vowed to live a life of poverty and service to others.

Included in most of those early expeditions—including Columbus's—were men of African ancestry. Some were descendants of the Moors who had once ruled Spain. Others were Africans who had been brought to Spain to work as laborers and slaves. They often provided labor for the expeditions, building settlements and planting crops. Some served as skilled seamen and officers aboard Spanish ships.

Columbus's Second Voyage

The first outpost of the new Atlantic world was in the West Indies, islands located in the Caribbean Sea. Ferdinand and Isabella had given Columbus the right to rule any lands he discovered and the right to half the wealth from those lands. On his second voyage in 1493, therefore, he set out to establish a kingdom. His seventeen ships carried those things needed to re-create Spain on the island of Hispaniola. (Today the nations of Haiti and the Dominican Republic are located on Hispaniola.)

Columbus began a cruel conquest of the people he had called "Indians," the island's Arawak people. "There is no better people or land in the world," Columbus had

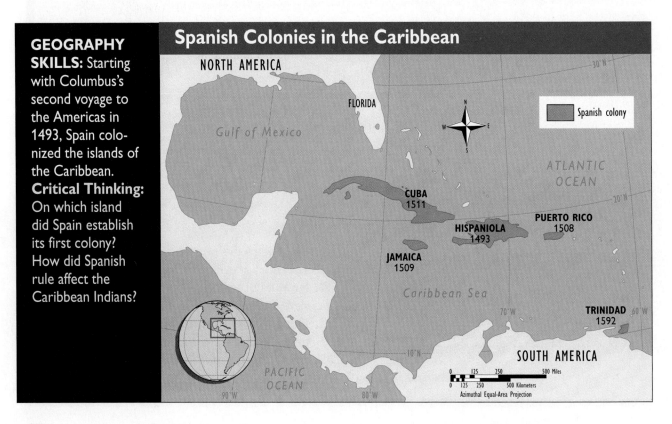

GEOGRAPHY SKILLS: Starting with Columbus's second voyage to the Americas in 1493, Spain colonized the islands of the Caribbean.
Critical Thinking: On which island did Spain establish its first colony? How did Spanish rule affect the Caribbean Indians?

Spanish Colonies in the Caribbean

NORTH AMERICA

FLORIDA

Gulf of Mexico

Spanish colony

ATLANTIC OCEAN

CUBA 1511

HISPANIOLA 1493

PUERTO RICO 1508

JAMAICA 1509

Caribbean Sea

TRINIDAD 1592

SOUTH AMERICA

PACIFIC OCEAN

0 125 250 500 Miles
0 125 250 500 Kilometers
Azimuthal Equal-Area Projection

written the king. "They love their neighbors as themselves and have the sweetest speech in the world and gentle, and are always smiling." Nevertheless, he was plotting to enslave them.

Columbus carried instructions from Ferdinand and Isabella. They said that he should "treat the Indians very well and affectionately without causing them any annoyance whatever. . . ." Furthermore, Columbus was to "mete out severe punishment" to any settlers who did mistreat the Indians.

Columbus did the reverse. First he demanded tribute from the Arawak in the form of gold or cotton. Those who failed to make the tribute had their hands cut off. Columbus also rounded up 500 Arawak and sent them to Spain to be sold as slaves. He said that they were cannibals. (Isabella had approved making slaves of Indians who were cannibals.)

Eventually Isabella realized that Columbus was lying and, in addition, was a very poor leader. He was stripped of his governing powers.

Abuse of the Indians

Removing Columbus from power, however, did not stop the abuse of the Indians. The Spanish Crown encouraged further mistreatment through the land system it established in the Americas. The Crown gave land grants to Spanish settlers and assigned Indians to that land. In return, the landholders promised to convert the Indians to Christianity, protect them, and look after their needs. In reality, the Indians were treated as slaves, with no rights.

On Hispaniola the Spanish forced local Indians to do the backbreaking labor of mining and farming. After about fifteen years, little gold was left. Most of the Indians had died. The Indian population in all Spanish-held areas fell from about 8 million to less than 100,000—a decline of about 99 percent.

This illustration shows the technology of grinding sugar cane, the first step in refining sugar. **Critical Thinking:** What kind of power is shown moving the machinery?

Wealth from Sugar Cane

Of all the plants Columbus carried with him on his second voyage, the most important for the future of the Caribbean was sugar cane. Throughout the Middle Ages the most common sweetener in Europe was honey. The small amount of sugar available was usually to be found in a monastery's medicine chest. Contact with the East during the Crusades, however, stimulated a new interest in sugar.

The Moors carried a knowledge of sugar-making with them into Spain. This knowledge was part of Spain's Islamic heritage. In their search for wealth, the Spanish brought the tradition to the Americas.

Most Spanish settlers regarded the Americas as a place to make money. The profits, as most saw it, came from two sources: (1) taking or mining precious metals such as gold and silver, and (2) growing crops, such as sugar cane, that could be sold in Europe. The large farm that grew such crops was called a **plantation.** The landowner of a plantation was a planter.

A Demand for Laborers

The Spanish soon turned from Hispaniola to neighboring islands in the search for both gold and laborers. The first to get Spanish attention was Puerto Rico, which Columbus had visited on his second voyage. A soldier and planter, Juan Ponce de

Sugar cane was brought by the Spanish to the Americas.

AFRICAN HERITAGE

For centuries, millions of Africans were torn from their homes and brought to the Americas in chains. Despite the hardships of slavery, they did not forget their African culture. Many elements of American life today have their roots in Africa. Katherine Dunham (shown performing in the 1940s), a dancer, choreographer, and teacher in East St. Louis, Illinois, bases her work on African forms of movement. For decades she has taught African cultural history and the importance of continuing those traditions.

Léon (PAWN-se duh LEE-uhn), led the first exploration to Puerto Rico in 1508. He found gold. Soon Indians were forced to mine streams for gold, to grow food for the Spaniards, and to carry their burdens. Ponce de Léon became one of the richest men in the West Indies.

The pattern continued. In 1509 Spanish conquistadors invaded Jamaica. In 1511 the ruthless Diego Velázquez (vuh-LAHS-kehs) conquered Cuba. He terrorized and massacred the Arawak. Among those who then received land grants and Indian slaves was Bartolomé de Las Casas, a soldier in the expedition.

Las Casas and the Indians

The father of Las Casas had sailed with Columbus in 1493. Las Casas himself had gone to Hispaniola as a planter in 1502. He no doubt shared the views of a fellow planter, Bernal Díaz, who said, "We came here to serve God, and also to get rich."

After settling in Cuba, Las Casas became a priest. He must have thought deeply on this question: How can you serve God and enslave Indians? In 1514 he gave up his land grant and freed his Indians. For the next 50 years Las Casas fought against those who abused the Indians. The Crown called him "Protector of the Indians."

When people argued that the best way to Christianize the Indians was to conquer them, Las Casas answered that peaceful persuasion was far better. When people said that Indians were naturally meant to be slaves, Las Casas replied, "Mankind is one, and all men are alike in that which concerns their creation. . . ." The views of Las Casas helped convince the Pope to forbid Indian slavery and led the king of Spain in 1542 to proclaim strict rules over how Indians should be treated.

The new rules came too late for the Indians. Most had already been wiped out by cruel treatment and disease.

Slavery in the Americas

As the Indians died off, the Spanish had to look elsewhere for laborers. They turned first to white slaves from Spain and then to Christian black slaves. Yet these were not enough to meet the demand.

Portugal and Spain looked briefly to Asia for slaves for their American colonies. Spain had conquered the Philippines, and in the late 1500s thousands of Filipinos were brought to Mexico. A few Japanese, Chinese, and Cambodians also served as slaves in Spain's American colonies. Yet the Asian slave trade was never very large. It ended with a royal ban in 1597.

In the 1400s Portugal had enslaved Africans to work on overseas plantations. Spain followed Portugal's lead. In the 1500s about 75,000 Africans were brought to the Americas to work as slaves.

The slave trade was conducted by African middlemen who delivered the slaves to ports on Africa's coasts. The trade enriched some members of African coastal states. In contrast, the societies of the interior, where most of the slaves came from, were weakened. In 1526 King Afonso, ruler of the Kongo kingdom at the mouth of the Congo River, protested the slave trade in a letter to the king of Portugal:

❝ Everyday these [slave] merchants take our people . . . to be sold as slaves. So great is this corruption and evil that our country is becoming completely depopulated. ❞

Afonso was a Catholic who had been educated in Portugal. Still, his appeal to the Portuguese king was in vain. He could not stop the **African diaspora** —the forced settlement of millions of Africans in the Western Hemisphere. (A *diaspora* is the scattering of a people outside their homeland.) Before the brutal trade ended, about 9.5 million Africans had been enslaved.

The slave trade had a great impact on Africa. In the words of poet Léopold Sédar Senghor, the trade "ravaged black Africa like a brush fire. . . ." The historian John Hope Franklin points out that "the traders would have none but the best available natives. . . . The removal of the best of the African population deprived the continent of an invaluable resource."

A Transfer of Cultures

One result of the African slave trade was that African ways were carried to the Americas. Coming from farming societies, Africans had knowledge and skills that helped plantations succeed. They were already used to year-round farm work and to caring for domestic animals.

Africans also brought a strong artistic heritage of dance, music, and storytelling. Though slave traders mixed up Africans from different regions in order to control them, many Africans still had much in com-

Bartolomé de Las Casas, a Roman Catholic priest, publicized Spain's cruel treatment of the Indians in its American colonies.

mon. From that common experience came an African-based culture in the Americas.

In the United States countless numbers of people are connecting with their African roots and taking pride in the triumph of their ancestors over slavery. One way they show this pride is by calling themselves *African Americans.*

SECTION REVIEW

1. Key Terms Columbian exchange, conquistador, missionary, plantation, African diaspora

2. People Bartolomé de Las Casas, King Afonso

3. Comprehension How was Las Casas's attitude toward the Caribbean Indians different from the attitude of other Spanish colonizers?

4. Comprehension Why did Spain turn to Africa to provide labor for its American colonies?

5. Critical Thinking How did the creation of an Atlantic world affect people in the Americas? Europe? Africa?

---

2 Spain Conquers Mexico and Peru

SECTION GUIDE

Main Idea
Spanish technology, and alliances with other Indians, helped Spain end the Aztec empire. In a further quest for gold, Spain conquered Peru.

Goals
As you read, look for answers to these questions:

1 What was the Aztec view of the Spanish?

2 How did Spain conquer Mexico and Peru?

Key Terms
colony
ally

THE STORY OF THE CONQUEST of Mexico is a rich tale, full of intrigue and passion, drama and tragedy. It begins with the restless, ambitious young men of Spain who had moved to Spanish lands in the Caribbean. Most quickly became bored with plantation life. They continued to dream of finding gold and glory for themselves.

The Invasion of Mexico

Hernán Cortés (kor-TEZ) was one of these men. Tired of studying law, Cortés sailed from Spain to Hispaniola in 1504. Hispaniola was one of Spain's colonies —areas controlled by a distant country. There Cortés became a rich and respected colonist. Still, he dreamed of being a conquistador.

In 1518 an expedition returned to Cuba with gold taken from the Indians on Yucatán. (The Yucatán Peninsula of Mexico was home to the Maya civilization.) Cortés organized an expedition to explore the mainland.

In 1519 Cortés landed on the coast of Yucatán. There he was challenged by a Maya army of 12,000. The Maya probably would have defeated the Spanish if Cortés had not sent his small cavalry onto the field. These armored men holding huge, metal-tipped lances galloped on horses toward the Maya. The Maya had never seen armored horses. Assuming the men on horseback to be monsters, they fled in terror.

The defeated Maya offered gifts to the conquerors. The Spanish received cotton cloth, gold ornaments, and female slaves. Among the slaves was Malinche (mah-LEEN-chay). Malinche was born an Aztec but was sold as a child to the Maya. The Spanish named her "Marina." Because she knew more than one Indian lan-

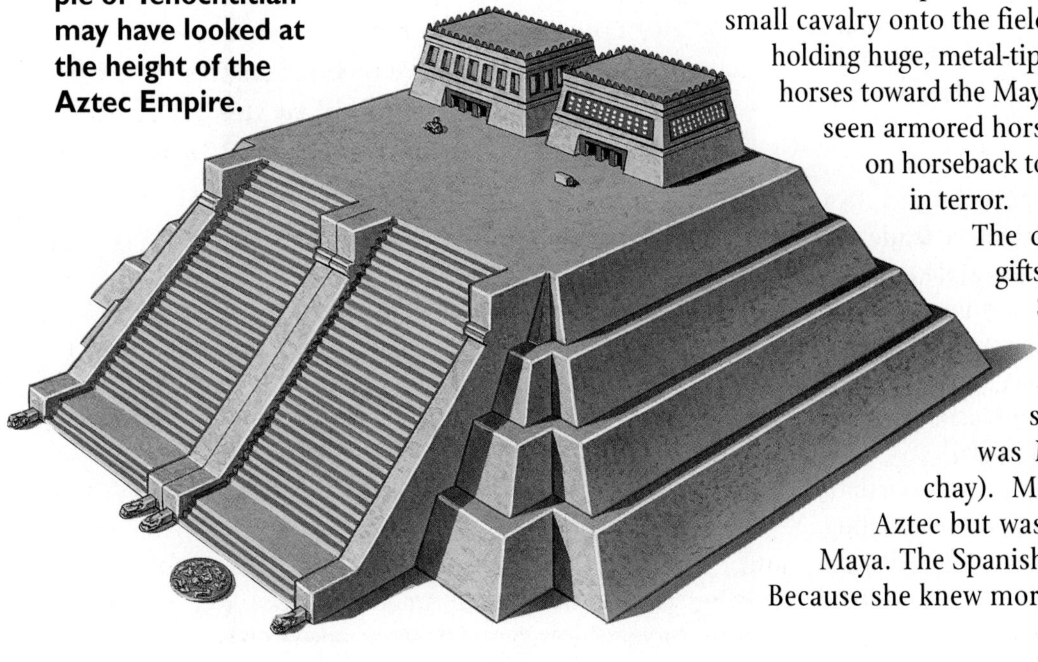

An artist's idea of how the Great Temple of Tenochtitlán may have looked at the height of the Aztec Empire.

The Spanish Invasion of Mexico

0 25 50 Miles
0 25 50 Kilometers
Conic Projection

N

Lake Texcoco

Tenochtitlán

Tlaxcala

Cholula

Cempoala

Veracruz

Gulf of Mexico

96°W
20°N

→ Route of Cortés's army

Lake Texcoco

Tenochtitlán

0 2.5 5 10 Miles
0 2.5 5 10 Kilometers

GEOGRAPHY SKILLS: As they crossed Mexico, Cortés and his men convinced the Indians of Cempoala and Tlaxcala to become allies of Spain. Before reaching the Aztec capital, Tenochtitlán (shown inset), the Spanish destroyed the sacred city of Cholula. **Critical Thinking:** What geographic features protected the Aztec capital?

guage, Marina became a valuable interpreter. Her loyalty to Cortés would help him conquer the Aztecs.

From Yucatán the Spanish sailed close to shore so that they could see and be seen. The land seemed so rich in resources that Cortés decided to make a permanent settlement. This was the port city of Veracruz.

Montezuma's Reaction

Meanwhile, swift runners carried news of Cortés to Montezuma (mahn-tih-ZOO-muh), emperor of the Aztecs. He lived in the Aztec capital of Tenochtitlán (teh-nawch-TEE-tlahn).

Montezuma believed in the legend of Quetzalcóatl (ket-sahl-ko-AHT-ehl), the god of civilization. Long before, it was said, a white, bearded man had ruled Mexico in the god's name. He had left, saying he would return in the year Reed 1. According to the Aztec calendar, Cortés had landed in Reed 1. Montezuma wondered: Had these men been sent by Quetzalcóatl?

Just in case, Montezuma had messengers greet the strangers at Veracruz. They were to bear gifts made of gold, feathers, gems, and shells. Montezuma told his messengers:

❝Come forward, my valiant Jaguar Knights. . . . It is said that our lord has returned to this land. Go to meet him. Go to hear him. Listen well to what he tells you; listen and remember.❞

Cortés received the gifts and gave others in return. He let it be known he wanted even more gold. Then Cortés showed off his cavalry and the power of his cannon.

The messengers returned to Montezuma. They told him of a weapon that could crack open a mountain and shatter a tree into splinters. "Their trappings and arms are all made of iron. . . . Their deer carry them on their backs wherever they wish to go."

Montezuma decided that Quetzalcóatl had sent Cortés to take back the throne of Mexico. He tried to bribe Cortés into staying away. Montezuma's messengers returned to Veracruz carrying dazzling gifts for the Spanish. Among the gifts were two plates as large as wagon wheels, one of gold and one of silver.

The March to Tenochtitlán

Such gifts only made Cortés more eager to conquer the Aztecs. In August 1519 Cortés set out for Tenochtitlán. Along the way he courted the many Indian groups that resented harsh Aztec rule. They became his **allies**—partners in a common cause.

Several months after leaving Veracruz, Cortés approached the magnificent city of Tenochtitlán. Montezuma's messengers again appeared. The Spanish must turn back, they told Cortés. Still, Cortés pushed ahead. Montezuma had enough warriors to stop Cortés, but he never used them.

When Cortés entered the heart of Tenochtitlán, Montezuma came to greet him. Montezuma housed the Spanish in his palace and showered them with gifts. Within a week Cortés took Montezuma hostage and ordered that his treasury be opened. It took the Spanish three days to divide up the great treasure.

This Aztec knife was a gift to the Spaniards.

La Noche Triste

Cortés had planned to rule Mexico with Montezuma as a puppet emperor (that is, a ruler in name only). This plan fell apart. Horrified by the Aztec practice of human sacrifice, some Spanish soldiers tried to stop it. The Aztec priests then led an uprising against the Spanish. When Montezuma tried to restore order, an angry Aztec mob stoned him to death. Then the Spanish tried to sneak out of the city at night with their loot. They were discovered. Fierce fighting broke out in what the Spaniards later called *La Noche Triste* (LAH NO-cheh TREES-teh), or "The Night of Sorrow."

Several hundred Spaniards and 4,000 of their Indian allies died. "Among our men," wrote one Spaniard, "those who were most [loaded down] with clothing, gold, and jewels were the first to die, and those were saved who carried the least and forged ahead fearlessly. So those who died, died rich, and their gold killed them."

The Aztecs Are Defeated

The survivors of *La Noche Triste* retreated to join their Indian allies in the nearby mountains. There Cortés rebuilt his forces. He also built boats that could attack Tenochtitlán from the water. In May 1521 Cortés launched a full-scale attack. In this Cortés had help from an unexpected source: smallpox. It entered Mexico with the arrival of additional Spaniards. The disease spread rapidly, greatly weakening Aztec resistance to the invaders.

Cortés set out to destroy Tenochtitlán house by house. The battle raged fiercely for more than three months. Finally, with the city in ruins, Aztec power crumbled.

An Aztec artist drew this meeting between Cortés and Montezuma. **Critical Thinking:** What might have impressed the artist most about the Spaniards?

Cortés himself wept to see the destruction of what he called the most beautiful city in the world. An Aztec poet cried:

> **Broken spears lie in the roads; We have torn out hair in our grief.**
>
> **The houses are roofless now, and their walls are red with blood. . . .**
>
> **We have pounded our hands in despair**
>
> **Against the adobe walls, for our inheritance, our city, is lost and dead.**

A New Society in Mexico

Mexico was now part of New Spain. On the rubble of Tenochtitlán, the Spanish built Mexico City.

The population of Mexico changed. Diseases from Europe killed millions of Indians. Historians estimate that Mexico's population shrank from 25 million in 1500 to less than 2 million in 1600.

Another result of the conquest of Mexico was the mixing of Spanish and Indian culture. The two cultures, the Spanish and the Indian, came together to produce a new society, that of present-day Mexico.

The Fall of Peru

News of the treasures of the Aztecs increased the Spanish desire for gold. In early 1531 Francisco Pizarro and 180 men set sail for the northern coast of Peru. The small force crossed into the mountains to make contact with Atahualpa (ah-tuh-WAHL-puh), ruler of the Inca Empire of Peru. This empire stretched for 2,000 miles along South America's west coast.

Pizarro invited Atahualpa to visit him, promising the Inca ruler complete safety. Thinking the tiny force of Spaniards could pose no threat, Atahualpa did so. With him went 6,000 servants, nobles, and warriors.

Once the Inca had entered the town square, the Spaniards attacked them. Trapped within the town walls, the unarmed Inca could not easily flee and were slaughtered by the Spanish.

Pizarro took Atahualpa prisoner. The emperor promised rooms full of gold and silver objects as ransom. Pizarro waited until the treasure had been collected. Then he had Atahualpa strangled.

The conquistadors proceeded to take control of all of Peru. To do so, they took advantage of the Inca's superb road system. The roads allowed the Spanish to establish their authority quickly. Pizarro, serving as governor of Peru, exercised that power from Lima, the new capital he founded in 1535.

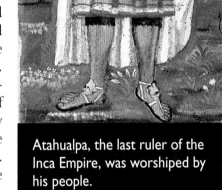

Atahualpa, the last ruler of the Inca Empire, was worshiped by his people.

SECTION REVIEW

1. Key Terms colony, ally

2. People and Places Hernán Cortés, Malinche, Montezuma, Pizarro, Tenochtitlán, Mexico, Peru

3. Comprehension Why did Montezuma send presents to Cortés?

4. Comprehension How did smallpox help Cortés conquer the Aztecs?

5. Critical Thinking How were a few hundred soldiers able to topple the great Aztec and Inca empires?

3 The Lure of North America

SECTION GUIDE

Main Idea

Spanish explorers made expeditions to North America in search of the same kinds of riches they found in Mexico.

Goals

As you read, look for the answers to these questions:

1. What was the result of the early explorations of North America?

2. What did the Spanish learn from their exploration of North America?

Key Terms

clergy
adobe

WOULD YOU answer an advertisement like this? Such an ad never appeared in the 1500s, but ambitious Spaniards set out for the Americas anyway.

> **HELP WANTED: ADVENTURERS**
> Must be ruthless and willing to leave friends and family—probably forever—to travel to distant land. Military experience required, physical hardship likely. Salary low, but great possibility of enormous wealth.

Exploring the Gulf Coast

The Spaniards saw themselves as brave explorers, bringing Christianity to the Indians. They often traveled with **clergy,** or religious officials. To the Indians, the Spaniards were cruel invaders. Some Indian groups developed a clever way to get rid of them. The Indians would agree that gold was to be found—but claimed that it was far away. Thus the Spaniards traveled North America, searching for wealth.

Juan Ponce de León, conqueror of Puerto Rico, was supposedly looking for a "fountain of youth" when he sailed north in 1513. Perhaps that was so. However, as a conquistador he was also looking for gold and Indian slaves. It was on this voyage that Ponce de Léon found the land he named Florida—"flower-covered."

In 1521, after hearing the news of gold in Mexico, Ponce de León returned to Florida. With 200 men he landed on Florida's west coast. Indians fiercely resisted the Spanish landing. The Spanish were forced to retreat to their ships. In the battle, Ponce de León

The Fountain of Youth appears in this fanciful drawing of the legendary island of Bimini. Ponce de Léon had hoped to find Bimini when he explored Florida.

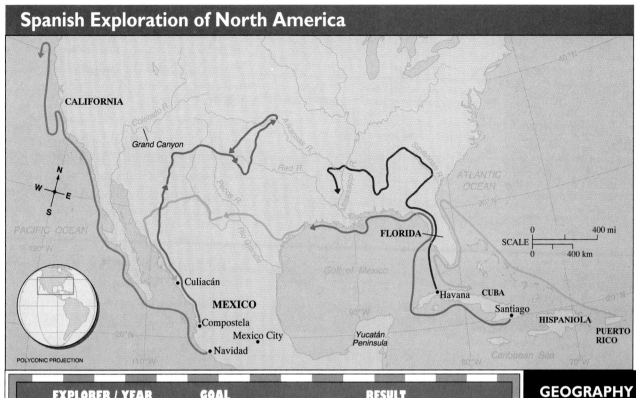

Spanish Exploration of North America

EXPLORER / YEAR	GOAL	RESULT
Ponce de León 1513	To find a "fountain of youth"	Explored Florida
Narváez 1527–1528	To reach the Rio Grande	Failure; four survivors
Cabeza de Vaca 1528–1536	Survivors of Narváez expedition	Traveled across Southwest
De Soto 1539–1542	To find the golden Cities of Cíbola	Explored Southeast
Coronado 1540–1542	To find the golden Cities of Cíbola	Explored Southwest, Great Plains
Cabrillo 1542–1543	To find the golden Cities of Cíbola	Explored as far north as Oregon

GEOGRAPHY SKILLS: Searching for gold and other riches, Spanish explorers traveled from Florida to California. **Critical Thinking:** Who was the first Spaniard to cross the Rio Grande? In your opinion, which explorer was the most successful? Why?

received an arrow wound from which he shortly died.

The Tragedy of Narváez

Another expedition to the Gulf Coast was led by Pánfilo de Narváez (nahr-VAH-ays). He had helped conquer the island of Cuba and had also fought alongside Cortés. In 1527, with a force of 400, Narváez set out for the Rio Grande, the western boundary of Spanish Florida. After leaving Cuba, the expedition ran into heavy storms that blew the ships off course. As a result, it ended

up at Tampa Bay, on the west coast of Florida. To see how far Narváez was from his goal, look at the map on this page.

In April 1528, Narváez divided his group. The ships were to continue on to the Rio Grande. The soldiers, with Narváez at their head, would reach the same place by land.

The Narváez group headed inland and wandered about for months, hoping to find riches. His men suffered from illness, battles with Indians, and lack of food. A year after he had landed, Narváez's goal

Estevanico, one of only four survivors of the Narváez expedition, learned many American Indian languages during the eight years he traveled through Indian-controlled lands. **Critical Thinking:** How might Estevanico's knowledge of Indian languages have helped him survive?

Spanish officials were most interested in one question: Were there riches in the north? They had not seen riches, Cabeza de Vaca said, but the Indians had told of rich cities. Cabeza de Vaca also reported that the mountains seemed to have ores of gold, iron, and copper.

Even the hint of gold was enough to inspire the Spanish. The report of rich cities brought back memories of the legend of the golden Seven Cities of Cíbola (SEE-buh-luh). In the years 1539–1542 three expeditions headed north. Each hoped to find Cíbola. Francisco Vásquez de Coronado led an expedition that would go to the interior. From Florida, Hernándo de Soto would explore the Southeast. Juan Rodríguez Cabrillo (kuh-BREE-yo) would travel up the California coast by sea.

was no longer riches but survival. He decided the only possible way to return to Mexico was by sea. Yet his ships were gone. (For a year the ships had sailed up and down the Gulf Coast looking for Narváez. They had given up.) He had no tools to build new ships.

Desperate, the Spanish decided to make do with what was available. Lacking axes, they cut trees with swords. They made nails out of stirrups. They used vines for ropes. They sewed together their shirts for sails. They killed horses and used the leg skins to make water containers. Then they built five rickety boats and the survivors, about 245 men, set off for Mexico.

The flimsy boats were not seaworthy enough. Narváez was drowned somewhere west of the Mississippi Delta. Two boats with roughly 80 men beached near present-day Galveston, Texas, in November 1528. By the following spring, only fifteen were still alive. The survivors spent years as slaves of different Indians. Finally some of these men planned an escape.

Cabeza de Vaca

The escaping survivors included Álvar Núñez Cabeza de Vaca (kuh-BAY-zuh DUH VAH-kuh) and Estevanico (es-tay-vahn-EE-ko). Cabeza de Vaca had been treasurer of the Narváez expedition. Estevanico was a slave of African and Arab descent.

Leaving the Texas coast, the survivors headed northwest. They crossed the Rio Grande near the site of present-day El Paso, Texas. From there they headed southwest on the long Indian trail that led to Mexico. Finally, in 1536, they reached a Spanish outpost. Welcomed as heroes, the four survivors were soon in Mexico City telling their tale.

The Coronado Expedition

Before exploring the interior, Coronado wanted more information. In the spring of 1539 he sent a small scouting party on the trail north. The head of this group was a friar, Marcos de Niza (NEE-zuh). People called him Fray Marcos. His guide was Estevanico. Taking on the role of healer, Estevanico was decked out with bells on his wrists and ankles. In his hand he rattled a "magic" gourd he had been given on his earlier journey.

Fray Marcos sent Estevanico on ahead. The two men communicated by sending Indian runners with messages. Near the border of present-day Arizona and New Mexico, Estevanico approached a Zuñi Indian town. He was certain it was Cíbola. From a distance the Zuñi pueblo (Indian village) looked grand. It was made of adobe (uh-DOH-bee)—sun-dried clay bricks. The Indians had plastered the bricks with a yellow soil full of shiny particles of mica. In a certain light the walls sparkled like gold.

Estevanico sent his gourd rattle into the town as a goodwill gesture, but the gesture

LEARN

You have probably looked at a bus map or a highway map or a subway map. These kinds of maps are route maps. They are full of numbers and symbols and lines. Finding which route goes where can seem to be a complex task. It does not have to be. Reading a map is easy once you figure out how it is set up.

Most maps have a title, a scale showing distance, a compass rose showing direction, and a key to any special symbols or markings. The most common marking in a key is a

Narváez and De Soto in America

color box to show a country or region. In an exploration chapter like this, you will also find route lines marked in color. The key tells you who followed the route and during what years.

Look at the map on this page. The route lines have arrows showing in what direction the explorers traveled. Consider what you have read about each explorer. Then trace the routes with your finger, thinking about what happened along the way.

PRACTICE

1. What is the color, on the map above, of the route that De Soto took?

2. Which explorer started out at the town of Santiago?

3. What natural features did each explorer follow?

APPLY

4. After reading the description of Juan de Oñate's expedition (at the end of this section), draw a map showing his route. Use an atlas if needed.

backfired. The gourd rattle had once belonged to Zuñi enemies. The Zuñi killed Estevanico. Fray Marcos viewed the pueblo from afar and then hurried back to Mexico City. He reported that Cíbola was even larger than Mexico City.

By February of 1540 Coronado was ready to head north. His expedition set off from the west coast of Mexico. It included about 300 soldiers, most of them Spanish cavalry. The youngest was seventeen, but most were in their early twenties. Hundreds of Mexican Indians, many with wives and children, went along as servants. Among their duties was tending the animals. These included 5,000 sheep, 500 head of cattle, 600 pack mules, and 552 horses.

Fray Marcos guided Coronado to what he claimed was Cíbola. Coronado was bitterly disappointed to find it only a mud-brick village. Tired and hungry, the Spanish drove the Zuñi from their town and feasted on the corn, beans, and turkeys they found there.

From this base, Coronado sent out scouting parties. At the head of one of these parties, García López de Cárdenas (KAHR-day-nahs) came upon the Grand Canyon.

The Search for Quivira

Coronado moved on to spend the winter of 1540–1541 at an Indian pueblo on the Rio Grande. There he first met the Plains Indian the Spanish called the Turk. The Turk, full of fancy talk, told about a place called Quivira (kee-VEER-uh). In Quivira, said the Turk, the Spanish could find as much gold, silver, and jewels as they desired. Other Indians said the Turk was lying, but the Spanish wanted to believe him.

The bulk of the expedition followed the Turk out onto the Great Plains. The Plains were like a sea. There were no landmarks by which to set one's course. One soldier had the job of counting the steps taken each day so the group could plot their course. "In all that wilderness, they were appalled at how little mark so great a throng of men and women and beast made upon the grasses of the plain," wrote the historian Paul Horgan. "They left no trail, for the grass in the wind waved over their path like the sea over a galleon's wake."

At last they reached Quivira, located in what is now central Kansas. Instead of a golden city, the Spaniards found Wichita Indian villages. Coronado, realizing he had been on a wild goose chase, headed toward the Rio Grande. Perhaps, he reasoned, the golden cities lay in another direction.

Before Coronado could find out, he was seriously injured when thrown from his horse. Disappointed and empty-handed, he led the expedition back to Mexico.

The De Soto Expedition

Hernándo de Soto had no better luck than Coronado. He had landed at Tampa Bay in 1539 with a force of 600 fighting men. In

This painting of Coronado's expedition to the American Southwest shows Spanish soldiers and the priests who traveled with them. **Critical Thinking:** Which members of the expedition have been left out of the painting?

his pursuit of gold, De Soto wandered through the Southeast for three years. Though we cannot be sure exactly where he traveled, historians suspect he got as far north as present-day Tennessee and as far west as Arkansas. He was the first European to see the Mississippi River.

The De Soto expedition attacked Indian settlements and enslaved Indians. De Soto was determined, ruthless, and cruel. To get rid of him, the Indians told him stories of riches to be found someplace far away.

In 1542 De Soto died of a fever along the lower Mississippi River. To prevent the Indians from learning of his death, De Soto's men buried him in the river. Then they made rafts and floated down to the Gulf. Only half of those who had started on the expedition made it back to Mexico.

Cabrillo and California

To learn about North America's west coast, Juan Rodríguez Cabrillo set sail from Navidad, Mexico, in 1542. This old conquistador had been with Cortés when he conquered the Aztecs.

As Cabrillo's expedition sailed north along the California coast, they came upon San Diego Bay. Continuing north, they camped on Catalina Island. There Cabrillo died from a fall. The expedition continued and sailed as far as Oregon and then returned to Mexico. Like those of Coronado and De Soto, the Cabrillo expedition found no gold.

The three expeditions, however, had greatly increased Spanish knowledge of North American geography. In the years to come, Spain would use this knowledge to conquer parts of North America.

Early Settlements

More than half a century after Coronado went looking for gold, Juan de Oñate (oh-NYUH-tay) led another group northward from Mexico. Unlike Coronado, he stayed on the eastern side of the Sierra Madre.

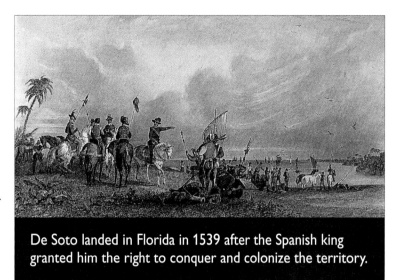

De Soto landed in Florida in **1539** after the Spanish king granted him the right to conquer and colonize the territory.

The expedition followed a low mountain pass that led to El Paso del Norte, a ford on the Rio Grande. From El Paso, Oñate headed north up the Rio Grande. There he took over an Indian town, renaming it San Juan. In 1609 the Spanish colonists of San Juan founded a new town, Santa Fe. It was to become a bustling outpost of the wealthy colony of New Spain.

SECTION REVIEW

1. Key Terms clergy, adobe

2. People Juan Ponce de León, Cabeza de Vaca, Estevanico, Francisco Vásquez de Coronado, Hernándo de Soto, Juan Rodríguez Cabrillo, Juan de Oñate

3. Comprehension Why was Cabeza de Vaca's report of his journey important?

4. Comprehension What regions of North America were explored by the Spanish in the 1530s and 1540s?

5. Critical Thinking Imagine that you are an American Indian in the 1500s. How might you respond to the arrival of a Spanish expedition on your lands?

4 The World of New Spain

SECTION GUIDE

Main Idea
Spain's government, religion, and culture spread throughout its American empire.

Goals
As you read, look for answers to these questions:

1 How did Spain organize and govern its empire?

2 What role did the Catholic Church play in the empire?

3 What ideas lay behind Spain's economic system?

Key Terms
tenant   export
mercantilism   import

THEY CALLED THEM the "singing wheels." To a Spanish colonist, it was a heavenly sound. It was the sound of mail bringing news of family and friends. It was the sound of new goods, perhaps a fine mirror or a crafted knife. The screeching made by the wooden cart wheels sent shivers up your back, and it could be heard for miles. An oxcart on a dusty road, a treasure laden ship—both are symbols of how Spain knit together its huge American empire.

Spain's Empire in the Americas

By 1700 Spain controlled much of the Americas (see the map on the opposite page). The Spanish were able to conquer and settle such vast territory for several reasons.

(1) The Spanish were good sailors. Their skill at navigation made it possible to maintain regular contact with the Americas.

(2) The Spanish had a long tradition of fighting and conquering. This tradition had been shaped during the *Reconquista.*

(3) The spread of European diseases killed millions of American Indians and seriously weakened their resistance to European armies.

(4) The Spanish made alliances with Indian nations when fighting against those nations' traditional enemies. Then the Spanish broke their agreements and conquered their former allies.

(5) The Spanish had experience in settling new territories.

The empire was divided into large parts. Each part, called a viceroyalty, was ruled by a viceroy, who was named by the king. As the king's representative, the viceroy had royal powers. The viceroyalty of New Spain is shown on the map on the opposite page. The hub of New Spain was Mexico City. There lived the viceroy.

Each viceroyalty was divided into smaller areas called provinces. The governor of each province reported to the viceroy. The governor in turn

This painting by Mexican artist Diego Rivera shows one type of Spanish settlement in the Americas.

ruled the alcaldes (al-KAHL-deez). The alcalde, a name from the Arabic word for "leader," was the top official in each town. The people had no say in forming the laws or choosing those who governed them.

Towns and Roads

From the first days of their conquest of Mexico, the Spanish had built outposts ever outward from Mexico City. The streets of each town were laid out on a square pattern called a grid. In the center of the grid was a plaza, or town square. Dominating the plaza was a cathedral or church.

The plaza was the focus of social activity. People gathered there to stroll or meet friends. On church holidays there were celebrations called fiestas. During fiestas the people gathered in the plaza to parade, eat, dance, and listen to music.

Like spokes of a wheel, roads linked Mexico City to the most remote parts of the empire. Once a year a baggage train of carts and mules made the 1,500-mile journey to these far-flung outposts. Each major road in the empire was called *El Camino Real* (EL kah-MEE-no reh-AHL)—"The King's Highway."

Large Estates

The Spanish divided the land into huge estates. In the 1600s, the system of binding Indians to the land was stopped. Under the new system, the *hacienda* system, the Indians were free to leave the land. Those who chose to stay became **tenants.** That is, they lived on and worked land they did not own, keeping some produce for themselves and giving some to the landowner.

Hacienda was also the name given to the owner's house, which was built around a courtyard with a well. (This style of building was learned from Spanish Muslims.) There, in nice weather, children played and women did their work.

People in the hacienda were largely self-sufficient. For instance, they raised and

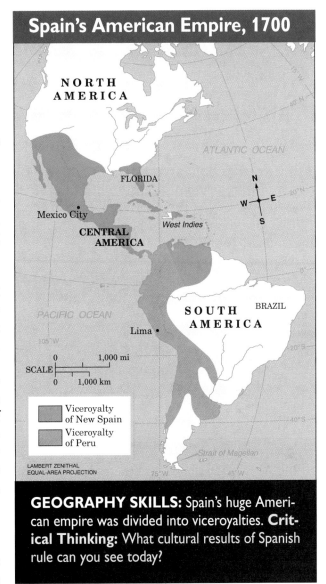

Spain's American Empire, 1700

GEOGRAPHY SKILLS: Spain's huge American empire was divided into viceroyalties. **Critical Thinking:** What cultural results of Spanish rule can you see today?

milled their own grain. From sheep and goats, residents spun wool and wove it into cloth. The women did the spinning, and the men did the weaving.

A New Society

Social classes had existed in Aztec and Spanish society, and a new set of social classes emerged in New Spain. At the top, holding the most important jobs in the Church and the government, were Spaniards born in Spain. Below them were the Creoles (KREE-olz). Creoles were people of Spanish ancestry who had been born in

JUANA INÉS DE LA CRUZ
(1651–1695)

As a teenager, Juana Inés de la Cruz believed women had as much right as men to develop their minds. The world of learning in colonial Mexico did not agree. To devote her life to study instead of marriage, she entered a convent. Even there she had to defend her right to study and write plays and poems. After many years, she sold her 4,000 books and scientific instruments and gave the money to the poor.

New Spain. Most of the landowners, merchants, and businessmen were Creoles.

Below the Creoles came the mestizos (mes-TEE-soz). They were the largest class. Mestizos were of mixed Spanish and Indian ancestry. They became parish priests, laborers, artisans, and hacienda tenants. They were much poorer than the classes at the top of society.

The bottom groups in New Spain were the Indians and enslaved Africans. Most enslaved Africans in Mexico worked on plantations along the eastern coast. Many more Africans were brought to Portugal's colony, Brazil. They mixed with Europeans and Indians to create an extremely diverse society.

Mission Settlements

Wherever the Spanish went, the Church followed. In New Spain there were both priests and friars. The priests set up parishes and ministered to the people there. On the frontier the missionary friars worked to convert the Indians and to teach them Spanish ways. The first northern missions were in New Mexico. In the 1700s the Spanish also built missions in Florida, Texas, and California.

The typical mission settlement consisted of several parts. The mission church was usually a simple building of stone or adobe. Its paintings and decorations combined Spanish and Indian art. The music, too, reflected both cultures. Most mission settlements had a presidio, or fort, of stone or adobe. It held quarters for the officers, barracks for the soldiers, and storerooms. Cannons were placed on its walls.

Each mission settlement also had a town and fields. Settlers and Indians lived in the town. Both men and women labored in the mission fields and tended the animals. Some of the villagers were blacksmiths or carpenters or weavers. They were important, for the frontier settlements had to make their own tools and clothing.

Once a mission was well established, the missionaries were supposed to turn it over to parish priests. Sometimes this did not happen. Particularly in California, the Indians were treated like slaves. If they ran away, the soldiers tracked them down and brought them back.

Popé's Rebellion

Indians and Africans rebelled against such cruel treatment. They were rarely successful against the Europeans' trained soldiers and advanced weapons. The Pueblo Indians, however, were able to force the Spanish from New Mexico for about a decade.

The rebellion was led by a Pueblo man, Popé, who organized his followers from his base at Taos pueblo. His chief adviser was a black man who had escaped from slavery in Mexico. In August 1680 Pueblo warriors encircled Santa Fe, demanding that the Spanish leave. After the Pueblos cut off their water supply, the Spanish fled to El Paso, in what is now Texas.

Popé ordered that churches and other Spanish buildings be destroyed. The Pueblo-controlled territory was soon weakened by Apache attacks. In 1692, the Spanish retook Santa Fe.

Colonial Trade

The wealth of the Americas was shipped to Spain in galleons. Galleons collected their cargo at various Caribbean ports and sailed to Havana, Cuba. There they formed a convoy—a group of ships traveling together for protection. Ships were safer in a convoy because they could help each other deal with pirates and other emergencies. From Havana, convoys caught the Gulf Stream as it swept around the tip of Florida into the Atlantic. The Caribbean Sea, with its busy Spanish ports and trade routes, was known as the Spanish Main. The name then, as now, evoked an image of great wealth.

Upon reaching Spain, the galleons would unload their cargoes of precious metals (gold and silver), tropical woods, hides, and other products. On the return trip to New Spain they carried elegant fabrics, guns, furniture, and iron and steel items.

This transatlantic trade was part of a new economic system called mercantilism. Two key ideas lay behind mercantilism:

(1) The purpose of colonies was to benefit the parent country. Spain controlled all trade with the colonies. This meant that products of the Americas could be shipped only to Spain. Spain even told the colonies what goods to produce. Also, the colonies were supposed to buy whatever they needed from Spain alone. No other country could trade with them.

(2) A country could become wealthy and powerful by building up its supply of precious metals. Spain did this in two ways. First, Spain made sure that its exports (goods shipped abroad) were larger than its imports (goods brought in from abroad). Because Spain was selling more to other nations than it was buying from them, it became richer. Second, Spain took vast amounts of gold and silver from the Americas and added them to its treasury.

American gold and silver made Spain a rich nation in the 1500s. Spain spent much

Portugal, another European power in the Americas, relied on African slave labor in its colony of Brazil. In the 1600s some Africans escaped to the jungle and founded Palmares. Attacked many times by the Portuguese, Palmares was undefeated until 1697. **Critical Thinking:** Why was rebellion against European rule difficult for Africans in the Americas?

of its wealth on wars, but was unable to force its will on Europe. In the meantime, other nations learned from Spain how to build an empire. They would challenge Spain's claim to North America. In time, they would become an important part of the Atlantic world.

SECTION REVIEW

1. Key Terms tenant, mercantilism, export, import

2. People Popé

3. Comprehension What factors helped the Spanish set up their American empire?

4. Comprehension Why did the Spanish government establish strict controls on trade in the empire?

5. Critical Thinking How did the Church and the government of New Spain help each other?

Summary

1. The Columbian exchange transported plants, animals, and diseases across the Atlantic. Spain conquered and settled the West Indies, enslaving the Indians there. When the Indian population was all but wiped out, Spain began the slave trade with Africa. Africans brought with them a rich cultural heritage that continues today.

2. Alliances with Indians living under harsh Aztec rule and Spanish technology helped Cortés conquer Mexico's Aztec Empire. Later, Pizarro conquered Peru.

3. Hoping to find riches similar to those in Mexico and Peru, Spanish explorers searched North America in the 1500s. They traveled the Gulf Coast, Great Plains, Southwest, and California coast, but did not find the wealth they sought.

4. Spain built an empire, called New Spain, out of its American territories, made up of missions, towns, and forts. Many Indians were put to work farming. Using mercantilist policies, Spain forced its colonies to trade only with Spain. It grew rich by taking huge amounts of precious metals out of New Spain.

Review

KEY TERMS

Define the terms in each of the following pairs.
1. Columbian exchange; African diaspora
2. conquistador; missionary
3. colony; ally
4. export; import

COMPREHENSION

1. What were the goals of the conquistadors?
2. How did Columbus treat the Indians on the islands that he governed?
3. What effect did the slave trade have on Africa? What effect did the African diaspora have on the Americas?
4. Describe what happened on *La Noche Triste*.
5. How did the Spanish defeat the Aztecs? What unexpected source helped Cortés succeed?
6. What was the goal of Spanish exploration in the Americas? Were their explorations successful?
7. Why did Coronado go to the Great Plains? What did he find?
8. List at least three reasons for Spain's success in conquering and settling the Americas.
9. What was the aim of building missions on the frontier?
10. Describe the economic relationship between Spain and its American colonies.

Graphic Summary

- Destruction of Native American way of life
- Establishment of New Spain based on mercantilism
- Growth of slave trade
- Spanish expansion in the Americas
- Exploration of North America
- Conquest of Aztec Empire in Mexico
- Conquest of Inca Empire in Peru

Places to Locate

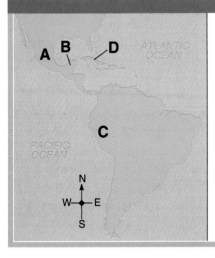

Match the letters on the map with the places listed below.
1. Peru
2. Mexico
3. Cuba
4. Yucatán Peninsula

Geographic Theme:
Movement Why did the Spanish and Portuguese take slaves from Africa?

Skill Review

Study the map of Spanish exploration below. Then answer the following questions.

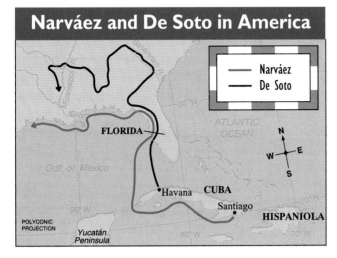

Narváez and De Soto in America

— Narváez
— De Soto

1. Which explorer traveled the farthest north?
2. Where did De Soto end his exploration?
3. Which explorer navigated the Gulf Coast?
4. Which explorer traveled mostly on land?

CRITICAL THINKING

1. Weighing Both Sides of an Issue Why did some Indians become allies of Cortés against the Aztecs? Why might it have been a bad idea for them to do this?

2. Forming a Hypothesis What *political* reason might Spain have had for trying to convert the Indians to Christianity?

PORTFOLIO OPTIONS

1. Civics Connection When it built its American empire, Spain was an absolute monarchy—a nation in which the ruler holds complete power. Create a chart outlining the government structure of New Spain. How did the structure resemble Spain's monarchy?

2. Writing Connection Write a play dramatizing one part of the struggle between the Spanish and the Aztecs for control of Mexico. Perform the play in class.

3. Contemporary Connection How did Spain's economic policies determine which natural resources it valued in the Americas? What other resources might a nation value today? Find pictures of natural resources in the United States. Create a collage showing which you think are most important.

4. Timeline Connection Copy the chapter timeline. Which event had the most influence on the Atlantic world? Why? Add other events from the chapter that should be included and explain why.

MORNING GIRL

MICHAEL DORRIS

Imagine that you are there as Columbus lands in the Americas in 1492. Are you on one of the Spanish ships as it nears land, or are you on the shore watching the ships approach? Michael Dorris, a Modoc Indian, described the scene from the perspective of a Native American girl who happened to be swimming that fateful day.

Dawn made a glare on the ocean, so I splashed through the shallow surf and dived without looking. I felt the hair lift from around my head, felt a school of tiny fish glide against my leg as I swam underwater. Then, far in the distance, I heard an unfamiliar and frightening sound. It was like the panting of some giant animal, a steady, slow rhythm, dangerous and hungry. And it was coming closer.

I forgot I was still beneath the surface until I needed air. But when I broke into the sunlight, the water sparkling all around me, the noise turned out to be nothing! Only a canoe! The breathing was the dip of many paddles! It was only *people* coming to visit, and since I could see they hadn't painted themselves to appear fierce, they must be friendly or lost.

I swam closer to get a better look and had to stop myself from laughing. The strangers had wrapped every part of their bodies with colorful leaves and cotton. Some had decorated their faces with fur and wore shiny rocks on their heads. Compared to us, they were very round. Their canoe was short and square, and, in spite of all their dipping and pulling, it moved so slowly. What a backward, distant island they must have come from. But really, to laugh at guests, no matter how odd, would be impolite, especially since I was the first to meet them. If I was foolish, they would think they had arrived at a fool-ish place. . . .

I kicked toward the canoe and called out the simplest thing.

"Hello!"

One of the people heard me, and he was so startled that he stood up, made his eyes small, as fearful as I had been a moment earlier. . . .

The man stared at me as though he'd never seen a girl before, then shouted something to his relatives. They all stopped paddling and looked in my direction.

"Hello," I tried again. "Welcome to home. My name is Morning Girl. My mother is She Wins the Race. My father is Speaks to Birds. My brother is Star Boy. We will feed you and introduce you to everyone."

All the fat people in the canoe began pointing at me and talking at once. In their excitement they almost turned themselves over, and I allowed my body to sink beneath the waves for a moment in order to hide my smile. One must always treat guests with respect. . . .

When I came up they were still watching, the way babies do: wide eyed and with their mouths uncovered. They had much to learn about how to behave.

"Bring your canoe to the beach," I shouted, saying each word slowly so that they might understand and calm themselves. "I will go to the village and bring back Mother and Father for you to talk to."

Finally one of them spoke to me, but I couldn't understand anything he said. Maybe he was talking Carib or some other impossible language. But I was sure that we would find ways to get along together. It never took that much time, and acting out your thoughts with your hands could be funny. You had to guess at everything and you made mistakes, but by midday I was certain we would all be seated in a circle, eating steamed fish and giving each other presents. It would be a special day, a memorable day, a day full and new.

I was close enough to shore now for my feet to touch bottom, and quickly I made my way to dry land. . . . "Leave your canoe right here," I suggested in my most pleasant voice. "It will not wash away, because the tide is going out. I'll be back soon with the right people."

The strangers were drifting in the surf, arguing among themselves, not even paying attention to me any longer. They seemed very worried, very confused, very unsure what to do next. It was clear that they hadn't traveled much before.

I hurried up the path to our house. . . . As I dodged through the trees, I hoped I hadn't done anything to make the visitors leave before I got back, before we learned their names. If they were gone, Star Boy would claim that they were just a story, just my last dream before daylight. But I didn't think that was true. I knew they were real.

From *Morning Girl* by Michael Dorris. Reprinted by permission of Hyperion Books for Children. Copyright ©1992 by Michael Dorris.

Analyzing Literature

1. Why does Morning Girl think that the visitors came from a backward island? Why does she think they have not traveled much before?

2. How does Morning Girl try to make the visitors feel welcome?

3. What might be the crew's reactions to seeing Morning Girl?

UNIT 2

Colonial Settlement (1497–1763)

UNIT OVERVIEW

Other nations, especially England and France, joined Spain in setting up colonies in the Americas. Rivalry between England and France led to war and thus to English control of eastern North America.

Chapter 5

Challenges to Spanish Power (1497–1610)
Europeans made new voyages to North America in search of a water route to Asia.

Chapter 6

English Colonies in North America (1607–1732)
England established colonies along the Atlantic coast of North America.

Chapter 7

Shaping of the American Colonies (1651–1740)
New England, the Middle Colonies, and the Southern Colonies developed distinct economies.

Chapter 8

The Clash of Empires (1668–1763)
France and Britain, each with Indian allies, fought for control of North America, a contest won by Britain.

Illustration: Detail of a colonial tapestry, c. 1740.

In the 1500s European struggles for power spilled over into the Americas. French navigators such as Jacques Cartier claimed territory in North America (map, below). King Philip of Spain (statue, below), his treasury filled with Aztec gold and silver, saw himself as the defender of Roman Catholicism throughout the world. Yet Protestant England, ruled by Queen Elizabeth (right), was more than a match for Spanish ships, and English interests spread to American shores.

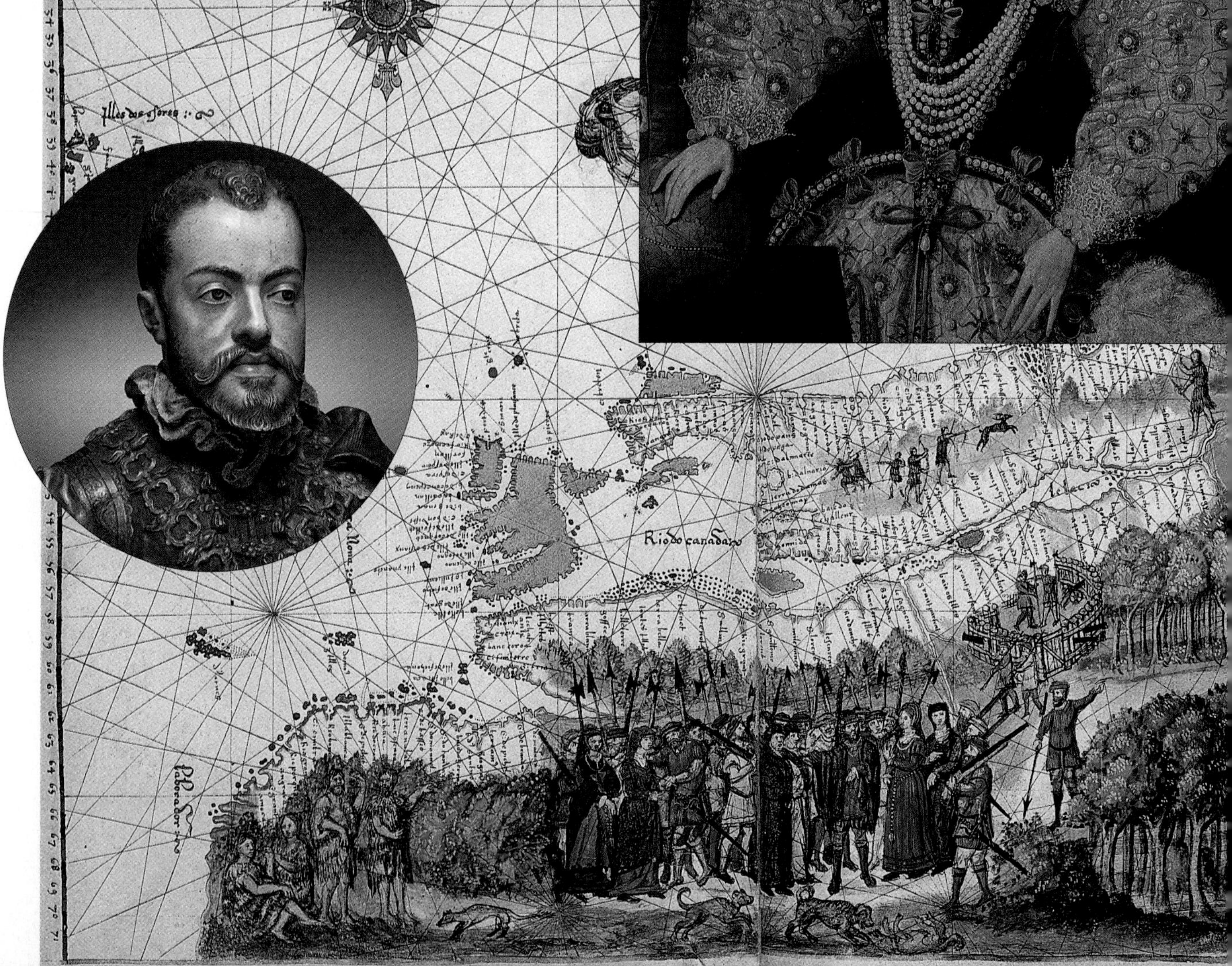

1500

1520

1540

1560

1497 Cabot sails to North America

1517 Reformation begins

1524 Verrazano searches for a Northwest Passage to Asia

1535 Cartier explores the St. Lawrence River

1565 St. Augustine, Florida, established

Challenges to Spanish Power (1497–1610)

1 Search for a Northwest Passage

SECTION GUIDE

Main Idea

Northern European explorers made important discoveries in North America while searching for a water route to Asia.

Goals

As you read, look for answers to these questions:

1 What was the outcome of John Cabot's voyage across the Atlantic?

2 What voyages of exploration did France support? What was their goal?

3 What areas of North America were explored by Henry Hudson?

Key Terms
Grand Banks
Northwest Passage

1580   **1600**

1588 Spanish Armada defeated

1585 First English settlement at Roanoke

1610 Henry Hudson reaches Hudson Bay

WAS CHRISTOPHER COLUMBUS a failure? He had landed in a part of the world unknown to Europeans, brought back important foods, and made it possible for Spain to gather wealth and power from new colonies. Columbus was honored with the title "Admiral of the Ocean Seas." Yet Columbus had failed in his goal. He never reached Asia by sailing west.

The Voyage of John Cabot

Columbus's attempt to reach Asia ended when he reached the Americas. These continents had rich American Indian cultures and many resources. Yet to some Europeans who followed Columbus, the Americas were not opportunities but obstacles. They wanted nothing more than to find a way past America.

If Columbus had not reached the Americas when he did, the honor might have gone to Giovanni Caboto, known in England as John Cabot. Like Columbus, Cabot was born in Genoa. They were about the same age. Cabot also dreamed of sailing west to Asia. While Columbus ended up in Spain, Cabot went to England looking for support. After news of Columbus's voyage reached England, the king of England approved Cabot's plan.

In 1497 Cabot set out from England with a crew of eighteen. He crossed the Atlantic Ocean in two months and reached the northeastern coast of North America. His map and journals are lost, but he probably landed at Newfoundland, Canada. Though he saw signs of people, he met no Indians there. He did sight plentiful forests. The ocean had so many fish that the English found they could simply lower baskets into the water and draw fish up. This rich fishing area was the Grand Banks.

Cabot was sure that he had reached Asia. Before leaving, he claimed the region for England. In 1498 Cabot again sailed west from England, hoping to reach Japan. He was never seen again.

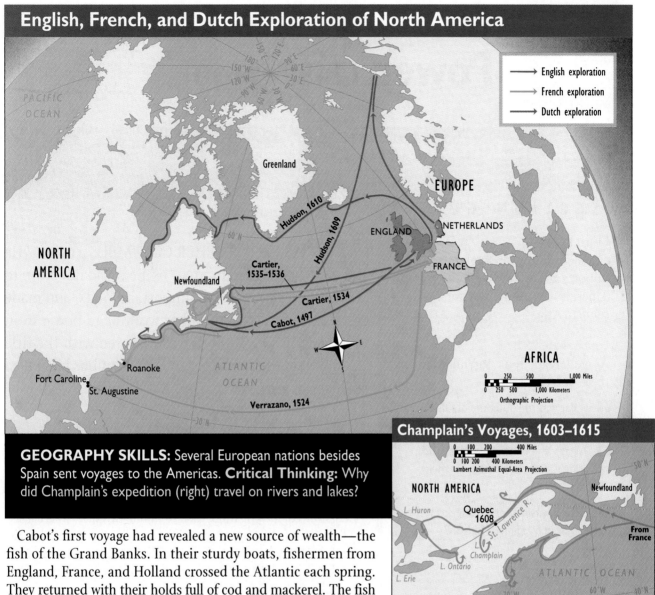

English, French, and Dutch Exploration of North America

Legend:
- English exploration
- French exploration
- Dutch exploration

PACIFIC OCEAN

Greenland

EUROPE

NETHERLANDS

ENGLAND

Hudson, 1610

Hudson, 1609

NORTH AMERICA

Cartier, 1535–1536

FRANCE

Newfoundland

Cartier, 1534

Cabot, 1497

AFRICA

Roanoke

ATLANTIC OCEAN

Fort Caroline

St. Augustine

Verrazano, 1524

0 250 500 1,000 Miles
0 250 500 1,000 Kilometers
Orthographic Projection

GEOGRAPHY SKILLS: Several European nations besides Spain sent voyages to the Americas. **Critical Thinking:** Why did Champlain's expedition (right) travel on rivers and lakes?

Champlain's Voyages, 1603–1615

0 100 200 400 Miles
0 100 200 400 Kilometers
Lambert Azimuthal Equal-Area Projection

NORTH AMERICA

Newfoundland

L. Huron

Quebec 1608

St. Lawrence R.

From France

L. Champlain

L. Erie

L. Ontario

ATLANTIC OCEAN

Cabot's first voyage had revealed a new source of wealth—the fish of the Grand Banks. In their sturdy boats, fishermen from England, France, and Holland crossed the Atlantic each spring. They returned with their holds full of cod and mackerel. The fish fed the hungry of Europe, and the profits paid for more ships.

French Explorations

Europeans still wanted to find a water route around or through North America. This hoped-for route, the Northwest Passage, was the goal of several voyages.

One of the first to seek a Northwest Passage was Giovanni da Verrazano (ver-uh-ZAH-no). Although Verrazano was Italian, his most important voyage was made for France. In 1524 Verrazano sailed westward to look for a Northwest Passage. He followed the Atlantic Coast of North America northward from present-day North Carolina. In doing so, he was the first European to visit New York Bay. However, Verrazano found no passage through the land.

Ten years later Jacques Cartier (kahr-TYAY), a Frenchman, sailed to America. He explored the Gulf of St. Lawrence, kidnapped two local Indians, and returned to France. When he sailed to America the next year, the Indians guided him up the St. Lawrence River. (See the map on this page.) Hoping this waterway might cut through the continent, Cartier followed the river for hundreds of miles. Finally he came to where the city of Montreal now stands. There rapids prevented Cartier's ships from going farther upstream. Cartier had to give up his pursuit of a Northwest Passage. His journey, however, was the basis of French claims to lands around the St. Lawrence River.

In the early 1600s Samuel de Champlain (sham-PLAYN), a French captain, explored the Atlantic Coast from the mouth of the St. Lawrence River to the southern part of present-day Massachusetts. In 1608, at a site on the St. Lawrence River, Champlain founded a fur-trading post that he named "Quebec." It was the first permanent French settlement in North America.

Champlain later traveled farther inland. (See map inset on facing page.) Champlain learned, and taught others, much about the Indians and the geography of the region. Although he found no shortcut to Asia, his activities were the beginning of French colonization in North America.

Henry Hudson's Voyages

Holland and England shared France's interest in a Northwest Passage. In 1609 Dutch merchants hired an Englishman, Henry Hudson, to find a route to China. In a small ship named the *Half Moon,* Hudson sailed west across the Atlantic until he reached North America. He came upon the river that now bears his name. He followed this river inland up to what is now Albany, New York. (Dutch colonists would later settle the region.)

Disappointed that the Hudson River was not a Northwest Passage, Hudson returned to Europe. In 1610, however, he made another trip to North America. This time he was sailing under the banner of his own country, England. Hudson and his crew headed to the northeast coast of present-day Canada. After traveling through an ice-blocked strait, they reached a great body of water, today called Hudson Bay.

All summer, Hudson sailed these waters in search of a Northwest Passage to Asia. When winter came, he and his crew had to

Henry Hudson brought his son with him on his voyages. They were set adrift to die in Hudson Bay after his crew rebelled. **Critical Thinking:** What search led Hudson to Canada?

camp on the bay's frozen shores. By spring, only a small amount of food was left. The crew could take no more. They forced Hudson, his young son, and a few loyal sailors into a small boat. Then they set it adrift. Hudson was never heard from again. Only a few members of his crew managed to make their way to England.

Hudson and other early navigators never found the waterway to Asia that they were seeking. However, they did do something more important. They turned the attention of Europe from Asia to the Americas.

SECTION REVIEW

1. Key Terms Grand Banks, Northwest Passage

2. People John Cabot, Giovanni da Verrazano, Jacques Cartier, Samuel de Champlain, Henry Hudson

3. Comprehension Where did John Cabot believe he had landed in 1497? Where had he actually landed?

4. Comprehension What was the aim of France's voyages of exploration?

5. Critical Thinking What do the fates of John Cabot and Henry Hudson tell you about the life of a navigator?

2 The Religious Challenge

SECTION GUIDE

Main Idea
Religious disputes during the 1500s challenged Spain's authority both in Europe and in the Americas.

Goals
As you read, look for answers to these questions:

1. How and why did a split in Christianity take place?

2. What effect did the religious disputes have on European history? On events in the Americas?

Key Terms
Reformation
Protestant

IN OCTOBER 1517 Johann Tetzel (TEHT-suhl), a Roman Catholic monk, was busy. A crowd had gathered around him to buy something very precious. Tetzel was selling forgiveness from sins. He explained that the people did not have to worry about repenting, confessing, or making amends for the wrongs they did. Money alone could free their souls to go to heaven.

The Reformation

Tetzel was in Germany, but such sales were going on across Europe. Many people were outraged that the Church allowed them. They did not believe that God's forgiveness could be sold for money.

Martin Luther, a Roman Catholic priest, lived in the German city of Wittenberg. Luther believed that Church leaders had become corrupt. In anger he wrote his protest, the Ninety-Five Theses, on a placard and marched to his church. He nailed the Theses to the church doors—and made public a debate that was to tear Europe apart and later spill over into the Americas.

Many scholars believe that the debate had its roots in the development of printing in the 1400s. For the first time, ordinary people could afford to own a copy of the Bible. As a result, many questioned the authority of the Roman Catholic Church. The Bible, they believed, described a simple religious faith, but the Church had grown rich, powerful, and corrupt. Critics also charged that the Church owned

The Roman Catholic monk Johann Tetzel sells forgiveness from sins (above). Martin Luther (right) protested such corruption. One change he called for was allowing clergy to marry. He later married Katherina von Bora (far right), a former nun.

PRESENT ▶ INFORMATION TECHNOLOGY

The development of the printing press was a revolution to Europeans in the 1400s. Information, published in books and periodicals, was now affordable and available to most people. Today, another information revolution is going on. A "data superhighway" is being built across the United States. Already, high-strength glass cables connected to television sets allow information to travel with the speed of a pulse of light. Experts predict that soon Americans will be able to shop, do research, and be entertained with the push of a button.

too much land and required too much money for support.

These people agreed with Luther's protests against corruption in the Church. Their desire to reform the Church began the **Reformation,** the revolt against the Catholic Church. Those who revolted were called **Protestants** because of their protests against Catholic practices.

Protestantism, the faith of the Protestants, spread rapidly in northern Europe. Europe became bitterly divided between Protestants, who did not recognize the Pope's authority, and Catholics, who did. The Spanish monarchs saw themselves as defenders of the Catholic Church against Protestants. They used the wealth of the Americas to finance campaigns against the Protestants. Religious wars swept through Holland, France, and Germany during the 1500s. The religious passions of Europe also spilled over to the Americas.

Protestants in Florida

In the 1500s, tensions between Catholics and Protestants in France grew. The French king was Catholic, but a growing number of French people had become Protestants. These French Protestants were known as Huguenots (HYOO-guh-nahts). Among the Huguenots was the Admiral of France, Gaspard de Coligny (kaw-lee-NYEE).

Coligny convinced royal officials to establish a Huguenot colony in the Americas. The colony would serve several purposes. Huguenots saw it as a place where they could freely practice their religion. Catholics liked the idea of getting the Huguenots out of France. The king of France was also happy that his flag would fly on American shores, challenging Spanish claims in the Americas.

In 1564 a group of French colonists established Fort Caroline near present-day Jacksonville, Florida. The group included Huguenots as well as young noblemen intent on finding gold and adventure. None of them had learned how to hunt, fish, or farm.

At first the Timucua (tim-uh-KOO-uh) Indians helped them. The Timucua got their food from hunting and fishing, and they grew two crops of corn a year. The settlers' many demands angered the Timucua, however, and they soon withdrew their help. The French had nothing to eat. To survive, they ground up fish bones into a powder and made bread of it. They waited in despair for new supplies from France.

The Spanish Respond

In September 1565 the longed-for help from France finally arrived. The little fort swarmed with activity. Then a week later "a huge hulk" approached the French ships anchored offshore. It was a warship from Spain.

The commander, Pedro Menéndez de Avilés, called out, "Gentlemen, whence does this fleet come?"

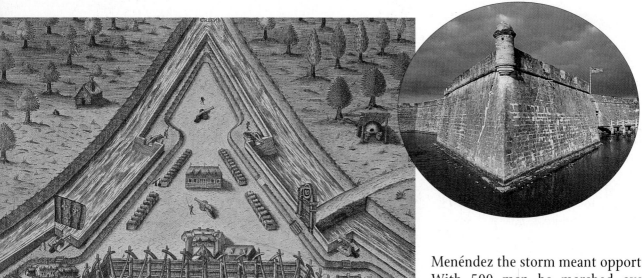

"From France," was the answer.

"What are you doing here?" Menéndez asked.

"Bringing soldiers and supplies for a fort which the king of France has in this country, and for many others which he soon will have."

"Are you Catholics or Lutherans [Protestants]?"

"Lutherans," they answered.

"I . . . have come to this country to hang and behead all Lutherans whom I shall find by land or sea, according to instructions from my king," said Menéndez.

The French quickly moved out to sea. After a short pursuit Menéndez gave up the chase. Returning to the coast, he sailed south a short distance and built a fort at St. Augustine. The fort took shape around a large structure that had been the dwelling of an Indian chief. (Today St. Augustine is the oldest permanent European settlement existing in the United States).

The French had hoped to destroy the Spanish fleet and thereby cut off Menéndez. However, a storm, the worst the Timucua could remember, roared out of the south. The French fleet was scattered. For Menéndez the storm meant opportunity. With 500 men he marched overland through marsh and forest and driving rain to attack Fort Caroline. He destroyed the fort, killing 142 men, but sparing about 50 women and children.

The massacre was not over. When the storm blew itself out, several French ships had been wrecked on the sandbars. The fate of the shipwrecked survivors was grim. Except for a few carpenters whom he needed, Menéndez killed the French. The reason, he made clear, was not that they were French, but that they were Protestant.

SECTION REVIEW

1. Key Terms Reformation, Protestant

2. People and Places Martin Luther, Fort Caroline, St. Augustine

3. Comprehension What was Spain's attitude toward the Reformation?

4. Comprehension What different purposes were served by the founding of Fort Caroline?

5. Critical Thinking What lessons can you draw from the failure of Fort Caroline regarding the requirements for a successful colony?

3 The English Challenge at Sea

SECTION GUIDE

Main Idea
Divided by issues of religion and power, Spain and England clashed during the 1500s. This conflict would affect the future of the Americas.

Goals
As you read, look for answers to these questions:

1. How and why did England raid Spanish shipping?

2. What was the outcome of Spain's attempt to conquer England?

Key Terms
armada
privateer

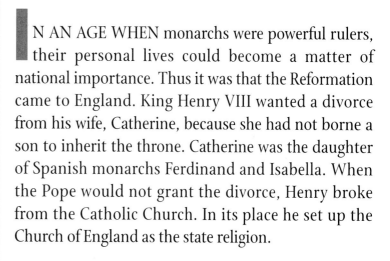

IN AN AGE WHEN monarchs were powerful rulers, their personal lives could become a matter of national importance. Thus it was that the Reformation came to England. King Henry VIII wanted a divorce from his wife, Catherine, because she had not borne a son to inherit the throne. Catherine was the daughter of Spanish monarchs Ferdinand and Isabella. When the Pope would not grant the divorce, Henry broke from the Catholic Church. In its place he set up the Church of England as the state religion.

Conflict with Spain

After Henry's death in 1547, the Spanish plotted to return England to Catholicism. Yet under the strong-willed, capable leadership of Queen Elizabeth I, England began to grow more powerful. Elizabeth vowed to keep England Protestant and independent. One of her tactics was to encourage the hopes of King Philip II of Spain for a union between them and their countries. Yet she never married him or any man. Elizabeth thus became known as the Virgin Queen.

Elizabeth's island kingdom developed its seapower during her reign. The fishing voyages that began with John Cabot's discovery of the Grand Banks helped. The fishing trips encouraged the development of fast, seaworthy craft—and sailors with skills to match. Such speedy craft were also just right for a pirate on the lookout for a Spanish treasure ship. The big, slow Spanish ships were easy targets for sea dogs—the name used to describe the captains of English pirate ships.

Pirates approach a Spanish galleon in this detail from a larger painting. **Critical Thinking:** Why might the smaller English ships have been effective in battle against Spain's larger galleons?

Drake and the Sea Dogs

The most famous of the sea dogs was Francis Drake. Drake felt a bitter hatred for the Spaniards. In 1567 his ship had been attacked by Spanish sailors pretending to be friendly. For many years afterward, Drake sought revenge by raiding Spanish vessels and Spanish towns. The Spanish feared him and called him "the Dragon." Spain's King Philip II offered a huge reward to anyone who could kill him.

Drake's most famous accomplishment was to sail through the Strait of Magellan in 1578 and up the coast of Peru. The Spanish had never been attacked in their "Spanish lake," as they proudly called the Pacific Ocean. Drake, however, stole so much Spanish treasure that his ship, the *Golden Hind,* rode low in the water from its load of gold, silver, and gems.

To evade Spanish warships, Drake sailed north. He touched briefly on the California coast, sailed west across the Pacific, and then on to Europe. Drake thus became the first Englishman to circle the world.

For years Queen Elizabeth had looked the other way while English sea dogs attacked Spanish ships. With Spanish loot flowing into her treasury, Elizabeth did not need to tax her own people. When Drake returned to England, Elizabeth received half the treasure. Furthermore, Drake had wounded Spanish pride and carried the English flag into new waters. For his achievements, Elizabeth made him a knight, a high honor.

The Spanish Armada

For King Philip of Spain, the attacks were intolerable. He decided that the time had come to teach the English a lesson. He assembled an **armada** —a giant fleet of warships—to conquer England and restore Catholicism to that nation. Some people called it the "Invincible Armada" because they believed it could not lose. Even brave Englishmen like Drake were worried. "There was never any force so strong as there is now . . . making ready against your Majesty," he warned Queen Elizabeth.

The armada of 130 ships sailed forth in the summer of 1588. It carried about 8,000 sailors, 19,000 soldiers, and hundreds of priests to reconvert the English to Catholicism. The Spanish commander was inexperienced and, worse, seasick. His ships were big and bulky. Waiting for them were England's small navy and numbers of **privateers** —privately operated armed ships. Old sea hands like Sir Francis Drake were junior admirals.

The English had fewer ships, but these were better than the Spanish ones. The Spanish had built big ships in order to carry heavy cannons. The English, however, had found a way to make small cannons that

Trophy given to Francis Drake to honor his circling the globe.

In 1581 Queen Elizabeth knighted Drake for his daring campaigns against the Spanish. **Critical Thinking:** How did the English people benefit from Drake's attacks on the Spanish?

The Spanish Armada relied on the traditional naval strategy of boarding an opponent's ships after closing in on them. The faster English fleet, with its long-range guns, easily avoided this maneuver. **Critical Thinking:** How did Spain's defeat shift the balance of power in Europe?

were just as powerful as the larger Spanish ones. As a result, the English were able to build ships that were lighter, faster, and more deadly.

The two fleets first met in the English Channel, the strait that separates Great Britain from Europe. The English ships darted back and forth around the Spanish, firing and then sailing out of reach of the Spanish guns.

The armada continued on its course for a French harbor, where it was supposed to pick up more soldiers for the invasion of England. However, the English sent burning ships into the French harbor, setting many Spanish ships aflame.

Thus crippled by English attacks, the Spanish decided to head for home. Then a terrible storm hit. The storm, known as the "Protestant wind," delivered a knockout punch to the weakened armada. Having lost half its ships to battle or storm, the Spanish fleet limped home to Spain.

The failure of the Spanish Armada meant that England would remain Protestant.

Spain's pride had also been dealt a serious blow. The world now knew that Spain, for all its wealth and might, was not all-powerful. Other nations became more brave about seeking commerce and empire in North America.

S E C T I O N   R E V I E W

1. Key Terms armada, privateer

2. People and Places Elizabeth I, Philip II, Francis Drake, English Channel

3. Comprehension Why did Queen Elizabeth make Francis Drake a knight?

4. Comprehension What technological advances helped the English defeat the Spanish Armada?

5. Critical Thinking In what way was the battle between England and Spain in 1588 a religious contest as well as a political one?

SKILLS: Reading a Line Graph

LEARN

We often hear about the way things are going—auto sales are down, movie ticket prices are up. A good way to show these directions, or trends, is with a line graph. All graphs are excellent ways to present data in a visual way. The line graph is especially helpful when we want to show the ups and downs of an event or situation over time.

Look at the graph to the right. The dates are shown along the bottom rule, called the horizontal axis. The vertical axis runs up the left side of the graph. To read a line graph, you should first look at the title. Then examine the labels on each axis. Once you know what the graph is about, you can examine individual dates for specific information. You can also look at the graph as a whole to determine the trend.

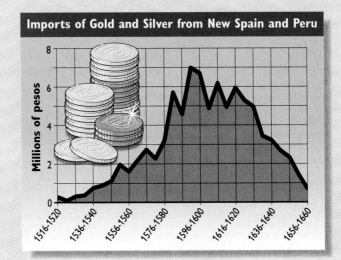

Imports of Gold and Silver from New Spain and Peru

PRACTICE

1. In the line graph above, what does the vertical axis represent?

2. What was the peak period for gold and silver imports?

3. Write a sentence or two describing the trend shown by this graph.

APPLY

4. Draw a line graph using the dates and figures below. Each figure gives the number of Spanish ships lost to pirates in that year.

Year	1536	1537	1538	1539	1540	1541	1542	1543	1544	1545	1546	1547
Ships Lost	1	24	4	5	3	3	4	4	12	1	1	4

4 The First English Colony

SECTION GUIDE

Main Idea
The first English efforts to establish a colony in North America failed. This failure taught the English valuable lessons for the future.

Goals
As you read, look for answers to these questions:

1. Why did the English decide to establish colonies?

2. What problems did the first English colony face?

3. What lessons did the English learn about building colonies?

Key Terms
sponsorship
Roanoke Island

I F YOU HAD BEEN English in the late 1500s, chances are you would have been proud. Your country had defeated the mighty Spanish fleet. English ships arrived in home ports heavy with riches. Your queen was a strong defender of the Protestant faith.

An English "Planting"

Richard Hakluyt (HAK-loot), an English geographer, believed the English were too smug. True, they had defeated the Spanish Armada, but Spain still had land throughout the Americas. How much American land did England control nearly a century after Columbus? Not one square foot. Hakluyt urged England to start a colony, or as he called it, a "planting." A "western planting" would have many advantages for England, said Hakluyt.

(1) It would provide a place to send petty criminals.

(2) It would allow England to build overseas bases.

(3) It would provide a market for English exports of manufactured goods and at the same time serve as an excellent source of raw materials.

(4) It would plant the Protestant faith in the Americas and keep the Roman Catholic Spanish from "flowing over all the face . . . of America."

In his writings, Hakluyt did not mention that such a colony should be able to feed itself. The English would have to learn that by experience.

The Founding of Roanoke

Sir Walter Raleigh, a soldier of sharp and witty mind favored by Queen Elizabeth, was the first Englishman to establish a colony across the seas. Raleigh claimed for England the Atlantic coast between the 34th and 45th parallels, roughly the area from present-day North Carolina to Maine. Raleigh named this region Virginia for England's Virgin Queen.

This map from the late 1500s shows the arrival of English colonists at Roanoke Island.

CULTURAL MOSAIC

SIR WALTER RALEIGH
(1554–1618)

Clever poet, youthful adventurer, and fancy dresser, Sir Walter Raleigh impressed Queen Elizabeth. She gave him permission to sponsor the unsuccessful colony at Roanoke. Raleigh's secret marriage angered the queen, and she sent the couple to the Tower of London. Though he was able to bribe their way out, Raleigh never returned to royal favor. Elizabeth's successor, James I, had Raleigh beheaded after the adventurer failed to capture gold mines in New Spain.

Under Raleigh's **sponsorship,** or backing, England's first colony began in 1585. It was at **Roanoke Island** off the coast of North Carolina.

The Roanoke and Croatoan Indians of the area were farmers who lived in towns surrounded by their corn fields. They valued justice and generosity. When the first English ships arrived in the area, a Roanoke man greeted them. The English took him aboard and gave him clothes and food. After leaving the ship, the Roanoke man went fishing nearby—and gave his entire catch to the colonists. During the winter, it was food provided by the local Indians that kept the colonists alive.

Good relations between the English and the Roanoke did not last. The English showed little respect to their neighbors. Misunderstandings between the English and the Indians often ended with violence. The colonists were soon starving because the Indians stopped giving them food. After a miserable year, the survivors begged passage home on a relief ship.

A Second Attempt

John White, a talented artist, convinced Sir Walter Raleigh to try again. White's idea was to attract settlers who would bring their families with them and invest some of their own money in the colony. Each settler would receive 500 acres of land.

In the spring of 1587, White set sail with his daughter, his son-in-law, and more than 100 other men, women, and children. When the group reached Roanoke, they started repairing the cottages left by the earlier settlers. It became clear to White that he would have to get more supplies.

White did not want to leave Roanoke. He now had a newborn granddaughter as well—Virginia Dare, the first English child born in America. The other Roanoke colonists, however, believed that White should make the trip back to England for supplies. He finally agreed and departed late in the summer of 1587.

White ended up stuck in England. A relief ship was supposed to have gone to Roanoke in 1588, but every seaworthy ship and sailor was needed to defend England against the Spanish Armada.

The Mystery of Roanoke

When White finally did reach Roanoke in 1591, he was shocked at what he found. Not a soul remained at the settlement. The only clues were the letters CRO carved on a tree and the word CROATOAN on a doorpost. White assumed that the settlers had gone to the friendly Croatoan Indians. Storms, however, kept him from reaching the Croatoan and forced his return to England. He was never able to discover the fate of his family and the other colonists.

Almost twenty years later, another English colony was started in Virginia. These colonists heard rumors about the "lost colonists." Indians said that the Roanoke

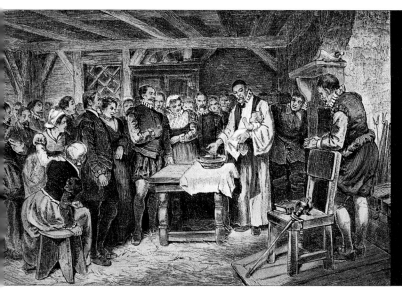

This illustration, drawn about 300 years after the English arrived at Roanoke, shows the artist's idea of the first English baptism in America, that of Virginia Dare. **Critical Thinking:** Why might the artist have considered this an important scene to illustrate?

Drawing of an Algonquin man by John White.

settlers had gone to live with the Chesapeake Indians. They had been killed when other Indians had attacked the Chesapeake. Others claimed that the colonists were victims of Spanish pirates. There was even reason to believe that some survivors remained among other Indian groups.

The truth was never discovered. To this day, no one knows for sure what really happened to the "lost colonists" of Roanoke.

The Lesson of Roanoke

The Roanoke colony had been a great financial loss for Raleigh rather than a source of profit. Yet in a broader sense, the English did gain from the experience. Their failure at Roanoke taught them some useful lessons about founding colonies.

Roanoke Island had been chosen as the site of the first English colony largely for geographic reasons. The island was far enough south to have a relatively warm climate. The English hoped that the climate would prove suitable for crops that could not be grown in England.

Though the weather was indeed mild, the colonists had overlooked a serious drawback of the island. Roanoke lacked a protected harbor. The shallow coastal waters and shifting tides put ships in danger of running aground.

Choosing a poor location for their colony was not the only mistake the English made. Perhaps the most important reason for Roanoke's failure was the lack of people, funds, and supplies. Raleigh and his backers had underestimated the problems of building a settlement so far from Europe. The English soon realized that if their American colonies were to thrive, better planning was necessary.

SECTION REVIEW

1. Key Terms sponsorship, Roanoke Island

2. People and Places Richard Hakluyt, Walter Raleigh, John White, Virginia

3. Comprehension What arguments did Richard Hakluyt use in favor of establishing overseas colonies?

4. Comprehension Why did the first English settlement at Roanoke Island fail?

5. Critical Thinking Why did the English make so many mistakes in the establishment of Roanoke?

Summary

1. In 1497, John Cabot claimed land in eastern North America for England. Other European explorers searched for a Northwest Passage to Asia. France sponsored voyages by Verrazano, Cartier, and Champlain. An Englishman, Henry Hudson explored parts of present-day New York and Canada in the 1600s.
2. Religious conflict in Europe spilled over into the Americas. The Reformation in Europe split Christianity. Spain saw itself as the defender of Catholicism and prevented France from establishing a Protestant colony at Fort Caroline in Florida.
3. England and Spain clashed over issues of religion and power during the 1500s. English pirates raided Spanish treasure ships returning from the Americas. In 1588 the Spanish Armada tried but failed to conquer England and return it to Catholicism.
4. England made its first attempt to build an American colony when Sir Walter Raleigh began a settlement on Roanoke Island in 1585. It failed. A second settlement there also failed. England learned valuable lessons from the experience.

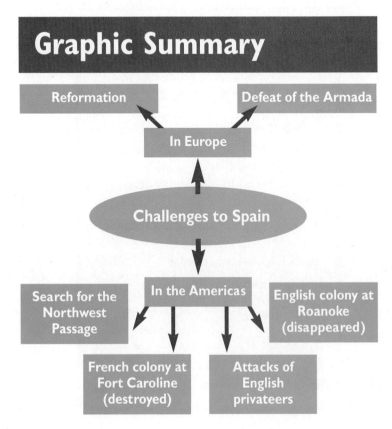

Graphic Summary

Reformation

Defeat of the Armada

In Europe

Challenges to Spain

In the Americas

Search for the Northwest Passage

French colony at Fort Caroline (destroyed)

Attacks of English privateers

English colony at Roanoke (disappeared)

Review

KEY TERMS

Define each of the following terms.
1. armada
2. Grand Banks
3. Northwest Passage
4. privateer
5. Protestant
6. Reformation
7. Roanoke Island
8. sponsorship

COMPREHENSION

1. What was the major accomplishment of John Cabot's voyage to the Americas? What had he hoped to accomplish?
2. What was the most important outcome of Champlain's explorations of North America?
3. What goal did Henry Hudson seek in his explorations of the Americas?
4. How did the development of the printing press help lead to the Reformation?
5. How did Spain react to the rise of Protestantism?
6. Why did Spain destroy the French settlement of Fort Caroline?
7. What actions of Francis Drake angered Spain? What was Queen Elizabeth's attitude toward Drake?
8. What happened to the Spanish Armada?
9. What happened to the first colony at Roanoke Island?
10. What lessons did the English learn from their failure at Roanoke?

Places to Locate

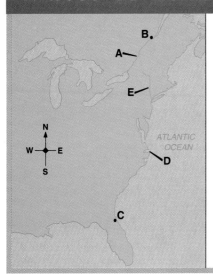

Match the letters on the map with the places listed below.

1. Hudson River
2. Quebec
3. Roanoke Island
4. St. Augustine
5. St. Lawrence River

Geographic Theme: Movement What reasons might have led English settlers to go to Roanoke? How did their reasons differ from those of the French Huguenots? Explain.

Skill Review

Study the line graph below. Then answer the questions that follow.

Spanish Ships Lost to Pirates, 1548–1556

1. What is the subject of the graph?
2. What does the horizontal axis represent?
3. During which years were the greatest number of Spanish ships lost? The least?

CRITICAL THINKING

1. **Making Comparisons** Compare Martin Luther's and Henry VIII's reasons for breaking with the Catholic Church.
2. **Forming a Hypothesis** What might the carving of the word CROATOAN at the site of the Roanoke colony tell about its fate?
3. **Expressing an Opinion** One reason England and France sought to build colonies in the Americas was to find a place for "undesirables." Do you approve of this practice? Explain.

PORTFOLIO OPTIONS

1. **Civics Connection** The invention of the printing press led to increased questioning of Church authority. Might it also have encouraged more people to question government power? Explain.
2. **Writing Connection** Imagine that you are trying to recruit people to settle in Roanoke. Write and illustrate an advertisement to persuade people to sail to America.
3. **Contemporary Connection** England's defeat of the Spanish Armada changed the course of history in the Americas as well as in Europe. How might American history have been different if the Spanish Armada had succeeded?
4. **Timeline Connection** Copy the chapter timeline. Add two other events from the chapter you think should be included and explain why.

Religion has played an important role in American life since colonial times. The painting below, "Pilgrims Going to Church," captures the devotion of the early settlers—men, women, and children walk through the snow on their way to worship.

1600   1620   1640   1660

1607 Jamestown founded

1619 House of Burgesses established

1634 Maryland founded

1620 Pilgrims settle Plymouth

1664 English seize
New Netherland

1630 Great Migration begins

English Colonies in North America (1607–1732)

1 Success at Jamestown

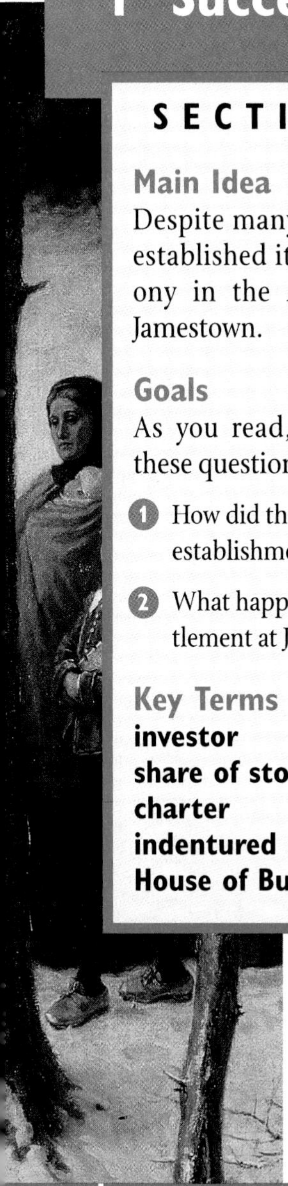

SECTION GUIDE

Main Idea
Despite many difficulties, England established its first permanent colony in the Americas in 1607 at Jamestown.

Goals
As you read, look for answers to these questions:

1 How did the English pay for the establishment of colonies?

2 What happened to the English settlement at Jamestown?

Key Terms
investor
share of stock
charter
indentured servant
House of Burgesses

ADVENTURE was what John Smith wanted. As a teenager, he left the family home in England to become a professional soldier in France. A few years later Smith was home again, but, becoming restless, he returned to being a professional soldier. This time he was captured by the Turks, who sold him into slavery. He was a slave several years before he killed his Turkish slaveowner and escaped by horseback into Russia. By 1606 he was back in England, famed as an experienced soldier and a man of action. More adventures awaited John Smith.

England Plans Colonies

Smith found that England had changed. "Good Queen Bess," as Elizabeth I was also called, had died. The new English monarch was her cousin, King James of Scotland. James had made peace with Spain. As a result, English privateers no longer had license to raid Spanish shipping. At the same time, Spain no longer claimed parts of North America. With peace secured, England again considered establishing colonies, thereby becoming part of the new Atlantic world.

Merchants were the most enthusiastic supporters of new colonies. Merchants believed that the Americas offered valuable trade opportunities. The most serious problem facing the

1680	1700	1720	1740

1682 Pennsylvania founded

1732 Georgia founded

107

would-be colonizers was how to pay for a colony. The English had learned from Raleigh's experience in Roanoke that one person could not finance a colony. The Spanish colonies had been financed by the monarchs, but English monarchs lacked such funds.

To raise money, therefore, the English turned to joint-stock companies, the form of business organization started by Genoese bankers in Italy. The joint-stock companies were backed by **investors,** people who put money into a project in order to earn profits. Each investor received **shares of stock** —pieces of ownership in the company. Thus the investors jointly accepted the risks of a new enterprise. They would split any profits they made and divide any losses they suffered.

A group of London merchants organized the Virginia Company of London. Plymouth merchants organized a similar company, the Virginia Company of Plymouth. In 1606 King James granted each company a **charter** to set up outposts in North America. (A charter is a written contract giving certain rights to a person or group.) The Virginia Company of London received the right to settle the southern part of England's claim. The Virginia Company of Plymouth would settle the northern part of the claim. The charters also granted each of the companies a monopoly on trade in its colony.

The Founding of Jamestown

The London investors immediately began organizing an expedition. They bought three ships and hired captains. They were delighted when John Smith assumed responsibility for buying supplies.

In late December 1606 the three ships set sail. On board were over 100 men and boys, all volunteers. The ocean voyage was particularly long. Smith, who thought very highly of himself, so angered the captains that they decided to hang him when they reached land. Later they changed their minds, partly because ex-soldier Smith was armed to the teeth.

Jamestown was England's first successful colony in North America. Its three walls made the fort easier to defend than four walls. **Critical Thinking:** How was the Jamestown fort protected?

In April 1607 the little ships entered the calm waters of a great bay. Smith would later name it Chesapeake Bay. There, near the mouth of the James River, they decided to settle. They named their outpost Jamestown, in honor of King James.

Terrible Hardships

From the start, the Jamestown settlers endured awful hardships. The site of the settlement was swampy and filled with mosquitoes. Many colonists fell sick from drinking the river water. As one colonist recalled, "There were never Englishmen left in a foreign country in such misery as we were in this newly discovered Virginia."

The settlers also feared the nearby Powhatan Indians, who were well organized and powerful. To make matters worse, Jamestown's settlers were greedy adventurers. They were more interested in hunting for gold than in building shelters or growing food. By autumn of the first year, food supplies were low and two-thirds of the Jamestown settlers had died.

The settlement would have failed had John Smith not taken control. Smith had settlers build defenses, including a wall around the colony. He persuaded the Powhatan Indians to trade corn to the colonists. Though Chief Powhatan distrusted the English, he respected Smith and may have wanted his help against his Indian rivals. To ensure that all settlers would work, Smith set a new rule: "He that will not work neither shall he eat."

Smith's leadership was short lived, however. Badly hurt in a gunpowder explosion, he returned to England in 1609. In the same year, 800 more settlers, including entire families, arrived. Yet the worst was yet to come. That winter the Indians stopped trading food, and the settlers did not dare leave the fort. It was a "starving time"—a time of eating rats and mice, a time of disease and death. Only 60 of the 838 settlers survived.

CULTURAL MOSAIC

POCAHONTAS
(1595?–1617)

Pocahontas married the colonist John Rolfe in 1614. Two years later they went to England to raise money for the struggling Jamestown colony. There she was treated as an Indian princess. While getting ready to sail back home, she developed smallpox and died. Her son, Thomas, was educated in England and later became a leading Virginia citizen.

Jamestown Grows

The Roanoke colony had collapsed from lack of overseas support. In contrast, the Virginia Company kept sending new supplies and new settlers to Jamestown. The marriage of colonist John Rolfe to Pocahontas, daughter of Chief Powhatan, led to peace between the colony and the Indians. Gradually the colonists learned from the Indians how to grow corn, catch fish, and capture wild fowl.

Rolfe's greatest contribution to the colony, however, was learning how to grow high-quality tobacco. Tobacco, a plant native to the Western Hemisphere, quickly became very popular in England. In vain

Elizabeth Canning of England was convicted of lying to a court. As her punishment, she was required to labor for seven years in America as an indentured servant.

King James complained that smoking was a "vile and stinking" habit.

The success of tobacco growing changed Jamestown in many ways. The Virginia Company considered the colonists to be employees. The colonists, however, did not want to grow tobacco that would benefit only the company. The tobacco harvest from an acre of land was worth ten times what a colonist was paid each year. Colonists wanted a larger share of the profits. The company responded by letting settlers own land. When the land became their own, settlers worked longer and harder.

To attract new settlers, the company offered a 50-acre land grant for each man, woman, or child who could pay his or her way to the colony. The population of Virginia quickly jumped from some 600 in 1619 to over 2,000 in 1621.

Still, more workers were needed. Those people who could not afford passage to America were encouraged to become indentured servants. Indentured servants sold their labor in exchange for passage to the colony. After laboring in the colony for an agreed-upon time, usually four to seven years, they were free to take up a trade of their own.

Not all indentured servants came from England. In 1619 a Dutch ship brought about twenty Africans to Jamestown, where they became indentured servants. They were the first Africans brought to the English colonies.

Changes in Government

The colonists soon became annoyed by the strict rule of the company governor. To provide for some local government, the Virginia Company decided that burgesses, or elected representatives of the settlers, would meet at least once a year in a colonial assembly. This House of Burgesses, created in 1619, would make laws for the colony. The company, however, could veto those laws. The House of Burgesses was the first representative assembly in the American colonies. It also was the first of many steps the colonists would take to establish their own identity as a people.

The success of the Jamestown colony depended upon one crop: tobacco.

SECTION REVIEW

1. Key Terms investor, share of stock, charter, indentured servant, House of Burgesses

2. People and Places John Smith, John Rolfe, Pocahontas, Jamestown

3. Comprehension Why were joint-stock companies better able than individual persons to finance colonies?

4. Comprehension What problems did Jamestown face at first?

5. Critical Thinking Explain how individual initiative helped ensure the survival of the Jamestown colony.

2 The Pilgrims at Plymouth

SECTION GUIDE

Main Idea
Started in 1620 by a small group of English settlers, the Plymouth colony survived its difficult first year.

Goals
As you read, look for answers to these questions:

1 Who settled at Plymouth and why?

2 Why did the Plymouth settlers establish their own rules for the colony?

Key Terms
persecution
Separatist
religious tolerance
Mayflower Compact

WHERE WILL YOU BE on the fourth Thursday in November this year? You will not be in school. If you are like many people in the United States, you will be enjoying a large meal with family and friends. Perhaps you will even be discussing the things for which you are grateful on Thanksgiving Day.

The Voyage of the Pilgrims

The tradition of a day of thanks dates back to ancient times. In the United States, however, we also recall a small settlement in New England where a group of plainly dressed English men and women sat down to a feast with American Indians. These settlers were the Pilgrims of Plymouth Colony, who were thanking God for a good harvest.

Pilgrims are people who make a journey for a religious reason. The Pilgrims of Plymouth Colony were seeking freedom from **persecution**—bad treatment. The Pilgrims belonged to a religious group called **Separatists** that had broken away from the Church of England. King James was persecuting the Separatists for rejecting the official church. In 1609, just two years after the settlement of Jamestown, the Separatists moved from England to the city of Leiden in Holland. They chose Holland as their destination because that country had the most **religious tolerance** of any place in Europe. Religious tolerance is the willingness to accept faiths different from one's own.

The Separatists lived and worshipped in Leiden for a few years, but they were not happy in their new home. Having been farmers in England, they had trouble finding work in the city. Also, their children began speaking Dutch instead of English. The Separatists again considered moving. They finally decided to ask the Virginia Company if they could settle in America "as a distinct body by themselves."

Thus it was on a cold, raw November day in 1620 that the ship *Mayflower* arrived off Cape Cod on the Massachusetts coast. The Virginia

The 90-foot ship *Mayflower*, shown here covered with ice, carried the Pilgrims to Massachusetts in 1620.

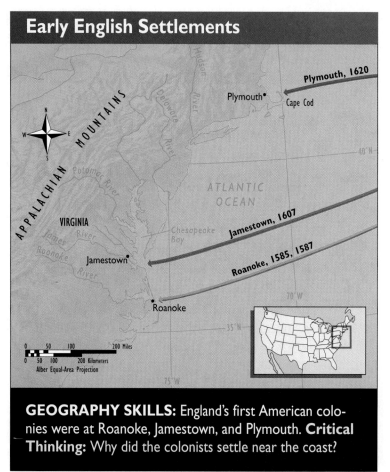

Early English Settlements

Plymouth, 1620

Plymouth • Cape Cod

Jamestown, 1607

Roanoke, 1585, 1587

APPALACHIAN MOUNTAINS

VIRGINIA

Jamestown •

Roanoke •

ATLANTIC OCEAN

Chesapeake Bay

James River

Roanoke River

Potomac River

Delaware River

Hudson River

40°N

70°W

35°N

75°W

0 50 100 200 Miles
0 50 100 200 Kilometers
Alber Equal-Area Projection

GEOGRAPHY SKILLS: England's first American colonies were at Roanoke, Jamestown, and Plymouth. **Critical Thinking:** Why did the colonists settle near the coast?

To ensure order, therefore, the men aboard the *Mayflower* signed an agreement, the Mayflower Compact. In it they vowed to obey any laws agreed upon for the general good of the colony. The Mayflower Compact was meant to be only an informal agreement. Still, it helped establish the idea of self-government in the colonies.

After exploring Cape Cod, the Pilgrims settled at the site named "Plymouth" on John Smith's map, which they carried. Plymouth had a harbor, cleared fields, and running brooks. "At least it was the best they could find, and the season and their present necessity made them glad to accept of it," wrote William Bradford. Bradford would later govern the colony and write its history.

Hard Times at Plymouth

Like the early settlers at Jamestown, the Pilgrims endured a starving time. That first winter, disease and death struck with such fury that "the living were scarce able to bury the dead." Half their number had died by spring.

With spring came energy, hope, and help. One day an Indian walked up to a group of settlers. To their astonishment, he called out, "Welcome, Englishmen." This was Samoset, a Pemaquid Indian who had learned to speak English from European fishermen.

Samoset introduced the settlers to an Indian named Squanto. Squanto was the last remaining member of the Patuxet, a nearby tribe that had been wiped out by disease. Earlier Squanto had been captured as a slave and then had returned as a sailor on a trading ship. Finding his kin all dead, Squanto set about helping the English plant corn, beans, and pumpkins in the tribal lands. He also acted as an interpreter to local Indians. Thanks to Squanto's efforts, the Pilgrims and Indians lived in peace for years.

Company had been eager to have the group settle near the mouth of the Hudson River, the northernmost area of its grant. During a rough, stormy passage, however, the *Mayflower* was blown north of its course. This was an area that John Smith, who had done so much to save Jamestown, had explored and mapped. He called it "New England" and had hoped to set up a settlement there. A storm and then pirates had upset his plans. Now storms brought the Pilgrims, weary and weak from the 66-day voyage, to New England. They decided to stay where they were.

Because the Pilgrims landed outside the limits of the Virginia Company, their charter did not apply. In effect, they had no authority to make or enforce rules. Yet they all knew that a society without rules would soon collapse.

This painting of the first Thanksgiving contains several historical inaccuracies. For example, Pilgrims lived in wood and sod houses, not log cabins. Nevertheless, the scene reflects the peace that existed at that time between Indians and Pilgrims.

While the corn grew, the colonists began trading with the Indians for furs and preparing clapboard (lumber used in building houses) to ship back to England. The Pilgrims had agreed to develop products to pay back the Virginia Company for its support.

Sometime in the fall of 1621—no one knows when—the Plymouth settlement celebrated the blessings of a good harvest by holding a three-day celebration. It was the first Thanksgiving. The only description of it is in a letter written back to England. According to the letter writer:

❝ **[Four men] in one day killed as much fowl as . . . served the company almost a week. At which time . . . many of the Indians [came] amongst us . . . whom for three days we entertained and feasted. . . .** ❞

Life for the infant colony, however, was still difficult. There was not enough corn to last the year. Some people disliked the arrangement in which each person worked for the whole and shared equally in the produce. Among them were women, who did not like to cook and wash for men other than their husbands. "They deemed it a kind of slavery," Bradford wrote.

Bradford thus decided to give each family a piece of land for its own use. In Plymouth, as in Jamestown, the switch to private property led to greater success for the colony and its people.

3 The Settlement of New England

SECTION GUIDE

Main Idea
The people who settled New England hoped to build a model society based on their religious views.

Goals
As you read, look for answers to these questions:

1. Why did thousands of English people choose to migrate to the Americas in the 1630s?

2. How did the Massachusetts colonists structure their society?

3. How did Massachusetts react to those who challenged their established views?

Key Terms
Puritan
Great Migration
commonwealth
dissenter

Puritan John Winthrop was the first governor of Massachusetts.

EACH YEAR the Plymouth colony sent back to England a cargo of furs and lumber. Then in 1628 the colonists sent back another kind of cargo. They sent their neighbor, Thomas Morton.

The Arrest of Thomas Morton

Morton had settled north of Plymouth, in a place he named Merrymount. Within a few years he was hunting, fishing, and trading guns to the Indians for furs. He also welcomed anyone who wanted to settle in Merrymount. This angered Governor Bradford of Plymouth. How could one keep servants, he complained, if they could flee to a place like Merrymount? How could settlers feel secure if the Indians were armed with guns? Disturbed by Morton's mischief, Bradford ordered his arrest.

Although sent to England, Morton was back in Massachusetts a year later. By that time, however, boatloads of religious-minded colonists had settled at Boston harbor north of Merrymount. Morton's rowdy days were over. The message was clear: New England was for the godly.

Unrest in England

During the 1620s the population of colonial New England had remained small, numbering only about 500 settlers. This figure ballooned in the 1630s when people began fleeing problems in England.

Some of this unrest was economic, for trade was down and times were hard. Another source of problems was the religious ideas of King Charles I. A stubborn ruler, Charles insisted that the people of England all worship in the same way—his way.

One hundred years after the English Reformation, the nation was at odds over the direction the Church of England should take. The Church was not under Catholic control, but it had kept many Catholic traditions. People known as **Puritans** wanted to rid the Church of such "Popish" traditions as the use of statues, paintings, and instrumental music. They also disliked such celebrations as Christmas and church marriage. To them, the English practice of playing sports and games on

Sunday was downright sinful. Why, they asked, could the Church not return to the ways of the early Christians as described in the Bible?

"No way," was the essence of the king's answer. He believed that religion and the state were one. If people started to question the authority of the Church, next they might question the power of the king.

The Great Migration

For devout Puritans the future looked bleak, and many chose to head to the Americas. Their leaving is known as the Great Migration. During the 1630s thousands of Puritan families poured out of England toward the Americas.

Most of these emigrants—40,000 of them—moved to England's new colonies in the West Indies. The Caribbean was no longer a Spanish sea, and other nations were laying claim to islands there. English settlers started plantations throughout the West Indies. They continued the pattern of raising subtropical crops—sugar, tobacco, cotton, and dyes—to sell abroad.

Another 20,000 Puritan emigrants chose New England. In 1629 the Massachusetts Bay Company had been given a royal charter to settle land in New England. Many Puritan merchants had invested in the company. It was only natural that the company began to recruit new settlers from among Puritans.

The leader of the Great Migration to New England was John Winthrop. A victim of the king's crackdown on English Puritans, Winthrop had been fired from his job as an attorney in the king's courts. The Massachusetts Bay Company knew of Winthrop's leadership skills and convinced him to become governor.

In March 1630 the migration began. A fleet of 11 ships carried 700 passengers, 240 cows, and 60 horses. The arrival of the fleet more than doubled the white population of New England.

CONNECTING WITH WORLD EVENTS

PURITANS IN THE CARIBBEAN

For every Puritan who settled in New England, two Puritans settled in the West Indies in the Caribbean Sea. There they found sugar cane (right), which grew well in the warm, moist climate. At that time the use of sugar as a sweetener was the latest craze in Europe. As the demand grew larger and larger, the Caribbean Puritans soon found themselves wealthy beyond belief. Some became owners of large plantations. Many growers imported slaves from Africa to work on the plantations.

Massachusetts Bay Colony

As governor for most of the next nineteen years, Winthrop helped set the course for the colony. In a sermon on his flagship, the *Arbella,* he had expressed the hopes for the new colony. Theirs would be a society, he said, of justice and mercy. It would be a commonwealth, a community in which people work together for the good of the whole. It would be a model for the whole world.

Massachusetts settlers believed they had a covenant, or agreement, with God to build a holy society. Covenants, whether written or unwritten, were important to the Puritans as a way of expressing community goals.

Colonial New England Towns

The basic unit of the commonwealth was the congregation—a group of people who belong to the same church. Each Puritan congregation set up its own town. Towns were built around an open field called a

A child when her family immigrated to America, Anne Pollard was reportedly the first Puritan ashore. She lived to be 105.

common. New England farmers lived in the towns and went out each day to work in the fields. At night they returned to their homes in town.

The most important building in each town was the meetinghouse, where people met for town meetings. At the town meeting, people made laws and other decisions for the community. They could grant land to newcomers, determine fees for workers, and even set the price for ale. They could also appoint people to perform tasks necessary to the community—repairing fences, operating a ferry, or serving in the militia. When the town's population grew too large for the meetinghouse, the congregation was likely to divide and start a new town.

The New England Way

The meetinghouse was also used for church services. By law, everyone in the town had to attend church. The church services were stricter than those of today. The meetinghouse had no heat, and the hard benches were uncomfortable. The men sat in one part of the church, and the women and girls in another. The boys usually sat together in the balcony. If there was any noise, the offenders were punished.

The raised platform called the pulpit was the central feature of the meetinghouse. There stood the minister, an important and respected man whose words carried great weight. From the pulpit he delivered the sermon, the most important part of the New England church service.

The sermon provided instruction in the "New England Way." This was the term used by the Puritans to describe both their beliefs and the society they were building. It was a society that emphasized duty, godliness, hard work, and honesty. The Puritans thought that amusements such as dancing and playing games would lead to laziness and sin.

The New England Way depended on education. The Puritans believed that the Bible was the source of truth. Therefore, each person should be able to read it. Laws required that each child learn to read. (It was not necessary, however, to know how to write.) Puritan life also depended on well-educated ministers to lead the society. To provide a future supply of ministers, Harvard College was founded in 1636.

The Massachusetts Puritans extended their influence by building towns farther and farther from Boston. Some Puritan congregations, however, set up colonies independent of Massachusetts. In the search for more fertile land, the minister Thomas Hooker and his congregation moved in 1636 to the gentle Connecticut Valley. There they wrote and adopted the Fundamental Orders of Connecticut. In effect, these laws were a constitution, the first in the American colonies.

Challenges to the Puritans

The Puritans did not believe in freedom of religion. They came to the Americas to worship in their own way. They did not tolerate dissenters. (A dissenter is someone who challenges the generally accepted views of Church or society.)

The first important dissenter was Roger Williams, a minister from the town of Salem. Massachusetts leaders thought it bad enough when Williams said that the king of England had no right to give away Indian land. They were outraged, however, when he claimed that government should have no power over religious matters. That challenged the very heart of the Puritan commonwealth.

As a result, the Puritan legislature, called the General Court, ordered him shipped back to England. Quickly Williams slipped away in the winter snows to Narragansett Bay. With a small group of followers, he founded a colony there in 1636 that would become Rhode Island.

Soon Massachusetts faced another dissenter, Anne Hutchinson. At weekly meetings she explained her belief that a person could find inner truth and divine guidance without the help of the ministry.

By challenging the religious leaders, Hutchinson was also challenging the basis of the commonwealth. This was treason, and she was brought to trial. At trial, pregnant with her sixteenth child, Hutchinson refused to change her views.

The court banished her from the colony. In 1638 Hutchinson left for Rhode Island. Rhode Island, called "Rogue Island" by people in Massachusetts, had become a refuge—a place of protection—for anyone seeking freedom of religion.

Quakers Face Persecution

Some years later the Massachusetts commonwealth was again challenged. This time it was the Quakers, a Puritan group that had arisen in England in the 1650s. The Quakers believed that each person could know God directly through "an inner light." Because all people were equal before God, they said, neither ministers nor the Bible was needed.

Such beliefs caused the Quakers to be persecuted both in England and in Massachusetts. In Massachusetts the laws against Quaker missionaries were harsh. Authorities whipped the Quakers and threw them in prison. They cut off parts of their ears and bored their tongues with hot irons. When those methods did not stop the Quakers, Massachusetts began to hang them. The king himself had to order the practice stopped.

The Puritan commonwealth lasted about 60 years. In 1691 the Crown forced a new charter on Massachusetts. As a result, the governor was chosen by the Crown, rather than elected by church members. Also, the right to vote was tied to ownership of property, not church membership. Massachusetts now had to tolerate dissenters.

Indians Help Europeans

The first contacts between Europeans and Indians often helped each side. The Indians valued the steel knives, iron pots, and guns of the Europeans. For these they eagerly traded furs. The survival of the Europeans depended upon Indian goodwill. From the Indians they learned about native plants and animals. In addition, colonists learned Indian methods of farming, fur trapping, and woodland survival.

The more the colonists learned from the Indians, however, the less dependent they became on the Indians' knowledge. At the same time, the growing colonial population began to pressure the Indians from their land.

Frontier Warfare

Europeans and Indians defined land ownership differently. In Europe, landowners completely controlled their land—they could cut down trees, plow the soil, and fence the pastures. For the Indians, land ownership meant having access to the things on the land whenever they wanted. No one could own the land itself.

Conflict over land resulted in frontier warfare between the Indians and the white settlers. In these wars each side used whatever means it had at its disposal to destroy

Wampum beads were used as currency in the Indian-European fur trade.

Roger Williams, like Anne Hutchinson, challenged the Puritan leaders of Massachusetts. Williams was sheltered by Narragansett Indians after fleeing to Rhode Island.

This 1810 engraving shows a battle during King Philip's War. **Critical Thinking:** Why did problems arise between the Indians and the English colonists?

the other side. In 1622 the Powhatan killed one-third of Virginia's colonists before they in turn were destroyed. In the next decade the Pequot Indians of the Connecticut Valley resisted the Puritan invasion of their land. The Pequot were also destroyed.

In 1675 the Puritan colonies went to war with the New England Indians over land. This was King Philip's War. "King Philip" was the English name of Metacom, leader of the Wampanoag.

Caught in the middle of this war was the peace-loving Roger Williams. Williams, who spoke Indian languages and was a friend of the Indians, had long tried to keep peace between settlers and Indians. But time worked against this peace.

King Philip's War would be one of the most deadly in American history. Almost every colonial town in Massachusetts and Connecticut was threatened. One-sixth of New England's male population was killed. Williams watched while his house—and the town of Providence, Rhode Island— were burned. It was a sad time for Williams. With a heavy heart, he joined the war against his Indian friends.

In the end the English destroyed the power of the New England Indians by destroying their corn fields and starving them into submission. About 500 Indians,

including Metacom's wife and son, were sold into slavery in the West Indies. Those who remained were put on reservations or forced to become laborers.

England's colonization of North America would be steady and relentless. Just as steadily, the Indians would continue to defend their right to live where they chose. For almost three centuries, frontier warfare would be part of the American experience.

SECTION REVIEW

1. Key Terms Puritan, Great Migration, commonwealth, dissenter

2. People Charles I, John Winthrop, Roger Williams, Anne Hutchinson, Metacom (King Philip)

3. Comprehension What caused the Great Migration?

4. Comprehension Who held political power in Massachusetts? When did this situation change?

5. Critical Thinking Why were the Puritans, who had migrated to North America for religious reasons, intolerant of religious dissenters?

SKILLS: Reading a Primary Source

LEARN

What do a shopping list, a newspaper article, and a personal journal have in common? To historians, these are primary sources—materials written or made at the time they tell about.

If you were a historian seeking information about American Indians in the English colonies, where would you look? You might read the letters and journals of colonists or accounts of personal interviews with Indians. Such primary-source documents would provide firsthand information about Indians and their lives.

When presenting primary sources, books such as this one use special kinds of punctuation. The set of dots you see here . . . is called an ellipsis (ih-LIP-sis). An ellipsis shows that some words have been left out. You may also see brackets such as [these] enclosing a helpful word or phrase not in the original.

When you read a primary source, take the following steps:

(1) Identify who wrote it, when, and where.

(2) Try to separate fact from opinion.

PRACTICE

Read the primary source at the right. Then answer the following questions.

1. Find two opinions in the description.

2. Find two facts that a historian might find valuable. Explain your choices.

3. Why is the word "colonists" enclosed in brackets?

APPLY

4. Read the Mayflower Compact and write a paragraph explaining why this document is so important to historians.

The following is a description of Pennsylvania Indians written by Englishman Gabriel Thomas in 1698.

"The natives of this country are very charitable to one another. The lame and the blind amongst them live as well as the best. They are also very kind and obliging to the [colonists].

In person they are ordinarily tall, straight, and well-formed. Their tread is strong, and they generally walk with the chin high up. . . . Their eyes are small and black. They have pleasing faces.

The boys fish till they are 15 years of age, then hunt. . . . The girls stay with their mothers, and help to hoe the ground, plant corn, and carry burdens."

4 An Expanding Empire

SECTION GUIDE

Main Idea

The colonies that became part of England's expanding American empire were different in many ways.

Goals

As you read, look for answers to these questions:

1 How did geographical factors influence life in the Chesapeake Tidewater?

2 How did New Netherland pass from Dutch to English rule?

3 What new English colonies were created?

Key Terms

patroon
proprietor

B Y THE MID-1600s there were two clusters of English colonists in America. One cluster was in New England, the other cluster in the lowlands around the Chesapeake Bay. This area, in present-day Maryland and Virginia, is called the Chesapeake Tidewater.

The Chesapeake Tidewater

Twenty-five years after its founding in 1607, Virginia's population had reached 2,500, and tobacco sales had soared. Through trial and error, the Virginia colonists had learned how to prosper in the Chesapeake Tidewater. (A tidewater is a region of low coastal land with rivers affected by ocean tides.) In doing so, Virginia set the pattern for its new neighbor, Maryland.

Maryland was established in 1634 by Lord Baltimore as a refuge for Catholics fleeing persecution in England. Yet the number of Catholics was small. To attract settlers, Lord Baltimore promised religious toleration to Protestants. During the Great Migration, thousands of Puritans moved to Maryland, where they soon outnumbered the Catholics.

The tobacco plantations of the Chesapeake Tidewater were strung out along the region's many waterways. To the dock of each plantation came ships that brought manufactured goods from England and in turn carried the tobacco to market. Towns were not necessary because there was no need for a place to buy and sell goods. Because the plantations were scattered, ministers found it hard to enforce Church rules of behavior. As a result, the Church had far less influence there than in New England.

Life for the early Chesapeake settlers was hard. Before tobacco could be planted, fields had to be cleared of trees and the stumps pulled. The planting and harvesting of tobacco demanded back-breaking labor. Within three or four years, tobacco used up the nutrients in the soil. Thus a tobacco farmer was always clearing new land. When there was no more land to clear, the farmer moved upriver and started over again.

Baltimore, Maryland, was a trading center for tobacco plantations in the Chesapeake Tidewater.

Disease took a high toll on Chesapeake settlers. Half of all children died. Even those who lived to age twenty could expect to live only half as long as New Englanders.

For much of the 1600s, thousands of immigrants came in response to the labor demands of the tobacco farms. Some were convicts sent to the colonies as punishment for their crimes. Others were jobless artisans who came in search of a better life.

Most laborers came as indentured servants. On arrival, they were auctioned off to those willing to pay their ocean passage. After their time of servitude, those who survived were given a hoe and a new suit of clothes and freed.

New Netherland

Between New England and the Chesapeake Tidewater was New Netherland. This colony of the Dutch West India Company included the Hudson River valley, Long Island, and land along the Delaware River.

The Dutch company had profited from fur trading at Fort Orange (Albany), Fort Nassau (Gloucester, New Jersey), and New Amsterdam (New York City), but it had few settlers. To make New Netherland a "proper" colony, therefore, the Dutch West India Company decided to encourage farming and settlement.

The way the Dutch company did so was through **patroons.** A patroon was a person who brought fifty settlers to New Netherland. The reward was a large land grant, a patroonship, along the Hudson River. The patroonships were in fact feudal estates. The patroon had special privileges in hunting, fishing, and the fur trade. He also had almost complete power over the people on his land—the same kind of power held by a feudal lord.

Eager to attract and keep settlers, the colony had welcomed different kinds of people. From its founding in 1626 New Amsterdam had included African indentured servants. (By the 1660s one-fifth of

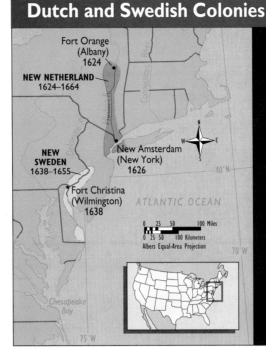

Dutch and Swedish Colonies

Fort Orange (Albany) 1624

NEW NETHERLAND 1624–1664

New Amsterdam (New York) 1626

NEW SWEDEN 1638–1655

Fort Christina (Wilmington) 1638

ATLANTIC OCEAN

0 25 50 100 Miles
0 25 50 100 Kilometers
Albers Equal-Area Projection

Chesapeake Bay

GEOGRAPHY SKILLS : The colonies of New Netherland and New Sweden were both established on rivers. **Critical Thinking:** Why were rivers important to early colonial settlements?

Seal of New York City, 1664.

New Amsterdam was African American.) Many Puritans moved there as well.

In May 1647 a Dutch ship arrived in New Amsterdam carrying a new governor. He was the cranky and strong-willed Peter Stuyvesant. Stuyvesant used a wooden peg to replace a leg lost in battle, thereby earning the nickname "Pegleg Peter."

Like many Christians during that time, Stuyvesant was suspicious of anyone who was not a Christian. He was not pleased in 1654 when 23 Jewish settlers arrived. Stuyvesant did allow the Jews to land, but then he wrote the Dutch West India Company asking what he should do. The company responded: Let the Jews remain there. The Jews were to have the same rights as other settlers of New Netherland.

Stuyvesant, wanting to expand New Netherland, attacked the neighboring colony of New Sweden in 1655. The Swedish colony consisted primarily of several fur-trading posts in the Delaware Valley. After a ten-day siege by the Dutch, the Swedes surrendered Fort Christina and gave up their American holdings.

The Thirteen English Colonies

Claimed by N.H. and N.Y.

FRENCH TERRITORY

NEW HAMPSHIRE

MASSACHUSETTS

Boston 1630
Plymouth 1620

NEW YORK

Hartford 1636

Providence 1636
RHODE ISLAND
CONNECTICUT

New York 1664

PENNSYLVANIA

Philadelphia 1682

NEW JERSEY

Wilmington 1664

MARYLAND

DELAWARE

ATLANTIC OCEAN

VIRGINIA

St. Mary's 1634

Jamestown 1607

Roanoke Island

APPALACHIAN MOUNTAINS

NORTH CAROLINA

SOUTH CAROLINA

Charles Town 1670 (Charleston)

GEORGIA

SPANISH TERRITORY

N W E S

0 50 100   200 Miles
0 50 100   200 Kilometers
Albers Equal-Area Projection

GEOGRAPHY SKILLS: English settlements dotted the eastern coast of North America in the 1600s. **Critical Thinking:** Why did the Appalachian Mountains form a logical western boundary for the colonies?

Seizure of New Netherland

English colonization stopped in the middle of the 1600s as a result of civil war and turmoil in England. The civil war started in 1642 with a Puritan rebellion against Charles I. After defeating and beheading the king in 1649, the Puritans ruled England until 1660. In that year Charles II reclaimed his father's throne. Colonization then resumed in North America.

Charles II decided that his brother, the Duke of York, should drive out the Dutch. When the duke's ships appeared off New Amsterdam in August 1664, the colony surrendered without a fight—much to the disgust of Peter Stuyvesant. The Duke of York was now the **proprietor,** or owner, of New Netherland, which was renamed "New York."

New Jersey and Pennsylvania

The Duke of York had become the largest single landowner in America. He gave a chunk of his claim, the province of New Jersey, to his friends Sir George Carteret and Lord John Berkeley. They encouraged settlers to come to their new land by promising freedom of religion, large grants of land, and a representative assembly.

The Duke of York gave up an even larger part of his estate when he paid off a debt to William Penn. Years before, the duke had borrowed money from Penn's father. Penn, an active Quaker, was seeking a refuge for Quakers being persecuted in England. By reminding the duke of the debt, Penn was granted the tract of land and in 1682 he founded Pennsylvania. That same year he was given more land by the duke, the three counties that became Delaware.

The Quakers believed that all people should live in peace and harmony. They welcomed different religions and ethnic groups. Pennsylvania thus kept an open door to the world. This policy, as well as its fertile land, would make Pennsylvania one of the wealthiest American colonies.

Land was of no use to a proprietor as wilderness. Settlers were needed to work the land. Thus William Penn, after first opening up Pennsylvania to Quaker settlement, went off to Germany to find more immigrants. In time, thousands of German settlers arrived in Pennsylvania. They brought with them craft skills and productive farming techniques that helped the colony thrive.

The Carolinas and Georgia

When Charles II became king, he owed a debt of gratitude to a number of people. Eight of them asked Charles for a grant of land between Virginia and Spanish Florida. This was to be Carolina (a feminine form of the name "Charles"). In 1663 Charles granted their request. The first settlers built Charles Town (Charleston) in 1670 and busied themselves cutting timber, raising cattle, and trading with the Indians for deerskins.

The settlement at Charleston soon lost its frontier character. In 1685 the king of France began persecuting the French Protestants, known as Huguenots. Thousands were forced to leave France, and a number found a new home in Carolina. There they farmed the lowlands and turned Charleston into one of the most attractive and charming cities of the colonies. The Huguenots achieved this prosperity, however, by heavy use of slave labor.

In 1729 the Crown took over Carolina from its proprietors. The colony was divided into North and South Carolina.

In 1732 one more colony, Georgia, was founded. The English government saw it as a military outpost and buffer against Spanish Florida. James Oglethorpe, founder of the colony, saw it as an opportunity to establish a model society.

Oglethorpe had long been upset by the number of people thrown into English prisons for debt. He hoped that debtors could gain economic freedom and self-respect in Georgia. He formed a charitable organization to help debtors. That organization then received a charter to settle Georgia. Oglethorpe and other officers of the organization had complete authority over the colony.

Oglethorpe set strict rules in Georgia. He limited the amount of land each settler could own. He outlawed trade with the Indians in order to avoid conflict. He also banned both slavery and alcohol. The rules were overturned by 1750 after settlers complained. With large plantations and slavery allowed, the colony grew rapidly.

William Penn, a Quaker, founded Pennsylvania. He is shown here signing a treaty with the Indians.

SECTION REVIEW

1. Key Terms patroon, proprietor

2. People Lord Baltimore, Peter Stuyvesant, Charles II, Duke of York, William Penn, James Oglethorpe

3. Comprehension For what different reasons did European immigrants come to the English colonies?

4. Comprehension What led to the founding of Pennsylvania? Georgia?

5. Critical Thinking Why might Penn's idealistic plan for Pennsylvania have had more success than Oglethorpe's idealistic plan for Georgia?

Summary

1. Despite many hardships, an English colony at Jamestown, Virginia, survived to become the first successful English colony in the Americas. By raising and exporting tobacco, Jamestown prospered.

2. The colony of Plymouth was started by Separatists who had fled England to escape religious persecution. The Separatists established a form of self-government. Starvation and disease threatened the colony. Yet with the aid of nearby Indians, Plymouth survived.

3. The Puritans left England in the 1630s and settled in New England, where they tried to build a society based on their religious beliefs. Laws were based on their interpretation of the Bible. The Puritans were intolerant of dissenters.

4. English colonies outside New England differed from one another in many ways. For example, colonists in the Chesapeake Tidewater lived on scattered farms, rather than in towns, as in New England. By the early 1700s, there were thirteen English colonies along the East Coast of North America.

Graphic Summary

Joint-stock companies help England finance colonies. The colony at Jamestown, Virginia, prospers from growing tobacco.

Separatists establish a colony at Plymouth, where they set up a system of self-government. Nearby Indians help Plymouth survive.

Puritans settle in Massachusetts to build a religious society. Conflict over land leads to warfare between settlers and Indians.

English colonies are settled outside of New England. By the early 1700s, there are thirteen English colonies on the East Coast of North America.

Review

KEY TERMS

Define the following terms.
1. indentured servant
2. House of Burgesses
3. patroon
4. Great Migration
5. persecution
6. religious tolerance

COMPREHENSION

1. Why were colonies like Jamestown and Plymouth financed by joint-stock companies rather than private individuals?

2. What problems did the Jamestown settlers face?

3. How did John Smith help save Jamestown?

4. Why did the Separatists journey to America?

5. How were relations between the Plymouth settlers and the nearby Indians? Why?

6. Describe the conflict between the Puritans and King Charles I.

7. What agreement did the Massachusetts settlers think they had with God?

8. What values did the New England Way represent?

9. Why was there such a great demand for labor in the Chesapeake Tidewater?

10. Briefly describe the founding of (a) Maryland, (b) New Netherland, (c) New Jersey, (d) Pennsylvania, (e) the Carolinas, (f) Georgia.

Places to Locate

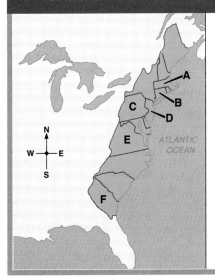

Match the letters on the map with the places that are listed below. Then explain the importance of each place.

1. Connecticut
2. Georgia
3. Massachusetts
4. New Jersey
5. Pennsylvania
6. Virginia

Geographic Theme: Movement Why did the Pilgrims leave England?

Skill Review

The anti-slavery resolution below was written in 1688 by a Protestant group. It is the earliest known anti-slavery protest in the American colonies. Read the passage and answer the questions that follow.

Against the Traffic of Slaves

"There is a saying that we shall do to all men like as we will be done ourselves, making no difference of what generation, descent, or color they are. And those who steal or rob men, and those who buy or purchase them, are they not all alike? Here is liberty of conscience, which is right and reasonable. Here ought to be likewise liberty of the body, except of evildoers, which is another case. But to bring men hither, or to rob and sell them against their will, we stand against."

1. How can you tell that this is a primary source?
2. What arguments are used to oppose the slave trade?
3. How might this document be valuable to historians?

CRITICAL THINKING

1. Identifying Significance What important idea was established after the Pilgrims landed outside the boundary of the Virginia Company's land in the Americas?

2. Analyzing a Quotation John Smith's rule for the Jamestown colony was, "He that will not work neither shall he eat." Do you think this was a fair rule? Explain.

3. Stating Both Sides of an Issue State (a) the argument that the governor of Massachusetts might have given for banishing Roger Williams or Anne Hutchinson, and (b) the reply those two might have given.

PORTFOLIO OPTIONS

1. Civics Connection Imagine that you and a group of colonists are settling in North America in the 1600s. Make up a plan of government for your colony. Share your plan with the rest of the class.

2. Writing Connection Support the following statement in a short essay: "By the early 1700s, the American colonies already contained a wide variety of peoples from different backgrounds."

3. Contemporary Connection How, if at all, did the qualities and skills needed by the Jamestown settlers differ from those needed by citizens today?

4. Timeline Connection Copy the chapter timeline. Which event do you think was most important? Explain.

Shaped by geography and by the labor of their settlers, England's American colonies grew more prosperous and diverse. Below are three re-creations of colonial life. The Massachusetts kitchen looks the same as it did around 1700. A master cooper (barrel maker) uses hand tools such as the cooper's hatchet (bottom left). Among the many chores for colonial women was churning butter (right).

1650

1670

1690

1710

1651 First Navigation Act

1676 Bacon's Rebellion

1688 Glorious Revolution in England

1689 English Bill of Rights

1692 Salem Witchcraft Trials

Shaping of the American Colonies (1651–1740)

1 Rights of the People

SECTION GUIDE

Main Idea
English colonists sailing to North America brought with them concepts such as limited government and self-rule, which became the basis of colonial government.

Goals
As you read, look for answers to these questions:

1 What basic ideas of freedom did English colonists bring to the Americas?

2 What issues caused political conflict in the colonies?

3 What kinds of government grew up in the English colonies?

Key Terms
Magna Carta
common law
Parliament
Glorious Revolution
English Bill of Rights

1730   1750

1740 Great Awakening

1735 Zenger trial

WHAT WOULD HAPPEN if you moved to a new place? You probably would not have space to pack everything, so you would leave some of your things behind. Would you also leave behind your way of looking at things, of thinking about things? You probably would not. Still, a new place would mean new experiences. Those experiences might cause you to start looking at things in a whole new way.

"Rights of Englishmen"
Life in the American colonies was shaped in the same way. People brought to the Americas old attitudes and ideas. The new environment, however, called into question some of these old ideas. As a result, colonists developed new ways. This was particularly true of the colonists' approach to government.

Most English colonists had arrived in the Americas with some basic ideas about freedom. These ideas about freedom were generally called the "rights of Englishmen."

The rights of Englishmen were first written down in the Magna Carta (Great Charter) of 1215. In this document the king of England was forced to observe rights claimed by the freemen. (A freeman was any person who was not a slave or a serf.) One of the most important of these rights was that a freeman should not be punished except by the judgment of his peers, or people of equal social status. Another right was that there should be no taxation except by legal means. The Magna Carta was important because it said there were laws even kings had to obey.

At first, the Magna Carta applied only to nobles and freemen. Yet in time, these rights were extended to all English people.

The rights of Englishmen also included a tradition of customs and law based on earlier court decisions. This was called the **common law.** Thus, when Englishmen moved to America, they carried with them the belief that they had certain rights by law and certain rights by tradition.

As for women, they had few rights. By law a married woman had no independent status. Her husband was responsible for her and spoke for her. By the 1700s, however, it was becoming more common for women to claim for themselves the "rights of Englishmen." A poem printed in 1736 called for equal laws: "More Freedom give to Womankind, Or give to Mankind less."

The Rights of Colonists

From the beginning, colonists had shown they wanted a say in the laws that affected them. Thus came into being the House of Burgesses and other colonial assemblies. Colonists also realized that they were far from the English government and often needed to make decisions on their own. The Mayflower Compact is an example of such self-government.

Remember, though, that the colonies had economic and political ties to England. England's political authority came in two forms: the laws passed by **Parliament** (England's lawmaking body) and the power held by governors appointed by the king. Conflicts often revolved around this issue: How much control would England have over the colonies?

This scene portrays Bacon's Rebellion.

Bacon's Rebellion

The first major challenge to English authority came from Virginia in 1676. Power in the colony was in the hands of the royal governor, Sir William Berkeley, and a handful of his planter friends. The House of Burgesses was under their complete control. No election had been held in fourteen years.

More and more settlers arrived in the colony. They seized Indian lands for tobacco plantations. Bloody clashes between the colonists and the Indians grew frequent.

Into the scene entered Nathaniel Bacon. Bacon was a new immigrant to Virginia and a tobacco planter. He organized some 300 colonists and they attacked and killed the first Indians they came across. These Indians, however, were peaceful friends of the governor.

Berkeley was furious, but Bacon had become so popular among the colonists that the governor felt helpless. Bacon and his followers then marched on Jamestown. In an attack known as Bacon's Rebellion, they forced Berkeley to flee and burned much of the town. Bacon then took control of Virginia's government.

The new government did not last long, however. Bacon grew sick and quickly died. Back in control, Berkeley took his revenge and had 23 of Bacon's followers hanged. The king of England was horrified by Berkeley's actions and appointed a new governor for the colony.

The House of Burgesses passed laws to prevent a royal governor from ever assuming such power again. An important step had been taken against tyranny and toward self-government.

The Glorious Revolution

The next gain for colonial rights came from England. King James II had claimed he had a God-given right to rule. As such, he said, he could ignore both popular opinion and Parliament. To strengthen his hold over New England, the king put all of the New England colonies under the control of one governor, Sir William Andros. To make matters worse, the colonial assemblies were abolished. The New England colonies might have soon rebelled against this

LEARN

Would your town or city be able to operate without some form of government? Probably it would not. Who would manage the area's businesses and provide needed services? Nearly every organization—from a school club to a town to the country as a whole—has some type of government.

Governments are formed to manage organizations. They also make and carry out the rules. In a democratic society, members of an organization help make the rules, and everyone is expected to obey them. The rules—or laws—exist for the benefit of the organization as a whole.

English government in colonial times was not a democracy. It was a monarchy. But it did employ certain democratic principles, as did England's colonies in the Americas. The actual forms of government varied from colony to colony, but all followed the same basic practices. Each had a governor, in charge of the colony. Each had a legislature, with some members elected by the people, to make the laws. And everyone had to obey those laws.

PRACTICE

This chart shows how the early colonial government of Pennsylvania was organized. Arrows represent power to elect or appoint. Other lines show working partnerships.

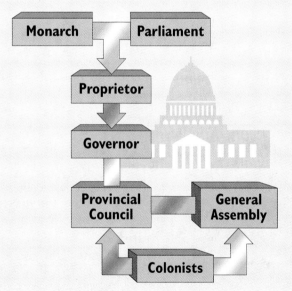

1. Who had supreme authority over the colony?

2. Who appointed the governor of Pennsylvania?

3. Where did the colonists have an input?

APPLY

4. Draw a chart showing how a student club, a parent-teacher organization, a local government, or a state government works.

TABLOID NEWS

Waiting in line at a store checkout counter, you spot a newspaper headline in huge type:

SPACE ALIEN ENDORSES BILL CLINTON

Common sense tells you that the story is not true. Why, then, is it legal to publish it?

Legal protection of newspapers that print the truth goes back to the 1735 Zenger case. There is no law, however, against printing an untruth.

A public figure can sue a newspaper that attacks his or her character with "reckless disregard for the truth." In recent years some people have sued tabloids—newspapers featuring large photos and sensational stories—and won. In the case above, the President could take the tabloid to court for printing a faked photo of him meeting with an alien. On the other hand, the court case probably would make the President look even more foolish than the photo did.

move, but a revolution in England made it unnecessary.

In 1688 the king was making plans to return England to Catholicism. Leaders of Parliament, most of whom were Protestant, were outraged. They turned to William of Orange, Protestant ruler of the Netherlands, whose wife was King James's daughter. Unable to find any popular support, James fled to France. Parliament then named William and Mary the new rulers of England. This was the **Glorious Revolution.** The Glorious Revolution made clear two things. First, government was to be based on law, not the whims of kings. Second, the authority of the king came from Parliament, not God.

To make this clear, the new rulers were forced to accept a bill of rights passed by Parliament in 1689. (*Bill* in this sense means a list.) The **English Bill of Rights** included: (1) no taxation without consent of Parliament, (2) no cruel or unjust punishment, (3) free speech in Parliament, (4) no imprisonment without a trial, (5) the right to petition, (6) the right to bear arms, and (7) the right to trial by jury.

Colonial Government

By 1700 the colonial governments all followed a similar pattern. Each colony was ruled by a governor, most of whom were appointed by the Crown. Each colony also had an elected assembly. Representatives to the assemblies were elected from towns, as in New England, or from counties, as in the other colonies. Voters usually had to be white, male, 21 years of age, Protestant, and property holders.

Assisting the governor was a council. Its members were usually appointed by the governor from among the wealthier colonists. In most colonies the council had to approve any laws passed by the assembly. In addition, the council acted as the highest court in the colony.

The governors were powerful. Royal governors had the ability to veto laws, to postpone or dismiss assemblies, and to appoint and dismiss all judges at will. Royal governors were responsible only to the Crown. They had no duty to observe the customs of the colonies nor the will of the people.

The Zenger Trial

In the 1730s New York's governor was William Cosby. Cosby was ill-tempered and, worse, not ethical. (An ethical person behaves according to accepted ideas of right and wrong.) The governor took bribes. He sold property that did not belong to him. He tried to rig elections. He tampered with the courts.

At John Peter Zenger's trial (left), Andrew Hamilton argued that newspapers had the right to print the truth. The flyer below announces Zenger's trial.

Opponents of the governor began to attack him in the *New-York Weekly Journal,* a newspaper started for the purpose. The editor of the newspaper was John Peter Zenger, a German immigrant and a printer by trade. It was risky attacking the governor. The law said that it was illegal for anything to be printed that expressed "an ill opinion" of the government or its officers. It did not matter if what was written was true or not. If it made the government look bad, it was illegal.

In 1734 the governor's supporters were defeated in a city election. In joy, the *New-York Weekly Journal* printed verses such as this:

&& To you good lads that dare oppose all lawless power and might,

You are the theme that we have chose, and to your praise we write. &&

The verses seem mild to us, but the governor had Zenger arrested and put in jail.

One of the best lawyers in America, Andrew Hamilton of Philadelphia, defended Zenger in his trial in 1735. He argued that a newspaper should have the right to print what was true, even if it criticized the government. The jury agreed. Zenger was freed.

From the Zenger trial a new right was born: freedom of the press to print the truth. Freedom of the press would become a crucial part of American liberty.

SECTION REVIEW

1. Key Terms Magna Carta, common law, Parliament, Glorious Revolution, English Bill of Rights

2. People Nathaniel Bacon, William and Mary, John Peter Zenger

3. Comprehension What were the rights of Englishmen?

4. Comprehension How did Bacon's Rebellion challenge England's authority over its American colonies? What was the result of the rebellion?

5. Critical Thinking How might American colonial rights have been different had the Magna Carta not existed?

2 Plantation Life in the Southern Colonies

SECTION GUIDE

Main Idea

Farming and trade became important parts of the southern economy. This economy relied heavily on slave labor.

Goals

As you read, look for answers to these questions:

1 How and why did farming thrive in the Southern Colonies?

2 Why did slavery expand in the Southern Colonies?

3 What was life like for slaves?

Key Terms
economy
Middle Passage
slave codes

IN 1621 ANTHONY JOHNSON, an African, arrived in Virginia and was sold to the highest bidder. Johnson was not a slave, but an indentured servant. When his term was up he was freed. He married and became a landholder himself. Thirty years after he arrived, Johnson lived in a community of free African Americans, owned 250 acres of land, and had five of his own indentured servants.

Laws in Virginia, however, were changing. Starting in 1660 it became harder for African Americans to gain their freedom. Black servants became slaves for life. Small communities of free blacks remained, but by 1700 slavery was strongly rooted in southern society. It was to make the South a distinctive region of the American colonies.

Colonial Regions

By the 1700s the colonies could be grouped into three regions: the New England Colonies, the Middle Colonies, and the Southern Colonies. Cutting through all the colonies was a fourth region, the backcountry.

Geography—the climate, the soil, and the resources—influenced the **economy** of a region. An area's economy refers to the way people use resources to make a living.

Each region also had a unique culture. One reason was economic differences among regions. Another was differences in the ways and attitudes of settlers.

Plantations Take Hold

The plantation economy shaped life in the Southern Colonies—Maryland, Virginia, the Carolinas, and Georgia. The soil and

The growth of slavery encouraged the expansion of plantations in the Southern Colonies. This painting shows the main residence and slave quarters of a southern plantation.

climate of this region were suited for warm-weather crops, like tobacco and rice, which could not be grown in Europe. The region's many waterways made it possible for oceangoing ships to tie up at plantation docks.

Toward the end of the 1600s, the Southern Colonies moved toward plantation agriculture, as it had been established in the West Indies. The plantation economy depended on growing crops for export and on slavery for laborers.

The Turn to Slavery

The number of Africans in Virginia, whether servants or free, remained small for the first half of the 1600s. Indentured servants, white and black, worked in the fields together. By 1665 fewer than 500 people of African descent had been brought into the colony.

Starting in the 1660s, the labor system in the South began to change. By 1700 there were few white servants on plantations.

This change occurred because of new leaders in Virginia, known as Cavaliers. They were well off. Most came from a part of England where people still lived much as in feudal times. Much of the land there was held in large estates owned by lords and worked by rural laborers.

William Berkeley was such a Cavalier. He arrived in 1642 as governor of Virginia. He encouraged other Cavaliers to move to Virginia by giving them both land and power. Many of them were younger sons who by English law could not inherit land. They wanted to remake in America the kind of society they had left behind.

In America there was so much available land that white people could not be held as servants forever as in England. So the Cavaliers turned to Indians for labor first. However, hard labor and European diseases caused many of the Indian population to die. The Cavaliers then turned to African slavery.

The Southern Colonies

[Map of the Southern Colonies showing Appalachian Mountains, Potomac River, Baltimore, MARYLAND, VIRGINIA, St. Mary's, James River, Richmond, Williamsburg, Jamestown, Roanoke R., Chesapeake Bay, 35°N, NORTH CAROLINA, SOUTH CAROLINA, Wilmington, Savannah River, GEORGIA, ATLANTIC OCEAN, Charles Town (Charleston), Savannah, Altamaha R., 80°W, 30°N. Scale: 0 50 100 200 Miles / 0 50 100 200 Kilometers, Albers Equal-Area Projection]

GEOGRAPHY SKILLS: Plantation agriculture shaped the life and economy of the Southern Colonies.
Critical Thinking: How might the economy of the Southern Colonies have developed without slave labor?

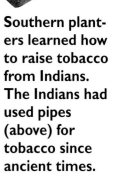

Southern planters learned how to raise tobacco from Indians. The Indians had used pipes (above) for tobacco since ancient times.

The Middle Passage

Since the early 1500s the African slave trade had been a part of the Atlantic world. To meet their need for farm labor, almost two centuries later, the English colonies joined that trade in earnest. As a result, thousands of Africans were brought directly to American shores. One of the kidnapped Africans, Olaudah Equiano, told what it was like.

Equiano was about eleven years old when he was taken from his home in Benin, West Africa, and sold into slavery. Later, after he bought his freedom, he wrote his life story.

Equiano's first fear, when imprisoned on a slave ship, was that he was to be eaten by those white men with horrible looks, red faces, and long hair. Assured not, he then feared death, for "the white people looked and acted, as I thought in so savage a manner; for I had never seen among any people such instances of brutal cruelty."

The most frightening part of Equiano's experience was the Middle Passage — the journey across the Atlantic. On board

The loading principle on slaves ships was simple—cram as many slaves into as little space as possible. **Critical Thinking:** Many Africans perished from the harsh conditions on these ships. Others tried to kill themselves by jumping overboard. Why do you think they did that?

Olaudah Equiano

the slaves were so crowded together that one "had scarcely room to turn himself," Equiano explained. The air became so foul and stinking that many died. "The shrieks of the women, and the groans of the dying . . . rendered the whole a scene of horror almost inconceivable." People were whipped for not eating. If they tried to jump overboard they were whipped "unmercifully for . . . attempting to prefer death to slavery."

An Elite Planter Class

Slavery allowed Cavaliers to become even richer. Those with money or credit were able to buy the most slaves. The more slaves one had, the more tobacco one could raise. Small landowners with just a servant or two could not compete. Many were forced to give up their land and move west. An elite planter class ended up controlling the land along the seaboard.

This small upper class held the political and economic power in the South. Its members were active in the management of their plantations and in colonial politics.

At their best, the planters felt responsible for the welfare of their slaves and believed in public service. The more power one had, they believed, the more responsibility one had to do good. At their worst, they were tyrants. They had complete authority over everyone in their households—slaves, wives, and children. Oftentimes planters used violence to enforce their will.

Growth of Plantations

In 1670 only about 6 percent of southerners were black. By 1700, more than 20 percent of southerners were black.

The growth of slavery encouraged the expansion of plantation farming in South Carolina and Georgia. Without slave labor, there probably would have been no rice plantations in the region's swampy lowlands. Growing rice required draining swamps, building dikes, planting, and harvesting. It required knowledge of rice growing and irrigation. Such knowledge came from Africa. South Carolina planters sought out slaves who came from Africa's rice-growing regions.

On the uplands, planters grew indigo. Indigo is a subtropical plant that yields a blue dye. (The first blue jeans were dyed with indigo. Today, jeans makers use chemical dyes to make the same color as indigo.)

Eliza Lucas was responsible for the success of indigo as a plantation crop. Lucas's father owned plantations both in the West Indies and in South Carolina. When she was seventeen, he sent her to South Carolina to supervise his plantations. Using seeds sent by her father, she began growing different kinds of indigo. In 1743, her dye was judged to be of the best quality. She then started giving seeds to neighbors and friends. Southern planters especially welcomed the crop because they could raise it on land not suitable for rice.

These restored slave quarters in Louisiana show the living conditions of plantation slaves. **Critical Thinking:** How did slave quarters differ from the houses of plantation owners?

Life Under Slavery

When a person had only a few slaves, master and slaves worked side by side in the fields or in the household and shared the same living area. This was common in slaveholding households outside the South. The slaves were more likely to be treated as indentured servants. They were often taught to read and write and given a chance to buy their freedom.

On the plantations, however, slaves worked in groups of about 20 to 25 men, women, and children. Slaves performed backbreaking work, often for more than 14 hours a day.

African Americans resisted slavery in a number of ways. Some used violence against their masters. Others worked slowly, damaged goods, or deliberately carried out orders incorrectly. A few ran away to mountainous areas and formed secret communities.

The fear of slave uprising prompted planters to pass slave codes—harsh laws controlling the treatment of slaves. Under the slave codes, slaves were not allowed to leave the plantation without permission. Nor were they allowed to meet with free blacks. Slaves were also forbidden to learn how to read and write.

On the plantations, Africans developed a new way of life in the "quarters"—the area on a plantation where slaves lived. Living in groups, they preserved many African beliefs and customs. These included the stories, music, dances, and crafts of their homelands. For a time, many held to their traditional African religions, and to Islam as well. The African kinship customs that you read about earlier became the basis of an African American family culture. A network of kin was a source of strength even when families were separated.

SECTION REVIEW

1. Key Terms economy, Middle Passage, slave codes

2. People and Places Olaudah Equiano, Eliza Lucas, Southern Colonies

3. Comprehension Who were the Cavaliers?

4. Comprehension Describe the southern plantation system.

5. Critical Thinking Why might slaves have been forbidden to meet with free blacks under the slave codes?

3 Life in Colonial New England

SECTION GUIDE

Main Idea
Aided by the success of fishing, whaling, and trade, the New England Colonies grew and prospered.

Goals
As you read, look for answers to these questions:

1. Why did New Englanders turn to the sea for a living?

2. What was the triangular trade?

3. What religious trends developed in New England?

Key Terms
apprentice
triangular trade
Navigation Acts
smuggling
Salem Witchcraft Trials
Great Awakening

Whaling, though dangerous, provided a living for New England colonists.

NEW ENGLAND is a region of low mountains and rocky soil. Winter lasts longer, with a longer period of freezing temperatures, than in the southern part of the Eastern Seaboard. It is a discouraging area for farmers, especially when compared to the warm, fertile fields of the South.

New Englanders have a different, rich resource: the ocean. In 1690, it is said, some persons were on a hill on Nantucket, a large island off Massachusetts. One of them pointed out to sea and said, "There is a green pasture where our children's grandchildren will go for bread." It was a prediction that came true.

Fishing and Shipbuilding in New England

Most early settlers in the New England Colonies—Massachusetts, New Hampshire, Connecticut, and Rhode Island—were farmers. Yet it did not take them long to discover the greener pasture of the Atlantic Ocean.

New England's coastline has many harbors. Not far off the coast lie some of the world's richest fishing grounds. All New Englanders needed were boats.

It was an age of wooden ships. The forests yielded a plentiful supply of trees with which to build and repair ships. Tall white pines provided masts that were straight-grained and strong. From other pines came turpentine and pitch, used to waterproof boats. The sturdy oaks were ideal for building ship hulls.

Fishing encouraged shipbuilding, and shipbuilding encouraged trade. By 1700, shipbuilding, fishing, and trade had made Boston the largest and richest of the American colonial towns.

Whaling on Nantucket

Nantucket Island is an example of how New England harvested the sea. When English Quakers arrived on the island, the Nattic Indians shared the island's main resource—shellfish—with them.

Then the newcomers to Nantucket discovered that their island was within easy reach of the main migration stream of whales. They built whale-watching towers on the outer coast of the island. As soon as the distinctive spray of a whale was sighted, the whalers were in their boats and away. Usually about five of the six crew members were Nattics.

The whalers killed the whales and towed the carcasses ashore. Whale blubber was turned into oil and burned in lamps. Whalebone was used in such products as umbrellas, hairbrushes, and corsets.

As whales became scarce near shore, whalers started going farther out to sea. In 1712 Christopher Hussey was caught in a storm and driven far out into the Atlantic. When the storm was over, Hussey found himself surrounded by the black shapes of sperm whales. Each whale was about the length of his 70-foot boat. Hussey killed one and towed it back to Nantucket. There it was found that the huge heads of sperm whales were filled with an oil, spermaceti. That oil made the finest of candles.

When the men were not at sea, they were coopers (barrel makers). Barrels were necessary to store and ship whale oil.

Boys on Nantucket went to school until they were twelve years old. Then for two years they served as **apprentices** to the cooper's trade. An apprentice was a young person who learned a skill from a master at his craft. Apprentices usually lived with the master's family for several years while they learned. During this time they received no wages.

When boys reached age fourteen, they went to sea. On sea they would learn sailing, navigation, and whaling.

The New England Colonies

Map showing: MAINE (part of Mass.), Kennebec R., Claimed by N.H. and N.Y., Lake Champlain, NEW HAMPSHIRE, ATLANTIC OCEAN, 44°N, MASSACHUSETTS, Salem, Massachusetts Bay, Springfield, Boston, 42°N, Providence, Plymouth, Hartford, Newport, Cape Cod, CONNECTICUT, New Haven, RHODE ISLAND, Nantucket I., Narragansett Bay. Scale: 0 25 50 100 Miles / 0 25 50 100 Kilometers, Albers Equal-Area Projection.

GEOGRAPHY SKILLS: New England prospered from fishing, whaling, and shipbuilding. **Critical Thinking:** How did New England's geography help support those activities?

Scrimshaw—decorated items carved from whale bone—were popular in New England.

Atlantic Trading Patterns

The people of Nantucket made their fortunes from whaling. Other Yankees (New Englanders) were traders. They became part of an Atlantic trading pattern that followed three courses. One was the Atlantic coastal trade among the colonies themselves. A second pattern was the simple exchange across the Atlantic of raw materials and manufactured goods.

A third trading pattern was known as the **triangular trade.** There were different triangular trade routes. In one, a ship leaving New England might take a cargo of rum and ironware. It would sell its cargo in Africa for slaves. The slaves then endured the dreadful Middle Passage across the Atlantic to the West Indies. The ship's captain sold the slaves in the West Indies and bought sugar and molasses. Back in the New England Colonies, the sugar and molasses were turned into rum. Through the triangular trade, New England traders profited enormously from the slave trade.

Triangular Trade Routes

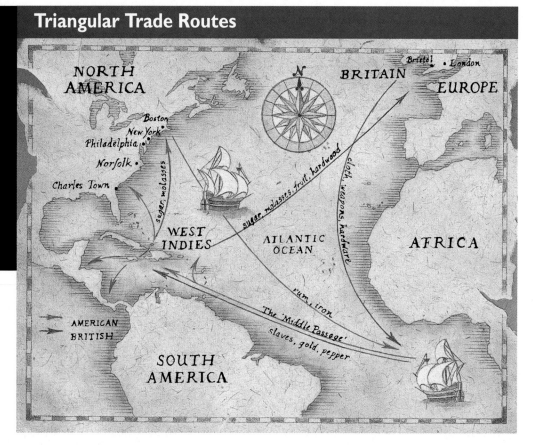

Policies of Empire

England's purpose in creating colonies was not to make the colonies rich, but to make England rich. Following the rules of mercantilism, England encouraged those activities that supplied the empire with food and raw materials.

Beginning in 1651 England's policy was spelled out in new laws called the Navigation Acts. According to these laws:

(1) all shipping was to be in English ships or in ships made in the English colonies;

(2) products such as tobacco, sugar, and cotton could be sold only to England or to another colony;

(3) all European imports to the colonies had to pass through England first;

(4) English tax officials were to collect duties (taxes) on any colonial goods not being shipped to England.

Because the Navigation Acts aimed to help England at the colonies' expense, colonists ignored them whenever possible. Smuggling —importing or exporting goods illegally— was everywhere. Many of the smuggled goods were brought into the colonies by pirates.

One of the most famous pirates was Edward Teach— known as Blackbeard. For several years this English pirate terrorized shipping off the Virginia and Carolina coasts. In this he was protected by the corrupt governor of North Carolina. Using his own money, the governor of Virginia sent an expedition against Blackbeard. In 1718 off the Carolina coast, Blackbeard was captured and beheaded. In the 1700s piracy gradually declined. (To learn about life on a pirate ship, turn to the Daily Life feature at the end of this section.)

Blacks in New England

There was little slavery in New England, mostly because the region had little need for large numbers of unskilled laborers. The few Puritan slaveowners in the New England Colonies were often different from slaveowners in the South. In New England, they gave their slaves religious instruction and sometimes taught them to read and write. Phillis Wheatley, a slave in the household of a Boston tailor, gained fame as a poet. A book of her poems was published in 1773.

Phillis Wheatley

More free blacks lived in New England than in any of the other regions. Free black men became merchants, sailors, printers, and carpenters. African Americans could also own land in New England. However, blacks were not treated as equals to whites.

The Role of Women

On farms the men and boys did the outdoor work. This included plowing, harvesting, and making farm tools. Women and girls did the jobs associated with the household. A list of household chores could fill this page. They included candle making, spinning, weaving, knitting, making soap, washing, making butter, and cooking.

In addition, a woman might share special skills with the community. She might help deliver babies. She might run a Dame School—a home where young children were taught to read and write.

Widows, women who never married, or the wives of sea-going husbands often entered business. Throughout the colonies one could find women who were printers, merchants, carpenters, and ship owners. Not until our own day have women played such an active role in the economy.

Changes in Puritan Society

Puritan New England was originally a church-centered society. By the late 1600s, however, this had begun to change. Growing prosperity and the end of Puritan political control led to new ideas and values. New generations of colonists did not share the strict religious views of their parents. To these younger people, wealth and the things it could buy seemed more important than religious faith. Puritan ministers began to complain that their "city on a hill" was full of greedy merchants.

One person whose ideas reflected both the old and the new was Cotton Mather, New England's leading minister in the late 1600s. A believer in witchcraft, Mather helped cause a panic in Massachusetts in 1692. Hundreds were accused of witchcraft, or dealing with the Devil. The accusations came at a time when people were upset about the changes in Puritan society.

In Salem, Massachusetts, charges by a group of young girls led to the Salem Witchcraft Trials. Nineteen persons were hanged, and another was pressed to death by heavy stones when he refused to enter a plea to the charge of witchcraft. The panic was short-lived, and Salem soon came to its senses. The experience shows, however, how a society can create scapegoats for its problems.

For all his interest in witchcraft, Mather was also a modern man, open to new ideas. In 1721 Mather led the campaign in New England for smallpox inoculation. This involved giving people a very mild case of smallpox in order to build up a resistance to the disease. Mather had read that people in Turkey did so. The only doctor willing to go along with Mather was Zabdiel Boylston. In this he was no doubt influenced by his slave, Onesimus. Onesimus told of similar inoculations being done in Africa. Smallpox inoculation was so controversial that people stoned the houses of both Mather and Boylston.

By the late 1600s the church had less influence on colonists' lives.

Witches and Witch Hunts

In every society there are words people use as labels for others they do not like. Centuries ago in Christian Europe, "witch" was one. To call someone a witch was to call that person an enemy of the Church. These enemies were burned or hanged. Tens of thousands died during the 1500s and 1600s. How could you spot a witch? Sometimes a mark on a person's body, like a mole or birthmark, or any sign of unusual power, like an ability to heal sick persons, was "proof" enough.

In 1692 a group of young girls in Salem, Massachusetts, fell into strange fits. They accused townspeople of being witches. Some historians believe the girls were faking. Maybe their families, to settle grudges and to gain land and belongings, coached the girls to accuse family rivals of witchcraft. Courts believed the girls. Of the hundreds who suffered in jail, twenty were executed.

There was no separation of religion and politics in Massachusetts. Salem clergymen were the judges in the witch trials. After the hunt was over, none of these judges expressed regret. Twelve jurors, however, later wrote of their deep sorrow for condemning innocent people:

"We do heartily ask forgiveness of you all, who we have justly offended: and do declare, according to our present minds, we would none of us do such things again, on such grounds, for the whole world."

How could this have happened? New England faced crop failures, a harsh winter, and smallpox. The French and Indians had joined to try to push the English out. Settlers had been killed. Shaken, the people of Salem looked for a scapegoat—someone to blame. The "witches," all innocent people, were Salem's scapegoat.

(Above, a Salem girl accuses a man of witchcraft.)

CRITICAL THINKING

1. Explain how the "witches" of Salem were victims of the town's fears.
2. What might have caused the jurors to change their minds later?
3. Describe another time in history in which a group of persons became a scapegoat.

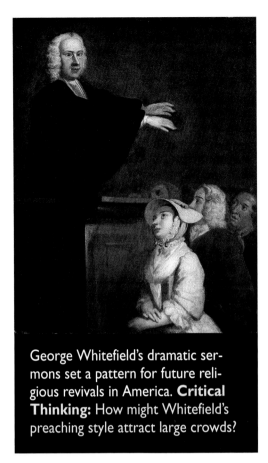

George Whitefield's dramatic sermons set a pattern for future religious revivals in America. **Critical Thinking:** How might Whitefield's preaching style attract large crowds?

The Great Awakening

In 1720 only about 25 percent of New Englanders belonged to a church. The figure was even lower in the other colonies. Educated men no longer became ministers but lawyers and merchants.

This changed around 1740 when a new religious movement "roared through the colonies like a sheet of flame." Ministers went from town to town, holding revival meetings and urging people to return to their faith. Many colonists eagerly responded. This movement became the Great Awakening.

The leader of the Great Awakening in New England was Jonathan Edwards. Like ministers in other colonies, he described the agonies of hell and urged people to repent their sins. "I think it is a reasonable thing," Edwards said, "to fright persons away from hell."

Another minister, George Whitefield, traveled the colonies giving "fire and brimstone" sermons. An observer noted Whitefield's effect on an audience:

❝ Some were struck pale as Death, . . . others sinking into the arms of their friends, and most lifting up their eyes toward heaven, and crying out to God. ❞

The effect of the Great Awakening was electric. People who had drifted away from the church responded to the energetic new preachers.

Along with this excitement came a sense of equality among Americans. Everyone was seen as equal in God's eyes. To stress this equality, many people began calling each other "brother" and "sister." The Great Awakening also encouraged people to reach out to African Americans and to Indians. Edwards himself became a missionary to the Indians in Massachusetts.

SECTION REVIEW

1. Key Terms apprentice, triangular trade, Navigation Acts, smuggling, Salem Witchcraft Trials, Great Awakening

2. People and Places Phillis Wheatley, Cotton Mather, Jonathan Edwards, New England Colonies, Nantucket Island

3. Comprehension In what ways did New Englanders harvest the sea?

4. Comprehension Describe the roles of women and African Americans in New England society.

5. Critical Thinking Why is the term *Great Awakening* a fitting name for the religious revival of the 1700s?

Daily Life

Tossed by winds and waves, those who climbed the rigging needed every finger and toe to hang onto the ropes.

ON A PIRATE SHIP

In 1701 the English government hanged William Kidd for piracy and murder. His body was displayed by the Thames River as a warning to other pirates (left). Firm action like this helped end the Golden Age of piracy, which lasted from the late 1600s to the early 1700s. During those roughly thirty years, however, crews of merchant ships lived in terror of seeing a skull-and-crossbones flag on the horizon. At right is William Kidd's *Adventure Galley*.

The captain's powers were limited. The crew had elected him and could elect a new one if they wished. He did, however, have a cabin with a fine view. The crew slept on the wet, slimy decks.

Pirates wanted to loot ships, not sink them, so they tried to frighten their targets into giving up without a fight. One way was to play loud, angry music as they approached.

Pirates carried pistols like this when boarding ships.

Below decks were ammunition, barrels of water, and food (often so rotten that men ate in the dark to avoid looking at it). Oars kept the ship moving on calm days.

4 Farm and City Life in the Middle Colonies

SECTION GUIDE

Main Idea
The economies of the Middle Colonies benefited from good farming conditions, harbors for shipping, and the growth of manufacturing.

Goals
As you read, look for answers to these questions:

1 Why was farming important in the Middle Colonies?

2 What factors encouraged the growth of trade and manufacturing?

3 What kinds of people settled in the Middle Colonies?

Key Terms
Conestoga wagon
mill

N 1723, a seventeen-year-old runaway apprentice stepped off a boat onto the bustling streets of Philadelphia. When he was a famous old man he recalled his arrival this way:

❝I was dirty from my journey; my pockets were stuffed out with shirts and stockings; I knew no soul nor where to look for lodging; I was very hungry; and my whole stock of cash consisted of a Dutch dollar and about a shilling in copper. ❞

The awkward youth was Benjamin Franklin. He had left his home city of Boston in New England to become a citizen of a very different region: the Middle Colonies.

A Wealth of Resources

In the mid-1700s a Frenchman, Michel Guillaume Jean de Crèvecoeur (krev-KUR), settled in the colony of New York. He later wrote about the colony:

❝[Here a visitor] beholds fair cities, substantial villages, extensive fields, an immense country filled with decent houses, good roads, orchards, meadows, and bridges, where a hundred years ago all was wild, woody, and uncultivated! ❞

The Middle Colonies were blessed with rich farmland. This early 1700s painting of a New York farm hung over the mantel of the house it shows.

The rich farming landscape Crèvecoeur described was typical of coastal parts of the Middle Colonies—New York, New Jersey, Delaware, and Pennsylvania. Local Indians, of course, had known for centuries of the area's natural resources. The region was blessed with rich soil, a good growing season, and a number of large rivers with good harbors. New York City grew at the mouth of the Hudson River. Philadelphia was located on the Delaware River, which drained into Delaware Bay.

Many of the colonists of the region came from the farming traditions of Germany, Switzerland, and Holland. Their skills, knowledge, and hard work would yield a bounty of agricultural products—fruits, vegetables, livestock, and grain. The Middle Colonies produced so much wheat that they became known as the "bread basket" colonies. They exported wheat and other foodstuffs to the other colonies, to the West Indies, and to England.

The Pennsylvania Germans

German-speaking people contributed much to Pennsylvania's farm wealth. Most arrived as indentured servants, fleeing religious persecution. Within a generation they had made their mark on the area. "German communities could be identified by the huge barns, the sleek cattle, and the stout workhorses," wrote one historian.

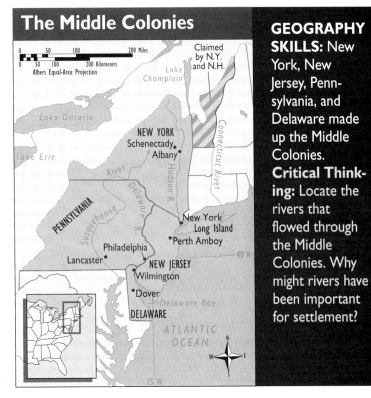

The Middle Colonies

0 50 100 200 Miles
0 50 100 200 Kilometers
Albers Equal-Area Projection

Claimed by N.Y. and N.H.
Lake Champlain
Lake Ontario
Lake Erie
NEW YORK
Schenectady
Albany
Connecticut River
Hudson R.
Delaware R.
River
PENNSYLVANIA
Susquehanna R.
New York
Long Island
Perth Amboy
Philadelphia
Lancaster
NEW JERSEY
Wilmington
Dover
Delaware Bay
DELAWARE
40° N
ATLANTIC OCEAN
75° W
N W E S

GEOGRAPHY SKILLS: New York, New Jersey, Pennsylvania, and Delaware made up the Middle Colonies.
Critical Thinking: Locate the rivers that flowed through the Middle Colonies. Why might rivers have been important for settlement?

To carry their flour, meat, fruit, and vegetables to town markets, they built Conestoga wagons. The team of four to six horses that pulled the wagons often wore bows of bells. The wagons had wide wheels suitable for roads of dirt and mud. The wagon bed was curved so that contents would not spill when the wagon went up or down hills. Canvas covers protected the contents. In time the Conestoga wagon would

A Pennsylvania German plate.

BENJAMIN FRANKLIN
(1706–1790)

God helps them that help themselves.
A penny saved is a penny earned.
Lost time is never found again.

These famous bits of wisdom and advice are from Benjamin Franklin's book, *Poor Richard's Almanack*. Born in Boston, Franklin moved to Philadelphia. There he worked hard, eventually opening a successful print shop. Indeed, he did so well that he was able to retire at age 42 and devote the rest of his life to public service and inventions. He invented an iron stove known as the Franklin stove (below). He experimented with electricity by flying a kite in a thunderstorm. Lightning struck the kite and passed down the wire to a key at the end, causing a spark. This proved that lightning was electricity. This led to another invention, the lightning rod.

As a public citizen, Franklin played an important role in improving the life of Philadelphia. In later years, as you will read, he helped in the birth of the United States.

The Franklin stove.

become the famous "covered wagon" that carried pioneers into new territory.

The Germans also brought a strong tradition of craftsmanship to the Middle Colonies. German gunsmiths first developed the long rifle. (The word *rifle* is itself German for "groove.") Other German artisans became noted as ironworkers, glass and furniture makers, and makers of kitchenware. Unlike the plain-living Puritans and Quakers, they took delight in decorating the things they made.

The Importance of Mills

Throughout the colonies one could find mills—machines that process materials such as grain. Some mills were run by wind or animal power, but most used running water for power. There were lumber mills, ironworks, paper mills, tanneries, breweries. Gristmills ground grain into flour. The largest gristmills were in Pennsylvania, Delaware, and New Jersey.

The gristmill was probably the most common and most important mill. It was to the gristmill that farmers brought their sacks of corn or wheat or rye. The grain was milled between heavy grinding stones that could be set to produce fine flour or coarse meal. Bread or meal was crucial to the colonists' diet. Each person ate about a pound of grain in some form each day—about three times as much as people eat today.

Philadelphia's Prosperity

Growing commerce and a supply of skilled artisans encouraged small-scale manufacturing in the Middle Colonies. Large-scale manufacturing was rare, except for shipbuilding. By 1720 Philadelphia had a dozen large shipyards. By 1750 the region led the colonies in shipbuilding.

Philadelphia's wealth paid for new improvements. Public buildings that were both large and graceful were constructed. They included Pennsylvania's state house, now Independence Hall. Public street lighting was introduced, streets were paved, a fire department established, and a library founded. Behind many of these improvements was Benjamin Franklin.

A Climate of Tolerance

The ways of New England were shaped by the English Puritans. The ways of the Southern Colonies were shaped by the English Cavaliers. Life in the Middle Colonies was shaped by a number of groups. The earliest settlers, the Dutch in

146

Colonial Philadelphia is shown in this 1700s painting. Philadelphia was one of the fastest growing cities of colonial times. **Critical Thinking:** How might Philadelphia's location have contributed to the city's prosperity?

New York and the Quakers in Pennsylvania, both practiced religious toleration. Later the Middle Colonies became home to peoples of different religions and from different nations. The languages one could study in Philadelphia in the mid-1700s included English, German, French, Spanish, Italian, Portuguese, Latin, Greek, Hebrew, and Arabic.

William Penn, who founded Pennsylvania, dreamed of a society in which there was "obedience to superiors, love to equals, and help . . . to inferiors." The Quakers recognized equality between men and women. As a result, Quaker women were active preachers. Female missionaries traveled the world to gain converts.

Quaker ideals would influence immigrants to the Delaware Valley—and eventually the whole nation. For instance, the first white voices to be raised against slavery came from Quakers. In Germantown, Pennsylvania, in 1688, a group of Quakers used the Biblical golden rule to condemn slavery and the slave trade:

❝There is a saying, that we shall do to all men like as we will be done ourselves; making no difference of what generation, descent, or color they are. And those who steal or rob men, and those who buy or purchase them, are they not all alike? ❞

SECTION REVIEW

1. Key Terms Conestoga wagon, mill

2. People and Places Benjamin Franklin, Middle Colonies, Philadelphia

3. Comprehension Why were the Middle Colonies called a "bread basket"?

4. Comprehension What different groups settled the Middle Colonies?

5. Critical Thinking How did society in the Middle Colonies differ from that in New England and the Southern Colonies?

5 In the Backcountry

SECTION GUIDE

Main Idea
The peoples who settled the backcountry developed a simple, self-sufficient lifestyle.

Goals
As you read, look for answers to these questions:

1. Who were the people who settled in the backcountry?

2. How did backcountry life differ from plantation life in the South?

Key Term
backcountry
fall line
piedmont

THE COLONISTS who moved west, away from the Atlantic coast, had sayings such as:

> **The rain don't know broadcloth from jeans. No man can help his birth. Any fool can make money.**

Let the New England merchants and the southern planters get decked out in finery. The inland settlers wore simple clothing and spoke plain talk. They believed in self-sufficiency, equality, and "elbow room"—room enough between homes that you would not see the smoke from your neighbors' chimney nor hear their dog bark.

Geography of the Backcountry

In the 1700s there was elbow room in the backcountry —an area along the Appalachian Mountains. In the South the backcountry started at the fall line —the point at which waterfalls made river navigation impossible for large boats. Beyond the fall line was the piedmont —a broad plateau leading to the Blue Ridge Mountains.

Crossing the Blue Ridge, one reached the Great Valley of the Appalachians. This was a valley several hundred miles long that stretched from the Hudson River Valley into the South. Numerous springs and streams in the backcountry made it easy for small family farms to prosper.

Settling the Backcountry

The first Europeans in the backcountry were Indian traders. Just as tobacco was used as currency in Virginia and Maryland, deerskins were common currency on the southern frontier. A unit of value was a buckskin or, for short, a "buck." Cattle ranchers and then settlers followed the traders. Violent clashes often erupted between Indians and the Europeans as the settlers moved onto Indian lands.

Many of the backcountry settlers became self-sufficient farmers. They were content to clear some land, build a log cabin, and plant a garden.

Backcountry settlers cleared the land and built log cabins for homes. The dulcimer provided the music for backcountry folksongs.

148

In the late 1600s many families had gone to the backcountry to escape plantation agriculture. Large estates were crowding out small farmers. Then in the 1700s a new group of people came to the backcountry directly from England. They were the Scots-Irish.

The Scots-Irish

The Scots-Irish came from the borderland between Scotland and England. (Some of them had settled for a time in northern Ireland before going to America.) For centuries, Scottish and English armies had swept back and forth across the borderland. To survive, the farmers and herders who lived there relied on family rather than government, distrusted outsiders, and were always ready to fight. They valued liberty, religion, and responsibility.

Then in 1707 England and Scotland merged to become the United Kingdom of Great Britain. Investors, land developers, and tax collectors invaded the borderlands. Poverty and crop failures added to the peoples' woes. They headed to America by the thousands. Most arrived in Philadelphia, from there they headed for the backcountry.

The Scots-Irish came as families. The family was the most important social unit in the backcountry. Although people lived in scattered settlements, they were linked to others by a network of kin relationships. "Family" was not just the immediate family but a whole clan of relatives. The clan included all those with common ancestors and the same last name. They banded together when danger threatened and were suspicious of outsiders. Even marriages were likely to occur within the clan.

Backcountry Life

Typical of backcountry homesteads was the log cabin. Although introduced by the Swedes, the log cabin was not common in America until the Scots-Irish came. It was ideal for the backcountry because it could be built rather quickly using only an axe. Inside the cabins, pegs lined the walls. Here were hung the family's clothes. So displayed, the clothes were a form of decoration as well as a sign of the wealth or poverty of the household.

Backcountry women wore homespun clothing. On their heads they were likely to wear bonnets. They went barefoot in warm weather. The men wore a long hunting shirt with large sleeves. In summer they usually wore linen hunting shirts and in winter, deerskin shirts tucked in with a belt. From the belt might hang a bullet bag, knife, and tomahawk. Backcountry men might wear loose trousers or leggings made of deerskin.

People in the backcountry treated each other as equals. Even though some were richer than others, they all dressed about the same and called each other by the first name.

Backcountry people generally did not use books to educate their children. Instead they spread knowledge through ballads, folksongs, and folktales.

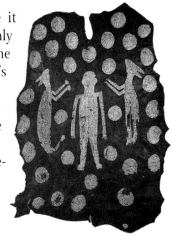

Deerskin was valuable to the settlers of the backcountry. It was used as currency, clothing, and during ceremonies.

Summary

1. English colonists brought with them ideas of limited government and self-rule. They kept their rights as English citizens when they moved to the colonies. Through elected assemblies, colonists exercised a certain amount of self-rule.
2. Plantations shaped the life and economy of the Southern Colonies. For labor, the colonists turned to Africa for slaves. On the plantations, slaves developed a new African American culture based on African beliefs and customs.

3. Though New England lacked good farming conditions, trade, fishing, and shipbuilding became profitable. The influence of religion, which had declined by the early 1700s, rose around 1740 with the Great Awakening.
4. In the Middle Colonies, farming and manufacturing prospered. The wealth of resources attracted people from many different nations.
5. Some colonists chose backcountry life to escape plantations. They cleared the land and built log cabins for homes. They valued independence and self-reliance.

Graphic Summary

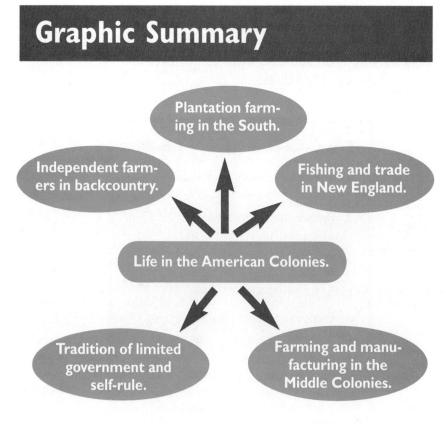

Plantation farming in the South.

Independent farmers in backcountry.

Fishing and trade in New England.

Life in the American Colonies.

Tradition of limited government and self-rule.

Farming and manufacturing in the Middle Colonies.

Review

KEY TERMS

Define the following terms
1. Magna Carta
2. English Bill of Rights
3. economy
4. Middle Passage
5. slave codes
6. triangular trade
7. Navigation Acts
8. Salem Witchcraft Trials
9. Great Awakening
10. backcountry

COMPREHENSION

1. Name and describe two documents that limited the power of the English monarch.
2. In what way was the Zenger trial a victory for freedom of the press?
3. How did the Cavaliers change the labor system in the Southern Colonies?
4. What was the Middle Passage?
5. What were some of the items traded in the triangular trade routes?
6. How did England try to protect its trade with the colonies?
7. Why was there less slavery in the New England Colonies?
8. What factors contributed to the prosperity of Philadelphia?
9. How did Quaker ideals encourage immigration to the Middle Colonies?
10. How did backcountry life differ from life in the Southern, New England, and Middle Colonies?

Places to Locate

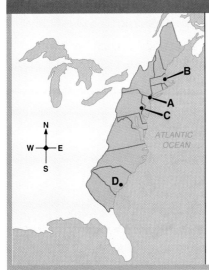

Match the letters on the map with the places listed below.
1. Charles Town
2. New York City
3. Philadelphia
4. Boston

Geographic Theme: Regions
Was the division of the colonies into three regions the result of geography, of colonists' efforts, or both? Explain.

Skill Review

The chart below shows one form of government in the American colonies. Compare this chart with the chart of Pennsylvania's colonial government on the Skill page. Then answer the following questions.

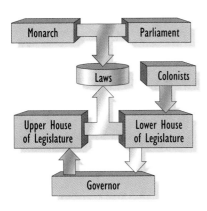

1. How are members of the colonial legislature chosen in each system of government?
2. How is the governor chosen in each system of government?
3. Under which system of government do colonists have greater power? Explain.

CRITICAL THINKING

1. **Making a Hypothesis** Why might voting rights in the English colonies have been limited to property owners?
2. **Analyzing a Quotation** Explain what Benjamin Franklin meant by the statements, "A penny saved is a penny earned," and "Lost time is never found again."
3. **Identifying Supporting Ideas** Find three facts that support the following statement: "Despite their many differences, the colonies had important things in common."

PORTFOLIO OPTIONS

1. **Civics Connection** Explain how a free press helps protect the rights of the people against abuses by the government.
2. **Writing Connection** Use reference books in the library to find out more about the Magna Carta and the English Bill of Rights. Write a two-page report on your findings.
3. **Contemporary Connection** Make a list of issues a New England town meeting might have considered in the early 1700s. Discuss in class which of the issues would still be relevant today.
4. **Timeline Connection** Copy the chapter timeline. Add other events from the chapter onto the timeline. Which event do you think was most significant for the American colonies? For the English government? Explain.

France began expanding its North American empire in the 1600s. At the same time, England was building colonies on the continent. The two powers eventually clashed in the French and Indian War. Native Americans were caught up in the struggle, fighting for both sides. In the painting below, a captured Iroquois warrior is about to be burned at the stake by the French governor-general of Canada and his Indian allies.

1660

1675

1690

1705

1673 Marquette and Joliet
explore the Mississippi

1689 King William's War begins

1682 La Salle reaches the
Gulf of Mexico

The Clash of Empires
(1668–1763)

1 The Expanding French Empire

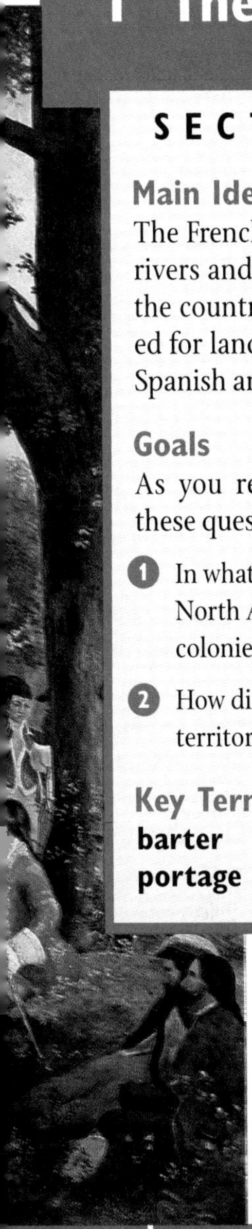

SECTION GUIDE

Main Idea
The French explored America's great rivers and claimed a huge section of the country's interior. They competed for land and trade rights with the Spanish and British.

Goals
As you read, look for answers to these questions:

1 In what ways did French colonies in North America differ from English colonies?

2 How did the French come to rule the territory of Louisiana?

Key Terms
barter
portage

WINTER WAS not far away that day late in 1668 as canoes of Indians paddled down the St. Lawrence River. They were headed for a French trading post just outside of Montreal. The Indians were strangers in these parts. They were Seneca Iroquois in a region dominated by the Algonquin.

La Salle's Search

At the trading post they spoke with the lean, sun-darkened Frenchman in charge. Yes, he said, the Seneca could camp there for the winter. The Frenchman was pleased they had come. From the Seneca he hoped to learn more about the lands to the south of the St. Lawrence.

Born Robert Cavelier, the Frenchman was known as La Salle. He had come to New France two years before to trade for furs with the Indians. La Salle had prospered as a trader. His great ambition, however, was to find a route to Asia through the interior of North America. This would be the Northwest Passage, for which European explorers had long searched in vain.

The St. Lawrence: Heart of New France

New France had begun with Samuel Champlain's founding of Quebec in 1608. Half a century later the French population in North America numbered about 2,000, mostly male. They were fur traders, government officials, and missionaries.

1720	1735	1750	1765

1754 Albany Plan of Union rejected

1756 Seven Years' War begins

1718 New Orleans founded

1759 British capture Quebec

1763 Treaty of Paris

Kateri Tekakwitha, a Mohawk, was converted to Christianity in 1676 by a French missionary.

Quebec was the capital of New France. The town sat upon rocky bluffs high above the St. Lawrence. Farther up river was the French settlement of Montreal. It started as a fur-trading post and became the center of the fur trade.

In the 1660s France became concerned about the growing number of English and Dutch colonists. They were beginning to compete with the French for the fur trade. As a result, France began to encourage French families to settle in New France. Unlike the English, who set up permanent settlements, most Frenchmen up to this point had come temporarily.

Now the French planned to establish a permanent colony of farming families in the St. Lawrence River valley. These families would raise crops and livestock for the colony. They would also raise children. The increased population would serve as a line of defense against English expansion.

The plan worked in that the population of New France grew to 15,000 by 1700. New France, however, never drew the numbers of new immigrants that were flowing into the English colonies.

A Trading Empire

The French based their North American empire on trade. They had not set out to conquer and rule like the Spanish. Nor had the French transplanted themselves and their institutions as had the English. Ordinary Frenchmen could not own land in New France. Land was granted only to nobles. They in turn brought settlers to the land. For most French, the riches of America lay not in gold mines, nor in farmland, but in pelts and hides.

The fur trade depended on Indian participation. The French got along with the Indians better than any other colonial power. French trappers and traders learned to live as the Indians did. The *voyageurs* (voy-uh-ZHUR), or canoeists, and *coureurs de bois* (koo-RUHR DUH BWAH), or fur traders, often lived in Indian villages and married Indian women.

French missionaries also treated the Indians with respect. They took the time to learn Indian languages. Although they hoped to convert Indians to Christianity, they did not try to force them to follow French ways. French missionaries needed no soldiers to protect them.

Both the French and the Indians benefited from the trading relationship. The Indians could **barter** —trade goods without exchanging money—furs and deerskins for manufactured items: iron pots, steel knives, glass beads, even guns. In turn, the French reaped great profits when shiploads of furs reached European markets.

To French fur traders, North America was a land of riches. Native Americans supplied furs to the traders in return for manufactured goods.

Reaching the Ohio

In the 1660s the French empire in North America included the land around the Great Lakes and the St. Lawrence Valley. Within two decades France would expand this empire to the Gulf of Mexico.

La Salle was the first Frenchman to head south. That winter of 1668–1669 La Salle took notes as the Seneca told him about their homeland. A great river called the Ohio ran through this land, they said. The river flowed into the sea, but it took eight or nine months to reach its mouth.

La Salle could hardly contain his excitement. Was it possible that the Ohio was the Northwest Passage? He was eager to find out. The next spring he headed southward from Lake Ontario until he reached the Ohio. He followed the great river almost to the Mississippi. Then he realized that the Ohio was heading south and was not likely to be the Northwest Passage.

Exploring the Mississippi

Meanwhile, Indians were telling of a "great water" that emptied into an even larger one. On that sea floated tall ships manned by white men. Jacques Marquette (mahr-KET), a missionary priest, and fur trader Louis Joliet (JOH-lee-et) set out in 1673 to find out the truth. They were also ordered to chart the course of the "great water."

Marquette and Joliet, taking two canoes and five men, paddled from Lake Michigan to the headwaters of the Fox River. There they made a **portage** —carrying boats overland—to the headwaters of the Wisconsin River. The Wisconsin flows into the Mississippi. Marquette and Joliet followed the Mississippi as far as the Arkansas River. Then, afraid they might run into the Spanish, they returned to Lake Michigan.

Claiming Louisiana

Back in Quebec, La Salle learned of what Marquette and Joliet had found. From his explorations of the Ohio River, La Salle had

CONNECTING WITH WORLD EVENTS

EUROPE'S HUNGER FOR FURS

Fur is sometimes called the oldest item of trade. It has been used for protective warmth by people for hundreds of centuries. During the Middle Ages in Europe, fur was in great demand both for warmth and decoration. Laws were even passed that determined which furs could be worn by which classes of people. The most expensive furs, such as ermine (a type of weasel), could only be worn by royalty.

In Europe in the 1600s, fur was not used on the outside of people's jackets. Rather, it was used to line their cloaks, gowns, boots, and mittens. After fur-bearing animals had been overhunted in Europe, fur traders turned to the vast continent of North America, where beaver, mink, and other animals were plentiful.

begun to dream of expanding New France to the west. He looked forward to the creation of permanent French trading settlements along the Ohio and Mississippi river valleys. Using this new information, La Salle was sure he could reach the mouth of the Mississippi. He asked permission to explore the Mississippi for purposes of colonization. In 1677 Louis XIV, king of France, granted La Salle's request.

In 1679 La Salle crossed the Great Lakes by boat. In December 1681 he set out with 23 French colonists and 31 Indians. Among the Indians were 10 women and 3 infants. From Lake Michigan they portaged to the Illinois River by dragging their canoes on sleds across the snow. Then the expedition paddled down to the Mississippi River. In the lower Mississippi Valley they met descendants of the mound builders and were impressed. "I cannot tell you the civility and kindness we received," wrote one of the priests on the expedition.

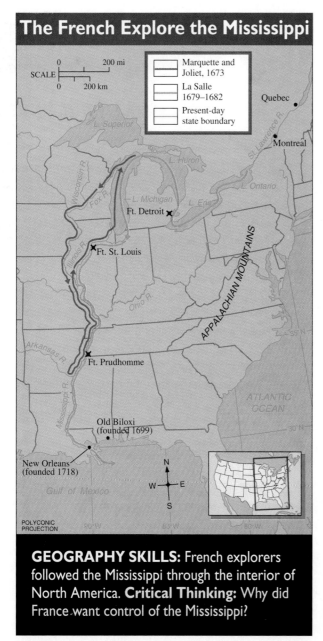

The French Explore the Mississippi

SCALE
0   200 mi
0   200 km

Marquette and Joliet, 1673
La Salle 1679–1682
Present-day state boundary

Quebec
Montreal
St. Lawrence R.
L. Superior
Wisconsin R.
Fox R.
L. Huron
L. Michigan
L. Erie
L. Ontario
Ft. Detroit ✕
Illinois R.
Ft. St. Louis ✕
APPALACHIAN MOUNTAINS
Ohio R.
Arkansas R.
Ft. Prudhomme ✕
35° N
Mississippi R.
Old Biloxi (founded 1699)
ATLANTIC OCEAN
New Orleans (founded 1718)
30° N
N
W   E
S
Gulf of Mexico
POLYCONIC PROJECTION
90° W   85° W   80° W

GEOGRAPHY SKILLS: French explorers followed the Mississippi through the interior of North America. **Critical Thinking:** Why did France want control of the Mississippi?

They reached the Gulf of Mexico in April 1682. There, at the mouth of the Mississippi, La Salle claimed "this country of Louisiana . . . in the name of the most high, mighty . . . Louis the Great, by Grace of God King of France."

La Salle defined the territory of Louisiana as the drainage of the Mississippi River from the Great Lakes to the Gulf of Mexico. This huge area stretched from the crest of the Appalachian Mountains to the crest of the Rocky Mountains. It was the heart of the North American continent.

La Salle planned to build a string of forts from the Great Lakes to the Gulf of Mexico. Around each fort there would be a French settlement. The Mississippi would be a water highway linking the settlements from the Great Lakes to the Gulf.

A Disastrous Expedition

With the king's blessing, La Salle set out from France in 1684 to establish a hold on the Mississippi Delta (the mouth of the river). He had four ships carrying over 300 colonists. The expedition was a disaster.

First of all, La Salle did not recognize the delta when he sailed by it on the Gulf of Mexico. This happened because by the time it discharges into the Gulf, the Mississippi has split into several different rivers.

La Salle was somewhere off the Texas coast when he realized he had overshot the mark. He was also out of food and had lost all but one of his ships during the voyage. La Salle landed, but Indians then wrecked the last remaining ship. Now La Salle was stranded.

With a small party he set out by land to find the Mississippi. La Salle had never been a popular or well-liked man. Now, on the hard march northward, grudges boiled over into hatred. A group of his followers rebelled. They killed La Salle north of the Brazos River in Texas. The year was 1687.

Controlling the Mississippi

For a while it looked as if La Salle's dream of a French empire in the Mississippi Valley would die. Shortly after La Salle's murder, the French government ordered settlers to stay close together. Later the government ordered trappers and traders out of the wilderness completely. "Their privilege of going into the woods is forever abolished," read the declaration by the Crown. The interior was to remain Indian territory permanently.

La Salle's friends continued to urge a settlement at the mouth of the Mississippi.

This painting shows a 1682 meeting between La Salle and a Taensa Indian chief in northern Louisiana. La Salle was killed five years later by a group of his followers.

Such a settlement could serve several purposes. (1) It would be a base of attack against Spanish-controlled Mexico. (2) It would function as a trading post for furs and minerals from the interior. (3) It would keep England from taking control of the Mississippi River.

The last argument was a strong one. Already the English were planning to plant a colony on the Mississippi. In 1699, therefore, the French king approved of settlements on the lower Mississippi. The French expedition first built a fort at Biloxi, in present-day Mississippi. Jean Baptiste de Bienville (byan-VEEL) was left in charge.

Bienville began exploring the Mississippi Delta. Imagine his surprise one day to round a bend and find an English ship filled with colonists. Was this the Mississippi River? asked the captain of the English ship. No, Bienville lied. The English believed him and turned back.

Bienville would oversee the building of more French settlements in southern Louisiana, including New Orleans in 1718. Other forts along the Mississippi helped link the two settled parts of New France. By the early 1700s, France held the two main access points to the American interior. The first of these was the St. Lawrence River, controlled by Quebec and Montreal. The second was the mouth of the Mississippi, controlled by New Orleans.

SECTION REVIEW

1. Key Terms barter, portage

2. People and Places La Salle, Jacques Marquette, Louis Joliet, Jean Baptiste de Bienville, New France

3. Comprehension How did France's approach to its North American colonies differ from England's?

4. Comprehension Why did the French decide to build a settlement at the mouth of the Mississippi?

5. Critical Thinking What helped France in exploring the interior of the North American continent?

SKILLS: Taking Notes

LEARN

Reporters always carry a pencil and pad for taking notes. They cannot afford to rely on memory alone. To them, taking notes is an art.

Whether you take notes on a pad or on note cards, you must remember two things. First, write down only the important ideas and details. Your notes on the clash of empires in this chapter should include the empires involved, when and why they clashed, the results, and any important people introduced. Second, write them in a form that will make sense to you later, when you try to read them.

You should learn to use abbreviations and symbols to save time and space. Abbreviations in history notes might include *Fr. & Ind.* for French and Indian, *PM* for prime minister, and *Miss. R.* for Mississippi River. Standard symbols include & (and), *w/* (with), and *w/o* (without). Remember, use abbreviations and symbols that you will recognize later.

PRACTICE

Study the notes on the card at the right to answer the questions.

1. Why is it important to show the title of the book and the chapter?

2. Rewrite the note for the 1682 entry without abbreviations.

3. How many bodies of water and waterways are mentioned in the notes? What are they?

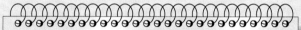

Am. Past and Promise, Ch. 8, Sect. 1
("Reach. the Ohio" to "A Disastrous Exp.")

1669 – La Salle (Fr.) seeks NW Pass. via Ohio R.

1673 – Marquette and Joliet (Fr.) go from L. Mich. to Wisc. R. to Miss. R.

1682 – La S. reaches mouth of Miss. R. at Gulf of Mex. & claims huge terr. of La. for Fr.

1687 – La S. killed in Tex. by own men.

APPLY

4. List ten terms from the Glossary at the back of the book. Then write your own abbreviations for the terms.

5. Using the skills you learned above, read and take notes on Section 2 of this chapter.

2 Rivalry over Furs and Land

SECTION GUIDE

Main Idea
France and Britain, competing for empire around the world, fought for valuable resources in the Americas.

Goals
As you read, look for answers to these questions:

1 Why did English-French rivalry develop in North America?

2 What role did Native Americans play in the rivalry?

Key Terms
League of the Iroquois
balance of power
land speculator
Albany Plan of Union

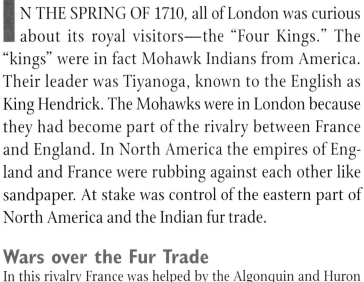

Mohawk statesman Tiyanoga (King Hendrick) wears clothes given to him by Queen Anne of England during his trip overseas in 1710.

IN THE SPRING OF 1710, all of London was curious about its royal visitors—the "Four Kings." The "kings" were in fact Mohawk Indians from America. Their leader was Tiyanoga, known to the English as King Hendrick. The Mohawks were in London because they had become part of the rivalry between France and England. In North America the empires of England and France were rubbing against each other like sandpaper. At stake was control of the eastern part of North America and the Indian fur trade.

Wars over the Fur Trade

In this rivalry France was helped by the Algonquin and Huron Indians of the lands bordering the St. Lawrence Valley. Siding with the English was the **League of the Iroquois.** The five nations of the League—the Cayuga, Mohawk, Oneida, Onondaga, and Seneca—would become six when the Tuscarora joined in 1722. They joined together to end the almost constant warfare that existed among the nations.

The League would become the most powerful union of Indian nations in America. Part of its power came from its control of the only fairly easy passage between New England and the St. Lawrence Valley. This passage extended from Albany along the Mohawk River to Lake Erie. (Later it would become the route of the Erie Canal.)

By 1640 all the beaver in the Hudson Valley had been trapped. The Iroquois then began warring on their northern neighbors in an attempt to gain control of their fur trade. Within a decade they had defeated the Huron. Through conquest, the Iroquois then extended their control over an area ranging from Maine to the Ohio Valley and north to Lake Michigan. By 1670, Iroquois trappers were hauling to the trading post at Albany a million pounds of beaver skins each year.

Iroquois expansion threatened the French fur trade. In 1687 France began to wage war on the League. The conflict broadened in 1689 when France and England went to war in the first of their struggles for world empire. (The wars fought in the Americas are named after the English ruler at the time.) In King

This toma-hawk from the 1600s had a stone blade.

William's War (1689–1697) the Iroquois defended the English frontier against the French and their Indian allies. A second war for empire, Queen Anne's War, was being fought when King Hendrick made his trip to London.

Queen Anne's War (1702–1713) and King George's War (1744–1748), did not change the balance of power in North America. (Balance of power among nations means that they have equal levels of strength.) One effect of the wars, however, was to unleash French-sponsored Indian raids on English settlements.

Frontier Brutality

The frontier wars were brutal. Consider the story of Hannah Duston of Haverhill, Massachusetts. This incident happened during King William's War. In March 1697 she, her week-old baby, and a nurse were in the house when a party of twenty Indians attacked the town. Her husband, in the field nearby, ran to save his wife. The Indians got there first.

The Indians forced Hannah Duston, her baby, and the nurse to join the other captives they had by then collected. Before they had gone many steps, they "dashed out the brains of the infant against a tree." As other captives tired, they were slain by a hatchet blow.

Duston and her nurse were assigned to an Indian family. Also with the family was a youth captured the year before. The captives accompanied the family 150 miles north to its home on the Merrimack River near present-day Concord, New Hampshire. The Indians intended to take the captives to Canada and sell them to the French. The prisoners were not guarded, for the Indians did not believe they would try to escape so far from home.

One day, Hannah Duston and her two companions rose just before daybreak. Seizing hatchets, they killed two men, two women, and six children. They had started on their way when Duston became fearful that her neighbors would not believe her story. So, they turned back, scalped the Indians, and returned to Haverhill with the bloody proof wrapped in a piece of cloth.

English Population Growth

By the 1750s, the growing population of the English colonies helped shift the bal-

The rivalry between France and England over furs and land led to frontier warfare. Here, Abenaki Indians and their French allies attack a British settlement in Massachusetts during Queen Anne's War.

ance between France and England. In 1750 French colonists numbered barely 80,000, compared with over 1,000,000 English. The English colonies were doubling their population every generation.

In response to this growth, English **land speculators** —people who buy and sell land in hopes of making a profit—began to plan for the settlement of the fertile Ohio Valley. The Ohio Company of Virginia had started to negotiate with the Indians in the Ohio Valley. Britain had already granted the company a half-million acres in the valley.

France became alarmed. A British presence along the Ohio River could threaten its claim to the Mississippi Valley and its valuable fur trade with the Indians. France began to rim the Ohio Valley with forts in order to protect its claims.

Franklin Urges Union

Both France and Britain were building forts on the territory of the Six Nations of the Iroquois. Yet no one really knew what the boundaries of that territory were. To discuss relations with the Iroquois, the British called a meeting at Albany in 1754.

Representing Pennsylvania at the conference was Benjamin Franklin. Franklin believed the British colonies had to join together for their mutual defense. He made that point just before the conference when he published the first political cartoon in America. It pictured a snake cut into pieces with the caption "JOIN, or DIE."

In Albany the Iroquois agreed with Franklin. Speaking for the Iroquois was King Hendrick, the Mohawk leader who had visited London more than 40 years earlier. Hendrick urged the colonists to strengthen themselves through unity, as the Iroquois had done. From the Iroquois' point of view, a strong union of colonies would bring stability to the frontier.

Franklin presented his **Albany Plan of Union** to the colonial delegates. The

Benjamin Franklin's political cartoon was based on the belief that a snake cut into pieces (colonies) would live again if the pieces were rejoined.

plan reflected Franklin's knowledge of and respect for the Iroquois League. It called for each colony to send representatives to a Great Council. The head of the council would be a president-general appointed by the Crown. The council would have the authority to make war and peace with the Indians. It would also have other powers to raise armies, construct forts, levy taxes, and found new settlements.

In the end, though, the colonies rejected the Albany Plan of Union. None of the colonies wanted to give up power to a central government. Nor did they want to pay taxes for a joint defense.

SECTION REVIEW

1. Key Terms League of the Iroquois, balance of power, land speculator, Albany Plan of Union

2. People and Places King Hendrick, Benjamin Franklin, Albany, Ohio Valley

3. Comprehension Over what issues did the rivalry between England and France grow in North America?

4. Comprehension What was the relationship between the League of the Iroquois and the Albany Plan of Union?

5. Critical Thinking How did European colonization affect the relationships among Indian nations?

3 The French and Indian War

SECTION GUIDE

Main Idea
The French-English rivalry exploded in the mid-1700s. France eventually lost its North American empire to Great Britain.

Goals
As you read, look for answers to these questions:

1 What advantages did each side have in the French and Indian War?

2 How did the war affect the fate of North America?

Key Terms
French and Indian War
casualty
prime minister
Battle of Quebec
Treaty of Paris (1763)

As a Virginia colonel, Washington wore a blue coat with red trim.

ON A SPRING MORNING in April 1754, a 22-year-old Virginian mounted his best horse. He gave a command. To the beat of drums, a single file of 132 soldiers followed the leader out of Alexandria, Virginia. Their orders were to drive the French from the upper Ohio Valley.

At the Forks of the Ohio

The young Virginian in charge was George Washington. Late in 1753, he had carried a message from Virginia's governor to the French whose forts dotted the Ohio River valley. The message informed the French they were on soil claimed by Virginia and requested their "peaceable departure." Not surprisingly, the French had refused.

The governor then ordered Washington to drive the French out. His first task was to secure the Forks of the Ohio. Here the Allegheny River, flowing from the north, and the Monongahela, flowing from the south, meet to form the Ohio River. Whoever controlled this site could control access to the Ohio Valley.

An advance party had been sent ahead to build a fort at the Forks. Washington was not far away when the fort commander appeared. He had just seen an armada of 350 canoes and other boats containing 1,000 Frenchmen. Faced with such power, the Virginians gave up the fort and left. The French then strengthened the fort and renamed it "Fort Duquesne" (doo-KAYN).

While he waited for reinforcements, Washington put his men to work. They widened a trail into a road for carts carrying supplies and artillery. They built a camp in a marshy valley where two streams joined. Washington thought it a "charming field for an encounter." They ringed the camp with a stockade of sharpened logs and called it "Fort Necessity."

The French and Indian War

The scene changed several weeks later. Early on a July morning, French soldiers advanced on Fort Necessity. Rather than charge the fort, the French lay in the surrounding woods and fired down onto the camp. Rain poured down, soaking the Virginians' gunpowder. It was "an unequal fight," Washington wrote, "with an enemy sheltered behind the trees, ourselves without shelter, in trenches full of water." Washington was forced to retreat to Virginia.

The fight at Fort Necessity was the first battle of the **French and Indian War.** This war would in turn become part of a larger, worldwide war known as the Seven Years' War (1756–1763). Britain and France fought each other in Europe and in India as well as in North America.

The French had four major advantages against the British. (1) France controlled access to the interior of North America. (2) New France had a single colonial government that could act quickly. The British, on the other hand, had to ask for help from the thirteen separate colonial governments. (3) France sent ships and professional soldiers to America rather than depend on military help from its colonists. (4) The French could count on help from such loyal Indian allies as the Huron and the Algonquin.

The British had strong points as well. (1) The population of the British colonies was far greater than the population of New France. (2) The British colonies, concentrated along the Atlantic coast, were easier to defend. (3) As permanent settlers, English colonists were fighting to save their homes and land.

In past wars the Iroquois had aided the British. After Washington's defeat at Fort Necessity, however, the British lost their Indian allies. The Iroquois wanted to avoid being on the losing side of a battle between Europeans. Within months many Iroquois were fighting with the French. Other Iroquois stayed on the sidelines.

The French and Indian War

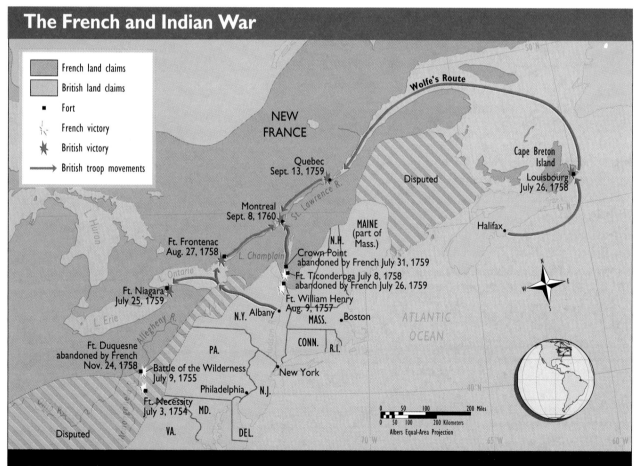

GEOGRAPHY SKILLS: This map shows the major battle sites of the French and Indian War. **Critical Thinking:** Why did the location of Ft. Louisbourg make it important for the British to capture it?

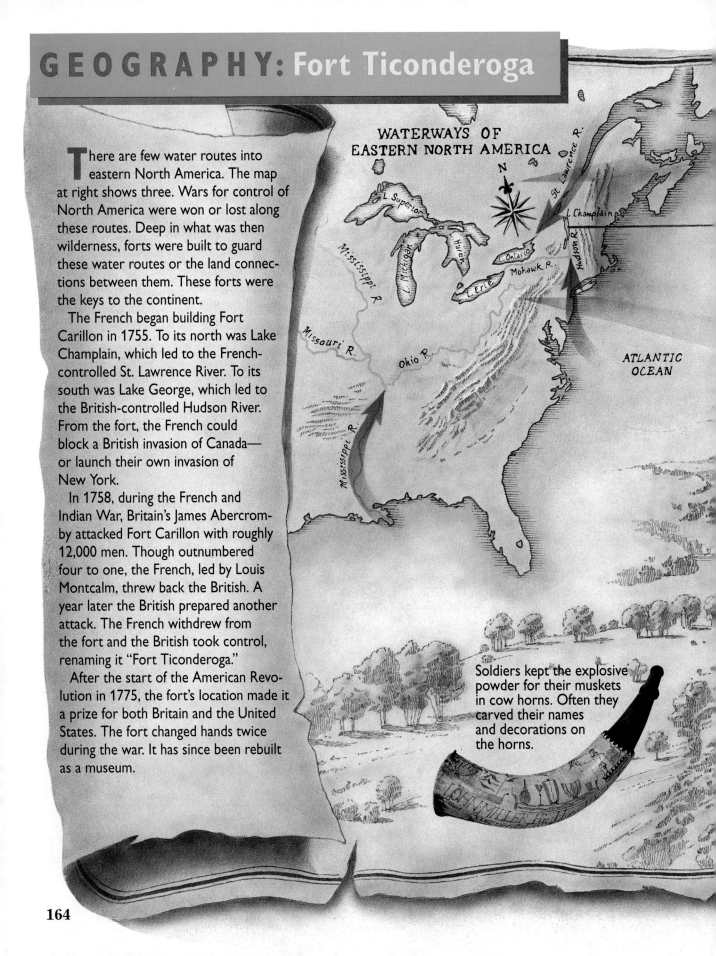

WATERWAYS OF EASTERN NORTH AMERICA

There are few water routes into eastern North America. The map at right shows three. Wars for control of North America were won or lost along these routes. Deep in what was then wilderness, forts were built to guard these water routes or the land connections between them. These forts were the keys to the continent.

The French began building Fort Carillon in 1755. To its north was Lake Champlain, which led to the French-controlled St. Lawrence River. To its south was Lake George, which led to the British-controlled Hudson River. From the fort, the French could block a British invasion of Canada—or launch their own invasion of New York.

In 1758, during the French and Indian War, Britain's James Abercromby attacked Fort Carillon with roughly 12,000 men. Though outnumbered four to one, the French, led by Louis Montcalm, threw back the British. A year later the British prepared another attack. The French withdrew from the fort and the British took control, renaming it "Fort Ticonderoga."

After the start of the American Revolution in 1775, the fort's location made it a prize for both Britain and the United States. The fort changed hands twice during the war. It has since been rebuilt as a museum.

Soldiers kept the explosive powder for their muskets in cow horns. Often they carved their names and decorations on the horns.

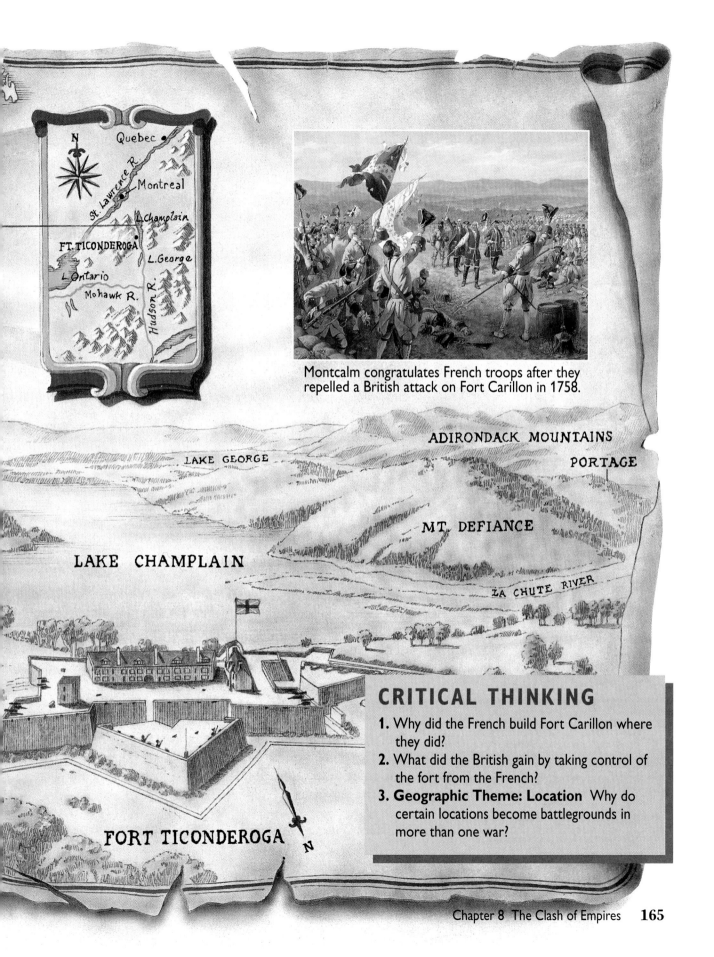

Quebec
St. Lawrence R.
Montreal
L. Champlain
FT. TICONDEROGA
L. George
L. Ontario
Mohawk R.
Hudson R.

N

Montcalm congratulates French troops after they repelled a British attack on Fort Carillon in 1758.

ADIRONDACK MOUNTAINS

LAKE GEORGE

PORTAGE

MT. DEFIANCE

LAKE CHAMPLAIN

LA CHUTE RIVER

FORT TICONDEROGA

N

CRITICAL THINKING

1. Why did the French build Fort Carillon where they did?
2. What did the British gain by taking control of the fort from the French?
3. **Geographic Theme: Location** Why do certain locations become battlegrounds in more than one war?

European Claims in North America

1754

Unclaimed by Europeans

NEW FRANCE

PACIFIC OCEAN

ATLANTIC OCEAN

FLORIDA

SOUTH AMERICA

100° W
120° W
100° W
80° W
40° N
20° N

	British		Russian
	French		Conflicting claims
	Spanish		

1763

Unclaimed by Europeans

PACIFIC OCEAN

ATLANTIC OCEAN

FLORIDA

SOUTH AMERICA

0   500   1,000   2,000 Miles
0 500 1,000   2,000 Kilometers
Azimuthal Equal-Area Projection

120° W
100° W
80° W

GEOGRAPHY SKILLS: The French and Indian War led to great changes on the North American continent. **Critical Thinking:** Why did the outcome of the war alarm many Indians?

Braddock's Defeat

George Washington had failed in his attempt to drive the French from the Ohio Valley. In 1755, General Edward Braddock made a second attempt. Leading an army of both Virginians and British troops, Braddock headed into the wilderness. As was common, several of the soldiers' wives traveled along with their husbands. Braddock's army arrived within ten miles of Fort Duquesne. They planned to bombard the fort with their cannons.

In desperation, the French commander at Fort Duquesne sent out his 250 soldiers dressed as Indians. With them were 600 real Indians. The French and Indians ambushed the British, who were an easy target in their bright red uniforms. The ambush threw the British forces into wild confusion. They were being shot at, but they could not see the enemy. Braddock had five horses shot out from under him before he himself was killed.

After three fierce hours of fighting, the British retreated. Their casualties —the wounded and dead—amounted to about two-thirds of the army. Among the dead were eight women.

As a result of Braddock's defeat, the French kept control of the Ohio Valley. For the next two years the French and their Indian allies won a string of victories against the British. Then, in 1757, the picture began to change.

British Victories

In 1757 William Pitt became Britain's secretary of state and the virtual prime minister —head of government. Pitt was a bold, confident leader. He poured vast amounts of money into the war, thereby throwing England into debt. Pitt also persuaded the colonies to furnish more troops and money.

In 1758 the British captured the important French fort at Louisbourg near the mouth of the St. Lawrence. The British also took several forts in the Ohio Valley, including Fort Duquesne. They renamed it "Fort Pitt" in honor of William Pitt. Today it is the site of Pittsburgh, Pennsylvania.

The fate of the Ohio Valley was to be settled by the fate of Canada. The crucial year was 1759. That summer the British, under James Wolfe, sailed up the St. Lawrence to attack the French stronghold of Quebec. Quebec was the head and heart of New France. Wolfe knew if he could conquer Quebec, New France would collapse. It would not be an easy task. Quebec sat high on cliffs above the St. Lawrence. Strong walls and many cannons protected it.

Two hundred ships carrying 18,000 men arrived at the foot of the cliffs. Waiting for them were 14,000 French troops under Louis Montcalm. Quebec seemed unconquerable. For three months Wolfe sailed up and down the river while the French matched his movements on land.

Finally, a British scout found a hidden path that led up the cliffs to the plateau above. On a September night, more than 4,000 British filed one-by-one up the steep passage. The French awoke the next day to find British troops waiting outside in battle formation. Both Wolfe and Montcalm lost their lives, but the British won a decisive victory at the **Battle of Quebec.**

The French Are Forced Out

The Battle of Quebec marked a turning point in North American history. The British went on to capture Montreal and the fighting ended. The British now controlled all of New France. The war continued in other parts of the world, with Britain finally defeating France. The Seven Years' War formally ended with the **Treaty of Paris (1763).**

By the terms of the treaty, Britain took from France its claims to land east of the Mississippi River except for New Orleans. Spain, which had sided with France in the war, had to give Britain its claim to Florida. To make up for this loss, France gave Spain New Orleans and its claim to all of Louisiana west of the Mississippi.

Pontiac's Uprising

For years the Indians of the Ohio River region had traded with the French. The French in turn had not taken Indian lands. After the British drove the French from North America, the Indians grew worried. Gone was their long-time trading partner and protector.

To many Indians, the future looked grim. Had not the English colonists steadily pushed westward? Their fences and guns had taken over Indian hunting grounds. Was it not just a matter of time before the British crossed the Appalachians?

Jeffrey Amherst, the British officer in charge of Indian affairs, thought of the Indians as no better than wild beasts. "Could it not be contrived," he wrote the

commander at Fort Pitt, "to send the Small Pox among [them]?" The commander then pretended to show goodwill to Indian leaders. He gave them blankets. But the blankets were a gift of death, for they came from a smallpox hospital and were infected with the disease.

The ink on the Treaty of Paris had barely dried when an Ottawa chief and holy man named Pontiac called together the Shawnee, Delaware, Chippewa, and Ottawa tribes. Pontiac's warriors drove the British from every outpost but Fort Detroit and Fort Pitt. White settlers in the Ohio Valley were killed and their cabins burned. The Indians would keep the British at bay for two years.

The uprising showed the British that it would not be easy to govern their huge American holdings. British leaders cast about for a way to keep peace on the American frontier. Their solution would set in motion the chain of events that led to the Revolutionary War.

The British met with France's Indian allies in 1764 to discuss peace. They gave the Indians medals as a symbol of their friendship.

SECTION REVIEW

1. Key Terms French and Indian War, casualty, prime minister, Battle of Quebec, Treaty of Paris (1763)

2. People and Places George Washington, Edward Braddock, William Pitt, Pontiac, Fort Duquesne

3. Comprehension What advantages did France have in its fight against the British in North America? What advantages did the British have?

4. Comprehension What were the terms of the Treaty of Paris?

5. Critical Thinking How might history have been different had a British scout not discovered a path up the cliffs of Quebec?

Summary

1. France set up colonies along the St. Lawrence River in the 1600s. Most early French colonists were fur trappers or traders. France sought to establish permanent settlements as English and Dutch settlements expanded. Marquette, Joliet, and La Salle used North America's river system to explore the interior of the continent.

2. Rivalry between Britain and France grew over competition for colonies and their wealth. The two countries competed on a worldwide scale. In North America, each side recruited Indian allies. The two countries fought a number of wars on the western frontier of Britain's colonies. Neither side had a clear advantage. British land speculators hoped to take control of the Ohio Valley.

3. The French and Indian War was a struggle for the rich lands along the Ohio River. The British suffered an early defeat at Fort Duquesne in 1755, but in 1759 they captured Quebec. This battle turned the tide of the war. In the Treaty of Paris of 1763, the French gave up their claims in North America. That same year, an Indian uprising against the British in the Ohio Valley raised new tensions.

Review

KEY TERMS

Define the terms in each of the following pairs.

1. balance of power; French and Indian War

2. League of the Iroquois; Albany Plan of Union

3. Battle of Quebec; Treaty of Paris (1763)

COMPREHENSION

1. Which explorer founded New France? When?

2. Why did French fur traders and trappers get along so well with the Indians?

3. What did La Salle claim for France? When did he claim it?

4. What gave the French a strong hold on the American interior in the early 1700s?

5. Why was the League of the Iroquois powerful?

6. Why were the French alarmed by English land speculators?

7. Why did the Iroquois desire a strong union of British colonies?

8. In what region did the first battles of the French and Indian War take place?

9. What was the effect of the war on France's North American empire? Which two countries gained French territory?

10. Why did Britain's victory in the war worry the Indians in the Ohio Valley?

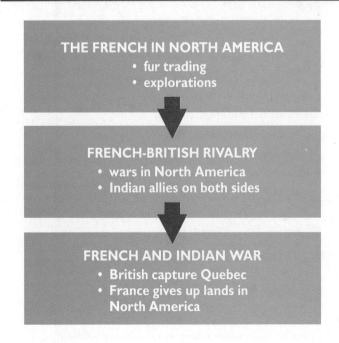

Graphic Summary

THE FRENCH IN NORTH AMERICA
- fur trading
- explorations

FRENCH-BRITISH RIVALRY
- wars in North America
- Indian allies on both sides

FRENCH AND INDIAN WAR
- British capture Quebec
- France gives up lands in North America

Places to Locate

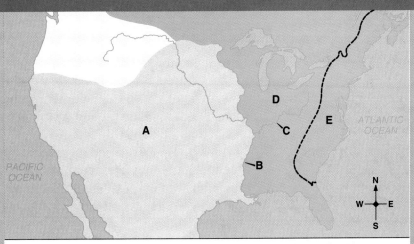

Match the letters on the map with the places that are listed below. Then explain the importance of each place.

1. Spanish land claims (1763)
2. British land claims (1763)
3. Ohio River
4. Thirteen British colonies
5. Mississippi River

Geographic Theme: Location What body of water connected the French settlements of Montreal and Quebec?

Skill Review

Read and take notes on the following paragraph. Then, using your notes, answer the questions that follow.

> The fate of the Ohio Valley was to be settled by the fate of Canada. The crucial year was 1759. That summer the British, under James Wolfe, sailed up the St. Lawrence to attack the French stronghold of Quebec. Quebec was the head and heart of New France. Wolfe knew if he could conquer Quebec, New France would collapse. It would not be an easy task. Quebec sat high on cliffs above the St. Lawrence. Strong walls and many cannons protected it.

1. What should you have written at the top of your notes? Which section is this paragraph taken from?
2. In what year did the British plan to attack Quebec? Who commanded British forces?
3. Why would attacking Quebec be difficult?

CRITICAL THINKING

1. Forming a Hypothesis If England and France had not been at war in North America, would relations between Indian nations have been different? Why or why not?

2. Making Judgments Imagine you are a citizen of Britain in 1757. Do you support William Pitt's war policy? Why or why not?

3. Drawing Conclusions It has been said that the French fur trade was one reason why France lost its North American territory. Explain why this may have been so.

PORTFOLIO OPTIONS

1. Civics Connection What was the objection of the thirteen colonies to the Albany Plan of Union? Discuss your answer with the class.

2. Writing Connection Research and write a report about one of the following topics: the League of the Iroquois, the French fur trade with the Indians, Braddock's defeat, the early history of New Orleans.

3. Contemporary Connection European powers once struggled for control of the Mississippi River, a vital water highway in the North American heartland. Write a report on the importance and impact of the Mississippi River in the United States today.

4. Timeline Connection Copy the chapter timeline. Add two events from the chapter that you think should be included and explain why.

THE INTERESTING NARRATIVE OF THE LIFE OF OLAUDAH EQUIANO

OLAUDAH EQUIANO

Olaudah Equiano, taken from his home in present-day Nigeria and sold into slavery in the mid-1750s, was later able to buy his freedom. He wrote a book in which he told of the horrors of the journey to America.

I loved my family, I loved my village, and I especially loved my mother because I was the youngest son and I was her favorite. She made great efforts to develop my mind. She trained me from my earliest years to be skilled in agriculture and war. She rewarded me whenever I did well on the lessons she gave me. I was very happy. But my happiness ended suddenly when I was eleven [and was captured by enemies and sold into slavery].

The first object which saluted my eyes when I arrived on the coast was the sea, and a slave ship, which was then riding at anchor and waiting for its cargo. The sight filled me with astonishment, then with a feeling of terror which I am still not able to describe.

I was soon put down under the decks, and then I received a salutation in the nostrils as I had never experienced in my life; so that with the loathsomeness of the stench, and crying, I became so sick and low that I was not able to eat. I now wished for the last friend, death, to relieve me. But soon, to my grief, two of the white men offered me eatables. On my refusing to eat, one of them held me fast by the hands and laid me across, I think, the windlass, and tied my feet, while the other flogged me severely. I had never experienced anything of this kind before, and, although not being used to the water, I naturally feared that element the first time I saw it; nevertheless, could I have got over the nettings, I would have jumped over the side. But I could not. Besides, the crew used to watch very closely those of us who were not chained down to the decks, lest we should leap into the water. I have seen some of these poor African prisoners most severely cut for attempting to do so and hourly whipped for not eating.

At last, when the ship we were in had got in all its cargo, they made ready with many fearful noises. We were all put under deck, so that we could not see how they managed the vessel. But this disappointment was the least of my sorrow. The closeness of the place and the heat of the climate, added to the

Packed tightly together, many Africans died on the slave ships.

number of people in the ship, which was so crowded that each had scarcely room to turn himself, almost suffocated all of us. This . . . brought on sickness amongst the slaves, of which many died. This wretched situation was aggravated by the rubbing of chains, and shrieks of the women, and the groans of the dying, all of which rendered the whole a scene of horror almost inconceivable. Often did I think many of the inhabitants of the deep much more happy than myself. . . .

At last, we came in sight of the island of Barbados, at which the whites on board gave a great shout and made many signs of joy to us. . . . As the vessel drew nearer, we plainly saw the harbor and other ships of different kinds and sizes; and we soon anchored amongst them off Bridge-Town. Many merchants and planters now came on board, though it was in the evening. They put us in separate parcels and examined us. . . . And, when soon after we were all put down under the deck again, there was so much dread and trembling among us . . . that at last the white people got some old slaves from the land to pacify us. They told us we were not to be eaten, but to work, and were soon to go on land, where we should see many of our countrypeople.

This report eased us much; and sure enough, soon after we landed there came to us Africans of all languages.

We were not many days in the merchant's custody before we were sold after their usual manner, which is this:—On a signal given (as the beat of a drum) the buyers rush at once into the yard where the slaves are confined, and make choice of that parcel they like best. The noise and clamor and the eagerness of the buyers serve not a little to increase the apprehension of the terrified Africans. In this manner . . . are relations and friends separated, most of them never to see each other again.

Adapted from *The Interesting Narrative of the Life of Olaudah Equiano, or Gustavus Vassa, the African* by Olaudah Equiano (W. Durrell, 1791).

Analyzing Literature

1. What kind of impression did the sight of the slave ship make on Equiano?

2. Describe the conditions on the slave ship.

3. Why might some people prefer death to slavery?

A New Nation (1763–1791)

UNIT OVERVIEW

In 1776 the American colonies formally broke with Britain. Several years after winning its war of independence, the United States established a new government under the Constitution.

Chapter 9

The Thirteen Colonies Rebel (1763–1776)
Angered by British efforts to tighten control over the colonies, Americans took up arms and declared independence.

Chapter 10

Americans Win Independence (1776–1787)
Americans defeated the British and set up a national government under the Articles of Confederation.

Chapter 11

Creating the Constitution (1786–1791)
Delegates from the states met in Philadelphia in the 1780s to create a stronger plan of government, which was approved by the states.

Illustration: Soldiers of the Continental Army, 1776.

By 1775 American colonists were fighting for the cause of independence. John Trumbull, who witnessed the Battle of Bunker Hill, painted this scene of the battle.

1761

1763 Proclamation of 1763

1764

1765 Stamp Act passed

1767

1767 Townshend Acts passed

The Thirteen Colonies Rebel (1763–1776)

1 Tighter British Control

SECTION GUIDE

Main Idea

Colonists resented new laws and taxes passed by the British after the French and Indian War and protested against them.

Goals

As you read, look for answers to these questions:

1. Why did Great Britain take measures to increase its control over the American colonies?

2. Why did the colonists object to British efforts to tax them?

Key Terms

alliance
Proclamation of 1763
revenue
Stamp Act
boycott
Sons of Liberty

BRITISH SOLDIERS and American colonists fought side by side against the French. When allies no longer have a common cause, however, their friendship often crumbles. The alliance between Britain and its American colonies is a case in point. (An alliance is an agreement to act together in a cause.) Once the French had been defeated, old problems resurfaced and new ones arose.

Halting Westward Movement

Pontiac's uprising in 1763 brought groans in London. British leaders wanted no more war. How, they asked, could they keep peace in the American colonies? They found the answer in the Proclamation of 1763. This law said colonists could not settle west of the Appalachian Mountains. That land would remain Indian.

Colonists felt cheated when they heard about the Proclamation of 1763. Owning land meant everything to a colonist. Those without land had no position in society. They could not even vote. The huge region west of the Appalachians was the land of opportunity, not only for people with no land but also for the young, the restless, and for those whose land was wearing out. They were angry that their own government would stop them from moving west. Many colonists ignored

1770	1773	1776
	1773 Boston Tea Party	1776 Declaration of Independence adopted
1770 Boston Massacre	1774 Intolerable Acts passed	1775 Battles of Lexington and Concord
	1774 First Continental Congress	1775 Second Continental Congress

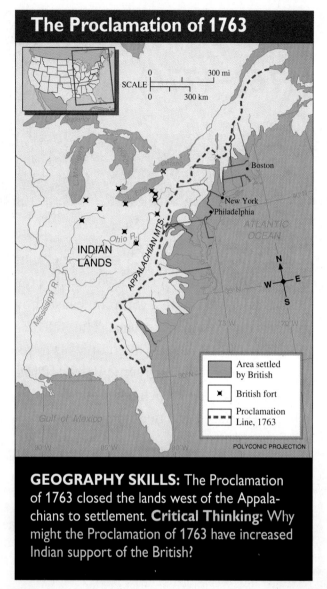

The Proclamation of 1763

SCALE

0 — 300 mi
0 — 300 km

Boston
New York
Philadelphia
ATLANTIC OCEAN

Ohio R.
INDIAN LANDS
APPALACHIAN MTS.
Mississippi R.

Gulf of Mexico

N E S W

Area settled by British

British fort

Proclamation Line, 1763

POLYCONIC PROJECTION

GEOGRAPHY SKILLS: The Proclamation of 1763 closed the lands west of the Appalachians to settlement. **Critical Thinking:** Why might the Proclamation of 1763 have increased Indian support of the British?

A British-issued stamp.

the order. They began to settle in the Ohio Valley.

To enforce the Proclamation of 1763, King George III decided to leave 10,000 British soldiers in the colonies. The Quartering Act was passed by Parliament in 1765. It required the colonies to quarter (provide housing and supplies for) the soldiers.

The general in charge of these soldiers was Thomas Gage. Gage decided to concentrate the British soldiers in New York. From there they could be sent to "hot spots" along the frontier.

Taxing the Colonies

Britain's war with France had caused Britain to go deeply into debt. British taxpayers had to repay that debt. Keeping an army on the American frontier would be an added expense for Britain. To meet the cost of its empire, Britain needed more revenue—income.

It seemed only logical to the British that the colonists should handle more of the empire's costs. Therefore, Parliament passed laws forcing the colonies to pay more for imported goods such as sugar and coffee. The extra money went to Britain. Also, British warships began to enforce the Navigation Acts by cracking down on smuggling.

The Stamp Act

In 1765 Parliament passed the Stamp Act and the colonists rioted. The Stamp Act was the first attempt of Britain to tax the colonists directly. The law required that each sheet of every legal document carry a stamp showing that a tax had been paid. Every copy of a newspaper, a diploma, a will, every advertisement, even playing cards were taxed. People had to use paper already marked with a stamp. This meant that they had to go to a special stamp-tax office to buy the stamped paper. Furthermore, the tax was to be paid in silver coins—a scarce item in the colonies. Those caught disobeying the law were to be tried in courts in which there was no trial by jury.

The colonists reacted with rage. For them the issue was clear. The American colonies had no representatives in Parliament, and Parliament therefore could not tax them. If Parliament could pass a stamp tax without the colonists' consent, what else might it tax in the future? "Why not our lands?" demanded Samuel Adams of Boston. "Why not the produce of our lands and everything we possess and make use of?"

176

Colonists in New York tear down a statue of King George III. Some 4,000 pounds of lead from the statue was later melted down and used for musket balls.

Protesting the Stamp Act

"No taxation without representation" became the protesters' rallying cry. In October 1765, nine colonies sent delegates to the Stamp Act Congress in New York City. There the delegates drew up a petition protesting the Stamp Act. The petition declared that the right to tax the colonists belonged to the colonial assemblies, not to Parliament. Later, colonial merchants organized a boycott of British goods. (To boycott is to refuse to buy.)

Meanwhile, some men and women in the American colonies formed secret societies. They called themselves the Sons of Liberty and the Daughters of Liberty. Most Sons of Liberty were lawyers, merchants, and artisans—the ones who were most affected by the Stamp Act. These groups staged protests against the Stamp Act. Not all their protests were peaceful. The Sons of Liberty burned the stamped paper wherever they could find it. They tarred and feathered customs officials. Many customs officials quit their jobs for fear of further attacks by the angry colonists.

The roar of protest, both from colonists and English merchants hurt by the boycott, had an impact. Parliament cancelled the Stamp Act in 1766. Yet Parliament was not about to give in to the colonists. It passed the Declaratory Act. This law declared Parliament's right to rule and tax the colonies "in all cases whatsoever." A great tug-of-war between Parliament and the colonies had begun. The central issue in this struggle was the authority of Parliament over the colonies.

A 1766 teapot celebrates the Stamp Act's repeal.

SECTION REVIEW

1. Key Terms alliance, Proclamation of 1763, revenue, Stamp Act, boycott, Sons of Liberty

2. People and Places George III, Appalachian Mountains, New York

3. Comprehension Why did colonists protest the Proclamation of 1763?

4. Comprehension How did colonists fight the Stamp Act?

5. Critical Thinking Was Britain justified in thinking that the colonies should pay for part of their own defense? Why or why not?

2 Colonial Resistance Grows

SECTION GUIDE

Main Idea
Colonial leaders resisted Britain's efforts to tighten control over the colonies. They began to organize to oppose British policies.

Goals
As you read, look for answers to these questions:

❶ Why did colonists object to British taxation policies?

❷ How did colonists attempt to resist British policies?

Key Terms
Townshend Acts
writs of assistance
propaganda
Boston Massacre
Boston Tea Party

British troops in Boston in 1768 enforce the writs of assistance.

CRISPUS ATTUCKS, the son of an African father and a Natick Indian mother, was born into slavery in Framingham, Massachusetts, around 1723. Determined not to spend his life as a slave, Attucks ran away to sea. March 1770 found him in Boston, where the words "liberty" and "freedom" seemed on everyone's lips. As you will read, Attucks gave his life for those words.

The Townshend Acts

First, however, let us turn back three years, to 1767. Parliament wanted no more trouble like that caused by the Stamp Act. On the other hand, it still badly needed new revenues to pay for the troops in America. Not even the Quartering Act was working. Most of the British army was in New York, and New York saw that as an unfair burden. New York's assembly refused to pay to house additional troops.

The king's finance minister, Charles Townshend (TOWN-zuhnd), was no friend of the colonists. He told Parliament that he had found a way to tax the colonies "without offense." In 1767 Parliament passed his plan. It was known as the Townshend Acts.

The first of the Townshend Acts suspended New York's assembly. Lawmakers were forbidden to do any business until they met the demands of General Gage to house his troops.

The Townshend Acts placed duties (taxes) on glass, paper, paint, lead, and tea brought into the colonies. The colonists had to pay these duties in gold or silver. The money would pay for the salaries of governors and other British officers. British officials would use writs of assistance to enforce the acts and to stop smuggling. A writ of assistance was a legal paper that gave officers the right to search any building for any reason.

Reasons for Protests

Protests immediately broke out at news of the Townshend Acts. New Yorkers were upset that their elected assembly had been suspended. Would this be a new pattern in dealing with the colonies? they wondered. Were their liberties at risk?

Colonists also realized that the new duties were just an excuse to raise revenue. True, the duties were not a direct tax, but did that matter? The issue, wrote John Dickinson of Pennsylvania, was "whether Parliament can legally take money out of our pockets without our consent."

The writs of assistance particularly upset anyone who believed in the traditional rights of Englishmen. Even earlier, in 1761, a group of Boston merchants went to court to challenge the legality of writs of assistance. The government had argued that collecting public taxes—and catching smugglers—were more important than the rights of one individual. Not so, colonist James Otis had argued. The writs of assistance, he said, were against the common law and against the law of nature.

Everyone knew what Otis meant by the law of nature. It was an idea best expressed by the English philosopher John Locke in the 1600s. The law of nature, said Locke, "teaches all mankind . . . that, being all equal and independent, no one ought to harm another in his life, health, liberty, or possessions." Locke's law of nature was probably influenced by reports of American Indian ideas of government, since he mentioned Indian groups in his works.

Tools of Protest

In summary, the Townshend Acts offended the colonists by challenging some of their basic notions of liberty. A Boston town meeting voted another boycott of British goods. The driving force behind this vote was Samuel Adams. A leader of the Sons of Liberty, he continued to urge resistance to British controls.

The boycott spread throughout the colonies. The Sons of Liberty pressured shopkeepers not to sell imported goods. The Daughters of Liberty held spinning bees, at which they spun their own cloth and drank herbal tea. Such activities publicized the goal of wearing and using only

CONNECTING WITH WORLD EVENTS

THE GASPEE INCIDENT

In June 1772, citizens in London were in an uproar. They had just heard about the *Gaspee* incident. This time the American colonists had gone too far!

The British ship *Gaspee* had been patrolling the coast of Rhode Island. On June 9, the *Gaspee* ran aground.

That evening eight colonists sat in a Providence tavern and plotted to burn the ship. At around 10 P.M., the men, armed with guns and stones, quietly rowed out and boarded the *Gaspee*. They tied up the crew, put them to shore, and set the ship on fire.

Back in London, the outraged king ordered a secret commission to find and arrest those guilty. Most of the people of Providence knew who the guilty men were. Yet when the British commission arrived, no one would talk. There were no arrests, and the commission returned empty-handed.

American-made goods. Trade between Britain and the colonies dropped sharply.

Colonial leaders asked that there be no violence in the protests. Articles in the *Boston Gazette* called for "no mobs, no confusions, no tumults. . . . Constitutional methods are the best."

However, tempers were high. When customs officials tried to seize the merchant ship *Liberty,* a riot broke out. John Hancock, a wealthy merchant, owned the ship. On board lay casks of wine from Portugal. The cargo had been smuggled and was illegal under British law. Even so, when customs officers tried to seize the ship, rioters forced the officers to flee.

The Boston Massacre

Fearing for their lives after the riot, the officials called for British troops to keep order in Boston. One thousand British soldiers (known as redcoats for their bright scarlet jackets) arrived under the command of General Thomas Gage.

The arrival of the troops only made things worse. Since the redcoats were poorly paid, they hired themselves out as workers, usually at rates lower than those American workers received. Resentment against the redcoats grew. The redcoats and street youths often taunted each other. "Lobsters for sale!" the youths would holler. "Yankees!" the soldiers jeered. *Yankee* was meant to be a term of ridicule, but colonists soon took pride in the name.

Tensions finally exploded. A gang of youths and dockworkers started throwing snowballs in front of the Boston Customhouse. A squad of soldiers showed up. As the crowd grew, the soldiers became nervous. They started firing. When the smoke cleared, Crispus Attucks and four other men lay dead or mortally wounded.

The Sons of Liberty used the shooting as propaganda —information designed to influence people's thinking or behavior. They referred to the shooting as the Boston Massacre and claimed it showed the dangers of having British troops in colonial towns.

The soldiers were arrested for murder. Two lawyers, John Adams and Josiah Quincy, Jr., defended them. Adams and Quincy were criticized for doing this, but Adams said the law should be "deaf . . . to the clamors of the populace." Their defense was successful. Six of the soldiers were acquitted (cleared of wrongdoing). Two others had their thumbs branded as a penalty for the shootings.

The Tea Act

Little more than a month after the Boston Massacre, Parliament repealed the Townshend Acts. The colonial boycott had hurt British trade. Parliament kept only the tax on tea, to show that it still had the right to tax the colonists.

For most Americans, the crisis was over. In Boston, however, Samuel Adams was not content to let people forget the cause of liberty. In 1772 Adams organized a Committee of Correspondence to keep up communication among leaders in Massachusetts towns. The idea quickly spread. Soon committees in all the colonies were corresponding with each other.

Parliament then opened up old wounds when it passed the Tea Act of 1773. This act aimed to help the British East India Company by giving it total control over the American tea trade. The tea would arrive in the colonies in the trading company's own ships and be sold there by its own merchants. This tea would be even cheaper than smuggled tea. Colonists, however, would still have to pay a tax on tea.

Shippers and merchants were enraged about the new law. It hurt their business. Other colonists also hated the law. They asked: If Parliament had a monopoly on tea, what monopoly might it create next?

Images such as these by Paul Revere stirred public anger over the Boston Massacre. Below are the coffins of the five men who died as a result of the Boston Massacre. **Critical Thinking:** How is Revere's painting an example of propaganda?

The Boston Tea Party

Colonists organized against the Tea Act. In Charleston, colonists unloaded cargoes of tea and stored it in damp cellars so it would rot. In New York City and Philadelphia, ships carrying tea were turned away from the harbor. In Boston, the Sons of Liberty planned what came to be known as the Boston Tea Party. George Hewes, who took part, gave this account of what happened:

Colonists dumped chests of tea into Boston's harbor. Later, a young boy recovered this chest (below) from the water.

❝It was now evening, and I immediately dressed myself in the costume of an Indian, equipped with a small hatchet . . . and a club. . . . I [went] to . . . where the ships lay that contained the tea. . . . I fell in with many who were dressed, . . . as I was, and marched . . . to the place of our destination [and boarded the ships]. . . .

We then were ordered by our commander to open the hatches, and take out all the chests of tea and throw them overboard. . . .

In about three hours from the time we went on board, we had thus broken and thrown overboard every tea chest to be found in the ship, while those in the other ships were disposing of the tea in the same way, at the same time. ❞

On that night in December 1773, Hewes and others destroyed 342 chests of tea. Many colonists rejoiced when they heard about the Boston Tea Party. John Adams believed Britain would now see how strongly colonists opposed taxation without representation.

Other colonists doubted that destroying property was the best way to settle the debate over the right to tax. Benjamin Franklin even offered to pay for the tea. His only condition was that the British repeal the Tea Act. The British ignored him. Britain's heavy-handed response to the Boston Tea Party would feed the fires of rebellion in the thirteen colonies.

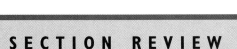

SECTION REVIEW

1. Key Terms Townshend Acts, writs of assistance, propaganda, Boston Massacre, Boston Tea Party

2. People Crispus Attucks, James Otis, John Locke, Samuel Adams

3. Comprehension Why, according to the colonists, did the Townshend Acts violate their liberties?

4. Comprehension How did colonists fight the Townshend Acts? The Tea Act?

5. Critical Thinking Why was it important for colonial leaders to unite the colonists against Britain?

Daily Life

IN BOSTON ON THE EVE OF REVOLUTION

"Passion governs, and she never governs wisely," Ben Franklin warned in 1775. Boston was in a tense, ugly mood. The Intolerable Acts had closed the port and forced people to house British soldiers. Patriots used the Acts to keep anti-British feelings high.

The closing of Boston's port hurt the free blacks, whites, and British soldiers who competed for jobs on the docks. The dockworker at right is carrying a tar brush.

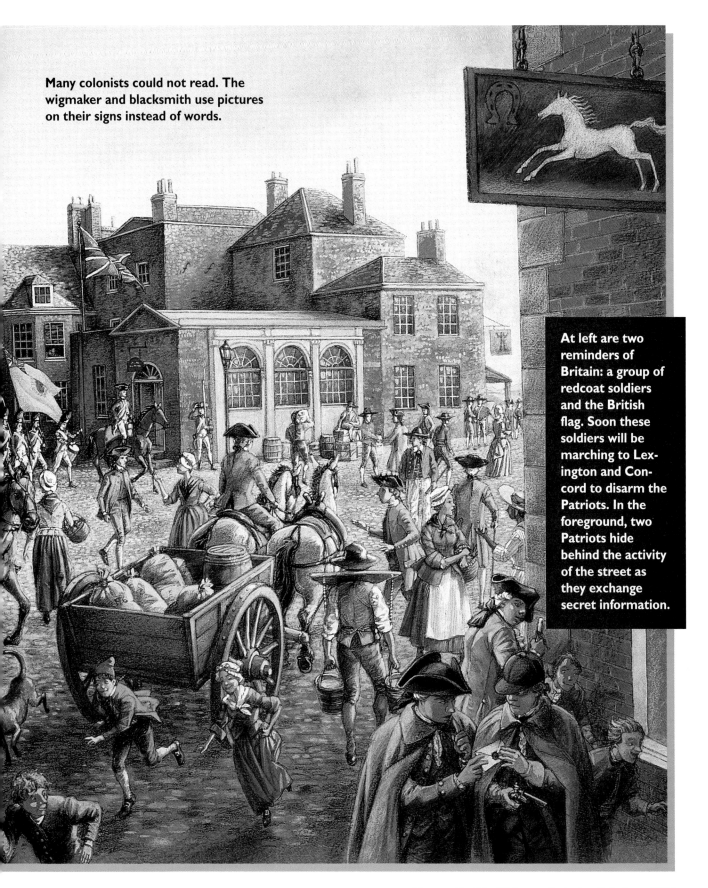

Many colonists could not read. The wigmaker and blacksmith use pictures on their signs instead of words.

At left are two reminders of Britain: a group of redcoat soldiers and the British flag. Soon these soldiers will be marching to Lexington and Concord to disarm the Patriots. In the foreground, two Patriots hide behind the activity of the street as they exchange secret information.

3 The Road to Lexington and Concord

SECTION GUIDE

Main Idea
Tensions between Britain and the colonies led to armed conflict in Massachusetts.

Goals
As you read, look for answers to these questions:

1 How did Britain respond to the colonists' refusal to obey British laws?

2 What events led up to the fighting at Lexington and Concord?

Key Terms
Intolerable Acts
First Continental Congress
militia
Minuteman
Loyalist
Patriot

WHEN KING GEORGE III heard of the Boston Tea Party, he was furious. As he saw it, there were two possible responses. "We must master them," he said of the colonists, "or totally leave them to themselves and treat them as aliens." Of course, leaving the colonists to themselves was never a serious choice. Britain had invested too much money in the colonies. There was also the matter of Britain's image. The world's most powerful nation simply did not let a group of colonists tell it what to do.

The Intolerable Acts

In 1774 King George took the first choice: mastering the colonies. To punish the colonists of Massachusetts, Parliament passed four harsh laws. The colonists found these laws so intolerable—unbearable—they called them the Intolerable Acts. The Intolerable Acts did the following:

(1) They closed the port of Boston to all ships until colonists paid for the destroyed tea.

(2) They greatly restricted representative government in Massachusetts. Town meetings could be held only with the governor's permission. Towns were forbidden to appoint Committees of Correspondence.

(3) They allowed British commanders to house troops wherever necessary.

(4) They allowed British officials accused of crimes to stand trial in Britain rather than in the colonies.

To enforce the Intolerable Acts, King George III named General Thomas Gage the governor of Massachusetts.

In 1773 Sam Adams had written, "I wish we could arouse the continent." The Intolerable Acts of 1774 answered his wish. Other colonies sent food and money to Boston. The Virginia assembly declared the day of the port closing to be a day of fasting and prayer. The Committees of Correspondence called for delegates from all the colonies to meet in Philadelphia.

The TIMES are
Dreadful,
Dismal
Doleful
Dolorous, and
DOLLAR-LESS.

A colonial newspaper (left) comments on tensions in the colonies. In a 1774 cartoon (right), colonists force a tarred-and-feathered British tax collector to drink tea.

The Continental Congress

Delegates from all colonies but Georgia met the call. In September and October of 1774, delegates from the Committees of Correspondence gathered in Philadelphia. The First Continental Congress, as it was called, voted a ban on all trade with Britain until the Intolerable Acts were repealed. The Congress also called on each colony to begin training soldiers.

The meeting of the First Continental Congress marked an important step in American history. At the time, most delegates did not want independence from Britain. They did, however, take their rights as British subjects seriously. Their gathering broke British law and carried the risk of further punishment It also planted the seed of a future independent government.

Before they broke up, the delegates agreed to meet again in seven months if conditions were not better. By the time the Second Continental Congress met, however, fighting with Britain had already begun.

Between War and Peace

Colonists expected that the ban on trade with Britain would force Parliament to repeal the Intolerable Acts. After all, past boycotts had led to the repeal of the Stamp Act and the Townshend Acts. This time, however, Parliament stood firm. It defeated a bill that would have repealed the Intolerable Acts. In fact, it added new limits on colonial trade and sent more troops to the colonies.

By the end of 1774, some colonists began preparing to fight. In Massachusetts, John Hancock headed a Committee of Safety with the power to call out the militia. (A militia is an army of ordinary citizens rather than professional soldiers.) Because the colonial militias needed to be ready to fight on a minute's notice, they were called the Minutemen.

The drums of war were beginning to beat. Most colonial leaders thought that any fight with Britain would be short. They believed a show of force by the colonists would once and for all make the British repeal the Intolerable Acts. Then the

Conflict Widens Between Britain and America

Date	Actions of the British Parliament	Reactions of the Colonists
1763	Issues Proclamation of 1763 to close frontier	Resent Proclamation
1765	Passes Stamp Act to pay for British troops in colonies	Boycott British goods; pass Stamp Act Resolves
1766	Repeals Stamp Act; passes Declaratory Act to assert its authority	End boycott
1767	Passes Townshend Acts to raise more money from colonial imports	Organize new boycotts; clash with British troops in Boston Massacre (1770)
1773	Passes Tea Act, giving East India Company a monopoly on tea trade	Protest Tea Act by boycotting British tea and staging Boston Tea Party
1774	Passes "Intolerable Acts" to tighten British control over Massachusetts	Establish First Continental Congress; boycott British goods
1775	Orders troops to Lexington and Concord, Massachusetts	Battle British troops; establish Second Continental Congress and Continental Army

Source: *Am. Heritage Book of the Revolution*

CHART SKILLS: Colonists' resentment of British rule began long before the outbreak of fighting. **Critical Thinking:** How might the Intolerable Acts be seen as a response rather than a cause?

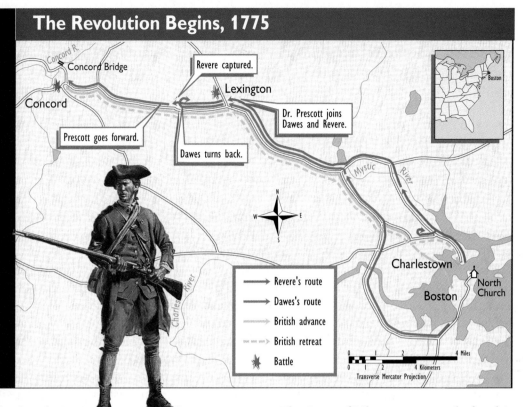

Map labels: Concord R. · Concord Bridge · Revere captured. · Lexington · Concord · Dr. Prescott joins Dawes and Revere. · Prescott goes forward. · Dawes turns back. · Mystic River · Charles River · Charlestown · Boston · North Church · Boston (inset)

Legend:
Revere's route
Dawes's route
British advance
British retreat
Battle

0 1 2 4 Miles
0 1 2 4 Kilometers
Transverse Mercator Projection

colonists would go back to being loyal British subjects. Few expected a war of independence. One who did, however, was Patrick Henry. He urged his fellow Virginians to call up a militia. In March 1775 Henry delivered his most famous speech:

> **"Gentlemen may cry, peace, peace but there is no peace. The war is actually begun! The next gale that sweeps from the north will bring to our ears the clash of resounding arms! Our brethren are already in the field! Why stand we here idle? . . . I know not what course others may take; but as for me, give me liberty or give me death!"**

Paul Revere's Ride

Spies were busy that spring of 1775. Samuel Adams had organized a spy network that used teams of men moving every hour throughout Boston to spot unusual British activity. The spy network included servants and barmaids—anyone who might have contact with the British.

General Gage learned from his own spies that the Minutemen were storing guns and ammunition in Concord. Concord was eighteen miles northwest of Boston. On the night of April 18, Gage ordered his troops to Concord to destroy the supplies.

The Sons of Liberty were ready for this move. Paul Revere, the "messenger of the Revolution," had already prepared to spread the word to the countryside. Revere arranged to have a horse waiting for him across the water from Boston at Charlestown. In case he was captured, he also arranged for signals to the opposite shore. If the British were leaving Boston by water, two lanterns would shine in the North Church steeple. If they were going by land, one lantern would shine.

Thus when the British started to move, so did the Bostonians. Two lanterns were lit in the North Church steeple. Revere was then rowed across the water to Charlestown. From there he took off at a gallop to rouse the countryside. Another messenger, William Dawes, set off for Lexington by land. (To trace their routes, see the map above.) They raced through the darkened countryside, pounding on doors, shouting the alarm.

In Lexington, Revere and Dawes warned Sam Adams and John Hancock. Hancock

At Lexington, British soldiers and the Minutemen engaged in the first military encounter of the Revolutionary War.

wanted to fight, but Adams persuaded him to head for safer quarters.

From Lexington, Revere and Dawes set off for Concord. Along the way they joined up with a doctor named Samuel Prescott. The three ran into a British patrol and split up. Prescott jumped his horse over a stone fence and carried the alarm to Concord. Dawes got away on foot. Revere was captured but let go without his horse. Revere's midnight ride thus ended with a walk along a moonlit country lane.

Lexington and Concord

At dawn, British troops reached Lexington and found the Minutemen ready to make a stand. British officers ordered the colonists to lay down their arms. The Minutemen would not. No one knows who fired the first shot, but within a few minutes eight colonists lay dead. The British then marched on Concord. They burned the courthouse and destroyed some of the militia's supplies. At the Old North Bridge over the Concord River, however, Minutemen forced the British to retreat.

Nearly 4,000 Minutemen had answered the alarm. They lined the road from Concord back to Lexington. From behind walls and trees, they peppered the British soldiers with musket fire.

The British soldiers were saved by the arrival of reserve troops from Boston. The British retreated to Boston, with Minutemen pressuring them the whole way.

The Revolutionary War began that day, April 19, 1775. For Americans the outbreak of war meant choosing sides. Those Americans who feared revolution and who supported the British were called Tories or Loyalists. Those who sided with the Minutemen were Patriots.

4 Declaring Independence

SECTION GUIDE

Main Idea

Fighting between Britain and colonial militias led colonists to form an army and declare their independence.

Goals

As you read, look for answers to these questions:

1. What decisions did colonial leaders make at the Second Continental Congress?

2. What were the arguments for and against American independence?

3. What ideas and beliefs were contained in the Declaration of Independence?

Key Terms
artillery
Second Continental Congress
Declaration of Independence

Ethan Allen lent Benedict Arnold his rifle *Blunderbuss* for the attack on Fort Ticonderoga in May 1775.

ON A SIMPLE STONE monument by a stream in Concord, Massachusetts, these words appear:

> **By the rude bridge that arched the flood,**
> **Their flag to April's breeze unfurled,**
> **Here once the embattled farmers stood**
> **And fired the shot heard round the world. . . .**
>
> **Spirit, that made those heroes dare**
> **To die, and leave their children free,**
> **Bid Time and Nature gently spare**
> **The shaft we raise to them and thee.**

Written by Ralph Waldo Emerson over 150 years ago, this poem describes the battle in 1775 that began the American Revolution.

The Continental Army

After the battles of Lexington and Concord in April 1775, thousands of militiamen began gathering at Patriot headquarters near Boston. Militias from other colonies prepared to join them. General Gage decided to remove his soldiers from the peninsula opposite Boston into the city itself. Because Boston was nearly surrounded by water, a land attack against the city was almost impossible.

That same spring of 1775, a band of rowdy backwoodsmen stormed Britain's Fort Ticonderoga on Lake Champlain. These were the Green Mountain Boys. Their leaders were Benedict Arnold and Ethan Allen.

The Green Mountain Boys seized Ticonderoga. Within its walls lay a valuable store of artillery —cannons and large guns. That artillery would drive the British from Boston.

In May 1775 the Second Continental Congress met in Philadelphia. The delegation from Massachusetts included John Adams, Samuel Adams, and John Hancock. Benjamin Franklin was part of the Pennsylvania delegation. From Virginia came George Washington, Richard Henry Lee, and Patrick Henry.

Henry and the two Adamses believed that the duty of Congress was to prepare for war. Other delegates hesitated. They favored peace talks, not war. Many delegates felt unsure about

Ethan Allen's action. They talked of giving Ticonderoga back to the British. "We find a great many bundles of weak nerves," John Adams wrote.

John Adams thought the troops gathering in Massachusetts needed experienced leadership. He persuaded his fellow delegates to set up a Continental Army and to name George Washington its leader. He pointed to Washington's experience fighting for the British during the French and Indian War. Washington had studied Indian war tactics that had worked against the redcoats. Washington was also wealthy. He had married the widow Martha Custis, one of the richest women in America. Southerners in particular considered wealth a requirement for leadership.

Not all New Englanders agreed with Adams. They doubted their militias would obey a southerner. After some debate, however, the Congress gave George Washington the job.

The Battle of Bunker Hill

In June 1775 Washington and his officers left on horseback for Massachusetts. They had gone less than twenty miles when a messenger galloped up with news. The Battle of Bunker Hill had just been fought.

This is what happened. Patriot troops moved to occupy the peninsula near Boston recently left by the British. On it were two hills, Breeds Hill and Bunker Hill. Overnight, the Patriots turned the peninsula into an armed camp. Stunned, the British hurried to retake it.

British General William Howe, with 2,200 men, crossed by boat to the beaches below Breeds Hill. There the redcoats formed assault lines, guns at the ready. Drums beat. Up the hill they marched. Tense, the Patriots waited. The redcoats were only fifteen paces away when the Patriots began firing.

Twice the British stormed the hill. Twice they were turned back. Then American gunpowder ran out. The British took the hill. Nevertheless, Patriots viewed the Battle of Bunker Hill as a victory. Over 1,000 redcoats had been killed or wounded. There were 400 Patriot casualties. The colonial militia had held its own against the world's most powerful army.

Although the British won the Battle of Bunker Hill, the Patriots fought so well that one British general described his casualties as "greater than we can bear." **Critical Thinking:** Why might an uphill assault result in high casualties?

ABIGAIL ADAMS
(1744–1818)

Separated for long periods by the demands of his political career, John and Abigail Adams stayed close through the mail. Abigail filled her letters to him with news from the family farm, which she ran while he was away. She told of the war's effects on Massachusetts. She also gave advice on a number of topics such as women's rights. "Remember all men would be tyrants if they could," she warned her husband. Abigail urged John to include rights for women in the Declaration of Independence. The idea was so far ahead of its time that he thought she was joking.

Petition and Response

In spite of the bloody battles at Lexington, Concord, and Bunker Hill, most colonists still hoped for peace. They believed that George III deserved their loyalty. They trusted that, like a good father, he would step in and settle the dispute.

Thus in July 1775 Congress sent off to London the Olive Branch Petition. (The olive branch is a symbol of peace.) In this letter Congress blamed Parliament for the war. They begged the king to stop the war and bring about "a happy and permanent reconciliation." John Adams was disgusted, but he signed the petition. What good, he thought, could it do?

No good at all, as it turned out. The king refused the petition and called the colonists rebels. He said he would blockade American shipping and send 10,000 hired German soldiers called Hessians to fight in America. "When once these rebels have felt a smart blow, they will submit," he declared.

The British Leave Boston

In Massachusetts, George Washington faced the task of forming an army without enough money, supplies, or weapons. There was so little ammunition that when the British fired a cannon ball, the Patriots ran after it, shoved it into one of their cannons, and fired it back.

Help was on the way, however. Patriots were hauling artillery from Fort Ticonderoga. This was a rough job, since there were no roads across the mountainous land. It took about 2 months to drag 59 cannons over the mountains to Boston.

With cannons available at last, Washington moved his army to Dorchester Heights overlooking Boston. The Patriots began bombarding the city. General Howe, who was now in charge of the British forces, decided he had to get out.

In March 1776 Abigail Adams, the wife of John Adams, watched the British go— 170 ships carrying 9,000 soldiers. With them went about 1,000 American Loyalists. Anti-British feeling in Boston was so strong that the Loyalists had feared for their safety. Among these Loyalists were some of Abigail Adams's closest friends.

Push for Independence

Most Americans still wanted to avoid a final break with Britain. Abigail Adams expressed some of their fears. "If we separate from Britain," she wrote, "what code of laws will be established? How shall we be governed so as to retain our liberties? . . . Who shall frame these laws? Who will give them force and energy?"

SKILLS: Primary and Secondary Sources

LEARN

What is the difference between an article about the Battle of Bunker Hill in a colonial newspaper and the discussion of the Battle of Bunker Hill in your textbook? The article is a primary source, and the textbook discussion is a secondary source. **Primary sources** are materials written or made at the time they describe. **Secondary sources** are descriptions or interpretations of the past, made by people not directly involved in the events described.

   Historians rely on both primary and secondary sources for information. A primary source can provide complete details of an event. It can also reflect the emotions and the atmosphere surrounding an event. A secondary source, written later, can be more objective. Both sources, however, can contain errors. The best policy is to check several different sources.

Braintree
[Massachusetts]
14 September, 1774

   About eight o'clock Sunday evening there passed by here about two hundred men, preceded by a horsecart, and marched down to the powder-house, from whence they took the [gun]powder, and carried it into the other parish and there [hid] it. . . . The reason they gave for taking it was that we had so many Tories [Loyalists] here, they dared not trust us with it. . . . This town appears as [excited] as you can well imagine, and, if necessary, would soon be in arms. Not a Tory but hides his head. The church parson [a Tory] ran up [to his attic]; they say another jumped out of his window and hid among the corn, whilst a third crept under his board fence.

PRACTICE

Read the excerpt at the right. It is a letter from Abigail Adams to her husband John, a Patriot leader. Then read the text section, "The British Leave Boston."

1. Which is the primary source? Explain.

2. What do you learn about Abigail Adams's relationship with the Loyalists in the text section that you do not learn from the letter?

3. Which source tells more of the emotions of the time? Explain.

APPLY

4. Read the Declaration of Independence at the end of this chapter. Write a paragraph describing what the Declaration meant to Americans in 1776. Then imagine it is 1776, and you are reading the Declaration for the first time. Describe who you are and where you live. Write a paragraph telling what the Declaration means to you.

In January 1776 a 46-page pamphlet jolted Americans out of their uncertainty. The pamphlet was *Common Sense*. Its author was Thomas Paine, a recent immigrant from Britain. Paine did what no one else had been able to do. He made a bold call for independence from Britain.

Many people of the time still believed that kings ruled by the will of God. Paine ridiculed this idea. He called George III "the Royal Brute." All monarchies, he argued, were in fact corrupt. Paine also disagreed with the economic arguments for remaining with Britain. "Our corn," he wrote, "will fetch its price in any country in Europe." America had its own destiny. "The blood of the slain, the weeping voice of nature cries, 'Tis time to part,' " he said.

Common Sense was an instant success. Never had a book sold so well in America. The call for independence became a roar.

A Time of Decision

In June 1776 Richard Henry Lee of Virginia presented the Continental Congress with several resolutions, or proposals to be voted on. Lee called for the colonies to do three things. (1) They should become independent states, (2) They should take steps to form their own foreign alliances, and (3) They should prepare a plan for joining together in a confederation.

Not all the delegates were ready to vote on Lee's resolutions. The Congress went ahead anyway and set up a committee to write a Declaration of Independence. It included Benjamin Franklin, John Adams, Roger Sherman, Robert Livingston, and Thomas Jefferson. At age 33, Jefferson was the youngest of the group and also the best writer. To him, therefore, went the task of writing the Declaration. At a portable desk of his own design, Jefferson

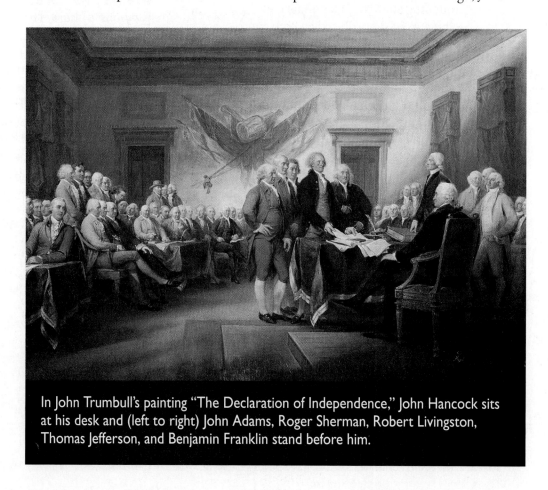

In John Trumbull's painting "The Declaration of Independence," John Hancock sits at his desk and (left to right) John Adams, Roger Sherman, Robert Livingston, Thomas Jefferson, and Benjamin Franklin stand before him.

went to work. In about two weeks, he had finished most of the Declaration.

On July 1, 1776, Congress began debating Lee's resolutions. Some delegates, including John Dickinson, were upset. How, he asked, could the states think of independence? It was "like destroying our house in winter . . . before we have got another shelter." When the vote was taken, however, the ayes had it. From then on, the colonies saw themselves as independent states.

The Declaration Is Adopted

On July 4, 1776, Congress adopted the Declaration of Independence. Its core idea was that people have rights that the government cannot take away. In what was to become the Declaration's best-known passage, Jefferson wrote:

> ❝ We hold these truths to be self-evident, that all men are created equal, that they are endowed by their Creator with certain unalienable Rights, that among these are Life, Liberty, and the pursuit of Happiness. ❞

If a government disregards these God-given rights, Jefferson explained, it loses its right to govern. The people then have the right to abolish that government, by force if necessary. They can form a new government that will protect their rights.

When Jefferson spoke of "the people," however, he meant only free white men. In Jefferson's time it was commonly believed that some people should rule and others should be ruled. Women were thought to be weaker and less intelligent than men. They had no place in politics.

Slaves made up about 20 percent of the population. Though a slaveowner himself, Jefferson had included a passage condemning the slave trade in the Declaration. Slaveowners complained about the passage. It was cut from the final document.

Declaring independence from Britain was not to be taken lightly. Therefore, in powerful language, Jefferson listed the reasons for the break with Britain.

In conclusion, the Declaration declared the colonies to be free and independent states. This was a very serious action—treason from the British point of view—and the delegates knew it. John Hancock warned the delegates that "there must be no pulling in separate ways; we must all hang together." "Yes," replied Benjamin Franklin, "we must all hang together, or . . . we shall all hang separately."

The Declaration closed with this pledge:

> ❝ And for the support of this Declaration, with a firm reliance on the protection of divine Providence, we mutually pledge to each other our Lives, our Fortunes and our sacred Honor. ❞

Americans had declared independence. Now they had to win it.

This etching, entitled "Warm'd by One Heart, United by One Band," celebrated the Declaration of Independence.

SECTION REVIEW

1. Key Terms artillery, Second Continental Congress, Declaration of Independence

2. People Ethan Allen, George Washington, Thomas Paine, Thomas Jefferson

3. Comprehension Why did some colonists question whether independence was a sensible policy?

4. Comprehension Summarize the message of *Common Sense*.

5. Critical Thinking Reread the passage from the Declaration beginning, "We hold these truths. . . ." Then restate the passage in your own words.

Summary

1. To pay its war debts and to maintain troops in the American colonies, Britain passed the Stamp Act of 1765. The Sons of Liberty organized protests and boycotts. Parliament repealed the Stamp Act.

2. The Townshend Acts brought more protests. Tensions between colonists and the British erupted in 1770 with the Boston Massacre. Parliament passed the Tea Act in 1773 to gain revenue. In protest, colonists in Boston dumped chests of tea into the harbor.

3. In response, Parliament passed the Intolerable Acts. The First Continental Congress organized a ban on trade with Britain. Colonial militias prepared to fight. When British troops marched on Lexington and Concord, they clashed with Patriot troops.

4. Although many colonists remained loyal to Britain, Patriot leaders declared America's independence and prepared to fight for it. The Second Continental Congress voted to form an army under George Washington. Though defeated in the Battle of Bunker Hill, Patriots killed and wounded over 1,000 British troops. Washington and his militia drove the British from Boston. The Congress issued the Declaration of Independence on July 4, 1776.

Review

KEY TERMS

Define the terms in each of the following groups.
1. revenue; Stamp Act
2. Townshend Acts; writs of assistance
3. Boston Massacre; Boston Tea Party
4. militia; Minuteman
5. Patriot; Loyalist

COMPREHENSION

1. Why did Britain pass the Proclamation of 1763? What objections did colonists raise to it?
2. Which method was most effective in combating the Stamp Act? Why?
3. What limits did the Townshend Acts place on the colonies?
4. What events led up to the Boston Massacre?
5. Why did Parliament pass the Tea Act of 1773? How did colonists react?
6. Describe the importance of the First Continental Congress.
7. Why did colonists think a ban on trade would force Parliament to repeal the Intolerable Acts?
8. For what reasons did some colonists oppose independence from Britain?
9. Why did the Patriots view the Battle of Bunker Hill as a victory?
10. How did the Declaration of Independence justify the decision to break with Britain?

Graphic Summary

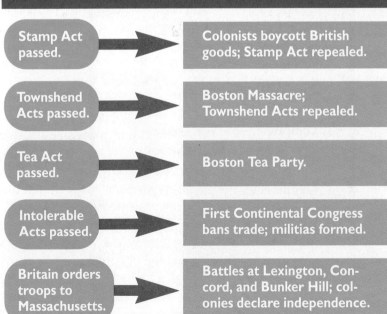

Stamp Act passed.	Colonists boycott British goods; Stamp Act repealed.
Townshend Acts passed.	Boston Massacre; Townshend Acts repealed.
Tea Act passed.	Boston Tea Party.
Intolerable Acts passed.	First Continental Congress bans trade; militias formed.
Britain orders troops to Massachusetts.	Battles at Lexington, Concord, and Bunker Hill; colonies declare independence.

Places to Locate

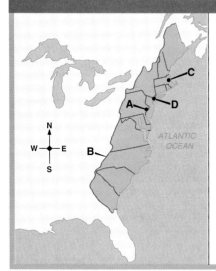

Match the letters on the map with the places listed below. Then explain the importance of each place.

1. New York City
2. Philadelphia
3. Proclamation Line of 1763
4. Boston

Geographic Theme:

Location What feature made Boston difficult to attack by land?

Skill Review

Read the excerpt below from a letter written in 1775 by an American woman. Then reread the subsection, "Tools of Protest," in Section 2, and answer the following questions.

> **"**My only brother I have sent to the camp with my prayers and blessings. . . . I have not drunk [tea] since last Christmas, nor bought a new cap or gown since your defeat at Lexington. . . . I know this, that as free I can die but once, but as a slave I shall not be worthy of life. . . . All my sister Americans . . . have sacrificed both assemblies, parties of pleasure, tea drinking, and finery to that great spirit of patriotism. . . .**"**

1. Which passage is the primary source? How do you know?
2. What do you learn about protests against the British in the text that is not in the letter?

3. Is the woman who wrote this letter a Patriot or a Loyalist? How can you tell?
4. Which source has more emotional appeal? Explain.

CRITICAL THINKING

1. Identifying Advantages and Disadvantages What were the advantages and disadvantages to the colonies of remaining in the British Empire?

2. Stating Both Sides of an Issue Write a paragraph in support of each of these statements: (a) Parliament had the right to govern the colonies in any way it pleased. (b) Parliament had no right to govern the colonies without colonial representation.

PORTFOLIO OPTIONS

1. Civics Connection Organize a class debate on the following question: Resolved, Britain could not have avoided the differences with its American colonies that led to the Declaration of Independence.

2. Writing Connection Write a newspaper account of the events at Lexington and Concord in April 1775 from the point of view of a Patriot. Try to persuade colonists to join the Patriot cause.

3. Contemporary Connection Read newspapers to learn about an independence movement taking place today. Write a report stating the reasons why the group wants independence and the difficulties the movement is facing.

4. Timeline Connection Copy the chapter timeline. Add other events from the chapter that you think should be included. Which event do you think had the greatest impact on the colonists? Why?

The Declaration of Independence

The first paragraph, known as the Preamble, explains why the American colonists thought it necessary to make a political break with Great Britain.

When in the Course of human events, it becomes necessary for one people to dissolve the political bands which have connected them with another, and to assume among the powers of the earth, the separate and equal station to which the Laws of Nature and of Nature's God entitle them, a decent respect to the opinions of mankind requires that they should declare the causes which impel them to the separation.*

[The Right of the People to Control Their Government]

This paragraph states that all people are born with certain God-given rights that are "unalienable." In other words, these rights cannot be given away or taken away by any government. Governments get their authority from the "consent" or approval of the people they govern. If a government lacks the consent of the people, then the people have a right to change or dissolve it. The people should, however, only resort to such change when the existing government has abused its powers.

endowed provided

We hold these truths to be self-evident, that all men are created equal, that they are endowed by their Creator with certain unalienable Rights, that among these are Life, Liberty and the pursuit of Happiness. That to secure these rights, Governments are instituted among Men, deriving their just powers from the consent of the governed, That whenever any Form of Government becomes destructive of these ends, it is the Right of the People to alter or to abolish it, and to institute new Government, laying its foundation on such principles and organizing its powers in such form, as to them shall seem most likely to effect their Safety and Happiness. Prudence, indeed, will dictate that Governments long established should not be changed for light and transient causes; and accordingly all experience hath shown, that mankind are more disposed to suffer, while evils are sufferable, than to right themselves by abolishing the forms to which they are accustomed. But when

*In punctuation and capitalization, the text of the Declaration follows accepted sources.

196

a long train of abuses and usurpations, pursuing invariably the same Object evinces a design to reduce them under absolute Despotism, it is their right, it is their duty, to throw off such Government, and to provide new Guards for their future security. Such has been the patient sufferance of these Colonies; and such is now the necessity which constrains them to alter their former Systems of Government. The history of the present King of Great Britain is a history of repeated injuries and usurpations, all having in direct object the establishment of an absolute Tyranny over these States. To prove this, let Facts be submitted to a candid world.

[Tyrannical Acts of the British King]

He has refused his Assent to Laws, the most wholesome and necessary for the public good.

He has forbidden his Governors to pass Laws of immediate and pressing importance, unless suspended in their operation till his Assent should be obtained; and when so suspended, he has utterly neglected to attend to them.

He has refused to pass other Laws for the accommodation of large districts of people, unless those people would relinquish the right of Representation in the Legislature, a right inestimable to them and formidable to tyrants only.

He has called together legislative bodies at places unusual, uncomfortable, and distant from the depository of their Public Records, for the sole purpose of fatiguing them into compliance with his measures.

He has dissolved Representative Houses repeatedly, for opposing with manly firmness his invasions on the rights of the people.

He has refused for a long time, after such dissolutions, to cause others to be elected; whereby the Legislative powers, incapable of Annihilation, have returned to the People at large for their exercise; the State remaining in the mean time exposed to all the dangers of invasion from without, and convulsions within.

He has endeavoured to prevent the population of these States; for that purpose obstructing the Laws for Naturalization of Foreigners; refusing to pass others to encourage their migrations hither; and raising the conditions of new Appropriations of Lands.

He has obstructed the Administration of Justice, by refusing his Assent to Laws for establishing Judiciary powers.

He has made Judges dependent on his Will alone, for the tenure of their offices, and the amount and payment of their salaries.

He has erected a multitude of New Offices, and sent hither swarms of Officers to harass our People, and eat out their substance.

He has kept among us, in times of peace, Standing Armies without the Consent of our legislatures.

He has affected to render the military independent of and superior to the Civil power.

He has combined with others to subject us to a jurisdiction

This section lists the colonial grievances against George III and his government. Each of these 27 British offenses occurred between 1763 and 1776. The language of this section is often very emotional. Words such as **despotism, annihilation, ravaged,** and **perfidy** express the seriousness of the King's offenses against the colonies. The list of grievances makes it clear that King George no longer has "the consent of the governed," and so should not continue to rule the colonies.

Arbitrary tyrannical
abdicated given up
ravaged destroyed
perfidy treachery
constrained forced
insurrections rebellions

foreign to our constitution, and unacknowledged by our laws; giving his Assent to their Acts of pretended Legislation:

For quartering large bodies of armed troops among us:

For protecting them, by a mock Trial, from Punishment for any Murders which they should commit on the Inhabitants of these States:

For cutting off our Trade with all parts of the world:

For imposing Taxes on us without our Consent:

For depriving us in many cases, of the benefits of Trial by Jury:

For transporting us beyond Seas to be tried for pretended offences:

For abolishing the free System of English Laws in a neighboring Province, establishing therein an Arbitrary government, and enlarging its Boundaries so as to render it at once an example and fit instrument for introducing the same absolute rule into these Colonies:

For taking away our Charters, abolishing our most valuable Laws, and altering fundamentally the Forms of our Governments:

For suspending our own Legislatures, and declaring themselves invested with power to legislate for us in all cases whatsoever.

He has abdicated Government here, by declaring us out of his Protection and waging War against us.

He has plundered our seas, ravaged our Coasts, burnt our towns, and destroyed the lives of our people.

He is at this time transporting large Armies of foreign Mercenaries to compleat the works of death, desolation and tyranny, already begun with circumstances of Cruelty and perfidy scarcely paralleled in the most barbarous ages, and totally unworthy the Head of a civilized nation.

He has constrained our fellow Citizens taken Captive on the high Seas to bear Arms against their Country, to become the executioners of their friends and Brethren, or to fall themselves by their Hands.

He has excited domestic insurrections amongst us, and has endeavoured to bring on the inhabitants of our frontiers, the merciless Indian Savages, whose known rule of warfare, is an undistinguished destruction of all ages, sexes and conditions.

[Efforts of the Colonies to Avoid Separation]

In every stage of these Oppressions We have Petitioned for Redress in the most humble terms: Our repeated Petitions have been answered only by repeated injury. A Prince, whose character is thus marked by every act which may define a Tyrant, is unfit to be the ruler of a free people.

Nor have we been wanting in attentions to our British brethren. We have warned them from time to time of attempts by their legislature to extend an unwarrantable jurisdiction over us. We have reminded them of the circumstances of our emigration and settlement here. We have appealed to their native justice and magnanimity, and we have conjured them by the ties of our common kindred to disavow these usurpa-

This section states that the colonists tried, without success, to settle their grievances with the king. George III ignored the colonists' repeated petitions for change. The British people, too, failed to listen to the colonists' pleas. The colonists must now look on them as enemies in war and friends in peace.

Oppressions unjust uses of power
Petitioned for Redress asked for the correction of wrongs
unwarrantable jurisdiction unjust control
magnanimity generous nature

tions, which, would inevitably interrupt our connections and correspondence. They too have been deaf to the voice of justice and of consanguinity. We must, therefore, acquiesce in the necessity, which denounces our Separation, and hold them, as we hold the rest of mankind, Enemies in War, in Peace Friends.

consanguinity blood relationship
acquiesce accept

[The Colonies are Declared Free and Independent]

We, therefore, the Representatives of the United States of America, in General Congress, Assembled, appealing to the Supreme Judge of the world for the rectitude of our intentions, do, in the Name, and by Authority of the good People of these Colonies, solemnly publish and declare, That these United Colonies are, and of Right ought to be Free and Independent States; that they are Absolved from all Allegiance to the British Crown, and that all political connection between them and the State of Great Britain, is and ought to be totally dissolved; and that as Free and Independent States, they have full Power to Levy War, conclude Peace, contract Alliances, establish Commerce, and to do all other Acts and Things which Independent States may of right do. And for the support of this Declaration, with a firm reliance on the protection of divine Providence, we mutually pledge to each other our Lives, our Fortunes and our sacred Honor.

The final paragraph states that the colonies are now free and independent states. All political ties between the United States of America and Great Britain are broken. The United States now has the power to declare war, make peace treaties, form political alliances, and establish trade. In the last sentence, the delegates (signers) pledge their support of the Declaration of Independence. They express their reliance on the protection of God.

rectitude honesty
Absolved freed
divine Providence God's guidance

Signers of the Declaration

NEW HAMPSHIRE
Josiah Bartlett
William Whipple
Matthew Thornton

MASSACHUSETTS
John Hancock
Samuel Adams
John Adams
Robert Treat Paine
Elbridge Gerry

RHODE ISLAND
Stephen Hopkins
William Ellery

CONNECTICUT
Roger Sherman
Samuel Huntington
William Williams
Oliver Wolcott

NEW YORK
William Floyd
Philip Livingston
Francis Lewis
Lewis Morris

NEW JERSEY
Richard Stockton
John Witherspoon
Francis Hopkinson
John Hart
Abraham Clark

PENNSYLVANIA
Robert Morris
Benjamin Rush
Benjamin Franklin
John Morton
George Clymer
James Smith
George Taylor
James Wilson
George Ross

DELAWARE
Caesar Rodney
George Read
Thomas McKean

MARYLAND
Samuel Chase
William Paca
Thomas Stone
Charles Carroll of Carrollton

VIRGINIA
George Wythe
Richard Henry Lee
Thomas Jefferson
Benjamin Harrison
Thomas Nelson, Jr.
Francis Lightfoot Lee
Carter Braxton

NORTH CAROLINA
William Hooper
Joseph Hewes
John Penn

SOUTH CAROLINA
Edward Rutledge
Thomas Heyward, Jr.
Thomas Lynch, Jr.
Arthur Middleton

GEORGIA
Button Gwinnett
Lyman Hall
George Walton

"The Spirit of '76" captures the proud determination of Patriot fighters: Troops march on as a fallen comrade salutes. The Patriots defeated a powerful British army and won America's independence.

1775

1777

1779

1781

1776 Battle of Trenton

1777 Battle of Princeton

1777 Battle of Saratoga

1778 France joins the war

1779 Spain joins the war

1780 British capture Charleston

1781 Articles of Confederation adopted

1781 Battle of Yorktown

Americans Win Independence (1776–1787)

1 Early Years of the War

SECTION GUIDE

Main Idea
During the Revolutionary War, inexperienced Patriot forces struggled with a lack of supplies and a divided society.

Goals
As you read, look for answers to these questions:

1. What difficulties did Washington face as head of the American army?

2. What were the major battles of the war in the North?

3. How did foreign nations affect the war?

Key Terms
enlist
mercenary
rendezvous
Battle of Saratoga

I N 1776 MERCY OTIS WARREN published *The Blockheads*, a play set in Boston during the British occupation. In the play a British officer, General Puff, complains, "We are shamefully confined within the bounds of three miles, wrangling and starving among ourselves."

The Country Divided

General Puff's complaint reflects the British situation throughout the Revolutionary War. The British were able to take and hold every city, except for Boston, that they wanted. They could do so because of their superior firepower, trained troops, and supply ships from Britain. However, British troops went into the countryside at their peril. As another character in Warren's play observed, "These Yankee dogs . . . divert themselves by firing at us, as at a flock of partridges. A man can scarcely put his nose over the entrenchments without losing it."

The Americans had problems of their own. Only a minority of Americans actively supported the Revolution. About two-fifths of them were Patriots. One-fifth were Loyalists, also called Tories. The rest did not take sides.

The American Revolution was thus a civil war that bitterly split families and neighbors. Patriots and Loyalists alike came from all walks of life and from all parts of America. In general, however, New England and Virginia had the greatest share of

1783	1785	1787
		1787 Northwest Ordinance
	1785 Ordinance of 1785	
1783 Treaty of Paris		

Patriots. Loyalists were most numerous in New York State. New York provided more troops for the British than for the Patriots.

Other Loyalist strongholds were found in the Carolinas and in cities near the Atlantic coast. Loyalists were often employees of the British government or clergy of the Church of England. Those who did not take sides included Quakers and the German population of Pennsylvania.

Most Indians living in the colonies sided with the British during the Revolution. They believed that if the Patriot forces won, they would be pushed off their land by land-hungry American settlers. Indeed, the Continental Congress had offered Indian land to men who enlisted —signed up—in the army.

Americans at War

George Washington had formed the Continental Army from the ranks of local militias. Throughout the war Washington struggled to hold his army together. The soldiers needed everything—blankets, shoes, soap, food, and even guns and ammunition. How, Washington worried, could a war be fought without guns—let alone wagons, horses, clothes, and tents?

Washington looked in vain to the Continental Congress, which had authorized the army. To raise funds, the Congress issued paper money. The British, however, were paying for goods in silver and gold. As the war dragged on, Continental paper money lost so much value that suppliers refused to accept it. The expression *not worth a Continental* came to mean "worthless."

Washington also had trouble getting men to enlist for long terms. Thus he often had to use inexperienced troops. On the other hand, the promise of land after the war lured many men to join the army. They also hoped to gain money and social standing by serving for a year or so.

George Washington's cooking supplies were carried in this mess kit.

Molly Pitcher, whose husband has fallen, takes his place at the cannon.

One group of Americans were eager to enlist for longer periods. These were free black men. At first Washington, a slaveholder himself, opposed enlistment by African Americans. He and others feared that arming African Americans could threaten the slave system. When the British governor of Virginia promised freedom to slaves who fought for the king, however, Washington announced that the Patriot forces would welcome free black soldiers. In all, about 5,000 African Americans served in the Continental Army.

The army relied on the efforts of Patriot women. Martha Washington was the most famous of those who joined their husbands in the army camps. Some women did so because they had no other way to survive. Women busied themselves with soldiers' washing, cooking, nursing, sewing, and mending. A few women even joined their men on the battlefield. Mary Hays was given the nickname "Molly Pitcher" for serving water from a nearby well to exhausted soldiers during one battle.

Women served in other ways as well. They gave up their pewter plate to be melted into musket balls. They spied. They forced merchants to set fair prices and not profit from the wartime shortage of goods.

New York City, 1776

The British had left Boston in March 1776. Washington guessed that they would reappear in New York City. Acting on this hunch, Washington hurried with his new army to New York City.

In July 1776 Britain's General William Howe finally made his move. He arrived from Nova Scotia with the largest seaborne army ever launched. It included 8,000 Hessian mercenaries —professional soldiers. There were so many ships that New York harbor looked like a forest of trees stripped of their bark.

All that summer the British and Americans struggled for New York in a "bloody game of cat-and-mouse." Washington lost the city but saved the army by retreating into New Jersey and then to Pennsylvania.

It was now winter—and a cold one. Howe ordered the Hessians to hold New Jersey. He and his army returned to New York. Howe hoped winter might destroy what was left of Washington's army.

New Jersey Victories

Howe's prediction nearly came true. Patriot spirits fell as low as the thermometer. Many volunteers went home. The army dwindled from 20,000 to a few thousand. To rekindle the patriotic fire, Thomas Paine wrote the first of a series of pamphlets called *The Crisis*. Paine declared:

> **❝These are the times that try men's souls: The summer soldier and the sunshine patriot will, in this crisis, shrink from the service of his country; but he that stands [by] it now, deserves the love and thanks of man and woman. ❞**

With the situation desperate, Washington was willing to gamble. "Victory or death" was the choice, he said. Late on December 25, 1776—Christmas Day—Patriot troops rowed across the icy Delaware River to the New Jersey shore.

"Washington Crossing the Delaware" is one of the most famous paintings in American history. **Critical Thinking:** Why was the Patriots' attack on Trenton so successful?

From there they marched in the bitter pre-dawn cold to catch the Hessians at Trenton sleeping off their Christmas celebration. The Patriots captured or killed over 1,000 Hessians. They also captured much-needed supplies, guns, and ammunition.

The Patriots won another victory at Princeton a week later. The New Jersey victories gave the Patriots new hope. The army attracted new recruits.

Philadelphia, 1777

The losses at Trenton and Princeton did not greatly discourage the British. The Patriot army still consisted of a mere 4,000 men. With winter's inactivity behind him, Howe set out in the summer of 1777 to take Philadelphia. His hope was that by seizing the American capital and its largest city he would destroy the Patriots' will to fight.

Howe easily captured the city in September. He failed, however, to stop the stubborn Patriot forces. The Continental Congress just picked up and moved to the town of York, located in the countryside.

British Strategy

Meanwhile the British were pursuing a grand strategy to seize the Hudson River valley. If successful, the British would isolate New England and divide the American colonies in two.

The British strategy called for three armies to meet at Albany, New York. General John Burgoyne would lead a force south from Canada. A second British force led by Barry St. Leger was supposed to move east from Lake Ontario down the Mohawk Valley. General Howe was supposed to head north up the Hudson from New York City.

According to plan, Burgoyne started south from Canada. His forces included German mercenaries as well as about 400 Indians. Nicknamed "Gentleman Johnny" by his soldiers, Burgoyne liked to travel slowly and throw lavish parties between battles. His slow pace gave the Patriots time to cut down trees to block his route. They also burned crops and drove off cattle, leaving the countryside bare of supplies for the advancing redcoats.

After capturing Fort Ticonderoga on Lake George, "Gentleman Johnny's" confidence grew. It was only twenty miles from Fort Ticonderoga to the Hudson River. On a map the march to the Hudson looked easy, but maps can be misleading.

The route Burgoyne chose was twenty miles of swampy wilderness. To cross it, the army had to build bridges and temporary roads for its wagons and cannons. It took Burgoyne about three weeks to reach the Hudson. Still confident, he looked forward to the rendezvous (RAHN-day-voo)—meeting—with St. Leger and Howe.

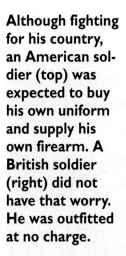

On August 3 a message was delivered to Burgoyne. It was from General Howe in Pennsylvania. He would not be coming north, Howe said, because he was sticking close to Washington's army. Howe explained that he would go north only if Washington moved northward. "Success be ever with you," he said. Yet General Burgoyne needed soldiers, not simply good wishes.

Although fighting for his country, an American soldier (top) was expected to buy his own uniform and supply his own firearm. A British soldier (right) did not have that worry. He was outfitted at no charge.

Battles Along the Mohawk

At that moment General St. Leger was trying to overcome a small Patriot force at Fort Stanwix (near present-day Rome, New York). St. Leger's army included British and Hessian troops. It also had a large number of Loyalist troops, and a force of 1,000 Iroquois. Leader of the Indians was the Mohawk chief Joseph Brant, also known as Thayendanegea.

Toward the end of August, General Benedict Arnold and a small army headed up the Mohawk River to help Patriot troops at Fort Stanwix. A clever leader, Arnold sent a few Indian allies ahead to spread rumors that he was coming with a very large army. The rumors worked. St. Leger's army retreated so fast it left behind tents, cannon, and supplies.

The flight of St. Leger left the British strategy in shambles, but it did not bring peace to the Mohawk Valley. For the rest of the war, bitter and murderous fighting raged between Patriot and Loyalist forces. The Mohawk Valley was the heartland of the Iroquois, and in this warfare most of the Iroquois, led by Joseph Brant, sided with the Loyalists.

Saratoga—A Turning Point

Burgoyne's army was running out of provisions by August, and it needed horses. A raiding party the general sent into Vermont was badly defeated at the Battle of Bennington. Despite this setback, Burgoyne's army crossed to the west bank of the Hudson and headed slowly toward Albany. At a place called Freeman's Farm there waited a powerful Continental force led by General Horatio Gates.

To proceed, Burgoyne would have to break through earthworks—a barrier made of earth—protecting the Continental Army. The earthworks had been put up under the supervision of Thaddeus Kosciuszko (kahs-ee-UHS-ko), a Polish engineer who had come to help the Patriots.

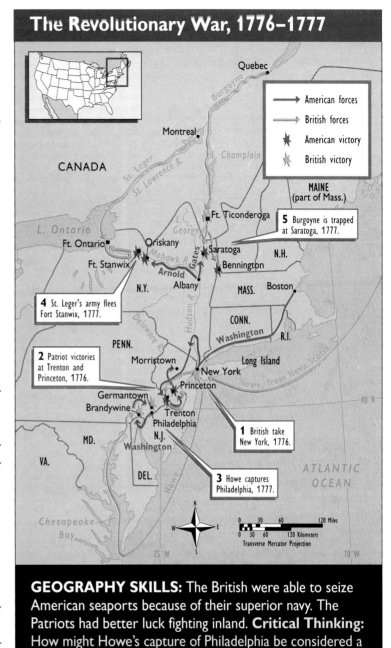

The Revolutionary War, 1776–1777

Legend:
→ American forces
⇢ British forces
✦ American victory
✦ British victory

CANADA

Quebec
Montreal
L. Champlain
L. Ontario
Ft. Ontario
Oriskany
Ft. Ticonderoga
Ft. Stanwix
Saratoga
Bennington
Albany
N.Y.
N.H.
MASS.
Boston
CONN.
R.I.
Long Island
New York
Morristown
Princeton
Germantown
Brandywine
Trenton
Philadelphia
N.J.
PENN.
MD.
DEL.
VA.
Washington
Chesapeake Bay
ATLANTIC OCEAN

5 Burgoyne is trapped at Saratoga, 1777.

4 St. Leger's army flees Fort Stanwix, 1777.

2 Patriot victories at Trenton and Princeton, 1776.

1 British take New York, 1776.

3 Howe captures Philadelphia, 1777.

MAINE (part of Mass.)

0 30 60 120 Miles
0 30 60 120 Kilometers
Transverse Mercator Projection

GEOGRAPHY SKILLS: The British were able to seize American seaports because of their superior navy. The Patriots had better luck fighting inland. **Critical Thinking:** How might Howe's capture of Philadelphia be considered a failure for the British?

Burgoyne halted to wait for reinforcements. Patriot forces fired constantly at Burgoyne's now-hungry army. Even the wolves boldly entered the camp. Burgoyne knew that conditions would worsen once winter set in, so he made the decision to fight. Twice his attempt to break through the earthworks failed. In both battles—the

Helmet belonging to a Hessian soldier.

General Burgoyne surrenders to George Washington following the Patriots' victory at the Battle of Saratoga. **Critical Thinking:** Why did the Patriots achieve more than a military victory at Saratoga?

Battles of Freeman's Farm—Benedict Arnold's courageous attacks were crucial in stopping Burgoyne. (Resentment that Gates received most of the credit for these victories is one reason Arnold turned traitor in 1780 and joined the British.)

Burgoyne started to retreat—but slowly. At Saratoga, the Continental Army trapped him, cutting off all retreat. "Gentleman Johnny" was forced to surrender his 6,000 troops.

Help from Abroad

The American victory in the Battle of Saratoga was a turning point in the war against the British. After Saratoga, a Patriot victory seemed possible. Now France recognized America's independence and in 1778 forged an alliance with the new nation. France also persuaded its ally, Spain, to join the American side a year later. France and Spain donated badly needed funds and supplies to the American side.

Spain also provided military help. In 1779–1780 General Bernardo de Gálvez, the Spanish governor of Louisiana, cap-

tured the British strongholds of Natchez and Baton Rouge in the lower Mississippi Valley. From there his forces went on to take Mobile and, in 1781, Pensacola in West Florida. These victories prevented the British from attacking the United States from the southwest. They also extended Spain's empire in North America.

SKILLS: Reading an Organization Chart

LEARN

You probably have a clear understanding of how most school clubs are organized. Usually there is a president to run the meetings, a secretary to take notes, and a treasurer to manage the money. But what about a large organization with hundreds or thousands of people? How could you ever understand how that is run? One way is to look at an organization chart.

An organization chart visually shows the structure of an organization.

Historians use organization charts as tools to study the past. Organization charts can provide a view of the way governments, businesses, armies, and other organizations operated. They do this by revealing how power, information, or supplies flowed from one place to another. Look at the chart at the right. It shows how the Continental Army was organized. There is a key to explain what the arrows and dashed lines mean. Notice that commands flow in one direction only, while information can travel both ways.

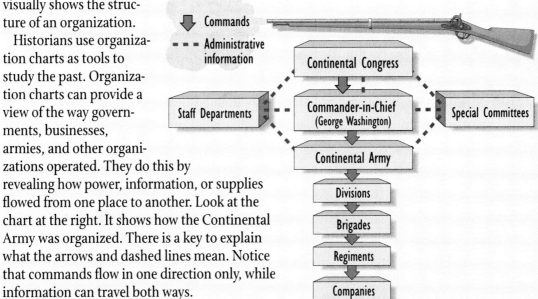

Commands

Administrative information

Continental Congress

Staff Departments

Commander-in-Chief
(George Washington)

Special Committees

Continental Army

Divisions

Brigades

Regiments

Companies

PRACTICE

1. What was the smallest organizational unit in the army?

2. Who gave commands to the head of the regiment—the brigade commander or the division commander? How do you know?

3. From what three sources could the Continental Congress get administrative information?

4. How does the chart help you better understand this organization?

APPLY

5. Draw an organization chart that shows the lines of authority in a school club. The club should include club officers, such as president, secretary, and treasurer, other members, and a teacher advisor.

2 The Path to Victory

SECTION GUIDE

Main Idea
After 1777 the war's focus shifted from the North to other areas: the frontier, the sea, and the South. The war's final battles took place in the South.

Goals
As you read, look for answers to these questions:

1. What strengthened Patriot forces?

2. Why did heavy fighting take place in the South?

3. What events led to the end of the war?

Key Terms
desert
bayonet
guerrilla
Battle of Yorktown

The bitter winter at Valley Forge brought much pain and suffering. Some of the soldiers marched with no jackets, others with no shoes.

DURING THE WINTER of 1777–1778, a young French volunteer walked into George Washington's camp at Valley Forge, near Philadelphia. The Frenchman had thought he would find "an army with uniforms, the glitter of arms, . . . military pomp of all sorts." What he found instead was "a few militiamen, poorly clad, and for the most part without shoes—many of them badly armed. . . ." It was, he said, the appearance of an armed mob.

Winter at Valley Forge
Driven from Philadelphia by Howe, Washington and his army spent the winter of 1777–1778 at Valley Forge. The name came to stand for the hunger and suffering the Patriots endured. "No pay, no clothes, no provisions, no rum," the soldiers grumbled.

Over the winter, nearly a quarter of the soldiers at Valley Forge died from the cold, from smallpox and typhoid, and from lack of food. Many soldiers **deserted** —left the army without permission—because of the terrible conditions. "The [lack] of clothing, added to the misery of the season," wrote Washington, "has [caused] them to suffer such hardships as will not be [believed] but by those who have been spectators."

Among the Europeans with Washington was the Marquis de Lafayette (mahr-KEE DUH laf-ee-ET), a nineteen-year-old

French nobleman. Lafayette had volunteered with Washington's men in the summer of 1777. He became one of the army's most popular leaders. With Lafayette came the Baron de Kalb, an able and experienced professional soldier.

Another European volunteer, Baron von Steuben (STOO-buhn), turned the ragged troops at Valley Forge into an effective fighting force. In his homeland of Prussia (now part of Germany), Von Steuben was a general. Impressed with Washington's strategy in winning the battles of Trenton and Princeton, he had offered his help to the Patriot forces. Von Steuben arrived at Valley Forge in the spring of 1778.

Von Steuben was kind, open-hearted, and competent. Washington asked him to drill the army. Working with 100 soldiers at a time, Von Steuben taught the troops about European military formations. They practiced making charges with **bayonets** —two-foot-long steel knives—attached to the ends of their muskets. Even if they only had rags to wear, Von Steuben insisted soldiers shave, wash, and keep a clean camp.

Within a month the troops were able to execute drills with speed and precision. In June the troops engaged the British army leaving Philadelphia and proved they could fight with the best.

War on the Frontier

In 1778 George Rogers Clark, a 26-year-old explorer, walked into the offices of Virginia's governor, Patrick Henry. He had come, he said, to take part in the defense of the land on America's western frontier against the British. Virginia had claimed land in what are now Indiana and Illinois. It therefore should defend that land against the British. "If a country is not worth protecting," he declared, "it is not worth claiming."

Governor Henry was impressed with the red-haired young man with black, spark-

ling eyes. The governor gave him money and told Clark to raise an army to capture British posts on the western frontier.

In the summer of 1778 Clark traveled down the Ohio River with 175 Virginians. After 900 miles on the river, Clark's men left their boats. They started on foot for Kaskaskia, a British fort on the Mississippi River in what is now southern Illinois. They captured Kaskaskia without a fight and then moved east to take the fort at Vincennes (vin-SENZ) on the Wabash River in present-day Indiana.

That winter, however, British forces under Henry Hamilton recaptured Vincennes. Hamilton was known as "Hair Buyer" because of the rewards he was supposed to have paid for American scalps.

Clark was determined to retake Vincennes. He and his men set out from Kaskaskia in February 1779. They slogged through miles of flooded swamps known as the "drowned lands," caught the British defenders at Vincennes off guard, and took "Hair Buyer" prisoner.

Clark's victory gave the Americans a hold on the vast region between the Great Lakes and the Ohio River—an area over half the total size of the thirteen states. Fort Detroit, however, remained in the hands of the British.

After leading his men through miles of swampland, George Rogers Clark recaptured the fort at Vincennes. His victory helped secure American control of the West.

Sailors at the time used an instrument called an octant to help them navigate.

War at Sea

By 1777 Britain had more than 100 warships off the American coast. This naval force gave Britain complete command of the Atlantic trade routes. There was no way the Americans could defeat the powerful British navy.

Instead the Americans continued the old tradition of privateering, or commerce raiding. After capturing an enemy trading ship and selling the cargo, the crew of a privateer shared in the prize. Recruiters for the privateers emphasized profits as well as patriotism. An advertisement for the privateer *Ranger* called for, "All gentlemen seamen and able-bodied landsmen who have a mind to distinguish themselves in the glorious cause of their country and make their fortunes."

Altogether the states and Congress commissioned more than 2,000 privateers to prey on the enemy. Their hit-and-run tactics disrupted British shipping.

The most famous of the privateer captains was the Scottish-born John Paul Jones. In 1779 he left a French port in command of a small fleet of privateers. His ship was the *Bonhomme Richard* (BAHN-om rih-SHAR), named after the French version of a character in Ben Franklin's almanac, Poor Richard. The *Bonhomme Richard* was a worn out, rotting ship.

Patrolling along the east coast of England in 1779, Jones's three vessels approached a convoy of trading ships guarded by two British warships. Jones boldly closed in on the *Serapis,* the larger of the two warships. What followed was the greatest sea fight of the Revolutionary War. Jones edged the *Bonhomme Richard* alongside the British vessel. His crew then tied the two ships together with rope. With the muzzles of their guns almost touching, the two warships blasted away at each other.

Seeing that Jones's damaged ship was leaking badly, the British commander challenged Jones to surrender. In words that have become famous, Jones is said to have replied, "I have not yet begun to fight!" After a bloody three-hour battle, the main-mast of the *Serapis* cracked and fell, and its captain surrendered. Jones took over the *Serapis.* The *Bonhomme Richard* sank two days later.

Setbacks in the South

After three years of fighting, the British faced some tough decisions. The battles in the North had brought them no nearer to victory than they had been in 1775.

British generals decided on a new strategy. They would shift the focus of the war to the South. There they hoped to benefit from the many southern Loyalists. They also expected slaves to join them in large numbers. Responding to the promise of freedom, at least 50,000 African Americans served the British as guides, spies, and laborers. (One of the war's tragedies was that thousands did not earn their freedom as they hoped. Instead British officers made fortunes by selling African Americans in the West Indies.)

The portrait of John Paul Jones also shows the *Bonhomme Richard–Serapis* battle in the background. The pistol below was awarded to Jones by the U.S. Navy.

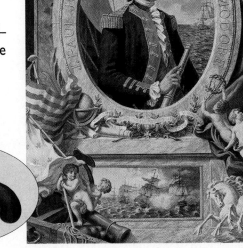

At first it seemed that the British had made the right decision. In November 1778 British forces sailed from New York and captured the port of Savannah, Georgia. Using Savannah as a base, the British soon took control of Georgia. Later efforts by French and American forces to retake Savannah failed.

In 1780 the British captured a second major port: Charleston, South Carolina. When the city's 5,500 defenders surrendered, the Patriots lost almost their entire southern army. For the Americans, it was the worst disaster of the war.

Washington asked General Gates, the victor at Saratoga, to form a new southern army. Its core was a force of several hundred men led by Baron de Kalb. Gates added several thousand new and untrained recruits to this core. He then headed for Camden, South Carolina, and a battle with the British army led by General Charles Cornwallis.

The "Swamp Fox"

On the way a ragged band of South Carolinians approached Gates. "Their number did not exceed twenty men and boys, some white, some black, and all mounted, but most of them miserably equipped," wrote an officer. Their leader was Francis Marion, known as the "Swamp Fox."

Marion and his band offered what few had—a thorough knowledge of South Carolina's coastal swamplands. Gates sent Marion and his small force to seize Santee River crossings behind Camden. In this way they cut off British communications with Charleston.

In August 1780, facing veteran British troops at Camden, Baron de Kalb's force of Americans panicked and ran. Among those killed was the baron himself. This defeat of a second American army in the South brought Patriot spirits to a new low.

After the Battle of Camden British troops set out for Charleston with a column of

CULTURAL MOSAIC

JAMES ARMISTEAD
(1760–1832)

James Armistead was a 21-year-old slave when he joined the Continental Army. He fooled the British into thinking he was on their side, when actually he was spying for the Marquis de Lafayette. The great risks he took won Lafayette's respect and friendship. When the war was over, Lafayette returned to France. Armistead, in contrast, had to return to slavery. In 1786, after the Virginia assembly read a letter Lafayette wrote to honor Armistead's service to the Patriot cause, it voted to free him by buying him from his master. In 1824 Lafayette returned to America. He traveled to Virginia and visited Armistead.

Patriot prisoners. Marion and his band launched an attack. The Americans captured the redcoats and freed the prisoners.

Guerrilla Fighting

Marion and his ragtag group were fighting as guerrillas. In other words, they carried out surprise hit-and-run attacks on the enemy. This small guerrilla force, with its base in the swamps, managed to cut off the British supply line between Charleston and the interior.

Other Patriots, as well as Loyalists, formed guerrilla bands in the region. They carried out vicious raids against each other in which all existing rules of warfare were cast aside. At the Battle of Kings Mountain, fought on the border between the Carolinas in October 1780, a Patriot force of frontier guerrillas slaughtered most of a British force of over a thousand men. It was one of the bloodiest battles of the war.

The Tide Turns in the South

In 1780 Washington put a new general, Nathanael Greene, in charge of the southern army. One of Washington's most able officers, Greene was the son of a Quaker preacher. He had been expelled from the Quakers for his belief in armed struggle against Britain. Greene began a policy of mercy toward Loyalists. He also won over the Cherokee Indians to the American side.

Under General Greene's command, the American army avoided full-scale battles, where Britain's superior firepower would give Britain the edge. Instead, the Patriot forces let the British chase them around the countryside and wear themselves out. When the Americans fought, even if they retreated, they made sure the British suffered heavily. "Another such victory will destroy the British army," grumbled a British leader on hearing of heavy losses after a battle.

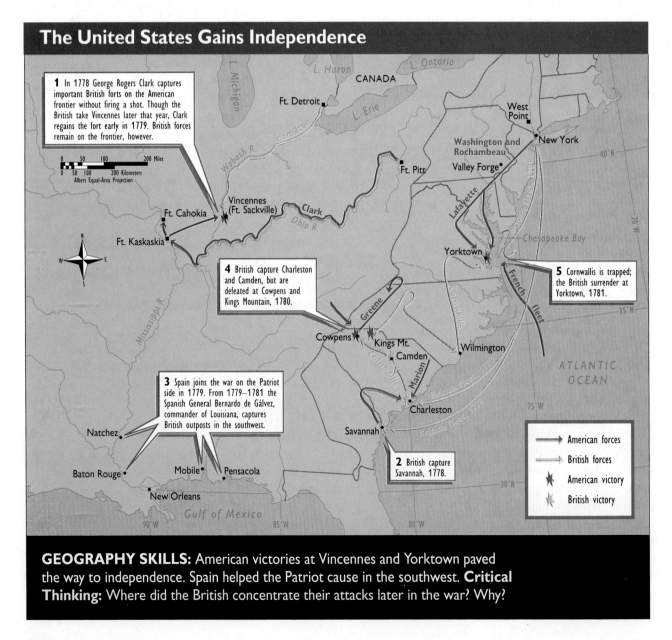

The United States Gains Independence

1 In 1778 George Rogers Clark captures important British forts on the American frontier without firing a shot. Though the British take Vincennes later that year, Clark regains the fort early in 1779. British forces remain on the frontier, however.

4 British capture Charleston and Camden, but are defeated at Cowpens and Kings Mountain, 1780.

5 Cornwallis is trapped; the British surrender at Yorktown, 1781.

3 Spain joins the war on the Patriot side in 1779. From 1779–1781 the Spanish General Bernardo de Gálvez, commander of Louisiana, captures British outposts in the southwest.

2 British capture Savannah, 1778.

→ American forces
⇢ British forces
★ American victory
✷ British victory

GEOGRAPHY SKILLS: American victories at Vincennes and Yorktown paved the way to independence. Spain helped the Patriot cause in the southwest. **Critical Thinking:** Where did the British concentrate their attacks later in the war? Why?

The victorious American forces accept the British surrender at Yorktown. George Washington appears to the left of the American flag. **Critical Thinking:** How did the Patriots benefit from having allies in the war?

The End of the War

The war dragged into its sixth year. In Britain opposition to the war grew. Some British leaders began to think American independence would not be so bad.

The last year of the war was fought mostly in Virginia. Britain's General Cornwallis had set up a base at Yorktown on Chesapeake Bay. From there his army could receive supplies by ship from New York.

Meanwhile, French forces under the command of General Jean Rochambeau (ro-sham-BO) arrived in Rhode Island to help the American troops. Washington learned that a large French fleet had also arrived from the West Indies. Here was a golden opportunity. The French fleet could cut Yorktown off from resupply by sea. At the same time, he could cut Cornwallis off from the North. Cornwallis would then be trapped on land.

Washington and Rochambeau marched south. When British ships tried to reach Cornwallis, French ships drove them back. The American and French troops began to bombard Yorktown. Cornwallis saw that he had no way out. On October 19, 1781, he surrendered his army of 8,000.

Back in London, British leaders took the news hard. "It is all over!" gasped Lord North. Indeed, he and other British leaders were soon forced to resign. The defeat at the Battle of Yorktown convinced Britain's new leaders to begin peace talks with the Americans.

SECTION REVIEW

1. Key Terms desert, bayonet, guerrilla, Battle of Yorktown

2. People and Places Marquis de Lafayette, George Rogers Clark, John Paul Jones, Francis Marion, Valley Forge, Vincennes, Charleston

3. Comprehension Why did the war shift to the South in its last stages?

4. Comprehension Describe the Patriot strategy that led to the British defeat at Yorktown.

5. Critical Thinking Using Marion and Greene as examples, explain how the Americans used effective defense strategies against the British.

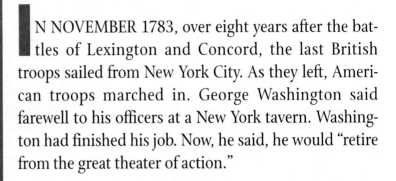

I N NOVEMBER 1783, over eight years after the battles of Lexington and Concord, the last British troops sailed from New York City. As they left, American troops marched in. George Washington said farewell to his officers at a New York tavern. Washington had finished his job. Now, he said, he would "retire from the great theater of action."

Why the Americans Won

As you have read, Patriot forces faced many obstacles in the Revolutionary War. They lacked training and experience. They were always short of supplies and weapons. They were loosely organized. By contrast, British forces ranked among the best trained in the world. They were professional soldiers, not volunteers, and their troops were well supplied.

The Patriots won the war in spite of these disadvantages. Several factors explain why.

(1) *Better leadership.* British generals made mistakes in judgment. Many had obtained their jobs through personal connections, not ability. Their overconfidence and bad judgment made possible Patriot victories at Saratoga and Yorktown. Washington, on the other hand, was an excellent leader. He had valuable experience from the French and Indian War. He also kept his spirit through such difficult times as the winter at Valley Forge.

(2) *Foreign aid.* Britain's rivals—especially France—helped the Patriots. Loans and military aid from nations opposed to Britain were essential to the American victory.

(3) *Knowledge of the land.* The Americans knew the land where the fighting took place,

Benjamin West's painting of the signing of the Treaty of Paris, the peace agreement ending the war, was left unfinished. The unhappy British delegation refused to pose.

and they made skilled use of that knowledge. The British could control cities on the coast, but they could not extend that control to the interior.

(4) *Motivation.* The Patriots had more to fight for. At stake were their property and their dream of liberty. Far from their homes, the British and Hessians fought with less motivation.

The Cost of the War

About 25,000 Americans and 10,000 British lost their lives in the fighting. Many Americans died in prison after being captured by the British. Others starved or froze to death in military camps. Many of the survivors left the army penniless. They had received little or no pay while they served. In return for food, many sold the titles to the western land they had received from the government.

The United States went deeply into debt to finance the war. Congress later gained the power to tax American trade and used such taxes to help pay off the war debt.

The Treaty of Paris

In 1782 American negotiators began meeting with British officials to work out a peace agreement. The final treaty, signed the next year, was very favorable to the United States. The Treaty of Paris (1783) established that:

(1) The United States was independent.

(2) The boundaries of the United States would extend west to the Mississippi River. The nation would border Canada to the north and Spanish Florida to the south. (The exact locations of these last two boundaries remained in dispute for some time.)

(3) The United States would receive fishing rights off Canada's Atlantic Coast, near Newfoundland and Nova Scotia.

(4) Each side would repay debts owed from before the war.

(5) The British would return any slaves they had captured.

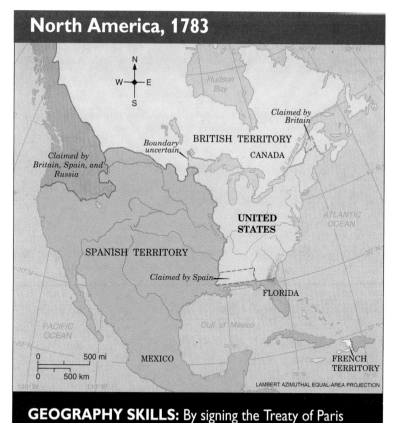

North America, 1783

GEOGRAPHY SKILLS: By signing the Treaty of Paris (below), Britain recognized American independence.
Critical Thinking: What hints does the map give that more conflicts with Britain lay ahead?

(6) Congress would recommend that property taken from the Loyalists by the states be returned.

Some Americans were unhappy with the treaty. Virginia tobacco planters, for example, owed Britain millions of dollars. They resented being told they would have to pay their debts. "If we are now to pay debts due the British merchants," one Virginian complained, "what have we been fighting for all this while?"

Neither Britain nor the United States fully lived up to the terms of the Treaty of Paris. Americans did not repay the prewar debts they owed to British merchants. Neither did they return Loyalist property.

New Homes for the Loyalists

Tories, with their brats and wives,
Should fly to save their wretched lives.

With rhymes like this one on the lips of Patriots, it was little wonder that tens of thousands of Loyalists fled the United States during and after the Revolutionary War.

Some chose Britain, where they asked the government to pay for their lost property. Parliament created a commission to hear the complaints. About two-thirds received payments for their losses.

Tens of thousands chose the British colony of Canada. Among them were Indians and free blacks. Led by Joseph Brant (below), a group of Iroquois settled in Quebec. Many black Loyalists later chose to leave Canada. In 1792 more than a thousand sailed to Sierra Leone, a British colony in West Africa. They founded Freetown, now the nation's capital, and became some of that country's most successful residents.

For their part, the British did not return slaves they had sold in the West Indies. They also refused to give up military outposts in the Great Lakes area, such as Fort Detroit. Britain's continued presence on the western frontier would be a source of tension in the years to come.

Fate of the Loyalists

"History is written by the winners," the writer Alex Haley once said. It is easy in telling the story of the winners to forget about the losers, such as the American Loyalists. Thousands had lost their property. Between 80,000 and 100,000 Loyalists left the United States during and just after the war. Among them were ex-soldiers, several thousand Indian allies, and about 4,000 African Americans.

Most of the Loyalists fled after the war's end to other parts of Britain's North American empire. Thousands of refugees went north to the Canadian provinces of Nova Scotia and Quebec. Their arrival created instant new towns. So many people settled in Quebec that the government divided the province in two. Among the new settlers were the Iroquois Loyalists led by Joseph Brant.

The Loyalist migration would change Canadian history. Until then Canada had been French in its ways and language. The Loyalists would bring English traditions. Even today, both French and English are Canada's official languages.

Thousands of Loyalists had also fled to East Florida. Yet after the war, Britain gave Florida to Spain. Thus they were forced to move once again. Many went to Caribbean islands such as the Bahamas.

New State Governments

With the Declaration of Independence, the American colonies became states. As states, they had to write new laws by which to govern themselves. The form of most colonial governments had been shaped by charters. These were written contracts that said how the colony was to be governed. It was only natural that Americans wanted to write down how the new state governments should work.

Between 1776 and 1780, during the American Revolution, each of the thirteen colonies formed a state government. Eleven of the colonies drew up new constitutions. Two states, Connecticut and Rhode Island, simply reworded their colonial charters. Never before in history had people written down the rules under which they were to be governed.

Several principles formed the basis of the new constitutions. One was the idea that people should work together to make an agreement for the common good. Another was that good government is based on the consent of the people. A third was that there are fundamental laws that differ from ordinary laws. These fundamental laws are so basic they should not be changed by lawmakers.

In all thirteen states, the duties of governing were divided among three branches. The most powerful of these branches was the legislative branch, which made the laws. The executive branch, made up of a governor or council, enforced these laws. Interpreting laws and punishing lawbreakers was the job of the judicial branch.

Forming a Republic

As the states were setting up their own governments, they debated the way the country as a whole should be run. Most Americans agreed that their new nation should be a republic. In a republic the voters choose representatives who make the laws. There is no king in a republic; never again would a king tell Americans what to do.

In 1776 the Continental Congress had begun work on a plan for a national government that would be a republic. Congress proposed that the states join together in a loose union, or confederation. (A model for such a confederation was the Iroquois Confederacy.) Congress's plan was called the Articles of Confederation. Under the Articles, the United States would have a national government, but the states would have most of the power.

By 1779, twelve states had ratified —approved—the Articles. Maryland refused. Its people were upset over the huge

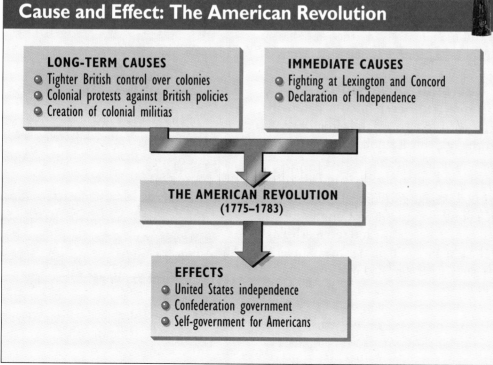

Cause and Effect: The American Revolution

LONG-TERM CAUSES
- Tighter British control over colonies
- Colonial protests against British policies
- Creation of colonial militias

IMMEDIATE CAUSES
- Fighting at Lexington and Concord
- Declaration of Independence

THE AMERICAN REVOLUTION
(1775–1783)

EFFECTS
- United States independence
- Confederation government
- Self-government for Americans

CHART SKILLS: Colonial resistance to Britain's attempts to tighten its control led to the Revolutionary War and American independence. **Critical Thinking:** Could the Revolution have been avoided? Why or why not?

chunks of western lands claimed by other states.

Control of this fertile land between the Appalachians and the Mississippi River would more than double the size of some states. People in Maryland saw this growth in size and power as a threat to their small state. They noted that the western lands had been won by the "common blood and treasury of the thirteen states." Maryland said it would not ratify the Articles of Confederation until these lands were turned over to the nation.

States such as New York and Virginia opposed Maryland's demands. Still, these large states understood the need for a central government. Virginia declared itself "willing to make great sacrifices to the common interests of America." One by one the larger states gave up their claims.

A National Government

In March 1781, seven months before the victory at Yorktown, Maryland ratified the Articles of Confederation. The new government was established.

The government of the Confederation was not like our government today. To run the country, there was a Congress. Each state sent between two and seven delegates to the Congress. No matter the number of delegates, each state had only one vote. As a result, small states had as much say in the government as large states.

Many Americans did not trust central government. They preferred that power be left to the states. The Articles of Confedera-

The Articles of Confederation set up a weak national government.

tion sharply limited Congress's powers. For instance, only the states had the power to tax and enforce laws. Congress, however, had more power over foreign affairs. Congress could wage war and make peace. It could also set up rules for trade with the Indian nations.

To create laws or make any other major decisions, nine of the thirteen states had to agree. All thirteen states had to vote in favor of any change in the Articles of Confederation themselves.

Americans had learned to fear the power of kings and royal governors. For this reason, the executive branch was not run by one person. There was no President with powers like those our modern Presidents have. A three-person committee, chosen by Congress, led the executive branch. Like Congress itself, the committee's powers were limited.

In sum, the Articles of Confederation created a weak union of independent states. The system set up to govern this union had very limited power over the states.

SECTION REVIEW

1. Key Terms Treaty of Paris (1783), legislative, executive, judicial, republic, Articles of Confederation, ratify

2. People and Places Joseph Brant, Newfoundland, Nova Scotia, Quebec

3. Comprehension List and explain the reasons why the United States defeated Britain in the Revolutionary War.

4. Comprehension Why did Americans want to limit the power of the new national government?

5. Critical Thinking Do you agree with the idea that there are fundamental laws so basic they should not be changed by lawmakers? Explain.

4 The Confederation: Successes and Problems

SECTION GUIDE

Main Idea

Under the Articles of Confederation, Congress passed laws to deal with western lands, but it lacked the power to deal with other problems.

Goals

As you read, look for answers to these questions:

① How did the Confederation Congress organize lands north of the Ohio?

② What kinds of problems faced the Confederation Congress?

Key Terms
Northwest Territory
ordinance
survey
Northwest Ordinance
republicanism

At right is a detail of the painting, "Daniel Boone Escorting Settlers Through the Cumberland Gap." His leather hunting bag is shown above.

ON A SPRING DAY in 1775, 30 men gathered in the mountains of Virginia. Their leader was Daniel Boone, a famous woodsman and scout. He had been hired by Virginia to build a road to Kentucky. Following Boone's orders, the axmen chopped down trees, connected trails, and widened buffalo paths. Working through the spring and summer, they created a wagon road over the Appalachian Mountains. This was the Wilderness Road.

Moving Westward

The Wilderness Road led through the Cumberland Gap into the land the Iroquois called *Kentake,* meaning "meadowland." In 1775 Kentucky had 100 white settlers. In 1780 the number had leaped to about 20,000.

The Treaty of Paris granted the United States the land between the Appalachians and the Mississippi River. In effect, this was the eastern drainage of the Mississippi River Valley. This region is cut in two by the Ohio River. The Ohio itself is a major river—one of the longest in the United States.

After 1775 thousands of pioneers settled south of the Ohio, in Kentucky, but few had moved north of the river. One reason was

GEOGRAPHY: The Northwest Territory

The U.S. government in the mid-1780s wanted to encourage settlement of the Northwest Territory. It needed the money from sale of the land, and it wanted to strengthen U.S. control over the Territory. To meet these goals it passed two laws, the Ordinance of 1785 and the Northwest Ordinance. The first said how the Territory would be divided. The second said how it would be governed.

In some other parts of the country, settlers themselves had set the boundaries of their plots. They used whatever landmarks were handy—trees, streams, rocks. Endless fights over boundaries resulted. To prevent this, the Ordinance of 1785 called for the Territory to be divided ahead of time into square lots (see diagram). This encouraged settlement by giving settlers clear ownership of their land.

Would these settlers remain loyal Americans or become, in George Washington's words, "a distinct people from us . . . a formidable and dangerous neighbor"? To keep their loyalty, the Northwest Ordinance gave settlers a voice in their government and protected their basic rights. It also promised that in time the Territory could join the Union as several states, with all the rights of the original states.

Americans responded by the thousands, settling what one called "a perfect paradise" of rich soil and good weather. The states of Illinois, Indiana, Michigan, Ohio, and Wisconsin joined the Union in the 1800s.

This aerial photograph of farmland in Indiana shows the "patchwork-quilt" land division created by the Ordinance of 1785.

QUARTER SECTION (160 ACRES)

HALF SECTION (320 ACRES)

HALF QUARTER

1 MILE

1 MILE

Each section, one mile square, could be divided into smaller lots.

Each township was divided into 36 sections, one being reserved to support education.

6 MILES

6 MILES

WIS. MICH. ILL. IND. OHIO

Public lands were divided into townships.

220

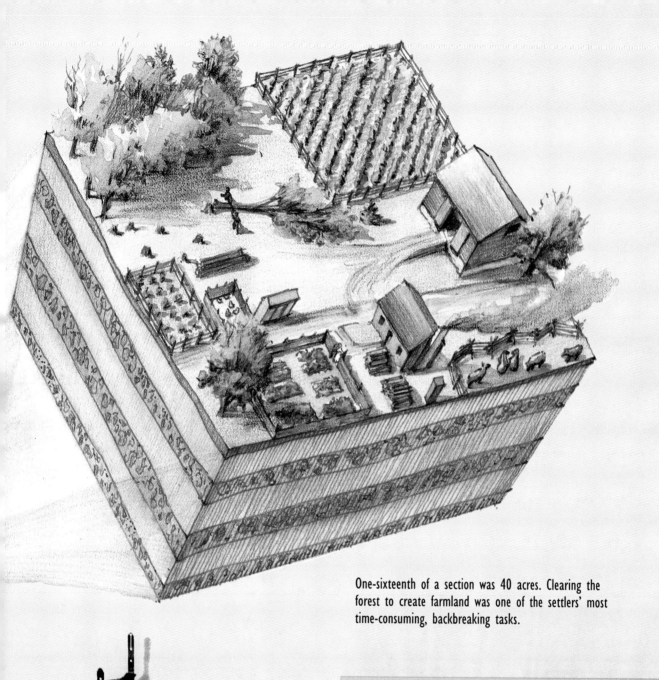

One-sixteenth of a section was 40 acres. Clearing the forest to create farmland was one of the settlers' most time-consuming, backbreaking tasks.

Surveyors used compasses like this to measure precise boundaries.

CRITICAL THINKING

1. How did a system of land division encourage settlement in the Northwest Territory?
2. How did the Ordinance of 1785 reflect the government's belief in public education?
3. **Geographic Theme: Region** Why was it a good idea for the government to treat the Northwest Territory as one region?

that the Indians there remained strong and determined to keep their land. Also, it was a land of no government. States had claimed the region north of the Ohio, but in name only. In order to pass the Articles of Confederation, they had given up their claims. This region, which was called the Northwest Territory, now belonged to the national government.

What was the best way to govern the Northwest Territory? Among the proposals was one by Thomas Jefferson, now a member of the Congress. Jefferson wanted to divide the region into fourteen territories. Westerners did not like his plan, however, because it called for rectangular boundaries. They wanted state boundaries based on natural features such as rivers and mountains.

Easterners objected to the number of states that might result from the plan. The West, they said, would soon gain control of Congress. They also doubted that settlers could rule themselves.

The Ordinance of 1785

From these debates emerged new laws on settling and governing the Northwest Territory. These new laws were called ordinances —government regulations.

The first of the ordinances had more to do with selling the land than governing it. Members of Congress were eager to raise money to pay off the nation's debts. In 1785 they passed an ordinance calling for the land to be surveyed. To survey means to measure land to determine the exact boundaries of a given area. (The Geography Feature in this section shows how the Northwest Territory was surveyed.) Once the land was surveyed, the Ordinance of 1785 called for the sections to be sold to the highest bidder.

The Northwest Ordinance

Congress next turned its attention to governing the Northwest Territory. In 1787 it passed the Northwest Ordinance. This law said that the Congress would choose a governor and three judges to rule the territory. Over time, the Northwest Territory was to be carved into not fewer than three and not more than five states.

The Ordinance also said a territory could become a state in two steps. The first step was for 5,000 free men to settle in the territory. Those settlers could then elect an assembly that would work with the governor and judges. When the territory had 60,000 free citizens, they could ask to

This detail of a painting of Cincinnati, Ohio, dates back to the early 1800s. Cincinnati, which today is one of Ohio's largest cities, had its beginnings as a small settlement in the Northwest Territory.

join the Union. If Congress voted to admit the area, it would become a state "on equal footing with the original states in all respects whatsoever."

The Ordinance set three other important conditions:

(1) The citizens in those lands would have freedom of religion and speech, the right to trial by jury, and protection from unfair punishments.

(2) Settlers had to treat Indians fairly.

(3) Slavery was banned in the territory. This meant that slavery would never exist in those states carved from the Northwest Territory—Wisconsin, Indiana, Ohio, Illinois, and Michigan.

The Northwest Ordinance proved to be a good plan that lasted longer than the Confederation. It protected settlers' freedom and allowed frontier governments to change as the population changed. As the United States grew, the Northwest Ordinance became a model for the settlement of other territories.

Toward Greater Equality

The conditions of the Northwest Ordinance are just one example of a feeling called **republicanism.** Republicanism was the idea that, for the country to thrive, its citizens needed certain virtues. These included a sense of equality, simplicity, and willingness to sacrifice for the public good.

Republicanism wore many faces. It was a lawyer complaining about the great wig worn by a judge. It was Benjamin Franklin hoping his daughter would not wear jewelry. It was the belief that people should not attend the theater because their time could be better spent doing good deeds.

The new spirit also called for greater religious freedom. Laws that had punished people because of the religion they followed were changed. Some states had not allowed Catholics, Jews, or atheists to hold

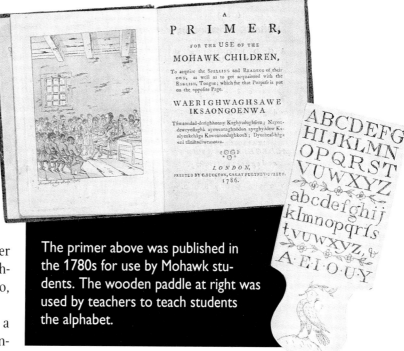

The primer above was published in the 1780s for use by Mohawk students. The wooden paddle at right was used by teachers to teach students the alphabet.

public office. After the war, states began to end those laws. Starting with Virginia, state after state also ended the old practice of supporting churches with tax money.

Still another effect of republicanism was the growing belief that the nation needed educated citizens. New secondary schools, colleges, and state universities were started. Women's education also received more attention. People realized that both men and women had important roles to play in society. Men were to be breadwinners and decision makers. Women were to manage the home and raise their children to become good citizens. To be wise mothers, it was thought, women needed a proper education.

African Americans

The republican spirit also caused Americans to reconsider slavery. The feeling grew that slavery was not in keeping with the new nation's ideals. "It did, indeed, . . . become very hard for us to listen each year to the Preamble to the Declaration of Inde-

Elizabeth Freeman challenged the institution of slavery in a Massachusetts court and won. Her victory in **1781** led to the end of slavery in that state.

This painted tray shows Reverend Lemuel Haynes preaching to a New England congregation. Haynes fought in the Revolution at Concord and Ticonderoga.

found the Free African Society, a self-help organization. The Society was a way for African Americans to work on their problems together. It also helped the needy and paid for the education of black children.

In 1794 Allen started a Methodist church for African Americans. No such church had existed before then. Allen's church, which helped educate adults and children, became a model for other African American churches.

pendence and still remain the owners and users and catchers of slaves," wrote a southern planter.

The antislavery movement grew during the years of the Revolution. Rhode Island and Connecticut had restricted the slave trade in 1774. Virginia, Pennsylvania, and Maryland followed their lead. Virginia, Delaware, and Maryland also passed laws saying that an owner could free a slave without government approval. Vermont banned slavery in its 1777 constitution.

With independence, free blacks began to think of themselves differently. A leader in the free black community was Richard Allen, a Methodist preacher. He helped

A Troubled Government

The Northwest Ordinance was the greatest triumph of the Confederation Congress. In dealing with other matters, however, Congress did poorly.

Perhaps the greatest problem facing the Confederation Congress was that it could not tax. It depended entirely on the states to give it the money it needed. The states had their own expenses and rarely sent money to the Congress.

Without money, the new nation was unable to pay its debts. The largest debt was the one that remained from the Revolution. Congress had borrowed large sums to fight the war. France, Holland, Spain, and European banks had made some of those loans.

Weaknesses of the Articles

CONGRESS
- Laws were hard to pass (needed approval of nine out of thirteen states for important laws)
- Lacked power to collect taxes, regulate trade, coin money, or establish armed forces
- Congress was responsible to the state legislatures, not to the people

EXECUTIVE
- No President or Chief Executive

COURTS
- No system of national courts

CHART SKILLS: The inability to tax hurt the national government under the Articles of Confederation.
Critical Thinking: Why did Americans fear strong central government?

The United States owed money to its own citizens as well. Many of the soldiers who had served in the war had not been paid. In June 1783 several hundred soldiers surrounded the state house in Philadelphia, where members of Congress were meeting. Angry soldiers thrust their bayonets through the windows. The legislators were forced to flee. The soldiers' actions symbolized the Congress's lack of power.

International Problems

Congress also found that it did not have the power to earn the respect of other nations. Having fought their way out of the British Empire, Americans were now shut out of old trading patterns. Britain made it hard for American ships to trade with the West Indies. Britain also refused to give up its forts in the West, and the United States could do little about it.

Spain and the United States quarreled over the boundary of Florida. Like Britain, Spain blocked American shipping in the West Indies. Even worse, Spain threatened to restrict American use of the lower Mississippi River. Development of the western lands depended on this water link with world markets.

The Not-So-United States

With the Revolution over, the threat of a common enemy no longer united the thirteen states. The Confederation Congress did not provide that unity. Just gathering enough delegates for a vote was hard. Getting them to agree was harder still.

No courts existed to settle disputes among member states. Pennsylvania and Connecticut nearly went to war over a disputed piece of land. Arguments and bad feelings also grew as each state began to pursue its own trade policy. The northern states imposed duties on imported goods. Delaware and the southern states did not. Many states placed heavy taxes on products from other states.

Thomas Jefferson saw that the states were drifting further and further apart. Worried that they might go to war with each other, he wrote, "I find . . . the pride of independence taking deep and dangerous hold on the hearts of individual states."

Yet the Articles of Confederation were not a complete failure. The years after the war were difficult times; it would not have been easy for *any* government to rule. The Confederation filled an important role by providing a national government in the years after the Revolution.

As time went on, however, growing numbers of Americans began to agree that the Confederation Congress needed more power. If not, they feared that the thirteen states might become thirteen separate nations. These small countries could become prey to the armies of Britain and Spain. The United States had won the war. Could it now survive the peace?

Paper money, like the colonial currency shown here, lost its value after the war. Many merchants stopped accepting bills issued by other states.

SECTION REVIEW

1. Key Terms Northwest Territory, ordinance, survey, Northwest Ordinance, republicanism

2. People and Places Daniel Boone, Wilderness Road

3. Comprehension Under the Northwest Ordinance, how could a region become a state?

4. Comprehension In what ways did American society move toward equality?

5. Critical Thinking How were the values expressed in Congress's plans for the Northwest Territory similar to values that had been fought for in the American Revolution?

Summary

1. The Revolutionary War divided American society. Washington's troops faced hardships and a powerful, experienced enemy in Britain. Yet the Americans won an important victory at the Battle of Saratoga and formed an alliance with France. Soon other Europeans came to America and joined the fight against the British.

2. The war's focus shifted from the North to the western frontier and the South. After heavy losses in the South, the Patriots began hit-and-run guerrilla attacks. The tide turned against Britain when French and American forces combined to defeat the British at Yorktown.

3. In 1783 Britain signed the Treaty of Paris, which recognized United States independence. States drew up constitutions that divided the duties of government among legislative, executive, and judicial branches. The states formed a loose union under the Articles of Confederation, which established a national government. However, most power was left to the states.

4. The Confederation Congress passed the Ordinance of 1785 and the Northwest Ordinance. Both laws dealt with the settling and governing of the Northwest Territory. The Confederation Congress had problems, however, including debt and a lack of power within the United States and abroad.

Review

KEY TERMS

Define the terms in each of the following pairs.

1. Battle of Saratoga; Treaty of Paris
2. legislative; executive
3. Articles of Confederation; ratify
4. Northwest Territory; Northwest Ordinance

COMPREHENSION

1. What were some of the problems that George Washington faced as commander of the Patriot forces?
2. Why was the Battle of Saratoga considered a turning point in the war?
3. Why was Clark's victory at Vincennes important?
4. IIow did the Patriots change their fighting style after their defeats at Charleston and Camden?
5. How was Cornwallis forced to surrender at Yorktown?
6. What were the costs of the war to the United States?
7. What parts of the Treaty of Paris did each side ignore?
8. Describe the organization of government under the Articles of Confederation.
9. Explain the importance of the Ordinance of 1785 and the Northwest Ordinance.
10. What were the major problems facing the Confederation Congress?

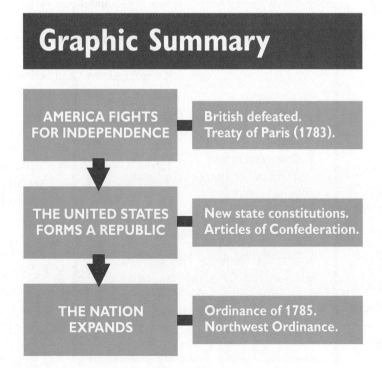

Graphic Summary

AMERICA FIGHTS FOR INDEPENDENCE — British defeated. Treaty of Paris (1783).

THE UNITED STATES FORMS A REPUBLIC — New state constitutions. Articles of Confederation.

THE NATION EXPANDS — Ordinance of 1785. Northwest Ordinance.

Places to Locate

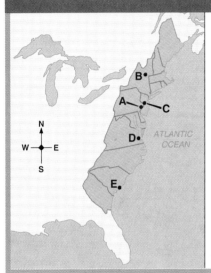

Match the letters on the map with the places that are listed below. Then explain the importance of each place.

1. Charleston
2. Philadelphia
3. Saratoga
4. Yorktown
5. Trenton

Geographic Theme: Location Explain the importance of Yorktown's location near the coast in deciding the Battle of Yorktown.

Skill Review

Study the chart below of a British infantry regiment. Then answer the questions that follow.

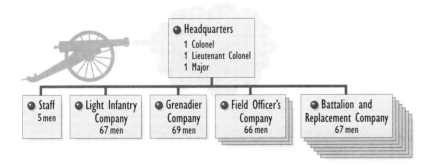

Headquarters
1 Colonel
1 Lieutenant Colonel
1 Major

Staff — 5 men
Light Infantry Company — 67 men
Grenadier Company — 69 men
Field Officer's Company — 66 men
Battalion and Replacement Company — 67 men

1. How many different types of companies did headquarters oversee? What other unit did headquarters oversee?
2. Which single company had the greatest number of people?
3. How many units of a battalion and replacement company were in a regiment? How can you tell?
4. How does the chart help you to understand the size of a British infantry regiment?

CRITICAL THINKING

1. **Making a Judgment** If you had been a slave during the Revolution, which side would you have supported? Why?
2. **Forming a Hypothesis** Other nations aided the Patriot cause. Could the Patriots have won the war without such aid? Explain.
3. **Making Comparisons** How were state governments stronger than the national government under the Articles of Confederation?

PORTFOLIO OPTIONS

1. **Civics Connection** Do you think those who supported the Revolution had the right to act for those who did not take sides? Organize a class debate on this issue.
2. **Writing Connection** Write down the journal entries for one week in the life of someone traveling west on the Wilderness Road.
3. **Contemporary Connection** With no power to tax citizens, the Confederation Congress could not repay its debts after the war. Look in newspapers and magazines for information on the national debt today. Discuss how the nation's debt increases and ways in which it might be reduced.
4. **Timeline Connection** Copy the chapter timeline. Which of the events do you think had the greatest impact on the war? Explain. Use an encyclopedia to create a timeline of important battles fought in the Revolutionary War.

More than 200 years after it was written, the Constitution of the United States remains the "supreme law of the land."

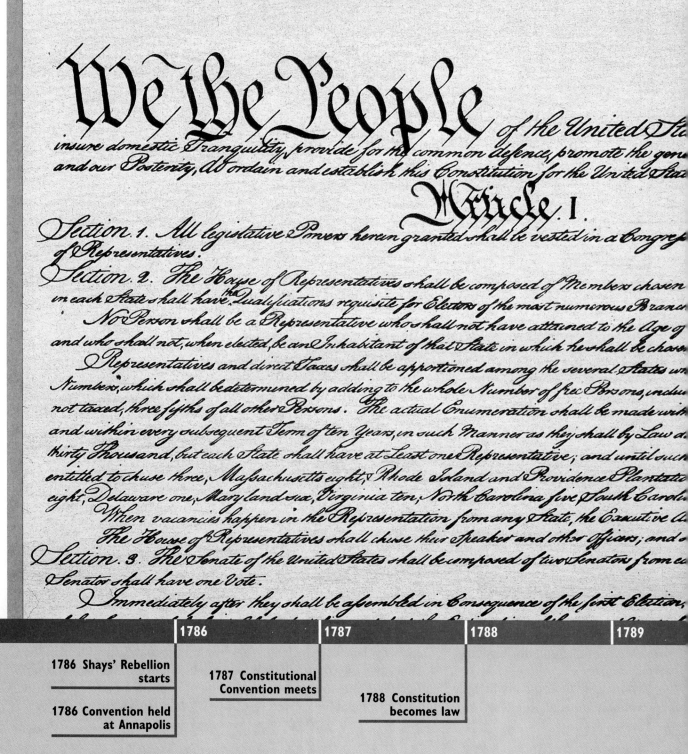

1786

1787

1788

1789

1786 Shays' Rebellion starts

1787 Constitutional Convention meets

1788 Constitution becomes law

1786 Convention held at Annapolis

Creating the Constitution (1786–1791)

1 The Call for Change

SECTION GUIDE

Main Idea

Political leaders assembled in Philadelphia in 1787 to work out a plan to strengthen the national government.

Goals

As you read, look for answers to these questions:

1. Why did farmers in Massachusetts rebel against the authorities?

2. Why did some Americans of the mid-1780s want changes in their government?

3. What were the men like who gathered to restructure the national government?

Key Terms

Shays' Rebellion
convention
Constitutional Convention
Founding Fathers

IMAGINE YOU ARE making a trip through the United States of the mid-1780s. When you cross a state border, you have to pay a tax on goods from another state. Paying for items with one kind of money, you might get change in another currency, which might not have any value anywhere else. Everywhere you go, you hear people bitterly complaining, "How can we pay our debts?"

Shays' Rebellion

The country was in trouble. The national government had little power. The states were free of British rule, but they were far from united.

Times were very tough in Massachusetts. Paper money in the state could buy little. Lawmakers had outlawed paper money in 1781, thereby forcing people to pay debts and taxes in gold or silver money. This law hurt farmers because farming brought in little gold or silver. Unable to pay their debts, many farmers lost their land. In those days, people who owed money could go to prison until they paid their debts. In one Massachusetts county, 80 percent of the men in jail were debtors.

In 1786, mobs of Massachusetts farmers protested loudly outside the courts. Using threats and violence, they stopped the sale of farms for nonpayment of debts. These protests became known as **Shays' Rebellion.** Daniel Shays, a former soldier in the American Revolution, was a leader of the movement.

The movement had little focus. One of Shays' men had urged on a mob by claiming that they were fighting for liberty. He then defined liberty as, "for every man to do what he pleases, to make other people do as you please to have them, and to keep folks from serving the devil."

1790

1791

1791 Bill of Rights added

State leaders in Boston declared that the rebels had to obey the law. They told farmers to use their votes, not their guns, if they wanted to change things. At the same time, many towns and merchants raised funds to send the state militia after the rebels.

Late in 1786, Shays and several hundred followers marched to Springfield, in the western part of the state. They planned to seize the United States arsenal, a storehouse for weapons. An army of state militia set out to meet the rebels and fought a short battle with them. Some 150 rebels were captured. Others, including Shays, fled to Rhode Island.

Reaction to the Rebellion

In the next Massachusetts election, the voters elected a new state government. The new leaders promised to change the strict laws against debtors. For governor the voters chose John Hancock, who pardoned the leaders of the revolt.

Thomas Jefferson, serving as U.S. minister in Paris, was not disturbed when he heard the news of Shays' Rebellion. He wrote:

> **"I hold it, that a little rebellion, now and then, is a good thing. . . . It is a medicine necessary for the sound health of government."**

Back in the United States, people were more concerned. Shays' Rebellion showed that the national government had no power to meet such a crisis. People worried about future revolts. What if others felt free to take the law into their own hands? John Locke, the British philosopher, had said, "Wherever law ends, tyranny begins." Had Americans thrown off the tyranny of the British king only to find themselves under the tyranny of mob rule?

A Call for a Convention

Tensions among the states over trade issues also worried many Americans. Lawmakers from Virginia called for a meeting of all the states to discuss trade disputes. This meeting of delegates, called a **convention,** was to be held at Annapolis, Maryland, in September 1786.

When the convention met, delegates from only five states showed up. Among the delegates were Alexander Hamilton from New York and James Madison from Virginia. They persuaded the other delegates that little could be done since so few of the states had sent people.

Hamilton went a step further. He wrote a report saying what he thought was wrong with the Articles of Confederation. The Confederation could not negotiate trade treaties, the report said. It could not pay its debts. It could not settle disputes between the states. Nor could it tax. To solve these problems, Hamilton called for a special convention to consider ways to strengthen the government. The delegates at Annapolis voted to support the report.

It was about this time that news of Shays' Rebellion swept through the states. This news convinced many people of another

Angered by tough economic times, Massachusetts farmers took part in Shays' Rebellion in 1786 (right). Today, a stone in a quiet field marks the conflict (above). **Critical Thinking:** Explain Jefferson's comment that "a little rebellion, now and then, is a good thing."

important reason to strengthen the government: to keep order. From his home at Mount Vernon, George Washington wrote:

❝No morn ever dawned more favorable than ours did and no day was ever more clouded than the present!❞

Responding to the national feeling that something had to be done, Congress called for another convention to be held. Delegates would meet, Congress said, "for the sole and express purpose of revising the Articles of Confederation." The convention would begin in May 1787 in Philadelphia.

The Convention Delegates

Twelve states responded to the call to send delegates to Philadelphia, to what is now called the **Constitutional Convention.** Only Rhode Island did not attend.

The 55 delegates who went were among the most educated men in America. About half were lawyers. Others were planters, merchants, and doctors. Three-fourths of them had sat in the Continental Congress. Many had been members of their state legislatures and had helped write their state constitutions. Several were state governors and judges. Along with other leaders of the time, these delegates are sometimes called the **Founding Fathers.**

For all their experience, the delegates were a young group. Although the average age was 43, most were under the age of 40. (Today, the average age of Congress is over 50.) It was mainly the younger men who took on the challenge of putting the nation on a firmer footing.

Gouverneur Morris of Pennsylvania, for example, was in his thirties. Alexander Hamilton was about 30. Hamilton had been raised on the Caribbean island of Nevis. Unlike many Americans whose first loyalty was to their state, Hamilton was interested in making the United States a strong and wealthy nation.

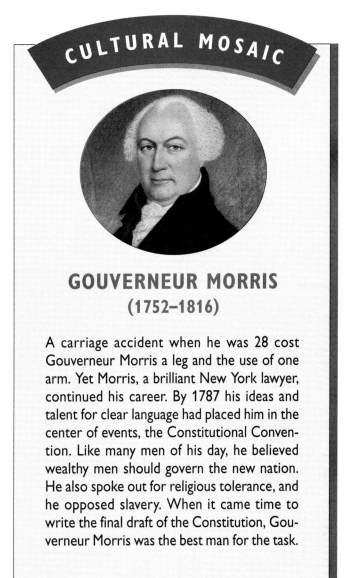

CULTURAL MOSAIC

GOUVERNEUR MORRIS
(1752–1816)

A carriage accident when he was 28 cost Gouverneur Morris a leg and the use of one arm. Yet Morris, a brilliant New York lawyer, continued his career. By 1787 his ideas and talent for clear language had placed him in the center of events, the Constitutional Convention. Like many men of his day, he believed wealthy men should govern the new nation. He also spoke out for religious tolerance, and he opposed slavery. When it came time to write the final draft of the Constitution, Gouverneur Morris was the best man for the task.

Not all the delegates were young men. The oldest, at 81, was Benjamin Franklin. Franklin brought experience, wisdom, and humor to the Convention. During the meetings he moved around the room, giving good advice. He often cooled hot tempers by making a joke at the right moment.

Some prominent men did not go to the Convention. Jefferson was still in Paris. John Adams was representing the nation in London. Patrick Henry refused to attend. He feared a strong central government and worried that the Convention would do more than simply revise the Articles of

Though James Madison lacked the commanding presence of George Washington or the wit of Benjamin Franklin, he used reason and quiet leadership to win arguments at the Constitutional Convention. **Critical Thinking:** What qualities make a person a natural leader?

honest can repair [rally around]." He finished by saying, "The event is in the hand of God."

The Historical Record

The Convention then decided on rules for its meetings. Delegates voted that all their discussions would be secret. To keep their talks from being overheard, the windows were nailed shut throughout the Convention. The heat of the closed room proved a terrible hardship for the delegates through the long summer.

The Convention had a secretary, but he did not keep a full record. Historians have relied more on the notes of James Madison. Madison's notes have allowed us to get past the secrecy of the Convention.

Madison also took an important part in the discussions. Many of the principles of the Constitution are based on his ideas. Historians call Madison the "Father of the Constitution" because of the important role he played.

Confederation. Henry's response to the idea of the Convention reportedly was that he "smelt a rat."

Also missing from the Convention were people who reflected the varied population of the United States in the 1780s. No African Americans or American Indians attended. None of the delegates were women. The absence of these groups most probably affected the decisions made.

The Convention Assembles

Rain poured down in Philadelphia on May 25, 1787. At the Pennsylvania state house, now known as Independence Hall, 29 delegates from 7 states gathered. The rest slowly arrived over the following weeks.

The first order of business was electing a president of the Convention. Robert Morris of Pennsylvania nominated George Washington. Every single delegate voted for the 55-year-old hero of the Revolution. Over six feet tall, Washington had the dignity and presence of a great leader. He rose to make his acceptance speech. It was in this room a dozen years earlier that Washington had been named commander-in-chief of the Continental Army. In this room, in 1776, the Declaration of Independence had been signed. Now the nation faced another crisis.

Washington was not very hopeful. "It is too probable that no plan we propose will be adopted," he said. Nevertheless, he urged the Convention "to raise a standard to which the wise and the

---

SECTION REVIEW

1. Key Terms Shays' Rebellion, convention, Constitutional Convention, Founding Fathers

2. People Alexander Hamilton, James Madison, George Washington

3. Comprehension What problems led to the call for a constitutional convention?

4. Comprehension In what ways were the delegates to the Convention similar in outlook and experience?

5. Critical Thinking Many Americans feared that if people took the law into their own hands, the result would be tyranny. Explain how this could have happened.

2 Conflict and Compromise

SECTION GUIDE

Main Idea
The delegates to the Constitutional Convention worked out a new form of government.

Goals
As you read, look for answers to these questions:

1. What was the basic structure of government adopted by the Constitutional Convention?

2. Why did states disagree about the make-up of the legislative branch?

3. Why is the Constitution a document of compromises?

Key Terms
compromise
impeach
Electoral College

THE CONVENTION WAS just a few days old when the governor of Virginia rose to speak. Edmund Randolph was a tall man. Unlike the fashionable men of the day, he wore his hair loose and unpowdered. He looked squarely at the delegates and said:

“Let us not be afraid to view with a steady eye the [dangers] with which we are surrounded. . . . Are we not on the eve of war, which is only prevented by the hopes from this convention? ”

Views on Government

Few delegates that hot summer of 1787 disagreed with Randolph that the nation was in danger. They were less sure about the solution. For weeks they argued how best to create a good and stable government.

The men who gathered in Philadelphia had many beliefs in common. They surely agreed with the "truths" set forth in the Declaration of Independence. One of these is that people have certain natural rights, among which are "life, liberty, and the pursuit of happiness." The delegates also agreed that people's natural rights could not exist without government. Government, therefore, was necessary to liberty.

The delegates believed that governments should be based on the consent of the governed. In that belief they reflected the principles of many American Indians. The five Iroquois nations lived under a government in which leaders were chosen by the people. Leaders of many other Indian societies were also strongly influenced by public feeling.

The delegates understood that government officials might use power for their own ends

Alexander Hamilton, James Wilson, James Madison, and Benjamin Franklin meet at the Constitutional Convention.

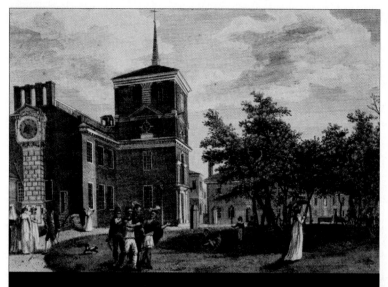

This 1799 engraving shows the back of the Pennsylvania state house in Philadelphia, now known as Independence Hall. **Critical Thinking:** Why might Philadelphia have been chosen as the location of the Constitutional Convention?

rather than for the people. Back in 1776, many of the delegates had thought that government had to rely on the goodness of people. By 1787, events had changed their minds. As George Washington said, "We have, probably, had too good an opinion of human nature in forming our confederation." Madison would write, "If men were angels, no government would be necessary. If angels were to govern men, neither external nor internal controls on government would be necessary." The delegates now assumed that people are by nature selfish.

The challenge was great. The delegates had to design a republic that would protect liberty and yet not depend on the virtue of the people.

The Virginia Plan

Just four days after the meetings began, Governor Randolph of Virginia presented a plan to the Convention. The Virginia Plan, as it was called, was drawn up chiefly by James Madison. It proposed a national government made up of three parts.

(1) Congress, the legislative branch, would make the laws.

(2) An executive branch would carry out the laws.

(3) United States courts would see that justice was done under the laws.

The Virginia Plan was more than just a slight change to the Articles of Confederation. It was a plan for an entirely new form of national government. Delegates voted to expand the original goal of the Convention and consider the plan.

The Debate Begins

The Virginia Plan called for Congress to be made up of two houses. The people would elect one house directly. The members of that house would then elect the members of the second house.

Some delegates were unhappy with this plan. They believed that ordinary people could not be trusted to elect good representatives. These delegates thought that state governments should be responsible for choosing members of Congress. Elbridge Gerry (GER-ee), from Massachusetts, noted that it was ordinary people who had caused Shays' Rebellion. "The evils we experience flow from [too much] democracy," Gerry said.

Many delegates disagreed with Gerry. James Wilson of Pennsylvania argued that government drew strength from the involvement of citizens. The more people who took part in choosing Congress, the stronger it would be, he said. Madison said that for a government to be free, the people must elect representatives. Disagreements over direct elections continued throughout the Convention.

The end to the arguments would come only with both sides giving in a little. This way of settling a problem is known as a **compromise.**

Large States Versus Small

Another part of the Virginia Plan sparked even hotter debate. It had called for representation in Congress to be based on population. A small state such as Delaware, for example, might have only one representative because it had so few people. A state with many people, such as Virginia, might have ten or more representatives.

Delegates from smaller states objected. They worried that the large states would end up ruling the rest. William Paterson of New Jersey was dramatic in his attack. "[I would] rather submit to a monarch," he warned, than to "such a fate."

SKILLS: Working Toward Compromise

LEARN

When you have a strong opinion on an issue, and a friend has the opposite opinion, how do you resolve the conflict? The ability to compromise is one of the most important skills a person can have.

A compromise is a settlement of differences by agreement. One of the keys is finding common ground—areas where both sides already agree. In other areas, where there is no agreement, each side must give up some of what it wants. Often the path to a compromise consists of a series of small steps. One side gives up something. The other side does the same. In this way the two sides inch toward agreement.

Nobody knew this better than the delegates to the Constitutional Convention. They came from different parts of the country and had different views. They faced the challenge of working together to create a lasting framework for governing the new nation. If they failed, the consequences could have been disastrous.

PRACTICE

Analyze the Great Compromise, described in this section.

1. What were the arguments on both sides?

2. What was the common ground?

3. How was the conflict resolved?

4. Based on your analysis, write a general statement about winners and losers when a compromise is reached.

APPLY

5. Role-play, within a group, the debate about how much power Congress should have over trade. Assign roles: northern delegate, southern delegate, and compromiser. Have one person take notes on the differences of opinion, the common ground, and how the issue is resolved.

Paterson offered a different plan to the Convention. Under this plan, called the New Jersey Plan, the legislature would have only one house. Each state, regardless of its population, would send the same number of representatives to Congress. This way a small state would have as many votes as a large state.

The Great Compromise

By now the humid days of summer had come to Philadelphia. Many said it was the worst heat they could remember. Northerners sweated out the days in wool clothing. The southern delegates were more comfortable in their lightweight suits.

For days the delegates argued. Feelings often ran as high as the temperature. The future of the Convention seemed unclear. Watching Washington leave the hall, a for-mer French officer reported, "The look on his face reminded me of its expression during the terrible months we were in Valley Forge Camp."

Connecticut's Roger Sherman offered what came to be called the Great Compromise. Under this plan, the people would be represented in the lower house of the legislature. This would be the House of Representatives. The states, meanwhile, would be represented in the upper house, the Senate. In other words, the larger states would have more representatives in the lower house. In the upper house, however, each state would have two votes.

The compromise also solved the problem of who would elect members of Congress. The people would vote for members of the lower house. The upper house would be chosen by state lawmakers.

Groups not represented at the Convention included women, who were not mentioned. Their rights were left to the states. In New Jersey, women were able to vote until 1807 (above). Enslaved African Americans (bottom right) were noted in the Three-Fifths Compromise and the compromise over the slave trade. In doing so, the Constitution officially recognized slavery. Indian groups were considered foreign nations with which officials negotiated (top right). Indians did not gain full citizenship rights until the 1920s.

Other Compromises

Having agreed to the Great Compromise, the delegates moved on to other matters.

(1) *Slavery.* The southern states had many more slaves than the northern states. Northerners argued that because slaves could not vote, they should not be counted in the figures determining representation in Congress. Southerners did want to include slaves in the figures.

Delegates worked out the Three-Fifths Compromise. They decided that five slaves would count as three persons for the purposes of representation. In doing so, the Constitution officially recognized that slavery was allowed in the United States. It was a compromise with tragic consequences.

(2) *Trade.* The delegates debated how much power Congress should have over trade. All of them agreed that the national government should control trade between states. The northern states wanted Congress to control foreign trade as well. Because many northerners made a living by shipping, they wanted the same trade laws in force everywhere. Southerners, however, preferred to let each state set its own rules. Southerners exported large amounts of rice, tobacco, and indigo. They worried about losing foreign customers if Congress taxed these goods.

Many of the most powerful men at the Convention were southerners. These men also feared that Congress might stop the slave trade. They knew that many northerners opposed slavery. Even southerners who owned slaves, such as George Mason, questioned the practice. "Every master of slaves is born a petty tyrant," he said. "They bring the judgment of heaven upon a country."

Again, the two sides compromised. The delegates gave Congress the power to control trade with other countries. Congress could tax imports but not exports. The delegates also said that Congress could end the slave trade in twenty years.

(3) *The Executive.* The Convention turned its attention to the executive branch. Should the executive be one person or a committee? Most delegates expected that the first executive would be George Washington, and they believed that he would use his powers wisely. They decided the executive branch would be headed by a single person, a President. To keep that person from becoming too powerful, Congress would have the power to impeach the President. (To impeach is to bring an official to trial for misconduct in office.)

Federal Powers Increase Under the Constitution

Powers of the Federal Government Under the Constitution	=	Powers Under Articles of Confederation	+	Additional Powers
		• Declare war, make peace • Direct military • Manage Indian affairs • Set standards of weights and measures • Establish postal services • Borrow money • Manage foreign affairs		• Prevent states from issuing money • Impose taxes • Call out state militias • Regulate all foreign trade • Organize a system of courts • Protect copyrights and patents • Govern territories and the capital city • Take actions to carry out above powers

CHART SKILLS: The Constitution grants the U.S. government many more powers than it had under the Articles of Confederation. **Critical Thinking:** Why did the delegates believe that they needed to increase the federal government's powers?

Some delegates did not trust the judgment of the people to choose a President. To lessen their fears, the Convention decided against direct election of the President. Instead, each state would choose electors—qualified voters. A state would have as many electors as it had senators and representatives combined. The electors would form the Electoral College and choose the President and the Vice President.

The Final Touches

The delegates worked all summer. Often, when tempers began to rise or agreement seemed unlikely, Benjamin Franklin would tell a story. A favorite was the tale of a woman who argued with her sister: "I don't know how it happens, Sister, but I meet with nobody but myself that's always in the right." The delegates would laugh, tensions would ease, and discussion would resume.

Finally, the delegates thought that they had done the best they could. They gathered for the last time on September 17, 1787. Of the 42 present, 39 signed the Constitution. Now it was up to the states to vote on the document.

SECTION REVIEW

1. Key Terms compromise, impeach, Electoral College

2. People Edmund Randolph, William Paterson, Roger Sherman

3. Comprehension What debates did the Great Compromise settle?

4. Comprehension How was the President to be chosen?

5. Critical Thinking Using the Three-Fifths Compromise as an example, explain why compromise might not always be the best solution.

3 Ratifying the Constitution

SECTION GUIDE

Main Idea
After much debate, the states approved the Constitution with the understanding that a bill of rights would be added to protect individual liberties.

Goals
As you read, look for answers to these questions:

1. How did the Constitution become law?

2. What were the concerns of the opponents of the Constitution?

3. How did supporters of the Constitution compromise in order to win its approval?

Key Terms
federalism
Federalist
Antifederalist

THE SECRET WAS OUT. In the autumn of 1787 the Constitution appeared in newspapers and leaflets across the United States. Its authors turned their attention to the states. All their work would be in vain unless nine of the thirteen states voted to accept this new idea of government.

A Federal System

The Constitutional Convention had created something very different from before. "This government is so new, it wants a name," said Patrick Henry. It was no longer a loose league of states. Neither was it a government that denied the states any power. It was a mixture of the two, based on a system called **federalism.** Federalism is the sharing of power between a central (or federal) government and its political subdivisions, in this case the states.

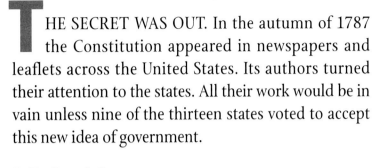

The Constitution became the hottest topic in the country. Some people, called **Federalists,** argued strongly in favor of the new plan of government. Others were against it.

This illustration celebrating the new Constitution includes the motto of the Great Seal of the United States: *E Pluribus Unum* (out of many, one).

The Antifederalists

The people who opposed the Constitution were known as **Antifederalists.** Antifederalists objected to the new plan for two main reasons:

(1) *Loss of states' power.* Antifederalists thought that the Constitution gave too much power to the national government. They feared a strong national government would swallow up the states.

(2) *Loss of individual freedom.* Liberty, the Antifederalists said, could only survive in a small republic. It would be easier in such a republic for people to keep watch over their leaders.

Patrick Henry had refused to attend the Convention. He remained dead set against the Constitution. "If a wrong step be now made," he warned, "the republic may be lost forever."

Thomas Jefferson, in France at the time, was not so doubtful. When he received a copy of the Constitution, he wrote a letter to James Madison expressing his views:

❝I like the organization of the government into legislative, judiciary, and executive [branches]. . . . I will now tell you what I do not like. First, [there is no] bill of rights. . . . A bill of rights is what the people are entitled to against every government on earth. . . .❞

The Federalists

In answer to these criticisms, Federalists insisted that citizens' rights were safe. After all, each state constitution already had a bill of rights. Also, the House of Representatives was to be elected directly by the people. Its members would be sure to protect the people's rights.

The Federalists argued their views in town meetings, newspapers, and pamphlets. The best-known writings were 85 essays collected under the title *The Federalist.* These essays were written by James Madison, Alexander Hamilton, and John Jay—all supporters of a strong central government. They clearly explained the Constitution and presented strong reasons for approving it. The essays argued that, "A nation without a national government is . . . an awful spectacle." Even today the essays in *The Federalist* remain the best explanation of federalism.

The States Decide

Among the first states to ratify the Constitution were the small states. Delaware, New Jersey, Georgia, Maryland, and Connecticut quickly approved it.

In Massachusetts, public opinion was divided. To gain support for the Constitution, Federalists came up with a plan. The state should ratify the Constitution, they argued. At the same time, Massachusetts should recommend that a bill of rights be added. Supporting that plan, Massachusetts voted to ratify.

New Hampshire was the ninth state to approve the Constitution, in June 1788. Nine states were needed to make it the law of the land. Yet New York and Virginia had still not approved. Without Virginia, the new government would lack the support of the largest state. Without New York, the nation would be separated into two parts.

In Virginia, Patrick Henry used all his powers of persuasion to fight against ratification of the Constitution. They were not

A Federalist (Hamilton) Against an Antifederalist (Henry)

"I am persuaded that this [plan] is the best which our political situation, habits, and opinions will admit, and superior to any the revolution has produced."

—*Alexander Hamilton*

"This proposal . . . is of a most alarming nature. . . . You ought to be extremely cautious, watchful, jealous of your liberty."

—*Patrick Henry*

enough, however, to counter the Federalist arguments of such Virginians as George Washington and James Madison. The promise of a bill of rights convinced the Virginia convention to accept the Constitution, 89 to 79.

The news of Virginia's vote arrived while the New York convention was in bitter and heated debates. When the ratification convention first met, the Antifederalists outnumbered the Federalists, 65–19. The leader of the New York Antifederalists was the state's powerful governor, George Clinton. Alexander Hamilton led the New York Federalists.

Over the course of six weeks, Hamilton's brilliant arguments gradually converted delegates to the Federalist point of view. Virginia's vote in favor of the Constitution greatly helped the Federalist cause. In the end the New York convention voted to ratify the Constitution, 30 to 27. They did so on the condition that the new government would respect all "essential rights." Those rights included freedom of the press.

North Carolina and Rhode Island did not ratify the Constitution until more than a year later. By then, the framework of government under which we live today was in place.

SECTION REVIEW

1. Key Terms federalism, Federalist, Antifederalist

2. People and Places Patrick Henry, Alexander Hamilton, New Hampshire

3. Comprehension In what way is a federal system of government a mixed government?

4. Comprehension What were the two main reasons for opposition to the Constitution?

5. Critical Thinking How did the Antifederalists have an impact on the Constitution?

Promises of the Constitution

"All men are created equal," says the Declaration of Independence. Equality is not mentioned, however, in either the Constitution or the Bill of Rights. Still, over time more and more Americans have pushed the Constitution toward a broader concept of equality under the law. Professor and writer Roger Wilkins (shown below) recalls his boyhood faith in the promises of the Constitution:

"When I tell people that I began my education in a one-room segregated schoolhouse in Kansas City, I feel like a fraud . . . because the emotional image it conveys—of a poor little four-year-old black child having his spirit crushed by segregation in the State of Missouri—is wrong. I was an optimistic and very lucky child who had an unshakable faith that America would keep her constitutional promise to us. . . .

The celebration of the 200th anniversary of the Constitution is, on one level, about pictures and memories. The dominant pictures are those of a group of . . . people dressed in eighteenth-century clothing in a room in Philadelphia 200 summers ago. . . .

[A] black American born in the twentieth century cannot avoid noticing that the people in the pictures are white and male. . . . After all, his American memory contains the possibility that one or more of the men in the picture actually owned one or more of his black ancestors. . . .

I viewed the Constitution as a Promise, a basket . . . of things I'd heard about: . . . 'We the people' and the commands of the First, Thirteenth, Fourteenth, and Fifteenth Amendments. All of that added up, in my young mind, to promises of freedom and equality and justice to all of us 'We the people,' in a country great enough to dream up those promises in the first place."

CRITICAL THINKING

1. Does the Constitution provide enough protection against discrimination? Explain.
2. In what ways might the Constitution be different if it were written today?
3. What did Wilkins mean by the statement, "a country great enough to dream up those promises in the first place"?

4 A More Perfect Union

SECTION GUIDE

Main Idea
The Constitution created a strong and balanced government with the flexibility to adjust to the nation's growth and changing needs.

Goals
As you read, look for answers to these questions:

1. How is power divided within the federal government and between the states and the federal government?

2. What is the purpose of the Bill of Rights?

3. How does the Constitution provide for change?

Key Terms
separation of powers
checks and balances
veto
Bill of Rights
amendment
due process
Cabinet

EVERY YEAR THOUSANDS of people visit the National Archives in Washington, D.C. There, carefully displayed, is the Constitution. People can still make out the words on this document written more than 200 years ago: "We the people . . . establish this Constitution for the United States of America." These opening lines declare that the United States is not ruled by a king, queen, or other individual. Instead, the Constitution created a country in which the supreme power rests with the nation's citizens.

The Structure of Government
The Constitution calls for the United States government to be divided into three separate branches.

(1) *The legislative branch makes laws.* It consists of the Senate and the House of Representatives. Senators are elected for six years, while representatives serve for two.

(2) *The executive branch enforces the laws.* The head of this branch is the President, who serves a four-year term. This branch includes such federal departments as the Department of Education.

(3) *The judicial branch interprets the laws.* It consists of the Supreme Court of the United States and other federal courts.

This **separation of powers** keeps any one branch from becoming too powerful. Imagine if one person or group of people had all the power of government in their hands. They could make a law and then arrest you if you broke it. If you appeared in court and claimed the law was unfair, you would be making your arguments to the same group that wrote the law.

The Bill of Rights is displayed at the National Archives in Washington, D.C.

CHART
SKILLS: The
Constitution
divides the pow-
ers of the federal
government into
three separate
branches. The
system of checks
and balances was
designed to pre-
vent any one of
those branches
from becoming
all-powerful.
Critical Think-
ing: Does the
system work?
What are some
of its flaws?

The System of Checks and Balances

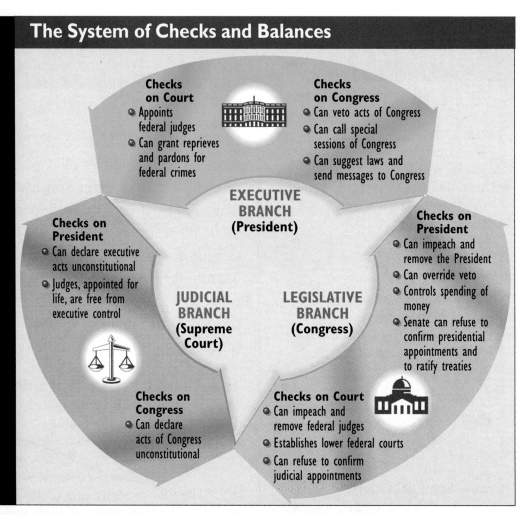

Checks on Court
- Appoints federal judges
- Can grant reprieves and pardons for federal crimes

Checks on Congress
- Can veto acts of Congress
- Can call special sessions of Congress
- Can suggest laws and send messages to Congress

EXECUTIVE BRANCH (President)

Checks on President
- Can declare executive acts unconstitutional
- Judges, appointed for life, are free from executive control

JUDICIAL BRANCH (Supreme Court)

LEGISLATIVE BRANCH (Congress)

Checks on President
- Can impeach and remove the President
- Can override veto
- Controls spending of money
- Senate can refuse to confirm presidential appointments and to ratify treaties

Checks on Congress
- Can declare acts of Congress unconstitutional

Checks on Court
- Can impeach and remove federal judges
- Establishes lower federal courts
- Can refuse to confirm judicial appointments

Checks and Balances

Separation of powers reduces the chance that government will abuse people's rights. It does not, however, prevent any branch of the government from misusing its power. For example, Congress could pass laws favoring one state over another. The executive branch and the federal courts could also at times act unfairly.

To prevent unfairness of this kind, the Constitution gives each branch some powers over the others. These checks keep the different branches in balance. The principle of checks and balances limits the power of the three branches by having each branch watch the others.

For example, the President must approve a proposed law, or bill, that Congress passes before it can take effect. If the President vetoes, or rejects, the bill, it does not become a law. The President also checks the power of the judicial branch, since it is the President who appoints federal judges.

The Senate, however, must approve the President's choices for federal judges. This

Ruth Ginsburg was named to the Supreme Court by President Bill Clinton and confirmed by the Senate.
Critical Thinking: How does Ginsburg's appointment illustrate the system of checks and balances?

is one way that Congress checks both the executive and the judicial branches. In addition, Congress may overturn a presidential veto if two-thirds of the House and Senate vote to do so. Congress also has the power to impeach and remove from office a President or federal judge who seriously misbehaves.

Federal courts have the power to strike down laws and actions of the other two government branches. The Supreme Court may decide that a law passed by Congress goes against the Constitution. The Court then declares the law unconstitutional. The Court can also declare a presidential order unconstitutional.

Sharing of Powers

In writing the Constitution, delegates took care that not all power rested in the federal (national) government. The federal govern-ment was given power over matters that concern the country as a whole. For example, only Congress can make treaties, coin money, put a tax on imported goods, and declare war. Yet the Constitution also allows for some powers to be shared by the federal and state governments. Both can tax, for example. Both can borrow money, build roads, and set up courts. The state militias (today's National Guard) are under the control of the states and the federal government. If conflicts develop between state and national laws, the states must follow the national laws.

States do have powers that are theirs alone. Each state can make its own laws about education and about trade within its borders. Each state can also set its own punishment for crimes.

The Bill of Rights

In 1791 Congress made the first ten additions to the Constitution. As a group, they are known as the Bill of Rights because they describe the rights Americans have under their government. Additions to the Constitution are known as amendments.

The First Amendment guards some of the liberties we cherish most. It protects freedom of religion, freedom of speech, and freedom of the press. It also says that citizens may meet peacefully in

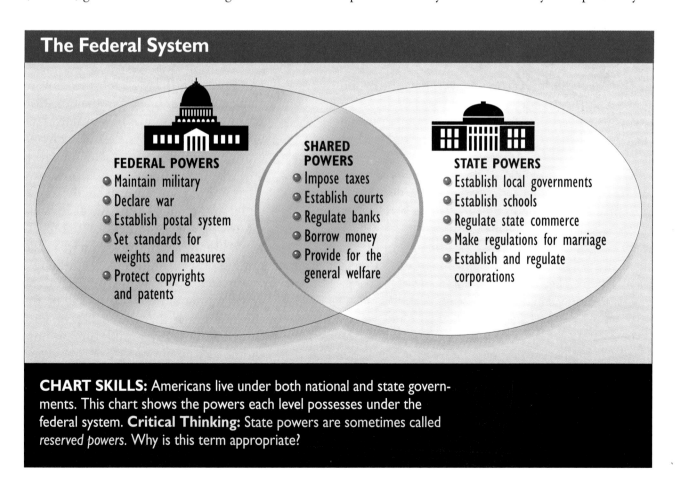

The Federal System

FEDERAL POWERS
- Maintain military
- Declare war
- Establish postal system
- Set standards for weights and measures
- Protect copyrights and patents

SHARED POWERS
- Impose taxes
- Establish courts
- Regulate banks
- Borrow money
- Provide for the general welfare

STATE POWERS
- Establish local governments
- Establish schools
- Regulate state commerce
- Make regulations for marriage
- Establish and regulate corporations

CHART SKILLS: Americans live under both national and state governments. This chart shows the powers each level possesses under the federal system. **Critical Thinking:** State powers are sometimes called *reserved powers*. Why is this term appropriate?

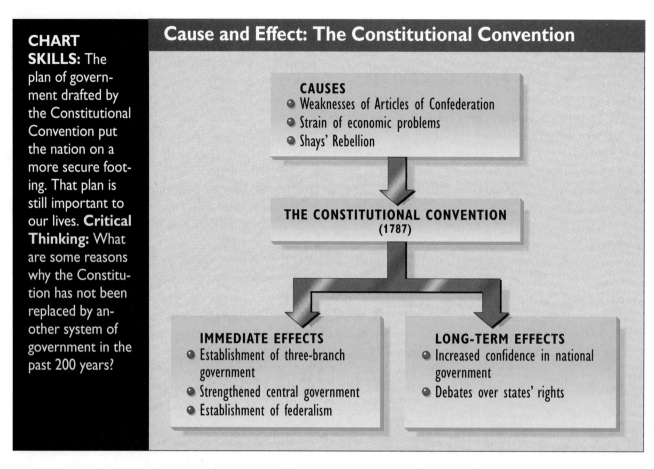

Cause and Effect: The Constitutional Convention

CAUSES
- Weaknesses of Articles of Confederation
- Strain of economic problems
- Shays' Rebellion

THE CONSTITUTIONAL CONVENTION (1787)

IMMEDIATE EFFECTS
- Establishment of three-branch government
- Strengthened central government
- Establishment of federalism

LONG-TERM EFFECTS
- Increased confidence in national government
- Debates over states' rights

groups. In addition, it gives people the right to ask the government to hear their complaints.

The next seven amendments guarantee other freedoms. These include the right to a fair trial. The Bill of Rights also protects us from having our property taken or homes searched without reason. It states that people accused or convicted of crimes must always be treated fairly and according to the law. This right to fair treatment under the law is called due process.

The first eight amendments are specific lists of what the government cannot do. The last two amendments in the Bill of Rights make it clear that there are many more restrictions on government actions. They grant to the states and to the people any powers not mentioned in the Constitution.

The Ability to Change

Delegates to the Constitutional Convention traveled to Philadelphia on horseback or by carriage. They could not have imagined today's world of cars and airplanes. Delegates communicated with their families through letters that took weeks to arrive. Today, telephones, computers, and fax machines send messages in seconds. Despite such mind-boggling changes, the Constitution has continued to serve brilliantly as the framework of our government.

One reason is that a way of amending, or making a change, is part of the Constitution. Article V describes how to amend the Constitution. Either Congress or state conventions can propose an amendment. It then goes to the states to be approved.

The first ten amendments to the Constitution were the Bill of Rights. James Madison wrote most of the Bill of Rights. He must have suspected that the future would bring more amendments. "In framing a system which we wish to last for ages," he said, "we should not lose sight of the changes which the ages will produce." However, in more than 200 years the Constitution has been amended only 27 times.

The Constitution can be changed in other ways as well. One way is through the Supreme Court. The language of the Constitution is often general. It is the Court's job to interpret that language. In one clause, for example, Congress is given the power to make any "laws necessary and proper" for carrying out its duties.

The Supreme Court has applied this "necessary and proper" clause to many different situations over the years. The Constitution says nothing about the airline business. Yet it does give Congress the right to control interstate trade. The Court thus decided that Congress can also regulate airlines. Because this clause has allowed the powers of Congress to expand, it is called the "elastic clause."

Change over Time

The Supreme Court can also change its interpretations over time. In 1896 (*Plessy v. Ferguson*) the Court decided that separate treatment for black and white citizens was constitutional. It was legal, said the Court, for African Americans to be forced to attend separate schools, sit in separate train cars, and use separate public facilities.

As time passed, this became less acceptable. In 1954 (*Brown v. Board of Education*) the Supreme Court declared that making white and black children go to separate schools was wrong. It ruled that laws separating people on the basis of race were unconstitutional.

Custom also affects the Constitution. Certain practices have been followed so long they have become an unwritten part of government. For example, all Presidents appoint a **Cabinet** —a formal group of advisers. The Constitution makes no mention of such a group. It simply says that the President may set up departments to help run the government. It is by custom, not by law, that the Cabinet has become an official part of the executive branch.

The Constitution continues to change through new customs, court decisions, and amendments. Yet its principles remain. The United States is ruled not by the whims of its leaders, but by a set of laws. These laws unite a diverse and changing population. One historian, Richard B.

The question of whether this prayer meeting at a public school is constitutional has been hotly debated for decades. **Critical Thinking:** How does the First Amendment support both sides of the argument?

Morris, has described the Constitution as the "symbol that unifies . . . people of different origins, races, and religions into a single nation."

SECTION REVIEW

1. Key Terms separation of powers, checks and balances, veto, Bill of Rights, amendment, due process, Cabinet

2. Comprehension What powers do the states and federal government share?

3. Comprehension What does the Bill of Rights protect?

4. Comprehension How can the Constitution be changed?

5. Critical Thinking Checks and balances discourage officials from acting rapidly. How might this be an advantage? How might it be a drawback?

Summary

1. Shays' Rebellion, combined with complaints about the government's inability to tax and control commerce, led to a convention to revise the Articles of Confederation.

2. The Constitution was made from a series of compromises on such issues as representation by population or by state. Delegates debated direct election versus states' choosing representatives. Southern and northern delegates argued about slavery. Compromises were also reached on congressional control of trade and the method for electing the President.

3. Antifederalists feared that the Constitution gave too much power to the federal government. Federalist arguments and the promise of a bill of rights helped convince such states as Virginia and New York to ratify the Constitution, and it became the law of the land.

4. For over 200 years, the Constitution has provided a strong but flexible framework for the United States. This framework has the ability to change over time. It is based on a division of powers between the federal and state governments, separation of powers within the federal government, and a system of checks and balances.

Graphic Summary

Weakness of Articles of Confederation

Trade Disputes → Annapolis Convention

Currency Problems → Shays' Rebellion

Constitutional Convention

Compromises

Constitution

Review

KEY TERMS

Define the terms in each of the following pairs.
1. Shays' Rebellion; Constitutional Convention
2. compromise; Electoral College
3. federalism; Antifederalist
4. separation of powers; checks and balances
5. Bill of Rights; due process

COMPREHENSION

1. What factor led to Shays' Rebellion? What were the consequences of the rebellion?
2. What problems led some Americans to call for revisions in the Articles of Confederation?
3. Describe the government proposed in the Virginia Plan.
4. What issues caused controversy in the debate over the legislative branch? How were they resolved?
5. What issue caused the greatest controversy in the debate over the executive branch? How was it resolved?
6. What were the concerns of the Antifederalists?
7. By what process did the Constitution became the law of the land?
8. How can the judicial branch check the powers of other branches of the federal government?
9. What powers are shared by both the federal and state governments?
10. How is a plan for dealing with change built into the Constitution?

Places to Locate

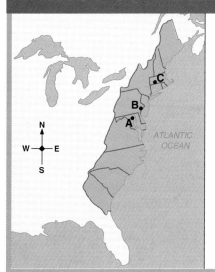

Match the letters on the map with the places listed below. Then explain the importance of each place.

1. Philadelphia, Pennsylvania
2. Springfield, Massachusetts
3. Annapolis, Maryland

Geographic Theme: Regions
Why did northern states want the federal government to control foreign trade? Why did southern states oppose the idea? What was the outcome?

Skill Review

Reread the suggestions for reaching compromises discussed on the skill page in this chapter. Then follow the directions below.

1. Describe the conflict the delegates to the Constitutional Convention had over the executive branch. Discuss with the class how a compromise was reached.

2. Look through recent newspapers and magazines for examples of conflicts over a bill being considered by Congress or your state government. Discuss how a compromise on the issue can be reached.

3. Imagine that your class is going on an educational field trip. Divide the class into five groups. Each group should think of one suggestion for a place to visit. The class as a whole should consider each idea and work together to agree on one place to go. Then each student should write a short paragraph describing how a compromise was reached.

CRITICAL THINKING

1. Forming a Hypothesis How might a case have been made that Shays' Rebellion was different from the Boston Tea Party?

2. Making Judgments What, in your opinion, were the most important arguments in favor of ratifying the Constitution? What were the most important arguments against ratification?

PORTFOLIO OPTIONS

1. Civics Connection At the close of the Constitutional Convention, Benjamin Franklin was approached by a woman who asked, "Well, Dr. Franklin, what kind of government have you given us?" He replied, "A republic, if you can keep it." What do you think he meant?

2. Writing Connection Under our system, citizens can inform their representatives of their concerns by writing letters. Write a letter to your representative about an issue that is important to you.

3. Contemporary Connection Choose one of the rights protected by the Bill of Rights. Then gather pictures, news articles, and other images of life in the United States today that illustrate that right.

4. Timeline Connection Study the chapter timeline. Explain the significance of Shays' Rebellion to the forming of a new government for the United States. How many years after the Constitution became law was the Bill of Rights added?

CONSTITUTION Handbook

The framers of the Constitution wanted to create a government powerful enough to protect the rights of citizens and defend the country against its enemies. They did not want a government, however, so powerful that it could become a tyranny. As James Madison observed, "In framing a government . . . the great difficulty lies in this: you must first enable the government to control the governed; and in the next place oblige it to control itself." As you study the Constitution, you will discover the many ways the framers sought to balance these diverse goals.

Principles of the American System of Government

The United States is dedicated to the proposition that people have the capacity to make wise decisions and govern themselves. Our country is a *republic* because we choose representatives to act for us in governing. It is also a democracy because all qualified citizens have the privilege of voting and therefore determining the kind of government we have.

French historian Alexis de Tocqueville studied systems of government in the 1830s. Compared to other forms of government, Tocqueville concluded, republics "will be less brilliant, less glorious, and perhaps less strong, but the majority of the citizens will enjoy a greater degree of prosperity, and the people will remain quiet . . . because it is conscious of the advantages of its condition."

What are some features of our form of government? Under the Constitution, states share power with the federal (national) government. Some powers are given only to the federal government; others belong to the states; some are held jointly. This division of powers, known as federalism, encourages each side to protect its special powers against intrusion by the other.

The Constitution provides for separation of powers within the federal government as well. Only the legislative branch of the government can make laws. The executive branch administers them. The judicial branch interprets laws when disagreements arise over their meanings.

In order to guard against any one branch of the federal government becoming too powerful, the Constitution specifies a system of checks and balances. Each branch of government possesses the power to check, or limit the actions of, the other two branches.

Thirteen Enduring Constitutional Issues

Our Constitution is the world's oldest written constitution. In the two centuries since its ratification, the Constitution has been changed through custom and through amendment, though these changes have been remarkably few. Arguments over how to interpret the language of the document, however, have been continual.

When disputes over the Constitution's meaning arise, the Supreme Court interprets and decides the issue. Supreme Court interpretations have changed over the years, and many unresolved issues remain.

The following thirteen issues have been sources of ongoing debates among legislators, legal scholars, and concerned citizens. The course of these debates shapes our system of government and the society in which we live.

1. National Power The framers of the Constitution carefully limited the power of the federal government. However, over time, the government has expanded its authority. In the course of the nation's expansion, the federal government has also taken possession of territories such as Puerto Rico, the Panama Canal, the Philippines and other Pacific islands, and land belonging to American Indians. During national emergencies, the government has tried to take over some businesses and forced others to close.

Has the expansion of federal power gone too far? Or is the federal government too weak to deal effectively with complex problems that the nation faces as it nears the twenty-first century?

2. Federalism The framers of the Constitution divided power between the state governments and the federal government to avoid the dangers of centralized authority. In doing so, however, they created what John Quincy Adams called "the most complicated government on the face of the earth."

The boundaries between state and federal power have been the subject of many lawsuits. Supporters of states' rights argue that state governments should have final authority within their state. Federalists believe that many state policies involve national issues and should be under the authority of the federal government. The Supreme Court has claimed the power to declare state laws unconstitutional.

In addition, the federal government controls most tax revenues. State governments depend on federal aid to carry out many of the powers reserved to them in the Constitution. The federal government has used the threat of withholding this aid to change state policies.

Is the increased power of the federal government necessary to enforce justice throughout the nation? Or does it endanger our liberties by destroying the balance of power in the federal system?

3. The Judiciary The Supreme Court is unique because it decides fundamental social and political questions. These include the boundaries between church and state, between legislative and executive power, and even between racial groups. The Court has the power to declare the acts of governors, Congress, or the President to be unconstitutional.

Tocqueville called this power of judicial review "one of the most powerful barriers that have ever been devised against the tyranny of political assemblies." But its opponents have challenged judicial review repeatedly since *Marbury v. Madison* helped establish it in 1803.

In the twentieth century, Supreme Court decisions have helped shape government policies in hotly debated areas such as school integration. Some scholars believe it is the Court's responsibility to act when Congress or the state legislatures do not. Others support "judicial self-restraint." They claim that the activism of the unelected federal judiciary represents a threat to the separation of powers and to democracy itself.

4. Civil Liberties The first ten amendments to the Constitution are known as the Bill of Rights. The First Amendment guarantees individual liberties such as freedom of speech, religion, and assembly. Questions of limits on these individual liberties have often been debated. For example, should the First Amendment right to freedom of speech prevail if it offends the values of the majority? What if it is racist speech? To what extent should human and civil rights be limited in the name of national security?

5. Suspects' Rights How can the government balance the rights of persons accused of crimes with the public's right to safety? For example, some believe the courts should allow guilty persons to go free if crucial evidence against them has been obtained without a warrant, or if they were not specifically informed of their constitutional rights. Others argue that these restrictions on law enforcement needlessly endanger the rest of the community.

Another area of debate concerns the widespread practice of "plea-bargaining" in criminal cases. In order to avoid costly trials, should prosecutors permit accused persons to plead guilty to lesser crimes? Or does this allow the guilty to escape the punishment they deserve?

6. Equality In what ways are all Americans equal? The Constitution guarantees equality before the law, as well as equal political rights. Traditionally, discriminatory political and legal practices have thwarted these goals.

Today, many people believe that the government should promote a more equal distribution of economic resources among citizens. For example, affirmative action programs require employers to promote a racial and sexual balance by favoring minority and female applicants. Supporters contend that without government help, the injustices of the past will continue to plague minorities. Opponents argue that affirmative action is a misguided attempt to guarantee equality of result rather than equality of opportunity.

7. Women's Rights Does the Constitution adequately protect the rights of women? The document does not mention women, but its use of the terms "person" and "citizen" does not exclude women either. In the past the nation has debated the merits of the Equal Rights Amendment. Is such an amendment necessary? Is it desirable? Short of a constitutional amendment, how can women be assured that they will not suffer from discrimination in the work force and other areas? How do Supreme Court decisions on a number of issues affect women's rights?

8. Minority Rights Slaves had no vote or other rights under the Constitution until passage of the Fourteenth Amendment in 1868. After World War II, the federal government took a larger role in protecting minority groups from discrimination. In *Brown v. Board of Education of Topeka* (1954), the Supreme Court outlawed school segregation.

Often, government decisions involving minority rights met fierce resistance from people who felt that their own rights and the principle of majority rule were threatened. Then, in the 1980s, there was a shift in government policy. Critics of Supreme Court decisions argued that minority gains from earlier decades were fast being eroded. Despite some gains, many minorities still suffer from discrimination. What is the federal government's role in protecting minority rights? What is the proper balance between majority rule and minority rights?

9. Foreign Policy Under the Constitution, Congress has the power to declare war. Yet the President is commander-in-chief of the armed forces. How should the government handle the conduct of war and foreign policy? Should the President have the power to send troops into combat without a declaration of war, as was done in Korea and Vietnam?

Some argue that the President needs to be able to act decisively to protect national security. Others state that without popular support, in the form of a congressional vote, military actions are illegitimate. In passing the War Powers Act of 1973, which limited the President's ability to use military power, did Congress unconstitutionally infringe on presidential power?

10. Separation of Powers Does the separation of powers make the federal government too inefficient to meet modern-day challenges? The framers deliberately pitted the branches of government against one another and, in effect, lessened their efficiency in order to guard against abuses. Some critics argue that these safeguards are not worth the price we pay for them in governmental inefficiency. Others contend that the history of abuse of governmental power proves the worth of the system of checks and balances.

11. Representation Our government is based on a system of representation. Does our current system of government provide fair and effective representation of our citizenry? The twentieth century has seen the growth of thousands of special interest groups, which often have political clout beyond the size of their memberships. Do these groups protect the rights of minorities? Or are they unacceptable limitations of democracy?

12. Government and the Economy Does the Constitution's encouragement of business and commerce help all Americans, or does it favor the interests of the wealthy? In this century, reformers have urged the government to limit the exercise of free enterprise in order to protect the public from a variety of abuses. These abuses include unfair pricing, unsafe products, and environmental destruction.

13. Constitutional Change How flexible is the Constitution? The framers included Article V so that the Constitution could be revised to suit future conditions. However, they deliberately made the amendment process difficult so that the Constitution would be more than temporary law.

Does the requirement of a two-thirds vote of Congress and a three-quarters vote of the state legislatures or state conventions benefit the nation by making its political system more stable? Or does it harm America by preventing the Constitution from adapting to changing times? If, in accordance with Article V, the states called a second constitutional convention, would the delegates have the right to frame an entirely new constitution?

Studying the Constitution

These thirteen enduring issues involve basic questions of law and policy. It is useful to keep them in mind as you study the Constitution, since they demonstrate the document's importance in the lives of American citizens.

The complete text of the Constitution of the United States begins on the next page. The actual text of the Constitution appears in the inside column on each page, while the other column explains specific parts or provisions.

Headings and subheadings have been added to the Constitution to help you find specific topics. Those parts of the Constitution that are no longer in effect are shown in lighter type. Some of the spellings and punctuation have been modified for modern readers.

The Constitution of the United States

The Preamble states the purposes for which the Constitution was written: (1) to form a union of states that will benefit all, (2) to make laws and establish courts that are fair, (3) to maintain peace within the country, (4) to defend the nation against attack, (5) to ensure people's general well-being, and (6) to make sure that this nation's people and their descendants remain free.

The opening words of the Constitution make clear that it is the people themselves who have the power to establish a government or change it.

Preamble

*W*e the people of the United States, in order to form a more perfect union, establish justice, insure domestic tranquility, provide for the common defense, promote the general welfare, and secure the blessings of liberty to ourselves and our posterity, do ordain and establish this Constitution for the United States of America.

The first branch described is the legislative, or law-making, branch. Congress is made up of two houses—the Senate and the House of Representatives.

ARTICLE I Legislative Branch

SECTION 1 Congress

All legislative powers herein granted shall be vested in a Congress of the United States, which shall consist of a Senate and House of Representatives.

SECTION 2 The House of Representatives

Clause 1. Election and term of members The House of Representatives shall be composed of members chosen every second year by the people of the several states, and the electors in each state shall have the qualifications requisite for electors of the most numerous branch of the state legislature.

Section 2
Note that the states establish qualifications for voting. Any person who has the right to vote for representatives to the state legislature has the right to vote for the state's representatives in the House of Representatives. This is the only qualification for voting listed in the original Constitution. It made sure that the House would be elected by the people themselves.

Clause 2. Qualification of members No person shall be a representative who shall not have attained to the age of twenty-five years, and been seven years a citizen of the United States, and who shall not, when elected, be an inhabitant of that state in which he shall be chosen.

254

Clause 3. Appointment of representatives and direct taxes Representatives [and direct taxes] shall be apportioned among the several states which may be included within this Union, according to their respective numbers, [which shall be determined by adding to the whole number of free persons, including those bound to service for a term of years, and excluding Indians not taxed, three-fifths of all other persons]. The actual enumeration shall be made within three years after the first meeting of the Congress of the United States, and within every subsequent term of ten years, in such manner as they shall by law direct. The number of representatives shall not exceed one for every thirty thousand, but each state shall have at least one representative; [and until such enumeration shall be made, the State of New Hampshire shall be entitled to choose three; Massachusetts, eight; Rhode Island and Providence Plantations, one; Connecticut, five; New York, six; New Jersey, four; Pennsylvania, eight; Delaware, one; Maryland, six; Virginia, ten; North Carolina, five; South Carolina, five; and Georgia, three].

Clause 4. Filling vacancies When vacancies happen in the representation from any state, the executive authority thereof shall issue writs of election to fill such vacancies.

Clause 5. Officers; impeachment The House of Representatives shall choose their Speaker and other officers; and shall have the sole power of impeachment.

SECTION 3   The Senate

Clause 1. Number and election of members The Senate of the United States shall be composed of two senators from each state, chosen [by the legislature thereof,] for six years; and each senator shall have one vote.

Clause 3
Several amendments have changed these provisions. All the people of a state are now counted in determining the number of representatives a state shall have, based on a census taken every ten years. The House of Representatives cannot have more than one member for every 30,000 persons in the nation. But each state is entitled to one representative, no matter how small its population. In 1910 Congress limited the number of representatives to 435.

Amendment 16 made the income tax an exception to the rule against direct taxes not based on population.

Clause 4
When a state does not have all the representatives to which it is entitled—for example, when a representative resigns or dies—the governor of the state may call an election to fill the vacancy.

Clause 5
Only the House can impeach, that is, bring charges of misbehavior in office against a U.S. official.

Section 3
Senators are no longer chosen by state legislatures but elected by the people (Amendment 17).

Senators in the 1st Congress were divided into three groups so that their terms would not all end at the same time. Today all senators are elected for six-year terms, but only one-third are elected in any election year.

A bird's-eye view of the nation's capital in 1880, when the Washington Monument was still being built.

Daniel Webster in a tense Senate debate, 1850.

Clauses 6 and 7

The Senate tries the case when a federal official is impeached by the House of Representatives. The Senators must formally declare that they will be honest and just. If the President of the United States is on trial, the Chief Justice presides over the Senate. Two-thirds of the senators present must agree that the charge is true for the impeached person to be found guilty.

If the Senate finds an impeached official guilty, the only punishment is removal from office and disqualification for ever holding a government job again. Once out of office, however, the former official may be tried in a regular court and, if found guilty, punished like any other person.

Clause 2. Choosing senators Immediately after they shall be assembled in consequence of the first election, they shall be divided as equally as may be into three classes. [The seats of the senators of the first class shall be vacated at the expiration of the second year, of the second class at the expiration of the fourth year, and of the third class at the expiration of the sixth year,] **so that one-third may be chosen every second year;** [and if vacancies happen by resignation, or otherwise, during the recess of the legislature of any state, the executive thereof may make temporary appointments until the next meeting of the legislature, which shall then fill such vacancies.]

Clause 3. Qualifications of members No person shall be a senator who shall not have attained to the age of thirty years, and been nine years a citizen of the United States, and who shall not, when elected, be an inhabitant of that state for which he shall be chosen.

Clause 4. Senate President The Vice President of the United States shall be President of the Senate, but shall have no vote, unless they be equally divided.

Clause 5. Other officers The Senate shall choose their own officers, and also a President pro tempore, in the absence of the Vice President, or when he shall exercise the office of President of the United States.

Clause 6. Impeachment trials The Senate shall have the sole power to try all impeachments. When sitting for that purpose, they shall be on oath or affirmation. When the President of the United States is tried, the Chief Justice shall preside; and no person shall be convicted without the concurrence of two-thirds of the members present.

Clause 7. Impeachment convictions Judgment in cases of impeachment shall not exceed further than to removal from office, and disqualification to hold and enjoy any office of honor, trust, or profit under the United States; but the party convicted shall nevertheless be liable and subject to indictment, trial, judgment, and punishment, according to law.

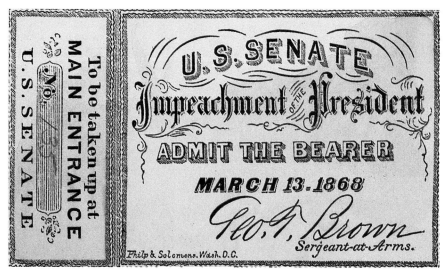

A visitor's ticket to the Senate gallery for the 1868 impeachment trial that acquitted President Johnson.

SECTION 4   Congressional Elections and Meetings

Clause 1. Elections   The times, places, and manner of holding elections for senators and representatives shall be prescribed in each state by the legislature thereof; but the Congress may at any time by law make or alter such regulations, [except as to the places of choosing senators.]

Clause 2. Meetings of Congress   The Congress shall assemble at least once in every year, [and such meeting shall be on the first Monday in December, unless they shall by law appoint a different day.]

SECTION 5   Organization and Rules

Clause 1. Organization   Each house shall be the judge of the elections, returns, and qualifications of its own members, and a majority of each shall constitute a quorum to do business; but a smaller number may adjourn from day to day, and may be authorized to compel the attendance of absent members, in such manner, and under such penalties as each house may provide.

Clause 2. Rules   Each house may determine the rules of its proceedings, punish its members for disorderly behavior, and with the concurrence of two-thirds, expel a member.

Clause 3. Journal   Each house shall keep a journal of its proceedings, and from time to time publish the same, excepting such parts as may in their judgment require secrecy; and the yeas and nays of the members of either house on any question shall, at the desire of one-fifth of those present, be entered on the journal.

Section 4
The legislature of each state has the right to determine how, when, and where senators and representatives are elected, but Congress may pass election laws that the states must follow. For example, a federal law requires that secret ballots be used. Congress must meet at least once a year. Amendment 20 made January 3 the day for beginning a regular session of Congress.

Andrew Johnson, the only U.S. President impeached.

Clause 3
Each house of Congress keeps and publishes a record of what goes on at its meetings. The *Congressional Record* is issued daily during sessions of Congress. Parts of the record that the members of Congress believe should be kept secret may be withheld. How members of either house vote on a question may be entered in the record if one-fifth of those present wish it.

Clause 4

When Congress is meeting, neither house may stop work for more than three days without the consent of the other house. Neither house may meet in another city without the consent of the other house.

Section 6

Senators and representatives are paid out of the United States Treasury and have a number of other privileges.

Until their terms have ended, senators or representatives may not hold offices created by the Congress of which they are members. The same restriction applies to jobs for which Congress has voted increased pay. No person may be a member of Congress without first giving up any other federal office he or she may hold.

Section 7

Bills for raising money for the federal government must start in the House of Representatives, but the Senate may make changes in such bills. Actually, the Senate now has as much influence over revenue bills as does the House. Other bills may start in either the Senate or the House of Representatives. However, exactly the same bill must be passed by a majority vote in both houses of Congress.

President Gerald Ford signs a tax bill into law.

Clause 4. Adjournment   Neither house, during the session of Congress, shall without the consent of the other adjourn for more than three days, nor to any other place than that in which the two houses shall be sitting.

SECTION 6   Privileges and Restrictions

Clause 1. Pay; Congressional immunity   The senators and representatives shall receive a compensation for their services, to be ascertained by law, and paid out of the Treasury of the United States. They shall in all cases, except treason, felony, and breach of the peace, be privileged from arrest during their attendance at the session of their respective houses and in going to and returning from the same; and for any speech or debate in either house, they shall not be questioned in any other place.

Clause 2. Restrictions   No senator or representative shall, during the time for which he was elected, be appointed to any civil office under the authority of the United States which shall have been created, or the emoluments whereof shall have been increased during such time; and no person holding any office under the United States shall be a member of either house during his continuance in office.

SECTION 7   Method of Passing Laws

Clause 1. Revenue bills   All bills for raising revenue shall originate in the House of Representatives; but the Senate may propose or concur with amendments as on other bills.

Clause 2. How bills become law   Every bill which shall have passed the House of Representatives and the Senate shall, before it become a law, be presented to the President of the United States; if he approves he shall sign it, but if not he shall return it, with his objections, to that house in which it shall have originated, who shall enter the objections at large on their journal, and proceed to reconsider it. If after such reconsideration two-thirds of that house shall agree to pass the bill, it shall be sent, together with the objections, to the other house, by which it shall likewise be reconsidered, and if approved by two-thirds of that house, it shall become a law. But in all such cases the votes of both houses shall be determined by yeas and nays, and the names of the persons voting for and against the bill shall be entered on the journal of each house respectively. If any bill shall not be returned by the President within ten days (Sundays excepted) after it shall have been presented to him, the same shall be a law, in like manner as if he had signed it, unless the Congress by their adjournment prevent its return, in which case it shall not be a law.

Clause 3. Presidential approval or disapproval Every order, resolution, or vote to which the concurrence of the Senate and House of Representatives may be necessary (except on a question of adjournment) shall be presented to the President of the United States; and before the same shall take effect, shall be approved by him, or being disapproved by him, shall be repassed by two-thirds of the Senate and House of Representatives, according to the rules and limitations prescribed in the case of a bill.

SECTION 8   Powers Granted to Congress

The Congress shall have power
Clause 1. To lay and collect taxes, duties, imposts, and excises; to pay the debts and provide for the common defense and general welfare of the United States; but all duties, imposts, and excises shall be uniform throughout the United States;

Clause 2. To borrow money on the credit of the United States;

Clause 3. To regulate commerce with foreign nations, and among the several states, and with the Indian tribes;

Clause 4. To establish a uniform rule of naturalization, and uniform laws on the subject of bankruptcies throughout the United States;

Section 8
This section lists the many delegated powers of Congress.

Clause 3
Under this "commerce clause," the national government has broadened its powers.

The harbor at Philadelphia — an important center for American commerce and shipping — in 1800.

Clause 8
Congress may pass copyright and patent laws that make it illegal for a person to use the work of an artist, musician, author, or inventor without permission.

U.S. gold "quarter eagle" coins, minted in 1796.

Clauses 11–16
These provisions ensure civilian control of the military.

Clause 5. To coin money, regulate the value thereof and of foreign coin, and fix the standard of weights and measures;

Clause 6. To provide for the punishment of counterfeiting the securities and current coin of the United States;

Clause 7. To establish post offices and post roads;

Clause 8. To promote the progress of science and useful arts by securing for limited times to authors and inventors the exclusive right to their respective writings and discoveries;

Clause 9. To constitute tribunals inferior to the Supreme Court;

Clause 10. To define and punish piracies and felonies committed on the high seas and offenses against the laws of nations;

Clause 11. To declare war, grant letters of marque and reprisal, and make rules concerning captures on land and water;

Clause 12. To raise and support armies, but no appropriation of money to that use shall be for a longer term than two years;

Clause 13. To provide and maintain a navy;

Clause 14. To make rules for the government and regulation of land and naval forces;

Clause 15. To provide for calling forth the militia to execute the laws of the Union, suppress insurrections, and repel invasions;

Clause 16. To provide for organizing, arming, and disciplining the militia, and for governing such part of them as may be employed in the service of the United States, reserving to the states respectively the appointment of the officers and the authority of training the militia, according to the discipline prescribed by Congress;

The first American dollar bill, an 1862 "greenback."

Clause 17. To exercise exclusive legislation in all cases whatsoever over such district (not exceeding ten miles square) as may, by cession of particular states and the acceptance of Congress, become the seat of the government of the United States, and to exercise like authority over all places purchased by the consent of the legislature of the states in which the same shall be for the erection of forts, magazines, arsenals, dock-yards, and other needful buildings; and

Clause 18. To make all laws which shall be necessary and proper for carrying into execution the foregoing powers, and all other powers vested by this Constitution in the government of the United States, or in any department or officer thereof.

SECTION 9 Powers Denied to the Federal Government

Clause 1. [The migration or importation of such persons as any of the states now existing shall think proper to admit shall not be prohibited by the Congress prior to the year one thousand eight hundred and eight, but a tax or duty may be imposed on such importation, not exceeding ten dollars for each person.]

Clause 2. The privilege of the writ of habeas corpus shall not be suspended, unless when in cases of rebellion or invasion the public safety may require it.

Clause 3. No bill of attainder or ex post facto law shall be passed.

Clause 4. No capitation or other direct tax shall be laid, unless in proportion to the census or enumeration herein before directed to be taken.

Clause 5. No tax or duty shall be laid on articles exported from any state.

Clause 6. No preference shall be given by any regulation of commerce or revenue to the ports of one state over those of another; nor shall vessels bound to or from one state be obliged to enter, clear, or pay duties in another.

Clause 7. No money shall be drawn from the treasury, but in consequence of appropriations made by law; and a regular statement and account of the receipts and expenditures of all public money shall be published from time to time.

Clause 8. No titles of nobility shall be granted by the United States; and no person holding any office of profit or trust under them shall, without the consent of Congress, accept of any present, emolument, office, or title, of any kind whatever, from any king, prince, or foreign state.

Clause 17
Congress has the power to make laws for the District of Columbia, the national capital. Congress also makes laws regulating the use of all other property belonging to the national government—forts, arsenals, national parks, etc.

Clause 18
The "necessary and proper" clause, or elastic clause, is the basis for the implied powers.

Section 9
This is the first list of prohibited powers—those denied to the federal government.

Clause 1
Congress could not take action against slavery until 1808, when it prohibited further importation of slaves.

The shelling of Ft. McHenry, Baltimore, in 1814, which inspired the words of the "Star-Spangled Banner."

Clause 8
The United States may not grant a title of nobility. Federal officials may not accept titles, gifts, or honors from any foreign ruler or government unless Congress gives its permission.

Section 10
This is the listing of powers prohibited to the states.

Clause 2
States cannot tax goods leaving or entering their territory but may charge fees to cover the costs of inspection. Any profit from such inspection fees must be turned over to the United States Treasury. Congress has the power to change the inspection laws of a state.

Clause 3
Unless Congress gives permission, a state may not tax ships entering its ports, keep an army or navy— except the militia — in time of peace, make treaties with other states or foreign countries, or make war except when it is invaded.

The second branch is the executive branch, which carries out the laws.

GENERAL ANDREW JACKSON.
The Hero, the Sage and the Patriot.

Clause 2
This provision sets up the Electoral College: The President and Vice President are elected by electors chosen by the states according to rules established by the legislatures. Each state has as many electors as it has senators and representatives in Congress.

This clause did not work well in practice and was changed by Amendment 12.

SECTION 10 Powers Denied to the States

Clause 1. No state shall enter into any treaty, alliance, or confederation; grant letters of marque and reprisal; coin money; emit bills of credit; make any thing but gold and silver coin a tender in payment of debts; pass any bill of attainder, ex post facto law, or law impairing the obligation of contracts; or grant any title of nobility.

Clause 2. No state shall, without the consent of the Congress, lay any imposts or duties on imports or exports, except what may be absolutely necessary for executing its inspection laws; and the net produce of all duties and imposts, laid by any state on imports or exports, shall be for the use of the treasury of the United States; and all such laws shall be subject to the revision and control of the Congress.

Clause 3. No state shall, without the consent of Congress, lay any duty of tonnage; keep troops or ships of war in time of peace; enter into any agreement or compact with another state or with a foreign power; or engage in war, unless actually invaded or in such imminent danger as will not admit of delay.

ARTICLE II Executive Branch

SECTION 1 President and Vice President

Clause 1. Term of office The executive power shall be vested in a President of the United States of America. He shall hold his office during the term of four years, and, together with the Vice President chosen for the same term, be elected as follows:

Clause 2. Electoral College Each state shall appoint, in such manner as the legislature thereof may direct, a number of electors, equal to the whole number of senators and representatives to which the state may be entitled in the Congress; but no senator or representative, or person holding an office of trust or profit under the United States, shall be appointed an elector.

[The electors shall meet in their respective states and vote by ballot for two persons, of whom one at least shall not be an inhabitant of the same state with themselves. And they shall make a list of all the persons voted for and of the number of votes for each; which list they shall sign and certify, and transmit sealed to the seat of government of the United States, directed to the President of the Senate. The President of the Senate shall, in the presence of the Senate and House of Representatives, open all the certificates, and the votes shall then be counted. The person having the greatest number of votes shall be the President, if such number be a majority of the whole number of electors appointed; and if there be more than one who have such majority, and have an equal number of votes, then the House of Representatives shall immediately choose by ballot one of them for President; and if no person have a majority, then from the five highest on the list the said house shall in like manner choose the President. But in choosing the President the votes shall be taken by states, the representation from each state having one vote; a quorum for this purpose shall consist of a member or members from two-thirds of the states, and a majority of all the states shall be necessary to a choice. In every case, after the choice of the President, the person having the greatest number of votes of the electors shall be the Vice President. But if there should remain two or more who have equal votes, the Senate shall choose from them by ballot the Vice President.]

Clause 3. Time of elections   The Congress may determine the time of choosing the electors, and the day on which they shall give their votes; which day shall be the same throughout the United States.

Clause 4. Qualifications for President   No person except a natural-born citizen, [or a citizen of the United States, at the time of the adoption of this Constitution] shall be eligible to the office of President; neither shall any person be eligible to that office who shall not have attained the age of thirty-five years, and been fourteen years a resident within the United States.

Clause 5. Succession   In case of the removal of the President from office or of his death, resignation, or inability to discharge the powers and duties of the said office, the same shall devolve on the Vice President; and the Congress may by law provide for the case of removal, death, resignation, or inability, both of the President and Vice President, declaring what officer shall then act as President; and such officer shall act accordingly, until the disability be removed or a President shall be elected.

An 1860 poster for candidates Lincoln and Hannibal Hamlin.

Clause 3
Congress determines when electors are chosen and when they vote. The day is the same throughout the United States. The popular vote for electors takes place on the Tuesday after the first Monday of November every four years. In mid-December the electors meet in their state capitals and cast their electoral votes.

Clause 5
If the presidency becomes vacant, the Vice President becomes the President of the United States. If neither the President nor the Vice President is able to serve, Congress has the right to decide which government official shall act as President. Amendment 25 practically assures that there always will be a Vice President to succeed to the presidency.

The White House — the presidential mansion — in 1848.

Section 2
Presidential powers are described very generally (unlike those of Congress).
Clause 1
The President is commander-in-chief of the armed forces and of the militia when it is called out by the national government. This is another provision to ensure civilian control of the military. No provision is made in the Constitution for the Cabinet or for Cabinet meetings, but the existence of executive departments is implied in this clause.

Clause 2
The President is the nation's chief diplomat, with the power to make treaties. All treaties must be approved in the Senate by a two-thirds vote of the senators present. The President also can appoint important government officials, who must be approved in the Senate by a majority.

Clause 6. Salary The President shall, at stated times, receive for his services a compensation, which shall neither be increased nor diminished during the period for which he shall have been elected, and he shall not receive within that period any other emolument from the United States, or any of them.

Clause 7. Oath of office Before he enter on the execution of his office, he shall take the following oath or affirmation: "I do solemnly swear (or affirm) that I will faithfully execute the office of President of the United States, and will to the best of my ability, preserve, protect, and defend the Constitution of the United States."

SECTION 2   Powers of the President

Clause 1. Military powers; Cabinet; pardons The President shall be Commander-in-Chief of the Army and Navy of the United States, and of the militia of the several states, when called into the actual service of the United States. He may require the opinion, in writing, of the principal officer in each of the executive departments, upon any subject relating to the duties of their respective offices, and he shall have power to grant reprieves and pardons for offenses against the United States, except in cases of impeachment.

Clause 2. Diplomatic powers; appointments He shall have power, by and with the advice and consent of the Senate, to make treaties, provided two-thirds of the senators present concur; and he shall nominate and, by and with the advice and consent of the Senate, shall appoint ambassadors, other public ministers and consuls, judges of the Supreme Court, and all other officers of the United States, whose appointments are not herein otherwise provided for, and which shall be established by law; but the Congress may by law vest the appointment of such inferior officers as they think proper in the President alone, in the courts of law, or in the heads of departments.

Past and future Presidents and their families at the inauguration of John F. Kennedy. (The front row includes the Eisenhowers, Lady Bird Johnson, Jacqueline Kennedy, Lyndon Johnson, Richard Nixon, and the Trumans.)

Clause 3. Filling vacancies The President shall have power to fill up all vacancies that may happen during the recess of the Senate, by granting commissions which shall expire at the end of their next session.

SECTION 3   Duties of the President

He shall from time to time give to the Congress information of the state of the Union, and recommend to their consideration such measures as he shall judge necessary and expedient; he may, on extraordinary occasions, convene both houses, or either of them, and in case of disagreement between them with respect to the time of adjournment he may adjourn them to such time as he shall think proper; he shall receive ambassadors and other public ministers; he shall take care that the laws be faithfully executed, and shall commission all the officers of the United States.

SECTION 4   Impeachment

The President, Vice-President, and all civil officers of the United States shall be removed from office on impeachment for, and conviction of, treason, bribery, or other high crimes and misdemeanors.

Clause 3
If the Senate is not meeting, the President may make temporary appointments to fill vacancies.

Section 3
The Constitution imposes only a few specific duties on the President. One is to give a "State of the Union" message, which Presidents now deliver once a year.

Section 4
This section makes all Federal officials subject to the impeachment process described in Article I.

The Supreme Court held its first two sessions in this New York building, known as the Exchange.

ARTICLE III   Judicial Branch

SECTION 1   The Federal Courts

The judicial power of the United States shall be vested in one Supreme Court and in such inferior courts as the Congress may from time to time ordain and establish. The judges, both of the Supreme and inferior courts, shall hold their offices during good behavior and shall, at stated times, receive for their services a compensation which shall not be diminished during their continuance in office.

Article III gives the power to interpret the laws of the United States to the third branch, the judicial, which includes the Supreme Court and the other federal courts established by Congress. District courts and courts of appeal are now part of the regular court system. Federal judges are appointed by the President with the approval of the Senate.

Section 2
The federal courts have jurisdiction in certain kinds of cases.

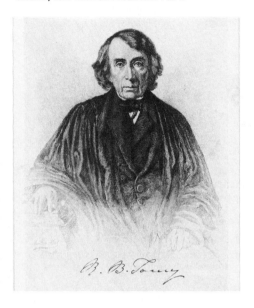

Roger B. Taney, Chief Justice of the United States in the crucial years between 1836 and 1864.

Section 3
The Constitution defines treason and places limits on how it can be punished.

The Supreme Court building today.

SECTION 2   Federal Court Jurisdiction

Clause 1. Federal cases   The judicial power shall extend to all cases, in law and equity, arising under this Constitution, the laws of the United States, and treaties made, or which shall be made, under their authority; to all cases affecting ambassadors, other public ministers, and consuls; to all cases of admiralty and maritime jurisdiction; to controversies to which the United States shall be a party; to controversies between two or more states; [between a state and citizens of another state;] between citizens of different states; between citizens of the same state claiming lands under grants of different states, and between a state, or the citizens thereof, and foreign states, citizens, or subjects.

Clause 2. Supreme Court jurisdiction   In all cases affecting ambassadors, other public ministers, and consuls, and those in which a state be a party, the Supreme Court shall have original jurisdiction. In all the other cases before mentioned, the Supreme Court shall have appellate jurisdiction, both as to law and fact, with such exceptions and under such regulations as the Congress shall make.

Clause 3. Trial rules   The trial of all crimes, except in cases of impeachment, shall be by jury; and such trial shall be held in the state where the said crimes shall have been committed; but when not committed within any state, the trial shall be at such place or places as the Congress may by law have directed.

SECTION 3   Treason

Clause 1. Definition   Treason against the United States shall consist only in levying war against them or in adhering to their enemies, giving them aid and comfort. No person shall be convicted of treason unless on the testimony of two witnesses to the same overt act, or on confession in open court.

Clause 2. Punishment   The Congress shall have power to declare the punishment of treason, but no attainder of treason shall work corruption of blood, or forfeiture except during the life of the person attainted.

ARTICLE IV The States and the Federal Government

SECTION 1 State Records

Full faith and credit shall be given in each state to the public acts, records, and judicial proceedings of every other state. And the Congress may by general laws prescribe the manner in which such acts, records, and proceedings shall be proved, and the effect thereof.

SECTION 2 Rights of Citizens

Clause 1. Privileges and immunities The citizens of each state shall be entitled to all privileges and immunities of citizens in the several states.

Clause 2. Extradition A person charged in any state with treason, felony, or other crime who shall flee from justice and be found in another state shall, on demand of the executive authority of the state from which he fled, be delivered up, to be removed to the state having jurisdiction of the crime.

[**Clause 3. Fugitive workers** No person held to service or labor in one state, under the laws thereof, escaping into another shall, in consequence of any law or regulation therein, be discharged from such service or labor, but shall be delivered upon claim of the party to whom such service or labor may be due.]

SECTION 3 New States and Territories

Clause 1. Admission of new states New states may be admitted by the Congress into this Union; but no new state shall be formed or erected within the jurisdiction of any other state; nor any state be formed by the junction of two or more states, or parts of states, without the consent of the legislatures of the states concerned, as well as of the Congress.

Clause 2. Federal territory The Congress shall have power to dispose of and make all needful rules and regulations respecting the territory or other property belonging to the United States; and nothing in this Constitution shall be so construed as to prejudice any claims of the United States, or of any particular state.

SECTION 4 Federal Duties to the States

The United States shall guarantee to every state in this Union a republican form of government, and shall protect each of them against invasion; and on application of the legislature, or of the executive (whom the legislature cannot be convened), against domestic violence.

Article IV sets out many of the principles of the federal system, describing relations among the states and between the national government and the states. Section 3 tells how new states may be admitted to the Union. Section 4 outlines the national government's duties to the states.

Section 2
The provisions of this section extend most privileges of state citizenship to *all* citizens. (Some exceptions are made.) It also establishes the extradition process.

Clause 3
Amendment 13 abolished slavery and made this clause obsolete.

Dakota Territory applying to Uncle Sam for statehood, in an 1880's cartoon.

Article V sets up two ways of amending the Constitution and two ways of ratifying amendments.

ARTICLE V Amending the Constitution

The Congress, whenever two-thirds of both houses shall deem it necessary, shall propose amendments to this Constitution, or, on the application of the legislatures of two-thirds of the several states, shall call a convention for proposing amendments, which, in either case, shall be valid to all intents and purposes, as part of this Constitution, when ratified by the legislatures of three-fourths of the several states or by conventions in three-fourths thereof, as the one or the other mode of ratification may be proposed by the Congress; provided that [no amendments which may be made prior to the year one thousand eight hundred and eight shall in any manner affect the first and fourth clauses in the ninth section of the first article; and that] no state, without its consent, shall be deprived of its equal suffrage in the Senate.

Article VI makes the Constitution the "supreme law of the land." If state law is in conflict with national law, it is the national law that must be obeyed.

ARTICLE VI Supremacy of National Law

Clause 1
The framers of the Constitution agreed that the United States would be responsible for all debts contracted by the government under the Articles of Confederation.

Clause 1. Public debt All debts contracted and engagements entered into, before the adoption of this Constitution, shall be as valid against the United States under this Constitution as under the Confederation.

Clause 2. Supreme law of the land This Constitution, and the laws of the United States which shall be made in pursuance thereof, and all treaties made, or which shall be made, under the authority of the United States, shall be the supreme law of the land; and the judges in every state shall be bound thereby, anything in the Constitution or laws of any state to the contrary notwithstanding.

Clause 3. Oath of office The senators and representatives before mentioned, and the members of the several state legislatures, and all executive and judicial officers, both of the United States and of the several states, shall be bound by oath or affirmation to support this Constitution; but no religious test shall ever be required as a qualification to any office or public trust under the United States.

Present-day courtroom, Newport, Rhode Island.

The signing of the Constitution, September 17, 1787.

ARTICLE VII Ratification of the Constitution

The ratification of the conventions of nine states shall be sufficient for the establishment of this Constitution between the states so ratifying the same.

Article VII established that the Constitution would go into effect when nine states voted to accept it. This occurred on June 21, 1788, with New Hampshire's ratification.

George Washington —
President and
delegate
from Virginia

New Hampshire
John Langdon
Nicholas Gilman

Massachusetts
Nathaniel Gorham
Rufus King

Connecticut
William Samuel
Johnson
Roger Sherman

New York
Alexander Hamilton

New Jersey
William Livingston
David Brearley
William Paterson
Jonathan Dayton

Pennsylvania
Benjamin Franklin
Thomas Mifflin
Robert Morris
George Clymer
Thomas FitzSimons
Jared Ingersoll
James Wilson
Gouverneur Morris

Delaware
George Reed
Gunning Bedford, Junior
John Dickinson
Richard Bassett
Jacob Broom

Maryland
James McHenry
Daniel of St. Thomas
Jenifer
Daniel Carroll

Virginia
John Blair
James Madison, Junior

North Carolina
William Blount
Richard Dobbs
Spaight
Hugh Williamson

South Carolina
John Rutledge
Charles Cotesworth
Pinckney
Charles Pinckney
Pierce Butler

Georgia
William Few
Abraham Baldwin

AMENDMENTS to the Constitution

Amendments 1–10 make up the Bill of Rights.

Amendment 1 protects citizens from government interference with their freedoms of religion, speech, press, assembly, and petition. These are the basic civil liberties.

AMENDMENT 1 Freedom of Religion, Speech, Press, Assembly, and Petition (1791)

Congress shall make no law respecting an establishment of religion or prohibiting the free exercise thereof; or abridging the freedom of speech, or of the press; or the right of the people peaceably to assemble, and to petition the government for a redress of grievances.

Amendment 2 guarantees that the federal government cannot deny states the right to enlist citizens in the militia and to provide them with training in the use of weapons.

AMENDMENT 2 Right to Bear Arms (1791)

A well-regulated militia being necessary to the security of a free state, the right of the people to keep and bear arms shall not be infringed.

Amendment 3 was included because of the troubles caused when the British sought to quarter and supply their troops in colonists' homes. The amendment guarantees that in time of peace the federal government may not force people to have soldiers live in their homes. Even in time of war, people cannot be compelled to do this unless Congress passes a law requiring it.

AMENDMENT 3 Quartering of Soldiers (1791)

No soldier shall, in time of peace, be quartered in any house without the consent of the owner, nor in time of war, but in a manner to be prescribed by law.

AMENDMENT 4 Search and Seizure (1791)

Amendment 4 extends the people's right to privacy and security by setting limits on authorities' power to search property and seize evidence.

The right of the people to be secure in their persons, houses, papers, and effects, against unreasonable searches and seizures, shall not be violated, and no warrants shall issue but upon probable cause, supported by oath or affirmation and particularly describing the place to be searched and the persons or things to be seized.

AMENDMENT 5   Rights of the Accused (1791)

No person shall be held to answer for a capital or otherwise infamous crime, unless on a presentment or indictment of a grand jury, except in cases arising in the land or naval forces, or in the militia, when in actual service in time of war or public danger; nor shall any person be subject for the same offense to be twice put in jeopardy of life or limb; nor shall be compelled in any criminal case to be a witness against himself, nor be deprived of life, liberty, or property, without due process of law; nor shall private property be taken for public use without just compensation.

Amendment 5 ensures certain rights for people accused of crimes. It says that no person may be tried in a federal court unless a grand jury decides that the person ought to be tried. (Members of the armed forces may be tried in military court under military law.) Other provisions guarantee due process of law. Finally, a person's private property may not be taken for public use without a fair price being paid for it.

AMENDMENT 6   Requirements for Jury Trial (1791)

In all criminal prosecutions, the accused shall enjoy the right to a speedy and public trial by an impartial jury of the state and district wherein the crime shall have been committed, which districts shall have been previously ascertained by law, and to be informed of the nature and cause of the accusation; to be confronted with the witnesses against him; to have compulsory process for obtaining witnesses in his favor; and to have the assistance of counsel for his defense.

Amendment 6 lists additional rights of an individual accused of a crime. A person accused of a crime is entitled to a prompt public trial before an impartial jury. The trial is held in the district where the crime took place. The accused must be told what the charge is. The accused must be present when witnesses give their testimony. The government must help the accused bring into court friendly witnesses. The accused must be provided with legal counsel.

AMENDMENT 7   Rules of Common Law (1791)

In suits at common law, where the value in controversy shall exceed twenty dollars, the right of trial by jury shall be preserved, and no fact tried by a jury shall be otherwise reexamined in any court of the United States than according to the rules of common law.

Amendment 7 is somewhat out of date. Today, cases involving lawsuits are not tried before federal courts unless large sums of money are involved.

The draft of the Bill of Rights — twelve amendments sent to the states in 1789 — only ten of which were approved.

Amendment 8 provides that persons accused of crimes may in most cases be released from jail if they or someone else posts bail. Bail, fines, and punishments must be reasonable.

Amendment 9 was included because of the impossibility of listing in the Constitution all the rights of the people. The mention of certain rights does not mean that people do not have other fundamental rights, which the government must respect. These include the right to privacy.

Amendment 10 establishes the reserved powers. It states that the powers that the Constitution does not give to the United States and does not deny to the states belong to the states and to the people.

This amendment was the first that was enacted to override a Supreme Court decision. It confirms that no federal court may try a case in which a state is being sued by a citizen of another state or of a foreign country. Amendment 11 changes a provision of Article III, Section 2.

AMENDMENT 8   Limits on Criminal Punishments (1791)

Excessive bail shall not be required, nor excessive fines imposed, nor cruel and unusual punishments inflicted.

AMENDMENT 9   Rights Kept by the People (1791)

The enumeration in the Constitution of certain rights shall not be construed to deny or disparage others retained by the people.

AMENDMENT 10   Powers of the States and the People (1791)

The powers not delegated to the United States by the Constitution, nor prohibited by it to the states, are reserved to the states respectively, or to the people.

AMENDMENT 11   Lawsuits Against a State (1798)

The judicial power of the United States shall not be construed to extend to any suit in law or equity commenced or prosecuted against one of the United States by citizens of another state or by citizens or subjects of any foreign state.

A southern jury in 1867 included blacks who, for the first time, had the rights of citizens.

AMENDMENT 12 Election of President and Vice President (1804)

The electors shall meet in their respective states and vote by ballot for President and Vice President, one of whom, at least, shall not be an inhabitant of the same state with themselves; they shall name in their ballots the person voted for as President, and in distinct ballots the person voted for as Vice President, and they shall make distinct lists of all persons voted for as President, and of all persons voted for as Vice President, and of the number of votes for each, which lists they shall sign and certify, and transmit sealed to the seat of the government of the United States, directed to the President of the Senate; the President of the Senate shall, in the presence of the Senate and House of Representatives, open all the certificates and the votes shall then be counted; the person having the greatest number of votes for President shall be the President, if such number be a majority of the whole number of electors appointed; and if no person have such majority, then from the persons having the highest numbers not exceeding three on the list of those voted for as President, the House of Representatives shall choose immediately, by ballot, the President. But in choosing the President, the votes shall be taken by states, the representation from each state having one vote; a quorum for this purpose shall consist of a member or members from two-thirds of the states, and a majority of all the states shall be necessary to a choice. And if the House of Representatives shall not choose a President whenever the right of choice shall devolve upon them, [before the fourth day of March next following] then the Vice President shall act as President, as in the case of the death or constitutional disability of the President. The person having the greatest number of votes as Vice President shall be the Vice President, if such number be a majority of the whole number of electors appointed, and if no person have a majority, then from the two highest numbers on the list, the Senate shall choose the Vice President; a quorum for the purpose shall consist of two-thirds of the whole number of senators, and a majority of the whole number shall be necessary to a choice. But no person constitutionally ineligible to the office of President shall be eligible to that of Vice President of the United States.

Amendment 12 changed the Electoral College procedure for choosing a President. The most important change made by this amendment was that the presidential electors would vote for President and Vice President on separate ballots. In 1800, when only one ballot was used, Thomas Jefferson and Aaron Burr received the same number of votes, and the election had to be decided by the House of Representatives. To guard against this possibility in the future, Amendment 12 calls for separate ballots.

Thomas Jefferson, third President of the United States.

AMENDMENT 13 Slavery Abolished (1865)

Section 1. Abolition of slavery Neither slavery nor involuntary servitude, except as a punishment for crime whereof the party shall have been duly convicted, shall exist within the United States or any place subject to their jurisdiction.

Section 2. Enforcement Congress shall have the power to enforce this article by appropriate legislation.

Amendment 13 is the first of three amendments that were a consequence of the Civil War. It states that slavery must end in the United States and its territories.

Congress may pass whatever laws are necessary to enforce Amendment 13. This statement, called an *enabling act*, is now commonly included in amendments.

By the definition of citizenship in Amendment 14, black Americans were granted citizenship. The first section provides that all persons born or naturalized in the United States and subject to this country's laws are citizens of the United States and of the state in which they live. State governments may not deprive anyone of due process of law or equal protection.

This section abolished the provision in Article 1, Section 2, which said that only three-fifths of the slaves should be counted as population.

Section 3 was designed to bar former leaders of the Confederacy from holding federal office.

Following emancipation, most Southern blacks became sharecroppers, working land owned by others.

AMENDMENT 14   Civil Rights Guaranteed (1868)

Section 1. Definition of citizenship   All persons born or naturalized in the United States, and subject to the jurisdiction thereof, are citizens of the United States and of the state wherein they reside. No state shall make or enforce any law which shall abridge the privileges or immunities of citizens of the United States; nor shall any state deprive any person of life, liberty, or property, without due process of law; nor deny to any person within its jurisdiction the equal protection of the laws.

Section 2. Apportionment of representatives   Representatives shall be apportioned among the several states according to their respective numbers, counting the whole number of persons in each state, [excluding Indians not taxed.] But when the right to vote at any election for the choice of electors for President and Vice President of the United States, representatives in Congress, the executive and judicial officers of a state, or the members of the legislature thereof, is denied to any of the [male] inhabitants of such state, [being twenty-one years of age] and citizens of the United States, or in any way abridged, except for participation in rebellion, or other crime, the basis of representation therein shall be reduced in the proportion which the number of such [male] citizens shall bear to the whole number of [male] citizens [twenty-one years of age] in such state.

Section 3. Restrictions on holding office   No person shall be a senator or representative in Congress, or elector of President and Vice President, or hold any office, civil or military, under the United States, or under any state, who, having previously taken an oath as a member of Congress, or as an officer of the United States, or as a member of any state legislature, or as an executive or judicial officer of any state, to support the Constitution of the United States, shall have engaged in insurrection or rebellion against the same, or given aid or comfort to the enemies thereof. But Congress may by vote of two-thirds of each house remove such disability.

THE FIRST COLORED SENATOR AND REPRESENTATIVES.

In the 41ˢᵗ and 42ⁿᵈ Congress of the United States.

Black members of Congress elected after the Civil War.

Section 4. Valid public debts of the United States The validity of the public debt of the United States, authorized by law, including debts incurred for payment of pensions and bounties for services in suppressing insurrection or rebellion, shall not be questioned. But neither the United States nor any state shall assume or pay any debt or obligation incurred in aid of insurrection or rebellion against the United States, or any claim for the loss or emancipation of any slave; but all such debts, obligations, and claims shall be held illegal and void.

Section 5. Enforcement The Congress shall have power to enforce by appropriate legislation the provisions of this article.

AMENDMENT 15   Black Voting Rights (1870)

Section 1. The right of citizens of the United States to vote shall not be denied or abridged by the United States or by any state on account of race, color, or previous condition of servitude.

Section 2. The Congress shall have power to enforce this article by appropriate legislation.

AMENDMENT 16   Income Tax (1913)

The Congress shall have power to lay and collect taxes on incomes, from whatever source derived, without apportionment among the several states and without regard to any census or enumeration.

This section was included to settle the question of debts incurred during the Civil War. All debts contracted by the United States were to be paid. Neither the United States nor any state government, however, was to pay the debts of the Confederacy. Moreover, no payment was to be made to former slave owners as compensation for slaves who were set free.

Amendment 15 sought to protect the right of citizens, particularly former slaves, to vote in federal and state elections.

Amendment 16 authorizes Congress to tax incomes. An amendment was necessary because in 1895 the Supreme Court had decided that an income tax law, passed by Congress a year earlier, was unconstitutional.

Amendment 17 changed Article I, Section 3, to allow the direct election of senators by popular vote. Anyone qualified to vote for a state representative may vote for United States senators.

AMENDMENT 17   Direct Election of Senators (1913)

Section 1. Election by the people The Senate of the United States shall be composed of two senators from each state, elected by the people thereof, for six years; and each senator shall have one vote. The electors in each state shall have the qualifications requisite for electors of the most numerous branch of the state legislatures.

Section 2. Senate vacancies When vacancies happen in the representation of any state in the Senate, the executive authority of such state shall issue writs of election to fill such vacancies: provided that the legislature of any state may empower the executive thereof to make temporary appointments until the people fill the vacancies by election as the legislature may direct.

Section 3. Effective date This amendment shall not be so construed as to affect the election or term of any senator chosen before it becomes valid as part of the Constitution.

AMENDMENT 18   Prohibition (1919)

[**Section 1.**   After one year from the ratification of this article the manufacture, sale, or transportation of intoxicating liquors within, the importation thereof into, or the exportation thereof from the United States and all territory subject to the jurisdiction thereof for beverage purposes is hereby prohibited.

Section 2.   The Congress and the several states shall have concurrent power to enforce this article by appropriate legislation.

Section 3.   This article shall be inoperative unless it shall have been ratified as an amendment to the Constitution by the legislatures of the several states, as provided in the Constitution, within seven years from the date of the submission hereof to the states by the Congress.]

Amendment 18 forbade the manufacture, sale, or shipment of alcoholic beverages within the United States. Importing and exporting such beverages was also forbidden. Amendment 18 was later repealed by Amendment 21.

Federal agents destroying a still to enforce Prohibition.

AMENDMENT 19   Women's Voting Rights (1920)

Section 1.   The right of citizens of the United States to vote shall not be denied or abridged by the United States or by any state on account of sex.

Section 2.   The Congress shall have power to enforce this article by appropriate legislation.

AMENDMENT 20   Terms of Office and Presidential Succession (1933)

Section 1. Terms of office   The terms of the President and Vice President shall end at noon on the 20th day of January, and the terms of senators and representatives at noon on the 3rd day of January, of the years in which such terms would have ended if this article had not been ratified; and the terms of their successors shall then begin.

Section 2. Sessions of Congress   The Congress shall assemble at least once in every year, and such meeting shall begin at noon on the 3rd day of January, unless they shall by law appoint a different day.

Section 3. Presidential succession   If, at the time fixed for the beginning of the term of the President, the President-elect shall have died, the Vice President-elect shall become President. If a President shall not have been chosen before the time fixed for the beginning of his term, or if the President-elect shall have failed to qualify, then the Vice President-elect shall act as President until a President shall have qualified; and the Congress may by law provide for the case wherein neither a President-elect nor a Vice President-elect shall have qualified, declaring who shall then act as President, or the manner in which one who is to act shall be selected, and such person shall act accordingly until a President or a Vice President shall have qualified.

Section 4. House election of President   The Congress may by law provide for the case of the death of any of the persons from whom the House of Representatives may choose a President whenever the right of choice shall have devolved upon them, and for the case of the death of any of the persons from whom the Senate may choose a Vice President whenever the right of choice shall have devolved upon them.

Section 5. Effective date   Sections 1 and 2 shall take effect on the fifteenth day of October following the ratification of this article.

[**Section 6. Ratification**   This article shall be inoperative unless it shall have been ratified as an amendment to the Constitution by the legislatures of three-fourths of the several states within seven years from the date of its submission.]

Amendment 19 provides that women citizens may not be denied the right to vote in a federal or state election.

A suffragist rally.

When the Constitution was written, transportation and communication were slow. There was a long period, therefore, between the President's election (November) and inauguration (March). One purpose of Amendment 20 was to shorten that waiting period. The amendment established that the terms of the President and Vice President end at noon on January 20 following a presidential election. The terms of one-third of the senators and of all representatives, meanwhile, end at noon on January 3 in years ending in odd numbers. The new terms begin when the old terms end.

Section 2 provides that Congress must meet at least once a year, with the regular session beginning on January 3 unless Congress sets a different day.

Section 3 provides ways of filling the office of President in several emergencies.

Because the House of Representatives chooses the President if no candidate receives a majority of the electoral votes, Section 4 also gives Congress power to make a law to decide what to do if one of the candidates dies.

Amendment 21 repealed Amendment 18, putting an end to Prohibition. It was the only amendment submitted to special ratifying conventions instead of state legislatures.

Section 2 allows states or local governments to continue prohibition if they wish.

Amendment 22 set limits on the time a President may serve. No person may be elected President more than twice. A person who has served more than two years in the place of an elected President may be elected President only once. This limitation did not apply to President Truman, who was in office when Amendment 22 was proposed.

Presidents Washington, Jefferson, and Madison set the pattern of serving only two terms in office. Although Ulysses S. Grant and Theodore Roosevelt sought third terms, the precedent of serving only two terms was not broken until 1940, when Franklin D. Roosevelt was elected for a third term.

AMENDMENT 21   Repeal of Prohibition (1933)

Section 1. The eighteenth article of amendment to the Constitution of the United States is hereby repealed.

Section 2. State laws. The transportation or importation into any state, territory, or possession of the United States for delivery or use therein of intoxicating liquors, in violation of the laws thereof, is hereby prohibited.

[**Section 3.** This article shall be inoperative unless it shall have been ratified as an amendment to the Constitution by conventions in the several states, as provided in the Constitution, within seven years from the date of the submission hereof to the states by the Congress.]

AMENDMENT 22   Limits on Presidential Terms (1951)

Section 1. No person shall be elected to the office of the President more than twice, and no person who has held the office of President, or acted as President, for more than two years of a term to which some other person was elected President shall be elected to the office of the President more than once. But this article shall not apply to any person holding the office of President when this article was proposed by the Congress, and shall not prevent any person who may be holding the office of President, or acting as President, during the term within which this article becomes operative from holding the office of President, or acting as President during the remainder of such term.

[**Section 2.** This article shall be inoperative unless it shall have been ratified as an amendment to the Constitution by the legislatures of three-fourths of the several states within seven years from the date of its submission to the states by the Congress.]

A victorious Franklin D. Roosevelt with congratulatory mail after his sweeping 1936 election victory.

Celebrating the bicentennial of the Constitution, 1987.

AMENDMENT 23 Voting in the District of Columbia (1961)

Section 1. The District constituting the seat of government of the United States shall appoint, in such manner as the Congress may direct:

A number of electors of President and Vice President equal to the whole number of senators and representatives in Congress to which the District would be entitled if it were a state, but in no event more than the least populous state; they shall be in addition to those appointed by the states, but they shall be considered, for the purposes of the election of President and Vice President, to be electors appointed by a state; and they shall meet in the District and perform such duties as provided by the twelfth article of amendment.

Section 2. The Congress shall have power to enforce this article by appropriate legislation.

This amendment gave the residents of the District of Columbia the right to vote in presidential elections. Before Amendment 23 was adopted, residents of the District of Columbia had not voted for President and Vice President because the Constitution provided that only states should choose presidential electors.

AMENDMENT 24 Poll Tax Illegal (1964)

Section 1. The right of citizens of the United States to vote in any primary or other election for President or Vice President, for electors for President or Vice President, or for senator or representative in Congress, shall not be denied or abridged by the United States or any state by reason of failure to pay any poll tax or other tax.

Section 2. The Congress shall have power to enforce this article by appropriate legislation.

Amendment 24 prohibited using the poll tax to deny voting rights in federal elections. (The poll tax was a device used in some southern states to keep black voters from the polls.) In 1966, the Supreme Court ruled that payment of poll taxes was also an unconstitutional precondition for voting in state and local elections.

AMENDMENT 25 Presidential Disability (1967)

Section 1. Vice President In case of the removal of the President from office or of his death or resignation, the Vice President shall become President.

Amendment 25 clarifies Article 2, Section 1, which deals with filling vacancies in the presidency. It also establishes procedures to follow when the President is too ill to serve and when there is a vacancy in the office of Vice President.

With ratification of the 26th Amendment, the voting age was lowered to eighteen years.

Section 2. Replacing the Vice President Whenever there is a vacancy in the office of the Vice President, the President shall nominate a Vice President who shall take office upon confirmation by a majority vote of both Houses of Congress.

Section 3. Presidential inability to act Whenever the President transmits to the President pro tempore of the Senate and the Speaker of the House of Representatives his written declaration that he is unable to discharge the powers and duties of his office, and until he transmits to them a written declaration to the contrary, such powers and duties shall be discharged by the Vice President as Acting President.

Section 4. Determining presidential disability Whenever the Vice President and a majority of either the principal officers of the executive departments or of such other body as Congress may by law provide, transmit to the President pro tempore of the Senate and the Speaker of the House of Representatives their written declaration that the President is unable to discharge the powers and duties of his office, the Vice President shall immediately assume the powers and duties of the office as Acting President.

Thereafter, when the President transmits to the President pro tempore of the Senate and the Speaker of the House of Representatives his written declaration that no inability exists, he shall resume the powers and duties of his office unless the Vice President and a majority of either the principal officers of the executive department or of such other body as Congress may by law provide, transmit within four days to the President pro tempore of the Senate and the Speaker of the House of Representatives their written declaration that the President is unable to discharge the powers and duties of his office. Thereupon, Congress shall decide the issue, assembling within forty-eight hours for that purpose, if not in session. If the Congress, within twenty-one days after receipt of the latter written declaration, or, if Congress is not in session, within twenty-one days after Congress is required to assemble, determines by two-thirds vote of both Houses that the President is unable to discharge the powers and duties of his office, the Vice President shall continue to discharge the same as Acting President; otherwise, the President shall resume the powers and duties of his office.

AMENDMENT 26   Voting Age (1971)

Section 1.   The right of citizens of the United States who are eighteen years of age or older to vote shall not be denied or abridged by the United States or by any state on account of age.
Section 2.   The Congress shall have power to enforce this article by appropriate legislation.

AMENDMENT 27   Congressional Pay (1992)

No law, varying the compensation for the services of the Senators and Representatives, shall take effect, until an election of Representatives shall have intervened.

REVIEW OF THE CONSTITUTION

KEY TERMS

Match the following words with the numbered definitions below: *ratification, impeachment, appropriation, jurisdiction, judicial review, democracy, Bill of Rights.*

1. Charges of crimes or misdeeds in office brought against a government official.

2. Money granted by a legislature to be used for a specific purpose.

3. The first ten amendments to the Constitution.

4. System in which people elect the government either directly or through representatives.

5. The act of giving approval to a document such as a treaty.

6. The limits within which a government body (such as a court) may act and make decisions.

7. The power of the court system to decide whether laws are constitutional.

COMPREHENSION

1. Who holds the office of President of the Senate? When can the President of the Senate cast a vote? Which house of Congress introduces bills needed to raise money for the government?

2. Name six of the specific powers given to Congress by the Constitution. What is the "elastic clause"?

3. According to Article II, what happens if the President dies in office? How did the Twenty-fifth Amendment provide additional measures in case of this event?

4. How are federal judges chosen? For how long do they hold office?

5. What freedoms are guaranteed by the First Amendment?

6. Under what circumstances may the Constitution be amended?

7. How does the Constitution limit the President's power to make treaties?

8. What three constitutional amendments were passed soon after the Civil War? What issues caused these amendments to be added?

9. Which branch of government has the power to declare war?

CRITICAL THINKING

1. Making Judgments The Founding Fathers sought both to create and to limit government power. Is this a contradiction in terms? Did they achieve their goal? Explain your answer.

2. Stating Both Sides of an Issue Write a response to the following statement: "Only the President has the information required to make decisions about war. Often he receives this information in secret. Therefore, we should not question his actions."

3. Making Judgments Supporters of constitutional protections for criminal suspects claim that it is better if some guilty people go free than if innocent people are convicted. Do you agree or disagree? Explain your reasons.

4. Forming a Hypothesis Does testing for drug use and AIDS violate Fourth Amendment restrictions on search and seizure? How might a lawyer make a case in favor of these tests?

PORTFOLIO OPTIONS

1. Civics Connection Research the history of the War Powers Act (1973). How does it illustrate the tension between the executive branch and the legislative branch under the separation of powers?

2. Writing Connection Research the following Supreme Court decisions on civil rights: *Dred Scott v. Sanford* (1857), *Plessy v. Ferguson* (1896), *Brown v. Board of Education of Topeka* (1954). Write a report describing how constitutional interpretation changed in each case.

3. Contemporary Connection Find out what constitutional amendments are currently under consideration. List the arguments both for and against two of the proposed amendments.

4. Timeline Connection Create a timeline of the United States Constitution. Start your timeline with the Constitutional Convention of 1787 and include constitutional amendments as well as important Supreme Court decisions.

CIVICS Handbook

> **"Proclaim Liberty throughout all the land unto all the inhabitants thereof."**

THIS INSCRIPTION ON THE LIBERTY BELL in Philadelphia is an enduring reminder of the American belief in the right of free people to govern themselves. The Constitution of the United States expresses this belief in its powers, in its laws, and in the rights it guarantees. The following pages will help you learn more about the American system of government and about the rights and responsibilities of citizens of our nation.

Learning how their government operates is a critical task for young Americans—tomorrow's voters and leaders. **Critical Thinking:** Why is it especially important for citizens of a free society to understand the workings of their government?

Rights and Responsibilities

The American government guarantees its citizens fundamental rights. These guarantees are found in the Constitution, the Bill of Rights, and other amendments to the Constitution. Along with these rights, however, come responsibilities. When Americans carry out their responsibilities, they help to preserve their freedom and the American system of government.

The Rights of Citizens

Every member of society is entitled to civil rights—the rights of a citizen. The Constitution and laws passed by Congress spell out many of these rights. They include freedom of speech, freedom of assembly (the right to meet with others peacefully for political or other purposes), freedom of the press, and freedom of religion. Others include the right to a fair trial and protection against illegal searches.

Civil rights also means that citizens are equal under the law. That is, each person's vote counts equally, and the government does not discriminate against certain individuals or groups. In a broader sense, citizens are also entitled to equal opportunity. That is, each citizen should have an equal chance to develop his or her capabilities without discrimination.

Responsibilities of a Good Citizen

In addition to rights, citizens also have responsibilities. These include paying taxes, defending the country, and obeying the laws.

A good citizen has many other duties. One of these is participating in government. There are many ways to participate.

The rights and responsibilities of citizenship unite Americans of all ages and backgrounds. Citizens' basic rights include freedom of speech, freedom of assembly, and freedom of religion.

One of the most important ways is by voting. When you turn eighteen, you will be given that right. Until then, there are many other ways you can effectively participate in government. Working for a political party or writing your representative in Congress are good examples.

Good citizens make an effort to keep up with the fast pace of events in their community and around the world. **Critical Thinking:** What have been some of the biggest headlines in world events recently?

What are some other characteristics of a good citizen? One is to be well-informed on important issues. This can be accomplished by regularly reading a newspaper or watching the news on television. Another is to respect people who may have a different way of life than you. Our nation is filled with citizens who have grown up in different cultures and who speak different languages. Understanding that there is no one "correct" cultural background is the mark of a good citizen. A third characteristic is helping your community. Examples include recycling paper and other products or volunteering at a local hospital.

There are many other qualities of citizenship that may come to your mind. By training to be an effective citizen, you will help to maintain the democratic values that this country is based upon.

Volunteering For a Cause

Suppose for a moment that you play basketball on your school team. A month before school is to begin, the school superintendent announces that the only way the school could afford to keep its sports programs would be if the people of the community donated a total of $10,000. Can you picture yourself volunteering, that is, working for no pay, to help raise the money? Would you sign a petition supporting the cause? Would you write letters to other citizens asking for their help? Would you go door-to-door to raise funds?

These are questions that may not be easy to answer without actually being in that type of situation. They may, however, help you to understand how and why many citizens become involved with community issues.

Small Volunteer Groups

There are thousands of small volunteer groups in the United States. Sometimes they have been in existence for years; other times they are formed for a specific purpose, such as in the example above. Examples of small groups include volunteer firefighters, hospital volunteers, and crossing-guard volunteers. Newspapers or your city hall are good sources of information about such local groups.

Large Volunteer Groups

Large national volunteer organizations are plentiful as well. They include groups ranging from the American Red Cross to the Little League. Other well-known groups include the League of Women Voters, the National Society for the Prevention of Cruelty to Animals, and the Girl Scouts. Your school or local library has information on those groups.

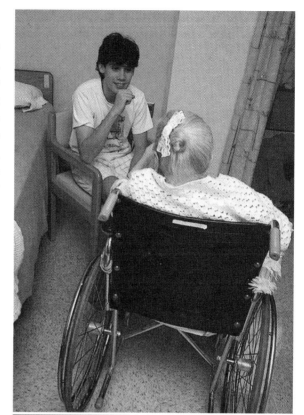

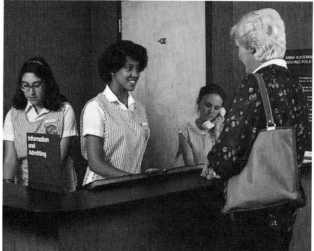

Hospitals benefit greatly from the dedication of volunteer workers. At top, a volunteer chats with a patient. Above, volunteers known as candy stripers (because of their colorful uniforms) help with office tasks. **Critical Thinking:** How do volunteers benefit from their efforts?

Expressing Your Political Opinions

One morning while listening to the news on the radio, you hear your member of Congress speaking in support of a bill that would cut one-half of the summer jobs in your community. After a minute you realize that the job you had lined up for the summer could be included in those cuts! You decide at that moment to let your representative know that you oppose the bill. How should you go about voicing your opposition?

Writing an Opinion Letter

The right to express your opinion about local, state, or national issues is one of the important rights you have as a citizen of a democracy. One of the ways to do this is by writing an opinion letter to a public official. The official may be the mayor of your town or your member of Congress. These officials welcome opinion letters, which allow them to remain in touch with those they represent.

Some Writing Guidelines

There are a few things to keep in mind when writing to a public official:

- Be sure of what you want to say. Look into the issue thoroughly and state your opinion thoughtfully.
- Write your opinions briefly and clearly. Three or four well-written paragraphs are more effective than several long pages that make the same point.
- Write your letter in the correct format. It should follow the format of a proper business letter. Guidelines for business letters can be found in your school or local library.

A letter following these guidelines will help you clearly state your point. It will also help ensure that your letter will be read—and that your opinion will be heard.

Kika de la Garza, a member of the House of Representatives, reads through his mail in his Washington, D.C., office. Elected officials pay careful attention to letters written by the people they represent. **Critical Thinking:** Why might letters to public officials not always give an accurate picture of public attitudes?

Great Words in American History

Americans are proud of their great nation and of the freedom for which it stands. Throughout the nation's history, that pride has been expressed in solemn pledges, memorable speeches, and rousing anthems, all of which celebrate freedom and express love of country.

The Pledge of Allegiance

I pledge allegiance to the flag of the United States of America and to the republic for which it stands; one nation under God, indivisible, with liberty and justice for all.

"America the Beautiful"

Oh beautiful for spacious skies, for amber
    waves of grain
For purple mountains majesties above the
    fruited plain
America! America! God shed his grace on
    thee
And crown thy good with brotherhood
    from sea to shining sea.

"My Country 'Tis of Thee"

My country `tis of thee, sweet land of liberty, of thee I sing.
Land where my fathers died, land of the pilgrims pride,
From every mountainside, let freedom ring.

"God Bless America"

God bless America, land that I love,
Stand beside her and guide her through
    the night with a light from above;
From the mountains, to the prairies to the
    oceans white with foam,
God bless America, my home sweet home.

Great Americans on Patriotism

God grants liberty only to those who live it, and are always ready to guard and defend it.

Daniel Webster
1782–1852

Our country, right or wrong. When right, to be kept right; when wrong, to be put right.

Carl Schurz
1829–1906

There are no days of special patriotism. There are no days when you should be more patriotic than on other days, and I ask you to wear every day in your heart our flag of the Union.

Woodrow Wilson
1856–1924

Ask not what your country can do for you—ask what you can do for your country.

John F. Kennedy
1917–1963

A nation is formed by the willingness of each of us to share in the responsibility for upholding the common good.

Barbara Jordan
1936–

In this two-hundredth anniversary year of our Constitution, you and I stand on the shoulders of giants—men whose words and deeds put wind in the sails of freedom. . . . We will be guided tonight by their acts, and we will be guided forever by their words.

Ronald Reagan
1911–

Symbols of Our Nation

The Liberty Bell

The Liberty Bell is one of America's most enduring symbols of freedom. It was rung on July 8, 1776, to celebrate Congress's adoption of the Declaration of Independence. It is inscribed with the words from the Bible, "Proclaim Liberty throughout all the land unto all the inhabitants thereof."

The Liberty Bell, first cast in England and weighing over 2,000 pounds, was shipped to Pennsylvania in 1752. After 1776 it rang on each anniversary of the adoption of the Declaration until 1835. In that year, the bell received its famous crack while being rung during the funeral of John Marshall, the first Chief Justice of the United States.

The Liberty Bell is now rung only on special occasions. On display in Philadelphia, it attracts thousands of visitors every year.

The Great Seal

Throughout history, governments have used official seals to signify that documents are authentic. The United States, wanting to show its equal rank with the governments of Europe, adopted the Great Seal in 1782. Both sides of the seal can be found on the back of a one dollar bill.

The face of the seal shows an American bald eagle with a shield on its breast. There are thirteen stripes to represent the thirteen original states. The thirteen leaves and olives in one claw and the thirteen arrows in the other symbolize the nation's desire for peace but its ability to wage war. The words *E pluribus unum* are Latin for "One [nation] out of many [states]."

The reverse side of the seal shows a pyramid with thirteen layers, representing the Union. The Eye of Providence guards the pyramid. The Latin motto *Annuit coeptis* means "He [God] has favored our undertakings." The motto *Novus ordo seclorum* means "New order of the ages."

Uncle Sam

The figure of Uncle Sam is a well-known patriotic symbol in the United States. He is generally shown as a tall figure with long white hair and a white beard. His costume is red, white, and blue, and decorated with stars and stripes.

Although the exact origin is unclear, the name "Uncle Sam" is thought to have originated with Samuel "Uncle Sam" Wilson, a resident of Troy, New York, who supplied the army with barrels of food stamped with the initials "U.S." Workers joked that the initials stood for Wilson's nickname, "Uncle Sam."

Following the Civil War, the cartoonist Thomas Nast began to draw Uncle Sam as he is pictured today. The symbol soon became widely known, and was heavily used on recruiting posters during World Wars I and II. In 1961 Congress officially recognized Samuel "Uncle Sam" Wilson as being the source of this patriotic symbol.

The Bald Eagle

The bald eagle is one of America's best-known symbols. It became the national bird of the United States in 1782, and appears on the face of the Great Seal. The eagle has been used as a symbol of strength and bravery dating back to Roman times.

The bald eagle is found only in North America. The eagle is not really bald, but has that appearance because white feathers cover its head. Bald eagles are protected by federal law.

Mount Rushmore

The Black Hills of South Dakota are home to a spectacular memorial. Carved into a granite cliff are the heads of George Washington, Thomas Jefferson, Theodore Roosevelt, and Abraham Lincoln, four of America's greatest Presidents. They were chosen to represent the nation's founding, philosophy, expansion, and unity.

The sculptures are approximately 60 feet high, and are 5,725 feet above sea level. On a clear day they can be seen from over 60 miles away.

Gutzon Borglum designed and supervised construction of the Mount Rushmore memorial, which was completed in 1941. The figures were cut from the stone by using drills and dynamite.

Statue of Liberty

The Statue of Liberty has become a symbol of the United States and a symbol of freedom to people all over the world. It stands on Liberty Island at the entrance of New York Harbor. The statue, one of the largest ever built, shows a proud woman in flowing robes holding a torch in her uplifted right hand. Her left hand holds a tablet with the date of the Declaration of Independence in Roman numerals. At her feet lies the broken chain of tyranny, or unjust rule. On her head rests a crown.

The Statue of Liberty was given to the United States by the people of France in 1884 as a symbol of the friendship between the two nations. The statue, which stands on a large concrete pedestal, rises over 150 feet high and is made of 300 copper sheets fastened together. A spiral staircase brings visitors up from the base of the statue to the crown. Windows in the crown give people an unforgettable view of the harbor.

Millions of immigrants passed the statue upon entering the United States. A poem by American poet Emma Lazarus is inscribed on a plaque on the pedestal. Its well-known lines, "Give me your tired, your poor, Your huddled masses yearning to breathe free," symbolize the nation's dedication to freedom.

Local Government

Think about one of your typical mornings. Do you wake up and take a shower? How did that water get to your house? Did you put out the trash in the morning? Who picked up the garbage? Did you take public transportation? Who runs the public transportation system?

In each of the above cases, you are relying on your local government. Good local governments protect their citizens and improve the quality of life in a community.

Local Governments Provide Needed Services

Protecting citizens is an important role for all local governments. One way this is accomplished is through a local police force. Police provide three basic services: preventing crime, enforcing the laws, and controlling traffic.

Fire protection is another important service provided by local governments. Firefighters may be full-time employees or volunteers. Finally, local governments protect the public health. This is achieved by such means as providing clean drinking water and maintaining hospitals.

Improving citizens' lives is the other main goal of local governments. Many governments help persons in need through cash assistance, free medical clinics, homeless shelters, and volunteer programs. Some communities provide public housing developments for low-income families. Improving public transportation and offering cultural and recreational activities also help to improve the quality of life in a community.

County Governments

Most states are divided into sections called counties, which are the basic unit of local

Shown here is Sharon Pratt Dixon, Mayor of Washington, D.C. Mayors, like other local officials, deal with many different issues that affect the daily lives of people in their communities. **Critical Thinking:** What are some of the qualities that make a local politician successful?

government. They vary widely in size and in number of residents. A rural county might have only a hundred or so residents. Some urban counties, on the other hand, have more than a million.

County governments are responsible for carrying out state government policies. At the head of the county government sits an elected board or committee, which oversees the operation of the county. Officials, such as a sheriff and treasurer, carry out the county's functions. Some of the services that counties provide their citizens are supervising elections, keeping records, and maintaining jails.

Towns, Townships, and Districts

The town is the most important form of government in some states. This form of government began in New England and still plays an important role there. One significant feature of towns is the town meeting. Once a year, and sometimes more frequently, the citizens of a town meet to decide the town's policies. Because citizens vote directly on issues rather than elect representatives to vote for them, the town meeting is an example of what is called "direct democracy."

Townships are still common in the Middle Atlantic states and the Midwest. Some are nothing more than lines on a map, while others function much as county governments. Districts serve a more specialized function. School districts are a common example. Most school districts are governed by an elected school board that determines school policies, such as hiring teachers.

City Government

Because about three-fourths of Americans now live in urban areas, city governments are an important local unit of government. Cities provide many of the necessary services, such as sewage treatment and police protection, that keep the lives of their citizens safe and enjoyable.

There are three main types of city government. The mayor-council form has a mayor as the chief executive and an elected council to perform legislative duties. The council-manager form of government runs a city more like a business might. An appointed city manager oversees the city's operations. Under the commission form of government, a commission of five to nine members is elected to run the city.

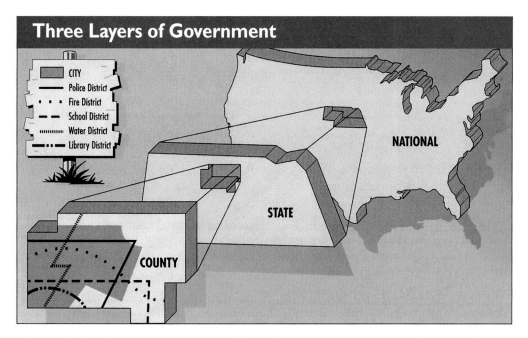

Three Layers of Government

CITY
Police District
Fire District
School District
Water District
Library District

NATIONAL

STATE

COUNTY

Chart Skills: This chart shows the different levels of government in the United States. Most public services are handled at the local level. **Critical Thinking:** Name one advantage and one disadvantage of local control over public services.

Johnny Tremain

ESTHER FORBES

Johnny Tremain, by Esther Forbes, tells the story of a fourteen-year-old apprentice silversmith in Boston during the early years of the American Revolution. Johnny becomes a spy for the Committee of Public Safety, a Patriot group preparing to fight the British. In the excerpt below, Johnny tries to get information about a British plan to stop the Patriots.

This very night—come darkness—the men would move, but in what direction? And who would be in charge of the expedition? Surely not more than one of the colonels would be sent. Johnny, who had his own colonel to watch, Colonel Smith, hardly left the Afric Queen all day and helped the pot-boy serve drinks to the officers in the dining room. A young officer sitting with Stranger did say, as he stirred his brandy-and-water with his thumb, that he hoped before long thus to stir Yankee blood—and what of that? Colonel Smith did have an army

chaplain to dine with him that day. Did that mean he was suddenly getting religious, as people are said to before they go into danger?

Of one thing Johnny was sure. Dove knew much less than he did. Dove was so thick-witted he had no idea anything unusual was afoot. He honestly believed that the grenadiers and light infantry were merely going to be taught "new evolutions." As usual, Dove was too wrapped in his own woes to think much of what was happening about him.

By five Johnny thought he would leave the Queen and report to Paul Revere that he had discovered nothing new. First one more glance at Dove.

For once he found him hard at work, his lower lip stuck out, his whitish piglashes wet. He was polishing a saddle.

"That guy," he complained, "hit me for nothing. He said I was to get to work on his campaign saddle."

"Who's he?"

"Colonel Smith, of course."

"Did you do as he told you?"

"I tried. I didn't know he had two saddles. So I went to work on the usual one. I shined it until you can see your face in it. And he takes it out of my hands and hit me on the head with it. Says I'm a stupid lout not to know the difference between a parade saddle and a campaign saddle. How'd I know? Why, he's been over here about a year and that campaign saddle hasn't ever been unpacked. I had to get it from Lieutenant Stranger. How'd I know?"

Johnny said nothing. He realized he had heard something which conceivably might be important. Careful . . . careful . . . don't you say anything to scare him.

"Where's your polish? I'll help with the stirrups."

The instant Johnny went to work, Dove as usual lay back on the hay.

"One of the stirrups wrapped 'round my head. Cut my ear. It bled something fierce."

Johnny was studying the saddle on his knees. It was of heavy black leather, brass (not silver) mountings. Three girths instead of two. All sorts of hooks and straps for attaching map cases, spy-glasses, flasks, kits of all sorts.

Colonel Smith is going on a campaign. But perhaps not. He might merely be riding down to New York.

He leaned back on his heels. "Say, what if you and I took time out to eat supper? The Queen's cook has promised me a good dinner, because I helped them at table this afternoon. Roast goose. I'll fix it so you can get in on it, too."

"Oh for goodness sake—no."

"It's past five o'clock. Colonel can't be going anywhere tonight."

"Oh, for land's sake, Johnny, he says I'm to show him that saddle by six sharp, and if he don't like its looks he's going to cut me to mince-meat. He's always saying things

like that. He's the . . ."

Johnny did not listen to what Colonel Smith was. He was thinking.

"Well after that—when Colonel Smith has settled down to play whist. Can you get off?"

"Tonight isn't like any other night. He told me to bring Sandy around for him, fed and clean and saddled with this old campaign saddle by eight o'clock tonight . . ."

Colonel Smith is going on a long journey. Starting tonight at eight. It might be a campaign.

From *Johnny Tremain*, by Esther Forbes. Copyright 1943 by Esther Forbes Hoskins. Copyright © renewed 1971 by Linwood M. Erskine, Jr., Executor of the Estate. Reprinted by permission of Houghton Mifflin Company.

Analyzing Literature

1. What is the importance of the colonel's choice of saddles?

2. Does Johnny get Dove to talk by asking direct questions? Explain.

3. What do you think Johnny will do with this information?

4

Building the Nation (1789–1840)

UNIT OVERVIEW

In its first half-century the United States grew in size, population, and economic power.

Chapter 12

Launching a New Government (1789–1801)
Early tests for the American government included repaying wartime debts and keeping the nation out of European conflicts.

Chapter 13

Expanding and Defending Boundaries (1800–1820)
Buying Louisiana from France gave the United States a vast new territory. Fighting Britain courageously in the War of 1812 gave the United States new respect.

Chapter 14

The Expanding Nation (1800–1840)
Even as a new spirit of national unity spread through the country, economic differences between the industrial North and the plantation South widened.

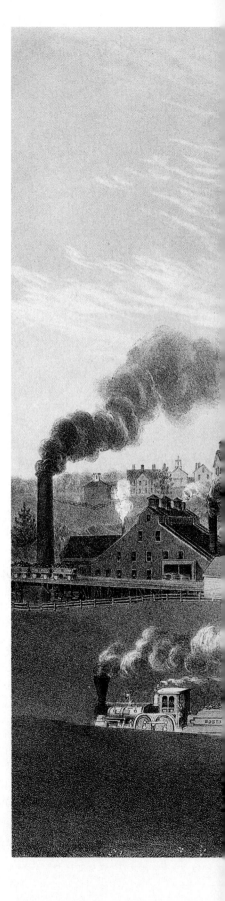

Illustration: "Bridgewater, Massachusetts" (detail).

The year 1789 marked the start of a new era. The nation's first President, George Washington, is saluted as he arrives in New York for his inauguration.

1789　　　1792　　　1795　　　1798

1789 Washington becomes President

1791 First Bank of the United States established

1789 French Revolution begins

1792 Washington re-elected

1794 Whiskey Rebellion

1797 John Adams becomes President

1798 Alien and Sedition Acts

Launching a New Government (1789–1801)

1 The Government Takes Shape

SECTION GUIDE

Main Idea
President Washington and his Treasury Secretary, Alexander Hamilton, designed financial policies that would strengthen the credit and authority of the government.

Goals
As you read, look for answers to these questions:

1 What steps did Congress take to organize the new government?

2 What views did Alexander Hamilton hold about money and business?

3 What financial policies did the government adopt?

Key Terms
inaugurate
precedent
capital
capitalism
tariff
strict construction
loose construction

1801

1801 Jefferson becomes President

NEW YORK CITY was festive on the last day of April 1789. At dawn thirteen cannons boomed. The streets were strung with banners. Church bells rang. Crowds gathered in front of Federal Hall, the temporary home of Congress. This was the day on which the first President of the United States would be sworn into office.

Washington Takes Office

At noon George Washington arrived. He was in formal dress: white silk stockings, silver buckles on his shoes, sword at his side, hair powdered white. His new suit was of a rare material: brown cloth made in the United States. Washington was *inaugurated* —sworn into office—on a balcony of Federal Hall. When the short ceremony ended, the crowd shouted, "God bless our President!"

Washington now began the task of leading the new republic. "I walk on untrodden ground," he wrote. "There is scarcely any part of my conduct which may not hereafter be drawn into precedent." (A *precedent* is an example that becomes standard practice.) Washington knew his actions would help define the office of President for generations to come.

Launching the Government

Washington had been elected only a few months before, after members of the Electoral College had prepared their ballots. Each elector had written down two names. The top vote getter would become the new President. The runner-up would be named Vice President. Washington's name was on every single ballot. He was the unanimous choice for President. John Adams of Massachusetts was elected Vice President.

The country now had a President, a Vice President, and the

297

President Washington (far right) chose leading political and military figures for his Cabinet. Shown here are (from left to right) Henry Knox, Thomas Jefferson, and Alexander Hamilton.

Congress. The Constitution also called for a Supreme Court and other courts. Yet it left many questions unanswered. How many judges should there be on the Supreme Court? How many other courts were needed by the federal government? The Constitution also mentioned executive departments to help the President. What should they be? The first task of the new Congress was to fill in the blanks left by the Constitution.

To set up a system of courts, Congress passed the Federal Judiciary Act. This law said that the Supreme Court would have five justices (judges) plus a Chief Justice. (Over time, that number has grown to nine.) Washington appointed John Jay, the lawyer who had negotiated the 1783 Treaty of Paris, as Chief Justice. The law also set up several other federal courts.

Washington's Cabinet

Congress created three departments to help the President. Washington chose talented men to run these departments. Thomas Jefferson, who had served as a diplomat in France, headed the Department of State. This office handled relations between the United States and other countries. Henry Knox, a trusted general during the Revolution, became Secretary of War. Alexander Hamilton ran the Treasury Department. His jobs were to raise money and handle government finances.

Washington named Edmund Randolph as Attorney General. Randolph's job was to advise the government on legal matters. The three department heads and the Attorney General made up Washington's Cabinet. Over the years, the number of departments has grown. Today there are fourteen members of the Cabinet.

Economic Problems

The new government's most pressing problem was money. The government needed a source of income, and it needed to pay its debts. The United States still had large debts from fighting the Revolution. It owed millions of dollars to France, the Netherlands, and Spain. It had also borrowed from private citizens. Individual states had borrowed, too, to pay for the Revolution.

By 1789 the United States owed more than $52 million. The states owed another $25 million. To gain the confidence of its people, the country needed to be able to pay this money back. "What are we to do with this heavy debt?" asked Washington.

For help, the President turned to his young Secretary of the Treasury, Alexander Hamilton. Hamilton believed in a strong central government that encouraged business and industry. Born poor, but now rich, Hamilton had little faith in ordinary people. As he saw it, what made a nation great was a powerful class of merchants and manufacturers.

Influence of Adam Smith

Hamilton's ideas showed the influence of Adam Smith. A Scottish economist, Smith published his *Wealth of Nations* in 1776. In it he described capital —money available for investment. Capital can produce wealth, Smith said. Smith pointed out that money that lies under a mattress does not make money. It is just being stored. On the other hand, money that is invested or lent produces wealth. (See the Skills feature.)

Adam Smith also favored private enterprise over mercantilism. He thought the government should set as few limits as possible on business, trade, and manufacturing. Today Smith's ideas go by the name of capitalism. This economic system has two main features. The first feature is that most businesses are privately owned and operated. The second feature is that competition and the free market most often determine what will be produced and at what price it will sell.

Hamilton's Financial Plan

In 1790 Hamilton presented a financial plan to Congress. The main goal of the plan was to build a strong national government. Hamilton believed this was necessary to the growth of business. In his plan Hamilton proposed: (1) paying off all war debts, (2) raising government revenues, and (3) creating a national bank.

(1) *War debts.* Hamilton wanted the government to pay off all Revolutionary War debts, state as well as national. Hamilton argued that if the nation did not pay off its debts, then no one would want to lend it money in the future. However, southern states balked at Hamilton's plan. Most of them had already paid their war debts. Why, they asked, should they help the northern states pay theirs?

To get southern support Hamilton turned to Thomas Jefferson. Jefferson was from Virginia and was respected among southerners. Taking a stroll one afternoon, the two discussed the debt issue. They also talked about Congress's failure to agree on a location for the national capital. For the time being it was New York City. However,

each region of the country wanted the honor of having the capital.

Hamilton and Jefferson struck a bargain. Jefferson would ask the southern states to support Hamilton's war-debt plan. In return, northerners would support having the nation's capital in the South. The site chosen would be along the Potomac.

(2) *Raising revenue.* Under Hamilton's plan, tariffs would become the main source of government revenue. A tariff is a tax on a foreign good. Tariffs would be highest on foreign products that could be made in America. By making foreign goods

Hamilton and Jefferson agreed to a national capital along the Potomac.

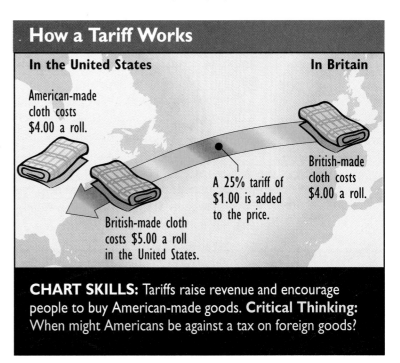

How a Tariff Works

In the United States   **In Britain**

American-made cloth costs $4.00 a roll.

British-made cloth costs $4.00 a roll.

A 25% tariff of $1.00 is added to the price.

British-made cloth costs $5.00 a roll in the United States.

CHART SKILLS: Tariffs raise revenue and encourage people to buy American-made goods. **Critical Thinking:** When might Americans be against a tax on foreign goods?

The Bank of the United States was created in 1791. The date on the front of the building (1795) refers to the year the building was erected.

expensive, the tariff would encourage people to buy American-made goods. Thus, the tariff filled two purposes: raising government money and helping American manufacturers.

(3) *A national bank.* Hamilton called for a main bank in Philadelphia with branches in other cities. The bank would give the government a safe place to keep its money. It would also issue paper money and make loans to the government and to people.

The bank proposal brought protest from Jefferson and James Madison. They believed the best kind of wealth was land. They were suspicious of people who held wealth in any other form, such as money. A national bank, they feared, would help create a new class of men with much money and power. Such a class could threaten the nation's liberty.

The debate over the bank brought into the open a sharp disagreement over how to interpret the Constitution. Madison and Jefferson believed in what is called strict construction of the Constitution. In other words, they argued that the

The half eagle was the nation's first official coin made of gold.

government has only the powers that the Constitution clearly says it has. The Constitution says nothing about a national bank. Therefore, said Madison and Jefferson, the government had no right to create one.

Hamilton, on the other hand, supported a loose construction of the Constitution. According to this view, the government can do anything the Constitution does not say it cannot do. Hamilton, pointing to the elastic clause, argued that the bank was "necessary and proper" to carry out the government's duties.

Jefferson and Hamilton went to President Washington. Each argued his point of view. Hamilton won the argument. The first Bank of the United States was established in 1791.

SECTION REVIEW

1. Key Terms inaugurate, precedent, capital, capitalism, tariff, strict construction, loose construction

2. People George Washington, John Adams, Henry Knox, Alexander Hamilton, Edmund Randolph, Adam Smith

3. Comprehension What economic problems did the new government face?

4. Comprehension How did Hamilton and Jefferson disagree on interpreting the Constitution?

5. Critical Thinking In what way did the arguments for and against the national bank resemble the arguments for and against the Constitution in 1787?

LEARN

Nearly everyone deals with a bank. Yet few understand how banks make the economy grow. This chart shows how banks help circulate money. Banks accept deposits from individuals and businesses. Then banks distribute this money to other individuals and businesses in the form of loans. Banks pay interest to depositors (a big reason why people deposit money in banks). Banks also receive interest from borrowers.

Money thus flows in a circular path from people like you—savers—into the general economy and back to you again. In the process, it can create goods and services, jobs, and profits.

Banks and businesses are partners in this system. Thus the establishment of a national bank in 1791 created a partnership between the federal government and American business.

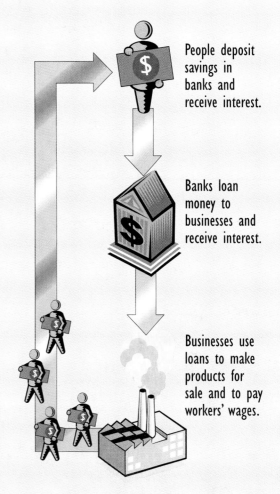

People deposit savings in banks and receive interest.

Banks loan money to businesses and receive interest.

Businesses use loans to make products for sale and to pay workers' wages.

PRACTICE

1. Using the chart as a guide, explain how banks help circulate money.

2. There is a saying, "It takes money to make money." Does the chart support this saying? Explain.

3. Do you think Americans who feared a strong central government favored a national bank? Explain your answer.

APPLY

4. Write a letter to the editor expressing your opinion about Hamilton's plan to create a national bank. Pretend you are either a southern farmer or a northern merchant in 1791.

2 Maintaining the Peace

SECTION GUIDE

Main Idea
Washington used firmness to assert American authority in the West and avoid war with the European powers.

Goals
As you read, look for answers to these questions:

1. What problems did the United States face in the West?

2. How did Americans react to the French Revolution?

3. How did the United States stay out of European conflicts?

Key Terms
Whiskey Rebellion
neutral
right of deposit

Many Westerners used flatboats to transport themselves and their goods down the Mississippi. This image shows the interior of a flatboat.

I N WAR, one fights to defeat an opponent. Peace takes another kind of struggle. It requires a skillful blend of diplomacy and firmness.

The biggest task facing President Washington and the young government was maintaining peace at home and abroad. The country needed peace in order to grow. As a general, Washington had worked to win the Revolutionary War. As President, he had to work just as hard to keep the peace.

Securing the West

In 1793 Spain, Great Britain, and Indian nations were all struggling with Americans. Each sought control of the Trans-Appalachian West—the land between the Appalachians and the Mississippi. Under the Treaty of Paris (1783), most of this land belonged to the United States. However, neither the Indians nor Spain felt it was necessary to honor the treaty. Neither did the British.

Spain claimed much of North America west of the Mississippi. In addition it controlled the Floridas and the crucial port of New Orleans. Westerners had only one way to get their goods to market: by flatboat down the Mississippi to New Orleans. Spain threatened to cut off this route. Also, Spain encouraged the Indians of the Southeast to resist white settlement.

The British still occupied forts north of the Ohio River. In fact, the governor of Canada plotted with the Indians to attack American settlements in the Northwest Territory. There the Indians hoped to set up their own nation under British protection.

Washington knew the Trans-Appalachian West was important for the security and growth of the new nation. His policy was to secure the West, whether by diplomacy or military action.

Battle of Fallen Timbers

The first army Washington sent to secure the Ohio Valley was soundly defeated by the Miami chief Little Turtle. Washington then sent a second army west, this one headed by Anthony Wayne. Wayne was both experienced and shrewd. His men called him "Mad Anthony" because of his reckless courage. At his headquarters near present-day Cincinnati, Wayne turned his raw recruits into a sturdy, disciplined force.

Meanwhile, the British had built Fort Miami on the Maumee River in Ohio. Expecting British help, Indian warriors from all over the Northwest Territory gathered at the site. There they prepared for battle against the Americans. Learning that the war drums were beating that summer of 1794, Washington ordered Wayne to march toward Fort Miami.

As many as 2,000 Shawnee, Ottawa, and Chippewa Indians planned to ambush Wayne's smaller force. The site they had chosen was littered with trees struck down by a tornado. As Wayne and his troop drew closer to Fort Miami, however, he stopped his march. Wayne knew that it was an Indian custom not to eat before a battle. The warriors waited three days for Wayne's force, all the time growing weaker and hungrier. When they finally met, Wayne's troop soundly defeated the Indians at the Battle of Fallen Timbers.

The Indians fled to Fort Miami, but the British closed the gates on them. Despite their talk, the British would not help the Indians if it meant risking a war with the United States. The Battle of Fallen Timbers crushed the Indians' hope of keeping their land. They signed the Treaty of Greenville, agreeing to surrender their homelands in what is now Ohio.

The Whiskey Rebellion

Washington faced another challenge in 1794. The tax on whiskey, part of Hamilton's financial plan, angered frontier farmers. They had trouble taking their crops to market because of poor roads. Therefore, they made their grain into whiskey. Whiskey was easier to carry than grain and brought a better price in the East. Backcountry settlers had little cash with which to buy goods, let alone pay the tax. They often used whiskey like money to buy salt, sugar, nails, and ammunition.

To many, the whiskey tax seemed as unfair as British taxes had been. Some

The Indians were defeated at the Battle of Fallen Timbers. As a result, they were forced to give up their rights to most of the land in what is now Ohio.

feared that even more taxes would follow. A group of farmers in western Pennsylvania refused to pay the tax. In what was called the Whiskey Rebellion, the farmers took up arms and chased away the tax collectors. Some even marched on Pittsburgh.

The farmers, poorly organized, were not really a threat to the nation. However, Hamilton wanted to prove the federal government's strength. He convinced Washington that troops should be sent to put down the uprising. In the fall of 1794 Washington himself—with Hamilton at his side—led an army of 13,000 soldiers into western Pennsylvania.

On the news of the army's approach, many rebels fled to Kentucky. By the time the army reached western Pennsylvania, the rebellion had ended. Washington's action, however, had shown that the federal government had the power and will to enforce its laws.

Jolts from French Revolution

A third challenge to Washington came from overseas. In the early 1790s France was in turmoil. In 1789 the French people had launched their own revolution, demanding liberty and equality. Americans cheered, believing the French were following their lead. Thomas Paine traveled to France to sit on their councils. Thomas Jefferson wrote a proposed bill of rights for the new French government.

By 1793, however, the revolution had grown bloody. The ruling group executed thousands of people, including the king and queen. Liberty and law seemed to disappear. The monarchs of Europe feared that the revolution would spread across the continent. They joined to defeat France and stamp out its revolution. Britain was a leader in this fight against France.

These events in Europe divided the American people. Growing numbers opposed the turn the French Revolution had taken. They agreed with Hamilton that the United States had to stay on good terms with Britain. British trade was too important to the American economy to risk war. On the other hand, Jefferson and others remained pro-French. Jefferson believed that the move to crush the French Revolution was an attack on liberty everywhere.

For Washington it was most important that the United States be neutral, or avoid siding with one country over another. In the spring of 1793 he announced that the United States would be "friendly and impartial" to both sides in the war. Congress then passed a law forbidding Americans to help either side.

Brandishing spears and pikes, women raid the palace of the French king. Americans were divided over the cause of the French revolutionaries.

This scene shows shipbuilders at work on the naval ship *Philadelphia*. **Critical Thinking:** How might building up armed forces help promote a policy of neutrality?

Remaining Neutral

With Europe armed and fighting, Washington worried about American defenses. Washington had not thought a navy necessary. He had kept to this view even when pirate states of North Africa captured American ships.

However, after Britain seized 250 American trading ships in the West Indies, the President changed his mind. In 1794 he asked Congress to start a navy and to buy warships. Called frigates, these warships turned out to be the best and fastest of their type on the seas.

Meanwhile, Britain stopped its policy of seizing American ships in the West Indies. Washington then sent Chief Justice John Jay to London for talks. During the talks, news came of the American victory at the Battle of Fallen Timbers. This helped Jay at the bargaining table. The result was Jay's Treaty, signed in late 1794.

In Jay's Treaty, Britain agreed to leave the Ohio Valley. Britain also agreed that under certain conditions, American ships could trade in the West Indies.

Jay's Treaty was followed by Pinckney's Treaty with Spain. It was negotiated by Thomas Pinckney in 1795. Pinckney's Treaty said Americans could navigate the Mississippi River. For three years westerners would also have the **right of deposit** in New Orleans. They were allowed, in other words, to store goods in New Orleans awaiting ocean transport.

In addition, Spain accepted the 31st parallel as the southern boundary of the United States. It also promised to stop helping the Indians fight American settlers.

Together, Jay's Treaty and Pinckney's Treaty had far-reaching effects. The United States managed to avoid war and preserve the boundaries set in 1783. The treaties also allowed Americans to move into the Trans-Appalachian West without fear of European attacks.

SECTION REVIEW

1. Key Terms Whiskey Rebellion, neutral, right of deposit

2. People and Places Little Turtle, Anthony Wayne, Trans-Appalachian West, New Orleans

3. Comprehension What military and diplomatic actions secured the West?

4. Comprehension How did the French Revolution divide Americans?

5. Critical Thinking Do you think that neutrality was a good policy in the 1790s? Why or why not?

3 The Federalists in Charge

SECTION GUIDE

Main Idea
The split between Alexander Hamilton and Thomas Jefferson led to the creation of political parties. Parties grew in importance after George Washington left the presidency.

Goals
As you read, look for answers to these questions:

1 What were the goals of the Federalist and Democratic-Republican parties?

2 What was Washington's Farewell Address to the nation?

3 What events during John Adams's presidency caused bitter debates among Americans?

Key Terms
political party
foreign policy
Alien and Sedition Acts
alien
sedition
states' rights

AS MEMBERS OF President Washington's Cabinet, Hamilton and Jefferson repeatedly argued over plans for the new nation. They disagreed on how to interpret the Constitution. They disagreed over Hamilton's financial plans. When war broke out between Great Britain and France, Hamilton favored Britain. Jefferson favored France. Finally, they each had a different vision of what the United States should be. Hamilton wanted an America of manufacturing, industry, and cities. Jefferson wanted a country of small, self-sufficient farmers.

Growth of Political Parties

Tensions between the two continued to grow. Each found it hard even to be in the same room as the other. By 1793 Jefferson had become fed up with the constant clashes with Hamilton. Jefferson thus quit his job as Secretary of State.

The basic differences between Hamilton and Jefferson led to the creation of **political parties.** A political party tries to influence government policy by promoting its ideas. Political parties also back candidates for office. With the help of James Madison, Jefferson formed the Democratic-Republican Party. The party name reflected their strong belief in both democracy and the republican system. Meanwhile, Hamilton and Vice President John Adams organized the Federalist Party.

Jefferson's followers were mainly farmers and artisans. They were often called "Republicans" (though they are not connected to today's Republican Party). Low taxes and small government were their aim. They supported a strict construction of the Constitution. Republicans believed that ordinary people and state lawmakers—not the United States Congress—should control most government matters. They opposed the idea of a national bank.

This detail of a painting shows farm life. Jefferson relied on support from farmers.

306

Following Hamilton's lead, the Federalists supported a loose construction of the Constitution and a strong national government. A strong national government could take steps, such as establishing banks, that would benefit the economy. Hamilton's ideas appealed mostly to business people from the Northeast.

Washington Retires

Washington had been re-elected President in 1792. After serving a second term, Washington decided that the time had come to leave office. In the summer of 1796 he published his Farewell Address, stating he would not run again. In it he urged Americans to avoid party politics. Political parties, he warned, could weaken the unity of the American people. Despite this advice, parties became a permanent part of American politics.

The nation paid more attention to Washington's advice on **foreign policy** —relations with the governments of other nations. In the Farewell Address, Washington advised the country to stay neutral. He warned against making long-term agreements with foreign nations. The United States would follow this principle for the next 150 years.

John Adams Takes Office

As Washington made his plans to retire to Mount Vernon, the question of who would be the next President took center stage. Vice President John Adams was the Federalists' choice. The Republicans wanted Jefferson. Jefferson was very popular around the country, but the Federalists were a more powerful party. When the votes of the Electoral College were counted, Adams received 71 to Jefferson's 68. Adams, therefore, became President in 1797, and Jefferson became Vice President. For the first and last time, the country had a President from one party and a Vice President from another.

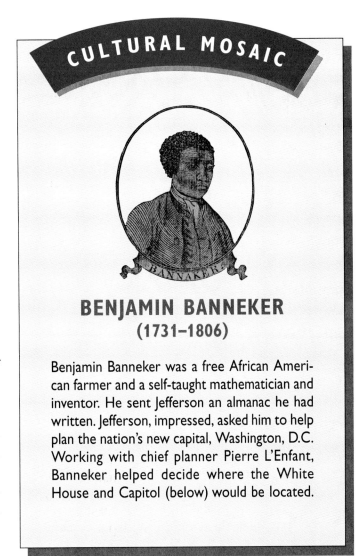

CULTURAL MOSAIC

BENJAMIN BANNEKER
(1731–1806)

Benjamin Banneker was a free African American farmer and a self-taught mathematician and inventor. He sent Jefferson an almanac he had written. Jefferson, impressed, asked him to help plan the nation's new capital, Washington, D.C. Working with chief planner Pierre L'Enfant, Banneker helped decide where the White House and Capitol (below) would be located.

In 1800 the Adamses moved to the newly built capital city, Washington, D. C. Abigail Adams described the city in November 1800. "Houses scattered over a space of ten miles, and [many] trees and stumps . . . with a castle of a house," she wrote. She was living in the still unfinished White House, hanging her washing to dry in the East Room. She had only to put up with  the discomforts of Washington for a short time. In less than a year, her husband would be out of office.

The Adamses moved into an unfinished White House in 1800. Here, Abigail Adams and her granddaughter, Susanna, watch as a servant hangs out laundry in the East Room. Today the East Room is open to the public.

Problems with France

In 1797 relations between the United States and France were tense. France, still fighting Britain, was angry that the United States and Britain had signed Jay's Treaty. The French navy began capturing American ships to keep them from trading with French enemies. In a short time the French had seized more than 300 American ships.

Talks and treaties, Adams hoped, would ease the tensions. To this end, Adams sent to Paris three ambassadors—Charles Pinckney, Elbridge Gerry, and John Marshall. There they hoped to meet with the French Minister of Foreign Affairs.

For weeks the three Americans sat in waiting rooms, ignored by the French. Then three French agents—later referred to as X, Y, and Z—approached them. The minister would speak with them about a treaty, the agents said. First, however, the minister wanted the United States to "loan" France $12 million and pay him $250,000. Pinckney realized they were being asked for a bribe. Somewhat deaf and unable to believe his ears, he answered, "No, no, not a sixpence."

The Americans sent Adams a full report of what became known as the XYZ Affair.

When Adams told Congress, the country exploded in anger. Pinckney's words were transformed into a popular slogan:

66 Millions for defense, not one cent for tribute! 99

In other words, Americans would rather pay for a war than pay a bribe. In 1798 Congress canceled the treaties it had made with France. It began to recruit an army and it said American ships could attack French ships.

The Alien and Sedition Acts

The problems with France sharpened the differences between the Federalists and the Republicans. The Republicans were attacking Adams and the Federalists. They disliked the government's new military spending. They were also sympathetic to France.

Feelings on both sides ran strong. Federalists accused Republicans of being "democrats, mobocrats, and all other kinds of rats." Republican newspapers fired back. One called Adams "the blasted tyrant of America." Adams was furious at such criticism in a time of near war. He blamed the Republican newspapers and the new immigrants. Most of the new immigrants were

Republicans. They included about 25,000 newcomers from France, as well as thousands of Irish.

To silence Republican critics, the Federalist Congress passed the Alien and Sedition Acts in 1798. Immigrants who are not yet citizens are called aliens. Until that time, it had taken five years for an alien to become a United States citizen. The new laws set fourteen years as the waiting period. In this way, Congress hoped to maintain Federalist power by reducing the number of new citizens.

The Alien and Sedition Acts also gave the President power to arrest disloyal immigrants or even order them out of the country. The acts outlawed sedition, which they defined as false or critical speech about the government. Federalists used this law to silence their critics. About 25 Republican newspaper editors were arrested and 10 sent to jail. One congressman was also locked up for speaking out against the President. In this way, the law restricted freedom of speech and of the press.

The Republican Response

Republicans believed that liberty itself was at stake. Jefferson and Madison challenged the Alien and Sedition Acts with a theory that came to be called states' rights. This theory claimed that states had the right to judge whether a law passed by Congress was constitutional. The Kentucky and Virginia legislatures agreed. In 1798–1799 they passed resolutions (statements) written by Jefferson and Madison. The Kentucky and Virginia Resolutions declared that the Alien and Sedition Acts had no legal force because they violated the Bill of Rights.

No other states sided with Kentucky and Virginia. Within a few years, a new Congress let the Alien and Sedition Acts expire. Yet the issue of states' rights would reappear in later years, especially in the decades leading to the Civil War.

Peace with France

In 1800 a new French leader, Napoleon Bonaparte, came to power. Napoleon had no wish to continue quarreling with the United States. The two countries signed an agreement to stop all naval attacks. Called the Convention of 1800, it cleared the way for American and French ships to sail the ocean in peace.

President Adams was proud of having saved the country from bloodshed. He later said that he hoped to be remembered as "John Adams, who took upon himself the responsibility of peace with France."

John Adams was a diplomat before becoming President. His peace-making skills helped keep the nation from going to war with France.

SECTION REVIEW

1. Key Terms political party, foreign policy, Alien and Sedition Acts, alien, sedition, states' rights

2. People and Places Alexander Hamilton, Thomas Jefferson, John Adams, Washington, D.C.

3. Comprehension What was George Washington's advice in his Farewell Address?

4. Comprehension Why did Congress pass the Alien and Sedition Acts? What was Kentucky and Virginia's response?

5. Critical Thinking How did relations with France affect political developments in the United States?

SECTION GUIDE

Main Idea

In 1801 the Republicans gained power with the election of Thomas Jefferson, who overturned Federalist programs.

Goals

As you read, look for answers to these questions:

❶ Why was the election of 1800 significant?

❷ What personal qualities did Thomas Jefferson have?

❸ What policies did Jefferson follow as President?

Key Terms
radical
administration

T he year 1801 marked the beginning of a new era for the United States. The 1800s was the century in which the United States would expand to the Pacific Ocean. It was the century in which democracy in the United States greatly expanded. The man who became President in 1801 had a powerful influence on these developments.

The Election of 1800

The election of 1800 was a contest between John Adams and Thomas Jefferson. It was also a bitter face-off between Federalists and Republicans.

Each party accused the other of endangering the Constitution and the American republic. The Republicans saw themselves as saving the nation from tyranny and monarchy. Again and again the Republicans argued that the Alien and Sedition Acts violated the Bill of Rights.

The Federalists thought that the nation was about to be undone by nonreligious radicals. (A radical is someone who takes an extreme position.) Fresh in the memory of the Federalists was the violence of the French Revolution, in which thousands had been executed in the name of "liberty."

In the first count of the electoral ballots, Jefferson had 73, to 65 for Adams. Yet there was a problem. Under the Constitution, electors cast two votes for President. The runner-up was supposed to become Vice President. However, Aaron Burr, who was intended to be the Republicans' candidate for *Vice* President, also got 73 votes, the same number as Jefferson. (This problem was resolved with the passage of the Twelfth Amendment in 1804. The Twelfth Amendment called for separate ballots for the President and Vice President.)

Breaking the Tie

Aaron Burr was the grandson of the fiery preacher Jonathan Edwards, who had helped lead the Great Awakening. Burr had fought bravely during the Revolutionary War. Like Alexander Hamilton, he was now a New York lawyer and politician.

According to the Constitution, the House of Representatives

Thomas Jefferson, the third U.S. President.

would have to break the tie between Burr and Jefferson. Republicans, it was clear, intended Jefferson to be President. Yet the Federalists held a majority in Congress. They, not the Republicans, would have the power to break the tie.

The Federalists were divided over whom to support. Some Federalists so feared Jefferson that they supported Burr. Alexander Hamilton, however, urged Jefferson's election. Hamilton wrote that Burr was as "unprincipled and dangerous a man. . . . If there be a man in the world I ought to hate, it is Jefferson. . . . But the public good must be paramount to [be more important than] every private consideration."

Voting on the issue, the House deadlocked for 35 ballots. On the 36th ballot 3 Federalists decided to follow Hamilton's advice and withdrew their support from Burr. Jefferson thus became the new President, and Burr the Vice President. (Burr never forgave Hamilton. For this and other "insults," Burr challenged Hamilton to a duel in 1804 and killed him.)

People were overjoyed by Jefferson's election. A Philadelphia newspaper reported, "The bells have been ringing, guns firing, dogs barking, cats mewling, children crying, and [Republican radicals] getting drunk ever since the news of Mr. Jefferson's election arrived in this city."

The Talented Jefferson

Our nation, in its more than 200 years of existence, has had more than 40 Presidents. They have included great leaders and men of good judgment. None of our Presidents, however, has matched Thomas Jefferson in the variety of his achievements.

You have already read about some of what Jefferson did. He wrote the Declaration of Independence. He served as ambassador to France and Secretary of State under Washington. He was leader of the Republican Party and Vice President under Adams. Yet Jefferson accomplished far more.

A Republican campaign flyer (left) warns voters against the Federalists.

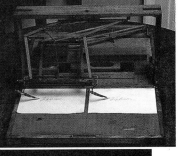

A man of many talents Jefferson designed and built Monticello (left), his Virginia plantation. Among his inventions was the polygraph (top). It allowed him to make an exact copy of letters as he wrote them.

JEFFERSON'S STAND AGAINST PIRACY

"Weakness provokes insult and injury." This was Thomas Jefferson's response to a government policy of paying pirates to leave American ships alone. For years pirates off the Barbary Coast—the North African states of Morocco, Algiers, Tunis, and Tripoli—had preyed on U.S. merchant ships in the Mediterranean.

In 1800 Tripoli demanded more "protection money" from the United States. Jefferson sent a fleet of warships to protect the merchant ships. These warships clashed with enemy ships in the Mediterranean.

In 1804 Lieutenant Stephen Decatur led a raid against the American ship, the *Philadelphia*. The pirates had captured the *Philadelphia*. Decatur's crew burned the ship to keep the pirates from using it. Eventually, the Barbary states signed a treaty promising not to interfere with American ships.

Jefferson was still a young lawyer when he also became an architect. Inspired by the buildings of classical Greece and Rome, he designed his home, Monticello. For the elegant mansion Jefferson invented a dumbwaiter (an elevator for food dishes), storm windows, and a seven-day clock. The look of the nation's capital also reflects Jefferson's interest in classical architecture. From the time the Potomac site was chosen, Jefferson worked closely with the architects and designers of Washington, D.C.

Jefferson was also a musician who loved to play the violin. An eager reader, he had one of the best libraries in America. After he died, his library became the core of the new Library of Congress.

As President, Jefferson dressed and behaved like a gentleman farmer. He refused to follow city fashions. He often wore green corduroy breeches, a red vest, and yarn stockings. Jefferson also did not like ceremony and show. Instead of riding in a fancy carriage to his inauguration, he walked. He entertained at the White House with friendly dinners instead of grand parties. He signed his invitations "Mr. Jefferson" rather than "The President of the United States."

Undoing Federalist Programs

For President Jefferson the first order of business was quieting the nation's political quarrels. In his Inaugural Address he called for unity:

❝ Let us unite with one heart and one mind. Every difference of opinion is not a difference of principle. We are all Republicans, we are all Federalists. ❞

Despite his words, Jefferson was no Federalist. He disagreed with Federalist ideas about a strong, active government. Jefferson believed in a small government. In Jefferson's mind, the federal government should have a limited role in people's lives.

During his administration —term of office—Jefferson undid as much of the Federalist program as he could. The new Congress, now controlled by Republicans, worked with him in this goal. At his urging, Congress allowed the Alien and Sedition Acts to expire. Jefferson released from prison any persons convicted under the Sedition Act. Congress also ended internal taxes, including the tax on whiskey.

In effect, Jefferson wanted to destroy the finance system set up by Hamilton.

In 1801 President Adams appointed John Marshall as Chief Justice of the United States. Marshall served as Chief Justice for 34 years—an all-time record.

Marshall had helped raise his fourteen younger brothers and sisters on their family farm. Marshall then served in the Continental Army and spent the winter of 1777–1778 with Washington at Valley Forge. After the war Marshall served in Congress and as Secretary of State under Adams. As a loyal Federalist, he disagreed heartily with Jefferson's policies.

Jefferson often felt frustrated by Federalist control of the courts. Yet there was little he could do. Judges were appointed for life. As he once remarked about judges, "Few die and none resign."

One reason Adams had chosen Marshall to be Chief Justice was that he was only 44 years old. Adams reasoned that Marshall would be around a long time to check the Republicans. He was right. Marshall would serve as Chief Justice until his death in 1835.

Hamilton's system depended on a certain amount of public and private debt. Jefferson opposed debt in any form. "Banking establishments are more dangerous than standing armies," he said. "The principle of spending money to be paid by posterity [future generations] . . . is swindling . . . on a large scale."

Jefferson's repeal of most taxes reduced the government's income. To cut spending, Jefferson lowered the number of its employees. With Congress's approval, he also reduced the size of the navy and army.

A Federalist Judiciary

The thorn in Jefferson's side was the judicial branch of government. Between the election of 1800 and Jefferson's inauguration, President Adams had appointed as many Federalist judges as he could. Among the appointments was John Marshall as Chief Justice.

Marshall was a Virginian and a distant relative of Thomas Jefferson. He had little formal schooling. Indeed, there was hardly time for school. Until he turned twenty,

---

SECTION REVIEW

1. Key Terms radical, administration

2. People Thomas Jefferson, Aaron Burr, John Marshall

3. Comprehension What events led to Jefferson's election as President?

4. Comprehension How and why did the Republicans try to undo Hamilton's financial program?

5. Critical Thinking What did Thomas Jefferson mean when he said, "We are all Republicans, we are all Federalists"?

Summary

1. President Washington worked to create a strong national government. Hamilton introduced a financial plan to do this. Jefferson and Hamilton disagreed over how to interpret the Constitution. This led to clashes over the creation of a national bank.

2. In the Battle of Fallen Timbers, Indians were forced to give up their lands in what is now Ohio. The American people were divided over the revolution in France. Washington decided the nation would be neutral on the issue. Jay's Treaty and Pinckney's Treaty further secured the West for Americans.

3. Hamilton and Jefferson's disagreements led to the creation of the political parties. Tensions with France grew after the XYZ Affair. Congress passed the Alien and Sedition Acts to silence Republican critics. Republicans responded with the Kentucky and Virginia Resolutions, which supported states' rights.

4. As President, Jefferson began undoing Federalist programs. He cut taxes and reduced the military. Jefferson could do little about Federalist control of the courts.

Graphic Summary

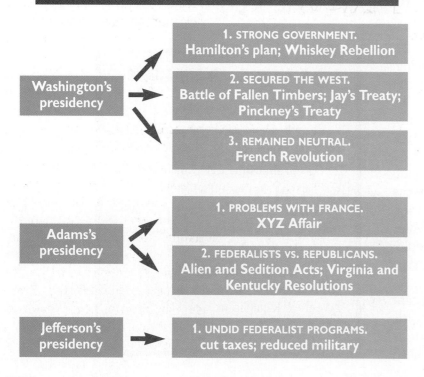

Washington's presidency
- **1. STRONG GOVERNMENT.** Hamilton's plan; Whiskey Rebellion
- **2. SECURED THE WEST.** Battle of Fallen Timbers; Jay's Treaty; Pinckney's Treaty
- **3. REMAINED NEUTRAL.** French Revolution

Adams's presidency
- **1. PROBLEMS WITH FRANCE.** XYZ Affair
- **2. FEDERALISTS VS. REPUBLICANS.** Alien and Sedition Acts; Virginia and Kentucky Resolutions

Jefferson's presidency
- **1. UNDID FEDERALIST PROGRAMS.** cut taxes; reduced military

Review

KEY TERMS

Define the terms in each of the following pairs.
1. capital; capitalism
2. strict construction; loose construction
3. neutral; foreign policy
4. Alien and Sedition Acts; states' rights

COMPREHENSION

1. What questions about the judiciary were left open by the Constitution? How were they answered?
2. What financial problems did the new nation face? How did Hamilton propose to solve them?
3. Describe the disagreement between those who believed in a strict construction of the Constitution and those who supported a loose construction.
4. How did Americans view the French Revolution?
5. What actions did Washington take to secure the West?
6. Why did Washington send troops to put down the Whiskey Rebellion?
7. What problems did Jay's Treaty address?
8. What was the XYZ Affair?
9. Why did Federalists pass the Alien and Sedition Acts? How did Republicans respond?
10. What changes in the Federalist government did Thomas Jefferson make when he became President?

Places to Locate

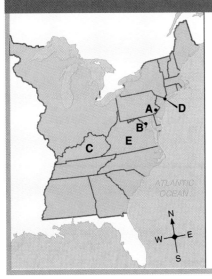

Match each of the letters on the map with the places that are listed below.
1. New York City
2. Kentucky
3. Philadelphia
4. Virginia
5. Washington, D.C.

Geographic Theme: Location What city was the first capital of the United States? To what site was the capital moved in 1800?

Skill Review

Use the skill lesson and the chart reproduced below to answer the following questions.

1. Define the following terms: deposit, withdrawal, interest, loan.
2. Explain the role of interest in creating money.
3. What would happen to the system if banks did not make loans?
4. What would happen to the system if a bank's loans were not repaid?
5. What would happen to the system if businesses shut down?

CRITICAL THINKING

1. **Analyzing a Quotation** "Merchants have no country. The mere spot they stand on does not constitute so strong an attachment as that from which they draw their gains." Who probably spoke these words, Jefferson or Hamilton? Explain your answer.
2. **Expressing an Opinion** Which group won the debate over how to interpret the Constitution, those who supported strict construction or those who supported loose construction? Cite examples to support your answer.

PORTFOLIO OPTIONS

1. **Civics Connection** Imagine that you are a U.S. citizen during the French Revolution. Create posters and pamphlets to show what action you think the U.S. government should take.
2. **Writing Connection** Research the platform of a U.S. political party today. List the party's views on major issues. Do you agree with the party's views? Explain.
3. **Contemporary Connection** Do you think Jefferson was wise to make cutbacks in the military? Explain. How much should the nation spend on the military today? Explain your answer.
4. **Timeline Connection** Copy the chapter timeline. Who was President during the Whiskey Rebellion? When were the Alien and Sedition Acts passed?

As the young nation grew in the early 1800s, conflicts arose between settlers and Indians in the West and between American and British sailors on the high seas. War with Britain broke out in 1812. In 1814 Fort McHenry outside Baltimore withstood a night of British shelling (below).

1800

1801 Jefferson becomes President

1803 Louisiana purchased

1804

1804 Lewis and Clark expedition begins

1808

1809 Madison becomes President

Expanding and Defending Boundaries (1800–1820)

1 Beyond the Mississippi

SECTION GUIDE

Main Idea
By 1800 the movement of people was bringing rapid change to North America. Thomas Jefferson, reflecting the concerns of westerners and southerners, bought new lands to add to the United States.

Goals
As you read, look for answers to these questions:

1 What changes were taking place on the Pacific Coast and on the Great Plains?

2 How did events in the West Indies affect American history?

3 What effect did the frontier have on Jefferson's foreign policy?

Key Terms
pioneer
Louisiana Purchase

I N THE LATE 1700s a variety of vessels could be found off the foggy northwest coast of North America. Richly decorated canoes carried Makah Indians who fished and hunted, as their ancestors had for thousands of years. Russian ships looking for furs sailed from settlements in Alaska. Spaniards, alarmed at Russian moves southward, came north from California. Large British ships of exploration searched the coast for the Northwest Passage. Into this mix came a new group: American traders in their small, fast ships. They represented the growing interests of the young republic on the other side of the continent.

The Pacific Coast in 1800

Spain had once claimed the entire Pacific coast of North America. In the 1740s, however, Russians set up trading posts on the Alaska coast. In response, Spain began settlement of the California coast. A mission was founded in 1769 at San Diego. By 1800 the Spanish had a chain of 21 mission outposts stretching from San Diego to San Francisco.

Meanwhile, British Canadians were pushing westward. In 1793 the great explorer Alexander Mackenzie became the first white man to cross North America and reach the Pacific. As a

1812	1816	1820

1812 War with Britain begins

1815 Battle of New Orleans

1814 British burn Washington, D.C.

1814 Treaty of Ghent

1811 Battle of Tippecanoe

result, the British laid claim to the Pacific Northwest.

From the United States, New England merchant ships sailed around the southern tip of South America. Like the Russians, they wanted furs. In 1792 Captain Robert Gray entered and explored the mouth of the great river that now divides the states of Washington and Oregon. He named the river "Columbia" after his ship. Gray also claimed the region for the United States. By 1800 so many New Englanders were trading along the Oregon coast that the Indian groups of the region called all white men "Bostons."

Changes on the Plains

Spain claimed much of the North American interior. Yet except for Spanish settlements in southeast Texas and the Rio Grande Valley, Spanish influence was absent. Meanwhile, rapid change was taking place on the Great Plains. This change was caused by the horse.

The first Spanish explorers, such as Coronado, had left horses behind. For a time, bands of horses roamed wild. Then the Indians learned to tame the horses and to ride them. This caused a social and economic revolution among the American Indians who lived on lands bordering the Great Plains. As more learned to ride, they moved onto the Plains. With the horse, the Indians could easily follow the buffalo herds. Horses also made it easier to chase down and kill buffalo. Because hunting buffalo took far less effort than farming, buffalo became the main food of the Plains Indians.

Plains Indians relied on the buffalo for more than just meat. Tissue from a buffalo serves as the string for this wooden bow.

George Catlin's painting suggests how the introduction of horses to the Great Plains transformed American Indian life there. **Critical Thinking:** How has new technology changed life in the United States in recent years?

Movement West

The Plains Indian culture was on a collision course with people moving west from the United States. Settlers by the thousands were spilling over the Appalachian Mountains. By 1800 Kentucky and Tennessee were both states. Ohio would enter the Union in 1803.

The settlers are often called **pioneers** because they were the first non-Indians to move into the area. Most people in the United States did not care that Indians already lived on these lands.

The new frontier west of the Appalachians differed from earlier frontiers. The frontier family was as distant in travel time from Boston or New York as those cities were from London or Paris. Far from the traditions and attitudes of the East Coast, frontier people developed their own.

"The Mississippi boatman and the squatter on Indian lands were perhaps the most distinctly American type then existing," wrote historian Henry Adams. "Their language and their imagination showed contact with Indians."

Most pioneers lived in crude log cabins set on an acre or two of cleared land. That was usually Indian land, so there was always the chance of Indian attack. There were opportunities for friendlier meetings as well.

Those who wanted adventure and independence were likely to pick up and move as soon as someone settled nearby. Those who had moved west because they were poor stayed to build a life for themselves. Their small communities began to show up as new dots on the map.

As the number of westerners grew, so did their political influence. Every state with a large frontier population, for example, had voted for Jefferson for President. Also in 1800, westerners had pressured Congress to sell public land at a low price. Cheap land, and plenty of it, continued to be part of the American dream.

In Hispaniola in the 1790s, enslaved Africans defeated French troops and planters. **Critical Thinking:** Who in the United States might have supported the revolt? Who might have opposed it? Why?

A Shifting Foreign Policy

When Jefferson became President, American foreign policy made a small but important shift. The concerns of the West and South carried more weight than the concerns of the North. An example was the change in policy toward the Caribbean island of Hispaniola.

More than one-third of U.S. trade was with the West Indies, and within those islands the most important market was Hispaniola. France controlled the western half of the island (now Haiti). Spain controlled the eastern half (now the Dominican Republic).

The French colony on Hispaniola was the jewel of the French empire. Its sugar, coffee, indigo, and cotton made up two-thirds of France's total trade. This rich trade in turn depended on the labor of half a million enslaved Africans.

News of the French Revolution caused turmoil on French Hispaniola. In 1791, inspired by the ideals of liberty and equality, the colony's slaves rebelled. By 1793 they had driven the French out and

Toussaint's dream of freedom has been long delayed. Haiti gained independence on January 1, 1804, but its troubles continue.

Revolts and civil war plagued Haiti throughout the 1800s. During the early 1900s, the United States occupied Haiti but did little to ease miserable living conditions there. From 1957 to 1986 two dictators, François Duvalier and his son, Jean-Claude, ruled Haiti with violence and repression. Haiti remained the poorest nation in the Western Hemisphere.

Today a new generation of Haitians is working to build democracy. Like the girl here, seated before a portrait of Toussaint, they remember their hero's dreams and await true freedom.

declared their freedom. It was the only successful slave revolt in the Americas. Their leader was Toussaint L'Ouverture (too-SAN loo-ve-TOOR). Toussaint, born a slave, was the grandson of an African chief.

The Federalist Party, backed by northern merchants who relied on trade, hoped to gain by the revolt. In the late 1790s, Federalist John Adams was President. He gave Toussaint military aid in exchange for trading rights. With such help, Toussaint then conquered the Spanish part of Hispaniola. By 1801 he ruled the whole island.

The news that slaves had rebelled and were governing Hispaniola alarmed southerners in the United States. Jefferson became President in 1801. As a slaveowner

himself, President Jefferson felt little sympathy for Toussaint L'Ouverture. Jefferson was also an admirer of France. Thus, when Napoleon, ruler of France, asked for American help in putting down the rebellion, Jefferson said yes. (Nothing, however, was to come from this promise.)

The Louisiana Purchase

Jefferson did not know that Napoleon's plans went further than Hispaniola. Most of Europe, including Spain, was in Napoleon's grip. In a secret treaty signed in 1800, he forced Spain to return the North American territory of Louisiana to France. (France had turned the region over to Spain after losing the French and Indian War.) Napoleon planned to re-establish white rule on Hispaniola. His next move would be to send an army to occupy Louisiana.

Meanwhile, Jefferson grew alarmed over two issues dear to every westerner. These were free navigation of the Mississippi River and the right of deposit in the Spanish port of New Orleans. (The right of deposit is the right to store goods for later shipment.) In late 1802 Spanish officials canceled the right of deposit. At about that time they were ordered to turn the colony over to France. Westerners were outraged. They had no other easy way to get their crops to market. Many of them called for war against both Spain and France.

To avoid war, Jefferson decided to offer to buy New Orleans from France. Behind the offer was a threat. If France should take possession of New Orleans, he wrote, "we [the United States] must marry ourselves to the British fleet and nation."

The French, meanwhile, were still fighting to restore slavery to Hispaniola. Even though they had captured Toussaint, resistance continued. To crush the rebellion, Napoleon had sent an army of nearly 34,000 men. Heavy fighting and an outbreak of yellow fever had reduced the

The eagle represents the United States in this 1803 painting of New Orleans, which celebrates the Louisiana Purchase. **Critical Thinking:** Why was it important for the United States to control New Orleans?

French force to 4,000. Disgusted, Napoleon decided to withdraw from Hispaniola. He also decided to sell Louisiana—all of it. Thus it was that for $15 million the United States made the Louisiana Purchase in 1803. This purchase doubled the area of the United States.

Jefferson agonized over the purchase. Was it legal? he asked. Jefferson believed in strict construction of the Constitution. According to that view, the President had only those powers specifically mentioned in the Constitution. Yet the Constitution said nothing about whether the President had the right to buy land. Among those urging Jefferson to make the deal was that old revolutionary Thomas Paine. Paine wrote Jefferson that buying Louisiana did not change the Constitution. Instead, he argued, "It only extends the principles of it over a larger territory."

Buying Louisiana was Jefferson's most important act as President. As a result of the purchase, the United States gained the western part of the Mississippi River basin. This was all the land between the Mississippi River and the Rocky Mountains. At the time no American knew how large the territory was, or even what it looked like. Soon, thanks to two men named Lewis and Clark, they would.

SECTION REVIEW

1. Key Terms pioneer, Louisiana Purchase

2. People and Places Alexander Mackenzie, Robert Gray, Toussaint L'Ouverture, Alaska, Columbia River, Hispaniola, Mississippi River, New Orleans

3. Comprehension Why were Europeans drawn to the Pacific Coast in the late 1700s?

4. Comprehension What events led to the Louisiana Purchase?

5. Critical Thinking Explain what Jefferson meant when he said the United States "must marry ourselves to the British fleet and nation."

2 Exploring the Far West

SECTION GUIDE

Main Idea
In the early 1800s American explorers learned valuable information about the West.

Goals
As you read, look for answers to these questions:

1 Why did President Jefferson encourage western exploration?

2 What regions of the West were explored during the early 1800s?

3 What were the effects of these western expeditions?

Key Terms
Lewis and Clark expedition
tributary

IN EARLY 1801 Meriwether Lewis was an officer with the army at Fort Detroit. He received a letter from Thomas Jefferson. Would Lewis, Jefferson asked, come to Washington to be his private secretary? The new President explained that he wanted a secretary who had knowledge of both the army and the "Western Country."

Lewis and Clark

If Jefferson had really wanted a secretary, he would not have chosen Lewis. Lewis had a limited education and was a poor speller. Jefferson was looking for someone to explore the West for him. Like most white Americans of the time, Jefferson viewed the West as empty and unknown. He ignored the American Indian cultures there. For years Jefferson had dreamed of an American expedition to explore beyond the Mississippi. As President, he had the chance to make his dream come true. In Jefferson's map-lined study, he and Lewis began to plan the trip.

The Thomas Gilcrease Institute of American History and Art, Tulsa

Lewis and Clark, with their guide Sacajawea and their servant York, stand at the Great Falls of the Missouri River in 1805. **Critical Thinking:** Why was their compass (right) a useful tool on the journey?

They called it the Corps of Discovery. ("Corps," pronounced "core," means a group of people acting together.)

Lewis decided he needed a partner who could recruit and oversee the volunteer force. He turned to his old friend, William Clark. Clark was a mapmaker, outdoorsman, and leader, and the younger brother of George Rogers Clark, a hero of the Revolution. With Clark sharing the lead, the Corps of Discovery became known as the **Lewis and Clark expedition.**

Accompanying Clark was York, his African American servant. York was a large, strong man skilled at hunting and in making contact with Indian groups. The first black man that many Indians had ever seen, York became a celebrity among western Indians.

The expedition was almost ready when news came that France was going to sell all of Louisiana to the United States. The purchase made it more urgent than ever to explore the West. Lewis and Clark set out in the summer of 1803. By winter they had reached St. Louis.

St. Louis sits on the western bank of the Mississippi, near its junction with the Missouri River. Its unique location would make St. Louis the gateway to the West. In 1803, however, St. Louis was just an outpost with 180 houses. Many of the town's citizens were French settlers who had lived for years under Spanish rule. Lewis and Clark spent the winter at St. Louis. There they waited for the ceremony to mark the transfer of Louisiana to the United States. In March 1804 the American flag was raised over St. Louis.

Up the Missouri

By May 1804 the expedition was finally on its way. About 40 men headed up the Missouri River, traveling in one flat-bottomed riverboat and two pirogues (pih-ROGS).

A pirogue was shaped like a canoe but was much larger.

By then Lewis knew by heart the President's instructions. He and his men were to explore the Missouri River and its tributaries. (A **tributary** is a river that flows into a larger river.) The explorers hoped to find a water route across the continent for the purpose of trade. At the same time they were to keep good relations with the Indians and to gather scientific information.

This was the first American scientific expedition. The explorers were expected to describe the land, the plants and animals, and the Indians. For this task, they carried scientific instruments, books, maps, and paper. For camping and traveling, they

Lewis and Clark kept detailed notes of the terrain, plants, and wildlife they saw during their travels. Their notebook (bottom) was bound in elkskin.

The Louisiana Purchase

BRITISH TERRITORY

OREGON COUNTRY

Columbia R.
Great Falls
Yellowstone R.
ROCKY MOUNTAINS
LOUISIANA TERRITORY
Lewis and Clark, 1804-1806
South Pass
Platte R.
Missouri R.
Pike, 1805-1806
Mississippi R.
UNITED STATES
St. Louis
Colorado R.
Pikes Peak
Arkansas R.
Long, 1820
Pike, 1806-1807
Canadian R.
Ft. Smith
Ohio R.
Santa Fe
Red R.
SPANISH TERRITORY
PACIFIC OCEAN
Rio Grande
Pike, 1807
Chihuahua
GULF OF MEXICO

N

LOUISIANA PURCHASE

GEOGRAPHY SKILLS: The United States sent explorers to territories purchased from France. Some traveled in pirogues (lower right). **Critical Thinking:** Why were many of the routes of the explorers along rivers?

Sacajawea

took guns, kettles, clothing, fishhooks, and oil lamps. To trade with the Indians, they had packed beads, fabric, needles, scissors, axes, and sheets of copper.

The expedition slowly made its way up the Missouri. Sometimes they had to pull, rather than row or sail, their big boats against the current. In late October they reached the Mandan Indian villages in what is now North Dakota.

The members of the expedition built a small fort and spent the winter at the Mandan villages. There they met a handful of French Canadian trappers and traders. The French Canadians acted as translators, but they were not happy to see the Americans. They suspected—rightly—that American traders would soon join the rich trade in beaver furs.

In the spring of 1805 the expedition set out again. In the company now was a French trapper, his wife Sacajawea (sak-uh-juh-WEE-uh), and their baby. Sacajawea was a Shoshone Indian who had been kidnapped from her people years before. Lewis and Clark wanted her to interpret for them when they reached the Rocky Mountain area where she was born.

On to the Pacific

The expedition had to stop at the Great Falls of the Missouri, a series of waterfalls ten miles long. To get around the falls, they had to carry their boats and supplies for eighteen miles. They built wheels of cottonwood and attached them to the boats. Even with wheels, the trek took almost two weeks. Rattlesnakes, bears, and even a hailstorm slowed their passage.

As they came to the Rocky Mountains, Sacajawea pointed out Shoshone lands. Eager to make contact with the Shoshone, Lewis and a small party went overland. Their route led to the headwaters of the Missouri. There the river was so small they could stand with a foot on each bank.

Lewis found the Shoshone, whose chief recognized Sacajawea as his sister. The chief traded horses to Lewis and Clark. Sinking their canoes for safekeeping, Lewis and Clark followed Shoshone guides across the mountains to the Clearwater River.

On reaching the river, the group built new boats. They followed the Clearwater and Snake Rivers to the mighty Columbia River, which empties into the Pacific Ocean. Lewis and Clark reached the mouth of the Columbia in November 1805. There they spent a rain-soaked winter before returning the next year to St. Louis.

The Lewis and Clark expedition brought back much valuable scientific and geographic information. Americans began to have a sense of what lay far to the west.

Search for the Red River

Lewis and Clark had set out to explore the northern part of the Louisiana Purchase. Two years later, in 1805, an expedition led by an army officer, Zebulon Pike, left St. Louis. It took a more southerly route to find the headwaters of the Red River. The Red River was supposed to be the boundary between New Spain and Louisiana.

From St. Louis, Pike's party of two dozen men headed westward across the Great

Lieutenant Zebulon Pike (above) explored the southern Rockies. He returned to the East in 1807 with valuable information for U.S. mapmakers (right).

Daily Life

AMONG THE MANDAN INDIÁNS

Lewis and Clark spent the winter of 1804–1805 with the Mandan Indians. The Mandan, who had a large corn surplus each year, traded widely with whites and Indians. In the 1830s a wave of smallpox brought by European traders would almost destroy the Mandan. Yet before that tragedy, artists like George Catlin and Karl Bodmer recorded scenes of life among the Mandan.

This robe of buffalo hide shows Mandan and other Indians at war. Note the many horses, used for warfare and hunting.

The Thomas Gilcrease Institute of American History and Art, Tulsa

Catlin painted the Mandan girl Sha-Ko-Ka (left). At the far left is a Hidatsa Indian painted by Bodmer. The Hidatsa, driven from Canada by other Indians, settled with the Mandan. This Hidatsa's headdress, topped by an eagle feather, was used for special ceremonies.

This Bodmer painting shows the inside of the hut of a Mandan chief. The Mandan used logs to support their houses, which they covered with twigs and mud for insulation. They also used logs to build forts protecting their settlements. The hole in the roof of the hut lets smoke out and sunlight in.

Here a group of Mandan, bundled against the cold, cross the frozen Missouri River. In the distance, overlooking the cliff, is a Mandan village. To its left is Fort Clark, where Bodmer spent the winter of 1833–1834.

Plains for the southern Rockies. While he was still 150 miles away, Pike could see the mountain peak that today bears his name, Pikes Peak.

Pike's exploring party headed into mountains frosted by winter. In their winter camp in a valley of the upper Rio Grande, they suffered terribly from hunger and frostbite.

Pike probably knew he was in Spanish territory. Thus he would not have been surprised when Spanish troops arrested him and his men. The Americans were taken south to Santa Fe, and then to Chihuahua, Mexico. The following year, 1807, they were released.

Pike had not even come close to the Red River. Still, the account of his expedition and his description of New Spain were important. They provided the first information in English on the Great Plains and the Rio Grande Valley.

Stephen Long's Expedition

In 1820 Stephen H. Long also tried to find the Red River. Both scientist and explorer, Long followed the Platte River westward from the Missouri River. He mapped the Great Plains, climbed Pikes Peak, and then headed south to find the Red River.

To Long's great disappointment, however, the river he followed eastward was the Canadian River, not the Red River. The Red River was located farther to the south. (See the map in this section.)

Effects of Exploration

The first American explorations of the West were more than tales of adventure and endurance. The knowledge the explorers gained had effects that would be felt for years to come.

(1) *Accurate maps.* The combined efforts of Lewis and Clark, Pike, and Long produced the first good maps of the Louisiana Purchase. These maps would be extremely valuable to later western travelers.

(2) *Growth of the fur trade.* Interest in the fur trade led John Jacob Astor in 1811 to establish a trading post at Astoria, at the mouth of the Columbia River in present-day Oregon. Mountain men—hunters and trappers—would add to the knowledge of the West as they searched for new routes and sources of furs.

(3) *An inaccurate view of the Great Plains.* Pike called the Plains the "Great American Desert." For decades, Americans believed that the Great Plains were not suited for farming and thus had no value.

Pike's view that the treeless Plains were useless led to the idea that all Indians should move—or be forced to move—from east of the Mississippi to the Plains. In general, exploration of the West ignored the Americans who already lived there and laid claim to it, the Indians.

Beavers were among the game that attracted American trappers to the West.

SECTION REVIEW

1. Key Terms Lewis and Clark expedition, tributary

2. People and Places Meriwether Lewis, William Clark, York, Sacajawea, Zebulon Pike, Stephen H. Long, St. Louis, Missouri River, Rocky Mountains

3. Comprehension What was the purpose of the Lewis and Clark expedition? What route did it follow?

4. Comprehension How was Pike's expedition of value to future Americans?

5. Critical Thinking How were Jefferson's aims in sending Lewis and Clark to the West similar to the aims of Ferdinand and Isabella in supporting Columbus's voyages across the Atlantic? How were they different?

3 The War of 1812

SECTION GUIDE

Main Idea

Pressure from westerners pushed the country into war with Britain in 1812. The war settled few issues but did prove American strength.

Goals

As you read, look for answers to these questions:

1. What caused the War of 1812?

2. What was the outcome of the war?

3. Why were Americans divided over the war?

Key Terms

War of 1812
impressment
War Hawk
blockade
Treaty of Ghent

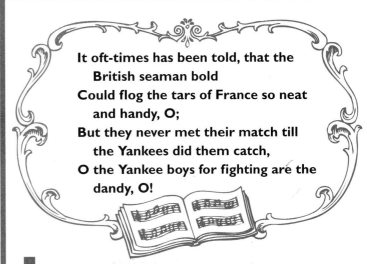

It oft-times has been told, that the
   British seaman bold
Could flog the tars of France so neat
   and handy, O;
But they never met their match till
   the Yankees did them catch,
O the Yankee boys for fighting are the
   dandy, O!

This drawing of a U.S. sailor illustrated another song from the early 1800s: "The Impressment of an American Sailor Boy."

F AMERICANS HAD TRACKED the popularity of music in 1812, then this song would have hit the charts. Many Americans sang it because it caught their fighting spirit. The country was going to war against Britain, and they looked forward to proving the power of their new nation.

Drifting Toward War

The conflict with Britain is known as the War of 1812. The resentments that led to the fighting started on the high seas. In 1803 France and Britain were at war. Each tried to prevent the other from getting food and supplies. Both France and Britain seized American ships and cargoes sailing toward their enemy's ports. Britain also stepped up the impressment (drafting by force) of American sailors into the British navy.

Americans were outraged. Jefferson, re-elected for a second term in 1804, could not ignore the British and French attacks. He wanted to avoid war. Yet how could he force European nations to respect the rights of American ships at sea?

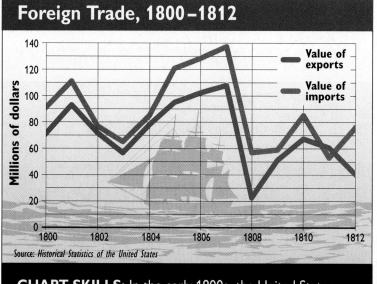

Foreign Trade, 1800–1812

Millions of dollars (y-axis: 0 to 140)

Years (x-axis): 1800, 1802, 1804, 1806, 1808, 1810, 1812

Legend:
— Value of exports
— Value of imports

Source: *Historical Statistics of the United States*

CHART SKILLS: In the early 1800s, the United States imported more than it exported. **Critical Thinking:** Why did exports drop between 1806 and 1808? Why would the drop in exports have hurt the U.S. economy?

Trade as a Weapon

Jefferson decided to ask Congress to pass a law stopping all foreign trade. The Embargo Act, passed in 1807, banned U.S. ships from sailing to any foreign port. It also closed American ports to ships from other countries. Jefferson thought that cutting off U.S. trade would make Britain and France promise to respect U.S. ships.

The act was a disaster. The nation's growing wealth was tied to commerce. To stop trade with other countries was to cripple the United States. Farmers suffered from the loss of their foreign customers. Sailors and shipbuilders had little work. The government lost income.

The embargo became a major issue in the election of 1808. The Republican Party's candidate was Jefferson's old friend James Madison. Madison won. It was clear, however, that the embargo could not continue. Congress repealed it in early 1809.

Madison's solution to the problem was a law that allowed merchants to trade with any country except France and Britain. Trade with these countries would start again when they agreed to respect American ships. However, this law proved no more effective than the embargo.

Tecumseh and Indian Unity

Meanwhile, American feeling toward Britain was growing more bitter. The loudest calls for war came not from eastern merchants, but from westerners. They claimed the British were encouraging Indian resistance to frontier settlements.

Since their defeat in the Battle of Fallen Timbers, fought in 1794, the Indian peoples of the Northwest Territory had continued to lose their lands. Thousands of white settlers had swarmed into Ohio and then into Indiana.

One Shawnee chief who vowed to stop the loss of Indian lands was Tecumseh (tih-KUHM-suh). To understand white people better, Tecumseh had learned English. He read the Bible, Shakespeare, and history books. From his reading, he concluded that the Indians had to do what white Americans had done: unite.

In 1809 William Henry Harrison, governor of the Indiana Territory, persuaded some Indians to sign a treaty selling land in the heart of the Indiana Territory. The Indians sold about 3 million acres. Tecumseh declared the treaty meaningless. He said:

❝ The white people have no right to take the land from the Indians, because the Indians had it first. It is theirs. The Indians may sell, but they must join together. Any sale not made by all is not valid. ❞

Tecumseh's efforts to halt white settlement failed. The Shawnee and forces under Harrison fought on November 7, 1811, in central Indiana. Known as the Battle of Tippecanoe, it was a crushing defeat for the Shawnee.

SKILLS: Using Special-Purpose Maps

LEARN

When you unfold a road map of your state, you know what to expect. Towns, roads, and bodies of water are labeled. A scale helps you figure distances. This is the standard tool that travelers use when they want to know how to go from one place to another. What if you want to know how each county voted in the last election? For this kind of special information you must turn to a special-purpose map.

Look at the special-purpose map at the right. It shows a number for each state. What do the numbers mean? When reading a special-purpose map, refer to the title and the key to figure out how to understand the map. In this map, the numbers tell how many representatives each state had in the U.S. House of Representatives in 1812.

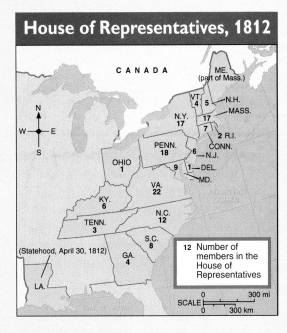

House of Representatives, 1812

PRACTICE

Look at the special-purpose map.

1. Which state had the most representatives in the House?

2. Did states in the West have more or fewer representatives than other regions?

3. Which states had frontiers that might have been subject to Indian raids? How many representatives did those states have?

APPLY

4. Draw a special-purpose map to help explain the events leading up to the Louisiana Purchase. Your map might focus on the United States, Louisiana Territory, New Orleans, Hispaniola, and France.

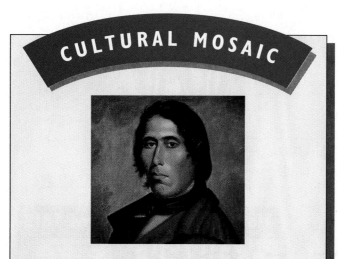

TECUMSEH
(1768–1813)

As a 15-year-old Shawnee warrior, Tecumseh spoke against cruel treatment of white captives. He never lost his belief in fairness as he grew into a great leader, even though he saw settlers taking Indian lands. With his brother, known as "The Prophet," Tecumseh worked to unite Indian peoples into a confederation. The confederation was based on the principle that Indian land would be held in common by all Indian peoples. Tecumseh's death in the War of 1812 ended his dream of confederacy.

The War Hawks

After the Battle of Tippecanoe, Tecumseh and his warriors found a warm welcome in Canada. At that point the British and Indians became allies.

Tecumseh's welcome in Canada raised even further the anti-British feelings in the West. Leaders such as Congressman Henry Clay of Kentucky called for war. Such westerners were called War Hawks. Not only did they want British aid to the Indians stopped, War Hawks wanted the British out of Canada altogether. "I am not for stopping at Quebec," said Clay, "but would take the whole continent."

Urged on by the War Hawks, Congress declared war on Britain on June 18, 1812. The reasons were (1) the impressment of American sailors, (2) violations of American rights at sea, and (3) British support of Indian resistance.

The War Begins

The War of 1812 had two main parts. During the first part, from 1812 to 1814, Britain was still tied up in its fight against France. Britain thus carried on only a limited war in North America. It did, however, set up a blockade. That is, the British navy blocked ships from entering or leaving American ports.

The American forces could do little at this time. The American army had fewer than 7,000 men at the war's start. Its leadership was poor. State militias provided help, but only for defense.

The navy, on the other hand, gave Americans something to cheer about. The navy's volunteer crews were dedicated. Its officers had experience fighting the French and pirates in the Mediterranean. Its warships were the fastest afloat. The frigates *Constitution, United States,* and *President* won stirring victories on the high seas.

The Battle of Lake Erie

The most important naval victory, however, took place on Lake Erie. In the winter of 1812–1813 the Americans had begun to build a fleet on the shores of Lake Erie. The man put in charge of the infant fleet was Oliver Hazard Perry. The son of a sea captain, Perry was an experienced seaman.

In September 1813 the small British fleet on the lake set out to destroy the American fleet. Perry lifted anchor and sailed out to meet it. Perry's ship, the *Lawrence,* flew a banner: "Don't give up the ship."

For two hours the British and Americans exchanged cannon shots. Perry's ship was demolished, the rigging destroyed, the guns put out of action. Perry could have

The War of 1812

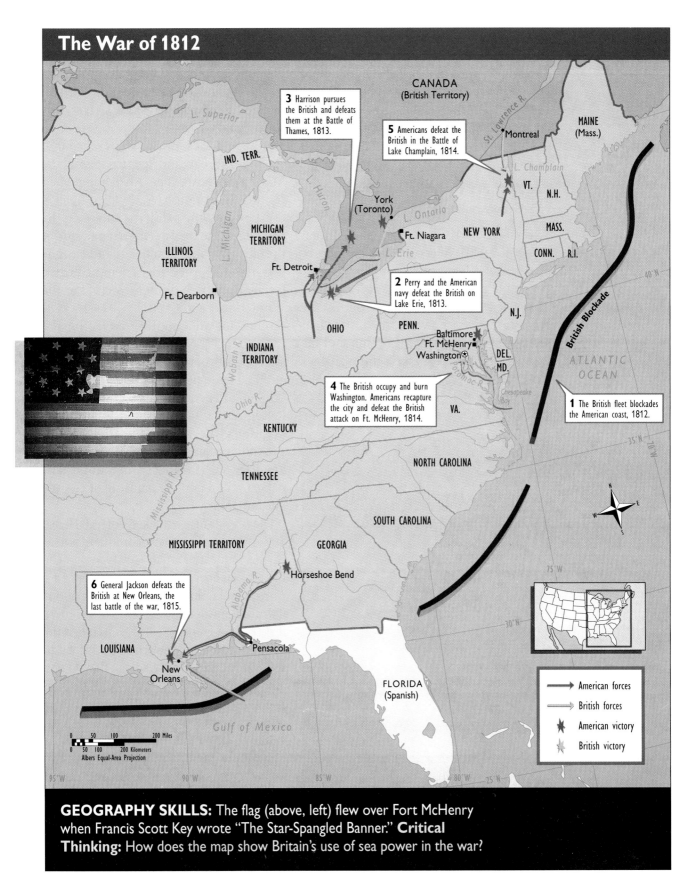

CANADA
(British Territory)

3 Harrison pursues the British and defeats them at the Battle of Thames, 1813.

5 Americans defeat the British in the Battle of Lake Champlain, 1814.

Montreal

MAINE (Mass.)

IND. TERR.

L. Superior

L. Huron

L. Michigan

York (Toronto)

L. Ontario

Ft. Niagara

MICHIGAN TERRITORY

ILLINOIS TERRITORY

Ft. Detroit

L. Erie

VT.

N.H.

NEW YORK

MASS.

CONN. R.I.

Ft. Dearborn

2 Perry and the American navy defeat the British on Lake Erie, 1813.

OHIO

PENN.

N.J.

40°N

INDIANA TERRITORY

Wabash R.

Ohio R.

Baltimore
Ft. McHenry
Washington

DEL.
MD.

British Blockade

ATLANTIC OCEAN

4 The British occupy and burn Washington. Americans recapture the city and defeat the British attack on Ft. McHenry, 1814.

Potomac R.

VA.

Chesapeake Bay

1 The British fleet blockades the American coast, 1812.

KENTUCKY

35°N

TENNESSEE

Mississippi R.

NORTH CAROLINA

SOUTH CAROLINA

75°W

MISSISSIPPI TERRITORY

GEORGIA

Alabama R.

Horseshoe Bend

6 General Jackson defeats the British at New Orleans, the last battle of the war, 1815.

30°N

LOUISIANA

Pensacola

New Orleans

FLORIDA (Spanish)

Gulf of Mexico

0 50 100   200 Miles
0 50 100   200 Kilometers
Albers Equal-Area Projection

95°W   90°W   85°W   80°W   25°N

N
W E
S

→ American forces
⇢ British forces
★ American victory
✦ British victory

GEOGRAPHY SKILLS: The flag (above, left) flew over Fort McHenry when Francis Scott Key wrote "The Star-Spangled Banner." **Critical Thinking:** How does the map show Britain's use of sea power in the war?

surrendered with honor. Instead he grabbed the ship's banner and jumped into a rowboat. Then, under British fire, he and five others rowed to another ship. Taking command of the second ship, Perry went on to destroy two British vessels.

The British surrendered. Perry scribbled a message to William Henry Harrison:

❝We have met the enemy, and they are ours.❞

General Harrison was waiting with an army of 3,000 soldiers on the Ohio shore of Lake Erie. When he received Perry's note, he made his move. Harrison ferried his army across Lake Erie to Detroit. By the time he arrived, however, the British had retreated into Canada. Harrison and his army followed. At the Battle of the Thames in October 1813, Harrison defeated the British and their Indian allies. One of the battle dead was Tecumseh.

When Perry's own vessel was destroyed during the Battle of Lake Erie, he moved to another ship and led American naval forces to victory. **Critical Thinking:** Why was this battle an important victory for the United States?

The British Burn the Capital

The second part of the war began after the British defeated Napoleon in April 1814. With the European war over, the British turned their complete attention to the Americans.

In August 1814, British ships sailed into Chesapeake Bay and left troops on the Maryland shore. The British marched toward Washington, D.C. They quickly overpowered the soldiers protecting the capital. As the British entered one side of the city, government officials and citizens fled from the other side. Then the British torched public buildings, including the White House and Capitol. This act was in revenge for an American attack on the Canadian city of York (Toronto). In that attack, U.S. troops had burned several government buildings.

Among the Americans who fled Washington during the invasion was President Madison's wife. Fortunately, Dolley Madison did not flee the White House empty-handed. She took with her important papers and a famous painting of George Washington.

The British next attacked Fort McHenry at Baltimore. The fort's commander had earlier requested a flag "so large that the British will have no difficulty in seeing it." The huge flag inspired the writing of our national anthem. Held prisoner on a British ship, Francis Scott Key watched the all-night battle. At dawn he was thrilled to see that the American flag still flew. On an old envelope he wrote a poem, "The Star-Spangled Banner."

Failed British Invasions

Meanwhile, the British were planning two invasions of U.S. territory. In September 1814 they sent a force from Canada across Lake Champlain. Its goal was to push south through the Hudson Valley and cut New England off from the rest of the country. (The British had tried this strategy dur-

Quick thinking by Dolley Madison (below), wife of President James Madison, saved important state papers as well as a portrait of George Washington when the British burned Washington, D.C. (left). **Critical Thinking:** How might the Americans have reacted to the burning of their capital?

ing the American Revolution.) This plan failed when American ships defeated the British at the Battle of Lake Champlain.

The next British move was at New Orleans. By December 1814 dozens of ships carrying 7,500 British troops were approaching Louisiana. To fight them the Americans patched together an army of militiamen, Indians, African Americans, and pirates. The army was under the command of General Andrew Jackson.

The British attacked in crisp formation on January 8, 1815. From behind earthworks, the American riflemen mowed down the advancing redcoats. It was a great victory for Jackson. American casualties were 21. The British lost about 2,030.

The Battle of New Orleans made Jackson a hero of the West. Yet the battle was not necessary. Neither side at New Orleans knew that the Treaty of Ghent, a peace treaty between Britain and the United States, had been signed two weeks earlier, on December 24, 1814. The treaty reflected the lack of a clear winner in the war. No territory changed hands. Border and trade disputes were resolved in later talks.

Since the Treaty of Ghent changed nothing, it is easy to forget that the War of 1812 was a serious crisis. If the British invasion strategy had worked, the United States might not have survived.

SECTION REVIEW

1. Key Terms War of 1812, impressment, War Hawk, blockade, Treaty of Ghent

2. People and Places James Madison, Tecumseh, William Henry Harrison, Oliver Hazard Perry, Francis Scott Key, Andrew Jackson, Lake Champlain

3. Comprehension Why did westerners want a war with Britain?

4. Comprehension How were the two parts of the War of 1812 different?

5. Critical Thinking The War of 1812 has been called "the unnecessary war." Do you agree or disagree? Explain.

Summary

1. In the late 1700s the West was changing with the growth of Spanish settlements, Russian interests, British exploration, and American trade. At the same time, the introduction of horses changed the lives of Plains Indians. When France offered to sell its western landholdings, President Jefferson made the Louisiana Purchase, greatly expanding U.S. territory.

2. Jefferson sent Meriwether Lewis and William Clark to explore and study the new lands in the West. Later expeditions led by Zebulon Pike and Stephen Long explored the southern Rockies. These explorations produced more accurate maps and created new interest in the fur trade. They also led Americans to believe that the Great Plains were unsuitable for farming.

3. The War of 1812 began because of British violations of U.S. sea rights and British aid to western Indians. Some British attacks on the United States were successful, and British troops burned Washington, D.C. Yet the United States won victories at sea and several land battles. The war ended with no change in territory.

Review

KEY TERMS

Write a sentence using each of the following terms.
1. blockade
2. Lewis and Clark expedition
3. Louisiana Purchase
4. tributary
5. War Hawk

COMPREHENSION

1. What nations were competing for influence in the Pacific Northwest in the 1790s?

2. How did the introduction of horses change life for Indians on the Great Plains?

3. Why did France sell the Louisiana Territory to the United States?

4. What were the goals of the Lewis and Clark expedition? Was the expedition successful in achieving them?

5. What caused Zebulon Pike to end his explorations?

6. List three effects of American explorations of the West.

7. How did Jefferson try to avoid war with Britain?

8. In which section of the country did people support the War of 1812 most strongly? Why?

9. What was the British strategy during the first part of the War of 1812? What actions did it take during the second part?

10. How did the Treaty of Ghent reflect the fact that neither side won the War of 1812?

Graphic Summary

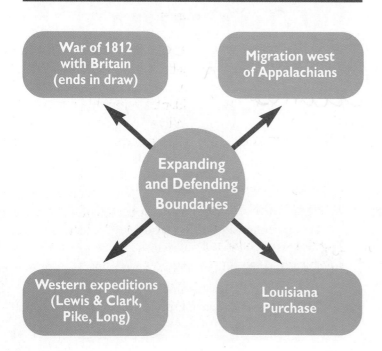

War of 1812 with Britain (ends in draw)

Migration west of Appalachians

Expanding and Defending Boundaries

Western expeditions (Lewis & Clark, Pike, Long)

Louisiana Purchase

Places to Locate

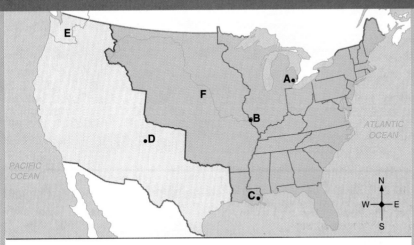

Match the letters on the map with the places that are listed below. Then explain the importance of each place.

1. Columbia River   3. Missouri River   5. St. Louis
2. Detroit   4. New Orleans   6. Santa Fe

Geographic Theme: Interactions Explain the significance of the Lewis and Clark exploration.

Skill Review

Study the map of the War of 1812 in the chapter. Then answer the following questions.

1. What do the numbered boxes show?

2. How did the British travel to Washington, D.C.? How might they have attacked the city? How can you tell?

3. Which side was victorious at Horseshoe Bend? How do you know?

4. How might this map be helpful to students examining the course of the War of 1812?

CRITICAL THINKING

1. **Understanding Other Points of View** Why might some people object to using the term *pioneer* to describe American settlers?

2. **Inferring** How did the Lewis and Clark expedition strengthen the American claim to the Pacific Northwest?

3. **Identifying Cause and Effect** Why did the British aid American Indians on the frontier?

PORTFOLIO OPTIONS

1. **Civics Connection** What was Jefferson's philosophy of government? Did the Louisiana Purchase and Embargo Act contradict that philosophy? Why or why not?

2. **Writing Connection** Imagine that you are traveling west with Lewis and Clark. Write a letter to a friend or member of your family describing your experiences.

3. **Contemporary Connection** Jefferson made cutbacks in the armed forces when he became President. Do you think that was wise? Why or why not? How should the nation decide how much to spend on defense today? Organize a class debate on the issue.

4. **Timeline Connection** Study the chapter timeline. Which event do you think had the most significance for the new nation? Explain why. Now find out the dates of important battles and events during the War of 1812. Create a new timeline to show this information.

In the early 1800s Americans began to take more pride in their country. Terence Kennedy's "Political Banner" shows some of the country's achievements: steam power, waterpower, railroads, and bridges. Overseeing all of these developments is the bald eagle, proud symbol of the new nation.

1800	1810	1820

1819 Adams-Onís Treaty

1803 *Marbury v. Madison*

1823 Monroe Doctrine

1807 Robert Fulton launches *Clermont*

1825 Erie Canal completed

chapter 14

The Expanding Nation
(1800–1840)

1 A Spirit of Nationalism

SECTION GUIDE

Main Idea
After the War of 1812 there was a new burst of nationalism. New roads and canals helped bind the nation together.

Goals
As you read, look for answers to these questions:

1 What were some examples of social, economic, and political nationalism?

2 How did the Supreme Court strengthen the power of the federal government?

3 What effect did the Erie Canal have on the nation's economic development?

Key Terms
Marbury v. Madison
judicial review
Monroe Doctrine
American System
National Road
Erie Canal

1830   1840

1831 Nat Turner's Rebellion

THE WAR OF 1812 achieved none of the demands of the War Hawks. Yet Americans celebrated the end of the war as a victory. Why? What had they gained? A Vermont newspaper summarized the answer:

❝The fear of our late enemy;
The respect of the world; and
The confidence we have acquired in ourselves. ❞

The Rise of Nationalism

Until 1815 it was not clear that the United States would survive. Wars in Europe and unrest at home were real threats to the republic. By 1815, however, Americans had fought what some called a "Second War of Independence." The war gave rise to a new and growing spirit of nationalism.

Nationalism was a mix of feelings and beliefs. It was patriotic pride in the achievements of the nation. It was also a belief that Americans were unique and did not have to follow the lead of other countries. History textbooks of the early 1800s praised the achievements of the United States. They claimed the United States was better than "worn-out" Europe. Books and newspapers preached patriotism. Noah Webster, a former teacher and newspaper editor, published a dictionary in 1806. Webster's dictionary went on to sell millions of copies. It helped create an *American* version of the English language by simplifying the spelling and pronunciation of many English words.

As nationalist feelings spread, people felt more loyalty toward the federal government and less toward state governments. People's focus changed to the nation as a whole. The political unrest of earlier years gave way to what one Boston newspaper called the "Era of Good Feelings."

CONNECTING WITH THE PRESENT

OBEYING THE COURT

The Supreme Court decides and the country obeys. Why? This handful of justices has no army to enforce its decisions. Yet the Court's power has grown over the last two centuries.

Presidents have often viewed the Court as a bother. In 1832 Georgia's Cherokee Indians asked the Court to stop the government from forcing them from their homelands. Led by John Marshall, the Court agreed. President Jackson, however, ignored the decision. The Cherokee won their case but lost their homes.

Unlike Jackson, most Presidents have bowed to the Court's will. In the 1970s President Nixon at first refused to give up secret tape recordings that would plunge him into scandal. Yet when the Court ordered him to, he did so. Modern-day Presidents may disagree with the Court, but like all people, they obey it.

Party politics in the years after the War of 1812 reflected this sense of national unity. In 1816 the Republicans swept to an easy victory. James Monroe, Madison's Secretary of State, was elected President. The Federalist Party made such a poor showing that it soon dissolved.

The Supreme Court

The new nationalism was helped by the decisions of an old Federalist. Under Chief Justice John Marshall, the Supreme Court upheld federal authority and strengthened the federal courts.

The first of the Marshall Court's landmark decisions came in the case of *Marbury v. Madison* (1803). Marshall declared that an act passed by Congress in 1789 was unconstitutional. This meant it violated the Constitution and thus could not stand. The *Marbury* case helped establish the principle of judicial review. Judicial review means that the Supreme Court has the final say in interpreting the Constitution. The Court decides what the Constitution means and whether a law violates it.

Using the principle of judicial review, the Court extended federal power in the case of *McCulloch v. Maryland* (1819). The state of Maryland claimed the right to tax the national bank. Maryland even argued that Congress did not have the right to create the bank in the first place. The Court declared that (1) Congress did have the right to create the bank, and (2) a state could not tax a national bank. It was a double victory for the federal government.

Marshall's reasoning in *McCulloch v. Maryland* was this. Congress had a right to create the bank, he said, because nothing in the Constitution forbids it. Marshall favored, in other words, a loose construction of the Constitution. Marshall also declared that the federal government was a government of people, not of states. Therefore, it had power over the states.

A Bold Foreign Policy

A bold foreign policy was another part of American nationalism. This policy aimed at (1) strengthening American land claims, and (2) ending European involvement in the Western Hemisphere.

Relations between the United States and Britain were smoothed by two agreements. The Rush-Bagot Treaty (1817) limited each side's naval forces on the Great Lakes. The Convention of 1818 set the 49th parallel as the border between the United States and Canada as far west as the Rocky Mountains.

The United States and Spain faced thornier problems. The two nations disagreed on the boundaries of the Louisiana Purchase. For example, who now owned West

The Supreme Court

American soldiers search for well-hidden Seminole Indians in Florida's swamplands. The Seminole fought to remain on their lands. Below, Tukosee Mathla, a Seminole chief, holds an English musket. It was prized by the Seminole for its light weight.

Florida? In addition, Spanish-held East Florida was a place of refuge for runaway slaves and pirates. The Seminole Indians of East Florida also raided white settlements in Georgia to reclaim lost lands.

In 1817 General Andrew Jackson was ordered to crush the Seminole. He followed them into Spanish territory and then claimed the Floridas for the United States. President Monroe, who had not called for Jackson's invasion, ordered him to withdraw. Yet the United States then offered Spain a tough choice: Police the Floridas or turn them over to the United States.

In the Adams-Onís Treaty of 1819, Spain gave the Floridas to the United States. The two countries also agreed on borders between Spanish and American lands from the Mississippi to the Pacific.

The Monroe Doctrine

Events elsewhere in the Americas also caught the nation's attention. An outburst of independence movements was causing the Latin American empires of Spain and Portugal to collapse. (Latin America refers to the nations of the Western Hemisphere south of the United States.) The monarchies of Austria, Russia, and Prussia, however, planned to help Spain and Portugal regain their colonies. By helping Spain and Portugal, they hoped to stop the "infection" of revolution from spreading to Europe.

Americans, meanwhile, were growing concerned about Russian colonies in the Pacific Northwest. By 1812 Russian trading posts reached almost as far south as San Francisco.

To deal with these concerns, President Monroe issued the **Monroe Doctrine** in 1823. As a warning to Russia, Monroe said that the Americas were closed to further colonization. Monroe also said that any European efforts to re-establish colonies would be considered "dangerous to our peace and safety." In sum, Europe was told to keep out of the Americas. Today the Monroe Doctrine is still a keystone of American foreign policy.

The American System

Two strong nationalists in Congress were John C. Calhoun of South Carolina and Henry Clay of Kentucky. Both were lawyers who had been elected to Congress at an early age. Both had been War Hawks. They wanted the United States to be a self-sufficient nation, one that did not need foreign products or foreign markets. They hoped that the United States would become a "world within itself."

In fact, this had already begun. During the War of 1812, Americans had begun to produce goods they once imported from Britain. With the return of peace, Congress wanted to protect these new industries. In 1816 it passed tariffs that made goods from Europe more costly. Americans were encouraged to buy American-made goods.

The new tariffs to protect American industry were part of a program, set forth by Clay, called the American System. The program also called for better transportation to help trade within the country.

The transportation problems facing the United States were as huge as the country itself. Only a few roads for coaches and wagons connected the states. The only other ways to travel or move goods were by small boats, on horseback, or on foot. Slow, costly transport was bad for business. It kept Americans in one region from dealing with those in another.

"Let us bind the Republic together with a perfect system of roads and canals," Calhoun said. "Let us conquer space." National roads were not a new idea. In 1806 Congress had promised to fund the building of a paved road linking Ohio with the East. By 1815, however, only 20 miles of it had been finished.

With a push from the nationalists, Congress then voted more money for the road. Within three years the Cumberland Road, or National Road, had crossed the Appalachians. It now connected Cumberland, Maryland, with Wheeling, on the Ohio River. By 1833 it would reach Columbus, Ohio. As the country's main east-west route, the road was soon jammed with everything from mail coaches to herds of cattle going to market.

The Erie Canal

The most successful improvement of this period was the Erie Canal. Paid for by New York State, it created an all-water transportation route between New York City and Buffalo, which was on Lake Erie.

When finished in 1825, the Erie Canal became the most important route between the Atlantic seaboard and the West. From New York City, passengers and cargo traveled northward up the Hudson River to Albany. Then they moved westward on the canal to Buffalo. On the return trip, boats brought products from the West to markets in New York City and beyond.

Before the canal opened, it cost about $100 to ship a ton of goods from Buffalo to New York City. The canal sliced this cost to $10. In addition, goods reached their markets twice as quickly.

The Thomas Gilcrease Institute of American History and Art, Tulsa

Traveling in the new nation was an adventure. Hard rains often turned unpaved roads into rivers of mud.

Canals Connect Rivers and Lakes

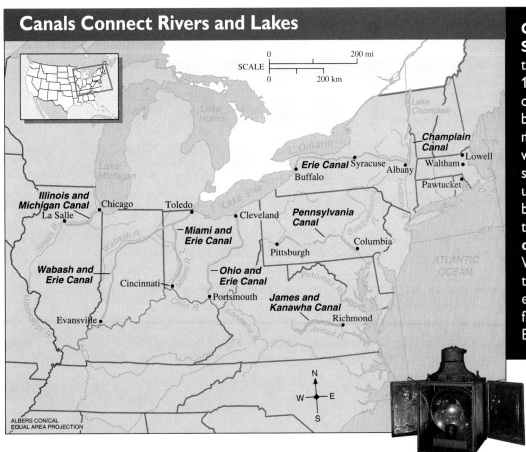

SCALE

0 — 200 mi
0 — 200 km

Lake Huron

Lake Michigan

L. Ontario

Lake Champlain

Champlain Canal

Erie Canal Syracuse • Lowell
Waltham •
Buffalo • Albany
Pawtucket

Illinois and Michigan Canal
La Salle
Chicago • Toledo
Lake Erie
• Cleveland **Pennsylvania Canal**

Miami and Erie Canal

Columbia

Pittsburgh •

Wabash and Erie Canal
Cincinnati •
Ohio and Erie Canal
• Portsmouth **James and Kanawha Canal**

ATLANTIC OCEAN

Evansville •
Richmond •

Mississippi R.

N
W — E
S

ALBERS CONICAL
EQUAL AREA PROJECTION

The Erie Canal opened the upper Ohio Valley and the Great Lakes region to settlement. Thousands of immigrants traveled the canal to homesteads in Ohio, Indiana, Illinois, and Michigan. Farm products from this rich region flowed eastward on the canal. These products helped eastern cities grow. Fed by the West, easterners could focus on trade and manufacturing. In turn, the westerners bought the goods of the East.

Trade on the canal drew more people to New York City and helped it become the nation's largest city. Between 1820 and 1830, the city's population swelled from less than 125,000 to more than 200,000.

The success of the Erie Canal encouraged canal building in other sections of the country. So many canals were built between 1825 and 1850 that the period has been called the Canal Era.

SECTION REVIEW

1. Key Terms *Marbury v. Madison*, judicial review, Monroe Doctrine, American System, National Road, Erie Canal

2. People Noah Webster, John Marshall, John C. Calhoun, Henry Clay

3. Comprehension How did the decisions of the Marshall Court strengthen the federal government?

4. Comprehension Describe the effect of the Erie Canal on the development of the West.

5. Critical Thinking Cite some examples of nationalism in the United States today. How are they similar to or different from the nationalism of the early 1800s?

GEOGRAPHY: The Erie Canal

Thomas Jefferson said the idea was "little short of madness." When the federal government refused to help, the people of New York built it themselves—a canal 40 feet wide, 4 feet deep, and 363 miles long from the Hudson River to Lake Erie.

What made a canal possible was the Mohawk Valley, which forms a passage through the Appalachians. The canal followed the Mohawk and other rivers, but remained separate from them. This was because a canal, unlike a river, could be kept level for boats. Sometimes the canal even crossed a river in an aqueduct, as in the photo.

The true genius of the canal, however, was its 83 locks. They dealt with changes in elevation along the course of the canal. At the far right you can see how the locks worked. When the canal was finished in 1825, Jefferson called DeWitt Clinton, the canal's designer, "the greatest man in America."

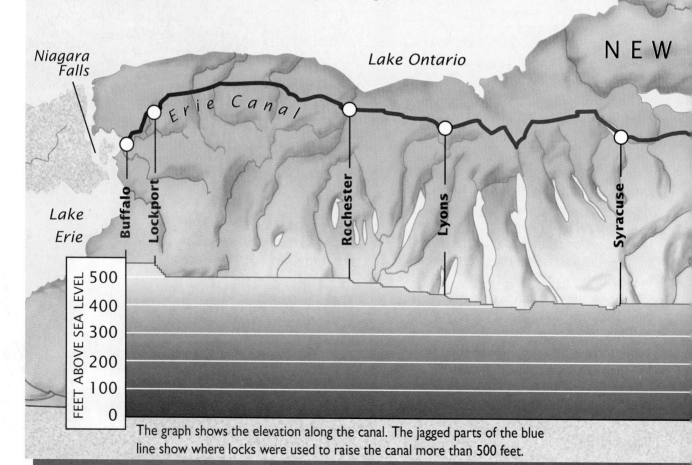

Niagara Falls

Lake Ontario

N E W

Lake Erie

Erie Canal

Buffalo

Lockport

Rochester

Lyons

Syracuse

FEET ABOVE SEA LEVEL

500
400
300
200
100
0

The graph shows the elevation along the canal. The jagged parts of the blue line show where locks were used to raise the canal more than 500 feet.

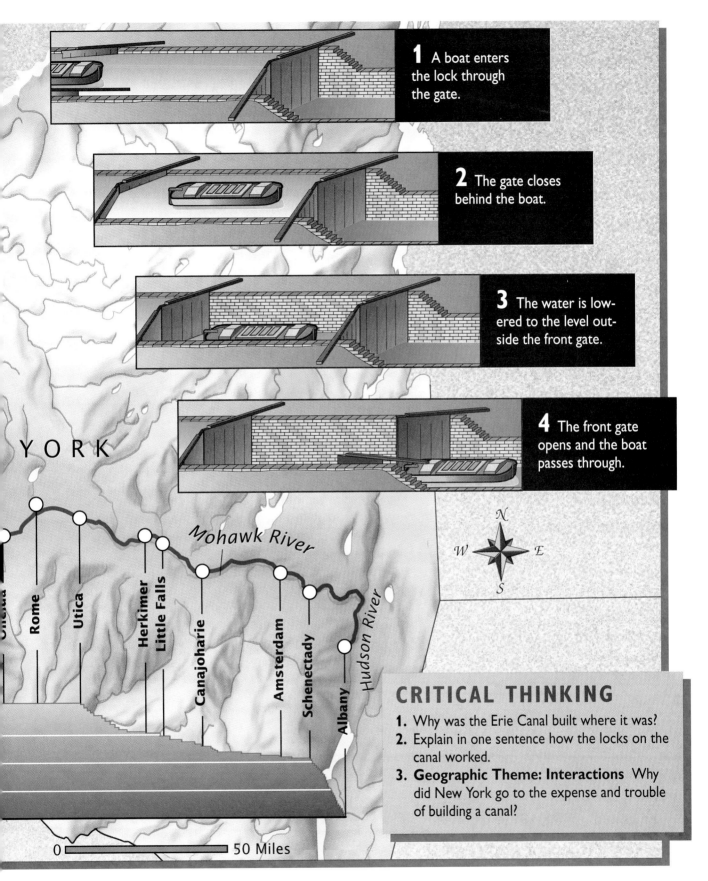

1 A boat enters the lock through the gate.

2 The gate closes behind the boat.

3 The water is lowered to the level outside the front gate.

4 The front gate opens and the boat passes through.

Y O R K

Mohawk River

Hudson River

Oneida
Rome
Utica
Herkimer
Little Falls
Canajoharie
Amsterdam
Schenectady
Albany

N
W E
S

0   50 Miles

CRITICAL THINKING

1. Why was the Erie Canal built where it was?
2. Explain in one sentence how the locks on the canal worked.
3. **Geographic Theme: Interactions** Why did New York go to the expense and trouble of building a canal?

2 The Industrial Revolution

SECTION GUIDE

Main Idea
During the late 1700s and early 1800s, inventions changed the way people lived and worked. The Northeast became the industrial center of the United States.

Goals
As you read, look for answers to these questions:

1 How did industry come to the United States?

2 How did machines change peoples' lives?

Key Terms
Industrial Revolution
standardization

Sun Monday Tue Wed Thu
Fri

A VISITOR TO LOWELL, Massachusetts, in the 1830s wrote the following: "Suddenly the stage stops amidst a throng of people of all tongues, the noise of rushing waters, and the rattling of a thousand machines." The visitor asked, "Driver, what city is this? There was nothing here 25 years ago." "No, nor 15, sir," the driver answered. "But it is no city; it is the village of Lowell."

The Industrial Revolution
What was taking place in Lowell was typical of changes in other northeastern towns. Factories, built along rivers and streams that provided water power, began to produce goods at a terrific rate. People moved from the countryside to work in the factories. Villages grew into towns and cities. These changes had their origins in the Industrial Revolution.

Strictly speaking, the Industrial Revolution marked the change from handmade goods to machine-made goods. Yet it was far more than a mere change in technology. The Industrial Revolution changed the way people used resources. It changed the way they worked and lived.

The Industrial Revolution started in Britain. There, inventions of machines that spun and wove cotton cloth completely changed the textile industry. Each worker could now produce much more than before.

The change to machines made different demands on workers. Factory workers, for example, did not need to be skilled. They

Textile mills like the ones shown here, in Lowell, Massachusetts, revolutionized the way Americans lived and worked.

346

could even be small children. Previously, textile workers worked at home on handlooms. Now they went to work in a factory and operated the machines that produced the goods.

Samuel Slater's Mill

The textile industry became so important to Britain's economy that Britain tried to keep the new process secret. The British government outlawed the sale of the machines to other countries. It even passed a law forbidding textile workers to leave the country. Laws, however, could not stop the ambitions of a man named Samuel Slater.

While working for a British spinning mill, Slater memorized its plan in detail. Then, with hopes of making his fortune, he set sail for America. Slater built a small spinning mill in Pawtucket, Rhode Island, in 1790. He then found investors willing to back construction of a much larger spinning factory. Slater's mill opened in 1793. The Industrial Revolution had come to the United States.

Factories Change New England

Two decades after Slater's first mill, a Boston merchant named Francis Cabot Lowell moved the textile industry a giant step further. In 1813 he built a factory at Waltham, Massachusetts. The factory combined all the steps of textile production. Raw cotton entered one end of the plant and emerged at the other end as finished goods. Lowell's factory would be the model for other textile operations.

Early factories used water power to run the machines. The first factories, therefore, were near the swiftly moving streams outside Philadelphia and in New England. Of the two regions, New England would end up as the manufacturing center of the United States. In addition to water power and ships for transportation, New England had a large labor force.

New England's first factory workers were farm families. Tired of scraping a living from New England's stony fields, they hoped for a better life in the factories. Two employment systems developed. In the Rhode Island system whole families were hired and housed. Even the young children worked in the textile mills.

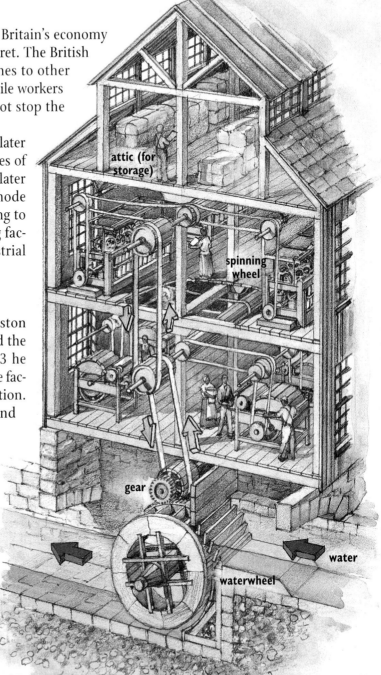

NEW ENGLAND MILL

attic (for storage)

spinning wheel

gear

waterwheel

water

How did factories use water power? Water flowed in and powered a large wheel, which turned gears. The gears operated pulleys and belts (see green arrows), which gave power to machines.

Lucy Larcom (below) was a "Lowell Girl" who went on to become a popular author. Her early writings were published in the *Lowell Offering*, a magazine written by mill girls.

Francis Cabot Lowell introduced another system, the Waltham system. He brought together young women from nearby farms to work in the factories. The "Lowell Girls," as they were called, made up around 90 percent of the factories' work force.

The young women lived in dormitories. During the early years of the mills, workers were encouraged to read and attend "mind-lifting" lectures. However, the owners' kindly attitudes toward mill workers gradually changed. Workers had to rise at five in the morning and work until seven at night with hardly a break. During these long hours they suffered through fast-paced production, loud noise, and a suffocating lack of fresh air. At the end of the day, the mill girls often received only bread and gravy.

Women workers in the mills were the first to feel the pain of the Industrial Revolution. They had to endure terrible working conditions while being paid half as much as men. Women would be among the first in New England to form unions and demand better working conditions and wages.

Advances in Production

In 1798 the United States government needed guns to supply its armed forces. It hired the inventor Eli Whitney to make the guns. Whitney's task was to make 10,000 muskets in two years. Until that time, skilled gunsmiths had started work on a new gun only after finishing the one before. Each gun differed slightly. If a part broke, a new one had to be custom-made to replace it.

By 1800 Whitney had not yet delivered the guns to the government. He was called to Washington to explain the delay. Whitney arrived with a box containing piles of

With smoke pouring from its engine, Robert Fulton's steamship *Clermont* chugs up the Hudson River. The *Clermont's* five-mile-an-hour speed was impressive in the early 1800s.

musket parts—barrels, triggers, and so on. He entered a room where Vice President Jefferson and other officials were waiting. As they watched, Whitney took one part at random from each pile and assembled a complete musket in seconds.

Eli Whitney had not wasted his time. He had spent the two years developing machines that could make parts that were exactly alike. For example, the trigger from one of Whitney's muskets would fit any of the other muskets. Whitney had shown the value of **standardization.** This means using interchangeable parts.

These interchangeable parts speeded up production and made repairs easy. Using an assembly line, Whitney could produce hundreds of muskets in the time it took a gunsmith to make one. Also, Whitney's machines could be run by unskilled workers. Standardized parts became the norm for goods and machinery.

Steam Power

America's first factories began by using water power. Before long they switched to steam power. More than any other invention, the steam engine symbolized the early Industrial Revolution.

The idea of putting a steam engine on a boat had been around since the 1780s.

CULTURAL MOSAIC

JOHN DEERE
(1804–1886)

Vermont farmers who wanted the best hay-fork or shovel sought out a young blacksmith named John Deere. When Deere moved to Illinois at age 32, farmers there told him they had trouble plowing the rich soil. He designed a steel plow that saved time and labor. Deere's plow helped farmers turn rugged prairie land into valuable farmland. His business soon grew into a large manufacturing company. By the late 1850s Deere was making more than 10,000 steel plows a year.

Robert Fulton, however, was the first to apply the idea successfully.

Fulton set out to invent a steam-powered boat that could move against the current or a strong wind. His attempts failed until he designed the *Clermont*. On the *Clermont* a steam engine turned a side paddle wheel, which pushed the boat through the water. People who watched it being built in New York City said it would never work.

Fulton launched the *Clermont* on the Hudson River in 1807. It made the 300-mile round-trip from New York to Albany in 62 hours. Afterwards Fulton wrote, "The morning I left New York there were not 30 persons in the city who believed the boat would ever move one mile."

In 1811 the *New Orleans* became the first steamship to travel down the Ohio and Mississippi rivers. Yet its engines were not

After their introduction in the 1830s, railroads fast became the nation's most important form of transportation. This painting shows one of the first trains. Note the conductor running along the train with a trumpet, which was used to announce the train's departure.

powerful enough to return against the river current. The man who solved this problem was Henry Miller Shreve.

Shreve, a Mississippi trader, designed a more powerful engine. He installed it on a double-decker boat with the paddle wheel in the back. Shreve's design opened up a new era of trade and transportation on the Mississippi. Steamboats turned New Orleans into a center of trade second only to New York City.

Railroads Take Over

In the 1830s inventors adapted steam power to another kind of transportation—the steam-powered locomotive. In a famous race near Baltimore in 1830, the locomotive *Tom Thumb* raced a horse and lost. The railroad's supporters, however, did not give up.

The first railroads were not exactly models of comfort. Nevertheless, trains were improved, and rail service spread. Rail transport moved people and goods faster than roads or canals. Railroads also provided transportation where water travel was impossible. In 1830 there were about 30 miles of railroad track in the United States. Ten years later there were 2,800 miles of track. By 1850 the number had jumped to 9,000 miles. The Canal Era was over. The Railroad Era was beginning.

SECTION REVIEW

1. Key Terms Industrial Revolution, standardization

2. People and Places Samuel Slater, Francis Cabot Lowell, Robert Fulton, Henry Miller Shreve, Lowell, Waltham

3. Comprehension Why did New England become the manufacturing center of the United States?

4. Comprehension What were some of the changes the Industrial Revolution made in society?

5. Critical Thinking Do you think children should be allowed to work in factories? List arguments on each side of the issue.

HISTORY AND YOU

Charles Dickens Visits America

Curious about the young American nation, European writers visited the United States in the early 1800s. Some returned home praising Americans' energy and confidence. To others, however, America was an uncivilized wilderness. They complained of overheated rooms, tobacco spitting, and bad manners. In *American Notes,* the great British writer Charles Dickens described a hair-raising train ride.

"Everybody talks to you, or to anybody else who hits his fancy. If you are an Englishman, he expects that the railroad is pretty much like an English railroad. . . . You say 'No'. . . . Then he guesses that you don't travel faster in England; and on your replying that you do, [doesn't] believe it. . . . Wherever you are going, you invariably learn that you can't get there without immense difficulty and danger, and that all the great sights are somewhere else. . . .

The train calls at stations in the woods, where the wild impossibility of anybody having the smallest reason to get out, is only to be equalled by the apparently desperate hopelessness of there being anybody to get in. It rushes across the turnpike road, where there is no gate, no policeman, no signal: nothing but a rough wooden arch, on which is painted 'WHEN THE BELL RINGS, LOOK OUT FOR THE LOCOMOTIVE.' On it whirls headlong, dives through the woods again, emerges in the light . . . unaccustomed horses plunging and rearing, close to the very rails—there—on, on, on—tears the mad dragon of an engine with its train of cars; scattering in all directions a shower of burning sparks from its wood fire; screeching, hissing, yelling, panting; until at last the thirsty monster stops beneath a covered way to drink, the people cluster round, and you have time to breathe again."

(Above, a poster warns of the danger of a new railroad line.)

CRITICAL THINKING

1. **What general impression does Dickens give of traveling in the United States?**
2. **Why might Britain's past ties to North America have led British visitors to look down on the United States?**
3. **Why are people often more critical of other nations than their own?**

SKILLS: Reading a Bar Graph

LEARN

It is said that a picture is worth a thousand words. A bar graph is a picture that represents not just words but statistical information in the form of easy-to-read bars. Bar graphs, like line graphs, have a vertical axis and a horizontal axis. Bar graphs show information in columns. They are best for presenting numbers and comparing quantities. The comparison is visual—you can see it immediately, even without reading any numbers.

Look at the purple bars in the graph at right. What do you see? One bar is tallest, one is shortest, and the others fall in between. The same is true for the green bars. It is easy to see how the quantities differ from each other.

Now study the rest of the graph. The title gives the subject of the graph. The dates are keyed to the colors. The towns being compared run along the horizontal axis. The vertical axis provides exact figures. Notice that this graph is really two graphs in one. It compares town populations, and it also shows how each town grew.

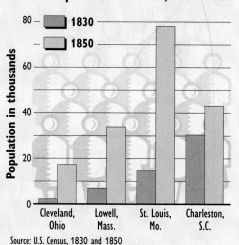

Urban Population Growth, 1830–1850

Source: U.S. Census, 1830 and 1850

PRACTICE

1. Which town had the smallest population in 1850?

2. Which town experienced the largest increase in population?

3. What factors might explain the growing population in each of these towns?

APPLY

4. Draw a bar graph to show the miles of railroad track in the United States in 1830, 1840, and 1850. You can find the data in Section 2 to construct your graph. Would a line graph show this data more effectively? Explain.

3 The Changing South

SECTION GUIDE

Main Idea

The invention of the cotton gin and the demand for cotton caused slavery to grow in the South.

Goals

As you read, look for answers to these questions:

1. In what way did cotton encourage westward expansion?

2. What was life like in the "Cotton Kingdom"?

3. How did slavery affect the lives of black and white Americans?

Key Terms

soil exhaustion
cotton gin

Whitney's cotton gin allowed one worker to clean as much cotton in a day as fifty workers could clean by hand.

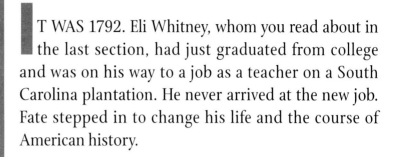

IT WAS 1792. Eli Whitney, whom you read about in the last section, had just graduated from college and was on his way to a job as a teacher on a South Carolina plantation. He never arrived at the new job. Fate stepped in to change his life and the course of American history.

Eli Whitney's Cotton Gin

On his way south, Whitney met Catherine Greene, widow of General Nathanael Greene of Revolutionary War fame. Mrs. Greene was now struggling to make her Georgia plantation profitable.

Mrs. Greene's problems were not unique. Few places in the South were prosperous. **Soil exhaustion**—the overuse of fertile soil—had reduced profits from tobacco, indigo, and rice. At the same time, the new English mills had created a huge demand for cotton.

Cotton grew easily in the South, but most of it was a short-staple cotton. The fibers of short-staple cotton stuck firmly to the seeds. Separating the fibers from the seeds had to be done by hand. A worker could clean just one pound of short-staple cotton a day.

While visiting Mrs. Greene, Whitney heard planters complain about the difficulties of cleaning short-staple cotton. Whitney had shown skill at making and fixing things since he was a child. Within ten days he had designed a cotton-cleaning machine. Whitney's **cotton gin** was a wooden box filled with stiff wire teeth. When the teeth brushed against the cotton, they picked up the cotton fiber and left the seeds behind. By April 1793 Whitney's gin was in operation. It could clean 50 pounds of short-staple cotton a day.

The Cotton Kingdom

The cotton gin changed life in the South in four ways:

(1) It triggered a vast move westward. Cotton farming moved from the Atlantic coastal states—the so-called "Old South"—into the uplands of Alabama, Mississippi, and northern Florida. Then it crossed the Mississippi River into Louisiana and Texas.

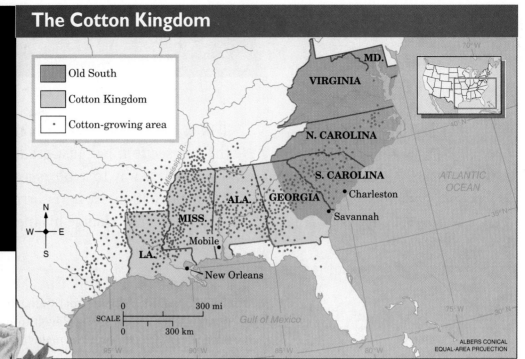

Old South

Cotton Kingdom

Cotton-growing area

VIRGINIA

MD.

N. CAROLINA

S. CAROLINA

Charleston

ALA. GEORGIA

MISS.

Savannah

Mobile

LA.

New Orleans

ATLANTIC OCEAN

Gulf of Mexico

SCALE 0 — 300 mi

0 — 300 km

ALBERS CONICAL EQUAL-AREA PROJECTION

(2) Because cotton was such a valuable crop, planters put all their efforts into growing it. In the years after 1812, cotton made up one-third of all exports from the United States. By 1830 it made up half of all exports. To southerners, cotton was king.

(3) Before the arrival of the cotton gin, slavery had been dying out. Growing cotton, however, required a large work force. Instead of dying out, slavery became more important than ever as a source of workers.

(4) The growing of cotton in the southern uplands led to the removal of the Indians living in those areas.

Who Held Slaves?

Growing cotton on large plantations worked by slaves was highly profitable. Slaves cost money, however, and most white southerners could not afford to buy any. In the mid-1800s, only about one white family in four in the South could afford to own slaves. In a white popula-tion of over 5 million, fewer than 10,000 planters owned 50 or more slaves. The number who owned more than 100 slaves was even smaller.

Planters with many slaves and much land came to control most of the South's wealth. In addition, many of these men represented the South in Congress. In con-trast to these powerful plantation owners, most southern farmers worked small farms with their own hands. Some of them owned a slave or two. Many poor white farmers dreamed that someday they too would own vast cotton fields and many slaves. This hope was one reason why small farmers supported the policies of the plantation owners.

Cotton and Slavery

Slaves made up over one-third of the South's population. They did all the hard work on the plantation. While some worked as house servants, most were field hands. Solomon Northrup, who was kid-napped and sold into slavery, later told of the life slaves led:

During all the hoeings the over-seer or driver follows the slaves with a whip. . . . The fastest hoer takes the lead row. He is usually about [fifteen feet] in advance of his companions. If one of them passes him, he [the fastest hoer] is whipped. If one falls behind or is a moment idle, he is whipped. In fact, the lash is flying from morning until night. . . .

The hands are required to be in the cotton field as soon as it is light in the morning, and, with the exception of 10 or 15 minutes, which is given them at noon to swallow their allowance of cold bacon, they are not per-mitted to be a moment idle until it is too dark to see.

The day did not end when the field work was over. There were still more tasks for slaves to do. "One feeds the mules," North-rup wrote, "another the swine—another cuts the wood." Slaves did not return to their cabins until evening. Then, before they could sleep, they had to prepare the next day's food.

Using slave labor, the South raised hun-dreds of thousands of tons of cotton each year for the textile mills of the North and Europe. As cotton profits rose, so did the

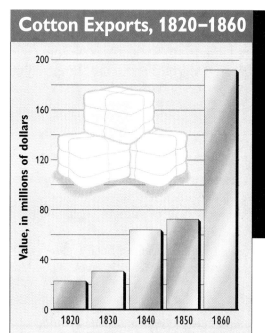

Cotton Exports, 1820–1860

Value, in millions of dollars

Source: *Historical Statistics of the United States*

CHART SKILLS: By the mid-1800s, cotton had become the most important crop in the South. **Critical Thinking:** How does this chart help explain why slavery did not die out in the South?

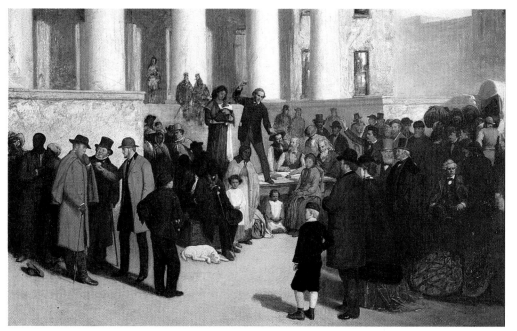

This detail of a painting shows a slave auction in Missouri. At these auctions, slaves were sold to the highest bidder. One result was that slave families were often broken apart.

price of slaves. A male field hand was worth $300 in the 1790s. By 1840 the price had jumped to $1,000. Slave trading had become big business. One slave-trading company, Franklin and Armfield, made over $500 million for each of its partners.

The Institution of Slavery

By 1860 nearly 4 million African Americans were laboring as slaves. Some were treated as members of their owners' families. Others were treated no better than work animals.

Even if all slaves had been treated well, however, they were still slaves. They had no freedom of choice because they were owned by others. Their parents, their children, their brothers and sisters could all be sold away at any time, and they were helpless to prevent it. Slaves had no rights. They could be tried in court only by whites. They could offer no evidence against a white person. While it was a crime to steal a slave, it was not a crime to kill one who tried to escape.

Although slavery put whites in a position of authority, they paid a price too. The planter class tried to convince itself that slaves were happy and cared for properly. Many planters, however, lived in fear of the day their slaves might revolt against them.

A Unique Culture

Slaves took refuge in their own culture and in religion. Whites hoped that Christian teaching would make the slaves accept their situation. White ministers often preached the virtues of obedience. However, slaves heard something else in the Bible stories. They heard about the enslavement of the Hebrews in Egypt and how Moses led the Hebrews to freedom. The story of Moses, told again and again by slave preachers, held out the hope that a new Moses would lead them to freedom.

A distinct African American culture had grown up by the early 1800s. In this, music played an important role. Visitors to plantations noted that slaves often sang as they worked. Partly this was because overseers

This painting, "The Old Plantation," shows the importance of music to African American slaves. Much of their culture, including music, came from Africa.

feared that silent slaves might be plotting against them. Most slave songs were versions of Christian hymns. The rhythms, however, came from African music. The emotions came from the slaves' experience. Frederick Douglass recalled the importance of that music:

❝ **[The songs] told a tale of grief and sorrow. In the most [joyful] outbursts . . . there was ever a tinge of deep [sadness]. . . . Every tone was a testimony against slavery, and a prayer to God for deliverance from chains.** ❞

Nat Turner preaches to fellow slaves. Turner, a Baptist, was inspired by the Bible's teachings. He led the most famous slave rebellion in U.S. history.

Resistance and Rebellion

Slaves resisted any way they could. They wrecked farm operations. Thousands ran away to escape the cruelty.

Slaves sometimes rebelled. A large revolt took place near New Orleans in 1811. About 450 slaves gathered together after a plantation revolt. Their numbers grew as they moved to other plantations. U.S. Army and Louisiana militia attacked the group and killed 66 slaves on the spot.

The most famous rebellion was led by Nat Turner in Virginia in 1831. Turner was a slave who was taught to read by his parents. He later became a preacher. Inspired by a dream of black and white angels fighting, Turner led about 60 fellow slaves on a revolt. They attacked several plantations and killed about 55 white men, women, and children. They were captured when their ammunition ran out.

Although Nat Turner was tried and hanged, his revolt sent shock waves through the South. Virginia became an armed camp. State legislatures began to pass harsh laws. As a result of these laws, slaves lost whatever freedom of movement they had. Slaves running errands, for example, now had to carry passes. In addi-

tion, whites were forbidden to teach a slave to read or write. Slaves were prevented from holding religious meetings. New restrictions were also placed on free blacks.

Before Nat Turner's Rebellion the Virginia legislature had thought of ending slavery. Now this movement to abolish slavery collapsed. Thus died any hope that the South itself would put an end to slavery.

SECTION REVIEW

1. Key Terms soil exhaustion, cotton gin

2. People and Places Eli Whitney, Nat Turner, New Orleans

3. Comprehension How did the cotton gin change the South?

4. Comprehension In what ways did slavery take away the basic rights of African Americans?

5. Critical Thinking How was the Cotton Kingdom a creation of the Industrial Revolution?

Summary

1. After the War of 1812, a new burst of nationalism took place. Under John Marshall, the Supreme Court strengthened the power of federal courts and the national government. American nationalism also led to a bold foreign policy. President Monroe issued the Monroe Doctrine, which warned European nations not to interfere in the Americas. Congress pushed for higher tariffs and improved transportation. The Erie Canal and other waterways helped make westward expansion possible.

2. The Industrial Revolution came to the United States in the late 1700s. New England became the center of the textile industry. Many families moved from their farms to work in factories. New technology, such as interchangeable parts and steam power, boosted industry and gave rise to steamships and trains. **3.** The South became a one-crop economy after the invention of the cotton gin. Cotton profits drew settlers westward and led to a rise in slavery. Slaves maintained their own culture and sometimes rebelled, but their efforts were usually crushed.

Review

KEY TERMS

Define the following terms.
1. cotton gin
2. Monroe Doctrine
3. National Road
4. standardization
5. *Marbury v. Madison*
6. soil exhaustion
7. Erie Canal
8. judicial review

COMPREHENSION

1. How did the Marshall Court increase the power of the federal government?
2. How did Andrew Jackson's actions lead to the transfer of Florida from Spain to the United States?
3. What was the American System?
4. How did the Erie Canal improve trade?
5. What was the Industrial Revolution? Why did New England become the country's main manufacturing center?
6. Who were the "Lowell Girls"? What kinds of conditions did they work under?
7. How did steam power contribute to the nation's economy?
8. In what ways did the cotton gin change life in the South?
9. How did slaves try to maintain their culture and dignity?
10. How did slaves actively resist slavery?

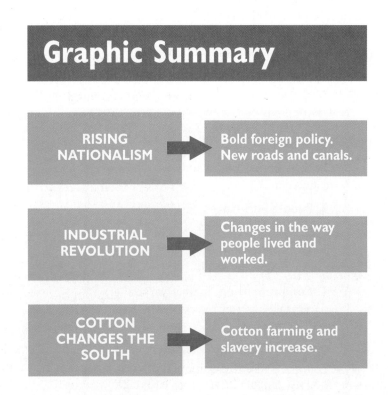

Graphic Summary

RISING NATIONALISM →	**Bold foreign policy. New roads and canals.**
INDUSTRIAL REVOLUTION →	**Changes in the way people lived and worked.**
COTTON CHANGES THE SOUTH →	**Cotton farming and slavery increase.**

Places to Locate

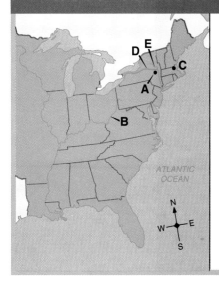

Match the letters on the map with the places that are listed below. Then explain the importance of each place.

1. Hudson River
2. Lowell, Massachusetts
3. Albany, New York
4. Ohio River
5. Erie Canal

Geographic Theme: Interactions What difficulties do you think were involved in digging a canal?

Skill Review

Study the bar graph below and answer the questions that follow.

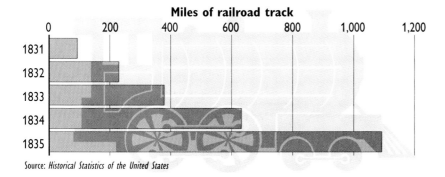

Miles of railroad track

Source: *Historical Statistics of the United States*

1. What is the subject of the graph? What years does it cover?
2. In which year shown was the amount of track the lowest? The greatest?
3. Between which years did the miles of track increase the most?
4. What factors do you think might account for the rapid growth of railroads during the mid-1800s?

CRITICAL THINKING

1. **Analyzing a Quotation** Former slave Frederick Douglass said, "No man can put a chain about the ankle of his fellow man without at last finding the other end fastened about his own neck." Explain what Douglass meant.
2. **Forming a Hypothesis** Which Americans might have opposed the decisions of the Marshall Court?
3. **Identifying Cause and Effect** Explain the political, economic, and social factors that caused slavery to become a way of life in the southern United States.

PORTFOLIO OPTIONS

1. **Civics Connection** Explain how the principle of judicial review fits into the Constitution's system of checks and balances.
2. **Writing Connection** Write a letter to the editor of a newspaper expressing your opinion on the Monroe Doctrine.
3. **Contemporary Connection** Research your local history to make a list of industries that were important to the local economy in the early 1800s. Then make a list of industries important to your community today. Compare the lists and write a paragraph to explain the similarities and differences.
4. **Timeline Connection** Copy the chapter timeline. Which event do you think was most significant for the United States? Why?

FOLK SONGS OF THE MOVE WEST

As the United States grew, a new tradition of folk songs arose to describe and celebrate the move west. Two are shown here. In the first song, a bargeman tells of his years towing barges on the Erie Canal. It was the bargeman's job to guide the mules or horses along a tow path at the side of the canal and to warn passengers to duck when a low bridge approached. In the second song, a restless farmer tries to convince his wife to move west.

"Low Bridge, Everybody Down"

I've got a mule and her name is Sal,
Fifteen miles on the Erie Canal.
She's a good old worker and a good
    old pal,
Fifteen miles on the Erie Canal.
We've hauled some barges in our
    day,
Filled with lumber, coal, and hay,
And we know every inch of the way
From Albany to Buffalo.

Chorus:
Low bridge! Everybody down!
Low bridge! We're a-coming to a
    town.
You'll always know your neighbor,
    you'll always know your pal
If you've ever navigated on the Erie
    Canal.

We'd better get on our way, old pal,
Fifteen miles on the Erie Canal.
You can bet your life I'd never part
    with Sal,
Fifteen miles on the Erie Canal.
Get us there, Sal, here comes a lock;
We'll make Rome 'for six o'clock.
One more trip and back we'll go,
Right back home to Buffalo.

Repeat chorus

"The Wisconsin Emigrant"

"Since times are so hard, I've
thought, my true heart,
Of leaving my oxen, my plough, and
my cart,
And a way to Wisconsin, a journey
we'd go
To double our fortune as other folks
do.
While here I must labor each day in
the field
And the winter consumes all the summer doth yield."

"Oh husband I've noticed with sor-
rowful heart
You've neglected your oxen, your
plough, and your cart.
Your sheep are disordered; at random they run,
And your new Sunday suit is now
every day on.
Oh, stay on the farm and you'll suffer no loss,
For the stone that keeps rolling will
gather no moss."

"Oh wife, let's go. Oh don't let us
wait.
Oh I long to be there. Oh I long to
be great!
While you some rich lady—and who
knows but I
Some governor may be before that I
die?
While here I must labor each day in
the field,
And the winter consumes all the
summer doth yield."

"O husband, remember that land is
to clear,
Which will cost you the labor of
many a year,
Where horses, sheep, cattle, and hogs
are to buy—
And you'll scarcely get settled before
you must die.
Oh, stay on your farm and you'll
suffer no loss,
For the stone that keeps rolling will
gather no moss."

"The Wisconsin Emigrant" published in *The Ballad of America* by John Anthony Scott. Bantam
Books, copyright ©1966, Southern Illinois University Press, ©1983 and copyright ©1937 (and
renewed) G. Schirmer, Inc. The source for the
lyric was A. L. Stewart and it was collected in the
early 1930s by Helen Hartness Flanders. "Low
Bridge, Everybody Down": traditional folk song.

Analyzing Literature

1. Why does the bargeman in "Low Bridge, Everybody Down" feel such loyalty and affection for his mule Sal?

2. In "The Wisconsin Emigrant," why does the farmer want to move? Why does his wife not want to move?

3. What does the farmer's wife mean by saying, "the stone that keeps rolling will gather no moss"?

UNIT 5

Expansion and Change (1810–1860)

Chapter 15

The Age of Jackson (1820–1840)

Though the United States was becoming more democratic, tensions among its sections were growing.

Chapter 16

Changes in American Life (1820–1860)

In the mid-1800s the United States benefited from immigration, reform movements, and a thriving culture.

UNIT OVERVIEW

Two important parts of the decades leading up to 1860 were territorial growth and reform.

Chapter 17

The Westward Movement (1810–1853)

Through settlement and war, the United States expanded to the Pacific Ocean.

Illustration: "The Old Scout's Tale" (detail).

The Thomas Gilcrease Institute of American History and Art, T

Democracy grew along with the nation, as George Caleb Bingham showed in this painting of a county election campaign. Yet differences among the nation's regions were growing too.

1820

1825

1830

1835

1829 Andrew Jackson becomes President

1830 Indian Removal Act

1820 Missouri Compromise

1832 South Carolina nullifies tariffs

1835 Seminole War begins

The Age of Jackson
(1820–1840)

1 A New Kind of Politics

SECTION GUIDE

Main Idea

Two signs of tension among regions were disputes over new states and a political split in the election of 1824. Andrew Jackson's election in 1828 reflected the growth of democracy in the country.

Goals

As you read, look for answers to these questions:

❶ What kinds of political disputes appeared in the early 1820s?

❷ What conflicts arose over the election of 1824?

❸ How did Andrew Jackson represent something new in American politics?

Key Terms

sectionalism
Missouri Compromise
Jacksonian democracy
spoils system

1840

1840 Harrison elected President

I N 1819 SENATORS AND REPRESENTATIVES gathered in Washington, D.C., for a new session of Congress. For five years they had been unable to meet in the Capitol because the British had burned it in the War of 1812. Now the rebuilt Capitol stood ready. Thick red curtains hung in the Hall of Representatives. Red silk was draped above the Speaker's desk. As the new session began, it became clear that the mood of the Congress was also new. The Era of Good Feelings was coming to a close. Tensions were growing that would set the course of the country for years to come.

The Missouri Compromise

Many of the divisions within the United States were the result of economic changes. White southerners relied on slaves to raise the cotton that enriched the region. In the Northeast, wealth was based on manufacturing and trade. In the West, settlers wanted cheap land and good transportation. The interests of these three sections of the country were often in conflict.

Loyalty to local interests is called sectionalism. Sectionalism replaced nationalism as the mood of Congress. It burst into the open when Missouri applied for statehood. People there wanted to allow slavery in their state. At the time, the United States was evenly split into eleven slave states and eleven free states. A new state would tilt the balance of power in Congress.

James Tallmadge of New York proposed that slavery be banned in Missouri. Southerners were angry. They asked: Did the Constitution give Congress the power to ban slavery? If nonslave states ever formed a majority in Congress, might they ban slavery altogether?

The Missouri Compromise

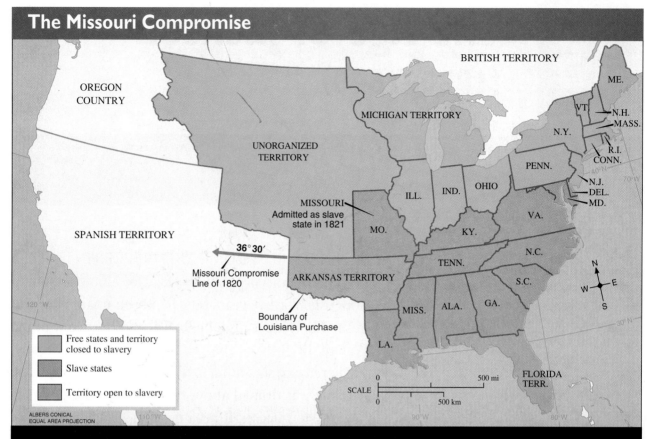

OREGON COUNTRY

BRITISH TERRITORY

ME.

MICHIGAN TERRITORY

VT

N.H.

MASS.

N.Y.

R.I.

CONN.

PENN.

UNORGANIZED TERRITORY

N.J.

DEL.

MD.

ILL. IND. OHIO

MISSOURI
Admitted as slave
state in 1821

SPANISH TERRITORY

MO.

VA.

KY.

36° 30'

N.C.

Missouri Compromise
Line of 1820

ARKANSAS TERRITORY

TENN.

S.C.

Boundary of
Louisiana Purchase

MISS. ALA. GA.

LA.

Free states and territory
closed to slavery

Slave states

Territory open to slavery

FLORIDA
TERR.

SCALE

0   500 mi

0   500 km

ALBERS CONICAL
EQUAL AREA PROJECTION

GEOGRAPHY SKILLS: Henry Clay (left) proposed the Missouri Compromise to maintain the balance of free and slave states. **Critical Thinking:** Why was the Missouri Compromise only a temporary solution?

For months the debate raged. Meanwhile, Maine declared itself ready for statehood. Henry Clay, now Speaker of the House, saw a chance for compromise. He suggested that Missouri be admitted as a slave state and Maine as a free state. Congress passed Clay's plan, known as the Missouri Compromise of 1820. It kept the balance of power in Congress between slave states and free states. It also called for slavery to be banned from the Louisiana Territory north of the parallel 36° 30', Missouri's southern border.

Thomas Jefferson, nearing 80 years old and living quietly in Virginia, was not happy with the Missouri Compromise. Worried that sectionalism would tear the country apart, Jefferson wrote:

❝In the gloomiest moment of the revolutionary war I never had any apprehension equal to what I feel from this source.❞

The Election of 1824

Jefferson had reason to worry. Just four years later, sectional differences led to a fight over the presidency. The Republican Party split apart, with four men seeking to replace Monroe as President. John Quincy Adams, Monroe's Secretary of State, was New England's choice. The South backed William Crawford of Georgia. Westerners supported Clay, the "Great Compromiser," and Andrew Jackson of Tennessee.

Jackson led the pack, but he failed to win a majority of the electoral vote. According to the Constitution, if no person wins a majority of the electoral vote, the House of Representatives chooses the President from the top three vote getters. Clay had come in fourth and was out of the running.

In the House vote, Clay threw his support behind Adams, who won.

John Quincy Adams was not a likable man. Stern and stubborn like his father, our nation's second President, Adams did not bargain easily. He ended up spending much of his four years as President quarreling with Congress.

A New Democratic Spirit

In 1828 all eyes were on the coming rematch between Jackson and Adams. Democrats saw the election as a chance for average people to show their political strength. They viewed Adams as corrupt, a man who worked for the rich. Adams's backers attacked Jackson as a gambler.

Jackson won the election of 1828 in a landslide. His victory has been called a triumph for democracy because it reflected changes in the country. Many states had once required that a man own property before he could vote. Members of the Electoral College had been chosen by state legislatures. Now, in the new western states, every adult white male could vote. Older states were lowering property requirements for voting. In all but two states, the people, rather than their lawmakers, voted for presidential electors.

There was a fresh democratic spirit in the country. Historians call this new spirit **Jacksonian democracy.** The mass of people once had been content to let their "betters" run the government. Andrew Jackson's election signaled new thinking in the land. Many Americans no longer thought of themselves as having "betters."

Jackson: An American Hero

On March 4, 1829, Washington, D.C., was full of excitement. Jackson was to be sworn in as President. From all over, people poured into the capital. "I never saw such a crowd before," observed Daniel Webster, a Massachusetts senator. "Persons have come 500 miles to see General Jackson, and they really seem to think that the country is rescued from some dreadful danger!"

Why was Jackson so popular? Americans saw him as one of them, a person who had risen above hardship and poverty. His father had died shortly before he was born. The Jacksons survived by farming on the Carolina frontier. At age thirteen, Jackson joined the militia. Taken prisoner by the British, he refused to shine the boots of an officer. The officer struck Jackson with a sword, leaving a scar that he bore for the rest of his life.

Jackson moved to the Tennessee frontier and became a wealthy planter. He then practiced law. After Tennessee became a state, he served as a member of Congress. In the War of 1812 his victory over the British at New Orleans made him a war hero.

Jackson's nickname was "Old Hickory," after one of the hardest types of wood. He was tough. He got things done. He also had a quick temper and had fought a number of duels. He was loyal toward his friends, and bitter toward his enemies.

Jackson's war record and humble background helped him become President. This walking stick (above) belonged to him.

Admirers sent Andrew Jackson a 1,400-pound cheese for his inauguration. The President got very little of it, however, because of the mobs of people.

Jackson Takes Office

Jackson looked thin and sad at his inauguration. His wife, Rachel, had died less than a month after his election. Political life had been hard on her. "I had rather be a doorkeeper in the house of God," she had said, "than to live in that palace at Washington."

The ceremony was held outdoors. This allowed the thousands present to see the inauguration. In the White House, long tables had been set with punch and cakes for those invited to the reception. Lack of invitations, however, did not stop the crowd. People pushed through the doors, breaking furniture and surrounding the food. "The reign of KING MOB seemed triumphant," a Supreme Court justice complained. The mob finally left, some through the windows, when drinks were moved out to the lawn.

A New Political Era

Jackson launched a new era of politics. He fired many government officials. Most of them were members of the upper classes. Jackson said that the duties of public office were so simple, any smart person could do the work. He followed an old saying, "To the victor belong the spoils [rewards]."

Jackson gave members of his party the jobs of those he had dismissed. This practice of giving government jobs to political backers is called the spoils system. Although subject to abuse, the spoils system did break the upper class's hold on government jobs.

SECTION REVIEW

1. Key Terms sectionalism, Missouri Compromise, Jacksonian democracy, spoils system

2. People and Places Henry Clay, John Quincy Adams, Andrew Jackson, Missouri, Maine

3. Comprehension Why was the outcome of the election of 1824 decided in the House of Representatives?

4. Comprehension Why did Americans admire Andrew Jackson?

5. Critical Thinking Why did Thomas Jefferson believe that the Missouri Compromise was a sign of future disaster for the nation?

2 Jackson's Harsh Indian Policy

SECTION GUIDE

Main Idea
President Jackson forced Indians west of the Mississippi River despite resistance.

Goals
As you read, look for answers to these questions:

1 What was Jackson's policy toward the Indians?

2 How did the new policy affect eastern Indians?

3 How did Indians respond?

Key Terms
literacy
Indian Removal Act
relocate
Trail of Tears

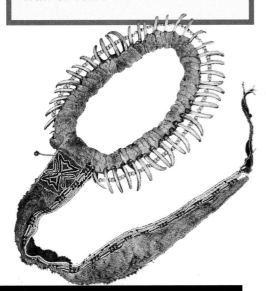

This necklace was made by Fox Indians from bear claws and otter fur. Like the Cherokee, the Fox were forcibly relocated.

MOST AMERICANS of European descent agreed on this: Their way of life was better than the Indians'. They were "civilized," and the Indians were not. Civilization, however, means more than cities and advanced technology. To be civilized also means to be humane, ethical, and reasonable. Shulush Homa, a Choctaw chief had this in mind in 1824. "It has been a great many years since our white brothers came across the big waters," he wrote, "and a great many of them have not got civilized yet." Indeed, American treatment of the Indians was not civilized. It was based on greed and ruthlessness. No story makes this clearer than President Jackson's Indian policy of forced removal.

The Cherokee Nation

Since the War of 1812, the government had been encouraging Indians to move west of the Mississippi River. Working for the government in 1817, Jackson had offered each Cherokee a choice. They could move west or settle down on 640 acres of land. To his surprise (and probably disappointment) most had decided to adopt the white peoples' way of life. The Cherokee acquired vast herds of cattle. They also had cotton gins, spinning wheels, and looms. Furthermore, some Cherokee owned African American slaves.

An important leader of the Cherokee during these years was Sequoya, son of a white trader and a Cherokee woman. Long interested in the "talking leaves" (books) of whites, Sequoya decided that Indian survival depended on literacy —being able to read and write. Sequoya created an alphabet for the Cherokee language. Within a few months, the Cherokee were reading and writing in their own language. Among their reading materials were Sequoya's newspaper, named the *Cherokee Phoenix*, and the Bible.

In 1827 the Cherokee went even further. They adopted a constitution, based on the United States Constitution, for a

SEQUOYA
(1770–1843)

Sequoya saw that literacy gave power to white people. He wanted that power for the Cherokee too. He studied European and Native American languages. Then he spent twelve years creating a Cherokee alphabet. The alphabet had 86 symbols that represented each of the sounds of the Cherokee language. Many of these symbols came from the Greek, Hebrew, and English alphabets.

The Cherokee council adopted Sequoya's alphabet. Soon thousands of Cherokee learned to read and write. They used their written language to begin a newspaper. The Cherokee also wrote and printed a constitution. Sequoya was the first person in history to invent an entire alphabet single-handedly. The giant redwood trees in California are named for him.

Cherokee Republic. Yet the Cherokee did not realize that regardless of what they did, they would not win the respect of white society. It did not matter how the Indians behaved, or what they accomplished. Most white people still considered them inferior simply because they were Indians. Furthermore, white people wanted Indian land, no matter what.

Jackson's Indian Policy

The southeastern states were often ruthless as they tried to pry Indians from their land. As President, Jackson backed laws in Georgia that seized Indian land. He also asked Congress to force southeastern Indians to move. Although religious and political groups protested, Congress passed the Indian Removal Act in 1830. It called for all Indians east of the Mississippi to move to public lands west of the Mississippi. The area had less rain and fewer trees than the Southeast and was seen by many as worthless.

Only one person from Jackson's home state of Tennessee voted against the Indian Removal Act. That was Davy Crockett. A backwoodsman, Crockett had become a legend in his own time. For his stand against Indian removal, however, he lost the next election to Congress.

The Trail of Tears

When Georgia decided to take over their lands, the Cherokee appealed to the Supreme Court. They pointed to the treaty with the federal government that guaranteed their lands. A state, they argued, could not break a federal treaty.

In 1832 Chief Justice John Marshall ruled in favor of the Cherokee. He declared that Georgia had no right to force the Cherokee to relocate, or move. Under the Constitution, President Jackson should have obeyed the Supreme Court decision. Instead he chose to ignore it. "John Marshall has made his decision," Jackson said. "Now let him enforce it." Never, before or since, has a President so openly defied a Supreme Court ruling.

Some Cherokee gave up and moved west to the Indian Territory (now Oklahoma). Most remained in Georgia. Their leader, John Ross, tried but failed to find a compromise with the government. In 1838, federal troops commanded by General Winfield Scott began to relocate some

15,000 remaining Cherokee. As one of the soldiers later told it:

>❝Men . . . were arrested and driven to the stockades. Women were dragged from their homes by soldiers whose language they could not understand. Children were often separated from their parents and driven into the stockades with the sky for a blanket and earth for a pillow.❞

From the stockades the troops moved the men, women, and children west. Forced to march in the cold and rain of winter, the Cherokee grew sick. Others starved. One survivor remembered reaching the icy Mississippi River and seeing "hundreds of sick and dying penned up in wagons or stretched upon the ground." The harsh journey became known as the Trail of Tears. Nearly one quarter of the Cherokee on the trail perished. The dead included John Ross's wife. She had given her blanket to a sick child and then herself died from the cold.

Indian Resistance

Not all the Cherokee moved west in 1838. That fall, soldiers had rounded up a farmer named Tsali, his family, and a few friends. The soldiers poked Tsali's wife with bayonets to make her walk faster. Exploding with anger, Tsali and the other men resisted. They killed a soldier and fled to the rugged Smoky Mountains.

General Scott did not want to chase them into the mountains. He offered a deal. If Tsali and his party would give themselves up, the remaining Cherokee could stay in the mountains. Tsali, his

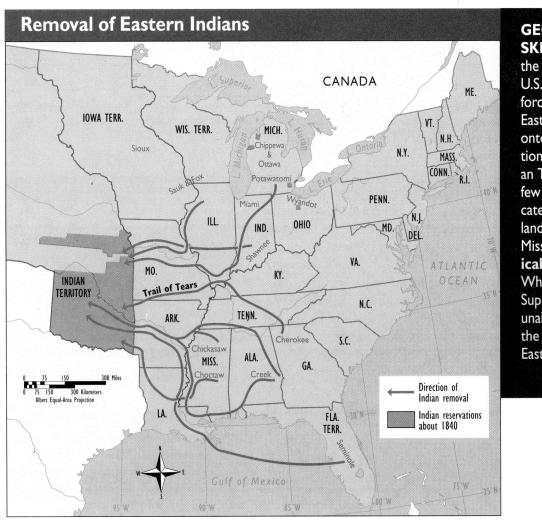

Removal of Eastern Indians

GEOGRAPHY SKILLS: During the 1830s, the U.S. government forced most Eastern Indians onto reservations in the Indian Territory. A few were relocated to other lands west of the Mississippi. **Critical Thinking:** Why was the Supreme Court unable to stop the relocation of Eastern Indians?

Direction of Indian removal

Indian reservations about 1840

In the Trail of Tears, the Cherokee were forced to relocate from Georgia to Indian Territory.

Chief Osceola led the Seminole fight against relocation.

brother, and his eldest son surrendered to the general and were shot. Their sacrifice allowed the survival of those Cherokee determined to remain in their homeland.

Resistance to the Indian Removal Act also flared up in other parts of the nation. The Sauk and Fox Indians of southern Wisconsin and northern Illinois were forced to move to the Iowa Territory after lead deposits were found on their land. In 1832 a Sauk chief named Black Hawk tried to lead his people back to their homes. The United States Army and the Illinois militia quickly crushed the uprising. The Black Hawk War was the last Indian war in the Midwest.

In 1835 the Seminole Indians refused to leave their lands in Florida. Told they must move west, they answered, "If suddenly we tear our hearts from the homes around which they are twined, our heart strings will snap." A young chief named Osceola (ahs-ee-O-luh) declared that his people would fight "till the last drop of Seminole blood has moistened the dust of his hunting ground."

In 1837 an American general called a truce to discuss peace with Osceola. During the meeting, the chief and his men were put in chains. Osceola was sent to prison,

where he later died. Many Americans were shocked by the trick that had been used to capture him.

The Seminole fought for seven years, until they were almost wiped out. Some retreated into the swamps of the Everglades, where their descendants live today. Others were forced to move west.

SECTION REVIEW

1. Key Terms literacy, Indian Removal Act, relocate, Trail of Tears

2. People and Places Sequoya, John Marshall, John Ross, Black Hawk, Osceola, Indian Territory, Florida

3. Comprehension What was the goal of Jackson's Indian policy?

4. Comprehension What happened to Indians who fought relocation?

5. Critical Thinking Historian Robert Remini called the forced relocation of the Indians "inevitable." Do you agree that Indian relocation could not be avoided? Explain your answer.

3 Sectional Divisions

SECTION GUIDE

Main Idea
As President, Andrew Jackson struggled to keep the nation from splitting apart over the issues such as tariffs.

Goals
As you read, look for answers to these questions:

1. What differences in economic goals divided the East, South, and West?

2. Why was the tariff a matter of sectional controversy?

Key Terms
credit
doctrine of nullification
secede

PICTURE THREE HORSES—West, Northeast, and South—in a harness pulling a wagon. That wagon is the United States. If the horses work together, all goes smoothly. What happens, however, if each horse decides to go in a different direction? The wagon could well overturn. The United States found itself in a similar position in the 1830s. In this section you will read how close the nation came to an armed conflict. You will also find out how the nation found a way out of that crisis.

Rising Sectional Differences

When Jackson took office, the Northeast, South, and West were arguing over three major issues. These were tariffs, internal improvements (such as new roads and canals), and the sale of public lands.

(1) *Tariffs.* Northerners supported high tariffs. The Northeast had most of the nation's manufacturing. The region had most of the banking and other business as well. Tariffs caused imported goods to be more expensive than American-made goods. This helped American manufacturers sell their products.

In contrast, southerners were beginning to hate tariffs. Tariffs had risen steadily since 1816. In that year, Congress had passed a tariff as part of the American System. Tariffs had become the government's main source of income.

The South opposed rising tariffs because tariffs made imported goods more expensive. Why did the South not buy more American-made goods? The answer is that planters usually received **credit,** rather than cash, for their cotton. Credit is an arrangement in which a person pays for something over time rather than all at once. Southerners, who sold most of their cotton overseas, gained credit from

Internal improvements were one issue that divided the nation along sectional lines. The North pushed Congress for better means of transportation such as this canal (detail). The South opposed such government spending.

those foreign buyers. They used that credit to buy foreign manufactured goods. Yet because of the tariff, those goods cost more.

(2) *Internal improvements.* Business leaders in the Northeast backed government spending on transportation. Good transportation would help bring raw materials to northeastern factories and take manufactured goods to western markets. It would also help bring food from the West to northeastern cities.

Southerners did not oppose roads and canals as such. They did oppose, however, anything that might cost the government money. They feared the government would raise tariffs to pay for these projects. In Congress, southerners began to vote against any internal improvements.

For westerners, living on the frontier, roads and canals were lifelines. They wanted the government to build as many as possible.

(3) *Sale of public lands.* Northeastern leaders did not want western land to be sold at low prices. Cheap land in the West would attract workers from the Northeast. Business owners in the Northeast would have to pay their workers higher wages to keep them from leaving.

Westerners wanted low prices for western lands because this would encourage settlement of the West. The more people who moved West, the more political power the region would have.

The Doctrine of Nullification

In the last months of John Quincy Adams's term, Congress passed a high tariff. Adams signed it into law. The South was outraged. In South Carolina, angry lawmakers spoke of leaving the Union.

Vice President John C. Calhoun had been born and raised in South Carolina. He loved his home state and the South. Calhoun also believed in a strong national government. (He had supported the 1816 tariff.) To prevent South Carolina from leaving the Union, Calhoun proposed the **doctrine of nullification.** Congress, said Calhoun, had no right to pass laws that favored one section of the nation at the expense of another. When it did, a state had the right to declare that law null and void within the state.

The Hayne-Webster Debate

Calhoun's arguments calmed southern leaders, though they still hated the high tariffs. To reduce the tariffs, southerners knew they needed help from the West. Then, in 1830, northerners called for limiting the sale of public land. Westerners protested. Here was the chance for which the South had waited!

Senator Robert Y. Hayne of South Carolina backed the West's call for a generous land policy. He argued that it was an abuse of federal power to cut off land sales. Each state had the right to make its own decisions, said Hayne.

This painting shows Senator Daniel Webster debating Senator Robert Hayne in 1830.

Hayne's argument shifted the topic of debate from land sales to states' rights. He claimed that the rights of the states came before the unity of the nation. A state could nullify any federal law it judged to be unfair, he said.

Hayne was an excellent speaker. The man who rose to answer him, however, was one of the greatest speakers of his time, Daniel Webster from Massachusetts.

Webster argued that laws made by Congress did need the approval of each state. The laws represented the will of the people as a whole. "It is, Sir," he declared, "the people's Constitution, the people's government, made for the people, made by the people, and answerable to the people." Webster scolded Hayne for wanting "Liberty first, and Union afterwards." He demanded "Liberty and Union, now and forever, one and inseparable!"

Webster's speeches lessened western support for the South. Southerners turned to President Jackson, hoping he would back them. They learned how he felt at the Jefferson Birthday Dinner of 1830.

Among the southerners attending the dinner were Hayne and Calhoun. Hayne was the main speaker. He reminded his audience that Jefferson had first raised the issue of states' rights in the Kentucky and Virginia Resolutions of 1798–1799. After the speech, Jackson gave a toast. He rose, looked at Calhoun, and said, "Our Federal Union—it must be preserved!" The room was silent. Calhoun's hand shook. He was called on to make the second toast. He replied, "The Union—next to our liberty, the most dear!"

South Carolina's Threat

Jackson understood the South's dislike of high tariffs. He suggested that the tariff be lowered. In 1832 Congress did so. South Carolina's legislature thought the tariff was still too high and voted to nullify the law. If the government tried to enforce the tariff,

the legislators said, South Carolina would **secede** — withdraw from the Union.

Jackson was furious. Calhoun defended his state. Since South Carolina had chosen to join the Union, he explained, it could choose to leave it. Jackson's reply was swift: "To say that any state may at pleasure secede from the Union is to say that the United States is not a nation."

Jackson was ready to enforce the tariff laws. He prepared to send troops to South Carolina. "If one drop of blood be shed [in South Carolina] in defiance of the laws of the United States," he said, "I will hang the first man of them I can get my hands on to the first tree I can find."

Armed conflict seemed possible. South Carolina readied its troops. Clay stepped in with a compromise. He suggested that tariffs be lowered over a ten-year period. Congress passed a compromise tariff in 1833 and South Carolina stayed in the Union.

Calhoun battled with Jackson over the doctrine of nullification. He resigned the vice presidency after winning a seat in the Senate.

SECTION REVIEW

1. Key Terms credit, doctrine of nullification, secede

2. People and Places John C. Calhoun, Robert Y. Hayne, Daniel Webster, South Carolina

3. Comprehension Why did the North and the South disagree over tariffs?

4. Comprehension Why did South Carolina threaten to secede?

5. Critical Thinking What did Calhoun mean when he said, "The Union—next to our liberty, the most dear!"

SKILLS: Interpreting Political Cartoons

LEARN

Cartoons found on the comics page of a newspaper or on television use humor to entertain. Political cartoons are often funny too, but they use humor to make a serious point. They usually appear on the editorial page of the newspaper because they express the cartoonist's opinion.

Look at the political cartoon of Andrew Jackson on this page. What do you see? Jackson is dressed like a king. Think about the American Revolution and the early political history of the United States. How did Americans of the time feel about kings, or people who acted like kings? Of course, Jackson did not really dress like a king. That is an exaggeration, one of the important tools of cartoonists.

Another tool cartoonists use is symbolism. For example, a dollar sign is a symbol for money. A sword or cannon suggests military might. Animals often stand for countries. To understand a political cartoon, you must interpret its exaggeration and decode its symbols.

King Andrew The First

PRACTICE

1. Is the comparison of Jackson to a king meant as praise or criticism? Explain.

2. There are two areas of paper on the floor, each labeled. What do they represent? What does it mean that they are torn up and that Jackson is standing on them?

3. What issue is the cartoonist examining in this cartoon?

4. What is the cartoonist's opinion about the issue?

APPLY

5. Draw your own political cartoon, based on a topic from this chapter.

4 Prosperity and Panic

SECTION GUIDE

Main Idea
Jackson's economic policies caused an economic downturn after he left office.

Goals
As you read, look for answers to these questions:

1. Why did Jackson oppose a national bank?

2. What were the results of Jackson's financial policies?

Key Terms
inflation
panic
depression

TODAY BANKS AND BANKERS are not often a subject of national debate. The biggest battle of Jackson's presidency, however, was his fight against the Bank of the United States. In this fight, bankers were seen as devils and the national bank as a monster. Jackson saw himself as a dragon slayer, fighting for right.

Jackson's War on the Bank

The original Bank of the United States had been Alexander Hamilton's idea. He had convinced Congress to charter the bank in 1791 for twenty years. After the War of 1812, the country's finances were a mess. Once again, Congress chartered a national bank, the Second Bank of the United States .

Jackson distrusted the bank. He believed that bank officers were influencing Congress to pass laws friendly to it. He was angry that the bank's high interest rates made it hard for the average person to borrow money.

In 1832 Congress voted to renew the charter of the bank. Jackson was sick in bed when he heard the news. The old soldier gathered strength at the thought of a battle against his rivals. "The Bank is trying to kill me," he declared, "but I will kill it." Jackson wrote a powerful veto message. In it he said the bank was a monopoly that favored the few at the expense of many.

This was the first time a President had vetoed a bill simply because he disagreed with it. Earlier Presidents had only vetoed bills they thought were unconstitutional. In effect, Jackson stated that a President had the right to veto any law for any reason. In this, Jackson had set a new precedent. The bank veto became a main issue in the election of 1832. Jackson presented himself as the defender of the American people against the bank.

Jackson won the election. He took this as a sign that the public approved of his war on the bank. In his second term he set out to destroy its power.

The bank's charter did not run out until 1836, but Jackson wanted to starve it to death in the meantime. He ordered all government money withdrawn from the

This cartoon shows Jackson (at left) attacking the Bank of the United States with a weapon labeled "VETO." Vice President Van Buren (in the middle) helps Jackson. The monster's heads represent bank branch directors.

CONNECTING WITH THE

POLITICAL PARTIES

Today's Democratic and Republican parties were born more than a century ago. Andrew Jackson's followers called themselves "Democratic-Republicans." During the 1830s they became known simply as "Democrats." Linked to the ideals of Thomas Jefferson, Democrats stood for states' rights and saw themselves as defenders of the common people.

The Republican Party of today was formed in 1854 to oppose slavery. Republicans, starting with Abraham Lincoln, dominated politics until well into the 1900s.

The donkey has come to symbolize the Democratic Party. The Republican Party is represented by the elephant.

In recent years the fastest-growing "party" in the United States has been no party at all. Many voters have decided to remain independent.

bank. These funds were then deposited in state banks that became known as "pet banks." The pet banks began to offer credit on easier terms.

The pet banks also printed more paper money. Each dollar bill was supposed to be worth a certain amount of gold or silver held by the bank. People could exchange their paper money for gold or silver. Yet the banks printed much more money than they could back with gold or silver.

Prosperity Becomes Panic

Most of the nation prospered during Jackson's last years in office. More money was available as a result of easy credit and the paper money printed by state banks. The rise in the supply of money made each dollar worth less. As a result, the price of goods rose. This rise in prices is called **inflation.** Inflation encouraged people to spend freely, before their dollars lost even more value.

Jackson left office proud of the nation's prosperity. But it was a puffed-up prosperity. Like a balloon, it had little substance.

Martin Van Buren, a Jacksonian Democrat, was elected President in 1836. Soon after he took office, the puffed-up economy collapsed. A **panic**—an economic crisis —spread throughout the country. People began taking their paper money to the banks and demanding gold or silver in exchange. The banks quickly ran out of their supplies of gold and silver.

Paper money quickly lost its value. When the government tried to get back its money from the state banks, the banks could not pay. Banks failed like falling dominoes. The collapse of the nation's money system caused the Panic of 1837. The Panic of 1837 was one of the first **depressions** in American history. A depression is a period of deep economic hardship.

Because people had no money, manufacturers no longer had customers for their goods. Almost 90 percent of the nation's factories closed down in 1837.

Jobless workers had no way of buying food or paying rent. In New York City workers met at City Hall to demand cheaper food. The crowd stormed a flour merchant. A newspaper described what happened:

❝Barrels of flour, by dozens, fifties and hundreds were tumbled into the street from the doors, and thrown . . . from the windows. . . .
Amidst the falling and bursting of the barrels and sacks of wheat, numbers of women were engaged . . . filling the boxes and baskets with which they were provided, and their aprons, with flour, and making off with it. . . .❞

Every section of the country suffered, but the depression hit hardest in the cities. Farmers were hurt less because they could at least grow their own food. Future economic depressions would be even more painful as more people took factory jobs.

The Whig Party

In the late 1830s Senators Henry Clay and Daniel Webster argued that the government needed to help the economy through the difficult times. President Van Buren disagreed. He believed that the economy would improve if left alone. "The less government interferes with private pursuits," Van Buren argued, "the better for the general prosperity."

The hungry, the poor, and the jobless did not care for Van Buren's theories. They wanted help. Many Americans blamed Van Buren for the Panic of 1837, though he had taken office only weeks before it started.

Opponents of Jackson and Van Buren had formed a political party called the Whigs. In 1840 the Whigs chose William Henry Harrison of Ohio to run for President and John Tyler of Virginia to run for Vice President. Harrison had led the army that defeated the Indians at Tippecanoe in 1811. He had also fought bravely in the War of 1812. The Whigs made the most of Harrison's military record and his nickname, "Old Tippecanoe." "Tippecanoe and Tyler too!" became their slogan.

The Election of 1840

In the election of 1840, image was much more important than issues. Harrison was the son of a Virginia plantation owner. However, because he had settled on a farm in Ohio, the Whigs said Harrison was a true westerner. They used symbols of the frontier to represent Harrision. The Whigs accused Van Buren of wearing "corsets and

To show that he was a true westerner, Harrison used a log cabin as the symbol of his presidential campaign.

silk stockings." In noisy parades and stirring rallies they shouted their slogans.

Harrison won. He was the first member of the Whig Party to be elected President. He also became the first President to die in office. Harrison died of pneumonia only one month after taking office. Vice President John Tyler took his place.

SECTION REVIEW

1. Key Terms inflation, panic, depression

2. People Andrew Jackson, Martin Van Buren, William Henry Harrison, John Tyler

3. Comprehension Why did Jackson wish to destroy the national bank?

4. Comprehension What caused the Panic of 1837?

5. Critical Thinking Which affected the economy more, Jackson's veto of the bank charter or his transfer of government money to state banks? Explain.

Summary

1. Tensions between regions of the country led to disputes over the admission of new states. The Missouri Compromise of 1820 allowed slavery in Missouri and states south of the Missouri Compromise line. The election of Andrew Jackson as President in 1828 reflected the growing democratic spirit in the United States.

2. Many Indian groups resisted the Indian Removal Act. President Jackson used the army to enforce his policy of making Eastern Indians relocate west of the Mississippi River. Many Cherokee died along the Trail of Tears.

3. Tension between the North and South grew greater. South Carolina threatened to nullify the tariff laws and to secede. A compromise tariff ended the threat.

4. Jackson set out to destroy the Bank of the United States. Americans went through deep economic hardship during the Panic of 1837. Voters blamed President Van Buren for it. They elected William Henry Harrison in 1840. Harrison died after only one month in office. Vice President John Tyler became President.

Graphic Summary

Admission of free and slave states is disputed.	Congress passes the Missouri Compromise of 1820.
Congress passes Indian Removal Act.	Eastern Indians are relocated to Indian Territory.
Congress passes high tariffs.	South Carolina threatens to nullify tariff and to secede.
Inflation encourages people to spend freely.	The nation's economy collapses, causing a depression.

Review

KEY TERMS

Write a sentence that defines each key term.
1. sectionalism
2. spoils system
3. Indian Removal Act
4. doctrine of nullification
5. secede
6. inflation
7. depression

COMPREHENSION

1. What issue did the Missouri Compromise resolve? How did it temporarily resolve that issue?
2. What changes in the United States did Jackson's election signal?
3. What did the Cherokee do to try to be accepted by white society?
4. Why did the Northeast support government spending to improve transportation? Why did the South oppose tariffs?
5. How did Webster respond to Hayne's argument that the states had the right to nullify federal laws?
6. What issue led South Carolina to threaten to secede in 1832?
7. What steps did Jackson take to destroy the Second Bank of the United States?
8. What caused the Panic of 1837?
9. What policies did the Democratic Party of the 1830s support?
10. What strategy did the Whigs use during the election campaign of 1840?

Places to Locate

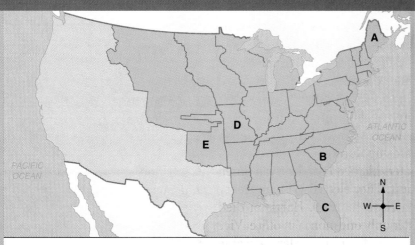

Match each of the letters on the map with the places that are listed below. Then explain the importance of each place.

1. Florida   3. Maine   5. South Carolina
2. Indian Territory   4. Missouri

Geographic Theme: Regions Why did northern states support high tariffs? Why did southern states oppose them? Explain.

Skill Review

This political cartoon comments on the spoils system. Study the cartoon and answer the questions.

1. What does the pig symbolize?
2. Do you think that the cartoonist supports or opposes the spoils system? Explain your answer.
3. Draw your own cartoon that shows your views on the spoils system.

CRITICAL THINKING

1. Identifying Advantages and Disadvantages What are the advantages and disadvantages of the spoils system? Does this system still exist today?

2. Identifying Trends Why has Andrew Jackson sometimes been called "the maker of the modern presidency"?

PORTFOLIO OPTIONS

1. Civics Connection Create a chart with two columns to show the arguments for and against the doctrine of nullification. Then write a short paragraph explaining your opinion on the doctrine.

2. Writing Connection What other methods, besides forced relocation, might the United States have used to end conflicts between settlers and Indians? Write a brief essay explaining your ideas.

3. Contemporary Connection Jackson's years as President are sometimes called the Age of Jackson. Is it possible today for one individual to stamp his or her image on an entire age in the same manner? Who in the United States today might have such an impact?

4. Timeline Connection Copy the chapter timeline. Which events had to do with the forced relocation of Indians? Which event had to do with slavery? Now add events from the chapter that you think should be included and explain why.

The painting below shows a common scene in New York harbor during the mid-1800s. A group of immigrants step off a ship, ready to start a new life in their adopted country. Immigration and new reform movements combined to bring great changes to American life.

1820

1830

1840

1850

1831 *The Liberator* begins publication

1845 Irish potato famine begins

1836 First women's college opens

1848 Seneca Falls Convention

1821 First public high school opens

1851 *Moby-Dick* published

1854 *Walden* published

Changes in American Life
(1820–1860)

1 The Impact of Immigration

THE SCENE WAS about as regular as the rising sun. A ship docks at an American port. People come down the gangplank. They are dazed from the ocean voyage and maybe hungry and sick. Many are men, sticking together in their loneliness and shared hopes. Others are family groups, clutching the suitcases, boxes, and sacks that hold their few possessions. The new sights and sounds confuse them. In the crowded port they strain to hear a voice speaking their language, a voice that will help them find shelter and a new life in America.

The Push-Pull of Immigration

The first steps of the immigrant on land may have been unsteady, but the effect was great. The millions of immigrants who arrived on these shores changed both a nation and a continent in the 1800s. These newcomers would enrich the country with their cultures and their labor.

The main immigrant groups in the mid-1800s were the British, Irish, Germans, and Scandinavians (people from Sweden, Denmark, and Norway). They usually came in **steerage,** the lowest deck on a ship. In steerage, hundreds were packed together for weeks at a time. The stench became so bad that harbor masters could smell these ships from miles away. Diseases spread rapidly. About 5 percent of the passengers died during the journey.

Immigration was a matter of "push-pull." There were a number of factors that "pushed" people out of Europe. Population was growing rapidly. As a result, land became overcrowded. Finding work became more and more difficult. Poor harvests caused hardships in some places. Another "push" was the desire

1860

Before they set foot in America, most immigrants first had to suffer through a long, crowded ocean journey. Joseph Gear, who came to America in 1824, made this sketch of immigrants lining up for a ship breakfast.

to flee governments that mistreated certain religious and ethnic groups.

The biggest "pull" factor in the United States was economic opportunity—jobs and land. Hope for a better life shone the brighter because of the freedom that went with it.

A Difficult Decision

In his novel *The Emigrants,* Vilhelm Moberg describes the push-pull factors affecting a group of Swedes in 1850. Plagued by drought and famine, Karl Oskar Nilsson one day saw a picture in a newspaper. The caption read: "A Wheat Field in North America." He stared at the picture, which showed an endless field of grain. "It was the fruit of the earth that he saw here," Moberg wrote, "an unmeasurable quantity of bread for man."

That winter Karl Oskar and his wife Kristina spent evenings talking about America. Karl Oskar wanted to move:

❝Perhaps [in America] they must face as much [difficulty] as here, but they would do it in another spirit. . . . Because the great difference between the two countries was this: *In America they could improve their [position] through their own work.* ❞

Kristina wanted to stay. She had heard about the dangers of traveling on ships. How would her children hold up on such a voyage and during the hardships that followed? They would have to live where they did not know the language. She imagined a lonely and difficult life in America.

That winter their young daughter died. She had eaten barley porridge too fast after months of a famine diet. (A famine is a severe food shortage.) Kristina changed her mind about coming to America, and they made plans to emigrate.

Like the real-life immigrants from Scandinavia, Karl Oskar and Kristina ended up in Minnesota. A Swedish writer, Frederika Bremer, explained the attraction: "The climate, the situation, the character of the scenery agrees with our people better than any other of the American states."

The Irish Flee Hunger

In the 1800s the Irish suffered under the iron-fisted rule of Britain. Irish Catholics

384

could not vote, hold office, buy or inherit land, go to school, or practice their faith. The census of 1841 reported that half the rural people lived in one-room, windowless, mud cabins. There was almost no furniture. One county of Ireland, for instance, had 9,000 people and only 10 beds and 93 chairs.

Yet the Irish maintained their faith. They developed ways to help each other, to worship, and to resist the British.

For food they relied on potatoes. Brought to Europe in the 1600s from Peru, potatoes were easy to grow in Ireland's rocky soil. Potatoes helped feed the growing population of Europe. In Ireland, potatoes made it possible for families to feed more children. In two centuries the population zoomed from half a million to about 8.5 million.

In 1845 disease attacked the potato crop. Famine and death came to Ireland. The Irish had already started to emigrate to America, but their numbers ballooned after the potato crop was destroyed. By 1854 some 1.25 million Irish had emigrated. Their journey was often paid for by relatives who had left Ireland earlier.

"Irish Power"

Once in America the Irish stayed in the great port cities of Boston, New York, Philadelphia, and Baltimore. By 1850 the populations of these cities were one-quarter Irish. By 1900 there were more Irish in America than in Ireland!

With little money and education and few skills, the Irish survived by doing unskilled work. Women took in washing and sewing or worked as cooks and servants. The men found jobs on the construction gangs building the nation's roads, canals, and railroads. These newcomers were often paid less than a dollar a day. "Waterpower, steam power, and Irish power" run the United States, a newspaper declared in 1850. "The last works hardest of all."

The Irish were used to sticking together to help each other out. In America they formed aid societies to help the newest arrivals. Many joined the Democratic Party, which they saw as the party of the common person. Irish political leaders helped their followers get jobs and find a place to live.

The church was also a powerful force in Irish neighborhoods. Almost all the Irish immigrants of the 1850s were Catholics. In addition to its religious tasks, the Catholic Church ran schools in which young Catholics were educated.

Anti-Immigrant Feelings

The coming of the Irish unleashed a wave of anger and prejudice. (Prejudice is an unfair opinion formed without facts.) Protestants feared that Catholics would

Catholic schools were a target of prejudice. In this cartoon, Catholic bishops are shown as crocodiles, coming out of the water to attack America's public school system.

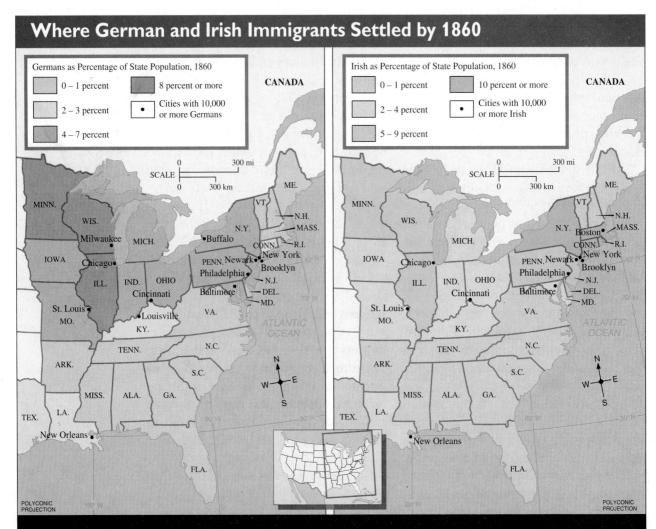

Where German and Irish Immigrants Settled by 1860

Germans as Percentage of State Population, 1860
- 0 – 1 percent
- 2 – 3 percent
- 4 – 7 percent
- 8 percent or more
- • Cities with 10,000 or more Germans

Irish as Percentage of State Population, 1860
- 0 – 1 percent
- 2 – 4 percent
- 5 – 9 percent
- 10 percent or more
- • Cities with 10,000 or more Irish

GEOGRAPHY SKILLS: German immigrants often settled where good farmland was available, while most Irish clustered in the cities. **Critical Thinking:** Which region of the country had the smallest percentage of German and Irish immigrants? Why might that have been the case?

obey only the Pope, the head of the Roman Catholic Church, even if his teachings conflicted with American political ideals. Native-born Americans also feared that Irish politicians would take over the cities.

Native-born Americans who wanted to restrict the influence of the foreign-born were called **nativists.** Some nativists refused to hire immigrants, putting up signs such as "No Irish Need Apply." In cities like New York and Boston, nativists formed a secret society. Members promised not to support any Catholics or immigrants running for office. If asked about their secret groups, they were to answer, "I know nothing about it."

In the 1850s nativists organized a political party, known as the Know-Nothing Party. Its aim was to limit the power of the immigrant Irish. It wanted to ban Catholics and the foreign-born from holding political office. The Know-Nothings also called for a cut in immigration and a 21-year-wait to become an American citizen.

The Know-Nothing Party lasted less than a decade. Immigrants continued to be a

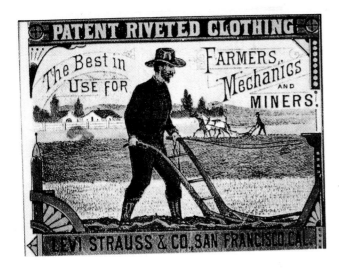

Levi Strauss wanted to make California miners clothes that would last. He began making blue jeans and jackets in 1874. Today the company is one of the world's largest clothing manufacturers.

target of prejudice in the United States. However, the hostility lessened as the children and grandchildren of immigrants became part of American life.

The Germans

With the acceptance of each immigrant group, American culture changed and expanded. By their numbers the group that probably had the greatest influence on American culture was the Germans, the largest immigrant group in the 1800s. Most arrived in the United States with good skills as farmers or artisans.

German immigrants settled both in cities and on farms. An especially large number moved to the midwestern states of Ohio, Illinois, Wisconsin, and Missouri. The German immigrants often built new industries. In doing so, they made their names household words—names like Steinway (pianos), Bausch and Lomb (eyeglasses), and Heinz (processed foods).

Much of German culture became part of American culture. The traditions of the Christmas tree, marching bands, musical societies, gymnasiums, kindergartens, and foods like the hamburger and frankfurter all came from Germany.

The German immigrants also included a number of German Jews. Many of them moved west, becoming peddlers and storekeepers on the frontier. One of the most famous of these was Levi Strauss, who came to the United States in 1847. He opened a business in San Francisco. Strauss's company was the first to make the blue denim work pants that today we call blue jeans.

2 A Spirit of Reform

SECTION GUIDE

Main Idea
In the early 1800s a number of reform movements worked to improve American society.

Goals
As you read, look for answers to these questions:

1. What role did religion play in the reform movements of the early 1800s?

2. What were the interests of the early labor movement?

3. What movements for social reform arose in the early 1800s?

Key Terms
Second Great Awakening
strike
rehabilitate
temperance
utopia

IN 1801 CANE RIDGE, Kentucky, was near the edge of the frontier. Yet in August more than 10,000 people gathered there, camping in the woods near a large clearing. Every day for a week these people met to hear sermons and sing religious songs. Many leaped up and cried out their newfound faith in God.

A New Awakening

The camp meeting at Cane Ridge was part of the Second Great Awakening, a revival of religious faith in the early 1800s. All over the country, Americans listened to Baptist, Methodist, and Presbyterian preachers. The preachers delivered the message that every person could be saved. Jesus Christ would come again, they said. First, Americans were told, they must cast out evil and create a heaven on earth.

One effect of the Second Great Awakening was a new spirit of reform. At first the reform took place within churches, with women taking a more active role. They set up Sunday schools, where children learned about their religion, and supported missionary societies. By the 1830s and 1840s women were often leaders in the efforts to reform other parts of society.

A Better Work Place

While the Second Great Awakening played a role in the new reform movement, changes in the way people worked also led to demands for reform. In earlier times, a worker learned a trade with the hope of becoming a master artisan. Artisans worked for themselves. In the factory system, workers did not learn a trade. They remained mostly unskilled, with little hope of ever working for themselves. Also, factory work was noisy, boring, and unsafe.

A preacher delivers a sermon at a religious revival meeting in the early 1800s. Many listeners were overwhelmed with emotion.

Public education played an important role in helping to unify the United States. A one-room schoolhouse, shown here in a painting by Winslow Homer, was common in many parts of the country. Below is a spelling book from the early 1800s.

By the 1830s American workers had begun to organize. The young women who worked the mills in Lowell, Massachusetts, started a group called the Factory Girls' Association. In 1836 the mill owners raised the rent of the boarding houses where these women lived. About 1,500 of them went on **strike**—they stopped working and demanded better conditions. Harriet Hanson, eleven years old, recalled her part in the walkout:

> **❝I marched out, and was followed by the others. As I looked back at the long line that followed me, I was more proud than I have ever been since.❞**

Sarah Bagley, another Lowell worker, became a leader of the movement to reduce the work day to ten hours. Other workers began to strike for higher wages. Male workers set up the Workingman's Party to win labor reforms. The depression caused by the Panic of 1837, however, caused the young labor movement to crumble.

Still, the early labor movement achieved a few of its goals. Some health and safety laws to protect workers were passed. In 1840 President Van Buren put in place a ten-hour day for all public workers. By the 1850s private employers were following the government's example.

Changes in Education

An important goal for workers was educating their children. Americans had long valued schooling, believing that a democracy needed well-informed citizens. Yet in the early 1800s, few American children were able to get a good education.

During the 1830s Americans began to demand change. Massachusetts set up a state board of education, the first in the United States. Its head, Horace Mann, called free public education "the great equalizer," meaning that it united the rich and the poor. By 1850 many northern states had elementary schools paid for by public taxes.

During this time of change, more young people gained the chance to attend high school and college. Boston set up the first public high school in 1821. Other northern cities soon followed its example. Some states founded universities and provided them with public funds.

In the mid-1800s women had little access to public education. Here women learn to draw in a private school. **Critical Thinking:** Why, do you think, was public education in the mid-1800s limited mainly to men?

Many other new colleges were founded by churches, especially in the states carved from the Northwest Territory. They included Northwestern, Antioch, Oberlin, and Notre Dame. Private colleges began to offer a wider range of subjects, including law, medicine, and business.

Young women could not attend public high schools and most colleges. Some went to private high schools. Wesleyan College, the first women's college, opened in Georgia in 1836. The following year another women's college, Mount Holyoke, opened in Massachusetts. Ohio's Oberlin College became the first college to accept women and men together. For most women, however, higher education remained out of reach until the 1880s.

African American Education

In northern states, African American families had to pay taxes to support public schools. Their children, however, were often barred from those schools. A few elementary schools for African Americans were opened in northern cities and in Washington, D.C.

In slave states there were no schools for the children of slaves. Teaching a slave to read had been illegal since Nat Turner's Rebellion in 1831.

Few colleges would accept African Americans. Those colleges that did often took only one or two black students at a time. One of the first black college graduates was John Russwurm, who finished his studies at Bowdoin College in Maine in 1826. Russwurm was a founder of the first African American newspaper in the United States.

The class of 1885 at Ohio's Oberlin College included one African American woman.

Newspapers and Magazines

The growth of public schools led to a growth in the number of people who could read. At the same time, new technology created new choices for people in reading material. In the 1830s cheaper newsprint and the invention of the steam-driven press lowered the price of newspapers to a penny. These "penny papers" made news available to the average American. By 1833 there were three times as many newspapers in the United States as in England.

Hundreds of new magazines also appeared. One such magazine was *Godey's Lady's Book*. Edited by Sarah Hale, *Godey's Lady's Book* advised American women on how they should dress and behave. The magazine also put forth the notion that men and women were responsible for different, but equally important, areas of life. A woman's area was the home and the world of "human ties." A man's area was politics and the business of earning a living to provide for his family.

Caring for the Needy

In 1841 Dorothea Dix, daughter of a wealthy Boston family, was teaching Sunday school at a women's prison. She discovered a group of insane women being kept in an unheated part of the prison. Upset by this cruel treatment, Dix began visiting jails and poorhouses. She learned that in many cases the mentally ill were forced to live "in cages, closets, cellars, stalls, pens! Chained naked, beaten with rods and lashed into obedience!"

Dix asked states to improve the care of the mentally ill. Her tireless efforts led to the building of 32 new hospitals. She became one of the most successful reformers in the country.

Dix was also a leader in the call for prison reform. Prisons in those days were poorly organized. Long-time criminals, debtors, and children who had committed crimes were all housed together.

Reformers demanded that special jails be set up for children. They also called for better treatment for adult prisoners. New prisons were built with the goal of rehabilitating prisoners— helping them return to normal, useful lives.

Reformers also worked to improve conditions for disabled people. In the 1830s Samuel G. Howe founded the Perkins School for the Blind, in Boston. At Perkins, Howe taught blind people skills to help them earn a living and lead independent lives. Another reformer, Thomas H. Gallaudet (gal-uh-DET) worked with the deaf. In 1817 Gallaudet started the first American school for deaf children.

Dorothea Dix devoted her life to helping prisoners and the mentally ill.

The Temperance Movement

Heavy drinking was common and widely accepted in the United States in the early 1800s. Some workers spent most of their wages on rum and beer, leaving their families with little on which to live. Children could buy alcohol as easily as adults.

Reformers blamed alcohol for increasing the misery of the poor. Reformers called for temperance —giving up the drinking of alcoholic beverages. The temperance movement was well organized. It sent speakers around the country who warned of the evils of alcohol. They urged people to sign pledges promising never to drink alcohol. By 1843 some 500,000 pledges had been signed.

Temperance societies had political success as well. Maine passed a law banning the sale of liquor in 1846, and twelve other states soon followed. Many people opposed these laws, however, and most of them were repealed. Still, the movement to ban alcohol remained powerful.

This signboard was made for the meeting house of a New Hampshire temperance society.

REDNESS OF EYES.

WOUNDS.

BABBLINGS.

CONTENTIONS

SORROW

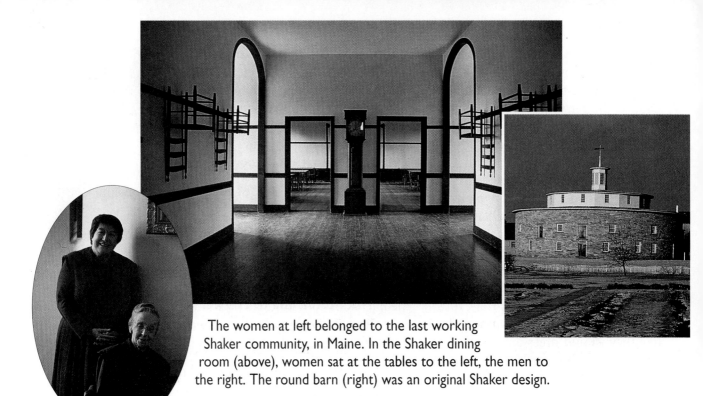

The women at left belonged to the last working Shaker community, in Maine. In the Shaker dining room (above), women sat at the tables to the left, the men to the right. The round barn (right) was an original Shaker design.

The Shakers

Most of the reform movements were attempts to improve society. Other reformers believed it was necessary to start from scratch and build a new society. These reformers tried to set up ideal communities, called **utopias.**

Religious principles were at the root of some utopian communities, such as those started by the Shakers. The founder of the Shakers, Ann Lee, came to the United States from England in 1774. She preached that all people were equal and should share in all aspects of life. In the next decades, Shakers set up communities in New York, New England, and on the frontier.

Life in these communities was strict. Men and women lived apart. They worked hard, farming and making simple, yet graceful furniture. On Sundays they worshipped, expressing deep religious emotions. They were called "Shakers" because the services were filled with shaking, dancing, and singing.

Because they had no children, the Shaker communities depended on gaining converts to grow. Membership reached its peak in the mid-1840s with about 6,000 members. Today the Shaker faith is only a memory. However, the graceful style of Shaker crafts and furniture is still copied.

SECTION REVIEW

1. Key Terms Second Great Awakening, strike, rehabilitate, temperance, utopia

2. People Sarah Bagley, Horace Mann, Sarah Hale, Dorothea Dix

3. Comprehension How was the labor movement a response to problems created by the Industrial Revolution?

4. Comprehension What changes took place in American education in the mid-1800s?

5. Critical Thinking Why might women have played a leading role in the reform movements of the early 1800s?

3 The Call for Equality

SECTION GUIDE

Main Idea
The spread of democracy to almost all white men led to calls for freedom for slaves and more opportunities for women.

Goals
As you read, look for answers to these questions:

1. How did democracy expand in the 1800s?

2. What groups called for the end of slavery?

3. What was the origin of the movement for women's rights?

Key Terms
caucus
abolitionist
Underground Railroad
suffrage

I N 1831 A YOUNG FRENCHMAN stepped off a boat onto United States soil. For one year Alexis de Tocqueville (tawk-VEEL) traveled all over the country, observing American culture. Tocqueville was impressed with the deep faith Americans had in their democracy.

After returning to France, Tocqueville wrote a book called *Democracy in America*. In it he said Americans' belief in equality helped make their democracy work. "The great advantage of the Americans," he wrote, is "that they are born equal instead of becoming so." Tocqueville was not blind, however, to the conditions of African Americans. "In one blow oppression has deprived the descendants of the Africans of almost all the privileges of humanity," he wrote.

Expanding Democracy

When Tocqueville arrived in the United States, most white men could vote. By that time almost all states had changed earlier laws that said only property owners could vote.

States also passed laws allowing voters more control over government. For example, state governors were once chosen by the state legislature. In the 1830s and 1840s laws were changed to allow voters to choose the governor in a direct election.

Until the 1830s each political party chose its presidential and vice-presidential candidates in a closed caucus —a meeting of important party members. In 1831 and 1832, however, the major parties held

Alexis de Tocqueville considered liberty to be a society's most important value. His life's goal was "to show man how to escape tyranny."

In this 1850s painting, African Americans escaping slavery in the South are given help at an Indiana farmhouse. **Critical Thinking:** Why did some people offer help to those who had escaped slavery?

William Lloyd Garrison and his newspaper, *The Liberator*, gave a powerful voice to the abolitionist movement.

national conventions to choose candidates. Members in each state elected delegates to represent them at the convention. These delegates then chose their party's candidates for President and Vice President. Conventions gave common people a stronger voice in the party's nominations.

Calls for Ending Slavery

African Americans were not included in the political life of the country. Almost all still worked as slaves in the South. More and more Americans, mostly in the North, thought that slavery was wrong. They believed it went against Christianity and against the principles the nation was founded upon.

A group of reformers who were called **abolitionists** sought to abolish, or put an end to, slavery. William Lloyd Garrison was perhaps the best known of these abolitionists. Son of a New England sea captain, Garrison was a newspaperman.

In Boston he started his own paper in 1831 to urge the abolition of slavery. In the first issue of *The Liberator*, he thundered, "I am in earnest—I will not retreat a single inch—*and I will be heard.*" For the next three decades Garrison's paper was a bugle call for freedom.

Another famous leader of the abolitionist movement was Frederick Douglass. Born into slavery in Maryland, Douglass escaped to Massachusetts when he was a young man. There he went to an antislavery meeting and gave a speech describing what freedom meant to him.

Douglass so impressed the audience that he was hired to lecture about his experience as a slave. A powerful speaker, Douglass also attacked the injustices faced by free blacks. He started a newspaper, the *North Star*. In later life, Douglass served as the United States' representative to Haiti.

394

Sojourner Truth was one of the first African American women to speak out against slavery. Originally named Isabella Baumfree, she was born a slave in New York. She gained her freedom when New York abolished slavery in 1827. She changed her name to reflect her life's work: to travel (or sojourn) and preach about the evils of slavery. Speaking throughout the North, Sojourner Truth was a tireless crusader for justice.

African American churches, which had their origins in the North, also played a role in the abolitionist movement. Many important leaders in the fight against slavery had their roots in these churches.

The antislavery movement was strongest in the North, but there were some southern abolitionists. Sarah and Angelina Grimké were raised on a South Carolina plantation. There the Grimké sisters saw that slavery went against Christian teachings. Moving north, they became Quakers and joined the American Anti-Slavery Society. They won over thousands of converts to the abolitionist cause.

The Underground Railroad

People who opposed slavery joined local antislavery societies. By 1840 more than 2,000 such groups stretched across the North. Their members included both blacks and whites.

For many people, merely joining a group or listening to speeches against slavery was not enough. These people took action by helping slaves escape to freedom along the **Underground Railroad.** This was a series of escape routes running from the South to the North.

Traveling the Underground Railroad, the former slaves moved at night and stayed during the day in hiding places called stations. The people who led the runaways to freedom were known as conductors. Harriet Tubman, a slave who had escaped to freedom herself, was one of the most

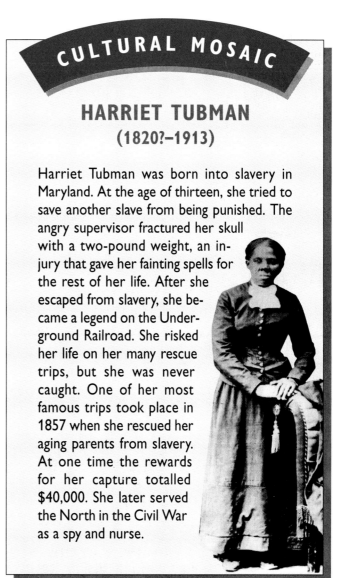

CULTURAL MOSAIC

HARRIET TUBMAN
(1820?–1913)

Harriet Tubman was born into slavery in Maryland. At the age of thirteen, she tried to save another slave from being punished. The angry supervisor fractured her skull with a two-pound weight, an injury that gave her fainting spells for the rest of her life. After she escaped from slavery, she became a legend on the Underground Railroad. She risked her life on her many rescue trips, but she was never caught. One of her most famous trips took place in 1857 when she rescued her aging parents from slavery. At one time the rewards for her capture totaled $40,000. She later served the North in the Civil War as a spy and nurse.

famous conductors. Tubman risked her life and freedom at least nineteen times by returning to the South to help others escape. She helped more than 300 slaves gain freedom.

The Call for Women's Rights

In 1840 leaders of the antislavery movement gathered in London, England. Among the American delegates were Lucretia Mott, Elizabeth Cady Stanton, and several other women. These women had been active in the struggle to end slavery and had much to say about their work.

GEOGRAPHY: The Underground Railroad

UNORGANIZED TERRITORY

NEBRASKA TERRITORY

KANSAS TERRITORY

INDIAN TERRITORY

TEX.

Austin

San Antonio

Houston

Galvest

To Mexico

Neither underground nor a railroad, the Underground Railroad was a network of people and places that hid escaping slaves and helped them reach safety in the North or in Canada. Both whites and blacks helped the slaves.

The map at right shows the main escape routes. Escape was least difficult for slaves living near northern states such as Ohio. The Ohio River froze in winter and was easy to cross. Slaves living in the Deep South—in states such as Mississippi and Alabama—had much farther to travel to freedom.

As the map shows, one escape route led through Florida. Florida's Seminole Indians welcomed escaped slaves. In contrast, slaves avoided Indian Territory (now Oklahoma). The Cherokee there supported slavery. While no one knows the exact number, around 50,000 people may have used the Underground Railroad on their journey from slavery to freedom.

Follow the Drinking Gourd

Follow the drinking gourd!
Follow the drinking gourd!
For the old man is a-waiting
  for to carry you to freedom
If you follow the drinking gourd.
When the sun comes back, and
  the first quail calls.
Follow the drinking gourd.
For the old man is a-waiting for to
  carry you to freedom
If you follow the drinking gourd.

The riverbank makes a very good road,
The dead trees will show you the way.
Left foot, peg foot, traveling on,
  Follow the drinking gourd.

The river ends between two hills,
  Follow the drinking gourd.
There's another river on the other side,
  Follow the drinking gourd.

When the great big river meets
  the little river,
  Follow the drinking gourd.
For the old man is a-waiting for to
  carry you to freedom
If you follow the drinking gourd.

The photo above shows Harriet Tubman (far left) and her husband (third from left) with former slaves. At left is a song that escaping slaves used to guide them. The "drinking gourd" is the Little Dipper, whose handle contains the North Star.

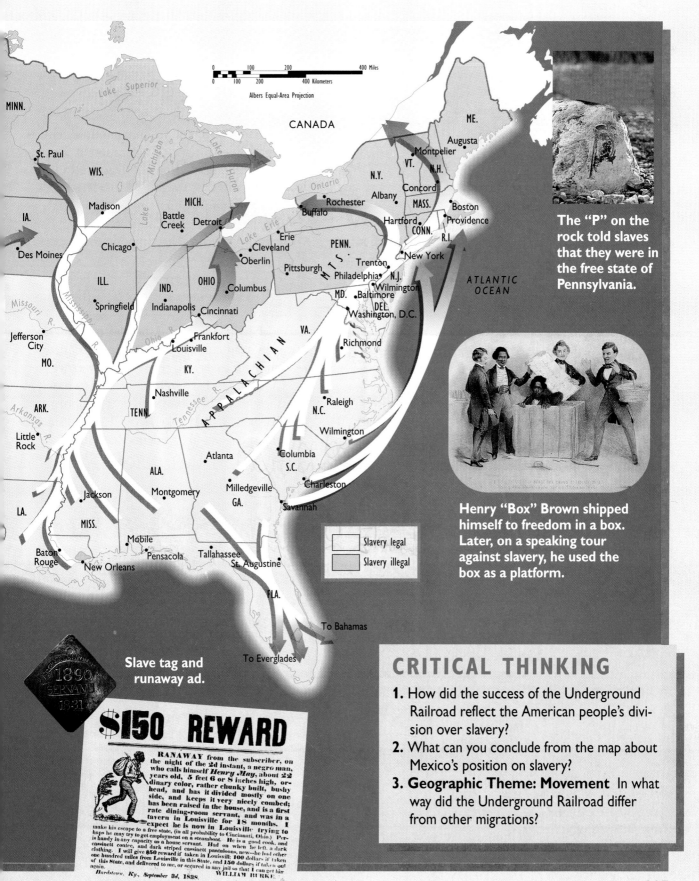

The "P" on the rock told slaves that they were in the free state of Pennsylvania.

Slavery legal
Slavery illegal

Henry "Box" Brown shipped himself to freedom in a box. Later, on a speaking tour against slavery, he used the box as a platform.

Slave tag and runaway ad.

$150 REWARD

RANAWAY from the subscriber, on the night of the 2d instant, a negro man, who calls himself *Henry May*, about 22 years old, 5 feet 6 or 8 inches high, ordinary color, rather chunky built, bushy head, and has it divided mostly on one side, and keeps it very nicely combed; has been raised in the house, and is a first rate dining-room servant, and was in a tavern in Louisville for 18 months. I expect he is now in **Louisville** trying to make his escape to a free state, (in all probability to Cincinnati, Ohio.) Perhaps he may try to get employment on a steamboat. He is a good cook, and is handy in any capacity as a house servant. Had on when he left, a dark cassinett coatee, and dark striped cassinett pantaloons, new—he had other clothing. I will give $50 reward if taken in Louisvill; 100 dollars if taken one hundred miles from Louisville in this State, and 150 dollars if taken out of this State, and delivered to me, or secured in any jail so that I can get him again.

Bardstown, Ky., September 3d, 1838. WILLIAM BURKE.

CRITICAL THINKING

1. How did the success of the Underground Railroad reflect the American people's division over slavery?
2. What can you conclude from the map about Mexico's position on slavery?
3. **Geographic Theme: Movement** In what way did the Underground Railroad differ from other migrations?

Times have changed since Susan B. Anthony's day—in some ways. Today as many as 7 million women run their own businesses in the United States. When they start their own businesses, many face problems. Marilu Meyer asked her bank for a loan to start a construction company. Bank officials denied her the loan. Meyer found the money elsewhere. Her Castle Construction Corporation, based in Chicago, now earns $7 million a year. Sally Fox (above) was given seeds in 1982 for colored cotton. She now runs a company called Natural Cotton Colours, Inc., that has among its customers Levi Strauss.

Yet when they tried to take part in the meeting, they found themselves silenced. Men angrily claimed that it was not a woman's place to speak in public. Instead, the women were forced to sit behind a heavy curtain.

The views of those men were not unusual for the time. Most people believed that women should not play a role in public life. In the 1800s women had few legal or political rights. Women could not vote, sit on juries, or hold public office. Many laws treated women—especially married women—as children. In most states, a husband controlled any property his wife inherited and any wages she earned. A husband could also punish his wife, as long as he did not seriously harm her.

Single women had greater freedom. They had more control over their own lives and could manage their own property.

Reformers who had called for equality for African Americans now began to push for women's equality as well. In 1848 Lucretia Mott and Elizabeth Cady Stanton organized a meeting at Seneca Falls, New York. Some 100 men and women gathered to discuss women's rights. Stanton delivered a speech titled "Declaration of Sentiments." Modeled on the Declaration of Independence, the speech declared that "all men and women are created equal." The convention delegates voted to approve this declaration. They went on to demand equality for women at work, school, church, and before the law. They also called for women's **suffrage**—the right to vote.

Many people found the idea of women's rights ridiculous. At a meeting in Ohio, a minister suggested that women were weak and helpless. Therefore, he said, women should not be allowed to vote. Sojourner Truth, who had spoken so well against slavery, spoke out for women:

This drawing shows a husband and wife struggling over who has the right to "wear the pants in the family," that is, who should rule the household.

Sojourner Truth (left), Elizabeth Cady Stanton (center), and Susan B. Anthony (right) were important leaders in the early struggle for women's rights.

“That man over there says women need to be helped into carriages and lifted over ditches, and to have the best place everywhere. Nobody ever helps me into carriages or over puddles, or gives me the best place. And ain't I a woman? Look at my arm! I have [plowed] and planted and gathered into barns. . . . And ain't I a woman?”

Among those who joined the growing women's movement was Susan B. Anthony. A Quaker, Anthony had been active in the temperance and antislavery movements. A skilled organizer, she built the women's movement into a national organization.

As a single woman, Anthony was particularly concerned that women get equal treatment in the workplace. To be free, she said, a woman "must have a purse of her own." To this end, Anthony worked for laws that would give married women rights to their own property and wages. New York passed the first such law in 1860.

Other states in the Northeast and Midwest soon passed similar laws.

The right of women to vote, however, stayed beyond reach. When Anthony tried to vote in the presidential election of 1872, she was arrested and fined. Women would be denied suffrage for years to come.

SECTION REVIEW

1. Key Terms caucus, abolitionist, Underground Railroad, suffrage

2. People and Places William Lloyd Garrison, Frederick Douglass, Sojourner Truth, Harriet Tubman, Susan B. Anthony, Seneca Falls

3. Comprehension How did abolitionists try to influence public opinion?

4. Comprehension What was the relationship between the abolitionist movement and the women's rights movement?

5. Critical Thinking What difficulties did women face in trying to gain equal rights with men in the mid-1800s?

SKILLS: Writing an Essay

LEARN

We all have ideas floating around in our heads. Some are simple, others more complex. These ideas represent our own personal views of life. One way to express your personal ideas about an issue is through an essay.

An essay begins with an **introduction**. This should clearly state the subject of the essay and suggest the author's viewpoint or opinion. It should also grab the reader's attention in an interesting way. The **body** of the essay is made up of one or more development paragraphs. Here the author presents facts and examples that support the opinion in the introduction. An essay should end with a **conclusion**. This should be one paragraph that restates and supports the author's opinion.

Your essay needs a beginning, middle, and ending. Within these guidelines there is still room for originality. You may want to use humor, personal stories, or other creative ways to gain the reader's interest.

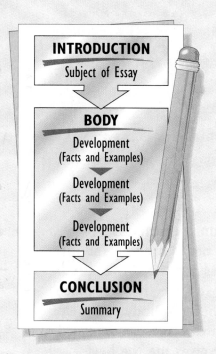

INTRODUCTION
Subject of Essay

BODY
Development
(Facts and Examples)

Development
(Facts and Examples)

Development
(Facts and Examples)

CONCLUSION
Summary

PRACTICE

Read the subsection titled "The Call for Women's Rights" in Section 3 of this chapter. Think about writing an essay on this subject.

1. Is this a good topic for an essay? Why or why not?

2. What is one argument in support of equal rights for women in the mid-1800s?

3. Who might have opposed equal rights for women? Why?

APPLY

4. Write an essay, choosing from the following chapter subjects: (1) anti-immigrant feelings in the mid-1800s; (2) the temperance movement; (3) the Underground Railroad; (4) women's rights. After you have finished the first draft, revise your essay. Make sure to check for grammar and spelling errors.

4 A New American Culture

SECTION GUIDE

Main Idea
American writers and artists began to create works reflecting American culture.

Goals
As you read, look for answers to these questions:

1 What was the inspiration for American writers and artists before the 1820s?

2 Who were some leading New England writers in the mid-1800s?

3 How did painters change their style to reflect new attitudes toward the nation?

Key Terms
passive resistance
Hudson River School

N 1818 A CRITIC wrote about American culture in a British magazine. The critic, Sydney Smith, decided that there was none. Americans were too busy clearing land and building towns to write books or create art, Smith wrote. After all, "In the four corners of the globe, who reads an American book? Or goes to an American play? Or looks at an American picture or statue?" Smith had a point. Yet even as Smith wrote, one writer was moving in a new direction. The writer was Washington Irving.

Early American Literature

Early American writers and artists copied European styles and subjects because they thought it was the only way to produce great works. They also viewed the United States as backward. The spirit of democracy and equality that swept through the country in the mid-1800s changed that attitude. American writers and painters began to take pride in their country. American history and scenery became subjects of their work.

Washington Irving wrote about the Dutch-English heritage of New York State. He first became popular in 1809 with a spoof of New York history and politics known as *A History of New York . . . by Diedrich Knickerbocker.* Eleven years later he published a book of short stories that included "Rip Van Winkle." In that story, the title character falls asleep for twenty years and wakes up to find everything has changed.

James Fenimore Cooper also helped create a unique American literature. In *The Leatherstocking Tales,* a collection of five novels, he wrote about a wilderness scout named Natty Bumppo. These books, published between 1823 and 1841, include *Last of the Mohicans*, *The Pathfinder,* and *The*

The painting "Ichabod Crane and the Headless Horseman" was inspired by one of Washington Irving's stories.

Deerslayer. In them, Cooper portrayed American Indians with dignity and showed the ways in which white settlers misused the wilderness.

Edgar Allan Poe, one of the greatest of the early American writers, wrote mysteries, short stories, and poems. His horror stories continue to terrify readers. Poe's series of stories about a French private detective made him the father of the modern detective story.

New England Authors

By the 1840s American scholars were taking pride in their nation's culture. A movement began to create works that reflected a unique American philosophy and style. The man who led that movement was Ralph Waldo Emerson.

Emerson taught that it was important for people to truly understand themselves. In doing so, they would develop a set of "inner rules" to guide their lives. In a 1837 speech, he urged American scholars to free themselves from their European roots and develop their own way of thinking. They should learn about life not just from books but from nature as well, he said.

Emerson's ideas attracted many young writers and thinkers. They made New England a center for American literature. Nathaniel Hawthorne wrote novels about spiritual conflict. The most famous of these, *The Scarlet Letter*, was set in Puritan Massachusetts and explored the human suffering that results from sin.

American history was an important theme in the work of a New England poet, Henry Wadsworth Longfellow. Another Massachusetts poet, John Greenleaf Whittier, wrote celebrations of country life. He also used his poetry to attack slavery.

Politics and Literature

One of the most original American thinkers of the mid-1800s was Henry David Thoreau (THAWR-o). A student of

Two New England authors, novelist Nathaniel Hawthorne (top) and poet Henry Wadsworth Longfellow (bottom).

Thoreau wrote *Walden* while living in a cabin he built by Walden Pond in Massachusetts.

Emerson's, Thoreau believed in living simply and in harmony with nature. In 1845 Thoreau moved into a a cabin on the wooded shores of Walden Pond near Concord, Massachusetts. He explained why:

❝I went to the woods because I wished to live deliberately, to front only the essential facts of life, and see if I could not learn what it had to teach, and not, when I came to die, discover that I had not lived.❞

For two years Thoreau lived alone, writing about his life and the nature around him. These writings were collected in a book entitled *Walden,* published in 1854.

Perhaps Thoreau's most powerful message was contained in his essay "Civil Disobedience." In it, he said that people should not obey laws they consider unjust. They should not protest with violence, he wrote. Rather, they should peacefully refuse to obey those laws. Thoreau practiced what he preached. Rather than pay taxes to support the Mexican War, Thoreau went to jail. This practice of passive resistance influenced future world leaders such as Mohandas K. Gandhi in India and Martin Luther King, Jr., in the United States.

Margaret Fuller was another New England writer whose work touched on political themes. Her cause was women's rights. Fuller was a friend of Emerson's and edited a magazine, *The Dial*. She also published a best-selling book, *Woman in the Nineteenth Century*. The book was a rallying cry for women's rights. "We would have every . . . barrier thrown down," she wrote. "We would have every path laid open to Woman as freely as to Man."

New York Writers

Herman Melville and Walt Whitman, two of the most original writers of the 1850s, were New Yorkers. Melville drew on his experience as a sailor in his books. *Moby-Dick*, published in 1851, is considered by many to be one of the greatest American novels of all time. *Moby-Dick* uses a whale hunt as a way of exploring the forces of good and evil in the human spirit.

Poet Walt Whitman wanted to create a special literature that would reflect the character of the country. His poetry expresses his faith in democracy, in the goodness of nature, and in the young American nation. In his introduction to *Leaves of Grass* he wrote, "The United States themselves are essentially the greatest poem."

The Visual Arts

In the mid-1800s American artists began to develop a unique style of painting landscapes. Their work reflected their pride in America's natural beauty.

Around 1825 Thomas Cole began painting landscapes in a simple, direct style.

Cole became a leader of a group of American artists who often painted the Hudson River valley in New York State. Called the Hudson River School, this group of artists painted quiet scenes of mountains, forests, and rivers.

George Caleb Bingham's paintings, on the other hand, reflected the energy of life on the frontier. He painted scenes of the Mississippi Valley. Other American artists began painting landscapes of the western plains and mountains.

John James Audubon used his talents to detail the birds and animals of America. Raised in France, Audubon moved to the United States at the age of eighteen. Audubon was fascinated by the birds and other wild creatures of his adopted country and traveled all over the continent to sketch them. Audubon's genius as an artist was in drawing wildlife as they appear in nature. His drawings were life-size and seemed to capture a "moment in time."

Audubon was famous for his detailed paintings of wildlife, such as the birds shown above.

SECTION REVIEW

1. Key Terms passive resistance, Hudson River School

2. People Edgar Allan Poe, Ralph Waldo Emerson, Henry David Thoreau, Margaret Fuller, Walt Whitman, John James Audubon

3. Comprehension Compare any two of the American writers described in this section. How were they alike? How were they different?

4. Comprehension How did American art change between the early 1800s and the mid-1800s?

5. Critical Thinking Why are Thoreau's ideas still powerful today?

Summary

1. In the mid-1800s famine and political and economic changes in Europe brought millions of immigrants to the United States. In response, some native-born Americans formed groups that opposed immigration.

2. The Second Great Awakening gave rise to reform movements in the 1830s and 1840s. Reformers pushed for better conditions for workers, free public education, better care for prisoners and the mentally ill, and temperance.

3. Many states ended property requirements for voters and gave more people a say in government. The abolitionist movement called for an end to slavery. The Underground Railroad helped slaves escape to freedom. Women began to question their own lack of rights. At the Seneca Falls Convention they called for equal rights and women's suffrage. However, progress on equal rights for women and African Americans was slow.

4. The new spirit of democracy and pride in the nation changed the attitudes of American artists and writers. They turned away from European styles and subjects and focused on scenes and stories of American life.

Graphic Summary

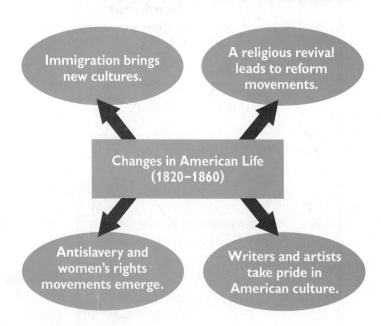

Immigration brings new cultures.

A religious revival leads to reform movements.

Changes in American Life (1820–1860)

Antislavery and women's rights movements emerge.

Writers and artists take pride in American culture.

Review

KEY TERMS

Define the terms in the following pairs.
1. prejudice; nativist
2. abolitionist; suffrage
3. strike; Second Great Awakening
4. steerage; famine

COMPREHENSION

1. What attracted European immigrants to the United States in the mid-1800s?
2. Why did Irish immigration show a sharp increase after 1845?
3. What steps did nativists take against immigrants in the mid-1800s?
4. How were educational opportunities limited for African Americans in the 1800s?
5. How were prisoners and the mentally ill treated in the 1840s? What changes did reformers try to make in those conditions?
6. What steps were taken in the 1830s and 1840s to expand democracy in the United States?
7. How did Frederick Douglass become a leader of the abolition movement?
8. What were the delegates' demands at the Seneca Falls Convention?
9. What was Ralph Waldo Emerson's message to American writers and scholars?
10. What is passive resistance? How did Henry David Thoreau practice it?

Places to Locate

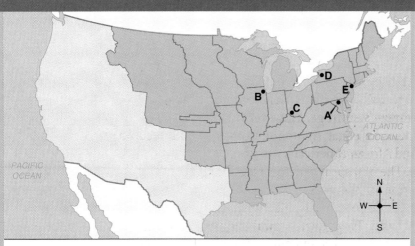

Match the letters on the map with the places that are listed below. Then explain the importance of each place.

1. Buffalo   3. Newark   5. Chicago
2. Baltimore   4. Cincinnati

Geographic Theme: Movement Explain the push-pull factors of immigration.

Skill Review

Write a short essay on how the spirit of democracy and equality in the mid-1800s influenced the writers and artists of that time. When you have completed your essay, check it by answering the following questions:

1. Does the introduction of the essay state the subject of the essay and your opinion on the subject?
2. Does the body of the essay provide details that support the opinion in the introduction?

3. Does the conclusion of the essay restate and support your opinion?
4. Is the essay written clearly and logically, with no grammar or spelling errors?

CRITICAL THINKING

1. Recognizing Cause and Effect How did the Second Great Awakening influence the reform movements of the 1830s and 1840s?
2. Making Judgments Reformers called for changes in the treatment of prisoners. Do you think these reforms were necessary? Explain.

PORTFOLIO OPTIONS

1. Civics Connection Horace Mann once said that an educated citizenry is more necessary to democracies than it is to other forms of government. Do you agree? Organize a class debate to argue the issue.
2. Writing Connection Imagine you are a slave escaping on the Underground Railroad. Write an account of your reasons for escaping and describe your experiences along the way.
3. Contemporary Connection What kinds of reform movements exist in American society today? What areas of American life are the movements trying to improve? Do you think they are succeeding? Choose one area that you think needs reform and write a paragraph explaining why.
4. Timeline Connection Copy the chapter timeline. Which events were connected to reform movements? Which event had an impact on immigration to the United States? Now add other events from the chapter you think should be included and explain why.

Go West! In the early to mid-1800s thousands of Americans heeded that call. Traveling in covered wagons, families headed for farmlands in Texas and Oregon. Gold seekers set off for California. Mormons in search of religious freedom settled in Utah. Meanwhile, a United States victory in the Mexican War brought the nation vast new lands.

1800

1811

1822

1833

1810 Mexican revolt against Spain begins

1821 Mexican independence

1836 Texas declares independence

1836 Battle of the Alamo

1836 Battle of San Jacinto

1836 Republic of Texas established

CHAPTER 17

The Westward Movement (1810–1853)

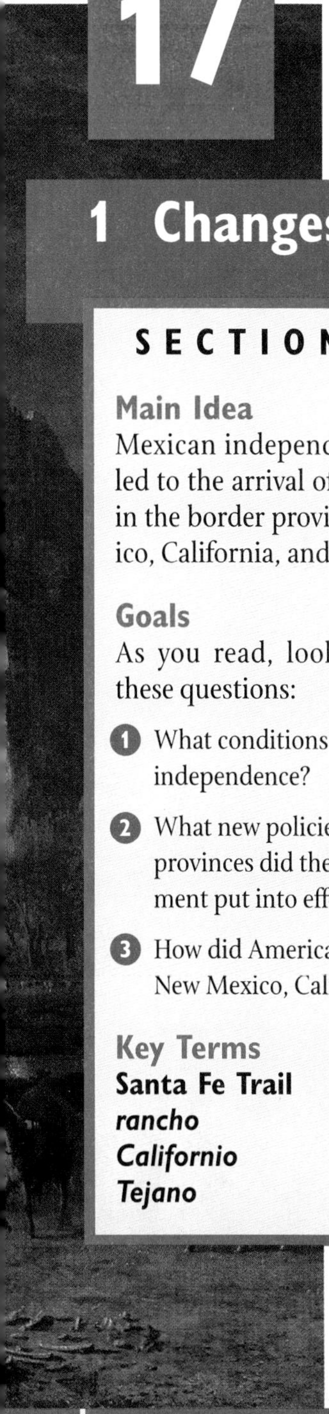

1 Changes in the Spanish Borderlands

SECTION GUIDE

Main Idea

Mexican independence from Spain led to the arrival of more Americans in the border provinces of New Mexico, California, and Texas.

Goals

As you read, look for answers to these questions:

1. What conditions led to Mexican independence?
2. What new policies toward the provinces did the Mexican government put into effect?
3. How did Americans change life in New Mexico, California, and Texas?

Key Terms

Santa Fe Trail
rancho
Californio
Tejano

1844 — 1855

- 1844 Polk elected President
- 1847 Mormon migration to Utah
- 1849 California Gold Rush
- 1853 Gadsden Purchase

FATHER MIGUEL HIDALGO, parish priest in the small Mexican town of Dolores, was upset. For years he had tried to improve the life of his people. He had taught them to keep honeybees, make tile, raise silkworms, tan leather, and make wine. However, all these went against the principle of mercantilism. By law, manufactured goods were supposed to come from Spain. To enforce the law, Spanish officials had come to Dolores and put an end to Hidalgo's activities.

Mexico's First Call for Revolt

In protest, early on September 16, 1810, Hidalgo rang the bells of his church. As the townspeople gathered, he asked, "Will you make the effort to get back from the hated Spaniards the land stolen from your forefathers three centuries ago?" Hidalgo's speech became known as the *Grito de Dolores,* or "Cry of Dolores." It was Mexico's first call for revolt.

Thousands rallied to Hidalgo's call for independence. The rebellion failed, however. Hidalgo was captured and executed by the Spanish army. (Today Hidalgo is remembered as the father of Mexican independence.)

Mexican Independence

The independence movement faded away, except for brief flare-ups. In 1821, Agustín de Iturbide (ee-toor-BEE-day) took over. He had so much support from the Mexican people that Spain had to give in. As of June 30, 1821, Mexico was independent—and not a shot had been fired. Iturbide made himself emperor.

A revolt broke out against Iturbide's harsh rule. It was led by Antonio López de Santa Anna. He would rule Mexico off and on for the next thirty years.

Opening Up the Border

Spain did not allow foreigners or foreign trade in its border provinces. With independence, Mexico opened up its borders to trade with the United States. Mexico also allowed foreigners to settle in its territory. The government did set two conditions. Settlers had to become citizens of Mexico, and they had to become Catholics.

American traders had seen the chance of profit in Santa Fe, in the province of New Mexico. Imported goods in the region came from Veracruz, some 1,500 miles away. Americans who had tried to enter Spanish territory, however, had been jailed or expelled.

An independent Mexico was just what trader William Becknell of Missouri wanted. As soon as he heard the news, he set out for Santa Fe with four companions and a caravan of goods such as hardware, cloth, needles, and china. Becknell made a handsome profit. He also earned the name of father of the Santa Fe Trail.

In 1824 Becknell became the first western trader to carry his goods in Con-

The Conestoga, or "covered wagon."

estoga wagons. As you read earlier, these huge wagons were first used in Pennsylvania. In the West they were known as "covered wagons" or "prairie schooners." (A schooner is a type of sailing ship.) Each wagon could carry about 5,000 pounds. Three pairs of oxen, mules, or horses were needed to pull a loaded wagon.

Many Americans who crossed into New Mexico's Rio Grande Valley decided to stay. The new settlers were often good with their hands. They built mills and brick kilns. They were blacksmiths, tinsmiths, and gunsmiths. Their skills and labor brought new prosperity to New Mexico.

Changing California

Mexican independence brought change to California's missions as well. In 1833 the Mexican Congress ordered the missions to turn over half their lands to the Indians.

Despite the order, most mission land ended up in the hands of *rancheros.* These landowners lived on ranchos, large land grants awarded by the government. There had been only twenty ranchos in California under Spanish rule. After Mexican independence this number rose to 500.

This painting from the late 1870s shows Mexican *vaqueros* in a horse corral. American cowboys of the West adopted *vaquero* clothing styles and ranching techniques.

The Thomas Gilcrease Institute of American History and Art, Tulsa

The *ranchos* were like feudal estates. Most of the mission Indians ended up working on the *ranchos* for no more than food, clothing, and shelter. The Indians did the hard work in tending fields and herds.

A person who had lived in California and had any Spanish ancestors was known as a *Californio.* The *Californios'* lives centered around community and family activities. Visiting and entertaining neighbors were common. Such entertaining usually included singing and dancing. Rodeos and fiestas drew neighbors from miles around.

Like the other Mexican provinces, California moved toward freer trade. Yankee ships began to arrive regularly on the California coast. From New England they brought a cargo of manufactured goods. They traded these goods for hides and tallow (animal fat). Tallow was used for candles and soap. A handful of the Yankee traders stayed in California and became Mexican citizens.

The Texas Borderland

In 1821 Texas had about 4,000 *Tejanos,* or Mexicans living in Texas. *Tejano* ranchers had grown rich by rounding up wild cattle and killing them for their hides. These cattle—the Texas longhorns—were descendants of cattle the Spanish had brought to the region in the early 1700s. The longhorns were a tough breed. They could travel miles without water, run fast, and survive extreme heat and cold.

On the ranches *vaqueros* (vah-KAYR-os) did the work. These cowhands worked on the open range. They herded cattle from horseback using lariats to rope them. *Vaqueros* wore practical clothes. To keep off the sun and rain they wore wide-brimmed sombreros on their heads. Leather chaps protected their legs from thorny brush. High-heeled boots with spurs helped *vaqueros* ride better. Cowboys of the American West would later adopt many of the styles and methods of the *vaqueros*.

CONNECTING WITH WORLD EVENTS

RUSSIANS IN CALIFORNIA

If not for some twists of history, today's Californians might be citizens of Russia. Led by explorer Vitus Bering, Russians first landed on the North American mainland in 1741. They hauled in what was probably the largest fur catch in history.

As the fur trade grew, Russia needed a settlement. In 1812, about 80 miles north of present-day San Francisco, builders raised the redwood walls of "Rossiya" (an ancient name for Russia). Later it was called Fort Ross.

Colonists built and tended farms and orchards. The population of Russian, Aleutian, and Indian families reached about 400. Over time, however, heavy fur hunting nearly wiped out the animal population. Also, American settlers spread across the region. In 1842 the Russians sold the contents of Fort Ross to an American, John Sutter, and left for home.

Anglo-Americans in Texas

Before Mexican independence, Moses Austin of Missouri had asked to settle in Texas. Spain granted his request and gave him a large land grant. Spain had hoped Austin would help defend the area from both illegal American settlers and Comanche Indians. Austin died before the move. Stephen Austin, his son, fulfilled his father's dream. In 1821 he led the first group of Americans to the Austin grant.

The Austin settlement opened a wedge on the Texas–United States border for further

Unlike Mexican towns, Anglo-American towns did not follow a grid pattern. This is what Austin, Texas, looked like in 1840.

Stephen Austin founded the first Anglo-American settlement in Texas.

settlement. Austin was just the first of about 25 people who were given large grants of land in return for bringing in settlers.

Texas boomed as a result of this policy. By 1830 the population had swelled to about 30,000. Anglo-Americans (English-speaking Americans) outnumbered *Tejanos* six to one. Free African Americans were among the settlers. However, nine out of ten African Americans in Texas were slaves.

Although Anglo-Americans had agreed to become Mexican citizens, they still thought like Americans. You could see this in the look of their towns. Mexican towns had a plaza (public square) and church in the center. Their buildings were of stone or adobe bricks plastered with mud. In contrast, Austin's town followed no overall plan. The houses were log cabins. It had the look of America's westward frontier.

Rising Tensions

Anglo-Americans also held onto strong ideas about their freedoms. They did not want Mexico's government meddling in their affairs. They were especially upset when the Mexican government ended slavery in 1829. Austin convinced the government not to apply the new law to Texas.

Mexico was beginning to have second thoughts about the Americans and about its settlement policy. In 1830 Mexico closed Texas to Anglo-American settlers and banned the introduction of more slaves. It also placed high tariffs on U.S. goods. Yet Mexico was unable to stop the Anglo-American population from growing. Illegal immigrants from the United States continued to cross the border into Texas.

SECTION REVIEW

1. Key Terms Santa Fe Trail, *rancho, Californio, Tejano*

2. People and Places Miguel Hidalgo, Agustín de Iturbide, William Becknell, Stephen Austin, New Mexico, California, Texas

3. Comprehension How did New Mexico and California change after Mexican independence?

4. Comprehension What factors contributed to the rapid population growth of Texas in the 1820s?

5. Critical Thinking How might trade bring about change to a community?

2 The Texas Revolution

SECTION GUIDE

Main Idea

Texans, led by Sam Houston, revolted against Mexico in 1835. After heavy fighting, Texas established an independent republic in 1836.

Goals

As you read, look for answers to these questions:

1. What caused the crisis in relations between Texas and Mexico?

2. How did the Texans achieve independence from Mexico?

3. Why did Texas not immediately join the United States?

Key Terms

Battle of the Alamo
Battle of San Jacinto
annex

TOUGHNESS AND INDEPENDENCE were part of Sam Houston's heritage. After his father died, his strong and spirited mother took her nine children and moved from Virginia to Tennessee in two Conestoga wagons. When Houston was sixteen, he left home to live with the neighboring Cherokee Indians. He spent most of the next three years with the Cherokee. Adopted into their tribe, he learned their customs and their language. For the rest of his life, Houston would be a friend to the Indians.

Texas in Upheaval

In 1832 Houston moved to Texas to practice law. He found the region in upheaval. Tensions between the Mexican government and Texas settlers were rising. Some people resented that Texas was not a separate state within Mexico. Texas was only part of the Mexican state of Texas-Coahuila. Anglo-Americans objected to being forced to become Catholics. They were unhappy that official documents were in Spanish. They hated the 1830 laws that banned American immigration and placed tariffs on American goods.

Although upset, people could not agree on what to do. The most recent immigrants were for war—for breaking from Mexico altogether. They had strong hopes that the U.S. government would help them. Others, on the other hand, listened to the calm, patient voice of Stephen Austin. He took seriously his promise to obey the Mexican government. He would not support the disloyal talk of separation. Hoping for peaceful change, Austin set off for Mexico City.

At Austin's request, President Santa Anna lifted the restrictions on immigration. Meanwhile, the legislature of Texas-Coahuila acted on other complaints. Lawmakers increased local self-government. They approved the use of English in public documents. They also allowed Texans to practice their own religion. Such moves might have kept the Texans happy, but Santa Anna triggered a crisis.

Sam Houston

War Breaks Out in Texas

By 1834 Santa Anna had become Mexico's dictator. He ruled without any regard to law or people's rights. To strengthen his control over Texas, Santa Anna sent more troops and tax collectors into the province. This led to a skirmish over a cannon. The army tried to take back a cannon used for protection against the Indians. The Texans refused to give it back. Flying over the cannon was a white flag with the words, "Come and Take It." This clear challenge to the Mexican army meant war.

In December the Texans drove the Mexican forces from the Alamo. The Alamo was an old mission in San Antonio that was used as a fortress. In response to this insult, Santa Anna headed for Texas with a force of about 6,000 troops. The Texans were not prepared for this military challenge.

Susanna Dickinson (above) was one of the few Texan survivors of the Battle of the Alamo.

The Fight for the Alamo

William B. Travis and about 150 men held the Alamo. The small force included such famous frontiersmen as Davy Crockett and Jim Bowie. Several hundred other Texans were 100 miles away at Goliad under the command of James W. Fannin.

The only Texan with real army experience was Sam Houston. He had served under Andrew Jackson in the War of 1812. When put in command, however, he had no real power. He ordered both Travis and Fannin to withdraw from their positions. Both refused.

On February 23, 1836, Santa Anna and his troops attacked San Antonio. Santa Anna flew a red banner—the sign that no mercy would be shown, no prisoners taken. Travis responded by firing a cannon. The siege against the Alamo began the next day. Travis penned a letter during the

The fierceness of the hand-to-hand fighting at the Alamo can be seen in this painting. In the center, with his rifle raised overhead, stands Davy Crockett. Crockett and 182 others died defending the Alamo.

siege. "I shall never surrender nor retreat!" he wrote. More men, one with a family, slipped into the Alamo to help its defense.

The defenders managed to hold off the Mexican attack for twelve days. Then on the thirteenth day, Santa Anna ordered his men to go over the walls. The Texans greeted the attackers with a rain of cannon and rifle fire. The air was full of sounds—of bullet whistles, cannon booms, the cries and groans of dying men.

Suddenly it became quiet. The Texans had run out of ammunition. As the Mexicans poured over the Alamo walls, the Texans fought on in hand-to-hand combat. At day's end 183 defenders of the Alamo were dead. The **Battle of the Alamo** was over. Women and children were spared. Susanna Dickinson, wife of one of the defenders, was one of the few survivors. Santa Anna sent her to Sam Houston with a message: any further revolt would be put down just as harshly.

The Defeat of Santa Anna

Soon after the fall of the Alamo, Mexican troops attacked Fannin's force at Goliad. Although the Texans surrendered, Santa Anna ordered them all killed. Santa Anna's officers objected to the order, but he insisted. It was the only way, he thought, to destroy Texas resistance. More than 300 prisoners were shot. Santa Anna's cruelty further aroused all Texans.

Next, Santa Anna and his troops went after the remaining force led by Sam Houston. This force included both Anglo-Americans and *Tejanos.*

On April 21 Santa Anna's force had camped near the San Jacinto (SAN juh-SIN-toh) River, which flowed into Galveston Bay. Santa Anna had expected Houston to attack at dawn, but the attack never came. The Mexicans relaxed, and by afternoon much of the camp was sound asleep. Then at four o'clock the Texans quietly advanced. When close to the camp,

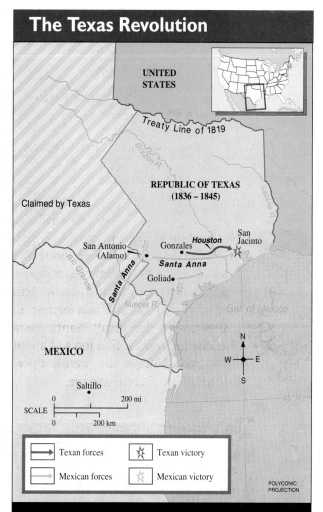

The Texas Revolution

GEOGRAPHY SKILLS: The Texas Revolution ended with the defeat of Santa Anna (below) and his troops at San Jacinto. **Critical Thinking:** How does the map suggest that tensions between Texas and Mexico continued after the war?

they came running and firing. "Remember the Alamo! Remember Goliad!" they screamed.

Santa Anna woke up to find the camp in turmoil. The Mexicans were quickly defeated, and Santa Anna himself was captured. With the **Battle of San Jacinto,** Texas won independence. Houston became a hero and a leader in the new Texas.

Despite Mexico's victories at the Alamo and Goliad, Sam Houston's surprise attack on Mexican troops at San Jacinto won Texas its independence. The battle lasted less than twenty minutes.

The Lone Star Republic

In September 1836 Texans raised a flag with a single star. They adopted a nickname, "Lone Star Republic" and proclaimed Texas a self-governing country. Sam Houston became its first president.

Many Texans did not plan to remain independent for long. They considered themselves Americans, and they wanted to be a part of the United States. They also felt unsafe because Mexico had refused to recognize their independence. In 1836 Texas asked Congress to be annexed, or added, to the Union. Many northerners objected. Texas, they argued, would become a slave state. They opposed any expansion of slavery. If Texas joined the Union, slave states would outnumber free states. This would give slave states a voting advantage in Congress. Some government leaders also feared that annexing Texas would mean war with Mexico. Congress refused Texas's request. Texas would remain an independent republic for almost ten more years.

Flag of the Lone Star Republic.

SECTION REVIEW

1. Key Terms Battle of the Alamo, Battle of San Jacinto, annex

2. People and Places Sam Houston, Santa Anna, William B. Travis, Alamo, Goliad

3. Comprehension What issues caused Texans to resent the Mexican government?

4. Comprehension How did the battles at the Alamo and San Jacinto differ? What was the outcome of each?

5. Critical Thinking Is there anything that Santa Anna could have done to prevent Texas's break with Mexico? Explain.

414

3 Across a Continent

SECTION GUIDE

Main Idea
Mountain men found routes to the West that later became trails for wagon trains of settlers crossing the continent.

Goals
As you read, look for answers to these questions:

1 What qualities did a mountain man need?

2 What was it like to travel on the Oregon Trail?

3 Why did Americans journey westward?

Key Terms
South Pass
Oregon Country
emigrant
Oregon Trail

Mountain men used traps like this to catch small animals.

I N 1822 ST. LOUIS was a rough young settlement on the very edge of the frontier. It was the place to go if you were heading farther west. If you wanted strong, able-bodied men for fur trapping, it was the place to advertise.

In February 1822 a small advertisement appeared in the St. Louis paper:

> **The subscriber wishes to hire 100 men, to ascend the river Missouri to its source, there to be employed for one, two, or three years.**

The ad was signed by William H. Ashley. Ashley headed one of four American fur-trading companies that had been formed after the Louisiana Purchase.

Jedediah Smith: Mountain Man

Sometime after that ad appeared, Jedediah (JED-uh-DY-uh) Smith, aged 23, knocked at Ashley's door. Smith told Ashley that he wanted to become a good hunter, learn about the Indians, explore the West, and make a living along the way. Ashley hired him, and Smith became a mountain man.

"Mountain men" was the name given to the adventurers who trapped furs and traded goods in and around the Rocky Mountains. Their lives were marked by hardship and danger. A mountain man spent much of the year alone or with a few companions, trapping animals such as mink, otter, and especially beaver. Beaver fur was valued for men's hats, both in the East and in Europe. To survive, the mountain men became skilled trackers and pathfinders. They were tough, able to get along with the Indians, and independent.

In the fall of 1823 Smith led a party of hunters to western Wyoming. In the winter snow Smith tried to cross the jagged peaks of the Teton Mountains, but had to give up and return to the Crow villages. Was there any other way west? he asked the Crow. Yes, they said. On a map marked out in sand, they pointed to a pass through the Rocky Mountains. It was south of the Tetons.

Braving a midwinter blizzard, Smith and his party set out and found South Pass. Unlike the more northern routes across the Rocky Mountains, South Pass was fairly low and open. It was a pass a wagon could get through. In the years to come, thousands would go through Wyoming's South Pass on their way west.

Smith headed for California in 1827. Some Mexicans were suspicious of him and jailed him as a spy. Released in 1828, Smith and his party headed northward along the coast toward Oregon. Along the way most of the party were killed by Umpqua Indians. Smith and a few others finally reached Fort Vancouver on the Columbia River.

The Oregon Country

Fort Vancouver was in the Oregon Country, a vast region of the Northwest. It included all the land surrounding the Columbia, Snake, and Fraser rivers. Since the 1790s both Britain and the United States had claimed the Oregon Country. In 1818 they had agreed to occupy the region together.

By the 1820s the Hudson's Bay Company of Canada had the region firmly in its control. Managing the company's fur-trading business in the Pacific Northwest was John McLoughlin. He ruled the territory firmly but fairly. The Indians respected him and called him "White Eagle." McLoughlin also made the outpost self-sufficient and prosperous.

Jedediah Smith was impressed with McLoughlin and with the country. Smith wrote a letter to the U. S. Secretary of War. The letter described the rich wheat crop, the fruit trees, and the fat livestock of Fort Vancouver. He also wrote about the many furs passing through Fort Vancouver.

Wagons rolling west left deep ruts along the Oregon Trail. These ruts are still visible today.

The British, Smith said, were taking over the Oregon Country, even though Americans could legally settle there. Smith made an important point. It was possible for Americans to cross the continent by wagons and thus reach Oregon Country.

The Oregon Trail

The first white migrants to cross the continent to Oregon were Methodist missionaries. Many came because of an 1833 article that appeared in a Methodist newspaper. The story told of a group of Nez Percé Indians who made a special trip to St. Louis. They had come in search of the "secret medicine" that allowed non-Indians to make such goods as guns, tools, and beads. The Nez Percé believed that through religious instruction they too could gain the power to make such goods.

The Methodists decided to send a missionary to Oregon. Jason Lee was the first. He settled in Oregon's fertile Willamette (wuh-LAM-it) Valley. Later missionaries included Marcus and Narcissa Whitman. They settled at Walla Walla, near the junction of the Snake and Columbia rivers.

In many ways, the Methodist missions were like those of the Spanish. Both tried to teach Indians the ways of white society as well as religion. The Methodist missionaries found few converts among the Indians. Their glowing reports of Oregon's rich farmland and forests, however, would draw thousands of newcomers.

The trickle of emigrants—people who leave one place for another—turned into a flood starting in 1843. To reach Oregon the emigrants traveled along the Oregon Trail. This trail started at Independence, Missouri. It crossed the Platte River and continued through South Pass into what is now northeast Utah. There the trail split. A branch of the trail, the California Trail, headed across the desert for California. The Oregon Trail continued north and west to the Columbia River.

Map labels:

CANADA

N

OREGON COUNTRY
Ft. Walla Walla
Columbia R.
Ft. Vancouver
Snake R.
Oregon Trail
Ft. Hall
ROCKY
South Pass
GREAT PLAINS
Missouri R.
Mississippi R.
Mormon Trail
Council Bluffs
California Trail
Ft. Bridger
Salt Lake City
Platte R.
Oregon Trail
Nauvoo
Carthage
ILL.
Sutter's Fort (Sacramento)
San Francisco
Monterey
M O U N T A I N S
Bent's Fort
Santa Fe Trail
St. Louis
Independence MO.
Old Spanish Trail
Colorado R.
Cimarron Cut-Off
Arkansas R.
Santa Fe
Cimarron R.
Los Angeles
San Diego
Gila R.
Red R.
Via Cape Horn
El Paso
MEXICO
PACIFIC OCEAN
Chihuahua
Rio Grande

SCALE
0 200 mi
0 200 km

GEOGRAPHY SKILLS: This map shows the major routes for traders and settlers heading west. **Critical Thinking:** Use the map scale to calculate the distance between Fort Walla Walla and Fort Vancouver. Why were forts built along the western trails?

This skillet was used by travelers heading West. Its "feet" allowed the travelers to cook over an open fire.

Life on the Trail

As of 1845, the travelers on the Oregon Trail had a guidebook to follow. The *Emigrants' Guide* explained everything. The biggest expense was getting a strong covered wagon and the animals to pull it. (Oxen were best because they were sturdier than horses.) Spare parts, heavy rope, and grease buckets were needed. For food, each adult was told to bring 200 pounds of flour, 150 pounds of bacon, 10 pounds of coffee, 20 pounds of sugar, and 10 pounds of salt. Other supplies might include dried beef, rice, dried beans, dried fruit, vinegar, and pickles.

People did not make the long journey alone. They traveled in wagon trains. Survival depended on working together. At the beginning of the journey one person was elected to be in charge. Rules were set and enforced. All of the men were expected to take turns on the night watch.

At the end of a day's travel, the wagons formed a large circle. Within the circle the

The Donner Party

During the winter of 1846–1847, far from the fighting of the Mexican War, a scene of horror and heroism was taking place in the Sierra Nevada. A group of 29 men, 15 women, and 43 children, led by George Donner, were heading for California by wagon. Using an untested route across the Sierra Nevada, the Donner Party became trapped in the mountains for the winter. William Eddy and others set out on foot to get help.

"On the night of [December] 15th the temperature dropped sharply," Eddy later wrote. "Dawn showed a thick crust upon the snow and ten men and five women uttered sad farewells to those who remained behind." For more than three weeks Eddy's group staggered through the snow. Finally, on January 10, they reached help:

> **"[W]e came to an open meadow and the brush shelters of a group of California Indians. The children were first to see us, rushing away in fright. . . . Their elders greeted us with extreme kindness. Tears actually coursed down their dark cheeks as they supported us to their huts and spread mats of woven rushes upon which we could rest. . . .**
>
> **They escorted us from one [Indian] village to the next, an Indian walking on either side of each one of us to support our faltering steps. . . . Their speech was [foreign] . . . yet every word and action conveyed their sympathy."**

The Indians guided Eddy to English-speaking settlers. A rescue team was sent into the mountains to save the others. Many there had died, including Eddy's wife and children. The survivors had eaten oxen, dogs, twigs, grass, mice, and their shoes. With nothing left, some had taken flesh from the dead in order to survive.

Forty-two people had died.

CRITICAL THINKING

1. How did the California Indians help Eddy and his companions?
2. Eddy also wrote that he could judge neither those who chose to eat human flesh nor those who chose not to. Why, in your opinion, did he feel this way?
3. Are there times when people do not have the right to judge others' actions? Explain.

oxen were herded and tents put up. The travelers might spend the evening gathered around a campfire to talk, sing, and dance.

The first travelers on the Oregon Trail were helped by the Indians along the way. Indians often brought game into their camps to exchange for cloth, needles, or other goods. As the number of travelers increased, however, the Indians, fearing the loss of their land, grew hostile. In time, Indian attacks became a further danger facing pioneers on the trail.

The Mormon Migration

In 1847 a different kind of wagon train set out on the Oregon Trail. Led by Brigham Young, this was a party of Mormons in search of a new home.

The Mormons belonged to the Church of Jesus Christ of Latter-Day Saints. This church had been founded by Joseph Smith in 1830. The Mormons believed in economic cooperation rather than competition. Cooperation helped the Mormons prosper. It also brought them conflict. Their neighbors viewed their cooperation as a form of monopoly. These neighbors were also upset by the Mormon practice of polygamy—allowing a man to have more than one wife at the same time.

Resentment turned to murder in 1844. An anti-Mormon mob in Illinois killed Joseph Smith. The next Mormon leader was Brigham Young. He decided to move his flock out of the United States.

In what became known as the Great Migration, the Mormons headed for Utah. They settled between the mountains and the desert near the Great Salt Lake. The Mormons hoped to be far from other settlements and free to live life as they chose. There they built Salt Lake City and started a prosperous community.

A key to success in Utah was sharing limited resources, such as water. This was new to people from the East, where there was plenty of rain. In the dry land of Utah,

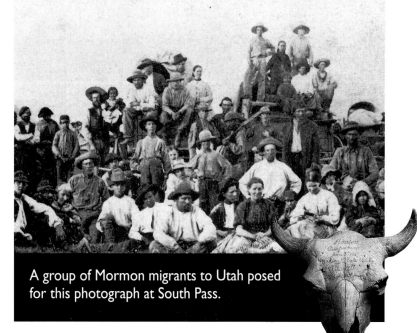

A group of Mormon migrants to Utah posed for this photograph at South Pass.

Brigham Young used buffalo skulls as trail markers during the Great Migration.

however, rivers were the main source of water. Indians, Spaniards, and Mexicans living in the dry Southwest had learned of the need to share water. The Mormons followed this practice.

The Mormons became expert at desert farming. With a system of canals, they diverted mountain streams to water their fields. They were the first Anglo-Americans to cooperate in the use of water.

SECTION REVIEW

1. Key Terms South Pass, Oregon Country, emigrant, Oregon Trail

2. People and Places Jedediah Smith, John McLoughlin, Marcus and Narcissa Whitman, Brigham Young, Rocky Mountains, Fort Vancouver, Utah

3. Comprehension How did Jedediah Smith help open up the West for the United States?

4. Comprehension Why did people migrate to Oregon and Utah?

5. Critical Thinking How did traveling west encourage both individual achievement and cooperation?

Daily Life

ON THE OREGON TRAIL

Their horse- or ox-drawn wagons inched forward at a couple of miles an hour, sometimes into a scorching sun or biting winter wind. People and possessions lurched each time the wagon hit a rock or a prairie dog hole. It was 2,000 miles and six months of discomfort—or worse. Between the 1840s and the 1870s some 350,000 people made this journey. At the end of the trail was a new life.

Re-creating life along the trail, a woman uses a campfire fueled by buffalo chips for cooking.

N

Fort Vancouver

Mt. Hood

Portland

Fort Walla Walla

Nez Percé Indians

BLUE MOUNTAINS

Shoshone Indians

Fort Boise

Snake R.

Fort Hall

South Pass

Great Salt Lake

Sublette Cut Off

Fort Bridger

THE NATIONAL Wagon Road Guide.

$420

"The living sea rolls onward, on!" proclaimed a guide for trail users (left). Herbal medicine, such as the kit at right, was one way the "sea" of migrants tried to deal with illness.

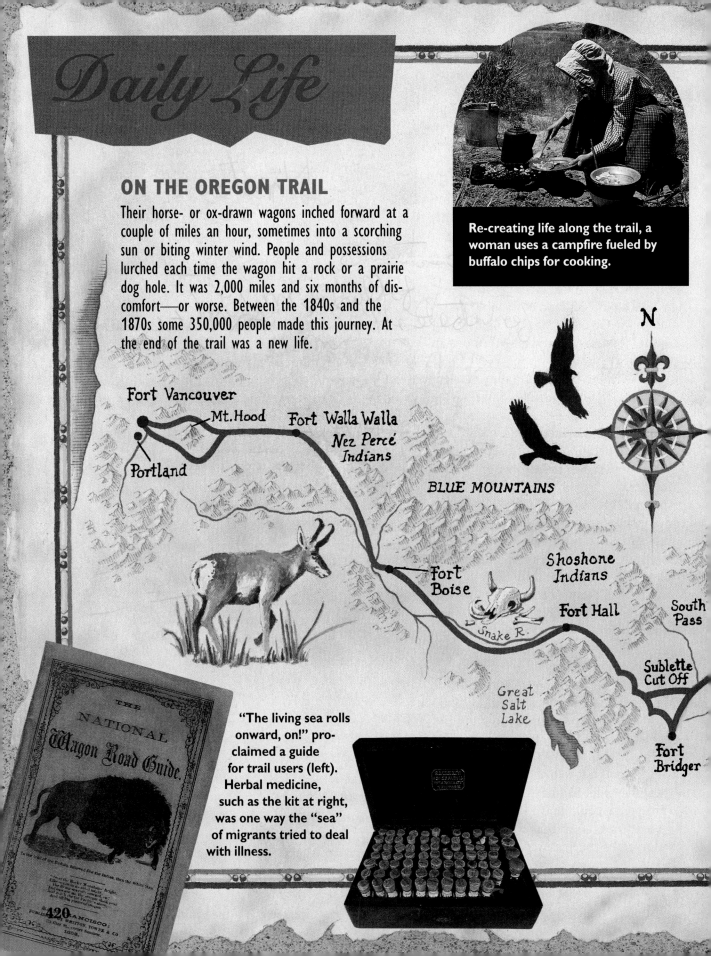

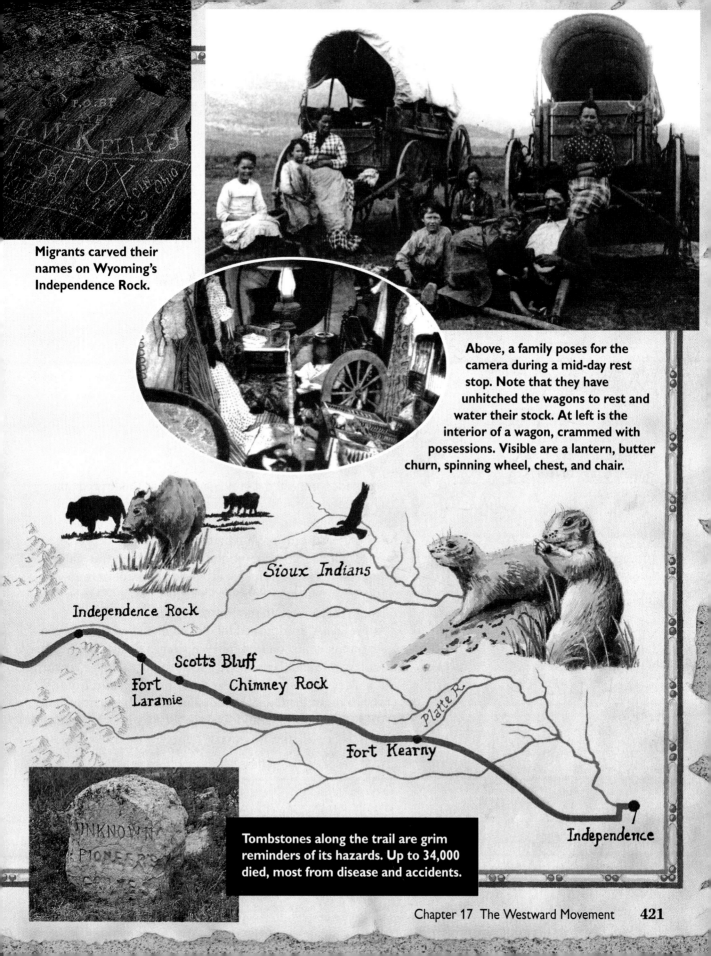

Migrants carved their names on Wyoming's Independence Rock.

Above, a family poses for the camera during a mid-day rest stop. Note that they have unhitched the wagons to rest and water their stock. At left is the interior of a wagon, crammed with possessions. Visible are a lantern, butter churn, spinning wheel, chest, and chair.

Sioux Indians

Independence Rock

Scotts Bluff

Fort Laramie

Chimney Rock

Platte R.

Fort Kearny

Independence

Tombstones along the trail are grim reminders of its hazards. Up to 34,000 died, most from disease and accidents.

4 The Mexican War

SECTION GUIDE

Main Idea
Through negotiation with Britain and war with Mexico, the United States expanded its borders to the Pacific Ocean.

Goals
As you read, look for answers to these questions:

1. Why was the presidential election of 1844 important?

2. What were the causes and effects of the Mexican War?

Key Terms
manifest destiny
Mexican War
Bear Flag Revolt
cede
Mexican Cession

A campaign poster from the 1844 election. Note the spelling error.

I N 1844 HENRY CLAY, the Great Compromiser, was running for President. People again raised the issue of annexing Texas. Clay opposed annexation. "Annexation and war with Mexico are identical," he said. Andrew Jackson, still the nation's leading Democrat, was delighted at Clay's unpopular stand. "Clay is a dead political duck," he said. Jackson was right.

Polk and Oregon

Jackson backed James K. Polk, a Tennessee slaveholder, for President. Polk believed that annexing Texas was both necessary and right. To gain northern support, he also urged "the re-occupation of Oregon." One of his campaign slogans was "Fifty-four forty or fight!" The parallel of 54°40′ was the northern boundary of the Oregon Country.

Polk's ideas reflected a growing feeling in the United States. Many Americans felt that it was the destiny of the nation to stretch from sea to sea. The Atlantic and the Pacific oceans, many felt, were our "natural boundaries." Taking Oregon, California, and Texas was, a newspaper wrote, the nation's **manifest destiny.** That is, expansion was not only good, it was bound to happen. After Polk's victory in the 1844 election, manifest destiny became government policy.

As President, Polk pushed the British into talks over Oregon. Each nation compromised. They agreed to divide the Oregon Country at the 49th parallel. The 49th parallel was already the border between Canada and the United States from the Great Lakes to the Rocky Mountains. The agreement of 1846 extended this line of latitude west to the Pacific Ocean. (Today this line is still the boundary between the United States and Canada.)

Trouble with Mexico

After Polk's election, Congress quickly voted to annex Texas. When Texas entered the Union in December 1845, the Mexican government was outraged. Adding to the tension was Texas's bold claim that the Rio Grande was its southern boundary. Mexico insisted that Texas included only the land as far south

This painting shows a battle in the Mexican War at Molino del Rey, a fortress outside Mexico City. The fortress contained an ammunition plant. The battle ended when the warehouse caught fire and the building blew up.

and west as the Nueces (noo-AY-sis) River. President Polk's efforts to negotiate with Mexico failed.

In January 1846 a new Mexican government came to power. It claimed that Mexican territory extended as far as the Sabine River. In effect, Mexico was claiming nearly all of Texas. Mexico announced it was ready to go to war to defend that claim. In response, Polk ordered General Zachary Taylor to move his troops to the Rio Grande, inside the disputed territory. Mexico saw that advance as an act of war.

A Mexican force crossed the river and attacked the American troops. Polk believed that the United States had to respond. Mexico, Polk told Congress, "has invaded our territory and shed American blood upon American soil." Congress reacted in May 1846 by declaring war on Mexico. The Mexican War had begun.

Early Phases of the War

Most Americans in the South and West eagerly supported the Mexican War. In the Northeast, however, people spoke angrily against it. The Massachusetts legislature called it a war of conquest.

Part of Polk's war plan was to seize New Mexico and California. Not long after the declaration of war, an American force led by Stephen Kearny (KAHR-nee) left Fort Leavenworth, Kansas, and headed for New Mexico. As the soldiers headed across the plains, they sang such verses as:

“Old Colonel Kearny, you can bet,
Will keep the boys in motion,
Till Yankee Land includes the sand
On the Pacific Ocean. ”

The Americans took Santa Fe, and with it all of New Mexico, without firing a shot. Kearny then headed for California.

The Bear Flag Revolt

In California, meanwhile, a group of newcomers led by John C. Frémont rebelled against Mexican authority. In

The Bear Flag

The Mexican War, 1846–1848

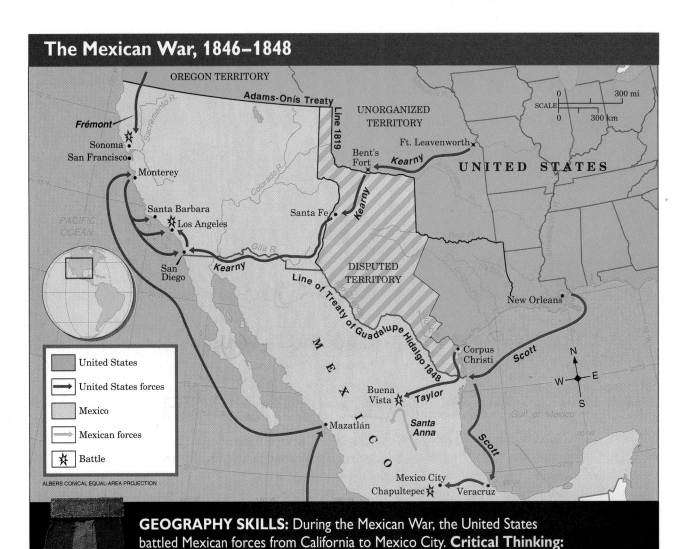

GEOGRAPHY SKILLS: During the Mexican War, the United States battled Mexican forces from California to Mexico City. **Critical Thinking:** Why might southerners and westerners have supported the war while northerners opposed it?

This medal was awarded to an American veteran of the Mexican War.

what was known as the Bear Flag Revolt they seized Mariano G. Vallejo, a leader in Mexican California, and threw him in jail. Then they made a flag showing a grizzly bear and a single star and declared California the Bear Flag Republic.

By the fall of 1846, Kearny's troops joined the Americans rebelling against Mexican rule. By 1847 American control of California was unchallenged.

Defeating Mexico

United States forces invaded Mexico from two directions. General Taylor moved south from Texas, defeating Santa Anna's troops at Buena Vista in February 1847. The following month, General Winfield Scott landed at Veracruz and battled inland toward Mexico City.

Outside Mexico City, Scott met fierce resistance from defenders of Chapultepec, (chuh-POOL-tuh-pek). Chapultepec was a fortress, Mexico's national military school was also located there. About 1,000 Mexican soldiers and 100 cadets from the military school fought to the death to defend the fortress. Despite such determined resistance, Mexico City fell to Scott's

Many young men volunteered to fight in the war with Mexico. Pictured here are an army private (left) and a cabin boy in the U.S. Navy (right). After the war some soldiers chose to remain in Mexico or California.

troops in September 1847. Most of the fighting was over.

The Mexican War ended with the Treaty of Guadalupe Hidalgo (gwah-duh-LOOP-ay hih-DAHL-go) in 1848. In the treaty Mexico agreed to accept the Rio Grande as its northern boundary. It also recognized that Texas was part of the United States.

In the treaty, Mexico also **ceded** —gave up—a vast stretch of land between Texas and the Pacific coast. This land, called the **Mexican Cession,** included the present-day states of California, Nevada, Utah, and parts of Arizona, New Mexico, Colorado, and Wyoming. In return, the United States agreed to pay Mexico $15 million in cash. The United States also paid $3.25 million to Americans who claimed that the Mexican government owed them money. The war was a bitter defeat for Mexico, which lost almost half of its territory.

In 1853 Mexico sold the United States a strip of land across what is now southern New Mexico and Arizona for $10 million. The deal was known as the Gadsden Purchase. The Gadsden Purchase completed the present-day southwestern boundary of the United States.

SECTION REVIEW

1. Key Terms manifest destiny, Mexican War, Bear Flag Revolt, cede, Mexican Cession

2. People and Places James K. Polk, Zachary Taylor, Stephen Kearny, John C. Frémont, Winfield Scott, Rio Grande

3. Comprehension How did the idea of manifest destiny lead to a division of the Oregon Country?

4. Comprehension What strategy did the United States use to defeat Mexico?

5. Critical Thinking How could the Mexican War have been avoided? Explain your answer.

5 The California Gold Rush

SECTION GUIDE

Main Idea
The discovery of gold in California resulted in a flood of newcomers to the region.

Goals
As you read, look for answers to these questions:

1 What cultures existed in California before the gold rush?

2 What was life like in the mining camps and gold fields?

3 What were the effects of the gold rush?

Key Terms
California Gold Rush
forty-niner
boomtown

These forty-niners are sifting through gravel and mud for gold. Raw gold appeared as nuggets (right), flakes, or dust. Nuggets were often turned into coins, such as this one minted in San Francisco in 1852.

IN JANUARY 1848 a man named James Marshall was building a sawmill for John Sutter on California's American River. One day Marshall was inspecting the stream of water that drove the mill. Then, as he said later, "My eye was caught by something shining in the bottom of the ditch. I reached my hand down and picked it up; it made my heart thump, for I was certain it was gold." It was gold. Three days later Marshall stumbled into Sutter's office to show him the gold nuggets. Sutter was not happy about the find.

Sutter's California Dream
In 1834 John Sutter, a bankrupt shopkeeper from Switzerland, had set out for America to make his fortune. First he settled near St. Louis and tried farming. That did not work. Then he tried making trading trips to Santa Fe. That failed too. Finally in 1838 he headed for California.

The Mexican governor gave Sutter permission to set up a colony on the American River. From his base, Sutter began to expand his land grant. The news of gold disappointed Sutter. "I was convinced," he wrote, "that it would greatly interfere with my plans." The discovery of gold not only interfered with Sutter's plans, it changed the whole country.

The Rush for Gold
Word of the discovery at Sutter's Mill quickly spread. Sutter's fears came true. Great crowds of people rushed onto his land. The **California Gold Rush** of 1849 was on.

People dreamed of instant riches. Some found them. A gold seeker wrote home, "You know Bryant, the carpenter who used to work for Ebenezer Dixon, well, he has dug more gold in the last six months than a mule can pack." Tens of thousands of forty-niners, as they were called, made their way to California by land and sea. By 1850 California had a non-Indian population of 93,000.

For Sutter, the forty-niners became a nightmare. They shot and ate his cattle, trampled his fields, and camped on his land. Sutter lost everything. "Sick at heart and body," he left California.

Life in the Mining Camps

Mining camps mushroomed along the streams and rivers of the Sierra Nevada foothills. The colorful names of the camps hinted at the ups and downs of the miners' lives. They included Poker Flat, Hangtown, Fiddletown, Angels Camp, Whiskey Flat, Happy Camp, Murderers' Bar, Poverty Hill, and Gouge Eye.

The population of these boomtowns, towns that grow quickly, could swell almost overnight to several thousand. The population might disappear as quickly with news of a new gold find.

Most of the forty-niners were men. They were adventurers determined to make a fortune and return home rich. Only a small number brought their families with them to California. Although some women could be found laboring in the mines, most earned money by cooking, washing, and running boarding houses.

Miners from Other Countries

People from all over the world, especially China, came to California. By the end of 1851 one of every ten Californians was Chinese. Tens of thousands of young Chinese men signed up as indentured servants. They came to California to work in the gold fields for Chinese labor lords. They called California *Gam Saan,* or "the Golden Mountain." Like other forty-niners, they dreamed of striking it rich and then returning home.

CULTURAL MOSAIC

YUNG WING
(1828–1912)

Many Chinese immigrants arrived in California during the gold rush. A few, however, headed to the eastern side of the United States. When Yung Wing was a young man, missionaries in China sent him to be schooled in America. He graduated from Yale University in 1854, becoming the first Chinese graduate of an American college. He stayed in America, working as a diplomat for China and helping to bring other Chinese to the United States. Years later, he married an American and wrote his autobiography, *My Life in China and America.* He was also the first Chinese to become a naturalized United States citizen.

Other gold seekers in California included immigrants from northern Mexico and Chile. Many of them ended up in the mining camp of Sonora, in central California. William Perkins, a Canadian forty-niner, wrote:

❝ Here were to be seen people of every nation in all varieties of costume, and speaking fifty different languages. ❞

SKILLS: Using a Diary as a Primary Source

LEARN

You might think that keeping a diary means simply writing down exactly what happens each day. That is partly true. A diary is a daily record. Details of people's lives, however, are often colored by their emotions and opinions.

Diaries contain ordinary facts about people's lives, such as where they went that day, what they ate, or whom they saw. For this reason alone, diaries are important primary sources for historians.

Factual statements can tell a lot about the culture and society of the period. Diaries often also include the writer's ideas, fears, opinions, and dreams. This information can help historians determine how people felt about events of the day. For example, the diary of a Texan in 1830 might reveal bitter feelings about Mexican laws banning American immigration. This clue might be helpful in establishing the causes of the Texas Revolution.

> " Tuesday, April 13th. Soon after we struck the Des Moines River . . . passing through Ottumwa, the prettiest place we have yet seen and have decided to come here and make our home when we return from California with a fortune. Camped this evening on the bank of a little stream. While we were eating supper a lady who lives close by came in to see, as she said, how campers did. On learning our name she and her husband, who are Scotch people, claimed [to know] our family in Scotland, and insisted on our going to their house to spend the night. They entertained us with the history of the McAuleys in Scotland, which we had never known before. "

PRACTICE

Read the excerpt at the right from a diary written by seventeen-year-old Eliza Ann McAuley. She traveled with her older brother and sister to California in 1852.

1. What facts do you learn from this diary entry?

2. What feelings and opinions do you find?

3. What picture does this entry paint of the life of the emigrants?

4. Would such a depiction be of interest to historians? Why or why not?

APPLY

5. Imagine an eventful day in the life of a forty-niner. Write a diary entry for that day.

Once word of a new gold find got out, a town's population could swell overnight. Once the gold ran out, people disappeared, leaving a ghost town behind.

Once in the gold fields, many of the foreign forty-niners faced prejudice. Their language, their food, their clothes, and their ways were different. As growing numbers of Yankees swarmed into California, they forced foreigners out of the gold fields.

Driven from the mining camps, many Chinese worked over old diggings and still made money. Some Chinese began to provide services such as cooking and washing clothes. In later years the Chinese served an important role in building railroads and drainage canals.

Effects of the Gold Rush

Between 1849 and 1852, about 250,000 people arrived in California. It was the largest migration, to that date, in American history. The effects were enormous. San Francisco swelled in size. It became a center of banking, manufacturing, shipping, and trade.

Most American newcomers to California who were white believed in the superiority of the white race, of the Anglo-American heritage, and of Protestant Christianity. As a result they looked down on Californians of Mexican heritage. Anglo-American culture and law quickly replaced that of Mexican California.

Another effect of the gold rush was the destruction of the California Indians. About 60 percent of the Indians died from disease. Large numbers, however, were hunted down and killed like animals. The reason was the Anglo-American belief that Indians stood in the way of progress. By 1870 the California Indian population had fallen from 150,000 to only 30,000.

A final effect of the gold rush was that by 1850 California was ready for statehood. This had great importance for the nation, because California applied to Congress for admission as a free state. As you will read in the next chapter, by the 1850s the issue of slavery was beginning to tear the United States apart.

SECTION REVIEW

1. Key Terms California Gold Rush, forty-niner, boomtown

2. People and Places John Sutter, American River, California

3. Comprehension What different peoples lived in California in the 1840s? What event brought new settlers to California?

4. Comprehension How did the gold rush change California?

5. Critical Thinking How might California have developed if there had not been a gold rush?

Summary

1. Mexico gained independence from Spain in 1821. Life in Mexico's northern provinces changed as Anglo-Americans settled in Texas and the Santa Fe Trail increased trade with New Mexico.

2. Tension between Mexico's government and American settlers led to the Texas Revolution. Texans were defeated at the Alamo and Goliad. Texas won independence after the Battle of San Jacinto. The United States, however, refused to allow Texas to enter the union.

3. Mountain men opened trails to the Oregon Country. Thousands went west in wagon trains along the Oregon Trail. In the Great Migration, Mormons seeking religious freedom headed to Utah.

4. The United States and Britain agreed to divide Oregon at the 49th parallel. War with Mexico erupted after Texas joined the Union in 1845. U.S. troops successfully invaded Mexico. Following the war, the United States acquired vast amounts of land from Mexico.

5. People headed to California after gold was discovered there in 1849. As the population grew, Mexican culture was replaced by Anglo-American ways. California joined the Union as a free state.

Graphic Summary

Americans move west.

- Mormons settle in Utah.
- Settlers seeking fertile lands settle Texas and Oregon.
- Gold seekers head to California.

The United States gains new lands.

- United States and Britain divide Oregon.
- United States annexes Texas.
- United States acquires lands in the Mexican Cession.

Review

KEY TERMS

Define the following key terms.
1. *Tejano*
2. annex
3. emigrant
4. Oregon Trail
5. manifest destiny
6. Bear Flag Revolt
7. Mexican Cession
8. forty-niner

COMPREHENSION

1. What two conditions did foreigners have to meet to settle in Mexican territory?
2. What caused tension between Anglo-American settlers in Texas and Mexico's government?
3. What effect did the defeat at the Battle of the Alamo have on Texans?
4. Why did Congress refuse at first to annex Texas?
5. What role did mountain men play in the settlement of the Oregon Country?
6. What were the basic rules that governed wagon trains on the Oregon Trail?
7. What were the causes of the Mexican War?
8. What territory did the United States gain as a result of the Treaty of Guadalupe Hidalgo?
9. What was life like in California's mining camps?
10. What effects did the gold rush have on California?

Places to Locate

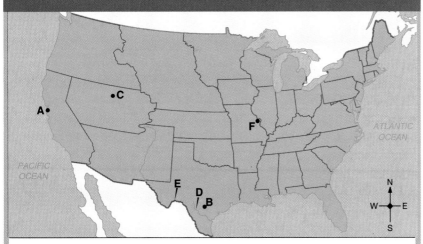

Match each of the letters on the map with the places that are listed below. Then explain the importance of each place.

1. San Antonio
2. Nueces River
3. Salt Lake City
4. St. Louis
5. Rio Grande
6. San Francisco

Geographic Theme: Movement What factors drew settlers to the West? What dangers did they face along the way?

Skill Review

The following passage is an entry from the diary of Amelia Stewart Knight, who traveled to Oregon in 1853. Read the entry and answer the questions that follow.

> "Tuesday, May 17th. We had a dreadful storm of rain and hail last night and very sharp lightning. It killed two oxen and one man. . . . As we could have no tents pitched, all had to crowd into the wagons and sleep in wet beds with their wet clothes on, without supper."

1. How did the storm described by Knight affect her wagon train?
2. How might Knight have felt about the journey west?
3. How might this diary entry be useful to historians? Explain.

CRITICAL THINKING

1. Making a Comparison Compare the Mexican independence movement with that of the American Revolution. In what ways were they similar? In what ways were they different?

2. Expressing an Opinion Many Americans in the mid-1800s believed it was the nation's manifest destiny to expand to the Pacific. Do you think U.S. expansion was good at that time? Is expansionism a good attitude for a nation to have? Explain.

PORTFOLIO OPTIONS

1. Civics Connection Imagine that you are living in California during the gold rush. Form a group to discuss the crime problem your town faces. Propose ways to maintain law and order.

2. Writing Connection Write a campaign speech for James K. Polk, explaining why he wants to annex Texas and acquire all of Oregon. Deliver your speech to the class.

3. Contemporary Connection In a short essay, compare the influence of Mexican culture on American society in the mid-1800s with Mexican influence on the United States today.

4. Timeline Connection Copy the chapter timeline. Choose one event and write a short description of its importance. Then add other events from the chapter you think should be included and explain why.

THE NARRATIVE OF THE LIFE OF
Frederick Douglass

FREDERICK DOUGLASS

Frederick Douglass, born into slavery in 1818, escaped to the North and became an abolitionist speaker and publisher. In these excerpts from his autobiography, Douglass describes his childhood as a slave and the start of his public speaking career.

My new mistress [Mrs. Auld] proved to be all she appeared when I first met her at the door,—a woman of the kindest heart and finest feelings. She had never had a slave under her control previously to myself, and prior to her marriage she had been dependent upon her own industry for a living. She was by trade a weaver; and by constant application to her business, she had been in a good degree preserved from the blighting and dehumanizing effects of slavery. I was utterly astonished at her goodness. I scarcely knew how to behave towards her. . . .

But, alas! this kind heart had but a short time to remain such. The fatal poison of irresponsible power was already in her hands, and soon commenced its infernal work. The cheerful eye, under the influence of slavery, soon became red with rage; that voice, made all of sweet accord, changed to one of harsh and horrid discord; and that angelic face gave place to that of a demon.

Very soon after I went to live with Mr. and Mrs. Auld, she very kindly commenced to teach me the A, B, C. After I had learned this, she assisted me in learning to spell words of three or four letters. Just at this point of my progress, Mr. Auld found out what was going on, and at once forbade Mrs. Auld to instruct me further, telling her, among other things, that it was unlawful, as well as unsafe, to teach a slave to read. To use his own words, further, he said, "If you give a [slave] an inch, he will take an ell. A . . . [slave] should know nothing but to obey his master—to do as he is told to do. . . . Now," said he, "if you teach . . . (speaking of myself) how to read, there would be no keeping him. It would forever unfit him to be a slave. He would at once become unmanageable, and of no value to his master. As to himself, it could do him no good, but a great deal of harm. It would make him discontented and unhappy." These words sank deep into my heart, stirred up sentiments within that lay slumbering, and called into an existence an entirely new train of thought. It was a new and special revelation, explaining dark and mysterious things, with which my youthful understanding had struggled, but struggled in vain. I now understood what had been to me a most perplexing difficulty—to wit, the white man's power to enslave the black man. It was a grand achievement, and I understood the pathway from slavery to freedom. It was just what I wanted, and I got it at a time when I least expected it. Whilst I was saddened by the thought of losing the aid of my kind mistress, I was gladdened by the invaluable instruction which, by the merest accident, I had gained from my master. Though conscious of the difficulty of learning without a teacher, I set out high hope, and a fixed purpose, at whatever cost of trouble, to learn how to read.

In 1847 Douglass founded an anti-slavery newspaper, the *North Star* (later called *Frederick Douglass' Paper*).

I had not long been a reader of the "Liberator," before I got a pretty correct idea of the principles, measures, and spirit of the anti-slavery reform. I took right hold of the cause. I could do but little; but what I could, I did with a joyful heart, and never felt happier than when in an anti-slavery meeting. . . . [W]hile attending an anti-slavery convention at Nantucket, on the 11th of August, 1841, I felt strongly moved to speak. . . . I spoke but a few moments, when I felt a degree of freedom, and said what I desired with considerable ease. From that time until now, I have been engaged in pleading the cause of my brethren. . . .

From: *The Narrative of the Life of Frederick Douglass, an American Slave,* by Frederick Douglass (Anti-Slavery Office, 1845).

Analyzing Literature

1. How does Douglass explain Mrs. Auld's kind treatment of him at first? How did becoming a slaveholder affect Mrs. Auld?

2. Why, according to Douglass, was it important for him to learn to read?

3. Why, do you think, did Douglass feel "strongly moved to speak" at the anti-slavery convention?

The Nation Divided and Rebuilt (1850–1896)

UNIT OVERVIEW

Southern states left the Union in 1860 and 1861, starting what would become the bloodiest war in our nation's history.

Chapter 18

The Nation Breaking Apart (1850–1861)
The issues of slavery and states' rights led to the outbreak of the Civil War in 1861.

Chapter 19

The Civil War (1861–1865)
The conflict between the North and South ended with a northern victory in 1865.

Chapter 20

Rebuilding the South (1865–1896)
The South's main tasks after 1865 were to deal with the war's destruction and the ending of slavery.

Illustration:
Fighting at Fair Oaks, Virginia, in 1862.

Slavery became one of the most controversial issues dividing the North and South during the mid-1800s. Plantations, like the one below, were maintained by slave labor and drove the South's economy. Few southerners wanted to end slavery.

1850

1852

1854

1856

1850 Compromise of 1850

1852 *Uncle Tom's Cabin* published

1854 Kansas-Nebraska Act

1857 Dred Scott case

The Nation Breaking Apart (1850–1861)

1 Growing Differences Between North and South

IMAGINE THAT it is the year 1850. You are taking a trip down the length of the Ohio River. As a tourist, you are on one of the paddle-wheel steamboats that regularly travel the river. From time to time, the steamboat pulls into one of the river towns. What you see on shore, however, depends on whether the boat docks on the right bank or the left bank of the river.

If the steamboat lands on the right bank—at Cincinnati, Ohio, for example—the dock workers are likely to be white men. If the steamboat lands on the left bank, at a place such as Louisville, Kentucky, the dock workers are likely to be slaves.

Contrasts Between North and South

The Ohio River—all 981 miles of it—was the boundary between slave and free states west of the Appalachian Mountains. (The Mason-Dixon Line, the border between Pennsylvania and Maryland, was the boundary east of the mountains.) On the north side of the river were Ohio, Indiana, and Illinois. These were free states as required by the Northwest Ordinance. On the south side of the river were Virginia (now West Virginia) and Kentucky. These were both slave states.

At the time of the American Revolution, slaves could be found in all the states. Since then, the northern states had gradually abolished slavery. Meanwhile, slavery had grown in the cotton-growing states of the South.

In the 1830s Alexis de Tocqueville, the French visitor you read about earlier, took a journey on the Ohio River. He saw many differences between the left bank and the right bank. "On the left bank of the river," Tocqueville wrote, ". . . one sees a troop

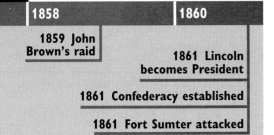

1858 | 1860

1859 John Brown's raid

1861 Lincoln becomes President

1861 Confederacy established

1861 Fort Sumter attacked

The economic differences between the North and South are highlighted in these images from the mid-1800s. Slaves harvest sugarcane in the rural South, while women work in textile mills (inset) in the industrial North.

of slaves loitering through half-deserted fields." On the right bank, however, "men are busily at work; fine crops cover the fields; elegant dwellings testify to the taste and industry of the workers."

Why, Tocqueville asked, was there such a difference between the two sides of the river? His answer was simple: slavery.

> **❝ On the left bank of the Ohio work is connected with the idea of slavery, but on the right with well-being and progress; . . . on the left bank no white laborers are to be found, for they would be afraid of being like the slaves; . . . but one will never see a man of leisure on the right bank. ❞**

Differences between North and South were nothing new. The two regions had been quite different even in colonial times. The Industrial Revolution, however, had made the differences greater. By the mid-1800s the North and South had separate economic systems and cultures. Northern cities were growing rapidly as a result of industry and immigration. Starting in the 1840s, thousands of Irish and German immigrants landed on American shores. Most stayed in the North, partly because they did not choose to compete with the slave labor of the South. By 1850 the North had more wealth, factories, more and bigger cities, and more people than the South. The South remained mostly rural.

Slavery and Racism

In the North the abolitionist movement, though small, gained strength. Abolitionists wanted to end slavery because they thought it morally wrong. Others had economic reasons for opposing slavery. Slavery was seen as a "blight" that "polluted" the soil and "paralyzed" economic growth.

Many southerners agreed that slavery was a moral and an economic evil. Yet they backed slavery because they did not know any other way in which whites and blacks could live in the same society. Most white southerners, rich and poor alike, held the racist belief that white people were superior to black people. If slavery were ended, white southerners worried, the social barriers separating whites and blacks would disappear. As one white farmer put it, "Now suppose they was free, you see they'd all think themselves as good as we."

Such racism existed at the very core of American society. In the North as well as the South, African Americans could not serve on juries or hold high public offices. Churches, schools, and even cemeteries would not accept them. Shut out of good jobs, most African Americans in the North lived in poverty.

Impact of the Mexican War

For decades the sectional divisions over slavery had been building. Lawmakers thought they had settled the issue with the Compromise of 1820. That law had said that slavery could continue in the Louisiana Territory south of the parallel 36°30'. The issue of slavery, however, would not go away.

By 1846 the North's growing population had tilted the balance of power in the House of Representatives toward the free states. Southerners feared that if the free states also gained control of the Senate, Congress would abolish slavery. Southern leaders reasoned, therefore, that their best defense was to extend slavery into new territories. If the territories became slave states, they might then hold on to their control of the Senate. If so, the balance of power between slave states and free states in Congress would be maintained.

In 1846 it was clear to Congress that President Polk intended to obtain California from Mexico. Gaining new territory, however, would raise the old question: slave or free? David Wilmot, a member of Congress from Pennsylvania, suggested that slavery never be allowed in any land gained from Mexico. This proposal, called the Wilmot Proviso, passed the House, but not the Senate. (The slave states were in the majority by one.) Still, the Wilmot Proviso did not die. It came up again and again. Each time it was defeated, with northerners in favor and southerners against.

When the Wilmot Proviso failed again in 1848, some northerners formed a new political party, the Free-Soil Party. The Free-Soil Party demanded an end to slavery. It also urged Congress to give western settlers free **homesteads**—land on which to settle and build houses. Candidates ran for office with the slogan, "Free Soil, Free Speech, Free Labor, and Free Men." The Free-Soil Party won thirteen seats in Congress in the election of 1848.

CONNECTING WITH WORLD EVENTS

WILLIAM WALKER'S DREAM OF EMPIRE

For some southerners, the desire to extend slavery was not limited to the new territories of the United States. One man wanted to expand slavery to lands south of the border. He was William Walker (1824–1860), a proslavery adventurer from Tennessee.

Walker set his sights on Central America. The small nation of Nicaragua was in the midst of a rebel take-over. In 1855, with a band of 58 men and help from Nicaraguans, Walker seized the country. He quickly rose to power, and in 1856 made himself president of Nicaragua.

Walker had grand dreams of creating a slave empire in Latin America. He also wanted his slave empire to be an ally of the American southern states. However, troops from neighboring countries squelched Walker's dreams when they drove him from power in 1857.

Three more times William Walker and his brigade tried to invade Nicaragua without success. On his final attempt, he was caught. Following a brief trial, Walker was executed by a firing squad.

For white southerners, the success of the Free-Soil Party was one more reason for alarm. Wisconsin had just entered the Union as a free state. There were now fifteen free states and fifteen slave states. As long as that balance held, no law could pass the Senate without southern support. If new territories in the West entered the Union as free states, however, the South would lose power in Congress.

After the Mexican War ended in 1848, the dispute over slavery heated up. California asked to be admitted as a free state. Southerners wanted to divide California in half, making the southern half a slave state.

Antislavery forces would have none of it. Southern talk of secession—withdrawing from the Union—became more frequent.

Forging a Compromise

Henry Clay of Kentucky, though old and ailing, rose once again to present a compromise. It included admitting California as a free state.

Extremists in both the North and the South opposed such a deal. The most conservative southerners also resisted compromise. They wanted to maintain a balance between slave states and free states. When they accused Clay of deserting the South, his answer electrified the Senate. "I know my duty and coming from a slave state as I do, no power on earth shall ever make me vote for the extension of slavery over one foot of territory now free. Never.—No, Sir, NO."

Daniel Webster, the Massachusetts politician, urged compromise:

> **❝I wish to speak today, not as a Massachusetts man, nor as a northern man, but as an American . . . I speak today for the preservation of the Union. Hear me for my cause. ❞**

Webster asked each side to bury the passions of the past. What was important, he said, was to preserve the Constitution. "Let us enjoy the fresh air of Liberty and Union," he urged.

It was one of Webster's most famous speeches. (American schoolchildren would recite it for years to come.) It appealed to the American people, most of whom wanted compromise. Business leaders, farmers, laborers—all were prospering. Public pressure forced Congress to vote for Clay's Compromise of 1850.

The Compromise of 1850 had several important provisions:

(1) California was admitted to the Union as a free state.

(2) The rest of the Mexican Cession was divided into the territories of New Mexico and Utah. People in these territories would follow a policy of popular sovereignty to resolve the issue of slavery. In other words, they would decide for themselves whether or not to allow slavery.

(3) The slave trade was abolished in Washington, D.C.

(4) Congress also passed the Fugitive Slave Law. This law said that people in the free states had to help catch and return fugitive (escaped) slaves. Anyone caught aiding a runaway slave could be jailed or given a heavy fine.

Few Americans liked the compromise. Southerners were so upset at the admission of California that four states threatened to secede. Northerners, many of whom supported the Underground Railroad, hated the Fugitive Slave Law. Still, both sides decided to give compromise a chance.

Flyers warn African Americans of the Fugitive Slave Law.

SECTION REVIEW

1. Key Terms Mason-Dixon Line, homestead, Compromise of 1850, popular sovereignty, Fugitive Slave Law

2. People and Places Henry Clay, Daniel Webster, Ohio River, California

3. Comprehension What economic differences existed between North and South by 1850?

4. Comprehension Why were passions so strong over the issue of allowing slavery in the territories?

5. Critical Thinking How might the South have developed differently had the Founding Fathers abolished slavery?

440

2 The Crisis Deepens

SECTION GUIDE

Main Idea
Several events during the 1850s increased the distrust between North and South.

Goals
As you read, look for answers to these questions:

1. How did the issue of slavery bring bloodshed to the frontier?

2. What events deepened the division between North and South?

Key Terms
Kansas-Nebraska Act
Dred Scott case

F OR A BRIEF time the Compromise of 1850 cooled hot tempers. Peace, however, did not last long. Events over the next decade caused the quarrels to become more frequent, more angry, and more bitter.

Uncle Tom's Cabin

Many fugitive slaves heading north tried to cross the Ohio River into the free states beyond. In Cincinnati, Harriet Beecher Stowe, the wife of a clergyman, watched the agony as part of the population helped slaves escape and another part tried to recapture them.

When the Fugitive Slave Law passed, Harriet received a letter from her sister. "Hattie," the letter read, "if I could use a pen as you can, I would write something that will make this whole nation feel what an accursed thing slavery is." Stowe took up the challenge:

> **The heroic element was strong in me, having come down . . . from a long line of Puritan ancestry, and just now it made me long to do something, I knew not what: to fight for my country, or to make some declaration on my own account.**

In 1852 Harriet Beecher Stowe published *Uncle Tom's Cabin*. The book told of a kind, hardworking slave, Uncle Tom, and his mistreatment by a cruel master. It gave a dramatic account of the sufferings of a beautiful young slave named Eliza and of her flight to freedom. The moving story touched the hearts of most northerners. The novel became an instant success, selling over 300,000 copies the first year.

Many opponents of the Fugitive Slave Law helped slaves escape. These photographs show a secret room behind a sliding panel that was used to hide fugitive slaves.

135,000 SETS, 270,000 VOLUMES SOLD.
UNCLE TOM'S CABIN
FOR SALE HERE.
The Greatest Book of the Age.

Uncle Tom's Cabin affected thousands who had not thought much about slavery one way or another. As a result, it set off a tidal wave of abolitionist feeling. Stowe pointed out that slavery was not just the South's problem; it was the nation's problem.

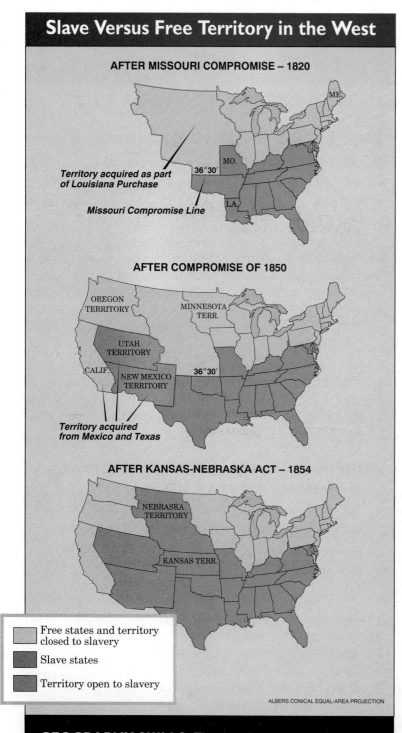

Slave Versus Free Territory in the West

AFTER MISSOURI COMPROMISE – 1820

ME.

MO.

36°30'

LA.

Territory acquired as part of Louisiana Purchase

Missouri Compromise Line

AFTER COMPROMISE OF 1850

OREGON TERRITORY

MINNESOTA TERR.

UTAH TERRITORY

CALIF.

NEW MEXICO TERRITORY

36°30'

Territory acquired from Mexico and Texas

AFTER KANSAS-NEBRASKA ACT – 1854

NEBRASKA TERRITORY

KANSAS TERR.

▢ Free states and territory closed to slavery

■ Slave states

■ Territory open to slavery

ALBERS CONICAL EQUAL-AREA PROJECTION

GEOGRAPHY SKILLS: These maps show the changing balance between slave and free states during the mid-1800s. **Critical Thinking:** After the Compromise of 1850, which new territories were open to slavery? How did the Kansas-Nebraska Act overrule the Missouri Compromise? Why did opponents of slavery find the Kansas-Nebraska Act a threat?

Everyone was responsible. She wrote:

" **The people of the free states have defended, encouraged, and participated; and are more guilty for it, before God, than the South, in that they have not the apology of . . . custom.** "

The nation could be saved, Stowe wrote, only "by repentance, justice, and mercy."

Angry southerners attacked the book for giving a false picture of the South. Resentful and defensive, white southerners repeated their argument that slavery was necessary and good. Planters even talked of re-opening the African slave trade.

The Kansas-Nebraska Act

In 1854 the slavery issue once more entered the halls of Congress. The cause was a proposal to build a transcontinental railroad (a railroad running completely across the continent). Stephen Douglas, a senator from Illinois, wanted the railroad to run through the Illinois city of Chicago. He knew, however, that a railroad heading west from Chicago would have to cross the unorganized territory of the Great Plains. He therefore proposed a new law, the **Kansas-Nebraska Act.**

Douglas's plan was to create two new territories, Kansas and Nebraska. Both territories would lie north of the Missouri Compromise line. By law they should have been closed to slavery. To win southern support, however, Douglas called for scrapping the Missouri Compromise. He proposed instead the principle of popular sovereignty. That is, the people in each territory would decide whether their territory was to be slave or free.

The Kansas-Nebraska Act passed with the solid backing of the South. Northern reaction, however, was divided. Some saw it as a useful compromise. Others opposed any move to extend slavery. This group of antislavery northerners banded together and organized the Republican Party in the summer of 1854. (This is the same Republican Party that exists today.) Its leaders shared one goal: keeping slavery out of the territories.

The new party quickly gained public support. In the 1854 congressional elections, Republicans defeated 35 of the 42 northern Democrats who had voted for the Kansas-Nebraska Act.

"Bleeding Kansas"

Kansas became a battleground over slavery. Both proslavery and antislavery forces sent settlers to Kansas. Each side hoped to "win" Kansas in the territorial election. However, there were more antislavery settlers than proslavery ones. Popular sovereignty was sure to make Kansas a free state. The proslavery settlers, however, had a plan. On Election Day, proslavery Missourians crossed the border into Kansas to stuff ballot boxes. "We had at least 7,000 men in the Territory on the day of the election, and one third of them will remain there," bragged a Missouri senator.

The proslavery Missouri toughs won that round. Congress found the election dishonest, however. It called for another election.

It was clear that popular sovereignty would not work where passions ran high. Each side boycotted the elections of the other. By early 1856 Kansas had two governments, an official proslavery government and an unofficial antislavery government.

Henry Ward Beecher, a clergyman from New York and brother of Harriet Beecher Stowe, suggested that rifles might be "a greater moral agency" in Kansas than the Bible. Funds were raised to send "Beecher's Bibles," as the rifles were then called, to the antislavery settlers.

In May 1856 a proslavery group attacked the Kansas town of Lawrence, burning homes and stores. Several people died in the blaze. An abolitionist named John Brown and several companions took revenge by killing five proslavery settlers. Several hundred settlers would die before peace was finally restored to "Bleeding Kansas." Even then, the issue of Kansas, slave or free, would not resolve itself until 1861, the year Kansas entered the Union as a free state.

The Dred Scott Decision

In 1857 a landmark case in the slavery debate came before the Supreme Court. This case concerned a Missouri slave named Dred Scott. Scott's master had taken him to live in Illinois and then in the Minnesota Territory before returning to Missouri. After his master's death, Scott sued for his freedom. He argued that living in a free territory had made him a free man.

In the Dred Scott case the Supreme Court ruled seven to two that Scott was still a slave. Chief Justice Roger B. Taney (TAW-nee) handed down the ruling. The Court had reached three important conclusions, Taney said. First, Dred Scott was not a citizen and therefore could not sue or be sued in the federal courts. Taney explained further that no person of African ancestry had the rights of citizenship under the Constitution. Taney's meaning was clear. Even if Scott had been born free, he could not sue in the courts.

Taney also said that Scott's stay in free territory had no bearing on the matter. Scott was now in Missouri, and Missouri law was what mattered.

Finally, the Chief Justice said that the Missouri Compromise was unconstitutional. Congress could not ban slavery in any part of the territories. Doing so would violate slaveholders' right to own property, a right protected by the Fifth Amendment. In other words, the territories were wide open to all settlers, including slaveholders. Once a territory entered the Union and became a state, it alone could decide whether or not to ban slavery.

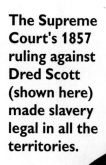

The Supreme Court's 1857 ruling against Dred Scott (shown here) made slavery legal in all the territories.

Southerners cheered the Court's decision. Republicans were outraged. They decided that their best course of action was to win the presidency. By choosing new justices, a Republican President could gradually change the make-up of the Supreme Court.

Lincoln and Douglas Debate

In the 1858 congressional elections, the Republicans again campaigned against northern Democrats willing to make a deal with the South. One of their targets was Senator Stephen Douglas, the powerful and popular Democrat from Illinois. To challenge Douglas, they chose Abraham Lincoln, a lawyer from Springfield.

Abraham Lincoln was known for his wit, his honesty, and his forceful oratory. He also was an experienced politician who had served both in the Illinois legislature and in the United States Congress. Accepting the Republican nomination for senator, Lincoln outlined the nation's dilemma:

❝A house divided against itself cannot stand. I believe this government cannot endure permanently half slave and half free. I do not expect the Union to be dissolved. I do not expect the house to fall but I do expect it will cease to be divided. It will become all one thing or all the other. ❞

When Douglas then accused Lincoln of urging a "war of the sections," Lincoln suggested a series of debates. Douglas accepted, and in seven Illinois towns the two men debated the issue of slavery. The debates drew large crowds and were printed in national newspapers.

Audiences immediately noticed differences in the way the two men looked. The tall, thin Lincoln cared little for fashion. His coat sleeves did not reach to his wrists,

nor his trousers to his shoes. He moved awkwardly and spoke with a country accent. Douglas, on the other hand, dressed stylishly and carried himself with grace. A short man, Douglas was called "The Little Giant" because of his sturdy build and powerful voice. (In those days there were no microphones or amplifiers to help a speaker be heard.) Douglas was famous throughout the nation. He even dreamed of becoming President one day.

Lincoln and Douglas differed almost as sharply in ideas as they did in appearance. Lincoln viewed slavery as "a moral, a social, and a political wrong." He did not suggest abolishing slavery where it already existed, but he opposed the spread of slavery. Douglas used the debates to defend the principle of popular sovereignty. The issue, as Douglas saw it, was not whether slavery was right or wrong. For him, the issue was the protection of democracy. The people's will was all that mattered.

Lincoln applied Douglas's reasoning to the Dred Scott decision. If the people's will is so important, he asked, could the people of a territory ban slavery if they chose to do so—in spite of the Dred Scott decision? Douglas answered that a territorial legislature could exclude slavery by passing laws that were "unfriendly" to slavery. For instance, it could refuse to hire law officers to catch runaway slaves.

While the voters re-elected Douglas, the debates cost him southern support. Southerners never forgave Douglas for showing how popular sovereignty could work against slavery. By losing influence in the South, Douglas lost his chance of one day becoming President. At the same time, the debates pushed Abraham Lincoln into the national spotlight.

John Brown's Attack

Sectional distrust was bad enough in 1859, but John Brown, the Kansas raider, made it much worse. Brown was consumed with the idea of starting a slave rebellion that would sweep through the South and destroy slavery once and for all. On October 16, 1859, Brown and eighteen followers—thirteen whites and five blacks—attacked the United States arsenal at Harpers Ferry in western Virginia. Brown

Was John Brown a "crucified hero" or a wild-eyed madman? A gentle Brown (left) is led to the gallows. Above, an angry Brown carries a rifle and Bible. **Critical Thinking:** How does each painting reflect the different perceptions of John Brown?

believed they could use the arsenal as a rallying point and supply station for a slave revolt. He was mistaken. After 36 hours of fighting, he and four survivors surrendered. Within six weeks John Brown had been tried for murder and treason, found guilty, and hanged.

That was not the end of it. Northerners began to praise John Brown for sacrificing himself to the antislavery cause. On the day he was hanged, bells tolled and guns fired in salute. Newspapers applauded his goal even though they condemned the way he tried to achieve it.

Northern praise of John Brown became as controversial as Brown's raid had been. Southerners had been stunned by Brown's attack on Harpers Ferry. Now they were horrified by the northern reaction to Brown's death. How, they asked, could they share the same government with people who regarded John Brown as a hero?

For many southerners it was the last straw. "I have always been a fervid Union man," a North Carolinian wrote, "but I confess the endorsement of the Harpers Ferry outrage . . . has shaken my [faith]." He stated that he would rather see the Union fall apart than "submit any longer to northern insolence."

SECTION REVIEW

1. Key Terms Kansas-Nebraska Act, Dred Scott case

2. People and Places Harriet Beecher Stowe, Stephen Douglas, Roger Taney, Abraham Lincoln, John Brown, Kansas Territory, Harpers Ferry

3. Comprehension How did *Uncle Tom's Cabin* raise North-South tensions?

4. Comprehension How did Lincoln and Douglas differ over the issue of slavery?

5. Critical Thinking Why was compromise over slavery so difficult by the late 1850s?

3 The Drums of War

SECTION GUIDE

Main Idea

With the election of Abraham Lincoln as President, southern states left the Union and formed their own government. The Civil War began when the South attacked Fort Sumter.

Goals

As you read, look for answers to these questions:

1 What was the main issue in the election of 1860?

2 Why did Lincoln's election cause southern states to secede?

3 What was Lincoln's attitude toward the seceding states?

Key Terms

platform
border state
Confederate States of America

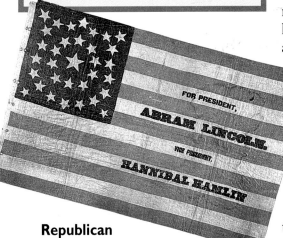

Republican banner from the 1860 presidential campaign.

A S THE ELECTION year of 1860 opened, the South was in an uproar. Thousands joined military companies. Rumors of slave revolts and abolitionist invaders abounded. Every northerner was considered an enemy. Some northerners were tarred and feathered. A few were hanged.

The Election of Lincoln

The widening gulf between North and South ripped apart the Democratic Party. At the party's national convention, southern Democrats insisted that the platform call for the protection of slavery in the territories. (A platform is a statement of beliefs.) Yet Stephen Douglas, who controlled most of the convention delegates, refused to abandon the principle of popular sovereignty.

The convention then split. Northern Democrats chose Douglas as their candidate. Southern Democrats moved to a convention hall across town. There they chose John C. Breckinridge, a Kentucky congressman, to run for President.

With the Democrats divided, the Republicans knew they had a good chance of winning the election. There was great excitement at their convention hall in Chicago. Spectators filled the hall and shouted for their favorite candidates. The delegates adopted a platform that called for limiting the spread of slavery. On the third ballot they nominated Abraham Lincoln as their candidate for President.

A fourth party, the Constitutional Union Party, nominated John Bell of Tennessee. Bell favored compromise as a way of saving the Union.

The election of 1860 could be seen as two different races, one in the North and one in the South. In the North the main contenders were Lincoln and Douglas. In the South they were Breckinridge and Bell. Lincoln and Breckinridge were viewed as the extremists. Lincoln was against any extension of slavery, and Breckinridge was for protecting slavery in the territories. The moderates, Douglas and Bell, looked for a compromise.

The election results made it clear that the nation was no longer in a mood to compromise. Lincoln won the election because he carried the more populous northern states.

LEARN

We all have suffered through debates that go nowhere. Often the problem is that everyone is talking and nobody is listening. Other times, people forget the issue at hand and start bringing up other issues. Respecting a few basic rules, listed below, can help prevent these problems.

1. *Do not interrupt someone else who is speaking.* Everyone must have a chance to give his or her opinions.

2. *Listen to what others are saying.* Sometimes we stop listening to someone because we think we know what that person is going to say. This shows a lack of respect for that person.

3. *Stick to the topic.* In formal debates, the topic for debate is explained in advance. Everyone must then speak only to that topic. In informal debates, we often lose track of the topic. It is tempting to criticize people personally rather than criticize their arguments.

These rules may sound simple. Yet when emotions run high, obeying them can be terribly difficult, even for people in high office. In the debate over slavery in the territories, southern Congressman Preston Brooks flew into a rage and attacked Senator Charles Sumner with a cane after Sumner gave an antislavery speech (illustration above).

PRACTICE

Review the following actions and tell whether each is an example of obeying, or disobeying, the rules of proper debating.

1. Using the time while someone else is speaking to read over your notes.

2. Looking for weaknesses in someone else's argument.

3. Suggesting that agreeing with your argument is a sign of intelligence.

APPLY

4. Review the last part of this section. Then hold a group discussion on the question, "Could the Civil War have been avoided?" Be sure that everyone obeys the rules outlined above.

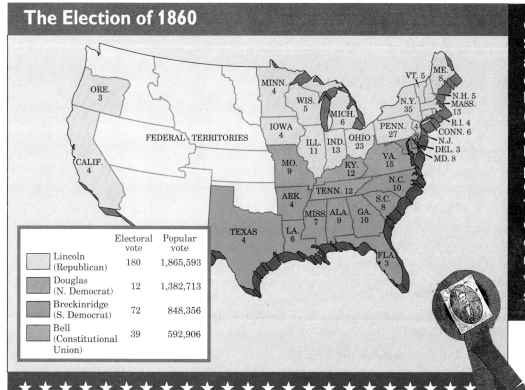

The Election of 1860

		Electoral vote	Popular vote
	Lincoln (Republican)	180	1,865,593
	Douglas (N. Democrat)	12	1,382,713
	Breckinridge (S. Democrat)	72	848,356
	Bell (Constitutional Union)	39	592,906

ORE. 3
CALIF. 4
FEDERAL TERRITORIES
MINN. 4
WIS. 5
IOWA 4
MO. 9
ARK. 4
TEXAS 4
LA. 6
MICH. 6
ILL. 11
IND. 13
OHIO 23
KY. 12
TENN. 12
MISS. 7
ALA. 9
GA. 10
FLA. 3
S.C. 8
N.C. 10
VA. 15
PENN. 27
N.Y. 35
VT. 5
ME. 8
N.H. 5
MASS. 13
R.I. 4
CONN. 6
N.J.
DEL. 3
MD. 8

GEOGRAPHY SKILLS: A split among Democrats in 1860 helped Lincoln (shown on the campaign ribbon below) win the presidency. **Critical Thinking:** Why did many northern states have more electoral votes than southern states?

Although he received only 40 percent of the popular vote, Lincoln won the most electoral votes, 180. Breckinridge carried most of the South. The compromisers, Douglas and Bell, did well only in the **border states,** the states between the North and South.

Mass hysteria swept through the South upon the Republican victory. Lincoln's election, many southerners were certain, meant their ruin. They feared more John Browns leading more slave revolts. They also dreaded the effect of northern majority rule in Congress. (There were now eighteen free states to fifteen slave states.) The vote for Lincoln had been, one southerner said, "a deliberate, cold-blooded insult and outrage" to southern honor.

Southern States Secede

Lincoln had never called for ending slavery altogether. He had said only that it should not spread to the territories. Few people in the South listened. They believed Lincoln planned to free the slaves. Southern radicals saw no choice but to secede from the Union.

South Carolina led the way, seceding from the Union on December 20, 1860. The South Carolina legislature feared what would happen when Lincoln took office. "The Slaveholding States will no longer have the power of self-government, or self-protection, and the Federal Government will have become their enemy," it argued.

South Carolina justified its secession on the basis of states' rights. The states had voluntarily joined the Union, South Carolina stated, and therefore had the right to leave the Union.

During the next six weeks Mississippi, Florida, Alabama, Georgia, Louisiana, and Texas voted to secede from the Union. It was a revolution fed by emotion. "You might as well attempt to control a tornado as to attempt to stop them," a southerner observed.

Some people wore ribbons like this to show their support for the Confederacy.

The Confederacy Established

In February 1861 the seceding states formed a new nation, the **Confederate States of America,** or the Confederacy. Its president was Jefferson Davis of Mississippi. Alexander H. Stephens of Georgia was the vice president. Secession, Davis stated, was necessary to maintain "the holy cause of constitutional liberty."

Yet how could the South talk about liberty while keeping millions of African Americans in bondage? Jefferson Davis spoke bluntly about the South's need for slaves. Southern agriculture could not survive without slaves, Davis argued. In his words, slavery was "absolutely necessary to the wants of civilized man."

However, only about one-fourth of the white families of the Confederacy owned slaves. What about the other three-fourths? Why should they fight the battles of the slaveholders? For many, the answer was to protect hearth and homeland. For others, the answer was status. Even very poor whites were likely to defend a system that gave them advantages over blacks.

The Northern Response

The idea that states had the right to defy the national government was hardly new. It had been asserted in the Kentucky and Virginia Resolutions of 1798 and 1799 and by South Carolina in 1828. Still, most northerners rejected it out of hand.

President Buchanan spoke for them. If secession were allowed, he said, the Union would become "a rope of sand." He warned that the 33 states could break up "into as many petty, jarring, and hostile republics." Abraham Lincoln, soon to take office, agreed with Buchanan. "The Union is older than any of the states," said Lincoln, "and, in fact, it created them as states."

In 1861 Jefferson Davis, a former senator, became president of the Confederacy. He is shown here with his wife, Varina.

Secession also raised the issue of democracy and majority rule. From the southerners' point of view, majority rule was a threat to liberty. They believed that the North, using its advantage in numbers, would trample on their rights.

To northerners, the South's argument sounded like sour grapes. Having lost out to the majority, southerners were questioning the right of the majority to govern. "Their quarrel is not with the Republican Party, but with the theory of democracy," penned the writer James Russell Lowell.

The Failure of Compromise

With war threatening, Congress made one last attempt at compromise. Senator John J. Crittenden of Kentucky proposed to restore the Missouri Compromise line of 36° 30' as the dividing line between free and slave states and territories. Lincoln, however, opposed the plan. From Springfield he wrote a friend, "The tug has to come, and better now than later." The Republicans refused to allow the spread of slavery, and the South would have no less. The deal failed.

The nation waited anxiously as Lincoln's inauguration drew near. What would he do? In his First Inaugural Address, Lincoln announced that he would not interfere with slavery in the states where it already existed. However, he also stated that "the Union of these states is perpetual." No state, he declared, could lawfully leave the Union.

Lincoln said that the federal government would not abandon its property and bases in southern states. On the other hand, Lincoln did not want to start a war. "There will be no invasion," Lincoln said, "no using of force against, or among the people anywhere." Lincoln appealed for calm. "We are not enemies, but friends," he concluded. "Though passion may have strained, it must not break our bonds of affection."

The Civil War began when Confederate troops attacked Fort Sumter in April 1861. **Critical Thinking:** How might events have turned out if Lincoln had withdrawn the garrison before the Confederate attack?

Crisis at Fort Sumter

Once in office, Lincoln faced a crucial decision. What should he do about Fort Sumter in Charleston harbor and Fort Pickens in the harbor of Pensacola, Florida? Each needed supplies. In January 1861 President Buchanan had sent a ship carrying men and supplies to Fort Sumter. It had turned back when fired upon by South Carolina gunners.

Now time was running out for Major Robert Anderson and his garrison at Fort Sumter. If Lincoln withdrew the garrison, he would be recognizing the Confederacy. If he supplied the garrison, he risked war. On April 4, 1861, Lincoln announced that he was sending relief expeditions to both Fort Sumter and Fort Pickens.

Lincoln's announcement meant he intended to fight if necessary. Confederate leaders decided to attack Fort Sumter before the supply ship arrived. At 4:30 A.M. on April 12, shore guns opened fire on the island fort. For 34 hours the Confederates fired shells into the fort. The fort's walls crumbled. The officers' quarters caught fire. Union soldiers were choking from smoke as the fire crept toward the fort's supply of gunpowder. Anderson lowered the Stars and Stripes and surrendered. No one had been killed, but the Civil War had begun.

Was War Avoidable?

Historians have long debated the causes of the Civil War. Was slavery the only cause? What role did economics play? Was bungling leadership responsible?

Some historians claim that better leadership could have prevented the war. Historian Arthur Schlesinger, Jr. disagrees. "Nothing exists in history to assure us that the great moral dilemmas can be resolved without pain," he wrote.

SECTION REVIEW

1. Key Terms platform, border state, Confederate States of America

2. People and Places John C. Breckinridge, John Bell, Jefferson Davis, John J. Crittenden, South Carolina, Fort Sumter

3. Comprehension What did the election of 1860 reveal about the political feelings of North and South?

4. Comprehension Why did the election of Lincoln alarm the South?

5. Critical Thinking Compare the South's reasons for leaving the Union with the American colonies' reasons for breaking with Britain.

Summary

1. Differences between North and South grew during the first half of the 1800s. The North, spurred by industry, prospered while the South relied on agriculture and slave labor. In the Compromise of 1850, Congress tried to end the dispute over slavery in new territories. Few were satisfied, however.

2. During the 1850s tensions increased between North and South. *Uncle Tom's Cabin*, published in 1852, turned many northerners against slavery. The 1854 Kansas-Nebraska Act led to violence in Kansas. In 1857 the Supreme Court ruled that the Constitution did not apply to African Americans. Two years later a radical abolitionist named John Brown tried to start a slave revolt. Southerners were appalled at Brown's action and at northern sympathy for Brown.

3. The election of Abraham Lincoln, an opponent of slavery, as President in 1860 led southern states to secede. They formed the Confederate States of America, with Jefferson Davis as president. In April 1861 Confederate forces attacked Union-held Fort Sumter, thereby beginning the Civil War.

Review

KEY TERMS

Define the following terms.
1. border state
2. Compromise of 1850
3. Confederate States of America
4. Dred Scott case
5. Fugitive Slave Law
6. homestead
7. Kansas-Nebraska Act
8. Mason-Dixon Line
9. platform
10. popular sovereignty

COMPREHENSION

1. Why was the Ohio River an important dividing line in the United States in the mid-1800s?
2. What were the social and economic differences between the North and South in the mid-1800s?
3. What were the provisions of the Compromise of 1850?
4. Why did white southerners object to *Uncle Tom's Cabin*?
5. How did passage of the Kansas-Nebraska Act lead to violence in Kansas?
6. Why was the Dred Scott case a defeat for abolitionists?
7. What was the outcome of the debates between Abraham Lincoln and Stephen Douglas?
8. Why did the Democratic Party split in 1860?
9. Why did southern states secede after Lincoln's victory in 1860?
10. What event marked the beginning of the Civil War?

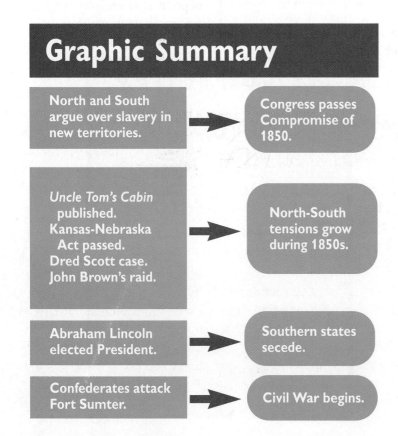

Graphic Summary

North and South argue over slavery in new territories. → Congress passes Compromise of 1850.

Uncle Tom's Cabin published. Kansas-Nebraska Act passed. Dred Scott case. John Brown's raid. → North-South tensions grow during 1850s.

Abraham Lincoln elected President. → Southern states secede.

Confederates attack Fort Sumter. → Civil War begins.

Places to Locate

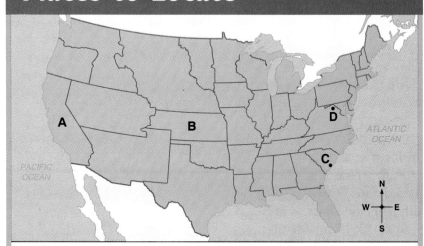

Match the letters on the map with the places that are listed below. Then explain the importance of each place.

1. California   3. Harpers Ferry
2. Fort Sumter   4. Kansas Territory

Geographic Theme: Regions Explain how regional differences between the North and South led to conflict.

Skill Review

Imagine that during a class debate on the issue, "Could the Civil War have been avoided?" one of your classmates begins a presentation by arguing that the Civil War could have been avoided because both sides agreed on the need to end slavery. For each of the responses listed below, write *Yes* if the response is an example of proper debating and *No* if it is not.

1. Before the speaker can go on to the next point, interrupt to say that the statement is incorrect.

2. Quietly review your notes during the first presentation so that you are well prepared to debate.

3. In your own presentation, state that there is no evidence that the South wanted to end slavery

4. In your own presentation, ask whether the first speaker even bothered to read the chapter.

CRITICAL THINKING

1. Analyzing a Quotation Reread Harriet Beecher Stowe's comment on who was responsible for slavery. Which region does she hold more accountable for slavery, the North or the South? Why? Do you agree with her? Explain.

2. Analyzing Factors Involved in a Decision Why did southern Democrats split from the party in the 1860 election? Why might this have been a short-sighted decision?

PORTFOLIO OPTIONS

1. Civics Connection Do you agree or disagree with the principle of popular sovereignty? Explain the reasons for your position.

2. Writing Connection People who disobeyed the Fugitive Slave Law and helped runaway slaves escape were breaking the law. Write a paragraph about whether or not you would have broken the law to help runaway slaves.

3. Contemporary Connection Read newspapers to learn about an issue that divides society in the United States today. Describe the positions of the opposing sides on this issue. Can a compromise be reached between the two sides? Explain.

4. Timeline Connection Copy the chapter timeline. Add other events from the chapter you think should be included. Which event do you think had the greatest impact on North-South relations? Explain.

After the Confederate capture of Fort Sumter in April **1861**, the armies of the North and South prepared for battle. Four years later, at a cost of over half a million lives on both sides, the North triumphed and the Union was preserved. This photograph by famed Civil War photographer Mathew Brady shows a Union camp in Virginia in **1862**.

1861 **1862** **1863** **1864**

1863 Emancipation
Proclamation

1861 Lincoln becomes
President

1862 *Virginia* and
Monitor clash

1863 Gettysburg
Address

1864 Sherman's march
through Georgia

1861 Civil War begins

The Civil War
(1861–1865)

1 Preparing for Battle

SECTION GUIDE

Main Idea
By calling out the state militias, Lincoln forced the states to choose sides. Both North and South prepared for war.

Goals
As you read, look for answers to these questions:

❶ What were the strengths and weaknesses of each side?

❷ How did geography affect each side's strategy for fighting the war?

❸ What roles did women have in the war?

Key Terms
front
antiseptic
anesthetic

1865

1865 Confederacy surrenders

1865 Lincoln assassinated

THE SOUTH'S ATTACK on Fort Sumter in 1861 started the Civil War. The Civil War would last for four years and result in the deaths of hundreds of thousands of soldiers. Almost every other American would be affected by the war in some way. The war would even change America itself.

Expecting a Short War
The war came as no surprise to Americans, in the North or the South. It had been brewing for years in the many angry fights over slavery. Americans did not expect, however, that the war would be so long and costly. They thought it would last only two or three months.

People on both sides responded with energy, even excitement, to the call to arms. A young Illinois recruit wrote that "it is worth everything to live in this time." A northern woman wrote, "It seems as if we never were alive till now; never had a country till now." In Washington, D.C., an office worker named Clara Barton took a pistol, put up a target, and fired away.

Lincoln Calls Out the Militia
On April 15, 1861, President Abraham Lincoln called on the states to provide 75,000 militiamen for 90 days. Throughout the North, volunteers hurried to sign up. Yet in the South there was anger and defiance. The governor of Kentucky telegraphed, "Kentucky will furnish no troops for the wicked purpose of subduing her sister southern states." In the days that followed, Virginia, North Carolina, Tennessee, and Arkansas voted to join the Confederacy.

With Virginia on its side, the South had a much better chance for victory. Virginia was wealthy and populous. It also was the home of Robert E. Lee. A brave and able leader, Lee had been

The States Choose Sides

CANADA

MINN.
WIS.
MICH.
IOWA
ILL. IND. OHIO
MO. KY.
KANSAS
TENN.
ARK.
MISS. ALA. GA.
LA.
TEXAS
FLA.
W. VA.
VA.
N.C.
S.C.
N.Y.
PENN.
VT. N.H. ME.
MASS.
R.I.
CONN.
N.J.
DEL.
MD.

OREGON

TERRITORIES UNDER FEDERAL CONTROL

CALIF.

PACIFIC OCEAN

Claimed by Confederacy

ATLANTIC OCEAN

MEXICO

Union state

Border state not seceding

Confederate state

ALBERS CONICAL EQUAL-AREA PROJECTION

GEOGRAPHY SKILLS: When the Civil War began, most southern states quickly joined the Confederacy. **Critical Thinking:** What special difficulties might border states have faced?

It was not just a war of men—boys as young as fifteen fought for their cause.

Lincoln's choice for head of the Union army. When Virginia seceded, Lee left the United States Army and joined the Confederacy. He wrote, "Save in defense of my native state I have no desire ever again to draw my sword." He soon found himself the commanding general of the Confederate forces.

In May 1861 the Confederate Congress voted to set up its capital in Richmond, Virginia. This was a gesture of defiance against the North. The city of Richmond stood only 100 miles away from the Union capital of Washington, D.C.

Choosing Sides

Both sides knew that the border states would play a key role in the war's outcome. From the Union's point of view, the most important of the border states was Maryland. If Maryland seceded, then Washington, D.C., would be cut off from the North. Thus Lincoln was determined to keep Maryland in the Union.

He ordered the arrest of Maryland lawmakers who backed the South. The remaining members of the Maryland legislature then voted to stay in the Union.

Federal troops helped a group of western counties break away from Virginia. These counties formed the state of West Virginia and returned to the Union. Delaware and Missouri also voted to side with the Union. A Confederate invasion prompted Kentucky to join the Union.

In the border states, war pulled families apart. Mary Todd Lincoln, wife of the President, had four brothers fighting for the South. Senator John Crittenden of Kentucky had one son who became a Confederate general and another who became a Union general.

Strengths and Weaknesses

On the face of it, the Union had huge advantages. It had about 22 million people. The Confederacy had roughly 9 million, of whom some 3.5 million were slaves. The Union had most of the mineral deposits—iron, coal, copper, and other precious metals. A full 86 percent of the nation's factories were located in the North. The North had 2.5 times the railroad mileage of the South. Almost every ship in the navy—90 of them—stayed with the Union.

The Union's greatest asset would turn out to be President Abraham Lincoln. Lincoln was able to convince northerners that the survival of democracy and freedom depended on preserving the Union. "Every war has its political no less than its military side," one historian has written. "Lincoln's genius was the management of the political side."

The Confederacy had its own advantages. It began the war with better generals. One-third of the career officers in the United States Army resigned to join the Confederacy. These officers had gained experience fighting in the Mexican War of 1846–1848. Foremost among them was Robert E. Lee.

The Confederacy had another advantage. It would be fighting a defensive war. "All we ask is to be let alone," Jefferson Davis said. An invading army is usually at a disadvantage. Invaders generally have less will to fight than soldiers defending their homes. Furthermore, maintaining the supply lines of an invading army takes great resources.

The Confederate soldiers never lost a battle for lack of ammunition. Still, other needs such as food and clothing were often in short supply. At times the southerners appeared to live only on spirit and courage. Well into the war a Union officer wrote, "How such men as the rebel troops can fight as they do; that, filthy, sick, hungry, and miserable, they should prove such heroes in fight, is past explanation."

Geography and Strategy

The two sides entered the war with different war aims and thus different strategies. The North aimed at conquering the Confederacy and bringing the southern states back into the Union. At first, Lincoln hoped to do this by smothering the South's economy. He made plans to seize Confederate strongholds along the Mississippi River. He also blockaded the Confederate coast, using the Union navy to keep ships from entering and leaving southern ports.

The South, in contrast, did not expect to conquer the North; it aimed only at staying independent. As historian James M. McPherson pointed out, "The South could 'win' the war by not losing; the North could win only by winning." Thus the South wanted to keep its army intact by avoiding large-scale battles. Southern leaders hoped that the North would soon tire of the war and accept southern independence.

The Confederate strategy also depended on King Cotton as a

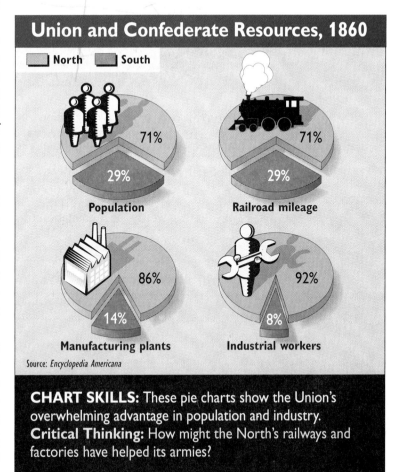

Union and Confederate Resources, 1860

North   South

Population: 71% North, 29% South

Railroad mileage: 71% North, 29% South

Manufacturing plants: 86% North, 14% South

Industrial workers: 92% North, 8% South

Source: *Encyclopedia Americana*

CHART SKILLS: These pie charts show the Union's overwhelming advantage in population and industry.
Critical Thinking: How might the North's railways and factories have helped its armies?

LEARN

You may have heard someone talk about receiving "a bigger piece of the pie." The pie represents the whole quantity of something. The piece represents a part of that whole.

A pie chart (also called a circle graph) is a useful way to show the parts that make up a whole. The whole pie is always 100 percent. Half a pie is 50 percent, a tenth is 10 percent, and so on. All the pieces of a pie must add up to 100 percent. In the chart at the right, for example, pieces of the pie are 87 percent and 13 percent. The title of this pie chart is at the bottom. The key to the colors is at the top.

In reading a pie chart, you first need to determine what the whole represents. Usually this information is in the title. Then you should see what each part of the whole stands for. By comparing the parts, you can learn how they relate to each other and to the whole quantity.

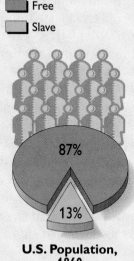

■ Free
■ Slave

U.S. Population, 1860

Source: *U.S. Census, 1860*

PRACTICE

Use the pie chart on this page to answer the following questions.

1. What is the whole quantity represented by the pie?

2. What does the smaller piece of the pie represent? What does the larger piece represent?

3. Summarize in your own words the information presented in the pie chart.

4. Is the pie chart an effective way to show this information? Could it be shown better by another kind of graph? Why or why not?

APPLY

5. Draw a chart showing what portion of the states in the United States joined the Confederacy. (Remember that the "whole" should be the United States as it existed then, not as it exists today.)

way to win foreign support. When the war broke out, southern planters withheld cotton from the world market. By doing so, they hoped to force France and Britain to aid the Confederate cause in order to keep their cotton mills running.

In 1861 Europe had plenty of cotton, and this plan failed. By the next year southern planters were again selling cotton if they could get it through the blockade. For the rest of the war they sought European support, but with little luck.

Before long, both North and South moved away from their cautious plans and looked for decisive victories on the battlefield. This happened for several reasons. People on both sides began to press their leaders for a knockout punch to end the war quickly. Also, the North came to believe that the South would give up only after its armies had been wiped out. The South, meanwhile, looked to military conquests to wreck northern morale and impress neutral Europe.

Much of the fighting took place on two **fronts** along the Confederacy's northern border, which stretched from Virginia to Arkansas. (A front is the area where two opposing armies meet.) The eastern front lay east of the Appalachian Mountains. The western front stretched from the Mississippi River to the Appalachians.

On the eastern front, the Confederate armies blocked the major routes southward. They were encamped in the Shenandoah Valley of central Virginia and on Virginia's coastal uplands.

In the West, the main access to the South was by river. Union forces were based at Cairo, Illinois, at the crucial junction of the Ohio and Mississippi rivers. Not far away were the mouths of the Tennessee and Cumberland rivers. These rivers led into one of the South's most productive regions. Here grain was grown, mules and horses bred, and iron produced. Much of the war on the western front would focus on the struggle for control of this region.

During the early years, northern support for the war was enthusiastic. In this painting by Thomas Nast, crowds cheer Union troops as they leave New York City for Washington, D.C. **Critical Thinking:** Do you think celebrations for soldiers leaving for battle were as enthusiastic toward the end of the war? Explain.

The Two Armies

In 1861 the Union was completely unprepared for war. Its forces had little training. Many soldiers were city residents who had never ridden a horse or fired a gun. In contrast, the southerners had begun organizing several months before Fort Sumter. They were used to outdoor life. They knew how to handle both horses and guns.

When the war started, there were no standards for uniforms. Men came dressed as their women had outfitted them. This caused confusion in battle because troops were not always certain who was friend or foe. As the war went on, textile mills on each side began to turn out uniforms for the troops. Union soldiers wore dark blue. Confederate soldiers wore gray.

The great killer of each army was not bullets but disease and infection. By the end of the war, some 140,000 Union soldiers had been killed in action or died of wounds. Yet many more, over 220,000, died of disease and other causes. Few doctors knew that cleanliness prevented infection, and antiseptics (germ-killing drugs) were unknown. Also rare were anesthetics, or pain-killers. Most soldiers endured operations by "biting the bullet"—braving the pain without the help of medication.

Women in the War

Women too prepared for war. Few plans had been made for the welfare of the soldiers. Women volunteered to do what the governments could not do.

Many women joined their husbands in the camps to cook and care for them. At least 600 Union soldiers were women who passed as men until illness or death revealed their disguise.

Thousands of women in the North and South organized aid societies. They raised funds for the war and made bandages and clothing for the soldiers. Clara Barton gained fame working as a one-person aid society throughout the war.

The women of the Soldiers' Aid Societies also formed the backbone of the Union's Sanitary Commission. It was organized with the help of Elizabeth Blackwell, the nation's first woman doctor. Over the army's objections, the government allowed the Sanitary Commission to inspect camps and hospitals.

The Commission's officers, agents, and inspectors were men. Supporting them were women volunteers. They raised money, sent supplies to the camps, aided escaped slaves, and recruited nurses.

The Civil War was the first war in which several thousand women served as nurses. Some people on each side did not approve of women's taking what had been considered a man's job. Yet altogether 3,000 women would serve as official Union army nurses. The Confederacy was slower to accept women nurses, but by 1862, they too were part of the Confederate army.

Women served in other ways. They ran plantations, farmed, and worked in factories. They spied for both sides. African American women were teachers, launderers, and cooks for Union troops.

Clara Barton was known as the "Angel of the Battlefield" for her work with wounded soldiers.

SECTION REVIEW

1. Key Terms front, antiseptic, anesthetic

2. People and Places Robert E. Lee, Clara Barton, Richmond

3. Comprehension What advantages did the North have over the South?

4. Comprehension Why was the blockade an important part of northern strategy?

5. Critical Thinking What opportunities did the war create for women? How might these opportunities have changed women's role in society?

2 The Agony of War

SECTION GUIDE

Main Idea
In the first two years of war, the Confederate army held its own on the eastern front. On the western front and at sea, however, the Union won several important victories.

Goals
As you read, look for answers to these questions:

1. What was the impact of the war's first major battle?

2. How did the Union triumph in the war at sea?

3. What was the impact of Union victories in the West?

Key Terms
First Battle of Bull Run
Battle of Shiloh
cavalry
Seven Days' Battle

Drums were more than musical instruments. During battle, drummers sounded the signal for charge and retreat.

O N TO RICHMOND! the northern papers cried. By capturing the Confederate capital, the Union might crush the rebellion in a single, swift blow. However, to win Richmond the Union army would first have to take Manassas Junction. This important railway center was only 30 miles south of Washington.

Marching to Manassas
On July 18, 1861, Union troops began the march to Manassas. They were raw recruits who had signed up for only 90 days of service. It took them three days to reach the battle site.

On July 21 a group of sightseers and picnickers rode out from Washington to watch the battle. Among them were society women who brought fancy gowns in trunks. They expected the day to end with a grand ball of celebration at Richmond.

The First Battle
The two armies met at the stream called Bull Run, just north of Manassas Junction. The Union forces outnumbered the Confederates 30,000 to 20,000. By midday they had driven a Confederate flank back a mile. At one point, a Confederate officer rallied his troops by pointing his sword toward General Thomas J. Jackson. He is said to have cried, "There is Jackson standing like a stone wall! Rally behind the Virginians!" Thus Jackson, one of the Confederacy's most able generals, won the nickname "Stonewall Jackson." Like a stone wall, Jackson's men held fast against the Union assault.

With the arrival of fresh troops, the Confederates launched a countercharge. Attacking the Union line, they let out a blood-curdling scream. The scream, later known as the "rebel yell," unsettled the Union troops. "There is nothing like it on this side of the infernal region," a northern veteran recalled. "The peculiar corkscrew sensation that it sends down your backbone under these circumstances can never be told. You have to feel it."

The Union troops, discouraged, tired, and hungry, broke ranks and scattered. For raw recruits they had fought well, but they had reached their limit.

The retreating soldiers became entangled with the sightseers. Convinced that the rebels were right behind them, the whole crowd panicked. Supplies were abandoned. Horses were cut loose, and soldiers began to run. Yet the Confederate army could not take advantage of the chaos. General Joseph Johnston later explained, "Our army was more disorganized by victory than that of the United States by defeat."

The **First Battle of Bull Run** was a great shock to the North. Confident of victory, it faced defeat instead. The day after the battle, Lincoln sent the 90-day militias home and called for a real army of 500,000 volunteers serving for three years. Three days later, he called for another 500,000. Lincoln made George B. McClellan head of this army. McClellan had won distinction fighting Confederate forces in West Virginia.

News of Bull Run electrified the South. "We have broken the backbone of invasion and utterly broken the spirit of the North," the *Richmond Examiner* rejoiced. More thoughtful southerners saw that the South had won only a battle, not the war. The victory "lulls us into a fool's paradise of conceit at our superior valor," Mary Chesnut wrote in her diary. She was right to be cautious. The war was far from over.

The Naval War

The great battles of the Civil War would take place on land. Still, the Union's choking off of southern shipping had a decisive effect on the war's outcome.

A number of southerners entered the profitable business of blockade-running. From bases in the Caribbean, the runners carried cargoes ranging from guns to hoop skirts. They used special ships that were low in the water, fast, quiet, and painted gray. On the return voyage the blockade runners carried southern cotton.

In the first year of the war the Union blockade was almost useless. Nine out of ten ships got through. However, northern shipyards were soon turning out a fleet of new boats, including deep-sea cruisers and gunboats that could operate in shallow

Following the First Battle of Bull Run, the size of both armies increased. This Mathew Brady photograph shows a Union soldier from Pennsylvania whose family has joined him in camp. **Critical Thinking:** What might the children have thought about joining their father in camp?

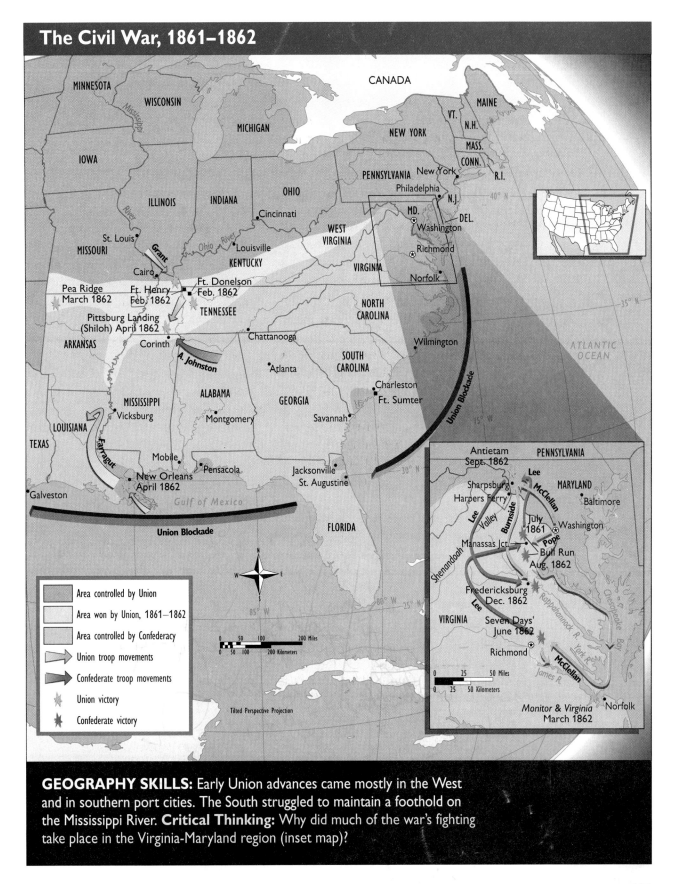

The Civil War, 1861–1862

MINNESOTA

WISCONSIN

CANADA

MAINE

MICHIGAN

VT.

N.H.

NEW YORK

MASS.

IOWA

CONN.

PENNSYLVANIA

New York

R.I.

ILLINOIS

INDIANA

OHIO

Philadelphia

N.J.

40° N

Cincinnati

MD.

DEL.

St. Louis

Louisville

WEST VIRGINIA

Washington

MISSOURI

KENTUCKY

Richmond

Grant

Cairo

VIRGINIA

Norfolk

Pea Ridge
March 1862

Ft. Henry
Feb. 1862

Ft. Donelson
Feb. 1862

35° N

TENNESSEE

NORTH CAROLINA

Pittsburg Landing
(Shiloh) April 1862

Chattanooga

Wilmington

ATLANTIC OCEAN

ARKANSAS

Corinth

A. Johnston

SOUTH CAROLINA

Atlanta

MISSISSIPPI

ALABAMA

Charleston

Union Blockade

Vicksburg

GEORGIA

Ft. Sumter

75° W

Montgomery

Savannah

LOUISIANA

Farragut

TEXAS

Mobile

Pensacola

Jacksonville

30° N

New Orleans
April 1862

St. Augustine

Galveston

Gulf of Mexico

FLORIDA

Union Blockade

N

W   E

S

85° W

80° W

25° N

Area controlled by Union

Area won by Union, 1861–1862

Area controlled by Confederacy

Union troop movements

Confederate troop movements

Union victory

Confederate victory

0   50   100   200 Miles

0   50   100   200 Kilometers

Tilted Perspective Projection

Inset map

Antietam
Sept. 1862

PENNSYLVANIA

Lee

Sharpsburg

McClellan

MARYLAND

Harpers Ferry

Baltimore

Lee

Valley

July 1861

Burnside

Washington

Shenandoah

Manassas Jct.

Pope

Bull Run
Aug. 1862

Fredericksburg
Dec. 1862

Rappahannock R.

Lee

Chesapeake Bay

VIRGINIA

Seven Days'
June 1862

York R.

Richmond

McClellan

James R.

0   25   50 Miles

0   25   50 Kilometers

Monitor & Virginia
March 1862

Norfolk

GEOGRAPHY SKILLS: Early Union advances came mostly in the West and in southern port cities. The South struggled to maintain a foothold on the Mississippi River. **Critical Thinking:** Why did much of the war's fighting take place in the Virginia-Maryland region (inset map)?

BELLE BOYD
(1844–1900)

Belle Boyd's career as a Confederate spy is full of tall tales—some of which she herself told. She claimed she shot a Federal soldier for insulting her mother during a Union raid on her hometown in West Virginia when she was seventeen.

What was true was her devotion to the South. For smuggling information to Confederate troops, Stonewall Jackson made her a captain. The Confederacy sent her to Europe in 1863 to recover from typhoid and to deliver documents. Her ship was captured, but the Union officer in charge fell in love with her and they married. After the war she began a successful acting career.

water. For the crews, blockade patrol meant months of boredom but offered the chance of riches. Each cargo captured was divided between the ship's crew and the government.

Enforcing the blockade became much easier as the Union took most of the Confederacy's major harbors. By April 1862, the Union had control of almost every important Atlantic harbor. Steadily, the blockade tightened. In 1864 a runner stood one chance in three of getting captured. By 1865 it was one chance in two.

The *Virginia* and the *Monitor*

The South's desire to break the northern blockade produced a revolution in naval technology: the ironclad warship. In 1861 the Confederates took the captured Union frigate *Merrimack* and refitted it with iron

sides. Sent into action off the coast of Virginia in March 1862, the *Merrimack* (now renamed the *Virginia*) destroyed two wooden Union warships and ran another one aground. On the following day the Union navy showed off its own ironclad, the *Monitor*. In the first fight ever between ironclad warships, the *Virginia* and *Monitor* hammered away at each other for two hours. Neither ship could sink the other, and the battle ended in a draw.

Although both sides built ironclads for bay and river fighting, the new ships were not a decisive factor in the war. The real importance of the ironclads is that they were the forerunners of future navies.

Union Victories in the West

Union troops in the West spent most of 1861 preparing for war. In February 1862 General Ulysses S. Grant made a bold move to take Tennessee.

Using new ironclad gunboats, Grant's forces captured two Confederate river forts. They were Fort Henry on the Tennessee and Fort Donelson on the nearby Cumberland. The seizure of Fort Henry opened up a river highway into the heart of

the South. Union gunboats could now travel on the river as far as northern Alabama. When the people of Nashville, Tennessee, heard the forts were lost, they fled the city in panic. A week later, Union troops marched into Nashville. It was the first major Confederate city to be captured.

Meanwhile, Earl Van Dorn, commander of a Confederate army in Arkansas, was organizing a surprise. He planned an end run around Union troops with the aim of taking St. Louis. With 16,000 soldiers, including some Cherokee Indians, Van Dorn headed north. Between Van Dorn and St. Louis, however, stood a Union army of 11,000. On March 7, 1862, the two armies collided at Pea Ridge, near the Arkansas-Missouri border. The Confederates could not hold out against the well-drilled and well-supplied Union troops. They broke ranks, scattering in all directions. It would take two weeks for Van Dorn to put his army back together.

The Battle of Shiloh

After Grant's river victories, Albert S. Johnston, Confederate commander on the western front, ordered a retreat to Corinth, Mississippi. Grant followed. By early April his troops had reached Pittsburg Landing on the Tennessee River. There he waited for more troops from Nashville. Johnston, however, was not about to wait for Grant to attack him. Marching his troops north from Corinth, on April 6, 1862, Johnston surprised the Union forces at the **Battle of Shiloh** (SHY-loh). It was the fiercest fighting the Civil War had yet seen.

Commanders on each side were in the thick of battle to rally their troops, most of whom had never fired at another human being. One Union general, William Tecumseh Sherman, had three horses shot out from under him. General Johnston was killed, and the southern command passed to General Pierre Beauregard. By the end of the day, each side believed that dawn would bring victory.

That night a terrible thunderstorm passed over the battlefield. Lightning lit up the battlefield, where soldiers dead and dying lay in water and mud. During that awful night, Union boats ran upriver to deliver fresh troops to Grant's camp. Grant made a surprise attack at dawn and forced the exhausted southerners to retreat.

The famous battle between the Union's *Monitor* and the Confederacy's *Virginia* revolutionized naval warfare. As word of the ironclads' fight reached other nations, one thing became clear: the days of wooden navies were numbered.

The cost of the Union victory was dreadful. Union casualties at Shiloh were 13,000, about one-fourth of those who had fought. The Confederates lost 11,000 out of 41,000 soldiers. Describing the piles of mangled bodies, General Sherman wrote home, "The scenes on this field would have cured anybody of war." There would be more such scenes—and worse—before the war was over.

The Fall of New Orleans

The South was just hearing the news of Shiloh when more bad news arrived. On April 25, 1862, a Union fleet led by David Farragut took New Orleans. Farragut's ships had to run through cannon fire and then dodge burning rafts in order to reach land. City folk stood on the docks and cursed the Yankee invaders, but were powerless to stop them.

In despair, Mary Chesnut wrote in her diary, "New Orleans gone—and with it the Confederacy. Are we not cut in two?" Indeed, after the victories of Grant and Farragut, only a 150-mile stretch of the Mississippi was left in southern hands. Guarding that section was the heavily armed fort at Vicksburg, Mississippi. Vicksburg would hold out for another year.

Lee Claims Victories

After Bull Run the eastern front had been fairly quiet. McClellan built up the new Army of the Potomac, preparing for the day when the North would try once again to capture the Confederate capital of Richmond. McClellan had more men than the Confederates, but he was slow to move. He was afraid, some said, of failure. Even Lincoln grew weary of McClellan's cautious approach. "If McClellan is not using the army, I should like to borrow it," he snapped.

In the spring of 1862 McClellan finally made his move. He planned to attack Richmond by way of the York Peninsula, a stretch of land between the York and James rivers.

Robert E. Lee was now in charge of the Army of Northern Virginia. Lee sent Jeb Stuart and his **cavalry** —soldiers on horseback—to spy on McClellan. With 1,200 men, the dashing Stuart rode around the whole Union army in four days and reported its size back to Lee. Lee then attacked McClellan's army. The two sides clashed for a week in what became known as the **Seven Days' Battle.** The Virginians suffered heavier losses, but McClellan's army was forced to retreat.

In late August the Confederates won a second victory at Bull Run. With Washington now in danger, Union troops withdrew from much of Virginia to protect the capital. By the end of the summer of 1862, southern troops once again stood on the banks of the Potomac.

These leather cavalry boots were worn by a Confederate soldier who saw action in 1863.

SECTION REVIEW

1. Key Terms First Battle of Bull Run, Battle of Shiloh, cavalry, Seven Days' Battle

2. People and Places Stonewall Jackson, George B. McClellan, Ulysses S. Grant, David Farragut, Manassas Junction, Shiloh, New Orleans

3. Comprehension What was the effect of the First Battle of Bull Run on the North?

4. Comprehension Why were Union victories in the West important?

5. Critical Thinking Explain why the naval war between North and South was as much an economic contest as a military one.

3 Turning the Tide

SECTION GUIDE

Main Idea
Union forces blocked Lee's invasions of the North and then invaded the South.

Goals
As you read, look for answers to these questions:

1 Why did Lee invade the North in 1862? In 1863?

2 Why did Lincoln issue an order freeing the slaves?

Key Terms
Battle of Antietam
Emancipation Proclamation
draft
Battle of Gettysburg
Battle of Vicksburg

RIDING A WAVE of Confederate victories, General Lee decided to invade the Union in the fall of 1862. It was a crucial time, for the fate of the Confederacy was at stake.

The Goals of Lee's Invasion

Lee had several reasons for taking the war north. A victory in the North would, he hoped, force Lincoln to talk peace. The invasion, too, would give northern Virginia a rest from war during the harvest season and let the hungry Confederates fill their stomachs with northern food. Finally, Lee hoped the invasion would show that the Confederacy could indeed win the war. This might convince Europe to side with the South.

By now, both Britain and France were leaning toward recognizing the Confederacy. They were impressed by Lee's military successes, and their textile mills were closing down for lack of southern cotton. The Confederates knew that European backing would help them. At the most, it would bring them money and guns. At the very least, it would pressure Lincoln to leave the South alone.

Antietam: A Turning Point

However, luck was not on Lee's side. A Confederate officer accidentally left a copy of Lee's battle plans wrapped around three cigars at a campsite. Soon after, a surprised Union corporal stumbled upon the plans. McClellan saw his chance to stop Lee and his army. "Here is a paper with which, if I cannot whip Bobbie Lee, I will be willing to go home," he said. Union forces went on the attack.

The clash came on September 17, 1862, at Antietam Creek near Sharpsburg, Maryland. The **Battle of Antietam** (an-TEE-tuhm) was the bloodiest of the war. The two armies fought all day, and at

These Confederate soldiers were killed at Antietam, Maryland. Though the battle was a draw, it marked the failure of the South's 1862 invasion of the North.

WARTIME TECHNOLOGY

In wartime, technology truly is a matter of life and death. Nations will spare no expense to create a "wonder weapon" that can help win the war. In the Civil War, as you read, ironclad ships first appeared. So too did underwater mines. The Union used hot-air balloons to view Confederate troops from the air.

Later wars would bring new advances. Ironclads gave way to steel-hulled battleships hundreds of feet long. Underwater mines were joined by submarines that could launch deadly torpedos. In place of balloons came sleek jets and, later, satellites that could spy from hundreds of miles away in space.

What will be the "wonder weapons" of tomorrow? Perhaps technology will be used to prevent wars as well as fight them. For example, satellites and sensors could guard borders and thus keep neighbors at peace.

nightfall they held the same ground that they had held in the morning. The only difference was that 23,000 men were dead or wounded. Lee, who lost one-third of his fighting force, withdrew to Virginia. The ever-cautious McClellan did not follow, missing a chance to finish off the crippled southern army.

Although a military draw, Antietam was a political victory for the Union. It caused the British and French to delay any plans to recognize the Confederacy. It also gave Lincoln the chance to tell the nation about his most fateful decision: to free the slaves.

A Document of Freedom

From the war's outset, Lincoln believed that the basic aim of the North was to preserve the Union, not to free the slaves. As he put it:

> **If I could save the Union without freeing any slave, I would do it; if I could save it by freeing all the slaves, I would do it; and if I could save it by freeing some and leaving others alone, I would also do that.**

Yet when Lincoln wrote these words, he had already decided to move against slavery. He saw that freeing the slaves would hurt the South. He knew that some in the North would be opposed to his bold decision. However, Lincoln was confident that many northerners would rally behind the Union cause.

After the Battle of Antietam, President Lincoln announced that he would emancipate, or free, all slaves in the rebelling states as of January 1, 1863. On New Year's Day in 1863, the President issued the Emancipation Proclamation. To an aide Lincoln said, "If my name ever goes into history, it will be for this act, and my whole soul is in it."

The call for emancipation changed the character of the war. The old South was to be destroyed and, in Lincoln's words, "replaced by new propositions and ideas." Abolitionists were overjoyed. "We shout for joy that we live to record this righteous decree," wrote Frederick Douglass.

Why, critics charged, did Lincoln free slaves in the South and not in the loyal border states? The answer was found in the Constitution. Freeing Confederate slaves weakened the South and thus was seen as a military action. As commander-in-chief of Union forces, Lincoln had the authority to do this. Yet the Constitution did not give the President the power to free slaves within the Union. Lincoln did recommend, however, that Congress gradually abolish slavery throughout the land.

Black Americans Join Up

The Emancipation Proclamation also declared that African American men willing to fight "will be received into the armed service of the United States." From the start of the war, African Americans had served in the navy, but the army had rejected black volunteers. As of 1863, however, free blacks in Louisiana, Kansas, and the South Carolina Sea Islands formed their own units. Massachusetts later raised two African American regiments. One of these, the 54th Regiment, gained fame for its heroic attempt to capture a South Carolina fort, Fort Wagner, in the summer of 1863.

African American regiments were led by white officers, and for most of the war were paid less than white regiments. Despite such unequal treatment, black leaders urged African Americans to enlist in the Union cause. Once the black man had fought for his country, Douglass said, "there is no power on earth which can deny that he has earned the right to citizenship."

By war's end about 200,000 African Americans had served in the Union army and navy. African American women, too, formed aid societies and worked behind the lines. Harriet Tubman, the famous conductor of the Underground Railroad, traveled with Union gunboats bringing slaves to freedom.

The Road to Gettysburg

Lincoln's great frustration was finding a general who would attack Lee. Lincoln tried one general after another. McClellan was put to pasture after he failed to pursue Lee at Antietam. The next Union general, Ambrose Burnside, also failed to impress Lincoln. He lost his job as commander of the Army of the Potomac after Lee defeated him in December 1862 at Fredericksburg, Virginia.

When General "Fighting Joe" Hooker took on Lee the next spring at Chancellorsville, Virginia, the result was a Union disaster. With fewer than half as many men as

Some 600 African American soldiers charged the Confederate position at Fort Wagner in 1863. Over one-third lost their lives. Sergeant William Carney of the 54th Massachusetts won the Congressional Medal of Honor for bravery during the battle (above).

Hooker, Lee still managed to cut the Union force to pieces and send it retreating north.

In the summer of 1863 Lee decided to head north once again, this time from the Shenandoah Valley into Pennsylvania.

Lee had two goals in heading north. First, he needed food and supplies for his army. His men were as thin and ragged as scarecrows, and horses were dying of starvation. Second, Lee hoped to force a peace settlement.

Time was running out for the Confederacy. The northern blockade was strangling the South. What had cost one dollar in 1861 now cost seven dollars. With the men gone, farm output dropped. Many of the men in gray deserted to help their families survive. "We are poor men and are willing to defend our country, but our families [come] first," a Mississippi soldier wrote the governor. Things were no better in the cities. Just a few months earlier a mob in Richmond had rioted, shouting for bread and breaking into stores.

Lee knew that northerners were also growing tired of the war. Lacking volunteers for the army, Congress had recently imposed a **draft.** (A draft, also called conscription, is a system of choosing people for required military service.) In July 1863 protesters against the draft battled police and soldiers in the streets of New York City.

In the North, more and more people were listening to the Copperheads—northern Democrats who called for peace and a compromise with the South. A successful invasion of the North, Lee figured, would encourage support for the Copperheads and thereby divide the enemy. Lee also hoped that an invasion would revive European interest in the South.

The Battle of Gettysburg

In late June 1863, Lee's army crossed into the fertile farmlands of southern Pennsylvania. "You never saw such a land of plenty," a Confederate soldier wrote home. "We could live here mighty well for the next twelve months. . . . Of course we will have to fight here, and when it comes it will be the biggest on record." The soldier's prediction held true.

In a line parallel to Lee's, the Army of the Potomac marched north along the east side of the Blue Ridge Mountains. "We cannot help beating them, if we have the man," Lincoln said. Still, Lincoln was not sure that he had the right general. Lee's army was already in Pennsylvania when Lincoln replaced General Hooker with a new leader, General George Meade.

Meanwhile, morale had risen in the Army of the Potomac. The men knew that they would be fighting on their own soil to protect their country. "They are more determined than I have ever before seen them," a Union doctor wrote.

Neither Meade nor Lee planned to fight at Gettysburg. It just happened. On July 1, 1863, Lee sent soldiers into the town of Gettysburg to get a supply of shoes. There they stumbled upon some Union cavalry, and the **Battle of Gettysburg** was on.

The fighting raged at Gettysburg for three days in what would be the greatest single battle of the Civil War. The most famous, and most crucial, moment of the battle was Pickett's Charge. For two days the armies had held their positions on opposite

This cannon was fired by the 1st Rhode Island Artillery during the Battle of Gettysburg.

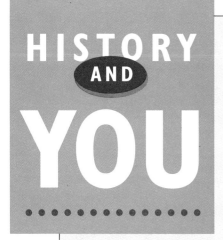

HISTORY AND YOU

A Soldier's Duty

In April 1863 Robert Gould Shaw (shown below) agreed to lead the 54th Massachusetts Infantry, a volunteer regiment of 1,000 African Americans. Some people wanted the 54th to fail, to show that black soldiers could not fight. Shaw knew his men would be held to higher standards than white soldiers.

After training in Boston, the 54th went to Georgia. The troops traveled on steamboats for their first expedition in June 1863. Shaw wrote about it to his wife:

"About noon we came in sight of Darien, a beautiful little town. Our artillery peppered it a little, as we came up, . . . and we landed the troops. The town was deserted. . . .

[Colonel James] Montgomery ordered all the furniture and movable property to be taken . . . and after . . . he said to me, "I shall burn this town." . . . I told him, "I do not want the responsibility of it," and he was only too happy to take it all on his shoulders; so [Darien] was burnt to the ground, and not a shed remains standing. . . . One of my companies assisted in it, because he ordered them out, and I had to obey. You must bear in mind, that not a shot had been fired at us from this place. . . .

The reasons he gave me for destroying Darien were, that the Southerners must be made to feel that this was a real war. . . .

I have not yet made up my mind what I ought to do. Besides my own distaste for this barbarous sort of warfare, I am not sure that it will not harm very much the reputation of black troops and of those connected with them. . . . There are two courses only for me to pursue: to obey orders and say nothing; or to refuse to go on any more such expeditions, and be put under arrest, probably court-martialled, which is a serious thing."

Shaw died in battle a month later and was buried alongside men in his company. To those who said that a white man should not be buried with blacks, Shaw's parents replied, "We can hope for no holier place for his body."

CRITICAL THINKING

1. List two reasons why Shaw was unhappy about the orders to burn the town.
2. What were Shaw's two options? Explain the drawback of each option.
3. What would you have done in Shaw's position? Why?

A monument stands today near a ridge at the Gettysburg battlefield. Labeled "The High-Water Mark of the Confederacy," it shows how far Confederate troops advanced against Union lines. On that spot, on July 3, 1863, the South came closest to winning the Civil War.

In the inset map at the right you can see that Lee's Confederate forces arrived at Gettysburg from the west and north. Meade's Union forces arrived from the east and south.

The fighting began on July 1. When a Confederate force captured Gettysburg, Union defenders took up new positions in the hills south of town.

On July 2 the Confederates attacked the wheat field and peach orchard (center bottom of the illustrated map). Their goal was to seize the hill called Little Round Top (bottom right), from which their cannons could pour fire down on Union positions. Yet Union troops held their ground.

July 3 was the decisive day. Lee, having failed to crack the side of the Union line, attacked its center. Some 15,000 men led by General George Pickett marched uphill across an open field toward the Union line—and Union guns. The Union rifles and cannons blanketed the field with fire. "Pickett's Charge" was torn to pieces.

Throughout the battle, both sides fought to control the high ground. At Gettysburg, Union control of the two "Round Top" hills, Cemetery Ridge and Culp's Hill, gave Meade the advantage.

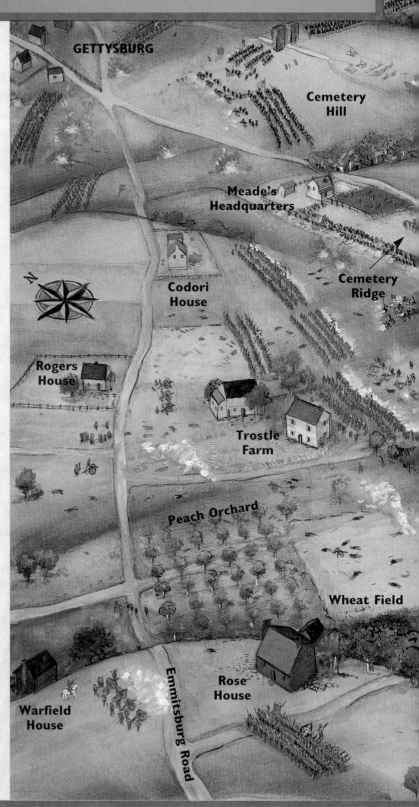

GETTYSBURG

Cemetery Hill

Meade's Headquarters

Codori House

Cemetery Ridge

Rogers House

Trostle Farm

Peach Orchard

Wheat Field

Warfield House

Emmitsburg Road

Rose House

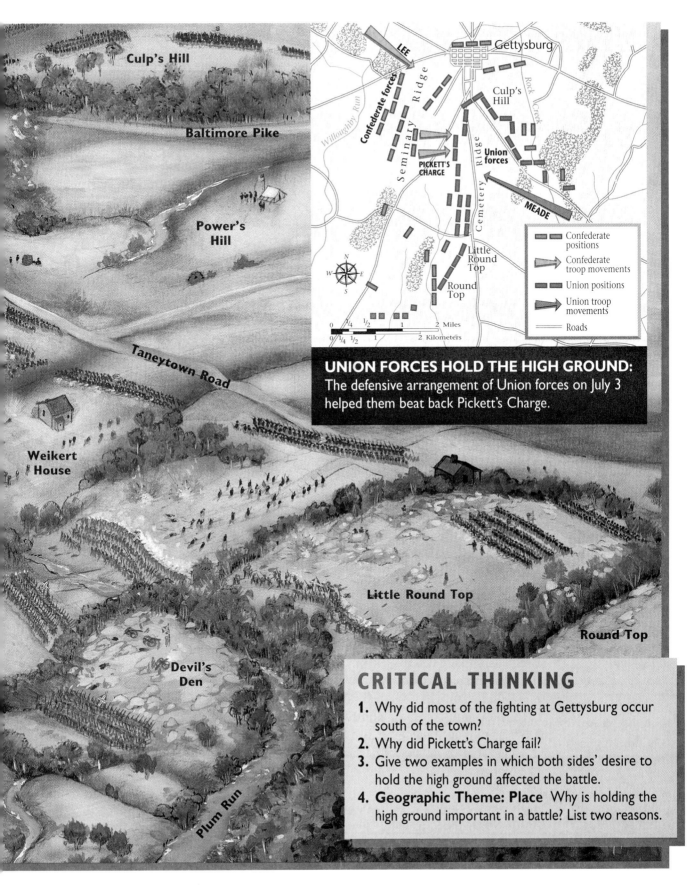

Culp's Hill

Baltimore Pike

Power's Hill

Taneytown Road

Weikert House

Little Round Top

Round Top

Devil's Den

Plum Run

LEE

Gettysburg

Confederate forces

Culp's Hill

Seminary Ridge

PICKETT'S CHARGE

Willoughby Run

Rock Creek

Cemetery Ridge

Union forces

MEADE

Little Round Top

Round Top

N
W E
S

0 ¼ ½ 1 2 Miles
0 ¼ ½ 1 2 Kilometers

Confederate positions

Confederate troop movements

Union positions

Union troop movements

Roads

UNION FORCES HOLD THE HIGH GROUND:
The defensive arrangement of Union forces on July 3 helped them beat back Pickett's Charge.

CRITICAL THINKING

1. Why did most of the fighting at Gettysburg occur south of the town?
2. Why did Pickett's Charge fail?
3. Give two examples in which both sides' desire to hold the high ground affected the battle.
4. **Geographic Theme: Place** Why is holding the high ground important in a battle? List two reasons.

Robert E. Lee's daring tactics and loyalty to his troops made him the South's most beloved general.

ridges. On the third day, Lee ordered General George Pickett to lead a charge of 15,000 men against the Union center. Pickett's troops had to cross a wide-open field in order to reach the Union army. Within half an hour, a blaze of Union gunfire had leveled half the attackers. Though Pickett's men reached the top of the ridge, they could not hold their position.

Pickett's Charge ended the Battle of Gettysburg. Lee's hopes of victory were dashed. "It's all my fault," he said, and ordered a retreat. Meade was amazed at his own success. "I did not believe the enemy could be whipped," he said.

The Confederates lost the Battle of Gettysburg largely because new technology had made Lee's tactics outdated. By 1863, rifles had replaced the old, inaccurate muskets that soldiers on both sides had carried at the start of the war. Rifling—the cutting of spiral grooves in a gun's bore—made guns more accurate and gave them a longer range. Soldiers marching in close formation, as they did in Pickett's Charge, could be mowed down far from enemy lines.

General Meade was so pleased with the Union victory that he did not pursue and finish off Lee's army. Lincoln was furious. When would he find a general who was a match for Lee?

Then good news came from the Battle of Vicksburg. On July 4, 1863, the day after Pickett's Charge, General Grant had finally taken Vicksburg after a three-month siege. The victory was even more important than Gettysburg, for it gave the Union complete control of the Mississippi. The Confederacy had been cut in half. "Grant is my man," declared President Lincoln.

The Gettysburg Address

In November 1863 President Lincoln made the sad journey to the Pennsylvania town of Gettysburg to dedicate the cemetery in which about 6,000 battle dead lay buried. The speech he gave that day was short, but powerful. Lincoln used simple language to make it clear that the Union soldiers were fighting to save democracy.

The nation, Lincoln said, was founded on "the proposition that all men are created equal." He continued:

> **It is . . . for us to be here dedicated to the great task remaining before us . . . that we here highly resolve that these dead shall not have died in vain—that this nation, under God, shall have a new birth of freedom—and that government of the people, by the people, for the people, shall not perish from the earth.**

No one has ever expressed better the spirit of democracy.

4 The Union Victorious

SECTION GUIDE

Main Idea
Led by Ulysses S. Grant, the Union armies bore down on Confederate forces in 1864 and 1865. The South was forced to surrender. The Civil War brought great changes to the nation.

Goals
As you read, look for answers to these questions:

1. How did the North defeat the South?

2. What were the results of the war?

Key Terms
total war
assassinate

THE BATTLES of Gettysburg and Vicksburg marked the turning point of the war. From then on, it was all downhill for the Confederacy. Late in 1863 Grant seized the important railroad center of Chattanooga, Tennessee. He thereby opened up another invasion route into the lower South.

Grant Takes Command
Impressed with Grant's ability to get things done, Lincoln gave him command of all the Union armies. Grant certainly did not look the part of a general. Unlike the formal and dignified Lee, Grant wore wrinkled uniforms. Yet like Lee, Grant knew how to lead an army. As Grant put it, "The art of war is simple enough. Find out where your enemy is. Get him as soon as you can. Strike at him as hard as you can and keep moving."

In the spring of 1864, Grant was in Washington. His plan was to attack the Confederacy on all fronts. He would go into the field himself to pursue Lee. Meanwhile, Admiral Farragut would go after Mobile, one of the few ports in Confederate hands. William Tecumseh Sherman was to move southeast from Chattanooga to Atlanta.

Sherman's Total War
Sherman took Atlanta in September 1864. He then set out on a march to the sea, cutting a path of destruction through Georgia. Leaving his supply trains behind, Sherman told his men to live off

General Ulysses S. Grant, shown riding with some of his generals, commanded all Union armies from 1864 until the war's end in 1865.

475

Daily Life

IN THE ARMY

Soldiers spent far more time preparing for battles than fighting them. One soldier described a typical day in camp: "Drill, drill, a little more drill. Then drill, and lastly drill." Yet still there was time for soldiers like those of the 5th Georgia Volunteers, shown at right, to relax.

Extra weight was a foot soldier's enemy. In his haversack he carried only a few essentials—toothbrush, comb, maybe a photo of his family or his hometown sweetheart.

Writing letters, smoking, and card games helped pass the time. Especially bored soldiers were even known to capture lice that infested the camps and stage lice races.

Confederate units short of supplies had to create their own uniforms. Some soldiers made shirts out of stolen drapes or tablecloths. Sergeant T.J. Duckett gave his hat a unique touch: a sign telling of his brush with death at Chickamauga.

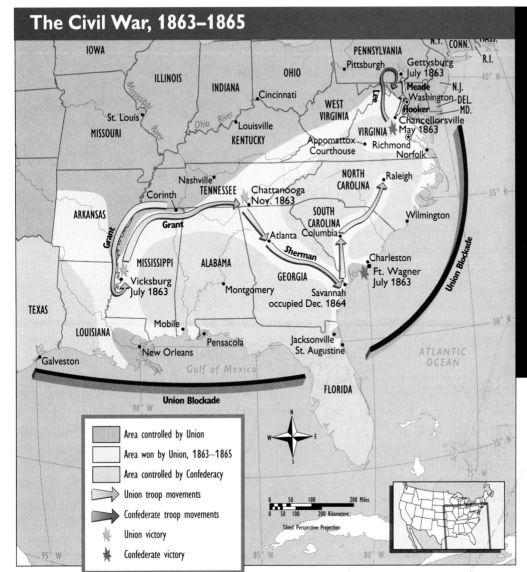

The Civil War, 1863–1865

IOWA
ILLINOIS
INDIANA
OHIO
PENNSYLVANIA
N.Y. CONN.
R.I.
Pittsburgh
Gettysburg July 1863
Meade
40° N
Cincinnati
WEST VIRGINIA
Washington DEL.
Hooker MD.
N.J.
St. Louis
Louisville
KENTUCKY
Chancellorsville May 1863
MISSOURI
Ohio River
VIRGINIA
Appomattox Courthouse
Richmond
Norfolk
Mississippi River
Nashville
TENNESSEE
Corinth
Chattanooga Nov. 1863
NORTH CAROLINA
Raleigh
35° N
ARKANSAS
Grant
SOUTH CAROLINA
Columbia
Wilmington
Atlanta
Sherman
MISSISSIPPI
ALABAMA
GEORGIA
Charleston
Ft. Wagner July 1863
Vicksburg July 1863
Montgomery
Savannah occupied Dec. 1864
Union Blockade
TEXAS
LOUISIANA
Mobile
Pensacola
Jacksonville
St. Augustine
ATLANTIC OCEAN
30° N
New Orleans
Galveston
Gulf of Mexico
FLORIDA
Union Blockade
90° W
75° W
25° N

Legend:
- Area controlled by Union
- Area won by Union, 1863–1865
- Area controlled by Confederacy
- Union troop movements
- Confederate troop movements
- ⭐ Union victory
- ✦ Confederate victory

0 50 100   200 Miles
0 50 100   200 Kilometers
Tilted Perspective Projection

95° W   85° W   80° W

GEOGRAPHY SKILLS: After cutting the Confederacy in two by taking Vicksburg, Union forces sliced through Georgia and moved north. Lee surrendered in Virginia in April 1865. **Critical Thinking:** How did Sherman's campaign in Georgia carry out the idea of total war?

the land. He was the first American general to wage **total war.** This kind of war is designed to destroy not only enemy troops but also enemy factories, farmland, railroads, and livestock.

A young Georgia woman described the scene after Sherman had passed through: "The fields were trampled down and the road was lined with carcasses of horses, hogs, and cattle. . . . The stench in some places was unbearable."

General Sherman made no apologies. "We are not only fighting hostile armies, but a hostile people, and must make old and young, rich and poor, feel the hard hand of war," he said. In December 1864 Sherman's army reached the port city of Savannah, Georgia. Behind him lay a corridor of devastation 60 miles wide and nearly 300 miles long.

The War Ends

The noose was tightening around the Confederacy. By the spring of 1865, Grant had an army twice the size of Lee's. In addition, Sherman was moving north from Savannah. Lee decided to leave Richmond and head for the mountains. Then he

Abraham Lincoln is considered by many scholars to be our nation's greatest President. His leadership during the nation's darkest days helped preserve the Union.

learned that Union General Sheridan was ahead of him. Trapped, Lee decided to surrender. "There is nothing for me to do but go and see General Grant, and I would rather die a thousand deaths," Lee said sadly.

On April 9, 1865, in the small Virginia town of Appomattox Courthouse, Lee and Grant arranged the terms of surrender. As Lincoln had ordered, Grant was generous. The Confederate soldiers were to lay down their arms. However, Lee's soldiers could return in peace to their homes, and those who owned horses or mules could keep them. Grant also told his men to supply food to the hungry Confederate soldiers.

The President Is Slain

The final act of the Civil War tragedy was now played out. A few days after Appomattox, President and Mrs. Lincoln went to the theater to see a popular comedy, *My American Cousin.* During the third act John Wilkes Booth, a Confederate supporter, crept through the theater to the door of Lincoln's box. Booth stepped into the box and shot Lincoln in the back of the head. Then he leaped over the railing and half-jumped, half-fell, to the stage. The fall broke his leg, but he was able to limp across the stage to the back door, mount his horse, and ride away. Booth was killed a few days later by soldiers who were sent to capture him.

Lincoln was carried to a house across the street from the theater. The bullet in his brain was too deep to be pulled out. Early the next morning, April 15, 1865, the President died. He was the first President to be assassinated. (Assassination is the murder of a public person.) With Lincoln's last breath rose up a cry of grief from freedom-lovers the world over.

Results of the War

The Civil War was the most wrenching experience in our nation's history. The Union was saved and slavery ended, but at a frightening cost. In four years 620,000 men died—360,000 for the Union, 260,000 for the Confederacy. No other war in our history caused such loss of life.

Throughout most of the war, the outcome was in doubt. Even today, historians cannot say exactly why the North won and why the South lost. They do agree, however, that final Union victory reflected Lincoln's leadership. During the nation's darkest hour, he held firm to the principles of freedom and democracy. As great leaders must, he bore the responsibility for the fate of his nation.

A tribute to the nation's fallen heroes, a statue is unveiled after the war.

478

Cause and Effect: The Civil War

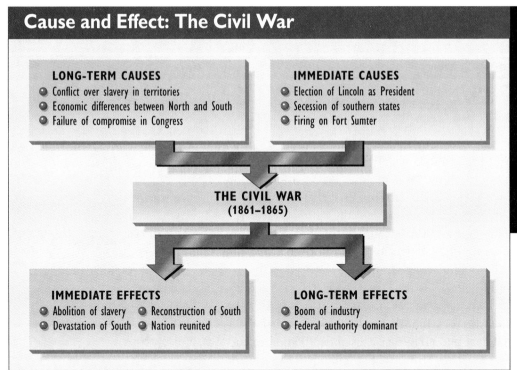

LONG-TERM CAUSES
- Conflict over slavery in territories
- Economic differences between North and South
- Failure of compromise in Congress

IMMEDIATE CAUSES
- Election of Lincoln as President
- Secession of southern states
- Firing on Fort Sumter

THE CIVIL WAR
(1861–1865)

IMMEDIATE EFFECTS
- Abolition of slavery
- Devastation of South
- Reconstruction of South
- Nation reunited

LONG-TERM EFFECTS
- Boom of industry
- Federal authority dominant

CHART SKILLS:
The North's victory in the Civil War preserved the Union and helped end slavery.
Critical Thinking:
If the North had lost, how might history have been different?

The consequences of the Civil War were enormous:

(1) *The war changed the way Americans thought about their nation.* In fighting to defend the Union, people accepted that the nation itself was more important than the states that formed it. After 1865, people no longer said "the United States are," but instead, "the United States is."

(2) *The war helped the federal government expand.* Before the Civil War, the federal government was a fairly small body with limited powers. By placing new demands on the government, the war made it necessary for government to grow.

To pay for the war, the government set up the first federal income tax in 1861. Congress also funded a transcontinental railroad, gave western land to settlers, and provided for state colleges. The growth in federal power would continue long after the guns of war had fallen silent.

(3) *The war spurred industry.* The war aided the early growth of several great postwar industries—petroleum, steel, food processing, manufacturing, and finance. This growth would continue for years.

For the South, of course, the war was a disaster. Defeated and occupied by Union forces, the South faced an uncertain future. The nation's next task was to rebuild the South and bring it back into the Union.

SECTION REVIEW

1. Key Terms total war, assassinate

2. People and Places William Tecumseh Sherman, John Wilkes Booth, Atlanta, Appomattox Courthouse

3. Comprehension What Union victories led to the South's surrender?

4. Comprehension List three consequences of the war.

5. Critical Thinking Explain this statement: "The war aims of North and South ensured that the war would continue until one side won total victory."

Summary

1. Early in 1861, North and South prepared for war. The North wanted the South to return to the Union. The South wanted independence. The North had more people and industry, greater wealth, and the leadership of Abraham Lincoln. The South had better generals and was fighting on its own soil.
2. In the early years of the war, the South held its own in the East but lost ground in the West. The Union's naval blockade of the South hurt the Confederacy. Union victories in the West, including the Battle of Shiloh and the capture of Nashville and New Orleans, weakened the South.
3. The turning point of the war came in July 1863, when Union forces triumphed at Gettysburg. A victory at Vicksburg gave the Union control of the Mississippi River. By 1865 the Union held the upper hand.
4. Led by Ulysses S. Grant, Union forces invaded the South. The South surrendered in April 1865. The war caused death and destruction. It also changed Americans' attitude toward their country, strengthened the federal government, and encouraged industrial growth.

Graphic Summary

North wants South to return to the Union; South wants independence.

Union blockades southern ports. Armies battle in Virginia, Maryland, Tennessee, and elsewhere.

Victories at Gettysburg and Vicksburg turn war in Union's favor.

South surrenders in April 1865.

War causes death and destruction, increases power of federal government, and spurs industry.

Review

KEY TERMS

Define the following terms.
1. Emancipation Proclamation
2. Battle of Gettysburg
3. front
4. First Battle of Bull Run
5. total war
6. Battle of Vicksburg
7. draft
8. antiseptic

COMPREHENSION

1. Where did Confederate leaders decide to establish their capital? Why was this a risky decision?
2. What were the strengths of the North and the South?
3. What were the war aims of the North and the South?
4. What factors led both sides to begin focusing more on winning decisive victories on the battlefield?
5. Why did the North blockade southern ports? How effective was the blockade by the end of the war?
6. Where was the western front in the war? Why was it important?
7. What battles marked the turning point in the war? Why were they significant?
8. When, where, and why did Lee finally surrender?
9. When was President Lincoln killed? Who killed him?
10. What were the consequences of the war?

Places to Locate

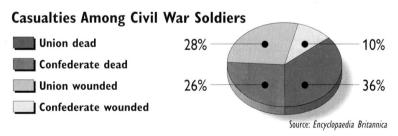

Match the letters on the map with the places listed below. Then explain the importance of each place.

1. Atlanta   **3.** Gettysburg   **5.** New Orleans
2. Vicksburg   **4.** Richmond

Geography Theme: Movement Explain the importance of rivers to both sides during the war.

Skill Review

The chart below shows casualties of the Civil War. Read it and answer the questions.

Casualties Among Civil War Soldiers

- Union dead
- Confederate dead
- Union wounded
- Confederate wounded

28%   10%
26%   36%

Source: *Encyclopaedia Britannica*

1. What is the whole quantity represented on the chart?
2. Which group made up the largest number of casualties? The smallest?

3. What percentage of Civil War casualties were deaths? What percentage were injuries?
4. What conclusions can you draw from this pie chart?

CRITICAL THINKING

1. Stating Both Sides of an Issue First defend, and then criticize, the idea that government should be given more power in wartime than in peacetime.

2. Identifying Cause and Effect Choose one of the battles discussed in this chapter and describe its effects on the South.

PORTFOLIO OPTIONS

1. Civics Connection The Civil War increased the power of the federal government. Do wars in general increase the power of the central government? Explain.

2. Writing Connection Find out about persons from your community or state who fought in the Civil War. Write a report on who they were, what units they joined, and what battles they fought.

3. Contemporary Connection Read newspapers to learn about a civil war taking place today. Create a chart showing similarities and differences between the opposing sides. Discuss how the emotions of a soldier involved in a civil war might differ from those of a soldier involved in a war between two or more different nations.

4. Timeline Connection Copy the chapter timeline. Add three other events from the chapter you think should be included and explain why. What effect did the Emancipation Proclamation have on the war? Explain.

When the Civil War ended, the nation was changed forever. The war had spurred the growth of northern industries and businesses. The South—like Richmond, shown below—lay in ruins. A great question faced the entire country: What sort of society would rise from the ashes of the former Confederacy?

1865

1870

1875

1865 Slavery ends

1866 Civil Rights Bill passed

1867 Reconstruction Act of 1867

1868 Fourteenth Amendment

1870 African Americans gain voting rights

1877 Federal troops leave the South

CHAPTER 20

Rebuilding the South
(1865–1896)

1 The Challenge of Freedom

SECTION GUIDE

Main Idea
After the Civil War, Americans had to work out a plan to rebuild the South.

Goals
As you read, look for answers to these questions:

1. What was the African American response to the ending of slavery?

2. What was President Johnson's plan for rebuilding the South?

3. How did southern states seek to restore the old order?

Key Terms
Reconstruction
amnesty
Thirteenth Amendment
black codes

THE DAY FREEDOM came was an event former slaves remembered for the rest of their lives. Years later one freedman (freed slave) described the feeling:

> **The end of the war, it come just like that—like you snap your fingers. . . . Soldiers, all of a sudden, was everywhere coming in bunches, crossing and walking and riding. Everyone was a-singing. We was all walking on golden clouds. Hallelujah! . . . We all felt like heroes, and nobody had made us that way but ourselves. We was free. Just like that, we was free.**

Responding to Freedom

African Americans' first reaction to freedom was to escape white control over their lives. Some returned to where they had been born. Others looked for family members, or just traveled for fun. "Right off colored folks started on the move," recalled one freedman. "They seemed to want to get closer to freedom, so they'd know what it was—like it was a place or a city."

Freedom allowed families to reunite and strengthened family ties. Under slavery, marriage had been an informal affair. With freedom, many couples went through marriage ceremonies.

African Americans also took steps to free their religion from white control. Throughout the South, they created their own

1880	1885	1890	1895	1900

1881 Tuskegee Institute established

1896 *Plessy v. Ferguson* decision

1890s Jim Crow laws passed

483

churches. The church then became the center of the African American community. It was a place for social events and political meetings. Often it was also a school.

Schools for African Americans sprouted up throughout the South. Both adults and children flocked to study at these schools. Reading and writing was, as many saw, the road to a new economic freedom. In the years after the war, African Americans raised over $1 million toward their own education. However, even this was not enough to meet the need. In the long run, government and private groups in the North would pay most of the cost of schooling for freedmen.

About 10 percent of the South's black adults could read. A number of them chose to become teachers. There were white teachers as well. Yet other, racist whites harassed teachers in African American schools. In some parts of the South, freedmen's schools were burned and teachers beaten or killed.

Issues of Land and Labor

More than anything else, freed slaves hoped to own land. General Sherman had ordered that coastal South Carolina be split into 40-acre parcels of land and given to freedmen. The rumor then spread through the South that all freedmen would be given 40 acres and a mule. That was, most believed, no more than their right. As one Virginian explained, "Didn't we clear the land, and raise the crops?" In fact, most freedmen never received land. Those who did often had to return it.

It was clear that the South needed a new system of labor. There were landowners with little cash and no laborers, and laborers without land.

Planters and freedmen alike had trouble getting used to their new working relationship. Planters were not used to bargaining with workers over hours and wages. Many freedmen assumed that the wage was an extra—that the landowner still had to clothe, house, and feed them.

Reconstruction Begins

When the Civil War ended in 1865, the South faced a great challenge: to build a new society, one not based on slavery. The federal government played an active role in this task. The government's plan to rebuild the ruined southern states is known as Reconstruction. Reconstruction took place during the years 1865–1877.

In the last year of the war, President Lincoln had begun to consider how the South should be treated when peace came. In his Second Inaugural Address in March 1865, Lincoln declared:

> **❝With malice toward none, with charity for all, with firmness in the right as God gives us to see the right, let us strive on to finish the work we are in, to bind up the nation's wounds . . . to do all which may achieve and cherish a just and a lasting peace among ourselves and with all nations. ❞**

On Lincoln's death, Vice President Andrew Johnson became President. Johnson, a Democrat, had been put on the Republican ticket in 1864 to broaden its appeal to the border states. A self-made man from Tennessee, Johnson was a former slaveholder. Unlike Lincoln, who knew how to compromise, Johnson was stubborn to a fault.

Johnson held that Reconstruction was the job of the President, not Congress. Johnson's policies were based on what he thought were Lincoln's goals. They included charity toward the former Confederates and the creation of new state governments. These governments, Johnson said, must forbid slavery. They must also accept the supreme power of the federal government.

To most white southerners Johnson offered amnesty, or official pardon. He also promised to restore their property. In return, they had to pledge their loyalty to the United States. The great planters, top military officers, and ex-Confederate leaders were not included in this offer. Even they, however, were able to win amnesty. Johnson was easily convinced when the once high-and-mighty asked him for pardon.

Reviving the Old South

Congress was not in session when Johnson took over as President in April 1865. It did not meet until the following December. During these eight months the former Confederate states rebuilt their societies. The problem was that the new states seemed too much like the old ones.

For example, nothing was done about black voting rights. Some states also refused to ratify the Thirteenth Amendment, which abolished slavery. "This is a white man's government," said the governor of South Carolina, "and intended for white men only."

Southern states began to pass laws limiting the freedom of African Americans. These laws, called black codes, aimed to return former slaves to plantation labor. In Mississippi, for instance, one law said that each person had to have written proof of employment. Anyone without such proof could be put on a plantation and forced to work there. In some states, children could be forced to work for their former owners, without their parents' approval. Other black codes said that African Americans could not meet in unsupervised groups or bear firearms. Those on

To regain captured property, white southerners, such as these residents of Charleston, South Carolina, had to swear loyalty to the United States.

A teacher conducts a class at a freedmen's school. Some of these schools developed into black colleges, such as Howard University. **Critical Thinking:** Why was education important for African Americans during Reconstruction?

plantations had to labor from sunup to sundown. They could not even leave the plantation without permission.

The Freedmen's Bureau

Opposition to the black codes came from the Freedmen's Bureau. This federal agency had been set up near the end of the war to distribute clothes, food, and fuel to the poor of the South. It ran schools for African American children. It was also in charge of land abandoned by Confederates or taken from them. It divided this land into 40-acre plots. These were to be rented to freedmen until the land could be sold.

All too often, however, freedmen had to give up their new farms. With Johnson's help, pardoned Confederate landowners were able to regain their land. Freedmen, their land gone, lost their best chance at economic freedom.

Congress Takes a Stand

When Congress met in December 1865, representatives from the South were there to take their seats. President Johnson was ready to welcome them. Yet the members of Congress were not willing to forget old differences quite so fast.

The problem was that many southern representatives had been officials in the Confederate government only the year before. This list included 9 officers, 6 cabinet members, and 58 congressmen. Even the former Confederate vice president was now about to enter Congress. Northern members of Congress were alarmed. They were also worried about conditions in the southern states. They asked: Had the Civil War been fought just to allow the South to return to its old ways?

Under the Constitution, Congress has the right to decide whether its members are qualified to hold office. Instead of admitting the southerners, therefore, Congress set up a committee. The committee would look into conditions in the South and decide whether the southern states should be represented in Congress. Congress thus let President Johnson know that it planned to play a role in Reconstruction.

SECTION REVIEW

1. Key Terms Reconstruction, amnesty, Thirteenth Amendment, black codes

2. People Andrew Johnson

3. Comprehension How did the lives of African Americans in the South change after they were freed?

4. Comprehension How did the South respond to President Johnson's reconstruction policies?

5. Critical Thinking President Johnson believed he was carrying out Lincoln's ideas on Reconstruction. Do you think Lincoln would have approved or disapproved of his policies? Explain.

2 Radical Reconstruction

SECTION GUIDE

Main Idea
Congress took over Reconstruction from the President and tried to give political equality to African Americans in the South.

Goals
As you read, look for answers to these questions:

1. How and why did Congress change its policy toward the South?

2. How did the efforts of Congress affect politics in the South?

3. Why did Congress try to limit the President's power?

Key Terms
moderate
civil rights
Fourteenth Amendment
scalawag
carpetbagger
Fifteenth Amendment

A S 1866 BEGAN, it was clear that the feelings that had led to war remained strong. A newspaper in Jackson, Mississippi, wrote, "We must keep the ex-slave in a position of inferiority. We must pass such laws as will make him *feel* his inferiority." The *Chicago Tribune* fired back. It wrote, "We tell the white men of Mississippi that the men of the North will convert the state of Mississippi into a frog pond before they will allow any such laws." The nation was in an angry mood as Congress began to consider the many problems of Reconstruction.

The Republicans in Congress

Republicans outnumbered Democrats in both houses of Congress. Most Republicans were moderates, or people who oppose great change. They wanted to work with the President.

Moderate Republicans were bothered by the number of ex-Confederates holding office. The abuses against African Americans in the South also concerned them. They did not believe the government could solve all of the South's problems. Like most Americans of the time, they wanted government to stay out of the affairs of individuals and the states.

The Radical Republicans felt differently. They had long urged the ending of slavery. They now called for full and equal citizenship for the freedmen. They argued that a true republic should grant citizenship to all.

The Radical Republicans had two leaders. One of them was Representative Thaddeus Stevens of Pennsylvania. The other was Senator Charles Sumner of Massachusetts.

The Radicals hoped that the federal government would remake southern politics and society. Their aim was to destroy the old ruling class. They wanted to turn the South into a place of small farms, free schools, respect for labor, and political equality.

Among the Republicans elected to Congress were the first black senators, Blanche K. Bruce (left) and Hiram R. Revels (right), shown here with Frederick Douglass.

SKILLS: Analyzing an Argument

LEARN

Most of us have heard or taken part in a heated argument. Such arguments often involve raised voices and hurt feelings, and they rarely help solve the problem at hand. There is, however, another kind of argument. The formal argument plays a vital role in the public discussion of important issues. It allows all sides of the issue to be aired. It is often written down.

A written argument has an introduction, a body, and a conclusion. The **introduction** expresses the main idea of the argument. The **body** contains the evidence or details that support the main idea. The **conclusion** restates the main idea and briefly summarizes the evidence. In an effective argument, these elements are presented in a convincing way.

PRACTICE

Read the excerpt at right. Senator Thaddeus Stevens is supporting a bill that would give the vote to African Americans living in the former Confederate states.

1. What is the main idea of Senator Stevens's argument?

2. What reasons does he offer to support his main idea?

3. Did Stevens follow the rules for creating an effective conclusion? Explain your answer.

APPLY

4. Write a formal argument to accept or reject the Fourteenth Amendment. Identify your viewpoint as that of a northerner or southerner, black or white, or male or female.

The following is an excerpt from an argument by Senator Thaddeus Stevens (shown right).

❝There are several good reasons for the passage of [the bill].

In the first place, it is just. . . . Have not loyal blacks as good a right to choose rulers and make laws as rebel whites? In the second place, it is [necessary] in order to protect the loyal white [Union] men in the seceded states. The white Union men are in a great minority in each of those states. With them the blacks would act in a body, . . . the two united would form a majority, control the states, and protect themselves. Now they are the victims of daily murder. . . .

For these, among other reasons, I am for Negro suffrage in every rebel state. If it be just, it should not be denied; if it be necessary, it should be adopted; if it be punishment to traitors, they deserve it.❞

The Civil Rights Act

Urged on by the Radicals, Congress did pass two bills in 1866. The first bill gave new powers to the Freedmen's Bureau. Congress also passed a bill dealing with civil rights —the rights of all citizens. This bill declared that all persons born in the United States (except American Indians) were citizens. It said that all citizens were entitled to equal rights regardless of their race.

Republicans were shocked when President Johnson vetoed both bills. Johnson tried to explain his position. He said that federal protection of black civil rights would lead "towards centralization" of the national government. He also argued that making African Americans full citizens would "operate against the white race."

Congress voted to override Johnson's veto of the Civil Rights Act. That is, two-thirds of the House and two-thirds of the Senate voted in favor of the bill after the President's veto. The bill thus became law. It was the first time Congress had passed a major law over a President's veto. Later, Congress also passed a new Freedmen's Bureau law over Johnson's veto. Congress had taken over Reconstruction.

The Fourteenth Amendment

Republicans were not satisfied with laws protecting the equality of all citizens. They wanted that equality to be protected by the Constitution itself. To do this they proposed the Fourteenth Amendment. It said that all people born in the United States were citizens and had the same rights as citizens. It also prevented states from depriving "any person of life, liberty, and property" without due process of law. All citizens were to be granted the "equal protection of the laws."

The Fourteenth Amendment stopped short of requiring black suffrage. Instead, it said that any state that kept African Americans from voting would lose representatives in Congress. This meant that the southern states would have less power if they did not grant black men the vote.

The year 1866 was a congressional election year. During the campaign, the President attacked the Fourteenth Amendment. He argued that southerners were loyal Americans. The real traitors, Johnson said, were the Radical Republicans. The voters, however, disagreed. They returned a 3 to 1 Republican majority in both houses of Congress.

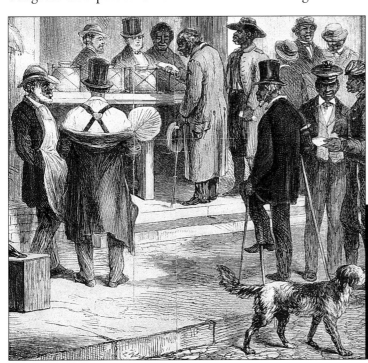

African Americans vote in an 1867 election in New Orleans. In the late 1860s, hundreds of thousands of black men registered to vote in the South. **Critical Thinking:** Why might the great majority of African Americans have backed Republican candidates?

BLANCHE KELSO BRUCE
(1841–1898)

Blanche Kelso Bruce, senator from Mississippi from 1875 to 1881, believed the rights of all citizens should be respected. He stood in the Senate chamber and spoke out: *Black people are being denied the right to vote. The government should be helping, not destroying, Native Americans. The United States should not exclude Chinese immigrants.* Bruce had been born into slavery. He was the first African American to serve a full term in the Senate. He worked for honest federal elections and urged better race relations. After his term, he was appointed register of the Treasury. For several years, his signature appeared on U.S. bills.

The Reconstruction Act of 1867

Encouraged by Johnson's support, each of the ex-Confederate states except Tennessee voted to reject the Fourteenth Amendment. This move so angered moderate Republicans that they agreed to work with the Radicals. Together, the two groups passed the tough Reconstruction Act of 1867. Thus began a period known as Radical Reconstruction.

The Reconstruction Act of 1867 divided the South into five military districts, each run by an army commander. Members of the prewar ruling class, about 10–15 percent of southern whites, lost their voting rights. The law also explained how the southern states could re-enter the Union. Voters in those states would have to do two things. (1) They would have to approve new state constitutions that gave the vote to all adult men. (2) They would have to ratify the Fourteenth Amendment.

A New Order in the South

In 1867, Freedmen's Bureau agents began to register voters in the South. About 735,000 blacks and 635,000 whites were registered to vote. The voters then chose delegates to the new state conventions. Three-fourths of them were Republicans.

Almost half of these Republican delegates were whites who had supported the North. Living in the upcountry, they were poor people who produced just enough food to feed themselves. Many of them had lost faith in the Confederate cause long before the war's end. Angry at the destruction of their farms and livestock, they blamed the plantation owners for starting what they called "a rich man's war." Now that the war was over, they were eager to take power from the old ruling class. The planters called them **scalawags** —meaning "scoundrels"—for going along with Radical Reconstruction.

Nearly one-fourth of the Republican delegates were white northerners who had moved south after the war. Many southerners thought that these northerners had come only for their own gain. They called them **carpetbaggers,** after a cheap kind of suitcase. The idea was that these northerners had quickly stuffed their belongings

Northerners who went south after the war were accused of seeking wealth and power, but possessing little more than could fit into a carpetbag.

into a suitcase and headed south to cash in on the South's distress. However, as one historian has pointed out:

> **[They] brought not skimpy carpetbags but rather considerable capital, which they invested in the South. They also invested human capital—themselves—in a drive to modernize the region's social structure, revive its crippled economy, and democratize its politics.**

African Americans made up close to one-third of the Republican delegates. Of these, half had been free before the war. Most were ministers, teachers, or skilled workers. Eighty percent of them could read, and some had gone to college.

The delegates wrote new constitutions based on northern examples. They set up public school systems and gave the vote to all adult males. By 1869, voters had approved all these constitutions. The ex-Confederate states were let back into the Union, and thus back into Congress. Fourteen African American congressmen and two African American senators would serve in Congress during Reconstruction.

Reconstruction Legislatures

More than 600 African Americans served in state legislatures during Reconstruction. These legislatures began rebuilding the South. Yet new schools, hospitals, and roads all cost money. To pay for them, the legislatures turned to property taxes (taxes based on the worth of a person's land). Thus plantation owners, who held the least political power in the new system, were paying the greatest share of the costs.

Some Republicans hoped that high taxes would force plantation owners to sell their land. Poor whites and blacks could then buy the land and set up farms. Though some landowners did have to give up their plantations, little of this land ended up belonging to the poor.

Johnson Is Impeached

Reconstruction faced problems in Washington, D.C., as well. President Johnson obeyed the letter of the Reconstruction laws, but he worked against them in spirit. For instance, he chose people friendly to the ex-Confederates to serve as military commanders in the South. Some in Congress would not stand for such an action. Finally there was a showdown between the President and Congress.

In 1867 Congress passed a law that challenged the President's power. It said that the President could not fire members of the Cabinet without the Senate's approval. This law broke with the tradition that a President controlled the Cabinet.

Johnson opposed the law. To test it, he fired Secretary of War Edwin Stanton in February 1868. Stanton and Johnson had clashed over Reconstruction. Three days later the House of Representatives voted to impeach the President. This means that the House formally accused him of improper conduct while in office.

The conflict between Congress and the President went far beyond the issue of the 1867 law. In the eyes of most members of Congress, Johnson's real crime was standing in the way of Congress's plans for Reconstruction. They hoped to convict Johnson and force him from office. In this way they would strengthen Congress's hold over Reconstruction.

In cases of impeachment, the Senate acts as the jury. A two-thirds vote is needed

To be taken up at MAIN ENTRANCE of the U.S. SENATE

U.S. SENATE
Impeachment OF THE President
ADMIT THE BEARER
MARCH 13. 1868
Geo. T. Brown
Sergeant-at-Arms
Philp & Solomons, Wash. D.C.

The cartoon, top, of Andrew Johnson pokes fun at his claim that it is the President's constitutional right to control the Cabinet. His refusal to accept congressional limits to that control led to his impeachment, which was open to the public (above). **Critical Thinking:** How did the Senate's failure to remove him from office strengthen the presidency?

This lithograph, honoring the passage of the Fifteenth Amendment, includes the text of the amendment, shown at the far right, above the picture of an African American soldier. **Critical Thinking:** In what ways was the Fifteenth Amendment a step beyond the Fourteenth Amendment?

before a President can be removed from office. After a full trial, the Senate fell one vote short of the two-thirds required. Johnson was acquitted. By one vote, the tradition of a strong presidency and the separation of powers had remained intact.

The Fifteenth Amendment

The Radical Republicans had more success with the Fifteenth Amendment, which became law in 1870. This amendment declared that the right to vote should not be denied "on account of race, color, or previous condition of servitude." (The Fifteenth Amendment, like the Fourteenth Amendment, did not apply to American Indians living on tribal lands.)

The Fifteenth Amendment was not only aimed at the South. Its supporters were concerned about black suffrage throughout the country. African American men could not vote in sixteen states. "We have no moral right to impose an obligation on one part of the land which the rest will not accept," one Radical wrote. By approving

the Fifteenth Amendment, the nation accepted the full consequences of ending slavery. It also committed itself once again to the principle of democracy.

3 The End of Reconstruction

SECTION GUIDE

Main Idea
White southerners limited black political power, ending Reconstruction. Despite the growth of industry in the late 1800s, the South suffered from poverty and segregation.

Goals
As you read, look for the answers to these questions:

1. What was the Ku Klux Klan? What was President Grant's response to it?

2. How did Democrats gain control of the southern political system?

3. What economic changes took place in the South in the late 1800s?

Key Terms
lynch
Compromise of 1877
sharecropping
Jim Crow laws
segregation
Plessy v. Ferguson

Republicans Ulysses S. Grant and Schuyler Colfax were elected President and Vice President in 1868.

D ELEGATES AT the Republican National Convention, meeting in Chicago in 1868, were wild with excitement. They had nominated Ulysses S. Grant, the great Union war hero, for President. With hundreds of thousands of African American men registered to vote in the South, Republicans were filled with hope for victory. They were not disappointed. African American votes helped power Grant into office.

The Rise of the Ku Klux Klan
The election brought a backlash against Reconstruction. Many members of the old planter class and ex-Confederate soldiers joined the Ku Klux Klan, a secret group formed just after the war. The Klan's first goal was to control elections.

Beyond that, the Klan aimed to keep African Americans powerless. It targeted blacks who owned their own land, any blacks who prospered, and teachers of black children. Such people were attacked by Klansmen. Some were even **lynched** —killed without a trial. The Klan was known to have murdered freedmen just because they could read and write.

The Klan's terrorist activities served the Democratic Party. The Democratic platform in 1868 had called reconstruction policies "unconstitutional, revolutionary, and void." It demanded that the Freedmen's Bureau be shut down. The white-robed, gun-toting, horse-riding Klansmen attacked Republicans. In the South, Klan raids killed hundreds of African Americans. The terror tactics worked. In every county where the Klan was active, Republican voters stayed away from the polls.

Grant Versus the Klan
At first, President Grant tried to avoid conflict with the Klan. By 1871, however, it became impossible to ignore the reign of terror that was sweeping the South. Grant asked Congress to pass a tough law against

PRESENT ▶ VICTORY AT THE POLLS

For a long time after Reconstruction, there were few African Americans in government. That is changing, as record numbers of African Americans are elected to local, state, and national office. In 1992 voting districts were redrawn to give all ethnic groups greater political power. That year five southern states elected their first black representatives to Congress since Reconstruction. Carol Moseley-Braun of Illinois (pictured above) became the first black woman to serve in the U.S. Senate.

the Klan. Joseph Rainey, a black congressman from South Carolina who had received death threats from the Klan, spoke of the fear of Klan violence:

❝When myself and colleagues shall leave these Halls and turn our footsteps toward our southern home we know not but that the assassin may await our coming. Be it as it may we have resolved to be loyal and firm, and if we perish, we perish! ❞

Congress did approve the anti-Klan bill. The federal government now moved against the Klan, as federal marshals arrested thousands of Klansmen. As a result, the 1872 election was both fair and peaceful in the South. Unfortunately, the same could not be said of later elections.

Reconstruction Ends

In 1876 the Democratic Party chose Samuel J. Tilden, governor of New York, to run for President. The Republicans nominated Rutherford B. Hayes, governor of Ohio. The race was so close that victory depended on the electoral votes of South Carolina, Louisiana, and Florida. Those results, however, were in dispute. It was up to Congress to settle the matter.

Congress appointed a special commission, which resolved the problem by an "understanding." Under the agreement, called the Compromise of 1877, Hayes was elected President. In return, Hayes agreed to remove the last troops from the South. As soon as he became President, Hayes did just that. The last few reconstruction governments then collapsed. With them went black southerners' best hope for political equality.

Sharecropping

African Americans in the South already suffered from economic inequality. Many engaged in sharecropping. Under this system, a farmer and his family rented a plot of land to farm. The landowner provided the tools, seed, and housing. When harvest time came, the sharecropper gave the landowner a share of the crop. This system allowed landowners to keep their land and gave landless families a place to farm.

The farmers and landowners had opposite goals. The farmers wanted to grow food to feed themselves. Yet landowners forced them to grow cash crops such as cotton. Farmers had to buy their food from the country store, which was often owned by the landlord. Most farmers got caught in a never-ending cycle of debt, in which this year's harvest went to pay last year's bills.

White farmers also became sharecroppers. Many had lost their land and livestock in the war. Others had lost their land to taxes. By 1880, one-third of the white farmers in the Deep South worked someone else's land.

The South paid a heavy price for depending on cotton. Growing cotton exhausted the soil and reduced the amount of land available for food crops. As a result, the South had to import half its food. Sharecroppers could barely afford to feed their families. The Deep South was doomed to years of rural poverty.

The Growth of Industry

The South's problems spurred calls for a shift away from farming. One of the best-known voices was that of Henry Grady, editor of the *Atlanta Constitution*. Grady urged the South to turn to industry. He wanted a "New South"—one that was more like the North, with large cities and factories. Aided by new leaders and by a nationwide boom in business, the South built new industries, including steel, cloth, and tobacco processing. It also repaired its war-damaged railroads and laid new track.

One of the most successful new businesses in the "New South" was the tobacco industry. James B. Duke of Durham, North Carolina, started out with a small, family-run tobacco business. In 1881 he bought the rights to the first cigarette-making machine. Sales of cigarettes made by his company soared. By the 1890s his American Tobacco Company controlled the tobacco industry.

Southern textile mills also grew. "Bring the cotton mills to the cotton," southern boosters declared. Textile mills began sprouting up in the piedmont region. By 1900 the South was producing almost a quarter of the nation's cotton cloth.

Laborers on a South Carolina rice plantation.

In the late 1800s, industries developed in some southern cities. Thanks to its huge steel mills, Birmingham, Alabama, became known as the "Pittsburgh of the South."
Critical Thinking: What other industries were important in the South?

Shown here is a chemistry class at Tuskegee Institute, founded by Booker T. Washington. Its faculty included George Washington Carver, a famous agricultural researcher. Students constructed the school buildings and farmed the surrounding fields.

The South had come a long way from the deep poverty that followed the war. Yet life there was in many ways more difficult than life in the North. White women and children in the North earned double the wages of their counterparts in the South.

The Segregated South

In the decades after Reconstruction, divisions between African Americans and whites in the South grew. In the 1890s Jim Crow laws began to rule southern life. (*Jim Crow* was a term commonly used to refer to African Americans.) These laws made segregation, or separation by race, official in streetcars, theaters, and even cemeteries.

On June 7, 1892, an African American named Homer Plessy boarded a train in Louisiana, taking a seat in a car labeled "whites only." He was promptly arrested for breaking a state law. Plessy took his case to the U.S. Supreme Court, arguing that the Fourteenth Amendment banned segregation.

In 1896 the Court issued its decision in *Plessy v. Ferguson.* It declared that segregation was lawful as long as facilities for blacks and whites were equal, a policy known as "separate but equal." One justice,

John Marshall Harlan, opposed this decision. He wrote, "Our Constitution is color-blind, and neither knows nor tolerates classes among citizens." His words were to be ignored for more than half a century, as African Americans were forced into a separate and very unequal life in the South.

The Solid South

One reason African Americans lost political power after Reconstruction was that they lacked economic power. Most still worked for whites. They could be fired if they voted, and they knew it.

In the years after Reconstruction, the old ruling class had tried to keep power by using the black vote or by controlling black officeholders. The next generation of southerners was even more racist. It tried to prevent African Americans from voting at all.

One way was to terrorize them. Jim Reeves, a black resident of Arkansas, remembered that in 1888 white people went around Union county ordering the blacks not to vote. One African American responded, "Well, I am going to the polls tomorrow if I have to crawl." On the day before the election, white gangs shot a number of blacks. "In that way," Reeves said, "quite a few of the Negroes [left] their

Booker T. Washington said economic success was more important than social equality for African Americans. **Critical Thinking:** Would you have agreed with him if you lived at that time? Explain.

homes and went into different counties and . . . different states." Those who stayed quit voting.

Beginning in 1890, Mississippi and other southern states also made it harder for African Americans to vote. In order to vote, people had to pay a fee (known as a poll tax) and prove that they could read. Many African Americans could not meet these conditions. Neither could many whites, but for them the rules were often relaxed. By 1900 politics in the South had become so Democratic that the region became known as the "solid South." It could be counted on to back solidly every Democratic candidate for office.

African Americans Organize

These were bitter days for African Americans in the South. The high hopes of the days of Reconstruction had been dashed. American society did not seem inspired by those words of the Declaration of Independence: "All men are created equal."

African Americans found hope in their own communities. Although short of funds, black schools and colleges educated the new generation of free black persons. Black churches provided leadership and gave aid to the needy. Groups like the National Negro Business League helped African Americans help each other.

The founder of the National Negro Business League was a former slave named Booker T. Washington. Washington be-

came one of the most noted African American leaders of his day. In 1881 he set up Tuskegee Institute in Alabama.

The school reflected Washington's view that African Americans needed to learn a useful trade instead of demanding social equality from the government. "It is at the bottom of life we must begin, and not at the top," he said. "The opportunity to earn a dollar in a factory just now is worth infinitely more than the opportunity to spend a dollar in an opera house."

In time, many African Americans came to doubt the wisdom of Washington's advice. Blacks could not make solid economic gains without political power, they argued. Winning this power, however, would take years of struggle.

SECTION REVIEW

1. Key Terms lynch, Compromise of 1877, sharecropping, Jim Crow laws, segregation, *Plessy v. Ferguson*

2. People Ulysses S. Grant, Rutherford B. Hayes, Henry Grady, Booker T. Washington

3. Comprehension How did the election of 1876 bring an end to Reconstruction?

4. Comprehension How did the sharecropping system contribute to poverty in the South?

5. Critical Thinking Was Reconstruction a success or a failure? Explain.

Summary

1. After the Civil War, the South's society and economy had to be rebuilt. This task was known as Reconstruction. The Thirteenth Amendment ended slavery, but President Johnson followed a cautious policy toward the ex-Confederate states.

2. In 1867, Congress imposed strict military rule on the South, thereby beginning a period known as Radical Reconstruction. It passed the Fourteenth Amendment, which protected the rights of African Americans. Tensions between the President and Congress rose. Johnson was impeached in 1868, though he was not convicted. Radical Republicans were successful in gaining passage of the Fifteenth Amendment, which gave African American men the vote.

3. During the 1870s, white Democrats regained control of the South and Reconstruction ended in 1877. A Supreme Court ruling upheld the official policy of racial segregation in the South. In the late 1800s, rural southerners, lacking their own land, became trapped in a vicious cycle of poverty. On the other hand, the growth of industry in parts of the south gave rise to a "New South."

Review

KEY TERMS

Write a sentence using each of the following terms.

1. amnesty
2. black codes
3. carpetbagger
4. civil rights
5. Fifteenth Amendment
6. *Plessy v. Ferguson*
7. scalawag
8. sharecropping

COMPREHENSION

1. What was President Johnson's attitude toward Reconstruction?
2. How did white southerners try to restore the prewar order?
3. What was the Freedmen's Bureau?
4. Why did moderate Republicans support the goals of the Radicals?
5. How did the Thirteenth, Fourteenth, and Fifteenth Amendments affect African Americans?
6. Why was President Johnson impeached? What was the outcome of the trial?
7. What were the aims of the Ku Klux Klan?
8. Why were U.S. troops removed from the South in 1877? How did that affect Reconstruction?
9. How did the Supreme Court affect African Americans in the late 1800s?
10. What economic changes took place in the postwar South?

Graphic Summary

Presidential Reconstruction: amnesty toward former Confederates.

Radical Reconstruction: military control, increased rights for African Americans.

Southern reaction: black codes, the Ku Klux Klan, attacks on Republicans.

End of Reconstruction: Compromise of 1877, U.S. troops leave, reconstruction governments collapse.

The New South: legal segregation, sharecropping system, some industry.

Places to Locate

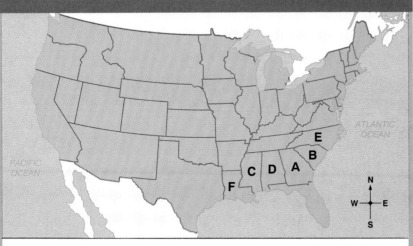

Match the letters on the map with the places that are listed below. Then explain the importance of each place.

1. Alabama   3. Louisiana   5. North Carolina
2. Georgia   4. Mississippi   6. South Carolina

Geographic Theme: Place How did the "New South" described by Henry Grady differ from the "Old South"?

Skill Review

Francis Cardoza, an African American member of South Carolina's constitutional convention, made the statement below in 1868. Read it and answer the questions that follow.

> "What is the main cause of the prosperity of the North? It is because every man has his own farm and is free and independent. Let the lands of the South be similarly divided. . . . If [the lands] are sold, . . . the chances are that the colored man and the poor [white] man would be the purchasers."

1. What is Cardoza proposing?
2. What sentence expresses the main idea behind Cardoza's argument?
3. How does Cardoza support his argument that dividing up southern plantations will help both black and white farmers?

CRITICAL THINKING

1. Analyzing Decisions Do you agree or disagree with Congress's decision in 1865 not to admit elected representatives with ties to the Confederacy? Explain your point of view.

2. Inferring Why was ending slavery only one step toward dealing with the nation's racial divisions?

3. Comparing Consider the Supreme Court's ruling in *Plessy v. Ferguson*. Is it possible for a society to be both segregated and free? Explain.

PORTFOLIO OPTIONS

1. Civics Connection During Radical Reconstruction, could white southern landowners justly object to property taxes on the grounds that there should be "no taxation without representation"? Why or why not?

2. Writing Connection Imagine that you are a member of the old upper class during Reconstruction. Write a letter to a relative outside the South explaining your views on Reconstruction.

3. Contemporary Connection Industry began to take hold in the South during Reconstruction. Do research to find out what industries the southern economy depends on today. How has the southern economy changed?

4. Timeline Connection Which event included on the chapter timeline was most significant? Why?

THE RED BADGE OF COURAGE STEPHEN CRANE

Stephen Crane's classic Civil War novel, *The Red Badge of Courage,* tells the story of Henry Fleming, a new recruit for the Union army. Henry volunteers to find adventure and glory, but the fury of the fighting makes him see the true horrors of war. The scene below takes place after Henry's first battle. Read the passage and answer the questions that follow.

At last an exultant yell went along the quivering line. The firing dwindled from an uproar to a last vindictive popping. As the smoke slowly eddied away, the youth [Henry] saw that the charge had been repulsed. The enemy were scattered into reluctant groups. He saw a man climb to the top of the fence, straddle the rail, and fire a parting shot. The waves had receded, leaving bits of dark debris upon the ground.

Some in the regiment began to whoop frenziedly. Many were silent. Apparently they were trying to contemplate themselves.

After the fever had left his veins, the youth thought that at last he was going to suffocate. He became aware of the foul atmosphere in which he had been struggling. He was grimy and dripping like a laborer in a foundry. He grasped his canteen and took a long swallow of the warmed water.

A sentence with variations went up and down the line. "Well, we've helt 'em back. We've helt 'em back; derned if we haven't." The men said it blissfully, leering at each other with dirty smiles.

The youth turned to look behind him and off to the right and off to the left. He experienced the joy of a man who at last finds leisure in which to look about him.

Under foot there were a few ghastly forms motionless. They lay twisted in fantastic contortions. Arms were bent and heads were turned in incredible ways. It seemed that the dead men must have fallen from some great height to get into such positions. They looked to be dumped out upon the ground from the sky.

From a position in the rear of the grove a battery was throwing shells over it. The flash of the guns startled the youth at first. He thought they were aimed directly at him. Through the trees he watched the black figures of the gunners as they worked swiftly and intently. Their labor seemed a complicated thing. He wondered how they could remember its formula in the midst of confusion. . . .

A small procession of wounded men were going drearily toward the rear. It was a flow of blood from the torn body of the brigade.

To the right and to the left were the dark lines of other troops. Far in front he thought he could see lighter masses protruding in points from the forest. They were suggestive of unnumbered thousands.

Once he saw a tiny battery go dashing along the line of the horizon. The tiny riders were beating the tiny horses.

From a sloping hill came the sound of cheerings and clashes. Smoke welled slowly through the leaves.

Batteries were speaking with thunderous oratorical effort. Here and there were flags, the red in the stripes dominating. They splashed bits of warm color upon the dark lines of troops.

The youth felt the old thrill at the sight of the emblem. They were like beautiful birds strangely undaunted in a storm.

As he listened to the din from the hillside, to a deep pulsating thunder that came from afar to the left, and to the lesser clamors which came from many directions, it occurred to him that they were fighting, too, over there, and over there, and over there. Heretofore he had supposed that all the battle was directly under his nose.

As he gazed around him the youth felt a flash of astonishment at the blue, pure sky and the sun gleaming on the trees and fields. It was surprising that Nature had gone tranquilly on with her golden process in the midst of so much devilment.

From *The Red Badge of Courage*, by Stephen Crane (D. Appleton, 1895).

"A Young Soldier," by Winslow Homer.

Analyzing Literature

1. Describe Henry's emotions.

2. Why did Henry think that all the fighting had been "directly under his nose"?

3. Why is Henry astonished as he gazes at the sky and the sun gleaming on the fields?

4. Do you think Henry has begun to see the harsh realities of war? Explain your answer, using examples from the passage.

UNIT 7

America Transformed (1860–1920)

Chapter 21

An Industrial Society (1860–1900)

Rising industries like steel powered American economic growth after 1860.

Chapter 22

The Rise of American Cities (1865–1900)

A new burst of immigration helped American cities grow in size and population.

UNIT OVERVIEW

Following the Civil War, the United States was transformed from a land of farms to a land with industry and cities.

Chapter 23

Forces Shaping a New West (1860–1900)

As American Indians were pushed off their lands, miners, ranchers, and farmers moved westward.

Chapter 24

Politics and Reform (1877–1919)

Several movements in the late 1800s and early 1900s worked to reform American politics and society.

Chapter 25

Becoming a World Power (1890–1920)

The United States became more involved around the world and gained overseas territories.

Illustration: "Washington Street, Indianapolis at Dusk" (detail).

503

American industry boomed in the late 1800s, and railroads and other technology were important reasons why. Trains played a key role in moving goods across the country. Shown here is a bustling railroad yard in Atlanta, Georgia.

1860

1865

1870

1875

1869 Transcontinental railroad completed

1876 Telephone invented

1862 Pacific Railroad Act passed

1876 Centennial Exposition opens in Philadelphia

An Industrial Society
(1860–1900)

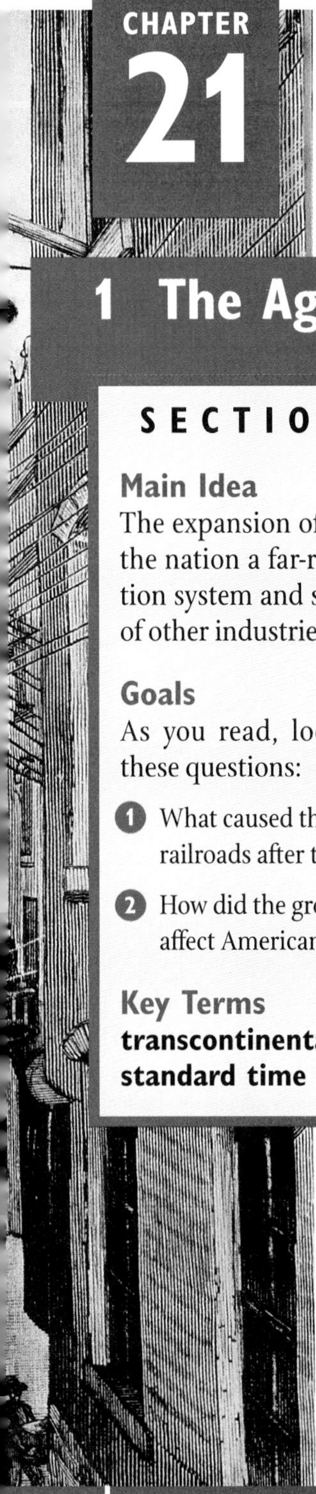

1 The Age of Railroads

SECTION GUIDE

Main Idea

The expansion of the railroads gave the nation a far-ranging transportation system and speeded the growth of other industries.

Goals

As you read, look for answers to these questions:

1. What caused the expansion of the railroads after the Civil War?

2. How did the growth of the railroads affect American life?

Key Terms

transcontinental
standard time

THERE WAS NOT A TREE to be seen. To the south shimmered the Great Salt Lake. In the east rose the bluish shapes of the Rocky Mountains. Across that space, from opposite directions, teams of workers sweated to build two lines of railroad. Both raced to see who could lay the most track before they met.

Rails Across the Continent

In 1860 Abraham Lincoln and the Republican Party had promised a transcontinental railroad if elected. (Transcontinental means "across the continent.") In 1862, therefore, Congress passed the Pacific Railroad Act, which provided for two companies to build a transcontinental line. The Central Pacific would build east from Sacramento, California. The Union Pacific would build west from Omaha, Nebraska.

It was an enormous job and required a huge amount of capital (money for investment). Congress, therefore, offered the railroad builders government land as well as loans. The railroads were to receive sections of land along the new tracks. In the end these land grants amounted to about 20 million acres.

Building the Railroads

The railroad companies needed a great many workers to lay the miles of track. They hired a variety of people, including African Americans, American Indians, and immigrants. For most of its

1880   1885   1890   1895

1886 Haymarket Riot

1894 Pullman Strike

1882 Chinese Exclusion Act

1892 Homestead Strike

1879 Light bulb invented

Brute strength built railroads, with workers like these often laying down tracks at a rate of four rails a minute. **Critical Thinking:** Why did most Chinese workers build railroads in the West? Why did Irish immigrants work mainly on eastern railroads?

gallons of it, and thus were less likely to get sick than workers who drank unboiled ditch water. Impressed, the railroad began a drive to bring Chinese laborers to the United States. At the peak of construction, more than 10,000 Chinese worked on the railroad.

The biggest challenge for the Central Pacific workers was to cross the Sierra Nevada. These mountains separate California from the desert lands to the east. At one place, workers had to lay track along a cliff face with a 1,400-foot drop. To blast out a roadbed from the cliff face, Chinese workers were lowered in baskets over the edge. There they drilled holes, put in sticks of dynamite, lit the fuse, and tugged the rope to be pulled up before the explosion.

There was no way over the mountains. The only answer was to tunnel through them. The engineers—a growing professional class in America—figured out how the tunnel would work. It would have to curve and at the same time change its level.

To build the tunnel, workers began drilling from each side of the mountain. After more than a year of round-the-clock drilling and blasting, the workers met in the middle of the mountain. The engineers figured that they were off by only two inches!

The Track Is Completed

Once through the Sierras, the Central Pacific moved fast. After all, it was racing with the Union Pacific to see who could lay the most track. (The Union Pacific had no such mountains to contend with.) Track was laid at an average of one to two miles a day. By May 1869, the Union Pacific had laid 1,086 miles of track. The Central Pacific had laid 690 miles of track.

On May 10, 1869, nothing but one span of track separated the two lines. On that day at Promontory, Utah, the rails were connected by a golden spike. A spike was attached to a telegraph wire so that when the spike was struck, the charge would be

laborers the Union Pacific turned to Irish immigrants. During this time about one of every five immigrants to the United States came from Ireland. These immigrants had few skills. They were qualified, however, for backbreaking labor on the railroads.

The Central Pacific relied on Chinese immigrants. Americans discriminated against the Chinese, and at first the construction manager of the Central Pacific had not welcomed them. They were small—weighing about 110 pounds—and in no way looked like the larger Irish laborers working on the Union Pacific. The manager soon discovered, however, that the Chinese were hard workers and fearless. They also drank tea—

This sign noted a record for the Central Pacific line.

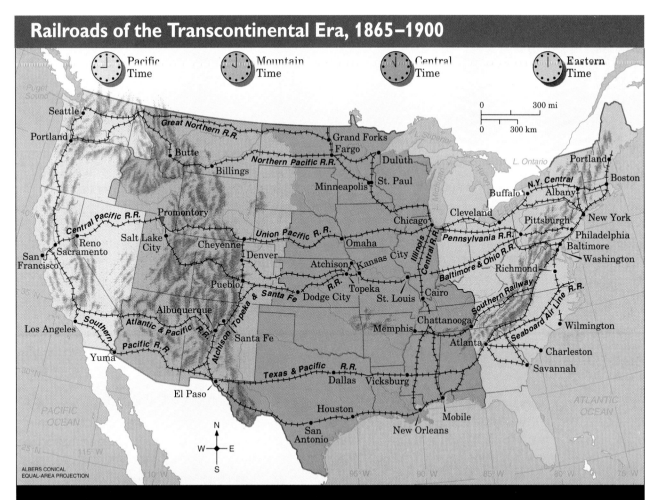

Railroads of the Transcontinental Era, 1865–1900

Pacific Time Mountain Time Central Time Eastern Time

GEOGRAPHY SKILLS: By 1900 the United States had almost 200,000 miles of track—about one-third of the world total. Railroads also contributed to the development of time zones. **Critical Thinking:** How did railroads contribute to the growth of such cities as Chicago and El Paso?

transmitted across the nation. Americans rejoiced at the news.

Combining the Railroads

In the years after the Civil War, railroad building became the nation's biggest business. By 1900 there were nearly six times as many miles of track as in 1865.

Because of government help, western railroads were big from the start. In contrast, the large rail systems of the East were formed by combining smaller companies that had been started earlier. For instance, Cornelius Vanderbilt created the New York

Central system by buying smaller railroads across the eastern half of the country. By 1873 the New York Central was providing direct rail service between New York City and Chicago.

Two other systems that tied together eastern and midwestern cities were the Pennsylvania Railroad and the Baltimore and Ohio. Meanwhile, the Southern Railway linked Washington, D.C., with such southern cities as New Orleans.

By 1893 there were five transcontinental railroad routes. Compared to the spiderweb look of eastern railways, the western

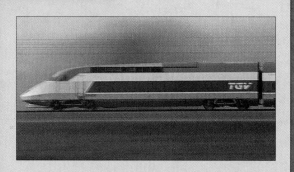

A new breed of trains is on its way to America, soaring at speeds never dreamed of by the railroaders of the 1800s. The Swedish-built X2000 races at a top speed of 155 miles per hour. It sweeps around curves at a breathtaking 112 m.p.h. Other trains must hold their speed to 75 m.p.h. or risk jumping the track. The wheels on the X2000 can adapt to the shape of the curves. To make passengers comfortable on those speedy curves, each train car tilts slightly, just as race cars do on a track. The tilt prevents luggage, cups, and people from tipping over as the car whips around a corner.

railways were straight. They pointed across deserts, prairies, and mountains on their way to Pacific Coast cities.

Impact of the Railroads

How did the railroads change American history?

(1) *The railroads helped end Indian control of the West.* The Plains Indians, across whose lands the railroads cut like knives, fought this invasion, but in vain. Indian fears were justified. The railroads brought the buffalo hunters, miners, and settlers who would destroy their world.

(2) *The railroads tied together the economies of the West and East.* From the West, the railroads carried eastward such raw materials as lumber, minerals, livestock, and grain. In midwestern cities like St. Louis, Chicago, Minneapolis, and Cleveland, the raw materials were processed. Grain was milled into flour. Hogs became bacon and hams. Cattle became beef. Iron ore was converted into steel. Lumber was cut into wood for housing. The processed goods were shipped by rail to eastern cities. From eastern cities, in turn, came manufactured goods, which were sold to westerners.

By turning the nation into a single giant marketplace, the railroads helped the growth of American industry. They also spurred the growth of those cities connected by railways.

(3) *The railroads helped people settle and farm the plains and valleys of the West.* The cattle and wheat these people raised would feed the cities. Many of these farm families had moved west with dreams of independence. Yet they often found themselves at the mercy of outside forces. Railroad companies controlled their ability to move their crops and the cost of transporting them. Eastern buyers determined how much they would pay for the crops.

(4) *Railroads changed the way people thought about the environment.* Until the age of railroads, people lived and worked mainly where there was water transport, such as rivers or the sea. Roads were primitive, following valleys from town to town. Snow, ice, rain, and floods could close down both water and road transportation. It was hard to keep to a schedule in the face of such hazards.

Railroads were different. Engineers and surveyors laid out the railroads in almost straight lines between cities. Railroads made possible cities like Denver, Colorado, and Cheyenne, Wyoming. These cities had no water transport at all.

Climate, too, had little effect on the trains. In summer storm and winter snow, in cold and in heat, the trains kept moving, delivering passengers and goods on time. Schedules became part of American life.

Railroads even broke free of what was called "sun time." Formerly wherever people had lived, noon was the time when the sun was highest in the sky. This system created a nightmare for the people who set railroad schedules.

At first the railroads set up "railroad time" along sections of the track. These time zones were so local, however, there were about 100 of them in 1883.

To deal with this problem, the railroads agreed to a system of standard time. They divided the United States into four time zones. Although the plan went into effect on November 18, 1883, many communities refused to accept it. Congress itself did not adopt the scheme until 1918. Today the country is divided into six time zones, the four original ones plus Alaska Time and Hawaii–Aleutian Time.

Railroad Heroes

Train workers also became heroes. One of the most famous was Casey Jones, engineer on a passenger train running from Chicago to New Orleans.

Freight trains always went on a side track to let passenger trains pass. On April 30, 1900, however, two freight trains in Mississippi blocked the main track. Jones's train was running at 70 miles an hour when he rounded a bend and saw the stalled freight cars. He told his fireman to jump as he hit the emergency brakes.

Jones was killed in the collision, but his was the only death. If he had jumped himself, all the passengers might have died.

An African American railroad worker, Wallace Saunders, wrote a ballad about Jones's heroic act. Later, two entertainers rewrote the ballad, turning it into a world-famous song about Jones's "farewell trip to the promised land."

Another kind of hero was the laborer on the track. As they worked, African American laborers sang a song about the mythical John Henry. John Henry, according to

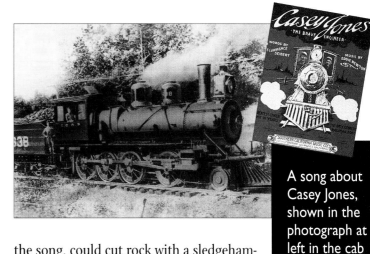

A song about Casey Jones, shown in the photograph at left in the cab of his engine, was published in the early 1900s (above).

the song, could cut rock with a sledgehammer faster than a steam drill could:

> **John Henry he told his Cap'n,
> Looky yonder, boy, what do I see?
> Your drill's done broke and your hole's done choke,
> And you can't drive steel like me, Lawd, Lawd,
> And you can't drive steel like me.**

SECTION REVIEW

1. Key Terms transcontinental, standard time

2. Places Sacramento, Omaha, Promontory (Utah)

3. Comprehension How did the federal government encourage the building of transcontinental railroads?

4. Comprehension How did transcontinental railroads affect the lands they crossed and the cities they connected?

5. Critical Thinking Explain how railroad technology changed the way people thought about the natural environment. What are some other examples of how technology has changed our relationship to the environment? Explain.

2 New Industries, New Inventions

SECTION GUIDE

Main Idea
The growth of industry in the years from 1865 to 1900 transformed American life.

Goals
As you read, look for answers to these questions:

1. What were the four main causes of industrial growth in the second half of the 1800s?

2. How did new innovations and inventions change Americans' ways of life?

Key Terms
centennial
patent

IN 1876 THE UNITED STATES was 100 years old. To celebrate, the nation gave itself a birthday party that lasted six months.

The Centennial

The great birthday party was a world's fair in Philadelphia. It was called the Centennial Exposition, or Centennial for short. (A centennial is a hundred-year anniversary.) The Philadelphia fair was both a party and a showcase of American achievement.

People came by the millions to see American advancements in art, science, and technology. What amazed visitors the most was the Corliss engine in Machinery Hall. This "athlete of steel and iron" was a giant steam engine. The Corliss supplied the power for 8,000 other machines in the hall.

The Corliss engine symbolized American achievements in industry by the 1870s. As one writer observed: "Yes, it is still in these things of iron and steel that the national genius most freely speaks. . . ."

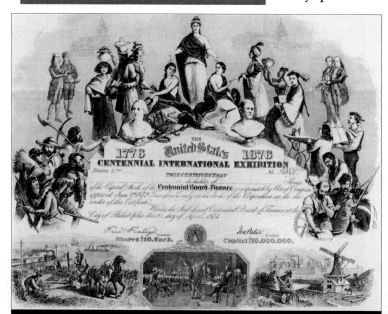

The Centennial Board of Finance issued stock to pay for the celebration of the nation's birthday. Symbols and scenes from American history decorated the stock certificate.

Why Did Industry Grow?

You have read about the Industrial Revolution. That great change in the way things were made got under way in the late 1700s and gathered speed in the first half of the 1800s. In those years it mainly affected life in the Northeast. One effect of the Civil War, however, was to spur the growth of a number of industries. By the 1870s industrial growth was transforming all of American society.

What made this rapid growth in industry possible? There were several factors.

(1) *Railroads.* As you have read, railroads made possible a vast national exchange of raw materials and goods.

(2) *Inventions.* New ideas and improvements helped the United States become an industrial giant. Before 1860 the government patent office had issued a total of only 36,000 patents. (A patent guarantees

an inventor all profits for his or her invention for a certain length of time.) From 1860 to 1900 it issued 650,000.

(3) *Natural resources.* The nation's vast mineral wealth, including coal, iron ore, and oil, was essential to the growth of industry. The forests, water resources, and fertile land also played a part.

(4) *Human talent and labor.* From 1860 to 1900 the nation's population more than doubled, from 31 million to 76 million. Much of the increase came from the arrival of about 14 million immigrants. Many of these people, and later their children, worked in the new industries.

(5) *Capital.* Large profits could be made from America's growing economy. This encouraged banks and wealthy people to lend their money to businesses for new factories, buildings, and railroads. Much of this capital came from European investors.

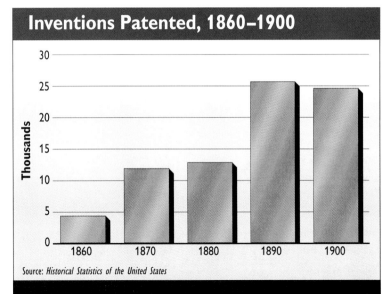

Inventions Patented, 1860–1900

Source: *Historical Statistics of the United States*

CHART SKILLS: This chart shows the number of inventions granted patents by the U.S. government between 1860 and 1900. **Critical Thinking:** How does the ability to patent an invention encourage people to invent things?

Steel: Backbone of Industry

Perhaps more than anything else, steel moved the United States into the industrial age. Steel is an iron alloy—that is, a mixture of iron and other metals. At its simplest, it is iron combined with a small amount of carbon. Other metals, such as copper, manganese, or nickel, may also be part of the alloy. Steel had long been used for knives, swords, or guns, but it was very expensive to make.

In the 1860s new techniques revolutionized the making of steel. The most important advance was the Bessemer process. It

Using the Bessemer process, these steelworkers in Bethlehem, Pennsylvania, pour red-hot iron into a converter. It was mixed with air, an alloy was added, and the iron became steel. **Critical Thinking:** Why was the development of the Bessemer process important?

Granville T. Woods patented 50 inventions in the late 1800s and early 1900s. Woods invented a telegraph system that allowed trains to communicate with railway stations. Thomas Edison took Woods to court to challenge that patent, but Woods won the case.

made iron into steel at a low cost. As a result, the nation's steel output increased by ten times between 1877 and 1892.

The greatest demand for the new steel came from the railroads. Nine-tenths of all the steel made in 1882, for instance, went into making railroad rails.

The production of steel required both iron and coal. Coal was a fuel as well as a source of carbon. Between 1870 and 1900 coal mining, iron mining, and steel making all greatly expanded, along with the railroads.

Inventions in Electricity

Also expanding in those years was Americans' use of electricity. In the 1800s scientists continued to learn about how electricity works. They also learned how to make electricity with an electrical generator. The type of generator that came into widest use was invented by Nikola Tesla, an immigrant from Croatia. In the 1890s his generators began to harness the power of Niagara Falls to create cheap electricity.

The inventor who made widest use of electricity was Thomas Edison. First a newsboy and then a telegraph operator, Edison wanted to invent practical things. "Anything that won't sell, I don't want to invent," he said.

In 1876 Edison set up his own barnlike workshop in the town of Menlo Park, New

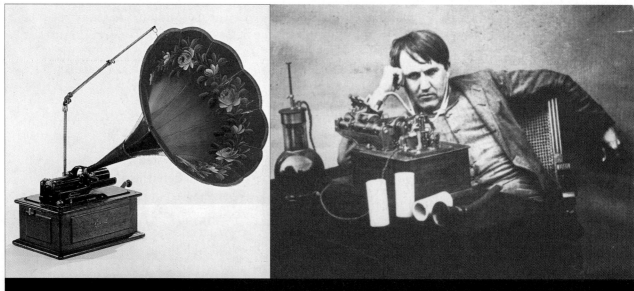

Thomas Edison lost his hearing as a boy but claimed that deafness made concentration easier. The phonograph (left) was his favorite invention.
Critical Thinking: What has replaced phonographs today?

Jersey. There he thought up hundreds of ways to use electricity. During one five-year period he took out a new patent almost every month.

His greatest invention was the light bulb (1879). By 1882 some New York City buildings were glowing with electric light. Electric lighting replaced gas lights so quickly that in 1899 Edison's factory produced 25 million light bulbs.

Edison helped shape life in the 1900s with his many inventions. He developed the dictating machine, motion-picture camera, and phonograph.

Bell and the Telephone

Electricity played an important role in other communication devices such as the telegraph. In the 1840s, telegraph stations multiplied in Europe and the United States. In 1866 a cable was laid under the Atlantic Ocean. Now the United States and Europe could communicate instantly.

Electrical communication underwent another revolution with the invention of the telephone by Alexander Graham Bell. Bell, a Scottish immigrant, had opened a school in Boston for training teachers of the deaf. At the same time he began to search for a way to transmit sound using

CULTURAL MOSAIC

ISAAC MERRIT SINGER
(1811–1875)

Inventors before him had created sewing machines, but Singer invented one that was easy to use. In a time before clothing stores were common, Singer's sewing machine saved hours of labor for tailors and for those who made clothes at home. Singer soon had a thriving sewing machine company in New York City. At $110, however, Singer's machine was too expensive for the average American. Many families only made $500 a year. The company set up ways for people to buy the machine by paying small amounts over a period of time—an idea that other companies quickly copied.

Alexander Graham Bell speaks into his invention as he holds the first telephone conversation between New York City and Chicago. (Bell was in New York.) **Critical Thinking:** What other inventions have telephones made possible?

electricity. His helper was a young mechanic named Thomas Watson. After working a full day in their jobs, Bell and Watson would meet in the evenings to experiment with a device to send sound.

Bell learned of the success of his experiments in a dramatic way. One evening he spilled acid on his clothes. Watson, working in another room, heard Bell shout over the transmitter he had been working on. "Mr. Watson, come here, I want you!" Bell called. Watson went running through the door. "I can hear the words!" he exclaimed.

Bell showed the new invention at the 1876 Centennial. A *New York Tribune* reporter said about it:

> ❝ **The telephone is a curious device that might fairly find place in the magic of the Arabian Tales. Of what use is such an invention?** ❞

People quickly realized the answer to that question. In 1877 telephone lines connected Boston and Salem in Massachusetts. By the 1890s many other American cities were connected by long-distance telephone lines.

Changes in Everyday Life

Out of the basic industries of coal, iron, and steel came everything from plows to bedsteads to zippers. Most of these items made daily life easier, more comfortable, or more pleasant—and at low cost.

Companies could now mass-produce items that people had once made for themselves at home. The advertising business grew in order to sell these products. In 1878, for instance, the Procter & Gamble

An 1899 Sears, Roebuck catalogue.

The advertising industry also grew in the late 1800s. **Critical Thinking:** What means does the soap advertisement above use to convince customers that its product is pure?

Company accidentally made a bath soap that floated. It called the bar "Ivory Soap" and advertised that unique quality.

Another great change for consumers was being able to buy ready-made clothing in stores. The first "ready-mades" were children's clothing and heavy coats. By the 1890s, however, manufacturers started to mass-produce women's clothing. With it, came a new awareness of style in clothing. Dressing in the latest fashion was no longer just for the rich.

A new business, the department store, developed to promote and sell the great variety of new goods. In cities, stores such as R. H. Macy in New York and Marshall Field in Chicago were founded. They offered customers a wide variety of brands. Chain stores, like Woolworth's, made low-cost goods available in small towns. Even those far from towns could order the latest products from the catalogs of Sears, Roebuck or Montgomery Ward.

3 The Rise of Big Business

SECTION GUIDE

Main Idea
Business leaders guided industrial expansion and created new ways of doing business.

Goals
As you read, look for answers to these questions:

1. How did business change in the late 1800s?

2. How did Andrew Carnegie and John D. Rockefeller gain control of the steel and oil industries?

Key Terms
business cycle   corporation
entrepreneur   philanthropist
refinery   trust

I N 1883 THE FANCIEST, most expensive party yet given in the United States was held. This costume ball for 1,200 guests was hosted by William K. and Alva Vanderbilt as a housewarming for their new home in New York City. The ball cost $250,000—more than $200 a guest. (This was at a time when the average nonfarm worker had a yearly income of $438.)

Entering the Gilded Age

The kind of wealth displayed at that party was new to the United States. With the growth of industry, a few people were growing rich almost beyond imagination. One feature of their palacelike homes was gilded decoration—decorations covered in gold. The times themselves are called the "Gilded Age."

During the Gilded Age, the nation's economy seesawed between boom and bust. The pattern of good times and bad times is called the business cycle. During business booms, people spend money and companies expand. When people spend less money, businesses lay off workers and make fewer goods. The country slides into recession. Depressions occur at the lowest part of the business cycle. The marks of a depression are many business failures, a slowdown in factory production, and high unemployment. Depressions end when people begin to buy more and companies hire back workers. (See the chart on the next page.)

William H. Vanderbilt and his family (including son William K., who stands at the back next to his sister) gather in their home in New York City in 1873.

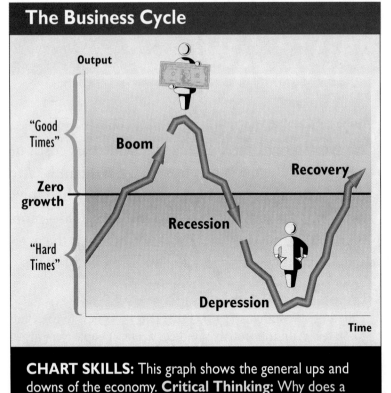

The Business Cycle

Output

"Good Times"

Boom

Zero growth

Recovery

Recession

"Hard Times"

Depression

Time

CHART SKILLS: This graph shows the general ups and downs of the economy. **Critical Thinking:** Why does a decrease in the amount of goods produced lead to an increase in unemployment?

The Rise of the Corporation

Until about 1880 most businesses were owned directly by one person or by a partnership. This kind of ownership caused a problem when a business needed to borrow large amounts of money. Often banks were afraid to lend millions to a business if the business might collapse with the death of the owner or a partner.

The solution was the **corporation.** A corporation is a company that has government permission to raise money by selling stock. Investors buy stock for two reasons: (1) they expect the value of the stock to rise, and (2) they wish to receive dividends (shares of the profits). The corporation can borrow money more easily because it continues to exist even when its owners die.

The Entrepreneurs

The founders of these corporations were **entrepreneurs** (ahn-truh-pruh-NURS)—people who start businesses. Entrepreneurs imagined a goal and then set out to achieve it. They took advantage of new inventions and new ways of doing things. Once established in business, they were skillful managers.

After they became rich, some also became **philanthropists.** In other words, they gave away millions of dollars to colleges, libraries, museums, orchestras, and opera companies. The entrepreneurs of the late 1800s are sometimes called "captains of industry" in honor of their leadership.

Critics, however, have another name for them: "robber barons." The entrepreneurs were ruthless in trying to destroy their competitors. When they succeeded, they raised prices and lowered the quality of their products. Their corporations paid low wages to their workers, who labored long hours in unsafe factories. They also fought workers who tried to organize for better conditions.

Two of the most famous entrepreneurs were Andrew Carnegie and John D. Rockefeller. Carnegie gained control of the steel business. Rockefeller ran the oil industry.

Andrew Carnegie

Carnegie, the son of a weaver, was born in Scotland. When weaving machines started replacing hand weavers, the Carnegie family joined relatives in the United States. While still a boy, Carnegie got a job in a textile mill. Then he went to work for the

In this cartoon, Andrew Carnegie's arms are filled with library buildings. He funded more than 2,500 libraries.

Pennsylvania Railroad as a telegraph messenger. He moved up to become a telegraph operator and then a clerk. All the while he saved money and invested it.

By the early 1870s Carnegie had decided that the future would be based on steel. He turned all his energy into building steel mills that used the latest technology.

To control costs, Carnegie bought iron-ore mines in the Mesabi Range of northern Minnesota. He bought ships to carry the ore across the Great Lakes. To get the ore from Lake Erie to his mills in Pittsburgh, Pennsylvania, he built a railroad. These moves reduced his costs and allowed him to keep lowering the price of his steel. Unable to meet Carnegie's low prices, most of his competitors went out of business. By 1900 Carnegie controlled the American steel business.

Carnegie did not believe in leaving his wealth to his family. "I started life a poor man, and I wish to end it that way," he said. He did not die poor, but he did give away $350 million for the "improvement of mankind."

John D. Rockefeller

Oil, or petroleum, became a business in the 1860s after a scientist discovered that the black gooey substance could be refined to make kerosene. Kerosene, in turn, could be used to light lamps.

John D. Rockefeller, a Cleveland produce merchant, bought a refinery in 1863. (Refineries are the plants that purify the crude oil.) From that base, he quickly expanded his business. He ended up owning not only oil refineries but barrel factories and pipelines.

To make sure of his control of the oil industry, Rockefeller formed the Standard Oil trust. A trust was a business organization that controlled many businesses in the same industry. By doing this, he was able to cut out any competition. The Standard Oil managers could charge whatever

John D. Rockefeller, the son of a peddler, became one of the world's richest men. **Critical Thinking:** How does this cartoon illustrate the way Rockefeller made his fortune?

prices they wanted to. Others followed Rockefeller's lead and formed trusts in a number of industries, including sugar, whiskey, and cotton.

SECTION REVIEW

1. Key Terms business cycle, corporation, entrepreneur, philanthropist, refinery, trust

2. People Andrew Carnegie, John D. Rockefeller

3. Comprehension Why do investors buy stock in corporations?

4. Comprehension How did Carnegie and Rockefeller each become industry leaders?

5. Critical Thinking In your opinion, do wealthy people have a duty to become philanthropists? Explain.

SKILLS: Analyzing Figures

LEARN

What's the connection? That is a question historians ask all the time. An important link they look for is between economic events and historical events. One way to do that is to analyze economic figures before, during, and after a historical event. Look at Table A. This table shows how many miles of railroad were built during a ten-year period. To analyze the figures, you might ask yourself these questions: Do the figures suggest a trend? What event during those years might have helped to cause that trend?

Except for the last two years, the general trend seems to suggest that Americans were building fewer miles of railroad during this time. You know that the Civil War took place from 1861 to 1865. Therefore, you might conclude that the Civil War had a negative effect on the railroad industry.

PRACTICE

1. What is the general trend suggested by the figures in Table B?

2. Which of the five-year periods shown in Table B goes against the trend? What event might explain this exception?

3. From your reading of the chapter, what would you expect the general trend to be for Table A if it showed figures for 1868 to 1900? Explain.

APPLY

4. Use your own knowledge and the information in Table C to draw some conclusions. Was the Bessemer process used more in 1960 or in 1870? Did manufacturers in the late 1800s prefer the Bessemer process over other ways of making steel? Did manufacturers in the mid-1900s prefer the Bessemer process? What might have affected the trends between the late 1800s and the mid-1900s?

5. Create three line graphs using the figures on these tables. Label any historical events that might have affected the trends on the graphs.

Table A

Miles of Railroad Built, 1858–1867	
1858	1,966
1859	1,707
1860	1,500
1861	1,016
1862	720
1863	574
1864	947
1865	819
1866	1,404
1867	2,541

Table B

Railroad Rails Produced, 1860–1900 (in tons)	
1860–1864	1,220,000
1865–1869	2,350,000
1870–1874	4,015,000
1875–1879	4,430,000
1880–1884	7,501,000
1885–1889	8,560,000
1890–1894	7,731,000
1895–1899	9,330,000

Table C

Raw Steel Produced, 1870–1960 (in tons)		
	Bessemer Process	Total
1870	42	77
1890	4,131	4,779
1900	7,481	11,227
1950	4,535	96,836
1960	1,189	99,282

4 Organizing Workers

SECTION GUIDE

Main Idea
To increase their bargaining power in disputes with management, workers tried to create large unions.

Goals
As you read, look for answers to these questions:

1. Why did violence sometimes break out between labor and business in the period 1865–1900?

2. What weapons did labor and big business use against each other in their disputes?

3. What unions were formed in the late 1800s?

Key Terms
sweatshop   socialist
labor union   anarchist

TIMES ARE HARD. You are one of the lucky ones, however, because you have a job sorting coal. The air is so thick with dust that you are always coughing. You must be alert the whole time or your fingers could be crushed. It has been months since you've seen the sun: It is dark when you leave for work in the morning and dark when you return. You make just two dollars a week, but your parents need every cent.

A Hard Life for Workers

This story is not a terrible fairy tale. It was true for thousands of American children in the late 1800s. In mines and factories across the United States, children as young as six labored long hours in unsafe conditions. Children often worked alongside adults in sweatshops, places where workers labor long hours under poor conditions for low wages. Few laws protected them. Those that existed were mostly ignored.

Conditions for adult workers were not much better. The rise of industry in the late 1800s changed the way many Americans made their living. In 1860 there were about an equal number of wage earners and self-employed people. By 1900, two of every three American workers were wage earners.

Earlier, skilled workers had made entire products from start to finish. In factories, however, workers usually did one small part of the work, over and over again. They lost the feeling of satisfaction that comes from making an entire product. Often they were treated like just another piece of machinery.

This photograph shows a few of the thousands of boys who worked in the coal mines. An observer described them as "shut out from everything that's pleasant, with no chance to learn, . . . grinding their little lives away in this dusty room."

Daily Life

IN A SWEATSHOP

The rooms were stuffy, dimly lit, and crowded. The work, which was mostly cutting and sewing clothing, cramped hands and strained eyes. The workday might last fifteen hours or more, and people were paid only by the number of items they produced. Yet, for immigrants and others, sweatshops provided much-needed jobs.

With so many immigrants needing jobs, employers took advantage of their workers. A worker might be fined for giggling or staring out the window.

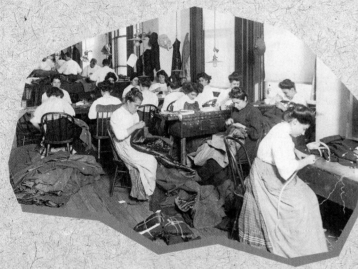

Clothing scraps litter the floor of the sweatshop at left. Most sweatshop workers were Italian or Jewish immigrants. Women, shut out of many other jobs, found low-paying work in the clothing industry.

Children as young as seven worked in the sweatshops with their families. Children's small fingers made them useful for detail work, such as making artificial flowers (left). Those children who attended school would work in the sweatshops in the morning and evening.

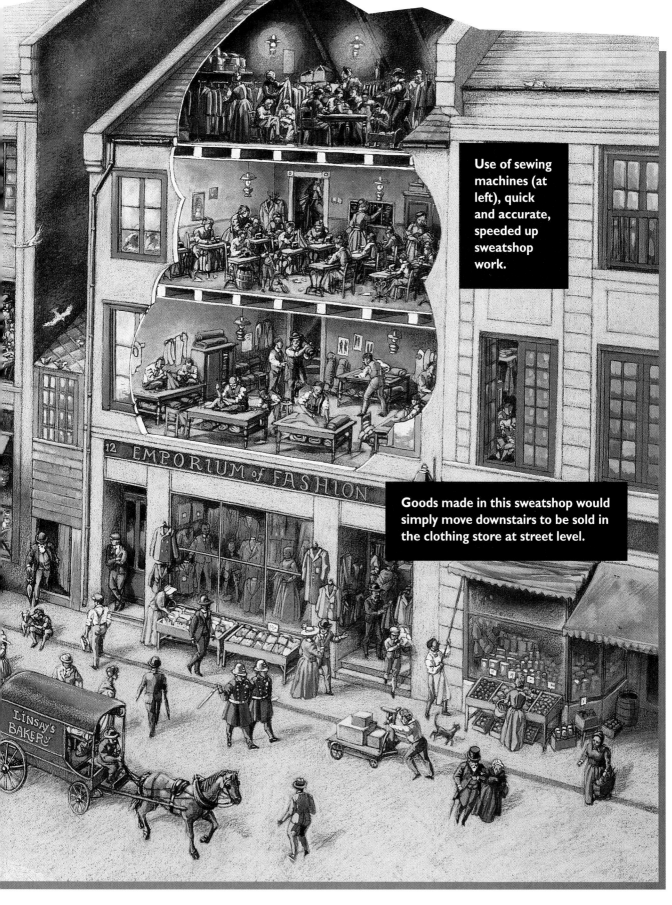

Use of sewing machines (at left), quick and accurate, speeded up sweatshop work.

Goods made in this sweatshop would simply move downstairs to be sold in the clothing store at street level.

In small businesses, workers and their bosses knew each other by sight and by name. This was no longer possible when the employer was a corporation with hundreds of employees. In a big business there was less understanding between managers and workers.

A Call for Action

In the late 1800s the government played almost no role in telling businesses how to run their companies in a fair and safe way. The goal of corporations was to make money, and they paid little attention to working conditions. Faced by powerful corporations and without government help, many workers decided to work together to better their lives. They wanted to establish labor unions, groups of workers that negotiate with company owners about wages and working conditions.

Unions were not a new idea in the United States. The women who worked in the textile mills of New England had organized before the Civil War. Skilled workers had banded together even earlier than that. Yet these workers' groups were usually small and local organizations.

The need for workers to organize became clear in 1877. In that year the railroads were losing money. To try to hold on to profits, railroad managers decided to cut workers' wages. Pushed to the limit, railroad workers in West Virginia went on strike and refused to go to work.

Strikes spread from West Virginia to every major industrial city. In several cities, state militias battled angry mobs. Federal troops were called in by President Rutherford B. Hayes. The Railroad Strike of 1877 lasted several weeks before state and federal troops smashed the strike and restored order.

Terence Powderly, shown surrounded by other leaders of the Knights of Labor, dreamed of a labor force in which "each man is his own employer."

The Knights of Labor

Two years after the 1877 strike, a machinist named Terence Powderly became the head of a workers' social club, the Knights of Labor. He turned the group into a national union of workers.

The Knights of Labor wanted to reform all of society. From employers it demanded a shorter work day (eight hours) and restrictions on child labor. It also urged equal pay for women and welcomed African Americans as members.

The Knights, however, did not welcome all groups. Many of its members, both skilled and unskilled, felt threatened by the great number of immigrants pouring into the country. In general, immigrants would work for less money than native-born workers. When native-born workers lost their jobs, they sometimes blamed the immigrants. On the West Coast the Knights excluded Chinese workers and called for an end to Chinese immigration. They applauded when the Chinese Exclusion Act was passed in 1882. This act stopped all Chinese immigration to the United States for ten years.

After the Knights helped railroad workers get better wages, their numbers grew fast. By 1886 there were about 15,000 local branches with between 700,000 and 1,000,000 members.

The Knights also became more political. Workingmen's political parties were started in many states. They called for restrictions on child labor, safety inspections of mines and factories, better conditions for women, and a way for states to help settle labor disputes.

Reacting to Unions

Meanwhile, business leaders saw labor's growing power as a threat to their ability to make profits. They blamed the labor movement on socialists and anarchists. The beliefs of both challenged capitalism. In general, socialists wanted workers to share in the ownership and profits of businesses. Some socialists even wanted the government to take over all important industries. Anarchists were far more extreme. They rejected all forms of government and authority.

In the late 1800s most Americans sided with the business leaders. They believed that an individual's success should only depend on his or her own labor, effort, and strength of character. The Knights' call for joint action seemed un-American.

Union Setbacks

Businesses fought back against the union. In Chicago, for instance, the McCormick Reaper Works called in strikebreakers in 1886 rather than talk with workers. When strikebreakers and union members clashed, labor leaders called for a protest rally in Chicago's Haymarket Square.

Held on a rainy day, the rally was small. As the police moved in to end it, someone threw a bomb. One policeman was killed. The police opened fire, and more were killed on both sides.

The Knights of Labor had not organized the Haymarket meeting. Yet the public blamed the union for the violence. Hundreds of radicals were arrested in Chicago. The membership of the Knights of Labor dropped steadily.

Labor conflicts grew increasingly bitter—and deadly. Consider the Homestead Strike of 1892. Steelworkers at Andrew Carnegie's Homestead mills in Pennsylvania had organized and had won higher wages. Carnegie, however, felt threatened by the strong union. In June 1892, the company announced that it would deal with workers only one person at a time.

When the workers protested, the company locked them out and re-opened the mills with nonunion labor. To protect the strikebreakers, the company hired 300 Pinkerton agents. The Pinkerton agents

Policemen and workers died in the 1886 riot in Chicago's Haymarket Square. Though four men accused of causing the riot were hanged, another three were pardoned by the governor of Illinois in 1893.
Critical Thinking: How did the Haymarket Riot hurt the labor movement?

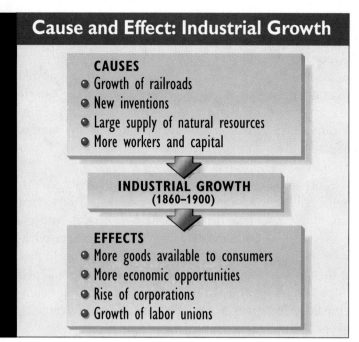

Cause and Effect: Industrial Growth

CAUSES
- Growth of railroads
- New inventions
- Large supply of natural resources
- More workers and capital

INDUSTRIAL GROWTH
(1860–1900)

EFFECTS
- More goods available to consumers
- More economic opportunities
- Rise of corporations
- Growth of labor unions

acted as private security guards and private detectives. When the armed Pinkerton men arrived, the locked-out workers met them with guns. They battled it out for twelve hours. Nine workers and seven agents were killed. The state governor then called in the militia, which escorted strikebreakers to work.

After four months the strike collapsed. The steelworkers' union was shattered.

The Pullman Strike

Workers also lost another bitter dispute in 1894. It was a depression year, the worst to date. Companies slashed wages to stay in business. The Pullman Palace Car Company, which made railroad sleeping cars, cut wages 25 to 40 percent. It also laid off workers at its plant in Pullman, Illinois.

Pullman was a "company town." That is, the company owned the houses, the stores, the land—even the churches. When the company cut wages, however, it refused to lower the rents it charged workers.

Desperate, most of the Pullman workers joined the new American Railway Union. Eugene V. Debs, a railroad fireman, had started the union the year before. Debs believed that only an industry-wide union of rail workers could stand up to the railroad managers.

When the company refused to negotiate, union members approved a boycott of Pullman cars. Railroad workers refused to handle the sleeping cars. The government got a court order demanding an end to the boycott. The President sent federal troops to Illinois to enforce the order. The railroad union was broken. Debs and other union leaders landed in jail.

Gompers and the AFL

In New York City, Samuel Gompers, leader of the Cigarmakers' Union, took a different point of view from earlier unions. He believed that the Knights of Labor had

Born in London to Dutch-Jewish parents, Samuel Gompers worked as a cigar maker before organizing the American Federation of Labor.

Women played an important role in the union movement. Here, the Women's Trade Union League demonstrates in New York City in the early 1900s. **Critical Thinking:** How might these women explain why they are marching?

been wrong to include both skilled and unskilled workers and wrong to try to reform society.

Gompers organized the American Federation of Labor (AFL). The AFL was open only to unions of skilled workers. Gompers reasoned that employers would bargain with skilled workers, since they were harder to replace than unskilled workers. He also thought that employers might listen more if workers limited their demands to issues of pay and working conditions.

By focusing on skilled labor, Gompers and the AFL separated themselves from the rest of the working force. The AFL barred nonwhites from membership. For the most part, it ignored women workers.

Mary Kenney served as an AFL organizer in 1892. She was concerned that the AFL paid little attention to working women's needs. At an AFL convention in 1903, she announced the start of an organization that would help women form unions: the National Women's Trade Union League.

Despite the fierce opposition of business, labor unions did grow. In 1870 one worker in a hundred had belonged to a union. By 1910 that number was up to ten workers in a hundred. There was some improvement in working conditions and wages. The government too was showing an interest in protecting workers. Laws were passed to increase the safety and health of workers. The struggles were not over, but the achievements were real. Both the public and businesses were beginning to accept unions as part of industrial life.

SECTION REVIEW

1. Key Terms sweatshop, labor union, socialist, anarchist

2. People and Places Terence Powderly, Eugene V. Debs, Samuel Gompers, Chicago, Pullman

3. Comprehension How were the Knights of Labor and the American Federation of Labor different?

4. Comprehension Why was there much distrust or fear of labor organizations in the 1800s?

5. Critical Thinking In the strikes discussed in this section, which side (workers or employers) benefited from the outbreak of violence? Why?

Summary

1. The transcontinental railroad was completed in 1869 and the U.S. rail network continued to expand. Railroads led to the defeat of the Plains Indians, connected regional economies, and made it possible to settle the West. They also changed the way people thought about the environment.

2. Industrialization took off in the late 1800s. Industrial expansion was helped by the growth of railroads and other technological advances, abundant natural resources, population growth, and available capital. New inventions led to the growth of industry and an improvement in everyday life for many Americans.

3. The development of corporations and the success of entrepreneurs increased the size of American industry. Andrew Carnegie played a leading role in the steel industry. John D. Rockefeller dominated the oil industry.

4. In the late 1800s poor working conditions and low wages convinced many industrial workers to organize labor unions. Labor strikes and other actions met with limited success.

Review

KEY TERMS

Define the terms in each of the following pairs.

1. transcontinental; standard time
2. patent; entrepreneur
3. corporation; trust
4. sweatshop; labor union
5. anarchist; socialist

COMPREHENSION

1. What challenges did companies and workers face in building the transcontinental railroad?
2. What were four major effects of the growth of the railroads?
3. What factors encouraged the growth of industry in the United States after 1860?
4. Name three important inventions of the late 1800s that relied on electricity.
5. Why did the advertising business grow in the late 1800s?
6. Why do investors buy stock in corporations?
7. Why were entrepreneurs in the late 1800s called "captains of industry"? Why were they called "robber barons"?
8. What were some of the problems that led workers to organize in the late 1800s?
9. What was the importance of the Haymarket Riot to the labor movement?
10. How did the American Federation of Labor differ from earlier unions?

Graphic Summary

Expansion of railroads

Goods for consumers

Growth of labor unions

Industrialization

Opportunities for entrepreneurs

Poor working conditions

Rise of corporations

Places to Locate

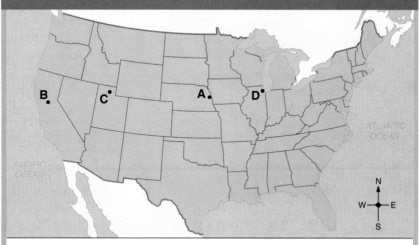

Match the letters on the map with the places listed below.
1. Chicago   3. Omaha
2. Promontory, Utah 4. Sacramento
Geographic Theme: Interactions What geographic barriers made railroad construction difficult?

Skill Review

Horsepower compares the power of another animal or an engine to the power of a horse. The table below compares the horsepower of work animals and railroads. Use the figures to answer the questions.

Year	Horsepower of Work Animals	Horsepower of Railroads
1860	8,630,000	2,156,000
1870	8,660,000	4,462,000
1880	11,580,000	8,592,000
1890	15,970,000	16,980,000
1900	18,730,000	24,501,000

Source: *Historical Statistics*

1. In which of the years shown was the horsepower of work animals greater than that of railroads?
2. Over what decade did the horse- power of work animals increase the least?
3. What is the general trend sug- gested by the figures in the table?

CRITICAL THINKING

1. Analyzing a Quotation In your own words, explain Thomas Edi- son's definition of genius as "one percent inspiration and ninety- nine percent perspiration."
2. Forming a Hypothesis How might Andrew Carnegie or John D. Rockefeller have responded to the charge that the concentration of wealth in the hands of a few indi- viduals was a threat to democracy?

PORTFOLIO OPTIONS

1. Civics Connection How might union leaders have reacted to the charge that unions were un-Ameri- can? Organize a class debate on the issue with half the class represent- ing union leaders and the other half representing business owners.
2. Writing Connection Imagine that you are a worker on the trans- continental railroad. Write a letter home describing your experiences.
3. Contemporary Connection Dis- cuss with the class what methods would have been used to send a message across the United States quickly in 1820, 1870, and 1900. What methods would be used today? Discuss how the increase in the speed of communication has affected society and the economy.
4. Timeline Connection Copy the chapter timeline. Which event do you think was more important, the completion of the transcontinental railroad or the invention of the light bulb? Explain.

In the late 1800s, more and more immigrants from southern and eastern Europe crossed the Atlantic for American shores. Other immigrants came from Asia and the Americas. Most tried to find work in America's growing cities, where they faced new challenges in their pursuit of a better life.

1865   1870   1875   1880

1869 First professional
baseball team is formed

1876 New York City's
Central Park opens

The Rise of American Cities (1865–1900)

1 Growing Immigration from Europe

SECTION GUIDE

Main Idea
Immigration to the United States grew in the late 1800s and early 1900s. Immigration from southern and eastern Europe increased.

Goals
As you read, look for answers to these questions:

1. Who were the new immigrants of the late 1800s and early 1900s?

2. What role did steamships play in immigration to the United States?

3. How did most immigrants decide where they would settle?

Key Terms
Ellis Island
nationality

IN THE EARLY 1890s, in the Italian city of Naples, a twelve-year-old orphan boy named Rocco Corresca worried about his future. He worked for an old man who beat him and forced him to beg as well as steal. Then Rocco met a young man who had traveled to the United States. Rocco had heard "that it was a far-off country where everybody was rich. . . ." Rocco and his friend Francisco decided to seek their fortune in America. They became part of a tidal wave of immigration that hit the shores of the United States in the late 1800s and early 1900s. Almost 24 million newcomers arrived between 1880 and 1920—an average of almost one each minute!

The New Immigrants

Though some of these new immigrants came from Asia and the Americas, most were Europeans. Immigrants from northern Europe—the English, Scots, Irish, Germans, and Scandinavians—had been crossing the Atlantic since before the American Revolution. By the late 1800s, however, fewer northern Europeans were coming to the United States. One reason was that they could now get jobs in new factories and mills in their own countries.

1885	1890	1895	1900

1888 Electric trolley set up in Richmond

1886 Statue of Liberty dedicated

1892 Immigration center opens on Ellis Island

1885 First skyscraper built

1891 Basketball invented

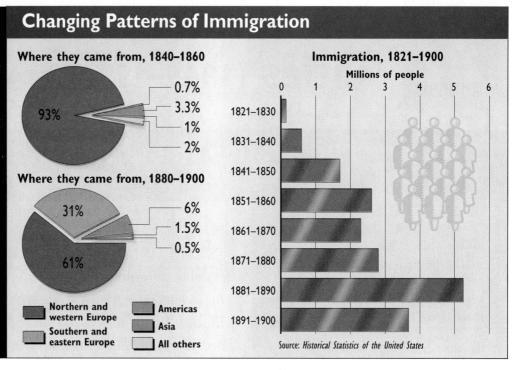

Changing Patterns of Immigration

Where they came from, 1840–1860

93%

0.7%
3.3%
1%
2%

Where they came from, 1880–1900

31%
61%

6%
1.5%
0.5%

■ Northern and western Europe
■ Southern and eastern Europe
■ Americas
■ Asia
□ All others

Immigration, 1821–1900

Millions of people

	0	1	2	3	4	5	6
1821–1830							
1831–1840							
1841–1850							
1851–1860							
1861–1870							
1871–1880							
1881–1890							
1891–1900							

Source: *Historical Statistics of the United States*

Beginning in the 1880s, other European groups began arriving on American shores. These groups came mainly from lands in southern Europe, eastern Europe, and the eastern Mediterranean. Except for Italy and Greece, most of these lands were controlled by the Russian Empire, the Austro-Hungarian Empire, or the Ottoman (Turkish) Empire. Within these empires were many peoples of different religions, languages, and traditions.

Starting in the 1880s, these empires allowed their people to leave. People left for a number of reasons—overpopulation, lack of jobs, and mistreatment by the government. America in turn offered jobs, opportunity, and freedom.

Eastern European Jews were one of the largest of these new immigrant groups. Next in numbers were Slavic peoples—Poles, Slovaks, Czechs, Croats, Serbs, Ukrainians, and Russians. The largest group, however, were southern Italians, like Rocco.

Steamships Cross the Ocean

Rocco and Francisco sailed across the Atlantic on a steamship. To pay their way, they were put to work on the ship. As Rocco told it:

❝The young man took us to a big ship and got us work way down where the fires are. We had to

The shoes of (left to right) Austrian, Greek, Chinese, and Albanian immigrants reflected the different cultures of the newest Americans.

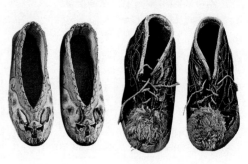

carry coal to the place where it could be thrown on the fires. Francisco and I were very sick from the great heat at first and lay on the coal for a long time, but they threw water on us and made us get up. 🙿

In the 1860s steamships had replaced sailing ships as the best way to travel across the Atlantic. Companies in Britain and Germany built passenger ships of iron and then steel. The companies competed to carry immigrants to America.

The coming of the steamships had a great effect on immigration. The steamships, which were strong and sturdy, took the danger out of crossing the ocean. They also made the journey faster than wooden sailing ships.

Steamships had the same advantages as those that made the railroads the best way to travel by land. Like the railroads, steamships did not have to worry about strong winds. Steamships also could operate on a schedule.

Steamship travel made it possible for a new kind of worker to come to America. This was the single male worker who came for a few months or a few years. These workers could come and earn money, and then return to their homelands.

Ellis Island: Gate to America

Nearly all the European immigrants arrived in New York City. Beginning in 1886 they were greeted by the powerful sight of the Statue of Liberty in New York harbor. Six years later an immigration center opened at **Ellis Island** in New York harbor. It was the first stop for most immigrants crossing the Atlantic.

At Ellis Island, immigrants had to have a medical checkup. If they passed it, they then had to answer a series of questions: Name? Occupation? Who paid your fare? Can you read and write? How much money

Immigrants arriving at Ellis Island had to have a medical checkup. If the official suspected a problem, he would draw a chalk symbol on the immigrant's coat and send him or her to a doctor. A large "H," for example, meant possible heart trouble.

do you have? Have you ever been in prison or in the poorhouse? Where are you going?

At this point, many immigrants received new names for a new life. Inspectors whose tongues stumbled over unfamiliar names often gave immigrants new "American" names. For example, the Jewish name "Buchenroth" might become "Roth." The Greek name "Stefanopoulous" might be shortened to "Stevens."

These young boys stand on a hill above a steel mill in Homestead, Pennsylvania. The booming factories of the industrial United States employed thousands of immigrants.

Shown from left to right on this page and the next: a Chinese drugstore, an Italian grocery, some German storefronts, and a Jewish outdoor market. Immigrant-owned businesses added new variety to America's cities.

In the end, most immigrants were allowed to stay on American soil. Only about 2 percent were sent home.

Where Immigrants Settled

The immigrants settled in areas where they could find work. At the time, the work was in the mines, mills, and factories of the industrial United States. By the beginning of the 1900s, half of the immigrants were in four industrial states: Massachusetts, New York, Pennsylvania, and Illinois. The cities of Boston, New York City, Philadelphia, Pittsburgh, and Chicago grew by leaps and bounds.

Most of the immigrants had their way paid by relatives who had come to the United States earlier. If the relative was working in the coal mines of Pennsylvania, that probably was where the immigrant ended up working. If the relative was a butcher in Chicago, the immigrant was likely to end up working in Chicago's stockyards. In other words, immigrants from the same village or family usually helped each other.

This led to a patchwork of ethnic neighborhoods in all the big cities of the United States. Of New York City, reporter Jacob Riis wrote in 1890, "A map of the city, colored to designate nationalities, would show more stripes than on the skin of a zebra and more colors than any rainbow."

Jobs for Immigrants

What if the immigrant did not know anyone or had no relatives to help? Let us return to the story of Rocco and Francisco after they reached New York. When they landed, officials at Ellis Island told them they must go back to Italy because they did not have enough money. However, a man named Bartolo told the officals he was their uncle and took them away.

Bartolo, of course, was not really Rocco's uncle. He was a padrone, a labor boss. Every nationality—group of people from the same nation—had its version of a padrone. The padrone found jobs for immigrants and gave them shelter and food. In return, the workers gave the padrone a large part of their wages.

Bartolo put Rocco and Francisco to work for him. Rocco tells what happened after leaving Ellis Island with Bartolo:

> **The next morning, early, Bartolo . . . gave us bags and hooks and showed us the [trash cans]. On the streets where the fine houses are, the people are very careless and put out good things like matresses and umbrellas, clothes, hats, and boots. We brought all these to Bartolo and he made them new again. . . .**
>
> **We were with Bartolo nearly a year, but some of our countrymen who had been in the place a long time said that Bartolo had no right to us and we could get work for $1.50 a day. . . . So we went away one day. . . .**

Rocco and Francisco got jobs working on the streets of Newark, New Jersey. As new, unskilled immigrants, Italians began to replace the Irish as the "pick-and-shovel" workers. It was often Italians who paved streets, dug sewers and subways, laid pipes, and built bridges in eastern cities. When Rocco and Francisco were laid off from the street job, they learned to shine shoes. Later, they opened a string of successful shoeshine parlors.

SECTION REVIEW

1. Key Terms Ellis Island, nationality

2. Places New York City, Boston, Philadelphia, Pittsburgh, Chicago

3. Comprehension How did immigration to the United States change in the late 1800s? Why did it change?

4. Comprehension How did most immigrants decide where they would settle in the United States?

5. Critical Thinking Do you think Rocco and Francisco made the right decision to come to the United States? Explain your answer.

2 New Life in the Promised Land

SECTION GUIDE

Main Idea
Though free public education greatly helped new immigrants, living and working conditions were often difficult.

Goals
As you read, look for answers to these questions:

❶ How did conditions in eastern Europe in the late 1800s lead to an increase in Jewish immigration?

❷ What role did public education play in immigrant life?

❸ What was life like for immigrants living in large American cities at the turn of the twentieth century?

Key Terms
pogrom
tenement
slum
piecework

IN THE CITY OF POLOTSK, Russia, Mary Antin was a young child the first time her playmate Vanka threw mud at her. When Mary ran home complaining, her mother said, "How can I help you, my poor child? Vanka is a Gentile [non-Jew]. The Gentiles do as they like with us Jews."

The prejudice that Mary Antin suffered was taking place across eastern Europe in the late 1800s. Sometimes this prejudice turned violent. In response, thousands of eastern European Jews fled Russia and Russian-ruled Poland. Between 1880 and 1920, about one-third of eastern European Jews—2 million in all—moved to the United States. Though many moved to cities throughout the East and Midwest, most settled in New York City. Their struggle to survive in their new country was similar to the experiences of other immigrants from eastern and southern Europe.

Reasons for Jewish Emigration

In the Russian Empire, Jews had long been denied equal rights. Laws said what kinds of jobs they could hold and where they could live. Education was often out of reach to Jews. Relations between Jews and Gentiles were often full of distrust.

As Mary Antin grew older, she understood that Polotsk was located in a region known as the Pale of Settlement. Speaking of Jews, Mary Antin wrote, "We must not be found outside the Pale, because we were Jews. . . . I accepted [bad treatment] from the Gentiles as one accepts the weather."

Life for eastern European Jews grew even worse beginning in 1881. In that year the Russian czar adopted anti-Jewish policies. At their worst, the czar's policies encouraged **pogroms,** organized robberies and massacres of Jews.

This menorah, used in Jewish ceremonies, was brought to the United States by a Polish Jew in the late 1800s.

Mary Antin remembered:

❝ Jews who escaped the pogroms came to Polotsk with wounds on them, and horrible, horrible stories. . . . Only to hear these things made one sob and sob and choke with pain. People who saw such things never smiled any more, no matter how long they lived: and sometimes their hair turned white in a day, and some people became insane on the spot. ❞

Eager to leave, Mary Antin's father made his way from Polotsk to Boston, Massachusetts. Three years later, when Mary was thirteen, she and the rest of her family joined him.

The Importance of Education

More than anything, Mary Antin's father wanted his children to receive an education. He believed that education was "the treasure no thief could touch, not even misfortune or poverty."

The American school system was expanding even faster than the nation's cities. In time, schools took over some of the tasks that had once belonged to parents and churches. Schools were expected to teach children citizenship, proper social behavior, and the skills to earn a living.

After 1870, cities and states began to pass laws requiring children to attend school until they reached a certain age. The number of children attending school more than doubled between 1870 and 1900.

Educators faced a difficult task. They had to educate children who came from different backgrounds and spoke different languages. To help schools become more efficient, educators looked to the factory as a model.

One result of this was a system of grades that organized students by age. Standards

CULTURAL MOSAIC

IRVING BERLIN
(1888–1989)

A Russian child named Israel Baline grew up to become one of America's great songwriters—Irving Berlin. Berlin's family fled the pogroms and came to New York City when he was a child. As a young man, he taught himself music and began writing popular songs. He was drafted into the army in 1918, where he entertained troops with his music. Americans sang his patriotic tunes during World Wars I and II, and his musicals were hits on Broadway. In his lifetime, Berlin wrote over 1,000 songs, such as "You'd Be Surprised" (below). His holiday classic, "White Christmas," is one of the most popular songs of all time.

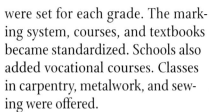

were set for each grade. The marking system, courses, and textbooks became standardized. Schools also added vocational courses. Classes in carpentry, metalwork, and sewing were offered.

Many working families needed the money earned by their children. So, despite new school attendance laws, these families chose not send their children to school. In Mary Antin's family, the oldest daughter, Frieda, went to work so that Mary could go to school. Mary understood the sacrifice her sister made for her:

Many immigrant parents felt that a good education was critical if their children were going to succeed. Here an Italian father watches as his son works on his homework.

❝I was led to the schoolroom, with its sunshine and its singing and the teacher's cheery smile; while [Frieda] was led to the workshop, with its foul air . . . and the foreman's stern command.❞

Sweatshop Labor

By 1890 half of all Jewish immigrants were clothing workers, many of them in sweatshops. Thousands of children also worked in sweatshops. At the Triangle Shirtwaist Company, a dressmaking sweatshop in New York City, one child said, "The corner of a shop would resemble a kindergarten because we were young, eight, nine, ten years old. . . ."

In 1911 one of New York City's worst tragedies took place at the Triangle Shirtwaist Company. A fire broke out and 146 employees—most of them young, immigrant women—died. Some of the exit doors to the factory, on the top three floors of a ten-story building, had been locked. Many workers jumped to their deaths. Others never made it out of the building.

Public anger led to a study of factory conditions in New York City. Investigators looked at 80 buildings in which 40,000 people worked. They found that 22 had no fire escapes, 26 had locked doors, and 51 had wooden stairways. As a result of the study, New York State established rules to protect workers.

Tenement Living

When workers left unsafe factories they returned home to unsafe tenements. Tenements were apartment buildings that were both overcrowded and unhealthy. Any neighborhood in a city that had these unsafe conditions was called a slum.

In large cities the poor and the newly arrived immigrants crowded into tenements. The buildings usually had neither indoor plumbing nor heating. There was little light or fresh air. One woman wrote: "In the summer the sidewalk, fire escapes, and the roof of the tenements became bedrooms just to get a breath of air."

Many immigrants, especially eastern European Jews, turned their tiny apartments into workplaces as well as living places. Most had come from places where it had been common for workers to live and work in the same building. Often they did piecework —work paid by the number of objects made.

A witness to the terrible fire at the Triangle Shirtwaist Company later painted this scene.

The unhealthy conditions of a city slum can be seen in the painting at left. Above, a group of immigrants are crowded into a filthy room in a New York City boarding house.

Family Tensions

Immigrants often had trouble adjusting to life in the United States. A common problem was tension between adult immigrants and their children. One reason was that children learned English faster than adults. This could be a source of embarrassment to parents. Another was that the authority of teachers over schoolchildren sometimes conflicted with the authority of parents.

Young people were also eager to adopt American ways. These new ideas often went against the ideas of immigrant parents. In the struggle, wrote reporter Jacob Riis, the father "loses his grip on the boy."

Riis believed that parents' loss of authority, plus poverty, led boys to join gangs. Gangs were a result of how little hope there was for boys in the slums. The writings of Riis, a Danish immigrant, helped fuel a reform movement to improve life for those in the slums of the inner city.

SECTION REVIEW

1. **Key Terms** pogrom, tenement, slum, piecework

2. **Places** Russia, Poland, New York City

3. **Comprehension** Why did eastern European Jews move to the United States in the late 1800s? Where did most of them settle?

4. **Comprehension** Describe the ways in which factories and tenements were unsafe and unhealthy.

5. **Critical Thinking** How did schools help immigrants adjust to life in the United States? Why did many immigrant families decide not to send their children to school?

SKILLS: Using a Map Grid

LEARN

Suppose you see a newspaper ad for a huge sale at a department store. Everything is on sale at rock-bottom prices—stereos, clothes, sports equipment. You want to go, but the store is at the intersection of two streets you are not familiar with. How can you find the store's location? You can read every street name on your city map, or you can narrow your search by using the map grid.

City maps use a grid system similar to the longitude and latitude grid on large-scale maps. The key to the grid system is a code made up of a letter and a number. Look at the map below of Philadelphia in 1896. The blue lines running left to right form four rows. Each row has a letter. The blue lines running up and down form four columns. Each column has a number. Together, these lines create a grid on the map.

Each letter-number code refers to a box on the grid. For example, South Street meets 4th Street in box D-4. Find D at the side and follow it across. Find 4 at the top and follow it down. In box D-4, you see the intersection.

PRACTICE

1. In which box does Vine Street meet the Schuylkill River?

2. Which streets intersect with South Street in box D-3?

3. In which box is Fairmount Park?

APPLY

4. Imagine that you are a newly arrived immigrant in Philadelphia. Write a journal entry describing how you wandered around the city your first day. For each intersection you walk through, provide the map grid code.

Philadelphia, 1896

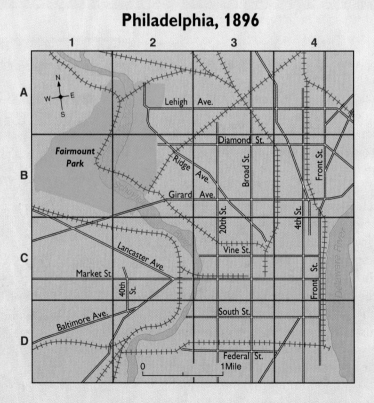

3 City Growth and Change

SECTION GUIDE

Main Idea
New technology and new attitudes changed city life in the late 1800s.

Goals
As you read, look for answers to these questions:

1 How did the look of the nation's big cities change in the late 1800s?

2 How did political organizations affect the lives of people in cities?

3 What role did women play in the settlement house movement?

Key Terms
skyscraper
suburb
political machine
ward
settlement house
Social Gospel

I N THE LATE 1800s American cities stank. "The river stinks. The air stinks," a New Yorker complained. "The stink is enough to knock you down." The smells came from everywhere: outhouses, raw sewage in rivers, piled-up garbage, factory smokestacks, and tons of horse manure.

Cities were not ignoring garbage and sewage. They were just growing so fast they could not keep up with basic services. Thousands of people were pouring into cities daily. They included rural, native-born Americans as well as immigrants. By 1890 New York City had 1.5 million people. Philadelphia and Boston each had more than 1 million.

The Size of Cities

Until the 1880s a city's physical size had been limited. Most people lived within walking distance of their jobs. Buildings were no higher than a person could comfortably walk up—four or five stories.

Many cities experienced difficult growing pains. Here, a horse-drawn buggy tries to navigate its way through mud and garbage on a New York City street.

Although railroads reached across the United States, the main form of transportation within cities—besides walking—was still provided by horses. Horse-drawn wagons, carts, and carriages were part of the street life in cities everywhere.

The technology of the industrial age allowed the city to grow both upward and outward. Electricity and the invention of the elevator allowed people to live and work in buildings higher than four or five stories. The use of steel for support made very tall buildings possible. They became known as **skyscrapers.**

This 1877 photo was taken to celebrate the first wire strung during construction of the Brooklyn Bridge. The bridge itself would eventually hang from steel cables supported by two stone towers. One of the towers is shown in the photo.

Cities tried to move people more efficiently with horse trolleys—streetcars drawn by horses. It was electricity, however, that really made a difference. The first practical electric trolley was set up in 1888 in Richmond, Virginia. Within just two years, there were more miles of electric streetcar lines than horse trolley lines.

In addition to new transportation systems, new bridges helped cities span rivers. The most impressive example was the steel-cabled Brooklyn Bridge, which connected Brooklyn with the island of Manhattan. It was completed in 1883.

Development of Suburbs

The electric streetcar made it possible to live farther than walking distance from work. As a result, cities expanded. New suburbs—areas at the edge of a city where people lived—arose farther and farther from the city's core.

Many city dwellers liked suburbs because they believed that city living was unhealthy. It was, at least in the crowded tenements at the heart of the nation's largest cities—New York, Chicago, and Philadelphia. Those who could afford it moved to the suburbs, where they could live in a single-family home with a lawn.

Technology made suburbs possible. Lawnmowers were a new invention—so one no longer needed animals to crop the grass. The invention of the icebox (with ice delivered daily), indoor plumbing, and the iron cooking range reduced the need for separate buildings.

Bringing Nature to the City

Of course, not everyone could afford to move out of the city. Very early in the industrial age, reformers began to worry about the loss of greenery and fresh air in the city. Thus was born a movement to create large city parks that would bring nature to the city.

In 1853 New York City became the first major city to plan such a park. Land was bought in the center of Manhattan. Frederick Law Olmsted and Calvert Vaux (VAWKS) won a contest to design and build what was later named Central Park.

Central Park succeeded in bringing nature to New York City. Millions of cartloads of dirt were shifted to create a landscape ranging from gentle hills to steep valleys. About 5 million trees and shrubs were planted. Walkways and roads were built in the park, which opened in 1876.

Olmsted designed similar parks for Brooklyn, Philadelphia, Detroit, Boston, and Chicago. He also designed the grounds of the nation's capitol building in Washington, D.C.

Running the Cities

Green parks could not mask the stink of the slums, however. The stink extended to the politics of big cities. Most immigrants came from countries where they had no say in running the government. Their limited

English skills also made it hard for them to understand citizenship in a democracy.

When Rocco Carresca, the Italian immigrant described in Section 1, had been in the United States for two years, a man offered to make him an American citizen for 50 cents. (The law said that it took five years to become a citizen.) Then, the man told him, Rocco could get $2 for voting for the "right" political candidate.

Buying votes was common practice for city politicians. Most belonged to a **political machine** —an informal organization designed to gain and keep power in city government. At the head of the political machine was the political "boss." Often the boss was the mayor.

Most cities were divided into sections called **wards.** Often a ward was made up heavily of a single ethnic group. In charge of each ward was the ward boss, who looked out for the people in the district. He found them jobs. If they were hungry, he got them food. In return for such favors he asked for only one thing: their votes at election time. Often people were paid for their votes by the political machine.

The power of the political machine rested on the spoils system. The explosive growth of cities had produced a growth in city jobs. Political machines controlled who got those jobs.

Political machines also controlled which companies got contracts to dig sewers, lay telephone lines, and build streetcar lines. To get such contracts, companies usually had to pay political bosses a "kickback" fee. Though political machines helped many immigrants, the machines' true goal was to gain power and wealth for political bosses.

New Roles for Women

In the late 1800s another force developed to bring relief to immigrants. This force

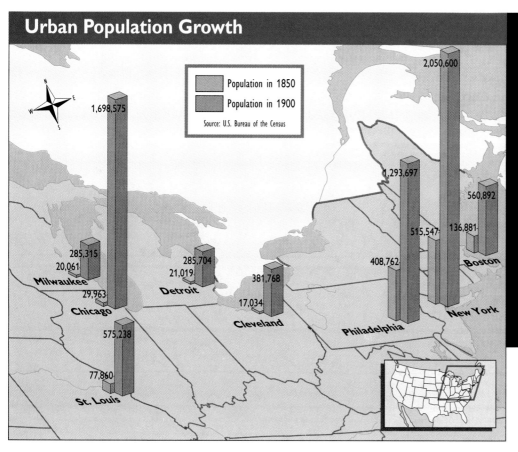

Urban Population Growth

Population in 1850
Population in 1900
Source: U.S. Bureau of the Census

2,050,600

1,698,575

1,293,697

560,892

515,547 136,881

408,762 **Boston**

285,315
20,061
Milwaukee

285,704
21,019
Detroit

381,768
17,034
Cleveland

New York

29,963
Chicago

575,238

Philadelphia

77,860
St. Louis

CHART SKILLS: The population of America's major cities skyrocketed between 1850 and 1900. **Critical Thinking:** Which cities increased by over a million people between 1850 and 1900? Why were the nation's largest cities during this period concentrated in the Northeast and Midwest?

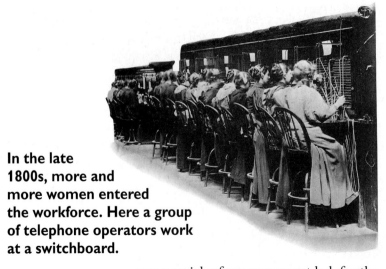

In the late 1800s, more and more women entered the workforce. Here a group of telephone operators work at a switchboard.

in the home. Immigration made inexpensive domestic help possible. Household equipment such as the icebox and washing machine saved housekeeping time.

Educated women also faced challenges. By 1890 one in four college graduates was a woman. Yet a woman's job choices were mostly limited to teaching or nursing. Jane Addams, born in Illinois, faced this problem. She wanted to make something of herself, but what she did not know.

Settlement Houses

After a visit to a settlement house in London, Jane Addams knew. Settlement houses supplied services such as daycare, adult education, and social clubs to the poor. On her return home, Addams, then 29, and her friend Ellen Gates Starr opened Hull House, a settlement house in Chicago.

Jane Addams felt that Hull House had two goals. One was to help the many immigrants in the city. There were, she said, "Germans and Bohemians and Italians and Poles and Russians and Greeks and Arabs in Chicago, vainly trying to adjust their [rural] habits to the life of a large city." The second goal was to provide a place where educated young people, especially women, could do useful work.

was a social reform movement led, for the most part, by educated women.

The role of women was changing in those years. Thousands of women were working in factories at low wages. Other women were taking jobs as telephone operators, store clerks, and typists.

Women who could afford to, however, were expected to quit their jobs when they married. In 1890, 30 percent of women between the ages of 20 and 24 worked. Only 15 percent between the ages of 25 and 44 worked.

At the same time, women's traditional skills became less important. Factories were producing goods women once made

Though jobs were opening up to women, many jobs were still restricted to men. Here telephone construction linemen, some of them newly arrived immigrants, pose for an 1889 photo.

Some settlement houses contained a gym like the one shown here. Settlement houses helped many poor immigrants make the adjustment to life in a large city.

By 1910 there were 400 settlement houses. Of those working in the houses, six out of ten were women.

Influence on City Life

Settlement houses helped change city government. For instance, Jane Addams persuaded the owner of a tenement to tear it down and build a playground. Hull House ran the playground for ten years until the city took it over.

In this way, Hull House and other settlement houses influenced life in the nation's cities. Hull House eventually owned thirteen buildings, including classrooms, a theater, music school, nursery, and gymnasium. Other settlement houses provided similar services.

By providing a model, settlement houses encouraged city governments to expand their social services, especially to the poor. In the process, a new profession was born: the social worker.

The Social Gospel

Not everyone agreed that the poor should be helped. Many people of the time believed that the world was set up to be competitive. Only the fittest people were supposed to survive. To help the poor, in other words, was to go against nature's law.

This view went against that of a new Protestant religious movement called the Social Gospel. Leaders of the Social Gospel movement urged Christians to help the poor, as Jesus had. The Social Gospel was an important reason many men and women went to work in settlement houses.

SECTION REVIEW

1. Key Terms skyscraper, suburb, political machine, ward, settlement house, Social Gospel

2. People and Places Frederick Law Olmsted, Jane Addams, Chicago

3. Comprehension How did new technology make it possible for cities to expand in the late 1800s?

4. Comprehension How did political machines influence elections?

5. Critical Thinking Do you think settlement houses could still play a role in poor communities today? Explain.

The Midwest grew in waves. The first wave came after 1825, when the Erie Canal linked the East with the Great Lakes region. (The map at right shows the resources of the lower Great Lakes.) The second wave began in the 1860s, caused by new Civil War investment. At this point mining, farming, and forestry were key areas of growth.

The third growth period began in the 1890s. By this time the Midwest, while still a processor of raw materials, was also becoming a manufacturing center. New industries included steel and steel products, such as train rails and skyscraper beams.

As the Midwest grew, so did its cities. Most great midwestern cities began life as little trading posts or forts. Chicago, Illinois, is one example. It was founded in 1779 by Jean Baptise Point Du Sable, a black trader born in Haiti. By 1848 Chicago had 30,000 people. It had 500,000 thirty years later and, by 1900, over 1.6 million.

The keys to Chicago's growth were resources and transportation. Goods shipped across the Great Lakes to Chicago could then pass by canal and river to the Mississippi River and south to New Orleans. Railroads brought grain and cattle from the West to Chicago, where they were processed into flour, beef, and leather. Trees from Michigan and Wisconsin, brought southward by river or rail, were processed into lumber.

This locomotive for the Chicago, Milwaukee, and St. Paul Line was built in 1860.

This bird's eye view of Chicago shows ships in the foreground as well as the tracks of the Illinois Central Railroad leading to large grain elevators.

The iron and steel industries became major sources of both prosperity and pollution.

CRITICAL THINKING

1. How did the Midwest's third period of growth differ from the first two?
2. Explain why Chicago was in an ideal position to benefit from the growth of the Midwest.
3. **Geographic Theme: Regions** Could the Midwest have prospered in the late 1800s if the West had not been expanding? Explain.

4 A New City Culture

SECTION GUIDE

Main Idea
Newspapers, department stores, sports, and popular entertainment helped bring diverse city populations together.

Goals
As you read, look for answers to these questions:

❶ How did newspapers attract wider readership in the late 1800s?

❷ How did leisure activities unify people living in cities?

Key Terms
circulation
vaudeville
nickelodeon

DESPITE THE POVERTY and poor working conditions you have read about, by the late 1800s Americans as a whole had more leisure time and money. This caused the growth of a new city culture in which everyone could share. Newspapers, department stores, sports, and variety shows were all exciting parts of city life.

The Popular Press
Newsboys once were on every city corner announcing special editions: "EXTRA! EXTRA! READ ALL ABOUT IT!" Before the arrival of home delivery and newsstands, newsboys performed the important job of getting newspapers to readers. By the 1880s newspapers had become more than papers filled with news. They had become entertainment.

Newspapers were designed to appeal to all kinds of people. Advances in technology made it possible to print them by the thousands, and newsboys sold them by the thousands.

Selling newspapers became big business. The higher the circulation (number of readers), the more companies would want to advertise in the newspaper. The greater the number of advertisers, the more money a newspaper made. Raising circulation, therefore, was the key to a newspaper's profits.

Joseph Pulitzer Changes Newspapers
Joseph Pulitzer, a Hungarian immigrant, understood the key to increasing circulation. After fighting in the Civil War, Pulitzer got into the newspaper business in St. Louis. He founded the successful St. Louis *Post-Dispatch*. Then he bought a paper in New York City—the *World*.

When he moved to New York, Pulitzer realized that New York had two halves. One half included the upper and middle classes. The other half was the poor. Pulitzer became a champion of the poor.

Pulitzer's *World* changed American journalism. He insisted on simple language most people could read. He included human-interest stories as well as news. Pulitzer added sections to his newspaper to appeal to different groups of readers. He

With a stack of newspapers tucked neatly under his arm, a young newsboy smiles for a camera.

was the first to bring together into one newspaper a women's section, a sports section, and comics.

The newspaper also became a way for immigrants to learn about their neighbors and to understand how the city worked. In other words, Pulitzer's *World* connected city people with each other.

Consider for instance, the story of the Statue of Liberty. France was presenting the Statue of Liberty to the United States as a symbol of the friendship betwen the two nations. Yet there was no base on which to place the statue, and Congress refused to pay for one. Pulitzer therefore asked his readers for the money. More than 120,000 people donated the necessary $100,000. The Statue of Liberty was dedicated in 1886.

Department Stores

Newspaper advertising was important to department stores. Through advertisements and window displays, department stores attracted a wide range of customers.

In the stores, sales clerks were expected to be as polite to a poor

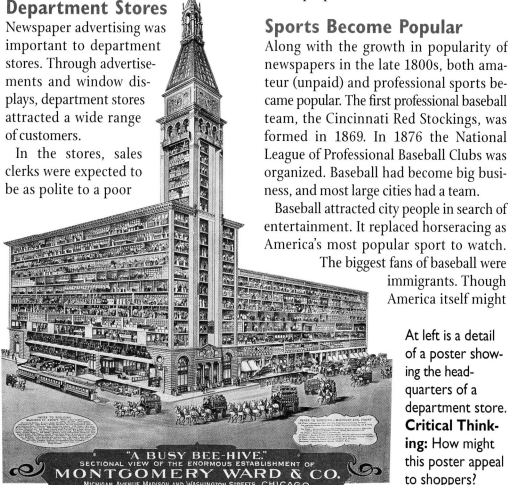

HOME WASHING MACHINE & WRINGER.

This 1869 advertisement shows some women using a home washing machine. **Critical Thinking:** Why, do you think, are no men pictured in this advertisement?

woman buying a piece of ribbon as to a rich woman buying a fur coat. Women of all classes thus shopped together in the new department stores.

Department stores also changed the downtown, once a place where only business people worked. With department stores, the downtown became a place for all the people.

Sports Become Popular

Along with the growth in popularity of newspapers in the late 1800s, both amateur (unpaid) and professional sports became popular. The first professional baseball team, the Cincinnati Red Stockings, was formed in 1869. In 1876 the National League of Professional Baseball Clubs was organized. Baseball had become big business, and most large cities had a team.

Baseball attracted city people in search of entertainment. It replaced horseracing as America's most popular sport to watch. The biggest fans of baseball were immigrants. Though America itself might

At left is a detail of a poster showing the headquarters of a department store. **Critical Thinking:** How might this poster appeal to shoppers?

"A BUSY BEE-HIVE."
SECTIONAL VIEW OF THE ENORMOUS ESTABLISHMENT OF
MONTGOMERY WARD & CO.
MICHIGAN AVENUE, MADISON AND WASHINGTON STREETS, CHICAGO.

BASEBALL'S OLDER COUSIN

This is no ordinary baseball game. The "diamond" is round or oval. The player facing you hurls a small red ball toward the ground. The ball takes a low bounce in front of you. You swing a flat, wide bat and the ball takes off.

Welcome to cricket, baseball's older cousin. The American game of baseball was based on the English game of "rounders," which in turn evolved from cricket. Cricket became a major sport in England in the 1700s. Today it is still a major sport in England and in some of the countries England once ruled, including South Africa, India, and Australia.

be confusing, baseball was a game of rules they could understand.

Rooting for a big-city team gave people a sense of belonging. According to historian Gunther Barth, "More often than not, . . . a trip to the ball park tied people, city life, and baseball together."

Two other American sports had their beginnings in the late 1800s: football and basketball. In the 1870s Americans took the English game of rugby and turned it into football. It was first played by college teams. Basketball was invented in Massachusetts in 1891 as a game to play indoors during the winter.

As sports became more popular, a small number of women began to challenge the idea that sports were for men only. Still in long skirts, they began to run races and play tennis. It was the bicycle, however, that gave women a new freedom to move.

The Impact of Bicycles

The development of the modern bicycle in the 1880s set off a craze that would last two decades. (Then a still newer invention, the automobile, would draw people away from their bicycles.) Although not cheap to buy, bicycles cost less than feeding and keeping a horse. Furthermore, bicycles were not just for men. Women could ride them as well. To do so, women started wearing bloomers—the baggy pants promoted in the 1850s by Amelia Bloomer.

Bicycles offered people a fun and easy way to get around. People could use them to go to work or to ride into the country for a picnic. The tandem bicycle—a bicycle built for two—inspired one of the period's most popular songs:

Daisy, Daisy, give me your answer, do!
I'm half crazy, all for the love of you!
It won't be a stylish marriage,
I can't afford a carriage,
But you'll look sweet upon the seat
Of a bicycle built for two!

A couple shows off their "high-wheeler" bicycle. The high-wheeler was difficult to ride.

Crowds flock outside a movie theater in Los Angeles in the early 1900s. The top photo shows a pianist playing music to accompany a silent film.

Vaudeville Theater

Many people first heard "A Bicycle Built for Two" sung in a **vaudeville** (VAWD-vil) theater. Vaudeville was a variety show that included a bit of everything—songs, skits, dances, comic routines, juggling, and gymnastics. In a vaudeville theater, it did not matter how rich you were, or what your religion was, or where your parents came from. When Boston's new playhouse opened in 1894, an actress told the opening-day crowd, "All are equals here."

Vaudeville used both song and comedy to explore human problems. Like television shows today, the subject of vaudeville was life at the time. Vaudeville helped define what was American about America.

Early Movies

In the 1890s one of the acts in a vaudeville show did not have any live performers. Instead a flickering light would project a few moments of "moving pictures" onto the stage. The audience would watch with excitement. These were the first movies.

By the early 1900s people were paying five cents to see short, silent films that told simple stories. The movies were shown in theaters called **nickelodeons.**

Huge audiences, many of them children, went to the nickelodeons. Soon filmmakers were using several reels of film to tell more complex stories. In this way the modern movie industry was born.

In time, movies would replace the live action of vaudeville theaters. Other forms of entertainment would appear—radio, musical theater, and television. Many of the great entertainers of the 1900s, however, had roots in vaudeville.

SECTION REVIEW

1. Key Terms circulation, vaudeville, nickelodeon

2. People Joseph Pulitzer

3. Comprehension What role did Joseph Pulitzer play in changing the newspaper business?

4. Comprehension Why were bicycles so popular in the late 1800s?

5. Critical Thinking What are some of today's forms of entertainments? In what ways might they unite Americans?

Summary

1. The United States experienced a huge wave of immigration in the late 1800s and early 1900s. Immigration from southern and eastern Europe increased. New York's Ellis Island was the first stop for many European immigrants. Most then moved to the cities of the industrial United States.

2. New immigrants, such as Jews fleeing mistreatment in eastern Europe, struggled to adjust to life in the United States. Free education helped immigrants, but working and living conditions were often difficult.

3. Immigration helped fuel the expansion of cities. Electric street-cars and bridges helped cities expand outward. Political machines controlled a number of city governments. They stayed in power by buying votes. Women began to enter the workforce in larger numbers. Many women also worked in settlement houses, which helped immigrants. The Social Gospel encouraged people to help the poor.

4. Advances in technology and advertising increased the circulation of newspapers. Department stores offered large varieties of goods. Sports and entertainment helped make city life exciting.

Review

KEY TERMS

Define the following terms.
1. political machine
2. nationality
3. vaudeville
4. suburb
5. tenement
6. pogrom
7. settlement house

COMPREHENSION

1. What factors encouraged southern and eastern Europeans to immigrate in the late 1800s?

2. What four states took in half of all immigrants in the early 1900s? Why did immigrants settle there?

3. What was the relationship between padrones and immigrants?

4. Why did so many eastern European Jews come to the U.S. in the late 1800s and early 1900s?

5. What factors caused tension between adult immigrants and their children?

6. What role did electricity play in expanding the size of cities in the late 1880s?

7. What role did ward bosses play in the running of political machines in cities?

8. How did the role of women change in the late 1800s?

9. How did advertising help the newspaper business?

10. Why was baseball a popular sport among immigrants?

Graphic Summary

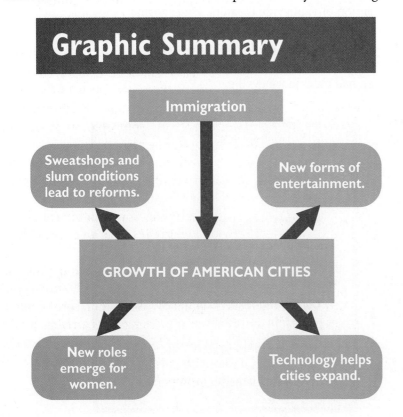

Immigration

Sweatshops and slum conditions lead to reforms.

New forms of entertainment.

GROWTH OF AMERICAN CITIES

New roles emerge for women.

Technology helps cities expand.

Places to Locate

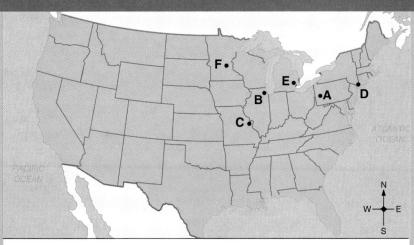

Match the letters on the map with the places that are listed below. Then explain the importance of each place.

1. Ellis Island
2. St. Louis
3. Detroit
4. Pittsburgh
5. Chicago
6. Minneapolis

Geographic Theme: Place Why do you think immigrants to the United States settled mostly in cities? Explain.

Skill Review

Study the street map of Chicago in 1890 and answer the questions below.

1. In what box does the Chicago River flow into Lake Michigan?

2. Which two streets intersect in box D-2?

3. In what box does the South Branch of the Chicago River cross 22nd Street? In what box does it cross 12th Street?

4. If you walked down Milwaukee Ave. toward the lake, through what boxes would you pass?

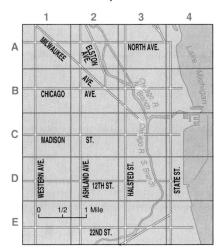

CRITICAL THINKING

1. Making a Judgment Do you think that immigrants found better lives in America than the ones they had left behind? Using information from the chapter, write a brief essay explaining your answer.

2. Forming a Hypothesis How might Jane Addams have responded to the charge that the Social Gospel went against nature's law?

PORTFOLIO OPTIONS

1. Civics Connection Imagine you are an immigrant from Europe in the late 1800s with no family or friends in America. Where could you turn for help in finding a job and a place to live? Discuss your options with the class.

2. Writing Connection Make a list of problems cities faced in the late 1800s and early 1900s. Then write a newspaper editorial expressing your opinion on how to solve one of the problems.

3. Contemporary Connection Millions of people still immigrate to the United States each year. Do you think that immigration should be restricted? Organize a class debate on the issue.

4. Timeline Connection Copy the chapter timeline. What do you think the Statue of Liberty symbolized to immigrants arriving at Ellis Island? Add other events from the chapter you think should be included and explain why.

On April 22, 1889, thousands of settlers rushed into Oklahoma Territory to stake their claims (below). This Oklahoma land rush symbolized the West in the late 1800s. Thousands came to find gold, raise cattle, or farm. The price of this settlement was paid by the original inhabitants, the American Indians.

1860　　　　　1864　　　　　1868　　　　　1872

1862 Homestead Act passed

1867 Alaska purchased

1864 Sand Creek Massacre

Forces Shaping a New West (1860–1900)

1 Changes Come to the West

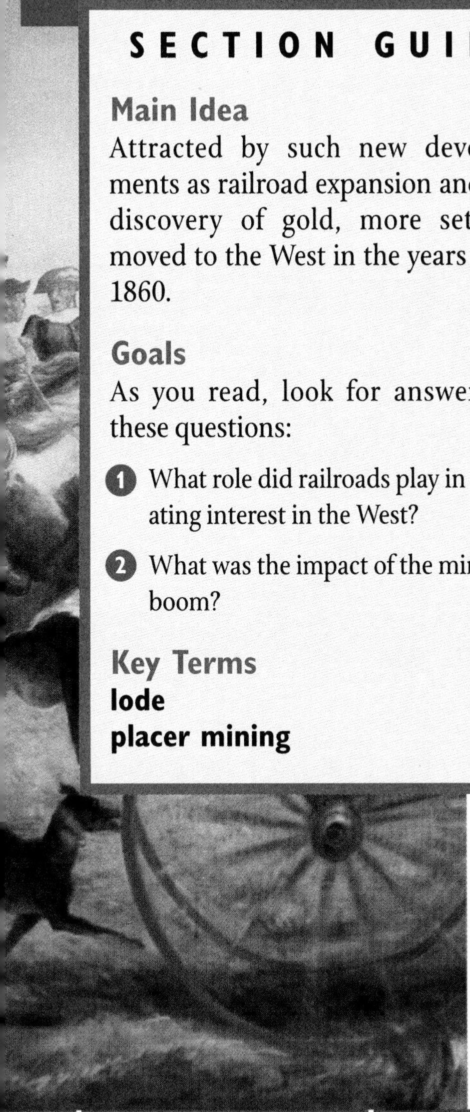

SECTION GUIDE

Main Idea
Attracted by such new developments as railroad expansion and the discovery of gold, more settlers moved to the West in the years after 1860.

Goals
As you read, look for answers to these questions:

❶ What role did railroads play in creating interest in the West?

❷ What was the impact of the mining boom?

Key Terms
lode
placer mining

I T IS 1859 and you have just arrived in St. Joseph, Missouri, the last stop for trains coming from the East. From here on you must travel west by stagecoach or wagon. You walk into the lobby of the City Hotel. There is Horace Greeley, publisher of the New York *Tribune*, who has come to see the West for himself. Another guest is an Indian trader from the Rockies who arrived by canoe. There are soldiers headed for forts far up the Missouri River. You also might see miners heading for Colorado's new goldfields or families on their way to new homes in the West.

The Geography of the West

In 1859 St. Joseph stood on the edge of the American frontier. The frontier was that area of the country where towns and cities gave way to lands where Indians and settlers lived. In the mid-1800s it lay between the Mississippi Valley and the mountains near the Pacific Coast. East of the Missouri River were factories, farms, and growing cities. These settled areas could also be found on the Pacific Coast. There, the new states of California (1850) and Oregon (1859) were growing rapidly.

The frontier included the Great Plains, treeless and full of buffalo. It included the Rocky Mountains and, farther west, the deserts and dry plateaus. This land was home to many Indians.

1876	1880	1884	1888

1876 Battle of Little Bighorn

1887 Dawes Act passed

1890 Battle of Wounded Knee

Generations of American children grew up playing "cowboys and Indians." In this game, Indians usually were bad guys who killed innocent pioneers. Cowboys were good guys. These images were myths created by books, radio, films, and television.

For many years, westerns presented a distorted view of history. In this view, Indians were cruel, Mexicans were bandits, women served their men, and African Americans did not exist.

Starting in the 1960s, westerns became more varied. One recent film, "A Thousand Pieces of Gold," tells of a Chinese woman in the West. Another film, "Posse," describes African American cowboys. "Unforgiven," which won several Academy Awards, portrays a cowboy not as a hero but as a bitter and lonely man.

Yet it had been claimed by France, Spain, Mexico, and now the United States.

By 1900 this frontier had disappeared. Thousands of settlers had moved west, pushing Indians off their lands. How had this happened?

The main cause was the transcontinental railroad, completed in 1869. The railroad did more than anything else to change the western United States. Trains carried the great resources of the region—mineral ores, timber, crops, and cattle. Trains also brought the miners, lumbermen, farmers, ranchers, and soldiers who would conquer the Indians.

Miners in the West

In 1859 a miner named George Jackson was about to give up his search for gold in the Rocky Mountains. After one last look at Clear Creek, he planned to head to Denver, 30 miles away. Jackson hacked out some frozen sand and water, swishing them in a cup. The light sand floated away, leaving behind heavy gold flakes.

Jackson's gold find started a rush for an area named for its most famous mountain, Pikes Peak. Prospectors from the East and

Deadwood, Dakota Territory, near the goldfields of the Black Hills was described as the one of the wildest towns in the West. **Critical Thinking:** Few women can be seen in this 1880 photograph. Why might that be true?

California slapped new signs on their wagons: "Pikes Peak or Bust."

The Clear Creek strike was just one of many discoveries in the West. The California gold rush of 1849 had long since ended because all the easy-to-find gold had been discovered. "Gold fever," however, did not end. Black Elk, a Sioux holy man, commented that "the yellow metal makes the Wasichus [white people] crazy."

The next big strike after Clear Creek came in June 1859 in Nevada. The Comstock Lode produced hundreds of millions of dollars of silver and gold. (A **lode** is a deposit of a valuable mineral buried between layers of rock.) Gold and silver were also found in Idaho, Wyoming, Montana, and Alaska.

Mining Life

Just as in the Gold Rush of 1849, boomtowns sprang up to serve the needs of the miners. This was one visitor's description:

❝ **The crack of the revolver was often heard above the merry notes of the violin. Street fights were frequent, and as no one knew when or where they would occur, everyone was on his guard. . . .** ❞

What sorts of people moved to such rough-and-tumble places? There were ex-California prospectors, adventurers from the eastern United States, and thousands of immigrants. Men from Cornwall, in southern England, came because they were experienced miners. Chinese immigrants also worked the mines.

Women worked in mining communities, though they were far outnumbered by the men. Many women took advantage of the mining boom to make money from cooking and washing for the miners. Others ran dance halls, hotels, stores, and boarding houses.

The Business of Mining

Few prospectors became rich. With each strike, prospectors would swarm into an area and try their luck. Then most would leave, disappointed and broke.

A big problem was technology. Most miners did placer mining. Placer mining meant washing the sand and gravel from a stream. The idea was to separate out any bits of gold or gold dust there might be. If you had a shovel, a washpan, and a good set of eyes, you could be a placer miner.

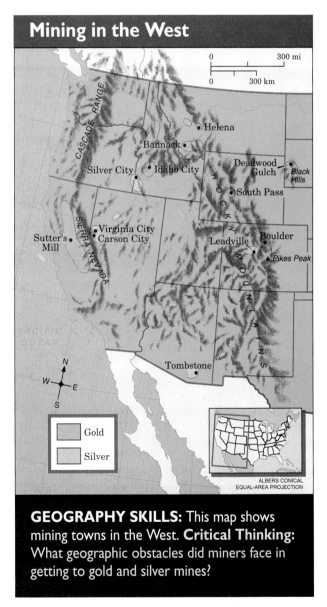

Mining in the West

GEOGRAPHY SKILLS: This map shows mining towns in the West. **Critical Thinking:** What geographic obstacles did miners face in getting to gold and silver mines?

More efficient methods of mining soon developed. In the 1870s miners turned to hydraulic mining—using water cannons to blast away at hillsides. This exposed any gold deposits that might exist below the surface. Another method was quartz mining. Rock was dynamited from a mountainside and then crushed to separate the gold ore.

While these new methods were more expensive than placer mining, they were more effective at getting out the ore. On the other hand, they were far more harmful to the environment. Hillsides were left stripped of plant life, and rivers were polluted.

Only companies, not individuals, had the money to buy the equipment needed for these new forms of mining. Many former prospectors started working for the mining companies. Working conditions were brutal. At the Comstock Lode in Nevada the temperature deep in the mines was well over 100 degrees. Miners wore thick boots to avoid being scalded by the hot water that might gush into underground passages.

Then there were the accidents. Cave-ins crushed miners or trapped them hundreds of feet below the surface. Dynamite, which was used to blast rock, sometimes exploded at the wrong time. In one accident, reported a Colorado paper, "arms and legs were torn from the bodies of all [four of] the men, and . . . scattered for a hundred feet along the tunnel."

The Mining Boom Ends

Few of the mining camps grew into permanent towns. They became ghost towns when the gold or silver ran out. As long as the mining rushes lasted, however, they created business for coach and freight companies. Wells Fargo captured most of the business in Colorado and Nevada. It had 6,000 wagons and 75,000 oxen to take supplies to the mining towns and haul the minerals to railroad stations.

The mining boom in most of the United States was over by 1890. Only a few miners had grown rich. Yet the boom had changed the map of the United States. Nevada's population grew so much after the Comstock strike that it was able to join the Union in 1864. Colorado joined in 1876. In 1889 North Dakota, South Dakota, and Montana became states. Idaho gained statehood in 1890.

This diagram of the Comstock Lode in Nevada illustrates the importance of lumber in supporting mines. The mines were dimly lit by lamps, such as the one above.
Critical Thinking: Using this diagram and your imagination, describe a day in the life of a miner.

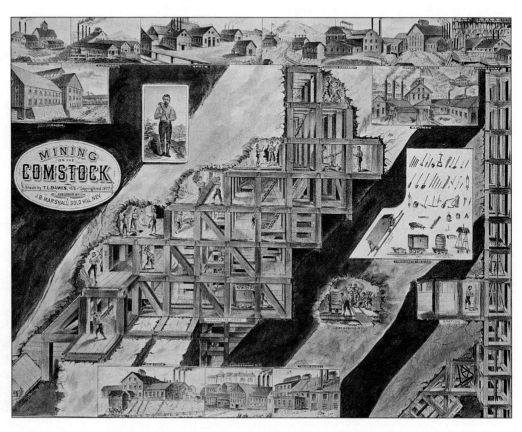

Chilkoot Pass, on the border of Alaska and Canada, was an important route to the northern goldfields.

The Lumber Industry

The natural resources of the West were not limited to gold and silver. California redwoods, Douglas fir, and other trees grew thick and tall in the Pacific Northwest. As settlers moved west, so did loggers. Rowdy lumber towns sprang up near forests.

The loggers found no shortage of work. The growing population of the West needed boards to build houses as well as logs to support mine tunnels. As early as 1865, a dozen or more sawmills buzzed away in Washington. By the 1880s the northwestern lumber industry was in full swing.

Lumbering required plenty of muscle. Loggers used special kinds of axes to chop down the huge trees. Horses or oxen dragged the trees to a river. Then the logs were floated downstream to a sawmill. From time to time the rivers became clogged with lumber.

Lumbering, like mining, required heavy investments in workers and machines. As in mining, a few large companies came to dominate the industry.

Alaska: The Last Frontier

Mining and lumbering played a big part in the development of the nation's last frontier, Alaska. In 1867 Secretary of State William Seward arranged for the purchase of Alaska from Russia. U.S. Senators howled when asked to pay for this land far to the north. They called it "Seward's Folly" and "Polar Bear Garden." Seward convinced them, however, and Russia lost its foothold in North America.

Seward's gamble paid off in many ways. In 1880 gold was discovered in southern Alaska. Another goldfield was found in Nome in 1899 and in Fairbanks in 1902. Thousands of prospectors from the lower states rushed north to make their fortune. Alaska was also rich in such natural resources as fur-bearing animals, timber, copper, coal, and oil. People continued to come to Alaska to take advantage of these rich resources, and it became a state in 1959. Even today the state is known as the "Last Frontier."

SECTION REVIEW

1. Key Terms lode, placer mining

2. People and Places William Seward, Great Plains, Comstock Lode, Pacific Northwest, Alaska

3. Comprehension What was the main cause of the great increase in the number of settlers who moved into the West from 1860 to 1900?

4. Comprehension Why did large businesses usually benefit more from gold and silver mining than individual prospectors?

5. Critical Thinking How did moving to the West create new opportunities for some people? Why might some people later have regretted moving west?

SKILLS: Identifying Fact and Opinion

LEARN

When a sales clerk tells you "This is the best pair of running shoes on the market today," can you believe her? The word "best" is a clue that the clerk's statement is an opinion. A good response to such a statement is, "Prove it." If the sales clerk then shows how well made the product is, you might just be persuaded that those running shoes are the best. This is still an opinion, but it is supported by facts.

Facts are pieces of information that can be checked for accuracy. **Opinions,** on the other hand, express people's feelings, beliefs, and attitudes. Historians rely not only on facts but also on opinions to get a full picture of an event.

Read the excerpt at the right. It appeared in a newspaper, the Arizona *Star,* in October 1895 and describes Nellie Cashman, a successful miner and businesswoman.

> "Yesterday Tucson was visited by one of the most extraordinary women in America, Nellie Cashman, whose name and face have been familiar in every important mining camp or district on the coast for more than twenty years. She rode into town from Casa Grande on horseback, a jaunt that would have nearly [overcome] the average man with fatigue. She showed no sign of weariness, and went about town in that calm businesslike manner that belongs particularly to her."

PRACTICE

1. Copy the excerpt onto a piece of paper. Circle the sentences or parts of sentences that are opinions.

2. Underline the words that suggest the sentences and parts of sentences you circled are opinions. Explain why you circled them.

3. Do you think a historian studying women in the West would benefit from examining this source? Why or why not?

APPLY

4. Imagine that you lived in the West between 1860 and 1900. Describe an exciting event from your life. Include facts, but also include opinions that would help a historian understand the West.

2 Indian Wars

SECTION GUIDE

Main Idea
As settlers poured onto their lands, the Plains Indians fought to maintain their way of life.

Goals
As you read, look for answers to these questions:

1. What caused conflicts between Plains Indians and white settlers?

2. What was the outcome of conflicts between white settlers and Indians?

3. What new policy toward Indians did the U.S. government adopt?

Key Terms
reservation
Battle of Little Bighorn
Wounded Knee Massacre
assimilation
Dawes Act

CHIEF CRAZY HORSE spoke for the Indians of the Great Plains when he said the following:

> *We did not ask you white men to come here. The Great Spirit gave us this country as a home. You had yours. We did not interfere with you. . . . But you have come here; you are taking my land from me.*

Government Policy

In the early 1800s the Plains Indians lived and hunted from southwestern Canada to northern Mexico and from the Mississippi to the Rocky Mountains. Beginning in the 1840s, white settlers passed through the Plains to reach the West Coast. The U.S. government asked the Plains Indians to let settlers through safely. It also asked the Indians to limit their hunting to certain areas. Yet the great herds of buffalo, on which the Indians depended, obeyed no such limits. To maintain their way of life, the Indians had to be free to follow the buffalo.

By the mid-1800s the federal government changed its policy. It began to set aside **reservations,** special areas used by a specific group. In return for agreeing to live on these reservations, the Indians were told that the land would be theirs forever. They were also promised food, money, and other help. Over the years, several treaties were signed, placing Indians on reservations.

Clash of Cultures

The Plains Indians and the white settlers who moved onto the Plains looked at the world in different ways. From the settlers' point of view, the resources of the West were there to be used. Getting at those

This photograph of a Blackfoot Indian camp in Montana was taken in 1900. Even after they were forced off most of their lands, the Plains Indians struggled to maintain their way of life.

Indians in the Western United States, 1860

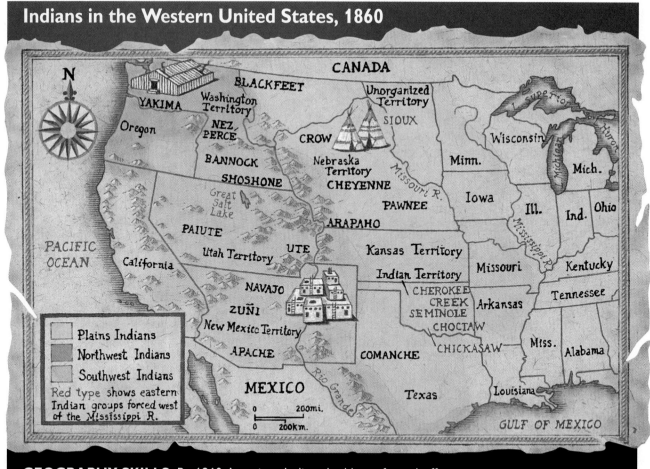

GEOGRAPHY SKILLS: By 1860 American Indians had been forced off their lands in most of California and east of the Mississippi River. **Critical Thinking:** Which groups had been forced westward? How might their westward movement have affected those Indians who already lived on the Plains?

resources meant mining, lumbering, hunting, and farming, all on a large scale.

The Plains Indians, in contrast, made use of animal or plant life only for their actual needs. They saw the settlers who cut down the forests, killed the buffalo, and dug up the land for gold as greedy and destructive.

Fighting Begins

By the 1860s, treaties between the United States and the Indians were being broken by both sides. Some settlers continued to pass through areas where they were not allowed. Some Indians raided white settlements and wagon trains.

In 1864 a band of Colorado state militia attacked Cheyenne and Arapaho Indians who had gathered at a camp on Sand Creek. The Indians had thought they were under the protection of a nearby government outpost. More than a hundred Indians, including women and children, were slaughtered in what became known as the Sand Creek Massacre.

In Montana a chief named Red Cloud had led the Oglala Sioux in resisting settlement of Sioux lands. His warriors followed and then attacked trains of settlers and construction parties. In 1866 a U.S. Army officer, Captain W. J. Fetterman, pursued a party of Sioux who had attacked a supply train. Fetterman led his 80 soldiers into a trap. A much larger band of Sioux fighters was waiting. In the battle, Fetterman's entire group was wiped out.

Little Bighorn

The most famous battle of the Indian Wars took place in June 1876 after tensions had arisen in the Black Hills of the Dakotas. These hills had been set aside by treaty for the Sioux and northern Cheyenne. In 1874, after a U.S. Army exploring party found gold in the Black Hills, miners arrived by the thousands. They cared little that this land was sacred to the Sioux.

Hoping to head off a clash, the government tried to buy the Black Hills from the Indians. The Sioux would not think of selling their land. As war fever mounted through the winter of 1875–1876, Sioux warriors left their reservations. They united under the leadership of two Sioux chiefs—Sitting Bull and Crazy Horse.

On June 25, 1876, George Armstrong Custer and several hundred soldiers came upon a Sioux camp on the bank of the Little Bighorn River. Custer was already famous. He had fought in many Civil War battles. To some he was a daring, brilliant officer. To others he was a dangerous showoff, with his colorful uniform and long blond hair.

Custer's orders were to attack if he found Indians. When he neared the camp on the Little Bighorn, however, he entered a trap set by Sitting Bull and Crazy Horse. A large force of Sioux and Cheyenne overpowered his forces. In what became known as "Custer's Last Stand," all of Custer's men—including Custer himself—were killed.

In the East, people were shocked by news of the **Battle of Little Bighorn.** The government sent thousands more soldiers west to fight the Indians.

Little Bighorn was the last Indian victory in the Indian Wars. Army forces defeated the Sioux in the fall of 1876. Sitting Bull and his followers fled to Canada. Crazy Horse and some 800 of his people surrendered. As Crazy Horse was being arrested, he was fatally stabbed. It was never determined if it was a guard who killed him or another Indian who opposed his aims.

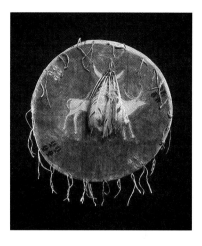

A Cheyenne war shield.

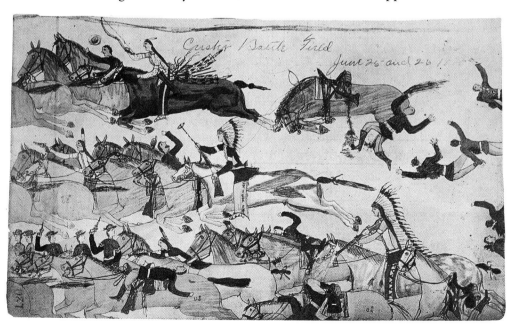

A Sioux artist painted this scene of the Battle of Little Bighorn. **Critical Thinking:** With what kinds of weapons did the Sioux fight?

Chief Joseph

A few months after the death of Crazy Horse, another war began—this one with the Nez Percé people. The Nez Percé were Northwest Indians. They fished for salmon, hunted, and gathered food from eastern Oregon to Idaho. Their leader was Chief Joseph, who refused to sell the lands where his people had lived for centuries.

When the government ordered the Nez Percé to move to a reservation in 1877, Chief Joseph and his followers fled. Army troops followed them. Over the next four months, the Nez Percé traveled some 1,300 miles through Oregon, Idaho, and Montana, looking for safety.

The Nez Percé were about 40 miles from the Canadian border when the army caught up with them. Cold, hungry, weary, and outnumbered, the Nez Percé surrendered. Chief Joseph spoke eloquently for many western Indians when he said:

> **Hear me, my chiefs. I am tired; my heart is sick and sad. From where the sun now stands, I will fight no more forever.**

Southwest Indians

The Indians of the Southwest were also forced onto reservations. In the 1860s the U.S. government ordered Colonel Kit Carson to move the Navajo from their traditional lands in Arizona to a reservation in eastern New Mexico on the Pecos River.

The Navajo refused to surrender. Carson waged total war against them. His soldiers burned their fields, cut down their trees, and slaughtered their animals. In January 1864, freezing and starving, the Navajo finally surrendered. Thus began what the Navajo call the "Long Walk" east, away from their rugged lands to the edge of the Great Plains. Hundreds died during the trip from lack of food and warm clothing.

Arrival at the reservation did not end their problems. Guarded and watched, the Navajo were forced to dig irrigation ditches and plant crops. Insects killed the crops and the Pecos River overflowed, destroying the irrigation system. Finally, the government admitted that the reservation was a failure. The Navajo returned home.

In the mid-1870s the Chiricahua Apache were moved onto land away from their traditional territory in the Southwest. Geronimo, an Apache leader, led his followers off the reservation. His knowledge of southern Arizona allowed them to escape the U.S. Army time and time again.

Geronimo was finally captured just north of the Mexican border in 1886. He spent the rest of his life forced to live far from his people.

A Way of Life Destroyed

The Indians lost more than battles. Their way of life was destroyed as well. Railroad crews seeking food killed thousands of buffalo. So did professional hunters. Buffalo hunting even became a sport. Settlers would shoot buffalo from passing trains, leaving the carcasses to rot in the sun.

The destruction of the buffalo herds meant another defeat for the Indians. They needed the buffalo for many uses, especially food. As a Lakota Sioux warrior put it:

> **Our living was their sport, and if you look at it one way, they might as well have been killing us as the buffalo.**

Destroying the Indians was what some whites had in mind. "Every buffalo dead is an Indian gone," said one army officer.

Faced with disaster, some Indians began to turn to the Ghost Dance religion. It taught that the spirits of dead Indians

Chief Joseph, leader of the Nez Percé.

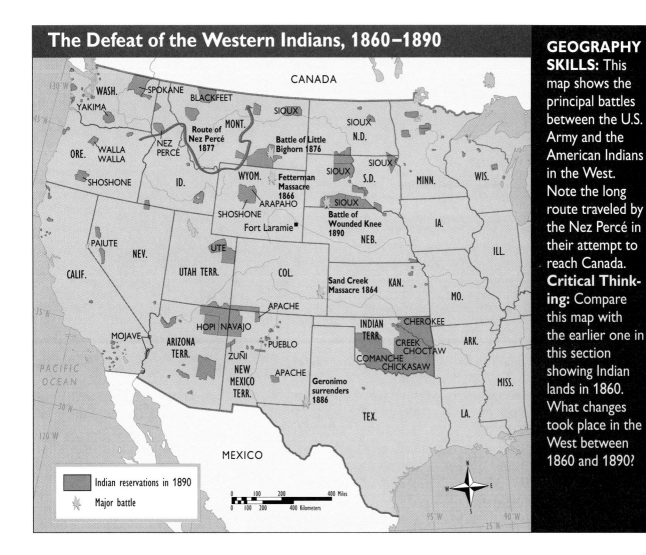

The Defeat of the Western Indians, 1860–1890

CANADA

WASH.
SPOKANE
YAKIMA
BLACKFEET
SIOUX
SIOUX
N.D.
ORE.
WALLA WALLA
NEZ PERCÉ
Route of Nez Percé 1877
MONT.
Battle of Little Bighorn 1876
SHOSHONE
ID.
WYOM.
Fetterman Massacre 1866
ARAPAHO
SIOUX
SIOUX
S.D.
MINN.
WIS.
SHOSHONE
Fort Laramie
Battle of Wounded Knee 1890
NEB.
IA.
ILL.
PAIUTE
NEV.
UTE
UTAH TERR.
COL.
Sand Creek Massacre 1864
KAN.
MO.
CALIF.
MOJAVE
ARIZONA TERR.
HOPI NAVAJO
PUEBLO
ZUÑI
NEW MEXICO TERR.
APACHE
APACHE
Geronimo surrenders 1886
INDIAN TERR.
CHEROKEE
CREEK
COMANCHE
CHOCTAW
CHICKASAW
ARK.
MISS.
TEX.
LA.

PACIFIC OCEAN
MEXICO

Indian reservations in 1890
Major battle

0 100 200 400 Miles
0 100 200 400 Kilometers

GEOGRAPHY SKILLS: This map shows the principal battles between the U.S. Army and the American Indians in the West. Note the long route traveled by the Nez Percé in their attempt to reach Canada. **Critical Thinking:** Compare this map with the earlier one in this section showing Indian lands in 1860. What changes took place in the West between 1860 and 1890?

would return to help living Indians win back their lands.

Fearful of this new movement, white settlers asked the army for help. In 1890 the cavalry responded by rounding up Sioux men on the Pine Ridge Reservation in South Dakota, at a place called Wounded Knee. Someone fired a rifle. Then all the soldiers began firing.

The result was a massacre. When the shooting ended, some 300 Sioux men, women, and children lay dead. "We tried to run," one Sioux woman later recalled, "but they shot us like we were buffalo." The Wounded Knee Massacre of 1890 is considered by many to have been the last "battle" of the Indian Wars.

The Dawes Act

As more and more Indians were forced onto reservations, conditions there grew worse. In time, reformers began to demand better treatment for Native Americans. In 1881 Helen Hunt Jackson published *A Century of Dishonor,* which recorded the failures of government policy. Speakers like Sarah Winnemucca, a Paiute, traveled across the country to advance the Indians' cause.

Many white Americans saw only one solution to the Indians' problems. They believed that Indians could survive only if they became more like whites. In line with this view, the government began a policy of assimilation. (To assimilate means to

Sarah Winnemucca

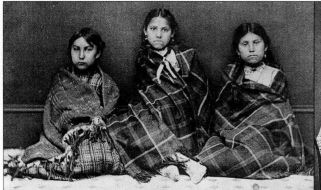

The photo above was taken when these three Plains Indian girls arrived at a school in Virginia in 1878. Fourteen months later, their photograph was taken again (right). **Critical Thinking:** How have the girls changed?

adopt the culture of the people around you.) Many reformers in those days believed that assimilation was the best way to help members of minority groups.

The Dawes Act, passed in 1887, was intended to make Indians give up their traditions and accept white culture. Under the Dawes Act, reservation lands were divided up. Indian families and individuals received farm plots of 40 to 160 acres. Any remaining land was sold to white settlers. The profits were used to support Indian schools that "civilized" the Indians—that is, taught them to live like whites. Indians who accepted the plots of land could, for the first time, become American citizens.

The Dawes Act failed. Not all western Indians wanted to settle down as farmers. Those who did lacked the tools and training to succeed. Many sold their plots of land to whites for a fraction of their real value. In this way, even more Indian land was lost.

Some Indians refused to accept the government offer. They tried to keep their traditions, continuing to live on reservations, where conditions remained harsh.

At the end of the 1800s the situation of American Indians in the United States was tragic. Their lands had been taken and their cultures scorned. Not until the twentieth century would the U.S. government recognize the importance of the Indian way of life.

SECTION REVIEW

1. Key Terms reservation, Battle of Little Bighorn, Wounded Knee Massacre, assimilation, Dawes Act

2. People and Places Crazy Horse, Sitting Bull, George Armstrong Custer, Chief Joseph, Geronimo, Black Hills

3. Comprehension In what way did the Indians and white settlers disagree about the use of land?

4. Comprehension Why did the destruction of the buffalo harm the Plains Indians?

5. Critical Thinking Present two arguments, one that assimilation was in the Indians' best interests and the other that it was not. With which do you agree?

3 Cowboys and Ranchers

SECTION GUIDE

Main Idea
Cattle ranching became a big business in the 1860s and 1870s as the railroads provided a new means of transport.

Goals
As you read, look for answers to these questions:

1. What part did the long drive and the open range play in the growth of the cattle industry?

2. Why did the cattle-raising business change after the mid-1880s?

Key Term
rodeo
long drive
vigilante

CLOSE YOUR EYES and think about a cowboy. What do you see? Do you imagine a young man in a tall hat on a horse? Is he shooting a "bad guy" or flirting with a pretty woman in a saloon?

Who Were the Cowboys?

The cowboy is perhaps this nation's best-known character. To many he symbolizes values that Americans respect, such as self-reliance and hard work. Cowboys are also celebrated as free-living souls who did not have to follow the rules of settled life. Today, people often use the term "cowboy" to describe an adventurous and reckless person.

What were the cowboys of the old West really like? About one in six or seven was Mexican American. In fact, the first American cowboys were Mexican: the *vaqueros* of Texas. The American cowboy's saddle was adapted from the Spanish horned saddle. From the *vaquero*, the cowboy borrowed the bridle, bit, and spur.

Some cowboys were African American. Nat Love, for example, was born in a Tennessee slave cabin. He moved west as a teenager, worked as a cowboy, and became famous performing in rodeos. (A rodeo, from the Spanish word for an enclosure, is a show at which cowboys demonstrate their skills.) After

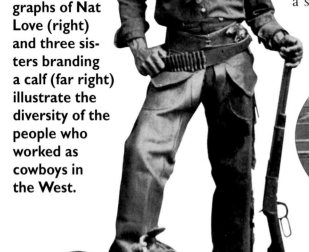

These photographs of Nat Love (right) and three sisters branding a calf (far right) illustrate the diversity of the people who worked as cowboys in the West.

Alligator Stampede!
Spanish Words in English

The language we use daily mirrors our society. When customs and ideas from different cultures become part of our lives, the language we speak changes. For example, over many generations our Spanish heritage has brought new words into American English. "Taco," "burrito," and "salsa" might come quickly to mind. Other words, such as "plaza," "tornado," and "cigar," also have Spanish origins.

El lagarto means "the lizard" in Spanish. If you say the two Spanish words quickly so that they run together, you can hear how the English word "alligator" came about.

Imagine the crashing sound of a cowherd in a headlong rush. Amid the noise, your Spanish friends yell *estampida!* You can hear only part of the word. You shout to your English-speaking friends, "stampede!"

Spanish culture and language shaped the American West, from Texas to the Pacific Coast. Like lands in central Spain, the western plains suited cattle raising. Spaniards brought horses to this new countryside and practiced ranching. Vaqueros, or cowboys, herded cattle on horseback (and sometimes saw stampedes). Several words now used in English come from this way of life—"ranch" (from *rancho* and *ranchero*), "bonanza," "lasso," "lariat," "corral," "bronco," "mustang," and "rodeo," for example.

Many place names in the United States reflect our Spanish heritage. City names, such as El Paso, Santa Fe, San Diego, Los Angeles; and state names, such as Texas, Colorado, California, Florida, and Montana, are a few examples. In 1513, even before Spanish explorer Ponce de León got off his ship, he named the new land he saw "Florida." From the ship, he could see the blooms of hundreds of flowers, or flora.

CRITICAL THINKING
1. What words and phrases from different languages do you use in everyday speech?
2. Why would you expect American English to contain words from many different languages?
3. Is the diversity of American English a strength or a weakness? Explain.

becoming a cowboy, Love explained why he had moved West:

> **The wild cowboy, prancing horses of which I was very fond, and wild life generally, all had their attractions for me.**

Other cowboys were descendants of Indians. Some were even cowgirls. Lucille Mulhall learned how to ride, shoot, and rope cattle on her family's Oklahoma ranch. She was good enough to perform in rodeos.

Birth of the Cattle Industry

Cowboys had their roots in Texas in the 1700s. Yet for more than a century, cowboys were not in great demand. Cattle herds were small. Cattle could only be sold locally since there were no good ways to transport beef to the cities.

In the mid-1800s a livestock dealer named Joseph McCoy came up with a plan. McCoy knew that cattle sold for $3 a head in Texas but up to $40 a head in the growing cities of the East. Why not use railroads to carry the cattle east? Since railroads did not extend to Texas, McCoy decided to drive cattle herds north to Abilene, Kansas. From there the cattle could be loaded on railroad cars and shipped to large cities. The profits, he realized, would be huge.

In 1867 McCoy persuaded a railroad to stop at the prairie town of Abilene, Kansas. The first train headed east, with twenty carloads of McCoy's Texas longhorns. Others quickly followed. Abilene was the first "cow town," followed by Wichita and Dodge City, also in Kansas. The shipment of cattle peaked in 1871. In that year 700,000 cattle were shipped by railroad.

The Long Drives

The success of McCoy's idea led to the long drives. On a long drive the cowboys herded cattle over the open plains to a stop on a railroad. Usually, twelve cowboys drove herds of up to 3,000 cattle.

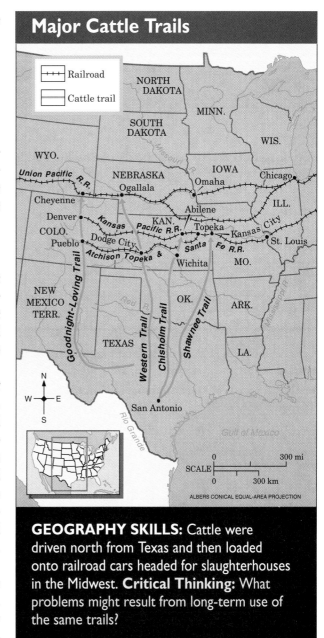

Major Cattle Trails

GEOGRAPHY SKILLS: Cattle were driven north from Texas and then loaded onto railroad cars headed for slaughterhouses in the Midwest. **Critical Thinking:** What problems might result from long-term use of the same trails?

The long drives followed trails that led from Texas to the cow towns. The first of these trails was the Chisholm Trail, followed by the Shawnee, Western, and Goodnight-Loving trails. (See the map above.) The trails crossed the open range, the vast grassland area owned by the government. Since heavier cattle were worth more, cowboys made sure the herds had plenty of grass to eat as they made their way to market.

ELFEGO BACA
(1865–1945)

The "wild West" was tamed by men like Elfego Baca, a sheriff, detective, politician, and folk hero of New Mexico. Baca's fame began when he was still a teenager. In 1884 Baca saw a group of cowboys harassing Mexican Americans. He took one cowboy prisoner and was attacked by about 80 more the next day. Fleeing to a friend's house, Baca killed several cowboys in the gun battle that followed. He refused to surrender until promised a fair trial. He was found innocent at that trial. Later he served as county clerk, mayor, district attorney, and superintendent of schools of Socorro County, New Mexico.

This "boot" is really a plaque that illustrates different kinds of barbed wire used for fences in the West. **Critical Thinking:** How did barbed wire help to bring about an end to the long drives?

It was a hard trip. The cowboys had to keep the longhorns together in the face of violent storms, severe heat, and swirling dust. At night they had to keep watch for "rustlers," or cow thieves. If something frightened the cattle, they might stampede. Chasing the frantic animals to round them up again was dangerous and exhausting.

The "Wild West"

At the end of a long drive the cowboys arrived in town, tired and filthy but with money in their pockets. They had spent a long time away from society, and their behavior could be far from law-abiding.

Cowboys were not the only group that gave the region its nickname, the "wild West." The frontier attracted many people who hoped to get rich quick. Some were honest and hardworking. Others were thieves.

The large spaces and thin settlement of the West made it difficult to catch the outlaws. Bank robbers such as Frank and Jesse James became legendary. So did cattle thieves like Belle Starr, who led a gang in Oklahoma Territory. No wonder a popular saying of the time was "Ain't no law west of St. Louis."

To keep the peace, westerners formed **vigilante** (vij-uh-LAN-tee) groups. A vigilante is someone who takes the law into his or her own hands. Vigilantes captured suspected lawbreakers and punished them without a trial. Sometimes they hanged suspects from a nearby tree.

End of the Long Drives

For a few years the open-range cattle industry did well. Some ranchers even made fortunes. Railroads built lines closer to Texas, and ranchers moved farther north. By the mid-1880s over 7 million head of cattle still grazed freely on the Great Plains.

After the mid-1880s, however, business fell off and the long

Chuck wagons served as portable kitchens for cowboys as they moved along the trail. **Critical Thinking:** How did conditions for cowboys change in the 1880s?

drives came to an end. There were several reasons. One was the spread of a disease called "tick fever" or "Texas fever." Trying to keep their livestock free of the disease, some Plains states closed their borders to cattle coming north from Texas.

The invention of barbed-wire fencing also played a part. Many farmers bought land from the government and used the barbed wire to fence off their property. Cattle could no longer pass through these lands. Angry at their loss of free range, cowboys sometimes cut down fences. Conflicts between ranchers and farmers were often bitter.

The final blow was a series of harsh winters in 1885–1886 and 1886–1887. The low temperatures and heavy snowfalls killed off large numbers of cattle. This disaster ended any hope of future profits from the open-range cattle business.

The ranchers who survived learned to change their ways. They fenced in their ranches and reduced their herds. Also, they grew hay for feed instead of relying on the natural grass of the range.

As for the cowboys, many took jobs on the new ranches, accepting the passing of their old way of life. Said one veteran cowboy in 1905, "I tell you, times have changed."

SECTION REVIEW

1. Key Terms rodeo, long drive, vigilante

2. People and Places Nat Love, Joseph McCoy, Texas, Abilene, Wichita, Dodge City

3. Comprehension What was the purpose of the long drives?

4. Comprehension What caused the decline of cattle ranching on the open range?

5. Critical Thinking How does the story of the long drive illustrate the importance of changes in technology in American history?

4 Farming the Plains

SECTION GUIDE

Main Idea
A wave of farmers moved onto the Plains in the late 1800s.

Goals
As you read, look for answers to these questions:

❶ Why did people move to the Plains region from the late 1860s to 1900?

❷ What was life like for the farm settlers on the Plains?

Key Terms
Homestead Act
Exoduster
sod

The J. W. Speese family, once enslaved in the South, sits proudly before their sod house in Westerville, Nebraska.

WHEN NANNIE T. ALDERSON was sixteen years old, her aunt invited her to go west. Nannie wrote:

❝What an experience that was! Kansas then was the West. I felt that the very air there was easier to breathe. In Union [West Virginia] you had to have your [family tree] with you to be accepted, but in Atchison it didn't matter who your ancestors were or what you did for a living.❞

The Government Encourages Settlement

From Kansas to Montana, a wave of new settlers arrived from the 1860s to 1900. Many moved west because the railroads made travel easier. Others had been encouraged by government policies.

For years, people had been calling on the government to sell western land at low prices. Before the Civil War, however, southern states blocked this policy. They feared that a big westward migration would create more nonslave states. When the southern states left the Union, the way was clear for a new land policy.

In 1862 Congress passed the **Homestead Act.** It offered 160 acres of land to the head of a family or any citizen 21 or older. In return, the settler had to live on the land for five years and improve it.

The federal government encouraged settlement in other ways as well. In 1862 it created a Department of Agriculture. The department began to introduce crops—such as Russian wheat—that could survive the harsh winters of the Plains. Its scientists taught farmers more efficient ways to raise crops. The department also set up experiment stations to study problems facing farmers.

Swedish American farmers sow their crops. After news of the Homestead Act reached Sweden in the late 1860s, more than 100,000 Swedes moved to the upper Midwest.

A Variety of Settlers

The western settlers were a cross-section of the American people. They included Civil War veterans and their families, as well as the sons and daughters of eastern farmers. There were honest business people and swindlers. Along with them came teachers, merchants, and others who hoped to fill the new settlers' needs.

Among the settlers were many African Americans, freed from slavery but disappointed with progress in the South. Benjamin "Pap" Singleton, from Tennessee, led a migration of African Americans out of the South in the "Exodus of 1879." They compared themselves to the Jews led out of slavery in Egypt by Moses and called themselves Exodusters.

The Exodusters started farming in Kansas and Nebraska. Some made a success of farming on the Plains. Others settled in growing towns such as Topeka and Kansas City. Unfortunately, African Americans still faced discrimination in their new homes in the West.

Settlers were also lured to the West by American railroad companies.

The companies had received land to build railroads. Now they wanted to resell the land at a profit.

To find customers, the railroad companies sent agents to Europe. They advertised for people willing to leave home and cross the ocean to start a new life. Company agents also greeted immigrants arriving at eastern ports with promises of cheap land. Among these immigrants were Germans,

A stove salesman shows a sample of his goods to farm women, who lived far from stores and show rooms.

Czechs, Ukrainians, Scandinavians, and Russians, eager for the chance to own good land.

Life on the Farming Frontier

The basics of food, fuel, and shelter did not come easily on the Plains. Because lumber was scarce, farmers often built houses with blocks of **sod.** (Sod is a section of earth held together by grass roots.) Sod houses were warm in the winter and cool in the summer. Yet sod roofs leaked both rain and melting snow. In dry weather, dust or grit coated the furniture, food, and dishes.

The lack of trees made fuel a problem. Farmers burned corn cobs and hay instead. They often collected and burned "cow chips" (the dried droppings of cows and buffalo). For water, the settlers dug deep wells. When they could afford it, they built windmills to pump the water to the surface.

Pioneer families fought a year-round battle against the weather. Blizzards, extreme heat, hailstorms, tornadoes, and drought (a long dry spell) were all part of the harsh Plains climate. At times of drought, people also had to be on guard for fires. Locusts and other grasshoppers destroyed crops. Fleas and bedbugs torment-ed the settlers. Rattlesnakes sometimes crept into cracks in the sod houses.

The farmers grew mainly cash crops of wheat and corn. New inventions helped them farm more efficiently. The steel plow, invented by John Deere in the 1830s, could cut through the tough Plains sod. Other new farm machines were reapers, threshers, hay mowers, and seed drillers.

Not all the Plains farmers could afford the new machinery. Those who could buy it grew more than they ever had before. From 1860 to 1890 wheat production went from 173 million bushels to 449 million.

Though the population of the Plains grew fast in the late 1800s, farmers and their families led lonely lives. Often the nearest neighbors were miles away. In her novel *My Ántonia* (1918), Willa Cather described a boy's first view of the Plains:

> **Cautiously, I slipped from under the buffalo hide, got up on my knees and peered over the side of the wagon. There seemed to be nothing to see; no fences, no creeks or trees, no hills or field. . . . There was nothing but land. . . . No, there was nothing but land. . . .**

North Dakota women gather in the 1890s to make a quilt and enjoy each other's company. The quilt at right was stitched by a New Hampshire woman when she moved west.
Critical Thinking: What rights did women in the West gain?

Women in the West

Life on homesteads was especially hard for women. While men sometimes worked in groups, women rarely saw their neighbors. Settlers were far from good medical care, and childbirth was dangerous. Social gatherings became special occasions. Quilting bees, barn raisings, even livestock butchering brought neighbors together.

Women bore their hardships bravely—and won a great deal of respect. They had more rights than their sisters to the east. Women had equal rights with men in receiving land grants. This was done to encourage as many families as possible to go west, since a husband and wife together could receive 320 acres. According to the Homestead Act, the wife's half of the property belonged to her, not to her husband. By 1890, a quarter of a million western women ran farms and ranches.

Women could also vote in many areas of the West. Wyoming Territory gave women the vote in 1869, and they served on juries there as well. Esther Morris of South Pass City, Wyoming, became a justice of the peace in 1870.

When Wyoming applied for statehood in 1890, members of Congress objected to Wyoming's guarantee of women's suffrage. Yet Wyoming stood firm. "We will remain out of the Union for 100 years rather than come in without the women," its leaders declared. Congress backed down, and Wyoming—with its women voters— became a state. Just a few months later, the women of Utah Territory gained the vote.

Closing the Frontier

By 1890 the stream of miners, ranchers, and farmers onto the Plains had greatly swelled the population of the West. Indians had been pushed off their land and onto the very edges of society.

Perhaps the closing of the frontier was best symbolized by the settlement of Oklahoma Territory in 1889. On April 22, at a given signal, thousands rushed into the area to stake out homesteads. By the end of the day, Oklahoma City had been laid out. By the end of the year, Oklahoma had a population of 60,000 people.

In 1890 the Census Bureau said that there was no longer a frontier line. In other words, for the first time since Europeans settlers had come to North America, there was no clear dividing line between areas populated by whites and areas populated by Indians.

To many, the frontier was what made America special. Frederick Jackson Turner,

a historian at the University of Wisconsin, published a paper in 1893 that made that claim. Turner said that the frontier was a promise to all Americans, no matter how poor, that they could advance as far as their abilities allow. In other words, the frontier meant opportunity.

To most Americans the West was not merely a land of opportunity but a place of excitement and bravery. They read stories about cowboys, Indians, and outlaws. They flocked to William F. "Buffalo Bill" Cody's Wild West show, which toured the country in the late 1800s. This image of the West continued into the 1900s in movies and later in television. It was a very unreal picture of the West that is being redrawn more accurately today. Still the ideal of the self-reliant westerner remains a powerful part of the American identity.

Annie Oakley was one of the most famous performers in Buffalo Bill's Wild West Show.

SECTION REVIEW

1. Key Terms Homestead Act, Exoduster, sod

2. People and Places Pap Singleton, Oklahoma Territory

3. Comprehension How did the government encourage western settlement? What kinds of people moved west?

4. Comprehension What was life like for the Plains farmers?

5. Critical Thinking Why might people have been willing to put up with the severe weather and other hardships of living on the Plains? What future did they hope for?

Summary

1. In the late 1800s the American frontier stretched between the Missouri River and the mountains near the Pacific Coast. Miners, attracted by gold and silver strikes, were early settlers in the region. Mining contributed to the population growth of many western territories, as did the lumber industry.

2. Government policies, wars, and the destruction of the buffalo led to the defeat of the Plains Indians by 1890. Indians were put on reservations, where living conditions were poor.

3. After railroads gave western ranchers access to eastern markets, cowboys and the cattle industry thrived. Lawlessness was such a problem that some people called the region the "wild West." New settlement, barbed wire, and bad weather ended the cattle boom.

4. Through the Homestead Act, the U.S. government made land available to new settlers on the Plains. Life for homesteaders was difficult, but they used new technologies to increase output. By 1890 the western frontier was considered closed, though the image of the western frontier continued.

Review

KEY TERMS

Define the following terms.
1. assimilation
2. Battle of Little Bighorn
3. Dawes Act
4. Exoduster
5. Homestead Act
6. long drive
7. placer mining
8. vigilante

COMPREHENSION

1. What was hydraulic mining? What was quartz mining?
2. Why were mining and lumbering more profitable for corporations than individuals?
3. What caused conflict between Indians and white settlers on the Great Plains?
4. How did U.S. policy towards the Plains Indians change in the mid-1800s?
5. What happened at Wounded Knee, South Dakota, in 1890?
6. Who were the first cowboys in America?
7. What was the goal of cattle drives? For what reason did they die out?
8. What steps did the U.S. government take to encourage people to settle the West?
9. Which groups of people moved onto the Great Plains in the late 1800s? Why did they come?
10. What hardships and rights existed for women in the West?

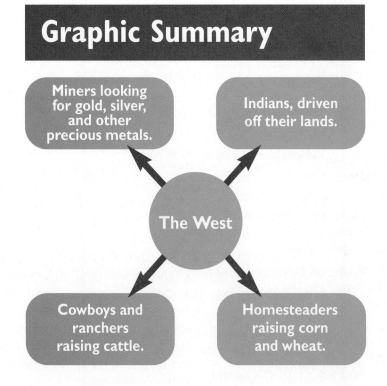

Graphic Summary

Miners looking for gold, silver, and other precious metals.

Indians, driven off their lands.

The West

Cowboys and ranchers raising cattle.

Homesteaders raising corn and wheat.

Places to Locate

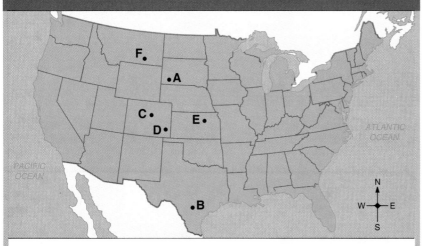

Match the letters on the map with the places that are listed below. Then explain the importance of each place.

1. Sand Creek   **3.** Wounded Knee   **5.** Denver
2. Little Bighorn   **4.** Abilene   **6.** San Antonio
Geographic Theme: Interactions What were some of the hardships faced by settlers on the frontier?

Skill Review

Attitudes toward cowboys varied. Read the two descriptions of cowboys below and answer the questions that follow.

> "A genuine cowboy is worth describing. In many respects he is a wonderful creature. He endures hardships that would take the lives of most men. . . ."—a Texas journalist

> "All . . . I got out of cowpunching is the experience. I paid a good price for that. I wouldn't take anything for what I . . . saw but I wouldn't care to travel the same road again."
> —a retired cowboy

1. Do you think the journalist's description is mainly fact or mainly opinion? Explain.

2. Do you think the cowboy's description is mainly fact or mainly opinion? Explain.

CRITICAL THINKING

1. Stating Both Sides of an Issue Make the best case you can to support each of the following statements: (a) White settlers had no right to settle on Indian lands. (b) White settlers were justified in taking Indian lands.

2. Forming a Hypothesis Why were frontier towns often violent?

PORTFOLIO OPTIONS

1. Civics Connection Discuss how the government's treatment of the Plains Indians changed. Then write a paragraph on how government policies affected the Indians.

2. Writing Connection Do research on a legendary figure of the West. Then write a biographical sketch to share with the class. How do the real facts of the person's life compare with the legend?

3. Contemporary Connection What impression do Americans today have of the old West? Look through magazines and books to find images that portray the West. Create a collage of pictures. Under each picture, explain whether you think it is accurate. Share your collage with the class.

4. Timeline Connection Copy the chapter timeline. Which event do you think was most significant? Using an encyclopedia, create a timeline of states that entered the Union between 1850 and 1890. What factors led to the admission of the western states?

Progressive reformers wanted a more active government. They gained national power when Theodore Roosevelt (below) became President. Suffrage for women (left) was a major progressive goal. Progressives also sought reforms in industry. The book *The Jungle* (below left) exposed problems in meat-packing plants.

VOTES FOR US WHEN WE ARE WOMEN

VOTES FOR US WHEN WE ARE WOMEN

THE JUNGLE
BY
UPTON SINCLAIR

DOUBLEDAY, PAGE & CO.
NEW YORK

1870

1880

1890

1900

1877 *Munn v. Illinois* permits business regulation

1883 Pendleton Civil Service Act

1890 Populist Party founded

1901 Theodore Roosevelt becomes President

Politics and Reform
(1877–1919)

1 A Deadlock in National Politics

SECTION GUIDE

Main Idea
Government at both the local and national levels suffered from corruption and deadlock.

Goals
As you read, look for answers to these questions:

1. What forms of corruption did local and national governments face?

2. What reforms were made to fight corruption in government?

Key Terms
patronage
civil service
Pendleton Civil Service Act
protectionist tariff

1910

1914 Clayton Antitrust Act

1913 Federal Reserve Act

1909 NAACP founded

WHAT WOULD YOU THINK if you found out your elected officials had charged taxpayers $11 million for a new courthouse that actually cost $3 million? Upset? Disgusted? You bet! That is exactly what many New Yorkers felt about William M. "Boss" Tweed. From about 1869 to 1871 Boss Tweed and his friends stole millions from New York City.

Big City Corruption
During the late 1800s cities faced many problems. As immigrants and farmers flocked to the cities, overcrowding and poverty became common. Cities needed better services like water, sewer, fire and police departments. Yet, most city governments did not have enough money to meet these needs.

Political bosses stepped in to do what city governments could not. They began giving the poor what they needed, such as food, housing, and loans. Often political bosses gave out government jobs or contracts. This power is called patronage. In return, the bosses expected the people they had helped to vote for them.

The Tweed Ring
The most famous political machine of the time was the Tweed Ring in New York City. The machine was named after the state senator and political boss William Marcy Tweed. Tweed and his friends in the Tweed Ring stole about $100 million from New York City's treasury. The city almost went bankrupt.

The political cartoonist Thomas Nast helped make the public aware of Tweed's crimes. Nast drew cartoons of Tweed and his friends as vultures, con artists, and money bags. His cartoons accused the Tweed ring of stealing the people's money. These cartoons were so damaging that Tweed offered Nast half a

577

MARK TWAIN
(1835–1910)

"It takes a heap of sense to write good nonsense," wrote Mark Twain, whose real name was Samuel Clemens. Few would call Twain's writing nonsense. Though he poked fun at nearly everything, he usually had an important point to make. In his amusing stories and books, he wrote against cruelty, racism, and war. Some of his favorite targets were greedy and corrupt politicians.

Twain grew up on the banks of the Mississippi. Later he piloted boats on the river. His most famous works, *Tales of Tom Sawyer* and *The Adventures of Huckleberry Finn*, capture a place and period in American history, but the books themselves are timeless.

million dollars to leave the country and stop drawing cartoons. "I don't care so much what the papers write about me," Tweed said, "My [supporters] can't read. But they can see pictures." Nast refused the money and continued to blast away at Tweed.

Tweed was later arrested, convicted, and put in prison. Although the Tweed Ring was broken, there were other corrupt political machines around the nation. Corruption existed at every level of government. At every level there were also people calling for reform.

A Thomas Nast cartoon of William "Boss" Tweed.

Attacking the Spoil System

Reformers began an attack on the spoils system. As you read earlier, the spoils system was the practice of giving government jobs to political backers. Not surprisingly, many government workers were not qualified for their jobs. A few could not read or write. Many were poorly trained. Often government workers were dishonest. Some put their families, and sometimes even their pets, on the payroll.

Reformers wanted to change the system of choosing people for the civil service. The civil service includes all those government jobs to which people are appointed rather than elected. Reformers wanted to get rid of the spoils system. They wanted government workers to be chosen on merit, or their abilities.

Speaking for civil service reform was Rutherford B. Hayes, Republican candidate for President in 1876. He attacked the spoils system during the campaign. "He serves his party best who serves the country best," he said. He won the election.

Civil Service Reform

As President, Hayes decided to clean up the Customhouse in New York City. When foreign goods came through the port of New York, tariffs on imports were collected at the Customhouse.

The Customhouse was an example of the spoils system at its worst. The job of Collector of the Port of New York was one of the most powerful in the nation. It was even more powerful than some positions in the President's Cabinet. The Collector, Chester A. Arthur, was also a leader of New York's Republican party machine. The machine boss, Roscoe Conkling, was a U.S. Senator. Conkling had used Customhouse money to support his political machine.

Hayes fired Arthur. Furious, Republicans dumped Hayes in the next election (1880). Their choice, James Garfield of Ohio, won the election. His Vice President was

Chester Arthur. Garfield had been in office for only four months, however, when he was shot by a disappointed office seeker.

After Garfield's death, Arthur became President. Public pressure led Arthur to back civil service reform. In 1883 Congress passed the **Pendleton Civil Service Act,** known also as the Pendleton Act. This law required people to take civil service exams for certain government jobs. Only people who proved their abilities on these tests could be hired. The law also forbid elected officials from firing civil service workers because of their political views.

National Deadlock

The Pendleton Act of 1883 was a rare accomplishment. At that time the federal government was stuck. Sometimes one party controlled the White House while the other party controlled Congress. At other times, control of Congress itself was split. Congress and the President could not agree on how to deal with the problems of the day. As a result of national deadlock, few laws were passed.

For the election of 1884 the Republican Party replaced Chester Arthur with James G. Blaine. The Democrats chose Grover Cleveland. As a sheriff, a mayor, and then governor of New York, Cleveland had rooted out corrupt officials. Cleveland won the election by a narrow margin.

The big issue for Cleveland was tariff reform. Taxes on foreign goods were high. They were called **protectionist tariffs** because they protected U.S. companies from foreign competition.

Cleveland wanted to lower tariffs. He pointed out that tariffs had brought in millions of dollars more a year than the government was spending. Congress, however, was split over the issue. The Democrats, who controlled the House of Representatives, and the Republicans, who controlled the Senate, each had their own tariff proposal.

The "Billion-Dollar Congress"

That brings us to the election of 1888. Republican candidate Benjamin Harrison defeated Cleveland. The Republicans gained control of Congress as well. The deadlock now over, the government began to act—and spend. Congress spent so much money that it became known as the "billion-dollar Congress."

The same Congress passed the McKinley Tariff in 1890. It set up a new protectionist tariff that raised taxes on most foreign goods. The tariff had two effects:

(1) It caused federal income to drop because the high tariffs discouraged imports.

(2) It made people pay more for almost everything they bought. Prices of imports rose because of the tariff. Also, U.S. companies raised their prices because the tariff protected them from foreign competition.

Voters were upset by the McKinley Tariff. In 1892 they voted Cleveland back into office. Meanwhile, voices calling for reform grew louder. In time they would be heard, and in time they would change the country.

A noisemaker from Cleveland's 1892 presidential campaign.

SECTION REVIEW

1. Key Terms patronage, civil service, Pendleton Civil Service Act, protectionist tariff

2. People Willam M. Tweed, Thomas Nast, Rutherford B. Hayes, Chester A. Arthur, James Garfield

3. Comprehension Why was corruption so common in cities?

4. Comprehension How did the Pendleton Act change the civil service?

5. Critical Thinking Can the public always prevent corruption in government? Explain your answer.

SECTION GUIDE

Main Idea
Farmers, facing economic problems, began organizing.

Goals
As you read, look for answers to these questions:

1 What problems did farmers face?

2 What steps did farmers take to improve their lives?

Key Terms
Grange   Populist Party
middleman   gold standard
cooperative

THE GROWTH OF URBAN AMERICA—and even urban Europe—was possible because American farmers were so productive. Yet there was unrest in rural America. Farm folk felt poor compared to city folk. Farm life seemed boring compared to the exciting opportunities of the city.

Hard Times for Farmers

In 1867 Oliver H. Kelley started the Patrons of Husbandry. Through his association Kelley hoped to fight the loneliness of farm life. He also sought to improve farming methods. Kelley's organization became known as the Grange. The Grange was open to both men and women. Meetings, often held at local schools, were both social and educational.

By the late 1800s most farmers were no longer self-sufficient. Instead they relied on cash crops. With the money they made from cash crops, farmers bought the food they were unable to grow for themselves. Most farmers were also in debt. Western farmers owed banks money for their land and farm equipment. Farmers in the South had taken on debt to rebuild the farms that were destroyed during the Civil War.

Low Prices and High Costs

Life for farmers was never easy. Drought, floods, insects, and crop or animal diseases could wipe out countless hours of work. By the 1870s farmers faced yet another danger—low prices for their crops. When farmers received less for their crops that meant they sank even deeper into debt.

One reason for low prices was the over-production of crops. As more farmland opened up in the West, more people became farmers. Also, farming methods had improved. With more farmers and better technology, more crops were produced. Food supplies jumped. Food prices fell.

This 1870s Granger poster shows the ideals of rural life.

Receiving less money for their crops was bad enough. Farmers also faced rising costs of running a farm. High tariffs on imported farm machines drove up the price of American-made machines.

Another high cost for farmers was railroad rates. Farmers paid railroads to move their crops to market. Railroads began charging whatever they wanted. Farmers had no choice but to pay. If not, their crops would not get to market and would rot. Railroads also owned grain elevators—places where grain was stored before it was shipped to market. Again, farmers had to pay the high cost of storage.

The Granger Movement

Faced with such difficult times, the Grangers (members of the Grange) turned their attention to economic and political goals. One economic goal was to avoid using middlemen. Middlemen make a living by storing, transporting, and selling products. The services of middlemen cut into a farmers' profits. They also added to the price of a product for buyers.

To bypass middlemen, the Grangers created cooperatives. A cooperative is an organization owned and managed by those who use its services. Granger cooperatives included businesses such as grain elevators and creameries. Cooperatives tried new ways to buy and sell goods. In some places Grangers shared their crops. This allowed them to set their own prices and sell directly to merchants.

To control railroad and storage costs, the Grangers turned to political action. On July 4, 1873, the "Farmer's Declaration of Independence" was read at Grange picnics. The document urged that states use their power to stop monopolies like railroads. Farmers began electing legislators that supported the Grangers. Illinois, Minnesota, Wisconsin, and Iowa passed "Granger laws." These laws put limits on railroad and storage rates.

Railroad companies fought the Granger laws all the way to the Supreme Court. In the 1877 case *Munn v. Illinois*, the Supreme Court ruled against the railroads. The Court stated that the government could control private businesses if public interest were involved. *Munn v. Illinois* thus cleared the way for state and federal regulation of businesses.

The price of storing crops in grain elevators was yet another high cost for farmers.

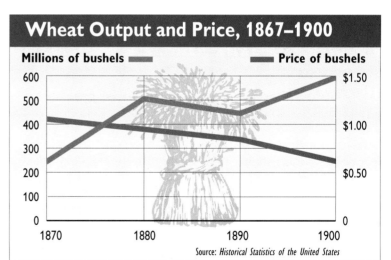

Wheat Output and Price, 1867–1900

Millions of bushels ▬▬ ▬▬ Price of bushels

Source: *Historical Statistics of the United States*

CHART SKILLS: This graph shows the tie between wheat production (in orange) and price (in blue). **Critical Thinking:** How many more bushels were produced in 1900 than in 1870? What happened to the price? How does the supply of and demand for wheat affect its price?

WHEAT, WHEAT EVERYWHERE

The rich, wheat-farming lands of the Great Plains do not stop at the U.S.-Canadian border. Canada's prairie spreads across modern-day Manitoba, Saskatchewan, and Alberta. In the 1870s Canadians rushed to settle these fertile lands. They feared the United States might try to annex them. Railroad lines pressed westward in the 1880s to bring in settlers.

Conditions were harsh, but the farmers stayed. Wheat from Canada and other producers—Argentina, India, and Australia—flooded the world market. American farmers suffered from the competition. Prices fell. California's huge wheat trade was almost wiped out.

The People's Party was a "patchwork" of several political groups.

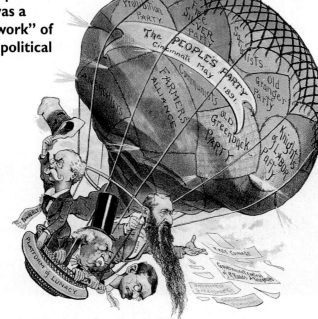

The Populist Party

In the 1880s more farmers turned their attention to politics. In 1890 several political groups came together to form the People's Party, also known as the Populist Party. It called for political and economic reforms.

Mary Ellen Lease of Kansas was a leader in the Populist Party. A fiery speaker, she was known as "Queen Mary" by her supporters. Her enemies called her "Mary Yellin'" because of her strong attacks on big business and the government:

❝ **Wall Street owns the country. It is no longer a government of the people, by the people, and for the people. . . . The parties lie to us, and the political leaders mislead us. . . . Let the bloodhounds of money who have dogged us . . . beware.** ❞

Lease is reported to have said, "What you farmers need to do is to raise less corn and more Hell."

Debate over Money Policy

The Populist movement pitted debtors against creditors. It was strongest in the West and South, the regions that were most in debt.

The debtors saw one solution to their problems. They wanted more money in circulation. That would produce inflation. Inflation would then make it easier to pay back loans, because the money that debtors repaid would be worth less than the money they borrowed.

To put more money in circulation, the Populists wanted the government to coin more silver. An 1878 law had allowed the government to coin a limited amount of silver. That amount was increased under an 1890 law, the Sherman Silver Purchase Act. Still, Populists wanted even more silver to be coined.

Opponents of this idea favored the gold standard. Under the gold standard, the government backs every dollar with a certain amount of gold. Since the supply of gold was limited, the gold standard would keep the money supply tight. Creditors liked the standard because it prevented inflation. Debtors disliked it for the same reason.

In 1892 the People's Party nominated James B. Weaver for President. As expected, the party platform demanded an expansion of the money supply. It also included a "wish list" to address a range of political and economic grievances.

Among the Populists' proposals were the following:

(1) They called for the government to own and operate the railroads and telegraph and telephone systems.

(2) They wanted a secret ballot to be used in elections.

(3) They called for a federal income tax.

(4) They demanded shorter working hours for labor.

(5) They wanted United States senators to be elected directly by the people rather than by state legislatures.

Cleveland won the election of 1892. Weaver, however, received 8 percent of the vote, a good showing for a third-party candidate. In the West and South the Populist movement grew even stronger as a result of the panic and depression of 1893. By 1896, the next presidential election year, the government's policy on money had become the major issue.

Gold Versus Silver

In 1896, Republicans chose William McKinley, a former governor of Ohio, as their candidate for President. McKinley supported the views of big business. This meant he supported the gold standard.

The Democratic convention was divided between the "gold bugs" and "silverites" Gold bugs supported the gold standard. Silverites, who were in the majority, called for the free coinage of silver. However, they had no candidate. Who would lead them?

The Two Sides in the Money Debate

	"GOLD BUG"	**"SILVERITE"**
Position	Favor gold standard	Favor coining silver
Reasons	Prevents inflation; protects value of money	Causes inflation; helps debtors to repay debts
Supporters	Business leaders, Republicans	Farmers, Democrats

CHART SKILLS: This chart shows two views on monetary policy, as well as the symbol of each side. **Critical Thinking:** Why is it difficult for the entire nation to agree on a policy on money?

William Jennings Bryan made over 600 speeches during the 1896 campaign. His voice was so powerful that, without straining, he made himself heard by a crowd of thousands.

The answer was clear as soon as William Jennings Bryan of Nebraska spoke. Bryan defended the platform's silver plank against the gold bugs. His speech became one of the most famous in U.S. history:

❝ . . . You [the gold delegates] come to tell us that the great cities are in favor of the gold standard; we reply that the great cities rest upon our broad and fertile prairies. Burn down your cities and leave our farms, and your cities will spring up again as if by magic; but destroy our farms and the grass will grow in the streets of every city in the country. ❞

Bryan ended his speech with a message to the gold bugs. "You shall not press down upon the brow of labor the crown of thorns," he warned. "You shall not crucify mankind upon a cross of gold." The delegates roared with approval. Bryan became the Populist candidate.

The Election of 1896

Never had there been such a difference in campaign styles as there was in 1896. McKinley followed tradition. He did not go out and campaign himself. That was considered undignified. He spent the campaign at home in Ohio, receiving guests and giving speeches from his front porch.

Bryan, on the other hand, launched something like a modern campaign. He traveled thousands of miles by train. He made hundreds of speeches to about 5 million Americans. He delivered slashing attacks on the rich and powerful. His audiences responded with cheers.

It was an emotional election. Republicans warned voters that a threat to the gold standard was a threat to their property. In the cities, industry leaders told their workers that factories would close down if Bryan was elected.

On Election Day, Bryan took the South and all the western states except California and Oregon. McKinley carried the Northeast and upper Midwest states. This was enough to give him an electoral victory. McKinley had won. Urban America had won out over rural America.

SECTION REVIEW

1. Key Terms Grange, middleman, co-operative, Populist Party, gold standard

2. People Oliver H. Kelley, Mary Ellen Lease, William McKinley, William Jennings Bryan

3. Comprehension What caused low prices for farmers?

4. Comprehension Why did farmers want the coining of more silver?

5. Critical Thinking Why did the Populists want the election of U.S. senators to be by direct vote of the people?

3 Roosevelt the Progressive

SECTION GUIDE

Main Idea

Theodore Roosevelt started national progressive reforms. His policies were based on his desire to be fair to all Americans.

Goals

As you read, look for answers to these questions:

1. What were the goals of the progressives?

2. What progressive reforms did Roosevelt make?

Key Terms

progressive
Sherman Antitrust Act
laissez faire
arbitration
conservation

Theodore Roosevelt's military career helped him gain national attention.

I N 1881 A NEW REPRESENTATIVE appeared in the New York legislature. He was young—23 years old—and fearless. He was a Republican. He was Theodore Roosevelt.

Roosevelt was able and confident. As a youth he had been skinny and sickly. With a routine that included weightlifting, rowing, and boxing, he had become healthy and strong. A man of many talents, Roosevelt was both a naturalist and a historian. Above all, he was a man of action. He wanted things done.

New Reformers

One of Roosevelt's first actions as a New York lawmaker was to challenge the power of corrupt money. Roosevelt did what no one else had dared do. He publicly called Jay Gould a crook. Gould was one of the most powerful men in the United States. Gould had made a fortune through dishonest deals in railroads and gold. The next day the *New York Times* said that "calling men and things by their right names in these days of . . . the robber-barons" took courage.

Roosevelt belonged to a new generation, one that grew up after the Civil War. It was a generation that wanted to do something about the wrongs it saw in American society. It was a generation of reformers.

Roosevelt's Career as President

With McKinley's election as President in 1896, Roosevelt became the assistant secretary of the Navy. He quit that job in 1898 to lead a volunteer cavalry unit to fight against Spain in Cuba. (You will read more about this in the next chapter.) Becoming a famous soldier in Cuba, he was easily elected governor of New York.

As governor, Roosevelt pushed through a civil service law. He appointed qualified people to state jobs. However, the state's Republican Party boss was upset at Roosevelt's actions. Wanting Roosevelt out of New York, he had him put on the Republican ticket in 1900 as McKinley's Vice President. Mark Hanna, the power behind McKinley, was upset at the choice. "Don't you realize," he said, "that there's only one life between this madman and the White House?" The election of 1900 was a replay of 1896. Again McKinley defeated William Jennings Bryan.

Roosevelt in the White House

In September 1901 McKinley went to Buffalo, New York, for the Pan-American Exposition. At a public reception, a man shot the President at close range. McKinley died from his wound more than a week later, and Roosevelt became President.

At age 42, Roosevelt was the youngest person ever to hold that office. When his family moved into the White House, the place shook with the joyous sounds of six children. The public adored reading such stories as the President having pillow fights with his children.

The public loved Roosevelt. They called him "Teddy." Once on a hunting trip he refused to shoot a cub bear. News of the event resulted in a new toy—the teddy bear.

The Progressives

With Roosevelt, a new generation of reformers achieved national power. These reformers were known as progressives.

The progressives believed in the basic goodness of people. They also believed in democracy. Evil and corruption in society, they believed, could be corrected by both moral behavior and good laws.

The progressives were mostly native-born and middle-class. Progressives could be found in either political party. In general the progressives had these goals:

(1) They wanted to expand democracy.

(2) They wanted to bring about good government.

(3) They wanted to limit the power of big business and big money.

(4) They wanted an increase in government regulation where the public interest was involved.

(5) They wanted to help the poor, the weak, and the unfortunate.

As President, Roosevelt had a great deal of power to push progressive ideas. To make progressive ideas into laws, however, he needed help. Roosevelt got it as voters began electing progressive senators and representatives. A progressive Congress would pass laws that would end up changing American society.

Progressives believed that the poor needed help to overcome poverty. Here a social worker pays a visit to a family who lives in a poor urban neighborhood.

Trustbusting

As you read earlier, many of America's big businesses were combining into trusts. Companies worked together to squeeze out their competitors. Then they raised their prices and made larger profits.

This trend had continued despite the **Sherman Antitrust Act** of 1890. This law had been passed to prevent corporations from gaining complete control of a type of business. However, many corporations ignored the law. No one had enforced it—no one, that is, until Roosevelt.

At the end of 1901 the nation's railroads were run by a handful of companies. The power of railroads continued to grow. It is not surprising, therefore, that one of Roosevelt's first targets was the railroads. He revived the Sherman Antitrust Act by using it to bust up a railroad trust.

Roosevelt was not against big business as such. He supported "good" trusts. He opposed any trust he thought worked against the public's interest. Altogether he would move against 44 trusts. His most famous case of trustbusting was against the Standard Oil Company in 1906.

The public learned about Standard Oil Company's ruthless practices through articles and a book written by Ida Tarbell. The daughter of an oilman, Tarbell accused Standard Oil of using unfair tactics to put her father and many small oil companies out of business. Her book caused a sensation. It led to calls for a government crackdown on trusts. In 1911 the Supreme Court ordered the Standard Oil Company to be broken up into small companies.

Ida Tarbell

In this political cartoon a monopoly is shown as a large octopus. **Critical Thinking:** Do you think the cartoonist supported or opposed trustbusting? How can you tell?

Roosevelt's trustbusting grew extremely popular with the people. In the poetry of Rosemary and Stephen Vincent Benét:

> **T.R. is spanking a Senator,**
> **T.R. is chasing a bear,**
> **T.R. is busting an Awful Trust**
> **And dragging it from its lair.**
> **They're calling T.R. a lot of**
> **things**
> **—The men in the private car—**
> **But the day-coach likes exciting**
> **folks**
> **And the day-coach likes T.R.**

Attack on Laissez Faire

Business leaders—the "men in the private car"—were shocked by the trustbusting. For years they had believed that the government was theirs to run. In fact, the Senate was known as the "Millionaire's Club." After making their millions in oil, steel, or lumber, many business leaders got their state legislators to elect them to the Senate.

In addition, many felt that government should not interfere in the economy. This

The National Park System

Alaska
- Kobuk Valley
- Gates of the Arctic
- Denali
- Lake Clark
- Katmai
- Kenai Fjords
- Wrangell-St. Elias
- Glacier Bay

0 — 400 mi
0 — 400 km

(Continental U.S. map)

- Olympic
- North Cascades — WA
- Mount Rainier
- Glacier
- Voyageurs
- Isle Royale
- ME
- Acadia
- OR
- MT
- ND
- Theodore Roosevelt
- MN
- VT
- NH
- NY
- MA
- CT
- RI
- Crater Lake
- ID
- Yellowstone
- Badlands
- SD
- WI
- MI
- PA
- Redwood
- Grand Teton
- Wind Cave
- NJ
- Lassen Volcanic
- NV
- WY
- IA
- OH
- DE
- MD
- UT
- Rocky Mountain
- NE
- IL
- IN
- WV
- Yosemite
- Great Basin
- Capitol Reef
- Arches
- Shenandoah
- VA
- Kings Canyon
- Bryce Canyon
- Canyonlands
- CO
- KS
- MO
- KY
- Mammoth Cave
- Zion
- NC
- Sequoia
- Mesa Verde
- Great Smoky Mountains
- TN
- CA
- Grand Canyon
- AR
- SC
- Channel Islands
- Petrified Forest
- NM
- OK
- Hot Springs
- AZ
- MS
- GA
- Carlsbad Caverns
- AL
- Guadalupe Mountains
- TX
- LA
- FL
- Big Bend
- Everglades
- Biscayne

National Park

National Forest

0 — 300 mi
0 — 500 km

Hawaii
- Haleakala
- Hawaii Volcanoes

0 — 300 mi
0 — 300 km

Virgin Islands
- Puerto Rico
- Virgin Islands

0 — 30 mi
0 — 30 km

GEOGRAPHY SKILLS: This map shows the location of the nation's parks and forests. **Critical Thinking:** In which regions are most of the nation's parks found? Why might this be?

"hands-off" approach toward business is called **laissez faire** (lehs-ay FAYR). (*Laissez faire* is French for "Let people do as they choose.")

To business leaders, laissez faire had built this nation. The economy performed best, they argued, when people were left free to create businesses and hire workers. To progressives, laissez faire caused high prices, low wages, and miserable working conditions. They did not want to do away with private business. They did want to regulate it.

The Square Deal

Roosevelt saw government somewhat as an umpire. Its purpose was to ensure fairness or, as Roosevelt put it, "a square deal."

An example of the square deal was Roosevelt's involvement in the anthracite coal strike of 1902. Miners walked off the job, demanding higher pay and shorter hours. Coal was the nation's main heating fuel. A shortage of coal would bring disaster if the strike continued into winter.

Earlier Presidents had sent in troops to break up strikes. Instead, Roosevelt, forced both the company and the union leaders to accept committee **arbitration.** In arbitration, two sides in a dispute let an impartial third party settle the issue. In the end, each side received some of what it wanted. Roosevelt had shown that the government could play a useful role in business.

Conservation

The controlled use of natural resources is called **conservation.** Conservation was not new when Roosevelt entered the White House. Roosevelt, however, believed strongly that the nation's water and timber resources should be maintained for the benefit of all people.

In the 1890s Congress had called for some federal land to be made into national

Conservationists (left) link hands around a tree to stop loggers from cutting it down. Roosevelt and conservationist John Muir at Yosemite (above).

forests. As President, Roosevelt transferred 150 million acres of federal land into the national forest system. Roosevelt also urged the creation of new national parks. Today, national parks such as Yellowstone, Yosemite, and the Grand Canyon continue to attract millions of vacationers each year.

SECTION REVIEW

1. Key Terms progressive, Sherman Antitrust Act, laissez faire, arbitration, conservation

2. People Theodore Roosevelt, Mark Hanna, Ida Tarbell

3. Comprehension Why did the progressives want to limit the power of big business?

4. Comprehension How was Roosevelt's handling of the 1902 coal strike a blow to supporters of laissez faire?

5. Critical Thinking In your opinion, what types of trusts might Roosevelt have considered "good"?

4 The Progressive Reforms

SECTION GUIDE

Main Idea
Progressives urged reforms that protected the public interest. Despite these reforms, immigrants and African Americans faced prejudice.

Goals
As you read, look for answers to these questions:

1 What progressive reforms were made at the state level?

2 What reforms did Woodrow Wilson achieve as President?

3 What steps did African Americans take to fight against discrimination?

Key Terms
muckraker   initiative
direct primary   recall
referendum   NAACP

SNAKE OIL was one of the great sellers at the turn of the century. Snake oil promised a cure for pain, coughs, warts, whatever. Of course, there is no such thing as snake oil. However, the term has come to mean any medicine making false claims.

Scientists investigated the snake oils. They found that they were mostly alcohol or were heavily mixed with the drug opium. Yet the scientists could do little about the problem because there was no law against it.

The Muckrakers

About 1900, however, a new group of writers began to expose corruption in American society. Roosevelt called them muckrakers, because they "raked" or searched through the dishonest "muck." The name stuck.

The muckrakers attacked corruption wherever they found it. They attacked labor unions as well big business. They exposed unhealthy conditions in the food industry. They also attacked misleading advertising. They spoke out against child labor and unfair treatment of women.

The muckrakers created a public demand for reforms. For instance, Upton Sinclair exposed the filthy conditions in the meat industry in his book *The Jungle.* The book caused people to pressure Congress into action. Congress passed the Pure Food and Drug Act and the Meat Inspection Act in 1906. These laws gave government inspectors the power to enforce safety and health standards in the making and selling of food and medicine.

State Reformers

Many important progressive reforms were made at the state level. Robert M. La Follette led the way after he was elected Wisconsin's governor in 1900. Under La Follette, Wisconsin passed laws to regulate railroads, banks, and lobbyists. It passed new taxes on railroads and corporations. To get rid of patronage, it passed its own civil service act.

The Jungle exposed unhealthy conditions of meat-packing plants such as this. The book led to the passage of health standard laws.

Other states soon followed Wisconsin's lead. By the early 1900s many state governments were passing laws to bring about social and economic change. New state laws protected women workers, outlawed child labor, and funded public education. They also helped women with dependent children and provided accident insurance.

Expanding Democracy

Wisconsin was also the first state to use a direct primary. In a direct primary the people, not party conventions, choose candidates for election.

Expanding democracy was important to editor William S. U'Ren, an Oregon progressive. In addition to the direct primary, he urged a trio of reforms. These were the referendum, the initiative, and the recall. A referendum allows legislatures to submit a law to the vote of the people. An initiative allows the people to propose and pass a law directly. A recall allows the people to vote an official out of office.

Many western states adopted U'Ren's reforms. This expansion of democracy, progressives hoped, would reduce the power of big business. They also hoped it would get rid of corrupt politicians.

For the same reason, progressives argued that U.S. senators should be elected directly by the people, not by state lawmakers. This became law in 1913 when the Seventeenth Amendment was adopted.

Changes in Leadership

The progressive agenda had become America's plan. In 1908 Roosevelt's hand-picked successor, William Howard Taft, was elected President. Taft backed Roosevelt's progressive policies. Yet Taft was no Roosevelt. He could not keep progressive and conservative Republicans from fighting each other. He lacked Roosevelt's ability to lead and to get things done.

Roosevelt was unable to stay on the sidelines. In the 1912 campaign he announced he was throwing his "hat in the ring" for

The Election of 1912

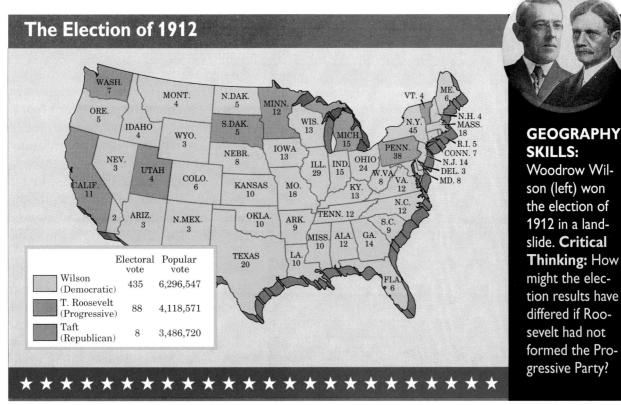

		Electoral vote	Popular vote
	Wilson (Democratic)	435	6,296,547
	T. Roosevelt (Progressive)	88	4,118,571
	Taft (Republican)	8	3,486,720

GEOGRAPHY SKILLS: Woodrow Wilson (left) won the election of 1912 in a landslide. **Critical Thinking:** How might the election results have differed if Roosevelt had not formed the Progressive Party?

the Republican nomination. Too many delegates, however, were already committed to Taft. Taft won the nomination. Roosevelt then formed a third party, the Progressive or "Bull Moose" Party. The result was predictable. The Republican vote split. Woodrow Wilson, the Democratic candidate, won the presidency.

Wilson and Big Business

Wilson had ideas very similar to those of Roosevelt. He too believed that the power of government should be used to protect the public's interest. However, unlike Roosevelt, Wilson did not believe "good trusts" existed. Wilson believed that "bigness" itself was wrong. Wilson wanted the government to use its powers to break up all monopolies. He also wanted government to help workers in their struggles against business owners.

Under the Clayton Act, picketing was no longer illegal. Here workers in New York City hold signs in Yiddish, Russian, Italian, and English that demand better working conditions.

At Wilson's urging, Congress passed the Clayton Antitrust Act of 1914. The new law laid down rules forbidding any business practice that "substantially" lessened competition. A business, for example, could no longer buy the stock of a competitor.

The Clayton Act has also been called the "Magna Carta" for labor. It got that name because it was the first national law to help labor unions. Until then the courts had ruled that strikes and boycotts violated the Sherman Antitrust Act. The Clayton Act was pro-labor because:

(1) It said labor unions and farm organizations were not covered by antitrust laws.

(2) It limited the ability of the courts to force workers to end strikes.

(3) It legalized such labor tactics as strikes, picketing, and boycotts.

Wilson's Financial Reforms

During Wilson's two terms, reforms to the nation's financial system also occurred. The income tax (another populist demand) was made possible in 1913 when the Sixteenth Amendment was ratified. The income tax gave the government another source of revenue besides tariffs. It was also a fairer way of raising revenue.

In 1913 the Federal Reserve Act was passed. This improved the nation's monetary and banking system. The law created the modern banking system, which resembles a pyramid. At the top is the Federal Reserve Board, which is appointed by the President. Next are twelve Federal Reserve Banks for different regions of the country. These are "bankers' banks." They serve the bottom level—the member banks.

The Federal Reserve Act created a more flexible currency system by allowing banks to control the money supply. To raise money, for example, the "Fed" lowers the interest rate that it charges member banks. These banks then borrow more from the Fed and thus have more money to lend to people and businesses.

Women's Suffrage

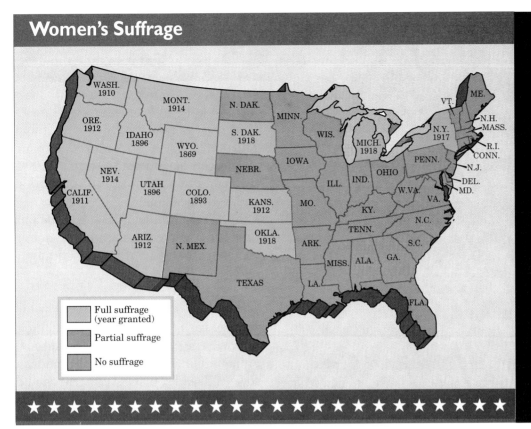

Full suffrage (year granted)

Partial suffrage

No suffrage

WASH. 1910
ORE. 1912
IDAHO 1896
MONT. 1914
N. DAK.
S. DAK. 1918
WYO. 1869
NEV. 1914
UTAH 1896
CALIF. 1911
COLO. 1893
ARIZ. 1912
N. MEX.
MINN.
WIS.
IOWA
NEBR.
KANS. 1912
OKLA. 1918
TEXAS
MICH. 1918
ILL.
IND.
OHIO
MO.
KY.
ARK.
MISS.
ALA.
GA.
LA.
FLA.
TENN.
N.C.
S.C.
PENN.
W.VA.
VA.
N.Y. 1917
VT.
ME.
N.H.
MASS.
R.I.
CONN.
N.J.
DEL.
MD.

GEOGRAPHY SKILLS: By 1919 women in many southern and eastern states still had no voting rights. In much of the Midwest, women had partial suffrage. They could vote only in primary or in presidential elections. **Critical Thinking:** Why, do you think, did western states allow women's suffrage before other regions?

Women's Suffrage

Another important event of Wilson's presidency concerned women's voting rights. Western states had been the first to grant women the right to vote. In 1900 four states—Wyoming, Utah, Idaho, and Colorado—allowed women to vote in all elections. Women in other states began to hold mass rallies and marches, demanding the right to vote. As a result, between 1910 and 1914 seven more western states approved full suffrage for women.

Meanwhile, suffragists urged a new amendment to the Constitution—one that would guarantee women's suffrage. In response, Congress passed the Nineteenth Amendment in 1919. It was a milestone in the struggle for equal rights for women.

The Progressives and Race

One of Roosevelt's first public moves had been to invite Booker T. Washington to the White House. African Americans had hoped that this signalled a new era in race relations. Yet despite Roosevelt's good intentions, the progressive record on racial issues was terrible.

Racism under the progressives took different forms. One form was discrimination against Jews. Progressives worked to keep Jews out of universities, housing, and jobs. Jewish bankers were often blamed for the nation's economic problems.

In California, racism under the progressives resulted in a law that denied Japanese immigrants the right to own land.

In the South racism resulted in the increased segregation of blacks from whites. One of Wilson's first acts as President was to segregate, or separate, black and white federal employees. African Americans protested that this was "a public humiliation and degradation." Wilson replied, "Segregation is not humiliating but a benefit. . . ." For African

Asian Americans were the victims of racism under the progressives.

The Crisis was the offical journal of the NAACP.

ment of Colored People, or the NAACP. (*Colored* was a term used to refer to African Americans.) The NAACP worked to secure equal rights for African Americans. It used the courts to seek an end to segregation and discrimination.

In 1910 the National Urban League was formed. It worked to improve economic conditions for urban African Americans.

The Progressive Impact

The coming of World War I brought the progressive era to an end. With their reforms, the progressives had made government a more active part of American society. The idea that government should serve and protect the public interest has had a lasting impact.

Americans, progressive talk about democracy was just another form of snake oil.

African Americans Organize

African Americans looked to new leaders to help them fight discrimination. As you have read, Booker T. Washington was one of the nation's best-known black leaders. He believed that African Americans should focus on jobs, not equal rights.

Yet many disagreed with Washington's views. One such person was W.E.B. Du Bois. A Harvard-trained professor, Du Bois believed that African Americans should focus on legal equality:

> **[African Americans] must insist continually . . . that voting is necessary . . . that color discrimination is barbarism, and that black boys need education as well as white boys. . . .**

In 1905 Du Bois and other leaders met at Niagara Falls, Canada. The "Niagara movement" demanded for African Americans "every single right that belongs to a freeborn American." In 1909, they and other reformers, both black and white, formed the National Association for the Advance-

SECTION REVIEW

1. Key Terms muckraker, direct primary, referendum, initiative, recall, NAACP

2. People and Places Upton Sinclair, Robert M. La Follete, William S. U'Ren, William Howard Taft, Woodrow Wilson, Booker T. Washington, W.E.B. Du Bois, Wisconsin, Niagara Falls

3. Comprehension What reforms did William S. U'Ren introduce that expanded democracy at the state level?

4. Comprehension What reforms in labor did the Clayton Act provide?

5. Critical Thinking How might the backgrounds of Du Bois and Washington have shaped each of their views on equal rights for African Americans?

LEARN

If you woke up one day and realized that your room was a complete mess, what would you do? Would you clean it up right away or put it off for a while? Some people—even entire nations—seem to be willing to live with a messy, dirty, or dangerous situation for a long time before they do something about it.

In the late 1800s and early 1900s, many Americans thought it was time to clean up. Important issues included dangerous factories, child labor, political corruption, and trusts. Reformers saw these problems as threats to society, and they took action to get them fixed.

We still have many problems today. Is there anything about your community that could be improved? Who is responsible for pointing out problems and acting to correct them? In the United States, all citizens share that responsibility. We are all potential reformers. You might wonder what you can do to make a difference. Think about these two sayings: "The pen is mightier than the sword" and "There is strength in numbers." Reformers have always found that writing letters and newspaper articles is an effective way to be heard. Another way is to organize—persuade other people to join your cause.

PRACTICE

1. If you lived near a dangerous intersection that needed a traffic light, to whom could you write a letter to get the problem fixed?

2. If your letter brought no results, where else might you send a letter?

3. Who else might be interested in joining your cause? Why?

APPLY

4. Choose a community problem that needs to be corrected. Briefly describe how you would go about fixing the problem. Then write a letter to a specific person or organization describing the problem. Describe ways in which you can get other people to join your cause.

Summary

1. Corruption was widespread at both the local and national levels in the late 1800s. To stop corruption, reformers called for an end to the spoils system. In response, Congress passed civil service reforms. Government workers were hired on their merit, not their political views. Congress, however, was deadlocked over other reforms.

2. Farmers faced difficult times. They united to deal with their political and economic problems. The nation's monetary policy had pitted debtors against creditors. Farmers wanted the coining of more silver, while business leaders favored the gold standard. The monetary policy became a major issue in the 1896 election.

3. With Theodore Roosevelt as President, reformers known as progressives came to national power. Roosevelt attacked monopolies. He also worked to preserve the nation's natural resources.

4. Progressives sought reforms in the food industry, labor, and politics. President Wilson attacked big business and reformed the nation's banking system. Women won the right to vote with the passage of the Nineteenth Amendment. Yet despite these reforms, racism and discrimination increased under the progressives.

Review

KEY TERMS

Write a sentence using each of the following groups of key terms.

1. patronage; Pendleton Civil Service Act

2. middleman; cooperative

3. Sherman Antitrust Act; laissez faire

4. referendum; initiative; recall

COMPREHENSION

1. What conditions allowed powerful political machines to arise in many of the nation's big cities?

2. What problem did the Pendleton Act try to fix?

3. What was the Grange? How did its members try to solve the problems facing farmers?

4. What were some of the goals of the Populist Party?

5. What actions did President Roosevelt take to regulate trusts?

6. Why did the progressives oppose the laissez faire approach to business?

7. How did Roosevelt affect the conservation movement in the United States?

8. What progressive reforms were made at the state level?

9. How did Roosevelt's Progressive Party affect the outcome of the 1912 election?

10. How did W.E.B. Du Bois's views on equal rights for African Americans differ from Booker T. Washington's beliefs?

Graphic Summary

Corruption plagues the government. →	Congress passes the Pendleton Civil Service Act.
Farmers face hard economic times. →	Farmers unite and form the Populist Party.
Theodore Roosevelt becomes President. →	Progressive reformers achieve national power.
Progressives push for reforms in industry, politics, business, and labor. →	Congress passes the Pure Food and Drug Act, the Seventeenth Amendment, the Clayton Act, the Federal Reserve Act, and the Nineteenth Amendment.

Places to Locate

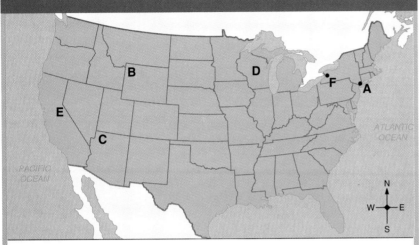

Match the letters on the map with the places that are listed below. Then explain the importance of each place.

1. Yellowstone National Park
2. Buffalo
3. Wisconsin
4. Grand Canyon National Park
5. New York City
6. Yosemite National Park

Geographic Theme: Interactions Do you think the establishment of national parks and forests was necessary? Explain your answer.

Skill Review

Look through your local newspaper to learn about problems your community is facing. Choose one issue that concerns you. Then answer the following questions.

1. To whom could you write a letter to get the problem fixed?
2. Who else might be interested in joining your cause?
3. Make a list of other ways to increase awareness of the problem.
4. Develop a detailed plan you think could help fix the problem. Share your plan with the class.

CRITICAL THINKING

1. Distinguishing Between Fact and Opinion In 1892 the Populist platform included the following statement: "The interest of rural and civic [urban] labor are the same: their enemies are identical." Was this a statement of fact or opinion. Explain your answer.

2. Forming a Hypothesis Why might progressive goals have been more attractive to the middle class than to the working class?

PORTFOLIO OPTIONS

1. Civics Connection Progressives increased the role of government in American life. Discuss with the class what role you think the government should play.

2. Writing Connection Imagine you are a progressive candidate for President in 1908. Draw up a list of goals. Now imagine you are an independent candidate for President today. Draw up another list of goals. Then write a paragraph comparing the two lists.

3. Contemporary Connection Discuss with the class areas of American life today that you think need reform. Then choose one area and write a newspaper editorial explaining why reform is needed. Include suggestions for reform in your editorial.

4. Timeline Connection Copy the chapter timeline. Choose two events and explain their significance in the reform movement.

As American industry grew in the late 1800s, so did American interest in world affairs. "The Great White Fleet" (below), sent around the world by President Theodore Roosevelt in 1906, was a symbol of American military power. The nation's new economic and military strength gave it influence in Asia and Latin America and victory in World War I.

1890　　　　1895　　　　1900　　　　1905

1904 Roosevelt Corollary announced

1898 Spanish-American War

1898 Hawaii annexed

Becoming a World Power
(1890–1920)

1 The United States Expands Overseas

SECTION GUIDE

Main Idea
After the Civil War, the United States expanded its interest in world affairs and acquired new territories.

Objectives
As you read, look for answers to these questions:

1. What were the reasons behind American expansion in the late 1800s?

2. What role did Secretary of State William Seward play in obtaining new territories?

3. How did the United States gain control of Hawaii?

Key Terms
imperialism
Social Darwinism

I T WAS A SIGHT TO BEHOLD! On December 16, 1906, sixteen sparkling white battleships steamed out of Virginia. This "Great White Fleet" crossed the Atlantic Ocean and continued around the globe. The fleet showed the world that the United States was a power to be reckoned with. It was an important step in expanding America's international interests.

Reasons for American Expansion

Expansion has always been part of this nation's history. At first, the expansion took place within North America as the United States spread westward to the Pacific. In the 1700s and 1800s, European countries practiced imperialism —one people ruling or controlling other peoples—in the Americas, Africa, Asia, and the Middle East. Some historians say that Americans practiced imperialism in those years against Indian nations.

At first Americans did not look to set up overseas colonies. They had been colonists themselves once and did not like it. Besides, involvement in foreign lands carried the risk of war. In 1797 George Washington said that the young nation could not afford such a risk. For many years Americans agreed.

Attitudes began to change in the late 1800s. The reasons were: (1) *Nationalism.* With the country united after the Civil War, nationalism once again became a powerful force. Americans saw European nations expanding their empires around the

1910	1915	1920

1914 Panama Canal completed

1914 World War I begins

1918 World War I ends

1917 Russian Revolution

1917 United States enters World War I

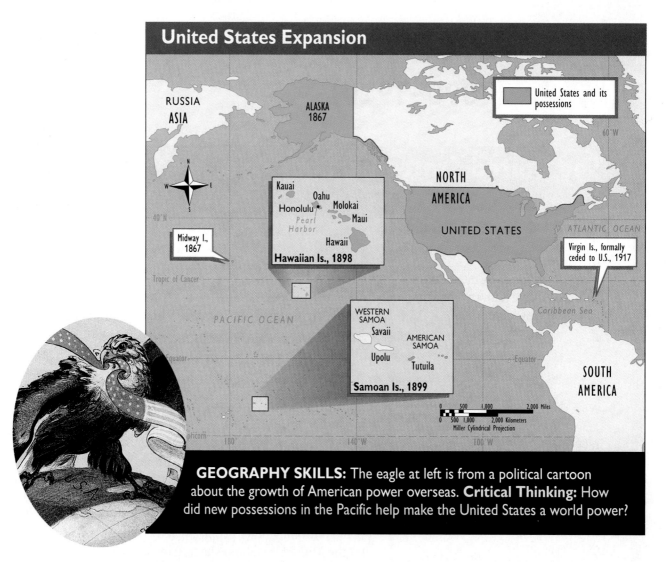

United States Expansion

RUSSIA
ASIA

ALASKA
1867

United States and its possessions

NORTH AMERICA

UNITED STATES

ATLANTIC OCEAN

60°W

40°N

Midway I., 1867

Kauai
Oahu
Honolulu •   Molokai
Pearl   Maui
Harbor
Hawaii

Hawaiian Is., 1898

Tropic of Cancer

Virgin Is., formally ceded to U.S., 1917

Caribbean Sea

PACIFIC OCEAN

WESTERN SAMOA
Savaii

AMERICAN SAMOA

Upolu
Tutuila

Samoan Is., 1899

Equator   Equator

SOUTH AMERICA

180   140°W   100°W

0   500   1,000   2,000 Miles
0 500 1,000   2,000 Kilometers
Miller Cylindrical Projection

GEOGRAPHY SKILLS: The eagle at left is from a political cartoon about the growth of American power overseas. **Critical Thinking:** How did new possessions in the Pacific help make the United States a world power?

globe. If the United States wanted to be a great world power, some people said, it needed its own colonies.

(2) *New ideas.* One of the most popular ideas of the time came from the work of Charles Darwin. Darwin was a British scientist who wrote that animal species change according to a natural law known as the "survival of the fittest." Only animals that are best suited to the environment survive and reproduce.

Social Darwinism developed from this theory. Social Darwinists believed that American democracy was the "fittest" form of government and would spread throughout the world. Social Darwinism was also used to support racism.

(3) *Foreign markets.* Leaders in farming and industry believed expansion would increase American wealth. After the Civil War, exports grew rapidly. In 1898, for the first time in its history, the United States exported more industrial products to other countries than it imported. At the same time, farms were expanding across the Great Plains as Indians were being pushed off their lands. Farmers wanted to sell their products overseas. Without new markets, some warned, the nation would have too many goods and too few buyers.

For all of these reasons—nationalism, Social Darwinism, and the desire for foreign markets—Americans were ready to play a larger role on the world stage.

Seward and Expansion

A strong backer of expansion was William Seward, U.S. Secretary of State under President Andrew Johnson. In 1867 Seward ordered the navy to occupy the Midway Islands, named for their location midway between California and Japan. He knew that Midway would be valuable as a coaling station to refuel both warships and merchant vessels on their way to and from Asia.

Seward's biggest move was in 1867 when he arranged the purchase of Alaska from Russia. As you have read, that purchase turned out to be a great bargain for the United States.

Throughout his term in office, Seward tried to gain new lands. He worked out a treaty with Denmark in which the United States would buy the Danish Virgin Islands in the Caribbean. (The United States did not actually buy the islands until 1917.) Before he retired in 1869, he considered adding the Hawaiian Islands to the United States. That would not happen, however, for almost 30 more years.

The Annexation of Hawaii

In the early 1800s, Christian missionaries from the United States had moved to the Hawaiian Islands to convert the local Polynesian population. Some of the missionaries' descendants had become wealthy sugar and pineapple planters. The planters dominated Hawaii's government.

In 1891 Liliuokalani (luh-LEE-uh-o-kuh-LAH-nee) became queen of Hawaii. She believed that the planters had too much control. She wanted to take back power for her people. This outraged the planters. They appealed to the United States government to protect their power.

The planters' timing was excellent. The United States had just set up joint control—with Britain and Germany—of the Samoan Islands in the Pacific. Samoa would serve as a refueling stop for American ships bound for Asia. Hawaii, closer to the mainland than Samoa, could be a much-needed link in the chain of stations stretching across the ocean.

In January 1893 a small group of U.S. Marines came ashore from a ship in Honolulu harbor. With the planters' help, they overthrew Queen Liliuokalani. The planters set up an independent republic with a planter, Sanford Dole, as president. They asked to be annexed by (joined to) the United States. President Benjamin Harrison supported the plan and sent a treaty to the Senate.

Before the Senate could act, Harrison left office and Grover Cleveland became President. Cleveland tried to persuade the planters to restore the queen to her throne. They refused. It was not until 1898, when the United States went to war with Spain, that Hawaii was annexed. It became a state in 1959. In 1993 the U.S. Congress apologized to the Hawaiian people for the American role in overthrowing Liliuokalani.

Liliuokalani (above) was the last queen of Hawaii. Her coat of arms (below) became the basis for the state seal.

SECTION REVIEW

1. Key Terms imperialism, Social Darwinism

2. People and Places William Seward, Queen Liliuokalani, Midway Islands, Hawaii, Samoa

3. Comprehension What were the three main reasons for the drive for American expansion in the late 1800s?

4. Comprehension What territories did William Seward acquire for the United States, and how did he acquire them?

5. Critical Thinking Why might President Cleveland have wanted to restore Liliuokalani to the Hawaiian throne?

2 The Spanish-American War

SECTION GUIDE

Main Idea
The United States went to war against Spain in 1898 and won new territories in the war.

Goals
As you read, look for answers to these questions:

1 Why did many Americans decide that the country should go to war against Spain?

2 What were the major battles of the Spanish-American War?

3 How did the war change the status of Cuba, Puerto Rico, and the Philippines?

Key Terms
yellow journalism
Spanish-American War

This cartoon of William Randolph Hearst shows him wearing the clothing of the "Yellow Kid," a character in a comic strip that ran in Hearst's newspaper, the New York *Journal*. **Critical Thinking:** What is the cartoonist saying about the American press?

IT IS 1897 and you want to find out the latest news. There are no televisions, radios, or fax machines. So you take a few pennies and buy some newspapers. The headlines scream about Spanish cruelty in one of its colonies, Cuba. The stories describe horrible scenes of suffering. The newspapers call for the United States to help the Cubans.

Rebellion Against Spain

The Spanish empire was crumbling. Once Spain had controlled most of the Americas, including land that became part of the United States. By the 1890s it owned just a few small colonies in Africa, the Philippine Islands and other islands in the Pacific, and Cuba and Puerto Rico in the Caribbean.

In 1868 unrest in Spain had led to uprisings in Cuba and Puerto Rico. Many Puerto Ricans called for complete independence. In 1897 Spain agreed to give Puerto Rico its own legislature. The governor would still be appointed by Spain.

People in Cuba and the Philippines also called for independence. In the 1890s both colonies burst into revolt. The revolt in Cuba, only 90 miles from Florida, attracted American attention. American business interests in Cuba had been growing, but the fighting had caused trade between the United States and Cuba to drop.

In 1896 Spain sent General Valeriano Weyler to crush the Cuban rebels. Weyler's methods were harsh. He forced people to leave their homes and move into camps, where they were guarded by Spanish troops. Thousands of Cubans died of starvation and disease in the camps.

The American press described the camps and called for the United States to take action. In particular, two New York City newspapers carried stories that stirred up people's emotions. The *World,* owned by Joseph Pulitzer, and the *Journal,* owned by William Randolph Hearst, were locked in a fierce battle for customers. Both papers tried to attract readers by printing stories about the terrible conditions in the Cuban camps.

Many Americans were convinced that Spain was behind the explosion of the U.S.S. *Maine* in Havana, Cuba. **Critical Thinking:** How might this kind of illustration have contributed to the call for war against Spain?

This type of newspaper writing was known as yellow journalism. The name comes from a comic strip called "The Yellow Kid." Yellow journalism aroused the emotions of many Americans.

America Goes to War

William McKinley, the U.S. President in 1898, did not want war. He believed that war would hurt American business interests and that the American economy could not support it. McKinley had served in the Civil War and fought in the bloody battle of Antietam. "I have been through one war," he told a friend. "I have seen the dead piled up, and I do not want to see another."

Yet public pressure forced McKinley to take action. He demanded that Spain stop its harsh treatment of the Cubans. Spain did bring General Weyler home, but did little to change its policies. In January 1898 McKinley sent the U.S.S. *Maine* to Cuba. Riots had broken out in the Cuban capital, Havana, and the battleship was there to protect American citizens.

On February 9, the New York *Journal* printed a letter written by a Spanish official in which he called McKinley "weak." The letter had been stolen by a spy. Its release forced McKinley to take an even tougher line against Spain.

Less than a week later, the *Maine* exploded in Havana harbor and sank. Of the roughly 350 men on the ship, some 260 were killed. No one knows what caused the explosion. Most historians today believe that it was an accident. For example, a spark might have set off the explosives stored in the ship.

At the time, however, Americans blamed Spain. The headlines in the *Journal* read, "WAR! SURE! *MAINE* DESTROYED BY SPANISH."

"Remember the *Maine*!" became a call to arms. On April 20, 1898, McKinley signed a congressional resolution declaring Cuba independent. He told Spain that it had three days to agree to leave Cuba. Spain broke relations with the United States. The Spanish-American War began.

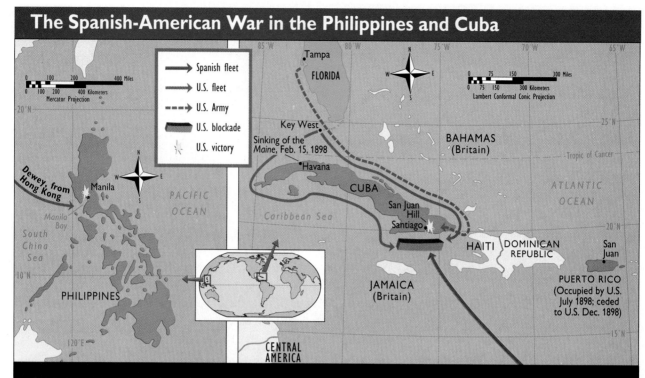

The Spanish-American War in the Philippines and Cuba

Spanish fleet
U.S. fleet
U.S. Army
U.S. blockade
U.S. victory

Tampa
FLORIDA
Key West
Sinking of the *Maine*, Feb. 15, 1898
Havana
BAHAMAS (Britain)
Tropic of Cancer
CUBA
San Juan Hill
Santiago
ATLANTIC OCEAN
HAITI
DOMINICAN REPUBLIC
San Juan
PUERTO RICO (Occupied by U.S. July 1898; ceded to U.S. Dec. 1898)
Caribbean Sea
JAMAICA (Britain)
CENTRAL AMERICA

Dewey from Hong Kong
Manila
Manila Bay
PACIFIC OCEAN
South China Sea
PHILIPPINES

Lambert Conformal Conic Projection
Mercator Projection

GEOGRAPHY SKILLS: The Spanish-American War was fought in two locations, the Pacific and the Caribbean. **Critical Thinking:** Should the United States have attacked the Philippines? Explain your answer.

The Pacific War

Although the United States had gone to war to fight for Cuban freedom, the first major battle took place on the other side of the world—in Manila Bay. Manila was the capital of the Philippines. Before the war began, Theodore Roosevelt, assistant secretary of the navy, had put a fleet of American ships in Hong Kong on alert. Their leader, Commodore George Dewey, trained his men, bought supplies, and changed the paint on his ships from white to battleship gray. He also made secret contact with the leader of the Philippine rebel forces, Emilio Aguinaldo (AH-gee-NAHL-doh).

At the start of the war, Dewey sailed for Manila.

Headlines celebrate the American victory in the Philippines.

The battle began early on the morning of May 1, 1898. By a little past noon, Dewey's four cruisers and two gunboats had destroyed the Spanish fleet in Manila Bay. About 380 Spanish sailors were dead or wounded. No Americans were killed. American troops, aided by Filipino rebels, completed Dewey's victory by taking control of Manila.

Dewey became an instant hero at home. Thousands of babies born at the time were named for him. A chewing gum named "Dewey's Chewies" became popular.

The War in the Caribbean

When the war began, the U.S. Army had only 28,000 men. Within six months, over 200,000 more joined up. Theodore Roosevelt had signed up and called for volunteers for a special regiment. Roosevelt picked a group that included cowboys,

New York policemen, athletes, and American Indians. He named his men the "Rough Riders."

The Rough Riders, along with 17,000 other men, set sail from Tampa, Florida, in June. They were wearing woolen clothing because lightweight uniforms had not arrived. Food spoiled in the heat. Thousands of the soldiers became sick with tropical fevers and other diseases.

The troops were heading for the port of Santiago, on the southern side of Cuba. To control the port, American troops had to capture San Juan Hill. They attacked on July 1, 1898. African American soldiers from the Tenth Cavalry began to drive the Spanish back. Roosevelt and the Rough Riders—minus their horses, which had been left behind in Florida—joined the other Americans. Together they rushed forward, capturing the hill.

The Spanish fleet in Santiago harbor was quickly defeated. The United States also seized Puerto Rico. On August 12, 1898, Spain signed a truce. To U.S. Secretary of State John Hay, it had been "a splendid little war." For Spain, as one Spanish captain explained, it was "the signal that the history of four centuries of grandeur [glory] was at an end."

Results of the War

At the treaty conference, held in Paris, the Americans shocked the Spanish. The war had been fought over Cuba, yet the United States demanded that Spain hand over Puerto Rico, the island of

A tin tray celebrates Theodore Roosevelt, leader of the Rough Riders.

The final capture of San Juan Hill in Cuba was achieved by a mixture of regular army troops and Rough Riders. Though they fought bravely and were well led, the Americans suffered high casualties in the battle because of poor planning and information. **Critical Thinking:** Why did Americans consider the war a great success?

PRESENT ▶ PUERTO RICO

Though the United States has controlled Puerto Rico since 1898, Puerto Ricans did not gain U.S. citizenship until 1917. In 1952 the island became a commonwealth. In 1993 Puerto Ricans voted on whether Puerto Rico should remain a commonwealth, become a state (above), or gain independence. Commonwealth supporters won.

As citizens of a U.S. commonwealth, Puerto Ricans elect their own leaders and can enter the rest of the United States without a passport. They cannot vote for President, and their representative in Congress has limited voting power. On the other hand, they do not pay U.S. taxes.

Guam, and the Philippines as well. Spain had no choice. The final treaty was signed in December 1898.

The United States did not grant Cuba immediate independence. First Cuba had to agree to the Platt Amendment. It gave the United States the right to interfere in Cuban affairs anytime there was a threat to "life, property, and individual liberty." Cuba also had to allow an American naval base at Guantánamo Bay until 1999.

Puerto Rico became a United States territory. It had its own elected legislature and a governor chosen by the President. Guam was controlled by the U.S. Navy.

President McKinley decided that the Philippines should become an American colony. Filipinos had hoped that Spain's defeat would bring them independence. Their leader, Emilio Aguinaldo, organized a bloody revolution against American con-

trol. Not until 1902 were American troops able to restore order.

The Anti-Imperialist League

Several well-known Americans opposed expansion overseas. Businessman Andrew Carnegie, reformer Jane Addams, and writer Mark Twain joined with others to form the Anti-Imperialist League. Members of the League believed that the United States should not deny other people the right to govern themselves. They declared:

❝We regret that it has become necessary in the land of Washington and Lincoln to reaffirm that all men, of whatever race or color, are entitled to life, liberty, and the pursuit of happiness.❞

The voice of the League was lost in the roar of popular approval of the Spanish-American War and its consequences. Many in the United States were eager to see the rise of an American power that would surpass the glory of Spain.

SECTION REVIEW

1. Key Terms yellow journalism, Spanish-American War

2. People and Places William McKinley, George Dewey, Theodore Roosevelt, Cuba, Philippines, Puerto Rico

3. Comprehension How did General Weyler's actions in Cuba increase the call for U.S. involvement there?

4. Comprehension Describe the major battles of the war.

5. Critical Thinking Has television increased or decreased the press's ability to shape public opinion? Explain.

3 American Involvement Overseas

SECTION GUIDE

Main Idea
Under President Theodore Roosevelt the United States became more active in world affairs, especially in Latin America.

Goals
As you read, look for answers to these questions:

1 What steps did the United States take to protect its interests in Asia?

2 How was the Panama Canal built?

3 How and why did the United States become involved in Latin America in the early 1900s?

Key Terms
Open Door Policy
Panama Canal
Roosevelt Corollary

READ THE FOLLOWING PHRASE: *A man, a plan, a canal—Panama!* Now read it backwards. If you rearrange the spaces between letters, it says the same thing. That phrase is a palindrome—something that reads the same backwards as frontwards. This palindrome describes a moment in American history when President Theodore Roosevelt planned to build a canal across the thin strip of land that connects North and South America. Such a canal would make it easier for American ships to travel from the Atlantic to the Pacific oceans. Among other things, it would help the United States maintain its position as a Pacific power.

A Power in the Pacific

The United States had a history of interest in the Pacific. In July 1853, four American warships had entered Tokyo Bay, Japan. Their commander, Commodore Matthew Perry, carried a letter from President Millard Fillmore asking that the Japanese open some of their ports to American trade. He also brought some gifts. He also made it clear that Japan should not refuse Fillmore's request.

The gifts and threats worked. After another visit by Perry in 1854, Japan signed a treaty of friendship with the United States. It allowed American merchants to set up trading companies in two Japanese port cities.

In the late 1800s the United States began to play an even larger role in Asia. Nations such as Britain, France, Germany, Russia, and Japan competed for control of China. U.S. Secretary of State John Hay called on nations to follow an **Open Door Policy** toward China. In other words, no single country should have a monopoly on trade with China. To further protect its interests,

This cartoon shows an American policeman (President Theodore Roosevelt) keeping order around the world.

the United States joined with other nations in 1900 to put down the Boxer Rebellion, an uprising in China against foreigners.

Roosevelt became President in 1901. He also believed that the American presence in Asia was important. He worried about growing Japanese power in the Pacific. After war broke out between Russia and Japan in 1904, Roosevelt agreed to serve as peacemaker. He hoped to keep Japan from winning a complete victory. The resulting treaty did not please many Japanese, but Roosevelt won the Nobel Peace Prize for his efforts.

The Panama Canal

Roosevelt is even better known for his efforts in Latin America—the part of the Americas south of the United States. Roosevelt wanted a shortcut to connect the Atlantic and Pacific oceans. The Spanish-American War, fought in both oceans, made clear the need for such a shortcut.

The South American nation of Colombia controlled the best spot for the canal—the Isthmus of Panama. (An isthmus is a narrow strip of land surrounded by water.) Columbia was unwilling to give the United States this land. Ignoring Colombia's right to control its territory, Roosevelt sent U.S.

Marines to support a revolution by people who lived on the isthmus. The new nation of Panama was created in 1903.

Panama's leaders gave the United States the rights to a ten-mile strip of land (later called the "Canal Zone") on which to build the Panama Canal. Roosevelt bragged that if he had asked Congress for approval, it would have taken years. Instead, he said, "I took the Canal Zone and let Congress debate; and while the debate goes on the Canal does also."

Building the canal was extremely difficult. The land was swampy and full of mosquitoes that carried the infection that causes malaria. First workers had to drain the swamps. Then they dug the canal.

More than 43,000 workers—many of them black West Indians and African Americans—labored for years. They did not finish until 1914. The canal cost $352 million, the most expensive project up to that time. It was expensive in human terms too. More than 5,000 workers died from disease or accidents.

Workers digging the Panama Canal used as many as 60 steam shovels a day. The painting (inset) shows ships moving through the canal. Today many ships are too wide to fit through the narrow locks. **Critical Thinking:** How did the canal affect relations between the United States and Latin America?

The United States and Latin America

N. MEX.
Columbus

UNITED STATES

SCALE 0 — 300 mi
0 — 300 km

U.S. troops, 1916–1917

S.C.

MISS. ALA. GA.

TEXAS LA.

•Santa Ysabel
•Parral

•New Orleans

FLORIDA

U.S. troops, 1898–1902, 1906–1909, 1912, 1917–1922
Platt Amendment, 1901–1934

Miami•

U.S. troops, 1915–1934
Financial supervision, 1916–1941

Americans controlled 43% of
Mexican property, 1910

MEXICO
Tampico •

U.S. troops, 1914

Mexico City•
Veracruz •

Havana

BAHAMA IS.
(Br.)

CUBA

U.S. naval base, 1903–

Guantanamo

U.S. troops, 1916–1924
Financial supervision, 1905–1941

HAITI

VIRGIN IS.

GUATEMALA

BR.
HONDURAS

U.S. troops,
1924–1925

DOMINICAN REP.

PUERTO
RICO

U.S. possession after 1898

HONDURAS

U.S. warns Germany against
attack on Venezuela, 1902

EL SALVADOR

NICARAGUA

COSTA
RICA

PANAMA

Caracas
•

U.S. troops, 1909–1910, 1912–1925, 1926–1933
Financial supervision, 1911–1924

VENEZUELA

U.S. acquired Canal Zone, 1903
Canal completed, 1914

COLOMBIA
• Bogota

BRAZIL

GEOGRAPHY SKILLS: The United States has a long history of involvement in Latin America. **Critical Thinking:** Why might the Caribbean Sea have been called an "American lake"?

Some people in Latin America and the United States opposed Roosevelt's actions. They believed that he had interfered in Colombia's affairs in order to cheat it out of its land. In 1921 the United States finally paid Colombia $25 million for the loss of Panama. In 1978 the United States signed a treaty promising to turn over the Canal Zone to Panama in the year 2000.

United States Involvement in Latin America

Much of Latin America had once been ruled by Spain. Under Spanish rule a few people, mostly of Spanish origin, held much of the power and wealth. The rest of the people, most of whom were of American Indian, African, and mixed ancestry, lived in poverty. Most Latin American nations gained independence in the 1800s. Yet their governments did little to help the common people.

The U.S. economy was growing in those years, and so was its interest in its southern neighbors. U.S. businesses found that they could buy food and materials—for example, bananas, coffee, and copper—cheaply from Latin America. They shipped these goods to the United States and sold them for higher prices. (More and more Americans were eager to buy these goods.)

U.S. companies bought large amounts of land in Latin America for farming and mining. Many Latin Americans lost their land and ended up in low-paying jobs for these companies.

Pancho Villa, shown leading his men, is remembered by Mexicans for his support of government reform.

action if unrest threatened these investments. He kept his word. Marines landed in Nicaragua to restore order in 1912. They did not leave until 1933.

In 1914 President Wilson sent a fleet to Mexico after U.S. Marines had been arrested there. Two years later, troops led by a Mexican revolutionary known as Pancho Villa (VEE-uh) killed eighteen Americans in Mexico and then raided a town in New Mexico, killing seventeen. Wilson ordered General John J. Pershing to "get Villa dead or alive." War did not break out between the two countries, and Pershing never captured Villa.

Actions in Latin America were rarely questioned in the United States. Americans saw their nation as a good police officer, keeping the peace and preventing disorder. Many Latin Americans believed the opposite. To them the United States was a bully more concerned with its business investments than with the people of Latin America. This deep mistrust continues to haunt U.S. relations with its neighbors.

Policing the Hemisphere

Roosevelt wanted it made clear that the United States was the leading power in the Americas. He quoted an African saying: "Speak softly, but carry a big stick." Roosevelt meant that the United States should not make loud threats when faced with world crises. Instead, it should take swift military action.

Roosevelt reminded European powers of the Monroe Doctrine. It declared that the United States would not stand for interference in the Americas. He added the Roosevelt Corollary in 1904. (A corollary is a statement that follows logically from an earlier statement—in this case, the Monroe Doctrine.) If a situation arose in the Western Hemisphere that required "international police power," he said, the United States would do the job.

Less than a year later, U.S. Marines were doing just that in the Dominican Republic. That Caribbean nation had been unable to pay its foreign debts. The United States took charge of the nation's finances and arranged payment of its debts. In 1906 U.S. troops landed in Cuba to prevent a revolution there.

Later Presidents expanded on Roosevelt's "big stick diplomacy." William Howard Taft urged American businesses to invest in Latin America, promising military

SECTION REVIEW

1. Key Terms Open Door Policy, Panama Canal, Roosevelt Corollary

2. People and Places Theodore Roosevelt, Pancho Villa, Japan, China, Colombia, Panama, Mexico

3. Comprehension Why did Roosevelt want to build the Panama Canal?

4. Comprehension Give an example of how Taft and Wilson followed the Roosevelt Corollary.

5. Critical Thinking Do you agree or disagree with how Theodore Roosevelt built the Panama Canal? Explain.

4 World War I Begins

SECTION GUIDE

Main Idea

Begun in 1914, World War I was a costly and terrible conflict. The United States was neutral at first but then entered the war in 1917.

Goals

As you read, look for answers to these questions:

1. What were the main causes of World War I?

2. How was the war fought?

3. Why was the United States unable to remain neutral throughout the war?

Key Terms

World War I   stalemate
militarism   communism

FRANCIS FERDINAND, Archduke of Austria-Hungary and heir to its throne, sat back in his open car. It was June 28, 1914, a lovely day in Sarajevo (SAR-uh-YAY-vo), capital of his empire's territory of Bosnia. Crowds lining the road smiled and waved as his car drove by. They did not seem to mind that their ruler was a German-speaking Austrian, while they spoke Slavic languages. Yet Francis Ferdinand knew that there were many in Bosnia who wanted to leave his empire and join with the Slavic country of Serbia.

Causes of World War I

The archduke's ride ended in tragedy. The route through the city had changed at the last moment, and the driver became confused. He stopped the car. A young Bosnian Serb stepped forward, a pistol in his hand. He shot twice, killing the archduke and his wife. Within two months, nations around the world were at war.

The assassination of the archduke was the immediate cause of World War I, as the conflict became known. The war had three major long-term causes:

(1) *Colonial rivalries.* France and Britain had many colonies. Germany felt that it deserved to have more colonies, where it could gain resources and sell its goods.

(2) *Alliances.* European nations were arranged into competing alliances. Nations pledged to fight if their allies were attacked. This meant that any small conflict could easily become a larger war.

(3) *Nationalism and militarism.* Europeans were proud of their nations and wanted to prove they

Minutes after assassinating the Archduke of Austria-Hungary, Gavrilo Princip was arrested. The Bosnian nationalist later died in prison.

were "the best." One way to compete was in the size and strength of their armed forces. **Militarism**—the belief that a nation should have and use a large military force—was common in Europe.

These factors were an explosive combination. President Woodrow Wilson sent an adviser to Europe to report on the situation. He wrote to Wilson that Europe was like an open keg of gunpowder. "It only requires a spark to set the whole thing off," the adviser said.

War Breaks Out in Europe

The assassination of Francis Ferdinand was that spark. The Austro-Hungarian emperor blamed Serbia for the murder of his nephew. On July 28, 1914, Austria-Hungary declared war on Serbia. Russia, a Slavic country, prepared to defend Serbia. In response, Germany—Austria-Hungary's ally—declared war on Russia and then on Russia's ally, France. German troops marched through neutral Belgium on their way to invade France. Britain, which had promised to protect Belgium, declared war on Germany. Like a tragic schoolyard match, the nations of Europe divided themselves into two opposing groups. The British foreign secretary warned:

> ❝ The lamps are going out all over Europe. We shall not see them lit again in our lifetime. ❞

Soon the world was divided. There were the Central Powers of Austria-Hungary, Germany, the Ottoman Empire, and Bulgaria. The Allied Powers consisted of Serbia, Russia, France, Great Britain, Japan, Italy, and fifteen smaller countries.

Fighting the War

Soldiers rushed to war, confident they would be home quickly. The war, however, became a **stalemate**—neither side was able to win a decisive victory. Battles were fought along several fronts in Europe. European colonies in Africa and Asia also sent troops to fight.

Most fighting against Germany occurred along the Western Front, which stretched across Belgium and France. Soldiers there on both sides huddled in ankle-deep mud at the bottom of deep, narrow trenches. Many died from diseases or the cold. Barbed wire was strung along the top of

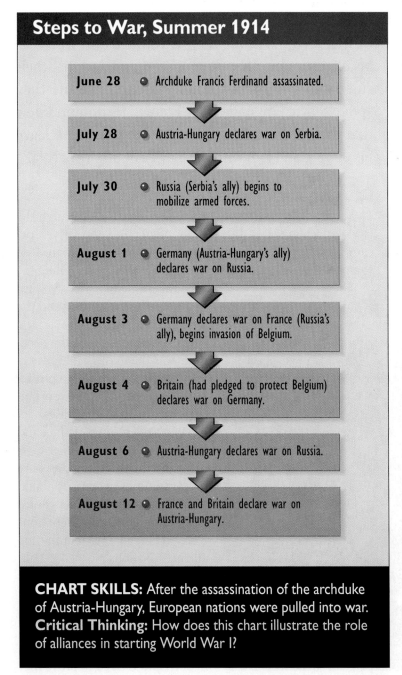

Steps to War, Summer 1914

June 28	● Archduke Francis Ferdinand assassinated.
July 28	● Austria-Hungary declares war on Serbia.
July 30	● Russia (Serbia's ally) begins to mobilize armed forces.
August 1	● Germany (Austria-Hungary's ally) declares war on Russia.
August 3	● Germany declares war on France (Russia's ally), begins invasion of Belgium.
August 4	● Britain (had pledged to protect Belgium) declares war on Germany.
August 6	● Austria-Hungary declares war on Russia.
August 12	● France and Britain declare war on Austria-Hungary.

CHART SKILLS: After the assassination of the archduke of Austria-Hungary, European nations were pulled into war. **Critical Thinking:** How does this chart illustrate the role of alliances in starting World War I?

the trenches. Artillery shelling turned the area between the two opposing armies into a "no man's land."

Battles began with hours or even days of steady shelling. Then one army would rush from its trenches toward the enemy. Thousands died in a hail of machine-gun bullets. In just one day during the First Battle of the Somme (sawm), July 1, 1916, the British lost 60,000 men—and gained not one inch of territory. That battle continued for months. When it ended in November, British casualties totaled 450,000, French losses were 195,000, and 650,000 Germans lay dead or wounded. For all their losses, the Allied Powers advanced less than eight miles during the battle.

Technology was a major reason for the killing. The British introduced tanks, for example, during the Battle of the Somme. Airplanes were also first used as offensive weapons—weapons used to attack the enemy—during World War I.

Defensive weapons like the machine gun, however, were more highly perfected than these offensive weapons and thus deadlier. Perhaps the most frightening new technology was poison gas, used by both sides to burn and blind enemy soldiers.

The War at Home

The home front was a different kind of battleground. World War I was a total war, requiring that civilians be as committed to victory as soldiers. Factories made weapons and farmers grew more crops to feed the soldiers.

Governments whipped up emotions, hoping to convince civilians to work harder and longer to destroy the enemy.

At first people were very patriotic. Yet as the war stretched on

The photograph, left, shows the misery of soldiers' lives in the trenches. When they finally went "Over the Top" (the title of the painting above), troops rushed into bullets, artillery, and poison gas. (A gas mask is at center.) **Critical Thinking:** How might conditions at the front have affected attitudes toward the war?

The Russian Revolution toppled the czars, and even their statues were torn down (above) after the Communists took over. Lenin (right), leader of the Communists, was a powerful speaker. He promised Russia's poor, "Bread, peace, land."

The Russian Revolution

In Russia the gloom was especially deep. The czar, or emperor, was a poor military leader. The army had few weapons and little training. Early on the Russians had achieved some victories against the Ottoman Empire to the south. Most of their soldiers, however, fought on the Eastern Front against Germany and Austria-Hungary. There, defeat followed defeat. In March 1917 food riots in Petrograd (now St. Petersburg) quickly turned into revolution, and the czar was forced from his throne.

The new government, led by Alexander Kerensky, hoped to make Russia more democratic. Kerensky also believed that Russia had to remain in the war. Most Russians, however, were tired of the fighting. Soldiers deserted their units and returned home. Nations controlled by the Russian Empire—Finland, Latvia, and Estonia, for example—demanded independence. The empire was falling apart.

Vladimir Lenin saw his chance to seize power. Lenin was the leader of the Bolsheviks, a political party dedicated to bringing communism to Russia. Communism is a system under which the government has complete control over the economy and people's lives.

In November 1917 the Communists seized power. Lenin began peace talks with Germany. The Treaty of Brest-Litovsk, signed in March 1918, gave Germany a large area of the former Russian Empire.

The treaty did not bring the Russian people the peace they so desperately wanted. Resistance to the Communist takeover led to civil war, which lasted for years before the Communists won.

The U.S. Stays Neutral

Many Americans had roots in the warring European nations. Yet most were against any involvement in the war. They agreed with President Wilson when he said:

and its horrors became known, some soldiers and civilians lost heart. One English poet, Rupert Brooke, had gone to war writing of his belief in the importance of fighting for his country. "If I should die, think only this of me:" he wrote, "That there's some corner of a foreign field that is forever England." Only a few years later, another British poet, Wilfrid Owen, described dying for his country in a different way: "What passing-bells for these who die as cattle?" Neither poet survived the war.

614

> **44 The United States must be neutral in fact as well as name. 77**

Both sides tried to persuade Americans to enter the war to help them. They used propaganda, information intended to convince people to think a certain way. Britain printed posters showing Germans killing babies in Belgium. Germany claimed that it was leading a fight to protect Europe and the United States from the "Slavic peril"—a reference to Russia and its allies.

Other pressures pushed the United States to become involved. American industry and farms were selling their products to both sides, though most of the business was with the Allied powers. Safe ocean travel was necessary if trade were to continue. Under international law, neutral nations could trade with warring nations as long as they did not sell such military goods as weapons or steel.

Both sides ignored the law. Britain blocked the entrance to the North Sea so that ships could not reach Germany. Wilson sent a strong protest to Britain and the blockade was lifted. The Germans, unable to match Britain's stronger navy, used a terrifying new weapon to halt trade: the submarine. The German submarines, called U-boats, could strike without warning.

Sheet music for a popular American song of 1916 reflected the antiwar mood of the nation.

In May 1915 a British ocean liner, the *Lusitania,* was torpedoed by a German U-boat. Nearly 1,200 of the 2,000 passengers, including 128 Americans, died. At the time, it was not publicly known that the *Lusitania* was also carrying war supplies to the Allies.

Americans were outraged at the sinking of an unarmed passenger ship. Public opinion turned against Germany. The Germans promised not to sink any more passenger ships without warning. Less than a year later, however, Germany torpedoed a French steamer. Congress agreed to President Wilson's request to build ships and increase the size of the U.S. Army. Again, Germany promised not to sink passenger or merchant ships.

The German poster (left) announces "U-boat, out!" German U-boats were responsible for sinking the *Lusitania* (above). **Critical Thinking:** How did German submarine warfare lead to the United States siding with the Allies?

President Woodrow Wilson addresses a joint session of Congress on April 2, 1917, asking for a declaration of war.

> **It is a fearful thing to lead this great peaceful people into war, into the most terrible and disastrous of all wars. . . . But the right is more precious than peace, and we shall fight for the things which we have carried nearest our hearts—for democracy . . . for the rights and liberties of small nations, for . . . peace and safety to all nations and make the world itself at last free.**

The German promise helped Wilson win re-election in 1916. Supporters proclaimed, "He kept us out of war." Germany did not believe that slogan, however. It was convinced that Wilson's re-election meant that the United States would enter the war on the Allied side. Germany stepped up its submarine attacks, hoping to defeat the Allies before the Americans could arrive.

America Enters the War

In March 1917, Wilson released a telegram captured by the British. The note had been sent by the German Foreign Minister, Arthur Zimmermann, to the German ambassador in Mexico. It told the ambassador to make an offer to the Mexican government. If Mexico joined the German side against the United States and if Germany won the war, the minister promised, Mexico would receive all the lands it had lost in the Mexican War.

The note caused an outcry in the United States. About six weeks later, after five more American ships were sunk by German submarines, Wilson called a special session of Congress. He asked it to vote for a declaration of war against the Central Powers. In his message Wilson said:

Not all Americans wanted to go to war. Some argued that the war was only helping war industries. Others were still against any overseas involvement. Six senators and 50 representatives (including the first woman in Congress, Jeannette Rankin of Montana) voted against the declaration.

Their opposition made little difference. On April 6, 1917, the United States entered World War I.

S E C T I O N   R E V I E W

1. Key Terms World War I, militarism, stalemate, communism

2. People and Places Francis Ferdinand, Woodrow Wilson, Vladimir Lenin, Sarajevo, Petrograd

3. Comprehension What were the three main causes of World War I?

4. Comprehension What were the causes of American entry into World War I?

5. Critical Thinking In your own words restate Wilson's message to Congress asking for a declaration of war. What was Wilson promising that the war would accomplish?

LEARN

Look at the posters and slogans in this chapter. They are examples of propaganda. **Propaganda** is communication that aims to influence people's opinions, emotions, or actions. It can be based on facts or on half-truths or entirely on lies. It often uses attractive people or striking symbols to grab your attention.

Governments have long used propaganda to sway public opinion. During World War I, both sides built support for their policies with propaganda. Some of it played on people's fear of the enemy. Much of it appealed to their patriotism. Look at the British poster at the right. It shows a scene that is supposed to be taking place after the war is over. How does the poster make you feel?

Daddy, what did YOU do in the Great War?

PRACTICE

1. What is the aim of the poster?

2. To what emotions does this poster appeal? Explain your answer.

3. Do you think this poster is effective? Why or why not?

APPLY

4. Write a journal entry describing your reaction to the poster, as if you were alive at the time.

5. Imagine that you work for one of the Allies or one of the Central Powers. Create your own propaganda poster. Try to persuade your own people to think or behave in a certain way.

SECTION GUIDE

Main Idea
The United States helped the Allies win World War I. Yet after the war, the United States refused to join an organization aimed at world peace.

Goals
As you read, look for answers to these questions:

1 How did involvement in World War I affect life in the United States?

2 Why did the Senate reject the Treaty of Versailles?

Key Terms
armistice
Fourteen Points
League of Nations
reparations
Treaty of Versailles

This became one of the most famous American posters of all time.

I N 1917 "Over There" was one of the most popular songs in the United States. Young men whistled it as they waited to sign up for the armed forces. Women hummed it as they traveled to jobs as factory workers.

> Over there, over there, send the word over there That the Yanks are coming . . . So prepare, say a prayer, send the word to beware, We'll be over, we're coming over, And we won't come back till it's over, over there.

Celebrities sang it at rallies organized to build support for the war. The song captured the patriotism and pride that were felt by many Americans as the country entered World War I.

The Home Front

Patriotic spirit alone would not win the war. President Wilson created the War Industries Board to organize and increase production of war materials. The Board made sure that iron and steel went into making weapons, not cars. Factories ran around the clock to produce arms, uniforms, and other equipment. Wilson also knew that workers had to be kept happy and productive. Other government agencies were given those tasks. The National War Labor Board helped prevent labor unrest. The War Labor Policies Board improved working conditions.

To pay for arms and soldiers, the government needed money —and lots of it. The United States issued Liberty Bonds, which were loans to the government that would be repaid in the future. Rallies, posters, and parades convinced more than 20 million people to buy war bonds.

The government also called for citizens to conserve food and fuel, work harder, and be more patriotic. People even renamed some German-sounding foods. "Sauerkraut" became "victory cabbage," for example.

The demand for loyalty had a dark side. Congress passed laws making it illegal to speak out against the war. Opponents of the war were jailed. President Wilson had said that America was at war to "make the world safe for democracy." Yet at the same time, freedom of speech at home was sharply limited.

Wartime Workers

Most Americans did support the war, and women played an important role in that support. The war had stopped immigration from Europe and pulled millions of men off the job and into the armed forces. Yet war production called for more workers. Large numbers of women entered the workforce. Thousands worked in steel mills and ammunition factories.

There was nothing new about women working in factories. Now, however, it was seen as patriotic and thus more acceptable. "A women's place is in the war" became a new and powerful slogan. Women also played important roles in raising money and support for the war.

Respect for women's abilities grew. Less than a year after the war ended, Congress passed the Nineteenth Amendment, giving women the right to vote.

The war affected other groups in the United States. Many Mexicans immigrated to the United States, fleeing revolution and looking for work.

The war also had a major impact on African Americans. More than half a million moved from southern states to work in northern factories. These jobs paid far more than the farm jobs they had in the South. African Americans still faced discrimination in the North. Many were fired from well-paying jobs when the war ended. Yet, as you will read later, this migration continued through the 1920s.

Soldiers for the War

In May 1917 Congress passed the Selective Service Act. All men between the ages of 21 and 30 had to sign up for military service. Later

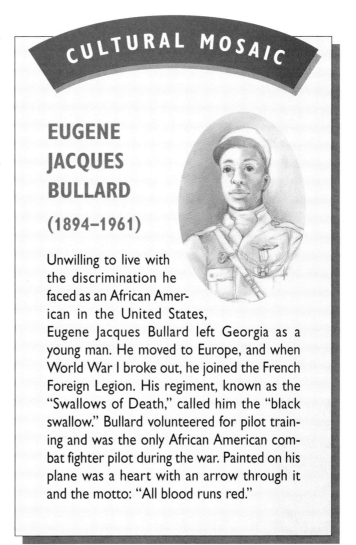

CULTURAL MOSAIC

EUGENE JACQUES BULLARD (1894–1961)

Unwilling to live with the discrimination he faced as an African American in the United States, Eugene Jacques Bullard left Georgia as a young man. He moved to Europe, and when World War I broke out, he joined the French Foreign Legion. His regiment, known as the "Swallows of Death," called him the "black swallow." Bullard volunteered for pilot training and was the only African American combat fighter pilot during the war. Painted on his plane was a heart with an arrow through it and the motto: "All blood runs red."

Women workers weld bomb casings in a wartime factory. **Critical Thinking:** Imagine you could interview these women. How might they explain their reasons for working?

the draft age was expanded to between 18 and 45. About 3 million men were drafted, joining about 2 million volunteers in the armed services. Women also joined the armed forces. Some worked as ambulance drivers and nurses near the front lines.

African American men were also drafted into the armed forces, and almost 400,000 draftees and volunteers served. Discrimination followed them into the military. Black soldiers served in separate units and rarely became officers. At first they were only allowed to work as laborers, unloading ships and digging ditches. Nevertheless, they played an important role in keeping American forces well supplied.

African Americans protested the treatment of black soldiers. In response, the army created black combat units. These troops were "loaned" to the French army. The French quickly put them on the front lines. One unit served in the trenches for more than six months, longer than any other American unit. Their bravery and ability won them the French Legion of Honor and the nickname the "Black Rattlers."

The War in Europe

The first Americans troops arrived in France in the summer of 1917. The most important role these troops played was to boost the spirits of the Allies.

It took more than a year for the bulk of the American troops to be trained and transported to Europe. They arrived just in time. The Allies had suffered several defeats. Russia had pulled out of the war, and Germany and the other Central Powers were massing all their forces on the Western Front for a final push.

A German attack began in March 1918 with early successes. The arrival of more American troops helped stop the German advance. Led by General John J. "Black Jack" Pershing, the Americans fought bravely at the Battle of Château-Thierry (shah-TOH tyeh-REE). The tide of war began to change in favor of the Allies.

In the Battle of the Argonne Forest, more than a million American troops began to push the Germans back. In one month, these troops fired more ammunition than had been used in the entire Civil War. By the end of the summer in 1918, Allied troops were defeating the Germans all along the front.

In November the Germans asked for an armistice, or an end to the fighting. The armistice became official on November 11, 1918. For many years, Armistice Day was celebrated as a holiday. Today, it is called Veteran's Day in honor of all veterans who have served in the armed forces.

Planning for Peace

In January 1918 President Wilson had issued a statement that included a list remembered as the Fourteen Points. These points represented American goals in the war. The first five points called for smaller military forces, an end to secret treaties, and freedom of the seas. Eight more points called for changes in national boundaries so that most European peoples could have their own nations. To Wilson, the most important point was the fourteenth. It called for the creation of a

An American SPAD-XIII (above) swoops down to fire on a German Fokker (right) in this illustration of a dogfight, a battle between airplanes. Before the development of a machine gun that could fire without hitting propellers, pilots shot at each other with pistols. **Critical Thinking:** What was the role of technology in the war?

World War I in Europe

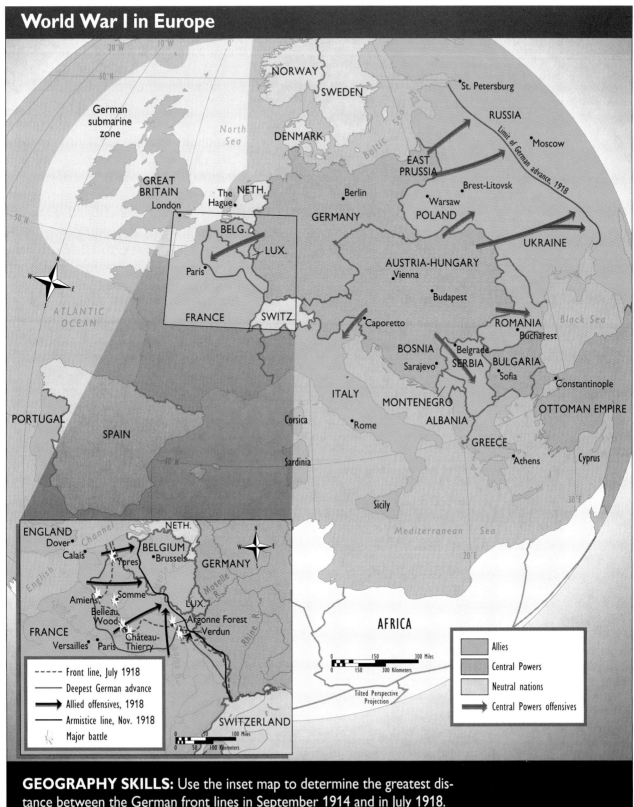

German submarine zone

GREAT BRITAIN
London

NETH.
The Hague

BELG.
LUX.

Paris

FRANCE
SWITZ.

ATLANTIC OCEAN

PORTUGAL

SPAIN

Corsica

Sardinia

NORWAY

SWEDEN

DENMARK

North Sea

Baltic Sea

GERMANY
Berlin

EAST PRUSSIA

POLAND
Warsaw

Brest-Litovsk

St. Petersburg

RUSSIA
Moscow

Limit of German advance, 1918

UKRAINE

AUSTRIA-HUNGARY
Vienna

Budapest

Caporetto

BOSNIA
Sarajevo

SERBIA
Belgrade

ROMANIA
Bucharest

BULGARIA
Sofia

Black Sea

Constantinople

ITALY

MONTENEGRO
ALBANIA

Rome

GREECE
Athens

OTTOMAN EMPIRE

Cyprus

Sicily

Mediterranean Sea

AFRICA

Inset map

ENGLAND
Dover
Calais

English Channel

NETH.

BELGIUM
Brussels

Ypres

GERMANY

Moselle R.

Amiens
Somme

Belleau Wood

LUX.

Argonne Forest
Verdun

Rhine R.

FRANCE
Versailles
Paris

Château-Thierry

Seine R.

SWITZERLAND

- - - - Front line, July 1918
——— Deepest German advance
——▶ Allied offensives, 1918
——— Armistice line, Nov. 1918
✳ Major battle

0   50   100 Miles
0   50   100 Kilometers

0   150   300 Miles
0   150   300 Kilometers

Tilted Perspective Projection

Allies

Central Powers

Neutral nations

Central Powers offensives

GEOGRAPHY SKILLS: Use the inset map to determine the greatest distance between the German front lines in September 1914 and in July 1918.
Critical Thinking: Why had the line moved so little in four years?

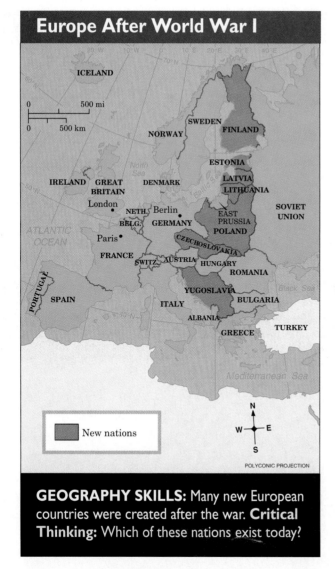

Europe After World War I

ICELAND

SWEDEN
NORWAY
FINLAND

ESTONIA

IRELAND GREAT
BRITAIN
DENMARK
LATVIA
LITHUANIA

London
NETH. Berlin
BELG. GERMANY
EAST
PRUSSIA
POLAND
SOVIET
UNION

ATLANTIC
OCEAN

Paris
CZECHOSLOVAKIA

FRANCE
SWITZ. AUSTRIA
HUNGARY

PORTUGAL
ROMANIA

SPAIN
YUGOSLAVIA

ITALY
BULGARIA
ALBANIA

GREECE
TURKEY

Mediterranean Sea

0   500 mi
0   500 km

North Sea

Baltic Sea

Black Sea

New nations

POLYCONIC PROJECTION

GEOGRAPHY SKILLS: Many new European countries were created after the war. **Critical Thinking:** Which of these nations exist today?

They demanded that Germany pay reparations—money that a defeated nation pays to make up for a war's destruction. The amount finally agreed upon was $33 billion, far more than Germany could afford.

The Treaty of Versailles, the formal agreement that ended the war, also changed the map of Europe. Gone were the great empires of Austria-Hungary and the Ottomans. New nations were created, such as Yugoslavia and Czechoslovakia. Allies gained land and control over former Ottoman land in the Middle East: Syria, Palestine, and Iraq. Germany was left smaller, poorer, and bitter.

Wilson did manage to convince the other Allied leaders to support a League of Nations. He returned home in July 1919, filled with hope that the League would bring an end to war.

The Treaty's Defeat

Wilson was more popular in Europe than in the United States. Though he had signed the Treaty of Versailles, the Senate had to agree for it to become law. Many senators opposed the treaty. They argued that joining the League of Nations would mean involvement in foreign conflicts. They might be convinced to support other

The cartoon shows President Wilson offering the League of Nations' olive branch to the dove of peace. Wilson hoped the League would make World War I the "war to end all wars."

League of Nations, an international organization that would settle disputes and keep the peace.

A month after the war ended, Wilson arrived in Europe to attend the peace conference. This was the first time that a President had ever left the country during his term of office. European crowds cheered the man they considered a hero.

Their leaders were less impressed. They thought that Wilson was lecturing them on how to keep the peace. The representatives from Britain, France, and Italy did not want to work with the nations they had defeated. They wanted to punish them.

parts of the treaty, but not the League.

Wilson refused to compromise on the treaty. He began a cross-country speaking trip to persuade Americans to support the treaty and the League. In September 1919, at a stop in Colorado, he suffered a stroke. He never really recovered. For the rest of his term his wife, Edith, handled many of his responsibilities.

Support for the League weakened. The Senate twice voted to reject the treaty as long as the League of Nations was part of it. The election of 1920 was seen as a test for the treaty and the League. The Democratic candidate, James M. Cox, supported Wilson's ideas. The Republican, Warren G. Harding, called for rejection of the League of Nations and a retreat from American involvement in world affairs. Harding won. Although the League of Nations was formed, the United States never joined.

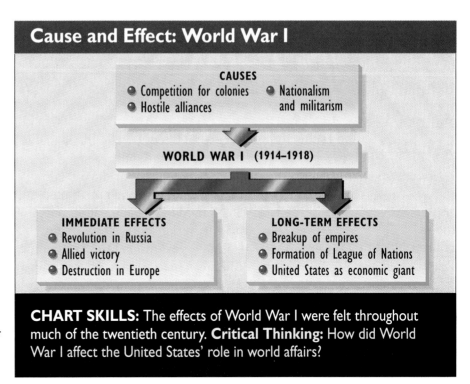

Cause and Effect: World War I

CAUSES
- Competition for colonies
- Hostile alliances
- Nationalism and militarism

WORLD WAR I (1914–1918)

IMMEDIATE EFFECTS
- Revolution in Russia
- Allied victory
- Destruction in Europe

LONG-TERM EFFECTS
- Breakup of empires
- Formation of League of Nations
- United States as economic giant

CHART SKILLS: The effects of World War I were felt throughout much of the twentieth century. **Critical Thinking:** How did World War I affect the United States' role in world affairs?

Results of the War

Far from solving Europe's problems, as many had hoped, World War I only made them worse. Nearly an entire generation of young European men had died. Germany was forced to admit guilt for the war and was burdened with an impossible debt. The Communist revolution in Russia threatened to spread to other nations. Britain's support of a Jewish homeland in Palestine led to fighting there. As the Ottoman empire collapsed, more than 1.5 million Armenians were killed by the Turkish government.

The United States suffered losses in the war, but not nearly as many as the European nations. The war had confirmed America's position as a major world power.

World War I had shaken up American society in many ways. Yet the war had also helped to make the United States the richest nation in the world. The country entered the 1920s prepared to enjoy that position.

Summary

1. New ideas and the need for new markets overseas increased interest in overseas expansion in the late 1800s.

2. The United States went to war against Spain in 1898. With victory came control of Puerto Rico, the Philippines, and Guam.

3. American relations with China and Japan broadened starting in the late 1800s. At the same time, the United States became the most powerful force in the Western Hemisphere, building and controlling the Panama Canal.

4. Colonial rivalries, alliances, nationalism, and militarism led to the outbreak of World War I in Europe in 1914. Though the United States tried to remain neutral, submarine warfare and actions by the German government led to an American declaration of war in April 1917.

5. A labor shortage caused by the war created new opportunities for women and African Americans. When the war ended, President Wilson's hope for a fair and lasting peace were frustrated by the Senate's opposition to the League of Nations.

Review

KEY TERMS

Define the following key terms.

1. armistice
2. imperialism
3. League of Nations
4. Open Door Policy
5. Panama Canal
6. Roosevelt Corollary
7. Treaty of Versailles

COMPREHENSION

1. What increased American interest in overseas expansion?

2. How did Hawaii become a U.S. territory?

3. Describe the course of the Spanish-American War. How did the war begin? Where were the main battles fought?

4. What territory did the United States win as a result of its victory in the Spanish-American War?

5. How did the United States open trade with Japan?

6. Why was there interest in building a canal across Central America?

7. How were the Latin American policies of Roosevelt, Taft, and Wilson similar?

8. What was the immediate cause of World War I? What were the other important causes of the war?

9. Why did the United States finally enter World War I? How did President Wilson present the war to the American people?

10. Why did the Senate reject the Treaty of Versailles?

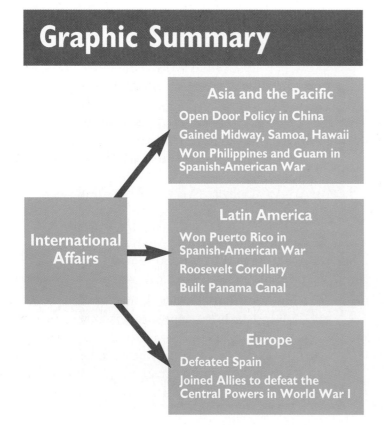

Graphic Summary

International Affairs

Asia and the Pacific
Open Door Policy in China
Gained Midway, Samoa, Hawaii
Won Philippines and Guam in Spanish-American War

Latin America
Won Puerto Rico in Spanish-American War
Roosevelt Corollary
Built Panama Canal

Europe
Defeated Spain
Joined Allies to defeat the Central Powers in World War I

Places to Locate

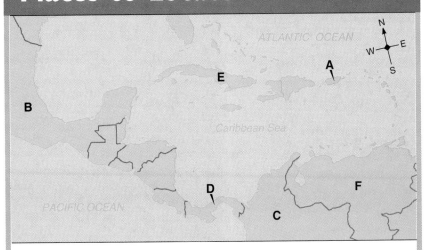

Match the letters on the map with the places that are listed below. Then explain the importance of each place.

1. Colombia   3. Mexico   5. Puerto Rico
2. Venezuela   4. Panama   6. Cuba

Geographic Theme: Movement What were the arguments in favor of United States expansion overseas?

Skill Review

The poster at right was used in Australia during World War I. Study the poster and answer the questions that follow.

1. How is the enemy represented?
2. What might the question mark on the poster mean?
3. Is the poster providing factual information or appealing to people's emotions? Explain.
4. Do you think this poster is effective? Why or why not?

CRITICAL THINKING

1. **Making a Judgment** Do you think the United States was justified in supporting the Panamanian revolution against Colombia? Explain.
2. **Recognizing Cause and Effect** Explain the role of nationalism in the outbreak of World War I.

PORTFOLIO OPTIONS

1. **Civics Connection** Imagine that you and your classmates are United States citizens in the 1890s. Do you believe that a policy of imperialism is best for the nation? Explain. Organize a class debate on the issue of United States imperialism.
2. **Writing Connection** Imagine that you are a member of the House of Representatives in April 1917. Write a letter to your constituents explaining how you voted on the declaration of war.
3. **Contemporary Connection** In the 1890s and early 1900s, the United States became known as the "police officer" of the Western Hemisphere. Today, the United States is often called the "police officer of the world." Do you think this description is accurate? Explain. What role, if any, do you think the United States should play in world affairs today?
4. **Timeline Connection** Copy the chapter timeline. Make a list of events that you think demonstrate United States imperialism and explain how.

TWO POEMS
BY PAUL LAURENCE DUNBAR

In the decades after the Civil War, some reform-minded Americans, both black and white, spread the knowledge that there was a distinctive African American culture, particularly in music, dance, and literature. The poet Paul Laurence Dunbar, born in 1872, was one of the earliest voices of modern black literature. Dunbar first became popular for his poems in black rural dialect. His later poems expressed some of the sorrows experienced by African Americans. These are two of the most famous.

We Wear the Mask

We wear the mask that grins and lies,
It hides our cheeks and shades our eyes,—
This debt we pay to human guile;
With torn and bleeding hearts we smile,
And mouth with myriad subtleties.

Why should the world be over-wise,
In counting all our tears and sighs?
Nay, let them only see us, while
   We wear the mask.

We smile, but, O great Christ, our cries
To thee from tortured souls arise.
We sing, but oh the clay is vile
Beneath our feet, and long the mile;
But let the world dream otherwise,
   We wear the mask.

Sympathy

I know what the caged bird feels, alas!
When the sun is bright on the upland slopes;
When the wind stirs soft through the
    springing grass
And the river flows like a stream of glass;
When the first bird sings and the first bud opes,
And the faint perfume from its chalice steals—
I know what the caged bird feels!

I know why the caged bird beats his wing
Till its blood is red on the cruel bars;
For he must fly back to his perch and cling
When he fain would be on the bough a-swing;
And a pain still throbs in the old, old scars
And they pulse again with a keener sting—
I know why he beats his wing!

I know why the caged bird sings, ah me,
When his wing is bruised and his bosom sore,—
When he beats his bars and would be free;
It is not a carol of joy or glee,
But a prayer that he sends from his heart's
    deep core,
But a plea, that upward to Heaven he flings—
I know why the caged bird sings!

"We Wear the Mask" and "Sympathy" from
*The Complete Poems of Paul Laurence
Dunbar* by Paul Laurence Dunbar.
Published by Dodd, Mead & Co.

Analyzing Literature

1. Why do you think African Americans had to wear a "mask" in the first decades following the Civil War?

2. In the poem "Sympathy," what are the "old, old scars" the poet refers to?

3. According to Dunbar's metaphor, how are African Americans like a "caged bird" even though they are no longer slaves?

UNIT 8

Troubled Decades (1900–1945)

UNIT OVERVIEW

After a time of prosperity, the nation endured a severe depression and then another world war.

Chapter 26

The Roaring Twenties (1919–1928)
For many Americans, the 1920s was a time of stable politics and economic prosperity.

Chapter 27

The Depression and the New Deal (1929–1941)
Following an economic crash in 1929, the United States entered the worst depression in its history.

Chapter 28

A More Diverse America (1900–1940)
Though many Americans faced discrimination, the nation's growing diversity was a source of strength.

Chapter 29

The Rise of Dictators and World War II (1930–1945)
The United States fought in Europe and Asia in World War II and emerged from the war as the world's greatest power.

Illustration: "The Docks, New York City" (detail).

629

The 1920s were an exciting, energetic period in American history. It was an age of prosperity for the nation. Americans had more money to spend and more time for entertainment. Jazz lovers flocked to hear Bessie Smith (right), a popular singer of the time. Young fans of actor Charlie Chaplin (below) enter a look-alike contest.

LIBERTY

Charles Chaplin
in his very latest
million dollar comedy

'THE
IDLE
CLASS'

	1919		1921		1923		1925

1919 Eighteenth Amendment (Prohibition) ratified

1920 Harding elected President

1923 Coolidge becomes President

1924 Nellie Tayloe Ross becomes first elected woman governor

1925 Scopes Trial

The Roaring Twenties (1919–1928)

1 A Look at Harding and Coolidge

SECTION GUIDE

Main Idea

Under Presidents Harding and Coolidge, the government supported business and kept a hands-off policy in other matters.

Goals

As you read, look for answers to these questions:

1 What political scandals troubled the Harding administration?

2 What were President Coolidge's policies and beliefs?

Key Terms

Teapot Dome scandal
isolationist
Kellogg-Briand Pact

1927

1928 Kellogg-Briand Pact signed

1927 Lindbergh makes first trans-Atlantic flight

1927 First sound movie, *The Jazz Singer*, released

PEOPLE WERE FED UP. By the start of the 1920s, Americans were tired of the progressives' crusade to help others at home and abroad. They were tired of the government sending their boys across oceans to fight "other people's wars." They were tired of government telling them to sacrifice. In fact, many were just plain tired of government. For all these reasons they elected Warren G. Harding as President.

The 1920 Election

Harding was not a man to rock the boat. As a U.S. senator from Ohio, he had never written an important law. He had few enemies and lots of friends. The Republican Party nominated him for President after neither of the two favored candidates could get enough votes. Harding was a compromise.

Harding and his running mate, Massachusetts governor Calvin Coolidge, faced a ticket with two progressive Democrats. They were James M. Cox, Governor of Ohio, and Franklin D. Roosevelt, Assistant Secretary of the Navy.

What America needed, said Harding, was "normalcy." He was not clear on what "normalcy" was, but to voters it rang true. The Republicans won by a landslide.

The Harding Presidency

History has been hard on Harding. He is not remembered as a man of great intellect. According to journalist H. L. Mencken, "No one hated him, and no one worshiped him. . . ."

Harding believed that the government was getting in the way of people's lives and businesses. Taxes and regulations were a burden. He wanted a Secretary of the Treasury who would get the hand of government out of people's pockets.

Harding chose banker Andrew W. Mellon, one of the six richest men in America. Mellon hated high taxes on the rich. He felt they discouraged businesses from investing profits and making the economy grow. Mellon convinced Congress to lower income taxes. His work paved the way for more tax cuts later in the 1920s.

Another Cabinet officer was Herbert Hoover. He was a mining engineer known for organizing aid to Europe during World War I. As the new Commerce Secretary, Hoover worked to cut government waste.

The Ohio Gang

Mellon and Hoover were both hard-working, able men. Many of the other men Harding appointed to the country's highest offices, however, were unqualified. Some were outright crooks. Yet they were Harding's pals. Most had been friends with him back in Ohio. The newspapers called them "the Ohio gang." Their misdeeds helped wreck Harding's presidency.

One scandal involved the head of the Veterans' Bureau. He stole millions of dollars worth of medical supplies meant for soldiers wounded in World War I. Soon after, members of the Ohio gang were caught illegally selling public property.

Harding was not directly involved in the corruption. However, he paid a steep price for it. Worried over the scandals, Harding decided to go on a speaking tour of the western United States. He wanted to improve his health and polish his image. On a trip from Alaska to California, he suffered a heart attack. Three days later, on August 2, 1923, the President died.

The Teapot Dome Scandal

After Harding's death, one of the most famous scandals of the century came to light. It involved Interior Secretary Albert Fall, head of the nation's land resources.

Fall had a salary of just $12,000 a year. Yet he was able to fix up his New Mexico ranch, pay overdue taxes on it, and buy up the land around it for $125,000. To a few suspicious senators, the numbers just did not add up.

Fall had made several secret, illegal deals with oil executives. One deal allowed a company to drill on oil-rich government land at Teapot Dome, Wyoming. In return the oilmen gave Fall thousands of dollars' worth of cash, bonds, and livestock for his ranch. Newspapers called the bribery scheme the **Teapot Dome scandal.**

When the truth came out, Fall did what his name suggests. He fell from office and resigned in disgrace. He was later convicted and fined $100,000. He spent a year in jail.

Coolidge Takes Over

At 2:47 A.M. on August 3, 1923, at the family home in Plymouth Notch, Vermont, John Coolidge lit two kerosene lamps. The Coolidges had just learned of Harding's death. John Coolidge, a justice of the peace, read his son the presidential oath of office. (Under the Constitution, Vice President Coolidge had already become President the moment Harding died.) The new President left for Washington, D.C., a few hours later.

Coolidge moved quickly to clean up the Ohio gang scandals. He stated:

> **If there has been any guilt, it will be punished. . . . If there has been any fraud, it will be revealed.**

His efforts limited any damage to the Republican Party.

The next year, 1924, the Democrats chose West Virginia businessman John W. Davis to face Coolidge. Progressives also jumped into the race, nominating Senator Robert M. La Follette of Wisconsin. The senator attracted many voters who were unhappy with the two major parties. In the end, however, Coolidge was re-elected.

Coolidge in Office

Coolidge reflected the values of his small, rural hometown. He was a hard-working, clean-living Yankee.

As governor of Massachusetts he had crushed a strike by the Boston police union in 1919. His actions earned him national fame during a time of growing fear of unions.

Unlike Harding, Coolidge was a man of few words. One critic joked that the President "could be silent in five languages." Yet he was an able speaker whose words were to the point.

Despite his no-nonsense habits, the President was a known practical joker. He once set off the White House burglar alarm and hid behind a curtain to watch the security guards scramble. Another time he rang for his secretary and then hid under his desk.

Some people called Coolidge "thrifty." Others called him "cheap." While many politicians surrounded themselves with luxury, Coolidge did not even own a car until he came to Washington. After walking with his bodyguard, Coolidge would make cheese sandwiches for the two of them in the White House kitchen. He watched the White House budget as

Calvin Coolidge (while governor of Massachusetts) sits with his wife Grace and two sons, Calvin, Jr., and John (left). President Coolidge poses with his family in the White House garden (right).

carefully as he did his own bank account. His method of managing money carried over into his management of the entire U.S. government.

Coolidge's Policies

Coolidge and those who voted for him believed that Americans who worked hard would enjoy prosperity. They also believed that it was not the job of the government to help people with special problems. Instead, private charities would help such people.

Farmers were one group that Coolidge refused to give any special treatment. Farmers were producing more food than the nation needed, and prices were dropping. Congress passed a bill that would have the government buy the extra food. Coolidge vetoed the bill.

Coolidge was a friend of big business. He believed in laissez faire—that business, if left alone, would act in a way that would benefit the entire nation. Under Coolidge, government agencies worked with business rather than against it. This was even true of agencies whose job it was to regulate business.

Relations with the World

The Republicans' hands-off approach also applied to relations with other nations. Harding and Coolidge were both isolationists. That is, they felt that this nation should stay out of other nations' affairs except in the defense of the United States. After the horror of World War I, many Americans agreed.

Harding and Coolidge supported efforts to avoid future wars. In 1921 and 1922,

Harding's Secretary of State, Charles Evans Hughes, organized the Washington Conference. These talks were aimed at reducing weapons worldwide. The result was the Five-Power Treaty. In it the United States, Britain, Japan, France, and Italy agreed to limit the number of ships in their navies.

Coolidge's major peace effort was the Kellogg-Briand Pact of 1928. (The pact was named after Coolidge's Secretary of State, Frank B. Kellogg, and French diplomat Aristide Briand.) Fifteen nations signed the pact, or treaty. They pledged not to make war against each other except in self-defense. By the early 1930s more than 60 countries had signed the treaty.

Some members of Congress criticized the Kellogg-Briand Pact. They felt that the treaty said nothing about how to enforce peace. They also pointed out that a country could attack another and simply claim to be acting in self-defense.

However, most Americans supported the Kellogg-Briand Pact. To them it represented the hope that if war could be outlawed, it would go away. This hope would all too soon vanish.

Not everyone supported the Kellogg-Briand Pact. This cartoon shows the reaction of some members of Congress to Secretary of State Frank B. Kellogg's treaty.

SECTION REVIEW

1. Key Terms Teapot Dome scandal, isolationist, Kellogg-Briand Pact

2. People Warren G. Harding, Calvin Coolidge, Andrew Mellon, Albert Fall

3. Comprehension How did members of the Ohio gang take advantage of their friendship with Harding?

4. Comprehension Describe Coolidge's policies as President.

5. Critical Thinking How is the belief in individualism shown in Coolidge's policies as President?

SKILLS: Outlining

LEARN

Think about giving a bath to an elephant. Where do you begin? Sometimes a task seems so huge that it can overwhelm you. Take the writing of a research paper, for example. You may have great ideas and piles of notes, but not a clue on how to start fitting them together. One helpful organizing tool is an outline.

An outline is a collection of ideas and notes organized by their importance. It is most useful when arranged into three categories: (1) **main points,** (2) **subtopics** that support the main points, and (3) **details** that add more information. A good outline is a guide for the writer to follow.

The outline here shows how the author might have arranged ideas and notes for the first part of Section 1. Because Harding is the main point, his name and a roman numeral appear at the top. The subtopics, which appear in order, are shown by capital letters. Arabic numerals and lowercase letters mark details.

Notice the use of abbreviations. You may prefer to spell out every word on your outline. You may also prefer to include more details. You should organize your outlines in a way that is most helpful to you, the writer.

> **I. Harding**
> **A. 1920 ELECTION**
> 1. Harding a compromise candidate
> 2. Campaign for "normalcy"
> **B. HARDING PRESIDENCY**
> 1. H. not intellectual
> 2. Mellon as Sec'y of Treasury
> a. One of six richest Americans
> b. Anti-tax
> 3. Hoover as Commerce Sec'y
> **C. OHIO GANG**
> 1. H. hires pals
> 2. Illegal sale of gov't property
> **D. TEAPOT DOME**
> 1. Albert Fall fixes N. Mex. ranch
> 2. Illegal deals with oil execs
> 3. F. fined $100,000 and jailed

PRACTICE

1. Which event came first: the campaign for "normalcy," Fall's imprisonment, or Hoover's appointment as Commerce Secretary? How do you know?

2. Which detail has details of its own?

3. Compare the outline with the actual text of Section 1. How would you have written the outline differently?

APPLY

4. Complete the outline for Section 1, as if you were the writer. First, create a set of notes that you would use to write about Coolidge. Then organize your notes into an outline.

2 A Decade of Business Growth

SECTION GUIDE

Main Idea
A number of factors helped business prosper in the 1920s.

Goals
As you read, look for answers to these questions:

1 How did new technology, management methods, and credit all play a part in the prosperity of the 1920s?

2 How did Henry Ford build a giant industry?

Key Terms
synthetic
installment buying
assembly line
social engineer

The switch to synthetic rubber made tires more affordable.

I F YOU WALKED into a store in the 1920s, you might think you had stumbled into the future. This is a partial list of the items that appeared in that decade: refrigerators, electric stoves, vacuum cleaners, wristwatches, foam rubber, disposable tissues, canned grape juice, and frozen foods.

Throughout the war years, people had sacrificed. Now, like a person coming off a bland diet, Americans began a decade-long buying binge.

Consumer Buying

Part of the "roar" in the "Roaring Twenties" was the growth in the nation's wealth. From 1921 to 1929, the average income per person rose from $522 to $716 a year. There was more money to spend and more to spend it on.

New technologies began making once-costly items available to the middle class. For instance, people who could not afford expensive fabrics could now buy artificial, or synthetic fabrics such as rayon. Synthetic materials replaced costly wood or metal in many products. This drove prices down. New machines turned out products faster and cheaper. This too caused prices to tumble. The cost of a tire and an inner tube, for example, dropped from $30 in 1914 to $15 in 1929.

Even those who did not see a rise in their incomes could join the buying spree. They were able to do this through a new option for consumers: installment buying. A family could now buy its first radio and pay for it over time in small monthly payments rather than all at once. One advertisement for tires told people that they could "Ride Now, Pay Later." As you will read in the next chapter, many people did pay dearly later on.

Powering the Nation

Cheap power fueled the new prosperity. During the 1920s, petroleum and electricity became widely available. They powered machines in the factories and tractors on the farms. They made possible new in-

636

ventions that made daily life easier. These included vacuum cleaners, washers, sewing machines, toasters, and fans.

You have already read about advances in the use of electricity in the late 1800s. By 1920 electricity flowed into the homes of most Americans.

The expansion of electricity was due largely to Samuel Insull. He worked as a secretary to Thomas Edison. Edison then made Insull a business partner. Together they built a company called General Electric (GE). The success of GE led Insull to break out on his own. He gained control of the Chicago Edison Company.

Insull had some 50,000 customers in Chicago by 1917. "We'll make electricity so cheap that only the rich will burn candles," he declared. Within 10 years, Insull had a $3 billion empire of more than 200 electric companies. These companies brought affordable power to more than thirty states.

Putting America on Wheels

Another man had a large impact on average citizens. His name was Henry Ford.

Ford was the son of an Irish immigrant who settled in Michigan. After quitting school at age 16, Ford found work as a mechanic. At age 28 he, like Insull, got a job in an Edison company. Now an engineer, in his spare time he tinkered with a gasoline engine in his garage. In 1896 he built his first successful automobile. Taking a chance, he left his job with Edison. In 1903 he formed the Ford Motor Company in Detroit.

Automobile Sales, 1921–1929

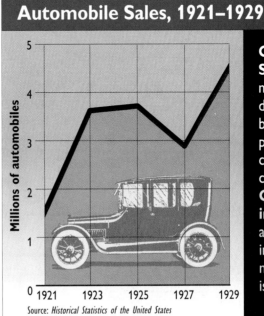

Source: *Historical Statistics of the United States*

CHART SKILLS: Automobile sales rose during the 1920s because of lower prices and new consumer purchasing options. **Critical Thinking:** How might automobile sales indicate how the nation's economy is doing?

Ford was determined to build a car that most people could afford. His dream came true with a design the company called the "Model T." Across the nation it became known as the "Tin Lizzie."

The Model T had a 20-horsepower engine and a body of steel. It was sturdy enough to handle the nation's rough roads. Its best feature was its price: $825 in 1908, the year it hit the market.

During that year Ford employed 350 workers at his Detroit plant and built 10,600 cars. In 1920 Ford produced more than a million automobiles, one per minute, each of which cost consumers $335 to $440.

He did this by using an assembly line. In the past, products were built by bringing the parts to one spot and putting them together there. In an assembly line, the product moves along a conveyor belt that runs across the factory. Workers at various stations add parts to it. By the mid-1920s, a Model T came off a Ford assembly line every ten seconds.

For starting his own business and working hard to make it succeed, Ford was hailed as a hero. With his wealth and power he tried to influence public opinion and politics. He published the newspaper the Dearborn *Independent.* He put some effort into running for President in 1924.

Ford's Beliefs

Ford believed that a business, if not bothered by government, would help its workers. The innovative Ford practiced what he preached. He made the eight-hour day a standard in American industry. He shortened the work week from six to five days. In 1914 he paid some of his workers $5 a day, far more than they could get elsewhere. By 1926 Ford employed more than 10,000 African Americans. He did this at a time when discrimination was still legal.

Yet in later years, people heard about another side to Ford. He was strongly anti-union. He could be a tyrant. He fired

A gasoline pump from the 1920s.

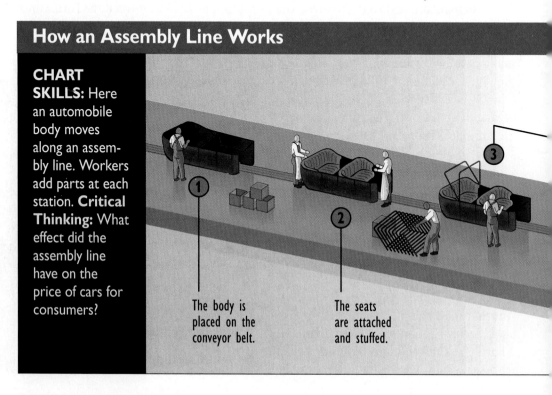

How an Assembly Line Works

CHART SKILLS: Here an automobile body moves along an assembly line. Workers add parts at each station. **Critical Thinking:** What effect did the assembly line have on the price of cars for consumers?

1. The body is placed on the conveyor belt.

2. The seats are attached and stuffed.

3.

nearly 1,000 Greek and Russian workers because they celebrated Christmas thirteen days later than other Christians. (The workers belonged to the Eastern Orthodox Church.) He accused the workers of not shedding their "foreign" ways and adapting to American life. Ford also had a deep hatred of Jews. He used the *Independent* to write numerous anti-Jewish articles.

Progress for Some

Calvin Coolidge once said, "The business of the United States is business." Republican policies loosened regulations on business. As a result, giant business empires arose during the 1920s. Ford and its competitors—General Motors, Chrysler, Studebaker, Packard, and Hudson—created a new market for steel, oil, rubber, and glass. Oil companies grew as the need for gasoline skyrocketed. American supplies of oil were still adequate to meet demand at home. The United States was also an exporter of oil. However, following the example of Europe, U.S. companies began to join the search for oil overseas.

Business leaders looked for ways to make workers more efficient. They hired people called social engineers to study how factories worked and to suggest ways to increase profits. Companies invested part of their profits in new machines to raise output and bring in even more money.

Yet where was all that money going? The "Roaring Twenties" did not roar for everyone. In 1929, according to one historian, some 60 percent of American families lived in poverty.

Those Left Behind

Two major groups of Americans suffered during the nation's rush to build and spend. The first were farmers. Farmers had

Ford and its competitors Packard (below) and Cadillac (bottom) grew into giant business empires during the 1920s.

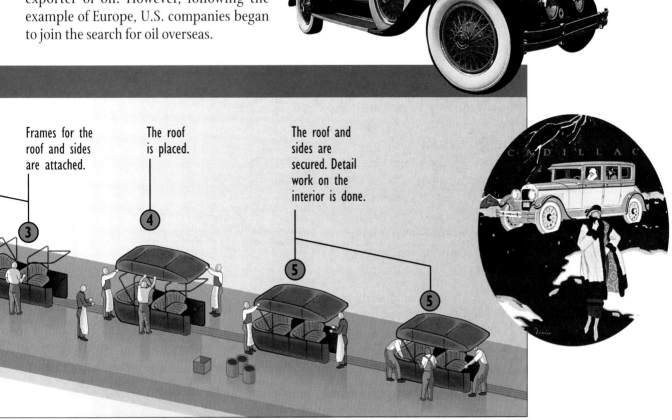

Frames for the roof and sides are attached.

③

The roof is placed.

④

The roof and sides are secured. Detail work on the interior is done.

⑤

Labor was one group of Americans that did not benefit from the prosperity of the 1920s. Violent strikes and protests, like the one shown here, spread a strong anti-union feeling across the nation.

profited from the demand for food in Europe during World War I. After the war, however, farmers watched the bottom drop out of the farm market. The value of farm products fell 50 percent in the 1920s. Synthetic fabrics hurt cotton sales. Machines sped up farm production. However, those farmers who could not afford the machines suffered. Drought and insects killed crops. Farmers begged for help, but the government did little.

The other group that watched its fortunes fall was labor. A series of violent strikes in 1919 led to strong anti-union feelings across the country. Court rulings in later years chipped away at the power of unions. In the coal industry, workers were hit hard by competition from oil.

Thinking about the great wealth created during the 1920s, U.S. Supreme Court Justice Louis Brandeis said:

❝I can't understand where all this . . . money comes from. . . . I think we must be exploiting about 80 percent of Americans, for the benefit of the other 20 percent. ❞

Indeed, throughout the United States, families were walking a dangerous line. Instead of building up savings, people were taking on debt. This debt was rising more than twice as fast as their incomes. Surely it could not last forever.

SECTION REVIEW

1. Key Terms synthetic, installment buying, assembly line, social engineer

2. People and Places Samuel Insull, Henry Ford, Detroit

3. Comprehension How did new technology and new management ideas help business grow in the 1920s?

4. Comprehension What new methods and ideas allowed Henry Ford to make a giant car industry?

5. Critical Thinking Since Ford was willing to pay his workers high wages and give them shorter working hours, why did he oppose unions?

3 A Decade of Change

SECTION GUIDE

Main Idea

Sweeping changes in American society during the 1920s brought new ideas, new forms of entertainment, and changes in literature.

Goals

As you read, look for answers to these questions:

1. How did women's lives change in the 1920s?

2. What changes came about in such areas as media, entertainment, and literature?

Key Terms

mass media
flapper
Lost Generation
expatriate

IT WAS 7:52 A.M. at Roosevelt Field in New York. Charles A. Lindbergh, a 25-year-old pilot, was about to do what no one had ever done before. He was going to fly nonstop across the Atlantic, alone. He lifted off in his single-engine airplane, the *Spirit of St. Louis*. Needing to save weight for extra fuel, he had no radio or parachute. He took only a few things, like a razor, a passport, five sandwiches and a quart of water.

Over 33 hours and 3,605 miles later, Lindbergh landed at Le Bourget Airport in France. America went wild. Few events have sparked the kind of pride and celebration that greeted "Lucky Lindy" when he came home.

Changes in Technology and Society

A year after Lindbergh's flight in 1927, a young woman pilot named Amelia Earhart became an American hero as well. She and two others also flew nonstop across the Atlantic. Earhart became the first woman to do so. These two events reflected the changes in technology and society taking place in the 1920s.

Many writers have said that the 1900s "began" in 1920. What they mean is that much of today's modern culture was born at that time. The pace of life became much quicker. Cars changed the look and size of cities. Suburbs grew. In 1927 the nation's first commercial airline, Pan American Airways, was founded. This drew distant cities closer together.

Other changes brought the nation together as well. Small general stores were replaced by giant, nationwide department store chains. Consumers from coast to coast could now buy the same products. The big business of national advertising got its start during this time. New types of mass media —communication that reaches a large public—began to take hold. New media, such as radio and movies, spread the latest ideas and fashions.

Lindbergh poses with his plane, the *Spirit of St. Louis*, after his historic flight across the Atlantic. His plane is now part of an exhibit at the National Air and Space Museum in Washington, D.C.

The attitudes of Americans changed during this era. After going through the hardships of war, many people demanded more freedom and more fun.

The Flapper

The image of the flapper is captured in magazine ads of the 1920s. She was a spirited young woman. She wore her hair in a "bob"—a short hairstyle. She wore masculine clothes or short dresses—that is, just below the knee. She had a powdered face and miles of necklaces. She went out to social events without a chaperone to watch over her. She was not like her mother.

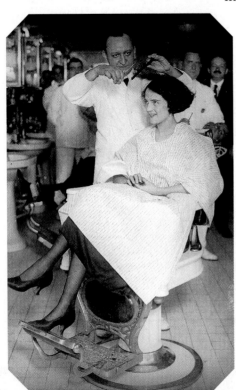

A flapper gets her hair "bobbed."

Most young women did not want or could not afford the flapper lifestyle. Still, the startling, rebellious image of the flapper remains one of the best-known features of the 1920s.

Flappers of the 1920s followed a generation of women who had fought for women's rights. Yet for many women's rights leaders, flappers marked a backwards step for women. Flappers seemed to think that beauty was a woman's main concern. One women's rights leader of the day, Charlotte Perkins Gilman, said, "A generation of white-nosed women who wear furs in summer cannot lay claim to any real progress."

Women and Politics

One small sign of change for women during this time was the Episcopal Church's decision to take the word "obey" out of a woman's wedding vow to her husband.

The 1920s brought other, much greater changes for women as well.

As you read earlier, Congress passed the Nineteenth Amendment in 1919. It guaranteed women the right to vote. It was ratified in time for the 1920 election.

While the law had changed, however, many peoples' attitudes had not. Most women did not use their hard-won right. In Chicago in 1924 only 39 percent of eligible women were registered to vote. (The figure for men was 62 percent.) When asked why they did not vote, some women said they had no interest in politics. Others said that their husbands had not reminded them to vote.

Still, women were taking a greater role in politics. In 1924 Wyoming elected Nellie Tayloe Ross, the nation's first woman governor. By 1928, 145 women held seats in state legislatures across the country.

A Major Controversy

One political issue that concerned both men and women was birth control. "No woman can call herself free until she can choose . . . whether she will or will not be a mother." These words were spoken by Margaret Sanger, a nurse in New York's Lower East Side. Sanger started a battle over birth control that would divide Americans and rage throughout this century.

In 1914 Sanger had launched a drive to spread information about birth control. This act was illegal at the time.

Opposition to Sanger and her ideas was fierce. Sanger's opponents felt that birth control was immoral and that it would weaken the family.

Sanger opened a clinic that gave out birth control information and devices. She was jailed several times. Then in 1918 a New York court ruled that doctors could give out birth control information. Other states, however, did not go along. The issue of birth control still produces bitter debates today.

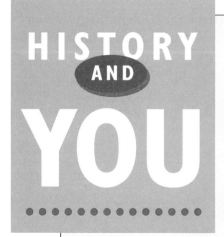

HISTORY AND YOU

Fitzgerald on the 1920s

In the 1920s, daring young women cut their hair and shortened their skirts. They flapped their arms and danced the Charleston. The older generation was shocked, which no doubt pleased the flappers.

In novels such as *The Great Gatsby*, F. Scott Fitzgerald wrote about this carefree and careless era. He called it the "Jazz Age." Here is a party scene from the novel:

"There was music from my neighbor's house through the summer nights. . . . At least once a fortnight a corps of caterers came down with several hundred feet of canvas and enough colored lights to make a Christmas tree of Gatsby's enormous garden. On buffet tables . . . spiced baked hams crowded against salads of harlequin designs and pastry pigs and turkeys bewitched to a dark gold. . . . By seven o'clock the orchestra has arrived. . . . [T]he cars from New York are parked five deep in the drive, and already the halls and salons and verandas are gaudy with primary colors and hair shorn in strange new ways. . . . Laughter is easier, minute by minute. . . . [A]lready there are wanderers, confident girls who weave here and there among the stouter and more stable, become for a sharp, joyous moment the center of a group and then excited with triumph glide on through the sea-change of faces and voices and color. . . .

Suddenly one of these gypsies in trembling opal . . . dances out alone on the canvas platform. A momentary hush; the orchestra leader varies his rhythm obligingly for her and there is a burst of chatter. . . . The party has begun."

A crowd watches young people dance the Charleston.

CRITICAL THINKING

1. Why, do you think, were the short hair and short skirts of flappers shocking?
2. What impressions of the party does Fitzgerald create?
3. Describe the behaviors of present-day youth that could be called rebellious. Do you think these are trends that will be forgotten or ones that will change society?

The Silver Screen

Of all the powerful new influences of the 1920s, none shaped the ideas and dreams of Americans like the "silver screen," or the movies.

Today's billion-dollar movie industry had its start in 1917. That year director Cecil B. De Mille sent a simple but historic message to his financial backers:

> **Flagstaff [Arizona] no good for our purpose. Have proceeded to California. Want authority to rent barn in place called Hollywood for $75 a month.**

Flagstaff's loss was California's gain. With its mountains, deserts, and year-round sunshine, Hollywood became the center of movie making in the United States. From the early 1900s motion-picture pioneers thought of themselves as carrying on a business. Their business was giving the public what it wanted. Movies gave people an escape into worlds they could never enter.

Charlie Chaplin made them laugh. His "tramp" character had big shoes, a tight-fitting coat, a mustache, a bowler hat, and a cane. He entertained moviegoers around the world. Young women wanted to look like Clara Bow, the movies' favorite flapper.

They loved actors Douglas Fairbanks and Rudolph Valentino, stars of romance and adventure films.

Movies of the early 1920s were in black and white. They also were silent. In 1927 the movie industry was transformed by something that many said would never happen. *The Jazz Singer,* the first full-length "talkie," or movie with sound, appeared. The movie was a hit. A year later another "talkie" caused a sensation. It was *Steamboat Willie,* featuring Mickey Mouse.

At 15 or 20 cents a ticket, an escape to the movies was a bargain. In 1929 there were almost 122 million Americans. Each week, an incredible 80 million movie tickets were sold.

Movie making giants like Samuel Goldwyn, Louis B. Mayer, William Fox, and the Warner brothers made millions overnight. The losers in "talkies" were silent film stars who had squeaky voices or could not memorize their lines. Many shining careers came to a sudden end.

Audiences in the 1920s flocked to movies theatres to see their favorite actors and actresses. Shown here are some of the stars of the "silver screen": Mickey Mouse (a colorized version of how he appeared in the late 1920s), Clara Bow, and Rudolph Valentino.

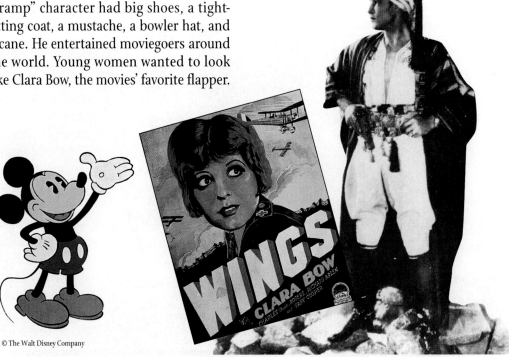

© The Walt Disney Company

644

The Radio

During World War I it was illegal for private citizens to own a radio. When the government lifted the ban in 1919, the radio industry took off.

The first coast-to-coast football broadcast from the West Coast took place on January 1, 1927. The event was the Rose Bowl. Fans were thrilled to be able to hear live, play-by-play accounts of sporting events.

Music lovers tuned in to hear symphony orchestras. Other new types of music reached their first large audiences through radio broadcasts.

Like modern television, radio offered situation comedies, soap operas, and comedians, like Jack Benny and Jimmy Durante. One of the most popular radio programs was the comedy show *Amos 'n Andy.* First broadcast in 1926, the program featured two African American cabdrivers and their friends Kingfish and Madame Queen. Few people realized that the show was performed by white actors. The show would later be condemned for its racism.

Duke Ellington (right photo) and Louis Armstrong (seated in left photo) were the founders of modern jazz. Their music captured the spirit of the 1920s.

The Birth of Jazz

In the 1920s a form of music called jazz burst onto the scene. Jazz was created by African American musicians in New Orleans in the late 1800s. It was a blend of two types of music, ragtime and blues. Both fast and energetic, jazz captured the spirit of the 1920s. For this reason the decade is also known as the Jazz Age.

In the early 1920s many African American musicians moved from New Orleans to northern cities. They brought jazz with them. Among the founders of modern jazz were musicians Louis Armstrong and Duke Ellington. Jazz singers such as Bessie Smith appeared on the scene. They played to sold-out crowds in the black nightclubs of New York City. Soon white musicians began playing jazz as well. Jazz quickly spread to the rest of the nation.

Jazz would also gain worldwide attention. Yet it is one of the few kinds of music that are considered uniquely "American."

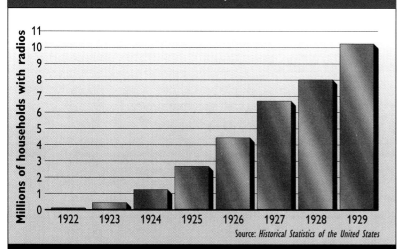

Households with Radios, 1922–1929

Millions of households with radios

Source: *Historical Statistics of the United States*

CHART SKILLS: Millions of households in the United States purchased radios in the 1920s. **Critical Thinking:** How did radio bring different parts of the nation closer together?

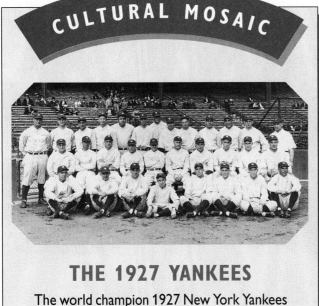

THE 1927 YANKEES

The world champion 1927 New York Yankees truly were a team for the record books. Slugger Babe Ruth hit 60 home runs, a record that has never been broken over a 154-game season. Lou Gehrig would play in 2,130 consecutive games from 1925 to 1939, another record. Other Yankees included "the Rifle" (Bob Meusel), "the Kentucky Colonel" (Earle Combes), "Jumping Joe" (Joe Dugan), "Schoolboy" (Waite Hoyt), and "Poosh 'Em Up" (Tony) Lazzeri. Together they made up what is widely seen as the best team of all time, helping give baseball its golden age.

Sports

Many Americans in the 1920s had more leisure time— that is, time to relax and have fun. One popular thing to do was to watch sports.

Professional baseball had started in the 1860s. In the 1920s the sport gained many new fans. Fans flocked to Yankee Stadium, which opened in 1922, to watch Babe Ruth and the rest of the "Bronx bombers." (See the box above.) Professional football and hockey also began in the 1920s. Baseball, however, remained the "national pastime."

Other sports in the 1920s also had their legends. Bobby Jones was the idol of golfers. People cheered Helen Willis

and Bill Tilden on the tennis courts. Boxing fans crowded to see Jack Dempsey and Gene Tunney in the ring. In 1926 New York City threw a homecoming parade for Gertrude Ederle. She had just become the first American and the first woman to swim across the English Channel.

Challenging Society's Values

Every era has its rebels—those who have different ideas than the rest of society. During the 1920s, rebellious artists, writers, and poets criticized the values of the day.

In the Greenwich Village section of New York City, a group of young writers and artists came to symbolize the spirit of rebellion. One of the group's best-known members, poet Edna St. Vincent Millay, commented on the 1920s lifestyle:

**❝ My candle burns at both ends;
It will not last the night;
But ah, my foes, and oh,
my friends—
It gives a lovely light! ❞**

In another part of New York, Harlem, a different group of artists made its mark on American culture of the 1920s. Its members were African Americans. You will read about their achievements, called the Harlem Renaissance, in a later chapter.

Heavyweight boxing champion Jack Dempsey was one of many sports idols of the 1920s. In 1927 he lost his title to Gene Tunney.

F. Scott and Zelda Fitzgerald led the fast-paced lifestyle of the Jazz Age. *The Smart Set* (below) was a magazine in which some of his works appeared.

The Lost Generation

For some artists, the postwar era was a time of deep despair. They had seen the ideals of the progressives end in a brutal and senseless war. They were filled with resentment toward the present age. They saw little hope for the future. These men and women came to be called the Lost Generation.

The woman who coined this phrase, writer Gertrude Stein, felt lost and limited in the United States. For her and many others, only one place offered freedom and tolerance. That was Paris, France. Stein's apartment in Paris became a gathering place for American expatriates. (Expatriates are people who choose to live in a country other than their own.)

Another member of the Lost Generation was the young novelist Ernest Hemingway. As an ambulance driver and newspaper reporter in Europe during World War I, he had seen the war's worst. His early novels, *The Sun Also Rises* and *A Farewell to Arms*, reflected the mood of despair that followed World War I.

One novelist knew both the excitement and the tragedy of his times. F. Scott Fitzgerald and his wife, Zelda, lived the whirlwind life of the Jazz Age—fast cars, nightclubs, wild parties, trips to Paris. Like many of their friends, the Fitzgeralds paid for their lifestyle. They endured nervous breakdowns, depression, and alcoholism.

Fitzgerald's masterpiece, *The Great Gatsby,* is a strange and tragic story of wealthy New Yorkers whose lives spin out of control. The novel is a dark postscript to the "Roaring Twenties."

SECTION REVIEW

1. Key Terms mass media, flapper, Lost Generation, expatriate

2. People and Places Charles Lindbergh, Amelia Earhart, Nellie Tayloe Ross, Charlie Chaplin, Louis Armstrong, Babe Ruth, Gertrude Stein, Ernest Hemingway, F. Scott Fitzgerald, Hollywood, Greenwich Village

3. Comprehension Name some examples of changes for women during the 1920s.

4. Comprehension What were some of the changes that came about in popular entertainment in the 1920s?

5. Critical Thinking The United States in the 1920s was more wealthy and powerful than ever before. What might explain the unhappiness of the Lost Generation?

4 Divisions in American Society

SECTION GUIDE

Main Idea
Reaction against many of the changes of the 1920s led to tension and conflict.

Goals
As you read, look for answers to these questions:

1. What were some examples of fear and intolerance during the 1920s?

2. What happened when the government tried to ban alcohol?

Key Terms
Red scare
prohibition
Scopes trial

IN APRIL 1920 two gunmen shot and killed a paymaster and his guard outside a Massachusetts shoe factory. The gunmen got away with the company's payroll. A few weeks later, Nicola Sacco, a shoemaker, and Bartolomeo Vanzetti, a fish seller, were charged with the crime. Over the next six years, Sacco and Vanzetti became the most famous prisoners in U.S. history.

The Red Scare

Sacco and Vanzetti were caught in a wave of fear that took hold of the nation during and after World War I. The Communist leaders of Russia (later renamed the Soviet Union) called on workers around the world to unite and overthrow their governments. Many Americans worried that workers were responding to that call.

Two Communist parties were started in the United States. Many of their members were foreign-born. Some were members of labor unions. Violent union strikes and bombings that took place in 1918 and 1919 had terrorized the nation. Many Americans thought that a foreign plot to overthrow the government was behind the labor unrest.

This period of fear and worry was called the Red scare. Any act of violence caused a wave of suspicion. The finger was usually pointed at radical politicians, union members, immigrants, Catholics, African Americans, or Jews. It did not matter if there was no proof against them.

Italian immigrants Nicola Sacco (right) and Bartolomeo Vanzetti (left) were victims of the Red scare. In this photograph, the two men await their trial.

Sacco and Vanzetti

Sacco and Vanzetti were perfect targets of a fearful public. They were Italian immigrants who had come to the United States in 1908. Both had been involved in union activities, strikes, and protests. Both said they were anarchists, or people who do not

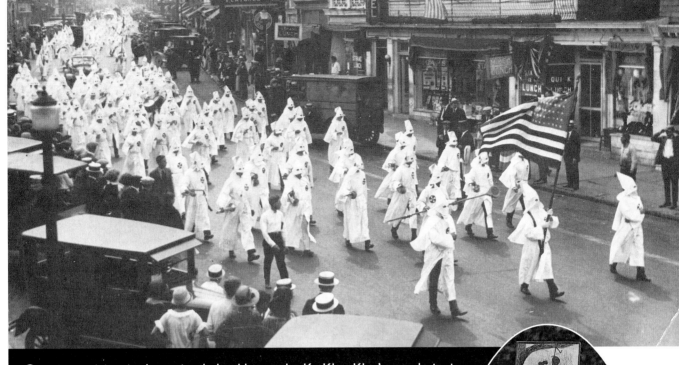

Growing nativism in the nation helped boost the Ku Klux Klan's popularity in the 1920s. Above, hooded Klan members march through a town in New Jersey. In a march (right), African Americans protest lynching and other acts of hate committed by the Klan.

believe in any form of government. At the time of their arrest they had been carrying guns. They were armed, they said, to protect themselves from attack while they handed out leaflets

During the trial it was clear that Sacco and Vanzetti were being judged for their views as well as their actions. The judge did not allow them to present a full defense. The jury found them guilty. They were sentenced to die in the electric chair.

Liberals, union leaders, workers, and Italian Americans raised thousands of dollars to pay for the appeals of the two men. When the appeals failed, demonstrators poured into Boston. They picketed the jail where Sacco and Vanzetti were being held. Protests were staged around the world. Bombs exploded in several cities.

The protests failed. On the night of August 23, 1927, as hundreds prayed and wept outside the prison walls, Sacco and Vanzetti were executed.

Rebirth of the KKK

As you have read, the fear of anything foreign is called nativism. In the minds of nativists, Jews were greedy for power and money. Asian Americans were seen as taking jobs from farmers. Immigrants, Catholics, and African Americans were also the objects of nativist fears.

Some nativist fears became laws. Iowa passed a law banning the teaching of all foreign languages in public schools. An Oregon law closed down all religious schools. The Supreme Court later ruled both laws unconstitutional.

Growing nativism fanned the hateful fires of the Ku Klux Klan. The Klan called for a "racially and morally pure" America. As you have read, the Klan attacked African Americans in the South in the years after the Civil War. In 1915 the Klan was revived in Georgia. It carried out beatings, lynchings, and other acts of hate against African Americans, Catholics, Jews, and many others.

By 1924 the Klan claimed about 4 million members. Nearly half lived in Indiana, Ohio, and Illinois. Local branches spread from Maine to Oregon. In Indiana Klan-backed candidates won the governor's race and most of the seats in the legislature.

After 1925 Klan membership dropped. Personal and financial scandals hurt Klan leaders. Also, Congress passed a law limiting immigration. This eased people's fears of foreign influence.

Prohibition

Fear of foreigners also breathed new life into an old issue, prohibition. For years progressives had tried to pass laws against making, selling, or drinking alcohol.

Reformers thought an alcohol ban would reduce poverty. Women's leaders argued that liquor added to unemployment and violence in the home. Business leaders saw that alcohol made workers less efficient.

In 1919 the Eighteenth Amendment, which banned alcohol, was ratified. It was seen by many as a victory of small-town, Protestant lifestyles over those of urban immigrant people. The nation became divided between the "wets" (who opposed prohibition) and the "drys" (who favored it).

The Volstead Act of 1919 gave the Treasury Department the power to enforce the ban. It was a thankless task. People who wanted alcohol found endless ways to get it. In Illinois in 1922, more than 2 million people got phony "prescriptions" for whiskey and gin. (Liquor was still legal for medical purposes.) Illegal nightclubs called "speakeasies" sold liquor freely. Club owners often bribed local police to protect them. "Bootleggers" made their living by moving and selling liquor illegally. Many people simply brewed their own "bathtub gin." More than a few people died from drinking homemade liquor.

Gangland Violence

Prohibition replaced the evils of alcohol with the evils of crime. It helped create a powerful network of organized crime. Members of organized crime sought to soak up profits from alcohol.

For years underworld gangs battled for control of the "booze racket." By the mid-1920s one gang leader had fought his way to the top by murdering everyone in his way. He was 23-year-old Al

The Volstead Act of 1919 authorized the enforcement of prohibition. Here a federal agent prepares to smash kegs of confiscated alcohol.

650

Capone. His business card said he was a "second-hand furniture dealer." In reality, Capone dealt in blood and greed.

By the late 1920s it had become clear that prohibition could not be enforced. Former supporters, like Herbert Hoover, began to urge its repeal. In 1933, the 21st Amendment repealed prohibition. Alcohol began flowing legally again.

The Scopes Trial

The tiny Tennessee town of Dayton was the setting for another clash of values. In 1925 a biology teacher named John Scopes broke a Tennessee law on purpose. The law was one that made it a crime to teach about evolution. Scopes did this to test whether the law could be enforced.

Evolution is the theory that all living things change over time. It states that humans evolved from lower forms of life. Opposing the theory are religious fundamentalists, who believe the Bible's story of creation to be true.

The Scopes trial brought two of the nation's most famous lawyers face to face. Clarence Darrow, from Chicago, was an agnostic—someone who believes the existence of God cannot be proven. He defended Scopes. William Jennings Bryan, from Nebraska, was a religious fundamentalist and former candidate for President. Bryan represented Tennessee.

The trial took place in July 1925. The judge opened the first session with a prayer. He did not allow Darrow's experts to testify about evolution.

Darrow did not expect to win the case. Scopes had admitted to breaking the law. Both did, however, hope to win public support for allowing evolution to be taught.

It took the jury just nine minutes to find Scopes guilty. However, he was fined only $100. Five days after the emotional battle, Bryan died in his sleep.

In a sense, both sides won. Scopes's fine was later overturned. The theory of evolu-

The Scopes trial drew to national attention the issue of teaching evolution in schools. Here, John Scopes's lawyer, Clarence Darrow, leans up against a table during the trial.

tion became a part of teaching in the United States. Yet Bryan's cause also lived on. After the trial, several states passed laws banning the teaching of evolution. Some of these laws remained until the 1970s.

SECTION REVIEW

1. Key Terms Red scare, prohibition, Scopes trial

2. People Nicola Sacco and Bartolomeo Vanzetti, Al Capone, John Scopes

3. Comprehension What was the connection between the Red scare and the Sacco and Vanzetti case?

4. Comprehension Why did the Ku Klux Klan gain popularity in the 1920s?

5. Critical Thinking Why was prohibition so difficult to enforce? How might the inability to enforce a law weaken respect for a government and its laws?

Summary

1. President Harding wanted to get government out of people's lives and businesses. He cut taxes and reduced government regulations. President Coolidge also took a laissez-faire attitude toward business. He also had a hands-off approach to relations with other nations.

2. The nation entered a period of prosperity during the 1920s. Consumer buying grew as new credit options were made available. The growth of the automobile industry added to the nation's prosperity. However, not all Americans did well. Farmers were hit hard as the value of farm products fell. Labor suffered as anti-union feelings swept across the nation.

3. Changes in society brought new attitudes and new lifestyles to the nation. Americans had more money to spend and more leisure time than ever before. Movies, radio, jazz, and sports became popular forms of entertainment. Some Americans, however, were disappointed with the changes in society. A group of writers, artists, and poets known as the Lost Generation used their works to criticize society's values.

4. The changes of the 1920s led to divisions and conflict. During the Red scare, the nation entered a period of fear and suspicion. Growing nativism led to the revival of the Ku Klux Klan. Also during this time a law banning alcohol caused a surge of crime.

Review

KEY TERMS

Write a sentence using each of the following key terms.
1. isolationist
2. Kellogg-Briand Pact
3. installment buying
4. assembly line
5. mass media
6. Lost Generation
7. Red scare
8. prohibition

COMPREHENSION

1. What were President Coolidge's policies toward farmers and businesses?
2. What was the Kellogg-Briand Pact? Why did some members of Congress criticize it?
3. How did new technologies affect the price of items in the 1920s?
4. Why did many businesses hire social engineers?
5. What gains in politics did women achieve during the 1920s?
6. What forms of entertainment became popular during the 1920s?
7. Why are the 1920s also called the Jazz Age?
8. Why did many Americans in the 1920s fear there was a plot to overthrow the government?
9. Why was prohibition difficult to enforce?
10. Define the theory of evolution. Why was the Scopes trial considered a victory for both supporters and opponents of evolution?

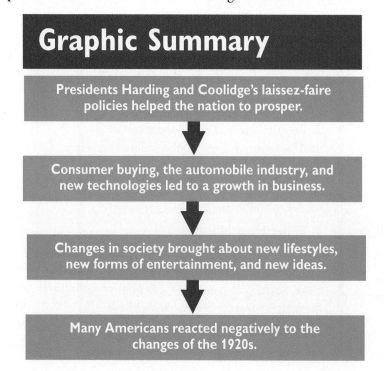

Graphic Summary

Presidents Harding and Coolidge's laissez-faire policies helped the nation to prosper.

Consumer buying, the automobile industry, and new technologies led to a growth in business.

Changes in society brought about new lifestyles, new forms of entertainment, and new ideas.

Many Americans reacted negatively to the changes of the 1920s.

Places to Locate

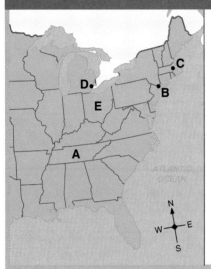

Match the letters on the map with the places that are listed below. Then explain the importance of each place.

1. Boston
2. New York City
3. Ohio
4. Detroit
5. Tennessee

Geographic Theme: Movement What impact do you think Lindbergh's and Earhart's trans-Atlantic flights had on the way Americans viewed the world around them? Explain.

Skill Review

This outline shows how the author might have arranged ideas and notes for the first part of Section 4. Copy the outline onto a separate sheet of paper. Complete the outline by filling in each blank entry. Then complete the outline for Section 4.

IV. Divisions in American Society
  A. RED SCARE
    1.
    2. Wave of fear in the U.S.
    3.
  B. SACCO AND VANZETTI
    1. S. and V. victims of
       Red scare
      a.
      b. anarchists
    2. Sentenced to die
    3. Protests staged
    4.

CRITICAL THINKING

1. **Understanding Economics** Explain the connection between advertising and installment buying. Why might this be dangerous for middle-class and poor families?

2. **Making a Judgment** What impact do you think the assembly line had on factory workers? Explain.

PORTFOLIO OPTIONS

1. **Civics Connection** The judge in the Sacco and Vanzetti case told the jury, "This man [Sacco], although he may not have actually committed the crime, is nevertheless morally culpable [guilty]." Write an essay on the constitutionality of this statement.

2. **Writing Connection** Discuss with other students the role advertising plays in determining what you buy. Find examples of magazine ads that you think are effective. Make a collage and write a paragraph describing the features used in each ad to convince you to buy.

3. **Contemporary Connection** The "roar" of the Roaring Twenties represented many different forces and voices. The same can be said for any era. Make a list of words that might describe American society today and explain each one.

4. **Timeline Connection** Copy the chapter timeline. Which event do you think best characterizes the "Roaring Twenties"? Explain. Add other events from the chapter that you think should be included and explain why.

During the Great Depression, millions of Americans were put out of work. This painting shows job seekers waiting at an employment agency. President Franklin Roosevelt's New Deal programs used federal government spending to help ease the nation's suffering.

1928
1930
1932
1934
1936

1929 Hoover becomes President

1929 Panic of 1929

1929 Great Depression begins

1933 New Deal begins

1932 Franklin Roosevelt elected President

1935 Second New Deal

1936 Roosevelt re-elected

The Depression and the New Deal (1929–1940)

1 The Great Depression

SECTION GUIDE

Main Idea
Following the stock market crash of 1929, the U.S. economy sank into the worst depression in its history.

Goals
As you read, look for answers to these questions:

1 What conditions brought about the stock market collapse in 1929?

2 What were the causes of the Great Depression?

3 What was Hoover's policy on the Depression?

Key Terms
brokerage house
Panic of 1929
Great Depression
relief
Bonus Army

AS HE ACCEPTED the Republican nomination for President in 1928, Herbert Hoover declared, "We shall soon . . . be in sight of the day when poverty will be banished from this country." Rarely has a President's prediction been so wrong.

Hoover Is Elected President

Hoover had served as Secretary of Commerce throughout the Harding and Coolidge years. His Democratic opponent in the 1928 election was New York governor Alfred E. Smith. Smith had an uphill battle ahead of him. He was a Roman Catholic, and a Catholic had never been elected President.

In his campaign speeches Hoover boasted of the nation's prosperity. He predicted that things would get even better. Hoover's now-famous campaign slogan was, "A chicken in every pot, a car in every garage." Before long those words would come back to haunt Hoover. In 1928, however, Americans felt confident under the Republicans. Hoover won by more than six million votes and captured 444 electoral votes to Smith's 87.

Prosperous Times

Indeed, there were many cars in many garages in America when Hoover took office in 1929. Millions of people also owned radios, washing machines, and refrigerators. Americans spent less of their income on food and clothing. They had more money for movies, sports events, and eating out.

The spread of chain stores and installment plans made it easier for people to buy things that in the past they could not afford. Yet there was another reason for the nation's prosperity: the stock market. As you read earlier, a share of stock is a piece of ownership in a corporation. As stock prices rose in the 1920s, more and more people began to buy shares.

1938   **1940**

1939 *The Grapes of Wrath* **published**

It looked like an easy way to make money. Buy some shares, watch the price climb, then sell the shares at a high price. People could buy stock on credit, so it cost them almost no money to make money. Some went heavily into debt in order to buy stock. They counted on using their profits to pay off the debt.

Buying stock was not limited to the wealthy. Americans from all walks of life bought stock. However, most people did not understand the dangers of these "easy" profits. They could sell their shares at high prices only if someone else was willing to buy them.

The 1929 Stock Market Crash

The value of stocks on the New York City stock exchange reached its highest point on September 3, 1929. The good times for Americans seemed here to stay.

Then on Wednesday, October 23, after a week of steadily falling stock prices, there was a sharp drop. The next morning, October 24, panic struck. Stockholders tried to sell thousands of shares before their value dropped even further, but there were few buyers. Prices plunged even lower. At the end of "Black Thursday," as it was called, a record number of nearly 13 million shares had been traded. Stockholders' losses stood at $3 billion. Try-

ing to stop the crisis, the big New York **brokerage houses** —businesses that buy and sell stocks—issued a public statement. "The worst has passed," they said.

In fact, the worst was yet to come. On October 29—"Black Tuesday"—the prosperity of the 1920s came screeching to a halt. By the end of the day, stocks were selling for a fraction of what they had cost a month earlier. Stock in the radio company RCA, which had peaked earlier at $450 a share, dropped to $32. Shares of White Sewing Company, which had been selling at $48 a share, could now be bought for $1 a share.

Terrified stockholders now tried to sell their stock for whatever they could get for it. The more stock people sold, the lower prices went. This week has become known as the **Panic of 1929.**

The Great Depression

For the nation's economy, the stock market crash was the beginning of a terrible chain reaction. The banks were the next to feel the impact. They began to demand that people pay back the money they had borrowed to buy stock. When people could not repay these loans, the banks ran short of money.

That news sent people running to the banks to get their money out. Banks do not usually keep enough cash on hand to pay all their customers at once. The result was that many banks simply closed their doors.

From the time of the Panic until early 1933, about 5,500 banks went out of business. Nothing Hoover did could save the banks—or the people whose life savings vanished when the banks failed.

The chain reaction caused by the crash helped spread financial disaster through the nation and the world. This economic collapse of the 1930s, which caused hardship for millions, is called the **Great Depression.**

A huge crowd swarmed into New York City's Wall Street on the day the stock market crashed. The cartoon at right shows the grief of one unlucky investor.

Causes of the Depression

Even before Hoover's election in 1928, there were signs of serious economic trouble. Few people saw them then, but they are easy to identify now:

(1) *Farm debt.* As you read, farmers had not shared in the prosperity of the 1920s. They could not sell all that they grew. Total farm income fell and farm debts grew. Many farmers had to sell their land, tools, and animals to pay off their debts.

(2) *Consumer debt.* Consumers were buying more and more goods on credit. This sent them deeper and deeper into debt.

(3) *More goods than buyers.* While wages of factory workers rose in the 1920s, the price of manufactured goods rose even faster. The result was that many workers were still too poor to buy the things they made. At the same time, companies were using new production methods to make goods faster. There were now more goods than buyers. As factories lost buyers for their goods, they closed down, and more workers lost their jobs.

(4) *Declining trade.* During the 1920s the United States raised tariffs on imports. Other nations fought back by raising their own tariffs. High tariffs meant less trade—and fewer markets for American goods. This trend continued even after the Depression started. In 1930 Congress passed the Hawley-Smoot Tariff, setting the highest tariff rate in history.

Hoover's Policies

Presidents are always blamed for hard times. As Americans began to feel the crushing impact of the Great Depression, they blamed President Hoover. They thought the government should do something to revive the nation's economy.

Hoover, however, believed the federal government should not interfere with business. Like Presidents before him, he believed the economy would fix itself in time. Hoover felt that government interfer-

CONNECTING WITH WORLD EVENTS

Economic Chaos in Germany

America's Great Depression spread disaster across Europe. In the 1920s the economies of Europe were still recovering from World War I. They relied on American banks for loans to rebuild their industries. When these banks crashed, money for the rebuilding of Europe dried up.

Hardest hit was Germany. It already was billions of dollars in debt from the war. German currency became so worthless some people used it as fuel for their stoves (right). These conditions allowed Adolf Hitler to become Germany's leader in 1933. He promised to restore Germany to its former greatness. The world would soon know the evils of his Nazi empire.

ence would hurt the economy even more. Like many Americans, Hoover worried that relief —aid—from the government would destroy people's spirit and make them dependent on government charity.

Hoover did encourage churches and private charities such as the Salvation Army and the Red Cross to help needy Americans. He asked businesses to work together to find solutions. None could be found.

The number of jobless workers rose from about 1.5 million in 1929 to more than 4 million in 1930. By 1933 one out of every four American workers was out of work. Local governments set up "soup kitchens" that served soup and bread to long lines of people. In some areas only seriously underweight children received free food.

In 1932, as the number of poor Americans continued to rise, Hoover softened his

Lines of unemployed people waiting for free soup and bread became a common sight during the Depression. Soup kitchens saved many people from starvation.

stand on government relief. He backed a law setting up an agency to lend money to states, cities, and towns. The money would be used for public works projects, such as building bridges, that would create jobs. Other money was given to states to pay directly to the needy.

Hoover's efforts, while sincere, were too little. By 1932 many Americans had lost faith in the President. They had also lost faith in the federal government.

The Bonus Army

An event in the summer of 1932 made Hoover even more unpopular. Congress had promised World War I veterans a bonus as a reward for their service. The bonuses were not supposed to be paid until the 1940s. However, since many of the soldiers had no jobs, they asked Congress to pay the bonuses now.

Some of the veterans decided to go to Washington and claim their bonuses in person. They started what was called the Bonus Army. Through May and June 1932 about 17,000 veterans, many with their families, streamed into Washington. They set up camps around the city, some near government buildings.

The House of Representatives passed a bill calling for payment of the bonuses. The Senate, backed by Hoover, rejected the bill. As the size of the Bonus Army grew, Hoover decided to take action. First the Washington police removed veterans from a government building, killing two of them. Hoover then ordered federal troops, some of them mounted on horses and others in tanks, to clear out the camps. Sixty-three people were injured.

Hoover said that he had met "a challenge to the authority of the United States." Yet to many Americans, Hoover's action was another sign that the government did not care about the people.

Two young boys at the Bonus Army camp sit next to signs critical of President Hoover.

SECTION REVIEW

1. Key Terms brokerage house, Panic of 1929, Great Depression, relief, Bonus Army

2. People Herbert Hoover, Alfred E. Smith

3. Comprehension How did the boom times of the 1920s lead to the collapse of the stock market?

4. Comprehension What were the four main causes of the Great Depression?

5. Critical Thinking In what ways might Hoover have handled the Bonus Army differently?

658

SKILLS: Expressing Ideas Through Numbers

LEARN

History books are full of statistics, with good reason. General statements do not paint as clear a picture of events. Read this generalization: "During the Great Depression many Americans lost their jobs." Now look at the chart below. You can make the statement more effective by using statistics from the chart: "During the Great Depression, unemployment increased from 1.6 million in 1929 to 12.8 million in 1933." The idea in the first statement is clear, but adding statistics makes the statement more meaningful. You can give your own history writing more impact if you learn to express ideas through numbers.

Some Economic Statistics of the Great Depression

	1928	1929	1930	1931	1932	1933
Unemployment (in millions of people)	2.0	1.6	4.3	8.0	12.1	12.8
Worker's average weekly wages	$27.80	$28.55	$25.84	$22.62	$17.05	$17.71
Bank closings	499	659	1,352	2,294	1,456	4,004
Federal spending (in billions of dollars)	$2.9	$3.1	$3.3	$3.6	$4.7	$4.6

Source: *Historical Statistics of the United States*

PRACTICE

Refer to the chart to complete the following exercises:

1. Write a general statement to express the change in government spending during the Depression.

2. Write another statement about government spending, but include specific numbers.

3. Write a statement about bank closings using specific numbers.

APPLY

4. Write two paragraphs about the American economy during the Depression. The first paragraph should contain general statements only. The second paragraph should include statistics from the chart.

2 Roosevelt's New Deal

SECTION GUIDE

Main Idea
Franklin D. Roosevelt put forth a new program of federal action to help the nation deal with the Great Depression.

Goals
As you read, look for answers to these questions:

1. What was the main issue in the 1932 election and what was the outcome?

2. What actions did the government take to fight the Great Depression?

Key Terms
fireside chat
New Deal
Hundred Days

IT WAS A HEARTBREAKING and painful disease, one of the most feared of his day. It cut down Franklin Delano Roosevelt at a critical moment of his career. In 1921, less than a year after losing his bid for Vice President on the Democratic ticket, Roosevelt was stricken with polio. The virus left him paralyzed from the waist down. Many people would have given up. Franklin Roosevelt went on to become one of the greatest leaders of this century.

From Governor to President

The newspaper headlines called him "FDR," in part to distinguish Franklin Roosevelt from his distant cousin Theodore, the former President. Like Theodore, he had grown up in a wealthy family. Both graduated from Harvard and studied law at Columbia University. In 1905 Franklin married Eleanor Roosevelt, a niece of Theodore Roosevelt. Franklin practiced law and became active in politics. Under President Wilson he served as Assistant Secretary of the Navy.

When polio struck, FDR drew on his own strength and his wife's to fight back. With exercise and physical therapy, he slowly regained the ability to walk with crutches and heavy braces.

In 1928 Roosevelt ran for governor of New York. In his campaign he showed his strength of character. When giving a speech, he would stand up in his braces, take the arm of his son James, and walk out on the platform. He won the election. In 1930 he was re-elected by a wide margin.

The next election for President came in 1932. With the Depression still dragging on, Hoover's chances for re-election seemed slim. The Democrats sensed victory. They chose Roosevelt as their candidate. In his acceptance speech to the Democratic convention, Roosevelt declared:

FDR is shown on his campaign train in 1932. Next to him is Albert Ritchie, the governor of Maryland, and John Nance Garner, FDR's vice-presidential candidate.

❝I pledge you, I pledge myself, to a new deal for the American people.❞

This painting shows a group of homeless men trying to keep warm in a field outside DeKalb, Illinois. Below, a man living in a Hooverville cooks a meal over an open fire.

FDR won by a landslide. Now the man who had taught himself to stand again would try to help the nation do the same.

A Nation in Crisis

When Franklin D. Roosevelt came into power, millions of families had little or no money for food or shelter. The stories were tragic. Hospitals reported cases of starvation in major cities. In Philadelphia, one family went without food for two days. Finally the father started pulling up dandelions from a local park for dinner. In a school in a coal-mining town, relief workers found that 99 percent of the children were underweight.

Chicago officials reported that several hundred homeless women were living in parks. In 1932 around 200,000 boys and girls, mostly teenagers, were living on their own throughout the nation. In cities and farm towns, the homeless built shacks of tin and cardboard. They nicknamed their shelters "Hoovervilles," a reference to the man they blamed for their misery.

This was the crisis that Roosevelt faced as he was sworn in as President on March 4, 1933. In his First Inaugural Address, Roosevelt offered something that people greatly needed: hope. In one of the most famous lines in American speechmaking, he declared:

❝ The only thing we have to fear is fear itself. ❞

Roosevelt Takes Action

The President had to act quickly. The first problem was the banking crisis.

More than 5,000 banks had shut down. Some had simply run out of money. Others—including all the banks in Illinois and New York—had been ordered closed in order to stop people from withdrawing all their money.

Roosevelt ordered a "bank holiday"—a four-day shutdown of all banks. During that time, federal officials spread out across the country to check the finances of every bank. Banks that were not in danger of failing were allowed to reopen. The government worked to help troubled banks to reopen later.

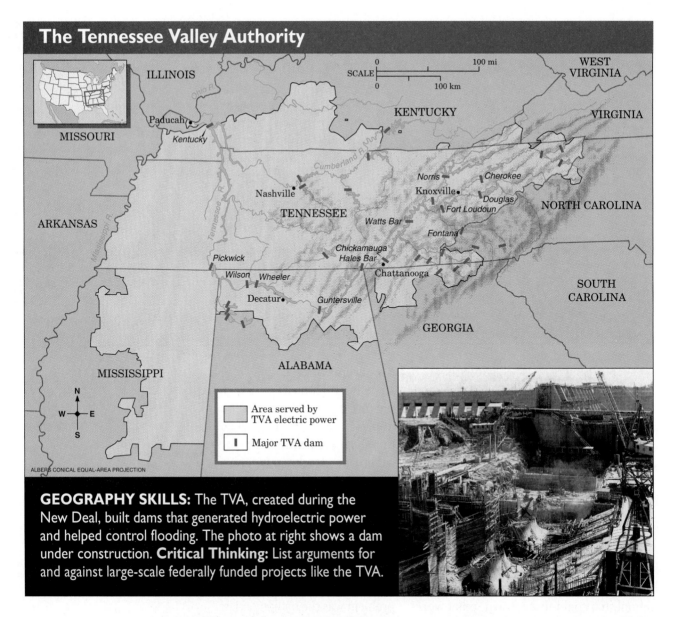

The Tennessee Valley Authority

ILLINOIS

MISSOURI

Paducah

Kentucky

ARKANSAS

Nashville

TENNESSEE

Pickwick

Wilson Wheeler

Decatur

Guntersville

MISSISSIPPI

ALABAMA

KENTUCKY

WEST VIRGINIA

VIRGINIA

Norris Cherokee

Knoxville Douglas

Fort Loudoun

Watts Bar

Fontana

NORTH CAROLINA

Chickamauga
Hales Bar

Chattanooga

GEORGIA

SOUTH CAROLINA

SCALE 0   100 mi
        0   100 km

Ohio R.

Cumberland R.

Tennessee R.

Mississippi R.

N
W — E
S

Area served by TVA electric power

Major TVA dam

ALBERS CONICAL EQUAL-AREA PROJECTION

GEOGRAPHY SKILLS: The TVA, created during the New Deal, built dams that generated hydroelectric power and helped control flooding. The photo at right shows a dam under construction. **Critical Thinking:** List arguments for and against large-scale federally funded projects like the TVA.

On Sunday, March 12, the day before the banks were to reopen, FDR gave the first of many fireside chats to the nation. These were radio talks in which he spoke to the American people in a simple, friendly style. FDR used the chats to explain and gain support for his policies. In his first fireside chat, he tried to convince Americans to return their money to the banks. "I can assure you that it is safer to keep your money in a re-opened bank than under the mattress," FDR said.

Roosevelt's speech helped restore public confidence in the banking system. Within a week, customers returned to the banks more than $600 million that they had been keeping in their homes. A top Roosevelt aide later said that American capitalism "was saved in eight days."

The New Deal

During the campaign FDR had said, "It is common sense to take a method and try it. If it fails, admit it and try another. But above all, try something." He also had pledged a "new deal" for Americans. Following this approach, Roosevelt and his advisers came up with programs that

Major Programs of the Hundred Days, 1933

FERA (Federal Emergency Relief Act)	Provided federal money for relief projects to the roughly 13 million unemployed.
PWA (Public Works Administration)	Created jobs by putting people to work building highways, bridges, and other public works.
AAA (Agricultural Adjustment Administration)	Regulated farm production and promoted soil conservation.
TVA (Tennessee Valley Authority)	Planned development of the Tennessee Valley region.
CCC (Civilian Conservation Corps)	Hired young men to plant trees, build dams, and work on other conservation projects.
FDIC (Federal Deposit Insurance Corporation)	Protected the money of depositors in insured banks.
NRA (National Recovery Administration)	Regulated industry and raised wages and prices.

CHART SKILLS: This chart shows the major programs of the Hundred Days. **Critical Thinking:** How did programs like the PWA and CCC help both those who were hired and the nation as a whole?

changed forever the federal government's relationship with its citizens. Roosevelt's program to end the Great Depression was called the New Deal.

Roosevelt sent Congress a pile of new bills, many of which were passed with little debate. This famous session of Congress from March 9 to mid-June of 1933 is called the Hundred Days.

The laws passed by Congress during the Hundred Days had three major goals, known as the "three R's." These were:

(1) *relief* programs to meet the needs of the hungry and jobless,

(2) *recovery* programs to help agriculture and industry, and

(3) *reforms* to change the way the nation's economy worked. FDR wanted to make sure that Americans would never again face a crisis like the Great Depression.

Voters Support Roosevelt

In its first year, the New Deal restored hope. It provided relief to thousands of desperate people. Said one cattle rancher, "I think we'd just pack up and move out and leave our stock to starve if the government hadn't stepped in." Many families regained their dignity with the help of new government-sponsored jobs.

In the 1934 congressional elections, voters had a chance to show what they thought of Roosevelt's New Deal. They signaled their approval by electing even more Democrats to Congress.

Yet while the Hundred Days legislation had bandaged the nation's most serious wounds, it had not cured the patient. Many Americans did not feel the relief that FDR had promised. They soon began to demand that the government do more.

SECTION REVIEW

1. Key Terms fireside chat, New Deal, Hundred Days

2. People and Places Franklin D. Roosevelt, New York

3. Comprehension Why did Roosevelt declare a bank holiday?

4. Comprehension What "three R's" were the goals of the Hundred Days?

5. Critical Thinking What psychological factors played a part in Franklin D. Roosevelt's victory in the 1932 presidential election?

3 The New Deal Continues

SECTION GUIDE

Main Idea
Despite opposition from different sources, more New Deal laws were passed in 1935.

Goals
As you read, look for answers to these questions:

1 Who opposed the New Deal and why?

2 What programs were adopted in the Second New Deal?

3 What were the issues and results of the court-packing fight?

Key Terms
Dust Bowl
Social Security Act
Second New Deal
Wagner Act

Huey Long, shown speaking at a rally, was a powerful rival of FDR.

N HARD TIMES, leaders sometimes gain power for themselves by playing on people's fears. Huey Long, "the Kingfish," was one of them. His rise to political power seemed unstoppable—until an assassin's bullet cut him down.

Huey Long Attacks the New Deal

Elected governor of Louisiana at age 35, Long built new schools, hospitals, and roads. However, as governor and later as a U.S. senator, Long ruled the state like a dictator. He smashed his enemies and controlled Louisiana's politics, courts, and police. He also bragged that he would be President one day.

The Kingfish saw his chance as FDR neared the end of his first term. The Depression had not ended and the effects of the New Deal still had not reached many parts of the nation. Long offered a solution more radical than the New Deal. He called it "Share Our Wealth." It guaranteed each family a yearly income, money to buy a home, free education, and low-cost food. To pay for the plan, the wealthy would be taxed heavily.

Share Our Wealth clubs formed throughout the country during 1935. More than 4.5 million people joined. FDR's followers were greatly concerned as Long stepped up his attacks on the New Deal. In his climb to power, however, Long had made one enemy too many. In September 1935 he was shot and killed by the son-in-law of a man whose political career Long had ruined.

Conservative Opponents

People like Long attacked the New Deal for not going far enough to help people hurt by the Depression. Other critics thought the New Deal went too far. They opposed the growth of the federal government that came with the New Deal. They warned that the powers of state and local governments were being weakened. They also asked how the government would pay for all the programs that Congress had passed. Lastly, they saw the New Deal approach as a threat to the American tradition of solving problems without government help.

In 1934 some wealthy Americans, business leaders, and conservative Democrats formed a group known as the Liberty League. The Liberty League declared that the New Deal was a

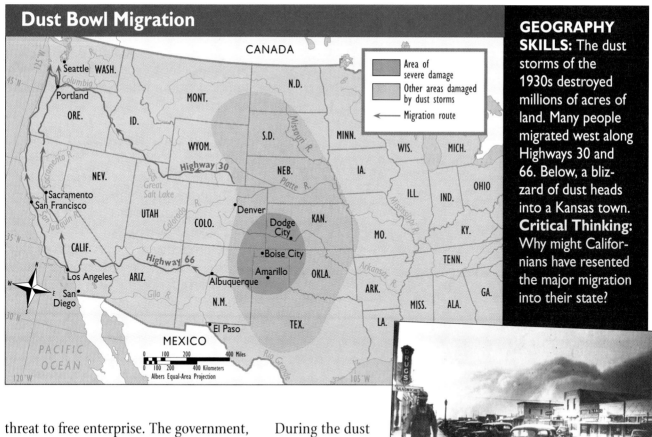

Dust Bowl Migration

CANADA

Legend:
- Area of severe damage
- Other areas damaged by dust storms
- ← Migration route

Seattle WASH.
Portland
ORE.
Columbia
N.D.
MONT.
ID.
S.D.
MINN.
WIS.
MICH.
WYOM.
Highway 30
NEB.
IA.
Missouri R.
Platte R.
NEV.
Great Salt Lake
Sacramento
San Francisco
UTAH
Colorado R.
COLO.
Denver
Dodge City
KAN.
ILL.
IND.
OHIO
MO.
KY.
CALIF.
Highway 66
Boise City
Amarillo
OKLA.
TENN.
Los Angeles
ARIZ.
Albuquerque
Arkansas R.
ARK.
Gila R.
N.M.
TEX.
MISS.
ALA.
GA.
San Diego
El Paso
LA.
PACIFIC OCEAN
MEXICO
Rio Grande
San Joaquin R.
Sacramento R.

0 100 200 400 Miles
0 100 200 400 Kilometers
Albers Equal-Area Projection

125°W · 45°N · 35°N · 30°N · 120°W · 105°W

GEOGRAPHY SKILLS: The dust storms of the 1930s destroyed millions of acres of land. Many people migrated west along Highways 30 and 66. Below, a blizzard of dust heads into a Kansas town. **Critical Thinking:** Why might Californians have resented the major migration into their state?

threat to free enterprise. The government, it said, should leave business alone.

The arguments of the Liberty League did little to change people's minds about the New Deal. Many Americans cared little about the rights of businesses at a time when families could barely keep food on the table.

The Dust Bowl

For many Americans, hunger was still a full-time problem. Nowhere was the threat worse in the mid-1930s than in the Midwest. Adding to the pain of the Depression, farmers in Kansas, Oklahoma, Texas, Colorado, and New Mexico were suffering a terrible drought that had lasted for years. The effects of the drought were made worse by farming methods unsuitable for the climate. As a result, winds whipped up the dry fields into sweeping curtains of dust. These dust storms buried farms throughout a 50-million acre region that became known as the Dust Bowl.

During the dust storms, day became night as the walls of dust rolled in on winds up to 60 miles an hour. In one such "black blizzard," Dodge City, Kansas, was in total darkness for 40 minutes. Semi-darkness lasted for another three hours. Dust storms ripped through the Plains for years until both rain and better farming methods brought relief.

The storms brought on a major migration. Acres and acres of crops had been buried under layers of dust. Ruined farmers loaded their belongings onto their trucks and set off with their families to find work. Many headed west along Route 66, the main highway to California. California's farms needed workers, they were told.

As newcomers poured in, however, California farm towns became overcrowded. Families lived in tiny shacks. By the end of the 1930s about a million Dust Bowl refugees had made their way to California

This mural by William Gropper was funded by the Works Progress Administration, a New Deal agency that created jobs for artists. It shows men building a dam.

and other Pacific states. Because many had come from Oklahoma, they were sometimes called "Okies."

Social Security

The suffering of Americans such as these, plus the attacks of critics such as Huey Long, led FDR to take further action. In 1935 he tackled the enormous question of how to take care of Americans who were most at risk.

At the top of the list were the nation's elderly. Many had watched as bank failures and the stock market crash took their life savings. Some became homeless. Some had to beg for food.

In August 1935 Congress passed one of the most important bills of the century—the Social Security Act. Under this act, workers and employers made payments into a special fund. Then, when workers retired, they received a monthly payment from the fund. The act also set up an insurance program for laid-off work-

ers. Finally, it gave help to disabled workers and to families of workers who died.

Social Security became a permanent program of the federal government. It continues to provide help to millions of Americans today.

The Second New Deal

Social Security was one of a list of reforms that FDR urged Congress to pass in 1935. That spring and summer Congress passed a flood of programs that became known as the Second New Deal.

The programs of the Second New Deal (see the chart on the next page) reshaped American life for the next half-century. Among those programs was the Wagner Act, or the National Labor Relations Act. This law protected the right of workers to form unions. It also set up a board to help settle problems between workers and employers.

Other laws put people to work building dams, parks, and bridges and bringing electricity to most of the country. Several of the key projects were aimed at protecting the nation's natural resources.

The Election of 1936

With the President still popular, the Democrats in 1936 nominated Roosevelt for a second term. The Republicans chose Kansas governor Alfred M. Landon to oppose him.

Republicans accused the Democrats of spending too much money and endangering private enterprise. "For the first time," the Republican Party stated, liberty and opportunity in America were "threatened by government itself."

Americans did not agree. FDR won by a landslide, which convinced him that Americans wanted the reforms to continue. In his Second Inaugural Address in 1937, Roosevelt said, "I see one third of a nation ill-housed, ill-clad, ill-nourished." He now set his sights on helping this "one third."

Major Programs of the Second New Deal, 1935

● **WPA** (Works Progress Administration)	Established large-scale national works programs to create jobs.
● **REA** (Rural Electrification Administration)	Brought electricity to rural areas.
● **NYA** (National Youth Administration)	Set up job programs for young people and helped them continue education.
● **Wagner Act**	Protected labor's right to form unions and set up a board to hear labor disputes.
● **Social Security Act**	Provided workers with unemployment insurance and retirement benefits.

CHART SKILLS: Social Security was one of the New Deal's most important programs. **Critical Thinking:** How do you think these programs helped FDR get re-elected in 1936?

Battling the Supreme Court

From the high point of the election, however, Roosevelt's presidency took a downturn. He had failed to win over nine very important people: the justices of the Supreme Court. These men threatened to destroy his New Deal programs.

One by one the Court had struck down laws and programs that it said would give the federal government too much power. To combat the Court, in 1937 the President asked Congress to pass a bill allowing him to increase the number of justices from nine to fifteen. He planned to appoint six new justices who shared his ideas about government. The additions would give him the majority votes he needed to save some of his programs from being overturned.

Roosevelt's "court-packing" bill, as it was called, met with harsh criticism. Opponents of the bill said it interfered with the system of checks and balances. Congress agreed and did not pass the bill.

As it turned out, retirements and deaths on the Court allowed Roosevelt to appoint seven new justices. FDR's image, however, was badly damaged by his proposed bill.

The New Deal Slows Down

Presidents, no matter how popular, often have trouble holding public support for their programs during their second term. Roosevelt was no different. People's hopes had soared so high in the early years that there was bound to be disappointment later on.

After the court-packing attempt, some people began to suspect that Roosevelt was power-hungry. Others questioned his political wisdom. In addition, the Depression still hung on to the country like a long-term illness. Excitement over the New Deal began to fade. FDR himself did not realize it at the time, but the New Deal was coming to an end.

SECTION REVIEW

1. Key Terms Dust Bowl, Social Security Act, Second New Deal, Wagner Act

2. People Huey Long, Alfred Landon

3. Comprehension What different arguments against the New Deal were raised by Huey Long and by business leaders?

4. Comprehension What were the main programs passed by Congress in the Second New Deal?

5. Critical Thinking How would Roosevelt's plan to "pack" the Supreme Court have challenged the principle of checks and balances?

4 Life in the Depression Years

SECTION GUIDE

Main Idea
Movies, sports, and other kinds of entertainment helped people escape from the grimness of their daily lives.

Goals
As you read, look for answers to these questions:

❶ How were families, women, and African Americans affected by the Depression?

❷ What kinds of entertainment were popular in the 1930s?

❸ What were the effects of the New Deal?

Key Terms
Black Cabinet
welfare state

ONE FACE MORE THAN ANY OTHER has become the symbol of the Great Depression. She is captured in a famous photograph, shown at the bottom of this page. The photographer was Dorothea Lange, who traveled the nation documenting the lives of Americans during the Depression. The woman's face is tanned and tired. There are lines around her troubled eyes. Her two young children are at her sides, hiding their faces from the camera. The woman's expression tells a story, a story of quiet despair.

A Difficult Time for Families

Family life was deeply shaken by the Depression. At a time when they were expected to provide for their families, many men were deeply ashamed when they lost their jobs and were forced to accept welfare. Some men had to leave home to find work in another city. This woman's story was not unusual: "My husband went north about three months ago to try his luck. . . . For five weeks we have had no word from him."

These strains took their toll on women. As men lost their jobs, working women came under pressure to give up their jobs to men. Some New Deal projects would not hire a woman if her husband had a job. A 1936 poll showed that 82 percent of Americans thought that wives of employed men should not work. Yet poverty often forced wives to take jobs, usually at low pay. About one-third of working wives took jobs as servants.

Women Leaders

A figure of hope to women of the time was Eleanor Roosevelt. The First Lady took an active role in New Deal planning. She visited coal mines, work camps, and hospitals around the nation to find out how New Deal projects were working. She told the President what she learned and suggested further action.

Franklin Roosevelt agreed with his wife that women should play a greater role in politics. In 1933 he named

Dorothea Lange's photo of a migrant mother with her children.

Frances Perkins the Secretary of Labor. Perkins was the first woman ever to serve in the Cabinet. FDR was also the first President to appoint a woman as minister to a foreign country.

African Americans

After the Civil War, African Americans for many years had voted Republican out of loyalty to the memory of Abraham Lincoln. By the mid-1930s, however, New Deal programs had won over many African Americans to the Democratic Party.

FDR made slow but steady progress in bringing African Americans into government. Again with the support of his wife, Roosevelt appointed several black advisers. These officials became known as the Black Cabinet. They included William H. Hastie and Robert C. Weaver, who worked in the Department of the Interior. Mary McLeod Bethune, a southern educator, ran the New Deal's job-training program for minority youth.

Art and Literature

The real-life dramas of the 1930s enriched the art and literature of the time. Painter William Gropper felt that America's capitalist system had failed. His paintings showed subjects such as corrupt politicians. Thomas Hart Benton, on the other hand, had great faith in the American spirit. His aim was to paint "American life as known and felt by ordinary Americans."

In 1936 writer James Agee and photographer Walker Evans traveled to the South to record the daily life of white tenant farmers. The results were published in 1941 as *Let Us Now Praise Famous Men.* Agee and Evans found people who lived in extreme poverty yet who valued their dignity.

Dignity in the face of disaster was also part of the most famous novel of the decade, John Steinbeck's *The Grapes of Wrath* (1939). Forced to move out of the Dust Bowl, the Joad family headed to California only to meet new hardships.

Entertainment

Not everyone suffered terribly during the Depression. Through luck, wisdom, hard work, the help of relatives, or help from the government, some Americans were able to hang on to whatever they had.

In New York City, hotels, restaurants, and shops continued to draw wealthy customers. Huge mansions were being built in the exciting young city of Hollywood. In clubs across the country, people danced the nights away to the magnificent music of Duke Ellington, George Gershwin, and Benny Goodman.

If most people could not enjoy this kind of life, they could at least watch it on the movie screen. The film industry boomed during the 1930s. At 25 cents for adults and a dime for children, a night at the movies was still affordable to most people. More than 100 million Americans went to the movies every week during the 1930s.

Movies portrayed both the hardship and the high living of the time. Following *The Grapes of Wrath,* another story of human tragedy was made into a movie. Margaret Mitchell's Civil War drama *Gone With the Wind* brought audiences to tears. For those who wanted to forget life's troubles, one could watch Fred Astaire and Ginger Rogers, the world's favorite dancers, spin gracefully across the screen.

For laughs a viewer could do no better than to see *My Little Chickadee,* starring Mae West and the comedian W. C. Fields. *The Wizard of Oz,* starring Judy Garland, was one of many musicals that were filmed

Mary McLeod Bethune was the first African American woman to head a federal agency.

Fred Astaire and Ginger Rogers

during this period. Adventure films such as *King Kong* were popular, as were cowboy and gangster movies. Walt Disney and his studio created cartoons featuring Mickey and Minnie Mouse and Donald Duck.

Sports Legends of the 1930s

On October 1, 1932, George Herman Ruth stepped to the plate in Wrigley Field in Chicago. After two strikes, some say he pointed at the pitcher. Others say he pointed to the center field wall to show where he was going to hit the ball. Whatever the truth, "the Babe" smacked a home run, helping the New York Yankees defeat the Chicago Cubs in the World Series.

Ruth's skill, wit, and love of the game of baseball made him a popular hero. When asked to justify how he could make more money than President Hoover, Ruth is said to have wisecracked, "I had a better year than he did."

The feats of Babe Ruth and other sports heroes of the 1930s are still thrilling to

sports fans today. For African Americans, it was a time of special pride, thanks to the triumphs of two remarkable athletes, Jesse Owens and Joe Louis.

The 1936 Olympic Games were being held in Berlin, Germany. Adolf Hitler and his Nazi Party ruled Germany. Hitler saw the Olympics as a way to prove his racist belief that the Germanic peoples were better than all others.

The Americans sent to the games one of the greatest athletes of all time—track and field star Jesse Owens, an African American from Cleveland, Ohio. With Hitler watching in the stands, Owens and his fellow black athletes left their opponents in the dust. Nine of ten African Americans in the Games came back with medals. A humiliated Hitler left the stadium before the awards ceremonies. African Americans celebrated the triumph of their athletes and the victory over racism.

That same year, a German and an African American faced off in another much-awaited contest. Germany's top heavyweight boxer, Max Schmeling, defeated U.S. champ Joe Louis in a 12-round bout. Louis "fought like an amateur," Schmeling sneered. The defeat was Louis's first.

In 1938 Louis, the son of an Alabama sharecropper, delivered a sharp blow to Germany's "master race." In a rematch,

Babe Didrikson, shown here throwing a javelin, is considered by many to be the greatest female athlete of this century.

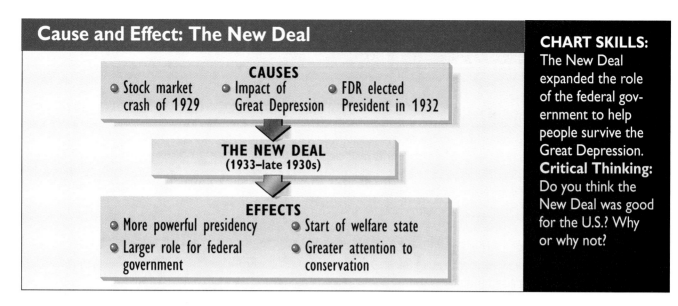

Cause and Effect: The New Deal

CAUSES
- Stock market crash of 1929
- Impact of Great Depression
- FDR elected President in 1932

THE NEW DEAL
(1933–late 1930s)

EFFECTS
- More powerful presidency
- Larger role for federal government
- Start of welfare state
- Greater attention to conservation

CHART SKILLS: The New Deal expanded the role of the federal government to help people survive the Great Depression. **Critical Thinking:** Do you think the New Deal was good for the U.S.? Why or why not?

Louis knocked out Schmeling in the first round. America's "Brown Bomber" would not be defeated again until 1950.

Effects of the New Deal

As the 1930s came to a close, the Depression still plagued the United States and nations around the world. Dictators took power in Germany and Japan by promising to build their countries into powerful empires. In 1939 Hitler's Germany invaded Poland, plunging Europe and later the United States into World War II. In the end it would be wartime spending, more than the New Deal, that finally lifted the nation out of the Great Depression.

While the New Deal did not solve all the nation's problems in the 1930s, it did help people survive the Depression. The New Deal had four major effects:

(1) It made the presidency more important and more powerful.

(2) It greatly expanded the role of the federal government in American life.

(3) It established the **welfare state** —a system in which the government takes on responsibility for the economic security of its people.

(4) It brought greater national attention to conservation and other environmental concerns.

To this day, the New Deal is both praised and criticized. Some people see FDR as the father of big, wasteful government. Others look to him as a model for strong, modern leadership.

A comment in a British magazine may have best summed up the impact of FDR and the New Deal: "Mr. Roosevelt may have given the wrong answers to many of his problems. But he is at least the first President of modern America who has asked the right questions."

SECTION REVIEW

1. Key Terms Black Cabinet, welfare state

2. People Eleanor Roosevelt, Frances Perkins, Mary McLeod Bethune, John Steinbeck, Babe Ruth, Jesse Owens

3. Comprehension How did the Depression harm family life?

4. Comprehension What were some highlights of the entertainment industry during the 1930s?

5. Critical Thinking List the four major effects of the New Deal. Which is the most important to you? Explain.

In the late 1800s African Americans were forced out of professional baseball. During that same period, black southerners began moving to northern cities for jobs in industry. These factors led to the rise of black baseball leagues.

This map shows major cities with black teams. Each city had a black population large and wealthy enough to support a team. Most teams were owned and run by African Americans.

To raise money, teams needed to play as many games as possible. Thus they traveled constantly. Stopping in big cities and small towns, they played other black teams or white semi-professional teams. During the winter off-season, some black players joined leagues in the Caribbean or Central America.

The integration of major league baseball in 1947 brought an end to the black leagues. Yet it also gave black players a new chance to show their abilities. Six of the first seven National League rookies of the year were former black league players.

Satchel Paige

BLACK BASEBALL CITIES

Mont.   N.D.   Min

Wyo.   S.D.

Ia

Neb.

Ut.   Colo.   Kansas City

Kan.

Ariz.

N.Mex.   Ok.

Tex.

Houston

MEXICO

This map shows major cities that had black baseball teams.

The Pittsburgh Crawfords and their team bus. Black teams sometimes ate and slept on their buses when white-owned businesses refused to serve them.

The Cincinnati Tigers in 1937.

Andrew 'Rube' Foster, founder of the first black baseball league.

James "Cool Papa" Bell, regarded as the fastest man in baseball.

A ticket for a 1919 league game and a press pass for the 1942 National Colored All Star game.

CRITICAL THINKING

1. How was the rise of black baseball leagues tied to migration patterns?
2. How did black teams survive financially?
3. **Geographic Theme: Movement** Would the rise of black baseball leagues have occurred without the migration of southern blacks to northern cities? Explain.

Summary

1. When Herbert Hoover took office in 1929, the economy was booming. However, a stock market crash that year helped drive the United States into the Great Depression. Millions of people were left jobless. Hoover believed the economy would fix itself, but Americans wanted more help from the federal government.

2. Franklin Roosevelt was elected President in 1932. He immediately took action to stop a banking crisis. Congress then passed most of the New Deal, which was FDR's program to end the Depression.

3. Some critics of the New Deal thought it did not go far enough to help people. Others thought it gave too much power to the federal government. In 1935 Congress passed the Second New Deal, which included Social Security. Excitement over the New Deal began to fade during FDR's second term.

4. FDR brought more women and African Americans into government. Movies, sports, and other forms of entertainment helped people forget the hard times. The New Deal had lasting effects, including a greater role for the federal government in people's lives and the establishment of a welfare state.

Review

KEY TERMS

Define the terms in each of the following pairs:
1. Hundred Days; New Deal
2. relief; welfare state
3. Panic of 1929; Bonus Army
4. Dust Bowl; Social Security Act

COMPREHENSION

1. What factors led to the stock market crash?
2. What were the four major causes of the Great Depression?
3. What did the members of the Bonus Army want? What was the outcome of the crisis?
4. What were the results of the "bank holiday" declared by Roosevelt in 1933?
5. What were the three major goals of the Hundred Days legislation?
6. What was Huey Long's response to the New Deal? What did conservative critics say about the New Deal?
7. How was Social Security funded? What was it set up to do?
8. Why did Roosevelt try to "pack" the Supreme Court? What were the results of his proposal?
9. How did Roosevelt bring women and African Americans into leadership positions in the federal government?
10. What were the four major effects of the New Deal?

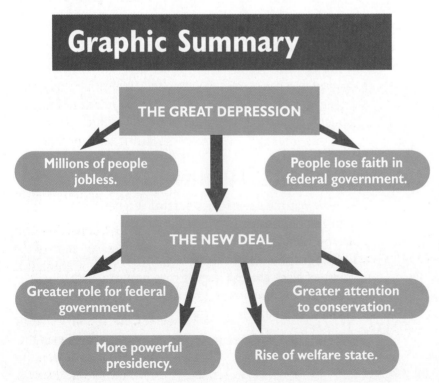

Graphic Summary

THE GREAT DEPRESSION

- Millions of people jobless.
- People lose faith in federal government.

THE NEW DEAL

- Greater role for federal government.
- More powerful presidency.
- Rise of welfare state.
- Greater attention to conservation.

Places to Locate

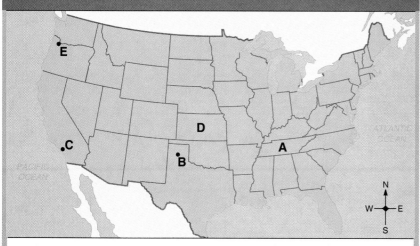

Match the letters on the map with the places that are listed below. Then explain the importance of each place.
1. Los Angeles, California
2. Portland, Oregon
3. Tennessee
4. Amarillo, Texas
5. Kansas

Geographic Theme: Regions Why were the 1930s especially hard on farmers of the Great Plains? Explain.

Skill Review

Study the paragraph below summarizing the stock market crash of 1929. Then rewrite the paragraph, using statistics from the chapter to make the paragraph more meaningful.

On Wednesday, October 23, stock market prices dropped sharply. The next day, "Black Thursday," stockholders panicked and began trading shares in record numbers. Total losses were huge. On October 29, "Black Tuesday," stocks dropped even further. People continued to sell their stocks for whatever price they could get. This frantic selling led to further price drops in the market. The week the stock market crashed became known as the Panic of 1929.

CRITICAL THINKING

1. Making a Judgment Do you agree with the way Hoover handled the Bonus Army? Why or why not?

2. Analyzing a Quotation Franklin Roosevelt once said, "To dole out relief is to administer a narcotic, a subtle destroyer of the human spirit." What did he mean? Do you agree or disagree? Explain.

3. Forming a Hypothesis How might Liberty Leaguers have defended their claim that New Deal programs were a threat to free enterprise? Explain.

PORTFOLIO OPTIONS

1. Civics Connection What role, if any, do you think the federal government should play in helping the poor and unemployed? Organize a class debate on the issue, with one side arguing in favor of government help and the other against.

2. Writing Connection Imagine that you are a speechwriter for one of the presidential candidates in the 1932 election. Write a speech to explain the candidate's views on how to help the nation recover from the Depression.

3. Contemporary Connection Discuss with the class the state of the economy today. Do you think it is possible for another Great Depression to occur? Explain.

4. Timeline Connection Copy the chapter timeline. Which event do you think was most significant for the recovery of the nation? Explain.

By the early 1900s, the United States was home to people from every corner of the world. Here a congregation of Chinese Americans poses in front of a church.

福音堂

1900

1910

1920

1908 Congress cuts Japanese immigration to the United States

1911 Society of American Indians formed

1917 Jones Act grants Puerto Ricans U.S. citizenship

A More Diverse America
(1900–1940)

1 Coming to America

SECTION GUIDE

Main Idea

Immigrants from overseas and from other nations in the Western Hemisphere sought new opportunities in the United States.

Goals

As you read, look for answers to these questions:

1 For what reasons did immigrants come to the United States, and what kind of life did they find here?

2 What limits did the United States put on immigration in the early 1900s?

Key Terms

anti-Semitism
Chinese Exclusion Act
Jones Act
quota
barrio

I N THE EARLY 1920s President Calvin Coolidge declared, "America must be kept American." People knew what Coolidge meant. The nation should be like most of the people he grew up with in rural Vermont. They were white, Protestant, and they farmed the land.

Yet what about African American auto workers in Detroit? Were they not Americans? Hollywood's Jewish filmmakers, New York's Italian restaurant owners—were they not Americans? Were Native Americans, Chinese Americans, and Puerto Ricans less "American" than Coolidge?

What Is an American?

America's diverse population is nothing new. If you traveled the country in Coolidge's day, you would have found that Americans came in all colors, religions, and cultures.

What worried Coolidge and many like him was a growth in immigration that had begun in the late 1800s. Also during this time, large numbers of African Americans in the South began moving to the North. These trends were changing the face of America. They forced the country to struggle with this question: What is an American?

1930	1940

1937 *Their Eyes Were Watching God* published

1924 Johnson-Reed Act passed

1924 Indian Citizenship Act passed

1934 Indian Reorganization Act

PRESENT ▶ A CHANGING AMERICA

CONNECTING WITH THE

If you could take a snapshot of America in 1920 and 1990 you would have two very different pictures. In 1920 the nation was at the end of a huge immigration wave. Most of those immigrants were European. Immigration was sharply reduced until the 1960s. Then waves of immigrants came from Mexico, South America, the Caribbean, and Asia.

As you can see from the charts, the 1920 Census did not even include a figure for Hispanics (people from Spanish-speaking countries). In 1990, Hispanics were the fastest-growing minority group. The charts also show that whites make up a smaller majority of Americans than they used to.

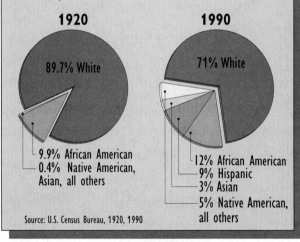

1920

89.7% White

9.9% African American
0.4% Native American, Asian, all others

1990

71% White

12% African American
9% Hispanic
3% Asian
5% Native American, all others

Source: U.S. Census Bureau, 1920, 1990

An Italian immigrant and her child in 1905.

New Immigrants

Most immigrants who came to America before the 1860s were the "old immigrants" from northern and western Europe. They were Irish, English, Swedish, and German. After 1860, however, "new immigrants" from eastern and southern Europe began arriving in large numbers.

Smaller numbers of immigrants crossed the Pacific to reach the western shores of the United States. They included Chinese, Japanese, and Filipinos. Their dream was to work hard, save their wages, and then bring their families to America.

In 1920, 14 million of the nation's 106 million people had been born outside the United States. Some newcomers found the land of their dreams. Others found new troubles. In the rest of this section you will read about some examples of these groups.

Italian Immigrants

Between 1880 and 1920 more than 4 million Italians entered the United States. No group had come in such large numbers in such a short time. Most Italian immigrants settled in cities along the East Coast, the Great Lakes, and the coast of California. By 1900 most big cities in the Northeast had a "Little Italy"—a neighborhood with large numbers of Italian Americans.

Italian immigrants began their life in the United States as unskilled workers. They worked for the railroads in the West, in the quarries and mills in New England, and in the coal and steel towns of Ohio and Pennsylvania. In time they opened shops, restaurants, and other businesses. Those with special skills became roofers, electricians, and plumbers. In time many Italians took important places in American society.

Because so many came so quickly, Italian immigrants stirred up fear among nativists. Italian Americans met with prejudice because they were Catholic. They were accused of spreading crime and taking jobs from other Americans.

678

Asian Immigrants

Italian and Jewish immigrants faced prejudice in the United States partly because they were not Protestant. Yet because they were white, many could assimilate and succeed. This was not true for immigrants of other races.

(1) *Chinese.* The first large group of Asians to immigrate to America were Chinese in the mid-1800s. As you have read, during the California Gold Rush of 1849 the trickle of Chinese immigrants to the United States turned into a flood. During the 1860s Chinese laborers came to the United States to help build the transcontinental railroad. When the railroad was completed, many decided to stay. Many Chinese immigrants became farmers, coal miners, and owners of small businesses.

(2) *Japanese.* The history of Japanese immigration to the United States begins in Hawaii. Starting in 1885 thousands of Japanese laborers came to Hawaii to work on U.S.-owned sugar plantations. The United States annexed Hawaii in 1898. By then nearly half of the people in Hawaii were Japanese immigrants.

Other Japanese immigrants settled on the U.S. mainland. Many became successful farmers in California. Some worked in fisheries in Washington. Others became miners in Wyoming. Japanese American communities across the nation included doctors, teachers, and business owners.

Jewish Immigrants

You have already read that millions of Jews fled Russia and Russian-ruled Eastern Europe to escape pogroms and other mistreatment. Jewish immigrants, mostly families, settled largely in New York City. They lived in crowded tenements and found low-paying jobs in sweatshops.

They also faced **anti-Semitism.** (Anti-Semitism is discrimination against Jews.) Jewish immigrants were barred from most housing, jobs, and social clubs. When faced with such barriers, however, Jews helped themselves. They enrolled in night schools and public schools. They later entered colleges and universities. Many Jewish immigrants found they could succeed if they gave up old-country customs for American ones. Others succeeded without giving up their culture.

Jews would become one of the highest-achieving groups in the country. They excelled in many fields. Many became leaders in business, banking, and many other professions. Jews played a large role in the rise of Hollywood's movie industry.

This 1920s photograph shows a market in New York City's Lower East Side, where many Jewish immigrants settled.

(3) *Filipinos.* Large numbers of Filipinos (people from the Philippines) began arriving in the United States after 1898. The United States took over the Philippines from Spain in that year. Filipinos were not U.S. citizens but they could enter the United States freely. Many Filipinos settled in Washington and Oregon.

Asian immigrants faced some of the worst treatment of any immigrants. They had appearances, languages, religions, foods, and holidays different from those common in the United States. Many whites looked down on Asian immigrants and shut them out of society.

As the number of Asian immigrants grew, a wave of anti-Asian feeling spread across the nation. In 1882 Congress passed the Chinese Exclusion Act. It banned Chinese immigration for ten years. In 1902 the ban was made permanent. Japanese immigration was cut sharply in 1908 and banned entirely in the 1920s. In 1934 Congress passed a law promising to grant the Philippines independence within ten years. Under this law, Filipinos in America were considered aliens, or foreigners. The law also limited Filipino immigration to 50 people a year.

Puerto Ricans

People who came from Puerto Rico in the early 1900s were not immigrants at all. The island became a possession of the United States after the Spanish-American War. In 1917 Congress passed the Jones Act. It granted all Puerto Ricans U.S. citizenship.

Driven by poverty on the island many Puerto Ricans headed to the U.S. mainland. By 1940 about 70,000 Puerto Ricans were living on the U.S. mainland, mostly in East Coast cities.

Puerto Ricans were racially mixed. They practiced their own form of Catholicism, and they spoke Spanish. For all these reasons, Puerto Ricans became frequent targets of racism.

Other Groups

The United States was becoming a home for people from troubled regions all over the world. The nation was known as a land with room for all to succeed.

Many smaller groups of immigrants came, such as Catholic Poles and Czechs from Eastern Europe, as well as Greeks, Turks, Armenians, and Arabs from the former Ottoman Empire. Each group settled down and deepened its roots in this nation. Each would go on to make important contributions to American life.

Arabs were among the many immigrant groups in the United States. Here a Syrian vendor sells pretzels in New York City.

Limiting Immigration

Fear of foreigners led to demands in the 1920s that the American door be closed to further immigration. In 1924 Congress passed the Johnson-Reed Act. The law set up a yearly quota, or limit, on the number of immigrants allowed from each country. Quotas for

The Jones Act in of 1917 gave Puerto Ricans U.S. citizenship. Thousands left Puerto Rico for the U.S. mainland to escape poverty. This photograph is of a Puerto Rican family who arrived in New York City in the 1940s. **Critical Thinking:** Why, do you think, did Puerto Ricans settle mainly on the East Coast?

southern and eastern European countries were much smaller than quotas for people from western and northern Europe. Most Asians were denied entry.

Not all Americans liked the new quotas. Some pointed out that the United States was, after all, a nation of immigrants. They had shared in making the nation great. Cultural diversity was a strength, they argued, not something to be feared.

French Canadians

The Johnson-Reed Act set no limits on immigrants from nations in the Western Hemisphere. Some people from the north who joined the immigration wave were French-speaking and Catholic. They were Canadians from the province of Quebec.

French Canadians, a minority group in Canada, were mostly farmers. As good farmland in Quebec grew scarce, they headed south. Some of them took up farming. Most found jobs in New England textile mills and factories.

As their numbers increased, French Canadians sometimes clashed with Irish Catholics. They also faced prejudice from English-speaking New Englanders. Yet over time, the French Canadians became more accepted in American society.

Mexican Immigrants

In 1910 a revolution began in Mexico. Its supporters, many of whom were poor farmers, wanted reforms that would give them more land. In 1917 Mexico adopted a new constitution that backed the goals of the revolution. Still, Mexico had few opportunities for its people. Between 1910 and 1930 about 700,000 Mexicans crossed the border to the United States.

Growers and ranchers in California and Texas were glad to get the cheap labor Mexican immigrants provided. Owners of copper mines in Arizona and Colorado hired Mexicans at low pay as well. Men, women, and children all performed ex-

hausting labor. Barred from good housing (as well as schools and jobs), Mexican immigrants often settled in separate communities known as barrios.

When the Great Depression struck in 1929, Mexicans became even less welcome. Whites accused Mexican immigrants of stealing jobs from them. Starting in 1931, President Hoover ordered hundreds of thousands of Mexican immigrants to be sent back to Mexico.

Many Mexican laborers found work in California on farms and ranches.

SECTION REVIEW

1. Key Terms anti-Semitism, Chinese Exclusion Act, Jones Act, quota, barrio

2. Places Hawaii, Philippines, Puerto Rico

3. Comprehension How did discrimination affect different immigrant groups in different ways?

4. Comprehension What limits on immigration did Congress pass on certain groups of immigrants?

5. Critical Thinking Why is the phrase *E pluribus unum,* or "from many, one," an appropriate motto for the United States?

SKILLS: Understanding Other Perspectives

LEARN

Have you ever heard a joke that you did not get? Others laugh, but all you can do is fake a smile. Most jokes are based on shared experiences. People with shared experiences often have similar views. Perhaps you have a different perspective, or point of view, from the ones who laughed.

In the early 1900s, immigrants brought their cultures and perspectives to America. They helped change the way we see our world.

Students bring their own perspectives to the classroom. In class discussions, you should encourage people to share them. Follow these steps to understand other perspectives.

(1) *Listen with an open mind*. Do not reject an opinion just because it sounds odd.

(2) *Ask follow-up questions.* This helps others make their opinions more clear. A good idea may be hidden in an unusual remark.

(3) *Express your own opinions*, even if others disagree with you. Exchanging opinions leads us to better understand one another.

PRACTICE

Immigrants often feel torn between the culture of their homeland and their new American culture. In the excerpt at right, from *Hunger of Memory,* Mexican American Richard Rodriguez describes the sense of conflict he felt when he began to learn English.

> "After dinner each night, the family gathered to practice "our" English. . . . Laughing, we would try to define words we could not pronounce. . . . One Saturday morning I entered the kitchen where my parents were talking in Spanish. . . . The moment they saw me, I heard their voices change to speak English. . . . I felt my throat twisted by unsounded grief. . . . I had no place to escape to with Spanish. . . .
>
> We remained a loving family, but one greatly changed. No longer so close. . . . The house would be empty of sounds . . . partly due to the fact that, as we children learned more and more English, we shared fewer and fewer words with our parents. . . ."

1. How did Rodriguez feel about learning English?

2. What might have been his parents' perspective on learning English?

3. What effect did learning English have on the Rodriguez family?

APPLY

4. Write two questions you would ask the Rodriguez family to understand their perspectives on learning English. Then express your own opinion on whether immigrants should learn English and speak it at home.

2 Changes for African Americans

SECTION GUIDE

Main Idea

Beginning around 1910, more than 2 million African Americans in the South began migrating to the North. Although they faced discrimination in the North, African Americans built a thriving culture in the 1920s and 1930s.

Goals

As you read, look for answers to these questions:

1. Why did many African Americans migrate from the South to the North?

2. What movements and organizations were started for African Americans?

3. What were the highlights of the Harlem Renaissance?

Key Terms
UNIA
Harlem Renaissance

THE TRAIN CLATTERED across the midpoint of a railroad bridge high above the Ohio River. Inside a group of African Americans rose from their seats and kneeled down in prayer. They gave thanks and raised their voices to sing. God had delivered them to the North. They were fleeing not slavery but poverty. Their goal was a chance at a better future.

Northern Migration

The hard life of southern blacks had become even harder in the early 1900s. Segregation was becoming the law of the land in many states. Between 1890 and 1910, southern states stripped away the right of African Americans to vote.

Parents saw a bleak future for their children. Whites had little interest in educating African American students. In Alabama, at least one-third of all black students had no chairs or desks. In the North, chances for education were better. Said one African American father, "I want to come north where I can educate my three little children, also my wife."

Millions did head north. In 1910, more than 90 percent of African Americans lived in the South. Over the next ten years, 1.4 million African Americans left the South. Most moved after 1915. By 1930, 2.3 million had migrated north. It was one of the biggest population shifts in this nation's history.

Large numbers of black southerners migrated north in search of better opportunities. This painting by African American artist Jacob Lawrence is part of a series of paintings that celebrate the migration.

A New Life in the North

Most African Americans who migrated to the North had been sharecroppers and farm workers. In the South they had faced attacks not only from whites, but also from nature. Insects and floodwaters ravaged southern crops. Many African Americans looked to the North, as they had since the days of slavery, as a place of opportunity.

The new arrivals settled mainly in the large cities of the North. They created large African American neighborhoods in cities such as New York City, Chicago, and Detroit.

For a time, African Americans were barred from jobs in northern factories. Then World War I ripped through Europe. The war cut the flow of European immigrants, who had filled unskilled jobs. Now companies were more than happy to hire African Americans. "Labor agents" toured the South, signing up any African American willing to jump on a train and migrate north.

Despite the need for labor, African Americans rarely found a warm welcome. Barred from joining unions, they often worked as strikebreakers. This, of course, only angered unions more. Also, many whites feared that blacks would take their jobs.

A woman greets a veteran of World War I at the parade of the "Negro Regiment," in New York City in 1919.

Rising Tensions

February 17, 1919, was a proud day for members of New York's "Negro Regiment." On that day one million people lined the streets to greet them. These soldiers were among the 400,000 African Americans to serve in World War I. They had fought as equals alongside French troops. They had fought for democracy and for their country. They were now eager to take an equal place in American society.

In fact, the returning soldiers found few signs of the democracy that they had fought to protect. During and after World War I, relations between blacks and whites grew ugly. In 1917 race riots broke out in Philadelphia, in East St. Louis, Illinois, and other cities. In 1919, 25 major riots erupted. A main cause was the move of African Americans into formerly white areas. Tensions were easily sparked. In Chicago a black swimmer on a raft drifted into a "whites only" area of a beach. Whites threw stones at him and he drowned. Thirteen days of rioting followed. Around 50 people, both black and white, died.

African Americans Resist

There were signs of hope for African Americans in the North. Living together in large neighborhoods, they gained some economic and political power.

One way African Americans exercised economic power was through boycotts. In black neighborhoods from St. Louis to New York, white-owned stores refused to hire black employees. With the rallying cry, "Don't Buy Where You Can't Work," African Americans boycotted such stores. In most cases, store owners gave in.

African Americans also used their influence to fight lynching, which the NAACP called the "shame of America." White mobs in many southern towns hunted down blacks accused (often falsely) of a crime. The mobs then tortured, burned, and hanged their victims.

Amazingly, in several states lynching was still legal. The Ku Klux Klan worked to prevent passage of anti-lynching laws. So many southern blacks had been lynched that the NAACP permanently hung the following banner outside its New York headquarters: "A MAN WAS LYNCHED TODAY." During the 1920s the NAACP worked to make people aware of these crimes. It was unable, however, to gain passage of a national anti-lynching law. Lynchings continued through the 1950s.

Marcus Garvey

Some blacks lost faith in the United States and its laws. One who did was Marcus Garvey. Born in Jamaica in 1887, Garvey traveled through Central America and Europe. There he saw blacks being treated unfairly by whites.

Garvey was greatly influenced by Booker T. Washington. He believed that blacks should work to help themselves. In Jamaica he started the Universal Negro Improvement Association, or UNIA.

Garvey called for the creation of a black homeland in Africa. He urged blacks worldwide to migrate to Africa:

&& We are the descendants of a people determined to suffer no longer. . . . If Europe is for the Europeans, then Africa shall be for the black peoples of the world. ""

Wishing to spread his "back to Africa" message, Garvey traveled to the United States in 1916. He settled in Harlem and opened a UNIA office.

Many African Americans supported Garvey and his message. By the 1920s UNIA was the nation's largest nonreligious black group. It claimed to have a million members. Garvey started *Negro World,* a newspaper that was read worldwide. To transport African Americans to Africa,

Millions of blacks around the world backed Marcus Garvey (second from right) and his "back to Africa" message. The stock certificate below was from the failed Black Star Line.

Garvey started his own shipping company, the Black Star Line.

Not all African Americans supported Garvey. Leaders of the NAACP and other organizations opposed UNIA. They believed that the best course for African Americans was not to be separate, but to fight for an equal place in American society.

Garvey's Example

Garvey's dream of a black homeland never came true. The Black Star Line went bankrupt. In 1922 he was charged with mail fraud. He was convicted and sentenced to prison. Five years later, he was sent back to Jamaica. During the 1930s Garvey and the UNIA lost influence and supporters. He died in 1940.

Although African Americans did not migrate to Africa, many blacks in Jamaica and Europe did. Garvey had set an example for future black political movements in the United States and around the world. Years later Martin Luther King, Jr., described Garvey as the "first man on a mass scale . . . to give millions of Negroes a sense of dignity and destiny."

In addition to artists and writers, Harlem was home to several wealthy African Americans. Here a group of high-society women meet for tea at Madame C. J. Walker's Beauty Salon in the late 1920s.

The Harlem Renaissance

As African Americans migrated North, they brought with them new ideas. In the 1920s and 1930s, New York's Harlem section enjoyed a burst of African American cultural activity. This movement was often called a "renaissance," since it symbolized a rebirth of hope. (*Renaissance* means "rebirth" in French.) The movement is now known as the **Harlem Renaissance.**

Just as Greenwich Village drew together the "Lost Generation" of white writers, Harlem became home to black writers, musicians, singers, painters, sculptors, and scholars. They found Harlem to be an exciting place where they could exchange ideas and develop their creative gifts.

James Weldon Johnson, a writer and leader of the NAACP, was one of the first Harlem writers to have his work published. Jamaican-born Claude McKay and Countee Cullen were other important writers of poetry and fiction.

Perhaps Harlem's best-known writer was Langston Hughes. When his father had offered to send him to college in Europe, Hughes chose New York's Columbia Univerisity. "More than Paris . . . or Berlin . . . I wanted to see Harlem, the greatest Negro city in the world," Hughes wrote. Using rhythms from blues and jazz, Hughes wrote about the difficult conditions under which African Americans lived. Hughes published poetry, short stories, essays, plays, and musicals.

Women wrote 8 of the 23 novels published by African American writers during the Harlem Renaissance. Of these writers, Zora Neale Hurston was the most active. She published four novels, as well as poetry and short stories. Her best-known novel, *Their Eyes Were Watching God,* was published in 1937.

Harlem was also the center of jazz and blues. The Cotton Club, the most famous nightclub, was a showcase for jazz greats like Duke Ellington, Louis Armstrong, Ella Fitzgerald, and Billie Holiday. They played to mostly white audiences. Although most of the entertainers were African American, many clubs barred African Americans from coming to the shows.

DURING THE HARLEM RENAISSANCE

For black writers of the 1920s, Harlem was the place to be. "In Harlem we were seen in a beautiful light," said Arna Bontemps. "We were the first-born of the dark renaissance." At fancy parties, writers mingled with black businessmen and other members of Harlem's elite. Writers also met working-class Harlem residents at "rent parties," held to raise rent money. Harlem's writers saw themselves as the voice of all African Americans.

Novelist Zora Neale Hurston (left) and poet Countee Cullen (above) both lived and worked in Harlem during the 1920s.

Poet Langston Hughes (right) attacked racism in "I, Too, Sing America."

I, Too, Sing America

I, too, sing America.

I am the darker brother.
They send me to eat in the kitchen
When company comes,
But I laugh,
And eat well,
And grow strong.

Tomorrow,
I'll be at the table
When company comes.
Nobody'll dare
Say to me,
"Eat in the kitchen,"
Then.

Besides,
They'll see how beautiful I am
And be ashamed–

I, too, am America.

645 OUR OWN COMMUNITY 645
GROCERY & DELICATESSEN
645 GROCERY · DELICATESSEN 645

MILK 6
SUGAR 5 lb 22
BACON ½ 10
STARCH 8
FOOD 3 13

Although African Americans were hit hard by the Great Depression, some were able to run businesses in African American neighborhoods.

The Harlem Renaissance Ends

By the mid-1930s the Harlem Renaissance was in decline. Artists, hurt by the Depression, took other jobs. Zora Neale Hurston spent her last years working as a maid. James Weldon Johnson died in 1938. He had already written his epitaph: "I will not let prejudice or any of its . . . injustices bear me down to spiritual defeat."

Even though the Harlem Renaissance lasted only about ten years, its impact was great. Before that time, few publishing companies would publish the works of black authors. The success of the Harlem Renaissance writers made it possible for later African American authors to be published.

In a 1926 essay, Langston Hughes summed up the spirit of the Harlem Renaissance. "We now intend to express our individual dark-skinned selves," he wrote, "without fear or shame."

Gains and Losses in the 1930s

As you read in the last chapter, African Americans suffered greatly during the Great Depression. Often the most recently hired workers, they were the first to be let go when hard times hit. As jobs in industries dried up, African American migration to the North in the 1930s fell by half.

Yet African Americans saw some gains during this time. The CIO, one of the nation's biggest unions, began a drive to represent all workers, not just whites. It refused to segregate its unions or accept different wages for blacks and whites.

The NAACP fought hard for political gains during the 1930s. It battled for years to force Texas to allow African Americans to vote in primary elections. The NAACP lost that case in the Supreme Court in 1935. Yet as in many battles, it continued to fight. The ruling was reversed in 1944.

Such victories marked progress toward the goals of returning veterans of World War I. Those goals were full integration and equality.

SECTION REVIEW

1. Key Terms UNIA, Harlem Renaissance

2. People and Places Marcus Garvey, James Weldon Johnson, Claude McKay, Countee Cullen, Langston Hughes, Zora Neale Hurston, Harlem

3. Comprehension Why did African Americans in the South see the North as a land of opportunity?

4. Comprehension What were the achievements of the Harlem Renaissance? What impact did it have?

5. Critical Thinking Many African Americans in the 1920s supported Marcus Garvey's "back to Africa" movement. Do you think such a movement would have similar support today? Explain your answer.

3 Progress for Native Americans

SECTION GUIDE

Main Idea
A change in government policy in the 1930s allowed American Indians to look forward to a better future.

Goals
As you read, look for answers to these questions:

1 What steps did Indians take to improve their lives?

2 What gains did Indians make under new government polices?

Key Terms
Society of American Indians
stereotype
Indian Citizenship Act
Indian Reorganization Act

Many Indians faced government pressure to live and work like whites. The Sioux man and child shown here farmed tiny plots of land. In the winter they lived in a house, and in the summer they returned to living in a teepee.

ROBERT SPOTT, a Yurok Indian, recalled, "My father was an Indian chief, and we used to own everything there." When reservation land was split under the Dawes Act, the government promised Spott's father horses, cows, and a plow to improve his poor land. "My father passed away when he was ninety years old. I am his son and I am waiting for it right now. If I ever will get the cows or the horses or the plow, I don't know."

The Dawes Act of 1887 tried to help Indians by forcing them to live and work like whites. Yet the Dawes Act brought only disaster. Indians, with poor land and little outside help, could not profitably farm their plots. Many Indians sold their land to white buyers. As one Crow elder said, it was a time when "our hearts were in the ground."

The Society of American Indians

In 1911 a group of Indian leaders met in Columbus, Ohio. They wanted to address the needs and rights of their people. They started a group called the Society of American Indians. They believed that Indians should govern themselves.

Members of the Society of American Indians included writers, artists, doctors, ministers, and lawyers. Many were graduates of the Carlisle Indian Industrial School. The government brought Indian children to the Carlisle School to teach them to live like whites.

The Society disagreed on how to improve Indian life. Some wanted to adopt white ways, while others did not. They all, however, agreed on the need to rebuild Indian pride. They also worked to correct stereotypes of Indians. (A stereotype is a judgment made about an entire group of people.) Indians were often stereotyped as "uncivilized."

One of the Society's key victories came about as a result of World War I. Some 12,000 Indians volunteered for the army and navy during World War I. Another 10,000 Indian women and men served in the Red Cross. American Indians were patriotic in their support of the war effort.

Although they helped fight America's battles, Native Americans still were not considered U.S. citizens at birth. The superb war record of Indian veterans helped lead Congress to pass the Indian Citizenship Act in 1924. This law granted U.S. citizenship to American Indians.

A New Deal for Native Americans

In 1920 a young social worker from New York, John Collier, spent his Christmas vacation among the Pueblo Indians of Taos, New Mexico. He became fascinated with the Pueblo people. Later he wrote, "They had what the world has lost . . . the ancient reverence and passion for the earth and the web of life."

By the 1920s Americans were paying more attention to nature. National parks had been created to preserve America's natural beauty. One result of this change was a growing understanding of what the Indians had been forced to give up.

Collier took up the cause of Indian rights during the 1920s. He opposed past efforts to assimilate Indians. In 1934 President Roosevelt appointed Collier as head of the Bureau of Indian Affairs. The Bureau was responsible for carrying out government policies toward Indians.

Collier gave the U.S. Senate a detailed plan for an all-new Indian policy. It was, he said, a "new deal" for Native Americans.

In his plan Collier proposed many changes:

(1) He pressed for a return to self-government for Native Americans.

(2) He pushed for an end to the land-allotment program.

(3) He wanted the government to give loans to Indian farmers and business owners.

(4) He urged the Bureau of Indian Affairs to hire Indians.

(5) He wanted an end to the practice of teaching Indian children to be ashamed of their culture.

Some white and Indian leaders were angry. Collier had not talked with Indians before forming his plan. Instead he presented the finished plan to Indian groups to ask for their reactions. One Creek Indian in Oklahoma accused Collier of wanting to return Indians to the Stone Age. Other Indians, however, saw in the new plan a chance for a better future.

One goal of the Society of American Indians and of the Bureau of Indian Affairs was to rebuild Indian pride. Here a group of Cherokee perform a ritual dance before a lacrosse game. **Critical Thinking:** How might negative stereotypes affect a people's pride in its heritage?

Changes in Indian Life

In 1934 the Collier plan became law as the Indian Reorganization Act, or IRA. (It was also known as the Wheeler Act.) Congress had made many changes to Collier's ideas. Yet the IRA did end allotment of Indian lands and gave Indians some self-government. It also helped to improve living conditions. For example, Indians could borrow money to launch their own businesses. Because of improved health care, the Indian death rate was cut in half.

Women benefited greatly from the IRA. New Indian constitutions, written to U.S. guidelines, gave women the right to vote and hold office. Collier also pressed for new education programs for women. He helped women find jobs on reservations and in New Deal projects.

Under Collier, the Bureau of Indian Affairs encouraged pride in Native American heritage. It published pamphlets about Indian life. It also issued textbooks printed in both English and the languages of Indian students. Children studied works of Indian culture in art classes.

The results of Collier's work were mixed. Some Indian groups received much-needed relief. Clarence Wesley, a leader of the San Carlos Apache, recalled when the IRA was explained to his people:

The Thomas Gilcrease Institute of American History and Art, Tulsa

Quanah Parker, principal chief of the Comanche.

Collier, however, was a tough person. He bullied some Indian groups into accepting his plan. Many Indians mistrusted him. In addition, Collier's plan was only a beginning. To this day, Indians still suffer injustices that Collier had hoped to correct.

❝ I remember that a prominent Indian stood up and said, 'This is what we have been waiting for. The white man has driven us around like cattle for many years. We need to take advantage of the opportunity to form our own government and run our own business.' I think the IRA was the best thing that ever happened to Indian tribes. It gave them the right to self-government. ❞

SECTION REVIEW

1. Key Terms Society of American Indians, stereotype, Indian Citizenship Act, Indian Reorganization Act

2. People John Collier, Clarence Wesley

3. Comprehension What were the goals of the Society of American Indians?

4. Comprehension What gains did Indians make under the Indian Reorganization Act?

5. Critical Thinking In what way was Collier's plan a "new deal" for American Indians?

Summary

1. Beginning in the mid-1800s a wave of "new immigrants" from eastern and southern Europe came to the United States. Also at this time, Asian immigrants began crossing the Pacific and settled along the nation's western coast. As the number of immigrants increased, however, many Americans began to call for limits on immigration. The Johnson-Reed Act, passed in 1924, limited the number of immigrants allowed from most nations, except those in the Western Hemisphere.

2. Life for African Americans in the South grew harder as the 1900s began. Around the year 1910, African Americans began migrating north in search of a better life. However, African Americans continued to face discrimination in the North. Despite rising racial tensions, African American art and culture flourished.

3. Through Indian organizations and changes made in government policies, Native Americans made gains in the 1930s. The Society of American Indians worked to improve Indian life. Congress passed the Indian Reorganization Act in 1934. Its goals were to improve economic conditions for Indians and to encourage pride in Indian heritage.

Graphic Summary

Immigrants come to the United States seeking better opportunities.	→	Congress passes laws that restrict immigration for certain groups.
Many African Americans in the South migrate to the North.	→	African Americans face prejudice in the North but still make economic, political, and cultural gains.
Congress passes laws to improve conditions for Native Americans.	→	Native Americans make gains in the 1930s.

Review

KEY TERMS

Define the following key terms.
1. anti-Semitism
2. quota
3. barrio
4. stereotype

COMPREHENSION

1. What groups were among the "new immigrants" to the United States?
2. What limits did the Johnson-Reed Act place on immigration?
3. Which immigrant groups came from nations of the Western Hemisphere? Why did each group come to the United States?
4. What was life like in the North for many African American immigrants?
5. What methods did African Americans use to fight discrimination in the North?
6. What action did Marcus Garvey believe African Americans should take to improve their lives? What course did his opponents believe was right for African Americans?
7. What was the Harlem Renaissance?
8. For what reasons was the Society of American Indians formed?
9. What changes in the government's Indian policy did John Collier propose?
10. What gains did American Indian women make under the Indian Reorganization Act?

Places to Locate

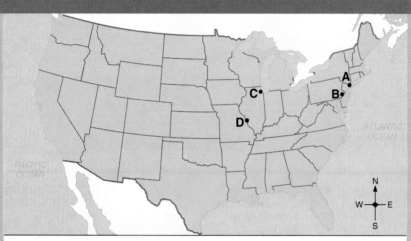

Match the letters on the map with the places that are listed below. Then explain the importance of each place.

1. Chicago
2. New York City
3. St. Louis
4. Philadelphia

Geographic Theme: Movement Why did many African Americans migrate to the North between 1910 and 1930? What were the advantages and disadvantages of life in the North?

Skill Review

Look through the editorial pages of a newspaper for different perspectives on an important national issue. Choose two editorials from a newspaper or magazine that express opposing viewpoints on an issue. Then answer the questions below.

1. What are the different viewpoints of the issue you chose?
2. Who are the supporters of this issue? Who are the opponents?
3. Make a list of questions you would ask that would help you better understand each perspective on the issue.
4. What is your viewpoint on the issue?

CRITICAL THINKING

1. Making a Judgment Why did many immigrants try to assimilate into American society? Do you think assimilation is helpful or harmful to immigrants? Explain.
2. Making Comparisons Compare and contrast the issue of restricting immigration in the 1920s with the issue as it exists today.

PORTFOLIO OPTIONS

1. Civics Connection In what ways were the problems of African Americans similar to those of Native Americans and immigrants? How were they different?
2. Writing Connection Imagine you are a Native American volunteer in the army or navy during World War I. Write a letter to your parents describing your experiences since you left home.
3. Contemporary Connection During the 1900s, Americans struggled with the question "What is an American?" Today, the nation's diverse population makes that question just as difficult to answer. Create a collage of American diversity. Include people, examples of cultures, and institutions. Celebrate American diversity with your classmates by displaying your collages on a bulletin board.
4. Timeline Connection Copy the chapter timeline. Choose two events and explain the impact each had on immigration or on the growing diversity in the United States.

On D-Day, June 6, 1944, almost 60,000 American troops landed on the beaches of France (below) as part of the largest invasion by sea in history. That day was a turning point in World War II. The United States' millions of soldiers and vast resources brought victory for the Allies and made the United States the world's most powerful nation.

1930 **1932** **1934** **1936**

1935 Italy invades Ethiopia

1931 Japan invades Manchuria

1936 Spanish Civil War

The Rise of Dictators and World War II (1930–1945)

1 Steps to War

SECTION GUIDE

Main Idea

Japan, Germany, and Italy threatened world peace during the 1930s. Germany's invasion of Poland in 1939 officially began World War II.

Goals

As you read, look for answers to these questions:

1 What conditions led to the rise of dictators in Europe and in Japan?

2 How did World War II begin?

Key Terms

aggression
fascism
Nazi
totalitarian
Axis Powers
appeasement
World War II
blitzkrieg

THE GREAT DEPRESSION of the 1930s struck the entire world. Americans responded to the Depression by voting in a New Deal and a new hope for the future. In some countries, however, desperate people turned to leaders who spoke out against democracy. These leaders told their people that they deserved to rule other nations. Their hate-filled voices led the world into the bloodiest war in history.

The Rise of Dictators

The roots of World War II went back to the end of World War I and the 1920s. The treaty that ended World War I had left the defeated nations bitter. In addition, three nations—Germany, Japan, and Italy—felt shut out of the economic growth of the 1920s. They envied Britain and France, which had overseas colonies. Colonies gave nations access to raw materials and customers. New leaders in Germany, Japan, and Italy promised to expand territory and improve living standards. They planned to do this through aggression —attacks on other nations.

In Italy, Benito Mussolini started a political movement called fascism (FASH-iz-uhm). Under fascism, the government rules through terror and by appealing to racism and nationalism. Mussolini came to power in 1922, promising to build a new Roman Empire. He said he would make the Mediterranean Sea an "Italian lake."

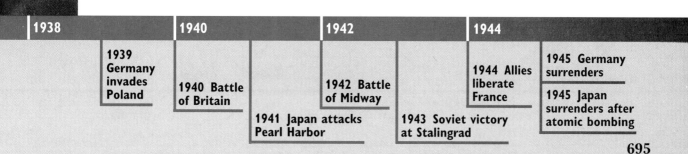

1938	1940	1942	1944
1939 Germany invades Poland	1940 Battle of Britain	1942 Battle of Midway	1944 Allies liberate France
	1941 Japan attacks Pearl Harbor	1943 Soviet victory at Stalingrad	1945 Germany surrenders / 1945 Japan surrenders after atomic bombing

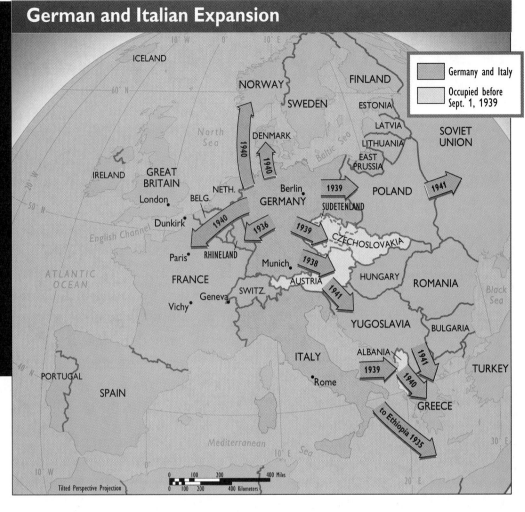

Adolf Hitler

In Japan, military leaders took more and more control of government decisions. Japan had conquered Korea and wanted to extend its power into China and Southeast Asia. This empire would supply Japan with the materials its growing industries needed.

Adolf Hitler began the National Socialist German Workers', or Nazi (NAHT-see), Party in Germany. The nation's defeat in World War I had taken a heavy toll. Germans had to accept blame for the war and pay large sums of money to the victors. Hitler told

Benito Mussolini

Germans that they should not be ashamed of their history, but proud of it. He blamed Jews and other groups for Germany's economic problems.

In 1933 Hitler won control of the German government. He set up totalitarian rule. (Under totalitarian rule, the government controls every aspect of life in the nation.) All Germans had to follow his orders. Critics of the government were imprisoned. Jews lost their rights as German citizens and were brutally mistreated by the Nazis.

In 1936 Hitler and Mussolini announced that they had signed an alliance called the "Rome-Berlin Axis." A few years later, Japan joined that alliance. Known as the Axis Powers, the three nations divided the world into three areas of influence.

Aggression Begins

In 1931 Japan invaded Manchuria, a coal-rich province of China. The League of Nations did little to stop it. Japan then set up a new government for the areas of China it controlled. This government would do what the Japanese wanted.

In 1935 Mussolini ordered Italian troops to invade Ethiopia, one of the few African nations not already a European colony. Using modern weapons such as tanks, airplanes, and poison gas against poorly armed soldiers, the Italians easily won. Again, the League of Nations did little.

After World War I, Germany had been forced to keep its military out of the Rhineland, a part of Germany on the French border. In 1936 Hitler ordered German troops into the Rhineland.

Later that year, Spain burst into civil war. Loyalists supported the elected government of the Spanish republic. They fought the Fascists, who were supported by Germany. The Loyalists received little outside aid. By 1939 the Fascists had won.

Hitler invaded and annexed Austria in 1938. He claimed that since most Austrians spoke German, Austria was really part of Germany. Soon Hitler declared that Germany should annex the parts of Czechoslovakia where many German speakers lived.

The Munich Conference

Prime Minister Neville Chamberlain of Britain and Premier Édouard Daladier (dah-lah-DYAY) of France met with Hitler in Munich, Germany, in late September 1938. Mussolini was also there. Chamberlain and Daladier agreed to allow Germany to take the parts of Czechoslovakia it

CONNECTING WITH WORLD EVENTS

INDIA'S FIGHT FOR INDEPENDENCE

Germany was not Britain's only worry in the 1930s. Britain faced a challenge to its rule of India. The leader of that challenge was Mohandas Gandhi. Indians who followed Gandhi fought British rule with nonviolent marches, boycotts, and strikes. They hoped to draw attention to the injustice of British rule of their country.

When World War II started, India helped Britain. The British jailed Gandhi for opposing India's involvement in the war. In 1947, after the war, India gained its independence. One year later Gandhi was assassinated. His ideas about nonviolent struggle lived on, most famously in civil rights leader Martin Luther King, Jr.

wanted. In return, Hitler promised that he would not demand any more land.

When Chamberlain returned to Britain, cheering crowds welcomed him. Chamberlain waved a paper with Hitler's signature on it. He declared that it represented "peace in our time."

Britain and France were following a policy of appeasement —giving in to someone's demands in order to avoid conflict. Among those who opposed appeasement was Winston Churchill, a British politician. He wrote about the Munich Conference:

❝ Britain and France had to choose between war and dishonor. They chose dishonor. They will have war. ❞

Steps to World War II

October 1922	Mussolini takes power in Italy.
September 1931	Japanese invade Manchuria.
January 1933	Hitler becomes chancellor of Germany.
October 1935	Italy invades Ethiopia.
March 1936	Germany reoccupies the Rhineland.
July 1937	Japanese forces move into China.
March 1938	Germany annexes Austria.
September 1938	Munich Conference.
August 1939	Nazi-Soviet Pact signed.
September 1939	German troops invade Poland.

CHART SKILLS: This timetable lists events leading up to the official start of World War II. **Critical Thinking:** In your opinion, why did other nations wait until the invasion of Poland to declare war on the Axis?

Six months later, in March 1939, Hitler broke his promise. German troops took the rest of Czechoslovakia. Hitler also demanded a section of Poland. Britain and France warned Germany that an attack on Poland would mean war.

On the eastern border of Poland lay the Soviet Union, led by Joseph Stalin. His Communist government had taken over all land and industries in the country. Millions of farmers and others who resisted had been killed or were imprisoned in labor camps.

Hitler and Stalin were bitter enemies. Thus the world was shocked when, in August 1939, the nations agreed to a Nazi-Soviet Pact. In one part of this pact, Germany and the Soviet Union agreed to divide Poland between them.

The Start of the War

On September 1, 1939, World War II officially began. German planes, tanks, and troops attacked Poland in a blitzkrieg ("lightning war" in German). The Polish army fought bravely. Yet its old guns and horse-mounted soldiers were no match for the well-trained German soldiers and their modern equipment. As German forces took over western Poland, Soviet troops moved in from the east. Within a month, Poland was defeated and occupied.

On September 3, Britain and France declared war on Germany. The Germans defeated Poland very quickly, however. France and Britain did little to help. They prepared for a German attack on the Allied forces of western Europe.

In April 1940, German troops parachuted into Denmark and Norway. Then, without warning, German forces invaded the Netherlands and Belgium. Using blitzkrieg tactics, the German army overran these nations and moved into France. Within a few weeks the large French army, supported by British soldiers, was defeated. Now Adolf Hitler was the ruler of most of western Europe. Only Britain and several neutral countries remained free of Nazi power.

In August 1940, Hitler began heavy bombing of Britain, hoping to pound it into surrender. The heroic efforts of the Royal Air Force (RAF) against the German warplanes became known as the Battle of Britain. Despite a nightly rain of bombs on its cities, Britain and its new prime minister, Winston Churchill, held firm.

SECTION REVIEW

1. Key Terms aggression, fascism, Nazi, totalitarian, Axis Powers, appeasement, World War II, blitzkrieg

2. People Benito Mussolini, Adolf Hitler, Winston Churchill, Joseph Stalin

3. Comprehension What countries or regions were victims of aggression in the 1930s?

4. Comprehension Describe the course of the first year of World War II.

5. Critical Thinking What connection is there between hard economic times and the rise of dictators?

2 The War Comes to America

SECTION GUIDE

Main Idea
The United States, though sympathetic to the Allied cause, stayed out of World War II until Japan attacked Pearl Harbor.

Goals
As you read, look for answers to these questions:

1 What was America's attitude toward the war, and how did it change over time?

2 When and why did the United States enter the war?

Key Terms
Four Freedoms
Lend-Lease
Atlantic Charter
Bataan Death March

IN THE 1920s AND 1930s most Americans had been isolationists. They hoped to avoid involvement in foreign affairs. When World War II broke out, some argued that the United States should stay neutral. Yet as Axis victory followed Axis victory, many Americans began to reconsider.

Preparing for War

The threat of war was reflected in the Selective Training and Service Act, passed by Congress in September 1940. This law allowed the government to start drafting men for the armed forces. It was America's first peacetime draft.

In 1940 Franklin Roosevelt was completing his second term of office. No President had served more than two terms. The world was in crisis, however, and Roosevelt decided to run again. Americans agreed that the nation needed an experienced leader. Roosevelt won a third term.

Aid to the Allies

Roosevelt spoke to Congress in early 1941 about why it was important to support Britain. He said that Britain was fighting to defend the **Four Freedoms:** freedom of speech, freedom of religion, freedom from want, and freedom from fear. He asked Congress to approve a plan to aid Britain in this fight. He called the plan **Lend-Lease.** Its purpose was to let the United States sell, lend, or lease arms and other war materials to any nation whose defense was considered vital to American security.

After a two-month debate, Congress approved Lend-Lease. With this action, the policy of isolationism came to an end. Although not yet in the war, the United States clearly had taken sides. Under Lend-Lease, billions of dollars worth of war goods were sent to Britain and other allies.

In June 1941 Hitler invaded the Soviet Union, breaking the Nazi-Soviet Pact. The Soviet Union joined the Allies. American lend-lease goods began to be shipped to the Soviet Union.

These volunteers line up at an army recruiting center in New York just days after Roosevelt signed the Selective Service Act of 1940.

Another sign of American support for the Allied cause was the **Atlantic Charter.** Roosevelt and Winston Churchill signed this document in August 1941. The charter spelled out the hopes of the two leaders for a better world. It recognized the right of all peoples to choose their own governments and to live in peace. It also called for nations to work together.

Japanese Expansion

Meanwhile, Japan's war against China continued. The Japanese were also threatening to invade European colonies in Asia. Roosevelt tried to warn Japan by cutting back trade with it.

In July 1941 the Japanese occupied French Indochina. Roosevelt responded by "freezing" (holding) all Japanese investments and property in the United States. He also cut off oil shipments to Japan. Japan had no oil of its own. Without imported oil, Japan's economy would collapse.

In October 1941 a new, even more warlike government came to power in Japan. Its leader was Hideki Tojo, an army general. The Tojo government began to plan an attack on the Dutch East Indies (a source of oil), British Malaya, and the Philippine Islands. The Philippines were at that time still an American possession. To ensure victory, Japanese leaders decided to cripple the U.S. Navy in one giant attack. They planned to destroy the huge navy base at Pearl Harbor in the Hawaiian Islands.

Pearl Harbor

December 7, 1941, dawned bright and clear in Hawaii. By 8:00 A.M., however, the sky was filling with smoke and flames. In a surprise attack, over 300 Japanese warplanes launched from carriers bombed American planes and ships at Pearl Harbor. Before the day was over, more than 2,400 Americans—both servicemen and civilians—died. Most of the American warplanes at the base were destroyed. Nineteen ships were sunk or damaged.

American officials had expected a Japanese attack somewhere in Asia. The United States had broken the code used by the Japanese to communicate with their ships. A few months before the attack, the U.S. Secretary of the Navy, Frank Knox, had

American sailors are rescued by motorboat after their battleship, the *West Virginia*, was bombed during the Japanese attack on Pearl Harbor. That surprise attack has been called the worst military defeat in American history. **Critical Thinking:** Imagine that you are one of these sailors. Write a letter to your family describing your experiences and your feelings about the attack.

said, "No matter what happens, the U.S. Navy is not going to be caught napping." That, however, is what happened. A radar operator saw blips on his screen that looked like incoming planes. Yet a series of errors kept the information from reaching the right people in time.

President Roosevelt spoke to Congress. Millions of Americans listened to his speech on the radio. Roosevelt called December 7, 1941, "a date which will live in infamy." He asked Congress to declare war against Japan. Every member but one voted to approve the declaration of war.

The attack on Pearl Harbor helped Roosevelt unite the nation behind him. Many former isolationists now supported an all-out American effort. On December 11, Germany and Italy declared war on the United States. America had become a full member of the Allies.

Defeats in the Pacific

At first the war news was bleak. The Allies could not stop Japanese advances. On December 8, 1941, the Japanese had attacked British and Dutch forces in Southeast Asia and U.S. forces in the Philippines. Within a few months, Japan held most of China and the Dutch East Indies. Many military leaders expected the Japanese to invade Australia.

The Japanese captured the Philippine capital, Manila, in January 1942. U.S. General Douglas MacArthur led a retreat of more than 12,000 American and 65,000 Filipino troops. They reached the Bataan Peninsula and the island of Corregidor (kuh-REG-i-dawr).

In February 1942 Roosevelt ordered MacArthur to Australia, to take command of all Allied forces in the Pacific. MacArthur left, promising, "I shall return."

Cut off from outside support, the Americans and Filipinos surrendered in April and May 1942. Allied prisoners, many of them injured or sick, were forced to march

Japanese soldiers guard Allied prisoners on the Bataan Death March. **Critical Thinking:** How might news of the march have affected attitudes toward the Japanese?

60 miles to a prison camp. Starving, thousands collapsed along the way. Many were shot, beaten, or bayoneted to death. The Bataan Death March, as this was known, horrified the American public.

SECTION REVIEW

1. Key Terms Four Freedoms, Lend-Lease, Atlantic Charter, Bataan Death March

2. People and Places Hideki Tojo, Douglas MacArthur, Philippines, Pearl Harbor

3. Comprehension What events of 1940 and early 1941 showed that the United States favored the Allies?

4. Comprehension How did the United States enter the war against the Axis?

5. Critical Thinking Would the United States have entered World War II if Japan had not attacked Pearl Harbor? Explain your answer.

3 The Home Front

SECTION GUIDE

Main Idea
World War II brought about many changes in American life.

Goals
As you read, look for answers to these questions:

1 How was everyday life in America changed by the war?

2 What great injustice was done to Japanese Americans during the war years?

Key Terms
internment camp
Nisei
rationing

O N SUNDAY NIGHT, DECEMBER 7, 1941, as American ships burned in Pearl Harbor, air-raid sirens sounded up and down the West Coast of the United States. A rumor spread that enemy planes were seen over San Francisco. (There were none.) In New York City, the mayor sent guards to protect the bridges, tunnels, and factories. The next morning, thousands of men stood outside military recruitment centers across the country. The United States had been attacked, and Americans everywhere prepared for war.

The Wartime Boom

One of the first steps the nation took was to enlarge the armed forces. Millions of men were drafted or volunteered to serve. More than 16 million men left their homes and jobs to serve during the war years.

Women also entered the armed forces. About 265,000 women served in the army, navy, and coast guard. These women performed important jobs that freed men for fighting. For example, they flew supply planes, taught young men to fly fighter planes, and ran field hospitals close to the battlefields.

The armed forces needed planes, tanks, uniforms, parachutes, bullets, and countless other supplies. Private industry, directed by the government's War Production Board, turned the United States into an "arsenal of democracy." In 1943 alone, defense plants made 86,000 planes and almost 2,000 merchant ships.

With so many people going off to war, there were jobs for those not in the armed services. Millions of women took jobs for the first time. Many former housewives worked in factories, shipyards, offices, or wherever they were needed. A popular song in 1942 was, "We're the Janes That Make the Planes." Yet the belief that "a woman's place was in the home" remained strong. Polls taken during the war showed that most Americans did not want married women to work outside their homes.

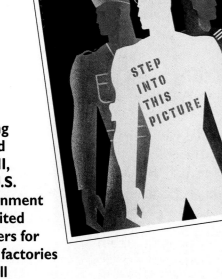

During World War II, the U.S. government recruited workers for arms factories as well as soldiers and sailors.

New Opportunities

The war also changed the lives of African Americans. Defense industries were hiring large numbers of workers for well-paying jobs. African Americans faced discrimination when they applied for these jobs.

In 1941 A. Philip Randolph, an African American labor leader, called on the government to ensure black workers a fair chance. To give his demand some teeth, Randolph announced that he would organize a protest march to take place in Washington, D.C. Roosevelt, hoping to get the march cancelled, issued Executive Order 8802. It outlawed job discrimination in industries that had contracts from the federal government. The order also set up the Fair Employment Practices Committee. It was given the power to look into charges of discrimination in defense industries.

Randolph called off the march after Roosevelt issued this order. A. Philip Randolph had won the first major civil rights victory since the days of Reconstruction.

More than 2 million African Americans worked in the defense industry during the war years. Thousands left the South to move to industrial centers such as Cleveland, Chicago, and Detroit. Unfair treatment continued in housing, education, and other areas of life. Still, the new jobs gave many African Americans their first chance to earn good wages.

Diversity in the Military

Nearly a million African Americans served in uniform. For the first time they were accepted into the Marine Corps and the Army Air Corps, though most units of all branches of the services were segregated. African American army units won awards for bravery in combat in both Europe and the Pacific.

In early 1945 the War Department announced that some units fighting in Germany would be integrated. These units, with black and white Americans fighting

Two women rivet (fasten metal) in an aircraft factory. About 18 million American women worked in war plants during World War II. **Critical Thinking:** Why might wartime open up new opportunities for women and other groups?

together, worked well. Yet the units were broken up when the European fighting ended. Meanwhile, African American servicemen and women were often reminded of their second-class status. They met unfair treatment in army camps or were turned away from movie theaters and lunch counters in nearby towns.

More than 300,000 Mexican Americans served in the U.S. armed forces during World War II. Though they were not segregated, they were mistreated in other ways. Hispanic civilians also faced prejudice. As one Hispanic Texan wrote:

❝ **We are being mistreated here every time we turn around. We are not allowed in cafes, movies, restaurants. Even Latin Americans in United States Army uniforms are sometimes told they can't see a show because the Mexican side is full.** ❞

In California and the Southwest, Hispanic Americans at times became the targets of mob actions. No other group of Americans, however, were as badly treated as those of Japanese descent.

442ND ARMY REGIMENT

Though some doubted the loyalty of Japanese Americans during World War II, most Nisei felt as patriotic as other Americans. Many joined the U.S. armed forces, some even enlisting from internment camps. In 1943 an all-Japanese-American unit, the 442nd Regiment, was formed. At first, the Nisei soldiers were given wooden rifles because they were not trusted. They later fought in Europe and were awarded thousands of medals for bravery. The 442nd became the most decorated unit in U.S. military history.

Japanese American families arrive at an internment camp in Wyoming. In 1988 Congress apologized and voted to pay survivors of the internment camps $20,000.

Japanese Americans

The Japanese attack on Pearl Harbor created anger toward Japanese Americans. Most lived in California, Oregon, and Washington. In February 1942, President Roosevelt signed an order calling for Japanese Americans to be moved away from the Pacific Coast. About 120,000 men, women, and children were rounded up. They had to sell their homes and possessions on very short notice, usually at great loss. Since no charges were brought against them, these people had no way to prove their loyalty.

The Japanese Americans were moved to internment camps, areas where they were kept under guard. In the camps entire families had to live in single rooms, with little privacy. One Japanese American woman later wrote:

> **There is no way that anyone who was not in one of the camps can understand the impact it had. . . . Non-internees cannot understand the extent of our anger, the height of our outrage, the depth of our despair.**

Two-thirds of the people interned were Nisei (nee-SAY)—Japanese Americans born in the United States. They argued that internment for racial reasons was unconstitutional. The Supreme Court, however, upheld internment throughout the war.

Shortages at Home

Since most resources were going to the armed services, Americans sometimes had to do without. For example, no automobiles were made from 1942 to 1945. Instead, the auto companies made tanks, jeeps, or airplanes. Gasoline was also in short supply. This meant the end of Sunday drives and long car trips. In fact, all pleasure travel became a thing of the past during the war. Trains and buses were always crowded.

To divide goods fairly, the government set up a system of rationing. (Rationing means to give a fixed amount of something.) Every family got ration books of stamps. Each time people bought such items as gasoline, tires, shoes, meat, and sugar, they gave up the required number of stamps.

To help the war effort, people saved kitchen grease, scrap metal, and rubber. Grease could be used in making explosives. Scrap metal and rubber were reused by war industries. A common slogan of the day was:

" Use it up
Wear it out
Make it do
Or do without! "

The Wartime Economy

Defense jobs gave Americans the money to buy goods they had been unable to afford during the Depression. Yet because of the war, there were few goods to buy. The result was inflation (an increase in prices). The government started an Office of Price Administration (OPA) to hold prices down. The OPA set limits on prices for items in short supply. Since housing too was scarce, limits were also placed on rents.

To help pay for the war, the government raised income taxes. It extended the tax to more people and started the payroll deduction plan. Under this plan, income taxes were deducted (taken out) from a person's wages or salary before they even got their paycheck. This was easier for people than paying all their taxes at once each year.

Another way the government paid for the war was by selling war bonds. The bonds were a kind of loan that the government promised to repay with interest. Movie stars traveled across the country to

Children in Montana flash the "V for Victory" symbol after a successful scrap drive. **Critical Thinking:** Compare wartime efforts with efforts today to conserve resources.

appear in war bond drives. These were huge rallies where the stars urged people to show their patriotism by buying bonds. Americans bought billions of dollars worth of bonds. It was a powerful expression of their support for the drive to victory.

SECTION REVIEW

1. Key Terms internment camp, Nisei, rationing

2. People A. Philip Randolph

3. Comprehension What effects did the war have on the lives of women, African Americans, and Japanese Americans?

4. Comprehension Why did wartime conditions create shortages and inflation? How did the government deal with these problems?

5. Critical Thinking Why was Randolph's plan to hold a mass march in Washington effective at the time? Would it have been as effective several years earlier? Explain your answer.

4 Toward Victory in Europe

SECTION GUIDE

Main Idea
After years of warfare, the Allies forced Germany to surrender in 1945.

Goals
As you read, look for answers to these questions:

1. How did the tide of the war turn in Europe?

2. What was decided at the Yalta Conference?

Key Terms
D-Day
summit conference

AS 1942 OPENED, the United States found itself at war with enemies in Europe and the Pacific. The United States and its allies decided that Hitler's Germany was a greater threat than the Japanese. The Allies agreed to halt Japan's advance, but to focus their efforts on defeating Germany.

The Soviet Union at War

The Soviet Union strongly backed this "Europe first" policy. In the summer of 1941 German troops had invaded the Soviet Union. Soviet forces fought bravely but were driven back by massive German firepower. Hitler had planned to defeat the Soviet Union by winter. Yet the Soviets held back the Germans at the gates of Moscow, the Soviet capital.

In 1942 the Germans pushed even deeper into the Soviet Union. They attacked the city of Stalingrad, a vital transportation center. In November 1942, as fighting raged at Stalingrad, Soviet forces encircled and trapped the German army near the city. German soldiers in summer uniforms froze to death in the bitter Russian winter. The German commander begged Hitler to let him break free of the Soviet trap. Hitler refused to allow retreat. In February 1943 the last of the German troops in Stalingrad surrendered. It was a turning point in the war.

The War in Africa and Italy

After defeating France in 1940, the Nazis had set up a French government centered in the town of Vichy (VISH-ee). The Vichy government also controlled French North Africa. In late 1942, Britain and the United States attacked North Africa. U.S. General Dwight D. Eisenhower led the combined Allied army. By May 1943 the Axis forces in North Africa had surrendered.

Southern Europe was now open to Allied attack. (See the map at right.) Allied forces landed on the Italian island of Sicily in July 1943 and took control. On July 25, the Italian ruling council arrested Mussolini. (He later escaped to Nazi-held territory.) A

Survivors of a Nazi attack in the Soviet Union search for relatives among the dead. About 20 million Soviet soldiers and civilians died in World War II.

World War II in Europe and North Africa

Legend:
- Allied nations
- Axis nations
- Axis-occupied, 1942
- Vichy French
- Neutral nations
- Allied advance
- Major battle

4 Battle of the Bulge, Dec. 1944–Jan. 1945

5 Fall of Berlin, May 1945

3 D-Day, June 6, 1944

1 Battle of Stalingrad, Nov. 1942–Feb. 1943

2 Invasion of Sicily, July 1943

ATLANTIC OCEAN

IRELAND, GREAT BRITAIN, London, Dunkirk, NORMANDY, NETH., BELG., LUX., Paris, FRANCE, Vichy, SWITZ., Milan, PORTUGAL, SPAIN, ITALY, Rome, Anzio, Salerno, Palermo, Sicily, Tunis, Casablanca, MOROCCO, ALGERIA, TUNISIA, LIBYA, EGYPT, Alexandria, El Alamein, Cairo

North Sea, Elbe R., Rhône R., DENMARK, GERMANY, Berlin, Potsdam, Prague, CZECHOSLOVAKIA, AUSTRIA, HUNGARY, Danube R., YUGOSLAVIA, ALBANIA, GREECE, Mediterranean Sea

NORWAY, SWEDEN, FINLAND, Leningrad, ESTONIA, LATVIA, LITHUANIA, EAST PRUSSIA, Warsaw, POLAND, ROMANIA, BULGARIA, Moscow, SOVIET UNION, Volga R., CRIMEA, Yalta, Black Sea, CAUCASUS, TURKEY, SYRIA, LEBANON, PALESTINE, TRANS-JORDAN, Red Sea

1944, 1943, 1945, 1942

GEOGRAPHY SKILLS: Allied forces moved against the Axis powers in Europe on several fronts. The photograph above shows American fliers in Italy. **Critical Thinking:** What advantages and disadvantages did Germany's central location in Europe present?

SKILLS: Drawing Conclusions from Maps

LEARN

You draw conclusions about your world every day, and you may not even realize it. On your way to school, for example, you may see bags of trash in front of people's homes. You think, "It must be trash day." Nobody has to tell you it is trash day. You have drawn a conclusion. Your eyes take in the picture, and your brain does the rest.

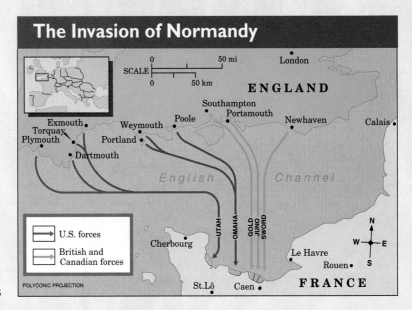

The Invasion of Normandy

You can draw conclusions from maps in the same way. Look at the map above. Read the title, the key, and the labels. You can use this information, along with what you already know, to get much more out of the map.

PRACTICE

Draw conclusions to answer the following questions.

1. Why might American forces have left from different places in England than British and Canadian forces? Why might the Americans have landed in different places than the British and Canadians?

2. At this time, was France in the hands of England's friend or enemy? How do you know?

3. Which French town on the map is the shortest distance from the English coast? Why did the Allies choose not to land there?

APPLY

4. The Germans expected an invasion of France, but they did not know where it would be. The Allies wanted to surprise the Germans. Use the map to help you imagine the invasion from start to finish. At each point, ask yourself "Why did they do this?" Write at least three "Why" questions that could help you figure out the Allied invasion strategy.

new government took control of Italy. The Allies moved onto the Italian mainland, and Italy surrendered on September 8, 1943.

German forces still held most of Italy. The Allies suffered heavy casualties as they cleared Italy from German control. It was not until June 1944 that Allied forces entered Rome, the Italian capital.

The D-Day Landing

While American and British forces fought in Italy, a huge army gathered in England. It prepared to cross the English Channel and liberate France.

On June 6, 1944, about 150,000 Allied troops landed in the region of France called Normandy. The day of this historic attack became known as **D-Day.** The attackers included American, British, Canadian, and French forces. Despite stiff resistance from the Germans, the Normandy landing succeeded. The Allies now had a foothold in western Europe.

The Allies moved eastward toward Germany. At the same time, Soviet forces moved west. In August 1944 Allied soldiers marched into Paris, freeing the French capital. In December 1944 Hitler ordered one last offensive, the Battle of the Bulge. German troops pushed the Allies back in Belgium, but soon the Allies regained control.

Winning the War in Europe

In February 1945 the Allied leaders met in the Soviet resort of Yalta. They held a **summit conference,** a meeting among the highest level of government leaders. With victory in sight, the "Big Three"—Roosevelt, Churchill, and Stalin—discussed the future. Stalin promised to declare war on Japan after Germany surrendered. All three agreed to set up a postwar peacekeeping organization. They also discussed the governments that would be set up in eastern Europe after the war.

Franklin Roosevelt (center) met with Winston Churchill (left) and Joseph Stalin (right) at Yalta in 1945 to plan for the postwar world.

For Roosevelt, the Yalta Conference came shortly after he was sworn in as President for a fourth time. The new Vice President was Harry S. Truman, a former senator from Missouri. Roosevelt was in poor health at the conference. Just a few months later, in April 1945, he died of a stroke. Truman became President.

Meanwhile, German forces were collapsing. On May 8, 1945, what was left of the German government surrendered. Hitler had committed suicide in Berlin a few days earlier. The war in Europe was over.

SECTION REVIEW

1. Key Terms D-Day, summit conference

2. People and Places Dwight D. Eisenhower, Harry S. Truman, Stalingrad, Normandy, Yalta

3. Comprehension What events in Europe in 1942 and 1943 turned the war in favor of the Allies?

4. Comprehension How was the Normandy landing in 1944 the beginning of the end for Germany?

5. Critical Thinking How, do you predict, would the defeat of Germany affect relations among the Allies?

5 Victory and Its Aftermath

SECTION GUIDE

Main Idea
U.S. victories and the atomic bombing of Japan led to Japan's surrender in 1945.

Goals

1 How did the United States take control of the Pacific War?

2 How did the United States develop and use the atomic bomb?

3 What was found out about the Nazi plan to destroy the Jews in Europe?

Key Terms
Battle of Midway
island-hopping
genocide
Holocaust
GI Bill of Rights

I N 1939 A GERMAN PHYSICIST, Albert Einstein, wrote a letter to President Roosevelt. Einstein had fled to America from Nazi Germany because he was Jewish. The Nazis, who claimed that Germanic peoples were a "master race," made Jews a special target of their racist hatred. In his letter, Einstein warned Roosevelt that the Nazis were developing an atomic bomb, a weapon more powerful than any known. With such a bomb, the Nazis could dominate the world. Roosevelt agreed that the United States needed to develop an atomic bomb of its own. Yet success was years away.

U.S. Victories in the Pacific

By mid-1942 Allied forces were finally able to halt the advance of Japanese power in the Pacific. In May the U.S. Navy clashed with Japanese forces in the Battle of the Coral Sea. For the first time in naval history, enemy ships fought a battle without coming within sight of each other. Warplanes launched from carriers fought the battle. The American victory at the Coral Sea blocked Japan's push toward Australia. In June 1942 the U.S. Navy defeated the Japanese navy at the **Battle of Midway.**

Bombardier steers during a bomb run and drops the bombs.

Flight engineer keeps track of engines and fuel supply.

Pilot—commander of the plane—and **copilot** control the aircraft.

Radio operator sits behind **navigator,** who plots route to target and back.

Three **gunners** in center (waist) of plane operate .50-caliber machine guns.

Radar operator helps navigate during bad weather.

American B-29 Bomber

American bombers sank four Japanese carriers. It was a crippling blow to Japan's navy. The battle marked the turning point of the war in the Pacific.

After Midway, U.S. forces took the offensive. They began to drive the Japanese back toward their home islands. Rather than attack every Japanese-held island, the Allies chose to invade a few key islands. This strategy was called **island-hopping.**

The Japanese fought fiercely. Thousands of American and Japanese soldiers died on islands across the Pacific. In the summer of 1944 the Allies captured the Mariana Islands. (See map on the next page.) Allied forces were now within striking distance of Japan. They began building airfields from which B-29 bombers could attack Japan.

In October 1944 General MacArthur fulfilled his promise to return to the Philippines. The U.S. Navy fought Japan there in the Battle of Leyte Gulf, the largest naval battle in history. During the battle, Japan began to use *kamikazes,* suicide pilots who crashed their planes into American ships.

The Atomic Bomb

Japan's determination to fight forced the United States to make a tough decision about use of the atomic bomb. Einstein's arguments had convinced Roosevelt to set up the

Two U.S. Marines transmit messages from a Pacific island in the Navajo language, a "code" the Japanese were unable to break. Some of the 300 Navajos who served as code talkers were as young as fifteen years old.

"Manhattan Project," the code name for secret work done by scientists and engineers. By mid-1945 they had developed the world's first atomic bomb. In a successful test, they exploded a bomb over the New Mexico desert in July 1945.

The project's engineers had built two more bombs. Should they be used in the war against Japan? American military leaders told President Truman that an invasion of Japan would take at least 18 months and might cost a million lives. Dropping an atomic bomb on Japan might end the war much more quickly, and with less life lost.

Truman sent a letter to the Japanese government. He declared that if Japan did not surrender, it would face destruction. The military leaders who ran the Japanese government refused.

On August 6, 1945, a U.S. bomber dropped an atomic bomb on the Japanese city of Hiroshima. About 80,000 Japanese people died in the blast. Tens of thousands were terribly injured. The destruction caused by one atomic weapon was enormous. Still, the Japanese leaders refused to surrender. Three days later an American plane dropped another atomic bomb—this time on the city of Nagasaki—with a loss of many more lives.

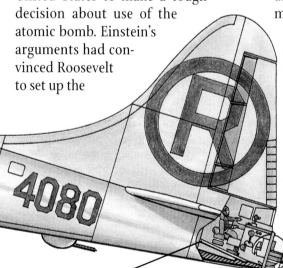

Tail gunner uses headsets to communicate with the rest of the crew.

Finally, Emperor Hirohito demanded that the Japanese military leaders surrender. He announced the decision by radio to a shocked Japanese people on August 15. The fighting stopped. Formal surrender papers were signed on September 2, 1945, on board the American battleship *Missouri* in Tokyo Bay.

The Holocaust

World War II was over, but with peace came details of its horrors. Allied troops found evidence of the Nazi treatment of Jews. In 1941 the Nazis decided to murder all Jews in the areas they controlled. This was a policy of genocide, the murder of an entire people. Throughout German-occupied Europe, millions of Jews were crammed into railroad boxcars and sent to concentration camps. Most of the able-bodied were put to work as slave laborers. All others—old people, young children, and the disabled—were killed.

By the end of the war, the Nazis were murdering thousands of these prisoners every day in gas chambers. More than 6 million Jews were killed in this campaign of terror now known as the Holocaust. Four million Gypsies, Russians, Poles, and others were also murdered.

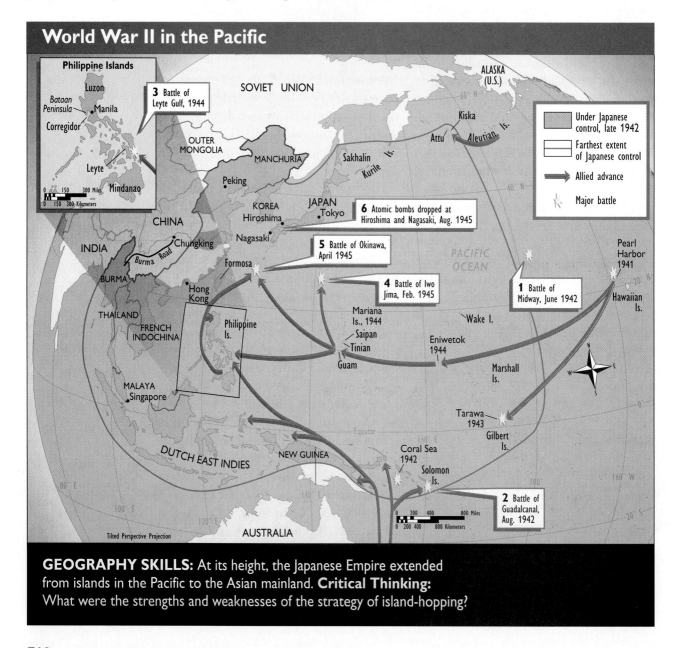

World War II in the Pacific

GEOGRAPHY SKILLS: At its height, the Japanese Empire extended from islands in the Pacific to the Asian mainland. **Critical Thinking:** What were the strengths and weaknesses of the strategy of island-hopping?

For the dead and the living we must bear witness

United States
Holocaust Memorial Museum

2122

In the photograph at the far left, Holocaust survivors are liberated from a concentration camp. At left is a pass to the United States Holocaust Memorial Museum, which opened in 1993 in Washington, D.C. **Critical Thinking:** Do you agree with the museum's motto? Explain.

After the war, an international court in Nuremberg, Germany, tried high Nazi officials for war crimes. Other courts tried less important officials. Many were found guilty, and 24 were executed.

The war trials upheld an important idea. People are responsible for their actions, even in wartime. Many Nazis said that they had simply been following orders when they herded people into the gas chambers. The Nuremberg trials established the principle that following orders was no excuse for taking part in genocide.

The Results of the War

World War II left much of the world in ruins. Perhaps as many as 60 million people were killed, many of them civilians. The war had shaken the empires of Britain and France. In the next decades, their overseas colonies would gain independence.

Except for Japan's attack on Hawaii and on Alaska's Aleutian Islands, no battles had been fought on American soil. American industry had boomed. After the war Americans looked forward to spending their savings on goods that had been scarce.

Returning soldiers took advantage of a 1944 law, the **GI Bill of Rights.** The GI Bill bought books, paid tuition, and provided living expenses for veterans who attended high school or college. It was one of several benefits offered to veterans.

The war had left the United States and the Soviet Union as the two great military powers in the world. With peace came distrust and tension between these former allies. Americans wondered about the burdens of world leadership that lay ahead.

SECTION REVIEW

1. Key Terms Battle of Midway, island-hopping, genocide, Holocaust, GI Bill of Rights

2. People and Places Albert Einstein, Hirohito, Hiroshima, Nuremberg

3. Comprehension How was the Battle of Midway a turning point in the war in the Pacific? What forced the Japanese finally to surrender?

4. Comprehension Contrast the situation in Europe and the United States after World War II.

5. Critical Thinking What principle was established in the Nuremberg trials? Describe a situation other than wartime in which this principle is relevant.

Summary

1. By the 1930s dictators had come to power in Italy, Germany, and Japan. Encouraged by the weakness of democracies, these nations captured lands in Europe, Africa, and Asia. When Germany invaded Poland in 1939, Britain and France declared war. By the end of 1940, Germany had conquered most of western Europe.

2. The United States took actions to support the nations opposing the Axis. After the Japanese attack on Pearl Harbor in December 1941, the United States joined the Allied side in the war.

3. In the United States, war production led to an economic boom that created new opportunities for women and African Americans. Fears of disloyalty led the government to move Japanese Americans into internment camps.

4. By 1943 the Allies had put Germany on the defensive. Invaded from east and west, Germany surrendered in 1945.

5. Island-hopping in the Pacific and the atomic bombing of Japan led to its surrender in 1945. The end of the war brought news of the Holocaust. The war left the United States prosperous and the greatest power in the world.

Review

KEY TERMS

Define the following pairs of terms and use them in a sentence.

1. aggression; appeasement
2. Axis Powers; blitzkrieg
3. Lend-Lease; Atlantic Charter
4. internment camp; Nisei
5. island-hopping; Battle of Midway
6. D-Day; summit conference

COMPREHENSION

1. What conditions in Europe and Japan led to the rise of dictators during the 1920s and 1930s?
2. Describe the course of Hitler's aggressions in the 1930s.
3. What finally caused the outbreak of World War II?
4. What steps did the United States take to help the Allies before December 1941?
5. What finally brought the United States into World War II?
6. Why were Japanese Americans sent to internment camps?
7. What effects did U.S. entry into the war have on the American economy?
8. What steps did A. Philip Randolph take to limit discrimination against African Americans in defense jobs?
9. What strategy did the Allies follow in the Pacific?
10. When and under what conditions did Italy, Germany, and Japan surrender?

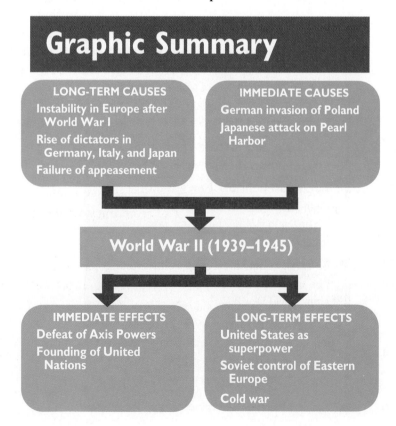

Graphic Summary

LONG-TERM CAUSES
Instability in Europe after World War I
Rise of dictators in Germany, Italy, and Japan
Failure of appeasement

IMMEDIATE CAUSES
German invasion of Poland
Japanese attack on Pearl Harbor

World War II (1939–1945)

IMMEDIATE EFFECTS
Defeat of Axis Powers
Founding of United Nations

LONG-TERM EFFECTS
United States as superpower
Soviet control of Eastern Europe
Cold war

Places to Locate

Match the letters on the map with the places that are listed below. Then explain the importance of each place.

1. Great Britain   3. Soviet Union   5. France
2. Germany   4. Italy

Geographic Theme: Movement What geographic factors helped the Soviet Union resist Germany's invasion?

Skill Review

Use the maps in this chapter to answer the following questions.

1. Why might Hitler have waited until 1941 to invade the Soviet Union?

2. How was Germany's location a factor in the war?

3. What conclusions can you draw about the Allies' strategy to defeat the Axis Powers in Europe?

4. Why was Japanese expansion in Asia a threat to the United States?

5. Why did the United States need a strong navy to fight in Europe and Asia?

6. What conclusions can you draw about the Allies' strategy to defeat Japan?

CRITICAL THINKING

1. Forming a Hypothesis In your opinion, why did the Allied leaders believe that Germany and Italy were more dangerous than Japan?

2. Making a Comparison What role did racism play in Hitler's treatment of the Jews? What role did racism play in the internment of Japanese Americans during the war? Explain why racism in Germany was different from racism in the United States.

PORTFOLIO OPTIONS

1. Civics Connection Many Americans believed Japanese Americans should show their loyalty to the United States by accepting relocation to internment camps. Failure to go peacefully, some said, was evidence of disloyalty. Discuss the problems with this argument.

2. Writing Connection Imagine that you are a woman who has found a job as a welder in a shipyard during the war. Write a diary entry describing the changes the war has brought to your life.

3. Contemporary Connection In 1988 Congress voted to pay Japanese Americans for property they had lost because of World War II. Do you agree with that decision? Explain.

4. Timeline Connection Copy the chapter timeline. Which event brought the United States into the war? Write a sentence next to each event, explaining its importance.

The House of Mirth

EDITH WHARTON

Edith Wharton grew up in New York City high society, but she could still view it with both humor and pity. In *The House of Mirth* (1905) Lily Bart, a young woman with little money, struggles to find a place among the wealthy. In this scene, Lily meets a friend and explains her situation.

*T*he walk up Fifth Avenue, unfolding before her, in the brilliance of the hard winter sunlight, an interminable procession of fastidiously-equipped carriages . . . this glimpse of the ever-revolving wheels of the great social machine made Lily more than ever conscious of the steepness and narrowness of Gerty's stairs, and of the cramped blind-alley of life to which they led. Dull stairs destined to be mounted by dull people. . . .

"You look horribly tired, Lily; take your tea, and let me give you this cushion to lean against."

Miss Bart accepted the cup of tea, but put back the cushion with an impatient hand.

"Don't give me that! I don't want to lean back—I shall go to sleep if I do."

"Well, why not, dear? I'll be as quiet as a mouse," Gerty urged affectionately.

"No—no; don't be quiet; talk to me—keep me awake! I don't sleep at night, and in the afternoon a dreadful drowsiness creeps over me. . . ."

"But you look so tired: I'm sure you must be ill—"

Miss Bart set down her cup with a start. "Do I look ill? Does my face show it?" . . . "After all I'd rather know the truth. Look me straight in the face, Gerty, and tell me: am I perfectly frightful?"

"You're perfectly beautiful now, Lily: your eyes are shining, and your cheeks have grown so pink all of a sudden—"

"Ah, they were pale, then—ghastly pale, when I came in? Why don't you tell me frankly that I'm a wreck? My eyes are bright now because I'm so nervous—but in the mornings they look like lead. And I can see the lines coming in my face—the lines of worry and disappointment and failure! Every sleepless night leaves a new one—and how can I sleep, when I have such dreadful things to think about?"

"Dreadful things—what things?" asked Gerty, gently detaching her wrists from her friend's feverish fingers.

"What things? Well, poverty, for one—and I don't know any that's more dreadful." Lily turned away and sank with sudden weariness into the easy-chair near the tea-table. . . . "You think we live *on* the rich, rather than with them: and so we do, in a sense—but it's a privilege we have to pay for! We eat their dinners, and drink their wine, and smoke their cigarettes, and use their carriages and their opera-boxes and their private cars—yes, but there's a tax to pay on every one of those luxuries. The man pays it by big tips to the servants, by playing cards beyond his means, by flowers and presents—and—and—lots of other things that cost; the girl pays it by tips and cards too—oh, yes, I've had to take up bridge again—and by going to the best dress-makers, and having just the right dress for every occasion, and always keeping herself fresh and exquisite and amusing!" . . .

"It doesn't sound very amusing, does it? And it isn't—I'm sick to death of it! And yet the thought of giving it all up nearly kills me—it's what keeps me awake at night, and makes me so crazy for your strong tea. For I can't go on in this way much longer, you know—I'm nearly at the end of my tether: And then what can I do—how on earth am I to keep myself alive? I see myself reduced to the fate of that poor Silverton woman—slinking about to employment agencies, and trying to sell painted blotting-pads to Women's Exchanges! And there are thousands and thousands of women trying to do the same thing already, and not one of the number who has less idea how to earn a dollar than I have!"

She rose again with a hurried glance at the clock. "It's late, and I must be off. . . . Don't look so worried, you dear thing—don't think too much about the nonsense I've been talking." She was before the mirror again, adjusting her hair with a light hand, drawing down her veil, and giving a dexterous touch to her furs.

"Of course, you know, it hasn't come to the employment agencies and the painted blotting-pads yet, but I'm rather hard-up just for the moment, and if I could find something to do—notes to write and visiting-lists to make up, or that kind of thing—it would tide me over till the legacy is paid. And Carry has promised to find somebody who wants a kind of social secretary—you know she makes a specialty of the help-less rich."

From *The House of Mirth* by Edith Wharton. Published by Bantam Books, Inc., 1984.

Analyzing Literature

1. How would you describe Lily Bart's mood? What was the cause of this mood?

2. What options for making a living did women like Lily have in this period?

3. According to Lily, why was it so costly for people with less money to keep up with their richer friends?

A Changing America
(1945–Present)

UNIT OVERVIEW

After World War II the U.S. government was active abroad, competing with the Soviet Union, and at home, where it sought to improve the lives of its citizens.

Chapter 30

The Cold War Era (1945–1991)
The United States and Soviet Union competed for influence around the world.

Chapter 31

Postwar America (1954–1992)
After a prosperous 1950s, the nation endured turmoil in the 1960s and early 1970s before stability returned in the 1980s.

Chapter 32

The Search for Equal Rights (1945–Present)
African Americans, Hispanic Americans, and other groups fought for legal and social equality.

Chapter 33

Patterns in Our Recent History (1990–Present)
Among the issues that this nation will face in the future are growing ethnic diversity and new changes in technology.

Illustration: Citizenship ceremony.

719

Soon after the fighting in World War II ended, a new war took its place: the cold war. Images of the cold war include a U.S. nuclear missile blasting out of the water, streetlights shining on the East German side of the Berlin Wall, and a Berlin Wall guard looking for signs of illegal activity.

1945

1955

1965

1945 United Nations formed

1947 Truman Doctrine

1947 Marshall Plan

1948 Berlin airlift begins

1950 Korean War begins

1962 Cuban missile crisis

1964 Gulf of Tonkin Resolution

The Cold War Era
(1945–1991)

1 A World Divided

SECTION GUIDE

Main Idea

After World War II, relations between the U.S. and the Soviet Union turned cold. The two superpowers often came close to direct warfare.

Goals

As you read, look for answers to these questions:

1 What events in Europe soured relations between the superpowers?

2 Why did war break out in Korea?

3 What crises did President Kennedy face in Cuba?

Key Terms

cold war
United Nations
containment
Truman Doctrine
Marshall Plan
NATO
Warsaw Pact
Korean War
Berlin Wall
Cuban missile crisis

THE SIREN PIERCED THE AIR. At their teacher's command, students ducked under their desks, preparing for nuclear attack. Such scenes were common during the cold war —the contest between the United States and the Soviet Union after World War II. The two sides never fought each other directly. Yet the cold war, a contest of will and nerves, shaped world events and people's lives for half a century.

The United Nations

In April 1945 delegates from 50 nations met in San Francisco to set up the United Nations (UN). In 1952 the UN moved to its permanent home in New York City. The main task of the UN was to work for world peace. The UN also aimed to help improve the lives of people around the world. It supplied food, capital, and technology to the world's poorer nations.

One of the UN's first challenges came in the Middle Eastern region of Palestine, which was ruled by Britain. Though most of the people in Palestine were Arabs, Jews from Europe and elsewhere had been settling there as well.

In 1947 the UN decided to split Palestine into two nations, one Arab and one Jewish. Britain withdrew from Palestine the following year. Jewish settlers then declared the founding of the nation of Israel. The Arab nations next to Israel invaded in hope

1975   **1985**   **1995**

1979 Americans taken hostage in Iran

1991 Soviet Union collapses

1978 Camp David Accords

1973 End of U.S. involvement in Vietnam War

1987 Reagan and Gorbachev sign historic arms treaty

1972 Nixon travels to China and Soviet Union

of destroying Israel. Israel won the war in 1949. Other major wars would occur in 1956, 1967, and 1973. These conflicts showed how difficult it would be for the UN to maintain world peace.

Soviet Expansion

Although France, England, and China were winners in World War II, they had been exhausted by the war. The Soviet Union too had suffered terribly, but it was by far the strongest power in Europe. It had huge armies and thousands of tanks. It was ruled by Joseph Stalin, whose very name meant "man of steel."

At the Yalta Conference in 1945, Stalin had agreed that there should be free elections in the nations of Eastern Europe. By the end of the war, Soviet troops occupied most of Poland, Romania, Bulgaria, Hungary, and the eastern third of Germany. If free elections were held, Stalin worried that these countries might elect anti-Soviet governments. To avoid that risk, the Soviets set up pro-Soviet Communist governments in Eastern Europe.

What was Stalin's goal? Some historians say that Stalin was determined to avoid another invasion from the West. Twice within 30 years the Soviet Union had been invaded. In World War II alone, an estimated 20 million Soviet citizens had died. According to this argument, Stalin wanted to use Eastern Europe as a buffer, or barrier, to protect the Soviet Union.

Other historians argue that Stalin wanted to spread communism throughout the world. That is what President Truman and

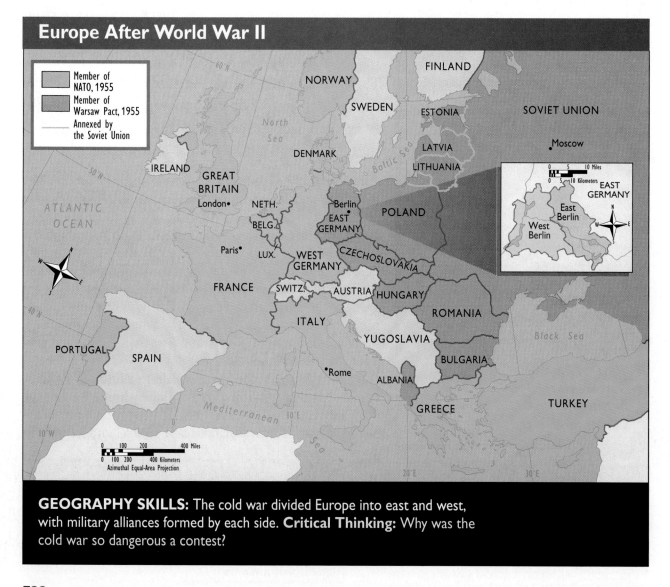

Europe After World War II

Member of NATO, 1955
Member of Warsaw Pact, 1955
Annexed by the Soviet Union

GEOGRAPHY SKILLS: The cold war divided Europe into east and west, with military alliances formed by each side. **Critical Thinking:** Why was the cold war so dangerous a contest?

his advisers thought. They became convinced that Stalin would take over Western Europe if he could. Ruined by war, Holland, Belgium, France, western Germany, and Italy all lay defenseless. Truman was determined to resist Soviet expansion. More than forty years later, Clark Clifford, a former Secretary of Defense, stated flatly, "Harry Truman saved the free world."

Containing the Soviets

The Truman government decided on a policy of **containment.** That meant that the United States would work in military and non-military ways to prevent communism from spreading around the world.

Containment was first announced in 1947. The Soviet government was trying to force Turkey to let it establish a naval base on Turkish territory. In addition, Truman believed that the Soviets were arming Greek Communists in a fierce civil war. Truman and his advisers thought that without American action, these nations might fall under Soviet control.

"I'm tired of babying the Russians," Truman told an adviser. In 1947 the President asked Congress to approve an aid package for Greece and Turkey. "I believe it must be the policy of the United States to support free peoples who are resisting attempted subjugation [enslavement] by armed minorities or by outside pressures," Truman boldly declared. This statement became known as the **Truman Doctrine.** It was the foundation of American foreign policy until the 1990s.

The Marshall Plan

Other European nations besides Greece and Turkey needed help too. In 1947 Truman's Secretary of State, George Marshall, announced a program of aid to Europe. It was called the **Marshall Plan.**

The goal of the Marshall Plan was to rebuild the cities, farms, and industries of Europe. American leaders hoped that if people's most basic needs for housing and food were met, they would be able to achieve prosperity. With healthy economies, people would resist communism.

The Marshall Plan was also offered to the Soviet Union and Soviet-controlled Eastern Europe. Stalin turned it down. He feared it would threaten Communist rule. In Western Europe, the Marshall Plan was wildly successful. By 1951 Western European economies were booming and democracy had been saved. British leader Winston Churchill called the Marshall Plan "the most unselfish act in history."

Airlift to Berlin

In 1945 Germany had been divided into zones. The parts occupied by troops from Britain, France, and the United States later became the nation of West Germany. The Soviet zone later became East Germany. The former capital of Germany, Berlin, was deep inside Soviet-controlled East Germany. Berlin was divided into halves—Soviet East Berlin and free West Berlin.

The Soviets wanted the Western powers out of Berlin. In 1948, Soviet troops closed off all ground routes into the city. In order

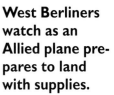

An overjoyed Austrian orphan hugs a new pair of shoes sent to him by the American Junior Red Cross.

West Berliners watch as an Allied plane prepares to land with supplies.

to save West Berlin, the United States and Britain began the Berlin airlift.

For nearly a year American and British cargo planes carried tons and tons of food, fuel, and other supplies to the more than 2 million citizens of West Berlin. Stalin's attempt to force the Western powers out of Berlin had failed. He finally ended the blockade. West Berlin had been saved.

The Beginning of NATO

During the Berlin blockade, the Western Powers called for the creation of **NATO** — the North Atlantic Treaty Organization. Nine European nations plus Canada, Iceland, and the United States promised to defend each other in case of attack.

The United States signed the treaty in 1949. This marked the first time in its history that the United States had joined a peacetime alliance that committed it to fight in Europe. A few years later the Soviet Union and nations of Eastern Europe formed an alliance similar to NATO called the **Warsaw Pact.** Europe was now divided into two armed camps.

American and South Korean troops search prisoners after the Inchon landing.
Critical Thinking: What part did the Korean War play in the cold war?

The Cold War in Asia

Meanwhile, the cold war had spread to Asia. It was in Asia that the cold war would turn "hot."

(1) *China.* In China, Communists led by Mao Zedong had been fighting for power since before World War II. In 1949 they overturned the government of Chiang Kai-shek. Chiang's government then fled to the small island of Formosa, now called Taiwan. Americans were shocked. A nation with one-fourth of the human race had become Communist. Many Americans saw the revolution as part of a Communist plot to rule the world.

(2) *Japan.* American troops occupied Japan at the end of World War II. General Douglas MacArthur became its military ruler. He had a new constitution written for Japan that created a democracy but also kept the Japanese emperor as a symbol of the nation. Massive American economic aid helped Japan rebuild its industry. Once bitter enemies, the United States and Japan became close allies.

(3) *Korea.* A colony of Japan since 1910, Korea was split in half after World War II. Communist North Korea was a Soviet ally. The United States backed South Korea.

In June 1950 North Korean forces swept over the border into South Korea. Truman called on the United Nations to help defend South Korea. The UN agreed. A total of sixteen nations sent soldiers to fight in the **Korean War.** About 90 percent of them were American. The commander of all UN forces was General MacArthur.

The Korean War

When MacArthur took over, the UN held barely a corner of the South Korean peninsula. In September 1950 MacArthur made a surprise move and landed forces behind the North Korean lines at Inchon. It was a daring, dangerous plan, but it worked. Within weeks, UN forces had retaken Seoul, South Korea's capital.

The Korean War

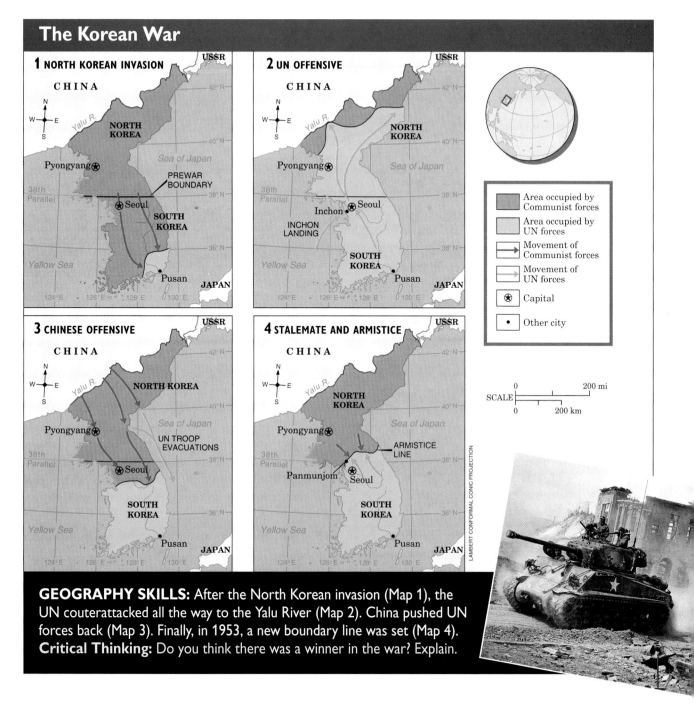

1 NORTH KOREAN INVASION

USSR
CHINA
Yalu R.
NORTH KOREA
Pyongyang ⊛
Sea of Japan
38th Parallel
PREWAR BOUNDARY
⊛ Seoul
SOUTH KOREA
Yellow Sea
• Pusan
JAPAN

2 UN OFFENSIVE

USSR
CHINA
Yalu R.
NORTH KOREA
Pyongyang ⊛
Sea of Japan
38th Parallel
Inchon ⊛ Seoul
INCHON LANDING
SOUTH KOREA
Yellow Sea
• Pusan
JAPAN

3 CHINESE OFFENSIVE

USSR
CHINA
Yalu R.
NORTH KOREA
Pyongyang ⊛
Sea of Japan
UN TROOP EVACUATIONS
38th Parallel
⊛ Seoul
SOUTH KOREA
Yellow Sea
• Pusan
JAPAN

4 STALEMATE AND ARMISTICE

USSR
CHINA
Yalu R.
NORTH KOREA
Pyongyang ⊛
Sea of Japan
ARMISTICE LINE
38th Parallel
Panmunjom • ⊛ Seoul
SOUTH KOREA
Yellow Sea
• Pusan
JAPAN

LAMBERT CONFORMAL CONIC PROJECTION

Area occupied by Communist forces
Area occupied by UN forces
Movement of Communist forces
Movement of UN forces
⊛ Capital
• Other city

SCALE
0   200 mi
0   200 km

GEOGRAPHY SKILLS: After the North Korean invasion (Map 1), the UN couterattacked all the way to the Yalu River (Map 2). China pushed UN forces back (Map 3). Finally, in 1953, a new boundary line was set (Map 4).
Critical Thinking: Do you think there was a winner in the war? Explain.

With the North Koreans in full retreat, MacArthur wanted to free North Korea from Communist rule. Truman agreed. UN forces pushed northward. To cut off Chinese help for North Korea, American planes bombed bridges on the Yalu River separating China from North Korea. China warned the UN to stop. Finally, as UN forces neared the Chinese border, China entered the war. The huge Chinese army began forcing the UN troops back.

MacArthur now asked for permission to bomb China. Truman, fearing that the bombing of China might lead to another global war, refused. In MacArthur's opinion, Truman was denying him the tools he needed to win the war. MacArthur said so—and he said it in public.

Truman Fires MacArthur

There were now two important issues at stake. The first one was whether the United States should pursue victory in Korea at all costs. The second issue concerned MacArthur's criticism of Truman. As President, Truman was commander-in-chief of the armed forces. Some people saw MacArthur's public attacks on his boss, President Truman, as an attack on the system of civilian control of the military.

In April 1951 Truman fired MacArthur and ordered him home. Supporters of MacArthur spoke of impeaching Truman. This talk grew as MacArthur received a hero's welcome at home. Truman, however, stuck to his position. In time the public came around to support him.

An End to the Korean War

As the unpopular war dragged on, Americans looked for new leadership. Truman decided to retire from politics. World War II hero Dwight D. Eisenhower, a Republican, won the 1952 presidential election. "I shall go to Korea," Eisenhower had promised during the campaign. Americans were hopeful that he could end the war.

The new President did go to Korea. He let it be known that he was willing to compromise to end the war. He also hinted to China that if the war continued, he might use the atomic bomb. In July 1953 both sides signed an armistice—halt in the fighting.

The war had cost the United States billions of dollars and 54,000 lives. Americans were glad the war was over, but there was no joy of victory. Neither side won. Though communism had been contained in Korea, it still dominated much of Asia and Europe.

Dwight D. Eisenhower, shown in Korea in 1952, took steps to end the fighting there the following year.

The "Balance of Terror"

During the 1950s new technology moved the cold war toward a new and more frightening phase, the "balance of terror." In 1949 the Soviet Union exploded its first atomic bomb. Three years later the United States built a hydrogen bomb, which was far deadlier than the atomic bomb. One year after that, in 1953, the Soviets had their own hydrogen bomb. By the end of the decade, both nations were developing missiles to carry their nuclear weapons.

The thought of nuclear war struck fear in the hearts of Americans. The government buried its military command post under a mountain in Colorado. Schoolchildren were told to duck under their desks during air-raid drills. Some American families bought backyard bomb shelters and stocked them with canned food.

Trouble in Berlin

In 1960 John F. Kennedy, a Democrat, was elected President. One of Kennedy's first tests as leader came over Berlin. West Berlin remained a thorn in the side of East Germany. Each year more and more East Germans fled to West Berlin. From there they traveled to West Germany and freedom. In the summer of 1961 East Germany built a wall between East and West Berlin.

West Berlin remained free, but East Germans could no longer reach it safely. East German guards patrolled the wall and shot anyone trying to flee. The Berlin Wall became a symbol of the cold war.

Two Crises over Cuba

Kennedy also faced trouble in Cuba. In 1959 Fidel Castro had taken power in Cuba. The next year he began taking over American-owned businesses. Cuba's relations with the United States soured. In 1961 Kennedy approved a plan for a group of anti-Castro Cuban exiles (Cubans living outside Cuba) to invade Cuba. The invaders were crushed at the Bay of Pigs.

Strengthened by his victory, Castro later declared himself a Communist. Kennedy, in contrast, looked weak and unsure of how to lead.

A more dangerous battle over Cuba took place in October 1962. American spy planes took pictures showing Soviet missiles being installed in Cuba. Faced with the prospect of nuclear missiles 90 miles from Florida, Kennedy knew he had to act.

Most of the President's advisers favored an air strike to destroy the missile sites. Kennedy, however, feared that if Soviet workers were killed, the Soviet Union might go to war. He chose instead a naval blockade of Cuba. He ordered the U.S. Navy to stop all Soviet ships headed for Cuba and search them. Those with missiles would be forced to return.

For six days after the blockade was announced, the world waited on the brink of a new world war. Just as war seemed likely, the Soviet ships heading for Cuba turned around. Soviet leader Nikita Khrushchev also agreed to remove the missile bases. In return, the United States promised not to invade Cuba. The Cuban missile crisis had ended.

The Cuban missile crisis was a turning point in the cold war. It showed the Americans and Soviets how close they could come to war, even if neither side wanted one. After the crisis, both sides worked to improve their relations. In 1963 they signed a treaty banning the testing of nuclear weapons in the air and under

Khrushchev and Kennedy (above) barely avoided war after Soviet ships were spotted carrying nuclear missiles (red arrows) to Cuba in 1962.

water. They also set up a "hotline," a way for American and Soviet leaders to communicate directly in times of trouble.

SECTION REVIEW

1. Key Terms cold war, United Nations, containment, Truman Doctrine, Marshall Plan, NATO, Warsaw Pact, Korean War, Berlin Wall, Cuban missile crisis

2. People and Places Joseph Stalin, George Marshall, Douglas MacArthur, Fidel Castro, Nikita Khrushchev, Israel, Berlin, Korea, Cuba

3. Comprehension Why did Stalin turn down the Marshall Plan?

4. Comprehension Why did war break out in Korea? How did the UN respond?

5. Critical Thinking Why did the U.S. and the Soviet Union want to improve relations after the Cuban missile crisis?

SECTION GUIDE

Main Idea
American involvement in the Vietnam War cost many thousands of lives and divided American society.

Goals
As you read, look for answers to these questions:

1 What steps led to U.S. involvement in Vietnam?

2 What effect did the Tet Offensive have on American society?

3 What eventually happened after U.S. troops left Vietnam?

Key Terms
Vietnam War
Geneva Accords
Vietcong
Gulf of Tonkin Resoultion
Tet Offensive
MIA

Two American soldiers see action near Saigon. The Vietnam War remains a painful memory for many Americans.

THE KOREAN WAR began as an attempt to prevent Communists from taking over a small, divided nation. That same goal would later draw America into the Vietnam War, which most historians believe was one of the worst foreign-policy mistakes in our history. It was America's longest war and its first defeat.

Background of the War

In 1950, three days before American ground troops began to fight in Korea, President Truman sent 35 military advisers to Vietnam. Vietnam was then part of the French colonial empire of Indochina. Truman needed France's help against the Soviet Union in Europe. In return, France demanded help in its struggle against the Vietnamese Communist leader, Ho Chi Minh.

The Vietnamese people wanted the French out of their country. They backed Ho Chi Minh and his army, led by the brilliant General Giap. Giap fought guerrilla-style, never letting his army become trapped in a battle against larger forces. His men struck quickly and then disappeared into the countryside.

The final blow to French hopes came in 1954 at Dien Bien Phu. Giap surrounded a large French army with a larger Vietnamese army and defeated the French in a huge battle. The French demanded that U.S. troops be sent to Vietnam to help them. President Eisenhower refused. France then decided to pull out of Vietnam.

The Geneva Accords

In 1954 diplomats meeting in Geneva, Switzerland, reached an international agreement called the Geneva Accords. It split Vietnam into two parts. The northern half of Vietnam was Communist, led by Ho Chi Minh. Its capital was Hanoi. The southern half, with its capital in Saigon, was non-Communist. It was led by Ngo Dinh Diem. The Geneva Accords called for free elections to be held in Vietnam in 1956.

Now came a major turning point. With U.S. support, Diem refused to hold the 1956 election. He knew, and Eisenhower knew, that Ho Chi Minh would win the election. Hoping that Diem would be an ally against communism, the U.S. government sent more military advisers and aid to South Vietnam.

The Vietcong

Diem's main opponent within South Vietnam was the National Liberation Front, or **Vietcong.** The Vietcong were South Vietnamese Communists backed by North Vietnam. Their goals were to drive out Diem and the Americans and to reunite South Vietnam with North Vietnam. They were disciplined soldiers with a strong will to win.

The South Vietnamese army, in contrast, was corrupt and frightened. Many South Vietnamese soldiers were sure the Vietcong would win and were afraid of them. Sometimes they would even sell their guns to the Vietcong. At other times, when the Vietcong attacked, the soldiers would drop their weapons and run away.

When Kennedy became President in 1961, Diem was losing the war in South Vietnam to the Vietcong. Kennedy sent many more military advisers to Vietnam. Believing that a better South Vietnamese leader could win the war, Kennedy did not interfere when the military overthrew Diem's government.

Deeper U.S. Involvement

Lyndon B. Johnson became President late in 1963. Advised by many of the same experts who advised Kennedy, Johnson was the first President to send American combat soldiers to fight in Vietnam.

In 1964 Johnson claimed that North Vietnam had attacked U.S. Navy ships in the Gulf of Tonkin, off the coast of North Vietnam. (It is not clear whether the attack took place.) He sent Congress the **Gulf of Tonkin Resolution.** This statement allowed Johnson to "take all necessary measures" to protect Americans in Vietnam. It was a turning point in American involvement in Vietnam. Johnson used the resolution as an unofficial declaration of war. The United States began bombing North Vietnam and sent troops into battle in South Vietnam.

CULTURAL MOSAIC

DITH PRAN (1943–)

Dith Pran was a Cambodian journalist who had helped foreign reporters cover the Vietnam War in his country. In 1975 he was captured by the cruel forces of the Khmer Rouge, who had taken power in Cambodia. He struggled to survive, sometimes eating as little as one spoonful of rice a day. Dith Pran eventually escaped. The 1984 film *The Killing Fields* is about his life. He now works in the United States as a photojournalist.

Debate over the War

Before 1967 American critics of the war, called "doves," were few in number. Most Americans accepted the arguments of the "hawks," those who supported the war. As the war continued, however, opposition grew. Many huge antiwar marches took place. Congress began to hold hearings critical of the war. Doubts about the war even surfaced among Johnson's aides.

By the end of 1967, Americans had been fighting in Vietnam for three years. Millions of young men had been sent there, and billions of dollars had been spent. Despite hopeful reports by American military leaders, the war did not seem to be going well. If we were winning, people wondered, why were more and more soldiers needed?

Some Americans believed that the way to win the war was to launch a full-scale invasion of North Vietnam. Without help from North Vietnam, they argued, the Vietcong could not survive.

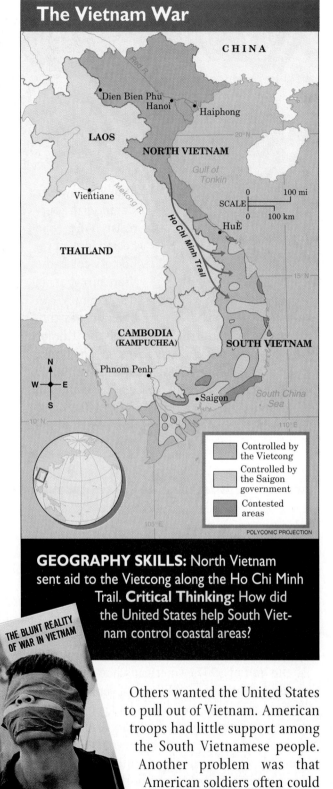

The Vietnam War

CHINA

Red R.

Dien Bien Phu
Hanoi
Haiphong

LAOS

NORTH VIETNAM

20°N

Gulf of
Tonkin

Vientiane

Mekong R.

SCALE
0   100 mi
0   100 km

HuÈ

Ho Chi Minh Trail

THAILAND

15°N

CAMBODIA
(KAMPUCHEA)

SOUTH VIETNAM

Phnom Penh

N
W   E
S

Saigon

South China
Sea

10°N

110°E

Controlled by
the Vietcong

Controlled by
the Saigon
government

Contested
areas

105°E

POLYCONIC PROJECTION

GEOGRAPHY SKILLS: North Vietnam sent aid to the Vietcong along the Ho Chi Minh Trail. **Critical Thinking:** How did the United States help South Vietnam control coastal areas?

LIFE

THE BLUNT REALITY
OF WAR IN VIETNAM

NOVEMBER 26 · 1965 · 35¢

Johnson chose a course somewhere in the middle. He resisted calls for a full-scale war or a complete pullout of American troops. Instead he steadily escalated, or increased, the number of troops and bombing raids. He hoped that North Vietnam would ask for peace talks. In early 1968, however, Johnson's middle course of action exploded like a land mine.

The Tet Offensive

January 30, 1968, was the beginning of Tet, the Vietnamese New Year. There was supposed to be a holiday ceasefire. Instead, Vietcong forces launched the Tet Offensive —surprise attacks on cities all over South Vietnam. In Saigon, the very heart of American power in Vietnam, American soldiers fought for their lives at the U.S. Embassy.

The Vietcong lost many troops in the fighting. Yet in political terms, the offensive was a huge victory for the Vietcong. It proved that they were still active throughout South Vietnam. In the United States, the much-trusted newscaster Walter Cronkite angrily reported that despite what the government said, the war had become a stalemate. Watching Cronkite's report, Johnson sadly remarked, "If I have lost Walter, I have lost America."

After the Tet Offensive, many Americans found it hard to believe official statements about the war. Ending the war was becoming more important to them than winning it. Americans wanted, above all else, for their sons and daughters to come home. Exhausted from the strains of the war, Johnson announced that he would not run for re-election.

Nixon Winds Down the War

Republican Richard Nixon was elected President in 1968, in part because he promised "peace with honor" in Vietnam. This policy meant withdrawing American soldiers and turning the war over to the

Others wanted the United States to pull out of Vietnam. American troops had little support among the South Vietnamese people. Another problem was that American soldiers often could not tell who supported the Vietcong and who did not. Many innocent people were killed.

CONNECTING WITH THE

WOMEN IN VIETNAM

They were said to have young faces and old eyes. The thousands of U.S. Army nurses who served in Vietnam walked among mangled bodies and felt the impact of falling bombs. Like other veterans, they received no hero's welcome when they returned home.

On Veteran's Day, in November 1993, a bronze statue (left) was dedicated in Washington, D.C. It shows two women helping a wounded soldier. At the ceremony, one veteran noted, "It took a long time to figure out that what we did during the Vietnam War was very important."

The decal above reminds Americans of the Vietnam War's POWs (Prisoners Of War) and MIAs (soldiers Missing In Action).

South Vietnamese army. It also meant bombing targets in North and South Vietnam to prove that the United States remained committed to the South. In the end, more bombs were dropped on Vietnam—a country the size of New Mexico—than were dropped in all of World War II.

Peace talks began in 1969. American combat troops were pulled out a few at a time, the last being withdrawn in 1972. In the meantime, heavy bombing of targets in North and South Vietnam continued. Finally, early in 1973 a peace agreement was signed.

The real end of the war came two years later. North Vietnam launched a giant offensive against the South. The South Vietnamese army and government collapsed. North and South Vietnam officially reunited under Communist rule in 1976. The neighboring countries of Laos and Cambodia fell to Communists as well.

The Vietnam War took the lives of more than 50,000 Americans. It drained billions of dollars from the nation's economy. It shook Americans' faith in their government and raised new doubts about whether the United States should be

involved in foreign conflicts. Relatives of MIAs —soldiers listed as Missing In Action—would pray for years that their loved ones would return alive. For all of these reasons, the Vietnam War remains a painful scar in American history.

SECTION REVIEW

1. Key Terms Vietnam War, Geneva Accords, Vietcong, Gulf of Tonkin Resolution, Tet Offensive, MIA

2. People and Places Ho Chi Minh, Ngo Dinh Diem, Lyndon Johnson, Richard Nixon, Hanoi, Saigon

3. Comprehension Why did Vietnam go to war with France?

4. Comprehension Why was the Gulf of Tonkin Resolution a turning point in U.S. involvement in the war?

5. Critical Thinking Compare and contrast the arguments "hawks" and "doves" might have made about the fighting in Vietnam.

Remembering Vietnam

The Vietnam Veterans Memorial in Washington, D.C., is often called "the Wall." It is simple and stark, a black granite scar in the green lawn near the Washington Monument. Some say that anyone who walks its length and sees the more than 58,000 names etched into it will never think the same

way about war again. The memorial lists the men and women in the armed forces who died during the Vietnam War. It also honors those who remain missing.

Visitors to the wall often leave objects at its base. The National Park Service collects them and keeps them in a safe place. These items are a kind of memorial too.

The items include everything from flags, flight jackets, and combat medals to a model ship, a wedding ring, and a stuffed bear. There are letters written to those whose names are on the wall. They come from parents, army buddies, and high-school friends.

Maya Ying Lin, an Asian American, designed the wall in 1981. She was 21. She believed that names alone could be a memorial. "I felt a memorial should be honest about the reality of war and be for the people who gave their lives. . . . I didn't want a static object people would just look at, but something they could relate to as on a journey, or passage. . . ."

It is a journey for all of us. More than a million Americans fought in Vietnam between 1965 and 1975, and veterans are a common sight at the wall. Yet the patriotism and sacrifice that the wall represents are ideals that every American should try to understand.

A veteran shows his child a name on the wall.

CRITICAL THINKING

1. Describe the emotions someone might feel visiting the Vietnam Memorial.
2. Why, in your opinion, do visitors leave things behind at the memorial?
3. Explain why war memorials are important for all Americans.

3 The End of the Cold War

SECTION GUIDE

Main Idea
Richard Nixon and the Presidents who followed him worked to smooth relations with the Soviet Union. The collapse of the Soviet Union in 1991 brought an end to the cold war.

Goals
As you read, look for answers to these questions:

1. How did Nixon improve relations with the Soviet Union?

2. How did Carter experience both success and failure in the Middle East?

3. How did Reagan deal with the cold war?

Key Terms
SALT
détente
human rights
Camp David Accords

RICHARD MILHOUS NIXON is the first President of the United States to be the subject of a grand opera. *Nixon in China* tells of Nixon's historic visit to Communist China early in 1972. That visit, the first by an American President, marked an important change in American cold war policies.

Nixon Eases the Cold War

Nixon and his chief foreign policy adviser, Henry Kissinger, were realists. They thought of foreign policy in terms of power, not morals or ideals. In this view, the enemies of your enemies were your friends, whether you liked them or not. Nixon used this strategy to try to divide China and the Soviet Union. Relations between the two largest Communist powers had been uneasy. By talking with both of them, Nixon tried to play the two powers off against one another.

Nixon's trip to China was the first step. Next he traveled to the Soviet Union. There he signed a treaty that grew out of the Strategic Arms Limitation Talks, or **SALT.** This was the first agreement between the United States and the Soviet Union to limit the growth of nuclear missiles. Still the limits were high. Under SALT the two nations were allowed roughly 4,000 missiles between them.

By ending the Vietnam War and improving relations with China and the Soviet Union, Nixon brought a period of **détente** to the cold war. (Détente is a French term meaning "relaxation of tensions.") Gerald Ford, who followed Nixon as President, continued Nixon's policy of détente for most of his term.

Carter's Foreign Policy

Jimmy Carter was President from 1977 to 1981. He supported détente but wanted to make further changes to U.S. cold war policies. Carter was concerned about nations making up the so-called "Third World"—the developing nations of Africa, Asia, and Latin America. Many of these nations suffered from extreme poverty. Often controlled by

President Nixon reviews Chinese troops during his 1972 visit. Behind him is First Lady Pat Nixon.

Egypt's Anwar el-Sadat (left), President Carter (middle), and Israel's Menachem Begin (right) speak to reporters during the peace talks at Camp David, Maryland.

Iranians demonstrate outside the U.S. embassy in Tehran. The sign refers to the U.S. economic boycott of Iran following the taking of the hostages.

dictators, these nations were neither Communist nor democratic.

Carter understood that the cold war had harmed Third World nations. To gain the support of the leaders of those nations, both superpowers bribed them with military aid. The dictators ruling in the Third World used this aid to keep themselves in power. Often this meant denying their own people **human rights.** These are the basic rights and freedoms to which all people are entitled.

Carter hoped to make human rights a centerpiece of U.S. foreign policy. He withheld U.S. aid from several nations that violated human rights.

One of Carter's biggest foreign policy successes came in Panama. The United States owned the Panama Canal and a strip of land on each side of it. Many Panamanians wanted control of these areas. In 1977 the United States and Panama signed a treaty calling for this to happen in the year 2000.

Some Americans fiercely opposed what they called the "giveaway" of the Panama Canal. "We built it, we paid for it, it's ours, and we're going to keep it," said Ronald Reagan. Yet to Carter, giving up the canal was one way of showing that the United States would treat Third World nations more fairly.

Carter's opponents said he worried too much about fairness and not enough about Soviet expansion. The Soviets, they argued, were using détente to gain an advantage over the United States among Third World nations.

In 1979 the Soviets invaded the neighboring nation of Afghanistan to help save a failing Communist government. The invasion killed détente. Carter declared an embargo on grain shipments to the Soviet Union and announced a boycott of the 1980 Summer Olympics in Moscow.

The Middle East

The Middle East was the subject of one of Carter's triumphs, a historic 1978 peace treaty between Egypt and Israel. Under this treaty, the Camp David Accords, Egypt became the first of Israel's neighbors to recognize its right to exist.

The Middle East, however, also gave Carter his biggest setback: Iran. Iran's U.S.-backed leader, the shah, had lost popular support. To stay in power, he became even harsher in his rule.

In 1979, under great pressure from the Iranian people, the shah fled the country. His government was replaced by a group of Muslim mullahs, or religious leaders. They shared a burning hatred of the United States. In 1979 a group of Iranians seized the American embassy in Tehran and held its employees hostage. Carter began secret talks for the release of the hostages.

For more than a year Americans watched the hostages being paraded before television cameras. Iranian crowds shouted, "Death to America!" Carter tried a rescue mission but it was a complete failure.

Finally the talks paid off. The hostages were released in January 1981. The crisis, however, had killed Carter's chances for re-election. On the very day the hostages were set free, a new President took office. The new President, Ronald Reagan, vowed that the United States would no longer be pushed around.

Reagan and the "Evil Empire"

Reagan wasted no time showing what he meant. He called the Soviet Union an "evil empire" and began the most expensive arms buildup in history, costing more than $2 trillion. One of Reagan's proposals, the Strategic Defense Initiative, was a space-based missile system to defend the United States from nuclear attack. It was nick-named "Star Wars" after a popular science fiction movie.

Reagan challenged communism everywhere. He smuggled arms to the rebels fighting the Soviet Union in Afghanistan. He aided the anti-Communist side in two Central American civil wars. In Nicaragua the United States backed rebels called *contras*. In El Salvador the United States backed the government against Communist-led rebels. Reagan also ordered the invasion of the Caribbean island nation of Grenada to overthrow a Communist government there.

Reforming the Soviet Union

By 1985 the Soviet Union was in deep trouble. Its top leaders were old and sick. Its Communist economy, based on central control rather than the free market, was falling apart. Its people had neither comfortable lives nor freedom. The Soviet army was bogged down in its own Vietnam, a no-win struggle in Afghanistan.

Ronald Reagan and Mikhail Gorbachev share a laugh after a meeting in Iceland in 1986. U.S. relations with the Soviet Union improved after Gorbachev came to power.

The Communist nations of Eastern Europe were restless because they could see how prosperous their Western neighbors were.

Desperate, the Soviet leadership turned to Mikhail Gorbachev. Gorbachev wanted to stop the arms race because it was bankrupting his country. More importantly, Gorbachev wanted to reform the Soviet system. He allowed people to criticize Communist Party officials and even to vote them out of local offices. These policies

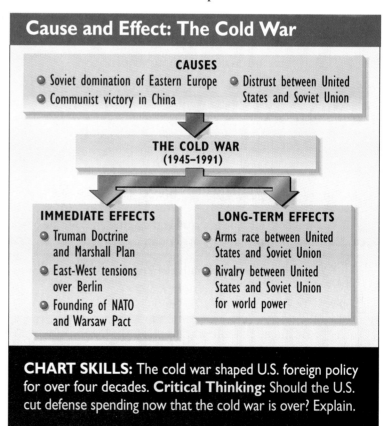

Cause and Effect: The Cold War

CAUSES
- Soviet domination of Eastern Europe
- Communist victory in China
- Distrust between United States and Soviet Union

THE COLD WAR (1945–1991)

IMMEDIATE EFFECTS
- Truman Doctrine and Marshall Plan
- East-West tensions over Berlin
- Founding of NATO and Warsaw Pact

LONG-TERM EFFECTS
- Arms race between United States and Soviet Union
- Rivalry between United States and Soviet Union for world power

CHART SKILLS: The cold war shaped U.S. foreign policy for over four decades. **Critical Thinking:** Should the U.S. cut defense spending now that the cold war is over? Explain.

SKILLS: Arranging Events in Sequence

LEARN

Suppose you decide to write your "life story." You begin with the day in fifth grade when your painting won a prize. Then you describe last week's soccer match. Next you tell about the day you took your first step. Then you recall your second-grade teacher.

What is wrong with your story? The events are out of sequence. Why is this confusing? Life is about connections. Things that happened earlier in our lives affect later events. When the events are out of sequence, the connections—causes and effects—get lost.

The same is true with history. The story of the past is best told with its events in sequence. Read the list of important cold war events at the right. The list suggests that the cold war was full of crises and conflicts. That is true. But because the events are in the wrong sequence, the connections are unclear. Without sequence, there is no story—and no history.

Events of the Cold War

- French withdraw from Vietnam.
- East Germany constructs Berlin Wall.
- North Korea and South Korea sign armistice.
- Vietcong launch Tet Offensive.
- United States and Soviet Union face off in Cuban missile crisis.
- Nixon visits China.
- Peace agreement ends Vietnam War.
- Fidel Castro takes power in Cuba.
- MacArthur lands at Inchon.
- Congress passes Gulf of Tonkin Resolution.
- Berlin Wall comes down.
- Bay of Pigs invasion fails.
- Reagan and Gorbachev sign treaty on medium-range nuclear missiles.
- Berlin airlift begins.
- Marshall Plan announced.

PRACTICE

1. Arrange, in proper sequence, the events of the "life story" described above. Do you see any possible connections between events? Explain.

2. Look at the list of cold war events. Find all the events related to Germany and arrange them in sequence.

3. Find the events related to Vietnam and arrange them in sequence.

APPLY

4. Find all the cold war events in the list that are related to one of the following countries: Germany, Vietnam, Korea, or Cuba. Write a paragraph or two presenting those events in sequence. Fill in any missing information so that the causes and effects are clear.

made Gorbachev the enemy of hard-line Communists but a hero in the West.

Reagan and Gorbachev met four times. They trusted and liked each other. Gorbachev promised not to use force to control Eastern Europe. He promised to end the war in Afghanistan. In return, Reagan agreed to end the arms race.

In 1987, at their final meeting, Reagan and Gorbachev signed a historic treaty. In it the United States and the Soviet Union agreed to destroy all their medium-range nuclear missiles.

The Soviet Union Collapses

In 1989 George Bush took office as President. During the next two years the Communist world fell apart.

Gorbachev pulled the last Soviet troops out of Afghanistan. In 1989 the Berlin Wall, long a symbol of the cold war, was torn down. In 1990 East and West Germany officially reunited. Across Eastern Europe, nations freed themselves from communism. They created new governments and introduced free market systems. In contrast to earlier times, when Soviet tanks had crushed reforms, the Soviets now stood aside.

Within the Soviet Union, the forces Gorbachev had set in motion swept him aside. In August 1991 a group of hard-line Communists tried to seize power from the government. The man who led the fight to defeat them was Boris Yeltsin, president of Russia. Yeltsin's popularity soared. He, unlike Gorbachev, was willing to break completely with communism. Gorbachev, trusted neither by the Communists nor by the people, lost power.

One by one the republics that made up the Soviet Union chose to become independent nations. On December 25, 1991, in the Kremlin—headquarters of the Soviet

government—the Soviet flag was lowered for the last time. The Soviet Union, once a world superpower, was no more.

The collapse of the Soviet Union meant the cold war was over after nearly half a century. The United States had won their long, costly struggle against Soviet communism. New challenges awaited the United States, but the end of the cold war brought new hopes for peace.

Boris Yeltsin triumphantly waves a Russian flag after Communists failed to regain power in the Soviet Union in 1991. Above, a statue of Lenin lies on its side, a sign of communism's collapse.

SECTION REVIEW

1. Key Terms SALT, détente, human rights, Camp David Accords

2. People and Places Richard Nixon, Jimmy Carter, Ronald Reagan, Mikhail Gorbachev, Boris Yeltsin, China, Soviet Union, Panama, Iran

3. Comprehension How did Nixon try to play off China against the Soviet Union?

4. Comprehension What was the Iran hostage crisis? How did it end?

5. Critical Thinking Do you think it is a safer world now that the cold war has ended? Why or why not?

Summary

1. After World War II ended, a new war took its place: the cold war. Truman's determination to resist Soviet expansion led to the Marshall Plan, which helped rebuild Western Europe. The cold war also spread to Asia, which led to the Korean War in 1950. The U.S. came close to war with the Soviet Union during the Cuban missile crisis of 1962. After that, the two nations worked to improve relations.

2. In the early 1960s the U.S. became involved in a conflict between Communist North Vietnam and non-Communist South Vietnam. The U.S. first sent advisers, then soldiers, to help South Vietnam. Protests against the war in the U.S. increased as the war dragged on. By the war's end in 1975, over 50,000 Americans had died in the conflict and South Vietnam had been conquered.

3. The cold war began to ease in the early 1970s under President Nixon. Yet by 1980 U.S.-Soviet tensions again grew. The renewed cold war eased again after Mikhail Gorbachev took power in the Soviet Union. It ended when the Soviet Union collapsed in 1991.

Review

KEY TERMS

Define the terms in each of the following pairs:
1. Truman Doctrine; United Nations
2. détente; SALT
3. cold war; NATO
4. Vietcong; Tet Offensive
5. human rights; containment

COMPREHENSION

1. What reasons do historians give for Stalin's creation of pro-Soviet Communist governments in Eastern Europe after World War II?
2. What were the goals of the Marshall Plan? Why did Stalin turn it down?
3. What two issues were at stake after General MacArthur publicly disagreed with President Truman over the bombing of China?
4. Describe the events that led to the Cuban missile crisis.
5. Why was the Gulf of Tonkin Resolution a turning point for U.S. involvement in the Vietnam War?
6. How was the Tet Offensive a victory for the Vietcong?
7. List the negative effects of the Vietnam War on the United States.
8. Why did President Carter agree to give up the Panama Canal?
9. Give three examples of how President Reagan fought communism around the world.
10. What happened to the Soviet Union between August and December 1991?

Graphic Summary

1940s: Truman Doctrine; Marshall Plan; Berlin airlift

1950s: Korean War ends in stalemate

1960s: Cuban missile crisis; Vietnam War at its height

1970s: Détente; Vietnam War ends; Carter's human rights policy

1980s: Arms race ends; communism collapses

Places to Locate

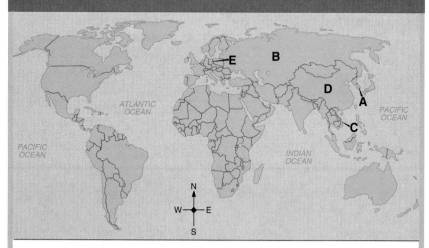

Match the letters on the map with the places that are listed below. Then explain the importance of each place.

1. Soviet Union   **3.** East Germany   **5.** Vietnam
2. Korea   **4.** China

Geographic Theme: Location Why did the United States demand that Soviet missiles be removed from Cuba in 1962?

Skill Review

Study the list of events below and answer the questions that follow.

Camp David Accords signed.
Soviet Union collapses.
George Bush becomes President.
American embassy in Tehran seized.

East and West Germany reunite.
Reagan becomes President.
Nixon visits China.
Carter becomes President.

1. Arrange the events in proper sequence.
2. Which event happened first, the Camp David Accords or Nixon's visit to China?
3. Which two events occurred while George Bush was President?

4. Use the events above and information from the chapter to write a brief essay discussing major cold war events during the presidencies of Nixon, Carter, Reagan, and Bush. Make sure the information in your essay is in proper sequence.

CRITICAL THINKING

1. Understanding the Main Idea Explain how U.S. involvement in Korea was an example of the Truman Doctrine in action.

2. Recognizing a Frame of Reference Describe the disagreement between Truman and MacArthur in terms of the different responsibilities and views each had during the Korean War.

PORTFOLIO OPTIONS

1. Civics Connection Imagine your classroom is a college campus during the early 1970s. Divide the class in half and hold a debate on the fighting in Vietnam.

2. Writing Connection Imagine you are an American soldier fighting in Vietnam in the early 1970s. Write a letter home explaining your position on U. S. involvement in the war.

3. Contemporary Connection Some analysts believe that television coverage of the Vietnam War turned Americans against the war. How might television have affected public opinion? What responsibilities do you think broadcasters have in reporting the news? Explain your views.

4. Timeline Connection Copy the chapter timeline. Which event do you think was most significant for American foreign policy? Explain. Then add events from the chapter you think should be included and explain why.

The years after World War II were a time of enormous economic growth. People could afford to buy more things, like houses in the suburbs, televisions, and cars. Though Americans continued to face challenges, millions of families from the 1950s (left) through the 1980s (right) enjoyed the benefits of living and working in the United States.

1945	1950	1955	1960	1965

1948 Truman elected President

1952 Eisenhower elected President

1956 Highway Act of 1956

1960 Kennedy elected President

1963 Kennedy assassinated

1964 Johnson's Great Society launched

Postwar America
(1945–1990)

1 Peace and Prosperity

SECTION GUIDE

Main Idea

Americans tried to maintain prosperity as they adjusted to peacetime. There were tremendous changes in where and how people lived.

Goals

As you read, look for answers to these questions:

1 What economic fears did Americans face after World War II?

2 How did fears of communism affect the United States?

3 What changes took place in postwar American society?

Key Terms

Taft-Hartley Act
Dixiecrat
Fair Deal
perjury
McCarthyism
baby boom
sunbelt
rock 'n' roll

AUGUST 14, 1945. "JAPAN SURRENDERS," "THE WAR IS OVER"—the newspaper headlines shouted. People danced in the streets and there was a two-day national holiday. Still, the joy of victory was mixed with uncertainty. Would the hard times of the Great Depression return?

Postwar Economic Fears

As World War II was nearing an end, Prime Minister Churchill told the British House of Commons, "America stands at this moment at the summit of the world." No one doubted Churchill's words. There were, however, many Americans who wondered whether Harry Truman would be as strong a leader as Franklin Roosevelt.

Mostly people worried about economic issues like jobs and inflation. During the war all the nation's resources had gone to making war supplies. Cars had not been built since 1941. Tires, gasoline, coffee, and many other products had been rationed— that is, people could buy only small amounts of them. Americans had worked long hours during the war and had put much of their money into savings accounts. They were ready for a spending spree.

When people have plenty of money and want to buy things that are in short supply, the result is inflation. During the war, the government had put controls, or limits, on prices. When

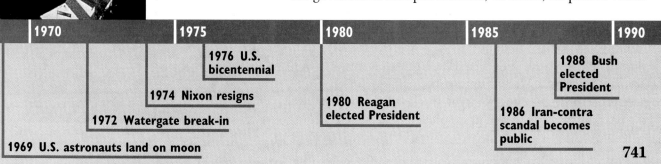

1970	1975	1980	1985	1990

1976 U.S. bicentennial

1974 Nixon resigns

1980 Reagan elected President

1988 Bush elected President

1986 Iran-contra scandal becomes public

1972 Watergate break-in

1969 U.S. astronauts land on moon

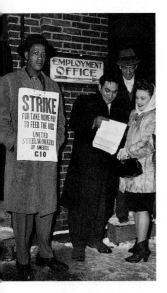

Unemployment and inflation after World War II led to strikes, such as this one by steelworkers in 1946.

"DEWEY DEFEATS TRUMAN" the headline of this newspaper screamed in November 1948. However, the paper had gone to press before the final results were in. A victorious Harry Truman, holding the newspaper, proved the headline wrong.

controls were removed in 1946, prices of new homes, clothing, and food skyrocketed.

Unemployment jumped too. Businesses that had made wartime goods now laid off workers. A Boeing aircraft plant in Washington let go more than 29,000 workers in a single day. Women, many of whom had worked in factories and offices during the war, were hit hardest. Between September 1945 and November 1946, over 3 million women lost their jobs.

Workers Go on Strike

During the war, unions had promised not to go on strike. Now they wanted better pay and working conditions. About 4.5 million workers went on strike in 1946.

The most serious strike was led by railroad workers. Travelers were stranded. Crops rotted in the fields because farmers could not get them to market.

Truman saw himself as a friend of workers. Still, he had had enough. He threatened to draft all railroad workers into the army and then have the army run the trains. When told such an action would be unconstitutional, Truman responded, "We'll draft 'em first and think about the law later." The strike was settled before Truman could carry out his threat.

A Republican Congress

Voters' fears about the economy hurt the Democrats. In 1946 the voters elected a Republican majority in both houses of Congress. Congress was determined to block Truman's programs. It rejected his plans to provide federal funds for housing, education, and health care.

Congress also took aim at the unions. In 1947 Congress passed the Taft-Hartley Act. It weakened unions by making closed shops illegal. (A closed shop is a place of employment in which

only union members are hired.) The law also gave the President the power to stop strikes for up to 80 days if public safety or health were threatened.

Congress also proposed the 22nd Amendment, which limits the President to two elected terms. The Republicans did not want another four-term President like Franklin Roosevelt. It was ratified in 1951.

Truman Wins in 1948

As the 1948 election campaign opened, strikes, inflation, and unemployment battered Truman. Truman's Republican opponent was New York Governor Thomas Dewey. Handsome and dignified, Dewey looked the part of a President.

Truman could not even control his own party. At the Democratic Convention, some southern delegates walked out because of Truman's support of civil rights. Calling themselves the States' Rights Party, or Dixiecrats, the southern Democrats nominated Strom Thurmond of South Carolina for President.

Another group of Democrats, upset by Truman's strong stand against the Soviet Union, called themselves the Progressive Party. They nominated Henry Wallace, who had been Vice President under Franklin Roosevelt.

With the three-way split in the Democratic Party, most Americans assumed that

Dewey would be elected. Yet Harry Truman was a fighter. He went on a "whistle-stop" tour of the country, taking a train through hundreds of cities and small towns. The train would stop, a crowd would gather around it, and Truman would blast the "do-nothing" Republican Congress for the nation's troubles. "Give 'em hell, Harry!" the crowds shouted.

When the early returns began to come in, it appeared that Dewey would win. Yet Truman's appeal to labor, African Americans, and average citizens carried the day. He defeated Dewey by winning 49.5 percent of the popular vote to Dewey's 45 percent. Democrats also regained control of both houses of Congress.

In his campaign, Truman had promised a Fair Deal for Americans. His Fair Deal program called on the government to create jobs, build public housing, and end job discrimination against African Americans. In the next few years, however, Republicans and southern Democrats blocked most of Truman's plans.

CULTURAL MOSAIC

LUIS MUÑOZ MARÍN
(1898–1980)

Another 1948 election winner was Luis Muñoz Marín, Puerto Rico's first elected governor. He headed a political party aimed at social and economic reform. Muñoz Marín promoted "Operation Bootstrap," which combined public and private enterprise to help improve the island's economy and slow the rate of poverty. In 1952, with his support, Puerto Rico became a U. S. commonwealth with its own constitution. Muñoz Marín served four terms, until 1965.

Luis Muñoz Marín — USA 05 — Governor, Puerto Rico

A New Red Scare

Meanwhile, a new concern was gaining more and more attention. Americans, fearful of communism around the world, feared it at home as well. Just as there was a "Red scare" after World War I, many Americans wondered after World War II if Communist spies were betraying the nation.

In 1938 the House of Representatives had set up the House Committee on Un-American Activities (HUAC). One of its jobs was to look for signs of Communist influence in the United States. In 1947 it began targeting the movie industry. HUAC believed Communists were sneaking propaganda into films. Dozens of actors, directors, and writers had their careers ruined, often on the basis of little or no proof.

Truman did not believe many of the stories about Communists. Yet he created a Loyalty Review Board to check the loyalty of federal employees. Thousands were forced to resign, again with little proof against them. The rest had to sign loyalty oaths in order to keep their jobs.

Two famous trials increased public fears. A government official named Alger Hiss was accused of spying for the Soviet Union. He was later convicted of perjury —lying under oath. A couple named Ethel and Julius Rosenberg were convicted of giving atomic secrets to the Soviet Union and executed. These cases strengthened fears that Communists were everywhere.

Public fears created an opening for Senator Joseph McCarthy, a Republican from Wisconsin. He claimed that there were hundreds of Communists and their supporters in the government. The Democrats, he argued, had backed "twenty years of treason." Secretary of State George Mar-

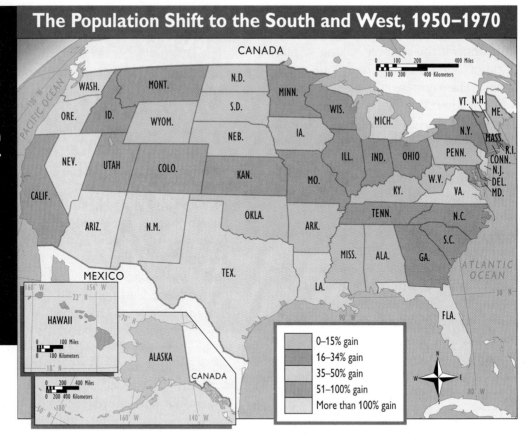

The Population Shift to the South and West, 1950–1970

0–15% gain
16–34% gain
35–50% gain
51–100% gain
More than 100% gain

Joseph McCarthy ruined many careers and reputations with his shocking claims about the Communist menace.

shall, a respected hero of World War II, was in McCarthy's opinion "an instrument of the Soviet conspiracy." A new word—**McCarthyism**—was coined to describe McCarthy's use of unproven charges against his opponents.

By 1954, though, McCarthy had become an embarrassment even to his supporters. Almost none of his charges had been proven. The Senate approved a statement criticizing his conduct. His career ruined, he faded from the public scene.

The Eisenhower Years

Truman, worn down by the war in Korea and issues at home, chose not to run for re-election in 1952. World War II hero Dwight D. Eisenhower, the Republican candidate, won in a landslide. He won by an even larger margin four years later.

During Eisenhower's two terms, the economy boomed. People had jobs, and prices did not rise too quickly. Although Eisenhower opposed large government, he left most existing social programs in place. He even backed some new spending. One of the highlights of his term of office was the Highway Act of 1956. It made auto travel easier by providing more than $30 billion to build more than 40,000 miles of new highways.

International trade was given a boost by the building of the St. Lawrence Seaway, which opened in 1959. Built along the St. Lawrence River, it connected Montreal, Canada, with Lake Erie.

Changes Sweep America

During the Depression and World War II, many Americans had put off getting married and having children. The end of the war changed all that. There was a "wedding boom" and, soon after, a **baby boom.** Between 1945 and 1960 the nation grew from 140 million to 180 million people. There were other changes as well:

(1) *People moved away from farms.* New technology and farming methods made farms more efficient than ever before. Small farmers who could not compete with larger farms moved to the cities.

(2) *Suburbs grew.* Many people who had lived in cities moved to suburbs. Shopping centers, movie theaters, restaurants, and houses sprouted up on what was once farmland. With the rise of suburbs, car sales exploded. People needed cars to get to offices and stores, which were often long distances from their homes. Car sales jumped from 2 million in 1946 to nearly 8 million in 1955.

(3) *Americans moved south and west.* They were heading for the sunbelt, the generally sunny states of the South and Southwest. Florida grew 79 percent between 1950 and 1960. In 1955 California passed New York as the most populated state.

(4) *Television boomed.* First tested successfully in the 1920s, television became widely available after World War II. By 1960 more homes in the United States had television sets than telephones.

(5) *Rock 'n' roll was born.* A new sound— a mix of African American blues and gospel, country, and pop—began to take the nation by storm. A young Cleveland disk jockey gave the new sound a name: rock 'n' roll.

In the mid-1950s African American rockers like Chuck Berry and Fats Domino held the spotlight with white rockers like Jerry Lee Lewis. The king of rock 'n' roll, though, was Elvis Presley. He would go on to sell over a billion records. The music of Presley, Berry, and others was rough, rhythmic, and loud. It helped give teenagers across the country a common identity, much to the dismay of many parents.

(6) *Religion grew.* Americans joined houses of worship in record numbers. Attendance grew twice as fast as the population.

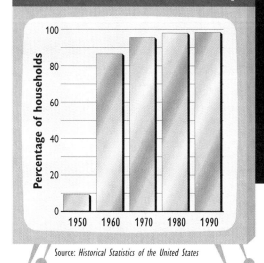

Television Set Ownership

Percentage of households

Source: *Historical Statistics of the United States*

CHART SKILLS: As television sets became cheaper to buy, their popularity skyrocketed. **Critical Thinking:** Why do you think the graph begins to level off around 1970?

In 1954 the Pledge of Allegiance was changed to include the words, "under God." Some historians think that the stresses of the cold war and the fear of a nuclear war were factors in the growth of religion during this period.

SECTION REVIEW

1. Key Terms Taft-Hartley Act, Dixiecrat, Fair Deal, perjury, McCarthyism, baby boom, sunbelt, rock 'n' roll

2. People Harry Truman, Thomas Dewey, Joseph McCarthy, Dwight D. Eisenhower, Elvis Presley

3. Comprehension Why were inflation and unemployment problems in the postwar economy?

4. Comprehension List six major changes that took place in postwar American society.

5. Critical Thinking Do you think another Red scare could take place in the United States? Why or why not?

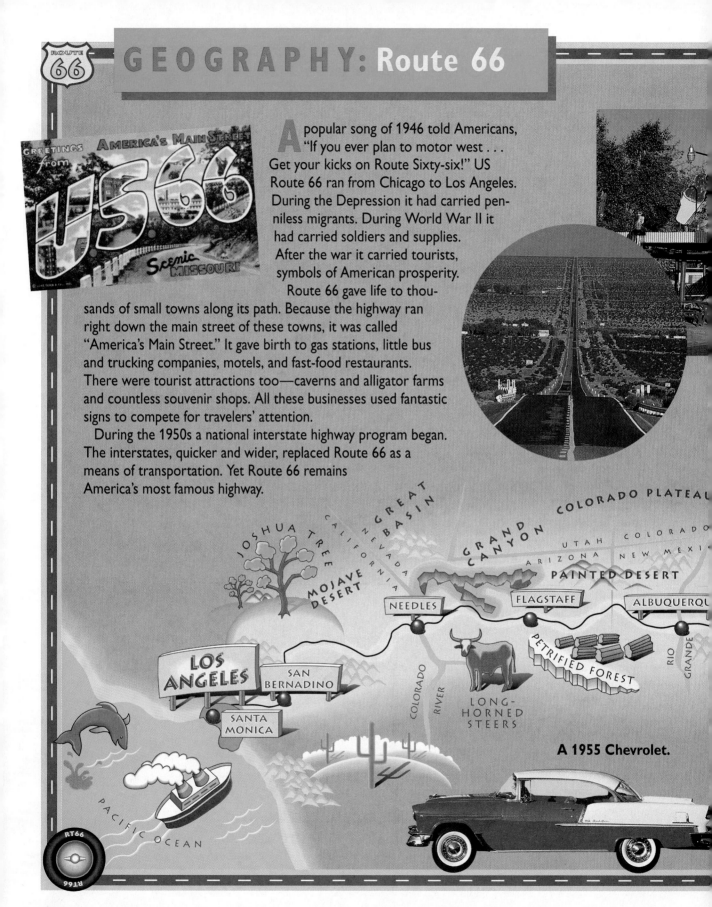

GEOGRAPHY: Route 66

A popular song of 1946 told Americans, "If you ever plan to motor west . . . Get your kicks on Route Sixty-six!" US Route 66 ran from Chicago to Los Angeles. During the Depression it had carried penniless migrants. During World War II it had carried soldiers and supplies. After the war it carried tourists, symbols of American prosperity. Route 66 gave life to thousands of small towns along its path. Because the highway ran right down the main street of these towns, it was called "America's Main Street." It gave birth to gas stations, little bus and trucking companies, motels, and fast-food restaurants. There were tourist attractions too—caverns and alligator farms and countless souvenir shops. All these businesses used fantastic signs to compete for travelers' attention.

During the 1950s a national interstate highway program began. The interstates, quicker and wider, replaced Route 66 as a means of transportation. Yet Route 66 remains America's most famous highway.

GREETINGS from AMERICA'S MAIN STREET US 66 Scenic MISSOURI

JOSHUA TREE CALIFORNIA NEVADA GREAT BASIN GRAND CANYON COLORADO PLATEAU UTAH COLORADO ARIZONA NEW MEXICO PAINTED DESERT MOJAVE DESERT NEEDLES FLAGSTAFF ALBUQUERQUE PETRIFIED FOREST RIO GRANDE

LOS ANGELES SAN BERNADINO SANTA MONICA COLORADO RIVER LONG-HORNED STEERS

PACIFIC OCEAN

A 1955 Chevrolet.

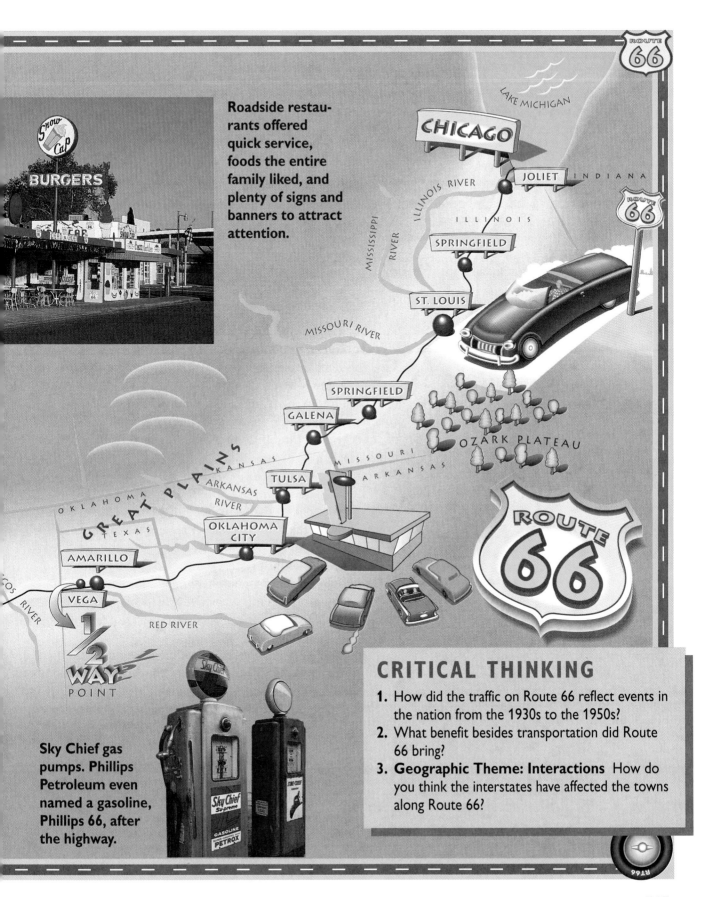

Roadside restaurants offered quick service, foods the entire family liked, and plenty of signs and banners to attract attention.

Sky Chief gas pumps. Phillips Petroleum even named a gasoline, Phillips 66, after the highway.

CRITICAL THINKING

1. How did the traffic on Route 66 reflect events in the nation from the 1930s to the 1950s?
2. What benefit besides transportation did Route 66 bring?
3. **Geographic Theme: Interactions** How do you think the interstates have affected the towns along Route 66?

2 The 1960s: A Time of Conflict and Hope

SECTION GUIDE

Main Idea
Under Kennedy and Johnson, the government began new social programs. Nixon faced the challenge of governing a deeply divided America.

Goals
As you read, look for answers to these questions:

1. What programs were put in place during Kennedy's term in office?

2. What was Johnson's Great Society?

3. What major problem did Nixon face after becoming President?

Key Terms
New Frontier	Medicare
Peace Corps	Medicaid
Great Society	

ON A COLD, SUNNY DAY in January 1961, John Fitzgerald Kennedy was sworn in as the nation's 35th President. Kennedy was both the first Catholic President and, at age 43, the youngest elected President. "The torch has been passed to a new generation of Americans," he declared.

The Election of 1960
Kennedy's victory in 1960 was one of the closest in U.S. history. His Republican opponent, Richard Nixon, was Eisenhower's Vice President. During televised debates—the first in a United States election—Kennedy appeared more forceful and confident than Nixon. Kennedy's charm and his promise to "get the country moving again" hit the right note with voters. His choice of Texas Senator Lyndon B. Johnson as his running mate helped him in the South.

Kennedy as President
Other chapters in this book describe the frightening days of the Cuban missile crisis and the early decisions that led to the Vietnam War. At home, the new President proposed a system of national health insurance for older Americans, more federal aid for education, and strong civil rights laws. He called his program the New Frontier. Congress passed only a few of Kennedy's proposals.

One program popular with Congress and most Americans was the space program. The Soviet Union had shocked the world by putting *Sputnik,* the first space satellite, into orbit in 1957. Kennedy boldly promised to put an American on the moon by 1970. Soon billions of dollars were being spent on space research. In 1962 John Glenn became the first American to orbit the earth.

Another popular Kennedy program was the Peace Corps, created in 1961. Made up of volunteers, mostly young people, the Peace Corps gave help to people in developing nations. Young Americans helped Africans, Asians, and Latin Americans build irrigation systems, schools, and roads.

President Kennedy hands a Christmas ornament to his son, John, Jr., in December 1962.

Kennedy Is Assassinated

By the fall of 1963, after some early setbacks, Kennedy appeared to be gaining the confidence of the nation. He and Vice President Johnson went to Texas to begin building support for re-election.

In Dallas on November 22, 1963, the President was greeted warmly by thousands of cheering people. As his motorcade passed through the city, shots rang out. The President slumped forward. Rushed to a hospital, Kennedy was soon pronounced dead.

Every American old enough to remember can tell you where he or she was when the news broke. For a President so young and full of life to die seemed unbelievable. The nation went into shock. In school, students and teachers wiped away tears as they were dismissed early. Factories and businesses closed. Some people gathered in houses of worship or outside public buildings to share their grief. Most simply went home.

Americans sat in stunned silence most of the weekend, watching the news on television. Two days after Kennedy's death, the nation was shocked again The accused assassin, Lee Harvey Oswald, was shot at point-blank range while being transferred to another jail. Millions watched it happen, live, on television.

Johnson's Great Society

"I will do my best. That is all I can do." Lyndon Johnson began his presidency with those words hours after Kennedy was killed. Johnson promised to continue Kennedy's policies. The nation's shock and grief led to broad support for his policies. More important, the new President was a skillful politician. He had served in the Senate for twelve years and knew how to move bills through Congress. Soon Johnson was going beyond Kennedy's proposals in civil rights and help for the poor.

In 1964 Johnson asked Americans to seek a Great Society. "The Great Society," he

Lyndon Johnson wanted his Great Society to be a place where people "are more concerned with the quality of their goals than the quantity of their goods."

said, "demands an end to poverty and racial injustice." His program provided job training, loans to poor farmers, and housing for migrant workers. He also pushed through important civil rights laws.

The Great Society, like Franklin Roosevelt's New Deal years earlier, had strong opponents. In the 1964 presidential election, the Republicans nominated Senator Barry Goldwater of Arizona to oppose Johnson. Goldwater wanted to reduce the size and cost of Johnson's Great Society. He also believed that the United States should be willing to use nuclear weapons in Vietnam. Yet with the economy strong and fears of nuclear war still high, voters chose Johnson in a landslide.

Now Johnson stepped up his war on poverty and his support for civil rights. A new Cabinet department, the Department of Housing and Urban Development, was created to deal with the problems of cities. It was led by Robert C. Weaver, the first African American to be appointed as head of a Cabinet department. Congress passed Johnson's Medicare program, which funded hospital care for people 65 and over, and Medicaid, which paid medical expenses for poor people. Congress also passed the Elementary and Secondary School Act, which provided new federal aid to education.

The Election of 1968

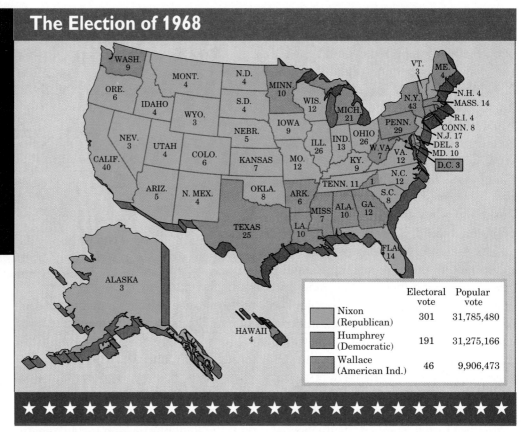

		Electoral vote	Popular vote
	Nixon (Republican)	301	31,785,480
	Humphrey (Democratic)	191	31,275,166
	Wallace (American Ind.)	46	9,906,473

1968 election campaign buttons.

Johnson Withdraws

Yet for all his victories, Johnson's popularity tumbled toward the end of his term. He realized that the Vietnam War was so unpopular he could not win re-election.

On March 31, 1968, Johnson made a televised speech from the White House. He announced he would seek peace talks to end the Vietnam War. Americans were then shocked to hear Johnson say, "I shall not seek, and I will not accept, the nomination of my party for another term as your President."

The Election of 1968

Three Democrats were left to fight for their party's nomination. John Kennedy's brother Robert, a senator from New York, challenged Eugene McCarthy, a Minnesota senator, and Johnson's Vice President, Hubert Humphrey.

In April 1968 civil rights leader Dr. Martin Luther King, Jr., was assassinated in Memphis, Tennessee. There were riots in the nation's cities. Many Americans began to see Robert Kennedy as the one who could pull the nation together. Then, after winning the California presidential primary in June, Kennedy too was gunned down by an assassin.

At the Democratic Convention in Chicago, Hubert Humphrey was nominated for President. The real story of the convention, however, took place outside on the streets. Thousands of antiwar protestors brawled with police as Americans, horrified, watched on television.

Such violent scenes boosted the chances of candidates promising law and order. The Republicans nominated Richard Nixon. Nixon claimed he spoke for the large number of Americans who were tired of violence and protests. Alabama governor George Wallace ran as an independent candidate with a message even tougher than Nixon's.

In terms of the popular vote, the election was almost as close as the 1960 election that Nixon had lost. In the Electoral College, however, Nixon won a decisive victory.

A Divided America

Richard Nixon became President of a deeply divided America. The Vietnam War and racial issues were tearing the nation apart. So was inflation. Caused in part by massive government spending on the war and social programs, inflation threatened Americans' economic security.

Yet Vietnam remained the nation's biggest concern, especially for young people. They were part of the baby boom that followed World War II. Many questioned their parent's values, which seemed too focused on money and conformity. They rebelled by praising love and individual freedom. To many young people, Vietnam was a brutal and senseless war that symbolized what was wrong with the nation.

At a student antiwar protest at Kent State University in Ohio in May 1970, National Guard troops shot and killed four students. Enraged, the antiwar movement called for more protests. Nixon's supporters, on the other hand, organized a huge march in New York City. They carried signs saying, "America, Love It or Leave It."

The war helped bring a change to the Constitution. In 1971 the 26th Amendment was ratified. It lowered the minimum voting age to 18. A major factor in its approval was the Vietnam War. Supporters of the amendment had argued that if 18-year-old Americans were "old enough to fight, they were old enough to vote."

Though the war continued to haunt the nation in the late 1960s, one event made Americans temporarily forget the nation's troubles. On July 20, 1969, six months after Nixon took office, astronauts Neil Armstrong and Edwin "Buzz" Aldrin walked on the surface of the moon. It was a triumph of American technology and courage.

The 1972 Election

Not surprisingly, Vietnam dominated the 1972 election campaign. Nixon's Democratic opponent was Senator George McGovern of South Dakota. McGovern wanted to pull American forces out of Vietnam. While Americans were tired of the war, most found McGovern too liberal. Nixon won one of the most lopsided victories in American history, carrying every state but Massachusetts.

In June 1972, just before the Democratic and Republican conventions, the *Washington Post* had run a small story on a break-in in Democratic National Headquarters. The headquarters was in a Washington, D.C., hotel called Watergate. The burglars, who were caught by police, turned out to have ties to Nixon's re-election campaign. Compared to stories like Vietnam and Nixon's huge lead in the polls, the Watergate story seemed unimportant. Yet within two years it would destroy a President.

Edwin Aldrin walks on the moon in 1969. The members of the Apollo 11 mission became national heroes.

SECTION REVIEW

1. Key Terms New Frontier, Peace Corps, Great Society, Medicare, Medicaid

2. People John F. Kennedy, Richard Nixon, Lyndon B. Johnson, John Glenn, Lee Harvey Oswald, Robert Kennedy, Hubert Humphrey, George Wallace

3. Comprehension What event cut short the Kennedy presidency?

4. Comprehension In what ways was American society divided when Nixon took office?

5. Critical Thinking Martin Luther King, Jr., once said, "The Great Society has been shot down on the fields of Vietnam." What do you think he meant?

3 An Unsettled Decade

SECTION GUIDE

Main Idea

The Watergate scandal forced Nixon to resign, which brought Ford to power. Ford and his successor, Carter, had troubled presidencies.

Goals

As you read, look for answers to these questions:

1. What events led Nixon to resign the presidency?

2. What two big problems did Ford face after becoming President?

3. How did being an outsider in Washington both help and hurt Carter?

Key Terms

Watergate scandal
bicentennial
OPEC

THE YEAR 1973 started well for Nixon. In January a ceasefire was signed in Vietnam. The same day, the military draft ended and the army became an all-volunteer force. Still, trouble loomed on the horizon.

The Watergate Scandal Grows

The deepening Watergate scandal haunted the Nixon White House. Four of the burglars were sentenced to prison. Another agreed to tell about the connections to Nixon's re-election campaign. The Senate set up a committee to investigate, headed by North Carolina Senator Sam Ervin. The President said he had first heard about the story when it broke in the papers. In a speech in Florida, Nixon said:

> **❝I welcome this kind of examination, because people have got to know whether or not their President is a crook. Well, I'm not a crook.❞**

More bad news came for Nixon. Spiro Agnew, his Vice President, was accused of improper actions while governor of Maryland. Agnew resigned. Nixon nominated Gerald Ford, the House Republican leader, to succeed Agnew. Ford became Vice President in December 1973. The Agnew scandal only deepened Americans' distrust of Nixon.

There was more to come. A Nixon aide told Ervin's committee that the President had secretly taped most conversations in the Oval Office. The committee wanted to listen to the tapes as part of its investigation, but Nixon did not want to turn them over. Late in 1973, after losing a court battle, the President began handing over the tapes.

Nixon Resigns

When the Watergate tapes were made public, it became clear that Nixon had tried to cover up the crime. He had talked about paying the burglars to keep quiet. He had also tried to keep the Federal Bureau of Investigation out of the case.

In October 1973 the House had started moving toward an impeachment hearing. It would have been

Richard Nixon bids goodbye following his resignation in 1974. Though painful for the nation, the Watergate scandal was a triumph for the rule of law.

Gerald Ford, shown here with First Lady Betty Ford, was the only President in American history not elected to either the presidency or the vice presidency.

the first one since Andrew Johnson was impeached after the Civil War. (In an impeachment, the House of Representatives accuses the President of crimes or other offenses. The Senate then holds a trial.) Even strong supporters of Nixon believed he should leave office.

When the House Judiciary Committee approved impeachment charges, Nixon knew that his presidency was over. On August 9, 1974, he became the first President in American history to resign. Gerald Ford took the presidential oath of office.

It was all so senseless. Nixon had been a sure winner in 1972. There was no need to break into the Democratic headquarters. As the tapes revealed, however, he wanted revenge against anyone who opposed him. This flaw helped ruin his presidency.

The Ford Presidency

When he was sworn in as President, Gerald Ford declared, "Our long national nightmare is over." In fact, there were two nightmares—Watergate and Vietnam. Their effects continued to be felt.

Only a month after taking office, Ford gave Nixon a full pardon for any crimes he might have committed in office. Many Americans reacted angrily. They thought that Nixon should have been forced to stand trial since so many of his aides had. Ford argued that the nation had been through two years of agony over Watergate. Putting Nixon on trial would only make it worse.

In Vietnam, the ceasefire signed in 1973 broke down and heavy fighting resumed. Ford asked Congress to help South Vietnam, but Congress refused. Without American help, South Vietnam surrendered to the North in 1975. Again President Ford tried to bring the nation together. "I ask all Americans," he said, "to close ranks, to avoid [blaming each other] about the past." Ford wanted a healing process for the nation to begin.

A Birthday for the Nation

In 1976 the United States celebrated the bicentennial —200th anniversary—of the Declaration of Independence. On July 4 over 33 tons of fireworks exploded above the Washington Monument. In Chicago, 1,776 immigrants from nations around the world were sworn in as American citizens.

In the midst of all the celebrating, some Americans asked whether freedom really applied to all citizens. African Americans, Native Americans, women, and other groups still faced discrimination. Still, Americans were proud of how far the nation had come. It seemed that the country needed a celebration to help move beyond the turmoil of the early 1970s.

The Election of 1976

Ford's pardon of Nixon hurt him as the 1976 election drew near. Ford barely survived a strong challenge by Ronald Reagan, a former movie actor and California governor, in the Republican primaries. Ford's Democratic opponent was a former peanut

As these photos show, the bicentennial was a time to celebrate and take pride in America's heritage.

The towers at the Three-Mile Island plant rise up in the darkness. Following the accident there, safety efforts at nuclear plants around the nation were increased.

farmer and Georgia governor, Jimmy Carter. Carter promised the American people clean, honest government. It was the message people wanted to hear. Carter won a narrow victory.

The Carter Years

Carter was an outsider in Washington, and proud of it. After all, one cause of Watergate was that top officials saw themselves as above the law. Carter showed through symbols that he would not lose touch with the people. He wore a cardigan sweater instead of a suit when giving a televised "fireside chat" to the nation. He stayed in the homes of average citizens when he traveled around the country.

Yet there was a drawback to being an outsider. Unfamiliar with the ways of Washington, Carter did not know how to get things done. He had trouble working with Congress. It seemed that a new crisis emerged every time another was settled.

One of Carter's most troublesome issues was the economy. **OPEC** (the Organization of Petroleum Exporting Countries) had begun charging higher and higher prices for its oil. Higher oil prices led to skyrocketing inflation. To deal with the energy crisis, Carter called on Americans to conserve energy. He urged Americans to turn down the heat in their homes and to conserve gasoline by driving less.

One way for the United States to reduce its dependence on foreign oil was through nuclear power. In March 1979, however, an accident at the Three-Mile Island nuclear power plant in Pennsylvania damaged those hopes. Only a small amount of radioactive gas escaped into the air. Yet the accident stirred the public's fears of the dangers of nuclear energy.

In July 1979 Carter made the most important speech of his presidency. Its main part addressed what he called a "crisis of the American spirit." He said Americans had lost "faith that the days of our

children will be better than our own." He also claimed that the nation had lost its sense of purpose. Many people rejected Carter's views. They said that the nation had lost faith not in itself, but in Carter.

The Reagan Triumph

Carter had entered the White House promising to return honesty and pride to government. Yet he seemed unable to solve any of the nation's biggest problems.

In 1980 the Republicans nominated Ronald Reagan to challenge Carter. Reagan called for less government and lower taxes. This conservative message appealed to many voters. At every campaign stop, Reagan asked, "Are you better off now than you were four years ago?" The crowd shouted back, "No! No!"

Poll watchers predicted a close race. Even in hard times, defeating a President is not easy. Yet on Election Day, Reagan scored a landslide victory. Republicans also made major gains in Congress, winning control of the Senate. To many historians, the 1980 election marked a shift in American politics from liberal to conservative.

SECTION REVIEW

1. Key Terms Watergate scandal, bicentennial, OPEC

2. People Sam Ervin, Spiro Agnew, Gerald Ford, Jimmy Carter

3. Comprehension What was the significance of the Watergate tapes?

4. Comprehension Why did Ford pardon Nixon? Why did many people react angrily to the pardon?

5. Critical Thinking Why, do you think, did many Americans reject the views expressed in Carter's July 1979 speech?

SKILLS: Exploring Local History

LEARN

Have you ever been curious about your family's past? How could you find out, for example, where your great-grandparents lived when they were first married? If they are no longer alive, the best source of information would be other relatives. They might have a wealth of family history in old letters or photographs—or in their memories.

The search for local history is much like the search for family history. First decide what era you wish to study. Then choose a subject that interests you, such as music or sports. You might already know that your town once had an orchestra or that it supported a semi-professional football team. You are ready to dig a little deeper.

Start your search at the library. You can find lots of information in old newspapers and books. They will give you the factual background. Then

turn to the most interesting source: people. Armed with a tape recorder and a list of thoughtful questions, you might interview people who lived during that time. They can tell you what it was really like to hear the orchestra play or to cheer the local football team to victory. Their memories can bring the era to life.

PRACTICE

Imagine you are going to do a local history project. Choose a subject appropriate to the years following World War II, for example, the 1950s.

1. What is your subject?

2. To what sources will you turn for help? Try to think of sources in addition to the ones mentioned above.

3. List each source you named in question 2, and explain how you think that source will help you.

APPLY

4. Write out a step-by-step plan for your local history project. Include your answers to questions 1–3. Also, write a list of interview questions you would like to ask someone about your subject.

4 The Reagan Revolution

SECTION GUIDE

Main Idea
The election of Ronald Reagan marked a shift in American politics from liberal to conservative.

Goals
As you read, look for answers to these questions:

1 What was Reaganomics? How did it affect the nation's deficit?

2 What scandal harmed Reagan's presidency?

3 How did the Savings and Loan crisis affect the deficit?

Key Terms
Reaganomics
national debt
Iran-contra affair
Savings and Loan crisis

S OME REVOLUTIONS, like the American Revolution, create new governments. Others, like the Industrial Revolution, make major changes in the way people live and work. Historians call the presidency of Ronald Reagan a "conservative revolution." Reagan's election in 1980 marked a shift in the way Americans thought about government. Americans were saying that after years of growth, government had become too big and too expensive.

Reagan's Economic Policies

Reagan had been speaking out against big government for years. In his 1981 Inaugural Address, he said, "Government is not the solution to our problem; government is the problem." He promised to cut taxes and reduce government's role in business.

His economic plan, which came to be called **Reaganomics,** had three parts. It called for (1) spending cuts on social programs, (2) lower taxes, and (3) increased military spending. During Reagan's first year in office, Congress passed much of his economic plan. Included were lower taxes and cuts in government programs such as Medicaid and student loans.

At first, things got worse. Inflation and unemployment stayed high. By 1983, however, the economy had improved. Inflation slowed and more people found jobs. Reagan claimed that his policies were working. As the recovery continued, Americans began to feel more confident about the nation's future.

The Growing Deficit

One problem, however, was still getting worse. The federal government was spending more money than it was taking in through taxes and other sources. The result was a huge budget deficit each year. These deficits caused a rise in the **national debt** —the money the government owes investors. To make up for overspending, governments sell bonds

Two students recite the Pledge of Allegiance with President Reagan during ceremonies in 1987 marking the 200th anniversary of the signing of the U.S. Constitution.

Federal Surplus or Deficit, 1960–1990

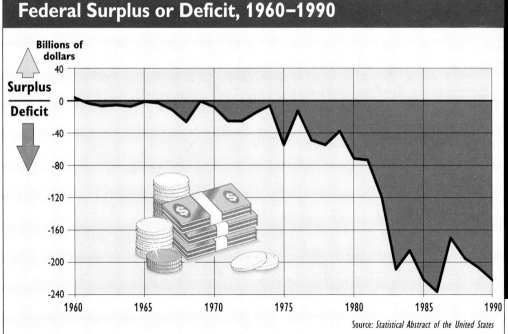

Billions of dollars

Surplus / Deficit

40
0
-40
-80
-120
-160
-200
-240

1960   1965   1970   1975   1980   1985   1990

Source: *Statistical Abstract of the United States*

(like U.S. Savings Bonds) to raise money. The buyer of the bond pays for it in the form of a loan. The government must then pay back the loan—with interest—to the bondholder in the future.

The U.S. government had a deficit during most of the years following World War II. Yet the deficit skyrocketed during the Reagan years. This was because lower taxes meant less income for the government. Though there were cuts in social programs, there was new spending on military programs. Reagan's supporters argued that the tax cut would give people more money to start businesses and create jobs. Others said that it would make the deficit grow.

First-Term Highlights

It was just another speech, one of many public events in the President's schedule. Yet as Reagan left a Washington hotel after making a speech in March 1981, a disturbed young man shot him in the chest. The President was rushed to a hospital. Doctors removed a bullet that had stopped three inches from his heart. Reagan was in good spirits when his wife, Nancy, arrived.

The good-humored President joked, "Honey, I forgot to duck!"

Within a few weeks the President was back at work. One of his first acts was to welcome back to earth the crew of *Columbia. Columbia* was a space shuttle, the world's first reusable spacecraft. Reagan also ended an embargo on grain shipments to the Soviet Union, a move that helped improve the farm economy.

Reagan made a historic appointment in the summer of 1981. He nominated Sandra Day O'Connor, an Arizona judge, to be the first woman on the U.S. Supreme Court. During his eight years as President, Reagan would appoint two more conservative Supreme Court justices, Antonin Scalia and Anthony Kennedy. Since Supreme Court justices can serve for life, Reagan was making sure that his conservative beliefs would have support on the Court long after he left office.

Reagan Wins Re-election

To challenge President Reagan in the 1984 presidential elections, the Democrats chose Walter Mondale. Mondale had

The shuttle *Columbia*, first flown in 1981, is shown blasting off on a 1992 mission.

One of the benefits of the growing world connections in the 1980s was the chance to hear music from other cultures. With rock music roughly 30 years old, American musicians at that time looked overseas for fresh inspiration. Paul Simon, for example, recorded music with the South African group Ladysmith Black Mambazo (below).

In the late 1980s new music companies began promoting what was called "world music." Today, Americans can hear Moroccan disco, Cambodian heavy metal, and selections from Zaire, Greece, Brazil, and the Caribbean. More than ever, music is becoming a language for the entire world.

served as Vice President under Jimmy Carter. One of the men Mondale defeated for the nomination was the Reverend Jesse Jackson, who had been a close ally and friend of Martin Luther King, Jr.

Mondale surprised the nation by picking congresswoman Geraldine Ferraro of New York as his running mate. Ferraro became the first woman to be chosen as Vice President on a major party ticket.

Reagan, however, remained popular. His conservative beliefs had gained him many supporters. As in 1980, Reagan was helped by the revival of religion across the nation. By 1980 a large number of Americans described themselves as "born-again" Chris-

tians. They were conservative on most major issues and joined the Republican Party in large numbers. Many working-class voters also joined the Republicans because they felt the Democrats had become too liberal on many social issues.

Reagan and his Vice President, George Bush, won in a landslide, taking 49 of 50 states. Reagan promised to continue his economic and military policies. He told a cheering crowd of supporters, "You ain't seen nothing yet!"

The Iran-contra Affair

As you read in the previous chapter, U.S.-Soviet relations were tense during Reagan's first term. They improved after Mikhail Gorbachev took power and began reforming the Soviet Union.

It was in the Middle East that Reagan suffered the worst embarrassment of his presidency. During Reagan's first term, groups friendly to the government of Iran were holding several Americans hostage in Beirut, Lebanon. In 1986 many Americans were shocked to learn that the U.S. government had made secret deals with Iran. The deals involved selling weapons to Iran in return for its help in gaining the release of the hostages.

It was then revealed that money from the sales had been used to help the *contras,* rebels fighting the left-wing Marxist Nicaraguan government. Congress had earlier cut off all funding to the *contras.* Reagan claimed that he did not know about this use of the money. He fired Colonel Oliver North, a national security aide who had been at the center of the deal.

Yet the issue, which became known as the Iran-contra affair, refused to go away. A congressional committee later accused the President of giving too much power to his advisers. The committee's report said, "If the President did not know what his national security advisers were doing, he should have."

Bush Wins in 1988

As Reagan's second term began to wind down, Vice President George Bush declared that he would run for the presidency. He had been a loyal Vice President, and he benefited from Reagan's popularity.

Bush promised to continue Reagan's policies and not to raise taxes. In speech after speech, he pledged, "Read my lips. No new taxes." Bush chose a senator from Indiana, Dan Quayle, as his running mate.

The Democrats thought they had a chance to defeat Bush. They nominated Massachusetts governor Michael Dukakis. He promised to reduce the federal budget deficit and improve education and other social programs. Dukakis chose Texas Senator Lloyd Bentsen as his running mate.

The 1988 campaign started with Dukakis leading Bush by a wide margin. By the end of the campaign, however, Bush's constant attacks on Dukakis for being too liberal worked with voters. Bush and Quayle won the 1988 election by a wide margin.

Bush as President

You read in the previous chapter about the collapse of communism in Eastern Europe and the Soviet Union. President Bush was widely praised for working to keep these changes peaceful. He was also praised for his handling of a war in the Persian Gulf, which you will read about later. At one point, nine out of ten Americans approved of the way he was doing his job.

Yet Bush lost his bid for re-election in 1992. The main reason was the sluggish economy. While Bush was in office, the national debt topped the $4 trillion mark. Most Americans agreed that the deficit needed to be reduced, but they were not sure how. Bush had promised not to raise taxes, and Americans did not favor large cuts in social programs.

Contributing to the deficit was the Savings and Loan crisis. In the early 1980s, Congress and President Reagan had agreed to allow Savings and Loan banks to make high-risk kinds of loans. (Banks earn more from risky loans because they can charge higher interest.) Many of these loans were never repaid, and bank after bank failed. The government was left to pay hundreds of billions of dollars to bail out the failed banks.

In 1990 Bush and Congress worked out a deal to cut the deficit. The deal included new taxes. Bush explained that he had no choice but to break his campaign promise. Many Americans were not so sure. Even with the budget agreement, the deficit remained high—and climbing. The economy entered a recession in 1990, and Bush had no way to end it. Though the worst of the deficit growth had occurred while Reagan was President, it was Bush who would pay at the polls.

Though George Bush was praised for his foreign policy successes, he was criticized for his handling of the economy.

SECTION REVIEW

1. Key Terms Reaganomics, national debt, Iran-contra affair, Savings and Loan crisis

2. People Ronald Reagan, Sandra Day O'Connor, Walter Mondale, Jesse Jackson, Geraldine Ferraro, George Bush, Oliver North, Michael Dukakis

3. Comprehension Why has the federal government had a budget deficit most years since World War II?

4. Comprehension Why did Reagan's conservative beliefs gain him many supporters in the 1980s?

5. Critical Thinking When the economy is bad, people often blame the President. Why do you think this is so?

Summary

1. Unemployment and inflation in the postwar economy led to labor unrest. Truman overcame these issues and won the 1948 election. Meanwhile, cold war fears were sweeping across the nation. Under Eisenhower, the economy boomed.
2. In 1960 John F. Kennedy became the youngest man ever elected President. Three years later, he was assassinated. Johnson put many of Kennedy's proposals into action with the Great Society, but his handling of the Vietnam War hurt his popularity. Nixon won the 1968 election and won again in a landslide four years later.
3. The Watergate scandal led to Nixon's resignation in 1974. Jimmy Carter won the 1976 election partly due to his promise to bring honest government to Washington. However, his status as an outsider hurt his presidency.
4. Ronald Reagan was swept into the presidency on the wave of a conservative revolution. Many Americans felt government had become too big. However, Reagan's economic program increased the deficit. Bush was unable to solve the nation's deficit problems.

Graphic Summary

1940s:	Truman faces labor unrest and cold war fears.
1950s:	The economy booms under Eisenhower.
1960s:	Kennedy is assassinated; Johnson's Great Society; Vietnam divides the nation; Nixon becomes President.
1970s:	Nixon resigns, succeeded by Ford; U.S. bicentennial; Carter deals with an energy crisis.
1980s:	Reagan leads a conservative revolution; deficit skyrockets; Iran-contra affair; sluggish economy hurts Bush.

Review

KEY TERMS

Define the following terms.
1. national debt
2. McCarthyism
3. Peace Corps
4. baby boom
5. Watergate scandal
6. perjury
7. Iran-contra affair
8. sunbelt

COMPREHENSION

1. Why did unemployment jump after World War II?
2. Who was Joseph McCarthy? How did he contribute to Americans' cold war fears?
3. What programs were put in place during Kennedy's presidency?
4. In what ways did Johnson's Great Society program fight poverty?
5. How did Richard Nixon benefit from the violent scenes at the 1968 Democratic Convention?
6. How did Nixon try to cover up the Watergate scandal?
7. What did Carter call on Americans to do to deal with the energy crisis?
8. How did the election of Ronald Reagan in 1980 mark a shift in the way many Americans thought about government?
9. Why did the deficit skyrocket during the Reagan years?
10. How did the state of the economy hurt Bush's re-election bid in 1992?

Places to Locate

Match the letters on the map with the places that are listed below. Then explain the importance of each place.

1. Memphis 3. Wisconsin 5. Detroit
2. Florida 4. Ohio 6. Chicago

Geographic Theme: Movement Why, do you think, did many Americans move to suburbs after the end of World War II? What factors made this movement possible?

Skill Review

Follow the steps below to create a scrapbook of the history of your community.

1. Visit a local library to research books and newspaper articles on important people and events.
2. Interview an older resident for his or her account of life in your community.
3. Photocopy drawings and photographs of your community over a broad period of time to show how your community has changed.
4. Assemble text and artwork to create your scrapbook. Be sure to write an introduction that provides an overview of your community.

CRITICAL THINKING

1. Making Comparisons Presidents Johnson and Nixon both had troublesome ends to their presidencies. Compare and contrast the reasons for their downfalls.
2. Understanding Advantages and Disadvantages In 1976 Jimmy Carter used his status as an outsider in Washington to gain voters' trust. What advantages might an outsider have as President? What might be some disadvantages?

PORTFOLIO OPTIONS

1. Civics Connection Organize a class debate on the issue of the economy today. Divide the class into four teams. Then have each team present a list of economic problems and suggest solutions.
2. Writing Connection Imagine that you are a speaker at the 1968 Democratic Convention in Chicago. Write a speech explaining your position on the most important issues of the campaign.
3. Contemporary Connection Some historians say that the Watergate scandal destroyed the trust Americans had in their elected officials. How do you think the scandal affected Americans' view of government? Conduct an informal survey of the attitudes voters have toward politicians today.
4. Timeline Connection Copy the chapter timeline. Then add events from the chapter you think should be included and explain why.

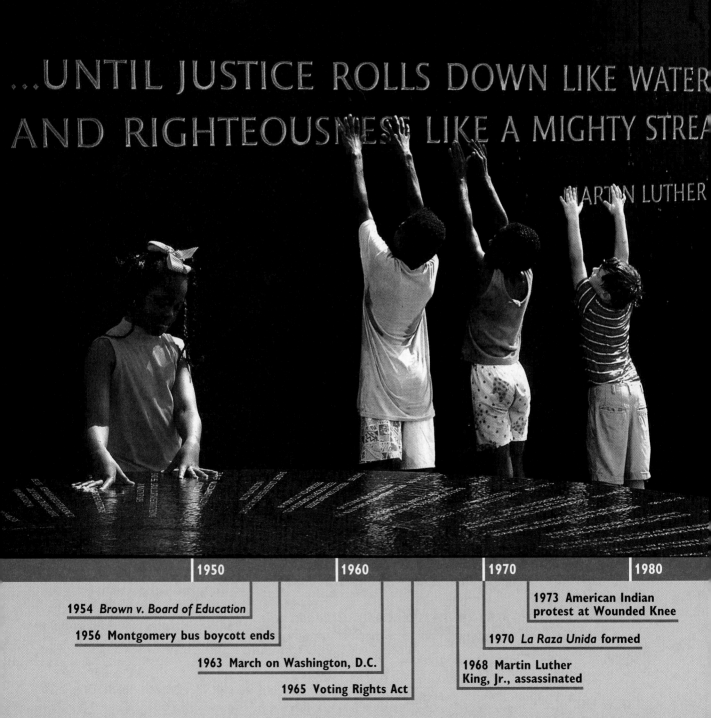

Children play at the Civil Rights Memorial, in Montgomery, Alabama, which honors those who died in the struggle to guarantee the rights of African Americans. That struggle has widened in recent decades to include many groups of Americans, reflecting the growing diversity of the nation.

...UNTIL JUSTICE ROLLS DOWN LIKE WATER
AND RIGHTEOUSNESS LIKE A MIGHTY STREA
MARTIN LUTHER

1950	1960	1970	1980

1954 *Brown v. Board of Education*

1956 Montgomery bus boycott ends

1963 March on Washington, D.C.

1965 Voting Rights Act

1968 Martin Luther King, Jr., assassinated

1970 *La Raza Unida* formed

1973 American Indian protest at Wounded Knee

The Search for Equal Rights (1954–Present)

1 The Start of the Civil Rights Movement

SECTION GUIDE

Main Idea
African Americans in the 1950s and 1960s organized to end segregation in the South.

Goals
As you read, look for answers to these questions:

1 How did the *Brown* decision of 1954 enable the civil rights movement to gather strength in the 1950s?

2 How did opponents of the civil rights movement respond?

Key Terms
Brown v. Board of Education
Montgomery bus boycott
sit-in
freedom ride

1990	2000

1990 Americans with Disabilities Act

KANSAS LAW IN 1952 required nine-year-old Linda Brown to go to a school for African American children miles from her Topeka home. She and her parents thought that she should be able to attend an all-white school closer to home. The Browns took their case all the way to the Supreme Court.

Brown v. Board of Education

Linda Brown's situation was not unique. In 1896 the Supreme Court had ruled that segregation was constitutional. "Separate but equal" facilities for black and white Americans were allowed, the Court had said in *Plessy v. Ferguson.*

The "separate but equal" ruling made segregation a fact of life in the South. There were two of everything: waiting rooms, restrooms, restaurants, and public schools. One was for whites, one for blacks. Segregation had the full force of state and local law. (Segregation was common in the North, too, but more often it was a matter of custom rather than law.)

The separate areas for African Americans were rarely equal to those for whites. Far less money was spent on schools for black children, for example. These schools had fewer books and seldom offered courses that prepared students for college.

On May 17, 1954, the Supreme Court struck down segregation in public schools. In *Brown v. Board of Education* the Court ruled that "segregation is a denial of the equal protection of the laws." Chief Justice Earl Warren wrote:

> **To separate [black children] from others of similar age . . . solely because of their race generates a feeling of inferiority . . . that may affect their hearts and minds in a way unlikely ever to be undone.**

Linda Brown can be seen near the front of this photograph of her classroom in a segregated school in Topeka, Kansas. **Critical Thinking:** How was *Brown v. Board of Education* a significant victory for the civil rights movement?

In other words, segregated schools told young African Americans that they were not good enough to mix with white children. It was therefore clearly unequal.

A year later, the Supreme Court ordered public schools to integrate, or accept black and white students, "with all deliberate speed." Washington, D.C., quickly integrated its schools. By 1956 about one-fifth of the African American students in Baltimore, Maryland, attended integrated schools. Oklahoma and Missouri also began to integrate their public schools.

The Roots of the Movement

Brown v. Board of Education was a great victory for the NAACP, whose lawyers had argued the case. The NAACP had long focused on the courts in the struggle for civil rights. Lawyers like Thurgood Marshall argued that the Constitution guaranteed the rights of African Americans. (Marshall later became the first African American member of the Supreme Court.) Starting in the 1940s, Supreme Court rulings supported those arguments.

Other factors strengthened the civil rights movement. By the 1950s many African Americans had moved to cities from small towns. In the cities they found it easier to unite to challenge unfair treatment. Television also played a role. People watched television newscasts of the civil rights struggle. Many were shocked to see violent racism and began to oppose it. Another important factor was taking place overseas, in Africa. In those years, Africans were demanding their independence from European nations. Their struggle for freedom inspired many African Americans.

Perhaps the greatest support for the civil rights movement came from black churches. Religious faith gave people the courage to fight for justice. Religious leaders were at the forefront of the movement.

Montgomery Bus Boycott

It was December 1, 1955, in Montgomery, Alabama. Rosa Parks, a 43-year-old seamstress, took a seat in the middle of a city bus. When the bus filled up, a white man was left standing. The driver ordered Parks and three other African Americans to move to the back of the bus. The others rose, but she stayed.

"If you don't stand up," the driver threatened, "I'm going to have to call the police and have you arrested."

"You may do that," Parks replied. He did. The police took her off to jail.

Parks was active in the local NAACP. Her challenge to the law was deliberate. News of her arrest soon reached her fellow members. They issued a notice to black churches and local groups. "If Negroes did not ride the buses, they could not operate," it said. "We are, therefore, asking every Negro to stay off the buses Monday in protest of the arrest and trial."

Parks was found guilty and told to pay $14 in fines and fees. That day the boycott began.

NAACP leaders tried to decide whether or not to continue the Montgomery bus boycott. They held a meeting to discuss the question. A young Baptist minister was asked to speak. His name was Martin Luther King, Jr.

Some whites organized to oppose integration. New groups called White Citizens Councils pressured lawmakers to support segregation. The most violent group was the Ku Klux Klan. It used threats, beatings, murder, and house burnings to deny African Americans their civil rights.

Rosa Parks refused to move to the back of a bus in 1955. Here she sits in the front after the Montgomery bus boycott succeeded in desegregating the city's buses.

The 26-year-old King moved the audience with his words. "There comes a time that people get tired," he said. "We are here this evening to say to those who have mistreated us so long that we are tired—tired of being segregated and humiliated; tired of being kicked about by the brutal feet of oppression. . . ."

The members vowed to continue the boycott. It went on for thirteen months, rain and shine. Former bus riders, including some whites, organized car pools, rode bikes, or walked to their jobs and schools. King and other black leaders endured death threats, bombings, and jailings. The violent reaction of angry whites to the nonviolent protests in Montgomery gained national attention.

Meanwhile, the NAACP pressed its case in court. On November 13, 1956, the Supreme Court ruled that Montgomery's bus segregation law was illegal. African Americans once again boarded the buses in Montgomery. This time they sat where they pleased.

White Opposition

These civil rights victories upset many southern whites. Polls showed that more than 80 percent opposed the decision to integrate public schools.

Little Rock

September 4, 1957, was no ordinary back-to-school day at Central High School in Little Rock, Arkansas. Under a court-ordered plan, nine African Americans were scheduled to attend the school, which had 2,000 white students. Governor Orval Faubus opposed the plan. He ordered the Arkansas National Guard to surround Central High School.

That morning, 15-year-old Elizabeth Eckford, one of the "Little Rock Nine," took the longest walk of her life. Getting off the school bus, she faced a mob of angry white

Days after the start of classes at Central High School in Little Rock, Arkansas, U.S. Army troops still escorted African American students to and from school. **Critical Thinking:** What might be the emotions of the students in this photograph?

Steps Toward Equal Rights

1863 ● Emancipation Proclamation frees slaves in the Confederacy.

1865 ● Thirteenth Amendment abolishes slavery.

1866 ● Civil Rights Act makes discrimination illegal.

1868 ● Fourteenth Amendment promises equal protection of the laws.

1870 ● Fifteenth Amendment assures right to vote regardless of race.

1909 ● National Association for the Advancement of Colored People (NAACP) founded.

1948 ● Truman issues executive order ending segregation in the military.

1954 ● Supreme Court rules segregation in public schools unconstitutional in *Brown v. Board of Education*.

1957 ● Southern Christian Leadership Conference (SCLC) founded.

CHART SKILLS: Several laws and organizations played important roles in advancing the cause of civil rights. **Critical Thinking:** In your opinion, which was most important?

parents. She thought the National Guard soldiers were there to protect her.

As Elizabeth headed toward the school, the crowd began to follow her. "Then my knees started to shake all of a sudden and I wondered whether I could make it to the center entrance a block away," she recalled.

She saw a guard let some white students pass, so she went up to him. He did not move. "When I tried to squeeze past him, he raised his bayonet. . . . Somebody started yelling, 'Lynch her! Lynch her!'"

Finally, a white woman came forward. She guided Elizabeth away from the crowd and took her home.

Governor Faubus continued to oppose the Supreme Court's order to integrate the schools. This put him in conflict with the federal government. Yet the President, Dwight D. Eisenhower, did not want to force the governor to obey. "You cannot change people's hearts merely by laws," he had once said.

As the crisis dragged on, however, Eisenhower realized that the federal government had to act. On September 24, 1957, he ordered soldiers of the 101st Airborne Division into Little Rock. In a television address to the nation, Eisenhower said that "mob rule cannot be allowed to override the decisions of our courts."

The nine children were driven to school, escorted by jeeps armed with machine guns. Hundreds of paratroopers lined the streets, but this time they turned their bayonets on the mob. The children walked bravely into their new school.

Sit-Ins at Lunch Counters

By 1960, victories like those in Montgomery and Little Rock filled civil rights workers with confidence. Now it was time to end segregation in all public places.

On February 1, 1960, four black college students walked into a Woolworth's store in Greensboro, North Carolina. They sat down at the lunch counter and ordered coffee. "I'm sorry," said the waitress, "but we don't serve colored [people] here."

The students began a **sit-in.** That is, they refused to move until their demands were met. The store closed, but the students were back again the next day.

Over the next few weeks, sit-ins spread to fifteen cities. The students, black and white, knew the risks they were taking. Many had taken months of training in nonviolent protest. They learned how to deal with the abuse they would face and to respond without violence.

Some whites covered the students with ammonia and itching powder. They yelled

SKILLS: Resolving Conflicts Peacefully

LEARN

Have you ever been so angry that you screamed at someone? Emotions can be powerful, but they do not have to be destructive. Even emotions such as anger can be useful. It all depends on how you express your anger.

Civil rights protesters worked to channel their emotions. They learned how to attack racism and segregation with nonviolence. Their behavior helped gain wide support for the cause of civil rights.

You can apply the principles of nonviolence to resolving personal conflicts. For example, what if someone makes a racist remark about a friend? How should you protest? You could call the person a name, which might lead to a shouting match or even a fight. A better response would be to take a moment to think. Count to ten if that helps. Then explain your feelings to the person in a calm way.

This nonviolent approach works in school too. Emotional reactions can ruin a class discussion.

> **"**Nonviolence is the answer to the crucial political and moral questions of our time; the need for man to overcome oppression and violence without resorting to oppression and violence. Man must [develop] for all human conflict a method which rejects revenge, aggression, and retaliation. The foundation of such a method is love.**"**
>
> —Martin Luther King, Jr.

PRACTICE

Read the excerpt on this page.

1. According to Martin Luther King, Jr., what was the purpose of nonviolent protest?

2. Explain the meaning of the last sentence of the excerpt.

3. How does the photograph on this page of a sit-in at a lunch counter illustrate Dr. King's method?

APPLY

4. Recall a situation in which someone you know lost control of his or her emotions. Describe what happened. Then explain how that person could have dealt with the situation better.

Police in Birmingham, Alabama, use dogs to attack civil rights protesters. **Critical Thinking:** How did state and local governments in the South respond to federal orders to integrate? What arguments might they have used to support their actions?

The freedom riders expected violence, and they got it. Riders were beaten. Buses were blown up. The rides continued, and so did the attacks.

Attacks were made on other civil rights workers. In May 1963, police in Birmingham, Alabama, turned fire hoses and snarling police dogs on protesters. In Jackson, Mississippi, an NAACP worker was murdered in his office.

One of the most shocking acts of violence was the bombing of an African American church in Birmingham. Four young children in a Sunday school class were killed in the attack.

President John F. Kennedy and his brother, Attorney General Robert F. Kennedy, sent federal agents to protect civil rights workers. State and local officials often refused to deal with them. "We do not recognize the federal marshals as law-enforcement officers in this matter," declared Alabama Governor John Patterson. Clearly, more action was needed.

at the students, beat them, and burned them with cigarettes. Protesters were pulled from their seats and hauled off to jail. Others replaced them.

The sit-ins attracted national sympathy. After months of protests, store owners gave in. Lunch counters began serving whites and blacks.

Riding to Freedom

Nonviolent protests spread. The Congress of Racial Equality (CORE), a major African American civil rights group, planned a series of freedom rides through segregated southern cities.

White freedom riders would sit in the back of a bus. Black freedom riders would sit in the front and refuse to move. At bus terminals along the route, black riders would try to use "whites only" waiting rooms, bathrooms, drinking fountains, and eating areas.

SECTION REVIEW

1. Key Terms *Brown v. Board of Education,* Montgomery bus boycott, sit-in, freedom ride

2. People and Places Earl Warren, Rosa Parks, Martin Luther King, Jr., Little Rock, Birmingham

3. Comprehension What different methods did civil rights workers use to fight segregation?

4. Comprehension How did some whites try to defend segregation?

5. Critical Thinking If black schools had received as much money for their students as white schools did, would segregation have been justified? Explain your answer.

2 New Directions for the Civil Rights Movement

SECTION GUIDE

Main Idea

In the mid-1960s the civil rights movement took new directions, and the federal government passed laws to guarantee rights.

Goals

As you read, look for answers to these questions:

❶ What laws were passed in the 1960s to guarantee the rights of African Americans?

❷ What challenges did the civil rights movement face in the North?

Key Terms

Civil Rights Act (1964)
Voting Rights Act (1965)

FROM THE STEPS of the Lincoln Memorial, Martin Luther King, Jr., looked out across a sea of hushed listeners. About 250,000 people stood before him on that hot August day in 1963. They were gathered at the end of the March on Washington. In the rolling rhythms of a preacher, King spoke of the importance of the civil rights struggle. His words are among the most famous in American history:

❝I have a dream that my four little children will one day live in a nation where they will not be judged by the color of their skin but by the content of their character. I have a dream today!❞

Civil Rights Laws

At the time King spoke, there was cause for such dreams. The civil rights movement had widespread support. The March on Washington had united many groups, all of which called for passage of a civil rights law to end racial injustice. President John F. Kennedy promised support.

In November 1963 Kennedy was assassinated. The new President, Lyndon Johnson, moved with great speed on civil rights. In July 1964 Congress passed the Civil Rights Act. The act barred states from using different voting standards for blacks and whites. It made discrimination in public places illegal. It gave the federal government the power to integrate schools and protect voting rights. It also banned job discrimination based on race, sex, or religion. Later in 1964 the 24th Amendment to the Constitution, outlawing poll taxes, was ratified. (Poll taxes are fees people must pay in order to vote.)

Still, many African Americans in the South found it difficult to vote. Civil

Martin Luther King, Jr., greets the crowd during the 1963 March on Washington. **Critical Thinking:** In your opinion, why did his "I Have a Dream" speech become so famous?

Martin Luther King, Jr., and his wife, Coretta Scott King (center), lead marchers into Montgomery, Alabama, on March 25, 1965.

rights leaders called for a federal law to guarantee the vote. To call attention to the issue, they planned a march in March 1965. Marchers planned to walk from Selma, Alabama, to the state capital, Montgomery.

On March 7, as the marchers crossed a bridge at the edge of Selma, state troopers on horseback attacked them. Two days later, marchers led by Martin Luther King, Jr., peacefully crossed the bridge, but they were ordered to go no farther. In the days that followed, a white minister who supported the civil rights movement was killed in Selma and others were attacked.

On March 15, 1965, President Lyndon Johnson introduced the **Voting Rights Act.** Its purpose was to end rules that southern states used to keep African Americans from voting. Congress passed the law that summer.

Malcolm X

Malcolm Little was a man who quickly outgrew his name. Malcolm was the son of the Reverend Earl Little, an organizer for Marcus Garvey's "Back to Africa" movement. The minister and his family were often terrorized by white hate groups. Earl Little was murdered. Malcolm got into

Malcolm X

trouble at a young age and spent time in prison for burglary. There he was introduced to a group called the Black Muslims.

The group declared its hatred for whites. Whites, it said, had enslaved blacks and deprived them of their true religion, Islam. The Black Muslims wanted not equality, but black supremacy. ("Supremacy" means being above.) Malcolm converted to Islam and took the name Malcolm X.

Malcolm X became a fiery spokesman for the Black Muslims. Rejecting King's idea of nonviolence, Malcolm urged blacks to defend themselves against whites.

In March 1964 Malcolm broke with the Black Muslims and formed his own group. Later that year he went to Mecca, a holy city of Islam in Saudi Arabia. There he met Muslims who taught that all races were equal. He wrote about what he saw:

> **There were tens of thousands of pilgrims, from all over the world. They were of all colors, from blue-eyed blonds to black-skinned Africans. But we were all participating in the same ritual, displaying a spirit of unity and brotherhood that my experiences in America had led me to believe never could exist between the white and the non-white.**

After Mecca, Malcolm X no longer spoke of black supremacy. Instead, he pictured a world where all races could live together in peace. He had little time to spread his new message. In 1965 he was gunned down by members of the Black Muslims. Today Malcolm X is remembered as an honored—and controversial—African American leader.

Violence in Northern Cities

Racial discrimination existed in the North as well as the South. Northern cities were often segregated in fact, if not in law. City schools with many black students were poorly funded. African Americans did not have a fair chance at most jobs.

President Johnson's "War on Poverty" helped some African Americans. Still, others saw little hope for the future. Summers were the worst time, as the heat made tempers flare. Anger turned into violence.

In the 1960s, smoke rose from cities across the United States. Harlem, in New York City, erupted in the summer of 1964. The following summer a riot took place in Watts, a mostly African American neighborhood in Los Angeles. Nationwide, 164 riots broke out in the first nine months of 1967. The worst, in Detroit, left 43 people dead. City neighborhoods, already in bad condition, were heavily damaged.

The violence peaked in 1968. On April 4, as he stood on the balcony of a motel in Memphis, Tennessee, Martin Luther King, Jr., was killed by a rifle shot. Black neighborhoods across the nation exploded in anger, and 46 people died in riots. King's message of nonviolence was lost in the smoke and rubble.

The Struggle Continues

King's death greatly weakened the civil rights movement. The movement had won historic victories in education and voting rights. It had brought about great change. For example, by 1968 the Voting Rights Act had helped add more than a million African Americans to voter lists in southern states. Yet civil rights leaders disagreed over what should be done next. Some argued that little more was possible.

In fact, there were many more battles to come. In the 1970s and 1980s, the battlefield would shift from lunch counters to colleges and corporation boardrooms. A new generation of black leaders would

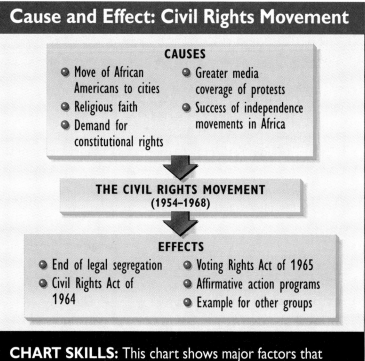

Cause and Effect: Civil Rights Movement

CAUSES
- Move of African Americans to cities
- Religious faith
- Demand for constitutional rights
- Greater media coverage of protests
- Success of independence movements in Africa

THE CIVIL RIGHTS MOVEMENT (1954–1968)

EFFECTS
- End of legal segregation
- Civil Rights Act of 1964
- Voting Rights Act of 1965
- Affirmative action programs
- Example for other groups

CHART SKILLS: This chart shows major factors that fueled the civil rights movement. **Critical Thinking:** In your opinion, was the civil rights movement a success? Explain the reasons for your answer.

emerge. They would work to defend and build on the gains of the 1960s.

SECTION REVIEW

1. Key Terms Civil Rights Act (1964), Voting Rights Act (1965)

2. People and Places Malcolm X, Washington, D.C., Selma, Detroit

3. Comprehension How did the civil rights laws of 1964 and 1965 guarantee the rights of African Americans?

4. Comprehension What were the reasons for the violence that broke out in northern cities in the mid-1960s?

5. Critical Thinking Reread the excerpt from King's speech at the start of this section. Then restate it in your own words.

SECTION GUIDE

Main Idea
The struggle for equal rights widened to include other groups such as Hispanic Americans, Native Americans, and American women.

Goals
As you read, look for answers to these questions:

1 How have Hispanic Americans worked to build better lives?

2 What gains have Native Americans made toward equality?

3 What were the goals of the women's movement?

Key Terms
Latino
American Indian Movement

S A YOUNG MAN, César Chavez listened to the speeches of Martin Luther King, Jr. He waited anxiously to hear of the fate of the sit-in protesters and the freedom riders. Chavez rejoiced as the walls of segregation fell. All the while, he thought about his own people, the Mexican Americans.

The Movement Catches On

The courageous battles of African Americans in the 1950s inspired other Americans to strengthen their fight for equality. During the 1960s the civil rights movement grew to include women, Native Americans, Hispanic Americans, and others.

Hispanic Americans trace their roots to a Spanish-speaking country or culture, such as Mexico, Puerto Rico, or countries in Central and South America. Since this region is also known as Latin America, immigrants from this area and their descendants often call themselves **Latinos.**

Since the 1950s, the Hispanic American population has grown rapidly. By 2010, Hispanic Americans are expected to be the nation's largest minority group. Most are Mexican American, like César Chavez.

Mexican Americans Organize

Chavez was born in Yuma, Arizona, in 1927. In the 1940s he and his family worked as migrant laborers in the California fields. (Migrant workers travel from place to place in search of work.) One time they found work picking peas. The whole family, parents and six children, worked. They walked down the long rows, bent at the waist in the hot sun. In three hours of back-breaking labor, the entire family earned just twenty cents.

In 1962 Chavez took on the challenge of his life: starting a union of farm workers. Farm owners would have nothing to do with Chavez's new farm workers' union. Chavez decided to change their minds by following Martin Luther King's example. Nonviolent protest, Chavez said, was "the truest act of courage."

Responding to Chavez's call, workers went on strike. Then Chavez asked consumers not to buy grapes, let-

César Chavez speaks to a meeting of the United Farm Workers of America.

tuce, and other produce harvested by non-union workers. The pressure tactics worked. In 1970, 26 major California growers agreed to talk with the farm workers. They later signed contracts. Chavez continued his work until he died in 1993.

The farm workers' struggles inspired other Mexican Americans. By the 1960s most lived in cities in the Southwest and California. Cultural pride grew in the barrios (Hispanic neighborhoods). In 1970 Mexican Americans formed *La Raza Unida* (lah RAH-zah oo-NEE-dah)—"the united people." The organization worked to get better jobs, pay, education, and housing for Mexican Americans and to elect them to public office.

One Mexican American who has worked to improve life in the cities is Henry Cisneros (sis-NEHR-os). Born in San Antonio, Texas, Cisneros decided at the age of 21 that he wanted to become his city's mayor. Just thirteen years later, in 1981, he achieved his goal, becoming the first Mexican American mayor of a large city in the United States. Cisneros won by gaining the support of both white and Mexican American voters. He was later named by President Bill Clinton as Secretary of Housing and Urban Development.

Puerto Ricans

Since 1917 people from the U.S.-controlled island of Puerto Rico have been American citizens. Puerto Ricans did not start moving to the United States mainland in large numbers, however, until the 1930s and 1940s. Most settled in New York City. About 1.5 million Puerto Ricans live in New York today.

The first Puerto Rican to become a voting member of Congress was Herman Badillo (bah-DEE-yoh). Badillo served as a representative from New York City in the 1970s.

Nydia Velázquez, from Brooklyn, New York, is the first Puerto Rican-born woman elected to the U.S. Congress.

Hispanic Diversity

In general, Cuban immigrants have had an easier time than other Hispanic newcomers in adjusting to American life. Just 90 miles off the Florida coast, Cuba once had close ties to the United States. Many Cubans had relatives here. Then Fidel Castro came to power in 1959 and set up a Communist government. The United States and Cuba became enemies. Travel between these countries was cut off.

Cubans began fleeing poverty and dictatorship. Between 1960 and 1973, over half a million Cubans came to the United States. Most settled in southern Florida. With their education, skills, and family ties, many Cuban refugees were able to buy homes and start businesses.

Other Hispanic newcomers have been less fortunate. Among them are refugees from Central America. The region has been torn by civil wars. Starting in the 1970s, thousands of people from El Salvador, Nicaragua, and Guatemala traveled north up the length of Mexico to reach safety in the United States.

DESFILE DEL DIA DE LA RAZA, INC.
UNITED HISPANIC AMERICAN PARADE

Hispanic Americans celebrate their diversity as well as their common heritage in this parade. **Critical Thinking:** Why might immigration policy be of special concern to Hispanic Americans?

American Indians occupied Alcatraz Island in San Francisco Bay for more than a year to call attention to their demands for fair treatment.

Native American Rights

The civil rights movement also inspired Native Americans, who faced many challenges in the 1960s. The U.S. government had a long history of breaking its treaties with the Indians. The Bureau of Indian Affairs, which ran Indian reservations, allowed crime and corruption. Discrimination against Native Americans went unpunished. Rivers that they had fished for centuries now ran foul with pollution.

Such injustices led Native Americans to join the battle for civil rights. They fought to preserve their cultures and gain greater control over their lands. The American Indian Movement (AIM), founded in 1968, became a voice for their rights.

On a November night in 1969, a group of Indians in small boats rowed to a slab of rock in the middle of San Francisco Bay. This was Alcatraz Island, once home to a prison. They chose Alcatraz to make the point that life on the island was like life on an Indian reservation. They noted that both places lacked clean water, good soil, health care, jobs, and schools.

Indians occupied the bleak island through June 1971. Their efforts got publicity but won few results.

Russell Means, a Sioux active in AIM, led a series of dramatic protests. On Thanksgiving 1970, he took over the *Mayflower II* in Plymouth, Massachusetts. Means and his followers briefly occupied the Bureau of Indian Affairs in 1972. Means explained AIM's demands:

> **We don't want civil rights in the white man's society—we want our own sovereign rights.**

In February 1973 Means led hundreds of American Indians into the town of Wounded Knee, South Dakota. (Wounded Knee had been the site of an American Indian massacre in 1890.) The Indians were armed and demanded that the Senate look into the government's treatment of Indians.

The protest was met with massive force. Armored vehicles, helicopters, and soldiers encircled the town. During the ten-week standoff, two Indians were killed. The government promised to address the Indians' demands. Yet it did very little.

Gains for Native Americans

Real victories came later, in the courts. Indians have won back some of their lands. They have also gone to court over rights to water, hunting, and fishing. Courts have

Members of the Navajo Tribal Council meet in Window Rock, Arizona. **Critical Thinking:** How does the Constitution guarantee Indians the right to their own governments?

forced some of the nation's top museums to return Indian remains for reburial.

In time, government policy began to change. More federal aid went to Indian programs in such areas as health, education, and housing. The Self-Determination Act of 1975 allows Indian tribal governments to run these programs.

Native American struggles are not over. Indian groups in the Pacific Northwest oppose the heavy logging of forests, which strips mountainsides and pollutes the water. They are angry at the illegal dumping of chemicals on their land. Native Americans want less government involvement in their affairs. Yet it is U.S. judges who will continue to have great influence over these issues.

The Women's Movement

In 1960 you rarely saw a woman police officer. Women could be telephone operators but were not allowed to climb telephone poles to repair the lines. Military jobs for women were limited. The business world was a man's world.

Women had limited legal rights as well. Married women faced problems in signing contracts, selling property, getting credit, and serving on juries. A woman could lose her job if she became pregnant. Society placed strong pressure on women to quit their jobs when they got married. Those who were interested in working outside their homes were seen as "unnatural."

Betty Friedan described this "problem that has no name" in her 1963 book *The Feminine Mystique.* She wrote, "We can no longer ignore that voice within women that says: 'I want something more than my husband and my children and my home.'"

Friedan's words shocked the nation. A women's liberation movement took shape. In 1966 Friedan helped found the National Organization for Women (NOW). Its top goal was to help women get good jobs and equal pay for their work.

The ERA Effort

Every term since 1923, Congress had considered an Equal Rights Amendment (ERA) to the Constitution. Every term the ERA had been killed. In 1972, however, Congress passed the ERA. It stated:

> **Equality of rights under the law shall not be denied or abridged [limited] by the United States or any State on account of sex.**

Now the ERA needed to be ratified by 38 of the 50 state legislatures.

Women Working Outside the Home

Percentage of women

60 — 50 — 40 — 30 — 20 — 10 — 0

1950   1960   1970   1980   1990

Source: *Statistical Abstract of the United States*

CHART SKILLS: The percentage of women in the labor force has been growing. **Critical Thinking:** Do you think that trend will continue? Explain.

Political and Legal Victories

Meanwhile, the situation for women in the United States was changing. The number of women in state legislatures roughly doubled from 1975 to 1988. In 1992 alone, four new women were elected to the Senate. President Bill Clinton named several women to his Cabinet and appointed a second woman to the Supreme Court.

In courtrooms across the nation, women sued companies for equal pay and an equal chance at every job. Some cases dragged on for years. Companies protested that women could not perform certain jobs. Some said they should not have to hire women because women would later quit to have babies. One by one, courts rejected these arguments.

Today, women are finding that laws alone do not wipe out old prejudices. Women who try to break into formerly male careers have been mistreated. Women still make less money than men. Yet like African Americans, Hispanic Americans, and Native Americans, women look back with pride on their civil rights victories.

Marchers relax after a pro-ERA demonstration in Washington, D.C.

Not everyone supported the ERA, however. Phyllis Schlafly, the ERA's best-known opponent, warned that it would destroy American families. Women would have to serve in combat, she said. Husbands would no longer have to support their families after divorce. She argued that women would be forced to work and would not be able to raise their children at home.

Schlafly and her supporters declared war on the ERA. She took her movement to "Stop ERA" to state after state. The deadline for passage of the Equal Rights Amendment was 1982. That year, three states short of final approval, the ERA died.

4 American Society's Many Faces

SECTION GUIDE

Main Idea
The U.S. population is becoming more diverse. This raises issues of immigration policy and the nation's ability to guarantee opportunities for all its people.

Goals
As you read, look for answers to these questions:

1 How has U.S. immigration policy changed since the 1960s?

2 What other changes in American society have taken place in recent years?

Key Terms
Immigration Reform and Control Act
Americans with Disabilities Act
affirmative action

I N THE FALL OF 1993, a special edition of *Time* magazine appeared on newsstands. The cover showed the face of a young woman. The face was a computer-generated image that mixed the features of many different types of Americans. *Time* proclaimed this "The New Face of America." In reality, our multicultural society has always included many different faces. The civil rights movements of recent decades have made these faces more visible.

A Nation of Immigrants

Immigration, of course, is the reason for the diversity of America. Congress has opened and closed the doors to immigrants many times in the 1900s. In 1965 Congress reformed U.S. immigration policy, which had favored immigrants from Europe. The 1965 law opened new doors to Asians and Latin Americans.

Before the laws changed, it had been difficult for most Asians to come to the United States. Filipinos had been able to move to America after their homeland became a U.S. territory in 1898. Yet laws and agreements made in the late 1800s and early 1900s limited Chinese and Japanese immigration. Asians who did settle here faced unfair treatment. Japanese Americans, for example, could not own land in some places and had to attend segregated schools.

The civil rights movement helped end these types of laws. Today Asian Americans enjoy full legal equality. Asian Americans serve in Congress and in state and local government.

The 1965 law opened the doors to immigrants from across Asia, including India, Pakistan, Indonesia, and the Middle East. Wars in Indochina in the 1960s led to a flood of refugees from Vietnam, Cambodia, and Laos. Today the Asian American community includes many cultures.

Some Asians have moved to this country illegally. They are among the thousands of illegal immigrants who arrive in the United States each

The cover of this issue of *Time* magazine shows a woman who combines the characteristics of many of the ethnic groups in the United States today.

AMERICANS WITH DISABILITIES ACT

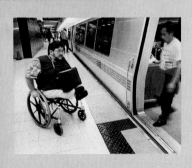

In 1990 the United States acknowledged the rights of its largest minority: the disabled. Congress passed the Americans with Disabilities Act (ADA), considered the most sweeping anti-discrimination law since the Civil Rights Act of 1964.

The ADA bans discrimination on the basis of physical or mental handicap in employment and public facilities. It sets up a timeline during which everything from new offices to telephone services must be made accessible to all Americans. (The train shown above, for example, has a handle by the door and a ramp that closes the gap between the platform and the train.) The law requires wheelchair ramps and elevators, but businesses have complied in other ways as well. Some schedule meetings on the ground floor and provide job information on telephone services for the hearing-impaired.

year. Illegal immigrants come in crowded vans in the middle of the night. They come in rafts across stormy seas. They include frightened families and orphaned children. Some are caught and sent home. Some die trying to get here.

Most illegal immigrants to the United States, however, come across the border from Mexico. Some have traveled north from Central American countries. "You can't stop them," said one border patrol agent. "It's like water in your hands, . . . it falls through your fingers."

Should the United States let anyone come who wants to? This has long been a nation of immigrants. Yet newcomers are often poor, and they need jobs, housing, and health care. Many people feel that we cannot afford to help everyone who comes knocking at America's door.

By 1985 an estimated 6 million illegal aliens lived in the United States. They filled many low-paying jobs that others refused to take. Yet some Americans claimed that illegal immigrants kept wages low. They were angry that illegal immigrants benefitted from public schools and social programs. These programs are paid for by American taxpayers.

In response to growing concerns, Congress passed the **Immigration Reform and Control Act** in 1986. It allowed illegal aliens to stay and become legal citizens if they had arrived before 1982. The law then tried to cut further illegal entry by fining businesses that hired illegals. Still, more than 300,000 illegal immigrants are estimated to arrive in the United States each year.

Changes in U.S. Society

The movement to expand rights for all Americans did not end in the 1970s. Many groups that had long felt ignored or mistreated began to speak out for their rights.

As a young man, Robert L. Burgdorf, Jr., was rejected for an electrician's job because his right arm, partly paralyzed, hung lower than his left. In 1990 a bill that Burgdorf wrote was signed by President George Bush. The **Americans with Disabilities Act** requires businesses to give disabled persons more access to the workplace.

Women also continued to call for equality of opportunity. In her Air Force officer training in 1989, Jeannie Flynn took backseat rides in "some very high-performance aircraft." Although she knew that the U.S. military barred women from flying in combat, she applied anyway. As expected, her request was rejected. Just a few years later, in 1993, the Defense Department ended the ban. Flynn took to the skies. In 1994 the Defense Department further expanded the types of jobs women could fill in the armed forces.

These changes have created tensions. Some have occurred because of the policy of affirmative action. This policy was introduced by the federal government. It requires businesses and schools that received federal funds to recruit women and members of different ethnic groups. This effort is meant to make up for past discrimination.

Opponents of affirmative action say that it discriminates against white men. They argue that it is no better than other forms of discrimination.

The American People

Take a look at the U.S. population. According to the 1990 Census, about three quarters of Americans are white —most of European descent. About 12 percent are African American and 9 percent are Hispanic American. Nearly 3 percent are Asian American. Native Americans make up about 1 percent of the U.S. population.

White people, however, are becoming a smaller slice of the population. Hispanic Americans are the fastest growing group. About half have settled in California and the Southwest. African Americans will make up about one-seventh of the U.S. population by the year 2025.

The number of Asian Americans more than doubled from 1980 to 1990. Most Asians live on the east and west coasts, especially in Los Angeles, San Francisco, and New York City.

The numbers, of course, are based on which groups people report they belong to. What should Roberto Chong of Lawrence, Massachusetts, tell the census takers? He was born to a Peruvian mother and Chinese father. That makes him an Asian American *and* an Hispanic American. As

ethnic groups grow and become more settled in this country, the lines between them will continue to blur.

The American People

Ancestry of Americans	(descendants, in millions)	Birthplace of Immigrants Today	(U.S. population, in thousands)
1. German	58	1. Mexico	4,298
2. Irish	39	2. Philippines	913
3. English	33	3. Canada	745
4. African	24	4. Cuba	737
5. Italian	15	5. Germany	712
6. Mexican	12	6. United Kingdom	640
7. French	10	7. Italy	580
8. Polish	9	8. Korea	568
9. Native American	9	9. Vietnam	543
10. Dutch	6	10. China	530

Source: U.S. Census Bureau

CHART SKILLS: These charts show the diversity of the American population today. **Critical Thinking:** Based on the list of immigrant groups shown above, how might the order of American ancestry groups change in the next 50 years?

SECTION REVIEW

1. Key Terms Immigration Reform and Control Act, Americans with Disabilities Act, affirmative action

2. Comprehension How was U.S. immigration policy changed in 1965?

3. Comprehension How do illegal immigrants come into the United States?

4. Comprehension How is the population of the United States changing?

5. Critical Thinking Explain how disagreements over immigration policy and affirmative action reflect the challenges of diversity.

Summary

1. Determined to overcome racial injustice, African Americans organized to win their civil rights. They pursued their goals through the courts, economic boycotts, and nonviolent protests such as freedom rides and sit-ins.

2. The civil rights movement had several important victories in the 1960s, especially in the area of federal laws. Still, violence took many lives. There were deadly summer riots in many U.S. cities. Malcolm X was killed in 1965, and in 1968 Dr. Martin Luther King, Jr., was assassinated.

3. Inspired by the black civil rights movement, other groups, including Hispanic Americans, American Indians, and women, became politically active.

4. Recent changes in American immigration policy have led to an even more diverse society.

Graphic Summary

African Americans use the courts and other nonviolent means to end segregation.

New federal laws ensure greater civil and political rights.

Civil Rights Movement

Hispanic Americans, American Indians, and women demand equality.

Greater respect for all Americans.

Review

KEY TERMS

Define the following key terms.

1. *Brown v. Board of Education*
2. Montgomery bus boycott
3. sit-in
4. Civil Rights Act (1964)
5. Latino
6. American Indian Movement
7. Americans with Disabilities Act

COMPREHENSION

1. Why did President Eisenhower decide to send federal troops to Little Rock, Arkansas, in 1957?
2. How did sit-ins and freedom rides promote civil rights during the 1960s?
3. How did white opponents respond to the civil rights movement?
4. What was the purpose of the Selma to Montgomery march?
5. What split developed in the civil rights movement in the mid-1960s?
6. What were the goals of Chavez's farm workers' union?
7. Why did American Indians take over Alcatraz Island in 1969?
8. What was the Equal Rights Amendment? What arguments were made for and against it? What happened to it?
9. Why did Congress pass the Immigration Reform and Control Act in 1986?
10. Give three examples of how employment practices today reflect America's diversity.

Places to Locate

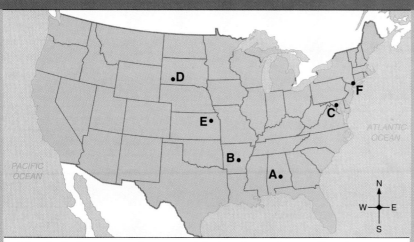

Match the letters on the map with the places that are listed below. Then explain the importance of each place.

1. Little Rock   4. Montgomery
2. New York City   5. Topeka
3. Wounded Knee   6. Washington, D.C.

Geographic Theme: Places What factors led to the eruption of violence in northern cities in the 1960s?

Skill Review

Reread the skill lesson in this chapter. Then answer the questions that follow.

1. Using the suggestions in the skill lesson and your own ideas, create a list of steps to take during a conflict that allow you to respond in a peaceful way.

2. Look through a newspaper or magazine or listen to a news broadcast and identify one or two stories about a conflict taking place somewhere around the world. Are the participants responding peacefully? If not, brainstorm to discover one or two possible ways they might try to resolve their conflict in a peaceful way.

3. Write the dialogue of an imaginary conversation between two of your classmates. The conversation should show them dealing with a conflict peacefully.

CRITICAL THINKING

1. **Identifying Significance** Why was nonviolent resistance so effective? How might the history of the civil rights movement have been different if the protesters had fought back when attacked?

2. **Forming an Opinion** How successful has the women's movement been in achieving its goals? Explain.

3. **Comparing and Contrasting** Compare the tactics of African Americans, Hispanic Americans, and Native Americans in their struggles for civil rights.

PORTFOLIO OPTIONS

1. **Civics Connection** Research and discuss the roles that students played in the civil rights movements of the 1960s. What impact do you think student involvement had? In what ways are students active today?

2. **Writing Connection** Imagine that you are a reporter listening to Martin Luther King, Jr.'s, speech in Washington. Write an editorial describing the scene and the reactions of the people around you.

3. **Contemporary Connection** What groups face discrimination in American society today? Discuss with the class the reasons behind such discrimination and ways in which it can be fought.

4. **Timeline Connection** Copy the chapter timeline. Write a brief paragraph explaining the significance of the Civil Rights Act and the Voting Rights Act.

We live in a world that is rapidly changing. What will the future bring as people around the world face new opportunities and challenges? Here students search for answers to these questions in the Earth Balloon—the world's largest (nearly exact) representation of the earth. Made out of sailcloth, the Earth Balloon expands to nearly 22 feet in diameter. Its colors and symbols are hand-painted and represent earth's landforms and population concentrations.

1991

1992

1993

1994

1991 Operation Desert Storm

1991 Four Yugoslav republics declare independence

1992 U.S. troops land in Somalia

1992 Bill Clinton elected President

1993 Israel-PLO agreement signed

1993 Congress approves NAFTA

1994 Congress rejects Clinton's health-care plan

Patterns in Our Recent History (1990–Present)

1 The Clinton Presidency

SECTION GUIDE

Main Idea

Demanding change, Americans voted Bill Clinton into the White House in 1992 and then reelected him in 1996.

Goals

As you read, look for answers to these questions:

1 What were the main issues in the presidential campaigns of 1992 and 1996?

2 What issues has Clinton faced as President?

3 How did the 1994 elections shift power in government?

Key Term
NAFTA

FOR THE 1992 ELECTION Americans had one major demand: change. There was plenty that needed changing, according to voters. Americans were worried about the huge federal debt, more than $3 trillion and growing at the rate of $240,000 per minute. Workers watched their jobs disappear as companies tried to cut costs. Families wondered why their standard of living seemed lower than that of their parents, even though two family members were holding down jobs. These concerns gave a central theme to the campaign—the economy.

The 1992 Election

The year before the election, Democrats were not eager to run against a popular President. The U.S. victory in the Gulf War (which you will read about later in this chapter) made President George Bush a hero in 1991. Fully 91 percent of Americans approved of the way he was doing his job. This was the highest percentage ever recorded for a President.

Yet Bush's advantage started to slip away. The public felt that he was not doing enough to help the economy. Soon several Democrats announced that they would enter the race. One candidate was Arkansas governor Bill Clinton. Though only in his mid-forties, Clinton was an experienced politician. At Yale Law School he had met and later married Hillary Rodham, also a law student. They returned to Arkansas, where Bill Clinton later became governor. He was seen as a hard-working governor who improved Arkansas' schools and economy. Hillary Rodham Clinton was his closest adviser. Later in the 1992 campaign, Bill Clinton joked that if American voters elected him, they would get a "two for one" deal.

1995	1996
1995 Million Man March	**1996 Bill Clinton reelected President**
1995 Bosnian peace treaty	

Ross Perot

By 1992 many voters were tired of traditional politics. They felt that politicians would not even discuss the nation's problems. By June it was not a Republican or a Democrat who led in the polls. It was billionaire H. Ross Perot, an independent candidate.

Perot gained national attention by appearing on television talk shows and on commercials. His straight talk about tough issues like the economy, unemployment, and education appealed to voters. Perot blasted the failure of the nation's leaders to deal with the most serious problems. People called this failure "gridlock." Perot promised to use his skills as a businessman to end it.

The Conventions

By the Democratic Convention in July 1992, Clinton had all but sewn up the nomination. An important goal for the Democratic Party was to win back its members who had voted Republican in the 1980, 1984, and 1988 elections. Clinton described himself as a new kind of Democrat, a person not tied to big government or big spending.

As expected, the Republicans nominated President Bush and Vice President Dan Quayle for a second term. Yet things did not go smoothly for the Republicans. Patrick Buchanan, a conservative journalist, had entered some Republican primaries against the President. Buchanan and other conservatives made fiery speeches at the convention. Voters remembered the conservatives' message more than Bush's speech defending his record.

In his speech Bush explained why he had raised taxes in 1990, breaking an earlier promise. "With my back against the wall, I agreed to a hard bargain," he said. Bush was caught between the moderate and conservative wings of the Republican Party. It was not a good place to be with Clinton leading in the polls and the election a little over two months away.

On the Campaign Trail

Soon after the Democratic Convention, Clinton and his running mate, Tennessee Senator Al Gore, chartered a bus and took a 1,000-mile campaign tour. They were greeted by large crowds as they stopped in small towns from Virginia to Missouri. The two candidates appeared on the evening news almost daily. They spoke to crowds or played touch football and miniature golf.

Clinton had taken a risk in picking Gore as his running mate. A candidate for President commonly chooses a running mate who has different strengths from the candidate himself. Yet both Clinton and Gore were from the South. Both were born after World War II. Both were moderate Democrats. Some critics remarked that the men were too similar to win the election.

The Debates

In October, Bush, Clinton, and Perot met in three television debates. Bush had three goals for the debates. He wanted to portray Clinton as a big-spending liberal. He wanted to point out Clinton's lack of experience in foreign affairs. He also wanted to argue that Americans could trust a proven leader like him more than Clinton.

Clinton, too, had three goals. He needed to look and act like a President. He wanted to show that he belonged to a new generation, with new energy and ideas. Finally, he wanted to blame Bush for the economy.

In the debates, as well as in the campaign as a whole, the economy was the main issue. Bush was haunted by his flip-flop on taxes and by the lack of economic growth. A poster in Clinton's main office served as a reminder of his campaign focus. It read, "IT'S THE ECONOMY, STUPID."

Clinton Wins

Clinton won the 1992 election with 43 percent of the popular vote. Bush won 37 percent and Perot won 19 percent.

The 1992 election brought more than a new President. Four new female senators were elected to Congress. Among them was Carol Moseley Braun, the first African American woman senator. Together with two incumbents, they became the largest group of women ever to serve in the Senate. Nineteen women entered the House of Representatives, bringing the total to 47. Voters also elected thirteen new African American representatives. Hispanic representatives increased from 7 to 17. California elected the first Korean American representative, and Colorado elected the first Native American to serve in the Senate in 60 years.

The Clinton Presidency

Clinton's first few months as President were difficult. He lost battles in Congress over his Cabinet appointments. The press accused him of being disorganized. According to one poll, only 36 percent of Americans approved of how he was handling his new job. That was a record low for a postwar President four months into his term.

The first important victory for Clinton was when Congress passed his federal budget plan. His plan, which squeaked through by only two votes in the House and one vote in the Senate, included cuts in government spending and new taxes. Clinton hoped his plan would help reduce the federal deficit. This narrow win in Congress made it possible for Clinton to proceed with another project: health-care reform.

Here Bill Clinton and Al Gore speak to a crowd of supporters in Georgia during a stop in the 1992 campaign bus tour.

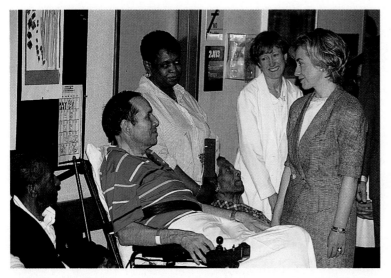

Hillary Rodham Clinton (above) visits a Washington, D.C., medical center to learn about the nation's health-care problems. Union members (below right) hold an anti-NAFTA rally in California.

Health-Care Reform

The President put his wife, Hillary Rodham Clinton, in charge of designing a health-reform plan. Rising costs for everything from medicine to hospital equipment had turned health care into a $1 trillion-a-year problem. The Clintons needed a plan that would answer two important questions: (1) How could the nation provide health insurance for the many millions of Americans who were without it? (2) How could the rising costs and waste in medical care be controlled?

In late 1993 Clinton presented the plan. It was the largest piece of legislation since Franklin Delano Roosevelt started Social Security in 1935. Clinton's health plan would guarantee every American a minimum package of health care. Congress began debating the plan in early 1994. Opponents criticized the reforms as too complicated. Further, they charged, covering every American was too expensive. By September, Clinton realized his plan would not pass the Senate and he withdrew it without a vote.

The insurance crisis continued, though. By the beginning of 1995, the number of Americans not covered by health insurance reached 41 million. About 11 million of these were children.

In August 1996 Congress and the President approved the Kassebaum-Kennedy bill. While this legislation did little for those without health coverage, it protects many from losing it. The key characteristic of the measure is "portability," which guarantees that individuals who lose or leave their jobs can maintain coverage.

The Debate over NAFTA

A year after his election, Clinton faced another uphill battle in Congress. This time it was over a trade agreement called the North American Free Trade Agreement, or NAFTA. It would lower tariffs and increase trade between Mexico, the United States, and Canada. This would form the biggest trading bloc in the world.

NAFTA caused a heated debate across the nation. Those opposed to NAFTA, such as labor unions, feared that it would lead U.S. companies to move to Mexico, where workers are paid less. This, they argued, would put many Americans out of work. People in favor of NAFTA argued that as Mexicans began buying more American-made goods, new jobs would be created in the United States.

The debate in Congress was heated as well. Most Republicans backed Clinton and NAFTA. Many Democrats opposed NAFTA, even though that meant voting against their President. In late 1993, Congress passed NAFTA. Clinton hailed the vote as a victory for free trade.

NAFTA, though, had little immediate impact. In its first year, it caused a loss of about 38,000 jobs in the United States. In Mexico, anger over NAFTA was just one of many causes that led to widespread political protests. The protests frightened investors who then pulled their money out of Mexico. As a result, Mexican wages fell and the price of foreign goods rose.

The 1994 Election

NAFTA was only one factor shaping the U.S. economy in the mid-1990s. For politicians, the key factor was that people did not feel prosperous. One poll in 1994 indicated that 70 percent of Americans worried about their future. Voters saw Clinton's policies as no better than Bush's. They were frustrated with him and with most politicians.

Voters expressed their frustration in the 1994 Congressional elections. Only 39 percent of voters went to the polls. Of those, 51 percent voted for a Republican in the House of Representatives races. This slim margin, though, gave the Republicans a stunning victory. They picked up 53 House seats and 7 Senate seats. For the first time since the elections of 1954, the Republicans controlled both houses of Congress.

The House Republicans moved quickly to reshape government. During the campaign, many of them were among the 300 signers of the Contract with America. In this document, they pledged to bring to a vote several key issues during their first 100 days in office. They fulfilled their pledge, voting on 28 bills. They passed 26 of them. Among these were bills to reduce regulations on businesses, to increase military spending, and to shift anti-poverty programs from federal to state control. However, most of these bills stalled in the Senate. A coalition of Democrats and some Republicans considered the changes in them too drastic. Only three had become law by the end of 1995.

The Budget Battle

On the budget, the Republicans and Clinton shared two basic goals: cutting taxes and balancing the federal budget. Both also agreed that balancing the budget required cuts in spending for two popular programs, Medicare and Medicaid. These programs provided health care for the elderly and the poor.

Despite their shared goals, the Republicans and Clinton could not agree on an overall budget. The Republicans called for $240 billion in tax cuts over seven years. Clinton offered cuts of $87 billion. For Medicare and Medicaid, the Republicans wanted spending cuts that were twice what Clinton supported. Neither side was willing to compromise enough to satisfy the other. The debate over the budget had become a deadlock.

By November 14, 1995, Congress and the President had agreed on budgets for only a few departments. On that day, most government agencies ran out of authority to spend money. Over 800,000 federal workers were sent home. National parks closed, environmental inspections halted, and passports were not issued. Six days later, an agreement reopened all agencies for a month. Then another shutdown closed agencies for 21 days. The shutdowns fueled the frustration that many citizens felt about politics and politicians.

Welfare Reform

During the 1992 campaign Clinton promised to "end welfare as we know it." On August 22, 1996, heavily influenced by the Contract with America and Republican governors, a welfare reform bill was signed into law by President Clinton.

Under the new legislation, the federal government gave states broader authority over their own welfare programs. In addition, the bill requires welfare recipients to work within two years of receiving benefits and it limits them to five years of benefits.

Bill Clinton and Bob Dole square off in the 1996 presidential debate.

It is projected that the measure will save approximately $54.6 billion through 2002. Most of this amount would be saved by reducing significantly the food stamp program and denying a variety of benefits to legal immigrants until they meet certain requirements.

Clinton Wins Reelection in 1996

A poll conducted in October 1996 revealed that 72 percent of the American population rated the economy as very good or fairly good. Most Americans saw a robust economy with lower average inflation, lower interest rates, low unemployment, and a stock market that kept hitting record highs. For an incumbent president seeking reelection this was good news.

The Republicans chose Bob Dole as their nominee. Dole, who resigned as Senate majority leader after three decades in Congress, attempted to convince voters that the economy was faltering and could do better. It was a difficult idea to sell.

Dole had never been much for supply-side economics or tax cuts. To the surprise of some, he chose former New York congressman Jack Kemp as his running mate. Kemp had long been a supporter of Reaganomics and believed in tax cuts.

While Clinton emphasized staying the course, Dole proposed an across-the-board tax cut of 15 percent over three years. Many were suspicious of a cut that Dole said would both balance the budget and protect Medicare and Social Security. When the promise of a tax cut failed to win him support, Dole attacked Clinton's ethics and character.

It was difficult to damage the President, who was presiding over a hardy peacetime economy. The Dole campaign even made an unsuccessful effort to win the support of Reform Party candidate Ross Perot. Perot, however, declined to quit the race.

When the 1996 election votes were tallied, Clinton received 49 percent of the popular vote, while Dole garnered 41 percent, and Perot 8 percent. Clinton became the first Democrat since Franklin Delano Roosevelt to win a second term. Voters did, however, return Republican control to both the House and the Senate.

Prior to his second inauguration Clinton began revamping his Cabinet. The most notable nominee was U. N. ambassador Madeleine Albright. In selecting Albright to be the first female secretary of state, Clinton said he hoped she would be an inspiration to women "across the world."

SECTION REVIEW

1. Key Term NAFTA

2. People and Places George Bush, Bill Clinton, Hillary Rodham Clinton, H. Ross Perot, Al Gore, Mexico, Bob Dole

3. Comprehension Why did Perot appeal to voters in the 1992 election?

4. Comprehension What is NAFTA, and why is it controversial?

5. Critical Thinking How would you balance the federal budget? What programs would you cut or reduce? Which programs would you maintain? Explain your reasons why.

2 The World After the Cold War

SECTION GUIDE

Main Idea
After the fall of communism around the world, the United States faced new international crises and new chances for peace.

Goals
As you read, look for answers to these questions:

1 What role did the United States and the UN play in regional crises?

2 What events signaled new chances for peace in the troubled regions of the world?

Key Terms
Operation Desert Storm
apartheid
political prisoner

WITH THE FALL of communism in the Soviet Union, President Bush declared the beginning of a "new world order." Yet what would that new world order mean? Would the end of the U.S.-Soviet rivalry bring peace, or would new conflicts arise? Both predictions were right. The United States faced both new conflicts and new chances for peace around the world.

Iraq Invades Kuwait

On August 2, 1990, troops from the Middle Eastern nation of Iraq stormed across their southern border into the nation of Kuwait. Iraqi forces conquered Kuwait and carried some of its vast wealth to Baghdad, Iraq's capital. The Iraqi leader, Saddam Hussein, announced that Kuwait was now a part of Iraq.

Iraq had long claimed Kuwaiti land. Small in size and population, Kuwait is rich in oil. Before the invasion, Hussein had demanded that Kuwait pay Iraq for oil wells that he said were on Iraqi land. He had also demanded that Kuwait not collect $15 billion in loans that it had made to Iraq. Kuwait had refused.

Iraq's invasion sent shock waves around the globe. President Bush and other world leaders demanded that Iraq leave Kuwait. When Iraq refused, the UN Security Council voted to use force to remove Iraqi troops if they did not leave before January 15, 1991. Iraq's invasion "will not stand," Bush vowed.

The Gulf War

Bush and his advisers prepared to free Kuwait. General Colin Powell, Chairman of the Joint Chiefs of Staff, led the military planning. Bush involved other UN nations. In Bush's view, more was at stake than having access to Kuwait's oil. Iraq had conquered an independent nation. Other nations should join to defend Kuwait.

The United States and its allies built up a force of about 500,000 troops near Kuwait. General Norman Schwarzkopf led those troops. Most of the soldiers were Americans. Yet many other nations provided troops, supplies, or money.

A group of U.S. Marines stationed in Kuwait patrol an oil field. Iraqi troops set the fire in the background.

On January 17, 1991, the United States and its allies began to bomb Baghdad. The code name for the offensive was Operation Desert Storm. After more than a month of heavy bombing, allied forces attacked Iraqi troops in Kuwait.

Americans watched on their television sets as the allied attack began. Allied tanks, planes, and helicopters swept into Kuwait. In just 100 hours, Kuwait was free. More than 200,000 Iraqi soldiers were killed or captured. Fewer than 300 Americans died.

The war's aftermath was less hopeful. Although Desert Storm had taken Hussein out of Kuwait and crippled his military machine, he remained in power. Hussein brutally crushed uprisings started in northern Iraq by Kurdish rebels and in the south by Shiite Muslims. Many had hoped the allied troops would help remove Hussein from power. President Bush argued that the goal of the war—to free Kuwait—had been achieved.

Other Conflicts

After Desert Storm the UN and the United States tried to take bigger roles in solving regional conflicts. In three other crises, UN or American military forces tried to promote peace.

(1) *Yugoslavia.* Ethnic rivalries caused four republics to leave the European country of Yugoslavia in 1991. One was Croatia. Another was Bosnia and Herzegovina. Remaining in Yugoslavia was Serbia. Battles for land between Croatians, Bosnians, and Serbians created the bloodiest fighting in Europe since World War II. In December 1995, the warring factions signed a peace treaty. To keep the peace, NATO sent 60,000 troops. This force included 20,000 Americans.

(2) *Somalia.* Civil war and famine broke out in the African nation of Somalia. In 1992 President Bush sent 28,000 U.S. troops to help deliver UN food aid and save thousands from starvation. While this

CULTURAL MOSAIC

COLIN POWELL
(1937–   )

From 1989 to 1993 Colin Powell was Chairman of the Joint Chiefs of Staff, this nation's highest military position. He was the youngest person ever to hold this post and the first African American.

The son of Jamaican immigrants, Powell grew up in New York City. He joined the U.S. Army in 1958. He served twice in the Vietnam War and became a four-star general.

Powell's role in the Gulf War, and later in Somalia, made him widely known and popular. When he retired from the military in 1993, many Americans considered him a hero. He briefly considered running for president. Polls showed he might win. However, Powell decided not to run in 1996.

part of the mission succeeded, the UN and U.S. forces could not restore peace in this troubled country. After a battle in which 17 Americans, as well as hundreds of Somalis, died, the United States decided to withdraw its troops. They returned home in the spring of 1994.

(3) *Haiti.* In the Caribbean island country of Haiti, the military removed President Jean-Bertrand Aristide from power in 1991. Aristide was the first democratically elected leader in Haiti's history. After three years in exile, Aristide returned to power, backed by 20,000 U.S. troops.

Nations of the Middle East

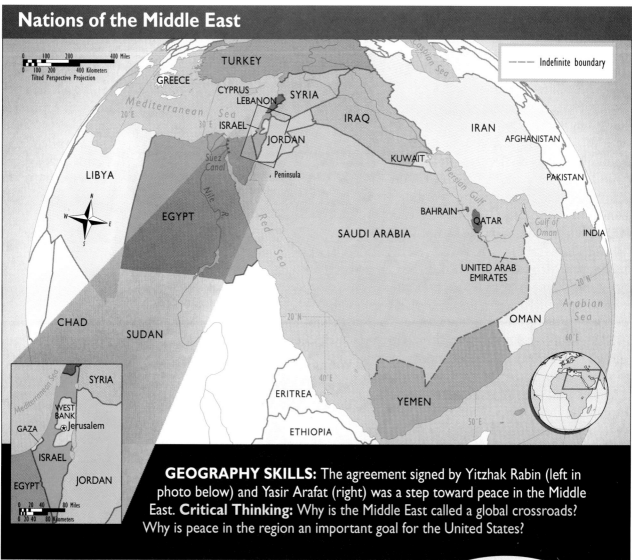

GEOGRAPHY SKILLS: The agreement signed by Yitzhak Rabin (left in photo below) and Yasir Arafat (right) was a step toward peace in the Middle East. **Critical Thinking:** Why is the Middle East called a global crossroads? Why is peace in the region an important goal for the United States?

New Hope in the Middle East

In September 1993 a handshake was world news. Newspapers ran stories describing it—who extended his hand first, what emotions were on the men's faces. Television news showed it over and over again. In the Middle East, and all over the world, people waited in hope and fear to see how it would change their lives.

The handshake was between Israel's prime minister, Yitzhak Rabin, and Yasir Arafat, head of the Palestine Liberation Organization (PLO). For years the PLO had used terrorism—attacks on civilians—against Israel. The PLO vowed to destroy Israel and gain self-rule for Palestinians living under Israeli rule. The Israeli government had refused to talk with the PLO.

The PLO and its Arab allies were not able to destroy Israel. On the other hand, Israel was unable to prevent Palestinian attacks and civilian protests.

In 1988 the PLO took steps to recognize Israel's right to exist. In 1991 Israel agreed to begin talks about the future of Palestinians on the West Bank and Gaza. (Israel had captured these areas from Jordan and Egypt in the 1967 Six-Day War.) These talks led to an agreement signed by Rabin and Arafat in 1993. It called for limited self-rule for part of the West Bank, as well as for Gaza. Though not a final settlement, it was an important step toward peace.

The peace movement received a jolt on November 4, 1995, when Rabin was assassinated by an Israeli Jew opposed to peace with the Palestinians. Rabin's successor, Shimon Peres, vowed to continue peace efforts. Peres, however, was defeated in the 1996 general election by hardliner Benjamin Netanyahu. To date, peace remains elusive in the Middle East.

Progress in South Africa

The Nobel Peace Prize in 1993 was awarded to two South Africans, President F. W. de Klerk and African National Congress (ANC) leader Nelson Mandela. They were chosen for their work to bring democracy to South Africa.

Since 1910 South Africa had been controlled by Afrikaners. (Afrikaners are descendants of Dutch, French, and German settlers.) In 1948 the government put into place laws known as apartheid (uh-PAHRT-hayt). These laws segregated blacks and whites and denied blacks such basic rights as the vote.

The ANC demanded fair treatment for blacks. It called for blacks to be given the right to vote and the right to move freely anywhere in the nation. Several nations urged South Africa to end apartheid.

In 1990, under President de Klerk, the government made major reforms. It legalized the ANC and other antigovernment groups. It also released Mandela after 27 years in prison. Mandela had been a political prisoner—someone jailed for his or her political views.

Mandela and de Klerk worked to bring a peaceful change of power. Not all South Africans shared this commitment. Yet the sight of blacks and whites working together for peace was cause for hope.

In a speech to the U.S. Congress in 1990,

F. W. de Klerk (left) and Nelson Mandela (right) worked to bring democracy to South Africa. For their efforts the two men were awarded the Nobel Peace Prize in 1993.

Mandela said that black South Africans had been inspired by several figures in U.S. history. Among them were George Washington, Abraham Lincoln, Thomas Jefferson, Sojourner Truth, W.E.B. Du Bois, and Martin Luther King, Jr. He went on to say:

❝We could not have known of your Declaration of Independence and not elected to join in the struggle to guarantee the [South African] people's life, liberty, and the pursuit of happiness.❞

SECTION REVIEW

1. Key Terms Operation Desert Storm, apartheid, political prisoner

2. People Saddam Hussein, Colin Powell, Norman Schwarzkopf, Yitzhak Rabin, Yasir Arafat, F.W. de Klerk, Nelson Mandela

3. Comprehension What reforms did Nelson Mandela and F. W. de Klerk seek for South Africa?

4. Critical Thinking Why, do you think, was the United States willing to send troops to Bosnia with UN troops? Do you agree with that decision? Explain.

3 Challenges of the Future

SECTION GUIDE

Main Idea
New developments in technology will transform the lives of Americans and people around the world.

Goals
As you read, look for answers to these questions:

1. How has technology changed Americans' lives?

2. What challenges do the nations of the world face?

3. What social challenges does the United States face?

Key Terms
telecommuting   **deforestation**
global warming

AS AMERICA and the world prepare to enter the 21st century, dramatic changes in technology and society continue. Some of these changes are already affecting the way we learn, work, and play.

A Communications Age

Recent inventions have made it possible for information to travel farther, faster, and in larger amounts than ever before. Fax machines can transmit words and pictures for about the cost of a phone call. Employees can exchange messages through "e-mail" (electronic mail). Modems allow computers around the world to "talk" to each other, sharing vast amounts of data.

Such inventions will change how we live our lives. Here is one example. Many people are already **telecommuting** —working at home while communicating with co-workers by computer. What will the nation be like if students and workers no longer have to gather in schools, offices, and factories?

Another way in which technology changes our lives is by making life-long education even more important. As businesses adopt new technology, they need workers who have the skills to use it. Education gives people those skills. It also allows people to shift from one kind of job to another as new jobs open up.

Cooperation in Space

Space exploration has shown both the risks and the rewards of technology. In the early 1970s scientists and engineers developed a reusable spaceship called a "space shuttle." In 1981 the United States launched *Columbia,* the first space shuttle. Since then the space shuttle program has had many successes but one tragic accident. In 1986 the shuttle *Challenger,* whose crew included New Hampshire schoolteacher Christa McAuliffe, exploded shortly after liftoff. The space shuttle program continued, however.

Technology has changed the way we work. An employee (above) conducts his work away from the office. An astronaut (right) repairs faulty equipment in space.

What is the next step for humans in space? The United States and Russia are working together to build a space station where humans can live for long periods. Other nations are also taking part. This cooperation lets nations share the knowledge and costs of space exploration.

Global Challenges

Nations around the world are also confronting new problems.

(1) *Environment.* Biologist Thomas Lovejoy of the Smithsonian Institution claims, "Most of the great environmental struggles will be either won or lost in the 1990s. By the next century it will be too late."

One threat to the environment is global warming, an increase in the earth's temperature. Global warming is caused by the burning of fossil fuels (oil, gasoline, and coal). This causes a gas called carbon dioxide to be released into the atmosphere. The gas acts as a blanket around the earth, trapping heat.

Scientists disagree on the effects of global warming. Some believe that a rise in the earth's temperature could wipe out whole species and melt enough ice to flood low-lying areas of the world. Others argue that the increase in temperature might even benefit the colder regions of the world.

Another environmental challenge is deforestation, the destruction of forests. Forests are important to all forms of life. Trees clean the air by turning carbon dioxide into oxygen. Also, thousands of species live in tropical rainforests around the world. Yet many of the world's forests are being rapidly destroyed to make way for farming, mining and grazing.

There are signs of progress. In 1990 President Bush signed the Clean Air Act. It aimed to reduce poisonous chemicals in the air. On a global level, an "Earth Summit" was held in 1992 in Rio de Janeiro, Brazil. Delegates from 178 nations discussed global environmental challenges.

PROTECTING NATURE

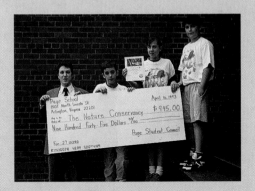

Students across America are helping the environment. Some have formed clubs to plant trees and to recycle bottles and cans. Some have saved acres of rainforest through The Nature Conservancy. This organization buys and protects lands where endangered plants and animals live. Since 1951 it has preserved millions of acres in the United States and other countries. Students from over 1,200 classrooms have joined the organization's Adopt-an-Acre program. They have raised money by performing plays, holding bake sales, and collecting pennies. Together they have bought over 4,000 acres of forest all over the world.

(2) *AIDS.* Acquired Immune Deficiency Syndrome, or AIDS, is one the earth's most frightening health problems. First identified in 1981, AIDS has killed more than 295,000 Americans. Some estimate that 15-20 million people throughout the world will have AIDS by the year 2000.

AIDS is caused by HIV—a virus that destroys the body's ability to fight diseases. AIDS is spread through sexual contact or by sharing unsterilized needles. Pregnant women with AIDS can pass the disease on to their babies. AIDS cannot be spread through activities such as hugging or kissing. A cure or a vaccine for AIDS is not expected for a decade or more.

(3) *Poverty.* The gap between the rich and the poor countries in the world remained large in the 1990s. In the United States and in a dozen other wealthy countries, total economic output per person was over $20,000. However, in most countries, output per person was less than half that. In poor countries such as Egypt, India, and the Philippines, output per person was less than $1,000. Higher rates of disease, shorter lives, and political instability often accompanied such poverty.

Facing the Nation's Problems

At different times in American history, one issue has been the focus of national attention. In the pre-Civil War years it was slavery. In the early 1900s it was political and social reform. During the Depression it was economic growth. Now our most critical problem may be damage to our "social fabric." This damage includes drugs, crime, and homelessness.

(1) *Drugs and crime.* Most alarming to many Americans is the number of young people involved in crime. In many cases, crime is linked to drugs. The debate in the nation is whether punishment or treatment will solve the drug problem.

Those who favor punishment believe that to reduce drug-related crimes the nation should hire more police and impose harsher prison sentences for criminals. Others argue that the number of people in prison has more than doubled since 1980. Yet drug use has not gone down. They say that money should be spent to reduce the demand for drugs.

(2) *Homelessness.* Homelessness strikes all Americans—male and female, young and old, rural and urban. No one knows exactly how many Americans are homeless. The 1990 Census estimated the figure to be almost 230,000 people. Many experts believe the number is much higher.

In most cases, the troubles of the homeless are much more than not having a place to live. Homelessness is combined with many other problems—poverty, unemployment, mental illness, crime, and drug and alcohol abuse.

(3) *Economic uncertainty.* While the economy grew overall during the 1980s and 1990s, many Americans felt less secure. One cause of this worry was that they were working harder but not making more money. The typical employee in the 1990s was working about 160 hours a year more than a typical worker in the 1960s. Yet incomes for most of the population had stagnated over that period. In terms of comparable dollars, the income of a typical family had remained about the same since the 1960s.

The only group whose income increased in the 1980s and early 1990s were the rich. During the 1980s, the richest fifth of Americans had increased their wealth, but the other four-fifths had not. In 1980, the chief executive officers of American's largest companies made, on average, 30 times the salary of the average worker. By 1990, the same CEOs were making 90 times more than the workers.

President Clinton greets members of City Year, a Boston youth organization dedicated to community service.

During the day of speeches at the Million Man March, participants had moments of intense pride and joy as well as of quiet reflection.
Critical Thinking: How should the success of a large rally be measured?

America's Promise

While the United States faces large problems, Americans are willing to struggle against them. For example, to show their commitment to overcoming the challenges facing the country, nearly one million African American men—maybe more—rallied in Washington, D.C. on October 16, 1995. The Million Man March, as the event was known, was organized by Nation of Islam leader Minister Louis Farrakhan. Individuals at the march pledged to take greater responsibility for themselves, their families, and their communities when they returned to their homes across the country.

As these words are being written, thousands of people around the world are dreaming about coming to America. Our nation—the United States of America—is the strongest and wealthiest nation in the world. It still offers the best hope of economic opportunity and political freedom for all of its citizens.

However large the challenges we face as a nation, they are not worse than those faced by earlier generations of Americans. Now that we are using, more than ever before, the talents of *all* Americans, we stand a better chance of solving our problems. President Clinton spoke of the promise always present in America when he said, "All of us—we need each other. We don't have a person to waste."

SECTION REVIEW

1. Key Terms telecommuting, global warming, deforestation

2. People Christa McAuliffe

3. Comprehension How has technology made life-long education important?

4. Comprehension What problems are created by global warming and deforestation?

5. Critical Thinking How might factors like poverty, unemployment, mental illness, crime, and drug and alcohol abuse lead to homelessness?

SKILLS: Considering Careers

LEARN

Adults often ask, "What do you want to be when you grow up?" Perhaps you have no idea what career you want, or maybe you are certain. In either case you can benefit from studying patterns of job growth.

The chart below shows some jobs with a future. Some of them are high-skill, high-wage. Others call for few skills and offer low pay.

As you consider a career, ask yourself these questions: Which job will make me happy? How much money do I need? Do I want to help people? Would I prefer to be my own boss? Your answers will reflect your needs, interests, and skills. The right job for you should suit all three. But remember, with experience and education, your needs, interests, and skills will change. The first career you choose may not be your last.

PRACTICE

1. In the year 2005, will there be more jobs for lawyers or teachers?

2. Which career on the chart is expected to grow the most?

3. Which career on the chart is expected to have the most jobs?

APPLY

4. Design your own career chart. Write a list of your needs, interests, and skills. Decide how much education you want to obtain. Then decide "what you want to be when you grow up."

Projected Job Growth, 1990–2005 (numbers in thousands)

Occupation	1990	Projected, 2005	Percent change
Computer programmers	565	882	56.1
General managers and top executives	3,086	3,684	19.4
Home health aides	287	550	91.7
Lawyers	587	793	35.1
Psychologists	125	204	63.6
Salespersons, retail	3,619	4,506	24.5
Teachers, secondary school	1,280	1,717	34.2
Travel agents	132	214	62.3
Waiters and waitresses	1,747	2,196	25.7

Source: U.S. Department of Labor

Summary

1. Worried about the economy, Americans elected Bill Clinton as President in 1992. Voters also elected a record number of women and minorities to Congress. Issues Clinton faced in the early months of his term included health-care reform and NAFTA. In 1996 voters reelected Clinton.

2. With the cold war over, new conflicts and opportunities for peace arose around the world. The Iraqi invasion of Kuwait rallied nations around the world to action. U.S. and allied troops ousted Iraq from Kuwait. A 1993 Israeli–PLO agreement signaled a step toward peace in the Middle East.

3. The lives of people around the world are being transformed by new developments in technology. Nations of the world are working together to solve global challenges related to the environment and AIDS. Americans are also working to solve social challenges.

Review

KEY TERMS

Write a sentence using each of the following terms.

1. NAFTA
2. Operation Desert Storm
3. apartheid
4. political prisoner
5. telecommuting
6. global warming
7. deforestation

COMPREHENSION

1. What was the main issue in the 1992 and 1996 elections?
2. What criticisms did each of the candidates have for one another in the 1992 debate?
3. What changes in Congress did the 1994 elections bring?
4. What caused the government shutdown in 1995 and 1996?
5. What effect did the end of the cold war have on the United States' role in world affairs?
6. Why did President Bush involve other nations in the decision to oust Iraq from Kuwait?
7. What agreement did Israel and the PLO reach in 1993?
8. What reforms were made in South Africa under President de Klerk?
9. What are the benefits of having nations work together in space exploration?
10. Why has AIDS become a major global challenge?

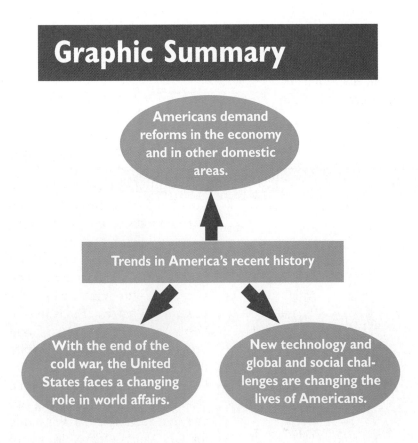

Graphic Summary

Americans demand reforms in the economy and in other domestic areas.

Trends in America's recent history

With the end of the cold war, the United States faces a changing role in world affairs.

New technology and global and social challenges are changing the lives of Americans.

Places to Locate

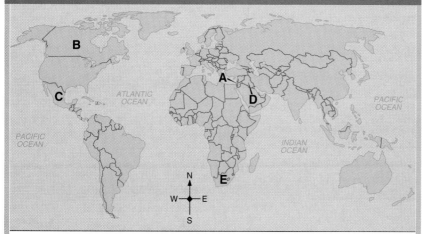

Match the letters on the map with the places that are listed below. Then explain the importance of each place.

1. Iraq   **3.** South Africa   **5.** Israel
2. Canada   **4.** Mexico

Geographic Theme: Interactions What environmental problems does the world face today? What progress is being made to solve some of the problems?

Skill Review

Refer to the career chart you created in this chapter's Skill lesson. Make a list of careers that appeal to you. Do research to determine which careers on your list are high-skill and which are low-skill. Then research which careers on your list are expected to grow the most by the year 2005.

CRITICAL THINKING

1. Analyzing Decisions Do you agree or disagree with the United States' decision to to free Kuwait from Iraqi occupation? Explain your point of view.

2. Expressing an Opinion Although the U.S. played a greater role in world affairs in the 1990s, the 1992 and 1996 elections showed that voters were most concerned about the economy at home. In your opinion, where should the government's focus be today—at home or abroad? Explain.

PORTFOLIO OPTIONS

1. Civics Connection Do research on third party and independent candidates in the 1990s. Who voted for Ross Perot? Why did people support Colin Powell? Predict whether a third large party will emerge.

2. Writing Connection Choose one social problem that affects America today. Write an editorial describing the causes of the problem and ways in which it is being addressed. Read your editorial to the class and answer any questions.

3. Contemporary Connection Discuss with the class what the promise of America means to you. Create a collage of words and images that you think symbolizes that promise.

4. Timeline Connection Copy the chapter timeline. Which events do you think signify a changing role for the United States in world affairs? Explain your answer.

The Joy Luck Club

AMY TAN

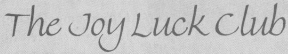

In *The Joy Luck Club*, Amy Tan describes the conflicts between Chinese immigrant women and their American-born daughters. Caught between two cultures, the mothers struggle to teach their daughters Chinese values and traditions. In the passage below, Lindo Sun tries to understand her daughter's feelings about her Chinese heritage. She then remarks on her own conflicting feelings.

My daughter wanted to go to China for her second honeymoon, but now she is afraid.

"What if I blend in so well they think I'm one of them?" Waverly asked me. "What if they don't let me come back to the United States?"

"When you go to China," I told her, "you don't even need to open your mouth. They already know you are an outsider."

"What are you talking about?" she asked. My daughter likes to speak back. She likes to question what I say.

"Aii-ya," I said. "Even if you put on their clothes, even if you take off your makeup and hide your fancy jewelry, they know. They know just watching the way you walk, the way you carry your face. They know you do not belong."

My daughter did not look pleased when I told her this, that she didn't look Chinese. She had a sour American look on her face. Oh, maybe ten years ago, she would have clapped her hands—hurray!—as if this were good news. But now she wants to be Chinese, it is so fashionable. And I know it is too late. All those years I tried to teach her! She followed my Chinese ways only until she learned how to walk out the door by herself and go to school. So now the only Chinese words she can say are *sh-sh, houche, chr fan,* and *gwan deng shweijyau.* How can she talk to people in China with these words? Pee-pee, choo-choo train, eat, close light sleep. How can she think she can blend in? Only her skin and her hair are Chinese. Inside—she is all American-made.

It's my fault she is this way. I wanted my children to have the best combination: American circumstances and Chinese character. How could I know these two things do not mix?

I taught her how American circumstances work. If you are born poor here, it's no lasting shame. You are first in line for a scholarship. If the roof crashes on your head, no need to cry over this bad luck. You can sue

anybody, make the landlord fix it. You do not have to sit like a Buddha under a tree letting pigeons drop their dirty business on your head. You can buy an umbrella. Or go inside a Catholic church. In America, nobody says you have to keep the circumstances somebody else gives you.

She learned these things, but I couldn't teach her about Chinese character. How to obey parents and listen to your mother's mind. How not to show your own thoughts, to put your feelings behind your face so you can take advantage of hidden opportunities. Why easy things are not worth pursuing. How to know your own worth and polish it, never flashing it around like a cheap ring. Why Chinese thinking is best.

No, this kind of thinking didn't stick to her. She was too busy chewing gum, blowing bubbles bigger than her cheeks. Only that kind of thinking stuck.

"Finish your coffee," I told her yesterday. "Don't throw your blessings away."

"Don't be so old-fashioned, Ma," she told me, finishing her coffee down the sink. "I'm my own person."

And I think, How can she be her own person? When did I give her up?

* * *

It's hard to keep your Chinese face in America. At the beginning, before I even arrived, I had to hide my true self. I paid an American-raised Chi-

nese girl in Peking to show me how.

"In America," she said, "you cannot say you want to live there forever. If you are Chinese, you must say you admire their schools, their ways of thinking. You must say you want to be a scholar and come back to teach Chinese people what you have learned."

"What should I say I want to learn?" I asked. "If they ask me questions, if I cannot answer. . ."

"Religion, you must say you want to study religion," said this smart girl. "Americans all have different ideas about religion, so there are no right and wrong answers. Say to them, I'm going for God's sake, and they will respect you."

Reprinted by permission of The Putnam Publishing Group from *The Joy Luck Club* by Amy Tan. Copyright ©1989 by Amy Tan.

Analyzing Literature

1. Why does Waverly now want to be thought of as "really" Chinese when she visits China? Why has she changed her mind about her heritage?

2. What kind of values did the narrator try to teach her daughter?

3. What does the narrator mean when she says, "It's hard to keep your Chinese face in America"?

The Magna Carta (1215)

English barons secured the Magna Carta (Great Charter) from King John in 1215. The charter provided a basis for guaranteeing the personal and political liberties of the people of England and placed kings and queens under the rule of law. The Magna Carta was, in short, an important step in establishing the principle of limited government.

Know ye, that we, in the presence of God, . . . have confirmed for us and our heirs forever:

1. That the English Church shall be free, and shall have her whole rights and liberties inviolable. . . . We have granted moreover to all the freemen of our kingdom, for us and our heirs forever, all the liberties, to be enjoyed and held by them and by their heirs, from us and from our heirs. . . .

39. No freeman shall be seized, imprisoned, dispossessed, outlawed, or exiled, or in any way destroyed; nor will we proceed against or prosecute him except by the lawful judgment of his peers, or by the law of the land.

40. To none will we sell, to none will we deny, to none will we delay right or justice.

60. Also all these customs and liberties which we have granted to be held in our kingdom, for so much of it as belongs to us, all our subjects, as well clergy as laymen, shall observe toward their tenants as far as concerns them. . . .

63. Wherefore our will is, and we firmly command that the Church of England be free, and that the men in our kingdom have and hold the aforesaid liberties, rights, and concessions, well and in peace, freely and quietly, fully and entirely, to them and their heirs, of us and our heirs, in all things and places forever, as is aforesaid.

From J. J. Bagley and P. B. Rowley, eds., *A Documentary History of England,* Vol. 1, pp. 91–113.

The Mayflower Compact (1620)

In 1620, shortly before they landed at Plymouth, 41 of the colonists aboard the Mayflower *drew up the Mayflower Compact. Under this written agreement, the colonists provided for self-government under majority rule of the male voters.*

We, whose names are underwritten, . . . having undertaken for the glory of God, and advancement of the Christian faith, and the honor of our King and country, a voyage to plant the first colony in the northern parts of Virginia, do by these presents, solemnly and mutually in the presence of God and one another covenant and combine ourselves together into a civil body politic, for our better ordering and preservation; and furtherance of the ends aforesaid . . . do enact, constitute, and frame such just and equal laws, ordinances, acts, constitutions, and offices from time to time as shall be thought most [proper] and convenient for the general good of the colony unto which we promise all due submission and obedience. In witness whereof we have hereunto subscribed our names at Cape Cod the eleventh of November, in the year of our sovereign lord King James of England . . . *Anno Domini* 1620.

From B. P. Poore, ed., *The Federal and State Constitutions,* Part I, p. 931.

The Northwest Ordinance (1787)

The Northwest Ordinance outlined a governmental structure for the Northwest Territory, the land north of the Ohio River and westward to the Mississippi River. Provisions in the Ordinance for freedom of religion, civil liberties, and free public education would eventually be incorporated into the constitutions of state governments across the nation.

That the following articles shall be considered as articles of compact between the original States and the people in the said territory, and forever remain unalterable, unless by common consent, to wit:

Article 1. No person . . . shall ever be molested on account of his mode of worship or religious sentiments. . . .

Article 2. The inhabitants of the said territory shall always be entitled to the benefits of habeas corpus, and of trial by jury. . . . No man shall be deprived of his liberty or property, but by the judgment of his peers or the law of the land. . . .

Article 3. Religion, morality, and knowledge being necessary to good government and the happiness of mankind, schools and the means of education shall forever be encouraged. The utmost good faith shall always be observed toward the Indians; their lands and property shall never be taken from them without their consent . . . .

Article 4. The said territory, and the States which may be formed therein, shall forever remain a part of . . . the United States of America. . . .

Article 5. There shall be formed in the said territory, not less than three nor more than five States.

Article 6. There shall be neither slavery nor involuntary servitude in the said territory, otherwise than in the punishment of crimes. . . .

From F. N. Thorpe, ed., *Federal and State Constitutions,* Vol. II, p. 57.

The Federalist, No. 10 *(1787)*

The basis of American government is representative government, rather than direct democracy. In The Federalist, No. 10, *James Madison put forth his arguments in support of electing representatives to Congress.*

The two great points of difference between a democracy and a republic are: first, the delegation of the government, in the latter, to a small number of citizens selected by the rest; secondly, the greater number of citizens and greater sphere of country, over which the latter may be extended.

The effect of the first difference is, on the one hand, to refine and enlarge the public views, by passing them through the medium of a chosen body of citizens, whose wisdom may best discern the true interest of their country and whose patriotism and love of justice will be least likely to sacrifice it to temporary or partial considerations. . . .

By enlarging too much the number of electors, you render the representative too little acquainted with all their local circumstances and lesser interests; as by reducing it too much, you render him unduly attached to these, and too little fit to comprehend and pursue great and national objects. . . .

Extend the sphere and you take in a greater variety of parties and interests; you make it less probable that a majority of the whole will have a common motive to invade the rights of other citizens.

From J. and A. McLean, eds., *The Federalist: A Collection of Essays,* Vol. 1, No. 10.

Washington's Farewell Address *(1796)*

At the end of his second term as President, George Washington spoke of three dangers facing the nation: the rise of political parties, sectionalism, and involvement in European affairs. He urged Americans to steer a neutral course in foreign relations.

A solicitude for your welfare which cannot end with my life . . . urges me on an occasion like the present . . . to recommend to your frequent review some sentiments which are the result of much reflection. . . .

The name of American, which belongs to you . . . , must always exalt the just pride of patriotism. . . . You have in a common cause fought and triumphed together. The independence and liberty you possess are the work of joint councils and joint efforts, of common dangers, sufferings and successes. . . . Every portion of our country finds the most commanding motives for carefully guarding and preserving the union of the whole. . . .

This government, the offspring of our own choice, . . . completely free in its principles, in the distribution of its powers, uniting security with energy, and containing within itself a provision for its own amendment, has a just claim to your confidence and your support. Respect for its authority, compliance with its laws, acquiescence in its measures, are duties enjoined by the fundamental maxim of liberty. . . .

Against the insidious wiles of foreign influence, the jealousy of a free people ought to be constantly awake, since history and experience prove that foreign influence is one of the most baneful foes of republican government. . . . The great rule of conduct for us in regard to foreign nations is in extending our commercial relations to have as little political connection as possible. . . . It is our true policy to steer clear of permanent alliances, with any portion of the foreign world. . . .

From J. D. Richardson, ed., *A Compilation of the Messages and Papers of the Presidents*, Vol. I, p. 213.

"The Star-Spangled Banner" *(1814)*

During the British attack on Fort McHenry in 1814, a young American lawyer named Francis Scott Key wrote the words to "The Star-Spangled Banner." In 1931 Congress made "The Star-Spangled Banner" the national anthem of the United States.

O say! can you see, by the dawn's early light,
What so proudly we hail'd at the twilight's last
   gleaming,
Whose broad stripes and bright stars, thro' the
   perilous fight,
O'er the ramparts we watch'd were so gallantly
   streaming?
And the rockets' red glare, the bombs bursting in
   air,
Gave proof thro' the night that our flag was still
   there.
O, say, does that Star-Spangled Banner yet wave
O'er the land of the free and the home of the
   brave?

From Francis Scott Key, "The Star-Spangled Banner," 1814.

The Monroe Doctrine *(1823)*

President Monroe's message to Congress in 1823, later to be called the Monroe Doctrine, proclaimed the dominance of the United States in the Western Hemisphere. The Monroe Doctrine has continued to influence American foreign policy to the present day.

The American continents, by the free and independent condition which they have assumed and maintain, are henceforth not to be considered as subject for future colonization by any European powers. . . .

The political system of the [European] powers is essentially different . . . from that of America. . . . We owe it, therefore, to candor . . . to declare that we should consider any attempt on their part to extend their system to any portion of this hemisphere as dangerous to our peace and safety. . . .

Our policy in regard to Europe, which was adopted [many years ago], nevertheless remains the same, which is, not to interfere in the internal concerns of any of its powers.

From J. D. Richardson, ed., *A Compilation of the Messages and Papers of the Presidents,* Vol. II, p. 207.

The Seneca Falls Declaration of Sentiments *(1848)*

For her opening address at the Seneca Falls Convention, Elizabeth Cady Stanton prepared a "Declaration of Sentiments." She modeled this appeal for women's rights on the Declaration of Independence.

When in the course of human events, it becomes necessary for one portion of the family of man to assume among the people of the earth a position different from that which they have hitherto occupied, but one to which the laws of nature and nature's God entitle them, a decent respect to the opinion of mankind requires that they should declare the causes that impel them to such a course.

We hold these truths to be self-evident: that all men and women are created equal; that they are endowed by their Creator with certain inalienable rights . . . that to secure these rights governments are instituted, deriving their just powers from the consent of the governed. . . .

The history of mankind is a history of repeated injuries and usurpations on the part of man toward woman, having in direct object the establishment of an absolute tyranny over her. . . .

Now, in view of not allowing one half the people of this country to vote, of their social and religious degradation . . . and because women do feel themselves aggrieved, oppressed, and fraudulently deprived of their most sacred rights, we insist that they have immediate admission to all the rights and privileges which belong to them as citizens of the United States.

In entering upon the great work before us, we anticipate mistaken ideas, misrepresentations, and ridicule; but we shall make every effort within our power to secure our object.

From E. C. Stanton, S. B. Anthony, and M. J. Gage, eds., *The History of Woman Suffrage,* Vol. 1, p. 70.

The Emancipation Proclamation *(1863)*

On January 1, 1863, President Lincoln proclaimed the freedom of all slaves in states in rebellion against the United States.

Whereas, on the twenty-second day of September, in the year of our Lord one thousand eight hundred and sixty-two, a proclamation was issued by the President of the United States containing among other things the following, to wit:

"That on the first day of January, in the year of our Lord one thousand eight hundred sixty-three, all persons held as slaves within any State, or designated part of a State, the people whereof shall then be in rebellion against the United States, shall be then, thenceforth and forever free; and the Executive Government of the United States, including the military and naval authorities thereof will recognize and maintain the freedom of such persons, and will do no act or acts to repress such persons, or any of them, in any efforts they may make for their actual freedom.

That the Executive will, on the first day, designate the States and parts of States, if any, in which the people therein respectively shall then be in rebellion against the United States, and the fact that any State . . . shall on that day be in good faith represented in the Congress of the United States by members chosen thereto . . . shall, in the absence of strong countervailing testimony, be deemed conclusive evidence that such State and the people thereof are not then in rebellion against the United States."

Now, therefore, I, Abraham Lincoln, President of the United States, by virtue of the power in me vested as Commander-in-Chief of the Army and Navy of the United States in time of actual armed rebellion against the authority and Government of the United States, and as a fit and necessary war measure for suppressing said rebellion, do, on this first day of January, in the year of our Lord one thousand eight hundred and sixty-three . . . designate, as the States and parts of States wherein the people thereof . . . are this day in rebellion against the United States, the following, to wit: Arkansas, Texas, Louisiana (except the parishes of St. Bernard, Plaquemines, Jefferson, St. John, St. Charles, St. James, Ascension, Assumption, Terre Bonne, Lafourche St. Mary, St. Martin, and Orleans, including the City of New Orleans), Alabama, Florida, Georgia, South Carolina, North Carolina, and Virginia (except the forty-eight counties designated as West Virginia and also the counties of Berkeley, Accomac, Northampton, Elizabeth City, York, Princess Ann, and Norfolk, including the cities of Norfolk and Portsmouth). . . .

And, by virtue of the power and for the purpose aforesaid, I do order and declare that all persons held as slaves within these said designated States and parts of States are, and henceforward shall be free; and that the Executive Government of the United States, including the military and naval authorities thereof, will recognize and maintain the freedom of said persons.

And I hereby enjoin [urge] upon the people so declared to be free, to abstain from all violence, unless in necessary self-defense, and I recommend to them, that in all cases, when allowed, they labor faithfully for reasonable wages.

And I further declare and make known that such persons of suitable condition will be received into the armed service of the United States to garrison forts, positions, stations, and other places, and to man vessels of all sorts in said service.

And, upon this, sincerely believed to be an act of justice, warranted by the Constitution, upon military necessity, I invoke the considerate judgment of mankind and the gracious favor of Almighty God.

From *United States Statutes at Large,* Vol. XII, p. 1268.

The Gettysburg Address (1863)

President Lincoln presented his memorable Gettysburg Address on November 19, 1863, at the dedication of a national cemetery on the battlefield of Gettysburg. His eloquent words express his hopes for a war-torn nation.

Four score and seven years ago our fathers brought forth on this continent, a new nation, conceived in liberty, and dedicated to the proposition that all men are created equal.

Now we are engaged in a great civil war, testing whether that nation or any nation so conceived and so dedicated, can long endure. We are met on a great battlefield of that war. We have come to dedicate a portion of that field, as a final resting place for those who here gave their lives that that nation might live. It is altogether fitting and proper that we should do this.

But, in a larger sense, we cannot dedicate—we cannot consecrate—we cannot hallow—this ground. The brave men, living and dead, who struggled here, have consecrated it, far above our poor power to add or detract. The world will little note, nor long remember what we say here, but it can never forget what they did here. It is for us the living, rather, to be dedicated here to the unfinished work which they who fought here have thus far so nobly advanced. It is rather for us to be here dedicated to the great task remaining before us—that from these honored dead we take increased devotion to that cause for which they gave the last full measure of devotion—that we here highly resolve that these dead shall not have died in vain—that this nation, under God, shall have a new birth of freedom—and that government of the people, by the people, for the people, shall not perish from the earth.

From *The Writings of Abraham Lincoln,* Constitutional ed., Vol. VIII, p. 20.

Abraham Lincoln's Second Inaugural Address (1865)

Lincoln delivered his Second Inaugural Address just before the end of the Civil War In it he recalls the circumstances that led the nation to war and his hope for the restoration of peace and unity.

Fellow Countrymen: At this second appearing to take the oath of the presidential office there is less occasion for an extended address than there was at the first. Then a statement of a course to be pursued seemed fitting and proper. Now, at the expiration of four years, during which public declarations have been constantly called forth on every point and phase of the great contest which still absorbs the attention and engrosses the energies of the nation, little that is new could be presented. The progress of our arms, upon which all else chiefly depends, is as well known to the public as to myself, and it is, I trust, reasonably satisfactory and encouraging to all. With high hope for the future, no prediction in regard to it is ventured.

On the occasion corresponding to this four years ago, all thoughts were anxiously directed to an impending civil war. All dreaded it, all sought to avert it. While the inaugural address was being delivered from this place, . . . insurgent agents were in the city seeking to destroy it without war—seeking to dissolve the Union. Both parties [disapproved of] war, but one of them would make war rather than let the nation survive, and the other would accept war rather than let it perish, and the war came.

One eighth of the whole population was colored slaves, not distributed generally over the Union, but localized in the southern part of it. These slaves constituted a peculiar and powerful interest. All knew that this interest was somehow the cause of the war. To strengthen, perpetuate, and extend this interest was the object for which the rebels would tear the Union even by war while the government claimed no right to do more than to restrict the territorial enlargement of it. Neither party expected for the war the magnitude or the duration which it has already attained. Neither anticipated that the cause of the conflict itself should cease. Each looked for an easier triumph, and a result less fundamental and astounding. . . . Fondly do we hope, fervently do we pray, that this mighty scourge of war may speedily pass away. Yet, if God wills that it continue until all the wealth piled by the slaves' two hundred and fifty years of unpaid toil shall be sunk, and until every drop of blood drawn with the lash shall be paid by another drawn with the sword. . . .

With malice toward none, with charity for all, with firmness in the right as God gives us to see the right, let us strive on to finish the work we are in, to bind up the nation's wounds, to care for him who shall have borne the battle and for his widow and his orphan—to do all which may achieve and cherish a just and a lasting peace among ourselves and with all nations.

From J. D. Richardson, ed., *A Compilation of the Messages and Papers of the Presidents,* Vol. VI, p. 276.

The Fourteen Points (1918)

Nine months after the United States entered World War I, President Wilson delivered to Congress a statement of war aims that became known as the "Fourteen Points." In the speech, the main parts of which are summarized below, the President set forth fourteen "points" or proposals for helping to reduce the risk of war in the future.

Open covenants of peace, openly arrived at, after which there shall be no private international understandings of any kind, but diplomacy shall proceed always frankly and in public view.

Absolute freedom of navigation upon the seas . . . in peace and in war. . . .

The removal, so far as possible, of all economic barriers and the establishment of an equality of trade conditions among all the nations. . . .

Adequate guarantees given and taken that national armaments will be reduced. . . .

A free, open-minded, and absolutely impartial adjustment of all colonial claims, based upon . . . the principle that . . . the interests of the populations concerned must have equal weight with the . . . claims of the government whose title is to be determined.

A general association of nations must be formed under specific covenants for the purpose of affording mutual guarantees of political independence and territorial integrity to great and small states alike.

From *Supplement to the Messages and Papers of the Presidents Covering the Second Administration of Woodrow Wilson.*

Franklin D. Roosevelt's First Inaugural Address (1933)

Taking office in the depths of the Great Depression, President Roosevelt sought in his First Inaugural Address to restore the public's confidence. His words electrified the nation and had the desired effect of boosting morale.

This is pre-eminently the time to speak the truth, the whole truth, frankly and boldly. Nor need we shrink from honestly facing conditions in our country today. This great nation will endure as it has endured, will revive and will prosper.

So first of all let me assert my firm belief that the only thing we have to fear is fear itself—nameless, unreasoning, unjustified terror which paralyzes needed efforts to convert retreat into advance. . . .

Our greatest primary task is to put people to work. This is no unsolvable problem if we face it wisely and courageously.

It can be accomplished in part by direct recruiting by the government itself, treating the task as we would treat the emergency of a war, but at the same time, through this employment, accomplishing greatly needed projects to stimulate and reorganize the use of our national resources. . . .

I am prepared under my constitutional duty to recommend the measures that a stricken nation in the midst of a stricken world may require.

These measures, or such other measures as the Congress may build out of its experience and wisdom, I shall seek, within my constitutional authority, to bring to speedy adoption.

From *The Public Papers and Addresses of Franklin D. Roosevelt*, Vol. I.

The Truman Doctrine *(1947)*

In February 1947, with the Greek government under attack by Communist rebels, President Truman announced that the United States would support not only Greece but free people anywhere in the world who were facing subversion. Thus was born the Truman Doctrine. This excerpt comes from Truman's memoirs.

Greece needed aid, and needed it quickly and in substantial amounts. The alternative was the loss of Greece and the extension of the iron curtain across the eastern Mediterranean. . . .

But the situation had even wider implications. Poland, Rumania, and the other satellite nations of Eastern Europe had been turned into Communist camps because, in the course of the war, they had been occupied by the Russian Army. We had tried, vainly, to persuade the Soviets to permit political freedom in these countries, but we had no means to compel them to relinquish their control, unless we were prepared to wage war.

Greece and Turkey were still free countries being challenged by Communist threats both from within and without. These free peoples were engaged in a valiant struggle to preserve their liberties and their independence.

America could not, and should not, let these free countries stand unaided. To do so would carry the clearest implications in the Middle East and in Italy, Germany, and France. The ideals and the traditions of our nation demanded that we come to the aid of Greece and Turkey and that we put the world on notice that it would be our policy to support the cause of freedom wherever it was threatened. . . .

On Wednesday, March 12, 1947, at one o'clock in the afternoon, I stepped to the rostrum in the hall of the House of Representatives and addressed a joint session of the Congress. I had asked the senators and representatives to meet together so that I might place before them what I believed was an extremely critical situation.

To cope with this situation, I recommended immediate action by the Congress. But I also wished to state, for all the world to know, what the position of the United States was in the face of the new totalitarian challenge. This declaration of policy soon began to be referred to as the "Truman Doctrine." This was, I believe, the turning point in America's foreign policy, which now declared that wherever aggression, direct or indirect, threatened the peace, the security of the United States was involved.

From Harry S. Truman, *Memoirs of Harry S. Truman. Years of Trial and Hope,* Doubleday & Co., Inc., Publishers, 1956, by permission of Margaret Truman Daniel.

Brown v. Board of Education
(1954)

In the years following the Supreme Court decision in Plessy v. Ferguson, *many areas of the nation maintained "separate-but-equal" education systems for whites and blacks. Then, in 1954, the Court set aside the 1896 decision when it unanimously ruled against school segregation in* Brown v. Board of Education.

Today, education is perhaps the most important function of state and local governments. Compulsory school attendance laws and the great expenditures for education both demonstrate our recognition of the importance of education to our democratic society. It is required in the performance of our most basic public responsibilities, even service in the armed forces. It is the very foundation of good citizenship. Today it is a principal instrument in awakening the child to cultural values, in preparing him for later professional training, and in helping him to adjust normally to his environment. In these days, it is doubtful that any child may reasonably be expected to succeed in life if he is denied the opportunity of an education. Such an opportunity, where the state has undertaken to provide it, is a right which must be made available to all on equal terms.

We come then to the question presented: Does segregation of children in public schools solely on the basis of race, even though the physical facilities and other "tangible" factors may be equal, deprive the children of the minority group of equal educational opportunities? We believe that it does. . . .

We conclude that in the field of public education the doctrine of "separate but equal" has no place. Separate educational facilities are inherently unequal. Therefore, we hold that the plaintiffs and others similarly situated for whom the actions have been brought are, by reason of the segregation complained of, deprived of the equal protection of the laws guaranteed by the Fourteenth Amendment.

From *Brown v. Board of Education of Topeka, United States Report,* Vol. 347 (Washington, D.C., 1954).

John F. Kennedy's Inaugural Address *(1961)*

President Kennedy's inauguration on January 20, 1961, set the tone for his administration. In his Inaugural Address, he stirred the nation by asking Americans to serve their country and their fellow human beings.

We observe today not a victory of party but a celebration of freedom—symbolizing an end as well as a beginning—signifying renewal as well as change. For I have sworn before you and Almighty God the same solemn oath our forebears prescribed nearly a century and three quarters ago.

The world is very different now. For man holds in his mortal hands the power to abolish all forms of human poverty and to abolish all forms of human life. And, yet, the same revolutionary beliefs for which our forebears fought are still at issue around the globe—the belief that the rights of man come not from the generosity of the state but from the hand of God.

We dare not forget today that we are the heirs of that first revolution. Let the word go forth from this time and place, to friend and foe alike, that the torch has been passed to a new generation of Americans—born in this century, tempered by war, disciplined by a cold and bitter peace, proud of our ancient heritage—and unwilling to witness or permit the slow undoing of those human rights to which this nation has always been committed, and to which we are committed today.

Let every nation know, whether it wish us well or ill, that we shall pay any price, bear any burden, meet any hardship, support any friend or oppose any foe in order to assure the survival and success of liberty.

This much we pledge—and more. . . .

In your hands, my fellow citizens, more than in mine, will rest the final success or failure of our course. Since this country was founded, each generation has been summoned to give testimony to its national loyalty. The graves of young Americans who answered the call encircle the globe.

Now the trumpet summons us again—not as a call to bear arms, though arms we need—not as a call to battle, though embattled we are—but a call to bear the burden of a long twilight struggle, year in and year out, "rejoicing in hope, patient in tribulation"—a struggle against the common enemies of man: tyranny, poverty, disease, and war itself. . . .

And so, my fellow Americans: Ask not what your country can do for you—ask what you can do for your country.

My fellow citizens of the world: Ask not what America will do for you, but what together we can do for the freedom of man.

From John F. Kennedy, Inaugural Address, *Department of State Bulletin* (February 6, 1961).

Martin Luther King, Jr.'s, "I Have a Dream" Speech *(1963)*

In August 1963, while Congress debated civil rights legislation, Martin Luther King led a quarter of a million demonstrators on a March on Washington. On the steps of the Lincoln Memorial he gave a stirring speech in which he told of his dream for America.

I say to you today, my friends, that in spite of the difficulties and frustrations of the moment, I still have a dream. It is a dream deeply rooted in the American dream. I have a dream that one day this nation will rise up and live out the true meaning of its creed: "We hold these truths to be self-evident: that all men are created equal. . . ."

I have a dream that one day on the red hills of Georgia the sons of former slaves and the sons of former slaveowners will be able to sit down together at the table of brotherhood. . . .

I have a dream that my four children will one day live in a nation where they will not be judged by the color of their skin but by the content of their character. I have a dream today.

I have a dream today. . . .

From every mountainside, let freedom ring. And when we allow freedom to ring, when we let it ring from every village, from every hamlet, from every state and every city, we will be able to speed up the day when all God's children, black men and white men, Jews and Gentiles, Protestants and Catholics, will be able to join hands and sing in the words of the old Negro spiritual: "Free at last! Free at last! Thank God almighty, we are free at last!"

From *I Have a Dream* by Martin Luther King, Jr. Copyright © 1963 by Martin Luther King, Jr. Reprinted by permission of Joan Daves.

PRESIDENTS	BORN/DIED	YEARS IN OFFICE	PARTY	ELECTED FROM
1 George Washington	1732–1799	1789–1797	None	Virginia
2 John Adams	1735–1826	1797–1801	Federalist	Massachusetts
3 Thomas Jefferson	1743–1826	1801–1809	Democratic–Republican	Virginia
4 James Madison	1751–1836	1809–1817	Democratic–Republican	Virginia
5 James Monroe	1758–1831	1817–1825	Democratic–Republican	Virginia
6 John Quincy Adams	1767–1848	1825–1829	National Republican	Massachusetts
7 Andrew Jackson	1767–1845	1829–1837	Democratic	Tennessee
8 Martin Van Buren	1782–1862	1837–1841	Democratic	New York
9 William H. Harrison	1773–1841	1841	Whig	Ohio
10 John Tyler	1790–1862	1841–1845	Whig	Virginia
11 James K. Polk	1795–1849	1845–1849	Democratic	Tennessee
12 Zachary Taylor	1784–1850	1849–1850	Whig	Louisiana
13 Millard Fillmore	1800–1874	1850–1853	Whig	New York
14 Franklin Pierce	1804–1869	1853–1857	Democratic	New Hampshire
15 James Buchanan	1791–1868	1857–1861	Democratic	Pennsylvania
16 Abraham Lincoln	1809–1865	1861–1865	Republican	Illinois
17 Andrew Johnson	1808–1875	1865–1869	Nat'l Unionist/Democratic	Tennessee
18 Ulysses S. Grant	1822–1885	1869–1877	Republican	Illinois
19 Rutherford B. Hayes	1822–1893	1877–1881	Republican	Ohio
20 James A. Garfield	1831–1881	1881	Republican	Ohio
21 Chester A. Arthur	1830–1886	1881–1885	Republican	New York
22 Grover Cleveland	1837–1908	1885–1889	Democratic	New York
23 Benjamin Harrison	1833–1901	1889–1893	Republican	Indiana
24 Grover Cleveland	1837–1908	1893–1897	Democratic	New York
25 William McKinley	1843–1901	1897–1901	Republican	Ohio
26 Theodore Roosevelt	1858–1919	1901–1909	Republican	New York
27 William H. Taft	1857–1930	1909–1913	Republican	Ohio
28 Woodrow Wilson	1856–1924	1913–1921	Democratic	New Jersey
29 Warren G. Harding	1865–1923	1921–1923	Republican	Ohio
30 Calvin Coolidge	1872–1933	1923–1929	Republican	Massachusetts
31 Herbert Hoover	1874–1964	1929–1933	Republican	California
32 Franklin D. Roosevelt	1882–1945	1933–1945	Democratic	New York
33 Harry S. Truman	1884–1972	1945–1953	Democratic	Missouri
34 Dwight D. Eisenhower	1890–1969	1953–1961	Republican	New York
35 John F. Kennedy	1917–1963	1961–1963	Democratic	Massachusetts
36 Lyndon B. Johnson	1908–1973	1963–1969	Democratic	Texas
37 Richard M. Nixon	1913–1994	1969–1974	Republican	New York
38 Gerald R. Ford	1913–	1974–1977	Republican	Michigan
39 Jimmy Carter	1924–	1977–1981	Democratic	Georgia
40 Ronald Reagan	1911–	1981–1989	Republican	California
41 George Bush	1924–	1989–1993	Republican	Texas
42 Bill Clinton	1946–	1993–	Democratic	Arkansas

	STATE NAME	DATE OF ADMISSION	POPULATION	NUMBER OF REPRESENTATIVES	CAPITAL
1	Delaware	1787	689,000	1	Dover
2	Pennsylvania	1787	12,009,000	21	Harrisburg
3	New Jersey	1787	7,789,000	13	Trenton
4	Georgia	1788	6,751,000	11	Atlanta
5	Connecticut	1788	3,281,000	6	Hartford
6	Massachusetts	1788	5,998,000	10	Boston
7	Maryland	1788	4,908,000	8	Annapolis
8	South Carolina	1788	3,603,000	6	Columbia
9	New Hampshire	1788	1,111,000	2	Concord
10	Virginia	1788	6,377,000	11	Richmond
11	New York	1788	18,119,000	31	Albany
12	North Carolina	1789	6,843,000	12	Raleigh
13	Rhode Island	1790	1,005,000	2	Providence
14	Vermont	1791	570,000	1	Montpelier
15	Kentucky	1792	3,755,000	6	Frankfort
16	Tennessee	1796	5,024,000	9	Nashville
17	Ohio	1803	11,016,000	19	Columbus
18	Louisiana	1812	4,287,000	7	Baton Rouge
19	Indiana	1816	5,662,000	10	Indianapolis
20	Mississippi	1817	2,614,000	5	Jackson
21	Illinois	1818	11,631,000	20	Springfield
22	Alabama	1819	4,136,000	7	Montgomery
23	Maine	1820	1,235,000	2	Augusta
24	Missouri	1821	5,193,000	9	Jefferson City
25	Arkansas	1836	2,399,000	4	Little Rock
26	Michigan	1837	9,437,000	16	Lansing
27	Florida	1845	13,488,000	23	Tallahassee
28	Texas	1845	17,656,000	30	Austin
29	Iowa	1846	2,812,000	5	Des Moines
30	Wisconsin	1848	5,007,000	9	Madison
31	California	1850	30,867,000	52	Sacramento
32	Minnesota	1858	4,480,000	8	St. Paul
33	Oregon	1859	2,977,000	5	Salem
34	Kansas	1861	2,523,000	4	Topeka
35	West Virginia	1863	1,812,000	3	Charleston
36	Nevada	1864	1,327,000	2	Carson City
37	Nebraska	1867	1,606,000	3	Lincoln
38	Colorado	1876	3,470,000	6	Denver
39	North Dakota	1889	636,000	1	Bismarck
40	South Dakota	1889	711,000	1	Pierre
41	Montana	1889	824,000	1	Helena
42	Washington	1889	5,136,000	9	Olympia
43	Idaho	1890	1,067,000	2	Boise
44	Wyoming	1890	466,000	1	Cheyenne
45	Utah	1896	1,813,000	3	Salt Lake City
46	Oklahoma	1907	3,212,000	6	Oklahoma City
47	New Mexico	1912	1,518,000	3	Santa Fe
48	Arizona	1912	3,832,000	6	Phoenix
49	Alaska	1959	587,000	1	Juneau
50	Hawaii	1959	1,160,000	2	Honolulu

435

The United States
Cities and States

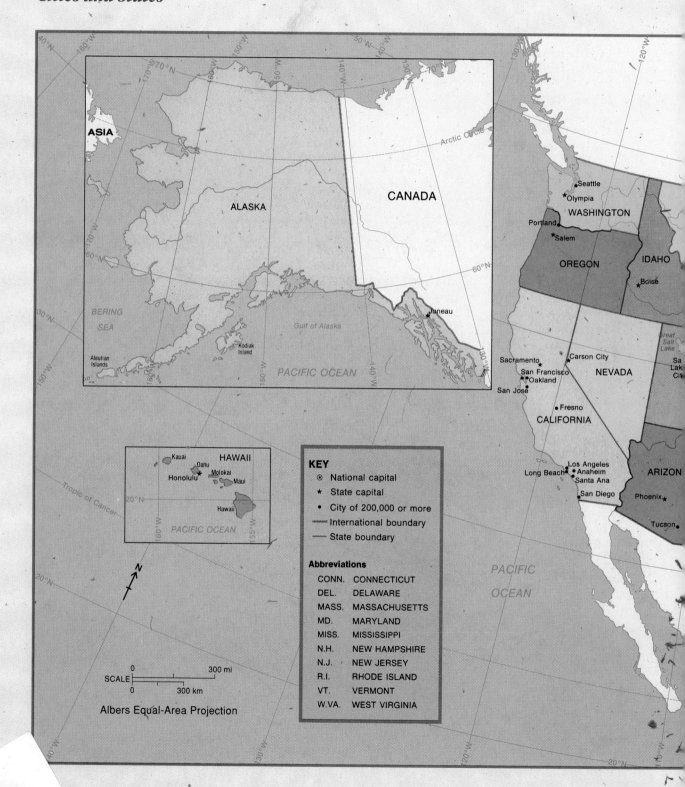

ASIA

ALASKA

CANADA

Arctic Circle

70°N

60°N

BERING
SEA

Gulf of Alaska

Juneau

Kodiak
Island

Aleutian
Islands

PACIFIC OCEAN

Seattle
Olympia
Portland
WASHINGTON
Salem
OREGON
IDAHO
Boise

Great
Salt
Lake

Sacramento
San Francisco
Oakland
San José
Carson City
NEVADA
Sa
Lak
Ci

Fresno

CALIFORNIA

Long Beach
Los Angeles
Anaheim
Santa Ana
San Diego
ARIZON
Phoenix
Tucson

HAWAII

Kauai
Oahu
Honolulu
Molokai
Maui
Hawaii

20°N

Tropic of Cancer

PACIFIC OCEAN

KEY
- ⊙ National capital
- ★ State capital
- • City of 200,000 or more
- ▦▦ International boundary
- —— State boundary

Abbreviations
CONN.	CONNECTICUT
DEL.	DELAWARE
MASS.	MASSACHUSETTS
MD.	MARYLAND
MISS.	MISSISSIPPI
N.H.	NEW HAMPSHIRE
N.J.	NEW JERSEY
R.I.	RHODE ISLAND
VT.	VERMONT
W.VA.	WEST VIRGINIA

PACIFIC

OCEAN

N

SCALE
0   300 mi
0   300 km

Albers Equal-Area Projection

CANADA

Hudson Bay

MAINE

★Augusta

Helena
MONTANA

NORTH DAKOTA
★Bismarck

MINNESOTA

Lake Superior

MICHIGAN

Montpelier★
NEW
YORK
VT. ★N.H.
★Concord

Lake Huron

★Boston
★Providence
R.I.
CONN.

WYOMING

SOUTH DAKOTA
★Pierre

Minneapolis●St. Paul
WISCONSIN
★Madison
●Milwaukee

Lake Ontario
●Rochester
●Buffalo

Albany★
Hartford●
MASS.

Lansing★

Lake Erie

Jersey City●●New York

Detroit●

Cleveland●
Akron●

Harrisburg★
PENNSYLVANIA

Newark●
Trenton
Philadelphia●
N.J.
★Dover
DEL.
Annapolis
MD.

Chicago●
ILLINOIS

Toledo●

INDIANA
Indianapolis●

OHIO
Columbus●
Dayton●
Cincinnati●

Pittsburgh●

Baltimore●
Washington, D.C.●

NEBRASKA
Omaha●
Lincoln★
●Des Moines

IOWA

UTAH
★Denver
COLORADO
●Colorado
Springs

Cheyenne●

Springfield●
Kansas
City
Topeka★
KANSAS
Jefferson★
City
St.
Louis

Frankfort★
Louisville●Lexington●

W.VA.
★Charleston

Richmond●

Norfolk●
Virginia
Beach●

VIRGINIA

ATLANTIC

OCEAN

Wichita●
MISSOURI

KENTUCKY

Raleigh●

●Nashville

NORTH CAROLINA
Charlotte●

Santa Fe●
Albuquerque●

Tulsa●
Oklahoma
City ★
OKLAHOMA

ARKANSAS
Memphis●

TENNESSEE

SOUTH
CAROLINA
●Columbia

NEW MEXICO

Little★
Rock

Birmingham●
MISS.
ALABAMA

★Atlanta

GEORGIA

El Paso●

Fort Worth●●Dallas
Arlington●

Shreveport●
Jackson★

Montgomery●

TEXAS

Baton●
Rouge
LOUISIANA
New Orleans●

Mobile●

Tallahassee●
●Jacksonville

★Austin

San Antonio●

●Houston

FLORIDA

BAHAMAS

●Corpus Christi

Tampa●
St. Petersburg●

Miami●

MEXICO

Gulf of Mexico

Tropic of Cancer

CUBA

The United States
Physical Features

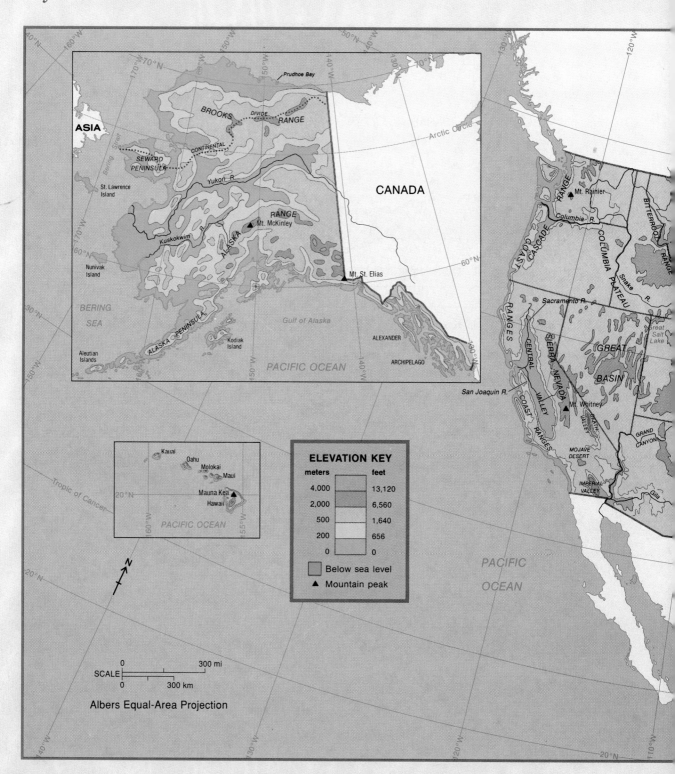

ASIA

BROOKS   DIVIDE   RANGE

Prudhoe Bay

CONTINENTAL

SEWARD
PENINSULA

CANADA

Arctic Circle

St. Lawrence
Island

Yukon R.

RANGE

Kuskokwim R.

Mt. McKinley

ALASKA

60°N

Nunivak
Island

70°N

Mt. St. Elias

**BERING
SEA**

Gulf of Alaska

ALASKA   PENINSULA

Kodiak
Island

ALEXANDER

Aleutian
Islands

PACIFIC OCEAN

ARCHIPELAGO

Mt. Rainier

COAST   RANGE

Columbia R.

BITTERROOT RANGE

COLUMBIA   PLATEAU

Snake R.

Sacramento R.

Great
Salt
Lake

COAST   RANGES

SIERRA   NEVADA

CENTRAL   VALLEY

**GREAT
BASIN**

San Joaquin R.

Mt. Whitney

DEATH VALLEY

GRAND
CANYON

COAST   RANGES

MOJAVE
DESERT

IMPERIAL
VALLEY

Gila R.

**PACIFIC
OCEAN**

Kauai

Oahu
Molokai
Maui

Mauna Kea
Hawaii

20°N

PACIFIC OCEAN

Tropic of Cancer

ELEVATION KEY

meters		feet
4,000		13,120
2,000		6,560
500		1,640
200		656
0		0

Below sea level
▲ Mountain peak

N

SCALE
0   300 mi
0   300 km

Albers Equal-Area Projection

CANADA

Hudson Bay

MEXICO

Gulf of Mexico

ATLANTIC OCEAN

BAHAMAS

CUBA

Tropic of Cancer

R O C K Y

GREAT

CONTINENTAL

DIVIDE

Missouri R.

Yellowstone R.

BLACK HILLS

MESABI RANGE

Lake Superior

Lake Michigan

Lake Huron

St. Lawrence R.

WHITE MTS

GREEN MTS

ADIRONDACK MTS.

Mohawk R.

CATSKILL MTS

Connecticut R.

Hudson R.

CAPE COD

M O U N T A I N S

Susquehanna R.

Delaware R.

Long Island

Platte R.

INTERIOR

Missouri R.

P L A I N S

Wabash R.

PLAINS

Colorado R.

Mt. Elbert

Pikes Peak

COLORADO

PLATEAU

M O U N T A I N S

Arkansas R.

OZARK PLATEAU

Ohio

R.

Cumberland R.

PLATEAU

CUMBERLAND

Potomac R.

James R.

A P P A L A C H I A N

BLUE RIDGE MTS.

CAPE HATTERAS

COASTAL

PLAIN

LLANO ESTACADO

OUACHITA MTS.

Mississippi R.

Tennessee R.

Alabama R.

Chattahoochee R.

Savannah R.

ATLANTIC COASTAL

Pecos R.

Red R.

GULF

Pearl R.

PLAIN

EDWARDS PLATEAU

Brazos R.

COASTAL

Rio Grande

Nueces R.

MISSISSIPPI DELTA

Appalachicola R.

CAPE CANAVERAL

EVERGLADES

FLORIDA KEYS

R15

Nations of the World

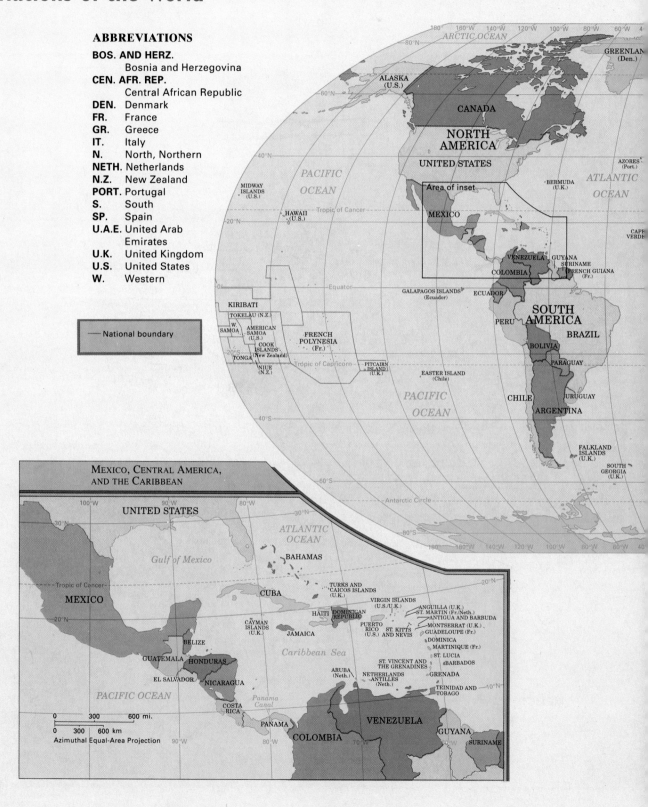

ABBREVIATIONS

BOS. AND HERZ.
    Bosnia and Herzegovina
CEN. AFR. REP.
    Central African Republic
DEN. Denmark
FR. France
GR. Greece
IT. Italy
N. North, Northern
NETH. Netherlands
N.Z. New Zealand
PORT. Portugal
S. South
SP. Spain
U.A.E. United Arab
    Emirates
U.K. United Kingdom
U.S. United States
W. Western

—— National boundary

Mexico, Central America, and the Caribbean

UNITED STATES

ATLANTIC OCEAN

Gulf of Mexico

BAHAMAS

MEXICO

Tropic of Cancer

CUBA

TURKS AND CAICOS ISLANDS (U.K.)

VIRGIN ISLANDS (U.S./U.K.)

ANGUILLA (U.K.)
ST. MARTIN (Fr./Neth.)
ANTIGUA AND BARBUDA

CAYMAN ISLANDS (U.K.)

HAITI

DOMINICAN REPUBLIC

PUERTO RICO (U.S.)

ST. KITTS AND NEVIS

MONTSERRAT (U.K.)
GUADELOUPE (Fr.)

JAMAICA

DOMINICA
MARTINIQUE (Fr.)

BELIZE

Caribbean Sea

ST. LUCIA

GUATEMALA

HONDURAS

ST. VINCENT AND THE GRENADINES

BARBADOS

EL SALVADOR

NICARAGUA

ARUBA (Neth.)

NETHERLANDS ANTILLES (Neth.)

GRENADA

TRINIDAD AND TOBAGO

PACIFIC OCEAN

COSTA RICA

Panama Canal

PANAMA

COLOMBIA

VENEZUELA

GUYANA

SURINAME

| 0 | 300 | 600 mi. |
| 0 | 300 | 600 km |

Azimuthal Equal-Area Projection

ARCTIC OCEAN

GREENLAND (Den.)

ALASKA (U.S.)

CANADA

NORTH AMERICA

UNITED STATES

AZORES (Port.)

BERMUDA (U.K.)

ATLANTIC OCEAN

PACIFIC OCEAN

MIDWAY ISLANDS (U.S.)

Area of inset

MEXICO

Tropic of Cancer

HAWAII (U.S.)

CAPE VERDE

Equator

VENEZUELA

GUYANA
SURINAME
FRENCH GUIANA (Fr.)

COLOMBIA

GALAPAGOS ISLANDS (Ecuador)

ECUADOR

KIRIBATI

TOKELAU (N.Z.)

W. SAMOA

AMERICAN SAMOA (U.S.)

COOK ISLANDS (New Zealand)

FRENCH POLYNESIA (Fr.)

Tropic of Capricorn

TONGA

NIUE (N.Z.)

PITCAIRN ISLAND (U.K.)

EASTER ISLAND (Chile)

PERU

SOUTH AMERICA

BRAZIL

BOLIVIA

PARAGUAY

PACIFIC OCEAN

CHILE

URUGUAY

ARGENTINA

Antarctic Circle

FALKLAND ISLANDS (U.K.)

SOUTH GEORGIA (U.K.)

R16

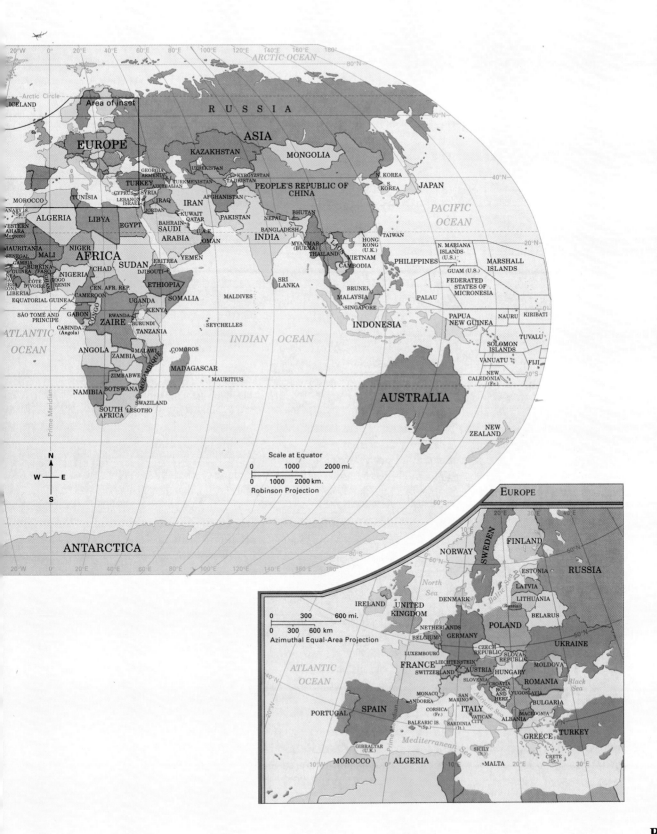

The gazetteer provides information about important places and geographical features in this book. Entries include a short description, a reference to a text page on which the entry is discussed, and a reference to a map on which the place appears. Latitudes and longitudes are approximate; for states and countries, they indicate the capital city, for other large areas, they are generally a central point.

A

Abilene city in Kansas. (39°N 97°W) *page 567; map, page 567*

Alabama 22nd state. Capital city: Montgomery (32°N 86°W) *map, page 354*

Alamo Texas mission captured by Mexico in 1836. (29°N 98°W) *page 412; map, page 413*

Alaska 49th state. Capital city: Juneau (58°N 134°W) *map, page 600*

Albany capital of New York. (43°N 73°W) *page 342; map, pages 344–345*

Antietam Maryland site of 1862 Union victory during the Civil War. (39°N 77°W) *page 467; map, page 463*

Appalachian Mountains mountain range that runs from Georgia into Canada. (38°N 80°W) *page 219; map, pages R14–R15*

Arizona 48th state. Capital city: Phoenix (33°N 112°W) *map, page 665*

Arkansas 25th state. Capital city: Little Rock (35°N 92°W) *map, page 371*

Atlanta capital of Georgia. (34°N 84°W) *page 475; map, page 477*

Atlantic Ocean ocean to the east of the United States. (35°N 30°W) *page 51; map, page 53*

B

Baltimore large city in Maryland. (39°N 77°W) *page 334; map, page 333*

Berlin capital of Germany, divided by the Berlin Wall from 1961 to 1989. (53°N 13°E) *page 723; map, page 722*

Boston capital of Massachusetts. (42°N 71°W) *page 178; map, page 186*

Buffalo large city in New York, on Lake Erie. (43°N 79°W) *page 342; map, pages 344–345*

Bull Run Virginia site of the first battle of the Civil War, won by the Confederacy in 1861. (39°N 78°W) *page 461; map, page 463*

C

California 31st state. Capital city: Sacramento (39°N 121°W) *map, page 563*

Cambodia nation in Southeast Asia. Capital city: Phnom Penh (120°N 105°E) *page 731; map, page 730*

Canada nation to the north of the United States. Capital city: Ottawa (45°N 76°W) *page 787; map, pages R16–R17*

Caribbean Sea tropical sea in the Western Hemisphere. (16°N 73°W) *page 66; map, page 66*

Central America area of North America between Mexico and South America. (14°N 86°W) *page 772; map, page 81*

Château-Thierry site in France of Allied victory during World War I. (49°N 3°E) *page 620; map, page 621*

Chicago Illinois city on Lake Michigan. (42°N 88°W) *page 544; map, pages 544–545*

China large, populous nation in Asia. Capital city: Beijing (40°N 116°E) *page 733; map, pages R16–R17*

Cleveland Ohio city on Lake Erie. (41°N 82°W) *page 508; map, page 507*

Colorado 38th state. Capital city: Denver (40°N 105°W) *map, page 563*

Concord Massachusetts site of first battle of the Revolutionary War in April 1775. (42°N 71°W) *page 186; map, page 186*

Confederate States of America nation formed by eleven southern states. Capital city: Richmond (38°N 77°W) *page 450; map, page 456*

Connecticut 5th state. Capital city: Hartford (42°N 73°W) *map, page 137*

Cuba island nation south of Florida. Capital city: Havana (22°N 82°W) *page 602; map, page 604*

D

Dallas large city in Texas. (33°N 97°W) *page 749; map, pages R12–R13*

Delaware 1st state. Capital city: Dover (39°N 76°W) *map, page 145*

Detroit large city in Michigan. (42°N 83°W) *page 637; map, pages 544–545*

District of Columbia (D.C.) seat of the federal government by the Potomac River. (39°N 77°W) *map, page 333*

Dust Bowl region that suffered from dust storms and erosion in the 1930s. (36°N 102°W) *page 665; map, page 665*

E

England part of Great Britain. Capital city: London (52°N 10°W) *page 101; map, page 101*

Erie Canal all-water route from the Hudson River to Lake Erie. (43°N 76°W) *page 342; map, pages 344–345*

F

Florida 27th state. Capital city: Tallahassee (30°N 84°W) *map, page 386*

Fort McHenry fort in Baltimore harbor attacked by the British in 1814. (39°N 77°W) *page 334; map, page 333*

Fort Sumter fort in Charleston harbor attacked by Confederates, beginning the Civil War. (33°N 80°W) *page 451; map, page 463*

Fort Ticonderoga fort between Lake Champlain and Lake George.

(44°N 73°W) *page 164; map, pages 164–165*

France nation in western Europe. Capital city: Paris (49°N 2°E) *page 612; map, page 621*

Fredericksburg Virginia site of 1862 Confederate victory during the Civil War. (38°N 78°W) *page 469; map, page 463*

G

Georgia 4th state. Capital city: Atlanta (34°N 84°W) *map, page 133*

Germany nation in central Europe. Capital city: Berlin (53°N 13°E) *page 612; map, page 621*

Gettysburg site of Pennsylvania battle in which Union forces halted invasion of North. (40°N 77°W) *page 470; map, pages 472–473*

Great Britain island European nation consisting of England, Scotland, and Wales. Capital city, London (52°N 10°W) *page 161; map, page 696*

Great Lakes group of five large freshwater lakes in the United States. (45°N 82°W) *page 343; map, pages 544–545*

Great Plains vast grassland region from Canada to Texas. (40°N 98°W) *page 318; map, pages R14–R15*

Great Salt Lake large salt lake in Utah. (41°N 112°W) *page 505; map, pages R14–R15*

Gulf of Mexico body of water south of the eastern United States. (28°N 90°W) *page 74; map, page 75*

H

Haiti nation on the Caribbean island of Hispaniola. Capital city: Port-au-Prince (19°N 72°W) *page 319; map, page 604*

Hawaii 50th state. Capital city: Honolulu (21°N 158°W) *map, page 600*

Hudson River large river in eastern New York. (42°N 74°W) *page 93; map, pages 344–345*

I

Idaho 43rd state. Capital city: Boise (44°N 116°W) *map, page 563*

Illinois 21st state. Capital city: Springfield (40°N 90°W) *map, pages 544–545*

Indiana 19th state. Capital city: Indianapolis (40°N 86°W) *map, pages 544–545*

Iowa 29th state. Capital city: Des Moines (42°N 94°W) *map, page 386*

Iraq Middle Eastern nation whose 1990 invasion of Kuwait led to the Gulf War. Capital city: Baghdad (33°N 44°E) *page 789; map, page 790*

Israel Jewish nation in the Middle East. Capital city: Jerusalem (32°N 35°E) *page 721; map, page 791*

Italy nation in southern Europe. Capital city: Rome (42°N 13°E) *page 45; map, page 48*

J

Jamestown English colony founded in Virginia in 1607. (37°N 77°W) *page 108; map, page 112*

Japan island nation in Asia. Capital city: Tokyo (36°N 140°E) *page 695; map, page 712*

K

Kansas 34th state. Capital city: Topeka (39°N 96°W) *map, page 563*

Kentucky 15th state. Capital city: Frankfort (38°N 85°W) *map, page 333*

Kuwait small, oil-rich nation in the Middle East. Capital city: Kuwait City (29°N 48°E) *page 789; map, page 791*

L

Lake Champlain large lake between New York and Vermont. (44°N 73°E) *page 335; map, page 333*

Laos landlocked nation in Southeast Asia. Capital city: Vientiane (18°N 103°E) *page 731; map, page 730*

Latin America Mexico, Central and South America, and the West

Indies. (14°N 86°W) *page 341; map, page 609*

Little Big Horn Montana site of Sioux and Cheyenne victory over U.S. forces in 1876. (46°N 107°W) *page 561; map, page 563*

Los Angeles large, populous city in southern California. (34°N 118°W) *page 566; map, page 665*

Louisiana 18th state. Capital city: Baton Rouge (30°N 91°W) *map, page 333*

Louisiana Purchase land west of the Mississippi River purchased from France in 1803. (40°N 94°W) *page 320; map, page 324*

Lowell industrial city in Massachusetts. (43°N 71°W) *page 346; map, page 343*

M

Maine 23rd state. Capital city: Augusta (44°N 70°W) *map, page 366*

Maryland 7th state. Capital city: Annapolis (39°N 76°W) *map, page 133*

Massachusetts 6th state. Capital city: Boston (42°N 71°W) *map, page 137*

Mexico nation to the south of the United States. Capital city: Mexico City (19°N 99°W) *page 407; map, page 424*

Michigan 26th state. Capital city: Lansing (43°N 85°W) *map, page 371*

Midway Island U.S. possession in the Pacific Ocean. (28°N 177°W) *page 711; map, page 600*

Minnesota 32nd state. Capital city: St. Paul (45°N 93°W) *map, page 386*

Mississippi 20th state. Capital city: Jackson (32°N 90°W) *map, page 354*

Mississippi River river that flows south from Minnesota to the Gulf of Mexico. (38°N 90°W) *page 155; map, page 156*

Missouri 24th state. Capital city: Jefferson City (39°N 92°W) *map, page 366*

Missouri River river that joins the Mississippi River near St. Louis.

(39°N 94°W) *page 323; map, page 324*

Montana 41st state. Capital city: Helena (47°N 112°W) *map, page 563*

N

Nebraska 37th state. Capital city: Lincoln (41°N 97°W) *map, page 563*

Nevada 36th state. Capital city: Carson City (39°N 120°W) *map, page 563*

New Hampshire 9th state. Capital city: Concord (43°N 72°W) *map, page 137*

New Jersey 3rd state. Capital city: Trenton (40°N 75°W) *map, page 145*

New Mexico 47th state. Capital city: Santa Fe (36°N 106°W) *map, page 665*

New Orleans Louisiana port city at the mouth of the Mississippi River. (30°N 90°W) *page 507; map, page 507*

New York 11th state. Capital city: Albany (43°N 73°W) *map, page 145*

New York City large, populous city at the mouth of the Hudson River. (41°N 74°W) *page 203; map, page 205*

Normandy region in northern France that was the site of the Allied invasion of June 6, 1944. (49°N 2°W) *page 709; map, page 708*

North Carolina 12th state. Capital city: Raleigh (36°N 79°W) *map, page 133*

North Dakota 39th state. Capital city: Bismarck (47°N 101°W) *map, page 563*

North Korea Communist nation in Asia. Capital city: Pyongyang (39°N 126°E) *page 724; map, page 725*

North Vietnam Communist nation in Southeast Asia that won a struggle for unification with South Vietnam. Capital city: Hanoi (21°N 106°E) *page 728; map, page 730*

Northwest Territory land north of the Ohio River to the Great Lakes and west to the Mississippi River.

(40°N 85°W) *page 222; map, pages 220–221*

O

Ohio 17th state. Capital city: Columbus (40°N 83°W) *map, pages 544–545*

Ohio River river that flows from western Pennsylvania to the Mississippi River. (38°N 86°W) *page 155; map, page 156*

Oklahoma 46th state. Capital city: Oklahoma City (35°N 98°W) *map, page 567*

Omaha Nebraska city on the Missouri River. (41°N 96°W) *page 505; map, page 507*

Oregon 33rd state. Capital city: Salem (45°N 123°W) *map, page 563*

Oregon Country Pacific Northwest area drained by the Columbia, Snake, and Fraser rivers. (45°N 120°W) *page 416; map, page 417*

Oregon Trail pathway from Missouri to the Pacific Northwest. (39°N 94°W) *page 416; map, page 417*

P

Pacific Ocean largest ocean in the world, to the west of the United States. (30°N 165°W) *page 710; map, page 712*

Panama Canal canal in Central America that links the Atlantic and Pacific oceans. (8°N 80°W) *page 607; map, page 609*

Pearl Harbor site of Hawaiian naval base attacked by Japan on December 7, 1941. (21°N 158°W) *page 700; map, page 712*

Pennsylvania 2nd state. Capital city: Harrisburg (40°N 77°W) *map, page 145*

Philadelphia large port city in Pennsylvania. (40°N 75°W) *page 204; map, page 205*

Philippine Islands Pacific islands off the coast of Asia. (12°N 123°E) *page 602; map, page 604*

Pittsburgh large city in Pennsylvania. (40°N 80°W) *page 532; map, pages 544–545*

Plymouth colony in New England founded by Pilgrims in 1620. (42°N 71°W) *page 111; map, page 112*

Puerto Rico Caribbean island transferred to the United States as a result of the Spanish-American War. Capital city: San Juan (18°N 66°W) *page 602; map, page 604*

R

Rhode Island 13th state. Capital city: Providence (42°N 71°W) *map, page 137*

Richmond Virginia capital that was the capital of the Confederacy. (38°N 77°W) *page 461; map, page 463*

Rio Grande river that forms part of the border between the United States and Mexico. (28°N 100°W) *page 422; map, page 424*

Roanoke Island island off the coast of North Carolina and the site of the first English colony in the Americas, started in 1585. (36°N 76°W) *page 101; map, page 112*

Rocky Mountains mountain range in the western United States. (39°N 107°W) *page 321; map, page 324*

Route 66 highway from Chicago to Los Angeles. (35°N 102°W) *page 746; map, pages 746–747*

Russia large nation in both Europe and Asia. Capital city: Moscow (56°N 38°E) *page 737; map, pages R16–R17*

S

St. Lawrence River river, primarily in Canada, that empties into the Atlantic Ocean. (45°N 75°W) *page 153; map, page 156*

St. Louis Missouri city at the junction of the Missouri and Mississippi rivers. (39°N 90°W) *page 415; map, page 417*

San Diego large city in southern California. (33°N 117°W) *page 79; map, page 665*

San Francisco major port city in northern California. (38°N 122°W) *page 429; map, page 665*

Santa Fe Trail wagon route from Missouri to New Mexico. (35°N 106°W) *page 408; map, page 417*

Saratoga New York site of important American victory during the Revolutionary War. (43°N 74°W) *page 205; map, page 205*

South Africa nation on the southern tip of Africa. Capital city: Pretoria (26°S 28°E) *page 792; map, pages R16–R17*

South Carolina 8th state. Capital city: Columbia (34°N 81°W) *map, page 133*

South Dakota 40th state. Capital city: Pierre (44°N 100°W) *map, page 563*

South Korea small nation in Asia. Capital city: Seoul (38°N 127°E) *page 724; map, page 725*

South Pass pass in Wyoming through the Rocky Mountains. (42°N 109°W) *page 416; map, page 417*

South Vietnam nation in Southeast Asia overtaken by Communist North Vietnam. Capital city: Saigon (11°N 107°E) *page 728; map, page 730*

Soviet Union large Communist nation that split into several republics in 1991. Capital city: Moscow (56°N 38°E) *page 735; map, page 722*

Spain nation in southwestern Europe. Capital city: Madrid (40°N 4°W) *page 52; map, page 722*

T

Tennessee 16th state. Capital city: Nashville (36°N 87°W) *map, page 662*

Texas 28th state. Capital city: Austin (30°N 98°W) *map, page 413*

Trenton New Jersey capital; site of Washington's 1776 victory during the Revolutionary War. (40°N 75°W) *page 204; map, page 205*

U

Utah 45th state. Capital city: Salt Lake City (41°N 112°W) *map, page 665*

V

Valley Forge Pennsylvania site of Continental Army's camp during the winter of 1777–1778. (40°N 76°W) *page 208; map, page 212*

Vermont 14th state. Capital city: Montpelier (44°N 73°W) *map, page 333*

Vicksburg site of Civil War battle in Mississippi that gave the Union complete control of the Mississippi River. (32°N 91°W) *page 474; map, page 477*

Virgin Islands United States territory in the Caribbean Sea. (18°N 65°W) *page 601; map, page 600*

Virginia 10th state. Capital city: Richmond (38°N 77°W) *map, page 133*

W

Washington 42nd state. Capital city: Olympia (47°N 123°W) *map, page 563*

Washington, D.C. capital of the United States since 1800. (39°N 77°W) *map, page 333*

West Virginia 35th state. Capital city: Charleston (38°N 82°W) *map, page 456*

Wisconsin 30th state. Capital city: Madison (43°N 89°W) *map, page 386*

Wounded Knee South Dakota site of 1890 massacre of Indians. (43°N 102°W) *page 563; map, page 563*

Wyoming 44th state. Capital city: Cheyenne (41°N 105°W) *map, page 563*

Y

Yorktown Virginia site of the last major battle of the Revolutionary War. (37°N 77°W) *page 213; map, page 212*

The glossary defines key terms in this book. Remember that many words have more than one meaning. The definitions given here are the ones that will be most helpful in reading this book, The page number in parentheses after each definition refers to the page on which each word or term is defined in the textbook.

A

abolitionist a person who worked in the movement to do away with slavery. *(page 394)*

administration term of office. *(page 312)*

adobe sun-dried clay brick. *(page 76)*

affirmative action a policy that requires businesses and schools that receive federal funds to recruit women and members of different ethnic groups to make up for past discrimination. *(page 779)*

African diaspora the forced settlement of millions of Africans in the Western Hemisphere. *(page 69)*

aggression attacks on other nations. *(page 695)*

Albany Plan of Union a plan proposed by Benjamin Franklin at the Albany Congress of 1754 under which the American colonies would form a loose confederation to promote mutual defense. *(page 161)*

alien an unnaturalized foreign resident of a country. *(page 309)*

Alien and Sedition Acts laws passed in 1798 to curb immigration and limit criticism of the government. *(page 309)*

alliance an agreement by two or more nations or parties to act together in a cause. *(page 175)*

ally a partner in a common cause. *(page 72)*

amendment a change or addition, as to a bill or constitution. *(page 245)*

American Indian Movement (AIM) an organization formed in 1968 to fight for better treatment for Indians. *(page 774)*

American System Henry Clay's program to spur national economic growth and national self-sufficiency. *(page 342)*

Americans with Disabilities Act a law passed in 1990 that requires businesses to give disabled persons more access to the workplace. *(page 778)*

amnesty official pardon. *(page 485)*

anarchist person who rejects all forms of government. *(page 522)*

anesthetic a pain-killer. *(page 460)*

annex to add to an existing country or area. *(page 414)*

Antifederalist a person who opposed ratification of the Constitution. *(page 239)*

anti-Semitism discrimination against Jews. *(page 679)*

antiseptic a germ-killing drug. *(page 460)*

apartheid laws put in place by the South African government in 1948 that denied blacks' basic civil rights. *(page 792)*

appeasement giving in to someone's demands in order to avoid conflict. *(page 697)*

apprentice a person learning a skill or trade from a master worker. *(page 137)*

arbitration the practice in which two sides in a dispute let an impartial third party settle the issue. *(page 589)*

armada a giant fleet of warships. *(page 98)*

armistice an end to the fighting in a conflict. *(page 620)*

Articles of Confederation the plan, ratified by the states in 1781, that established a national congress with limited powers. *(page 217)*

artifact an item made by humans. *(page 5)*

artillery cannons and large guns. *(page 188)*

assassinate to murder a public person. *(page 478)*

assembly line process of assembling a product whereby workers at various stations add parts to it. *(page 638)*

assimilation the adoption of the dominant culture. *(page 563)*

Atlantic Charter the 1941 agreement between FDR and Churchill that outlined their ideas for the postwar world. *(page 700)*

Axis Powers the alliance of Germany, Italy, and Japan during World War II. *(page 697)*

B

baby boom the rapid population increase that took place between 1945 and 1960. *(page 744)*

backcountry the region between the fall line and the Appalachians. *(page 148)*

balance of power an equal distribution of strength among nations. *(page 160)*

barrio a Mexican community. *(page 681)*

barter to trade goods without exchanging money. *(page 154)*

Bataan Death March the brutal forced march of Allied prisoners after the surrender of the Philippines to Japan in World War II. *(page 701)*

Battle of the Alamo the 1836 attack on the Alamo mission in San Antonio by Mexican forces during the Texas Revolution. *(page 413)*

Battle of Antietam a Civil War battle, a military draw but a political victory for the Union, near Sharpsburg, Maryland, in 1862. *(page 467)*

Battle of Gettysburg the greatest single battle of the Civil War, won by the Union in Pennsylvania in 1863. *(page 470)*

Battle of Little Bighorn the 1876 battle between U.S. forces and Sioux Indians that was the last Indian victory in the Indian wars. *(page 561)*

Battle of Midway the turning point in the Pacific in World War II, in which the U.S. Navy defeated the Japanese navy in 1942. *(page 710)*

Battle of Quebec the decisive battle of the French and Indian War in 1759, won by Britain. *(page 167)*

Battle of San Jacinto the 1836 battle in which Texan forces under Sam Houston defeated Santa Anna's forces to win independence for Texas. *(page 413)*

Battle of Saratoga the American victory over the British in 1777, which led to French entry into the war on the American side. *(page 206)*

Battle of Shiloh the fierce Civil War battle at Pittsburg Landing on the Tennessee River, won by Union forces in 1862. *(page 465)*

Battle of Vicksburg the Union capture of Vicksburg, Mississippi, during the Civil War in 1863. *(page 474)*

Battle of Yorktown the last major battle of the Revolutionary War, won in 1781 by combined American and French troops. *(page 213)*

bayonet a long knife attached to a gun for use in close combat. *(page 209)*

Bear Flag Revolt the 1846 uprising in which Americans living in California rebelled against Mexican rule and formed an independent republic. *(page 424)*

Berlin Wall a wall separating East and West Berlin built by East Germany in 1961 to keep citizens from escaping to the West. *(page 726)*

bicentennial a 200-year anniversary. *(page 753)*

Bill of Rights the first ten amendments to the Constitution, guaranteeing the basic rights of American citizens. *(page 245)*

Black Cabinet the group of black advisers appointed by FDR to government positions. *(page 669)*

black codes laws limiting the freedom of African Americans, passed by southern states after the Civil War. *(page 485)*

blitzkrieg the swift attacks by German forces during World War II. *(page 698)*

blockade the blocking off of a city or port by enemy ships or other forces. *(page 332)*

Bonus Army the group of veterans who set up camps in Washington, D.C., in 1932 to demand payment of their war bonuses. *(page 658)*

boomtown a town that grows rapidly in population as a result of sudden prosperity. *(page 427)*

border state around the Civil War, a state between the North and the South. *(page 449)*

Boston Massacre the clash in 1770 between British troops and a group of Bostonians in which five colonists were killed. *(page 180)*

Boston Tea Party the 1773 protest against British trade policies in which Patriots boarded vessels of the East India Company and threw the tea cargo into Boston Harbor. *(page 181)*

boycott a refusal to buy. *(page 177)*

brokerage house a business that buys and sells stocks. *(page 656)*

Brown v. Board of Education the 1954 Supreme Court decision that declared racial segregation in public schools unconstitutional. *(page 763)*

business cycle the economic pattern of good times and bad times. *(page 515)*

C

Cabinet the group of presidential advisers made up of the heads of the executive departments. *(page 247)*

California Gold Rush the mass migration to California following the discovery of gold in 1849. *(page 426)*

Californio in the 1800s, a person who lived in California and had Spanish ancestors. *(page 409)*

Camp David Accords the 1978 plan for peace between Egypt and Israel. *(page 734)*

capital money used for investment. *(pages 47 and 299)*

capitalism the economic system characterized by private enterprise, competition, and the free market. *(page 299)*

caravan a group of traders and pack animals loaded with trade goods. *(page 28)*

caravel a double-rigged ship, used by Portuguese sailors in the 1400s, that could sail with the wind or against it. *(page 48)*

carpetbagger insulting term used to describe a northerner who moved to the South during Reconstruction. *(page 490)*

casualty a person wounded or killed in battle. *(page 166)*

caucus a meeting of the members or leaders of a political party. *(page 393)*

cavalry soldiers on horseback. *(page 466)*

cede to give up. *(page 425)*

centennial a 100-year anniversary. *(page 510)*

charter a written contract, issued by a government or other authority, giving the holder the right to establish a colony, corporation, or other organization. *(page 108)*

checks and balances a system that allows each branch of government to limit the powers of the other branches. *(page 244)*

Chinese Exclusion Act 1882 law that banned Chinese immigration for ten years. *(page 680)*

circulation the number of readers of a newspaper or magazine. *(page 546)*

circumnavigate to sail completely around. *(page 59)*

civil rights the rights of all citizens. *(page 489)*

Civil Rights Act (1964) an act that banned discrimination in public places, on the job, and at the polls. *(page 769)*

civil service government jobs to which people are appointed rather than elected. *(page 578)*

civilization a distinct and highly developed culture. *(page 7)*

clergy religious officials. *(page 74)*

cold war the rivalry between the United States and the Soviet Union after World War II. *(page 721)*

colony a settlement ruled by a distant parent country. *(page 70)*

Columbian exchange the transfer of plants, animals, and diseases between the eastern and western hemispheres after Columbus reached the Americas. *(page 63)*

common law a system of law developed in England in medieval times, based on customs and previous court decisions. *(page 128)*

commonwealth a community in which people work together for the good of the whole. *(page 115)*

communism a system under which the government has complete control over the economy and people's lives. *(page 614)*

compromise a settlement of differences in which each side gives up some of its demands in order to reach an agreement. *(page 234)*

Compromise of 1850 the agreement between proslavery and antislavery forces over the extension of slavery. *(page 440)*

Compromise of 1877 the agreement that resolved an 1876 election dispute: Rutherford B. Hayes became President and then removed the last federal troops from the South. *(page 494)*

Conestoga wagon a horse-pulled covered wagon with wide wheels, a curved wagon bed, and an arched canvas top. *(page 145)*

Confederate States of America the nation formed by eleven southern states in 1861. *(page 450)*

conquistador a Spanish adventurer or conqueror. *(page 66)*

conservation the controlled use of natural resources. *(page 589)*

constitution a framework for government. *(page 21)*

Constitutional Convention the meeting of state delegates in Philadelphia in 1787 that resulted in the writing of the Constitution. *(page 231)*

containment the post–World War II American foreign policy designed to prevent the spread of communism throughout the world. *(page 723)*

convention a meeting of representatives or delegates. *(page 230)*

convert to change someone's beliefs. *(page 59)*

cooperative an organization owned and managed by those who use its services. *(page 581)*

corporation a business chartered by a state and owned by shareholding investors. *(page 516)*

cotton gin a machine designed to separate cotton seeds from cotton fiber, invented by Eli Whitney. *(page 353)*

credit an arrangement to make a delayed payment over time on a loan or purchase. *(page 373)*

Crusades wars between Christians and Muslims over the Holy Land during the Middle Ages. *(page 45)*

Cuban missile crisis the 1962 confrontation between the United States and the Soviet Union over Soviet missiles in Cuba. *(page 727)*

culture a way of life shared by people who have similar arts, beliefs, customs, and methods of doing things. *(page 6)*

D

Dawes Act the 1887 law that sought to make Indians give up their traditions and accept white culture. *(page 564)*

D-Day the Allied invasion of German-occupied France on June 6, 1944, during World War II. *(page 709)*

Declaration of Independence the document adopted by the Continental Congress on July 4, 1776, establishing the United States as a nation independent of Great Britain. *(page 192)*

deforestation the destruction of forests. *(page 794)*

depression a period of deep economic hardship. *(page 378)*

desert to leave without permission. *(page 208)*

détente a relaxing of tensions between nations. *(page 733)*

direct primary a primary in which the people, not party conventions, choose candidates for election. *(page 591)*

dissenter a person who challenges the generally accepted views of an established church or society. *(page 116)*

Dixiecrat a member of a dissenting group of southern Democrats who formed the States' Rights Party in 1948. *(page 742)*

doctrine of nullification the theory that a state could declare a federal law null and void within its borders if the

law favored one sectional interest over another. *(page 374)*

domestication the breeding of plants or animals to meet specific human needs. *(page 7)*

draft a system of choosing people for required military service. *(page 470)*

Dred Scott case the 1857 case in which the Supreme Court ruled that slaves were not citizens and that Congress could not forbid slavery in the territories. *(page 444)*

due process the right to fair treatment under the law. *(page 246)*

Dust Bowl an area of the south-central United States that suffered from dust storms in the 1930s. *(page 665)*

E

economy the way people use resources to make a living. *(page 132)*

Electoral College the group of delegates from each state who cast the official votes that elect the President and Vice President. *(page 238)*

Ellis Island the immigration center in New York City's harbor. *(page 531)*

Emancipation Proclamation the announcement on January 1, 1863, by President Lincoln that all slaves in Confederate territory would be considered free. *(page 468)*

emigrant a person who leaves one place for another. *(page 416)*

empire a number of people or lands controlled by one nation or ruler. *(page 10)*

English Bill of Rights the document signed in 1689 that guaranteed English citizens certain rights. *(page 130)*

enlist to sign up. *(page 202)*

entrepreneur a person who starts a business. *(page 516)*

Erie Canal the New York canal, finished in 1825 that connected Albany and Buffalo, New York. *(page 342)*

executive concerning the branch of government that enforces laws. *(page 217)*

Exoduster a black southerner who migrated to the Great Plains in the 1870s. *(page 571)*

expatriate a person who chooses to live in another country. *(page 647)*

export something sent to another country for trade or sale. *(page 83)*

F

fascism system under which the government rules through terror and by appealing to racism and nationalism. *(page 695)*

Fair Deal President Truman's program of social reform. *(page 743)*

fall line point at which waterfalls make river navigation impossible for large boats. *(page 148)*

famine a severe food shortage. *(pages 10 and 384)*

federalism the sharing of power between a central government and its political subdivisions. *(page 239)*

Federalist a person who favored the plan of government created by the Constitution. *(page 239)* Also, member of a political party during the late 1700s and early 1800s. *(page 306)*

feudalism a system in which people exchanged loyalty to a lord in exchange for land and protection. *(page 44)*

Fifteenth Amendment amendment to the Constitution that declared that the right to vote should not be denied "on account of race, color, or previous condition of servitude." *(page 492)*

fireside chat one of Franklin Roosevelt's radio talks to the American people. *(page 662)*

First Battle of Bull Run the first major battle of the Civil War, won by the Confederates in 1862. *(page 462)*

First Continental Congress the group of colonial delegates who met in Philadelphia in 1774 to discuss opposition to British policies. *(page 185)*

flapper spirited young woman of the 1920s whose hair, clothes, and behavior symbolized the rebellious attitude of many youths of the time. *(page 642)*

foreign policy a nation's way of dealing with other nations. *(page 307)*

forty-niner a person who took part in the California Gold Rush. *(page 427)*

Founding Fathers the delegates to the Constitutional Convention, as well as other American leaders of the time. *(page 231)*

Four Freedoms the freedoms FDR encouraged Congress to help Britain defend against the Axis Powers. *(page 699)*

Fourteen Points President Wilson's list of American goals for the post–World War I period. *(page 620)*

Fourteenth Amendment the constitutional amendment declaring that all native-born or naturalized persons were citizens and had the same rights as citizens. *(page 489)*

freedom ride a bus or train ride through segregated southern cities organized by a civil rights group to protest segregation. *(page 768)*

French and Indian War the conflict between France and Britain in North America between 1754 and 1763. *(page 163)*

front the area where two opposing armies meet. *(page 459)*

Fugitive Slave Law the law, part of the Compromise of 1850, that said people in free states had to help catch and return fugitive slaves. *(page 440)*

G

Geneva Accords the 1954 international agreement that split Vietnam into two parts—Communist North Vietnam and non-Communist South Vietnam. *(page 728)*

genocide the murder of an entire people. *(page 712)*

GI Bill of Rights the 1944 law providing financial aid to veterans. *(page 713)*

global warming an increase in the earth's temperature. *(page 794)*

Glorious Revolution the change of monarchs in England in 1689, in which James II was removed from power and Parliament offered the throne to William and Mary of Orange. *(page 130)*

gold standard the money policy in which the government backs every dollar with a certain amount of gold. *(page 583)*

Grand Banks the rich fishing area near Newfoundland. *(page 91)*

Grange the organization formed by Oliver H. Kelley in 1867 to fight the loneliness of farm life and improve farming methods. *(page 580)*

Great Awakening the religious movement in the colonies around 1740 that emphasized personal religious experience. *(page 141)*

Great Depression the economic collapse of the 1930s that caused hardship for millions. *(page 656)*

Great Migration the emigration to America by English Puritans during the 1630s. *(page 115)*

Great Society President Lyndon Johnson's 1964 program to end poverty and racial injustice. *(page 749)*

guerrilla a member of a band of fighters who use surprise raids and ambushes to harass their enemy. *(page 211)*

Gulf of Tonkin Resolution the resolution passed by Congress in 1964 that authorized President Johnson to increase American military involvement in Vietnam. *(page 729)*

H

Harlem Renaissance the period of African American cultural activity in Harlem in the 1920s and 1930s. *(page 686)*

Holocaust Nazi Germany's systematic murder of millions of European Jews. *(page 712)*

homestead land on which to settle and build a house. *(page 439)*

Homestead Act the 1862 law that offered western land for settlement in return for improvement of the land. *(page 570)*

House of Burgesses the Virginia legislature, founded in 1619, that served as an early step in the establishment of representative government in America. *(page 110)*

Hudson River School a group of artists in the mid-1800s that painted quiet scenes of nature. *(page 403)*

human rights the basic rights and freedoms to which all people are entitled. *(page 734)*

Hundred Days the session of Congress in 1933 in which the first bills of the New Deal were passed. *(page 663)*

I

Immigration Reform and Control Act law passed in 1986 to deal with the problem of illegal immigration. *(page 778)*

impeach to bring an official to trial for misconduct in office. *(page 237)*

imperialism one people ruling or controlling other peoples. *(page 599)*

import something brought from another country for trade or sale. *(page 83)*

impressment the practice of drafting sailors by force. *(page 329)*

inaugurate to swear into office. *(page 297)*

indentured servant an individual who worked without wages for a specified number of years in exchange for transportation to the American colonies. *(page 110)*

Indian Citizenship Act 1924 law that granted U.S. citizenship to American Indians. *(page 690)*

Indian Removal Act the 1830 law that authorized the President to move eastern Indians to public lands west of the Mississippi. *(page 370)*

Indian Reorganization Act the 1934 law that ended allotment of Indian lands, gave Indians some self-government, improved living conditions, and gave Indian women the right to vote. *(page 691)*

Industrial Revolution the period of rapid industrial growth that began in Britain in the 1700s and then spread to other nations. *(page 346)*

inflation a rise in prices. *(page 378)*

initiative the practice in which a state allows the people to propose and pass a law directly. *(page 591)*

installment buying making small payments for a product over time. *(page 636)*

internment camp an area kept under guard, especially during wartime. *(page 704)*

Intolerable Acts laws enacted by Parliament in 1774 severely restricting the rights of Massachusetts colonists. *(page 184)*

investor a person who puts money into a product in order to earn profits. *(page 108)*

Iran-contra affair a scandal uncovered in 1986 that involved a secret arms deal with Iran and the diversion of money to support Nicaraguan rebels. *(page 758)*

irrigation the practice of bringing water to crops. *(page 10)*

island-hopping the American strategy to win World War II in the Pacific by using islands as stepping stones to reach Japan. *(page 711)*

isolationist person who believes his or her country should avoid involvement in world affairs. *(page 634)*

J

Jacksonian democracy the emerging democratic spirit in the United States after Andrew Jackson's election as President in 1828. *(page 367)*

Jim Crow laws laws that made segregation official in public facilities in the South. *(page 496)*

Jones Act the 1917 law passed by Congress that granted all Puerto Ricans U.S. citizenship. *(page 680)*

judicial concerning the branch of government that interprets laws and punishes lawbreakers. *(page 217)*

judicial review the power of the Supreme Court to declare laws unconstitutional. *(page 340)*

K

Kansas-Nebraska Act the 1854 law creating the territories of Kansas and Nebraska and allowing settlers there to decide whether to permit slavery. *(page 442)*

Kellogg-Briand Pact the 1928 treaty, signed by the United States and other nations, that outlawed war. *(page 634)*

kinship a relationship based on common ancestors. *(page 35)*

Korean War the cold war conflict in which UN soldiers fought to defend South Korea from takeover by Communist North Korea, ending in a stalemate in 1953. *(page 724)*

L

labor union an organization of workers that negotiates with company owners about wages and working conditions. *(page 522)*

laissez faire a government's practice of not interfering in business. *(page 589)*

land speculator a person who buys land in order to sell it later for a profit. *(page 161)*

Latino an immigrant or descendant of an immigrant from a Spanish-speaking country in the Americas. *(page 772)*

League of the Iroquois the association of Indian nations formed to improve relations among them. *(page 159)*

League of Nations an organization of nations established at the end of World War I to maintain world stability. *(page 622)*

legislative concerning the branch of government that makes laws. *(page 217)*

Lend-Lease the policy approved by Congress in 1941 that allowed the U.S. to sell, lend, or lease war materials to any nation whose defense was considered vital to U.S. security. *(page 699)*

Lewis and Clark expedition the expedition in 1804–1806 that explored the Louisiana Territory. *(page 323)*

Line of Demarcation the imaginary line around the earth's poles established in 1493 to divide non-Christian lands between Spain and Portugal. *(page 56)*

literacy the ability to read and write. *(page 369)*

lode a deposit of a valuable mineral buried between layers of rock. *(page 555)*

long drive the herding of cattle over the open plains to a stop on a railroad. *(page 567)*

loose construction an interpretation of the Constitution that argues that the government can do anything the Constitution does not plainly forbid it to do. *(page 300)*

Lost Generation the name coined by Gertrude Stein for the U.S. artists of the 1920s who saw little hope for the future. *(page 647)*

Louisiana Purchase the United States' purchase from France in 1803 of land west of the Mississippi River. *(page 321)*

Loyalist a colonist who remained loyal to Britain during the Revolutionary War. *(page 187)*

lynch to kill without a trial. *(page 493)*

M

McCarthyism unfairly accusing others of disloyalty and subversion. *(page 744)*

Magna Carta the charter of English liberties granted by King John in 1215. *(page 127)*

manifest destiny the idea that it was the nation's destiny to expand across the continent to the Pacific Ocean. *(page 422)*

Marbury v. Madison the 1803 case in which the Supreme Court asserted its right to declare laws passed by Congress unconstitutional. *(page 340)*

Marshall Plan a massive American aid program announced in 1947 to help European nations recover from World War II. *(page 723)*

Mason-Dixon Line the border between Pennsylvania and Maryland that divided the slave and free states. *(page 437)*

mass media communication that reaches a large public. *(page 641)*

Mayflower Compact an agreement signed by the male passengers aboard the *Mayflower* in which they vowed to respect laws agreed upon for the general good of the colony. *(page 112)*

Medicaid Lyndon Johnson's program to fund medical expenses for poor people. *(page 749)*

Medicare Lyndon Johnson's program to fund hospital care for people 65 and older. *(page 749)*

mercantilism an economic policy based on a state monopoly over trade and an attempt to transfer wealth from colonies to the parent country. *(page 83)*

mercenary a soldier who serves in a foreign army for pay. *(page 203)*

Mexican Cession the land that Mexico ceded to the United States in 1848 under the terms of the Treaty of Guadalupe Hidalgo. *(page 425)*

Mexican War the 1846–1848 war with Mexico, ending in a United States victory. *(page 423)*

MIA a soldier listed as Missing In Action. *(page 731)*

Middle Ages roughly the thousand years between the 400s and 1400s. *(page 43)*

middle class in the Middle Ages, merchants, artisans, and others who did not have feudal obligations; later, those who were socially and economically between the working class and the upper class. *(page 45)*

Middle Passage the journey of slave ships across the Atlantic. *(page 133)*

middleman a person who makes a living by storing, transporting, and selling other people's products. *(page 581)*

migrate to move from one region to another. *(page 6)*

militarism the belief that a nation should have and use a large military force. *(page 612)*

militia an army of ordinary citizens rather than professional soldiers. *(page 185)*

mill a machine that processes materials such as grain. *(page 146)*

Minuteman a member of a colonial militia who needed to be ready to fight given only a minute's notice. *(page 185)*

missionary a person sent to do religious work. *(page 66)*

Missouri Compromise act in 1820 admitting Missouri as a slave state, Maine as a free state, and forbidding slavery north of the parallel 36°30′. *(page 366)*

moderate a person who opposes extreme change. *(page 487)*

monarch a king or a queen. *(page 52)*

monopoly complete control over a product or service. *(page 30)*

Monroe Doctrine President Monroe's 1823 warning against new European colonization in the Americas. *(page 341)*

Montgomery bus boycott the successful 1955-1956 boycott by African Americans of the Montgomery, Alabama, bus system to protest segregated seating. *(page 764)*

mosque a Muslim place of worship. *(page 31)*

muckraker the name given to writers who exposed corruption in American society around 1900. *(page 590)*

Muslim a follower of the teachings of Islam. *(page 31)*

N

NAACP (National Association for the Advancement of Colored People) the organization formed in 1909 to secure equal rights for African Americans. *(page 594)*

NAFTA (North American Free Trade Agreement) the 1992 trade agreement between the United States, Canada, and Mexico to lower tariffs and increase trade. *(page 786)*

national debt the money a government owes investors. *(page 756)*

National Road the road, financed by the federal government and built in the early 1800s, that became the country's main east-west route. *(page 342)*

nationalism love for and loyalty to one's country. *(page 46)*

nationality groups of people from the same nation. *(page 532)*

nativist a person hostile to immigrants. *(page 386)*

NATO (North Atlantic Treaty Organization) defensive alliance formed in 1949 by the United States, a group of European nations, and Canada. *(page 724)*

Navigation Acts laws begun in 1651 by England to tax and regulate trade in the colonies. *(page 138)*

navigator someone who can plan and control the course of a ship. *(page 48)*

Nazi (National Socialist German Workers' Party) political party founded by Adolf Hitler that set up a totalitarian government in Germany in the 1930s. *(page 696)*

neutral taking no side in a disagreement. *(page 304)*

New Deal President Franklin Roosevelt's program to end the Great Depression. *(page 663)*

New Frontier President Kennedy's reform program of the early 1960s. *(page 748)*

nickelodeon an early movie theater. *(page 549)*

Nisei a Japanese American born in the United States. *(page 704)*

Northwest Ordinance the 1787 law that set forth a plan of government for the Northwest Territory. *(page 222)*

Northwest Passage a water route sought by European explorers around or through the Americas. *(page 92)*

Northwest Territory the land north of the Ohio River to the Great Lakes and west to the Mississippi River. *(page 222)*

O

OPEC (Organization of Petroleum Exporting Countries) organization of major oil-producing nations formed in 1960. *(page 754)*

Open Door Policy a policy set forth by the United States advocating equal trading opportunity for all nations dealing with China. *(page 607)*

Operation Desert Storm the 1991 offensive by the U.S. and other allied nations against Iraq after Iraq's 1990 invasion of Kuwait. *(page 790)*

ordinance a government regulation. *(page 222)*

Oregon Country the vast region of the Northwest surrounding the Columbia, Snake, and Fraser rivers. *(page 416)*

Oregon Trail the route to the Pacific Northwest from Independence, Missouri, to the Columbia River. *(page 416)*

P

Paleo-Indian a member of the first group of humans in the Americas. *(page 5)*

Panama Canal the canal built by the United States in Panama to connect the Atlantic and Pacific oceans, finished in 1914. *(page 608)*

panic an economic crisis. *(page 378)*

Panic of 1929 the week of frantic selling of stocks, resulting in lower and lower prices, that helped lead to the Great Depression. *(page 656)*

Parliament the assembly of representatives who make laws in England. *(page 128)*

passive resistance the practice of peacefully refusing to obey a given law. *(page 403)*

patent a guarantee issued by the government giving an inventor all profits from his or her invention for a certain length of time. *(page 510)*

Patriot a colonist who supported American independence at the time of the Revolutionary War. *(page 187)*

patronage the power to give government jobs and contracts and to provide services in exchange for votes. *(page 577)*

patroon a person who brought fifty settlers to New Netherland in return for a large land grant from the Dutch government. *(page 121)*

Peace Corps a volunteer organization formed in 1961 to provide help to developing countries. *(page 748)*

Pendleton Civil Service Act the 1883 law passed by Congress that required people to take exams for certain government jobs. *(page 579)*

perjury lying under oath. *(page 743)*

persecution bad treatment of a person or group, often based on race, religion, or beliefs. *(page 111)*

pharaoh a ruler in ancient Egypt. *(page 29)*

philanthropist a wealthy person who donates money to educational and cultural institutions. *(page 516)*

piecework work paid by the number of objects made. *(page 536)*

piedmont a plateau at the foot of a mountain or mountain range. *(page 148)*

pilgrimage a journey to a sacred place. *(page 32)*

pioneer an early settler of a frontier region. *(page 319)*

placer mining washing the sand and gravel from a stream to find small amounts of minerals. *(page 555)*

plantation a large farm. *(page 67)*

platform a statement of the goals and principles of a group, especially a political party. *(page 447)*

Plessy v. Ferguson the 1896 Supreme Court decision declaring that segregation was lawful as long as blacks and whites had access to equal facilities. *(page 496)*

pogrom an organized robbery and massacre of Jews. *(page 534)*

political machine organization designed to gain and keep power in government. *(page 541)*

political party organization that tries to influence government policy by promoting its ideas and backing candidates for office. *(page 306)*

political prisoner someone jailed for his or her political views. *(page 792)*

popular sovereignty the pre–Civil War policy of allowing the voters in a territory to decide whether or not to allow slavery. *(page 440)*

Populist Party the political party formed in 1890 that called for political and economic reforms. *(page 582)*

portage the act of carrying boats overland. *(page 155)*

precedent an act or decision that serves as a standard for later acts or decisions. *(page 297)*

prehistory the period of time before history was recorded in writing. *(page 27)*

prejudice an unfair opinion formed without facts. *(page 385)*

prime minister the chief executive in a parliamentary system. *(page 166)*

privateer an armed, privately owned ship enlisted by a government to attack enemy vessels. *(page 98)*

Proclamation of 1763 the British decree prohibiting colonial settlement west of the Appalachians. *(page 175)*

profit money left over after costs are paid. *(page 47)*

progressive a reformer in the early 1900s. *(page 586)*

prohibition a ban on the manufacture and sale of alcohol. *(page 650)*

propaganda information designed to influence people's thinking. *(page 180)*

proprietor an owner. *(page 122)*

protectionist tariff high taxes on foreign goods that protect domestic companies from foreign competition. *(page 579)*

Protestant someone who rebelled against the Catholic Church in the 1500s, or a member of one of the Christian groups founded after that rebellion. *(page 95)*

Puritan a member of an English religious group that believed the Anglican Church should purify itself by abandoning much of its ritual and ceremony. *(page 114)*

Q

quota a limit. *(page 680)*

R

racism the belief that one's own racial group is superior to others. *(page 49)*

radical one who takes an extreme position. *(page 310)*

rancho large land grant awarded by Spain and then Mexico to landowners in California. *(page 408)*

ratify to approve. *(page 217)*

rationing giving a fixed amount of something. *(page 705)*

Reaganomics President Reagan's economic plan of budget cuts, tax cuts, and increased military spending. *(page 756)*

recall reform that allows the people to vote an official out of office. *(page 591)*

Reconquista struggle by Spanish Christians, completed in 1492, to recapture Spain from the Muslims. *(page 52)*

Reconstruction the period after the Civil War, lasting from 1865 to 1877, when the federal government took action to rebuild the South. *(page 485)*

Red scare the 1919-1920 panic over communism in the United States. *(page 648)*

referendum reform in which a legislature is allowed to submit a law to the vote of the people. *(page 591)*

refinery a plant that purifies crude oil. *(page 517)*

Reformation the revolt against the Catholic Church begun by Martin Luther in 1517. *(page 95)*

rehabilitate to help a prisoner return to a normal, useful life. *(page 391)*

relief aid. *(page 657)*

religious tolerance the willingness to accept faiths different from one's own. *(page 111)*

relocate to move to another location. *(page 370)*

Renaissance the cultural and intellectual "rebirth" of Europe that began in the 1300s. *(page 46)*

rendezvous a meeting. *(page 204)*

reparations money that a defeated nation pays to the victor to make up for a war's destruction. *(page 622)*

republic a nation or state in which the power is held by citizens who elect representatives to manage the government. *(page 217)*

republicanism a belief after the Revolution that a virtuous life embracing simplicity, sacrifice, and freedom of conscience was necessary for the nation to thrive. *(page 223)*

reservation an area designated for use by a special group. *(page 559)*

revenue income. *(page 176)*

right of deposit the right to store goods in a given place for later shipment. *(page 305)*

Roanoke Island site of first English colony in the Americas, started in 1585. *(page 102)*

rock 'n' roll a popular style of music that emerged during the 1950s, combining elements of pop, country, and African American blues and gospel music. *(page 745)*

rodeo a show at which cowboys demonstrate their skills. *(page 565)*

Roosevelt Corollary the 1904 corollary to the Monroe Doctrine in which the United States claimed the right to intervene in the affairs of other nations of the Western Hemisphere. *(page 610)*

S

Salem Witchcraft Trials trials in Salem, Massachusetts, in 1692, that led to the death of twenty people after young girls charged people with practicing witchcraft. *(page 139)*

SALT (Strategic Arms Limitation Talks) the first agreement between the United States and the Soviet Union to limit nuclear missiles. *(page 733)*

Santa Fe Trail the westward route from Independence, Missouri, to Santa Fe, New Mexico, in the 1800s. *(page 408)*

savanna a flat, open grassland with scattered clumps of trees and shrubs. *(page 28)*

Savings and Loan crisis a string of bank failures in the late 1980s that required a huge government bailout. *(page 759)*

scalawag an insulting term used to describe a white southerner who supported Reconstruction. *(page 490)*

Scopes trial the famous 1925 trial in which a Tennessee biology teacher was convicted of teaching the theory of evolution. *(page 651)*

secede to withdraw from the Union. *(page 375)*

Second Continental Congress the assembly of colonial delegates in Philadelphia in 1775 that organized a Continental Army. *(page 188)*

Second Great Awakening a revival of religious faith in the early 1800s. *(page 388)*

Second New Deal programs passed by Congress starting in mid-1935 that created jobs, protected workers' rights, and protected natural resources. *(page 666)*

sectionalism loyalty to local interests. *(page 365)*

sedition saying or doing anything to bring down a government. *(page 309)*

segregation separation by race. *(page 496)*

self-sufficient able to make the things one most needs for survival. *(page 44)*

separation of powers the division of governmental power into executive, legislative, and judicial branches. *(page 243)*

Separatist an individual in England who called for a total break with the Anglican Church. *(page 111)*

settlement house a center that provided services to the poor in a city. *(page 542)*

Seven Days' Battle a week-long battle on Virginia's York Peninsula in which the Confederates forced Union forces to retreat in 1862. *(page 466)*

share of stock a piece of ownership in a company. *(page 108)*

sharecropping a system in which a farmer rented land, tools, seed, and housing from a landowner in return for a share of the crop. *(page 494)*

Shays' Rebellion the attempt by Massachusetts farmers in 1786–1787 to stop local courts from imprisoning debtors. *(page 229)*

Sherman Antitrust Act law passed in 1890 to prevent corporations from gaining complete control of a type of business. *(page 587)*

sit-in a method of nonviolent protest whereby people sit down in a public place and refuse to move. *(page 766)*

skyscraper a very tall building made of steel. *(page 539)*

slash-and-burn a way of clearing land for farming by cutting strips of bark from trees to kill them and then burning the undergrowth. *(page 19)*

slave codes the laws controlling the treatment of slaves. *(page 135)*

slum a crowded, unsafe, and unhealthy neighborhood in a city. *(page 536)*

smuggling illegal trade. *(page 138)*

social engineer a person who studies how factories worked and suggests ways to increase profits. *(page 639)*

Social Darwinism the application of Darwin's law of "survival of the fittest" to human societies. *(page 600)*

Social Gospel religious movement of the late 1800s that urged Christians to help the poor. *(page 543)*

Social Security Act the 1935 act that provided a fund for retired workers, disabled workers, and families of workers who died. *(page 666)*

socialist a person who wants workers to share in the ownership and profits of businesses. *(page 522)*

Society of American Indians the organization founded in 1911 to address the needs and rights of American Indians. *(page 689)*

sod a section of earth held together by grass roots. *(page 572)*

soil exhaustion the overuse of fertile soil. *(page 353)*

Sons of Liberty a secret citizens' group organized in the American colonies during the 1760s to protest the Stamp Act. *(page 177)*

South Pass a pass through the Rocky Mountains in Wyoming. *(page 416)*

Spanish-American War the 1898 war in which the United States defeated Spain. *(page 603)*

spoils system the practice of giving government jobs to political backers. *(page 368)*

sponsorship backing or official support. *(page 102)*

stalemate the point in a conflict in which neither side is able to win a decisive victory. *(page 612)*

Stamp Act the 1765 British decree taxing all legal papers issued in the colonies. *(page 176)*

standard time the division of the United States into time zones, first introduced in 1883. *(page 509)*

standardization the practice of using interchangeable parts. *(page 349)*

states' rights the theory that states have the right to judge whether a law passed by Congress is unconstitutional. *(page 309)*

steerage the lowest deck on a ship. *(page 383)*

stereotype a judgment made about an entire group of people. *(page 689)*

strait a narrow passage of water. *(page 58)*

strict construction an interpretation of the Constitution that argues that the government has only the powers that the Constitution specifically gives it. *(page 300)*

strike a stoppage of work. *(page 389)*

suburb a residential area at the edge of a city. *(page 540)*

suffrage the right to vote. *(page 398)*

summit conference a meeting among the highest level of government leaders. *(page 709)*

sunbelt the sunny states of the South and Southwest. *(page 745)*

survey to measure land to determine the exact boundaries of a given area. *(page 222)*

sweatshop a place where workers labor long hours under poor conditions for low wages. *(page 519)*

synthetic artificial. *(page 636)*

T

Taft-Hartley Act the 1947 law that weakened unions by making closed shops illegal and giving the President the power to stop strikes. *(page 742)*

tariff a tax on foreign goods brought into a country. *(page 299)*

Teapot Dome scandal the secret, illegal leasing of government oil reserves to oil companies during the Harding administration. *(page 632)*

technology the use of tools to do things. *(page 15)*

Tejano a Mexican living in Texas in the 1800s. *(page 409)*

telecommuting working at home while communicating with co-workers by computer. *(page 793)*

temperance refusal to drink alcoholic beverages. *(page 391)*

tenant a person who works another person's land in exchange for part of the produce. *(page 81)*

tenement an apartment building designed to house large numbers of people as cheaply as possible. *(page 536)*

Tet Offensive the January 1968 surprise attacks by Vietcong forces on cities and towns throughout South Vietnam. *(page 730)*

Thirteenth Amendment the constitutional amendment that abolished slavery. *(page 485)*

total war a war aimed at the total destruction of the enemy. *(page 477)*

totalitarian controlling every aspect of life in a nation. *(page 696)*

totem an animal spirit that has a special meaning to a person. *(page 15)*

Townshend Acts British decrees of 1767 levying duties on important items in the colonies, such as tea, paper, and glass. *(page 178)*

trading post a fortified station where a country exchanges goods with local traders. *(page 37)*

Trail of Tears the forced journey of Cherokee Indians from their homes in Georgia to lands in the West in 1838–1839. *(page 371)*

transcontinental across the continent. *(page 505)*

Treaty of Ghent the 1814 treaty between the U. S. and Britain that ended the War of 1812. *(page 335)*

Treaty of Paris (1763) the treaty in which France gave up its North American empire to Britain, ending the French and Indian War. *(page 167)*

Treaty of Paris (1783) the treaty ending the Revolutionary War. *(page 215)*

Treaty of Versailles the peace agreement that formally ended World War I. *(page 622)*

triangular trade a trade route connecting three different places, such as the route connecting the English colonies, England, and Africa. *(page 137)*

tributary a river that flows into a larger river. *(page 323)*

Truman Doctrine President Truman's 1947 promise that the United States would defend peoples from subversion or outside pressure. *(page 723)*

trust a business organization that controls many businesses in the same industry. *(page 517)*

tundra a treeless region with permanently frozen subsoil. *(page 14)*

U

Underground Railroad escape routes and hiding places that moved escaped slaves north. *(page 395)*

UNIA (Universal Negro Improvement Association) the organization founded by Marcus Garvey to encourage blacks to help themselves and to create a homeland in Africa. *(page 685)*

United Nations (UN) an international organization founded in 1945 to promote world peace and progress. *(page 721)*

utopia an ideal community. *(page 392)*

V

vaudeville a form of variety show entertainment that became popular in the late 1800s. *(page 549)*

veto to reject. *(page 244)*

Vietcong South Vietnamese Communists who fought for the reunification of Vietnam. *(page 729)*

Vietnam War the conflict in which South Vietnam, supported by the United States, was defeated by Communist North Vietnam. *(page 728)*

vigilante someone who takes the law into his or her own hands. *(page 568)*

Voting Rights Act (1965) a law designed to end rules that southern states used to keep African Americans from voting. *(page 770)*

W

Wagner Act the 1935 law that protected the right of workers to form unions and set up a board to help settle disputes between workers and employers. *(page 666)*

War Hawk in the early 1800s, a southern or western leader who favored war with Britain. *(page 332)*

War of 1812 the war between the United States and Britain from 1812 to 1815. *(page 329)*

ward a political subdivision of a city, often made up of a single ethnic group. *(page 541)*

Warsaw Pact alliance formed in 1949 by the Soviet Union and nations of Eastern Europe. *(page 724)*

Watergate scandal the public exposure of a burglary and its coverup by the Nixon administration that eventually led to Nixon's resignation in 1974. *(page 752)*

welfare state a system in which the government takes on responsibility for the economic security of its people. *(page 671)*

Whiskey Rebellion the 1794 refusal by western farmers to pay the federal tax on whiskey. *(page 304)*

World War I a global conflict between 1914 and 1918 in which the Allied Powers defeated the Central Powers. *(page 611)*

World War II a global conflict between 1939 and 1945 in which the Allied Powers defeated the Axis Powers. *(page 698)*

Wounded Knee Massacre the 1890 massacre in which U.S. soldiers killed 300 Sioux Indians. *(page 563)*

writs of assistance legal papers that gave officers the right to search any building for any reason. *(page 178)*

Y

yellow journalism journalism that exaggerates events in order to attract readers. *(page 603)*

The purpose of the index is to help you quickly locate information on any topic in this book. The index includes references not only to the text but to maps, pictures, and charts as well. A page number with *m* before it, such as *m143*, refers to a map. Page numbers with *p* and *c* before them refer to pictures and charts.

660, 668, 669; Grace Coolidge, *p633*; Betty Ford, *p753*; Hillary Rodham Clinton, 783, 786, *p786*

fishing, 91–92, 97; of Northwest Coast Indians, 15; in New England Colonies, 136–137, *p136, p137, m137*; Canada and, 215

Fitzgerald, F. Scott and Zelda, 643, *p647*, 647

Five-Power Treaty, 634

flappers, 642, *p642*, 644

flatboats, 302, *p302*

Florida, R11; discovery of, 74–75, *m75*; Spanish exploration of, 78–79, *p79*, 302; missions in, 82; Protestants in, 95–96; in French and Indian War, 167; in Revolution, 206; Loyalists in, 216; boundaries of, 225; Native Americans in, 341, *p341*; cotton farming in, 353, *m354*; in Civil War, 449, 451; election of 1876, 494; naming of, 566; population of, 745; Cubans in, 773

Flynn, Jeannie, 778–779

folk songs, 360–361

Forbes, Esther, 292–293

Ford, Betty, *p753*

Ford, Gerald, R10, *p258*, 733, 752, 753, *p753*

Ford, Henry, 637–639, *p639*

Ford Motor Company, 637

foreign policy, 307; Constitution and, 252–253; of Jefferson, 319; Spain and, 340–341; of T. Roosevelt, 608–610; of Coolidge, 634; of Truman, 723; of Nixon, 733, *p733*; détente, 733; of Ford, 733; of Carter, 733–734, *p734*; of Reagan, 735, *p735*; of Clinton, 791–792

foreign trade, 600; Jefferson and, 329–330; with Japan, 607; with China, 607–608; Latin America and, 608–610, *m609*; NAFTA, 786–787, *p786. See also* trade

Formosa, 724

Fort Carillon, 164–165

Fort Caroline, 95, 96, *p96*

Fort Castillo de San Marcos, *p96*

Fort Christina, 121

Fort Detroit, *m156*, 167, 209, *m212*, 216

Fort Donelson, 464–465

Fort Henry, 464–465

Fort McHenry, *p261, p316, m333*, 334

Fort Miami, 303

Fort Nassau, 121

Fort Necessity, 162–163

Fort Orange, 121

Fort Pickens, 451

Fort Pitt, 166, 167

Fort Prudhomme, *m156*

Fort Ross, *p409*

Fort St. Louis, *m156*

Fort Stanwix, 205

Fort Sumter, 451, *p451*, 455

Fort Ticonderoga, *p164–165*, 188, 190, 204

Fort Wagner, 469, *p469*

forty-niner, 427

Founding Fathers, 231

Fountain of Youth, 74–75, *p74, m75*

Four Freedoms, 699

Fourteen Points, 621, 622; excerpts from, R6

Fourteenth Amendment, 274–275, 489, 490, 496, *c766*

Fourth Amendment, 270

Fox, William, 644

Fox Indians, *m371*, 372

Fox River, 155, *m156*

France, explorations by, 92–93, *m90, m92*, 153–157, *p154, m156, p157*; Reformation in, 95–96; conflicts with England, 157, 159–160, *p160*; French and Indian War, *p152*, 162–167, *m163, m166, m167*; and American Revolution, 206, 213, 214; French Revolution, 304, *p304*, 319; XYZ Affair, 308; Jay's Treaty, 308; immigrants from, 308–309; in West Indies, 319; and Civil War, 459, 467, 468; Statue of Liberty and, 547; in World War I, 611, 612, *c612*, 613, 620, *m621*, 622, *m622*; Five-Power Treaty, 634; expatriates in, 647; in World War II, 695, 697, 698, 709; Vietnam and, 728

Franklin, Benjamin, 144, 146, *p146*, 161, 181, *p182*, 192, *p192*, 193, 210; at Second Continental Congress, 188; at Constitutional Convention, 231, *p233*, 238

Franklin, John Hope, 69

Free African Society, 224

Freedmen's Bureau, 486, *p486*, 489, 490, 493

freedom of assembly, 245–246, 270

freedom of press, 130–131, *p131*, 241, 245, 270, 309

freedom of religion, 95, 116–117, 245, 270. *See also* religion

freedom of speech, 130, 245, 270, 309

freedom rides, 768

Freeman's Farm, Battle of, 205–206

Free-Soil Party, 439

free states, 366, 437, 439–440, 442, *m442*

Frémont, John C., 423–424, *m424*

French and Indian War, *p152*, 162–167, *m163, m166, p167*

French Revolution, 304, *p304*

Friedan, Betty, 775

frigates, 305

Fugitive Slave Law, 440, *p440, p441*

Fuller, Margaret, 403

Fulton, Robert, 349

Fundamental Orders of Connecticut, 116

fur trade, *p117*, 121, 154, *p154*, 155, 415–416; Native Americans and, 154,

p154; wars over, 159–160, *p160*; in Oregon, 328, *p328*; in California, *p409*

G

Gadsden Purchase, 425

Gage, Thomas, 176, 178, 180, 186, 188

Gallaudet, Thomas H., 391

galleons, 83, *p97*

Galveston, Texas, 76

Gálvez, Bernardo de, 206, *m212*

Gandhi, Mohandas K., 403, *p697*

Garfield, James, R10, 578–579

Garner, John Nance, *p660*

Garrison, William Lloyd, 394, *p394*

Garvey, Marcus, 685, *p685*, 770

Gaspee (ship), 179

Gates, Horatio, 205, *m205*, 211

Gear, Joseph, *p382*

Geneva Accords, 728–729

Genoa, Italy, 47, *m48*, 51

genocide, 712

geography, parts of a map, G1; glossary of geographic terms, G2–G3; map projections, G4; five geographic themes, G5; of Alaska, 14, *m17*; of Africa, 28, *m28, m31*; trade networks, *m48, m50*, 52; strait, 58; circumnavigation, 59; Columbian exchange, 63–65; of North America, 79; of Roanoke Island, 103; economics and, 132; of backcountry, 148; in Civil War, 457, 459; railroads and, 508–509; of the West, 553–554; Great Plains, 572; national parks, *m588*, 589

George III, King of England, 176, 192; colonies and, 184–185, 190

Georgia, R11; founding of, 123; plantations in, 132–133, *m133*, 134; and Continental Congress, 185; in Revolution, 211, *m212*; ratifies Constitution, 240; Native Americans in, 340, 370; secedes, 449; in Civil War, 471, 475, *p476*, 477–478, *m477*; railroads in, *p504*; Klan in, 649–650

Germany, immigrants from, 123, 145–146, 202, 383, *m386*, 387, 438, 530, *c530, p533*, 571; American Revolution, 190; in World War I, 611, 612, *c612*, 613–616, *p616*, 620, *p620, m621*, 622, *m622*; Olympic Games (1936), 670; in World War II, 695, 696–698, *m696*, 701, 706, 712–713, *p713*; in cold war, 723–724, *p723*; 726, 737; reunification of, 737

Geronimo, 562

Gerry, Elbridge, 234, 308

Gettysburg, Battle of, 469–470, 472–474, *m472–473, p474*

Gettysburg Address, 474; text of, R5

Ghana, 30–31

GI Bill of Rights, 713

Gilded Age, 515

Gilman, Charlotte Perkins, 642

Ginsburg, Ruth, *p244*

Hudson Bay, 93
Hudson Bay Company, 416
Hudson River, 121, 145, 148, 204, *m205, g344, p345*
Hudson River School, 403
Hughes, Charles Evans, 634
Hughes, Langston, 686, 687
Huguenots, 95, 123
Hull House, 542–543
human rights, 734
Humphrey, Hubert, 750
hunter-gatherers, 6–7, 15–16
Huron Indians, 159, 163
Hurston, Zora Neale, 686, 687
Hussein, Saddam, 789–790
Hussey, Christopher, 137
Hutchinson, Anne, 117
hydraulic mining, 556
hydrogen bomb, 726

I

Iceland, 45
Idaho, R11; gold in, 555, *m555*; gains statehood, 556; Native Americans in, 562; women's right to vote in, 593, *m593*
Illinois, R11; mound cultures in, 12; in Revolution, 209; and Northwest Ordinance, 220; gains statehood, 220; immigrants in, 343, *m386*, 387, 532; Native Americans in, 372; Mormons in, 419; as free state, 437; railroad in, 442; Civil War in, 459; union riots in, 523, *p523*; Granger laws, 581; prohibition in, 650; Ku Klux Klan in, 650; Great Depression in, 661, *p661*
Illinois River, 155, *m156*
immigrants, 383–387, *p384, p385, m386, p528*; in Chesapeake Tidewater, 121; from Germany, 123, 145–146, 202, 383, *m386*, 387, 438, 530, *c530, p533*, 571; from Switzerland, 145; from Holland, 145; from Scotland,149; from Ireland, 149, 309, 383, 384–386, *m386*, 438, 506; Alien and Sedition Acts, 308–309; from France, 308–309; from Sweden, 383, 384, *p571*, 572; from England, 383; from Denmark, 383; Catholic, 384–386, *p385*; Jewish, 387, *p520–521*, 530, 534–536, *p533, p534, p535*, 678; from China, 427, *p427*, 429, 506, 522, *p532*, 678, 679, 777, 800–801; from Mexico, 427, 681, *p681*, 778; from Chile, 427; in northern states, 438; from Italy, *p520–521, p526*, 529, 530–531, 532–533, *p532, p678*, 679, *p679*; European, *p528*, 529–533, *c530, p531, p532, p533*, 678–680; from Greece, 530, *c530*, 680; from Poland, 530; from Russia, 530, 534–535, 572, 678; Ellis Island, 531, *c531*; employment for, 532–533, *p542*; education of, 535–536, *p536*; city government and, 540–541; settlement houses and, 542–543, *p543*; sports and, 547–548; from Japan, 593, *p593*, 678,

679, 777; limitation of, 650, 680–681; from Philippines, 678, 680, 777; Johnson-Reed Act, 680–681; from Canada, 681; literature about,716–717; diversity and, 777–778, *p777*; from Cuba, 773; from Vietnam, 777; Immigration Reform and Control Act, 778–779; illegal, 778
Immigration Reform and Control Act, 778–779
impeachment, 237, 245, *p257*, 265, 491–492, *p491*
imperialism, 599
imports, 83, *g100*, 237, 657
impressment, 329
Incan culture, 73, *p73*
income tax, 275, 479, 592, 705
indentured servants, 110, *p110*, 121, 132, 133
India, *p697*, 777
Indiana, R11; in Revolution, 209; and Northwest Ordinance, 220; gains statehood, 220; Battle of Tippecanoe, 330; immigrants in, 343; abolitionists in, *p394*; as free state, 437; Ku Klux Klan in, 650
Indian Citizenship Act, 690
Indian Removal Act, 370, 372
Indians. *See* Native Americans
Indian Territory, 370, *m371*
Indian Wars, 559–564, *p559, m560, p561, m563*
indigo, 134
Indochina, 728
Indonesia, 777
Industrial Revolution, 346–350, *p346, p347, p348–349, p350*, 438
industry, 479; in Middle Colonies, 146; in southern states, 495–496, *p495*; Corliss engine, 510; growth of, 510–511, *c524*; in Midwest, 544; business, *c663*
inflation, 378, 582, 705, 741–742, 751, 756
information technology, 95, 792, *p792*
installment buying, 636, *p636*, 657
Insull, Samuel, 637
internment camps, 704, *p704*
Intolerable Acts, *p182*, 184–185, *c185*
Inupiat, 14, *m17*
inventions, 510–514, *p512, p513, p514*; in 1920s, 637–639, *g637, p638, p639*
Invincible Armada, 98–99, *p99*
Iowa, R11; Granger laws, 581; nativism in, 649
Iowa Territory, 372
Iran, 734, *p734*; Iran-contra affair, 758
Iraq, 622, *m622*, 789–790, *p789, m791*
Ireland, 149, 309, 384–386, *m386*, 438, 506
ironworking, 28, 29
Iroquois Indians, 20, *p20*, 22, *p22*, 160, 161, 163, 205, 216, 233
irrigation, 10–11
Irving, Washington, 401, *p401*
Isabella, Queen of Spain, 52–53, *p52*, 54,

66, 67, 97
Islam, 26, *p26*, 34, 35; trade and, 31, 32, 43; African Americans and, 32, *p32*, 770; Crusades and, 45; *Reconquista,* 52–53
island-hopping, 711
isolationism, 634, 699
Israel, 734, *p734*, 790–791, *m790, p790*
Italy, trade with, 47, *m48*; immigrants from, *p520–521, p526*, 529, 530–531, 532–533, *p532, p678*, 679, *p679*; in World War I, 612, 622, *m622*; Five-Power Treaty, 634; in World War II, 695, *m696*, 697, 700, 706, 709
Iturbide, Agustín de, 407
ivory, 37, 38, *m50*

J

Jackson, Andrew, *p262*, 341, 366–368, *p367, p368*, 422, R10; banks and, 377–378, *p377*; Indian policy of, 369–372, *m371*; in War of 1812, 335
Jackson, George, 554
Jackson, Helen Hunt, 563
Jackson, Jesse, 758
Jackson, Rachel, 368
Jackson, Thomas J. (Stonewall), 461, 464
Jacksonian democracy, 367
Jamaica, *m66*, 68
James, Jesse, 568
James, King of England, 102, 107, 108, 109, 110, 111
James II, King of England, 128, 129
Jamestown, 107–110, *p108*
Japan, immigrants from, 593, *p593*, 678, 679, 777; trade with, 607; in World War I, 612; Five-Power Treaty, 634; in World War II, 696, 697, 700–701, *p700, p701*, 710–712, *m712*; cold war and, 724
Japanese Americans, 777; in internment camps, 704, *p704*
Jay, John, 240, 298
Jay's Treaty, 305, 308
Jazz Age, 643, *p643*, 645, *p645*
Jefferson, Thomas, 225, 231, 240, 273, *p273*, R10; writing of Declaration of Independence, 192–193, *p192*; Shays' Rebellion and, 230; as Secretary of State, 298, *p298*, 299, 300; French Revolution and, 304; forms Democratic-Republican Party, 306; differences with Hamilton, 306–307; as Vice President, 307; election of 1800, 310–311, *p311*; presidency of, 311–313, *p311*; piracy and, *p312*; foreign policy of, 319; slave revolt and, 320; Louisiana Purchase and, 320–321, *p321*, 322–325, *m324*; foreign trade and, 329–330; and Erie Canal, 344; Missouri Compromise and, 366; political parties and, 378
Jews, in Spain, 52, 66; in New Netherland, 121; as immigrants, 387, *p520–521*, 530, *p533*, 534–536, *p534, p535*, 678; racism

and, 593; Henry Ford and, 639; anti-Semitism, 678; in World War II, 696; Holocaust, 712–713, p713; Palestine and,
721–722
Jim Crow laws, 496
John, Prester, 37
Johnny Tremain (Forbes), 292–293
Johnson, Andrew, p257, R10; Reconstruction under, 485–486; Civil Rights Act and,
489; impeachment of, 491–492, p491;
expansion under, 601
Johnson, Anthony, 132
Johnson, James Weldon, 686, 687
Johnson, Lady Bird, p264
Johnson, Lyndon Baines, p264, R10; Viet-
nam War and, 729–730; as Vice President,
748; presidency of, 749–750, p749; civil
rights movement and, 749, 769, 770; War
on Poverty, 771
Johnson-Reed Act, 680–681
Johnston, Albert S., m463, 465
Johnston, Joseph, 462
joint-stock companies, 47, 108
Joliet, Louis, 155, m156
Jones, Bobby, 646
Jones, Casey, 509, p509
Jones, John Paul, 210, p210
Jones Act, 680
The Joy Luck Club (Tan), 800–801
judicial branch, 217, 243, 244–245, c244;
in the Constitution, 251, 265–266, p266;
Jefferson and the, 313. *See also* Supreme
Court
judicial review, 340
The Jungle (Sinclair), 590, p590
jury, 127

K

kamikazes, 711
Kansas, R11; Spanish exploration of, 78;
Kansas-Nebraska Act, 442–443, m442;
admitted to Union, 443; Bleeding Kansas,
443; free blacks in, 469; cattle industry
and, 567; Exodusters in, 571; Dust Bowl
migration from, 665, m665, p665
Kansas-Nebraska Act, 442–443, m442
Karenga, Maulana, 36
Kearny, Stephen, 423, m424
Kelley, Oliver H., 580
Kellogg, Frank B., 634, p634
Kellogg-Briand Pact, 634, p634
Kemp, Jack, 788
Kennedy, Anthony, 757
Kennedy, Jacqueline, p264
Kennedy, John F., p264, R10; Berlin Wall,
726; Cuban missile crisis, 727, p727; Viet-
nam War and, 729; presidency of, 748,
p748; assassination of, 749; civil rights
movement and, 768; text of Inaugural
Address, R8–R9
Kennedy, Robert F., 750, 768

Kennedy, Terence, p338
Kenney, Mary, 525
Kent State University, 751
Kentucky, 304, 456, m456, R11; settlers in,
219–220; Kentucky and Virginia Resolu-
tions, 309; gains statehood, 319; as a slave
state, 437
Kentucky and Virginia Resolutions,
309, 375, 450
Kerensky, Alexander, 614
Key, Francis Scott, m333, 334
Khmer Rouge, p729
Khrushchev, Nikita, 727, p727
Kidd, William, p142–143
King, Coretta Scott, p770
King, Martin Luther, Jr., 403, 685, p697;
Montgomery bus boycott, 764–765; non-
violence, 767; March on Washington,
769–771, p770; text of "I Have a Dream"
speech, R9
King George's War, 160
King Hendrick, 159, p159, 160, 161
King Philip's War, 117–118, p118
King's Highway, 81
Kings Mountain, Battle of, 212, m212
King William's War, 159–160
kinship, 35, 135. *See also* families
KKK. *See* Ku Klux Klan
knights, 44
Knights of Labor, 522–523, 524
Know-Nothing Party, 386–387
Knox, Frank, 700–701
Knox, Henry, 298, p298
Korea, 724
Korean Americans, 786
Korean War, 724–726, p724, m725, p725,
p726, 744
Kosciuszko, Thaddeus, 205
Ku Klux Klan, 493–494, 649–650, p649,
685, 765
Kush, 28
Kuwait, 789–790, p789, m791
Kwanzaa, 36

L

labor and labor unions, 519–525, p522,
p523, p524, c525, p525; after Civil War,
484; setbacks for, 523; women and, 525,
p525, 542, p542; Clayton Antitrust Act,
592, p592; strikes by, 640, 742, p742; Red
scare and, 648; Wagner Act and, 666,
c667; Taft-Hartley Act, 742; farm workers
and, 772–773. *See also* employment
Lafayette, Marquis de, 208–209
La Follette, Robert M., 590, 633
laissez-faire policy, 587, 589, 634
Lake Champlain, Battle of, 334
Lake Erie, 159; Battle of, 332, 334, m333,
p334; Erie Canal, m344–345
Lake Michigan, 155, m156, 159
Lakota Sioux Indians, 562

Landon, Alfred M., 666
land ownership, at Plymouth colony, 113;
European and Indian ideas about,
117–118; in New France, 154; Proclama-
tion of 1763, 175–176, m176; in Northwest Territory, 220–221; voting and, 393;
homesteads, 439; of freed slaves, 484;
sharecropping and, 494–495
Lange, Dorothea, 668, p668
languages, Native American, 22–23, p22,
p370; Arabic, 35; Portuguese, m57; Eng-
lish, 339; Spanish, 566
La Noche Triste, 72
Laos, 731, 777
La Raza Unida, 773
Larcom, Lucy, p348
La Salle, Robert, 153, 155–156, p157, m156
Las Casas, Bartolomé de, 68, p69
Last of the Mohicans (Cooper), 401
Latin America, 608–610, m609; indepen-
dence movements in, 341; slavery in,
p439–440; in cold war, 733–734
Latinos. *See* Hispanic Americans
Latvia, 614
Lawrence, Jacob, p683
Lawrence, Kansas, 443
Lawrence (ship), 332
League of Nations, 622–623, p622, 697
League of the Iroquois, 20–21, 159
Lease, Mary Ellen, 582
Leaves of Grass (Whitman), 403
Lee, Ann, 392
Lee, Jason, 416
Lee, Richard Henry, 188, 192, 193
Lee, Robert E., 455–456, 457, 466, 467; at
Gettysburg, 469–470, 472–474,
m472–473, p474
legislative branch, 217, 243, 244–245,
c244; in the Constitution, 254–262. *See
also* Congress, U.S.; federal government;
House of Representatives; Senate
Leiden, Holland, 111
Lend-Lease Act, 699
L'Enfant, Pierre, 307
Lenin, Vladimir, 614, p614
Lewis, Meriwether, 322–325, p322, p323,
m324, p326–327
Lewis and Clark expedition, 322–325,
p322, p323, m324
Lexington, Battle of, 186–187, m186, p187
Leyte Gulf, Battle of, 711, m712
The Liberator (newspaper), 394
Liberty Bonds, 618
Liberty League, 664–665
Liberty (ship), 179
Library of Congress, 312
Liliuokalani, 601, p601
Lin, Maya Ling, 732
Lincoln, Abraham, p263, R10; political par-
ties and, 378; Lincoln-Douglas debates,
444–445, p445; on slavery, 445, 450, 468,

Pierce, Franklin, R10
Pigafetta, Antonio, 58
Pike, Zebulon, 325–326, *p325*
Pikes Peak, 328, 554
Pilgrims, *p106*, 111–113, *p111, m112, p113*
Pinckney, Charles, 308
Pinckney, Thomas, 305
Pinckney's Treaty, 305
Pinta (ship), *p42*, 53, 54
pioneers, 319
piracy, 97–99, *p97, p99, c105, p142–143*; Navigation Acts, 138
Pitcher, Molly, 202, *p202*
Pitt, William, 166
Pittsburgh, Pennsylvania, 166
Pizarro, Francisco, 73
placer mining, 555–556
Plains Indians, *m17*, 18, *p18*, 78, 318–319, *p318*, 508, 559–560, *p559*
plantations, 67, 132–135, *p132, m133, p135*; Portugal and, 49; slavery and, 68–69; of Chesapeake Tidewater, 120; in Georgia, 123; property taxes and, 491
Platt Amendment, 606, *m609*
Pledge of Allegiance, 745
Plessy, Homer, 496
Plessy v. Ferguson, 247, 496
PLO. *See* Palestine Liberation Organization
Plymouth Colony, 111–113, *p111, m112, p113*
Pocahontas, 109, *p109*
Poe, Edgar Allan, 402
pogroms, 534
Poland, immigrants from, 530; in World War II, 671, 698
political action committees, 632
political cartoons, 161, *p161, p184, p267*, 376, *p376, p377, p381, p491*, 577–578, *p578, p600, p602, p607, p634*
political parties, 306–307, 378. *See also names of individual parties*
political prisoners, 791
Polk, James K., 439, R10; Mexican War and, 422–425, *m424*
Pollard, Anne, *p116*
poll tax, 279, 497, 769
Polo, Marco, 45–46, *p46*, 51, *p51*
Ponce de Léon, 67–68, 74–75, 566
Pontiac, 167
Poor Richard's Almanack (Franklin), 146
popular sovereignty, 440, 442, 443, 445, 447
population, ancient African, 29; of Arawak Indians, 67; of Mexico, 73; of Jamestown, 109; of Plymouth colony, 112; of colonial New England, 114; colonial Virginia, 133; of South Carolina, 134; of New France, 154; of English and French colonies, 161; effects of economy on, 343; urban, *c352*, 539, *c541*; slave, 355, 356; of Irish immigrants, 385; of Texas, 410; in boom-

towns, 427; during Civil War, 457, 478; industry and growth of, 511; immigrant, 529; cultural diversity and, 677, *c678*; during northern migration, 683; baby boom and, 744–745; of southern states, *m744*, 745; of western states, *m744*, 745; of Hispanic Americans, 772, 779; of Puerto Rico, 773; illegal aliens, 778; of Native Americans, 779; of African Americans, 779; of Asian Americans, 779; 1990 Census, *c779*; homeless, 796; of states, R11
Populist Party, 582–583, *p582*
Portugal, slavery and, 37–38, *p37*, 68–69; explorations by, 48–50, *m48, m50*, 51–52, 56–57, *m57*; Line of Demarcation and, 56, *p56, m57*, 58; conquest of Brazil, *p83*
Potawatomi Indians, *m371*
Powderly, 522, *p522*
Powell, Colin, 789, *p790*
Powhatan Indians, 109, 118
Pran, Dith, *p729*
prejudice, 385–386; religious, 534, 679
Prescott, Samuel, 187
President, U.S., 237–238, 243, 244–245, *c244*, 297–300, R10; Cabinet of, 247; in the Constitution, 262–265; impeachment of, 265; term of office, 277, 278, *p278*; Twelfth Amendment and, 273; electing, 393–394
President (ship), 332
presidios, 82
printing press, 46, 94, 95
prison reform, 391
private enterprise, 299
privateers, 98, 210
Proclamation of 1763, 175–176, *m176, c185*
Progressive Party, 586, *p586*, 591–592, *m591*, 742
Prohibition, 276, *p276*, 278, 650–651, *p650*
Promontory, Utah, 506–507, *m507*
propaganda, 180, 615
property taxes, 491
protectionist tariffs, 579
Protestants, 95–96, 101; Social Gospel, 543
public education, 389–390, *p389, p390*
Public Works Administration, *c663*
Pueblo Bonito, 10–11, *p11*
Pueblo Indians, 16, *p16, m17*, 82, 690
Puerto Rico, *m66*, 74, *m609*; exploration of, 68; gains independence from Spain, *m602*, 604; in Spanish-American War, 605–606; as commonwealth, *p606*; immigrants from, 680, *p680*; Jones Act, 680; government in, *p743*; population of, 773; citizenship in, 773
Pulitzer, Joseph, 546–547, 602
Pullman Strike, 524–525
Puritans, 114–117; Great Migration, 120; in England, 122

PWA. *See* Public Works Administration
pyramids, 29, *p29*

Q

Quakers, 117, 122–123, *p123*, 147, 202
Quayle, Dan, 759, 784
Quartering Act, 176, 178
Quebec, 93, 153–154, 157, 216, 681; in French and Indian War, 166–167, *m166*
Queen Anne's War, 160, *p160*
Quetzalcóatl, 9, 71
Quivira, 78

R

Rabin, Yitzhak, 791–792, *p792*
racism, 49, 450; slavery and, 438; after Civil War, 484; Jim Crow laws, 496; Social Darwinism and, 600; Puerto Ricans and, 680; riots and, 684; in northern states, 771; in Africa, 792. *See also* civil rights movement; Ku Klux Klan
Radical Reconstruction, 490–492
radio, 549, 645, *c645*, 662
railroads, 350, *p350, g359*, 479, *p504, g527*; in Illinois, 442; in Civil War, 475; transcontinental, 505–509, *p506, m507, p508, p509*; growth of industry and, 510–511, 512; strikes against, 522, 524–525, 742; in Midwest, *p544–545*; Native Americans and, 554; cattle industry and, 567; settlers and, 571; farming and, 581; Sherman Antitrust Act and, 587; Gold Rush and, 679
railroad time, 509
Rainey, Joseph, 494, *p494*
Raleigh, Sir Walter, 101–102, *p102*
ranching, 408–409, *p408, p565*, 567–569, *m567, p569*
Randolph, Edmund, 233, 234
Randolph, Philip, 703
Ranger (ship), 210
Rankin, Jeannette, 616
Reagan, Ronald, R10; on Panama Canal, 734; foreign policy of, 735, *p735*, 737; election of 1976, 753; election of 1980, 754; economy under, 756–757, *c757*; Supreme Court appointments, 757; election of 1984, 757–758; Iran-contra affair, 758; Savings and Loan crisis and, 759
Reaganomics, 756–757, *c757*
Reconquista, 52–53, 80
Reconstruction, 485–494, *p485, p486, p487, p489, p490*
The Red Badge of Courage (Crane), 500–501
Red Cloud, 560–561
redcoats, 180
Red River, 325, 328
Red scare, 648, 743–744
Reeves, Jim, 496–497
Reformation, 94–96

Acknowledgments

Text Credits

Grateful acknowledgment is made to authors, publishers, and other copyright holders for permission to reprint (and in some cases to adapt slightly) copyright material listed below.

21 "Heritage" from *On These I Stand* by Countee Cullen. Copyright 1925 by Harper & Row, Publishers, Inc., renewed, 1953 by Ida M. Cullen. The selection is printed by permission. **39** Reprinted by permission from Weekly Reader Corporation. Copyright © 1993 by Weekly Reader Corporation. All Rights Reserved. **188** From "Concord Hymn" by Ralph Waldo Emerson sung July 4, 1837, at the completion of the battle monument commemorating the battles of Lexington and Concord, April 19, 1775. **242** From "A Child's Faith" by Roger Wilkins, *The Washington Post Magazine,* June 28, 1987. Reprinted by permission of the author. **396** From *Get on Board: The Story of the Underground Railroad* by Jim Haskins. Copyright © 1993 Scholastic Inc. **418** From *The Grim Journey* by Hoffman Birney. Copyright 1934 by Hoffman Birney. **438** From *Democracy in America,* by Alexis de Tocqueville, translated by George Lawrence and edited by J.P. Mayer. Copyright © 1969, copyright © 1966 in the English translation by Harper & Row, Publishers. **471** From *Blue-Eyed Child of Fortune: The Civil War Letters of Colonel Robert Gould Shaw* edited by Russell Duncan. Copyright © 1992 by The University of Georgia Press. The letter was originally published in 1864 in *Letters: RGS* by Harvard University Press. **533** "The Biography of Bootblack" by Rocco Corresa, from *The Independent, Vol. LIV,* December 4, 1902. **534** From *The Promised Land* by Mary Antin. Houghton Mifflin Company, 1912. **548** From *City People: The Rise of Modern City Culture in Nineteenth-Century America* by Gunther Barth. Oxford University Press, 1980. **548** *A Bicycle Built for Two* by Hary Dacre. This song was originally published in 1892 under the title *Daisy Bell.* **582** From "The Populist Uprising" by Elizabeth N. Barr, in *History of Kansas, State and People, Vol. 2* edited by W. E. Connelly, American Historical Society, 1928. **587** From *A Book of Americans,* by Rosemary and Stephen Vincent Benet. Copyright 1933, by Rosemary and Stephen Vincent Benet. Copyright renewed © 1961, by Rosemary Carr Benet. Reprinted by permission of Brandt & Brandt Literary Agents, Inc. **614** "The Soldier" by Rupert Brooke published in *The New Oxford Book of English Verse*, edited by Helen Gardner, copyright © 1972, Oxford University Press. **614** "Anthem for Doomed Youth" by Wilfred Owen. From *Collected Poems*. Copyright Chatto & Windus Ltd. 1944, © 1963. **618** "Over There" by George M. Cohan. Copyright 1917 (Renewed 1945) LEO FEIST, INC. All rights assigned to EMI CATALOGUE PARTNERSHIP. All rights Controlled and Administered by EMI FEIST CATALOG INC. International Copyright secured. Made in USA. All Rights Reserved. **643** From *The Great Gatsby* by F. Scott Fitzgerald. Copyright 1925 by Charles Scribner & Sons. Copyright renewed 1953 by Frances Scott Fitzgerald Lanahan. **646** From "First Fig" by Edna St. Vincent Millay. From *Collected Poems,* HarperCollins. Copyright 1922, 1950 by Edna St. Vincent Millay. Reprinted by permission of Elizabeth Barnett, literary executor. **682** From *Hunger of Memory: The Education of Richard Rodriguez* by Richard Rodriguez, Copyright © 1982 by David R. Godine Publisher, Inc., Copyright © 1983 by Bantam Books, Inc. **687** Copyright 1926 by Alfred A. Knopf, Inc. and renewed 1954 by Langston Hughes. Reprinted from *Selected Poems of Langston Hughes* by permission of Alfred A. Knopf, Inc. **765** From *Stride Toward Freedom* by Martin Luther King Jr., Copyright © 1958 by Martin Luther King Jr. Copyright renewed 1986 by Coretta Scott King. **770** From *The Autobiography of Malcolm X* by Malcolm X and Alex Haley, Copyright © 1964 by Alex Haley and Malcolm X. Copyright © 1965 by Alex Haley and Betty Shabazz.

Art Credits

Cover design: Corey McPherson Nash
Cover image: Tony Rinaldo (eagle: Tom and Pat Leeson)
Text design: Corey McPherson Nash
Text maps: RR Donnelley: xiv **BR**, 6, 28, 31, 66, 71, 92, 112, 121, 122, 133, 137, 145, 163, 186, 205, 212, 333, 371, 396–397, 473, 541, 544–545, 563, 604, 621, 665, 696, 702, 712, 722, 744, 791; Ellen Jane Kuzdro: xiv T, xv, 138, 164–165, 324, 417, 560; John Sanderson: 17, 25, 41, 48, 50, 53, 57, 61, 64, 75, 77, 81, 85 **T**, **B**, 105, 125, 151, 156, 166, 176, 195, 215, 227, 249, 315, 331, 337, 343, 354, 359, 366, 381, 386, 405, 413, 424, 431, 442, 449, 453, 499, 507, 527, 538, 551, 555, 567, 575, 588, 591, 593, 597, 609, 622, 625, 653, 662, 675, 693, 708, 715, 725, 730, 739, 750, 761, 781, 799
Text charts, graphs and informationgraphics: Neil Pinchin Design
Illustrations: Ernest Albanese: 618, 620; Francis Back: 142–143, 182–183, 520–521; Kirk Caldwell: 64–65; Chris Costello: 329 **T**, 556 **L**, 710; Randall Enos: 360–361; Dale Glasgow: 746–747; Ellen Jane Kuzdro: 420–421; Joe Le Monnier: 344–345, 672–673; John Nelson: xvi **BC**, 95; Raymond Ortiz Godfrey: 86–87; Stephen Patricia: 20, 220–221, 347; Linda Phinney-Crehan: 74 **T**, 170–171 (background), 292–293 (background), 311, 432–433 (background), 500–501 (background), 716–717 (background); Tony Smith: 472–473; Cynthia Von Buhler: 626–627
Photo Research: 1–740: Linda L Rill; 741–799: Martin A. Levick
Positions are shown in abbreviated form as follows: **T**–top; **B**–bottom; **C**–center; **L**–left; **R**–right
Key: **BB**–Brown Brothers; **CP**–Culver Pictures, Inc.; **GC**–Granger Collection

vi R Michael C. Rockefeller Memorial Collection, The Metropolitan Museum of Art, Gift of Nelson A. Rockefeller, 1972. [1978.412.323]; **vi B** G. Dagli Orti; **vii T** Mansell Collection, London; **vii B** Sarah Warner "The Fishing Lady" Museum of Fine Arts, Boston. Seth K. Sweetser Fund [21.2233]; **viii T** GC; **viii R** Painting by Don Troiani, photo courtesy of Historical Art Prints, Inc.; **ix T** I.N. Phelps Stokes Collection, Miriam and Ira D. Wallace, New York Public Library (Dear 290, Stokes C.1813-E-91). Astor, Lenox and Tilden Foundations; **ix B** "Oberlin Class of 1855". Oberlin College; **x T** from THE OLD WEST: The Pioneers. Photograph by Harold Sund. © 1974 Time-Life Books, Inc. By permission of the Oregon Historical Society; **x C** Cook Collection, Valentine Museum, Richmond; **x B** By permission of the Rhode Island State House, Providence, photograph by Mark Sexton; **xi TR** GC; **xi TL** Theodore Groll "Washington Street, Indianapolis at Dusk" ca. 1892–1895, oil on canvas, 76×98 1/2. IMA72.133. © 1993 Indianapolis Museum of Art, Gift of a Couple of Old Hoosiers; **xi B** Ernest Albanese; **xii T** UPI/Bettmann; **xii B** Margaret Bourke-White, Life Magazine©Time Warner; **xiii T** NASA; **xiii C** Ivan Massar/Black Star; **xiii B** © Richard Hutchings/Photo Edit; **xiv BL** Painting by Don Troiani, photo courtesy of Historical Art Prints, Ltd.; **xvi BL** © A. Tannebaum/Sygma; **xvi T** Jonathan Kerr/The Nature Conservancy; **xvi BR** Reuters/Bettmann; **xvii T** Karl Bodmer: "Mih-Tutta-Hang-Kusch, Mandan Village." Joslyn Art Museum, Omaha, Nebraska; **xvii B** Phil Dixon's Negro Baseball Photographic History; **xix** Curt Teich Postcard Archives, Lake County (IL) Museum; **xx T** GC; **xx B** Francis Miller, Life Magazine © Time Warner, Contributors: Miller, Francis; **xxi T** GC; **xxi B** Reuters/Bettmann; **G10** Rohan/TSI **2** Aspect Picture Library, London; **4** Courtesy, Colorado Historical Society [WHJ 113]; **7 C** © Jerry Jacka; **7 R** Robert S. Peabody Museum of Archaeology, Phillips Academy, Andover, MA. All rights reserved; **8** © Michael D. Coe; **9 L** © Justin Kerr; **9 T** Denver Art Museum [1965.0202]; **10** © Jonathan Daniel/Allsport USA; **11 B** © David Muench; **11** (inset) © Richard Townsend; **12** John J. Egan "Panorama of the Monumental Grandeur of the Mississippi Valley, 1850" [detail:Dr. Dickerson Excavating a Mound] Saint Louis Art Museum, Eliza McMillan Fund; **14** © Clark Mishler/Alaska Stock Images; **15 L** © John W. Warden/Alaska Stock Images; **15 R** Collected by George T. Emmons at Klukwan, Alaska, before 1905; Thomas Burke Memorial Washington State Museum (cat. no. 2291); **16 TL** Yosemite National Park Service Research Library [neg.#16,590]; **16 TR** © Jerry Jacka, private collection; **16 B** Southwest Museum, Los Angeles; **17** Thomas Burke Memorial Washington State Museum [4516]; **18 L** Buffalo Bill Historical Center, Cody, WY, Gift of Mr. & Mrs. Larry Larom, photo by Devendra Shrikhande; **18 B** Painting © Roy Anderson, photo courtesy of the Pecos National Historic Park; **19** © James Schnepf/Gamma-Liaison Network; **21** © 1993 Steve Wall; **22 TL** © Steve Wall; **22 BL** Photo by Woodenturtle (Christopher Nyerges); **22 B** Alan Berner/Seattle Times; **23 TL** © Jerry Jacka; **23 TR** © Walter P. Calahan/Folio, Inc; **23 CR** © Monty Roessel; **26** © Georg Gerster/Comstock; **26 T** British Museum, © Michael Holford; **28** Museum Expedition, Courtesy of Museum of Fine Arts, Boston. [23.731]; **29** © Stephen Studd/Tony Stone Images; **30 L** Hoa-Qui, Paris; **30 R** Musee Barbier-Mueller, Geneve. Photo P.A. Ferranzzini; **32 R** Detail from the Catalan Atlas, by Abraham Cresques, 1375. Bibliotheque Nationale [RCC 14596]; **32 T** © Steven Rubin/JB Pictures, Inc; **34** GC; **35** © Fred Mayer/Magnum Photos; **36** (all) © Lawrence Migdale; **37** Michael C. Rockefeller Memorial Collection, The Metropolitan Museum of Art, Gift of Nelson A. Rockefeller, 1972. [1978.412.323]; **38** © Chuck Fishman 1986/Woodfin Camp & Associates; **39** © Olivier Rebbot/Stock,Boston; **42 B** © Bob Sacha; **42** (inset) Ministere de la Defense-Service Historique de l'Armee de Terre/Art Resource, New York; **44 T** Academic head post from the Oseberg find. Copyright University Museum of National Antiquities, Oslo, Norway; **44 B** Musee de l'Assistance Publique, Paris; **45** © Michael Holford; **46** Bodleian Library, Oxford; **47** Siena, Archivio di Stato/Scala,Florence/Art Resource, New York; **49 L** Flemish School, 17th Century, "Interior of an Art Gallery" (detail) Courtesy of the Trustees of the National Gallery, London; **49 R** Science Museum, © Michael Holford; **51** Livre des Merveilles, Ms. fr.2810,fol.84r. Bibliotheque Nationale, Paris; **52 C** Museo Navaledi Pegli/Scala/Art Resource, New York; **52 C** GC; **53 T** © Bob Sacha; **54** GC; **56** Museu de Marinha, Lisbon; **58** Courtesy of The Trustees of the British Museum, Franks Bequest, 1897; **62** Copyright National Maritime Museum, London; **67 R** "Camamelle sucre," Pl.283 from M.E. Descourtilz, 1827. Flore Pittoresque et Medicale des Antilles, ou Traite des Plantes Usuelles des Colonies Francaises, Anglaises, Espagnoles et Portugaises. vol.4, courtesy of the Botony Libraries, Harvard University; **67 T** From John Baptiste Labat, Nouveau voyage aux isles de l'Amerique, vol.3, 1722, courtesy of the John Carter Brown Library, Brown University; **68** The Bettmann Archive; **69** GC; **72 L** Courtesy of the Trustees of the British Museum; **72 B** Biblioteca Nacional, Madrid; **73** Louis Nicolas "Atahualpa" The Thomas Gilcrease Institute of American History and Art, Tulsa, Oklahoma; **74** "Tèrre Bieme" (detail) from Miller Atlas, 1519, [RcR 1264] Bibliotheque Nationale **76** GC; **78** GC; **79** GC; **80** Diego Rivera, La Era, 1904, oil on canvas, 100 x 114.5 cm., Marte R. Gómez Collection, Museo Diego Rivera, Guanajuato, photo by Dirk Bakker, courtesy of the Founders Society Detroit Institute of Arts, reproduction authorized by the Instituto Nacional de Bellas Artes y Literatura, Mexico; **82** Laura Winfrey Platt, Inc.; **83** GC; **88** Sarah Warner "The Fishing Lady" Museum of Fine Arts, Boston. Seth K. Sweetser Fund [21.2233]; **90 TR** Woburn Abbey, Bedforshire/Bridgeman Art Library/Art Resource, New York; **90 TL** Kunsthistorisches Museum, Vienna; **90** (background) The Huntington Library, San Marino, CA; **93** "The Last Voyage of Henry Hudson" by J. Collier. Tate Gallery, London/Art Resource, New York; **94 L** Lutherhalle, Wittenberg; **94 TR** Uffizi/Alinari/Art Resource, New York; **96 R** © Robert Frerck/Odyssey Productions; **96 L** Museum Service Histoire de la Marine/Giraudon/Art Resource, New York; **97** Howard Pyle "An Attack on a Galleon" (detail) Howard Pyle collection, Delaware Art Museum, Museum Purchase, 1912; **98 B** Mansell Collection, London; **98 L** Derek Bayes/Aspect Picture Library/City Museum and Art Gallery, Plymouth; **99** Hendrik Cornelius Vroom "The Battle between the Spanish and English" Naval Forces (detail) photograph by Erich Lessing, Vienna, courtesy of the Landesmuseum Ferdinandeum, Innsbruck, Austria/Art Resource, New York; **101** G. Dagli Orti; **102** (detail) Nicholas Hilliard "Sir Walter Raleigh" miniature on vellum. By courtesy of the National Portrait Gallery, London; **103 R** Courtesy of The Trustees of the British Museum; **103 L** GC; **106** Collection of The New-York Historical Society; **108** Colonial Williamsburg Foundation; **109** (detail) National Portrait Gallery of Art, gift of Andrew W. Mellon, 1942/Art Resource, New York; **110 T** The Historical Society of Pennsylvania; **110 B** GC; **111** "The Mayflower" (detail) by Halsall. Courtesy of the Pilgrim Society, Plymouth, MA.; **113** Courtesy of the Pilgrim Society, Plymouth, MA.; **114** Courtesy of the American Antiquarian Society; **115** GC; **116** Courtesy of the Massachusetts Historical Society; **117 B** GC; **117 T** Courtesy, Peabody & Essex Museum, Salem, Mass. Photo by Mark Sexton; **118** Courtesy of the American Antiquarian Society (handtinted by Ron Kyle); **120** I.N. Phelps Stokes Collection, Miriam and Ira Wallach Division of Art, Prints and Photographs. New York Public Library, Astor, Lenox and Tilden Foundations; **121** Collection of the Museum of the City of New York; **123** Photographed by The Shelburne Museum, Shelburne, VT; **126** (both insets) David Hiser/Photographers Aspen; **126** (background) GC; **128** GC; **130** © Weekly World News; **131 L** Collection of The New-York Historical Society; **131** (inset) Courtesy The Newberry Library; **132** Thomas Coram "View of Mulberry Plantation (House and Street)" oil on paper. Carolina Art Association/Gibbs Art Museum, Charleston; **133 R** Courtesy of The Trustees of the British Museum, Museum of Mankind [MM032887]; **134** (both) Courtesy of the American Antiquarian Society; **135** © Louis Psihoyos/Contact Press Images; **136** Photographed by The Shelburne Museum, Shelburne, VT; **137** (both) Mariners Museum, Newport News, VA; **139 L** Courtesy of The New-York Historical Society; **140** T.H. Matteson "The Accusation of George Jacobs, August 5, 1692" Oil on canvas, 1855. Courtesy of the Peabody Essex Museum, Salem, Massachusetts, photo by Mark Sexton; **141** John Wollaston "George Whitefield" By courtesy of the National Portrait Gallery, London; **142 L** Copyright National Maritime Museum, Greenwich; **143 R** Copyright National Maritime Museum, Greenwich; **144** Copyright, New York State Historical Association, Cooperstown, New York 13326 **145 R** Philadelphia Museum of Art:Given by John T. Morris; **146 T** Robert Feke "Benjamin Franklin" (detail). Harvard University Portrait Collection. Bequest of Dr. John C. Warren in 1856; **146 B** © Jim Abbott, collection of the Franklin Institute; **147** Rare Book Department, Free Library of Philadelphia; **148 C** © Bob Brudd/Tony Stone Images; **148 B** Photo courtesy Museum of Appalachia, Norris, Tennessee, photo by Frank Hoffman; **149** Ashmolean Museum, Oxford; **152** Onondaga Historical Association, Syracuse, New York; **154 B** The Mansell Collection (handtinted by Ron Kyle); **154 T** Kateri Center, Mission Saint-Francois-Xavier, Kahnawake, Quebec; **157** George Catlin "Chief of the Taensa Indians Receiving La Salle, March 1682" (detail) National Gallery of Art, Washington, D.C.; **159** Courtesy of the Trustees of the British Library [Sloan 5253]; **160 B** "The Deerfield Massacre, February 29, 1704" by Henry H. Brooks and Theodore B. Pitman, 1960. Oil on canvas. Fruitlands Museums, Harvard, MA; **160 T** The National Museum of Denmark, Department of Ethnography, Copenhagen; **161** GC; **162** John G. Chapman "George Washington" The West Point Museum, United States Military Academy, West Point, New York; **164** Fort Ticonderoga Museum; **165** Harry Ogden "The Marquis de Montcalm Congratulating his Troops After the Battle of Carillon, July 8, 1758" Fort Ticonderoga Museum; **167** Courtesy of the Massachusetts Historical Society; **170** Copyright National Maritime Museum, Greenwich; **171** GC; **172** Maryland National Guard, Fifth Regiment Armory, Baltimore. Photo by Jeff D. Goldman; **174** John Trumbull "The Death of General Warren at the Battle of Bunker's Hill, 17 June 1775" (detail) Yale University Art Gallery, Trumbull Collection; **176** Courtesy of the Massachusetts Historical Society; **177 L** GC; **177 R** Courtesy, Peabody Essex Museum, Salem, Mass. Photo by Mark Sexton; **178** GC; **179** Charles DeWolf Brownell: "The Burning of the Gaspee" Rhode Island Historical Society; **180** "The Bloody Massacre" by Paul Revere. 1770. Mezzotint. H. 10-3/8 in. W. 9 in. Metropolitan Museum of Art, Gift of Mrs. Russell Sage, 1909; **181 T** GC; **181 R** Daughters of the American Revolution, Boston Tea Party Chapter; **184 R** Courtesy of the John Carter Brown Library at Brown University; **186** Painting by Don Troiani, photo courtesy of Historical Art Prints, Ltd.; **187** GC; **188** Fort Ticonderoga, Ticonderoga, New York; **189** "Attack on Bunker's Hill, with the Burning of Charles Town" anonymous. American School, National Gallery of Art, Washington, D.C., Gift of Edgar W. and Bernice C. Garbisch; **190** (detail) "Portrait Traditionally Said That to be of Abigail Adams" by unknown artist. Copyright New York State Historical Association, Cooperstown, New York; **191** Independence National Historical Park Collection; **192** John Trumbull "The Declaration of Independence, 4 July 1776" Yale University Art Gallery, Trumbull Collection; **193** Courtesy, Winterthur Museum; **200** Archibald M. Willard "The Spirit of '76" Abbott Hall, Marblehead, MA; **202 T** GC; **202 B** National Museum of American History, Division of Armed Forces, Smithsonian Institution [76-3258]; **203** Emanuel Gottieb Leutze "Washington Crossing the Delaware" Oil on canvas. H. 149 in. W. 255 in. Signed and dated (lower right): E. Leutze/Dusseldorf 1851. The Metropolitan Museum of Art, Gift of John Stewart Kennedy, 1897 [97.34]; **204** Paintings by Don Troiani, photo courtesy of Historical Art Prints, Inc; **205** Peabody Essex Museum, Salem, MA, photograph by Mark Sexton; **206** John Trumbull "The Surrender of General Burgoyne at Saratoga 16 October 1777" oil on canvas. Trumbull Collection. Yale University Art Gallery [1832.7]; **208** "Washington Reviewing His Troops" by William Trego. The Valley Forge Historical Society; **209** CP; **210 BR** Pierpont Morgan Library; **210 BL** Massachusetts Historical Society, Gift of Theodore Chase, 1977; **210 T** Peabody Essex Museum [M1932]; **211** Valentine Museum, Richmond; **213** John Trumbull "The Surrender of Lord Cornwallis at Yorktown, 19 October 1781" oil on canvas. Trumbull Collection. Yale University Art Gallery [1832.4]; **214** Benjamin West "Preliminary Peace Negotiations with Great Britain." Courtesy of the Winterthur Museum; **215** National Archives; **216** William Berczy "Thayendanegea" (Joseph Brandt). National Gallery of Canada, Ottawa, (#5777); **217** Architectural ornament: eagle, unknown artist. Carved wood, iron. 69-7/8" × 44" × 50" deep. Collection of the Museum of American Folk Art, New York, N.Y. Gift of William Engvick [1966.2.1]; **218** National Archives; **219 R** George Cabel Bingham: "Daniel Boone Escorting Settlers Through the Cumberland Gap." Washington University Art Gallery, St. Louis, Gift of Nathaniel Phillips, Boston, 1890; **219 L** © William Strode/Woodfin Camp & Associates; **220** © Jon Feingersh/Stock, Boston; **221** Courtesy the Museum of Science and Industry, Chicago; **222** John C. Wild "View of Cincinnati from Covington, KY, 1835" Cincinnati Historical Society; **223 TL** A Primer for the Use of Mohawk Children, London: C. Buckton, 1786, frontispiece and title page. © The Pierpont Morgan Library 1994. [PML 85496 ECB68]; **223 B** Massachusetts Historical Society; **223 TR** From Original in the Rare Book Department of The Free Library of Philadelphia, photography by Studio Lux; **224 T** "Reverend Lemuel Haynes in the Pulpit" anonymous, on painted tray. Museum of Art, Rhode Island School of Design, Gift of Miss Lucy T. Aldrich; **225** Historical Society of Pennsylvania collection. Photograph by Victor Boswell, © National Geographic Society; **228** GC; **230 L** © Sam Abell; **230 B** GC; **231** James Sharples "Governeur Morris." (detail) National Portrait Gallery, Washington, D.C./Art Resource, New York; **232** Charles Willson Peale "James Madison" 1792 (detail). Thomas Gilcrease Institute of History and Art, Tulsa, Okalahoma; **233** Architect of the Capitol; **234** Rare Book Department, Free Library of Philadelphia; **235** © Jeffrey W. Myers/Stock,Boston; **236** The Bettmann Archive; **237 C** National Museum of the American Indian, Smithsonian Institution, photograph by Janine Jones; **237 B** Benjamin Henry Latrobe "An Overseer Doing His Duty" Collection of The Maryland Historical Society, Baltimore; **239** GC; **240** AP/Wide World Photos; **241 R** Shelburne Museum, Shelburne, Vermont, photograph by Ken Burris; **241 L** Independence National Historical Park; **242** © Ben Boblett; **243** Sam Abell, © National Geographic Society; **244** © Brad Markel/Gamma-Liaison Network; **247** Ted Thai, Time-Warner, Inc; **255** GC; **256 B** © Robert Llewellyn; **256 T** GC; **257 B** CP; **257 T** GC; **258** © Dennis Brack/Black Star; **259** GC; **260 B** The Bettmann Archive; **260 T** GC; **261** GC; **262** Library of Congress; **263 B** GC; **263 T** The Bettmann Archive; **264 B** Frank Scherschel, Life Magazine © Time-Warner, Inc. **264 T** The Bettmann Archive; **266 B** © Randy Duchain/The Stock Market; **266 T** GC; **267** Historical Pictures Services; **269** Historical Pictures Services; **271** GC; **272** GC; **273** GC; **274** Library of Congress; **275** GC; **276** The Bettmann Archive; **278** UPI/Bettmann Newsphotos; **279** © Robert Llewellyn; **282** Don Smetzer/Tony Stone Worldwide; **283** Bob Daemmrich; **284 T** Charles Gupton/Picturesque; **284 B** Rhoda Sidney/Photo Edit; **285 T** Michal Heron/Woodfin Camp & Associates; **285 B** Paul Conklin/Photo Edit; **286** Courtesy of Congressman Kika de la Garza; **288 TL** Ed Wheeler/The Stock Market; **288 R** GC; **288 BC** GC; **289 TL** FPG/The Stock Directory; **289 R** Rohan/Tony Stone Worldwide; **289 BL** Bruce Roberts/Photo Researchers; **290** © Larry Downing/Sygma; **294** Robertson, Seibert & Shearman. Lazell, Perkins & Co. Bridgewater, Mass. Yale University Art Gallery, Mabel Brady Garven Collection [1946.9.1746]; **296** L.M.Cooke "Salute to General Washington in New York Harbor" Gift of Edgar William and Bernice Chrysler Garbisch, © 1993 National Gallery of Art, Washington [1953.5.7.(1203)/PA]; **298** GC; **299** Library of Congress, photograph courtesy of the National Geographic Society; **300 T** Rare Book Department, Free Library of Phildelphia; **300 C** GC; **302** Museum d'Histoire Naturelle, Le Havre, France; **303** "Charge of the Dragoons at the Battle of Fallen Timbers" Ohio Historical Society; **304** J.E. Bulloz, Paris; **305** Rare Book Department, Free Library of Phildelphia; **306** Anonymous "He That Tilleth the Land Shall be Satisfied" (detail) Philadelphia Museum of Art: Edgar William and Bernice Chrysler Garbisch Collection ['65-209-5]; **307 T** Maryland Historical Society, Baltimore; **307 B** Library of Congress; **308** Gordon Phillips "Abigail Adams and Grand-Daughter Susanna Supervise as a Servant Hangs the Wash in the East Room." Copyrighted by the White House Historical Association, Photograph by the National Geographic Society; **309** GC; **310** (detail) Thomas Jefferson Memorial Foundation; **311 T** Collection of The New-York Historical Society; **311** (both-bottom) © Robert Llewellyn; **312** Anonymous: "Burning of the Frigate Philadelphia." Mariners Museum of Newport News, VA; **313** Architect of the Capitol; **316** GC; **318 B** Neg.# Tr.#1900(2) - "Buffalo Hunt" by George Catlin. Courtesy of the Department of Library Sciences, American Museum of Natural History; **318 R** Neg.# Tr.#3273(3) - Photo by Lee Boltin. Courtesy Department Library Services, American Museum of Natural History; **319** GC; **320** © Maggie Steber, New York; **321** "Boqueto Under My Wings," 1803. Chicago Historical Society; **322** (left) Olaf C. Seltzer "Lewis and Clark with Sacajawea at the Great Falls of Missouri, 1804" The Thomas Gilcrease Institute of American History and Art, Tulsa, Oklahoma **322 R** National Museum of American History, Smithsonian Institution [# 75-2348]; **323 C** American Philosophical Society; **323 B** Missouri Historical Society, Neg. CT LA 109; **324** From the Picture Collection of the State Historical Society of North Dakota [#800-45]; **325 L** Independence National Historical Park Collection; **325 B** from Zebulon Montgomery Pike, "An account of expeditions to be the sources of the Mississippi, and through the western parts of Louisiana" Philadelphia, 1810, Smithsonian Institition Libraries, photo by Ed Castle; **326 BC** George Catlin "Sha-Ko-Ka." Thomas Gilcrease Institute of American History and Art, 0226.1545; **326 C** Copyright © President and Fellows of Harvard College. Peabody Museum of Archaelogy and Ethnology, Harvard University, photo by Hillel Burger; **326 BL** Karl Bodmer: "Pehriska-Ruhpa Hidatsa Man." Gift of the Enron Art Foundation, Joslyn Art Museum, Omaha, Nebraska; **327 T** Karl Bodmer: "Interior of a Hut of a Mandan Chief, c. 1836." Thomas Gilcrease Institute of American History and Art, 0476.7; **327 B** Karl Bodmer:"Mih-Tutta-Hang-Kusch, Mandan Village." Joslyn Art Museum, Omaha, Nebraska; **328** CP; **329** Collection of The New-York Historical Society; **332** Field Museum of Natural History, transparency # A93851.1c, Chicago; **333** Smithsonian Institution; **334** GC; **335 L** GC; **335 R** (detail) "Dolley Madison" by unknown artist (has been attributed to James Peale and Anna Claypole Peale). Watercolor on ivory. Yale University Art Gallery, Lelia A. and John Hill Morgan Collection; **338** © C. Bruce Foster/Allstock; **338** Copyright New York State Historical Society, Cooperstown, N.Y.; **340** © Art Stein/Folio, Inc; **341 B** Library of Congress; **341 T** National Archives, (NA # 127-G-10H)/photo courtesy of Smithsonian Press; **342** William Tylee "Ranney Crossing the Ferry 1846" The Thomas Gilcrease Institute of American History and Art, Tulsa, Oklahoma; **343** Pennsylvania Canal Society Collection. Hugh Moore Historical Park and Museums; **345** Photo collection of the Erie Canal Museum, Syracuse, N.Y.; **346** E.A. Farrar: "View of Lowell" Museum of American Textile History; **348 TR** The Bettmann Archive; **348 TL** Massachusetts Historical Society; **348 B** I.N. Phelps Stokes Collection, Miriam and Ira D. Wallace, New York Public Library (Dear 290, Stokes C.1813-E-91), Astor, Lenox and Tilden Foundations; **349 T** GC; **350** Edward Lamson Henry "First Railroad Train on the Mohawk and Hudson" (detail). Collection of the Albany Institute of History and Art, Gift of Friends of the Institute (photo by Joseph Levy); **351** Copyright Union Pacific Railroad Museum Collection; **353** National Museum of American History, Smithsonian Institution [# 73-11287]; **354** Benjamin L.C. Wailes, "Report of the Agriculture and Geology of Mississippi, 1854." Library Company of Philadelphia; **355** T.S. Noble "The Last Sale of Slaves in Saint Louis" Missouri Historcial Society; **356** "The Old Plantation" c.1800. The Abby Aldrich Rockefeller Folk Art Center, Williamsburg, VA; **357** GC; **362** William Tylee Ranney, "The Old Scout's Tale," ca. 1853, oil on canvas. The Thomas Gilcrease Institute of American History and Art, Tulsa, Oklahoma; **364** George Caleb Bingham "County Election" Saint Louis Art Museum; **366** GC; **367 R** The Hermitage Home of Andrew Jackson; **367 L** J. H. Whitcomb "Our President, Old Hickory" M. & M. Karolik Collection, Courtesy Museum of Fine Arts, Boston; **368** GC; **369** University of Iowa Museum of Natural History; **370** "Se-Quo-Yah" (detail) printed by Lehman & Duval, after a painting by Charles Bird King. Philadelphia Museum of Art, Given by Mis Willian Adger ['37-40-1d]; **372 B** GC; **372 T** Robert Lindneux "The Trail of Tears," 1942. Woolaroc Museum, Bartlesville, OK; **373** "Before the Days of Rapid Transit" published by Charles Klackner after a painting by Edward Lamson Henry. Chicago Historical Society; **374** City of Boston Art Commission; **375** John C. Calhoun, daguerreotype by unknown artist. The Gibbes Museum of Art/Carolina Art Association; **376** GC; **377** Collection of The New-York Historical Society; **378** Thomas Nast drawings in Harper's Weekly; **379** Collection of The New-York Historical Society [1944.270]; **381** The Bettmann Archive; **382** Samuel Waugh "The Bay and Harbor of New York," 1855 (detail). Museum of the City of New York, Gift of Mrs. Robert M. Littlejohn; **384** Joseph W. Gear "Half past Eight O'Clock" Chicago Historical Society; **385** GC; **387 R** © Bob Dammerich/Stock,Boston; **387 L** Courtesy, Levi Strauss & Company; **388** New Bedford Whaling Museum; **389 L** Winslow Homer "The Country School," 1871. Saint Louis Art Museum, Museum Purchase **389 R** GC; **390 B** "Oberlin Class of 1855." Oberlin College; **390 T** Anonymous, American, 19th century, "The Drawing Class" watercolor, c. 1820, 36.5 × 56 cm, Gift of Emily Crane Collection, 1951.202. Photograph © 1993, The Art Institute of Chicago. All Rights Reserved; **391 T** Harrisburg State Hospital, photo by Ken Smith, courtesy of LLR Research Collection; **391 B** Courtesy of Sandwich Historical Society, Sandwich Center, N.H. **392** (all) Sam Abell, © National Geographic Society; **393** GC; **394 T** "The Underground Railroad" (detail), by Charles T. Webber. Cincinnati Art Museum; **394 B** GC; **394 L** Friends Historical Library, Swarthmore College; **395** GC; **396 TL** Eastman Johnson "The Ride for Liberty-The Fugitive Slaves" Brooklyn Museum; **396 BC** (detail) Sophia Smith College, Smith College; **397 BC** GC; **397 TR** © Louis Psihoyos/Contact Press Images; **397 BL** Special Collections Department, Chicago Public Library Cultural Center, © Louis Psihoyos/Contact Press Images; **397 CR** GC; **398 T** © 1992 Beth Brookhart; **398 B** Collection of The New-York Historical Society [neg.51038]; **399 L** GC; **399 R** CP; **401** J. Wilgus "Ichabod Crane and the Headless Horseman" National Gallery of Art, Washington D.C. [1971.83.21]; **402 TR** © John Wells/New England Stock Photo; **402 CL** Charles Osgood "Nathaniel Hawthorne" Peabody & Essex Museum, Salem, Mass.; **402 BL** Theodore Wust "Henry Wadsworth Longfellow" National Portrait Gallery, gift of Gary J. Polinsky in memory of his mother, Lily Esther Rose./Art Resource, New York; **403** © J.J. Audubon, Photo Researchers,Inc.; **406** Albert Bierstadt "Emigrants Crossing the Plains." National Cowboy Hall of Fame and Western Heritage Center; **408 L** from THE OLD WEST: The Pioneers. Photograph by Harald Sund. © 1974 Time-Life Books Inc. By permission of the Oregon Historical Society; **408 B** James Walker "Vaqueros in a Horse Corral" The Thomas Gilcrease Institute of American History and Art, Tulsa; **409** CP; **410 L** GC; **410 R** Eugene C. Barker Texas History Center, The University of Texas at Austin; **411** San Jacinto Museum of History, Houston, Texas; **412 B** Robert Jenkins Onderdonk "Fall of the Alamo" 1903, courtesy of Friends of the Governor's Mansion, Austin; **412 L** Courtesy of the Daughters of the Republic of Texas, at the Alamo, San Antonio, Texas; **413** Courtesy, The New-York Historical Society [1878.3]; **414 T** Detail of "The Battle of San Jacinto" by Charles Shaw, San Jacinto Museum of History, Houston, Texas; **414 B** Courtesy of the Texas Memorial Museum; **415 L** Alfred Jacob Miller "Rocky Mountain Trapper" Buffalo Bill Historical Center, Cody, Wyoming, Gift of the Coe Foundation; **415 B** The Museum of the Fur Trade; **416** © David Hiser/Photographers Aspen; **417** from THE OLD WEST:The Pioneers. Photograph by Harald Sund. © 1974 Time-Life Books, Inc. By permission of the Oregon Historical Society; **418** William Gilbert Gaul "On the Way to the Summit" Collection of the Oakland Museum, Gift of The Kahn Foundation [65.98]; **419** (inset) Church of Jesus Christ of Latter-Day Saints. Photo: Ronald Read, courtesy Museum of Church History and Art, Salt Lake City; **419 T** Utah State Historical Society; **420 BR** from THE OLD WEST:The Pioneers. Photograph by Harald Sund. © 1974 Time-Life Books, Inc. By permission of the Oregon Historical Society; **420 T** © Bill and Jan Moeller, Omaha; **420 BL** Western History Department, Denver Public Library; **421 TL** © David Hiser/Photographers Aspen; **421 B** © David Hiser/Photographers Aspen; **421 CR** Collection of the New-York Historical Society [20019]; **421 TR** Western History Department, Denver Public Library [#11188]; **422** Museum of American Political Life, University of Hartford. Photograph by Sally Anderson-Bruce; **423 B** California State Library, Sacramento; **423 T** C. Escalante "Battle at Molina del Rey" Museo Nacional de Historia/Laurie Platt Winfrey, Inc. **424** from MEXICAN WAR. Photograph by Tom Tracy. © 1978 Time-Life Books, Inc; **425 L** Courtesy of Michael F. Bremer with permission and from the Collection of Dr. William Schultz; **425 R** Courtesy the Collection of Michael F. Bremer; **426 L** California State Library, Sacramento; **426** (inset) Courtesy of Wells Fargo Bank; **427** Yung Wing and students (detail) Courtesy Connecticut Historical Society, Hartford [neg.1491]; **429** © Ellis Herwig/Stock, Boston; **432** GC; **433** American Antiquarian Society; **434** Bucks County Historical Society, Doylestown, PA; **436** Charles Giroux "Cotton Plantation" Oil on canvas. M. & M. Karolik Collection, Courtesy Museum of Fine Arts, Boston; **438 L** Glenbow Collection, Calgary, Alberta, Canada; **438** (inset) Stock Montage, Inc.; **439** CP; **440** (both) CP; **441 R** GC; **441** (both-left) Louis Psihoyos/Contact Press Images; **443** The Stowe-Day Foundation, Hartford, CT; **444** Louis Schultze "Dred Scott" Missouri Historical Society, Neg. # S-8; **445** Robert M. Root "Lincoln-Douglas Debate" (detail) Illinois State Historical Library; **446 L** Thomas Hovenden "The Last Moments of John Brown" (detail) Oil on canvas. H 77-3/8 in. W. 63-1/4 in. The Metropolitan Museum of Art, gift of Mr. and Mrs. Carl Stoeckel, 1987; **446 R** Photo by Photo 1,Inc. Topeka; **447** Museum of American Political Life, University of Hartford, photography by Steven Laschever; **448** New York Public Library; **449 R** Illinois State Historical Library, Springfield, IL, (#LR-72); **450 B** The Bettmann Archive; **450 T** The Museum of the Confederacy, Richmond, Virginia. Photography by Katherine Wetzel; **451** GC; **454** The Bettmann Archive; **456** Cook Collection, Valentine Museum, Richmond; **459** The Seventh Regiment

Fund,Inc. **460** GC; **461** Courtesy of Don Troiani Collection, from ECOHES OF GLORY: Arms & Equipment of the Union, photograph by Larry Sherer © 1991 Time-Life Books Inc.; **462** Library of Congress; **464 L** GC; **464 B** Peabody Museum of Salem, photo by Mark Sexton; **466** Confederate Memorial Hall, New Orleans. From ECHOES OF GLORY: Arms & Equipment of the Confederacy, photograph by Larry Sherer © 1991 Time-Life Books Inc; **467** Library of Congress; **468** © Joe Towers/The Stock Market; **469 B** GC; **469 R** Courtesy of the Stamatelos Brothers Collection. From ECHOES OF GLORY: Arms & Equipment of the Union, photograph by Larry Sherer © 1991 Time-Life Books Inc; **470** By permission of the Rhode Island State House, Providence, photograph by Mark Sexton; **471** Boston Athenaeum; **474** Library of Congress; **475** Balling, Ole Peter Hansen. "Grant and His Generals." National Portrait Gallery, Washington,D.C./Art Resource, New York; **476 TR** Courtesy of Joseph Canole; **476 BR** Museum of the Confederacy. From ECHOES OF GLORY: Arms & Equipment of the Union, photograph by Larry Sherer © 1991 Time-Life Books Inc; **476 BC** Museum of the Confederacy. From ECHOES OF GLORY: Arms & Equipment of the Union, photograph by Larry Sherer © 1991 Time-Life Books Inc; **476** (far right center Museum of the Confederacy. From ECHOES OF GLORY: Arms & Equipment of the Union, photograph by Larry Sherer © 1991 Time-Life Books Inc; **476** (far right) Collection of Dean E. Nelson. From ECHOES OF GLORY: Arms & Equipment of the Confederacy, photograph by Larry Sherer © 1991 Time-Life Books Inc; **476** (far left-center) Museum of the Confederacy. From ECHOES OF GLORY: Arms & Equipment of the Confederacy, photograph by Larry Sherer © 1991 Time-Life Books Inc; **476** (right far left) Museum of the Confederacy. From THE CIVIL WAR: Tenting Tonight, photograph by Larry Sherer © 1984 Time-Life Books Inc; **476** (far left) Collection of Ann Louise G. Gates. From THE CIVIL WAR: Tenting Tonight, photograph by Larry Sherer © 1984 Time-Life Books Inc; **478 T** GC; **478 B** Massachusetts Commandery, Military Order of the Loyal Legion and the U.S. Army Military History Institute, Carlisle, PA; **482** The Valentine Museum, Richmond, Virginia; **484** Brooke, Richard Norris. "A Pastoral Visit, Virgina, 1881." oil on canvas, 47-3/4 × 65-3/4 in (121.29 × 167.01 cm) In the Collection of the Corcoran Gallery of Art, Museum Purchase, Gallery Fund; **485** Stock Montage; **486** GC; **487** The Bettmann Archive; **488** CP; **489** GC; **490 T** The Bettmann Archive; **490 B** Joseph H. Bailey, © National Geographic Society; **491 C** Culver Pictures; **491 T** Harper's Weekly; **492** Missouri Historical Society; **493** New Hampshire Historical Society, #F326; **494** Reuters/Bettmann; **495 T** From the Collections of the South Carolina Historical Society; **495 B** CP (handtinted by Ron Kyle); **496** CP; **497** The Bettmann Archive; **500** Stock Montage; **501** Winslow Homer "Young Soldier; Separate Study of a soldier giving water to a wounded companion," 1861. Oil, gouache, black crayon on canvas. Gift of Charles Savage Homer, Jr., 1912-12-110. Courtesy of Cooper-Hewitt, National Museum of Design, Smithsonian Institution/Art Resource, NY. Photo: Ken Pelka; **502** Theodore Groll "Washington Street, Indianapolis at Dusk" ca. 1892–1895, oil on canvas, 76 × 98-1/2. IMA72.133. © 1993 Indianapolis Museum of Art, Gift of a Couple of Old Hoosiers; **504** GC; **506 T** Special Collections Division, University of Washington Libraries, photo by Frank Nowell, negative No. UW 2315; **506 B** Courtesy of Southern Pacific Lines; **508** © Yves Forestier/Sygma; **509 L** The Bettmann Archive; **509 R** GC; **510** From p.30 of "Frank Leslie's illustrated historical register of the Centennial Exhibition" The Free Library of Philadelphia; **511** Courtesy of Bethlehem Steel; **512 BR** U.S. Department of the Interior, National Park Service, Edison National Historic Site; **512 BL** Henry Ford Museum & Greenfield Village; **512 T** CP; **513 T** Edward Harrison May "Isaac Merrit Singer" (detail) National Portrait Gallery, Smithsonian Institution, Gift of the Singer Company/Art Resource, New York; **513 B** Courtesy of AT&T Archives; **514 L** Warshaw Collection, Smithsonian Institution [# 93-14069]; **514 T** GC; **515** Courtesy of Biltmore Estate. Asheville. North Carolina; **516** GC; **517** The Newberry Library, Chicago; **519** Lewis Hine "Breaker Boys" George Eastman House; **520 C** BB; **520 B** Jacob A. Riis Collection. Photograph by Jessie Tarbox Beals. Museum of the City of New York; **522** GC; **523** GC; **524** CP; **525** Amalgamated Clothing Workers, print courtesy of Cornell University; **528** (background) National Park Service, Augustus F. Sherman Collection; **528 BL** GC; **528 TR** GC; **528 TL** PhotoWorld/FPG International Archive; **528 TC** National Park Service, Augustus F. Sherman Collection; **528 BC** National Park Service, Augustus F. Sherman Collection; **529** Karen Yamauchi for Chermayeff & Geismar Inc./Metaform Inc; **530 B** Karen Yamauchi for Chermayeff & Geismar Inc./Metaform Inc; **530 B** Karen Yamauchi for Chermayeff & Geismar Inc./Metaform Inc; **531 B** Library of Congress; **531 T** The Bettman Archive; **532 L** Keystone View Co/FPG International Archive; **532 R** FPG International; **533 L** Cincinnati Historical Society; **533 R** CP; **534** © Metaform, Inc./National Park Service, Gift of the Jewish Museum; **535 R** LLR Collection; **535 C** The Bettmann Archive; **536 T** Museum of the City of New York, Jacob Riis Collection 160; **536 B** Museum of the City of New York, Gift of Mrs. Henry L. Moses; **537 R** Museum of the City of New York, The Jacob A. Riis Collection 155; **537 R** Charles W. Witham, "Baxter Street" Museum of the City of New York; **539** CP; **540** Division of Engineering and Industry, Smithsonian Institution [48618]; **542 B** Courtesy of AT&T Archives; **542 T** Courtesy of AT&T Archives; **543** Collection of the Museum of the City of New York; **544 TC** State Archives of Michigan, Bureau of History Division; **544 B** Stock Montage, Inc; **545 TR** "Chicago" on stone by Christian Inger after a drawing by James Palmatary, 1857. Chicago Historical Society; **545 L** The Bettmann Archive; **546** GC; **547 B** "A Busy Bee Hive" (detail) Chicago Historical Society; **547 T** Library of Congress; **548 B** National Archives; **548 T** © David Simson/Stock,Boston; **549 R** The Bettmann Archive; **549 L** CP; **552** John Steuart Curry "Rush for the Oklahoma Land - 1894" Department of the Interior; **554** Courtesy of the Nebraska State Historical Society [S726:G3]; **556 B** Courtesy, The Bancroft Library; **557** Special Collections Division, University of Washington Libraries, photo by Eric A. Hegg, Negative No. 101; **559** Courtesy of The Southwest Museum, Los Angeles. Photo #[Ls.7458]; **561 B** From a Pictographic History of the Oglala Sioux, by Amos Bad Heart Bull, Plate No.147. Courtesy of the University of Nebraska Press" **561 T** Denver Art Museum [1968.330]; **562** Smithsonian Institution, National Anthropological Archives [neg.#2906]; **563** Nevada State Museum; **564 L** Smithsonian Institution, National Anthropological Archives [neg.15,516]; **564 R** Smithsonian Institution, National Anthropological Archives [neg.15,517]; **565 L** Library of Congress; **565 R** Colorado Historical Society; **568 B** © H. Brooks Walker; **568 C** Photo by Joseph E. Smith, Courtesy of the Museum of New Mexico, Neg. 75265; **569** GC; **570** Nebraska State Historical Society, Solomon Butcher Collection; **571 T** Olof Krans "Sowing Grain at Bishop Hill," 1896. Bishop Hill State Historic Site; **571 B** David Phillip Collection, Chicago Architectural Photographing Company; **572 C** From the Picture Collection of the State Historical Society of North Dakota [#neg B-338]; **572 B** © Tom Tracy, from the San Joaquin County Historical Museum in Lodi, California; **573** GC; **576** (background) GC; **576** (bottom inset) Breton Littlehales, © National Geographic Society; **576** (top inset) GC; **578 T** GC; **578 B** GC; **579** The Museum of American Political Life, University of Hartford. Photograph by Sally Andersen-Bruce; **580** Library of Congress; **581** Kansas State Historical Society, Topeka, Kansas; **582 B** GC; **582 T** © George Hunter/Tony Stone Images; **583 L** The Museum of American Political Life, University of Hartford. Photograph by Sally Andersen-Bruce; **583 R** John M. Heninger; **584** BB; **585** The Museum of American Political Life, University of Hartford. Photograph by Sally Andersen-Bruce; **586 L** From "National Museum of American History" by Shirley Abbott, courtesy of Harry N. Abrams, Inc.; **586 B** BB; **587 T** Collection of The New-York Historical Society; **587 L** Library of Congress; **588 BR** © John Warden/Tony Stone Images; **589 TR** CP; **589 TC** Gilbert H. Grosvenor, © National Geographic Society; **590** BB; **591 R** The Museum of American Political Life, University of Hartford. Photograph by Sally Andersen-Bruce; **592** BB; **593** Holt Atherton Center for Western Studies, University of the Pacific; **594 T** Schomberg Center for Research in Black Culture, The New York Public Library [SC-CN-79-0018]; **594 C** Schomberg Center for Research in Black Culture, The New York Public Library [SC-CN-93-0922]; **595** © Bob Daemmrich/Stock, Boston; **598** H. Reuterdahl "U.S. Fleet Entering Golden Gate, San Francisco" Courtesy United States Naval Academy Museum; **600** GC; **601 C** Seth Joel, Bishop Museum; **601 T** GC; **602** CP; **603** "Destruction of the U.S. Battleship Maine in Havana Harbor, Feb. 15, 1898" (detail) Chicago Historical Society; **604** Steve Adams, © National Geographic Society; **605 B** "Charge of the 24th & 25 Colored Infantry and Rescue of Rough Riders at San Juan Hill, July 2nd, 1898" (detail) Chicago Historical Society; **605 C** Collection of David J. and Janice L. Frent; **606** © Tony Pachecho/Sygma; **607** GC; **608** (inset) Charles Sheeler "Panama Canal" 1946, Courtesy of Citibank Art Collection [photo by Tony Cretaro]; **608 B** GC; **610** BB; **611** Camera Press Ltd, London; **613 C** From WORLD IN ARMS, photo by Michael Freeman. © Time-Life Books; **613 R** John Nash "Over the Top" Courtesy of the Trustees of the Imperial War Museum; **613 L** Courtesy of the Trustees of the Imperial War Museum [Q 872]; **614 T** The David King Collection; **614 C** GC; **615 T** The Bettmann Archive; **615 BR** The Bettmann Archive; **615 L** Courtesy of the Trustees of the Imperial War Museum; **616** BB; **617** Courtesy of the Trustees of the Imperial War Museum; **618 B** GC; **619** ; **619 B** GC; **622** "Punch", 1919; **625** Courtesy of the Trustees of the Imperial War Museum; **628** Everett Shinn "The Docks, New York City," 1901 (detail) Munson Williams Proctor Institute, Museum purchase 55.35; **630** Image #203, J.W. Sandison Collection. Whatcom Museum of History and Art, Bellingham, WA; **630** (inset) CP; **632** © Ed Castle/Folio, Inc.; **633 L** UPI/Bettmann; **633 R** UPI/Bettmann; **634** The Library of Congress; **636** Caufield & Shook Collection, Photographic Archives, University of Louisville [neg. # CS 32280]; **637 T** Caufield & Shook Collection, Photographic Archives, University of Louisville [neg. # CS 33925]; **638 T** Collection of the Museum of Transportation, St. Louis, MO; **639 C** Joseph H. Bailey, © National Geographic Society; **639 BR** LLR Collection; **640** CP; **641** GC; **642** UPI/Bettmann; **643** Missouri Historical Society; **644 C** GC; **644 L** © The Walt Disney Company. All rights reserved; **644 R** BB; **645 R** AP/Wide World Photos; **645 L** The Bettmann Archive; **646 L** National Baseball Library & Archive, Cooperstown, New York; **646 R** AP/Wide World Photos; **647 L** Princeton University Library, F. Scott Fitzgerald Papers; **647 R** GC; **648** BB; **649 C** UPI/Bettmann; **649 T** BB; **650** CP; **651** The Bettmann Archive; **654** Isaac Soyer "Employment Agency," 1937. Oil on canvas. 34-1/4 × 45 inches. Collection of Whitney Museum of American Art. Purchase 37.44, photograph by Geoffrey Clements; **656 L** UPI/Bettmann; **656 C** GC; **657** UPI/Bettmann; **658 T** The Bettmann Archive; **658 B** The Bettmann Archive; **660** UPI/Bettmann; **661 L** Oil on canvas painting by J. Porter from a photograph taken by Ivan E. Prall in 1938. Courtesy of Ivan E. Prall; **661 R** UPI/Bettmann; **662** Tennessee Valley Authority; **663** The Bettmann Archive; **664** UPI/Bettmann; **665** Library of Congress; **666** William Gropper "Construction of a Dam" Department of the Interior. Photo by Edward Owen; **667** Franklin D. Roosevelt Library; **668** Library of Congress; **669 T** UPI/Bettmann; **669 B** Shooting Star, Hollywood; **670 T** CP; **670 B** UPI/Bettmann; **672 T** UPI/Bettman; **672 B** Phil Dixon's Negro Baseball Photographic History; **673** Phil Dixon's Negro Baseball Photographic History; **676** National Anthropological Archives, Smithsonian Institution [89-1584]; **678** GC; **679 L** National Museum of American History, Division of Transportation, Smithsonian Institution [32602-B]; **679 R** The Bettmann Archive; **680 T** BB; **680 B** CP; **681** BB; **682** © Paul Fusco/Magnum Photos; **683** Jacob Lawrence "Panel 23: And the Migration Spread" Tempera on masonite. The Phillips Collection, Washington, D.C.; **684** UPI/Bettmann Newsphotos; **685 T** BB; **685** (inset) Schomberg Center for Research in Black Culture, The New York Public Library [SC CN-91-0390]; **686** The Metropolitan Museum of Art, New York; gift of the James VanDer Zee Institute, 1970 [1970.539.10]. By permission of Donna VanDerZee, New York; **687 C** Schomberg Center for Research in Black Culture, The New York Public Library [SC-CN-83-0269]; **687 B** UPI/Bettmann; **687 T** The Bettmann Archive; **688** Aaron Siskind "Untitled" From the project The Most Crowded Block, 1939–40.[1990.73.1] National Museum of American Art, Washington, D.C., gift of Tennyson and Fern Schad/Art Resource, New York. © 1940, Aaron Siskind; **689** John A. Anderson Collection. Nebraska State Historical Society; **690** National Anthropological Archives, Smithsonian Institution [1044-B]; **691** Thomas Gilcrease Institute of American History and Art, Tulsa, Oklahoma [4336.3854]; **694** National Archives (U.S. Army photo); **696 L** AP/Wide World Photos; **696 R** UPI/Bettmann ; **697** Margaret Bourke-White, Life Magazine © Time Warner; **699** UPI/Bettmann; **700** AP/Wide World Photos; **701** Fujiphotos, courtesy of LLR Research; **702** GC; **703** Special Collections, The New York Public Library; **704 B** Myron Davis, Life Magazine © Time Warner. Contributors: Davis Myron H; **704 T** UPI/Bettmann Newsphotos; **705** Library of Congress; **706** Sovfoto; **707** The Bettmann Archive; **709** The Trustees of the Imperial War Museum, London; **711** National Archives [127-GR-137-69889A]; **713 L** Margaret Bourke-White, Life Magazine © Time Warner; **713 R** United States Holocaust Memorial Museum, Washington, D.C." **716** © Steve Dunwell/The Image Bank; **718** Michael Evans, Time Magazine © Time Warner; **720** (Missile) Bill Sikes/Florida Union/Sygma; **720** (Berlin Wall) © Howard Sochurek. All rights reserved; **720** (guard) Emory Kristof, © National Geographic Society; **723 B** Walter Sanders, Life Magazine © Time Warner; **723 C** American Red Cross photo by Waller; **724** The Bettmann Archive; **725 R** GC; **726 R** UPI/Bettmann; **726 L** UPI/Bettmann; **727 T** © Cornell Capa/Magnum Photos; **727 C** AP/Wide World Photos; **728** © Don McCullin/Camera Press, Ltd.; **729** © A. Tannenbaum/Sygma; **730 BL** Paul Schutzer, Life Magazine © 1965 Time Warner. Contributors: Schutzer Estate of Paul; **731 R** National League of POW/MIA Families, Washington, D.C.; **731 L** © 1993 Tomas Muscionico/Contact Press Images; **732 B** Jeff Tinsley, Smithsonian Institution [87-4914/19]; **732 T** © David Burnett/Woodfin Camp & Associates; **733** © Wally McNamee 1972/Woodfin Camp & Associates; **734 L** © Robert Rathe/FPG International; **734 R** © Ledru/Sygma; **735** © Martti Kainulainen Lehtikuva/Woodfin Camp & Associates; **737 L** © Roberto Koch/Contrasto/Saba; **737 R** © Regis Bossu/Sygma; **740** (background) © Van Bucher/Photo Researchers, Inc; **740** (inset-right) © 1990 Tom McCarthey/Black Star; **740** (inset-left) The Bettmann Archive; **742 R** UPI/Bettmann; **742 L** UPI/Bettmann; **743** United States Postal Service; **744** © 1979 Robert Phillips/Black Star; **746 T** Curt Teich Postcard Archives, Lake County (IL) Museum; **746 CR** © Michael Dwyer/Stock,Boston; **746 B** Michael Medford/Image Bank **747 B** © Terrence Moore, Tucson; **747 TL** © Michael Dwyer/Stock, Boston; **748** John F. Kennedy Library; **749** © Fred Ward/Black Star; **750 L** CP; **750 L** CP; **750 L** CP; **751** NASA; **752** UPI/Bettmann; **753 TL** © Dennis Brack/Black Star; **753 CR** © Dan McCoy/Black Star; **753 BR** © 1976 Martin A. Levick, Scarsdale, NY; **754** © Robin Moyer/Black Star; **755 T** © Richard Hutchings/Photo Edit; **755 C** © Tony Freeman/Photo Edit; **756** UPI/Bettmann; **757** NASA; **758** © Gamma Liaison Network; **759** UPI/Bettmann; **762** © Richard Howard; **764** Carl Iwasaki, Life Magazine © 1953 Time Warner Inc.; **765 T** UPI/Bettmann Newsphotos; **765 B** UPI/Bettmann; **767** UPI/Bettmann; **768** © 1963 Charles Moore/Black Star; **769** Francis Miller, Life Magazine © Time Warner, Contributors: Miller, Francis; **770 T** © Ivan Massar/Black Star; **770 B** © 1969 John Launois/Black Star; **772** © Bob Fitch/Black Star; **773 T** © Carol Halebian/Gamma Liaison Network; **773 B** © 1979 Martin A. Levick, Scarsdale, NY; **774 B** © Jerry Jacka; **774 T** UPI/Bettmann; **775** © Lester Sloan/Woodfin Camp & Associates; **776 B** © 1981 Martin A. Levick, Scarsdale, NY; **777** Copyright 1993 Time, Inc. Reprinted by permission; **778** Sarah Fawcett, AP/Wide World Photos; **782** © Jeff Davis/Black Star; **784 T** © Glenn James/Sygma; **785** © Ira Wyman/Sygma; **785** Ken Karp; **786 T** © 1993 John Harrington/Black Star; **786 C** © J. Patrick Forden/Sygma; **788** AP/Wide World Photos; **789** © Bruno Barbey/Magnum Photos; **790** UPI/Bettmann; **791** Reuters/Bettmann; **792** Reuters/Bettmann; **793 L** © Thomas Hoepker/Magnum Photos; **793 R** NASA; **794** Jonathan Kerr/The Nature Conservancy; **795** The Boston Globe, photo by Tom Lander; **796** AP/Wide World Photos; **799** © Richard Hutchings/Photo Edit; **800** The Boston Globe, photo by Tom Herde